Advanced
Java™ 2 Platform
How to Program

Deitel™ Books, Cyber Classrooms, Complete Training Courses and Web-Based Training published by Prentice Hall

How to Program Series

Advanced Java™ 2 Platform How to Program
C How to Program, 3/E
C++ How to Program, 3/E
C# How to Program
e-Business and e-Commerce How to Program
Internet and World Wide Web How to Program, 2/E
Java™ How to Program, 4/E
Perl How to Program
Visual Basic® 6 How to Program
Visual Basic® .NET How to Program
Visual C++® .NET How to Program
Wireless Internet & Mobile Business How to Program
XML How to Program

Multimedia Cyber Classroom and Web-Based Training Series

(for information regarding Deitel™ Web-based training visit **www.ptgtraining.com**)
Advanced Java™ 2 Platform Multimedia Cyber Classroom
C++ Multimedia Cyber Classroom, 3/E
C# Multimedia Cyber Classroom, 3/E
e-Business and e-Commerce Multimedia Cyber Classroom
Internet and World Wide Web Multimedia Cyber Classroom, 2/E
Java™ 2 Multimedia Cyber Classroom, 4/E
Perl Multimedia Cyber Classroom
Visual Basic® 6 Multimedia Cyber Classroom
Visual Basic® .NET Multimedia Cyber Classroom
Visual C++® .NET Multimedia Cyber Classroom
Wireless Internet & Mobile Business Programming Multimedia Cyber Classroom
XML Multimedia Cyber Classroom

The Complete Training Course Series

The Complete Advanced Java™ 2 Platform Training Course
The Complete C++ Training Course, 3/E
The Complete C# Training Course, 3/E
The Complete e-Business and e-Commerce Programming Training Course
The Complete Internet and World Wide Web Programming Training Course
The Complete Java™ 2 Training Course, 3/E
The Complete Perl Training Course
The Complete Visual Basic® 6 Training Course
The Complete Visual Basic® .NET Training Course
The Complete Visual C++® .NET Training Course
The Complete Wireless Internet & Mobile Business Programming Training Course
The Complete XML Training Course

.NET Series

C# How to Program
Visual Basic® .NET. How to Program
Visual C++® .NET How to Program

Visual Studio Series

Getting Started with Microsoft® Visual C++™ 6 with an Introduction to MFC
Visual Basic® 6 How to Program
C# How to Program
Visual Basic® .NET How to Program
Visual C++® .NET How to Program

For Managers Series

e-Business and e-Commerce for Managers

Coming Soon

e-books and e-whitepapers

To communicate with the authors, send email to:

   deitel@deitel.com

For information on corporate on-site seminars and public seminars offered by Deitel & Associates, Inc. worldwide, visit:

   www.deitel.com

For continuing updates on Prentice Hall and Deitel & Associates, Inc. publications visit the Prentice Hall Web site

Advanced
Java™ 2 Platform
HOW TO PROGRAM

H. M. Deitel
Deitel & Associates, Inc.

P. J. Deitel
Deitel & Associates, Inc.

S. E. Santry
Deitel & Associates, Inc.

Prentice
Hall

PRENTICE HALL, Upper Saddle River, New Jersey 07458

Library of Congress Cataloging-in-Publication Data

Deitel, Harvey M
    Advanced Java 2 platform: how to program / H.M. Deitel, P.J. Deitel, S.
    Santry.--1st ed.
        p. cm.
    Includes bibliographical references and index.
    ISBN 0-13-089560-1
     1. Java (computer program language) I. Deitel, Paul J. II.Santry, S.
    III. Title
    QA76.73.J38 D445 2001
    005.13'3--dc21

                                          2001045145

Vice President and Editorial Director: *Marcia Horton*
Acquisitions Editor: *Petra J. Recter*
Assistant Editor: *Sarah Burrows*
Project Manager: *Crissy Statuto*
Editorial Assistant: *Karen Schultz*
Vice President and Director of Production and Manufacturing, ESM: *David W. Riccardi*
Executive Managing Editor: *Vince O'Brien*
Managing Editor: *David A. George*
Assistant Managing Editor: *Camille Trentacoste*
Formatters: *Kathryn Gesing, Victoria Johnson*
Software Production Editor: *Bob Engelhardt*
Director of Creative Services: *Paul Belfanti*
Creative Director: *Carole Anson*
Chapter Opener and Cover Designer: *Tamara L. Newnam*
Cover Illustration: *Tamara L. Newnam, Steve Lefkowitz*
Manufacturing Manager: *Trudy Pisciotti*
Manufacturing Buyer: *Lisa McDowell*
Marketing Manager: *Jennie Burger*

Prentice Hall

© 2002 by Prentice-Hall, Inc.
Upper Saddle River, New Jersey 07458

The authors and publisher of this book have used their best efforts in preparing this book. These efforts include the development, research, and testing of the theories and programs to determine their effectiveness. The authors and publisher make no warranty of any kind, expressed or implied, with regard to these programs or to the documentation contained in this book. The authors and publisher shall not be liable in any event for incidental or consequential damages in connection with, or arising out of, the furnishing, performance, or use of these programs.

Many of the designations used by manufacturers and sellers to distinguish their products are claimed as trademarks and registered trademarks. Where those designations appear in this book, and Prentice Hall and the authors were aware of a trademark claim, the designations have been printed in initial caps or all caps. All product names mentioned remain trademarks or registered trademarks of their respective owners.

Printed in the United States of America

10 9 8 7 6 5 4 3 2 1

ISBN 0-13-089560-1

Prentice-Hall International (UK) Limited, *London*
Prentice-Hall of Australia Pty. Limited, *Sydney*
Prentice-Hall Canada Inc., *Toronto*
Prentice-Hall Hispanoamericana, S.A., *Mexico*
Prentice-Hall of India Private Limited, *New Delhi*
Prentice-Hall of Japan, Inc., *Tokyo*
Pearson Education Asia Pte. Ltd., *Singapore*
Editora Prentice-Hall do Brasil, Ltda., *Rio de Janeiro*

In loving memory of our Uncle and Granduncle
Joseph Deitel:

"His pleasure was giving."

Harvey and Paul Deitel

For my brother Tim, who, by his example, always has
challenged me to excel.

Sean

Trademarks

Contents

11   Case Study: Servlet and JSP Bookstore   660

12   Java-Based Wireless Applications Development and J2ME   716

27 Common Object Request Broker Architecture (CORBA): Part 2 (on CD)   1508

28 Peer-to-Peer Applications and JXTA   1548

Preface

Live in fragments no longer. Only connect.
Edward Morgan Forster

Welcome to *Advanced Java 2 Platform How to Program* and the exciting world of advanced-programming concepts with the three major Java platforms—*Java™ 2 Enterprise Edition* (*J2EE*), *Java 2 Standard Edition* (*J2SE*) and *Java 2 Micro Edition* (*J2ME*). Little did we know when we attended the November 1995 Internet/World Wide Web conference in Boston what that session would yield—four editions of *Java How To Program* (the world's best-selling Java textbook), and now this book about Java software-development technologies for upper-level college courses and professional developers.

Before Java appeared, we were convinced that C++ would replace C as the dominant application-development language and systems-programming language for the next decade. However, the combination of the World Wide Web and Java now increases the prominence of the Internet in information-systems planning and implementation. Organizations want to integrate the Internet "seamlessly" into their information systems. Java is more appropriate than C++ for this purpose—as evidenced by Sun Microsystems' announcement in 2001 that over 96% of enterprise application servers support J2EE.

Advanced Java 2 Platform How to Program is the first book in our *Advanced How to Program* series. We discuss Java technologies that may be unfamiliar and challenging to the average Java programmer. We structured each chapter discussion to provide the reader with an introduction to leading-edge and complex Java technologies, rather than provide a detailed analysis of every nuance of each topic. In fact, each topic we present could be a 600–800 page book in itself.

We use a different approach with the examples in this book than that of programming examples in our previous books. We provide fewer programs, but these programs are more substantial and illustrate sophisticated coding practices. We integrate many technologies to create a book for developers that enables you to "go beyond" and experiment with the most up-to-date technologies and most widely employed design concepts. What better way to learn than to work with actual technologies and code?

When determining the appropriate topics for this book, we read dozens of journals, reviewed the Sun Microsystems Web site and participated in numerous trade shows. We audited our material against the latest technologies presented at the JavaOne conference—the leading Java-developer conference sponsored by Sun Microsystems—and at other popular Java conferences. We also reviewed books on specialized Java topics. After this extensive research, we created an outline for this book and sent it for professional review by Java experts. We found so many topics we wanted to include that we wound up with over 1800 pages of material (several hundred of those pages appear as PDF documents on the CD that accompanies this book). We apologize if this is inconvenient, but the material and the number of topics are voluminous. We will most likely split the next edition into two volumes.

This book benefitted from an unusually large pool of excellent reviewers and the detailed documentation that Sun makes available on their Web site (**www.sun.com**). We were excited to have a number of reviewers from Sun and many other distinguished industry reviewers. We wanted experienced developers to review our code and discussions, so we could offer "expert advice" from people who actually work with the technologies in industry.

We are pleased to include a discussion of application servers in Chapter 21. The three most popular application server software products are BEA's *WebLogic,* IBM's *Web-Sphere* and Sun/Netscape's *iPlanet*. Originally, we had planned to include all three on the book's accompanying CD, but we have included only WebLogic and WebSphere. iPlanet was about to publish a new version as this book went to publication. By mutual agreement between iPlanet and Deitel & Associates, Inc., we decided not to include this software, but iPlanet provides a link to a site specific to this book—**www.iplanet.com/ ias_deitel**—where readers can download the latest iPlanet software. We also include a discussion of how to deploy our case study on the iPlanet server. You can find this discussion on our Web site—**www.deitel.com.**

We moved four chapters from *Java How to Program, Third Edition*—RMI, Servlets, JavaBeans and JDBC—to *Advanced Java 2 Platform How to Program*. Prentice Hall has published a paperback supplement (ISBN: 0-13-074367-4) containing these four chapters for readers who have purchased *Java How to Program, Fourth Edition.*

The world of Java is growing so rapidly that *Advanced Java 2 Platform How to Program* and its companion text, *Java How to Program, Fourth Edition,* total 3400 pages! The books are so large that we had to put several chapters from each on the accompanying CDs. This creates tremendous challenges and opportunities for us as authors, for our publisher—Prentice Hall, for instructors, for students and for professionals. We hope you enjoy the results of these challenges as much as we have enjoyed the process of tackling them.

Features of *Advanced Java 2 Platform How to Program*

This book contains many features including:

- *Full-Color Presentation.* This book is in full color to enable readers to see sample outputs as they would appear on a color monitor. Also, we now syntax color all the Java code, as do many of today's Java integrated development environments and code editors. Our syntax-coloring conventions are as follows:

```
comments appear in green
keywords appear in dark blue
constants and literal values appear in light blue
JSP delimiters appear in red
all other code appears in black
```

- *"Code Washing."* This is our own term for the process we use to format the programs in the book with a carefully commented, open layout. The code is in full color and grouped into small, well-documented pieces. This greatly improves code readability—an especially important goal for us given that this book contains almost 40,000 lines of code.

- *Advanced Graphical User Interface (GUI) Design.* Starting with Chapter 2, we use advanced Java Swing features to create real-world Java components, including a Web-browser application with a multiple-document interface. In Chapter 3, we introduce the Model-View-Controller (MVC) architecture and its implementation in the Swing API. In Chapters 4 and 5, we create 2D graphics and 3D worlds. The Java 2D Drawing Application with Design Patterns Case Study in Chapter 5 presents a complex drawing program with which the user can create shapes in various colors and gradients. We are also pleased to add Java 3D coverage. One of the book's adopters said these chapters were ideal for a course in advanced GUI programming. (We wanted to include multimedia programming with the Java Media Framework, but instead we decided to include this material in the companion book, *Java How to Program, Fourth Edition.*)

- *Enterprise Java and Our Enterprise Java Case Study.* Developers use Java for building "heavy-duty" enterprise applications. Chapters 7–11, 14–16 and 21 explore the necessary components for implementing enterprise solutions—including security, database manipulation, servlets, JavaServer Pages, distributed transactions, message-oriented middleware and application servers. In Chapter 7, Security, we discuss secure communications and secure programming. Chapters 17–20 showcase an Enterprise Java Case Study that integrates many technologies, such as Enterprise JavaBeans, servlets, RMI-IIOP, XML, XSLT, XHTML, (and for wireless application development) WML and cHTML—into an online-bookstore application. The Deitel Bookstore demonstrates how to use the MVC architecture introduced in Chapter 3 to build enterprise applications. This bookstore uses technologies to provide support for almost any type of client, including cell phones, mobile devices and Web browsers. In this world of networks and wireless networks, business information must be delivered securely and reliably to the intended recipients.

- *Distributed Systems.* Enterprise applications are usually so complex that they run more efficiently when program components are distributed among different machines in organizations' networks. This book introduces several technologies for building distributed systems—Remote Method Invocation (RMI), Jini, JavaSpaces, Java Management Extensions (JMX), Jiro and Common Object Request Broker Architecture (CORBA). CORBA, controlled by the Object Management Group (OMG), is a mature distributed computing technology for integrating distributed components written in many disparate languages. Java was originally intended for networks of programmable devices—Jini assumes that technology role now. JMX and Jiro are technologies specifically for network management (LANs, WANs, intranets, the Internet, extranets, etc.).

- ***Java 2 Micro Edition (J2ME) and Wireless Applications.*** It is estimated that by 2003, more people worldwide will access the Internet through wireless devices than through desktop computers. The Java platform for wireless devices with limited capabilities such as cell phones and personal digital assistants is Java 2 Micro Edition (J2ME). Chapter 12, Wireless Java-Based Applications Development and J2ME, contains a case study that sends content from a centralized data store to several wireless clients, including a J2ME client.

- ***Web Services.*** Web services are applications that expose public interfaces usable by other applications over the Web. The area of Web services builds on existing protocols, such as HTTP, and communicate with XML-based messages. Directory services enable clients to perform lookups to discover available Web services. The Simple Object Access Protocol (SOAP) uses XML to provide communication in many Web services. Many of the technologies in this book can be used to build Web services.

- ***Employing Design Patterns.*** The book's largest case studies—such as the Java 2D drawing program in Chapter 5, the three-tier servlet and JavaServer Pages case study in Chapter 11, the three-tier wireless application in Chapter 12 and the Deitel Bookstore Enterprise Case Study in Chapters 17–20—each contain thousands of lines of code. Larger systems, such as automated teller machines or air-traffic control systems, can contain hundreds of thousands, or even millions, of lines of code. Effective design is crucial to the proper construction of such complex systems. Over the past decade, the software engineering industry has made significant progress in the field of *design patterns*—proven architectures for constructing flexible and maintainable object-oriented software.[1] Using design patterns can substantially reduce the complexity of the design process. We used many design patterns when building the software in this book. Chapter 1 introduces design patterns, discusses why they are useful and lists those design patterns we use throughout this book

- ***XML.*** XML (Extensible Markup Language) use is exploding in the software-development industry and we use it pervasively throughout the text. As a platform-independent syntax for creating markup languages, XML's data portability integrates well with Java's portable applications and services. If you do not know XML, Appendices A–D of this book provide an introduction to XML. Appendices A and B introduce XML basics and DTDs, which define standard XML document structures. Appendix C introduces the Document Object Model (DOM) API for manipulating XML documents. Appendix D covers XSLT (Extensible Stylesheet Language Transformations—an XML vocabulary for transforming XML documents into other text-based documents.

- ***Peer-to-Peer Applications.*** Peer-to-peer (P2P) applications—such as instant messaging and document-sharing programs—have become extremely popular. Chap-

---

1. Gamma, Erich, Richard Helm, Ralph Johnson, and John Vlissides. *Design Patterns; Elements of Reusable Object-Oriented Software.* (Massachusetts: Addison-Wesley, 1995).

ter 28, Peer-to-Peer Applications and JXTA, introduces this architecture, in which each node performs both client and server duties. JXTA (short for the term "Juxtapose"), defines protocols for implementing peer-to-peer applications. This chapter includes two P2P application case studies—one written with Jini and RMI and the other written in multicast sockets and RMI. Both implement a P2P instant messaging application. We wanted a capstone example for Jini and decided this chapter should have it. The first case study is somewhat centralized—and therefore not a "true" P2P application (some developers think that Jini has too much overhead for a peer-to-peer application). We developed the second to demonstrate a lighter-weight, decentralized implementation.

- ***Appendix H, Career Opportunities.*** This appendix introduces career services on the Internet. We explore online career services from both the employer's and employee's perspectives. We suggest Web sites at which you can submit applications, search for jobs and review applicants (if you are interested in hiring someone). We also review services that build recruiting pages directly into e-businesses. One of our reviewers told us that he had just gone through a job search largely using the Internet and this chapter would have expanded his search dramatically.

- ***Appendix I, Unicode.*** This appendix overviews the *Unicode Standard.* As computer systems evolved worldwide, computer vendors developed numeric representations of character sets and special symbols for the local languages spoken in different countries. In some cases, different representations were developed for the same languages. Such disparate character sets made communication between computer systems difficult. Java supports the Unicode Standard (maintained by a non-profit organization called the *Unicode Consortium*), which defines a single character set with unique numeric values for characters and special symbols in most spoken languages. This appendix discusses the Unicode Standard, overviews the Unicode Consortium Web site (**unicode.org**) and shows a Java example that displays "Welcome" in many different languages.

- ***Bibliography and Resources.*** Chapters in this book contain bibliographies when appropriate and URLs that offer additional information about the technologies. We did this so those readers who would like to study a topic further could begin with the resources we found helpful when developing this book.

Some Notes to Instructors

A World of Object Orientation

When we wrote the first edition of *Java How to Program*, universities were still emphasizing procedural programming in languages like Pascal and C. The leading-edge courses were using object-oriented C++, but these courses were generally mixing a substantial amount of procedural programming with object-oriented programming—something that C++ lets you do, but Java does not. By the third edition of *Java How to Program*, many universities were switching from C++ to Java in their introductory curricula, and instructors were emphasizing a pure object-oriented programming approach. In parallel with this activity, the software engineering community was standardizing its approach to modeling object-oriented systems with the UML, and the design-patterns movement was taking shape. This book takes a 100% object-oriented approach and emphasizes Java design patterns and adherence to Java idiom.

The prerequisite for this book is *Java How to Program, Fourth Edition* (or equivalent Java knowledge), which provides a solid foundation in Java programming. *Java How to Program, Fourth Edition* includes the following chapters and appendices, for a more detailed Table of Contents, visit **www.deitel.com**: Introduction to Computers, the Internet and the Web; Introduction to Java Applications; Introduction to Java Applets; Control Structures: Part 1; Control Structures: Part 2; Methods; Arrays; Object-Based Programming; Object-Oriented Programming; Strings and Characters; Graphics and Java 2D; Graphical User Interface Components: Part 1; Graphical User Interface Components: Part 2; Exception Handling; Multithreading; Files and Streams; Networking; Multimedia: Images, Animation, Audio and Video; Data Structures; Java Utilities Package and Bit Manipulation; Collections; Java Media Framework and Java Sound; Java Demos; Java Resources; Operator Precedence Chart; ASCII Character Set; Number Systems; Creating HTML Documentation with **javadoc**; Elevator Events and Listener Interfaces; Elevator Model; Elevator View; Career Opportunities; Unicode; Bibliography.

Students Like Java

Students are highly motivated by the fact that they are learning a leading-edge language (Java) and a leading-edge programming paradigm (object-oriented programming) for building entire systems. Java immediately gives them an advantage when they head into a world in which the Internet and the World Wide Web have a massive prominence and corporations need enterprise systems programmers. Students quickly discover that they can do great things with Java, so they are willing to put in the extra effort. Java helps programmers unleash their creativity. We see this in the Java and advanced Java courses Deitel & Associates, Inc. teaches.

Focus of the Book

Our goal was clear—produce an advanced Java textbook for higher-level university courses in computer programming for students with intermediate-level Java programming experience, and offer the depth and the rigorous treatment of theory and practice demanded by professionals. To meet these goals, we produced a book that challenges Java programmers. We present clear examples of advanced topics and often overlooked topics. We adhere to Java idiom and follow sophisticated coding style and practices (i.e., not just the code formatting, but the idiomatic use of Java API's, constructs and technologies). This book presents substantial Java applications that readers can use to start working with these technologies immediately.

Evolution of Advanced Java 2 Platform How to Program

Advanced Java 2 Platform How to Program was finished fresh on the heels of *Java How to Program, Fourth Edition*. Hundreds of thousands of university students and professionals worldwide have learned Java from our texts. Upon publication in September 2001, *Advanced Java 2 Platform How to Program* will be used in universities, corporations and government organizations worldwide. Deitel & Associates, Inc. taught Java courses internationally to thousands of students as we were writing the various editions of *Java How to*

Program and *Advanced Java 2 Platform How to Program*. We carefully monitored the effectiveness of material and tuned the books accordingly.

Conceptualization of Java

We believe in Java. Its conceptualization by Sun Microsystems, the creator of Java, was brilliant. Sun based the new language on C and C++, two of the world's most widely used implementation languages. This immediately gave Java a huge pool of highly skilled programmers who were implementing most of the world's new operating systems, communications systems, database systems, personal-computer applications and systems software. Sun removed the more complex and error-prone C/C++ features (such as explicit pointers, operator overloading and multiple inheritance, among others). They kept the language concise by removing special-purpose features used by only small segments of the programming community. They made the language truly portable for implementing Internet-based and Web-based applications, and they included features developers need such as strings, graphics, GUI components, exception handling, multithreading, multimedia (audio, images, animation and video), prepackaged data structures, file processing, database processing, Internet and Web-based client/server networking, distributed computing and enterprise computing. Then they made the language available *at no charge* to millions of potential programmers worldwide.

2.5 Million Java Developers

Java was promoted in 1995 as a means of adding "dynamic content" to Web pages. Instead of Web pages with only text and static graphics, Web pages could now "come alive" with audios, videos, animations, interactivity—and soon, 3D imaging. But we saw much more in Java than this. Java's features are precisely what businesses and organizations need to meet today's information-processing requirements. So we immediately viewed Java as having the potential to become one of the world's key general-purpose programming languages. In fact, Java has revolutionized software development with multimedia-intensive, platform-independent, object-oriented code for conventional, Internet-, Intranet- and Extranet-based applications and applets. Java now has 2.5 million developers worldwide—a stunning accomplishment when considering that it has been available publicly for only six years. No other programming language has ever acquired such a large developer base so quickly.

Teaching Approach

Advanced Java 2 Platform How to Program, First Edition contains a rich collection of examples, exercises and projects drawn from many fields to provide readers with a chance to solve interesting real-world problems. The book concentrates on the principles of good software engineering and stresses program clarity, especially important when creating substantial programs like those covered in this book. We avoid arcane terminology and syntax specifications in favor of teaching by example. Our code examples have been tested on popular Java platforms. We are educators who teach edge-of-the-practice topics in industry classrooms worldwide. The text emphasizes good pedagogy.

Learning Java via the live-code™ Approach

The book is loaded with live-code™ examples. This is how we teach and write about programming, and is the focus of each of our multimedia Cyber Classrooms and Web-based training courses. We present each new concept in the context of a complete, working Java program, immediately followed by screen captures that show the program's output. We call this style of teaching and writing our **live-code™ approach**. *We use the language to teach the language.* Reading these programs (almost 40,000 lines of code) is much like entering and running them on a computer.

Java Programming from Chapter Two

Advanced Java 2 Platform How to Program, "jumps right in" with substantial programs right from Chapter 2. This is the beginning of an aggressive pace that challenges readers with graphical, multithreaded, database-intensive, network-based programming. Throughout the book, readers learn by implementing impressive projects.

World Wide Web Access

All the code for *Advanced Java 2 Platform How to Program* is on the CD that accompanies this book. The code also is available at the following Web sites:

```
www.deitel.com
www.prenhall.com/deitel
```

Objectives

Each chapter begins with *Objectives* that inform the reader what to expect and provides an opportunity, after reading the chapter, to determine if the reader has met these objectives. It is a confidence builder and a source of positive reinforcement.

Quotations

The learning objectives are followed by quotations. Some are humorous, some are philosophical and some offer interesting insights. Our readers enjoy relating the quotations to the chapter material. The quotations are worth a "second look" after you read each chapter.

Outline

The chapter outline helps the reader approach the material in top-down fashion. This, too, helps students anticipate what is to come and set a comfortable and effective learning pace.

Almost 40,000 Lines of Code in 126 Example Programs (with Program Outputs)

We present Java features in the context of complete, working Java programs. The programs in this book are substantial, with hundreds to thousands of lines of code (e.g., 10,000 lines of code for the bookstore case study example). Students should use the program code from the CD that accompanies the book and run each program while studying that program in the text.

841 Illustrations/Figures

Many of the figures are code examples, but this book still offers many charts, line drawings and program outputs. For example, Chapter 4 and 5, Graphics Programming with Java 2D and Java 3D, provides stunning graphics, and the architectural overview of the Enterprise Java case study in Chapter 17 is impressive.

235 Programming Tips

We have included programming tips to help students focus on important aspects of program development. We highlight numerous tips in the form of *Good Programming Practices, Common Programming Errors, Testing and Debugging Tips, Performance Tips, Portability Tips, Software Engineering Observations* and *Look-and-Feel Observations*. These tips and practices represent the best we have gleaned from decades of programming and teaching experience. One of our students—a mathematics major—told us that she feels this approach is like the highlighting of axioms, theorems and corollaries in mathematics books; it provides a basis on which to build good software.

Good Programming Practices

We highlight Good Programming Practices *techniques for writing programs that are clearer, more understandable, more debuggable and more maintainable.*

Common Programming Errors

Focusing on these Common Programming Errors *helps readers avoid making the same errors.*

Testing and Debugging Tips

When we first designed this "tip type," we thought we would use it strictly to tell people how to test and debug Java programs. In fact, many of the tips describe aspects of Java that reduce the likelihood of "bugs" and thus simplify the testing and debugging process.

Performance Tips

We have included 13 Performance Tips *that highlight opportunities for improving program performance—making programs run faster or minimizing the amount of memory that they occupy.*

Portability Tips

One of Java's "claims to fame" is "universal" portability, so some programmers assume that if they implement an application in Java, the application will automatically be "perfectly" portable across all Java platforms. Unfortunately, this is not always the case. We include Portability Tips *to help readers write portable code and to provide insights on how Java achieves its high degree of portability.*

Software Engineering Observations

The object-oriented programming paradigm requires a complete rethinking about the way we build software systems. Java is an effective language for performing good software engineering. The Software Engineering Observations *highlight architectural and design issues that affect the construction of software systems, especially large-scale systems.*

Look-and-Feel Observations

We provide Look-and-Feel Observations *to highlight graphical user interface conventions. These observations help readers design their own graphical user interfaces in conformance with industry norms.*

Summary (949 Summary bullets)

Each chapter ends with additional pedagogical devices. We present a thorough, bullet-list-style summary of the chapter. On average, there are 26 summary bullets per chapter. This helps the readers review and reinforce key concepts.

Terminology (1904 Terms)

We include in a *Terminology* section an alphabetized list of the important terms defined in the chapter—again, further reinforcement. On average, there are 51 terms per chapter.

394 Self-Review Exercises and Answers (Count Includes Separate Parts)

Self-review exercises and answers are included for self-study. These reinforce the knowledge the reader gained from the chapter.

189 Exercises (Count Includes Separate Parts)

Each chapter concludes with a set of exercises. The exercises cover many areas. This enables instructors to tailor their courses to the unique needs of their audiences and to vary course assignments each semester. Instructors can use these exercises to form homework assignments, quizzes and examinations. The solutions for most of the exercises are included on the *Instructor's Manual* CD that is *available only to instructors* through their Prentice-Hall representatives. [*NOTE:* **Please do not write to us requesting the instructor's manual. Distribution of this publication is strictly limited to college professors teaching from the book. Instructors may obtain the Instructor's manual only from their Prentice Hall representatives. We regret that we cannot provide the solutions to professionals**.] Solutions to approximately half of the exercises are included on the *Advanced Java 2 Platform Multimedia Cyber Classroom* CD, which also is part of *The Complete Advanced Java 2 Platform Training Course*. For ordering instructions, please see the last few pages of this book or visit **www.deitel.com**.

Approximately 3,080 Index Entries (with approximately 4648 Page References)

This book includes an extensive index. This helps the reader find any term or concept by keyword. The index is useful to developers who use the book as a reference. The terms in the Terminology sections generally appear in the index (along with many more index items from each chapter).

"Double Indexing" of Java live-code™ Examples and Exercises

Advanced Java 2 Platform How to Program has 126 live-code™ examples and 189 exercises (including parts). Many exercises are challenging problems or projects that require substantial effort. We have "double indexed" the live-code™ examples. For every Java source-code program in the book, we took the file name with the **.java** extension, such as **WebBrowser.java** and indexed it both alphabetically (in this case under "W") and as a subindex item under "Examples." This makes it easier to find examples using particular features.

Software Included with *Advanced Java 2 Platform How to Program*

There are a number of for-sale Java products available. However, you do not need them to get started with Java. We wrote *Advanced Java 2 Platform How to Program* using the *Java 2 Software Development Kit (J2SDK) Standard Edition Version 1.3.1 for Windows and Linux (Intel x86)* and other software programs that we include on the CD that accompanies this book. For your convenience, Sun's J2SDK also can be downloaded from the Sun Microsystems Java Web site **java.sun.com/j2se**. We include some of the most popular server software so you can set up and run live systems. This software includes *BEA We-bLogic Server™, Version 6.0 (Windows/Linux) with Service Pack 2, 30-Day Trial, Enterprise Edition, 6.0, Testdrive*; *IBM® WebSphere® Application Server, Advanced Single Server Edition, Version 4.0 for Windows NT® and Windows® 2000 Evaluation Copy,* and *Apache Tomcat 3.2.3 from the Apache Software Foundation.* We also include Informix Software's *Cloudscape 3.6.4* database software. With Sun's cooperation, we also were able to include on the CD a powerful Java integrated development environment (IDE)—Sun Microsystem's *Forte for Java Community Edition. Forte* is a professional IDE written in Java that includes a graphical user interface designer, code editor, compiler, visual debugger and more. J2SDK 1.3.1 must be installed before installing *Forte.* If you have any questions about using this software, please read the introductory *Forte* documentation on the CD. We will provide additional information on our Web site **www.deitel.com**.

The CD also contains the book's examples and a Web page with links to the Deitel & Associates, Inc. Web site (**www.deitel.com**), the Prentice Hall Web site (**www.prenhall.com/deitel**) and the many Web sites listed at the end of each chapter. If you have access to the Internet, this Web page can be loaded into your Web browser to give you quick access to all the resources. Finally, because we wrote much more than we originally intended, a number of chapters and appendices have been off-loaded to the CD.

Ancillary Package for *Advanced Java 2 Platform How to Program*

Advanced Java 2 Platform How to Program has extensive ancillary materials for instructors teaching from the book. The Instructor's Manual CD contains solutions to the vast majority of the end-of-chapter exercises. We also provide PowerPoint® slides containing all the code and figures in the text. You are free to customize these slides to meet your own classroom needs. Prentice Hall provides a *Companion Web Site* (**www.prenhall.com/deitel**) that includes resources for instructors and students. For instructors, the Web site has a *Syllabus Manager* for course planning, links to the PowerPoint slides and reference materials from the appendices of the book (such as the character sets and Web resources). For students, the Web site provides chapter objectives, true/false exercises with instant feedback, chapter highlights and reference materials. [*NOTE*: **Please do not write to us requesting the instructor's manual. Distribution of this publication is strictly limited to college professors teaching from the book. Instructors may obtain the solutions manual only from their regular Prentice Hall representatives. We regret that we cannot provide the solutions to professionals.**]

Advanced Java 2 Platform Multimedia Cyber Classroom (CD and Web-Based Training Versions) and *The Complete Advanced Java 2 Platform Training Course*

We have prepared an interactive, CD-based, software version of *Advanced Java 2 Platform How to Program,* called the *Advanced Java 2 Platform Multimedia Cyber Classroom.* It is loaded with features for learning and reference. The *Cyber Classroom* is wrapped with the textbook at a discount in *The Complete Advanced Java 2 Platform Training Course.* If you already have the book and would like to purchase the *Advanced Java 2 Platform Multimedia Cyber Classroom* (ISBN: 0-13-091276-x) separately, please visit **www.infor-**

mit.com/cyberclassrooms. All Deitel *Cyber Classrooms* are generally available in CD and Web-based training formats.

The CD has an introduction with the authors overviewing the *Cyber Classroom*'s features. Many of the live-code™ examples in the textbook truly "come alive" in the *Cyber Classroom*. If you are viewing a program and want to execute it, you click the lightning bolt icon and the program will run. You will immediately see—and hear for the audio-based multimedia programs—the program's outputs. If you want to modify a program and see and hear the effects of your changes, simply click the floppy-disk icon that causes the source code to be "lifted off" the CD and "dropped into" one of your own directories so you can edit the text, recompile the program and try out your new version. Click the audio icon and one of the authors will talk about the program and "walk you through" the code.

The *Cyber Classroom* also provides navigational aids including extensive hyperlinking. The *Cyber Classroom* is browser based, so it remembers recent sections you have visited and allows you to move forward or backward among these sections. The thousands of index entries are hyperlinked to their text occurrences. You can search for a term using the "find" feature and the *Cyber Classroom* locates its occurrences throughout the text. The Table of Contents entries are "hot"—so clicking a chapter name takes you to that chapter.

Students tell us that they particularly like the fact that solutions to about half the exercises in the book are included with the *Cyber Classroom*. Studying and running these extra programs is a great way for students to enhance their learning experience.

Students and professional users of our *Cyber Classrooms* tell us they like the interactivity and that the *Cyber Classroom* is an effective reference because of the extensive hyperlinking and other navigational features. We received an email from a person who said that he lives "in the boonies" and cannot take a live course at a university, so the *Cyber Classroom* was the solution to his educational needs.

Professors tell us that their students enjoy using the *Cyber Classroom*, spend more time on the course and master more of the material than in textbook-only courses. We have published (and will be publishing) many other *Cyber Classroom* and *Complete Training Course* products. For a complete list of the available and forthcoming *Cyber Classrooms* and *Complete Training Courses*, see the *Deitel*™ *Series* page at the beginning of this book or the product listing and ordering information at the end of this book. You can also visit **www.deitel.com** or **www.prenhall.com/deitel** for more information.

Acknowledgments

One of the great pleasures of writing a textbook is acknowledging the efforts of the many people whose names may not appear on the cover, but whose hard work, cooperation, friendship and understanding were crucial to the production of the book.

Several people at Deitel & Associates, Inc. devoted long hours to this project. We would like to acknowledge the efforts of our full-time Deitel & Associates, Inc. colleagues Jonathan Gadzik, Tem Nieto, Su Zhang, Kyle Lomeli, Matthew Kowalewski,　Rashmi Jayaprakash, Kate Steinbuhler, Abbey Deitel and Betsy DuWaldt.

- Jonathan Gadzik, a graduate of the Columbia University School of Engineering and Applied Science (BS in Computer Science) co-authored Chapter 1, Introduction, and Chapter 12, Java-Based Wireless Applications Development and J2ME, and contributed to Chapter 4 and the design patterns material throughout the book. He also reviewed Chapter 28, Peer-to-Peer Applications.

- Tem Nieto, a graduate of the Massachusetts Institute of Technology, is Director of Product Development at Deitel & Associates. Tem teaches XML, Java, Internet and Web, C, C++ and Visual Basic seminars and works with us on textbook writing, course development and multimedia-authoring efforts. He is co-author with us of *Internet & World Wide Web How to Program (Second Edition), XML How to Program, Perl How to Program* and *Visual Basic 6 How to Program*. In *Advanced Java 2 Platform How to Program, First Edition* Tem updated Chapters 5, 6, 8 and 12 of *XML How to Program* for inclusion as Appendices A–D—Creating Markup with XML, XML Document Type Definitions, XML Document Object Model (DOM) and XSL (Extensible Stylesheet Language Transformations)—respectively.

- Su Zhang, a graduate of McGill University with a Masters in Computer Science, co-authored Chapters 22, 23, 24 and 25—Jini, JavaSpaces, Jiro and JMX, respectively.

- Kyle Lomeli, a graduate of Oberlin College in Computer Science co-authored Chapters 24 and 25 (JMX and Jiro). He contributed to Chapter 3, MVC; Chapter 7, Security; Chapter 13, RMI and Chapter 23, JavaSpaces, and he reviewed Chapter 12.

- Matthew Kowalewski, a graduate of Bentley College with a major in Accounting Information Systems and Director of Wireless Development at Deitel & Associates, Inc., contributed to Chapter 12.

- Rashmi Jayaprakash, a graduate of Boston University with a major in Computer Science, co-authored Appendix I, Unicode.

- Kate Steinbuhler, a graduate of Boston College with majors in English and Communications, co-authored Appendix H, Career Opportunities, and managed the permissions process.

- Abbey S. Deitel, a graduate of Carnegie Mellon University with a BS in Industrial Management and President of Deitel & Associates, Inc., co-authored Chapter 7, Security.

- Betsy DuWaldt, a graduate of Metropolitan State College of Denver with a degree in Technical Communications (Writing and Editing Emphasis) and a minor in Computer Information Systems, is Editorial Director at Deitel & Associates, Inc. She co-authored the Preface, helped prepare the manuscript for publication and edited the index.

We would like to thank the participants in our Deitel & Associates, Inc. College Internship Program.[2]

- Chris Henson, a Masters student at Brandeis University (Computer Science), co-authored Chapter 6, JavaBeans Component Model, and Chapter 29, Web Services. He contributed to the accessibility section of Chapter 2, reviewed Chapters 21

---

2. The *Deitel & Associates, Inc. College Internship Program* offers a limited number of salaried positions to Boston-area college students majoring in Computer Science, Information Technology, Marketing, English or Technical Writing. Students work at our corporate headquarters in Sudbury, Massachusetts full-time in the summers and part-time during the academic year. Full-time positions are available to college graduates. For more information about this competitive program, please contact Abbey Deitel at **deitel@deitel.com** and check our Web site, **www.deitel.com**.

and 22, 23, 25 and Appendix I and applied technical reviews to Chapters 2, 6, 8, 14, 15 and 29.

- Audrey Lee, a Senior at Wellesley College in Computer Science and Mathematics, co-authored Chapter 16, Java Message Service and contributed to Chapters 7, 13, 18 and Appendices F and I.

- Jeffrey Hamm, a Sophomore in Computer Science at Northeastern University, co-authored Chapter 21, Appendix E and Appendix G, Java Native Interface (JNI).

- Varun Ganapathi, a Sophomore in Computer Science and Electrical Engineering at Cornell University, co-authored Chapter 28, contributed to Chapter 12 and implemented the i-mode and WML clients in the Chapter 18 case study.

- Sasha Devore, a graduate of Massachusetts Institute of Technology in Electrical Engineering and Electrical Science, 2001, co-authored Chapter 4, Graphics Programming with Java 2D and Java 3D.

- A. James O'Leary, a sophomore in Computer Science and Psychology at Rensselaer Polytechnic Institute, co-authored Chapter 7, Security.

- Susan Warren, a Junior in Computer Science at Brown University, worked on the Instructor's Manual and ancillary materials for Chapters 9 and 10.

- Eugene Izumo, a Sophomore in Computer Science at Brown University, worked on the Instructor's Manual and ancillary materials for Chapters 9 and 10.

- Vincent He, a Senior in Management and Computer Science at Boston College, worked on the Instructor's Manual for Chapter 8.

- Christina Carney, a Senior in Psychology and Business at Framingham State College helped prepare the Preface and the bibliography for several chapters.

- Amy Gips, a Sophomore in Marketing and Finance at Boston College, co-authored Appendix F, Java Community Process, and researched URLs for several chapters. Amy also researched the quotes for the entire book and helped prepare the Preface.

- Fabian Morgan (a Summer 2000 intern from MIT) wrote the initial versions of the examples for Chapters 5, 8, 14, 15 and the Enterprise Java case study in Chapters 17–20.

- Josh Gould (a Summer 2000 intern from Clark University) worked on Chapters 9 and 10.

We also would like to thank two business colleagues who contributed to the book.

- Carlos Valcarcel co-authored Chapters 26 and 27. Carlos is an independent OO/Java/CORBA architect with EinTech, Inc., in New York. Carlos has been working with Java since November 1995 and CORBA since mid-1996. His clients range from investment banks and insurance companies to software vendors. Please feel free to send questions and comments to Carlos at **carlos@eintech.com**. Carlos would like to thank his wife Becky and daughter Lindley for their patience and understanding during the writing of these two chapters.

"If there is a bright center to the universe, the two of you are it."

- Kelby Zorgdrager served as a technical consultant on Chapter 22, Jini, Chapter 23, JavaSpaces, Chapter 24, JMX and Chapter 25, Jiro. He has been working with Java since its beginning stages of JDK 1.0. Over the past 5 years, Kelby has worked for Sun Microsystems as a Java Instructor where he developed course materials and presented to over 3500 students worldwide. During Kelby's last year at Sun, he worked as a Software Engineer on the development of the Jiro Technology. Kelby has spoken at internationally recognized industry conferences, including JavaOne. Currently, Kelby is working as the Director of Architecture for **eCarCredit.com**, where he uses Java to create cutting-edge technological solutions for the Auto Finance Industry. In Kelby's spare time, he provides independent consulting services, and enjoys spending time with his wife Beth, daughter Aubreigh, and Winston the St. Bernard. Kelby can be reached at **advanced_java@zorgdrager.org**.

We also would like to thank those people who helped us obtain commercial application server software for the CD that accompanies this book and those people who helped us complete the deployment instructions for our Deitel Bookstore case study on the three most popular application servers. Our thanks to Katherine Barnhisel of BEA Systems; Sheila Richardson, John Botsford, Jason McGee and Kevin Vaughan of IBM; and Holly Sharp, Heather Sutherland, Sharada Achanta, Patrick Dorsey and Deepak Balakrishna of iPlanet.

We are fortunate to have been able to work on this project with the talented and dedicated team of publishing professionals at Prentice Hall. We especially appreciate the extraordinary efforts of our computer science editor, Petra Recter and her boss—our mentor in publishing—Marcia Horton, Editor-in-Chief of Prentice-Hall's Engineering and Computer Science Division. Vince O'Brien and Camille Trentacoste did a marvelous job handling production.

The *Advanced Java 2 Platform Multimedia Cyber Classroom* was developed in parallel with *Advanced Java 2 Platform How to Program*. We sincerely appreciate the "new media" insight, savvy and technical expertise of our e-media editor-in-chief, mentor and friend Mark Taub. He and our e-media editor, Karen McLean, did a remarkable job bringing the *Advanced Java 2 Platform Multimedia Cyber Classroom* to publication under a tight schedule. Michael Ruel did a marvelous job as Cyber Classroom project manager.

We owe special thanks to the creativity of Tamara Newnam Cavallo (**smart_art@earthlink.net**) who did the art work for our programming tips icons and the cover. She created the delightful bug creature who shares with you the book's programming tips. Barbara Deitel contributed the bugs' names on the front cover.

We sincerely appreciate the efforts of our reviewers:

Jeff Allen (Sun Microsystems)
Dibyendu Baksi (Sun Microsystems)
Tim Boudreau (Sun Microsystems)
Paul Byrne (Sun Microsystems)
Onno Kluyt (Sun Microsystems)
Peter Korn (Sun Microsystems)
Petr Kozel (Sun Microsystems)
Jon Nyquist (Sun Microsystems)
Tomas Pavek (Sun Microsystems)

Martin Ryzl (Sun Microsystems)
Davanum Srinivas (JNI-FAQ Manager, Sun Microsystems)
Brandon Taylor (Sun Microsystems)

Vicki Allan (Utah State University)
Javaid Aslam (Analyst/Application Developer, Tektronix)
Henry Balen (CORBA author)
Kathy Barshatzky (**Javakathy.com**)
Don Benish (Ben-Cam Intermedia)
Keith Bigelow (Lutris)
Darrin Bishop (Levi, Ray and Shoup, Inc.)
Ron Braithwaite (Nutriware)
Carl Burnham (Southpoint)
John Conley (DeVry Institute)
Charles Costarella (Antelope Valley College)
Jonathan Earl (Technical Training Consultants)
Jesse Glick (NetBeans)
Ken Gilmore (Amdocs, Inc.)
Jason Gordon (Verizon)
Christopher Green (Colorado Springs Technical Consultants)
Michele Guy (XOR)
Deborah Hooker (Mnemosyne Consulting)
Elizabeth Kallman (Los Alamos National Library)
Salvi Karuppaswamy (EDS)
Jodi Krochalis (Compuware)
Anthony Levensalor (Compuware)
Derek Lane (President of Gunslinger Software and Consulting, Inc.)
Rick Loek (Callidus Software)
Ashish Makhijani (Senior Analyst, Programmer)
Paul McLachlan (Compuware)
Randy Meyers (NetCom)
Paul Monday (Imation)
Steven Newton (Lead Programmer/Analyst, Standard Insurance Company)
Victor Peters (NextStepEducation)
Bryan Plaster (Valtech)
Brian Pontarelli (Consultant)
Srikanth Raju (Staff Engineer, Sun Microsystems)
Robin Rowe (**MovieEditor.com**)
Michael Schmaltz (Accenture)
Joshua Sharff (Joshua Sharff Associates)
Dan Shellman (Software Engineer)
Jon Siegel (OMG)
Uma Subbiah (Unigraphics)
Arun Taksali (jataayusoft)
Vadim Tkachenko (Sera Nova)
Kim Topley (Author of *Core Java Foundation Classes* and *Core Swing: Advanced Programming*, both published by Prentice Hall)
John Varghese (University of Rochester)
Xinju Wang (Emerald Solutions)
Karen Wieslewski (Titan Insurance)
Jesse Wilkins (Metalinear Media)

Under a tight time schedule, they scrutinized every aspect of the text and made countless suggestions for improving the accuracy and completeness of the presentation.

We would sincerely appreciate your comments, criticisms, corrections, and suggestions for improving the text. Please address all correspondence to:

`deitel@deitel.com`

We will respond immediately. Well, that's it for now. Welcome to the exciting world of Java programming. We hope you enjoy this look at leading-edge computer applications development. Good luck!

Dr. Harvey M. Deitel
Paul J. Deitel
Sean E. Santry

About the Authors

Dr. Harvey M. Deitel, CEO of Deitel & Associates, Inc., has 40 years experience in the computing field including extensive industry and academic experience. He is one of the world's leading computer science instructors and seminar presenters. Dr. Deitel earned B.S. and M.S. degrees from the Massachusetts Institute of Technology and a Ph.D. from Boston University. He has 20 years of college teaching experience including earning tenure and serving as the Chairman of the Computer Science Department at Boston College before founding Deitel & Associates, Inc. with his son Paul J. Deitel. He is author or co-author of dozens of books and multimedia packages and is currently writing many more. With translations published in Japanese, Russian, Spanish, Italian, Basic Chinese, Traditional Chinese, Korean, French, Polish and Portuguese, the Deitel's texts have earned international recognition. Dr. Deitel has delivered professional seminars internationally to major corporations, government organizations and various branches of the military.

Paul J. Deitel, Chief Technical Officer of Deitel & Associates, Inc., is a graduate of the Massachusetts Institute of Technology's Sloan School of Management where he studied Information Technology. Through Deitel & Associates, Inc. he has delivered Internet and World Wide Web courses and programming language classes for industry clients including Sun Microsystems, EMC^2, IBM, BEA Systems, Visa International, Progress Software, Boeing, Fidelity, Hitachi, Cap Gemini, Compaq, Art Technology, White Sands Missile Range, NASA at the Kennedy Space Center, the National Severe Storm Laboratory, Rogue Wave Software, Lucent Technologies, Computervision, Cambridge Technology Partners, Adra Systems, Entergy, CableData Systems, Banyan, Stratus, Concord Communications and many other organizations. He has lectured on Java and C++ for the Boston Chapter of the Association for Computing Machinery, and has taught satellite-based courses through a cooperative venture of Deitel & Associates, Inc., Prentice Hall and the Technology Education Network. He and his father, Dr. Harvey M. Deitel, are the world's best-selling Computer Science textbook authors.

Sean E. Santry, Director of Software Development with Deitel & Associates, Inc., is a graduate of Boston College where he studied computer science and philosophy. At Boston College he performed original research on the application of metaphysical systems to object-oriented software design. Through Deitel & Associates, Inc. he has delivered advanced and introductory courses for industry clients including Sun Microsystems,

EMC^2, Dell, Compaq, Boeing and others. He has contributed to several Deitel publications, including *Java How to Program, Fourth Edition*; *XML How to Program*; *C++ How to Program, Third Edition*; *C How to Program, Third Edition*; *e-Business and e-Commerce How to Program* and *e-Business and e-Commerce for Managers*. Before joining Deitel & Associates, he developed e-business applications with a leading Boston-area consulting firm.

About Deitel & Associates, Inc.

Deitel & Associates, Inc. is an internationally recognized corporate training and content-creation organization specializing in Internet/World Wide Web software technology, e-business/e-commerce software technology and computer programming languages education. Deitel & Associates, Inc. is a member of the World Wide Web Consortium. The company provides courses on Internet and World Wide Web programming, object technology and major programming languages. The founders of Deitel & Associates, Inc. are Dr. Harvey M. Deitel and Paul J. Deitel. The company's clients include many of the world's largest computer companies, government agencies, branches of the military and business organizations. Through its publishing partnership with Prentice Hall, Deitel & Associates, Inc. publishes leading-edge programming textbooks, professional books, interactive CD-ROM-based multimedia *Cyber Classrooms*, *Complete Training Courses* and Web-based training courses. Deitel & Associates, Inc. and the authors can be reached via e-mail at

deitel@deitel.com

To learn more about Deitel & Associates, Inc., its publications and its worldwide corporate on-site curriculum, see the last few pages of this book and visit:

www.deitel.com

Individuals wishing to purchase Deitel books, *Cyber Classrooms*, *Complete Training Courses* and Web-based training courses can do so through

www.deitel.com

Bulk orders by corporations and academic institutions should be placed directly with Prentice Hall. See the last few pages of this book for worldwide ordering details.

The World Wide Web Consortium (W3C)

Deitel & Associates, Inc. is a member of the *World Wide Web Consortium (W3C)*. The W3C was founded in 1994 "to develop common protocols for the evolution of the World Wide Web." As a W3C member, we hold a seat on the W3C Advisory Committee (our Advisory Committee representative is our Chief Technology Officer, Paul Deitel). Advisory Committee members help provide "strategic direction" to the W3C through meetings around the world. Member organizations also help develop standards recommendations for Web technologies (such as HTML, XML and many others) through participation in W3C activities and groups. Membership in the W3C is intended for companies and large organizations. For information on becoming a member of the W3C visit **www.w3.org/Consortium/Prospectus/Joining**.

1

Introduction

Objectives

- To understand the organization of the book.
- To understand various setup issues in deploying the book's examples.
- To understand the elements of design patterns and how they are used throughout the book.
- To tour the book.

Before beginning, plan carefully.
Marcus Tullius Cicero

Things are always at their best in the beginning
Blaise Pascal

High thoughts must have high language.
Aristophanes

Our life is frittered away be detail ... Simplify, simplify
Henry Thoreau

Look with favor upon a bold beginning.
Virgil

I think I'm beginning to learn something about it.
Auguste Renoir

Outline

1.1 Introduction

Welcome to the world of advanced Java 2 Platform programming! We have worked hard to create what we hope will be an informative, entertaining and challenging learning experience for you.

The Java technologies you will learn are intended for developers and software engineers. *Advanced Java 2 Platform How to Program* presumes knowledge of either *Java How to Program: Fourth Edition* (ISBN: 0-13-034151-7) or *The Complete Java Training Course, Fourth Edition* (ISBN: 0-13-064931-7), which teach the fundamentals of Java and object-oriented programming. *Advanced Java 2 Platform How to Program* presents many advanced Java topics and introduces many new topics, using almost 40,000 lines of complete, working code and numerous illustrations to demonstrate the concepts. We integrate these technologies into substantial applications and enterprise systems that demonstrate how the pieces fit together. We call this our *Live-Code™ approach.*

We introduce technologies from the three Java editions—*Java 2 Standard Edition* (*J2SE*), *Java 2 Enterprise Edition* (*J2EE*) and *Java 2 Micro Edition* (*J2ME*). The beginning chapters of this book demonstrate several high-end concepts from J2SE (*Java How to Program, Fourth Edition* presents J2SE through the intermediate level). *Advanced Java 2 Platform How to Program* highlights many advanced features of J2EE, providing enterprise applications as examples. Finally, we introduce the exciting, leading-edge technologies of J2ME and wireless applications programming.

Object-oriented programming and design patterns are essential for building applications using the many technologies introduced in this book. These tools encourage modularity, allowing programmers to design classes and programs effectively. Design patterns in particular have proven critical to producing the substantial programs we present in this book.

Many of the book's applications integrate the *Extensible Markup Language* (*XML*), the standard for creating markup languages that describe structured data in a platform-independent manner. Everything from common Web pages to complex order-tracking and *business-to-business* (*B2B*) systems can use XML. XML's data portability complements the portability of programs built for the Java 2 Platform. XML's capabilities for describing data enable systems built with disparate technologies to share data without concerns for binary compatibility, which is key to developing interoperable distributed systems in Java. We assume knowledge of XML and Java's XML APIs. However, Appendices A–D also provide an introduction to XML and Java's XML APIs for those of you who are not yet familiar with these topics. It is highly recommended that you read these appendices first, if you are not already familiar with XML.

As you read this book, you may want to refer to our Web site `www.deitel.com` for updates and additional information on the cutting-edge technologies you will be learning.

1.2 Architecture of the Book

There are several broad technology categories that comprise *Advanced Java 2 Platform How to Program*. Many of these technologies are inter-related. We begin with a discussion of these categories and an overview of the architecture of the book. The chapters can be grouped into several advanced topics—advanced GUI and graphics, distributed systems, Web services, Enterprise Java and XML technologies.

1.2.1 Advanced GUI, Graphics and JavaBeans

Chapters 2–6
Graphical user interfaces help users interact effectively and efficiently with applications. When creating substantial client applications, it is important to create simple and attractive user interfaces that enable users to work with your application in an intuitive and convenient manner. Java's Swing API provides graphical user interface components common to many windowed applications and platforms. *Java How to Program, Fourth Edition* provides an introduction to GUI concepts with Swing. In Chapter 2 of *Advanced Java 2 Platform How to Program*, we introduce several more advanced Swing components and use them to create substantial applications such as a Web browser with a multiple-document interface. We also introduce Java's capabilities for building applications for global deployment (through *internationalization)* and for building accessible applications for people with disabilities (using the *Accessibility* APIs).

A fundamental theme in *Advanced Java 2 Platform How to Program* is the importance of design patterns for building object-oriented systems. We use several design patterns when building the programming examples in this book. This chapter (Section 1.5) introduces design patterns, discusses why they are important and lists by chapter those design patterns we use in the book. Chapter 3 introduces the *Model-View-Controller* (*MVC*) architecture, which is based on several design patterns. This widely applicable architecture separates the presentation of data (e.g., a bar-chart showing bank-account information) from the underlying data representation (e.g., tables in a database) and the control logic for those data (e.g., event handlers for buttons and text fields in a user interface). In Chapter 3, we discuss the MVC architecture and its implementation in the Swing API. In later chapters, we revisit the MVC architecture and use it to build substantial Enterprise Java applications.

In Chapter 4, we present Java's support for graphics. Java provides the Java 2D™ API for creating two-dimensional graphics and the Java 3D™ API for creating three-dimensional, virtual worlds. We introduce and demonstrate these APIs and provide examples including a three-dimensional game.

Chapter 5 contains a substantial case study—a Java 2D drawing application with design patterns—in which we present a complex drawing program as a capstone for the advanced GUI portion of the book. Using MVC and several other design patterns, and the capabilities of Java's Swing components and Java 2D, our drawing application provides several types of shapes, various colors, gradients, image capabilities and more. Users can choose multiple views for a drawing, including a zoomed detail view.

The *JavaBeans component model* enables developers to "componentize" their applications, making those applications more flexible and the application components more reusable. We introduce JavaBeans (often called simply *beans*) in the context of an animation application in Chapter 6. JavaBeans allow programmers to create components for building applications; programmers called *component assemblers* then can assemble these components, along with existing components, to create applications, applets or even new beans. In fact, most of the GUI components presented in earlier chapters are JavaBeans.

1.2.2 Distributed Systems

Chapters 13, 22–28
When creating substantial applications, often it is more efficient, or even necessary, for concurrent tasks to be performed on different computers. Distributed systems technologies enable applications to execute across several computers on a network. For a distributed system to function correctly, application components executing on different computers throughout a network must be able to communicate with one another. *Advanced Java 2 Platform How to Program* presents several technologies for building distributed systems.

Chapter 13 introduces Remote Method Invocation (RMI), which allows Java objects located on different computers or executing in different virtual machines to interact as if they were on the same computer or in the same virtual machine. Each object invokes methods on the other objects and RMI handles the *marshalling* (i.e., collecting and packaging) of arguments and return values passed between *remote objects*. We present several RMI examples, including a distributed chat application.

Java also provides higher-level APIs for building distributed systems, including Jini and JavaSpaces. Jini (Chapter 22) enables devices or software programs on a LAN to interoperate without the need to install special device drivers, and with reduced administrative overhead. Jini provides true "plug-and-play" support for devices—just plug a printer into a network and that printer's services become available to everyone on that network. JavaSpaces is a Jini service that provides a simple but powerful API for building distributed systems. We demonstrate JavaSpaces technology by building a distributed image processing application.

As networks grow in complexity and as companies depend on those networks more heavily for conducting business, network management grows in importance. The Java Management Extensions (JMX, Chapter 24) and Jiro (Chapter 25) are two complementary technologies for building distributed network management applications in Java.

In Chapters 26–27, we introduce *CORBA*—the *Common Object Request Broker Architecture*. CORBA allows programs written in various languages, with varying implementations running in disparate locations, to communicate with each other as easily as if they were in the same process address space. In these chapters, we introduce the fundamentals of CORBA and compare CORBA with other distributed-systems technologies, such as RMI. We also introduce *RMI-IIOP*, which enables RMI to interoperate with CORBA.

In Chapter 28, we discuss fundamental concepts of peer-to-peer (P2P) applications, where each application performs both client and server functions, thus distributing processing and information across many computers. We present two different implementations of a P2P instant-messaging application. The first implementation uses Jini technology and the second uses multicast sockets and RMI.

1.2.3 Web Services

Chapters 9–12, 29
The popularity of the Web and its importance for conducting business have exploded in recent years. The field of *Web services* is concerned with building services that enable information sharing, commerce and other interactions between businesses, between businesses and consumers, etc., using standard Web protocols. Web services have come about through an evolution of existing Web technologies, such as HTML forms, and enterprise technologies, such as messaging and Electronic Document Interchange (EDI) systems. Web services rely upon existing protocols and standards.

Chapter 9 introduces *servlets*. Servlets can generate documents dynamically (e.g., XHTML documents) to send to clients in response to requests for information. Chapter 10 introduces *Java Server Pages (JSP)*, which also deliver dynamic content to clients. JSPs dynamically serve Web content by using *scriptlets* and JavaBeans components in the context of a document. These documents are translated into servlets by the *JSP container*—i.e., the server application responsible for handling requests for JSPs. Chapter 11 presents a case study that serves as a capstone to the technology presented in Chapters 9 and 10. The case study integrates JavaBeans, servlets, JSPs, XML and XSLT to create an online bookstore.

Several new technologies, such as the *Wireless Application Protocol (WAP)*, *Wireless Markup Language (WML)*, *i-mode* and Java 2 Micro Edition (J2ME) have emerged for use with wireless devices. Chapter 12 introduces these wireless technologies, and uses them to construct a three-tier application that uses servlets and XML to deliver content to several wireless devices.

Chapter 29 introduces *Web services*—applications that expose public interfaces usable by other applications over the Web. Web services are accessible through HTTP and other Web protocols, and communicate with XML-based messages. Directory services enable clients to perform lookups to discover available Web services. The *Simple Object Access Protocol (SOAP)* uses XML to provide communication in many Web services. SOAP allows applications to make remote procedure calls to a Web service's public methods. In this chapter, we implement a weather service that provides local forecasts from the National Weather Service, using SOAP.

1.2.4 Enterprise Java

Chapters 7, 8, 14–16, 21

Java has become enormously popular for building enterprise applications. Sun originally conceived of Java as a programming language for building small programs embedded in Web pages; since its inception, Java has grown into an industrial strength, enterprise-development language. At the 2001 JavaOne conference, Sun Microsystems announced that over 96% of enterprise application servers support the Java 2 Enterprise Edition.

Security is a primary concern for Java applications of all types, including enterprise applications. In Chapter 7 we introduce the fundamentals of security, including cryptography, digital signatures, authentication, authorization and public-key infrastructure. We also introduce Java's *sandbox security model*, the *Java Cryptography Extensions* (*JCE*), the *Java Secure Sockets Extensions* (*JSSE*) and the J*ava Authentication and Authorization Services* (*JAAS*).

An integral part of powerful software applications is the storage, retrieval and display of data. Substantial amounts of data are organized and stored in databases. Programmers often need to interact with databases to update or retrieve information. Chapter 8 introduces Java Database Connectivity (JDBC) for manipulating databases. We present examples that interact with the Cloudscape database management system from Informix Software. Cloudscape is available for download at **www.cloudscape.com**.

Business logic forms the core functionality of an enterprise application. Business logic is responsible for implementing the complex business rules that businesses require for transaction and information processing. In Chapter 14, we introduce the *Enterprise Java-Bean* (*EJB*) component model for building enterprise application business logic. In particular, we discuss *session EJBs* for business logic, and *distributed transactions*, which enable EJBs to work across multiple databases and still maintain data integrity. In Chapter 15, we present *entity EJBs*, which enable developers to build and object-based layer for accessing information in long-term storage, such as a database.

Enterprise applications require extensive services and support at runtime for accessing databases, enabling distributed transactions, maintaining performance, etc. Application servers provide a rich runtime environment for enterprise application components. In Chapter 21, we introduce the three most popular commercial application servers—BEA's WebLogic, IBM's WebSphere and the iPlanet Application Server. We also provide complete instructions for deploying an enterprise-application case study on BEA's WebLogic and IBM's WebSphere.

1.2.5 Enterprise Case Study

Chapters 17–20

Chapters 17–20 present a capstone application for the Enterprise Java topics presented in *Advanced Java 2 Platform How to Program*—an Enterprise Java case study that integrates many Java technologies into a substantial 10,000 lines of code online bookstore application. In this case study, we build the Deitel Bookstore enterprise application using Enterprise JavaBeans with container-managed persistence, servlets, RMI-IIOP, XML, XSLT, XHTML, WML and cHTML. A fundamental feature of this example is that the bookstore uses XML and XSLT to provide support for virtually any type of client, including standard

Web browsers and mobile devices, such as cell phones. The modular, extensible architecture enables developers to implement support for additional client types simply by providing appropriate XSLT documents that translate XML documents into content appropriate for those client types. The Deitel Bookstore case study also demonstrates the Model-View-Controller (MVC) architecture in the context of an Enterprise Java application.

1.2.6 XML

Appendices A–D

Many examples throughout *Advanced Java 2 Platform How to Program* use XML. As a platform-independent language for creating markup languages, XML integrates well with Java applications. Unlike HTML, with which Web designers use to format information for display, XML provides structure and semantics for application data, but it does not format data. Developers can create XML grammars that define the structure for data and make those data interoperable with other applications. The *Java API for XML parsing (JAXP)* provides the Java 2 Platform with a common API for manipulating XML parsers and XML data across platforms. The *Document Object Model, Level 2 API (DOM)* is backed by the World Wide Web Consortium (W3C) as a standard API for building and manipulating XML documents. Using this API, developers can leverage the cross-platform capabilities of Java and XML to build powerful distributed systems.

We introduce the basics of XML in Appendix A, Creating XML Markup. Appendix B introduces Document Type Definitions (DTDs) for defining standard document structures against which XML parsers can validate XML documents. DTDs are crucial for building XML documents that interoperate across many applications. Appendix C introduces the Document Object Model (DOM) API and its use in the Java API for XML Processing (JAXP). Appendix D introduces Extensible Stylesheet Language Transformations (XSLT), which is an XML grammar for transforming XML documents into other XML documents. We use XSLT in several examples to transform raw XML data into appropriate markup for Web clients, such as standard Web browsers and cell phones.

1.3 Tour of the Book

In this section, we include walkthroughs of each chapter and outline the many Java technologies discussed in *Advanced Java 2 Platform How to Program*. There will be terms in these sections that are unfamiliar to you—they will be defined in the chapters of the book. Many chapters end with an Internet and World Wide Web Resources section that provides a listing of Web sites you should visit to enhance your knowledge of the technologies discussed in that chapter. You may also want to visit the Web sites **www.deitel.com** and **www.prenhall.com/deitel** to keep informed of the latest information, book errata and additional teaching and learning resources.

Chapter 1—Introduction

This chapter overviews the technologies presented in *Advanced Java 2 Platform How to Program* and introduces the architecture of the book—advanced GUI and graphics, distributed systems, Web services, Enterprise Java and XML technologies. We include a tour of the book with a brief overview of each chapter. We provide installation, and execution instructions for the examples in this book. We also discuss design patterns and how we use them to architect our examples.

Chapter 2—Advanced Swing Graphical User Interface Components
Advanced Swing components enable developers to build functionally rich user interfaces. The Swing graphical user interface components were introduced with the Java Foundation Classes (JFC) as a downloadable extension to Java 1.1 and became standard in the Java 2 Platform. Swing provides a much richer set of GUI components than Java's original Abstract Windowing Toolkit (AWT), including advanced features such as a pluggable look-and-feel, lightweight component rendering and an enriched component set. This chapter introduces Swing components with which you can enrich your application GUIs.

Many of the examples in this chapter use the **JEditorPane** class extensively, which is capable of rendering styled content, such as HTML pages. We also present the first of our inline design patterns discussions. Swing **Action**s implement the Command design pattern to build reusable user interface logic. We also introduce useful Swing components such as **JSplitPane**, **JTabbedPane** and multiple-document-interface components for organizing GUI elements. Swing provides mechanisms for building applications for multiple languages and countries, and for disabled users. Building internationalized applications ensures that applications will be ready for use around the world in many languages. Accessibility ensures that users with disabilities will be able to use applications through commonly available utilities, such as screen readers. We show how developers can use Swing to build Java applications that are accessible to users in other countries and users with disabilities.

Chapter 3—Model-View-Controller
Advanced Swing components, including the **JTree** and **JTable** components enable developers to build flexible, data-driven graphical user interfaces in Java. The *Model-View-Controller (MVC)* architecture abstracts the GUI (the *view*) from the underlying data (the *model*). A *controller* determines how the application handles user interactions, such as mouse and keyboard events. The Swing components implement a variation of the MVC architecture that combines the view and controller to form a *delegate*. For example, a **JTree** is a delegate (i.e., combined view and controller) for its **TreeModel** (the model). The **TreeModel** contains the raw data to be presented in, and modified by, the **JTree**. The **JTree** provides a visual representation of the data and processes user interactions, such as renaming nodes in the tree. The benefit of this architecture is that each component can change without requiring changes in the other components. Furthermore, several delegates, views and controllers may be associated with a single model. MVC has many uses in desktop applications, enterprise applications, simulations and other types of programs. In this chapter, we discuss MVC in general and its variant, the *delegate-model architecture*. We also introduce the Observer design pattern, which is one part of the MVC architecture. After reading this chapter, you will be able to take advantage of advanced Swing components that use the delegate-model architecture, such as **JList**, **JTable** and **JTree**.

Chapter 4—Graphics Programming with Java 2D™ and Java 3D™
The graphical features provided by the Java 2D API and the graphical user interface enhancements available in the Swing GUI components provide many tools for developing rich graphical content by incorporating line art, text and imaging in a single graphics mod-

el. Developers can use these tools to build custom graphics and images as well as visual representations of data. The Java 2D API also provides advanced capabilities for text layout and manipulation. Imaging technology in the Java 2D API allows for manipulation of fixed resolution images, and includes filters for blurring and sharpening images as well as other image-processing tools. The Java 2D API also provides support for delivering graphical content to different devices by defining a logical coordinate system that is translated appropriately for a given output device such as a printer or monitor. We also introduce the Java 3D API for developing three-dimensional, virtual worlds in Java. The Java 3D API provides technologies for manipulating 3D objects. For example, the programmer can rotate, scale and translate 3D objects. Other advanced features include applying textures to 3D objects using texture mapping and varying the lighting effects on 3D objects by changing the colors and positions of light sources. We implement an application that allows the user to manipulate a 3D object with the mouse. We then present a substantial 3D game in which the user navigates a shape through a 3D scene full of "flying" obstacles. The goal of the game is to move this shape to a specific target point without colliding with any of the moving obstacles.

Chapter 5—Case Study: Java 2D Drawing Application with Design Patterns

The case study in this chapter implements a substantial Java application that integrates the many Java features and techniques presented in Chapters 2–4. We present a graphics application case study that uses the GUI capabilities of Chapters 2 and 3 and the two-dimensional graphics capabilities of Chapter 4, as well as the flexible capabilities of XML. The case study emphasizes the Model-View-Controller architecture (Chapter 3) to provide multiple views of a single drawing such as a detail view and a complete view. A multiple document interface (Chapter 2) allows users to modify multiple drawings in parallel. Swing Actions (Chapter 2) provide reusable user-interaction logic for menu and toolbar functionality. The case study also uses the Drag-and-Drop API to enable users to move shapes between drawings and to drop JPEG images onto a drawing from the local file system. We use several design patterns including the Factory Method, Adapter State and Template Method design patterns.

Chapter 6—JavaBeans Component Model

In this chapter, we take a deeper look into developing Java components based on the *JavaBeans component architecture*. JavaBeans (*beans*) allow developers to reap the benefits of rapid application development in Java by assembling predefined software components to create powerful applications and applets. *Graphical programming and design environments* (often called *builder tools*) that support beans provide programmers with tremendous flexibility by allowing programmers to reuse existing components. A programmer can integrate these components to create applets, applications or even new beans for reuse by others. JavaBeans and other component-based technologies have led to a new type of programmer—the *component assembler*, who uses pre-built components to create richer functionality. Component assemblers do not need to know the implementation details of components, but they need to know what services the components provide. Component assemblers can make beans communicate through the beans' well-defined services (i.e., methods), typically without writing any code (the builder tool often generates code, which is sometimes hidden from the component assembler—depending on the tool). Indeed, a component assembler can create complex applications simply by "connecting the dots."

This chapter shows you how to use existing beans and how to create new beans. After studying this chapter, you will have a foundation in JavaBeans programming that will enable you to develop applications and applets rapidly using the more advanced features of integrated development environments that support beans.

Chapter 7—Security

Security is a primary concern in the development of software systems. This chapter discusses the issues associated with security and introduces Java technologies to that ensure successful, secure transactions. Among these technologies is the *Java Cryptography Extension (JCE)*, which supports *secret-key encryption* and *digital signatures*. The *Java Secure Socket Extension (JSSE)* supports the *Secure Sockets Layer (SSL)* protocol—one of the most widely used tools for securing Internet communications. JSSE provides encryption, message integrity checks and authentication of servers and clients. Java also provides the *Java Authentication and Authorization Service (JAAS)* for authenticating users and granting permissions. The basis for Java security is the *sandbox security model* in which applets and applications execute. The sandbox is a protected environment that prevents Java programs from accessing protected resources. The program must be granted specific permissions to access system resources, such as the files on a user's computer and servers on the Internet. Permissions may be granted through *policy files*.

Chapter 8—Java Database Connectivity (JDBC)

Access and storage of data are integral to creating powerful software applications. This chapter discusses Java's support of database manipulation. Today's most popular database systems are *relational databases*. We present examples using *Cloudscape 3.6.4*—a pure-Java database management system from Informix Software. Cloudscape is available free for download (for learning and development purposes) at **www.cloudscape.com** and is on the CD that accompanies this book. Java programmers communicate with databases and manipulate their data using the *Java Database Connectivity (JDBC) API*. A *JDBC driver* implements the interface to a particular database. This chapter introduces JDBC and uses it to connect to a Cloudscape database, then to manipulate its content. We use the *Structured Query Language (SQL)* to extract information from, and insert information into, a database. We then use JDBC and SQL to create an address-book application that stores, updates and deletes addresses. Several later chapters use the techniques shown in this chapter to build data-driven Web and enterprise applications.

Chapter 9—Servlets

Servlets extend the functionality of servers—typically Web servers. Servlets are effective for developing Web-based solutions that interact with databases on behalf of clients, dynamically generate custom content to be displayed by browsers, and maintain unique session information for each client. Many developers feel that servlets are the right solution for database-intensive applications that communicate with so-called *thin clients*—applications that require minimal client-side processing capability. Clients connect to the server using standard protocols, such as *HyperText Transfer Protocol (HTTP)*, available on most client platforms through Web browsers (and other applications). Thus, the application logic can be written once and reside on the server for access by clients. The *Java Servlet API* allows developers to add functionality to Web servers for handling client requests. Unlike the *Common Gateway Interface (CGI)*, in which a separate process may be started for each client request, servlets typically are threads in a single JVM process. Servlets also are reusable across Web servers and across platforms. This chapter demonstrates the Web's request/response mechanism (primarily with HTTP *get* and *post* requests), session-tracking capabilities, redirecting requests to other resources and interacting with databases through JDBC.

Chapter 10—Java Server Pages (JSP)
This chapter introduces an extension of servlet technology called *Java Server Pages (JSP)*. JSPs enable delivery of dynamically generated Web content and are used primarily for developing presentation logic in Enterprise Java applications. JSPs may contain Java code in the form of *scriptlets* and may also use JavaBeans components. *Custom tag libraries* enable Web-page designers unfamiliar with Java to enhance Web pages with powerful dynamic content and processing capabilities created by Java developers. To increase performance, each JSP is compiled into a Java Servlet—this normally occurs the first time each JSP is requested by a client. Subsequent client requests are fulfilled by the compiled servlet.

Chapter 11—Case Study: Servlets and JSP Bookstore
This chapter is a capstone for our presentation of JSPs and servlets. Here, we implement a bookstore Web application that integrates JDBC, XML, JSP and servlet technologies. We discuss additional servlet features as they are encountered in the case study. This chapter deploys the bookstore application on the J2EE 1.2.1 reference implementation application server software. The J2EE 1.2.1 reference implementation includes the Apache Tomcat JSP and servlet container. After reading this chapter, you will be able to implement a substantial distributed Web application with many components, and you will be able to deploy that application on the J2EE 1.2.1 application server.

Chapter 12—Java-Based Wireless Applications Development and J2ME
One topic of particular interest in e-business and e-commerce applications is wireless Internet technology. Wireless technology turns e-business into *m-business*, or *mobile business*. It allows you to connect to the Internet any time from almost any place. You can use it to conduct online transactions, make purchases, trade stocks and send e-mail. New technologies already enable the wireless office, where computers, phones and other office equipment are networked without cables. This chapter introduces some of the more popular wireless technologies, including WAP, i-mode and the *Java 2 Platform Micro Edition™ (J2ME)*. J2ME brings Java technology to embedded devices and consumer devices that have limited processing power and memory. J2ME includes specialized APIs for many consumer devices, including cellular phones, smart cards, Internet appliances and PDAs (personal digital assistants), such as Palm™ and PocketPC. The *K Virtual Machine*—a trimmed-down version of the Java virtual machine for consumer devices—provides the essential features for executing Java code on these devices. Using servlets and XML, we present a case study of a three-tier application that sends a game for several wireless device types.

Chapter 13—Remote Method Invocation (RMI)
This chapter introduces *Remote Method Invocation (RMI)*—a technology for building *distributed systems* in Java. Using RMI, Java objects can be located on computers across a network, yet still interact as if they resided on a single computer. Java objects can perform *lookups* to find remote objects on the network and invoke methods across a *local area net-*

work (LAN) or even the Internet. RMI allows Java-object-to-Java-object distributed communication. Once a Java object registers as being remotely accessible (i.e., it is a *remote object*), a client can "look up" that Java object and obtain a reference that allows the client to use that object remotely. The method call syntax is identical to the syntax for calling methods of other objects in the same program. RMI handles the marshalling (i.e., collecting and packaging) of data across the network; RMI also enables Java programs to transfer complete Java objects using Java's object-serialization mechanism. The programmer need not be concerned with the details of transmitting data over the network.

Chapter 14—Session Enterprise JavaBeans (EJBs) and Distributed Transactions

Enterprise JavaBeans (EJBs) enable Java developers to build robust *multi-tier applications*. In a multi-tier application the responsibilities of providing services to a *client* can be divided among multiple servers. A typical *two-tier* application consists of the *client-tier* and the *server-tier*. A *three-tier* architecture often makes use of an *application server* as a middle-tier between the *client Web browser* and a *database server*. Enterprise JavaBeans provide a framework for building middle-tier business-logic implementations. Using RMI and *EJB Containers*, Enterprise JavaBeans also allow for business logic to be distributed across a network. We introduce *Enterprise JavaBeans (EJBs)*, which provide a component model for building business logic in enterprise Java applications. We discuss *session EJBs* in their two forms: *stateful* and *stateless*. We demonstrate how to develop both stateless and stateful session EJBs. We also introduce EJB support for *distributed transactions*, which help to ensure data integrity across databases and across application servers. We show how to build EJBs that take advantage of J2EE's distributed transaction support to update data across multiple databases atomically.

Chapter 15—Entity Enterprise JavaBeans (EJBs)

This chapter continues our discussion of Enterprise JavaBeans with an introduction to *entity Enterprise JavaBeans*. Unlike session EJBs, entity EJBs store data in long-term storage, such as in a database. Entity EJBs provide an object-oriented representation of persistent data, such as data stored in an RDBMS or legacy application. Entity EJBs can be used to build powerful and flexible data applications. There are two types of entity EJBs—those that use *bean-managed persistence* and those that use *container-managed persistence*. Entity EJBs that use bean-managed persistence implement code for storing and retrieving data from the persistent data sources they represent. For example, an entity EJB that uses bean-managed persistence might use the JDBC API to store and retrieve data in a relational database. Entity EJBs that use container-managed persistence rely on the EJB container to implement the data-access calls to their persistent data sources. The developer must supply information about the persistent data source when deploying the EJB. This chapter provides a demonstration of both types of entity EJBs.

Chapter 16—Java Message Service (JMS)

The *Java Message Service (JMS)* provides an API for integrating enterprise Java applications with *message-oriented middleware (MOM)* systems. Message-oriented middleware enables applications to communicate by sending messages to one another. Message-oriented middleware is a popular technology for building loosely coupled applications. This chapter introduces the two basic messaging system models—*point-to-point* and *publish/subscribe*. We demonstrate Java's interfaces for both of these models. We also provide an introduction to *message-driven EJBs*—a new feature of J2EE version 1.3.

Chapter 17—E-Business Case Study: Architectural Overview

The technologies that comprise the Java 2 Enterprise Edition (J2EE) enable developers to build robust, scalable enterprise applications. In this case study, we build an e-business application using several features of J2EE, including servlets, Enterprise JavaBeans, XML and XSLT. We also integrate wireless technology, including WAP/WML and i-mode/cHTML. In this chapter, we present an overview of the Deitel Bookstore case study architecture, which uses the MVC design pattern in an enterprise application context. In the following chapters, we present the controller logic implementation with servlets (Chapter 18) and the business logic and data abstraction implementation with EJBs (Chapters 19 and 20).

Chapter 18—E-Business Case Study: Presentation and Controller Logic

This chapter presents the implementation of the controller and presentation logic for the Deitel Bookstore case study. *Controller logic* in an application is responsible for handling user requests. The Java servlets in the Deitel Bookstore implement the controller logic for the application. Every user request is handled by a servlet that takes the appropriate action, based on the request type (e.g., a request to view the store catalog) and presents content to the client. We use XSLT transformations to implement the *presentation logic* for the application—the view in MVC. After invoking business-logic methods to process a client request, the servlets generate XML documents that contain content to be presented to the client. These XML documents are not specific to any particular type of client (e.g., Web browser, cell phone, etc.); they simply describe the data supplied by the business logic. An XSL transformation is applied to the XML documents to present the information to the user in the appropriate format. For example, an XSL transformation might generate an XHTML document to present to a Web browser, or a WML document to present to a WAP browser. XSL transformations are needed for each type of client the application supports. We could enable the application to support other types of clients simply by implementing additional sets of style sheets and editing a configuration file.

Chapter 19—E-Business Case Study: Business Logic Part I

In this chapter, we present the EJB business logic for the shopping-cart e-business model and entity EJBs for maintaining product inventory of the Deitel Bookstore case study. The primary goal of an on-line store application is to enable customers to purchase products. EJB business logic implements the business rules that govern this process. We implement the business logic for managing the set of products a customer wishes to purchase as a **ShoppingCart** EJB. The **ShoppingCart** EJB enforces business rules that define how products are added to the shopping cart, how shopping carts are created and how customers complete their purchases. We also present entity EJBs that represent on-line store products and orders. After reading this chapter, you will understand the use of EJBs in an e-business application context, as well as more advanced EJB topics, such as custom primary-key classes and many-to-many relationships.

Chapter 20—Enterprise Java Case Study: Business Logic Part 2

In this chapter we present the business logic for managing customers in our Deitel Bookstore case study. Maintaining information about the customers of an online store can make purchases more convenient by storing billing and shipping information on the server. The online store's marketing department may also use gathered data for distribution of marketing materials and analyzing demographic information. We also present an entity EJB that generates unique IDs for the Customer, Order and Address EJBs. Instances of these EJBs are created when new customer's register and when customer's place new orders. Relational databases require unique primary keys to maintain referential integrity and perform queries. We provide the **SequenceFactory** EJB to generate these unique IDs because not all databases can generate these primary-key values automatically.

Chapter 21—Application Servers

This chapter introduces several commercial *application servers*—an application server is software that integrates server-side logic components to allow communication between components and tiers of a software architecture. Application servers also manage the persistence, life cycles, security and various other services for logic components. We discuss the concepts behind application servers and introduce three popular commercial application servers, including BEA's WebLogic, IBM's WebSphere and the iPlanet Application Server. We present a detailed walkthrough of deploying the Deitel Bookstore application on BEA's WebLogic and IBM's WebSphere, both of which we include on the CD-ROM that accompanies this book. As we went to publication, iPlanet was about to release a new version of their application server. Please visit **www.iplanet.com/ias_deitel** to download the latest version. We also will provide complete deployment instructions for the Deitel Bookstore case study on iPlanet at our Web site, **www.deitel.com**.

Chapter 22—Jini

Jini Technology is an advanced set of network protocols, programming models and services that enable true plug-and-play interactions between networked Jini-enabled devices and software components. Jini technology allows distributed-systems developers to discover and use Jini-enabled resources on the network. The heart and soul of Jini comes from its robust and standardized network protocols, including multicast request protocol, multicast announcement protocol and unicast discovery protocol. Jini-enabled resources—or *services*—use these three protocols to locate and interact with other services. Beyond the network protocols, Jini technology provides the infrastructure required to use the protocols. This infrastructure exists as a set of classes that hide the low-level details of the protocols, allowing developers to focus on functionality instead of implementation. This chapter overviews Jini technology, introduces the network protocols that support Jini services and demonstrates Jini technology with a substantial Jini application. Later in the book (Chapter 29, Peer-to-Peer Applications and JX-TA) we use Jini to build and instant-messaging application.

Chapter 23—JavaSpaces

Objects that take part in distributed systems must be able to communicate with one another and share information. The *JavaSpaces service* is a Jini service that implements a simple, high-level architecture for building distributed systems using a distributed repository for objects and three simple operations—*read*, *write* and *take*. JavaSpaces services support transactions through the Jini transaction manager, and a notification mechanism that notifies an object when an entry that matches a given template is written to the JavaSpaces service. In the first half of this chapter, we present fundamental JavaSpaces technology concepts and use simple examples to demonstrate operations, transactions and notifications. The case study at the end of this chapter uses JavaSpaces services to build an image-processing application that distributes the work of applying filters to images across many programs on separate computers.

Chapter 24—Java Management Extensions (JMX) (on CD)

This chapter introduces the *Java Management Extensions* (*JMX*), which were developed by Sun and other network-management industry leaders to define a component framework for building intelligent network-management applications. JMX defines a three-level management architecture—*instrumentation level*, *agent level* and *manager level*. The instrumentation level allows clients to interact with objects (called *managed resources*) by exposing public interfaces to those objects. The agent level contains *JMX agents*, which enable communication between remote clients and managed resources. The manager level contains applications (clients) that access and interact with managed resources via the JMX agents. JMX also provides support for existing management protocols—such as SNMP—so developers can integrate JMX solutions with existing management applications. This chapter discusses JMX architecture and presents a case study that uses JMX capabilities to manage a network printer simulator.

Chapter 25—Jiro (on CD)

This chapter serves as an introduction to Sun's *Jiro* technology, a Java-based technology that provides infrastructure for developing management solutions for distributed resources on heterogeneous networks. Jiro is an implementation of the *Federated Management Architecture (FMA)* specification, which defines a standard protocol for communication between heterogeneous managed resources (such as devices, systems, applications). Jiro technology supports a three-tier architecture of management solutions. The top tier is the *client tier*. The client locates and communicates with the management services. The *middle tier* provides both static and dynamic management services. The *bottom tier* consists of the heterogeneous managed resources. Jiro is a complementary technology to JMX and can be used to build management solutions. The chapter concludes with a similar case study to the JMX case study presented in Chapter 24.

Chapter 26—Common Object Request Broker Architecture (CORBA): Part 1 (on CD)

In this chapter, we introduce the *Common Object Request Broker Architecture (CORBA)*. CORBA is an industry-standard, high-level distributed object framework for building powerful and flexible service-oriented applications. We investigate the essential details of CORBA as defined in the *Object Management Group (OMG)* specifications. We discuss the *Object Request Broker (ORB)*—the core of the CORBA infrastructure—and describe how it makes CORBA a powerful distributed object framework. We discuss the *Java Interface Definition Language (JavaIDL)*—the official mapping of Java to CORBA. Livecode examples demonstrate how to write CORBA-compliant distributed code using Java. Both client-side and server-side JavaIDL are demonstrated. A feature of the chapter is a case study that implements the Deitel Messenger application using CORBA.

Chapter 27—Common Object Request Broker Architecture (CORBA): Part 2 (on CD)

This chapter continues the discussion of CORBA. We introduce the Dynamic Invocation Interface as well as CORBA services, including the Naming, Security, Object Transaction and Persistent State services. The discussion continues with a comparison of RMI and CORBA; we also introduce RMI-IIOP, used to integrate RMI with CORBA. Finally, we present an alternate implementation of the Deitel Messenger application using RMI-IIOP.

Chapter 28—Peer-to-Peer Applications and JXTA

Instant-messaging applications and document-sharing systems such as AOL Instant Messenger™ and Gnutella have exploded in popularity, transforming the way users interact with one another over networks. In a *peer-to-peer (P2P) application*, each node performs both client and server functions. Such applications distribute processing responsibilities and information to many computers, thus reclaiming otherwise wasted computing power and storage space, and eliminating central points of failure. In this chapter, we introduce the fundamental concepts of peer-to-peer applications. Using Jini (Chapter 22), RMI (Chapter 13) and multicast sockets, we present two peer-to-peer application case studies of instant-messaging systems. The first implementation uses Jini and RMI, and the second uses multicast sockets and RMI. Finally, we introduce JXTA (short for "juxtapose")—a new open-source technology from Sun Microsystems™ that defines common protocols for implementing peer-to-peer applications.

Chapter 29—Introduction to Web Services with SOAP

Interoperability, or seamless communication and interaction between different software systems, is a primary goal of many businesses and organizations that rely heavily on computers and electronic networks. This chapter introduces *Web services* with *Simple Object Access Protocol (SOAP)*, a protocol designed to address this issue. Web services can be Web accessible applications, such as Web pages with dynamic content. More specifically, Web services expose public interfaces for Web-based applications to use. SOAP is a protocol that uses XML to make remote-procedure calls over HTTP to provide interoperability between disparate Web-based applications.

Appendix A—Creating Markup with XML (on CD)

XML is enormously important in *Advanced Java 2 Platform How to Program* and is integrated into examples throughout the book. We have included a substantial introduction to XML in Appendices A–D. Appendix A introduces the fundamentals of XML. We discuss the properties of the XML character set, called *Unicode*—the standard aimed at providing a flexible character set for all the world's languages. (Appendix I introduces Unicode.) We provide a brief overview of *parsers*—programs that process XML documents and their data. We also overview the requirements for a *well-formed document* (i.e., a document that is syntactically correct). We discuss *elements*, which hold data in XML documents. Several elements can have the same name (resulting in *naming collisions*); we introduce *namespaces*, which differentiate these elements to avoid these collisions.

Appendix B—XML Document Type Definitions (on CD)

A *Document Type Definition (DTD)* is a structural definition for an XML document, specifying the type, order, number and attributes of the elements in an XML document as well as other information. By defining the structure of an XML document, a DTD reduces the validation and error-checking work of the application using the document. We discuss well-formed and valid documents (i.e., documents that conform to a DTD). This appendix shows how to specify different element and attribute types, values and defaults that describe the structure of the XML document.

Appendix C—XML Document Object Model (DOM) (on CD)

The W3C *Document Object Model (DOM)* is an API for XML that is platform and language independent. The DOM API provides a standard API (i.e., methods, objects, etc.) for manipulating XML-document contents. The *Java API for XML Processing (JAXP)* provides DOM support for Java programs. XML documents are hierarchically structured, so the DOM represents XML documents as tree structures. Using DOM, programs can modify the content, structure and formatting of documents dynamically. This appendix examines several important DOM capabilities, including the ability to retrieve data, insert data and replace data. We also demonstrate how to create and traverse documents using the DOM.

Appendix D—XSLT: Extensible Stylesheet Language Transformations (on CD)

XSL was designed to manipulate the rich and sophisticated data contained in an XML document. XSL has two major functions: formatting XML documents and transforming them into other data formats such as XHTML, Rich Text Format (RTF), etc. In this appendix, we discuss the subset of XSL called XSLT. XSLT uses XPath—a language of expressions for accessing portions of XML documents—to match nodes for transforming an XML document into another text document. We use JAXP—which includes XSLT support—in our examples. An XSL stylesheet contains *templates* with which elements and attributes can be matched. New elements and attributes can be created to facilitate a transformation.

Appendix E—Downloading and Installing J2EE (on CD)

We use the Java 2 Enterprise Edition extensively in this book to create substantial enterprise applications. This appendix provides instructions for downloading and installing Sun's reference implementation of the J2EE.

Appendix F—Java Community Process (JCP) (on CD)

This appendix provides an overview of the *Java Community Processes (JCP)*, which Sun Microsystems started in 1998. The JCP (**www.jcp.org**) allows Java individuals, organizations and corporations to participate in the development of new technologies and APIs for the Java Platform. Sun has integrated a number of technologies developed through the Java Community Process into the Java 2 Platform Software Development Kits, including the XML parsing specification.

Appendix G—Java Native Interface (JNI) (on CD)

The *Java Native Interface (JNI)* allows programmers to access pre-built applications and *libraries* written in other languages. JNI allows programmers to work in Java without requiring developers to rebuild existing libraries. JNI can be useful in time-critical applications—programmers may write a piece of the application in assembly code and link this program with Java to provide better performance. In this appendix, we explain how to integrate Java with C++ libraries. Included are the most common uses and functions of JNI. We show how Java programs can call *native* functions stored in compiled libraries, and how native code can access Java objects, methods and member variables from C++. Understanding these examples requires familiarity with C++.

Appendix H—Career Opportunities (on CD)

The Internet presents valuable resources and services for job seekers and employers. Automatic search features allow employees to scan the Web for open positions. Employers also can find job candidates using the Internet. This greatly reduces the amount of time spent preparing and reviewing resumes, as well as travel expenses for distance recruiting and interviewing. In this chapter, we explore career services on the Web from the perspectives of job seekers and employers. We introduce comprehensive job sites, industry-specific sites (including site geared specifically for Java and wireless programmers) and contracting opportunities.

Appendix I—Unicode (on CD)

This appendix introduces the *Unicode Standard*—a character-set-encoding standard that facilitates the production and distribution of software. As computer systems evolved worldwide, computer vendors developed numeric representations of character sets and special symbols for the local languages in different countries. In some cases, different representations were developed for the same languages. Such disparate character sets made communication between computer systems difficult. XML and XML-derived languages, such as WML, support the *Unicode Standard*, which defines a single character set with unique numeric values for characters and special symbols for most of the world's languages. In this appendix, we discuss the Unicode Standard and the *Unicode Consortium* (**www.unicode.org**)—a non-profit organization that maintains the Unicode Standard.

1.4 Running Example Code

Many example programs in *Advanced Java 2 Platform How to Program* are quite complex and require special software to execute. For example, Chapters 17–20 present a J2EE case study that requires an application server, which provides a runtime environment and services for an enterprise application. This case study also requires a database. For this and many other programs we provide installation, deployment and execution instructions in the text and at our Web site, **www.deitel.com**.

At the time of this writing, Java 2 Enterprise Edition reference implementation version 1.2.1 was the current, released version of J2EE, and version 1.3 was in beta release. We will update installation instructions on our Web site when Sun releases version 1.3, which will include several enhancements and updates. For example, version 1.3 implements the Java messaging Service (JMS 1.0.2), J2EE Connector Technology and the Java API for XML Processing (JAXP 1.1). Java Servlets (version 2.3) implement filters, a lightweight transfer framework for requests and responses, monitoring application lifecyles and better internationalization support. The Java Server Pages implementation (version 1.2) features improved runtime support for tag libraries and translation time JSP page validation. The 1.3 Enterprise JavaBeans implementation (EJB 2.0) supports message-driven enterprise beans, interoperability between EJB containers and Container-Managed Persistence 2.0.

The examples in *Advanced Java 2 Platform How to Program* use Sun's standard naming convention for packages. We place each example in an appropriately named sub-package of package **com.deitel**. For example, the **WebBrowser** example in Chapter 2, Advanced Swing Graphical User Interfaces, contains the package declaration

```
package com.deitel.advjhtp1.gui.webbrowser;
```

The acronym **advjhtp1** in the package name indicates that this package is from *Advanced Java 2 Platform How to Program, First Edition*. This package structure requires that you compile the examples into the corresponding directory structure.

Managing packages with Java's command-line compiler and tools can be cumbersome, so we recommend that readers use an integrated development environment to simplify the development and execution of the examples and exercises in this book. We used Sun's Forte for Java Community Edition—which derives from the open-source NetBeans IDE (**www.netbeans.org**)—to develop the code examples for this book. We have included Forte for Java, Community Edition version 2.0 and the Java 2 Standard Edition SDK version 1.3.1 on the CD that accompanies this book. For tutorials on how to install Forte and how to develop applications with it, please refer to Forte's help system or the documentation at:

> **www.sun.com/forte/ffj/documentation/index.html**

Most Java development environments enable developers to load directory structures containing Java packages directly into those environments. To facilitate working with the code in this way, we have provided the complete directory structure, with source files in the appropriate locations, on the CD-ROM that accompanies this book. We recommend that you copy this directory structure from the CD-ROM that accompanies this book to your hard drive. Once you have copied the directory structure, you can load the examples according to the instructions for your development environment.

For readers who wish to use command-line tools for compiling and executing the programs in this book, we also provide separate folders with the examples for each chapter. To compile and execute the examples from the command line, copy the folder for the particular chapter or example onto your hard drive. For example, if you copy the **ch02** directory to the **C:\examples** directory on your hard drive, you can compile the **WebBrowser** example using the commands

```
cd C:\examples\ch02\fig02_01
javac -d . WebBrowser.java WebBrowserPane.java WebToolBar.java
```

The command-line argument **-d .** specifies that the Java compiler should create the resulting **.class** files in the appropriate directory structure. To execute the example, you must provide the fully qualified package name for the class that defines method **main**. For example,

```
java com.deitel.advjhtp1.gui.webbrowser.WebBrowser
```

1.5 Design Patterns

Most code examples presented in introductory Java books—such as our *Java How to Program, Fourth edition*—contain fewer than 150 lines of code. These examples do not require an extensive design process, because they use only a few classes and illustrate rudimentary programming concepts. However, most of the programs in *Advanced Java How to Program*, such as the Java 2D case study (Chapter 5), the three-tier Wireless application (Chapter 12) and the Deitel Bookstore (Chapters 17–20), are much more complex. Such large applications can require thousands of lines of code, contain many interactions among objects and involve many user interactions. For such software, it is important to employ proven, effective design strategies. Systems such as automated-teller machines and air-traffic control systems can contain millions, or even hundreds of millions, of lines of code. Effective design is absolutely crucial to the proper construction of such complex systems.

Over the past decade, the software engineering industry has made significant progress in the field of *design patterns*—proven architectures for constructing flexible and maintainable object-oriented software.[1] Using design patterns can reduce the complexity of the design process substantially. Well-designed object-oriented software allows designers to reuse and integrate pre-existing components into future systems. Design patterns benefit system developers by

- helping to construct reliable software using proven architectures and accumulated industry expertise

- promoting design and code reuse in future systems

- helping to identify common mistakes and pitfalls that occur when building systems

- helping to design systems independently of the languages in which they will ultimately be implemented

- establishing a common design vocabulary among developers

- shortening the design phase in a software-development process

The notion of using design patterns to construct software systems originated in the field of architecture. Architects use established architectural design elements, such as arches and columns, when designing buildings. Designing with arches and columns is a proven strategy for constructing sound buildings—these elements may be viewed as architectural design patterns.

1.5.1 History of Object-Oriented Design Patterns

During 1991–1994, Erich Gamma, Richard Helm, Ralph Johnson and John Vlissides—collectively known as the "gang of four"—combined their expertise in writing the book *Design Patterns, Elements of Reusable Object-Oriented Software (Addison-Wesley: 1995).* This book showed that design patterns evolved naturally through years of industry experience. John Vlissides states that "the single most important activity in pattern writing is reflection."[2] This statement implies that to create patterns, developers must reflect on, and document, their successes (and failures) when designing and implementing software systems. Developers use design patterns to capture and use this collective experience, which ultimately helps them share similar successes with other developers.

The gang-of-four book described 23 design patterns, each providing a solution to a common software design problem. The book groups design patterns into three categories—*creational*, *structural* and *behavioral design patterns*. Figure 1.1 lists these design patterns.

Creational design patterns describe techniques for instantiating objects (or groups of objects). These design patterns address issues related to the creation of objects, such as preventing a system from creating more than one object of a class (e.g., Singleton) or deferring until execution time the decision as to what types of objects are created (e.g., Factory Method). For example, suppose we are designing a 3-D drawing program, in which the user can create several 3-D geometric objects, such as cylinders, spheres, cubes, tetrahedrons, etc. At compile time, the program does not know what types of shapes the user will choose to add to the drawing. Based on user input at runtime, this program should determine the class from which to instantiate an object. If the user chooses to create a cylinder, the program should "know" to instantiate an object of class **Cylinder** and add it to the drawing.

When the user decides what geometric object to draw, the program should determine the specific subclass from which to instantiate that object.

Structural design patterns describe common ways to organize classes and objects in a system. Developers often find two problems with poor organization. The first is that classes are assigned too many responsibilities. Such classes may damage information hiding and violate encapsulation, because each class may have access to information that belongs in a separate class. The second problem is that classes can overlap responsibilities. Burdening a design with unnecessary classes wastes time for designers because they will spend hours trying to extend or modify classes that should not even exist in the system. As we will see, structural design patterns help developers avoid these problems.

Behavioral design patterns assign responsibilities to objects. These patterns also provide proven strategies to model how objects collaborate with one another and offer special behaviors appropriate for a wide variety of applications. The Observer pattern is a classic example of collaborations between objects and of assigning responsibilities to objects. For example, GUI components use this patterns to communicate with their listeners, which respond to user interactions. A listener observes state changes in a particular component by registering to handle that component's events. When the user interacts with the component, that component notifies its listeners (also known as its *observers*) that the component's state has changed (e.g., a button has been pressed).

1.5.2 Design Patterns Discussion

Design patterns are implemented in code as sets of classes and objects. To use design patterns effectively, designers must familiarize themselves with the most popular and effective patterns used in the software-engineering industry. Throughout this book, we discuss fundamental object-oriented design patterns and architectures, as well as their importance in constructing well-engineered software. We discuss each design pattern as it is used in a particular code example or case study. Figure 1.2 lists those design patterns that we used and in which chapter we used them.

Creational	Structural	Behavioral
Abstract Factory	Adapter	Chain-of-Responsibility
Builder	Bridge	Command
Factory Method	Composite	Iterator
Prototype	Decorator	Interpreter
Singleton	Facade	Observer
	Flyweight	Mediator
	Proxy	Memento
		State
		Strategy
		Template Method
		Visitor

Fig. 1.1   Gang-of-four 23 design patterns.

Chapter	Creational design patterns	Structural design patterns	Behavioral design patterns
2			Command
3			Observer
5	Factory Method Singleton	Adapter	State Template Method
7		Decorator	
12	Factory Method		Command
24		Facade	Chain-of-Responsibility

Fig. 1.2   Gang-of-four design patterns used in *Advanced Java 2 Platform How to Program.*

Note that Fig. 1.2 does not include every design pattern specified in Fig. 1.1. We used only those patterns that were appropriate for solving specific design problems that we encountered when writing the examples and case studies in this book. We now list other popular "gang-of-four" design patterns that are useful in building software, even though we did not use them when building the examples for this book.

Prototype

Sometimes, a system must make a copy of an object but will not know that object's class until run time. For example, consider a drawing program that contains several "shape" classes (e.g., classes **Line**, **Oval** and **Rectangle**, etc.) that extend an abstract super-class **Shape**. The user of this program should, at any time, be able to create, copy and paste new instances of **Shape** classes to add those shapes to drawings. The *Prototype design pattern* enables the user to accomplish this. This design pattern allows an object—called a *prototype*—to clone itself. The prototype is similar to a rubber stamp that can be used to create several identical "imprints." In software, every prototype must belong to a class that implements a common interface that allows the prototype to clone itself. For example, the Java API provides method **clone** from interface **java.lang.Cloneable**—any object from a class that implements interface **Cloneable** uses method **clone** to make a copy of itself. Specifically, method **clone** creates a copy of an object, then returns a reference to that object. In the drawing program, if we designate class **Line** as the prototype, then it should implement interface **Cloneable**. To create a new line in our drawing, we clone the **Line** prototype—this prototype will return a reference to a different **Line** object. To copy a preexisting line, we clone that **Line** object. Developers often use method **clone** to prevent altering an object through its reference, because method **clone** returns a reference to an object's copy, rather than return the object's actual reference.

Bridge

Suppose we are designing a **Button** class for both the Windows and Macintosh operating systems. Class **Button** contains specific button information such as an **ActionListener** and a **String** label. We design classes **Win32Button** and **MacButton** to extend class **Button**. Class **Win32Button** contains "look-and-feel" information on how to display a

Button on the Windows operating system, and class **MacButton** contains "look-and-feel" information on how to display a **Button** on the Macintosh operating system.

Two problems arise from this approach. First, if we create new **Button** subclasses, we must create corresponding **Win32Button** and **MacButton** subclasses. For example, if we create class **ImageButton** (a **Button** with an overlapping **Image**) that extends class **Button**, we must create additional subclasses **Win32ImageButton** and **Mac-ImageButton**. In fact, we must create **Button** subclasses for every operating system we wish to support, which increases development time. The second problem is that when a new operating system enters the market, we must create additional **Button** subclasses specific to that operating system.

The *Bridge design pattern* avoids these problems by separating an abstraction (e.g., a **Button**) and its implementations (e.g., **Win32Button**, **MacButton**, etc.) into separate class hierarchies. For example, the Java AWT classes use the Bridge design pattern to enable designers to create AWT **Button** subclasses without needing to create corresponding subclasses specific to each operating system. Each AWT **Button** maintains a reference to a **ButtonPeer**, which is the superclass for platform-specific implementations, such as **Win32ButtonPeer**, **MacButtonPeer**, etc. When a programmer creates a **Button** object, class **Button** determines which platform-specific **ButtonPeer** object to create and stores a reference to that **ButtonPeer** object—this reference is the "bridge" in the Bridge design pattern. When the programmer invokes methods on the **Button** object, the **Button** object invokes the appropriate method on its **ButtonPeer** object to fulfill the request. If a designer creates **Button** subclass **ImageButton**, the designer does not need to create a corresponding **Win32ImageButton** or **MacImage-Button** class. Class **ImageButton** "is a" **Button**, so when a programmer invokes an **ImageButton** method—such as **setImage**—on an **ImageButton** object, the **Button** superclass translates that method invocation into an appropriate **ButtonPeer** method invocation—such as **drawImage**.

Portability Tip 1.1

*Designers often use the Bridge design pattern to enhance the platform independence of their systems. We can design **Button** subclasses without worrying about how an operating system implements each subclass.*

Iterator

Designers use data structures such as arrays, linked lists and hash tables to organize data in a program. The *Iterator design pattern* allows objects to access individual objects from data structures without knowing that data structure's implementation or how it stores object references. Instructions for traversing the data structure and accessing its elements are stored in a separate object called an *iterator*. Each data structure has an associated iterator implementation capable of traversing that data structure. Other objects can use this iterator, which implements a standard interface, regardless of the underlying data structure or implementation. Interface **Iterator** from package **java.util** uses the Iterator design pattern. Consider a system that contains **Set**s, **Vector**s and **List**s. The algorithm for retrieving data from each structure differs among the classes. With the Iterator design pattern, each class contains a reference to an **Iterator** that stores traversal information specific to each data structure. For objects of these classes, we invoke an object's **iterator** method to obtain a reference to an **Iterator** for that object. We invoke method **next** of the

Iterator to receive the next element in the structure without having to concern ourselves with the details of traversal implementation.

Memento

Consider a drawing program that allows a user to draw graphics. Occasionally the user may position a graphic improperly in the drawing area. The program can offer an "undo" feature that allows the user to unwind such errors. Specifically, the program would restore the drawing area's original state (before the user placed the graphic). More sophisticated drawing programs offer a *history*, which stores several states in a list, so the user can restore the program to any state in the history. The *Memento design pattern* allows an object to save its state, so that—if necessary—the user can restore the object to its former state.

The Memento design pattern requires three types of objects. The *originator object* occupies some *state*—the set of attribute values at a specific time in program execution. In our drawing-program example, the drawing area is the originator, because it occupies several states. The drawing area's initial state is that the area contains no elements. The *memento object* stores a copy of all attributes associated with the originator's state. The memento is stored as the first item in the history list, which acts as the *caretaker object*—the object that contains references to all memento objects associated with the originator.

Now, suppose the user draws a circle in the drawing area. The area now occupies a different state—the area contains a circle object centered at specified *x-y* coordinates. The drawing area then uses another memento to store this information. This memento is stored as the second item in the history list. The history list displays all mementos on screen, so the user can select which state to restore. Suppose the user wishes to remove the circle—if the user selects the first memento from the list, the drawing area uses the first memento to restore itself to a blank area.

Strategy

Package **java.awt** offers several **LayoutManager**s, such classes **FlowLayout**, **BorderLayout** and **GridLayout**, with which developers build graphical user interfaces. Each **LayoutManager** arranges GUI components in a **Container** object—however, each **LayoutManager** implementation uses a different algorithm to arrange these components. A **FlowLayout** arranges components in a left-to-right sequence, a **BorderLayout** places components into five distinct regions and a **GridLayout** arranges components in row-column format. Interface **LayoutManager** plays the role of the *strategy* in the *Strategy design pattern*.

The Strategy design pattern allows developers to encapsulate a set of algorithms—called a strategy—that each have the same function (e.g., arrange GUI components) but different implementations. For example, interface **LayoutManager** (the strategy) is the set of algorithms that arranges GUI components. Each concrete **LayoutManager** subclass (e.g., the **FlowLayout**, **BorderLayout** and **GridLayout** objects) implements method **addLayoutComponent** to provide a specific component-arrangement algorithm.

1.5.3 Concurrency Patterns

Many additional design patterns have been created since the publication of the gang-of-four book, which introduced patterns involving object-oriented systems. Some of these new patterns involve specific types of object-oriented systems, such as concurrent, distributed or parallel systems. Multithreaded programming languages such as Java allow designers to specify concurrent activities—that is, activities that operate in parallel with one another. Improper design of concurrent systems can introduce *concurrency problems*. For example, two objects attempting to alter shared data at the same time could corrupt that data. In addition, if two objects wait for one another to finish tasks, and if neither can complete their task, these objects could potentially wait forever—a situation called *deadlock*. Using Java, Doug Lea and Mark Grand created a set of *concurrency patterns* for multithreaded design architectures to prevent various problems associated with multithreading. We provide a partial list of these design patterns:

- The *Single-Threaded Execution design pattern* prevents several threads from invoking the same method of another object concurrently.[3] In Java, developers can use the **synchronized** keyword to apply this pattern.

- The *Balking design pattern* ensures that a method will *balk*—that is, return without performing any actions—if an object occupies a state that cannot execute that method.[4] A variation of this pattern is that the method throws an exception describing why that method is unable to execute—for example, a method throwing an exception when accessing a data structure that does not exist.

- The *Read/Write Lock design pattern* allows multiple threads to obtain concurrent read access on an object but prevents multiple threads from obtaining concurrent write access on that object. Only one thread at a time may obtain write access on an object—when that thread obtains write access, the object is *locked* to all other threads.[5]

- The *Two-Phase Termination design pattern* ensures that a thread frees resources—such as other spawned threads—in memory (phase one) before terminating (phase two).[6] In Java, a **Thread** object can use this pattern in method **run**. For instance, method **run** can contain an infinite loop that is terminated by some state change—upon termination, method **run** can invoke a **private** method responsible for stopping any other spawned threads (phase one). The thread then terminates after method **run** terminates (phase two). In Chapter 13, the **ChatServerAdministrator** and **ChatServer** classes of the RMI Deitel Messenger application use this design pattern, which we describe in greater detail.

1.5.4 Architectural Patterns

Design patterns allow developers to design specific parts of systems, such as abstracting object instantiations, aggregating classes into larger structures or assigning responsibilities to objects. *Architectural patterns*, on the other hand, provide developers with proven strategies for designing subsystems and specifying how they interact with each other.[7]

For example, the Model-View-Controller architectural pattern separates application data (contained in the *model*) from graphical presentation components (the *view*) and input-processing logic (the *controller*). In the design for a simple text editor, the user inputs text from the keyboard and formats this text using the mouse. The program stores this text and format information into a series of data structures, then displays this information on screen for the user to read what has been inputted. The model, which contains the application data, might contain only the characters that make up the document. When a user provides some input, the controller modifies the model's data with the given input. When the model changes, it notifies the view of the change so the view can update its presentation with the changed data—e.g., the view might display characters using a particular font, with a particular size. Chapter 3 discusses Model-View-Controller architecture in detail, and our Java 2D drawing application in Chapter 5 and the Enterprise Java case study in Chapters 17–20 use this architecture extensively.

The Layers architectural pattern divides functionality into separate sets of system responsibilities called *layers*. For example, *three-tier applications*, in which each tier contains a unique system component, is an example of the Layers architectural pattern. This type of application contains three components that assume a unique responsibility. The *information tier* (also called the "bottom tier") maintains data for the application, typically storing the data in a database. The *client tier* (also called the "top tier") is the application's user interface, such as a standard Web browser. The *middle tier* acts as an intermediary between the information tier and the client tier by processing client-tier requests, reading data from and writing data to the database. In this book, the three-tier architectures in the Deitel bookstore application (Chapter 11), the wireless application case study (Chapter 12) and the Enterprise Java case study (Chapters 17–20) all use the Layers architectural pattern. We discuss the nuances of each architecture in its respective chapter.

Using architectural patterns promotes extensibility when designing systems, because designers can modify a component without having to modify another. For example, a text editor that uses the Model-View-Controller architectural pattern is extensible; designers can modify the view that displays the document outline but would not have to modify the model, other views or controllers. A system designed with the Layers architectural pattern is also extensible; designers can modify the information tier to accommodate a particular database product, but they would not have to modify either the client tier or the middle tier extensively.

1.5.5 Further Study on Design Patterns

We hope that you will pursue further study of design patterns. We recommend that you visit the URLs and read the books we mention below as you study patterns throughout this book. We especially encourage you to read the gang-of-four book.

Design Patterns

www.hillside.net/patterns
This page has links to information on design patterns and languages.

www.hillside.net/patterns/books/
This site lists books on design patterns.

www.netobjectives.com/design.htm
This site overviews design patterns and motivates their importance.

umbc7.umbc.edu/~tarr/dp/dp.html
This site links to design patterns Web sites, tutorials and papers.

www.links2go.com/topic/Design_Patterns
This site links to sites and information on design patterns.

www.c2.com/ppr/
This site discusses recent advances in design patterns and ideas for future projects.

Design Patterns in Java

www.research.umbc.edu/~tarr/cs491/fall00/cs491.html
This site is for a Java design patterns course at the University of Maryland. It contains numerous examples of how to apply design patterns in Java.

www.enteract.com/~bradapp/javapats.html
This site discusses Java design patterns and presents design patterns in distributed computing.

www.meurrens.org/ip-Links/java/designPatterns/
This site displays numerous links to resources and information on Java design patterns.

Architectural Patterns

compsci.about.com/science/compsci/library/weekly/aa030600a.htm
This site provides an overview the Model-View-Controller architecture.

www.javaworld.com/javaworld/jw-04-1998/jw-04-howto.html
This site contains an article discussing how Swing components use Model-View-Controller architecture.

www.ootips.org/mvc-pattern.html
This site provides information and tips on using MVC.

www.ftech.co.uk/~honeyg/articles/pda.htm
This site includes an article on the importance of architectural patterns in software.

www.tml.hut.fi/Opinnot/Tik-109.450/1998/niska/sld001.htm
This site provides information about architectural patterns, design patterns and idioms (patterns targeting a specific language).

WORKS CITED

1. E. Gamma, et al, Design Patterns; Elements of Reusable Object-Oriented Software (Boston, MA: Addison-Wesley, 1995) 1–31.

2. J. Vlissides, Pattern Hatching; Design Patterns Applied (Boston, MA: Addison-Wesley, 1998) 146.

3. M. Grand, Patterns in Java; A Catalog of Reusable Design Patterns Illustrated with UML (New Yor, NY: John Wiley and Sons, 1998) 399–407.

4. M. Grand, 417–420.

5. M. Grand, 431–439.

6. M. Grand, 449–453.

7. R. Hartman. "Building on Patterns." *Application Development Trends* May 2001: 19–26.

BIBLIOGRAPHY

Carey, J., B. Carlson and T. Graser. *San Francisco*^{TM} *Design Patterns: Blueprint for Building Software*. Boston, MA: Addison-Wesley, 2000.

Coad, P., M. Mayfield and Jon Kern. *Java Design; Building Better Apps and Applets, Second Edition*. Englewood Cliffs, NJ: Yourdon Press, 1999.

Cooper, J. *Java Design Patterns; A Tutorial*. Boston, MA: Addition-Wesley, 2000.

Lea, D., *Concurrent Programing in Java, Second Edition: Design Principles and Patterns*. Boston, MA: Addison-Wesley, 1999.

Gamma, R., R. Helm, R. Johnson and J. Vlissides. *Design Patterns; Elements of Reusable Object-Oriented Software*. Boston, MA: Addison-Wesley, 1995.

Vlissides, J. "Composite a la Java, Part 1." *Java Report,* 6: no. 6 (2001): 69–70, 72.

Vlissides, J. "Pattern Hatching; GoF a la Java." *Java Report Online* (March 2001) <**www.javareport.com/html/from_pages/article.asp?id=355**>.

Advanced Swing Graphical User Interface Components

Objectives

- To be able to use Swing components to enhance application GUIs.
- To be able to use Swing text components to view styled documents.
- To understand the Command design pattern and its implementation in Swing.
- To be able to develop applications with multiple-document interfaces.
- To understand how to implement drag-and-drop support.
- To learn how to prepare internationalized applications.
- To understand how to use Swing to create accessible applications for people with disabilities.

The best investment is in the tools of one's own trade.
Benjamin Franklin

Every action must be due to one or other of seven causes: chance, nature, compulsion, habit, reasoning, anger or appetite.
Aristotle

Happiness, like an old friend, is inclined to drop in unexpectedly—when you are working hard on something else.
Ray Inman

2.1 Introduction

In this chapter, we introduce Swing components that enable developers to build functionally rich user interfaces. The Swing graphical user interface components were introduced with the Java Foundation Classes (JFC) as a downloadable extension to the Java 1.1 Platform, then became a standard extension in the Java 2 Platform. Swing provides a more complete set of GUI components than the Abstract Windowing Toolkit (AWT), including advanced features such as a pluggable look and feel, lightweight component rendering and drag-and-drop capabilities.

We introduce the **JEditorPane** class for rendering styled content, such as HTML pages, and build a simple Web browser. We continue our discussion of design patterns by introducing Swing **Action**s, which implement the Command design pattern. Swing **Action**s enable developers to build reusable, user-interface logic components. We also introduce **JSplitPane**, **JTabbedPane** and multiple-document-interface components for organizing GUI elements.

Java provides mechanisms for building applications for multiple languages and countries, and for disabled users. Building internationalized applications ensures that applications will be ready for use around the world in many languages and countries. Accessibility ensures that disabled users will be able to use applications through commonly available utilities, such as screen readers. We show how Swing components enable Java developers to build applications that are accessible to users with disabilities.

2.2 WebBrowser Using JEditorPane and JToolBar

In this section, we use Swing components to build a simple Web browser. We introduce Swing's advanced text-rendering capabilities and containers for grouping commonly used interface elements for convenient user access.

2.2.1 Swing Text Components and HTML Rendering

Many applications present text to the user for viewing and editing. This text may consist of plain, unformatted characters, or it may consist of richly styled characters that use multiple fonts and extensive formatting. Swing provides three basic types of text components for presenting and editing text. Class **JTextComponent** is the base class for all Swing text components, including **JTextField**, **JTextArea** and **JEditorPane**.

JTextField is a single-line text component suitable for obtaining simple user input or displaying information such as form field values, calculation results and so on. **JPasswordField** is a subclass of **JTextField** suitable for obtaining user passwords. These components do not perform any special text styling. Rather, they present all text in a single font and color. **JTextArea**, like **JTextField** and **JPasswordField**, also does not style its text. However, **JTextArea** does provide a larger visible area and supports larger plain-text documents.

JEditorPane provides enhanced text-rendering capabilities. **JEditorPane** supports styled documents that include formatting, font and color information. **JEditorPane** is capable of rendering HTML documents as well as Rich Text Format (RTF) documents. We use class **JEditorPane** to render HTML pages for a simple Web-browser application. **JTextPane** is a **JEditorPane** subclass that renders only styled documents, and not plain text. **JTextPane** provides developers with fine-grained control over the style of each character and paragraph in the rendered document.

WebBrowserPane (Fig. 2.1) extends class **JEditorPane** to create a Web-browsing component that maintains a history of visited URLs. Line 16 creates a **List** for keeping track of visited URLs. Line 23 invokes method **setEditable** of class **JEditorPane** to disable text editing in the **WebBrowserPane**. **JEditorPane** enables hyperlinks in HTML documents only if the **JEditorPane** is not editable.

```
1   // WebBrowserPane.java
2   // WebBrowserPane is a simple Web-browsing component that
3   // extends JEditorPane and maintains a history of visited URLs.
4   package com.deitel.advjhtp1.gui.webbrowser;
5
6   // Java core packages
7   import java.util.*;
8   import java.net.*;
9   import java.io.*;
10
11  // Java extension packages
12  import javax.swing.*;
13
14  public class WebBrowserPane extends JEditorPane {
15
16      private List history = new ArrayList();
17      private int historyIndex;
```

Fig. 2.1   **WebBrowserPane** subclass of **JEditorPane** for viewing Web sites and maintaining URL history (part 1 of 3).

```
18
19   // WebBrowserPane constructor
20   public WebBrowserPane()
21   {
22      // disable editing to enable hyperlinks
23      setEditable( false );
24   }
25
26   // display given URL and add it to history
27   public void goToURL( URL url )
28   {
29      displayPage( url );
30      history.add( url );
31      historyIndex = history.size() - 1;
32   }
33
34   // display next history URL in editorPane
35   public URL forward()
36   {
37      historyIndex++;
38
39      // do not go past end of history
40      if ( historyIndex >= history.size() )
41         historyIndex = history.size() - 1;
42
43      URL url = ( URL ) history.get( historyIndex );
44      displayPage( url );
45
46      return url;
47   }
48
49   // display previous history URL in editorPane
50   public URL back()
51   {
52      historyIndex--;
53
54      // do not go past beginning of history
55      if ( historyIndex < 0 )
56         historyIndex = 0;
57
58      // display previous URL
59      URL url = ( URL ) history.get( historyIndex );
60      displayPage( url );
61
62      return url;
63   }
64
65   // display given URL in JEditorPane
66   private void displayPage( URL pageURL )
67   {
```

Fig. 2.1   **WebBrowserPane** subclass of **JEditorPane** for viewing Web sites and maintaining URL history (part 2 of 3).

```
68          // display URL
69          try {
70              setPage( pageURL );
71          }
72
73          // handle exception reading from URL
74          catch ( IOException ioException ) {
75              ioException.printStackTrace();
76          }
77      }
78  }
```

Fig. 2.1   **WebBrowserPane** subclass of **JEditorPane** for viewing Web sites and maintaining URL history (part 3 of 3).

Method **goToURL** (lines 27–32) navigates the **WebBrowserPane** to the given URL. Line 29 invokes method **displayPage** of class **WebBrowserPane** to display the given URL. Line 30 invokes method **add** of interface **List** to add the URL to the browser history. Line 31 updates the **historyIndex** to ensure that methods **back** and **forward** navigate to the appropriate URL.

Method **forward** (lines 35–47) navigates the **WebBrowserPane** to the next page in the URL history. Line 37 increments **historyIndex**, and lines 43–44 retrieve the URL from the **history List** and display the URL in **WebBrowserPane**. If the **historyIndex** is past the last page in the **history**, line 41 sets **historyIndex** to the last URL in **history**.

Method **back** (lines 50–63) navigates **WebBrowserPane** to the previous page in the URL history. Line 52 decrements **historyIndex**, and lines 55–56 ensure that **historyIndex** does not fall below **0**. Lines 59–60 retrieve the URL and display it in the **WebBrowserPane**.

Method **displayPage** takes as an argument a **URL** to display in the **WebBrowserPane**. Line 70 invokes method **setPage** of class **JEditorPane** to display the page that the URL references. Lines 74–76 catch an **IOException** if there is an error loading the page from the given **URL**.

2.2.2 Swing Toolbars

Toolbars are GUI containers typically located below an application's menus. Toolbars contain buttons and other GUI components for commonly used features, such as cut, copy and paste, or navigation buttons for a Web browser. Figure 2.2 shows toolbars in Internet Explorer and Mozilla.

Class *javax.swing.JToolBar* enables developers to add toolbars to Swing user interfaces. **JToolBar** also enables users to modify the appearance of the **JToolBar** in a running application. For example, the user can drag the **JToolBar** from the top of a window and "dock" the **JToolBar** on the side or bottom of the window. Users also can drag the **JToolBar** away from the application window (Fig. 2.4) to create a *floating* **JToolBar** (i.e., a **JToolBar** displayed in its own window). Developers can set **JToolBar** properties that enable or disable dragging and floating.

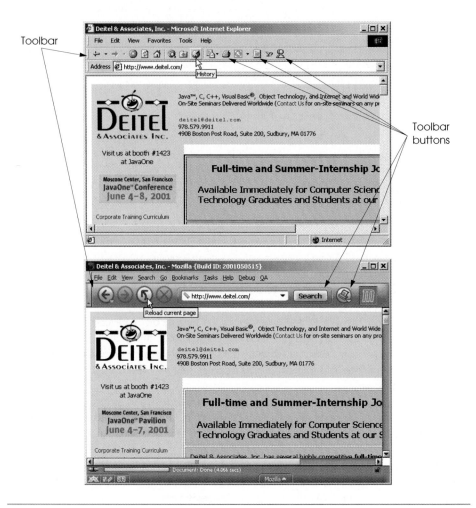

Fig. 2.2   Toolbars for navigating the Web in Internet Explorer and Mozilla.

WebToolBar (Fig. 2.3) extends class **JToolBar** to provide commonly used navigation components for a **WebBrowserPane**. **WebToolBar** provides **backButton** (line 20) for navigating to the previous page, **forwardButton** (line 21) for navigating to the next page and **urlTextField** to allow the user to enter a URL (line 22).

The **WebToolBar** constructor (lines 25–96) takes as an argument a **WebBrowserPane** for displaying Web pages. Lines 34–53 create **urlTextField** and its associated **ActionListener**. When a user types a URL and hits the *Enter* key, line 44 invokes method **goToURL** of class **WebBrowserPane** to display the user-entered URL.

Lines 56–57 create **backButton**, which allows the user to navigate to the previously viewed Web site. Recall that class **WebBrowserPane** maintains a history of visited URLs. When the user selects **backButton**, line 65 invokes method **back** of class **Web-**

BrowserPane to navigate to the previous URL. Method **back** returns the destination URL, which line 68 displays in **urlTextField**. This ensures that **urlTextField** shows the proper URL for the Web site displayed in the **WebBrowserPane**.

Lines 74–75 create **forwardButton**, which allows the user to navigate forward through the **WebBrowserPane**'s history of visited URLs. When the user activates **forwardButton**, line 83 invokes method **forward** of class **WebBrowserPane** to navigate to the next URL in the **WebBrowserPane**'s URL history. Line 86 displays the URL in **urlTextField**.

```
1   // WebToolBar.java
2   // WebToolBar is a JToolBar subclass that contains components
3   // for navigating a WebBrowserPane. WebToolBar includes back
4   // and forward buttons and a text field for entering URLs.
5   package com.deitel.advjhtp1.gui.webbrowser;
6
7   // Java core packages
8   import java.awt.*;
9   import java.awt.event.*;
10  import java.net.*;
11
12  // Java extension packages
13  import javax.swing.*;
14  import javax.swing.event.*;
15
16  public class WebToolBar extends JToolBar
17     implements HyperlinkListener {
18
19     private WebBrowserPane webBrowserPane;
20     private JButton backButton;
21     private JButton forwardButton;
22     private JTextField urlTextField;
23
24     // WebToolBar constructor
25     public WebToolBar( WebBrowserPane browser )
26     {
27        super( "Web Navigation" );
28
29        // register for HyperlinkEvents
30        webBrowserPane = browser;
31        webBrowserPane.addHyperlinkListener( this );
32
33        // create JTextField for entering URLs
34        urlTextField = new JTextField( 25 );
35        urlTextField.addActionListener(
36           new ActionListener() {
37
```

Fig. 2.3 **WebToolBar JToolBar** subclass for navigating URLs in a **WebBrowserPane** (part 1 of 3).

```
38                   // navigate webBrowser to user-entered URL
39                   public void actionPerformed( ActionEvent event )
40                   {
41                      // attempt to load URL in webBrowserPane
42                      try {
43                         URL url = new URL( urlTextField.getText() );
44                         webBrowserPane.goToURL( url );
45                      }
46
47                      // handle invalid URL
48                      catch ( MalformedURLException urlException ) {
49                         urlException.printStackTrace();
50                      }
51                   }
52                }
53             );
54
55             // create JButton for navigating to previous history URL
56             backButton = new JButton( new ImageIcon(
57                getClass().getResource( "images/back.gif" ) ) );
58
59             backButton.addActionListener(
60                new ActionListener() {
61
62                   public void actionPerformed( ActionEvent event )
63                   {
64                      // navigate to previous URL
65                      URL url = webBrowserPane.back();
66
67                      // display URL in urlTextField
68                      urlTextField.setText( url.toString() );
69                   }
70                }
71             );
72
73             // create JButton for navigating to next history URL
74             forwardButton = new JButton( new ImageIcon(
75                getClass().getResource( "images/forward.gif" ) ) );
76
77             forwardButton.addActionListener(
78                new ActionListener() {
79
80                   public void actionPerformed( ActionEvent event )
81                   {
82                      // navigate to next URL
83                      URL url = webBrowserPane.forward();
84
85                      // display new URL in urlTextField
86                      urlTextField.setText( url.toString() );
87                   }
88                }
89             );
```

Fig. 2.3   **WebToolBar JToolBar** subclass for navigating URLs in a
WebBrowserPane (part 2 of 3).

```
90
91          // add JButtons and JTextField to WebToolBar
92          add( backButton );
93          add( forwardButton );
94          add( urlTextField );
95
96      } // end WebToolBar constructor
97
98      // listen for HyperlinkEvents in WebBrowserPane
99      public void hyperlinkUpdate( HyperlinkEvent event )
100     {
101         // if hyperlink was activated, go to hyperlink's URL
102         if ( event.getEventType() ==
103             HyperlinkEvent.EventType.ACTIVATED ) {
104
105             // get URL from HyperlinkEvent
106             URL url = event.getURL();
107
108             // navigate to URL and display URL in urlTextField
109             webBrowserPane.goToURL( url );
110             urlTextField.setText( url.toString() );
111         }
112     }
113 }
```

Fig. 2.3   WebToolBar JToolBar subclass for navigating URLs in a
WebBrowserPane (part 3 of 3).

Based on class **JToolBar**'s inheritance hierarchy, each **JToolBar** also is a
java.awt.Container and therefore can contain other GUI components. Lines 92–94
add **backButton, forwardButton** and **urlTextField** to the **WebToolBar** by
invoking method **add** of class **JToolBar**. A **JToolBar** has property **orientation**
that specifies how the **JToolBar** will arrange its child components. The default is horizontal orientation, so the **JToolBar** lays out these components next to one another, left to
right.

Class **WebBrowserPane** renders HTML pages, which may contain hyperlinks to
other Web pages. When a user activates a hyperlink in a **WebBrowserPane** (e.g., by
clicking on the hyperlink), the **WebBrowserPane** issues a **HyperlinkEvent** of type
HyperlinkEvent.EventType.ACTIVATED. Class **WebToolBar** implements
interface **HyperlinkListener** to listen for **HyperlinkEvent**s. There are several
HyperlinkEvent types. Method **hyperlinkUpdate** (lines 99–112) invokes method
getEventType of class **HyperlinkEvent** to check the event type (lines 102–103)
and retrieves the **HyperlinkEvent**'s URL (line 106). This is the URL of the user-
selected hyperlink. Line 109 invokes method **goToURL** of class **WebBrowserPane** to
navigate to the selected URL, and line 110 updates **urlTextField** to display the
selected URL.

Class **WebBrowser** (Fig. 2.4) uses a **WebBrowserPane** and **WebToolBar** to create a simple Web-browser application. Line 26 creates a **WebBrowserPane**, and line 27 creates a **WebToolBar** for this **WebBrowserPane**. Lines 31–33 add the **WebBrowserPane** and **WebToolBar** to the **WebBrowser**'s content pane.

```
1   // WebBrowser.java
2   // WebBrowser is an application for browsing Web sites using
3   // a WebToolBar and WebBrowserPane.
4   package com.deitel.advjhtp1.gui.webbrowser;
5
6   // Java core packages
7   import java.awt.*;
8   import java.awt.event.*;
9   import java.net.*;
10
11  // Java extension packages
12  import javax.swing.*;
13  import javax.swing.event.*;
14
15  public class WebBrowser extends JFrame {
16
17     private WebToolBar toolBar;
18     private WebBrowserPane browserPane;
19
20     // WebBrowser constructor
21     public WebBrowser()
22     {
23        super( "Deitel Web Browser" );
24
25        // create WebBrowserPane and WebToolBar for navigation
26        browserPane = new WebBrowserPane();
27        toolBar = new WebToolBar( browserPane );
28
29        // lay out WebBrowser components
30        Container contentPane = getContentPane();
31        contentPane.add( toolBar, BorderLayout.NORTH );
32        contentPane.add( new JScrollPane( browserPane ),
33           BorderLayout.CENTER );
34     }
35
36     // execute application
37     public static void main( String args[] )
38     {
39        WebBrowser browser = new WebBrowser();
40        browser.setDefaultCloseOperation( EXIT_ON_CLOSE );
41        browser.setSize( 640, 480 );
42        browser.setVisible( true );
43     }
44  }
```

Fig. 2.4   **WebBrowser** application for browsing Web sites using **WebBrowserPane** and **WebToolBar** (part 1 of 2).

Fig. 2.4   WebBrowser application for browsing Web sites using
WebBrowserPane and **WebToolBar** (part 2 of 2).

2.3 Swing Actions

Applications often provide users with several different ways to perform a given task. For
example, in a word processor there might be an **Edit** menu with menu items for cutting,
copying and pasting text. There also might be a toolbar that has buttons for cutting, copying
and pasting text. There also might be a pop-up menu to allow users to right click on a document to cut, copy or paste text. The functionality the application provides is the same in
each case—the developer provides the various interface components for the user's convenience. However, the same GUI component instance (e.g., a **JButton** for cutting text)

cannot be used for menus and toolbars and pop-up menus, so the developer must code the same functionality three times. If there were many such interface items, repeating this functionality would become tedious and error-prone.

The *Command design pattern* solves this problem by enabling developers to define the functionality (e.g., copying text) once in a reusable object that the developer then can add to a menu, toolbar or pop-up menu. This design pattern is called Command because it defines a user command or instruction. The **Action** interface defines required methods for the Java Swing implementation of the Command design pattern.

An **Action** represents user-interface logic and properties for GUI components that represent that logic, such as the label for a button, the text for a tool tip and the mnemonic key for keyboard access. The logic takes the form of an **actionPerformed** method that the event mechanism invokes in response to the user activating an interface component (e.g., the user clicking a **JButton**). Interface **Action** extends interface **ActionListener**, which enables **Action**s to process **ActionEvent**s generated by GUI components. Once a developer defines an **Action**, the developer can add that **Action** to a **JMenu** or **JToolBar**, just as if the **Action** were a **JMenuItem** or **JButton**. For example, when a developer adds an **Action** to a **JMenu**, the **JMenu** creates a **JMenuItem** for the **Action** and uses the **Action** properties to configure the **JMenuItem**.

Actions provide an additional benefit in that the developer can enable or disable all GUI components associated with an **Action** by enabling or disabling the **Action** itself. For example, copying text from a document first requires that the user select the text to be copied. If there is no selected text, the program should not allow the user to perform a copy operation. If the application used a separate **JMenuItem** in a **JMenu** and **JButton** in a **JToolBar** for copying text, the developer would need to disable each of these GUI components individually. Using **Action**s, the developer could disable the **Action** for copying text, which also would disable all associated GUI components.

ActionSample (Fig. 2.5) demonstrates two **Action**s. Lines 15–16 declare **Action** references **sampleAction** and **exitAction**.

```
1   // ActionSample.java
2   // Demonstrating the Command design pattern with Swing Actions.
3   package com.deitel.advjhtp1.gui.actions;
4
5   // Java core packages
6   import java.awt.*;
7   import java.awt.event.*;
8
9   // Java extension packages
10  import javax.swing.*;
11
12  public class ActionSample extends JFrame {
13
14      // Swing Actions
15      private Action sampleAction;
16      private Action exitAction;
17
```

Fig. 2.5   **ActionSample** application demonstrating the Command design pattern with Swing **Action**s (part 1 of 4).

```
18      // ActionSample constructor
19      public ActionSample()
20      {
21         super( "Using Actions" );
22
23         // create AbstractAction subclass for sampleAction
24         sampleAction = new AbstractAction() {
25
26            public void actionPerformed( ActionEvent event )
27            {
28               // display message indicating sampleAction invoked
29               JOptionPane.showMessageDialog( ActionSample.this,
30                  "The sampleAction was invoked" );
31
32               // enable exitAction and associated GUI components
33               exitAction.setEnabled( true );
34            }
35         };
36
37         // set Action name
38         sampleAction.putValue( Action.NAME, "Sample Action" );
39
40         // set Action Icon
41         sampleAction.putValue( Action.SMALL_ICON, new ImageIcon(
42            getClass().getResource( "images/Help24.gif" ) ) );
43
44         // set Action short description (tooltip text)
45         sampleAction.putValue( Action.SHORT_DESCRIPTION,
46            "A Sample Action" );
47
48         // set Action mnemonic key
49         sampleAction.putValue( Action.MNEMONIC_KEY,
50            new Integer( 'S' ) );
51
52         // create AbstractAction subclass for exitAction
53         exitAction = new AbstractAction() {
54
55            public void actionPerformed( ActionEvent event )
56            {
57               // display message indicating exitAction invoked
58               JOptionPane.showMessageDialog( ActionSample.this,
59                  "The exitAction was invoked" );
60               System.exit( 0 );
61            }
62         };
63
64         // set Action name
65         exitAction.putValue( Action.NAME, "Exit" );
66
67         // set Action icon
68         exitAction.putValue( Action.SMALL_ICON, new ImageIcon(
69            getClass().getResource( "images/EXIT.gif" ) ) );
```

Fig. 2.5   **ActionSample** application demonstrating the Command design pattern with Swing **Action**s (part 2 of 4).

```
70
71        // set Action short description (tooltip text)
72        exitAction.putValue( Action.SHORT_DESCRIPTION,
73           "Exit Application" );
74
75        // set Action mnemonic key
76        exitAction.putValue( Action.MNEMONIC_KEY,
77           new Integer( 'x' ) );
78
79        // disable exitAction and associated GUI components
80        exitAction.setEnabled( false );
81
82        // create File menu
83        JMenu fileMenu = new JMenu( "File" );
84
85        // add sampleAction and exitAction to File menu to
86        // create a JMenuItem for each Action
87        fileMenu.add( sampleAction );
88        fileMenu.add( exitAction );
89
90        fileMenu.setMnemonic( 'F' );
91
92        // create JMenuBar and add File menu
93        JMenuBar menuBar = new JMenuBar();
94        menuBar.add( fileMenu );
95        setJMenuBar( menuBar );
96
97        // create JToolBar
98        JToolBar toolBar = new JToolBar();
99
100       // add sampleAction and exitAction to JToolBar to create
101       // JButtons for each Action
102       toolBar.add( sampleAction );
103       toolBar.add( exitAction );
104
105       // create JButton and set its Action to sampleAction
106       JButton sampleButton = new JButton();
107       sampleButton.setAction( sampleAction );
108
109       // create JButton and set its Action to exitAction
110       JButton exitButton = new JButton( exitAction );
111
112       // lay out JButtons in JPanel
113       JPanel buttonPanel = new JPanel();
114       buttonPanel.add( sampleButton );
115       buttonPanel.add( exitButton );
116
117       // add toolBar and buttonPanel to JFrame's content pane
118       Container container = getContentPane();
119       container.add( toolBar, BorderLayout.NORTH );
120       container.add( buttonPanel, BorderLayout.CENTER );
121    }
```

Fig. 2.5 **ActionSample** application demonstrating the Command design pattern with Swing **Action**s (part 3 of 4).

```
122
123      // execute application
124      public static void main( String args[] )
125      {
126          ActionSample sample = new ActionSample();
127          sample.setDefaultCloseOperation( EXIT_ON_CLOSE );
128          sample.pack();
129          sample.setVisible( true );
130      }
131  }
```

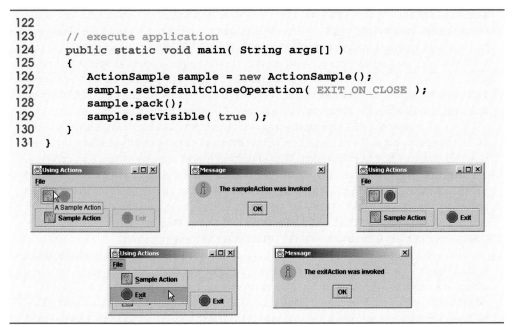

Fig. 2.5   `ActionSample` application demonstrating the Command design
pattern with Swing `Action`s (part 4 of 4).

Lines 24–35 create an anonymous inner class that extends class **AbstractAction**
and assigns the instance to reference **sampleAction**. Class **AbstractAction** facilitates creating **Action** objects. Class **AbstractAction** implements interface **Action**,
but is marked **abstract** because class **AbstractAction** does not provide an implementation for method **actionPerformed**. Lines 26–34 implement method **action-**
Performed. The Swing event mechanism invokes method **actionPerformed** when
the user activates a GUI component associated with **sampleAction**. We show how to
create these GUI components shortly. Lines 29–30 in method **actionPerformed** display a **JOptionPane** message dialog to inform the user that **sampleAction** was
invoked. Line 33 then invokes method **setEnabled** of interface **Action** on the **exi-**
tAction reference. This enables the **exitAction** and its associated GUI components.
Note that **Action**s are enabled by default. We disabled the **exitAction** (line 80) to
demonstrate that this disables the GUI components associated with that **Action**.

After instantiating an **AbstractAction** subclass to create **sampleAction**, lines
38–50 repeatedly invoke method **putValue** of interface **Action** to configure **sam-**
pleAction properties. Each property has a key and a value. Interface **Action** defines
the keys as **public** constants, which we list in Fig. 2.6. GUI components associated with
sampleAction use the property values we assign for GUI component labels, icons, tooltips and so on. Line 38 invokes method **putValue** of interface **Action** with arguments
Action.NAME and **"Sample Action"**. This assigns **sampleAction**'s name, which
GUI components use as their label. Lines 41–42 invoke method **putValue** of interface
Action with key **Action.SMALL_ICON** and an **ImageIcon** value, which GUI components use as their **Icon**. Lines 45–46 set the **Action**'s tool tip using key

Action.SHORT_DESCRIPTION. Lines 49–50 set the **Action**'s mnemonic key using key **Action.MNEMONIC_KEY**. When the **Action** is placed in a **JMenu**, the mnemonic key provides keyboard access to the **Action**. Lines 53–80 create the **exitAction** in a similar way to **sampleAction**, with an appropriate name, icon, description and mnemonic key. Line 80 invokes method **setEnabled** of interface **Action** with argument **false** to disable the **exitAction**. We use this to demonstrate that disabling an **Action** also disables the **Action**'s associated GUI components.

Line 83 creates the **fileMenu JMenu**, which contains **JMenuItem**s corresponding to **sampleAction** and **exitAction**. Class **JMenu** overloads method **add** with a version that takes an **Action** argument. This overloaded **add** method returns a reference to the **JMenuItem** that it creates. Lines 87–88 invoke method **add** of class **JMenu** to add **sampleAction** and **exitAction** to the menu. We have no need for the **JMenuItem** references that method **add** returns, so we ignore them. Line 90 sets the **fileMenu** mnemonic key, and lines 93–95 add the **fileMenu** to a **JMenuBar** and invoke method **set-JMenuBar** of class **JFrame** to add the **JMenuBar** to the application.

Line 98 creates a new **JToolBar**. Like **JMenu**, **JToolBar** also provides overloaded method **add** for adding **Action**s to **JToolBar**s. Method **add** of class **JToolBar** returns a reference to the **JButton** created for the given **Action**. Lines 102–103 invoke method **add** of class **JToolBar** to add the **sampleAction** and **exitAction** to the **JToolBar**. We have no need for the **JButton** references that method **add** returns, so we ignore them.

Class **JButton** provides method **setAction** for configuring a **JButton** with properties of an **Action**. Line 106 creates **JButton sampleButton**. Line 107 invokes method **setAction** of class **JButton** with a **sampleAction** argument to configure **sampleButton**. Line 110 demonstrates an alternative way to configure a **JButton** with properties from an **Action**. The **JButton** constructor is overloaded to accept an **Action** argument. The constructor configures the **JButton** using properties from the given **Action**.

> **Software Engineering Observation 2.1**
>
> *According to the Java 2 SDK documentation, it is preferable to create **JButton**s and **JMenuItem**s, invoke method **setAction** then add the **JButton** or **JMenuItem** to its container, rather than adding the **Action** to the container directly. This is because most GUI-building tools do not support adding **Action**s to containers directly.*

Lines 113–120 add the newly created **JButton**s to a **JPanel** and lay out the **JToolBar** and **JPanel** in the **JFrame**'s content pane. Note that in the first screen capture of Fig. 2.5, the **JButton**s for **exitAction** appear grayed-out. This is because the **exitAction** is disabled. After invoking the **sampleAction**, the **exitAction** is **enabled** and appears in full color. Note also the tool tips, icons and labels on each GUI component. Each of these items was configured using properties of the respective **Action** object.

Figure 2.6 summarizes **Action** properties. Each property name is a **static** constant in interface **Action** and acts as a key for setting or retrieving the property value.

In the following sections we demonstrate two alternative ways to create Swing **Action** instances. The first uses named inner classes. The second defines a generic **AbstractAction** subclass that provides a constructor for commonly used properties and *set* methods for each individual **Action** property.

Name	Description
NAME	Name to be used for GUI-component labels.
SHORT_DESCRIPTION	Descriptive text for use in tooltips.
SMALL_ICON	**Icon** for displaying in GUI-component labels.
MNEMONIC_KEY	Mnemonic key for keyboard access (e.g., for accessing menus and menu items using the keyboard).
ACCELERATOR_KEY	Accelerator key for keyboard access (e.g., using the *Ctrl* key).
ACTION_COMMAND_KEY	Key for retrieving command string to be used in **ActionEvent**s.
LONG_DESCRIPTION	Descriptive text, e.g., for application help.

Fig. 2.6   **Action** class **static** keys for **Action** properties.

2.4 JSplitPane and JTabbedPane

JSplitPane and **JTabbedPane** are container components that enable developers to present large amounts of information in a small screen area. **JSplitPane** accomplishes this by dividing two components with a divider users can reposition to expand and contract the visible areas of the **JSplitPane**'s child components (Fig. 2.7). **JTabbedPane** uses a file-folder-style tab interface to arrange many components through which the user can browse.

Look-and-Feel Observation 2.1

JSplitPanes can contain only two child components. However, each child component may contain nested components.

FavoritesWebBrowser (Fig. 2.7) is an application that uses a **JSplitPane** to show two **WebBrowserPane** components side-by-side in a single application window. On the left side, the **JSplitPane** contains a **WebBrowserPane** that displays a static HTML page containing links to the user's favorite Web sites. Activating the links in this favorites page displays the URL contents in the **WebBrowserPane** on the right side of the **JSplitPane**. This is a common user interface arrangement in Web browsers, such as Internet Explorer and Netscape Navigator.

```
1   // FavoritesWebBrowser.java
2   // FavoritesWebBrowser is an application for browsing Web sites
3   // using a WebToolBar and WebBrowserPane and displaying an HTML
4   // page containing links to favorite Web sites.
5   package com.deitel.advjhtp1.gui.splitpane;
6
7   // Java core packages
8   import java.awt.*;
9   import java.awt.event.*;
10  import java.net.*;
11
```

Fig. 2.7   **FavoritesWebBrowser** application for displaying two Web pages side-by-side using **JSplitPane** (part 1 of 3).

```
12   // Java extension packages
13   import javax.swing.*;
14   import javax.swing.event.*;
15
16   // Deitel packages
17   import com.deitel.advjhtp1.gui.webbrowser.*;
18
19   public class FavoritesWebBrowser extends JFrame {
20
21      private WebToolBar toolBar;
22      private WebBrowserPane browserPane;
23      private WebBrowserPane favoritesBrowserPane;
24
25      // WebBrowser constructor
26      public FavoritesWebBrowser()
27      {
28         super( "Deitel Web Browser" );
29
30         // create WebBrowserPane and WebToolBar for navigation
31         browserPane = new WebBrowserPane();
32         toolBar = new WebToolBar( browserPane );
33
34         // create WebBrowserPane for displaying favorite sites
35         favoritesBrowserPane = new WebBrowserPane();
36
37         // add WebToolBar as listener for HyperlinkEvents
38         // in favoritesBrowserPane
39         favoritesBrowserPane.addHyperlinkListener( toolBar );
40
41         // display favorites.html in favoritesBrowserPane
42         favoritesBrowserPane.goToURL(
43            getClass().getResource( "favorites.html" ) );
44
45         // create JSplitPane with horizontal split (side-by-side)
46         // and add WebBrowserPanes with JScrollPanes
47         JSplitPane splitPane = new JSplitPane(
48            JSplitPane.HORIZONTAL_SPLIT,
49            new JScrollPane( favoritesBrowserPane ),
50            new JScrollPane( browserPane ) );
51
52         // position divider between WebBrowserPanes
53         splitPane.setDividerLocation( 210 );
54
55         // add buttons for expanding/contracting divider
56         splitPane.setOneTouchExpandable( true );
57
58         // lay out WebBrowser components
59         Container contentPane = getContentPane();
60         contentPane.add( toolBar, BorderLayout.NORTH );
61         contentPane.add( splitPane, BorderLayout.CENTER );
62      }
63
```

Fig. 2.7   **FavoritesWebBrowser** application for displaying two Web pages side-by-side using **JSplitPane** (part 2 of 3).

```
64      // execute application
65      public static void main( String args[] )
66      {
67          FavoritesWebBrowser browser = new FavoritesWebBrowser();
68          browser.setDefaultCloseOperation( EXIT_ON_CLOSE );
69          browser.setSize( 640, 480 );
70          browser.setVisible( true );
71      }
72  }
```

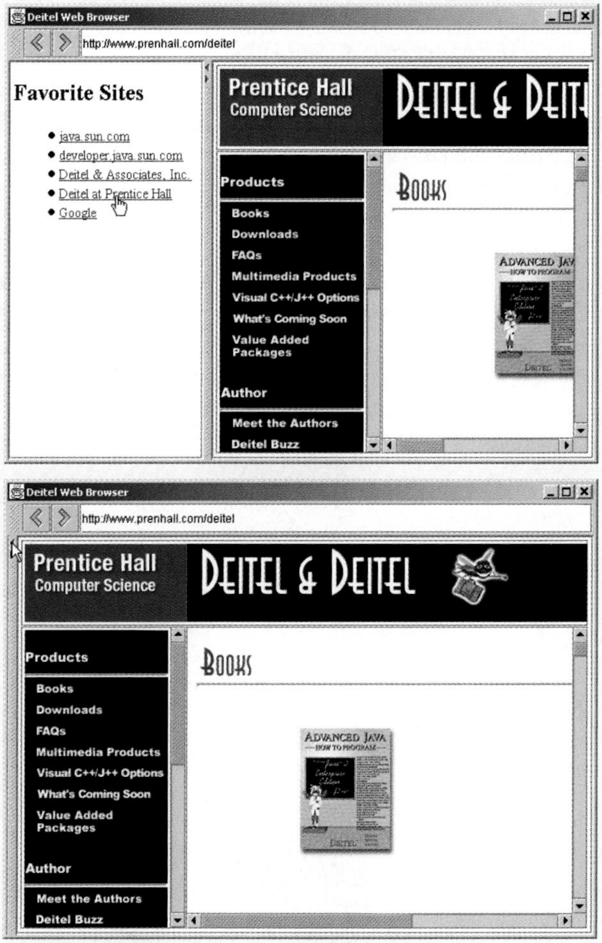

Fig. 2.7   **FavoritesWebBrowser** application for displaying two Web pages side-by-side using **JSplitPane** (part 3 of 3).

Lines 31–32 create a **WebBrowserPane** for displaying Web pages and a **WebToolBar** for navigating this **WebBrowserPane**. Line 35 creates an additional **WebBrowser** pane called **favoritesBrowserPane**, which the application will use to display **favorites.html**. This HTML document contains hyperlinks to some favorite Web sites. Line 39 invokes method **addHyperlinkListener** of class **WebBrowser-**

Pane to register the **toolBar** as a **HyperlinkListener** for **favorites-BrowserPane**. When a user activates a link in **favoritesBrowserPane**, **toolBar** will receive the **HyperlinkEvent** and display the activated URL in **browserPane**. This way the user can activate links in **favoritesBrowserPane** and display those links in **browserPane**. Lines 42–43 invoke method **goToURL** of class **WebBrowserPane** to load **favorites.html** in **favoritesBrowserPane**.

Lines 47–50 create a **JSplitPane**. This **JSplitPane** constructor takes as its first argument an integer that indicates the **JSplitPane** orientation. The constant **JSplitPane.HORIZONTAL_SPLIT** specifies the **JSplitPane** should display its child components side-by-side. The constant **JSplitPane.VERTICAL_SPLIT** would specify that the **JSplitPane** should display its child components one on top of the other. The second and third arguments to this **JSplitPane** constructor are the components to be divided in the **JSplitPane**. In this case, we add **favoritesBrowserPane** to the left side of the **JSplitPane** and **browserPane** to the right side of the **JSplitPane**. We place each **WebBrowserPane** in a **JScrollPane** to allow the user to scroll if the content exceeds the visible area.

Line 53 invokes method **setDividerLocation** of class **JSplitPane** to set the exact divider position between **favoritesBrowserPane** and **browserPane**. Line 56 invokes method **setOneTouchExpandable** of class **JSplitPane** to add two buttons to the divider that enable the user to expand or collapse the divider to one side or the other with a single click. Note the arrows on the divider in Fig. 2.7.

Good Programming Practice 2.1

*Place child components in **JScrollPane**s before adding the components to a **JSplitPane**. This ensures that the user will be able to view all the content in each child component by scrolling if necessary.*

JTabbedPane presents multiple components in separate tabs, which the user can navigate using a mouse or keyboard. Dialog boxes often use components similar to **JTabbedPane**s. For example, Fig. 2.8 shows the **Display Properties** tabbed dialog in Windows 2000.

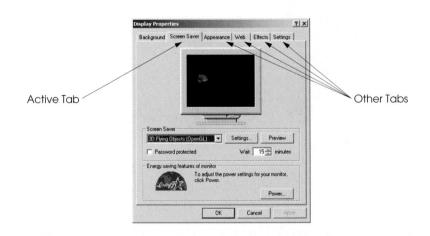

Fig. 2.8   Tabbed interface of **Display Properties** dialog box in Windows 2000.

TabbedPaneWebBrowser (Fig. 2.9) uses a **JTabbedPane** to enable users to browse multiple Web pages at once in a single application window. The user invokes an **Action** to add a new **WebBrowserPane** to the **JTabbedPane**. Each time the user adds a new **WebBrowserPane**, the **JTabbedPane** creates a new tab and places the **WebBrowserPane** in this new tab.

```java
1   // TabbedPaneWebBrowser.java
2   // TabbedPaneWebBrowser is an application that uses a
3   // JTabbedPane to display multiple Web browsers.
4   package com.deitel.advjhtp1.gui.tabbedpane;
5
6   // Java core packages
7   import java.awt.*;
8   import java.awt.event.*;
9
10  // Java extension packages
11  import javax.swing.*;
12
13  // Deitel packages
14  import com.deitel.advjhtp1.gui.webbrowser.*;
15
16  public class TabbedPaneWebBrowser extends JFrame {
17
18     // JTabbedPane for displaying multiple browser tabs
19     private JTabbedPane tabbedPane = new JTabbedPane();
20
21     // TabbedPaneWebBrowser constructor
22     public TabbedPaneWebBrowser()
23     {
24        super( "JTabbedPane Web Browser" );
25
26        // create first browser tab
27        createNewTab();
28
29        // add JTabbedPane to contentPane
30        getContentPane().add( tabbedPane );
31
32        // create File JMenu for creating new browser tabs and
33        // exiting application
34        JMenu fileMenu = new JMenu( "File" );
35        fileMenu.add( new NewTabAction() );
36        fileMenu.addSeparator();
37        fileMenu.add( new ExitAction() );
38        fileMenu.setMnemonic( 'F' );
39
40        JMenuBar menuBar = new JMenuBar();
41        menuBar.add( fileMenu );
42        setJMenuBar( menuBar );
43
44     } // end TabbedPaneWebBrowser constructor
45
```

Fig. 2.9   TabbedPaneWebBrowser application using **JTabbedPane** to browse multiple Web sites concurrently (part 1 of 3).

```
46     // create new browser tab
47     private void createNewTab()
48     {
49        // create JPanel to contain WebBrowserPane and WebToolBar
50        JPanel panel = new JPanel( new BorderLayout() );
51
52        // create WebBrowserPane and WebToolBar
53        WebBrowserPane browserPane = new WebBrowserPane();
54        WebToolBar toolBar = new WebToolBar( browserPane );
55
56        // add WebBrowserPane and WebToolBar to JPanel
57        panel.add( toolBar, BorderLayout.NORTH );
58        panel.add( new JScrollPane( browserPane ),
59           BorderLayout.CENTER );
60
61        // add JPanel to JTabbedPane
62        tabbedPane.addTab( "Browser " + tabbedPane.getTabCount(),
63           panel );
64     }
65
66     // Action for creating new browser tabs
67     private class NewTabAction extends AbstractAction {
68
69        // NewTabAction constructor
70        public NewTabAction()
71        {
72           // set name, description and mnemonic key
73           putValue( Action.NAME, "New Browser Tab" );
74           putValue( Action.SHORT_DESCRIPTION,
75              "Create New Web Browser Tab" );
76           putValue( Action.MNEMONIC_KEY, new Integer( 'N' ) );
77        }
78
79        // when Action invoked, create new browser tab
80        public void actionPerformed( ActionEvent event )
81        {
82           createNewTab();
83        }
84     }
85
86     // Action for exiting application
87     private class ExitAction extends AbstractAction {
88
89        // ExitAction constructor
90        public ExitAction()
91        {
92           // set name, description and mnemonic key
93           putValue( Action.NAME, "Exit" );
94           putValue( Action.SHORT_DESCRIPTION, "Exit Application" );
95           putValue( Action.MNEMONIC_KEY, new Integer( 'x' ) );
96        }
97
```

Fig. 2.9   **TabbedPaneWebBrowser** application using **JTabbedPane** to browse multiple Web sites concurrently (part 2 of 3).

```
98          // when Action invoked, exit application
99          public void actionPerformed( ActionEvent event )
100         {
101             System.exit( 0 );
102         }
103      }
104
105      // execute application
106      public static void main( String args[] )
107      {
108          TabbedPaneWebBrowser browser = new TabbedPaneWebBrowser();
109          browser.setDefaultCloseOperation( EXIT_ON_CLOSE );
110          browser.setSize( 640, 480 );
111          browser.setVisible( true );
112      }
113  }
```

Fig. 2.9　　**TabbedPaneWebBrowser** application using **JTabbedPane** to browse multiple Web sites concurrently (part 3 of 3).

Line 19 creates a new **JTabbedPane**, to which the user will add **WebBrowser-Panes**. Line 27 invokes method **createNewTab** of class **TabbedPaneWebBrowser** to create the first **WebBrowserPane** and place it in the **JTabbedPane**. Line 30 adds the **JTabbedPane** to the **TabbedPaneWebBrowser**'s content pane. Lines 34–42 create the **File** menu, which contains an **Action** for creating new **WebBrowserPane**s (line 35) and an **Action** for exiting the application (line 37). We discuss these actions in detail momentarily.

Method **createNewTab** (lines 46–64) creates a new **WebBrowserPane** and adds it to the **JTabbedPane**. Line 50 creates a **JPanel** for laying out the **WebBrowser-Pane** and its **WebToolBar**. Lines 53–59 create a **WebBrowserPane** and a **Web-ToolBar** and add them to the **JPanel**. Lines 62–63 invoke method **addTab** of class **JTabbedPane** to add the **JPanel** containing the **WebBrowserPane** and **WebT-oolBar** to the application's **JTabbedPane**. Method **addTab** of class **JTabbedPane** takes as a **String** argument the title for the new tab and as a **Component** argument the **Component** to display in the new tab. Although a developer may add any **Component** instance to a **JTabbedPane** to create a new tab, developers most commonly lay out components in a **JPanel** and add the **JPanel** to the **JTabbedPane**.

Figure 2.9 also demonstrates a second way to create **Action** instances. Lines 67–84 define inner class **NewTabAction**, which extends **AbstractAction**. The **New-TabAction** constructor (lines 70–77) configures the **Action** by invoking method **putValue** for the **Action** name, tool tip and mnemonic key. Lines 80–83 define method **actionPerformed** and invoke method **createNewTab** (line 82) to create a new tab in the **JTabbedPane** containing a **WebBrowserPane** and **WebToolBar**.

Lines 87–103 define inner class **ExitAction**, which also extends **AbstractAc-tion**. The **ExitAction** constructor (lines 90–96) configures the **Action** name, tool tip and mnemonic key by invoking method **putValue**. Method **actionPerformed** (lines 99–102) invokes **static** method **exit** of class **System** to exit the application.

2.5 Multiple-Document Interfaces

Most applications provide a single-document interface—users can view and edit only one document at a time. For example, most Web browsers allow users to view only one Web page. To view multiple Web pages, users must launch additional Web browsers. *Multiple document interfaces* allow users to view multiple documents in a single application. Each document appears in a separate window in the application. The user can arrange, resize, iconify (i.e., minimize) and maximize these separate document windows like application windows on the desktop. For example, a digital photograph-editing application could use a multiple document interface to enable users to view and edit multiple photographs at once. The user could place the photograph windows side-by-side to compare the photographs or copy part of one photograph and paste it into the other.

Java Swing provides classes **JDesktopPane** and **JInternalFrame** for building multiple-document interfaces. These class names reinforce the idea that each document is a separate window (**JInternalFrame**) inside the application's desktop (**JDesktop-Pane**), just as other applications are separate windows (e.g., **JFrame**s) on the operating system's desktop. **JInternalFrame**s behave much like **JFrame**s. Users can maximize, iconify, resize, open and close **JInternalFrame**s. **JInternalFrame**s have title bars with buttons for iconifying, maximizing and closing. Users also can move **JInternal-Frame**s within the **JDesktopPane**.

MDIWebBrowser (Fig. 2.10) uses **JInternalFrame**s and a **JDesktopPane** to enable users to browse multiple Web sites within a single application window. Line 20 creates a **JDesktopPane**, which is a container for **JInternalFrame**s. Line 32 adds the **JDesktopPane** to the **JFrame**'s content pane. Lines 36–44 construct the application menu. The **File** menu includes an **Action** for creating new browser windows (line 37) and an **Action** for exiting the application (line 39).

```
1   // MDIWebBrowser.java
2   // MDIWebBrowser is an application that uses JDesktopPane
3   // and JInternalFrames to create a multiple-document-interface
4   // application for Web browsing.
5   package com.deitel.advjhtp1.gui.mdi;
6
7   // Java core packages
8   import java.awt.*;
9   import java.awt.event.*;
10
11  // Java extension packages
12  import javax.swing.*;
13
14  // Deitel packages
15  import com.deitel.advjhtp1.gui.webbrowser.*;
16
17  public class MDIWebBrowser extends JFrame {
18
19      // JDesktopPane for multiple document interface
20      JDesktopPane desktopPane = new JDesktopPane();
```

Fig. 2.10 **MDIWebBrowser** application using **JDesktopPane** and **JInternalFrame**s to browse multiple Web sites concurrently (part 1 of 4).

```
21
22      // MDIWebBrowser constructor
23      public MDIWebBrowser()
24      {
25          super( "MDI Web Browser" );
26
27          // create first browser window
28          createNewWindow();
29
30          // add JDesktopPane to contentPane
31          Container contentPane = getContentPane();
32          contentPane.add( desktopPane );
33
34          // create File JMenu for creating new windows and
35          // exiting application
36          JMenu fileMenu = new JMenu( "File" );
37          fileMenu.add( new NewWindowAction() );
38          fileMenu.addSeparator();
39          fileMenu.add( new ExitAction() );
40          fileMenu.setMnemonic( 'F' );
41
42          JMenuBar menuBar = new JMenuBar();
43          menuBar.add( fileMenu );
44          setJMenuBar( menuBar );
45      }
46
47      // create new browser window
48      private void createNewWindow()
49      {
50          // create new JInternalFrame that is resizable, closable,
51          // maximizable and iconifiable
52          JInternalFrame frame = new JInternalFrame(
53              "Browser", // title
54              true,      // resizable
55              true,      // closable
56              true,      // maximizable
57              true );    // iconifiable
58
59          // create WebBrowserPane and WebToolBar
60          WebBrowserPane browserPane = new WebBrowserPane();
61          WebToolBar toolBar = new WebToolBar( browserPane );
62
63          // add WebBrowserPane and WebToolBar to JInternalFrame
64          Container contentPane = frame.getContentPane();
65          contentPane.add( toolBar, BorderLayout.NORTH );
66          contentPane.add( new JScrollPane( browserPane ),
67              BorderLayout.CENTER );
68
69          // make JInternalFrame opaque and set its size
70          frame.setSize( 320, 240 );
71
```

Fig. 2.10 **MDIWebBrowser** application using **JDesktopPane** and **JInternalFrame**s to browse multiple Web sites concurrently (part 2 of 4).

```
72          // move JInternalFrame to prevent it from obscuring others
73          int offset = 30 * desktopPane.getAllFrames().length;
74          frame.setLocation( offset, offset );
75
76          // add JInternalFrame to JDesktopPane
77          desktopPane.add( frame );
78
79          // make JInternalFrame visible
80          frame.setVisible( true );
81       }
82
83    // Action for creating new browser windows
84    private class NewWindowAction extends AbstractAction {
85
86       // NewWindowAction constructor
87       public NewWindowAction()
88       {
89          // set name, description and mnemonic key
90          putValue( Action.NAME, "New Window" );
91          putValue( Action.SHORT_DESCRIPTION,
92             "Create New Web Browser Window" );
93          putValue( Action.MNEMONIC_KEY, new Integer( 'N' ) );
94       }
95
96       // when Action invoked, create new browser window
97       public void actionPerformed( ActionEvent event )
98       {
99          createNewWindow();
100      }
101   }
102
103   // Action for exiting application
104   private class ExitAction extends AbstractAction {
105
106      // ExitAction constructor
107      public ExitAction()
108      {
109         // set name, description and mnemonic key
110         putValue( Action.NAME, "Exit" );
111         putValue( Action.SHORT_DESCRIPTION, "Exit Application" );
112         putValue( Action.MNEMONIC_KEY, new Integer( 'x' ) );
113      }
114
115      // when Action invoked, exit application
116      public void actionPerformed( ActionEvent event )
117      {
118         System.exit( 0 );
119      }
120   }
121
```

Fig. 2.10 **MDIWebBrowser** application using **JDesktopPane** and **JInternalFrame**s to browse multiple Web sites concurrently (part 3 of 4).

```
122     // execute application
123     public static void main( String args[] )
124     {
125         MDIWebBrowser browser = new MDIWebBrowser();
126         browser.setDefaultCloseOperation( EXIT_ON_CLOSE );
127         browser.setSize( 640, 480 );
128         browser.setVisible( true );
129     }
130 }
```

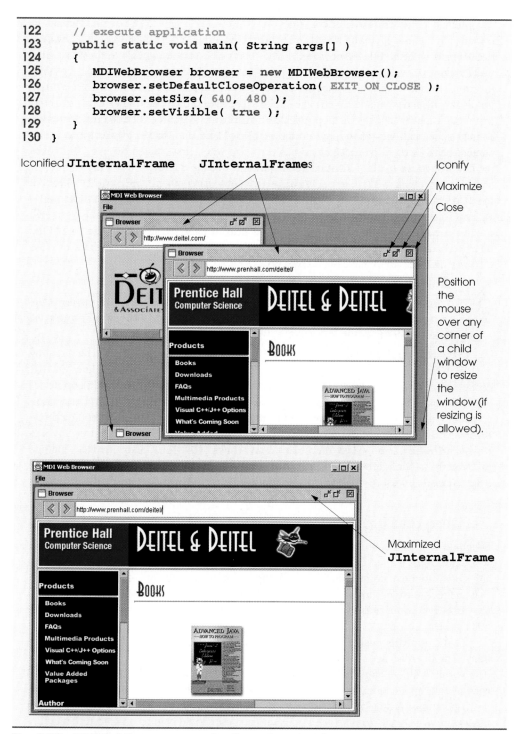

Iconified **JInternalFrame**   **JInternalFrame**s   Iconify

Maximize

Close

Position the mouse over any corner of a child window to resize the window (if resizing is allowed).

Maximized **JInternalFrame**

Fig. 2.10 **MDIWebBrowser** application using **JDesktopPane** and **JInternalFrame**s to browse multiple Web sites concurrently (part 4 of 4).

Method **createNewWindow** (lines 48–81) creates a new **JInternalFrame** in response to the user invoking **NewWindowAction**. Lines 52–57 create a new **JInternalFrame** with the title **"Browser"**. The four **boolean** arguments to the **JInternalFrame** constructor specify that the **JInternalFrame** is resizable, closable, maximizable and iconifiable. Lines 60–61 create a **WebBrowserPane** and **WebToolBar** for displaying and navigating Web pages. Like a **JFrame**, a **JInternalFrame** has a content pane. Line 64 invokes method **getContentPane** to get the **JInternalFrame**'s content pane, and lines 65–67 lay out the **WebToolBar** and **WebBrowserPane** in the content pane. A **JInternalFrame** has zero size when first created, so line 70 invokes method **setSize** of class **JInternalFrame** to size the **JInternalFrame** appropriately. To prevent new **JInternalFrame**s from obscuring other **JInternalFrame**s in the **JDesktopPane**, lines 73–74 invoke method **setLocation** of class **JInternalFrame** to position the new **JInternalFrame** at an offset from the previously created **JInternalFrame**. Line 77 invokes method **add** of class **JDesktopPane** to add the **JInternalFrame** to the display, and line 80 invokes method **setVisible** of class **JInternalFrame** to make the **JInternalFrame** visible.

Look-and-Feel Observation 2.2

JInternalFrames have no size and are invisible by default. When creating a new JInternalFrame, be sure to invoke method setSize to size the JInternalFrame and setVisible(true) to make the JInternalFrame visible.

Class **MDIWebBrowser** uses two **Action**s—**NewWindowAction** for creating new Web browser windows and **ExitAction** for exiting the application. Lines 84–101 declare inner class **NewWindowAction**, which extends class **AbstractAction**. Lines 90–93 invoke method **putValue** of interface **Action** to configure **NewWindowAction** properties. Method **actionPerformed** (lines 97–100) invokes method **createNewWindow** to create a new Web browser window each time the user invokes **NewWindowAction**. Class **ExitAction** (lines 104–120) also invokes method **putValue** to configure the **Action** (lines 110–112) and implements method **actionPerformed** (lines 116–119) to exit the application (line 118) when invoked.

2.6 Drag and Drop

Drag and drop is a common way to manipulate data in a GUI. Most GUIs emulate real-world desktops, with icons that represent the objects on a virtual desk. Drag and drop enables users to move items around the desktop and to move and copy data among applications using mouse *gestures*. A gesture is a mouse movement that corresponds to a drag-and-drop *operation*, such as dragging a file from one folder and dropping the file into another folder.

Two Java APIs enable drag-and-drop data transfer between applications. The data transfer API—package **java.awt.datatransfer**—enables copying and moving data within a single application or among multiple applications. The drag-and-drop API enables Java applications to recognize drag-and-drop gestures and to respond to drag-and-drop operations. A drag-and-drop operation uses the data transfer API to transfer data from the *drag source* to the *drop target*. For example, a user could begin a drag gesture in a file-manager application (the drag source) to drag a file from a folder and drop the file on a Java application (the drop target). The Java application would use the drag-and-drop API to recognize that a drag-and-drop operation occurred and would use the data transfer API to retrieve the data transferred through the drag-and-drop operation.

DnDWebBrowser (Fig. 2.11) is a Web-browsing application that also allows users to drop a file onto the **WebBrowserPane** to view the file contents. For example, a user could drag an HTML file from the host operating system's file manager and drop the file on the **WebBrowserPane** to render the HTML. **DnDWebBrowser** uses the drag-and-drop API to recognize drag-and-drop operations and the data transfer API to retrieve the transferred data. Lines 32–33 create a **WebBrowserPane** component for viewing Web pages and a **WebToolBar** to provide navigation controls.

The **WebBrowserPane** in class **DnDWebBrowser** acts as a drop target (i.e., a user can drop a dragged object on the **WebBrowserPane**). Lines 37–38 invoke method **set-DropTarget** of class **WebBrowserPane** and create a new **DropTarget** object. The first argument to the **DropTarget** constructor is the **java.awt.Component** that provides the GUI target onto which a user can drop objects. In this case, the **Component** is a **WebBrowserPane**. The second argument specifies the types of drag-and-drop operations that the **DropTarget** supports. Class **DnDConstants** specifies constant **ACTION_COPY** for allowing a **DropTarget** to accept a drag-and-drop operation for copying a dragged object. Other operations include **ACTION_MOVE** for moving an object and **ACTION_LINK** for creating a link to an object (e.g., a symbolic link on a UNIX filesystem). The third argument to the **DropTarget** constructor is the **DropTargetListener** to be notified of drag-and-drop operation events.

Class **DropTargetHandler** (lines 48–126) implements interface **DropTargetListener** to listen for drag-and-drop operation events related to a **DropTarget**. The drag-and-drop subsystem invokes method **drop** (lines 51–100) of interface **DropTargetListener** when the user drops an object on a **DropTarget**. Line 54 invokes method **getTransferable** of class **DropTargetDropEvent** to retrieve the *Transferable* object that the user dropped. Interface **java.awt.datatransfer.Transferable** declares methods that represent an object that can be transferred among applications. As part of the datatransfer API, interface **Transferable** represents objects that may be transferred through the system clipboard (e.g., via cut-and-paste operations) and objects that are transferred through drag and drop.

```
1   // DnDWebBrowser.java
2   // DnDWebBrowser is an application for viewing Web pages using
3   // drag and drop.
4   package com.deitel.advjhtp1.gui.dnd;
5
6   // Java core packages
7   import java.awt.*;
8   import java.awt.dnd.*;
9   import java.awt.datatransfer.*;
10  import java.util.*;
11  import java.io.*;
12  import java.net.*;
13
```

Fig. 2.11   **DnDWebBrowser** application for browsing Web sites that also accepts drag-and-drop operations for viewing HTML pages (part 1 of 5).

```
14   // Java extension packages
15   import javax.swing.*;
16   import javax.swing.event.*;
17
18   // Deitel packages
19   import com.deitel.advjhtp1.gui.webbrowser.*;
20
21   public class DnDWebBrowser extends JFrame {
22
23      private WebToolBar toolBar;
24      private WebBrowserPane browserPane;
25
26      // DnDWebBrowser constructor
27      public DnDWebBrowser()
28      {
29         super( "Drag-and-Drop Web Browser" );
30
31         // create WebBrowserPane and WebToolBar for navigation
32         browserPane = new WebBrowserPane();
33         toolBar = new WebToolBar( browserPane );
34
35         // enable WebBrowserPane to accept drop operations, using
36         // DropTargetHandler as the DropTargetListener
37         browserPane.setDropTarget( new DropTarget( browserPane,
38            DnDConstants.ACTION_COPY, new DropTargetHandler() ) );
39
40         // lay out WebBrowser components
41         Container contentPane = getContentPane();
42         contentPane.add( toolBar, BorderLayout.NORTH );
43         contentPane.add( new JScrollPane( browserPane ),
44            BorderLayout.CENTER );
45      }
46
47      // inner class to handle DropTargetEvents
48      private class DropTargetHandler implements DropTargetListener {
49
50         // handle drop operation
51         public void drop( DropTargetDropEvent event )
52         {
53            // get dropped Transferable object
54            Transferable transferable = event.getTransferable();
55
56            // if Transferable is a List of Files, accept drop
57            if ( transferable.isDataFlavorSupported(
58               DataFlavor.javaFileListFlavor ) ) {
59
60               // accept the drop operation to copy the object
61               event.acceptDrop( DnDConstants.ACTION_COPY );
62
63               // process list of files and display each in browser
64               try {
65
```

Fig. 2.11   **DnDWebBrowser** application for browsing Web sites that also accepts drag-and-drop operations for viewing HTML pages (part 2 of 5).

```
66                      // get List of Files
67                      java.util.List fileList =
68                         ( java.util.List ) transferable.getTransferData(
69                            DataFlavor.javaFileListFlavor );
70
71                      Iterator iterator = fileList.iterator();
72
73                      while ( iterator.hasNext() ) {
74                         File file = ( File ) iterator.next();
75
76                         // display File in browser and complete drop
77                         browserPane.goToURL( file.toURL() );
78                      }
79
80                      // indicate successful drop
81                      event.dropComplete( true );
82                   }
83
84                   // handle exception if DataFlavor not supported
85                   catch ( UnsupportedFlavorException flavorException ) {
86                      flavorException.printStackTrace();
87                      event.dropComplete( false );
88                   }
89
90                   // handle exception reading Transferable data
91                   catch ( IOException ioException ) {
92                      ioException.printStackTrace();
93                      event.dropComplete( false );
94                   }
95                }
96
97                // if dropped object is not file list, reject drop
98                else
99                   event.rejectDrop();
100            }
101
102            // handle drag operation entering DropTarget
103            public void dragEnter( DropTargetDragEvent event )
104            {
105                // if data is javaFileListFlavor, accept drag for copy
106                if ( event.isDataFlavorSupported(
107                   DataFlavor.javaFileListFlavor ) )
108
109                   event.acceptDrag( DnDConstants.ACTION_COPY );
110
111                // reject all other DataFlavors
112                else
113                   event.rejectDrag();
114            }
115
116            // invoked when drag operation exits DropTarget
117            public void dragExit( DropTargetEvent event ) {}
```

Fig. 2.11   **DnDWebBrowser** application for browsing Web sites that also accepts drag-and-drop operations for viewing HTML pages (part 3 of 5).

```
118
119        // invoked when drag operation occurs over DropTarget
120        public void dragOver( DropTargetDragEvent event ) {}
121
122        // invoked if dropAction changes (e.g., from COPY to LINK)
123        public void dropActionChanged( DropTargetDragEvent event )
124        {}
125
126     } // end class DropTargetHandler
127
128     // execute application
129     public static void main( String args[] )
130     {
131        DnDWebBrowser browser = new DnDWebBrowser();
132        browser.setDefaultCloseOperation( EXIT_ON_CLOSE );
133        browser.setSize( 640, 480 );
134        browser.setVisible( true );
135     }
136 }
```

Drag source

Drop target

Mouse cursor dragging **favorites.html**.

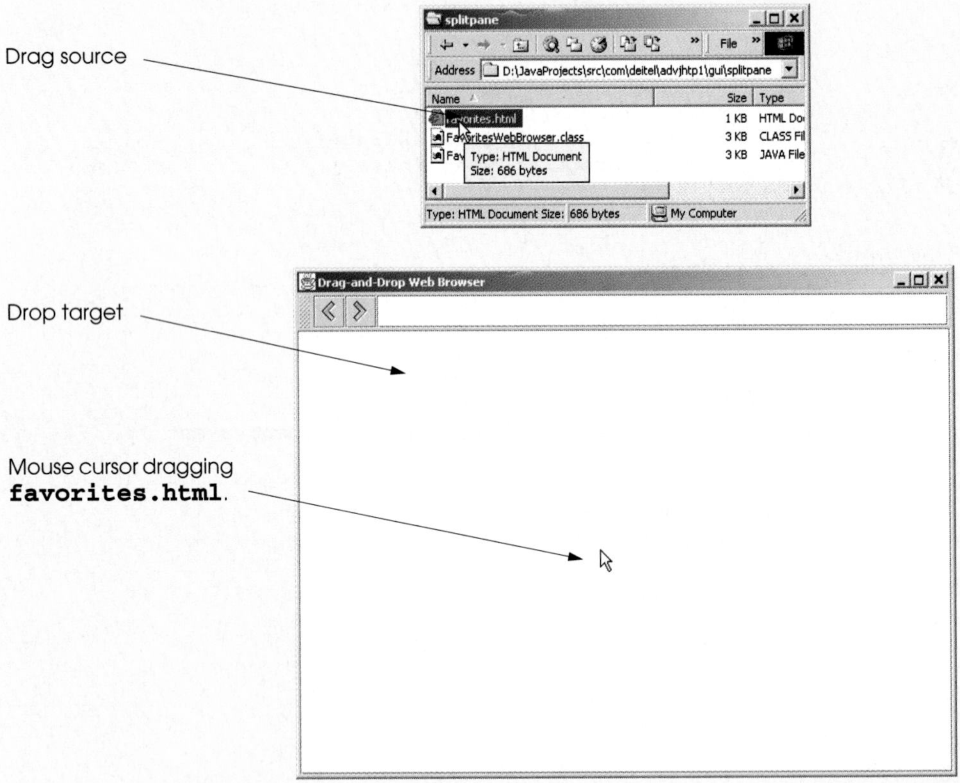

Fig. 2.11   **DnDWebBrowser** application for browsing Web sites that also accepts drag-and-drop operations for viewing HTML pages (part 4 of 5).

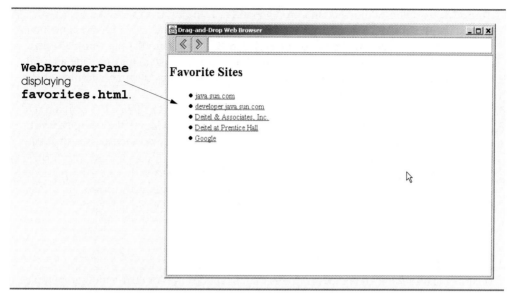

WebBrowserPane displaying **favorites.html**.

Fig. 2.11   **DnDWebBrowser** application for browsing Web sites that also accepts drag-and-drop operations for viewing HTML pages (part 5 of 5).

Lines 57–58 invoke method **isDataFlavorSupported** of interface **Transferable** to determine the type of data the **Transferable** object contains. The datatransfer API defines class **DataFlavor** to represent types of data contained in a **Transferable** object. Class **DataFlavor** provides several **static** constants that developers can use for comparison to common **DataFlavor**s. Lines 57–58 determine if the **Transferable** object supports **DataFlavor.javaFileListFlavor**, which represents a **List** of **File**s. If a user drags one or more **File**s from the host operating system's file manager, the dropped **Transferable** object will support **DataFlavor.javaFileListFlavor**. If the **Transferable** object supports this **DataFlavor**, line 61 invokes method **acceptDrop** of class **DropTargetDropEvent** to indicate that the drop operation is allowed for this **DropTarget**.

Lines 67–69 retrieve the **List** of **File**s from the **Transferable** object by invoking method **getTransferData** of interface **Transferable**. Lines 73–78 iterate the **List** of **File**s, displaying each by invoking method **goToURL** of class **WebBrowserPane**. Line 80 invokes method **dropComplete** of class **DropTargetDropEvent** with a **true** argument to indicate that the drag-and-drop operation was successful. If the **DataFlavor** was not **DataFlavor.javaFileListFlavor**, line 99 invokes method **rejectDrop** of class **DropTargetDropEvent** to reject the drag-and-drop operation.

The drag-and-drop subsystem invokes method **dragEnter** of interface **DropTargetListener** (lines 103–114) when a drag-and-drop operation enters a **DropTarget** (e.g., the user drags the mouse into the **DropTarget**). Lines 106–107 check the **DataFlavor**s that the **Transferable** object supports. If the **Transferable** object supports **DataFlavor.javaFileListFlavor**, line 109 invokes method **acceptDrag** of class **DropTargetDragEvent** to indicate that this

DropTarget allows the drag-and-drop operation. If the **Transferable** object does not support **DataFlavor.javaFileListFlavor**, line 113 invokes method **rejectDrag** of class **DropTargetDragEvent** to indicate that the **DropTarget** does not allow this drag-and-drop operation. The operating system may provide a visual cue to the user to indicate that the **DropTarget** does not allow the drag-and-drop operation, for example, by changing the mouse cursor.

The drag-and-drop subsystem invokes method **dragExit** (line 117) of interface **DropTargetListener** when the drag-and-drop operation leaves the **DropTarget** and method **dragOver** (line 120) when the drag-and-drop operation passes over the **DropTarget**. If the user changes the drop action (e.g., from **DndConstants.ACTION_COPY** to **DndConstants.ACTION_MOVE** by pressing the *Ctrl* key), the drag-and-drop subsystem invokes method **dropActionChanged** (line 123). We provide empty implementations of these methods because we do not require any special handling for these events.

2.7 Internationalization

Internationalization is the process of preparing an application for distribution in multiple *locales*. A locale identifies the language, currency, character set, date formats and other items most widely used for presenting information in a particular country or region. For example, in the U. S. locale, the language is English, the currency is the U. S. dollar and the date format is *month/day/year*. In the United Kingdom locale, the language also is English, but the currency is the British pound and the date format is *day/month/year*. Applications to be distributed in multiple locales must display information in the correct language and with appropriate date, currency and other formats.

To internationalize an application, a developer must replace hard-coded strings that the user might see, such as labels, tooltips and error messages, with strings contained in a **ResourceBundle**. A **ResourceBundle** is a Java properties file that maps keys to string values. For example, a **ResourceBundle** could contain the key **exitButtonLabel** with the string value **Exit**. Instead of hard coding the string **Exit** on a **JButton**'s label, the developer could retrieve the label from the **ResourceBundle**. The developer could then provide multiple versions of the **ResourceBundle** that use the same keys, but provide string values in different languages. For example, the developer could provide a **ResourceBundle** that contains French translations of each string value.

The developer also must use locale-sensitive classes to format data, such as dates, times and currencies, using locale-specific formats. There are several locale-sensitive classes that can perform this formatting, such as **NumberFormat** and **DateFormat**. A locale-sensitive class uses information about the appropriate locale to produce its output. For example, method **format** of class **DateFormat** takes as arguments a **Date** and a **Locale** and returns an appropriately formatted **String** for the given **Locale** (e.g., the string **3/8/2001** for the U. S. **Locale**).

Internationalized applications also must use *Unicode* characters. Unicode is a standard for encoding characters for most of the world's languages. Java uses Unicode to represent all characters, but it is possible that data generated by other applications may not use Unicode. Such data would need to be converted to Unicode before including it in an internationalized application. For more information about Unicode, please see Appendix I, Unicode.

Figure 2.12 presents an internationalized **WebToolBar** class. The **WebToolBar** constructor (lines 27–104) takes as an additional argument the **Locale** for which the **WebToolBar** should be localized. Lines 30–31 load the **ResourceBundle** named **StringsAndLabels** for the given **Locale** by invoking **static** method **get-Bundle** of class **ResourceBundle**. Line 33 invokes method **getString** of class **ResourceBundle** to retrieve the **toolBarTitle** string from the **Resource-Bundle**. Line 33 also invokes method **setName** of class **JToolBar** to set the **JToolBar**'s name to the retrieved value.

```
1   // WebToolBar.java
2   // Internationalized WebToolBar with components for navigating
3   // a WebBrowserPane.
4   package com.deitel.advjhtp1.gui.i18n;
5
6   // Java core packages
7   import java.awt.*;
8   import java.awt.event.*;
9   import java.net.*;
10  import java.util.*;
11
12  // Java extension packages
13  import javax.swing.*;
14  import javax.swing.event.*;
15
16  // Deitel packages
17  import com.deitel.advjhtp1.gui.webbrowser.WebBrowserPane;
18  import com.deitel.advjhtp1.gui.actions.MyAbstractAction;
19
20  public class WebToolBar extends JToolBar
21     implements HyperlinkListener {
22
23     private WebBrowserPane webBrowserPane;
24     private JTextField urlTextField;
25
26     // WebToolBar constructor
27     public WebToolBar( WebBrowserPane browser, Locale locale )
28     {
29        // get resource bundle for internationalized strings
30        ResourceBundle resources = ResourceBundle.getBundle(
31           "StringsAndLabels", locale );
32
33        setName( resources.getString( "toolBarTitle" ) );
34
35        // register for HyperlinkEvents
36        webBrowserPane = browser;
37        webBrowserPane.addHyperlinkListener( this );
38
39        // create JTextField for entering URLs
40        urlTextField = new JTextField( 25 );
```

Fig. 2.12   **WebToolBar** that uses **ResourceBundle**s for internationalization (part 1 of 3).

```
41          urlTextField.addActionListener(
42             new ActionListener() {
43
44                // navigate webBrowser to user-entered URL
45                public void actionPerformed( ActionEvent event )
46                {
47                   // attempt to load URL in webBrowserPane
48                   try {
49                      URL url = new URL( urlTextField.getText() );
50                      webBrowserPane.goToURL( url );
51                   }
52
53                   // handle invalid URL
54                   catch ( MalformedURLException urlException ) {
55                      urlException.printStackTrace();
56                   }
57                }
58             }
59          );
60
61          // create backAction and configure its properties
62          MyAbstractAction backAction = new MyAbstractAction() {
63
64             public void actionPerformed( ActionEvent event )
65             {
66                // navigate to previous URL
67                URL url = webBrowserPane.back();
68
69                // display URL in urlTextField
70                urlTextField.setText( url.toString() );
71             }
72          };
73
74          backAction.setSmallIcon( new ImageIcon(
75             getClass().getResource( "images/back.gif" ) ) );
76
77          backAction.setShortDescription(
78             resources.getString( "backToolTip" ) );
79
80          // create forwardAction and configure its properties
81          MyAbstractAction forwardAction = new MyAbstractAction() {
82
83             public void actionPerformed( ActionEvent event )
84             {
85                // navigate to next URL
86                URL url = webBrowserPane.forward();
87
88                // display new URL in urlTextField
89                urlTextField.setText( url.toString() );
90             }
91          };
92
```

Fig. 2.12 **WebToolBar** that uses **ResourceBundle**s for internationalization (part 2 of 3).

```
93              forwardAction.setSmallIcon( new ImageIcon(
94                 getClass().getResource( "images/forward.gif" ) ) );
95
96              forwardAction.setShortDescription(
97                 resources.getString( "forwardToolTip" ) );
98
99              // add JButtons and JTextField to WebToolBar
100             add( backAction );
101             add( forwardAction );
102             add( urlTextField );
103
104         } // end WebToolBar constructor
105
106         // listen for HyperlinkEvents in WebBrowserPane
107         public void hyperlinkUpdate( HyperlinkEvent event )
108         {
109             // if hyperlink was activated, go to hyperlink's URL
110             if ( event.getEventType() ==
111                 HyperlinkEvent.EventType.ACTIVATED ) {
112
113                 // get URL from HyperlinkEvent
114                 URL url = event.getURL();
115
116                 // navigate to URL and display URL in urlTextField
117                 webBrowserPane.goToURL( event.getURL() );
118                 urlTextField.setText( url.toString() );
119             }
120         }
121 }
```

Fig. 2.12 **WebToolBar** that uses **ResourceBundle**s for internationalization (part 3 of 3).

Lines 62–78 create an instance of class **MyAbstractAction** (Fig. 2.13) for the **WebToolBar**'s **backAction**. Lines 64–71 implement method **actionPerformed**. Lines 74–75 load the **Icon** for **backAction**, and lines 77–78 retrieve the internationalized tooltip text for **backAction** from the **ResourceBundle**. Lines 81–97 create the **forwardAction** in a similar manner.

The internationalized **WebToolBar** class also replaces the forward and back **JButton**s with **Action**s. Abstract class **MyAbstractAction** (Fig. 2.13) extends class **AbstractAction** to provide *set* methods for commonly used **Action** properties. The **MyAbstractAction** constructor (lines 19–27) takes as arguments the name, **Icon**, description and mnemonic key for the **Action**. Lines 23–26 invoke the appropriate *set* methods to configure the **Action** to the given values. Each *set* method invokes method **putValue** of interface **Action** with the appropriate key and the given value.

Figure 2.14 presents an internationalized **WebBrowser** class. Class **WebBrowser** has a single user-visible string, which is the application window title. The **WebBrowser** constructor (lines 26–42) takes as an argument the **Locale** for which the application should be localized. Lines 28–29 invoke **static** method **getBundle** of class **Resour-**

ceBundle to load the **ResourceBundle** containing the appropriate internationalized strings. Line 31 invokes method **getString** of class **ResourceBundle** to retrieve the **applicationTitle** string.

```java
1   // MyAbstractAction.java
2   // MyAbstractAction is an AbstractAction subclass that provides
3   // set methods for Action properties (e.g., name, icon, etc.).
4   package com.deitel.advjhtp1.gui.actions;
5
6   // Java core packages
7   import java.awt.event.*;
8
9   // Java extension packages
10  import javax.swing.*;
11
12  public abstract class MyAbstractAction extends AbstractAction {
13
14      // no-argument constructor
15      public MyAbstractAction() {}
16
17      // construct MyAbstractAction with given name, icon
18      // description and mnemonic key
19      public MyAbstractAction( String name, Icon icon,
20          String description, Integer mnemonic )
21      {
22          // initialize properties
23          setName( name );
24          setSmallIcon( icon );
25          setShortDescription( description );
26          setMnemonic( mnemonic );
27      }
28
29      // set Action name
30      public void setName( String name )
31      {
32          putValue( Action.NAME, name );
33      }
34
35      // set Action Icon
36      public void setSmallIcon( Icon icon )
37      {
38          putValue( Action.SMALL_ICON, icon );
39      }
40
41      // set Action short description
42      public void setShortDescription( String description )
43      {
44          putValue( Action.SHORT_DESCRIPTION, description );
45      }
46
```

Fig. 2.13   MyAbstractAction AbstractAction subclass that provides *set* methods for **Action** properties (part 1 of 2).

```
47      // set Action mnemonic key
48      public void setMnemonic( Integer mnemonic )
49      {
50         putValue( Action.MNEMONIC_KEY, mnemonic );
51      }
52
53      // abstract actionPerformed method to be implemented
54      // by concrete subclasses
55      public abstract void actionPerformed( ActionEvent event );
56   }
```

Fig. 2.13 **MyAbstractAction AbstractAction** subclass that provides *set* methods for **Action** properties (part 2 of 2).

```
1    // WebBrowser.java
2    // WebBrowser is an application for browsing Web sites using
3    // a WebToolBar and WebBrowserPane.
4    package com.deitel.advjhtp1.gui.i18n;
5
6    // Java core packages
7    import java.awt.*;
8    import java.awt.event.*;
9    import java.net.*;
10   import java.util.*;
11
12   // Java extension packages
13   import javax.swing.*;
14   import javax.swing.event.*;
15
16   // Deitel packages
17   import com.deitel.advjhtp1.gui.webbrowser.WebBrowserPane;
18
19   public class WebBrowser extends JFrame {
20
21      private ResourceBundle resources;
22      private WebToolBar toolBar;
23      private WebBrowserPane browserPane;
24
25      // WebBrowser constructor
26      public WebBrowser( Locale locale )
27      {
28         resources = ResourceBundle.getBundle(
29            "StringsAndLabels", locale );
30
31         setTitle( resources.getString( "applicationTitle" ) );
32
33         // create WebBrowserPane and WebToolBar for navigation
34         browserPane = new WebBrowserPane();
35         toolBar = new WebToolBar( browserPane, locale );
36
```

Fig. 2.14 **WebBrowser** that uses **ResourceBundle**s for internationalization (part 1 of 2).

```
37              // lay out WebBrowser components
38              Container contentPane = getContentPane();
39              contentPane.add( toolBar, BorderLayout.NORTH );
40              contentPane.add( new JScrollPane( browserPane ),
41                 BorderLayout.CENTER );
42          }
43      }
```

Fig. 2.14 **WebBrowser** that uses **ResourceBundle**s for internationalization (part 2 of 2).

Class **BrowserLauncher** (Fig. 2.15) provides a **JComboBox** for selecting a **Locale** and launching an internationalized **WebBrowser**. Line 25 creates the **JComboBox** and lines 28–34 add sample **Locale**s to the **JComboBox**. When the user selects a **Locale** from the **JComboBox**, lines 43–44 invoke method **launchBrowser** of class **BrowserLauncher** to launch a new **WebBrowser**. Method **launchBrowser** (lines 57–63) creates a new **WebBrowser** for the given **Locale**, sets its size and displays it.

The properties files of Fig. 2.16 and Fig. 2.17 contain internationalized strings for the default **Locale** (**Locale.US**) and the French Locale (**Locale.FRANCE**). In a properties file, the **#** character begins a single-line comment. Each property has a key, followed by an equals sign, followed by a value.

Note in Fig. 2.17 that the **backToolTip** value represents special characters (e.g., characters with accents) as *Unicode escape sequences* (line 3). Unicode can represent over 65,000 unique characters. A Unicode escape sequence begins with **\u** and contains four hexadecimal digits that represent the special character. Java uses Unicode characters by default and requires Unicode characters for proper internationalization.

```
1   // BrowserLauncher.java
2   // BrowserLauncher provides a list of Locales and launches a new
3   // Internationalized WebBrowser for the selected Locale.
4   package com.deitel.advjhtp1.gui.i18n;
5
6   // Java core packages
7   import java.awt.*;
8   import java.awt.event.*;
9   import java.util.*;
10
11  // Java extension packages
12  import javax.swing.*;
13
14  public class BrowserLauncher extends JFrame {
15
16      // JComboBox for selecting Locale
17      private JComboBox localeComboBox;
18
19      // BrowserLauncher constructor
20      public BrowserLauncher()
21      {
```

Fig. 2.15 **BrowserLauncher** application for selecting a **Locale** and launching an internationalized **WebBrowser** (part 1 of 3).

```
22            super( "Browser Launcher" );
23
24            // create JComboBox and add Locales
25            localeComboBox = new JComboBox();
26
27            // United States, English
28            localeComboBox.addItem( Locale.US );
29
30            // France, French
31            localeComboBox.addItem( Locale.FRANCE );
32
33            // Russia, Russian
34            localeComboBox.addItem( new Locale( "ru", "RU" ) );
35
36            // launch new WebBrowser when Locale selection changes
37            localeComboBox.addItemListener(
38               new ItemListener() {
39
40                  public void itemStateChanged( ItemEvent event )
41                  {
42                     if ( event.getStateChange() == ItemEvent.SELECTED )
43                        launchBrowser( ( Locale )
44                           localeComboBox.getSelectedItem() );
45                  }
46               }
47            );
48
49            // lay out components
50            Container contentPane = getContentPane();
51            contentPane.setLayout( new FlowLayout() );
52            contentPane.add( new JLabel( "Select Locale" ) );
53            contentPane.add( localeComboBox );
54         }
55
56         // launch new WebBrowser for given Locale
57         private void launchBrowser( Locale locale )
58         {
59            WebBrowser browser = new WebBrowser( locale );
60            browser.setDefaultCloseOperation( DISPOSE_ON_CLOSE );
61            browser.setSize( 640, 480 );
62            browser.setVisible( true );
63         }
64
65         // execute application
66         public static void main( String args[] )
67         {
68            BrowserLauncher launcher = new BrowserLauncher();
69            launcher.setDefaultCloseOperation( EXIT_ON_CLOSE );
70            launcher.setSize( 200, 125 );
71            launcher.setVisible( true );
72         }
73      }
```

Fig. 2.15   BrowserLauncher application for selecting a **Locale** and launching an internationalized **WebBrowser** (part 2 of 3).

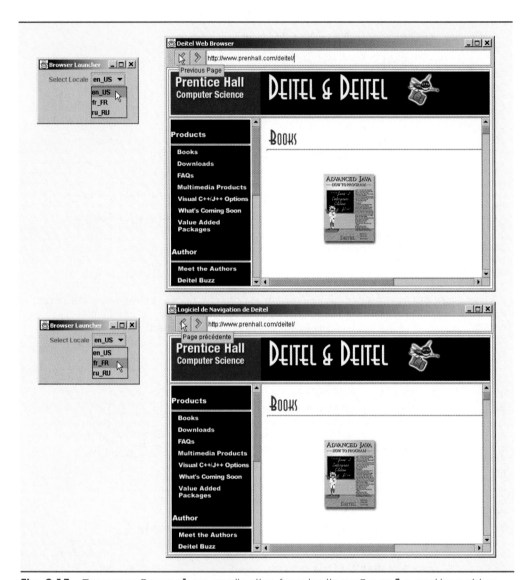

Fig. 2.15 **BrowserLauncher** application for selecting a **Locale** and launching an internationalized **WebBrowser** (part 3 of 3).

```
1   # English language strings for internationalized WebBrowser
2   # application title
3   applicationTitle = Deitel Web Browser
4
5   # title for WebToolBar
6   toolBarTitle = Web Navigation
7
```

Fig. 2.16 Properties file for default **Locale** (US English)— **StringsAndLabels.properties** (part 1 of 2).

```
 8   # tooltip for forward toolbar button
 9   forwardToolTip = Next Page
10
11   # tooltip for back button
12   backToolTip = Previous Page
```

Fig. 2.16 Properties file for default **Locale** (US English)—
StringsAndLabels.properties (part 2 of 2).

```
 1   # French language strings for internationalized WebBrowser
 2   # tooltip for back button
 3   backToolTip = Page pr\u00E9c\u00E9dente
 4
 5   # application title
 6   applicationTitle = Logiciel de Navigation de Deitel
 7
 8   # title for WebToolBar
 9   toolBarTitle = Navigation des Pages sur la Toile
10
11   # tooltip for forward toolbar button
12   forwardToolTip = Prochaine Page
```

Fig. 2.17 Properties file for French **Locale**—
StringsAndLabels_fr_FR.properties.

The filenames for properties files enable internationalized applications to load the proper resources for the selected **Locale**. Note the names in the above figure captions for the properties files. The properties file for the default **Locale** (i.e., the **Locale** used if there is none specified) is named **StringsAndLabels.properties**. The properties file for **Locale.FRANCE** is named **StringsAndLabels_fr_FR.properties**. This name specifies that this is an internationalized version of the **StringsAndLabels** properties file for the French language (**fr**) in the country of France (**FR**). The lowercase language abbreviation is an *ISO Language Code* for the French language. The uppercase country abbreviation is an *ISO Country Code* for the country of France. Together, the ISO Language Code and ISO Country Code specify a locale. The list of ISO Language codes is available at **www.ics.uci.edu/pub/ietf/http/related/iso639.txt**. The list of ISO Country Codes is available at **www.chemie.fu-berlin.de/diverse/doc/ISO_3166.html**.

2.8 Accessibility

Accessibility refers to the level of an application's usability for people with disabilities. To make an application accessible means to ensure that the application works for people with disabilities. Many software applications are inaccessible to people with visual, learning or mobility impairments. A high level of accessibility is difficult to achieve because there are many different disabilities, language barriers, hardware and software inconsistencies and so on. As greater numbers of people use computers, it is imperative that application designers increase the accessibility of their applications. Recent legislation in the United States has brought accessibility to the forefront of Web and application development.

The Swing API designers took advantage of the Java Accessibility API to build accessibility features into every Swing component to facilitate creating accessible Java applications. As a result, Java developers who use the Swing APIs to build application GUIs need only use the Swing APIs properly to enable most accessibility features. For example, when creating GUI elements such as **JButton**s and **JMenuItem**s, developers should provide tooltip text that describes the component and mnemonic keys or accelerator keys for enabling keyboard access. These simple properties enable accessibility tools, such as screen readers, to convey important descriptive information to the user. Enabling keyboard access makes applications easier to navigate for all users, and also allows accessibility tools to navigate the application more easily.

When it is not appropriate for a GUI component to have a tooltip or label, developers can use methods **setAccessibleName** and **setAccessibleDescription** of class **AccessibilityContext** to provide descriptive text. Each Swing component contains an **AccessibilityContext** for enabling the component's accessibility features. Assistive technologies (e.g., screen readers, input devices) then use the Java Access Bridge to interact with the Java application to take advantage of the developer-provided descriptive text.

Class **ActionSample2** (Fig. 2.18) modifies class **ActionSample** (Fig. 2.5) to demonstrate adding accessible component names and descriptions to Swing components.

Action actionSample (lines 26–50) now contains accessible text in the dialog box that opens when **actionSample** is fired. Lines 36–37 declare an **AccessibleContext** object for the **JOptionPane action** by calling method **getAccessibleContext** on **action**. Line 38 calls method **setAccessibleName** to set **action**'s name in **AccessibleContext actionContext**. Lines 39–41 call method **setAccessibleDescription** of class **AccessibleContext** to set **actionSample**'s description. Line 53 specify a name for **actionSample** and lines 60–61 specify a short description. Lines 64–65 assign a mnemonic key to **actionSample**.

Action exitAction (lines 68–92) now contains accessible text in the dialog box that opens when **exitSample** is fired. Lines 78–79 obtain an **AccessibleContext** for the **JOptionPane** by invoking method **getAccessibleContext**. Line 80 calls method **setAccessibleName** to specify a name for the JOptionPane's **AccessibleContext**. Lines 81–83 call method **setAccessibleContext**. Line 96 specifies a name for **exitAction** by invoking method **putValue** of interface **Action**. Lines 102–103 associate a short description with **exitAction**. Lines 106–107 assign a mnenonic key to **exitAction**.

```
1   // ActionSample2.java
2   // ActionSample2 demonstrates the Accessibility features of
3   // Swing components.
4   package com.deitel.advjhtp1.gui.actions;
5
6   // Java core packages
7   import java.awt.*;
8   import java.awt.event.*;
9
```

Fig. 2.18 ActionSample2 demonstrates **Accessibility** package (part 1 of 5).

```
10   // Java extension packages
11   import javax.accessibility.*;
12   import javax.swing.*;
13
14   public class ActionSample2 extends JFrame {
15
16      // Swing Actions
17      private Action sampleAction;
18      private Action exitAction;
19
20      // ActionSample2 constructor
21      public ActionSample2()
22      {
23         super( "Using Actions" );
24
25         // create AbstractAction subclass for sampleAction
26         sampleAction = new AbstractAction() {
27
28            public void actionPerformed( ActionEvent event )
29            {
30               // display message indicating sampleAction invoked
31               JOptionPane action = new JOptionPane(
32                  "The sampleAction was invoked." );
33
34               // get AccessibleContext for action and set name
35               // and description
36               AccessibleContext actionContext =
37                  action.getAccessibleContext();
38               actionContext.setAccessibleName( "sampleAction" );
39               actionContext.setAccessibleDescription(
40                  "SampleAction opens a dialog box to demonstrate"
41                  + " the Action class." );
42
43               // create and display dialog box
44               action.createDialog( ActionSample2.this,
45                  "sampleAction" ).setVisible( true );
46
47               // enable exitAction and associated GUI components
48               exitAction.setEnabled( true );
49            }
50         };
51
52         // set Action name
53         sampleAction.putValue( Action.NAME, "Sample Action" );
54
55         // set Action Icon
56         sampleAction.putValue( Action.SMALL_ICON, new ImageIcon(
57            getClass().getResource( "images/Help24.gif" ) ) );
58
59         // set Action short description (tooltip text)
60         sampleAction.putValue( Action.SHORT_DESCRIPTION,
61            "A Sample Action" );
```

Fig. 2.18 ActionSample2 demonstrates **Accessibility** package (part 2 of 5).

```
62
63     // set Action mnemonic key
64     sampleAction.putValue( Action.MNEMONIC_KEY,
65        new Integer( 'S' ) );
66
67     // create AbstractAction subclass for exitAction
68     exitAction = new AbstractAction() {
69
70        public void actionPerformed( ActionEvent event )
71        {
72           // display message indicating sampleAction invoked
73           JOptionPane exit = new JOptionPane(
74              "The exitAction was invoked." );
75
76           // get AccessibleContext for exit and set name and
77           // description
78           AccessibleContext exitContext =
79              exit.getAccessibleContext();
80           exitContext.setAccessibleName( "exitAction" );
81           exitContext.setAccessibleDescription( "ExitAction"
82              + " opens a dialog box to demonstrate the"
83              + " Action class and then exits the program." );
84
85           // create and display dialog box
86           exit.createDialog( ActionSample2.this,
87              "exitAction" ).setVisible( true );
88
89           // exit program
90           System.exit( 0 );
91        }
92     };
93
94     // set Action name
95     exitAction.putValue( Action.NAME, "Exit" );
96
97     // set Action icon
98     exitAction.putValue( Action.SMALL_ICON, new ImageIcon(
99        getClass().getResource( "images/EXIT.gif" ) ) );
100
101     // set Action short description (tooltip text)
102     exitAction.putValue( Action.SHORT_DESCRIPTION,
103        "Exit Application" );
104
105     // set Action mnemonic key
106     exitAction.putValue( Action.MNEMONIC_KEY,
107        new Integer( 'x' ) );
108
109     // disable exitAction and associated GUI components
110     exitAction.setEnabled( false );
111
112     // create File menu
113     JMenu fileMenu = new JMenu( "File" );
```

Fig. 2.18 ActionSample2 demonstrates **Accessibility** package (part 3 of 5).

```
114
115        // add sampleAction and exitAction to File menu to
116        // create a JMenuItem for each Action
117        fileMenu.add( sampleAction );
118        fileMenu.add( exitAction );
119
120        fileMenu.setMnemonic( 'F' );
121
122        // create JMenuBar and add File menu
123        JMenuBar menuBar = new JMenuBar();
124        menuBar.add( fileMenu );
125        setJMenuBar( menuBar );
126
127        // create JToolBar
128        JToolBar toolBar = new JToolBar();
129
130        // add sampleAction and exitAction to JToolBar to create
131        // JButtons for each Action
132        toolBar.add( sampleAction );
133        toolBar.add( exitAction );
134
135        // get AccessibleContext for toolBar and set name and
136        // description
137        AccessibleContext toolContext =
138           toolBar.getAccessibleContext();
139        toolContext.setAccessibleName( "ToolBar" );
140        toolContext.setAccessibleDescription( "ToolBar contains"
141           + " sampleAction button and exitAction button." );
142
143        // create JButton and set its Action to sampleAction
144        JButton sampleButton = new JButton();
145        sampleButton.setAction( sampleAction );
146
147        // get AccessibleContext for sampleButton and set name
148        // and description
149        AccessibleContext sampleContext =
150           sampleButton.getAccessibleContext();
151        sampleContext.setAccessibleName( "SampleButton" );
152        sampleContext.setAccessibleDescription( "SampleButton"
153           + " produces a sampleAction event." );
154
155        // create JButton and set its Action to exitAction
156        JButton exitButton = new JButton( exitAction );
157
158        // get AccessibleContext for exitButton and set name and
159        // description
160        AccessibleContext exitContext =
161           exitButton.getAccessibleContext();
162        exitContext.setAccessibleName( "ExitButton" );
163        exitContext.setAccessibleDescription( "ExitButton"
164           + " produces an exitAction event." );
165
```

Fig. 2.18 `ActionSample2` demonstrates `Accessibility` package (part 4 of 5).

```
166         // lay out JButtons in JPanel
167         JPanel buttonPanel = new JPanel();
168         buttonPanel.add( sampleButton );
169         buttonPanel.add( exitButton );
170
171         // add toolBar and buttonPanel to JFrame's content pane
172         Container container = getContentPane();
173         container.add( toolBar, BorderLayout.NORTH );
174         container.add( buttonPanel, BorderLayout.CENTER );
175
176     }
177
178     // execute application
179     public static void main( String args[] )
180     {
181         ActionSample2 sample = new ActionSample2();
182         sample.setDefaultCloseOperation( EXIT_ON_CLOSE );
183         sample.pack();
184         sample.setVisible( true );
185     }
186 }
```

Fig. 2.18 `ActionSample2` demonstrates `Accessibility` package (part 5 of 5).

Line 120 adds a mnemonic key for the **File** menu to enable keyboard access to this menu. Lines 137–138 obtain the **AccessibleContext** for **toolBar**. Line 139 sets a name for **toolBar** by invoking method **setAccessibleName**. Lines 140–141 set a description for **toolBar** by invoking method **setAccessibleDescription**. Lines 149–150 obtain an **AccessibleContext** for **JButton sampleButton**. Line 151 sets a name for **sampleButton** by invoking method **setAccessibleName**. Lines 152–153 set a description for **sampleButton** by invoking method **setAccessible-Description**. Lines 160–161 obtain an **AccessibleContext** for **JButton exitButton**. Line 162 sets a name for **exitButton** by invoking method **setAccessibleName**. Lines 163–164 set a description for **exitButton** by invoking method **setAccessibleDescription**.

We will download the *Java Access Bridge* and a demonstration of *JAWS for Windows 3.7* to demonstrate the accessibility features of **ActionSample2**. The Java Access Bridge allows assistive programs in Windows to use the accessibility information of a Java program. The Java Access Bridge can be downloaded at

> **java.sun.com/products/accessbridge**

JAWS for Windows is a screen reader from Henter-Joyce (**www.hj.com**). A demonstration version of JAWS can be downloaded at

> **www.hj.com/JAWS/JAWS37DemoOp.htm**

Download and install both programs to try the rest of the example in this section.

With the Access Bridge installed and JAWS running in the background, execute **ActionSample2**. JAWS reads the name of the new window that opens. The GUI of **ActionSample2** (Fig. 2.19) is identical to the original **ActionSample** (Fig. 2.5).

Switch between the buttons by pressing *Tab* to move forward or *Shift + Tab* to move backward. JAWS reads the name of the new button whenever the focus changes. To press the button that holds the focus, press the space bar. The **sampleAction** dialog opens and JAWS reads its name. Pressing the space bar or the *Enter* key closes the dialog. The **Exit** button is now available in the GUI. Switch the focus to the larger button labeled **Sample Action** (not the one in the tool bar) and press *Insert + F1*. This JAWS command reads the description attached to the button's **AccessibleContext** (Fig. 2.20). Do the same command on the **Exit** button to hear its description (Fig. 2.21). **ActionSample2**'s **Action**s are also available through the **File** menu. The **File** menu's mnemonic key is the underlined letter **F**. Pressing *Alt + F* opens the **File** menu and causes JAWS to read the menu name (Fig. 2.22). The arrow keys move the cursor within the menu. JAWS reads the name of each menu item as it is selected (Fig. 2.23). Pressing the space bar, *Enter* key, or a mnemonic key activates one of the **Action**s.

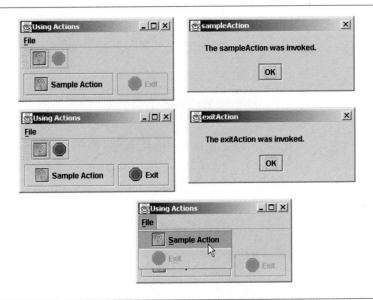

Fig. 2.19 Actions **sampleAction** and **exitAction** of **ActionSample2**.

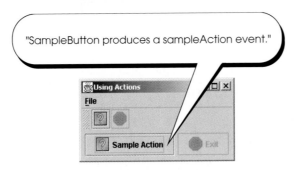

Fig. 2.20 AccessibleDescription of **sampleButton**.

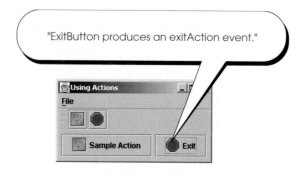

Fig. 2.21   `AccessibleDescription` of `exitButton`.

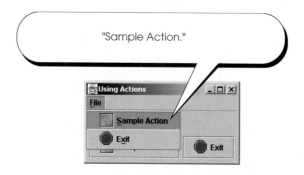

Fig. 2.22   **Sample Action** menu item description.

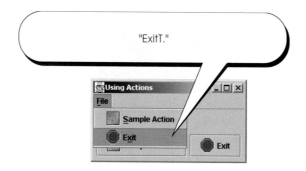

Fig. 2.23   **Exit** menu item description.

2.9 Internet and World Wide Web Resources

Swing

java.sun.com/products/jfc/tsc
The Swing Connection contains technical articles and documentation for Swing components.

www.javaworld.com/javaworld/topicalindex/jw-ti-foundation.html
JavaWorld collection of Swing-related articles.

Internationalization

www.ibm.com/developerworks/theme/international-index.html
IBM offers links to internationalization resources including multilingual software and international calendars.

developer.java.sun.com/developer/technicalArticles/Intl/index.html
This site provides numerous articles on learning how to localize and internationalize various Java programs.

www.onjava.com/pub/a/onjava/2001/04/12/internationalization.html
This article, *Java Internationalization and Localization*, by Jaric Sng describes the steps for accessing, installing, and determining fonts, focusing on Japanese, Chinese, and Korean.

java.sun.com/j2se/1.3/docs/guide/intl
This site supplies a guide to Java internationalization. It includes a detailed section on formatting currencies, time zones, dates, texts, messages and other international dissimilarities.

Accessibility

java.sun.com/products/jfc/jaccess-1.3/doc/guide.html
Sun Microsystems has improved Java accessibility through Java Accessibility API and Java Accessibility Utilities. Check out a detailed description of these packages at this site.

developer.java.sun.com/developer/earlyAccess/jaccesshelper
The Java Accessibility Helper examines Java programs for accessibility issues and provides a report that details changes needed to be made. This is an early-access download and requires a free registration with the Java Developer Connection Web site.

www.ibm.com/able/snsjavag.html
"IBM Guidelines for Writing Accessible Applications Using 100% Pure Java," by Richard S. Schwerdtfeger, states the necessary features that should be provided to create full accessibility. In addition, this online guidebook discusses the various programs to achieve accessibility.

www.sun.com/access/developers/access.quick.ref.html
This site simply emphasizes the importance of accessibility and gives tips on making applications accessible.

www.w3.org/WAI
The World Wide Web Consortium's *Web Accessibility Initiative* (*WAI*) site promotes design of universally accessible Web sites. This site will help you keep up-to-date with current guidelines and forthcoming recommendations for Web accessibility.

www.sun.com/access/gnome
GNOME Developer's Site provides information on various assistive technologies, such as screen magnifiers and screen keyboards for Linux and Unix platforms that use the GNOME user interface.

www.voice-assistant.com
The Voice Mate V4 assists the blind with using a computer. It speaks the menu options and characters as they are typed.

www.magnifiers.org
On this site, you can find information and downloads for screen magnifiers.

www.voicerecognition.com
This site contains information on various voice-recognition products.

trace.wisc.edu/world/web
This site explains how to make Web sites more accessible to disabled users. It also gives multiple references to other sites on Web accessibility.

www.access-board.gov/508.htm
Electronic version of Section 508 of the Rehabilitation Act, which mandates that government agencies provide accessible electronic access to information from federal agencies.

SUMMARY

- Swing provides three basic types of text components for presenting and editing text. Class **JTextComponent** is the base class for all Swing text components, including **JTextField**, **JTextArea** and **JEditorPane**.

- **JTextField** is a single-line text component suitable for obtaining simple user input or displaying information such as form field values, calculation results and so on. **JPasswordField** is a subclass of **JTextField** suitable for obtaining user passwords.

- **JEditorPane** provides enhanced text-rendering capabilities. **JEditorPane** supports styled documents that include formatting, font and color information. **JEditorPane** is capable of rendering HTML documents as well as Rich Text Format (RTF) documents.

- Toolbars are GUI containers typically located below an application's menus. Toolbars contain buttons and other GUI components for commonly used features, such as cut, copy and paste, or navigation buttons for a Web browser.

- Class **javax.swing.JToolBar** enables developers to add toolbars to Swing user interfaces. **JToolBar** also enables users to modify the appearance of the **JToolBar** in a running application.

- Users can drag a **JToolBar** from the top of a windows and "dock" the **JToolBar**s on the side or bottom. Users also can drag the **JToolBar** away from the application window to create a floating **JToolBar**.

- Based on **JToolBar**'s inheritance hierarchy, each **JToolBar** also is a **java.awt.Container** and therefore can contain other GUI components.

- A **JToolBar** has property **orientation** that specifies how the **JToolBar** will arrange its child components. The default is horizontal orientation, which indicates that the **JToolBar** lays out its child components next to one another.

- The Command design pattern enables developers to define requests (e.g., a user request to copy text) once in a reusable object that the developer then can add to a menu, toolbar or pop-up menu. This design pattern is called Command because it defines a user command or instruction.

- An **Action**, which implements the Command design pattern, represents user-interface logic and properties for GUI components that represent that logic, such as the label for a button, the text for a tool tip and the mnemonic key for keyboard access.

- The logic for an **Action** takes the form of an **actionPerformed** method that the event mechanism invokes in response to the user activating an interface component (e.g., the user clicking a **JButton**).

- Interface **Action** extends interface **ActionListener**, which enables **Action**s to process **ActionEvent**s generated by GUI components. **Action**s provide an additional benefit in that the developer can enable or disable all GUI components associated with an **Action** by enabling or disabling the **Action** itself.

- that **sampleAction** was invoked. Line 33 then invokes method **setEnabled** of interface **Action** on the **exitAction** reference. This enables the **exitAction** and its associated GUI components. Note that **Action**s are enabled by default. We disabled the **exitAction** (line 80) to demonstrate that this disables the GUI components associated with that **Action**.

- **JSplitPane** and **JTabbedPane** are container components that enable developers to present large amounts of information in a small screen area.

- **JSplitPane** divides two components with a divider that users can reposition to expand and contract the visible areas of the **JSplitPane**'s child components. **JSplitPane**s can contain only two child components, although each child component may contain nested components.

- The constant **JSplitPane.HORIZONTAL_SPLIT** specifies the **JSplitPane** should display its child components side-by-side. The constant **JSplitPane.VERTICAL_SPLIT** specifies that the **JSplitPane** should display its child components one on top of the other.

- Adding child components to **JScrollPane**s before adding those components to a **JSplitPane** ensures that the user will be able to view all the content in each child component by scrolling if necessary.

- **JTabbedPane** presents multiple components in separate tabs, which the user can navigate using a mouse or keyboard. Dialog boxes often use components similar to **JTabbedPane**s.

- Multiple document interfaces allow users to view multiple documents in a single application. Each document appears in a separate window in the application. The user can arrange, resize, iconify (i.e., minimize) and maximize these separate document windows like application windows on the desktop.

- **JInternalFrame**s behave much like **JFrame**s. Users can maximize, iconify, resize, open and close **JInternalFrame**s. **JInternalFrame**s have title bars with buttons for iconifying, maximizing and closing. Users also can move **JInternalFrame**s within the **JDesktopPane**.

- **JInternalFrame**s have no size and are invisible by default. When creating a new **JInternalFrame**, be sure to invoke method **setSize** to size the **JInternalFrame** and **setVisible(true)** to make the **JInternalFrame** visible.

- Drag and drop enables users to move items around the desktop and to move and copy data among applications using mouse gestures. A gesture is a mouse movement that corresponds to a drag-and-drop operation, such as dragging a file from one folder and dropping the file into another folder.

- The data transfer API—package **java.awt.datatransfer**—enables copying and moving data within a single application or among multiple applications. The drag-and-drop API enables Java applications to recognize drag-and-drop gestures and to respond to drag-and-drop operations.

- A drag-and-drop operation uses the data transfer API to transfer data from the drag source to the drop target. Applications can use the drag-and-drop API to recognize drag-and-drop operations and use the data transfer API to retrieve the data transferred through those drag-and-drop operations.

- The drag-and-drop subsystem invokes method **drop** of interface **DropTargetListener** when the user drops an object on a **DropTarget**.

- Interface **java.awt.datatransfer.Transferable** declares methods that represent an object that can be transferred among applications. As part of the datatransfer API, interface **Transferable** represents objects that may be transferred through the system clipboard (e.g., via cut-and-paste operations) and objects that are transferred through drag and drop.

- Internationalization is the process of preparing an application for distribution in multiple locales. A locale identifies the language, currency, character set, date formats and other items most widely used for presenting information in a particular country or region.

- Applications to be distributed in multiple locales must display information in the correct language and with appropriate date, currency and other formats.

- A **ResourceBundle** is a Java properties file that maps keys to string values. For example, a **ResourceBundle** could contain the key **exitButtonLabel** with the string value **Exit**. Instead of hard coding the string **Exit** on a **JButton**'s label, the developer could retrieve the label from the **ResourceBundle**. The developer could then provide multiple versions of the **ResourceBundle** that use the same keys, but provide string values in different languages.

- The developer also must use locale-sensitive classes to format data, such as dates, times and currencies, using locale-specific formats. There are several locale-sensitive classes that can perform this formatting, such as **NumberFormat** and **DateFormat**.

- Internationalized applications also must use Unicode characters. Unicode is a standard for encoding characters for most of the world's languages. Java uses Unicode to represent all characters.

- The filenames for properties files enable internationalized applications to load the proper resources for the selected **Locale**. These filenames must use a lowercase language abbreviation—called an ISO Language Code—and an uppercase country abbreviation—called an ISO Country Code.

- *Accessibility* refers to the level of an application's usability for people with disabilities. To make an application accessible means to ensure that the application works for people with disabilities.

- Many software applications are inaccessible to people with visual, learning or mobility impairments. A high level of accessibility is difficult to achieve because there are many different disabilities, language barriers, hardware and software inconsistencies and so on.

- Recent legislation in the United States has brought accessibility to the forefront of Web and application development.

- The Swing API designers took advantage of the Java Accessibility API to build accessibility features into every Swing component to facilitate creating accessible Java applications. As a result, Java developers who use the Swing APIs to build application GUIs need only use the Swing APIs properly to enable most accessibility features.

- Developers should provide tooltip text that describes each component and mnemonic keys or accelerator keys for enabling keyboard access. These simple properties enable accessibility tools, such as screen readers, to convey important descriptive information to the user. Enabling keyboard access makes applications easier to navigate for all users, and also allows accessibility tools to navigate the application more easily.

- Methods **setAccessibleName** and **setAccessibleDescription** of class **AccessibilityContext** enable developers to provide descriptive text for components. Each Swing component contains an **AccessibilityContext** for enabling the component's accessibility features.

- Assistive technologies (e.g., screen readers, input devices) can use the Java Access Bridge to interact with Java applications to take advantage of the developer-provided descriptive text.

TERMINOLOGY

AbstractAction class
accessibility
AccessibleContext class
Action interface
Action.ACCELERATOR_KEY constant
Action.ACTION_COMMAND_KEY constant
Action.MNEMONIC_KEY constant
Action.NAME constant
Action.SHORT_DESCRIPTION constant
Action.SMALL_ICON constant
addHyperlinkListener method of class
    JEditorPane
Command design pattern
DataFlavor.javaFileListFlavor
    constant
DnDConstants class

drag and drop
drag-and-drop gesture
drag-and-drop operation
DropTarget class
DropTargetDragEvent class
DropTargetDropEvent class
DropTargetListener interface
HyperlinkEvent class
HyperlinkEvent.EventType.
    ACTIVATED constant
HyperlinkListener interface
iconify
internationalization
Java Access Bridge
JDesktopPane class
JEditorPane class

JInternalFrame class	**putValue** method of interface **Action**
JPasswordField class	**ResourceBundle** class
JSplitPane class	screen reader
JSplitPane.HORIZONTAL_SPLIT constant	**setAccessibleDescription** method of
JSplitPane.VERTICAL_SPLIT constant	class **AccessibleContext**
JTabbedPane class	**setAccessibleName** method of class
JTextArea class	**AccessibleContext**
JTextComponent class	**setEditable** method of class **JEditorPane**
JTextField class	**setEnabled** method of interface **Action**
JToolBar class	tab
Locale class	toolbar
maximize	tooltip
multiple-document interface	**Transferable** interface
orientation property of class **JToolBar**	

SELF-REVIEW EXERCISES

2.1 State which of the following are *true* and which are *false*. If *false*, explain why.
a) The Abstract Windowing Toolkit provides a richer set of components than the Swing component set.
b) Swing provides a pluggable look and feel that enables components to change their appearance.
c) **JEditorPane** is capable of rendering only plain text, not richly styled text.
d) Toolbars—implemented by class **JToolBar**—enable developers to provide users with quick access to commonly used user-interface elements, such as cut, copy and paste.
e) Interface **Action** provides set and get methods for each **Action** property.
f) **JSplitPane**s can contain any number of child components.

2.2 Fill in the blanks in each of the following:
a) The drag-and-drop API uses the _____ API to transfer data through drag-and-drop operations.
b) A multiple document interface uses instances of class _____ for individual windows, which are contained in a _____.
c) The **JInternalFrame** constructor takes four boolean arguments that indicate whether the window is _____, _____, _____ and _____..
d) A _____ identifies the language, currency, character set, date formats and other items most widely used for presenting information in a particular country or region.
e) _____ refers to the level of an application's usability for people with disabilities.

ANSWERS TO SELF-REVIEW EXERCISES

2.1 a) False. Swing provides a richer set of components than the older AWT. b) True. c) False. **JEditorPane** can render HTML and RTF documents, which can contain rich styling information. d) True. e) False. Interface **Action** provides method **putValue**, which enables programmers to specify the property name and value as a key/value pair. f) False. Each **JSplitPane** may contain exactly two child components, but each child component may contain its own child components.

2.2 a) data transfer API. b) **JInternalFrame**, **JDesktopPane**. c) resizable, closable, maximizable, iconifiable. d) **Locale**. e) Accessibility.

EXERCISES

2.3 Modify class **WebToolBar** (Fig. 2.3) to include a **JComboBox** from which the user can select URLs from the history.

2.4 Create an image-viewing application that supports drag-and-drop loading of images. When the user drags and drops a image file onto the application window, load that image in an **ImageIcon** and display the **ImageIcon** in a **JPanel**.

2.5 Modify class **ActionSample2** (Fig. 2.18) to use **ResourceBundle**s for all user-visible **String**s in the application. If you know a language other than English, provide a **ResourceBundle** that contains Strings in that language.

2.6 Making an application accessible requires that the application provides keyboard navigation for all the application's functionality. Unplug your mouse from your computer and try using various programs, such as word processors, Web browsers and the Java programs in this chapter. What about these applications makes it difficult to navigate without a mouse? Is there functionality that you cannot access using a keyboard?

Model-View-Controller

Objectives

- To understand the model-view-controller (MVC) architecture for separating data, presentation and user input logic.
- To understand the Observer design pattern.
- To understand MVC's use in Java's Swing GUI components.
- To understand the default model implementations for Swing components.
- To understand the use of **TableModel**s to represent tabular data for **JTable**s.
- To understand tree data structures and their use as **TreeModel**s for **JTree**s.

The universe is wider than our views of it.
Henry David Thoreau

Let all your views in life be directed to a solid, however moderate, independence; ...
Junius

I think that I shall never see
A poem as lovely as a tree.
Joyce Kilmer

Outline

3.1 Introduction

In this chapter, we introduce the *model-view-controller architecture* (MVC) and its particular application in Java's Swing classes. The MVC architecture uses object-oriented design principles to modularize applications into data components, presentation components and input-processing components. Data components maintain the raw application data, such as the text of a document in a word processor or the locations of the pieces in a game of chess. The presentation components most commonly provide a visual representation of application data—for example a 3D graphic showing the chessboard and the arrangement of pieces. The input-processing components handle input from the user, such as dragging the mouse to move a piece on the chess board.

MVC has many uses in desktop applications, enterprise applications, simulations and other types of programs. In this chapter, we discuss MVC in general and its variant, the *delegate-model architecture*. We also introduce the Observer design pattern, which is a design pattern built into the MVC architecture. After reading this chapter, you will be able to design your own programs using MVC. You also will be able to take advantage of advanced Swing components that use the delegate-model architecture, such as **JList**, **JTable** and **JTree**.

3.2 Model-View-Controller Architecture

The *model-view-controller* architecture (MVC) separates application data (contained in the *model*) from graphical presentation components (the *view*) and input-processing logic (the *controller*). MVC originally appeared in Smalltalk-80 as a method for separating user interfaces from underlying application data.[1] Figure 3.1 shows the relationships between components in MVC. In our Enterprise Java case study (Chapters 17–20), we will show that MVC is applicable across a wide range of problems and can make applications easier to maintain and extend.

The controller implements logic for processing user input. The model contains application data, and the view generates a presentation of the data stored in the model. When a

---

1. E. Gamma et al., *Design Patterns* (New York: Addison-Wesley Publishing Company, 1995), 4.

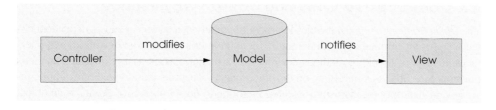

Fig. 3.1   Model-view-controller architecture.

user provides some input (e.g., by typing text in a word processor,) the controller modifies the model with the given input. It is important to note that the model contains only the raw application data. In a simple text editor, the model might contain only the characters that make up the document. When the model changes, it notifies the view of the change, so that the view can update its presentation with the changed data. The view in a word processor might display the characters on the screen in a particular font, with a particular size, etc.

MVC does not restrict an application to a single view and controller. In a word processor, for example, there might be two views of a single document model. One view might display the document as an outline, and the other might display the document in a print-preview window. The word processor also may implement multiple controllers, such as a controller for handling keyboard input and a controller for handling mouse selections. If either controller makes a change in the model, both the outline view and the print-preview window show the change immediately, because the model notifies all views of any changes. A developer can provide additional views and controllers for the model without changing the existing components.

Java's Swing components implement a variation of MVC that combines the view and controller into a single object, called a *delegate* (Fig. 3.2). The delegate provides both a graphical presentation of the model and an interface for modifying the model. For example, every **JButton** has an associated **ButtonModel** for which the **JButton** is a delegate. The **ButtonModel** maintains state information, such as whether the **JButton** is pressed and whether the **JButton** is enabled, as well as a list of **ActionListener**s. The **JButton** provides a graphical presentation (e.g., a rectangle on the screen with a label and a border) and modifies the **ButtonModel**'s state (e.g., when the user presses the **JButton**). We discuss several Swing components that implement the delegate-model architecture throughout this chapter.

Fig. 3.2   Delegate-model architecture in Java Swing components.

3.3 Observable Class and Observer Interface

The *Observer design pattern* enables loose coupling between an object and its dependent objects.[2] Loosely coupled objects interact by invoking methods declared in well-known interfaces, instead of invoking methods declared in particular classes. Using interface methods prevents each object from relying on the other objects' concrete class type. For example, Java's event-handling mechanism uses loose coupling to notify objects of events. If an object needs to handle certain events, it implements the appropriate listener interface (e.g., **ActionListener**). Objects that generate events invoke listener interface methods to notify listening objects of events. This loose coupling enables a **JButton**, for example, to send an **ActionEvent** to a **JFrame** subclass that implements **ActionListener**. The **JButton** interacts with the **JFrame** subclass only through method **actionPerformed** of interface **ActionListener**, and not through any method that is specific to the **JFrame** subclass. The **JButton** can send **ActionEvent**s to other objects that also implement interface **ActionListener** (e.g., a programmer-defined class or an inner class).

Class ***java.util.Observable*** represents a model in MVC, or the *subject* in the Observer design pattern. Class **Observable** provides method ***addObserver***, which takes a ***java.util.Observer*** argument. Interface **Observer** represents the view in MVC and enables loose coupling between an **Observable** object and its **Observer**s. When the **Observable** object changes, it notifies each registered **Observer** of the change. The **Observer** can be an instance of any class that implements interface **Observer**; because the **Observable** object invokes methods defined in interface **Observer**, the objects remain loosely coupled. We discuss the details of this interaction in the example that follows.

The example in Fig. 3.4–Fig. 3.10. uses the MVC architecture, class **Observable** and interface **Observer** to implement an **AccountManager** application for managing bank account information. Figure 3.3 illustrates the application's MVC architecture. The **AccountController** accepts user input in the form of dollar amounts entered in a **JTextField**. The user then selects a **JButton**, either to withdraw or deposit the given amount, and the **AccountController** modifies the **Account** to execute the transaction. Class **Account** is an **Observable** object that acts as the application's model. When the **AccountController** performs the withdrawal or deposit, the **Account** notifies each view (**AccountTextView**, **AccountBarGraphView** and **Account-PieChartView**) that the **Account** information has changed. Each view updates its display with the modified **Account** information.

Class **Account** (Fig. 3.4) represents a bank account in the **AccountManager** application (Fig. 3.10). Class **Account** extends class **Observable** (line 9) and acts as a model in the application. Class **Account** has **balance** and **name** properties that represent the amount of money in the **Account** and a short description of the **Account**. The **Account** constructor (lines 18–22) initializes the **name** and **balance** properties.

Method **setBalance** (lines 25–35) changes the model by updating the account **balance**. The MVC architecture requires the model to notify its views when the model changes. Line 31 invokes method ***setChanged*** of class **Observable** to set the model's ***changed*** flag. Line 34 invokes method ***notifyObservers*** of class **Observable** to notify all **Account Observer**s (i.e., views) of the change. An **Observable** object

---

2. E. Gamma et al., *Design Patterns* (New York: Addison-Wesley Publishing Company, 1995), 293.

must invoke method **setChanged** before invoking method **notifyObservers**. Method **notifyObservers** invokes method **update** of interface **Observer** for each registered **Observer**. Method **getBalance** (lines 38–41) simply returns the current **Account** balance. Method **getBalance** does not modify the model, so method **getBalance** does not invoke **setChanged** or **notifyObservers**.

> ### Common Programming Error 3.1
> *Failing to invoke method **setChanged** before invoking method **notifyObservers** is a logic error. If method **setChanged** has not been invoked, method **notifyObservers** considers the **Observable** object unchanged and will not invoke each **Observer**'s **update** method.*

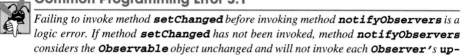

AccountController modifies **Account** by withdrawing and depositing funds.

AccountController → **Account**

Account notifies each view that the **Account** has changed.

AccountTextView

AccountBarGraphView

AccountPieChartView

Each view updates its display to reflect the new **Account** information.

Fig. 3.3   **AccountManager** application MVC architecture.

```
1   // Account.java
2   // Account is an Observable class that represents a bank
3   // account in which funds may be deposited or withdrawn.
4   package com.deitel.advjhtp1.mvc.account;
5
6   // Java core packages
7   import java.util.Observable;
8
9   public class Account extends Observable {
10
11      // Account balance
12      private double balance;
13
14      // readonly Account name
15      private String name;
16
17      // Account constructor
18      public Account( String accountName, double openingDeposit )
19      {
```

Fig. 3.4   **Account Observable** class that represents a bank account (part 1 of 2).

```
20          name = accountName;
21          setBalance( openingDeposit );
22       }
23
24       // set Account balance and notify observers of change
25       private void setBalance( double accountBalance )
26       {
27          balance = accountBalance;
28
29          // must call setChanged before notifyObservers to
30          // indicate model has changed
31          setChanged();
32
33          // notify Observers that model has changed
34          notifyObservers();
35       }
36
37       // get Account balance
38       public double getBalance()
39       {
40          return balance;
41       }
42
43       // withdraw funds from Account
44       public void withdraw( double amount )
45          throws IllegalArgumentException
46       {
47          if ( amount < 0 )
48             throw new IllegalArgumentException(
49                "Cannot withdraw negative amount" );
50
51          // update Account balance
52          setBalance( getBalance() - amount );
53       }
54
55       // deposit funds in account
56       public void deposit( double amount )
57          throws IllegalArgumentException
58       {
59          if ( amount < 0 )
60             throw new IllegalArgumentException(
61                "Cannot deposit negative amount" );
62
63          // update Account balance
64          setBalance( getBalance() + amount );
65       }
66
67       // get Account name (readonly)
68       public String getName()
69       {
70          return name;
71       }
72    }
```

Fig. 3.4   **Account Observable** class that represents a bank account (part 2 of 2).

Software Engineering Observation 3.1

*Method **notifyObservers** does not guarantee the order in which it notifies **Observers**. Method **notifyObservers** as implemented in class **Observable** notifies **Observers** in the order the **Observers** were registered, but this behavior may be different in **Observable** subclasses or in different Java implementations.*

Software Engineering Observation 3.2

*Method **notifyObservers** has no relation to methods **notify** and **notifyAll** of class **Object**. Multithreaded programs use methods **notify** and **notifyAll** to wake up **Threads** waiting to obtain an **Object**'s monitor.*

Method **withdraw** (lines 44–53) subtracts the given **amount** from the **Account balance**. If the given **amount** is negative, lines 48–49 **throw** an **IllegalArgumentException**. Line 52 subtracts the withdrawn **amount** from the current **balance** and invokes method **setBalance** to update the **Account**. Method **setBalance** will notify **Observers** that the model was changed, so that the **Observers** can update their displays.

Method **deposit** (lines 56–65) adds the **amount** input to the **Account** balance. If the **amount** is negative, lines 60–61 **throw** an **IllegalArgumentException**. Line 64 adds the deposit **amount** to the current **balance** and invokes method **setBalance** to update the **Account**. Method **getName** (lines 68–71) returns the **Account name**.

Application **AccountManager** presents **Account** information to the user through three views: **AccountTextView**, **AccountBarGraphView** and **AccountPie-ChartView**. Each view presents a different visual representation of the **Account** information. **AbstractAccountView** (Fig. 3.5) is an **abstract** base class for these **Account** views that provides common functionality, such as registering as an **Account** observer. Class **AbstractAccountView** implements interface **Observer**, which allows each **AbstractAccountView** subclass to register as an **Observer** of an **Account**. .

```
1   // AbstractAccountView.java
2   // AbstractAccountView is an abstract class that represents
3   // a view of an Account.
4   package com.deitel.advjhtp1.mvc.account;
5
6   // Java core packages
7   import java.util.*;
8   import java.awt.*;
9
10  // Java extension packages
11  import javax.swing.JPanel;
12  import javax.swing.border.*;
13
14  public abstract class AbstractAccountView extends JPanel
15     implements Observer {
16
17     // Account to observe
18     private Account account;
19
```

Fig. 3.5　**AbstractAccountView** abstract base class for observing **Account**s (part 1 of 2).

```
20      // AbstractAccountView constructor
21      public AbstractAccountView( Account observableAccount )
22          throws NullPointerException
23      {
24          // do not allow null Accounts
25          if ( observableAccount == null )
26              throw new NullPointerException();
27
28          // update account data member to new Account
29          account = observableAccount;
30
31          // register as an Observer to receive account updates
32          account.addObserver( this );
33
34          // set display properties
35          setBackground( Color.white );
36          setBorder( new MatteBorder( 1, 1, 1, 1, Color.black ) );
37      }
38
39      // get Account for which this view is an Observer
40      public Account getAccount()
41      {
42          return account;
43      }
44
45      // update display with Account balance
46      protected abstract void updateDisplay();
47
48      // receive updates from Observable Account
49      public void update( Observable observable, Object object )
50      {
51          updateDisplay();
52      }
53  }
```

Fig. 3.5   **AbstractAccountView** abstract base class for observing **Account**s (part 2 of 2).

Class **AbstractAccountView** extends **JPanel** because **AbstractAccount-View** implementations provide graphical presentations of **Account** data. Line 18 declares a **private** member variable for the **Account** that the **AbstractAccount-View** will observe. The constructor (lines 21–37) sets the **account** member variable to the new **Account** (line 29). Line 32 invokes method **addObserver** of class **Observable** to register the newly created **AbstractAccountView** instance as an **Observer** of the new **Account**. The **Account** will now notify this **AbstractAccountView** of any modifications to the **Account**. Lines 35–36 set the **AbstractAccountView**'s background color and border.

Method **getAccount** (lines 40–43) returns the **AbstractAccountView**'s **account**. Method **updateDisplay** (line 46) is marked **abstract**, requiring each **AbstractAccountView** subclass to provide an appropriate implementation for displaying the **Account** information. For example, **AbstractAccountView** subclass **AccountTextView** provides an **updateDisplay** implementation that shows the

Account balance in a **JTextField**. Method **update** (lines 49–52) invokes method **updateDisplay** each time an **Account** notifies the **AbstractAccountView** of a change. Interface **Observer** defines method **update**, which takes as an **Observable** argument a reference to the **Observable** instance that issued the **update**. An **Observable** object issues an **update** by invoking method **notifyObservers** of class **Observable**. Method **notifyObservers** invokes method **update** for each registered **Observer**. An **Observer** that listens for updates from multiple **Observable** objects can use the **Observable** argument to determine which **Observable** object issued the **update**. The **Object** argument (line 50) contains optional data the **Observable** object may pass to an overloaded version of method **notifyObservers**. This **Object** could contain information about the specific data that changed in the model.

    AccountTextView (Fig. 3.6) extends **AbstractAccountView** to provide a text-based view of **Account** data. Line 16 creates a **JTextField** in which **AccountTextView** displays the **Account** balance. Lines 19–20 create a **NumberFormat** field to format the **Account** balance as U. S. dollars. The **AccountTextView** constructor (lines 23–35) invokes the **AbstractAccountView** constructor with the given **Account** to perform required initialization (line 25). Line 28 makes the **balanceTextField** uneditable to prevent users from modifying the balance directly. Lines 31–32 add a **JLabel** and the **balanceTextField** to the **AccountTextView**. Line 34 invokes method **updateDisplay** to display the current **Account** balance.

```
1   // AccountTextView.java
2   // AccountTextView is an AbstractAccountView subclass
3   // that displays an Account balance in a JTextField.
4   package com.deitel.advjhtp1.mvc.account;
5
6   // Java core packages
7   import java.util.*;
8   import java.text.NumberFormat;
9
10  // Java extension packages
11  import javax.swing.*;
12
13  public class AccountTextView extends AbstractAccountView {
14
15     // JTextField for displaying Account balance
16     private JTextField balanceTextField = new JTextField( 10 );
17
18     // NumberFormat for US dollars
19     private NumberFormat moneyFormat =
20        NumberFormat.getCurrencyInstance( Locale.US );
21
22     // AccountTextView constructor
23     public AccountTextView( Account account )
24     {
25        super( account );
26
```

Fig. 3.6   **AccountTextView** for displaying observed **Account** information in a **JTextField** (part 1 of 2).

```
27            // make balanceTextField readonly
28            balanceTextField.setEditable( false );
29
30            // lay out components
31            add( new JLabel( "Balance: " ) );
32            add( balanceTextField );
33
34            updateDisplay();
35        }
36
37        // update display with Account balance
38        public void updateDisplay()
39        {
40            // set text in balanceTextField to formatted balance
41            balanceTextField.setText( moneyFormat.format(
42                getAccount().getBalance() ) );
43        }
44    }
```

Fig. 3.6   **AccountTextView** for displaying observed **Account** information in a **JTextField** (part 2 of 2).

Method **updateDisplay** (lines 38–43) implements abstract method **updateDisplay** of class **AbstractAccountView**. Lines 41–42 set the **balanceTextField**'s text to the formatted **Account** balance. Recall that method **update** of class **AbstractAccountView** invokes method **updateDisplay** each time method **update** receives a notification from the **Account** model.

AccountBarGraphView (Fig. 3.7) extends **AbstractAccountView** to provide a bar-graph view of **Account** data. Method **paintComponent** (lines 21–57) draws a bar graph for the current **Account** balance. Line 24 invokes method **paintComponent** of the superclass to follow the proper painting sequence. Line 27 gets the current **Account** balance. Line 32 calculates the length in pixels of the **Account**'s bar graph. The entire graph is 200 pixels wide and represents -$5,000 to +$5,000, so we divide the **Account** balance by $10,000 and multiply by 200 pixels to calculate the length of the the bar. If the **Account** balance is positive, lines 36–37 draw the bar graph in black. If the **Account** balance is negative, lines 42–43 draw the bar graph in red.

```
1    // AccountBarGraphView.java
2    // AccountBarGraphView is an AbstractAccountView subclass
3    // that displays an Account balance as a bar graph.
4    package com.deitel.advjhtp1.mvc.account;
5
6    // Java core packages
7    import java.awt.*;
8
9    // Java extension packages
10   import javax.swing.*;
11
```

Fig. 3.7   **AccountBarGraphView** for rendering observed **Account** information as a bar graph (part 1 of 3).

```
12   public class AccountBarGraphView extends AbstractAccountView {
13
14       // AccountBarGraphView constructor
15       public AccountBarGraphView( Account account )
16       {
17           super( account );
18       }
19
20       // draw Account balance as a bar graph
21       public void paintComponent( Graphics g )
22       {
23           // ensure proper painting sequence
24           super.paintComponent( g );
25
26           // get Account balance
27           double balance = getAccount().getBalance();
28
29           // calculate integer height for bar graph (graph
30           // is 200 pixels wide and represents Account balances
31           // from -$5,000.00to +$5,000.00)
32           int barLength = ( int ) ( ( balance / 10000.0 ) * 200 );
33
34           // if balance is positive, draw graph in black
35           if ( balance >= 0.0 ) {
36               g.setColor( Color.black );
37               g.fillRect( 105, 15, barLength, 20 );
38           }
39
40           // if balance is negative, draw graph in red
41           else {
42               g.setColor( Color.red );
43               g.fillRect( 105 + barLength, 15, -barLength, 20 );
44           }
45
46           // draw vertical and horizontal axes
47           g.setColor( Color.black );
48           g.drawLine( 5, 25, 205, 25 );
49           g.drawLine( 105, 5, 105, 45 );
50
51           // draw graph labels
52           g.setFont( new Font( "SansSerif", Font.PLAIN, 10 ) );
53           g.drawString( "-$5,000", 5, 10 );
54           g.drawString( "$0", 110, 10 );
55           g.drawString( "+$5,000", 166, 10 );
56
57       } // end method paintComponent
58
59       // repaint graph when display is updated
60       public void updateDisplay()
61       {
62           repaint();
63       }
```

Fig. 3.7 **AccountBarGraphView** for rendering observed **Account** information as a bar graph (part 2 of 3).

```
64
65        // get AccountBarGraphView's preferred size
66        public Dimension getPreferredSize()
67        {
68            return new Dimension( 210, 50 );
69        }
70
71        // get AccountBarGraphView's minimum size
72        public Dimension getMinimumSize()
73        {
74            return getPreferredSize();
75        }
76
77        // get AccountBarGraphView's maximum size
78        public Dimension getMaximumSize()
79        {
80            return getPreferredSize();
81        }
82    }
```

Fig. 3.7   **AccountBarGraphView** for rendering observed **Account** information as a bar graph (part 3 of 3).

Method **updateDisplay** (lines 60–63) invokes method **repaint** (line 62) to update the bar graph's display. **AbstractAccountView** method **update** invokes method **updateDisplay** each time the **Account** model notifies the view of a change in the model. Method **getPreferredSize** (lines 66–69) overrides method **getPreferredSize** of class **JPanel**. Line 68 returns a new **Dimension** object that specifies the **AccountBarGraphView**'s preferred size as 210 pixels wide by 50 pixels tall. Most **LayoutManager**s use method **getPreferredSize** to determine how much space to allocate for each component. Lines 72–81 override methods **getMinimumSize** and **getMaximumSize** to return the **AccountBarGraphView**'s preferred size.

AssetPieChartView (Fig. 3.8) provides a pie-chart view of multiple asset **Account**s. **AssetPieChartView** shows the percentage of total assets held in each **Account** as wedges in the pie chart. **AssetPieChartView** defines method **addAccount** (line 25–42), which adds an **Account** to the **List** of **Account**s shown in the pie chart. If the given **Account** reference is **null**, line 29 throws a **NullPointerException**. Otherwise, line 32 adds the **Account** to **accounts**. Line 35 invokes method **getRandomColor** and adds the random **Color** to the **colors Map**. **AssetPieChartView** uses this color to draw the **Account**'s wedge in the pie chart. The **Account** object itself is the **Color**'s key in the **Map**. Line 38 invokes method **addObserver** of class **Account** to register the **AssetPieChartView** for **Account** updates. Line 41 invokes method **repaint** the display the pie chart with the new **Account**'s information.

Method **removeAccount** (lines 45–58) removes an **Account** from the pie chart. Line 48 invokes method **deleteObserver** of class **Account** to unregister the **AssetPieChartView** as an **Observer** of the **Account**. Line 51 removes the **Account** from **List accounts**, and line 54 removes the **Account**'s color from **HashMap colors**. Line 57 invokes method **repaint** to update the pie-chart display.

```
1   // AssetPieChartView.java
2   // AssetPieChartView is an AbstractAccountView subclass that
3   // displays multiple asset Account balances as a pie chart.
4   package com.deitel.advjhtp1.mvc.account;
5
6   // Java core packages
7   import java.awt.*;
8   import java.util.*;
9   import java.util.List;
10
11  // Java extension packages
12  import javax.swing.*;
13  import javax.swing.border.*;
14
15  public class AssetPieChartView extends JPanel
16     implements Observer {
17
18     // Set of observed Accounts
19     private List accounts = new ArrayList();
20
21     // Map of Colors for drawing pie chart wedges
22     private Map colors = new HashMap();
23
24     // add Account to pie chart view
25     public void addAccount( Account account )
26     {
27        // do not add null Accounts
28        if ( account == null )
29           throw new NullPointerException();
30
31        // add Account to accounts Vector
32        accounts.add( account );
33
34        // add Color to Hashtable for drawing Account's wedge
35        colors.put( account, getRandomColor() );
36
37        // register as Observer to receive Account updates
38        account.addObserver( this );
39
40        // update display with new Account information
41        repaint();
42     }
43
44     // remove Account from pie chart view
45     public void removeAccount( Account account )
46     {
47        // stop receiving updates from given Account
48        account.deleteObserver( this );
49
50        // remove Account from accounts Vector
51        accounts.remove( account );
52
```

Fig. 3.8   **AssetPieChartView** for rendering multiple observed asset **Account**s as a pie chart (part 1 of 5).

```
53              // remove Account's Color from Hashtable
54          colors.remove( account );
55
56              // update display to remove Account information
57          repaint();
58      }
59
60      // draw Account balances in a pie chart
61      public void paintComponent( Graphics g )
62      {
63          // ensure proper painting sequence
64          super.paintComponent( g );
65
66          // draw pie chart
67          drawPieChart( g );
68
69          // draw legend to describe pie chart wedges
70          drawLegend( g );
71      }
72
73      // draw pie chart on given Graphics context
74      private void drawPieChart( Graphics g )
75      {
76          // get combined Account balance
77          double totalBalance = getTotalBalance();
78
79          // create temporary variables for pie chart calculations
80          double percentage = 0.0;
81          int startAngle = 0;
82          int arcAngle = 0;
83
84          Iterator accountIterator = accounts.iterator();
85          Account account = null;
86
87          // draw pie wedge for each Account
88          while ( accountIterator.hasNext() ) {
89
90              // get next Account from Iterator
91              account = ( Account ) accountIterator.next();
92
93              // draw wedges only for included Accounts
94              if ( !includeAccountInChart( account ) )
95                  continue;
96
97              // get percentage of total balance held in Account
98              percentage = account.getBalance() / totalBalance;
99
100             // calculate arc angle for percentage
101             arcAngle = ( int ) Math.round( percentage * 360 );
102
103             // set drawing Color for Account pie wedge
104             g.setColor( ( Color ) colors.get( account ) );
```

Fig. 3.8   **AssetPieChartView** for rendering multiple observed asset
Accounts as a pie chart (part 2 of 5).

```
105
106          // draw Account pie wedge
107          g.fillArc( 5, 5, 100, 100, startAngle, arcAngle );
108
109          // calculate startAngle for next pie wedge
110          startAngle += arcAngle;
111       }
112    } // end method drawPieChart
113
114    // draw pie chart legend on given Graphics context
115    private void drawLegend( Graphics g )
116    {
117       Iterator accountIterator = accounts.iterator();
118       Account account = null;
119
120       // create Font for Account name
121       Font font = new Font( "SansSerif", Font.BOLD, 12 );
122       g.setFont( font );
123
124       // get FontMetrics for calculating offsets and
125       // positioning descriptions
126       FontMetrics metrics = getFontMetrics( font );
127       int ascent = metrics.getMaxAscent();
128       int offsetY = ascent + 2;
129
130       // draw description for each Account
131       for ( int i = 1; accountIterator.hasNext(); i++ ) {
132
133          // get next Account from Iterator
134          account = ( Account ) accountIterator.next();
135
136          // draw Account color swatch at next offset
137          g.setColor( ( Color ) colors.get( account ) );
138          g.fillRect( 125, offsetY * i, ascent, ascent );
139
140          // draw Account name next to color swatch
141          g.setColor( Color.black );
142          g.drawString( account.getName(), 140,
143             offsetY * i + ascent );
144       }
145    } // end method drawLegend
146
147    // get combined balance of all observed Accounts
148    private double getTotalBalance()
149    {
150       double sum = 0.0;
151
152       Iterator accountIterator = accounts.iterator();
153       Account account = null;
154
```

Fig. 3.8 **AssetPieChartView** for rendering multiple observed asset **Account**s as a pie chart (part 3 of 5).

```
155        // calculate total balance
156        while ( accountIterator.hasNext() ) {
157           account = ( Account ) accountIterator.next();
158
159           // add only included Accounts to sum
160           if ( includeAccountInChart( account ) )
161              sum += account.getBalance();
162        }
163
164        return sum;
165     }
166
167     // return true if given Account should be included in
168     // pie chart
169     protected boolean includeAccountInChart( Account account )
170     {
171        // include only Asset accounts (Accounts with positive
172        // balances)
173        return account.getBalance() > 0.0;
174     }
175
176     // get a random Color for drawing pie wedges
177     private Color getRandomColor()
178     {
179        // calculate random red, green and blue values
180        int red = ( int ) ( Math.random() * 256 );
181        int green = ( int ) ( Math.random() * 256 );
182        int blue = ( int ) ( Math.random() * 256 );
183
184        // return newly created Color
185        return new Color( red, green, blue );
186     }
187
188     // receive updates from Observable Account
189     public void update( Observable observable, Object object )
190     {
191        repaint();
192     }
193
194     // get AccountBarGraphView's preferred size
195     public Dimension getPreferredSize()
196     {
197        return new Dimension( 210, 110 );
198     }
199
200     // get AccountBarGraphView's preferred size
201     public Dimension getMinimumSize()
202     {
203        return getPreferredSize();
204     }
205
```

Fig. 3.8   **AssetPieChartView** for rendering multiple observed asset
Accounts as a pie chart (part 4 of 5).

```
206    // get AccountBarGraphView's preferred size
207    public Dimension getMaximumSize()
208    {
209       return getPreferredSize();
210    }
211 }
```

Fig. 3.8   **AssetPieChartView** for rendering multiple observed asset **Account**s as a pie chart (part 5 of 5).

Method **paintComponent** (lines 61–71) invokes methods **drawPieChart** (line 67) and **drawLegend** (line 70) to draw the pie chart and chart legend, respectively. Method **drawPieChart** (lines 74–112) draws a pie-chart wedge for each **Account**. Line 77 invokes method **getTotalBalance** to get the total balance for all **Account**s. Lines 80–111 calculate the percentage of the total balance held in each **Account** and draw the wedges. Line 91 gets the next **Account** from **accountIterator**. Line 94 invokes method **includeAccountInChart** to determine if the pie chart should include the current **Account**. If the chart should not include the **Account**, line 95 **continue**s the **while** loop to the next iteration. Line 98 calculates the percentage of the total assets held in the current **Account**. Line 101 calculates the size of the **Account**'s pie wedge. Line 104 gets the **Account**'s color from **Map colors** and invokes method **setColor** of class **Graphics**. Line 107 invokes method **fillArc** of class **Graphics** to draw the **Account**'s pie wedge. The first four arguments to method **fillArc** specify the position and diameter of the arc, respectively. The third argument—**startAngle**—specifies the angle at which the arc should begin. The fourth argument—**arcAngle**—specifies the degrees of arc sweep. Line 101 sets the **startAngle** for the next pie wedge.

Method **drawLegend** (lines 115–145) draws a legend (shown in Fig. 3.10) to show which color represents each **Account**. The legend shows each color square and **Account** name in a list along the right side of the pie chart. Lines 137–138 set the **Font** in which to draw the **Account**. Lines 121–128 use a **FontMetrics** object to calculate the heights of characters in the current **Font**. Line 127 invokes method **getMaxAscent** of class **FontMetrics** to get the *maximum ascent* (i.e., maximum height above the baseline) of characters in the current **Font**. Line 128 calculates **offsetY** by adding **2** to the **Font**'s maximum ascent. We use **offsetY** to determine the position at which to draw each **Account**'s color square and name. Lines 131–144 draw the legend item for each **Account**. Line 134 gets the next **Account** from **accountIterator**. Lines 137–138 draw the color square, and lines 141–143 draw the **Account** name.

Method **getTotalBalance** (lines 148–165) calculates the total balance for all included **Account**s. Line 160 invokes method **includeAccountInChart** to determine whether the calculation should include the current **Account**. If the calculation should include the **Account**, line 161 adds the **Account**'s balance to variable **sum**.

Method **includeAccountInChart** (lines 169–174) returns a **boolean** indicating whether the **Account** should be included in the pie chart. **AssetPieChartView** shows only asset **Account**s (i.e., **Account**s with positive balances). Line 173 returns **true** only if the **Account** balance is greater than zero. Subclasses can override this method to include and exclude **Account**s based on other criteria.

Method **getRandomColor** (lines 177–186) generates a random **Color**. **Asset-PieChartView** uses this method to generate a different **Color** for each **Account** in the pie chart. Lines 180–182 calculate random values for the **red**, **green** and **blue Color** components. Line 185 creates a new **Color** object using the random **red**, **green** and **blue** values and returns the new **Color** to the caller.

Method **update** (lines 189–192) invokes method **repaint** to update the pie-chart display. Method **getPreferredSize** (lines 195–198) returns the **AssetPieChart-View**'s preferred size, which provides enough space to draw the pie chart and legend.

AccountController (Fig. 3.9) implements the controller in the MVC architecture. **AccountController** provides a user interface for modifying **Account** data. **AccountController** extends **JPanel** (line 14), because it provides a set of GUI components for depositing and withdrawing **Account** funds.

Line 28 sets the **account** member variable to the **Account** that **AccountController** will control. Line 31 creates a **JTextField** into which users can enter an amount to withdraw from, or deposit in, the controlled **Account**. Line 34 creates a **JButton** for depositing the given amount into the **Account**. The **depositButton**'s **ActionListener** (lines 37–55) invokes method **deposit** of class **Account** to deposit the amount entered in **amountTextField** (lines 44–45). If method **parseDouble** (line 44) throws a **NumberFormatException** because the text entered was not a valid number, lines 48–53 **catch** the exception and display an error message to the user.

```
1   // AccountController.java
2   // AccountController is a controller for Accounts. It provides
3   // a JTextField for inputting a deposit or withdrawal amount
4   // and JButtons for depositing or withdrawing funds.
5   package com.deitel.advjhtp1.mvc.account;
6
7   // Java core packages
8   import java.awt.*;
9   import java.awt.event.*;
10
11  // Java extension packages
12  import javax.swing.*;
13
14  public class AccountController extends JPanel {
15
16     // Account to control
17     private Account account;
18
19     // JTextField for deposit or withdrawal amount
20     private JTextField amountTextField;
21
22     // AccountController constructor
23     public AccountController( Account controlledAccount )
24     {
25        super();
26
```

Fig. 3.9   **AccountController** for obtaining user input to modify **Account** information (part 1 of 3).

```
27              // account to control
28              account = controlledAccount;
29
30              // create JTextField for entering amount
31              amountTextField = new JTextField( 10 );
32
33              // create JButton for deposits
34              JButton depositButton = new JButton( "Deposit" );
35
36              depositButton.addActionListener(
37                 new ActionListener() {
38
39                    public void actionPerformed( ActionEvent event )
40                    {
41                       try {
42
43                          // deposit amount entered in amountTextField
44                          account.deposit( Double.parseDouble(
45                             amountTextField.getText() ) );
46                       }
47
48                       catch ( NumberFormatException exception ) {
49                          JOptionPane.showMessageDialog (
50                             AccountController.this,
51                             "Please enter a valid amount", "Error",
52                             JOptionPane.ERROR_MESSAGE );
53                       }
54                    } // end method actionPerformed
55                 }
56              );
57
58              // create JButton for withdrawals
59              JButton withdrawButton = new JButton( "Withdraw" );
60
61              withdrawButton.addActionListener(
62                 new ActionListener() {
63
64                    public void actionPerformed( ActionEvent event )
65                    {
66                       try {
67
68                          // withdraw amount entered in amountTextField
69                          account.withdraw( Double.parseDouble(
70                             amountTextField.getText() ) );
71                       }
72
73                       catch ( NumberFormatException exception ) {
74                          JOptionPane.showMessageDialog (
75                             AccountController.this,
76                             "Please enter a valid amount", "Error",
77                             JOptionPane.ERROR_MESSAGE );
78                       }
```

Fig. 3.9   **AccountController** for obtaining user input to modify **Account** information (part 2 of 3).

```
79                } // end method actionPerformed
80            }
81        );
82
83        // lay out controller components
84        setLayout( new FlowLayout() );
85        add( new JLabel( "Amount: " ) );
86        add( amountTextField );
87        add( depositButton );
88        add( withdrawButton );
89    }
90 }
```

Fig. 3.9   **AccountController** for obtaining user input to modify **Account** information (part 3 of 3).

Line 59 creates a **JButton** for withdrawing the given amount from the **Account**. The **withdrawButton**'s **ActionListener** (lines 62–80) invokes method **withdraw** of class **Account** to withdraw the amount entered in **amountTextField** (lines 69–70). If method **parseDouble** (line 69) throws a **NumberFormatException**, because the text entered was not a valid number, lines 73–78 **catch** the exception and display an error message to the user. Lines 84–88 lay out **amountTextField**, a **JLabel**, **depositButton** and **withdrawButton**.

AccountManager (Fig. 3.10) is an application that uses MVC to manage **Account** information. Lines 22 creates a new **Account** with the name **Account 1** and a $1,000.00 balance. Line 25 invokes method **getAccountPanel** of class **AccountManager** to create a **JPanel** containing view and controller components for **account1**. Line 28 creates a new **Account** with the name **Account 2** and a $3,000.00 balance. Line 31 invokes method **createAccountPanel** to create a **JPanel** containing view and controller components for **account2**. Lines 34–35 create an **AssetPieChartView** for displaying **account1** and **account2** information in a pie chart. Lines 38–39 invoke method **addAccount** of class **AssetPieChartView** to add **account1** and **account2** to the pie chart. Lines 42–47 create a **JPanel** with a **TitledBorder** for the **AssetPieChartView**. Lines 50–54 lay out the **JPanel**s for each account and **AssetPieChartView**.

Method **createAccountPanel** creates a **JPanel** containing an **AccountController**, **AccountTextView** and **AccountBarGraphView** for the given **Account**. Lines 64–68 create a **JPanel** with a **TitledBorder** to contain the **Account**'s GUI components. Lines 71–72 create an **AccountTextView** for the **Account**. Lines 75–76 create an **AccountBarGraphView** for the **Account**. Lines 79–80 create an **AccountController** for the **Account**. Lines 83–85 lay out the **AccountTextView**, **AccountBarGraphView** and **AccountController** components on **accountPanel**.

Figure 3.10 shows sample **AccountManager** output. Notice as you run the program that the views reflect each withdrawal or deposit immediately. For example, depositing **1500.00** in **Account 1** causes the **AccountTextView** for **Account 1** to display **$2,500.00**, the **AccountBarGraphView** for **Account 1** to display a larger bar graph and **AssetPieChartView** to display a larger wedge for **Account 1**. Withdrawing **4623.12** from Account 2 causes a new balance of **($1,623.12)** (parentheses indicate a negative balance) to be shown, a red bar graph to be displayed and the **Account 2** wedge from **AssetPieChartView** to be removed. If both **Account**s have negative balances, **AssetPieChartView** removes both **Account**s from the pie chart.

```
1   // AccountManager.java
2   // AccountManager is an application that uses the MVC design
3   // pattern to manage bank Account information.
4   package com.deitel.advjhtp1.mvc.account;
5
6   // Java core packages
7   import java.awt.*;
8   import java.awt.event.*;
9
10  // Java extension packages
11  import javax.swing.*;
12  import javax.swing.border.*;
13
14  public class AccountManager extends JFrame {
15
16     // AccountManager no-argument constructor
17     public AccountManager()
18     {
19        super( "Account Manager" );
20
21        // create account1 with initial balance
22        Account account1 = new Account( "Account 1", 1000.00 );
23
24        // create GUI for account1
25        JPanel account1Panel = createAccountPanel( account1 );
26
27        // create account2 with initial balance
28        Account account2 = new Account( "Account 2", 3000.00 );
29
30        // create GUI for account2
31        JPanel account2Panel = createAccountPanel( account2 );
32
33        // create AccountPieChartView to show Account pie chart
34        AssetPieChartView pieChartView =
35           new AssetPieChartView();
36
37        // add both Accounts to AccountPieChartView
38        pieChartView.addAccount( account1 );
39        pieChartView.addAccount( account2 );
40
41        // create JPanel for AccountPieChartView
42        JPanel pieChartPanel = new JPanel();
43
44        pieChartPanel.setBorder(
45           new TitledBorder( "Assets" ) );
46
```

Fig. 3.10 **AccountManager** application for displaying and modifying **Account** information using the model-view-controller architecture (part 1 of 3).

```
47            pieChartPanel.add( pieChartView );
48
49            // lay out account1, account2 and pie chart components
50            Container contentPane = getContentPane();
51            contentPane.setLayout( new GridLayout( 3, 1 ) );
52            contentPane.add( account1Panel );
53            contentPane.add( account2Panel );
54            contentPane.add( pieChartPanel );
55
56            setSize( 425, 450 );
57
58        } // end AccountManager constructor
59
60        // create GUI components for given Account
61        private JPanel createAccountPanel( Account account )
62        {
63            // create JPanel for Account GUI
64            JPanel accountPanel = new JPanel();
65
66            // set JPanel's border to show Account name
67            accountPanel.setBorder(
68                new TitledBorder( account.getName() ) );
69
70            // create AccountTextView for Account
71            AccountTextView accountTextView =
72                new AccountTextView( account );
73
74            // create AccountBarGraphView for Account
75            AccountBarGraphView accountBarGraphView =
76                new AccountBarGraphView( account );
77
78            // create AccountController for Account
79            AccountController accountController =
80                new AccountController( account );
81
82            // lay out Account's components
83            accountPanel.add( accountController );
84            accountPanel.add( accountTextView );
85            accountPanel.add( accountBarGraphView );
86
87            return accountPanel;
88
89        } // end method getAccountPanel
90
91        // execute application
92        public static void main( String args[] )
93        {
94            AccountManager manager = new AccountManager();
95            manager.setDefaultCloseOperation( EXIT_ON_CLOSE );
96            manager.setVisible( true );
97        }
98  }
```

Fig. 3.10   AccountManager application for displaying and modifying **Account** information using the model-view-controller architecture (part 2 of 3).

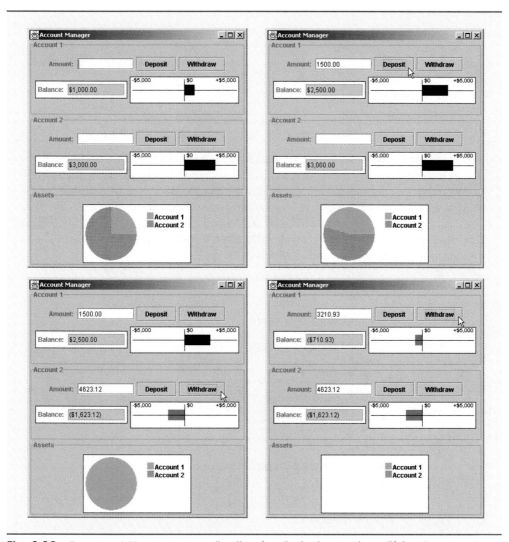

Fig. 3.10 **AccountManager** application for displaying and modifying **Account** information using the model-view-controller architecture (part 3 of 3).

3.4 JList

JList is a Swing component that implements the delegate-model architecture. **JList** acts as a delegate for an underlying **ListModel** (Fig. 3.11). Interface **ListModel** defines methods for getting list elements, getting the size of the list and registering and unregistering **ListDataListener**s. A **ListModel** notifies each registered **ListDataListener** of each change in the **ListModel**.

Class **PhilosophersJList** (Fig. 3.12) uses a **JList** and **DefaultListModel** to display a list of philosophers. Class **DefaultListModel** provides a basic **List-Model** implementation. Line 23 creates a new **DefaultListModel**, and lines 24–31 add several philosophers to the **DefaultListModel**. Line 34 creates a new **JList** and

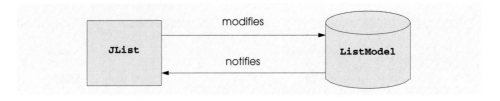

Fig. 3.11 **JList** and **ListModel** delegate-model architecture.

passes the **philosophers DefaultListModel** to the **JList** constructor. The
JList constructor registers the **JList** as a **ListDataListener** of the **Default-**
ListModel, so that updates to the **DefaultListModel** will be reflected in the
JList. Lines 37–38 set the **JList**'s selection mode to allow the user to select only one
philosopher at a time. The selection modes are constant integer values defined in interface
ListSelectionModel. For example, **MULTIPLE_INTERVAL_SELECTION** allows
the user to select multiple, separate intervals in the **JList**.

```
1    // PhilosophersJList.java
2    // MVC architecture using JList with a DefaultListModel
3    package com.deitel.advjhtp1.mvc.list;
4
5    // Java core packages
6    import java.awt.*;
7    import java.awt.event.*;
8
9    // Java extension packages
10   import javax.swing.*;
11
12   public class PhilosophersJList extends JFrame {
13
14      private DefaultListModel philosophers;
15      private JList list;
16
17      // PhilosophersJList constructor
18      public PhilosophersJList()
19      {
20         super( "Favorite Philosophers" );
21
22         // create a DefaultListModel to store philosophers
23         philosophers = new DefaultListModel();
24         philosophers.addElement( "Socrates" );
25         philosophers.addElement( "Plato" );
26         philosophers.addElement( "Aristotle" );
27         philosophers.addElement( "St. Thomas Aquinas" );
28         philosophers.addElement( "Soren Kierkegaard" );
29         philosophers.addElement( "Immanuel Kant" );
30         philosophers.addElement( "Friedrich Nietzsche" );
31         philosophers.addElement( "Hannah Arendt" );
32
```

Fig. 3.12 **PhilosophersJList** application demonstrating **JList** and
DefaultListModel (part 1 of 3).

```
33        // create a JList for philosophers DefaultListModel
34        list = new JList( philosophers );
35
36        // allow user to select only one philosopher at a time
37        list.setSelectionMode(
38           ListSelectionModel.SINGLE_SELECTION );
39
40        // create JButton for adding philosophers
41        JButton addButton = new JButton( "Add Philosopher" );
42        addButton.addActionListener(
43           new ActionListener() {
44
45              public void actionPerformed( ActionEvent event )
46              {
47                 // prompt user for new philosopher's name
48                 String name = JOptionPane.showInputDialog(
49                    PhilosophersJList.this, "Enter Name" );
50
51                 // add new philosopher to model
52                 philosophers.addElement( name );
53              }
54           }
55        );
56
57        // create JButton for removing selected philosopher
58        JButton removeButton =
59           new JButton( "Remove Selected Philosopher" );
60
61        removeButton.addActionListener(
62           new ActionListener() {
63
64              public void actionPerformed( ActionEvent event )
65              {
66                 // remove selected philosopher from model
67                 philosophers.removeElement(
68                    list.getSelectedValue() );
69              }
70           }
71        );
72
73        // lay out GUI components
74        JPanel inputPanel = new JPanel();
75        inputPanel.add( addButton );
76        inputPanel.add( removeButton );
77
78        Container container = getContentPane();
79        container.add( list, BorderLayout.CENTER );
80        container.add( inputPanel, BorderLayout.NORTH );
81
82        setDefaultCloseOperation( EXIT_ON_CLOSE );
83        setSize( 400, 300 );
84        setVisible( true );
```

Fig. 3.12 **PhilosophersJList** application demonstrating **JList** and **DefaultListModel** (part 2 of 3).

```
85
86       } // end PhilosophersJList constructor
87
88       // execute application
89       public static void main( String args[] )
90       {
91           new PhilosophersJList();
92       }
93   }
```

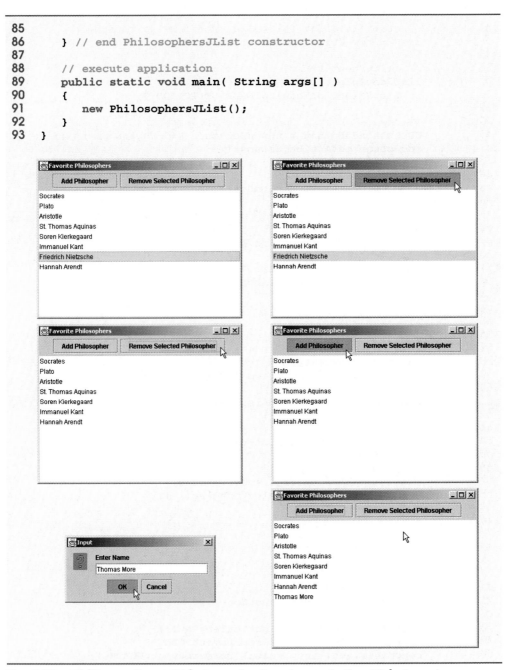

Fig. 3.12 PhilosophersJList application demonstrating **JList** and **DefaultListModel** (part 3 of 3).

Lines 41–55 create a **JButton** for adding new philosophers to the **DefaultList-Model**. Lines 48–49 in method **actionPerformed** invoke **static** method **show-InputDialog** of class **JOptionPane** to prompt the user for the philosopher's name.

Line 52 invokes method **addElement** of class **DefaultListModel** to add the new philosopher to the list. The **DefaultListModel** will notify the **JList** that the model changed, and the **JList** will update the display to include the new list item.

Lines 58–71 create a **JButton** for deleting a philosopher from the **DefaultList-Model**. Lines 67–68 in method **actionPerformed** invoke method **getSelected-Value** of class **JList** to get the currently selected philosopher and invoke method **removeElement** of class **DefaultListModel** to remove the philosopher. The **DefaultListModel** will notify the **JList** that the model changed, and the **JList** will update the display to remove the deleted philosopher. Lines 74–84 lay out the GUI components and set **JFrame** properties for the application window.

3.5 JTable

JTable is another **Swing** component that implements the delegate-model architecture. **JTable**s are delegates for tabular data stored in **TableModel** implementations. Interface **TableModel** declares methods for retrieving and modifying data (e.g., the value in a certain table cell) and for retrieving and modifying metadata (e.g., the number of columns and rows). The **JTable** delegate invokes **TableModel** methods to build its view of the **TableModel** and to modify the **TableModel** based on user input.

Figure 3.13 describes the methods defined in interface **TableModel**. Custom implementations of interface **TableModel** can use arbitrary internal representations of the tabular data. For example, the **DefaultTableModel** implementation uses **Vector**s to store the rows and columns of data. In Chapter 8, JDBC, we implement interface **TableModel** to create a **TableModel** that represents data stored in a JDBC **ResultSet**. Figure 3.14 illustrates the delegate-model relationship between **JTable** and **TableModel**.

Method	Description

void addTableModelListener(TableModelListener listener)

        Add a **TableModelListener** to the **TableModel**. The **TableModel** will notify the **TableModelListener** of changes in the **TableModel**.

void removeTableModelListener(TableModelListener listener)

        Remove a previously added **TableModelListener** from the **TableModel**.

Class getColumnClass(int columnIndex)

        Get the **Class** object for values in the column with specified **columnIndex**.

int getColumnCount()

        Get the number of columns in the **TableModel**.

String getColumnName(int columnIndex)

        Get the name of the column with the given **columnIndex**.

int getRowCount()

        Get the number of rows in the **TableModel**.

Fig. 3.13 TableModel interface methods and descriptions (part 1 of 2).

Method	Description

Object getValueAt(int rowIndex, int columnIndex)

Get an **Object** reference to the value stored in the **TableModel** at the given row and column indices.

void setValueAt(Object value, int rowIndex, int columnIndex)

Set the value stored in the **TableModel** at the given row and column indices.

boolean isCellEditable(int rowIndex, int columnIndex)

Return **true** if the cell at the given row and column indices is editable.

Fig. 3.13 TableModel interface methods and descriptions (part 2 of 2).

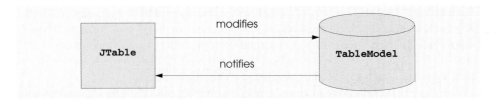

Fig. 3.14 JTable and **TableModel** delegate-model architecture.

PhilosophersJTable (Fig. 3.15) displays philosopher information in a **JTable** using a **DefaultTableModel**. Class **DefaultTableModel** implements interface **TableModel** and uses **Vector**s to represent the rows and columns of data. Line 24 creates the **philosophers DefaultTableModel**. Lines 27–29 add columns to the **DefaultTableModel** for the philosophers' first names, last names and years in which they lived. Lines 32–53 create rows for seven philosophers. Each row is a **String** array whose elements are the philosopher's first name, last name and the year in which the philosopher lived, respectively. Method **addRow** of class **DefaultTableModel** adds each philosopher to the **DefaultTableModel**. Line 56 creates the **JTable** that will act as a delegate for the **philosophers DefaultTableModel**.

Lines 59–72 create a **JButton** and **ActionListener** for adding a new philosopher to the **DefaultTableModel**. Line 66 in method **actionPerformed** creates a **String** array of three empty elements. Line 69 adds the empty **String** array to the **DefaultTableModel**. This causes the **JTable** to display a blank row at the bottom of the **JTable**. The user can then type the philosopher's information directly into the **JTable** cells. This demonstrates the **JTable** delegate acting as a controller, because it modifies the **DefaultTableModel** based on user input.

```
1    // PhilosophersJTable.java
2    // MVC architecture using JTable with a DefaultTableModel
3    package com.deitel.advjhtp1.mvc.table;
```

Fig. 3.15 PhilosophersJTable application demonstrating **JTable** and **DefaultTableModel** (part 1 of 4).

```
4
5   // Java core packages
6   import java.awt.*;
7   import java.awt.event.*;
8
9   // Java extension packages
10  import javax.swing.*;
11  import javax.swing.table.*;
12
13  public class PhilosophersJTable extends JFrame {
14
15     private DefaultTableModel philosophers;
16     private JTable table;
17
18     // PhilosophersJTable constructor
19     public PhilosophersJTable()
20     {
21        super( "Favorite Philosophers" );
22
23        // create a DefaultTableModel to store philosophers
24        philosophers = new DefaultTableModel();
25
26        // add Columns to DefaultTableModel
27        philosophers.addColumn( "First Name" );
28        philosophers.addColumn( "Last Name" );
29        philosophers.addColumn( "Years" );
30
31        // add philosopher names and dates to DefaultTableModel
32        String[] socrates = { "Socrates", "", "469-399 B.C." };
33        philosophers.addRow( socrates );
34
35        String[] plato = { "Plato", "", "428-347 B.C." };
36        philosophers.addRow( plato );
37
38        String[] aquinas = { "Thomas", "Aquinas", "1225-1274" };
39        philosophers.addRow( aquinas );
40
41        String[] kierkegaard = { "Soren", "Kierkegaard",
42           "1813-1855" };
43        philosophers.addRow( kierkegaard );
44
45        String[] kant = { "Immanuel", "Kant", "1724-1804" };
46        philosophers.addRow( kant );
47
48        String[] nietzsche = { "Friedrich", "Nietzsche",
49           "1844-1900" };
50        philosophers.addRow( nietzsche );
51
52        String[] arendt = { "Hannah", "Arendt", "1906-1975" };
53        philosophers.addRow( arendt );
54
```

Fig. 3.15 **PhilosophersJTable** application demonstrating **JTable** and **DefaultTableModel** (part 2 of 4).

```
55          // create a JTable for philosophers DefaultTableModel
56          table = new JTable( philosophers );
57
58          // create JButton for adding philosophers
59          JButton addButton = new JButton( "Add Philosopher" );
60          addButton.addActionListener(
61             new ActionListener() {
62
63                public void actionPerformed( ActionEvent event )
64                {
65                   // create empty array for new philosopher row
66                   String[] philosopher = { "", "", "" };
67
68                   // add empty philosopher row to model
69                   philosophers.addRow( philosopher );
70                }
71             }
72          );
73
74          // create JButton for removing selected philosopher
75          JButton removeButton =
76             new JButton( "Remove Selected Philosopher" );
77
78          removeButton.addActionListener(
79             new ActionListener() {
80
81                public void actionPerformed( ActionEvent event )
82                {
83                   // remove selected philosopher from model
84                   philosophers.removeRow(
85                      table.getSelectedRow() );
86                }
87             }
88          );
89
90          // lay out GUI components
91          JPanel inputPanel = new JPanel();
92          inputPanel.add( addButton );
93          inputPanel.add( removeButton );
94
95          Container container = getContentPane();
96          container.add( new JScrollPane( table ),
97             BorderLayout.CENTER );
98          container.add( inputPanel, BorderLayout.NORTH );
99
100         setDefaultCloseOperation( EXIT_ON_CLOSE );
101         setSize( 400, 300 );
102         setVisible( true );
103
104      } // end PhilosophersJTable constructor
105
```

Fig. 3.15 **PhilosophersJTable** application demonstrating **JTable** and **DefaultTableModel** (part 3 of 4).

```
106    // execute application
107    public static void main( String args[] )
108    {
109        new PhilosophersJTable();
110    }
111 }
```

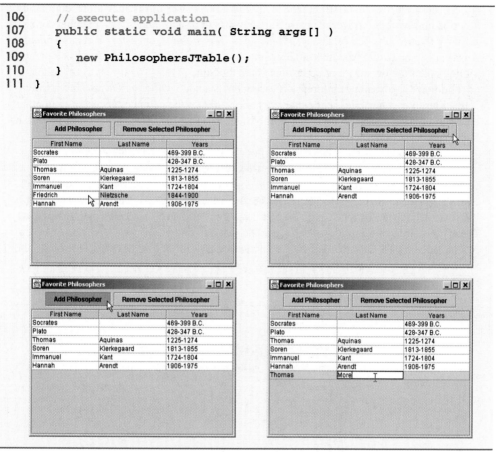

Fig. 3.15   **PhilosophersJTable** application demonstrating **JTable** and **DefaultTableModel** (part 4 of 4).

Lines 75–88 create a **JButton** and **ActionListener** for removing a philosopher from the **DefaultTableModel**. Lines 84–85 in method **actionPerformed** retrieve the currently selected row in the **JTable** delegate and invoke method **removeRow** of class **DefaultTableModel** to remove the selected row. The **DefaultTableModel** notifies the **JTable** that the **DefaultTableModel** has changed, and the **JTable** removes the appropriate row from the display. Lines 96–97 add the **JTable** to a **JScrollPane**. **JTables** will not display their column headings unless placed within a **JScrollPane**.

3.6 JTree

JTree is one of the more complex Swing components that implements the delegate-model architecture. **TreeModel**s represent hierarchical data, such as family trees, certain types of file systems, company management structures and document outlines. **JTree**s act as delegates (i.e., combined view and controller) for **TreeModel**s.

To describe tree data structures, it is common to use terms that more commonly describe family trees.[3] A tree data structure consists of a set of nodes (i.e., members or elements of the tree) that are related as *parents*, *children*, *siblings*, *ancestors* and *descendents*. A parent is a node that has other nodes as its children. A child is a node that has a parent. Sibling nodes are two or more nodes that share the same parent. An ancestor is a node that has children that also have children. A descendent is a node whose parent also has a parent. A tree must have one node—called the *root node*—that is the parent or ancestor of all other nodes in the tree. [*Note*: Unlike in a family tree, in a tree data structure a child node can have only one parent.]

Figure 3.16 shows the relationships among nodes in a tree. The **JTree** contains a hierarchy of philosophers whose root is node **Philosophers**. Node **Philosophers** has seven child nodes, representing the major eras of philosophy—**Ancient**, **Medieval**, **Renaissance**, **Early Modern**, **Enlightenment**, **19th Century** and **20th Century**. Each philosopher (e.g., **Socrates**, **St. Thomas Aquinas** and **Immanuel Kant**) is a child of the philosopher's era and is a descendent of node **Philosophers**. Nodes **Socrates**, **Plato** and **Aristotle** are sibling nodes, because they share the same parent node (**Ancient**).

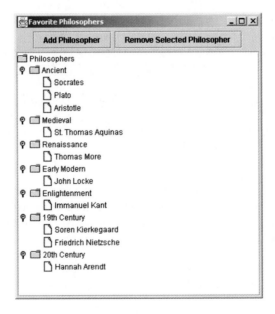

Fig. 3.16   **JTree** showing a hierarchy of philosophers.

---

3. Note that nodes in the tree data structures we discuss in this section each have only a single parent, unlike a family tree.

3.6.1 Using `DefaultTreeModel`

Interface **_TreeModel_** declares methods for representing a tree data structure in a **JTree**. Objects of any class can represent nodes in a **TreeModel**. For example, a **Person** class could represent a node in a family tree **TreeModel**. Class **_DefaultTreeModel_** provides a default **TreeModel** implementation. Interface **TreeNode** defines common operations for nodes in a **DefaultTreeModel**, such as **_getParent_** and **_getAllowsChildren_**. Interface **_MutableTreeNode_** extends interface **TreeNode** to represent a node that can change, either by adding or removing child nodes or by changing the **Object** associated with the node. Class **_DefaultMutableTreeNode_** provides a **MutableTreeNode** implementation suitable for use in a **DefaultTreeModel**.

Software Engineering Observation 3.3

*Although a **TreeModel** implementation can use objects of any class to represent the **TreeModel**'s nodes, the **TreeModel** implementation must be able to determine the hierarchical relationships among those objects. For example, a **Person** class would have to provide methods such as **getParent** and **getChildren** for use in a family tree **TreeModel**.*

JTree employs two interfaces to implement the **JTree**'s delegate functionality. Interface **TreeCellRenderer** represents an object that creates a view for each node in the **JTree**. Class **DefaultTreeCellRenderer** implements interface **TreeCell-Renderer** and extends class **JLabel** to provide a **TreeCellRenderer** default implementation. Interface **TreeCellEditor** represents an object for controlling (i.e., editing) each node in the **JTree**. Class **DefaultTreeCellEditor** implements interface **TreeCellEditor** and uses a **JTextField** for the **TreeCellEditor** default implementation.

PhilosophersJTree (Fig. 3.17) uses a **DefaultTreeModel** to represent a set of philosophers. The **DefaultTreeModel** organizes the philosophers hierarchically according to their associated eras in the history of philosophy. Lines 26–27 invoke method **createPhilosopherTree** to get the root, **DefaultMutableTreeNode**, which contains all the philosopher nodes. Line 30 creates a **DefaultTreeModel** and passes the **philosophersNode DefaultMutableTreeNode** to the **DefaultTreeModel** constructor. Line 33 creates a **JTree** and passes **DefaultTreeModel philosophers** to the **JTree** constructor.

```
1   // PhilosophersJTree.java
2   // MVC architecture using JTree with a DefaultTreeModel
3   package com.deitel.advjhtp1.mvc.tree;
4
5   // Java core packages
6   import java.awt.*;
7   import java.awt.event.*;
8   import java.util.*;
9
10  // Java extension packages
11  import javax.swing.*;
12  import javax.swing.tree.*;
```

Fig. 3.17   **PhilosophersJTree** application demonstrating **JTree** and **DefaultTreeModel** (part 1 of 6).

```
13
14   public class PhilosophersJTree extends JFrame {
15
16       private JTree tree;
17       private DefaultTreeModel philosophers;
18       private DefaultMutableTreeNode rootNode;
19
20       // PhilosophersJTree constructor
21       public PhilosophersJTree()
22       {
23           super( "Favorite Philosophers" );
24
25           // get tree of philosopher DefaultMutableTreeNodes
26           DefaultMutableTreeNode philosophersNode =
27               createPhilosopherTree();
28
29           // create philosophers DefaultTreeModel
30           philosophers = new DefaultTreeModel( philosophersNode );
31
32           // create JTree for philosophers DefaultTreeModel
33           tree = new JTree( philosophers );
34
35           // create JButton for adding philosophers
36           JButton addButton = new JButton( "Add" );
37           addButton.addActionListener(
38               new ActionListener() {
39
40                   public void actionPerformed( ActionEvent event )
41                   {
42                       addElement();
43                   }
44               }
45           );
46
47           // create JButton for removing selected philosopher
48           JButton removeButton =
49               new JButton( "Remove" );
50
51           removeButton.addActionListener(
52               new ActionListener() {
53
54                   public void actionPerformed( ActionEvent event )
55                   {
56                       removeElement();
57                   }
58               }
59           );
60
61           // lay out GUI components
62           JPanel inputPanel = new JPanel();
63           inputPanel.add( addButton );
64           inputPanel.add( removeButton );
```

Fig. 3.17 **PhilosophersJTree** application demonstrating **JTree** and **DefaultTreeModel** (part 2 of 6).

```
65
66          Container container = getContentPane();
67
68          container.add( new JScrollPane( tree ),
69             BorderLayout.CENTER );
70
71          container.add( inputPanel, BorderLayout.NORTH );
72
73          setDefaultCloseOperation( EXIT_ON_CLOSE );
74          setSize( 400, 300 );
75          setVisible( true );
76
77       } // end PhilosophersJTree constructor
78
79       // add new philosopher to selected era
80       private void addElement()
81       {
82          // get selected era
83          DefaultMutableTreeNode parent = getSelectedNode();
84
85          // ensure user selected era first
86          if ( parent == null ) {
87             JOptionPane.showMessageDialog(
88                PhilosophersJTree.this, "Select an era.",
89                "Error", JOptionPane.ERROR_MESSAGE );
90
91             return;
92          }
93
94          // prompt user for philosopher's name
95          String name = JOptionPane.showInputDialog(
96             PhilosophersJTree.this, "Enter Name:" );
97
98          // add new philosopher to selected era
99          philosophers.insertNodeInto(
100            new DefaultMutableTreeNode( name ),
101            parent, parent.getChildCount() );
102
103      } // end method addElement
104
105      // remove currently selected philosopher
106      private void removeElement()
107      {
108         // get selected node
109         DefaultMutableTreeNode selectedNode = getSelectedNode();
110
111         // remove selectedNode from model
112         if ( selectedNode != null )
113            philosophers.removeNodeFromParent( selectedNode );
114      }
115
```

Fig. 3.17 **PhilosophersJTree** application demonstrating **JTree** and **DefaultTreeModel** (part 3 of 6).

```
116    // get currently selected node
117    private DefaultMutableTreeNode getSelectedNode()
118    {
119       // get selected DefaultMutableTreeNode
120       return ( DefaultMutableTreeNode )
121          tree.getLastSelectedPathComponent();
122    }
123
124    // get tree of philosopher DefaultMutableTreeNodes
125    private DefaultMutableTreeNode createPhilosopherTree()
126    {
127       // create rootNode
128       DefaultMutableTreeNode rootNode =
129          new DefaultMutableTreeNode( "Philosophers" );
130
131       // Ancient philosophers
132       DefaultMutableTreeNode ancient =
133          new DefaultMutableTreeNode( "Ancient" );
134       rootNode.add( ancient );
135
136       ancient.add( new DefaultMutableTreeNode( "Socrates" ) );
137       ancient.add( new DefaultMutableTreeNode( "Plato" ) );
138       ancient.add( new DefaultMutableTreeNode( "Aristotle" ) );
139
140       // Medieval philosophers
141       DefaultMutableTreeNode medieval =
142          new DefaultMutableTreeNode( "Medieval" );
143       rootNode.add( medieval );
144
145       medieval.add( new DefaultMutableTreeNode(
146          "St. Thomas Aquinas" ) );
147
148       // Renaissance philosophers
149       DefaultMutableTreeNode renaissance =
150          new DefaultMutableTreeNode( "Renaissance" );
151       rootNode.add( renaissance );
152
153       renaissance.add( new DefaultMutableTreeNode(
154          "Thomas More" ) );
155
156       // Early Modern philosophers
157       DefaultMutableTreeNode earlyModern =
158          new DefaultMutableTreeNode( "Early Modern" );
159       rootNode.add( earlyModern );
160
161       earlyModern.add( new DefaultMutableTreeNode(
162          "John Locke" ) );
163
164       // Enlightenment Philosophers
165       DefaultMutableTreeNode enlightenment =
166          new DefaultMutableTreeNode( "Enlightenment" );
167       rootNode.add( enlightenment );
```

Fig. 3.17 PhilosophersJTree application demonstrating **JTree** and
DefaultTreeModel (part 4 of 6).

```
168
169        enlightenment.add( new DefaultMutableTreeNode(
170           "Immanuel Kant" ) );
171
172        // 19th Century Philosophers
173        DefaultMutableTreeNode nineteenth =
174           new DefaultMutableTreeNode( "19th Century" );
175        rootNode.add( nineteenth );
176
177        nineteenth.add( new DefaultMutableTreeNode(
178           "Soren Kierkegaard" ) );
179
180        nineteenth.add( new DefaultMutableTreeNode(
181           "Friedrich Nietzsche" ) );
182
183        // 20th Century Philosophers
184        DefaultMutableTreeNode twentieth =
185           new DefaultMutableTreeNode( "20th Century" );
186        rootNode.add( twentieth );
187
188        twentieth.add( new DefaultMutableTreeNode(
189           "Hannah Arendt" ) );
190
191        return rootNode;
192
193     } // end method createPhilosopherTree
194
195     // execute application
196     public static void main( String args[] )
197     {
198        new PhilosophersJTree();
199     }
200  }
```

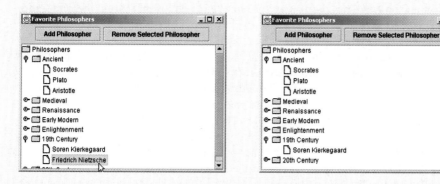

Fig. 3.17   PhilosophersJTree application demonstrating **JTree** and **DefaultTreeModel** (part 5 of 6).

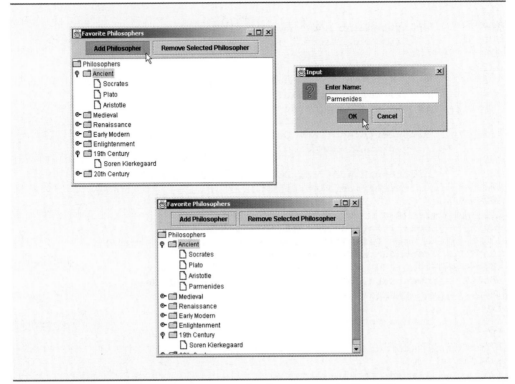

Fig. 3.17   **PhilosophersJTree** application demonstrating **JTree** and **DefaultTreeModel** (part 6 of 6).

Lines 36–45 create a **JButton** and an **ActionListener** for adding a philosopher to the **philosophers DefaultTreeModel**. Line 42 in method **actionPerformed** invokes method **addElement** to add a new philosopher. Lines 48–59 create a **JButton** and an **ActionListener** for removing a philosopher from the **philosophers DefaultTreeModel**. Line 56 invokes method **removeElement** to remove the currently selected philosopher from the model.

Method **addElement** (lines 80–103) gets the currently selected node in the **JTree** by invoking method **getSelectedNode** (line 83). Method **addElement** inserts the new philosopher node as a child of the currently selected node. If there is no node currently selected, line 91 returns from method **addElement** without adding a new node. Lines 95–96 invoke **static** method **showInputDialog** of class **JOptionPane** to prompt the user for the new philosopher's name. Lines 99–101 invoke method **insertNodeInto** of class **DefaultTreeModel** to insert the new philosopher in the model. Line 100 creates a new **DefaultMutableTreeNode** for the given philosopher. Line 101 specifies the parent node to which the new philosopher should be added. The final argument to method **insertNodeInto** specifies the index at which the new node should be inserted. Line 101 invokes method **getChildCount** of class **DefaultMutableTreeNode** to get the total number of children in node **parent**, which will cause the new node to be added as the last child of **parent**.

Method **removeElement** (lines 106–114) invokes method **getSelectedNode** (line 109) to get the currently selected node in the **JTree**. If **selectedNode** is not **null**, line 113 invokes method **removeNodeFromParent** of class **DefaultTree-Model** to remove **selectedNode** from the model. Method **getSelectedNode** (lines 117–122) invokes method **getLastSelectedPathComponent** of class **JTree** to get a reference to the currently selected node (line 121). Line 120 casts the selected node to **DefaultMutableTreeNode** and returns the reference to the caller.

Method **createPhilosopherTree** (lines 125–192) creates **DefaultMu-tableTreeNode**s for several philosophers and for the eras in which the philosophers lived. Lines 128–129 create a **DefaultMutableTreeNode** for the tree's root. Class **DefaultMutableTreeNode** has property **userObject** that stores an **Object** that contains the node's data. The **String** passed to the **DefaultMutableTreeNode** constructor (line 129) is the **userObject** for **rootNode**. The **JTree**'s **TreeCellRenderer** will invoke method **toString** of class **DefaultMutableTreeNode** to get a **String** to display for this node in the **JTree**.

Software Engineering Observation 3.4

*Method **toString** of class **DefaultMutableTreeNode** returns the value returned by its **userObject**'s **toString** method.*

Lines 132–134 create a **DefaultMutableTreeNode** for the **ancient** era of philosophy and add node **ancient** as a child of **rootNode** (line 134). Lines 136–138 create **DefaultMutableTreeNode**s for three ancient philosophers and add each **Default-MutableTreeNode** as a child of **DefaultMutableTreeNode ancient**. Lines 141–189 create several additional **DefaultMutableTreeNode**s for other eras in the history of philosophy and for philosophers in those eras. Line 191 returns **rootNode**, which now contains the era and philosopher **DefaultMutableTreeNode**s as its children and descendents, respectively.

3.6.2 Custom **TreeModel** Implementation

If the **DefaultTreeModel** implementation is not sufficient for an application, developers also can provide custom implementations of interface **TreeModel**. **FileSystem-Model** (Fig. 3.18) implements interface **TreeModel** to provide a model of a computer's file system. A file system consists of directories and files arranged in a hierarchy. Line 17 declares a **File** reference **root** that serves as the root node in the hierarchy. This **File** is a directory that contains files and other directories. The **FileSystemModel** constructor (lines 23–26) takes a **File** argument for the **FileSystemModel** root. Method **get-tRoot** (lines 29–32) returns the **FileSystemModel**'s root node.

```
1   // FileSystemModel.java
2   // TreeModel implementation using File objects as tree nodes.
3   package com.deitel.advjhtp1.mvc.tree.filesystem;
4
5   // Java core packages
6   import java.io.*;
```

Fig. 3.18   FileSystemModel implementation of interface **TreeModel** to represent a file system (part 1 of 5).

```
7    import java.util.*;
8
9    // Java extension packages
10   import javax.swing.*;
11   import javax.swing.tree.*;
12   import javax.swing.event.*;
13
14   public class FileSystemModel implements TreeModel {
15
16      // hierarchy root
17      private File root;
18
19      // TreeModelListeners
20      private Vector listeners = new Vector();
21
22      // FileSystemModel constructor
23      public FileSystemModel( File rootDirectory )
24      {
25         root = rootDirectory;
26      }
27
28      // get hierarchy root (root directory)
29      public Object getRoot()
30      {
31         return root;
32      }
33
34      // get parent's child at given index
35      public Object getChild( Object parent, int index )
36      {
37         // get parent File object
38         File directory = ( File ) parent;
39
40         // get list of files in parent directory
41         String[] children = directory.list();
42
43         // return File at given index and override toString
44         // method to return only the File's name
45         return new TreeFile( directory, children[ index ] );
46      }
47
48      // get parent's number of children
49      public int getChildCount( Object parent )
50      {
51         // get parent File object
52         File file = ( File ) parent;
53
54         // get number of files in directory
55         if ( file.isDirectory() ) {
56
57            String[] fileList = file.list();
58
```

Fig. 3.18 **FileSystemModel** implementation of interface **TreeModel** to
represent a file system (part 2 of 5).

```
59              if ( fileList != null )
60                  return file.list().length;
61          }
62
63          return 0; // childCount is 0 for files
64      }
65
66      // return true if node is a file, false if it is a directory
67      public boolean isLeaf( Object node )
68      {
69          File file = ( File ) node;
70          return file.isFile();
71      }
72
73      // get numeric index of given child node
74      public int getIndexOfChild( Object parent, Object child )
75      {
76          // get parent File object
77          File directory = ( File ) parent;
78
79          // get child File object
80          File file = ( File ) child;
81
82          // get File list in directory
83          String[] children = directory.list();
84
85          // search File list for given child
86          for ( int i = 0; i < children.length; i++ ) {
87
88              if ( file.getName().equals( children[ i ] ) ) {
89
90                  // return matching File's index
91                  return i;
92              }
93          }
94
95          return -1; // indicate child index not found
96
97      } // end method getIndexOfChild
98
99      // invoked by delegate if value of Object at given
100     // TreePath changes
101     public void valueForPathChanged( TreePath path,
102         Object value )
103     {
104         // get File object that was changed
105         File oldFile = ( File ) path.getLastPathComponent();
106
107         // get parent directory of changed File
108         String fileParentPath = oldFile.getParent();
109
```

Fig. 3.18 **FileSystemModel** implementation of interface **TreeModel** to represent a file system (part 3 of 5).

```
110        // get value of newFileName entered by user
111        String newFileName = ( String ) value;
112
113        // create File object with newFileName for
114        // renaming oldFile
115        File targetFile = new File(
116           fileParentPath, newFileName );
117
118        // rename oldFile to targetFile
119        oldFile.renameTo( targetFile );
120
121        // get File object for parent directory
122        File parent = new File( fileParentPath );
123
124        // create int array for renamed File's index
125        int[] changedChildrenIndices =
126           { getIndexOfChild( parent, targetFile) };
127
128        // create Object array containing only renamed File
129        Object[] changedChildren = { targetFile };
130
131        // notify TreeModelListeners of node change
132        fireTreeNodesChanged( path.getParentPath(),
133           changedChildrenIndices, changedChildren );
134
135     } // end method valueForPathChanged
136
137     // notify TreeModelListeners that children of parent at
138     // given TreePath with given indices were changed
139     private void fireTreeNodesChanged( TreePath parentPath,
140        int[] indices, Object[] children )
141     {
142        // create TreeModelEvent to indicate node change
143        TreeModelEvent event = new TreeModelEvent( this,
144           parentPath, indices, children );
145
146        Iterator iterator = listeners.iterator();
147        TreeModelListener listener = null;
148
149        // send TreeModelEvent to each listener
150        while ( iterator.hasNext() ) {
151           listener = ( TreeModelListener ) iterator.next();
152           listener.treeNodesChanged( event );
153        }
154     } // end method fireTreeNodesChanged
155
156     // add given TreeModelListener
157     public void addTreeModelListener(
158        TreeModelListener listener )
159     {
160        listeners.add( listener );
161     }
```

Fig. 3.18 FileSystemModel implementation of interface **TreeModel** to represent a file system (part 4 of 5).

```
162
163      // remove given TreeModelListener
164      public void removeTreeModelListener(
165         TreeModelListener listener )
166      {
167         listeners.remove( listener );
168      }
169
170      // TreeFile is a File subclass that overrides method
171      // toString to return only the File name.
172      private class TreeFile extends File {
173
174         // TreeFile constructor
175         public TreeFile( File parent, String child )
176         {
177            super( parent, child );
178         }
179
180         // override method toString to return only the File name
181         // and not the full path
182         public String toString()
183         {
184            return getName();
185         }
186      } // end inner class TreeFile
187  }
```

Fig. 3.18 **FileSystemModel** implementation of interface **TreeModel** to represent a file system (part 5 of 5).

When building its view of a **TreeModel**, a **JTree** repeatedly invokes method **get-Child** (lines 35–46) to traverse the **TreeModel**'s nodes. Method **getChild** returns argument **parent**'s child node at the given **index**. The nodes in a **TreeModel** need not implement interface **TreeNode** or interface **MutableTreeNode**; any **Object** can be a node in a **TreeModel**. In class **FileSystemModel**, each node is a **File**. Line 38 casts **Object** reference **parent** to a **File** reference. Line 41 invokes method **list** of class **File** to get a list of file names in **directory**. Line 45 returns a new **TreeFile** object for the **File** at the given **index**. **JTree** invokes method **toString** of class **TreeFile** to get a label for the node in the **JTree**.

Method **getChildCount** (lines 49–64) returns the number of children contained in argument **parent**. Line 52 casts **Object** reference **parent** to a **File** reference named **file**. If **file** is a directory (line 55), lines 57–60 get a list of file names in the directory and return the **length** of the list. If **file** is not a directory, line 63 returns **0**, to indicate that **file** has no children.

A **JTree** invokes method **isLeaf** of class **FileSystemModel** (lines 67–71) to determine if **Object** argument **node** is a *leaf node*—a node that does not contain children.[4] In a file system, only directories can contain children, so line 70 returns **true** only if argument **node** is a file (not a directory).

---

4. Leaf node controls the initial screen display of the expand handle.

Method **getIndexOfChild** (lines 74–98) returns argument **child**'s index in the given **parent** node. For example, if **child** were the third node in **parent**, method **getIndexOfChild** would return zero-based index **2**. Lines 77 and 80 get **File** references for the **parent** and **child** nodes, respectively. Line 83 gets a list of files, and lines 86–93 search through the list for the given **child**. If the filname in the list matches the given child (line 88), line 91 returns the index **i**. Otherwise, line 95 returns **-1**, to indicate that **parent** did not contain **child**.

The **JTree** delegate invokes method **valueForPathChanged** (lines 101–135) when the user edits a node in the tree. A user can click on a node in the **JTree** and edit the node's name, which corresponds to the associated **File** object's file name. When a user edits a node, **JTree** invokes method **valueForPathChanged** and passes a **TreePath** argument that represents the changed node's location in the tree, and an **Object** that contains the node's new value. In this example, the new value is a new file name **String** for the associated **File** object. Line 105 invokes method **getLastPathComponent** of class **TreePath** to obtain the **File** object to rename. Line 108 gets **oldFile**'s parent directory. Line 111 casts argument **value**, which contains the new file name, to a **String**. Lines 115–116 create **File** object **targetFile** using the new file name. Line 119 invokes method **renameTo** of class **File** to rename **oldFile** to **targetFile**.

After renaming the file, the **FileSystemModel** must notify its **TreeModelListener**s of the change by issuing a **TreeModelEvent**. A **TreeModelEvent** that indicates a node change includes a reference to the **TreeModel** that generated the event, the **TreePath** of the changed nodes' parent node, an integer array containing the changed nodes' indices and an **Object** array containing references to the changed nodes themselves. Line 122 creates a **File** object for the renamed file's parent directory. Lines 125–126 create an integer array for the indices of changed nodes. Line 128 creates an **Object** array of changed nodes. The integer and **Object** arrays have only one element each because only one node changed. If multiple nodes were changed, these arrays would need to include elements for each changed node. Lines 132–133 invoke method **fireTreeNodesChanged** to issue the **TreeModelEvent**.

Performance Tip 3.1

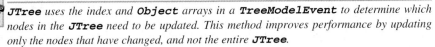

*JTree uses the index and **Object** arrays in a **TreeModelEvent** to determine which nodes in the **JTree** need to be updated. This method improves performance by updating only the nodes that have changed, and not the entire **JTree**.*

Method **fireTreeNodesChanged** (lines 139–154) issues a **TreeModelEvent** to all registered **TreeModelListener**s, indicating that nodes in the **TreeModel** have changed. **TreePath** argument **parentPath** is the path to the parent whose child nodes changed. The integer and **Object** array arguments contain the indices of the changed nodes and references to the changed nodes, respectively. Lines 143–144 create the **TreeModel** event with the given event data. Lines 150–153 iterate through the list of **TreeModelListener**s, sending the **TreeModelEvent** to each. Methods **addTreeModelListener** (lines 157–161) and **removeTreeModelListener** (lines 164–168) allow **TreeModelListener**s to register and unregister for **TreeModelEvent**s.

Inner-class **TreeFile** (lines 172–186) overrides method **toString** of superclass **File**. Method **toString** of class **File** returns a **String** containing the **File**'s full path name (e.g., **D:\Temp\README.TXT**). Method **toString** of class **TreeFile** (lines 182–185) overrides this method to return only the **File**'s name (e.g.,

README.TXT). Class **JTree** uses a **DefaultTreeCellRenderer** to display each node in its **TreeModel**. The **DefaultTreeCellRenderer** invokes the node's **toString** method to get the text for the **DefaultTreeCellRenderer**'s label. Class **TreeFile** overrides method **toString** of class **File** so the **DefaultTreeCell-Renderer** will show only the **File**'s name in the **JTree**, instead of the full path.

   FileTreeFrame (Fig. 3.19) uses a **JTree** and a **FileSystemModel** to allow the user to view and modify a file system. The user interface consists of a **JTree** that shows the file system and a **JTextArea** that shows information about the currently selected file. Lines 33–34 create the uneditable **JTextArea** for displaying file information. Lines 37–38 create a **FileSystemModel** whose root is **directory**. Line 41 creates a **JTree** for the **FileSystemModel**. Line 44 sets the **JTree**'s editable property to **true**, to allow users to rename files displayed in the **JTree**.

```
1    // FileTreeFrame.java
2    // JFrame for displaying file system contents in a JTree
3    // using a custom TreeModel.
4    package com.deitel.advjhtp1.mvc.tree.filesystem;
5
6    // Java core packages
7    import java.io.*;
8    import java.awt.*;
9    import java.awt.event.*;
10
11   // Java extension packages
12   import javax.swing.*;
13   import javax.swing.tree.*;
14   import javax.swing.event.*;
15
16   public class FileTreeFrame extends JFrame {
17
18      // JTree for displaying file system
19      private JTree fileTree;
20
21      // FileSystemModel TreeModel implementation
22      private FileSystemModel fileSystemModel;
23
24      // JTextArea for displaying selected file's details
25      private JTextArea fileDetailsTextArea;
26
27      // FileTreeFrame constructor
28      public FileTreeFrame( String directory )
29      {
30         super( "JTree FileSystem Viewer" );
31
32         // create JTextArea for displaying File information
33         fileDetailsTextArea = new JTextArea();
34         fileDetailsTextArea.setEditable( false );
35
```

Fig. 3.19 **FileTreeFrame** application for browsing and editing a file system using **JTree** and **FileSystemModel** (part 1 of 3).

```
36         // create FileSystemModel for given directory
37         fileSystemModel = new FileSystemModel(
38            new File( directory ) );
39
40         // create JTree for FileSystemModel
41         fileTree = new JTree( fileSystemModel );
42
43         // make JTree editable for renaming Files
44         fileTree.setEditable( true );
45
46         // add a TreeSelectionListener
47         fileTree.addTreeSelectionListener(
48            new TreeSelectionListener() {
49
50               // display details of newly selected File when
51               // selection changes
52               public void valueChanged(
53                  TreeSelectionEvent event )
54               {
55                  File file = ( File )
56                     fileTree.getLastSelectedPathComponent();
57
58                  fileDetailsTextArea.setText(
59                     getFileDetails( file ) );
60               }
61            }
62         ); // end addTreeSelectionListener
63
64         // put fileTree and fileDetailsTextArea in a JSplitPane
65         JSplitPane splitPane = new JSplitPane(
66            JSplitPane.HORIZONTAL_SPLIT, true,
67            new JScrollPane( fileTree ),
68            new JScrollPane( fileDetailsTextArea ) );
69
70         getContentPane().add( splitPane );
71
72         setDefaultCloseOperation( EXIT_ON_CLOSE );
73         setSize( 640, 480 );
74         setVisible( true );
75      }
76
77      // build a String to display file details
78      private String getFileDetails( File file )
79      {
80         // do not return details for null Files
81         if ( file == null )
82            return "";
83
84         // put File information in a StringBuffer
85         StringBuffer buffer = new StringBuffer();
86         buffer.append( "Name: " + file.getName() + "\n" );
87         buffer.append( "Path: " + file.getPath()  + "\n" );
```

Fig. 3.19 **FileTreeFrame** application for browsing and editing a file system using **JTree** and **FileSystemModel** (part 2 of 3).

```
88              buffer.append( "Size: " + file.length() + "\n" );
89
90              return buffer.toString();
91          }
92
93          // execute application
94          public static void main( String args[] )
95          {
96              // ensure that user provided directory name
97              if ( args.length != 1 )
98                  System.err.println(
99                      "Usage: java FileTreeFrame <path>" );
100
101             // start application using provided directory name
102             else
103                 new FileTreeFrame( args[ 0 ] );
104         }
105     }
```

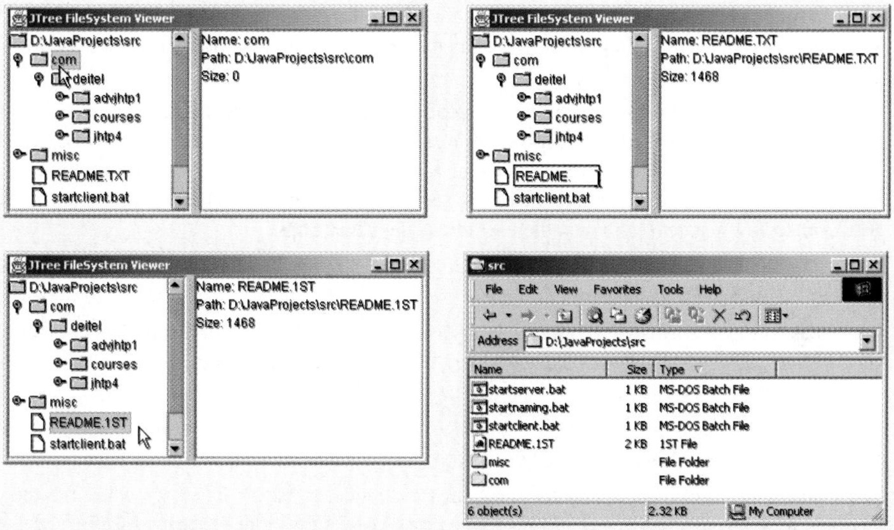

Fig. 3.19 `FileTreeFrame` application for browsing and editing a file system using `JTree` and `FileSystemModel` (part 3 of 3).

Lines 47–62 create a `TreeSelectionListener` to listen for `TreeSelection-Event`s in the `JTree`. Lines 55–56 of method `valueChanged` get the selected `File` object from the `JTree`. Lines 58–59 invoke method `getFileDetails` to retrieve information about the selected `File` and to display the details in `fileDetailsTextArea`. Lines 65–69 create a `JSplitPane` to separate the `JTree` and `JTextArea`. Lines 67 and 68 place the `JTree` and `JTextArea` in `JScrollPane`s. Line 70 adds the `JSplitPane` to the `JFrame`.

Method `getFileDetails` (lines 78–91) takes a `File` argument and returns a `String` containing the `File`'s name, path and length. If the `File` argument is `null`, line 81 returns an empty `String`. Line 85 creates a `StringBuffer`, and lines 86–88 append the **File**'s name, path and length. Line 90 invokes method **toString** of class **String-Buffer** and returns the result to the caller.

Method **main** (lines 94–104) executes the **FileTreeFrame** application. Lines 97–99 check the command-line arguments to ensure that the user provided a path for the **FileTreeModel**'s root. If the user did not provide a command-line argument, lines 98–99 display the program's usage instructions. Otherwise, line 103 creates a new **FileTreeFrame** and passes the command-line argument to the constructor.

In this chapter, we introduced the model-view-controller architecture, the Observer design pattern and the delegate-model architecture used by several Swing components. In later chapters, we use MVC to build a Java2D paint program (Chapter 6), database-aware programs (Chapter 8, JDBC) and an Enterprise Java case study (Chapters 16–19).

SUMMARY

- The model-view-controller (MVC) architecture separates application data (contained in the model) from graphical presentation components (the view) and input-processing logic (the controller).

- The Java Foundation Classes (more commonly referred to as Swing components) implement a variation of MVC that combines the view and the controller into a single object, called a *delegate*. The delegate provides both a graphical presentation of the model and an interface for modifying the model.

- Every **JButton** has an associated **ButtonModel** for which the **JButton** is a delegate. The **ButtonModel** maintains the state information, such as whether the **JButton** is clicked, whether the **JButton** is enabled as well as a list of **ActionListener**s. The **JButton** provides a graphical presentation (e.g., a rectangle on the screen, with a label and a border) and modifies the **ButtonModel**'s state (e.g., when the user clicks the **JButton**).

- The *Observer design pattern* is a more general application of MVC that provides loose coupling between an object and its dependent objects.

- Class **java.util.Observable** represents a model in MVC, or the subject in the Observer design pattern. Class **Observable** provides method **addObserver**, which takes a **java.util.Observer** argument.

- Interface **Observer** represents the view in MVC, or the observer in the Observer design pattern. When the **Observable** object changes, it notifies each registered **Observer** of the change.

- The model-view-controller architecture requires the model to notify its views when the model changes. Method **setChanged** of class **Observable** sets the model's *changed* flag. Method **notifyObservers** of class **Observable** notifies all **Observer**s (i.e., views) of the change.

- An **Observable** object must invoke method **setChanged** before invoking method **notifyObservers**. Method **notifyObservers** invokes method **update** of interface **Observer** for each registered **Observer**.

- **JList** is a Swing component that implements the delegate-model architecture. **JList** acts as a delegate for an underlying **ListModel**.

- Interface **ListModel** defines methods for getting list elements, getting the size of the list and registering and unregistering **ListDataListener**s. A **ListModel** notifies each registered **ListDataListener** of each change in the **ListModel**.

- **JTable** is another **Swing** component that implements the delegate-model architecture. **JTable**s are delegates for tabular data stored in **TableModel** implementations.

- **JTree** is one of the more complex Swing components that implements the delegate-model architecture. **TreeModel**s represent hierarchical data, such as family trees, file systems, company management structures and document outlines. **JTree**s act as delegates (i.e., combined view and controller) for **TreeModel**s.

- To describe tree data structures, it is common to use family-tree terminology. A tree data structure consists of a set of nodes (i.e., members or elements of the tree) that are related as parents, children, siblings, ancestors and descendents.

- Interface **TreeModel** defines methods that describe a tree data structure suitable for representation in a **JTree**. Objects of any class can represent nodes in a **TreeModel**. For example, a **Person** class could represent a node in a family tree **TreeModel**.

- Class **DefaultTreeModel** provides a default **TreeModel** implementation. Interface **TreeNode** defines common operations for nodes in a **DefaultTreeModel**, such as **getParent** and **getAllowsChildren**.

- Interface **MutableTreeNode** extends interface **TreeNode** to represent a node that can change, either by addition or removal of child nodes or by change of the **Object** associated with the node. Class **DefaultMutableTreeNode** provides a **MutableTreeNode** implementation suitable for use in a **DefaultTreeModel**.

- Interface **TreeCellRenderer** represents an object that creates a view for each node in the **JTree**. Class **DefaultTreeCellRenderer** implements interface **TreeCellRenderer** and extends class **JLabel** to provide a **TreeCellRenderer** default implementation.

- Interface **TreeCellEditor** represents an object for controlling (i.e., editing) each node in the **JTree**. Class **DefaultTreeCellEditor** implements interface **TreeCellEditor** and uses a **JTextField** to provide a **TreeCellEditor** default implementation.

- If the **DefaultTreeModel** implementation is not sufficient for an application, developers can also provide custom implementations of interface **TreeModel**.

TERMINOLOGY

ancestor
child
controller
DefaultListModel class
DefaultMutableTreeNode class
DefaultTableModel class
DefaultTreeCellEditor class
DefaultTreeCellRenderer class
DefaultTreeModel class
delegate
delegate-model architecture
descendent
getChild method of interface **TreeModel**
getChildAtIndex method of
    interface **TreeModel**
getChildCount method of interface
    TreeModel
getIndexOfChild method of
    interface **TreeModel**
isLeaf method of interface **TreeModel**
JList class
JTable class
JTree class

ListModel interface
ListSelectionModel interface
model
model-view-controller architecture
MutableTreeNode interface
notifyObservers method of
    class **Observable**
Observable class
Observer design pattern
Observer interface
parent
setChanged method of class **Observable**
sibling
TableModel interface
TreeCellEditor interface
TreeCellRenderer interface
TreeModel interface
TreeNode interface
update method of interface **Observer**
valueForPathChanged method of
    interface **TreeModel**
view

SELF-REVIEW EXERCISES

3.1   What more general design pattern does the model-view-controller (MVC) architecture use?

3.2   How does the variation of MVC implemented in the Swing packages differ from regular MVC?

3.3   List the Swing classes that use MVC.

3.4   What type of data does a **TableModel** contain, and what Swing class is a **TableModel** delegate?

3.5   What interfaces does a **JTree** employ to provide its delegate functionality for a **TreeModel**?

ANSWERS TO SELF-REVIEW EXERCISES

3.1   The model-view-controller architecture uses the more general Observer design pattern to separate a model (i.e., a subject) from its views (i.e., its observers).

3.2   The Swing packages use a version of MVC known as the delegate-model architecture, in which the view and controller are combined into a single object to form a delegate.

3.3   Most Swing classes use MVC, including **JButton**, **JList**, **JTable** and **JTree**.

3.4   A **TableModel** contains tabular data, such as data from a database table or spreadsheet. **JTable** is a delegate for **TableModel**s.

3.5   A **JTree** uses a **TreeCellRenderer** to provide a view of its nodes and a **TreeCellEditor** to provide a controller for its nodes.

EXERCISES

3.6   Create class **LiabilityPieChartView** as a subclass of class **AssetPieChartView** (Fig. 3.8) that includes only liability **Account**s (i.e., **Account**s with negative balances). Modify class **AccountManager** (Fig. 3.10) to include a **LiabilityPieChartView**, in addition to the **AssetPieChartView**.

3.7   Create a new version of class **AccountBarGraphView** (Fig. 3.7) that shows multiple **Account**s in a single bar graph. [*Hint*: Try modeling your class after **AssetPieChartView** to include multiple **Account**s.]

3.8   Enhance your solution to Exercise 3.7 to allow transfers between accounts. Modify class **AccountController** (Fig. 3.9) to include a **JComboBox** to select the destination account and a **JButton** to perform the transfer.

3.9   Create a **TreeModel** implementation named **XMLTreeModel** that provides a read-only model of an XML document. Create a program that uses a **JTree** to display the XML document. If you are not familiar with XML, please see Appendices A–D.

4

Graphics Programming with Java 2D and Java 3D

Objectives

- To be able to use the Java 2D API to draw various shapes and general paths.
- To be able to specify **Paint** and **Stroke** characteristics of shapes displayed with **Graphics2D**.
- To be able to manipulate images using Java 2D image processing.
- To use the Java 3D API and Java 3D Utility classes to create three-dimensional graphics scenes.
- To manipulate the texture and lighting of three-dimensional objects with Java 3D.

Sit in reverie and watch the changing color of the waves that break upon the idle seashore of the mind.
Henry Wadsworth Longfellow

Art is not a mirror to reflect the world, but a hammer with which to shape it.
Vladimir Mayakovsky

… work transforms talent into genius.
Anna Povlova

A work that aspires, however humbly, to the condition of art should carry its justification in every line.
Joseph Conrad

Outline

4.1 Introduction

Over the past few years, developers have strived to integrate cutting-edge graphics and animation in their applets and applications. However, the original Java AWT graphics packages have provided a limited means to achieve such goals. Now, with the *Java 2D™ API* and *Java 3D™ API*, developers can implement more sophisticated graphics applications—such as games, screen savers, splash screens and 3D GUI's.

This chapter overviews several of Java's 2D and 3D graphics capabilities. We begin with a brief introduction to fundamental graphics topics, such as coordinate systems and graphics contexts. Next, we discuss several Java 2D capabilities, such as controlling how to fill shapes with colors and patterns. We also introduce how to blur, invert, sharpen and change the color of an image using Java 2D's image processing capabilities. In the second half of our graphics discussion, we present the Java 3D API. Using the Java 3D utility classes, we build an application that allows the user to manipulate (rotate, scale and translate) 3D objects with a mouse. The application has a control panel that allows the user both to apply textures to 3D objects using texture mapping and to vary the lighting effects on 3D objects by changing the color of a light source.

4.2 Coordinates, Graphics Contexts and Graphics Objects

Java's 2D *coordinate system* (Fig. 4.1) is a scheme for identifying every point on the screen. By default, the upper left corner of a GUI component has the coordinates (0, 0). The *y*-coordinate is the vertical distance moving down from the upper left corner. The *x*-coordinate is the horizontal distance moving right from the upper left corner.

A Java *graphics context* enables drawing on the screen. A **Graphics** object manages a graphics context by controlling how information is drawn. **Graphics** objects contain methods for drawing, font manipulation, color manipulation and the like. Every application that performs drawing on the screen uses **Graphics** object to manage the application's graphics context.

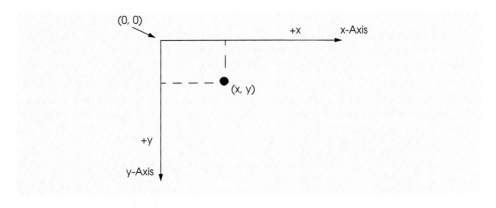

Fig. 4.1   Java coordinate system. Units are measured in pixels.

Class **Graphics** is an **abstract** class (i.e., a **Graphics** object cannot be instantiated). This contributes to Java's portability. Drawing is performed differently on each platform that supports Java so there cannot be one class that implements drawing capabilities on all systems. For example, the graphics capabilities that enable a PC running Microsoft Windows to draw a rectangle are different from the graphics capabilities that enable a UNIX workstation to draw a rectangle—and those are both different from the graphics capabilities that enable a Macintosh to draw a rectangle. For each platform, a **Graphics** subclass implements all the drawing capabilities. This implementation is hidden by the **Graphics** class, which supplies the interface that enables us to write programs that use graphics in a platform-independent manner.

Class **Component** is the superclass for many of the classes in the **java.awt** package. Method **paint** of class **Component** is called when the contents of the **Component** should be painted—either in response to the **Component** first being shown or damage needing repair—such as resizing the **Component** window. Method **paint** takes a **Graphics** reference as an argument. When a **Component** needs to be painted, the system passes a **Graphics** reference to method **paint**. This **Graphics** reference is a reference to the platform-specific **Graphics** subclass. The developer should not call method **paint** directly, because drawing graphics is an *event driven process*. To request the system to call **paint**, a developer can invoke method **repaint** of class **Component**. Method **repaint** requests a call to method **update** of class **Component** as soon as possible, to clear the **Component**'s background of any previous drawing. Method **update** then calls **paint** directly.

Class **JComponent**—a **Component** subclass—is the superclass for many of the classes in the **javax.swing** package. The Swing painting mechanism calls method **paintComponent** of class **JComponent** when the contents of the **JComponent** should be painted. Method **paintComponent**—which takes as an argument a **Graphics** object—helps the Swing components paint properly. The **Graphics** object is passed to the **paintComponent** method by the system when a **paintComponent** operation is required for a **JComponent**. The developer should not call method **paintComponent** directly. If the developer needs to call **paintComponent**, a call is made to method **repaint** of class **Component**—exactly as discussed earlier for method **repaint** of class **Component**.

4.3 Java 2D API

The *Java 2D™ API* provides advanced 2D graphics capabilities for developers who require detailed and complex graphical manipulations in their programs. The Java 2D API is part of the Java 2 Platform, Standard Edition. The Java 2D API includes features for processing line art, text and images in packages **java.awt.image**, **java.awt.color**, **java.awt.font**, **java.awt.geom**, **java.awt.print** and **java.awt.image.renderable**. Figure 4.2 describes several of the Java 2D classes and interfaces covered in this chapter.

Class/*Interface*	Description
Classes and interfaces from package **java.awt**	
Graphics2D	**Graphics** subclass for rendering 2D shapes, text and images.
BasicStroke	Defines a basic set of rendering attributes for the outlines of graphics primitives.
GradientPaint	Provides a way to fill and outline 2D shapes with a linear color gradient.
TexturePaint	Provides a way to fill and outline shapes with texture images.
Paint	Defines how color patterns can be generated for rendering operations.
Shape	Provides definitions for geometrical objects.
Stroke	Provides methods for obtaining the outline of a geometrical shape.
Classes and interfaces from package **java.awt.geom**	
GeneralPath	Represents a path constructed from straight lines, quadratic curves and cubic curves.
Line2D	Represents a line in coordinate space.
RectangularShape	Base class for geometrical shapes with rectangular frames. Subclasses include **Arc2D**, **Ellipse2D**, **Rectangle2D** and **RoundRectangle2D**.
BufferedImage	Describes an **Image** with a buffer of colored pixel data composed of a **ColorModel** and a **Raster**.
ColorModel	Defines methods for translating a numerical pixel value to a color.
Classes and interfaces from package **java.awt.image**	
Raster	Is part of a **BufferedImage** that describes sample values in a rectangular array of pixels.
Kernel	Describes a 2D array used for filtering **BufferedImage**s.

Fig. 4.2   Some Java 2D classes and interfaces (part 1 of 2).

Class/*Interface*	Description
BufferedImageOp	Defines methods that perform operations on **BufferedImage**s (e.g. blurring a **BufferedImage**)
RasterOp	Describes single-input/single-output processes performed on **Raster**s.

Fig. 4.2   Some Java 2D classes and interfaces (part 2 of 2).

Class **java.awt.Graphics2D** enables drawing with the Java 2D API. Class **Graphics2D** is a subclass of class **Graphics**, so it has all the capabilities for managing the application's graphics context discussed earlier in this chapter. To access the **Graphics2D** capabilities, we cast the **Graphics** reference passed to **paint** to a **Graphics2D** reference.

Java 2D can render three types of built-in graphics objects—termed *graphics primitives*—images, text and geometrical shapes. There are seven **Graphics2D** state attributes that determine how graphics primitives are rendered—*clipping, compositing, font, paint, rendering hints, stroke* and *transforms*. Figure 4.3 describes each of these seven attributes. The attributes form a pipeline that processes the graphics primitives to produce the final image. The first stage in the pipeline determines which of the primitives to render. A *draw method* then draws the primitive—method **draw** for shapes, method **drawString** for text and method **drawImage** for images. The pipeline applies any transformations, fills and strokes during the drawing process. The next stage is to *rasterize* the drawn shape—convert the shape to a two-dimensional array of numerical pixel values called a *raster*. At this stage, the pipeline invokes any image-processing operations on the raster. The raster is then clipped, colored and combined with the current drawing—known as compositing. Finally, the image is *rendered*—drawn—on an output device, such as a screen or printer.

Attribute	Description
Clipping	Defines the area in which rendering operations take effect. Any geometrical shape, including text, can be used as a clipping region.
Compositing	Is a Set of *blending rules* that control how the pixels in a source image mix with the pixels in a destination image.
Font	Fonts are created from shapes that represent the characters to be drawn—called *glyphs*. Text is rendered by drawing and filling the glyphs.
Paint	Determines the colors, patterns and gradients for filling and outlining a shape.
Rendering Hints	Specify techniques and methods that help to optimize drawing.

Fig. 4.3   The seven state attributes of a Java 2D graphics context (part 1 of 2).

Attribute	Description
Stroke	Determines the outline of the shape to be drawn.
Transform	Defines ways to perform linear transformations—an operation that changes the shape of an image.

Fig. 4.3   The seven state attributes of a Java 2D graphics context (part 2 of 2).

The Java 2D API provides hints and rules that instruct the graphics engine how to perform these operations. The following sections present several features of image and geometrical shape-rendering processes.

4.3.1 Java 2D Shapes

In this section, we present several Java 2D shape classes from package **java.awt.geom**, including **Ellipse2D.Double**, **Line2D.Double**, **Rectangle2D.Double**, **RoundRectangle2D.Double** and **Arc2D.Double**. Each class represents a shape with dimensions specified as double-precision floating-point values. Each class can also be represented with single-precision floating-point values (e.g., **Ellipse2D.Float**). In each case, class **Double** is a **static** inner class contained in the class to the left of the dot operator (e.g., **Ellipse2D**).

Class **Shapes** (Fig. 4.4) demonstrates several Java 2D shapes and rendering attributes (such as thick lines), filling shapes with patterns and drawing dashed lines. These are just a few of the many capabilities Java 2D provides.

```
1   // Shapes.java
2   // Shapes demonstrates some Java 2D shapes.
3
4   // Java core packages
5   import java.awt.*;
6   import java.awt.event.*;
7   import java.awt.geom.*;
8   import java.awt.image.*;
9
10  // Java extension packages
11  import javax.swing.*;
12
13  public class Shapes extends JFrame {
14
15      // constructor method
16      public Shapes()
17      {
18          super( "Drawing 2D shapes" );
19      }
20
```

Fig. 4.4   Demonstrating some Java 2D shapes (part 1 of 3).

```
21      // draw shapes using Java 2D API
22      public void paint( Graphics g )
23      {
24          // call superclass' paint method
25          super.paint( g );
26
27          // get Graphics 2D by casting g to Graphics2D
28          Graphics2D graphics2D = ( Graphics2D ) g;
29
30          // draw 2D ellipse filled with blue-yellow gradient
31          graphics2D.setPaint( new GradientPaint
32              ( 5, 30, Color.blue, 35, 100, Color.yellow, true ) );
33          graphics2D.fill( new Ellipse2D.Double( 5, 30, 65, 100 ) );
34
35          // draw 2D rectangle in red
36          graphics2D.setPaint( Color.red );
37          graphics2D.setStroke( new BasicStroke( 10.0f ) );
38          graphics2D.draw(
39              new Rectangle2D.Double( 80, 30, 65, 100 ) );
40
41          // draw 2D rounded rectangle with BufferedImage background
42          BufferedImage bufferedImage = new BufferedImage(
43              10, 10, BufferedImage.TYPE_INT_RGB );
44
45          Graphics2D graphics = bufferedImage.createGraphics();
46          graphics.setColor( Color.yellow ); // draw in yellow
47          graphics.fillRect( 0, 0, 10, 10 ); // draw filled rectangle
48          graphics.setColor( Color.black );  // draw in black
49          graphics.drawRect( 1, 1, 6, 6 );   // draw rectangle
50          graphics.setColor( Color.blue );   // draw in blue
51          graphics.fillRect( 1, 1, 3, 3 );   // draw filled rectangle
52          graphics.setColor( Color.red );    // draw in red
53          graphics.fillRect( 4, 4, 3, 3 );   // draw filled rectangle
54
55          // paint buffImage into graphics context of JFrame
56          graphics2D.setPaint( new TexturePaint(
57              bufferedImage, new Rectangle( 10, 10 ) ) );
58          graphics2D.fill( new RoundRectangle2D.Double(
59              155, 30, 75, 100, 50, 50 ) );
60
61          // draw 2D pie-shaped arc in white
62          graphics2D.setPaint( Color.white );
63          graphics2D.setStroke( new BasicStroke( 6.0f ) );
64          graphics2D.draw( new Arc2D.Double(
65              240, 30, 75, 100, 0, 270, Arc2D.PIE ) );
66
67          // draw 2D lines in green and yellow
68          graphics2D.setPaint( Color.green );
69          graphics2D.draw( new Line2D.Double( 395, 30, 320, 150 ) );
70
71          float dashes[] = { 10, 2 };
72
73          graphics2D.setPaint( Color.yellow );
```

Fig. 4.4   Demonstrating some Java 2D shapes (part 2 of 3).

```
74        graphics2D.setStroke( new BasicStroke(
75           4, BasicStroke.CAP_ROUND, BasicStroke.JOIN_ROUND,
76           10, dashes, 0 ) );
77        graphics2D.draw( new Line2D.Double( 320, 30, 395, 150 ) );
78
79     } // end method paint
80
81     // start application
82     public static void main( String args[] )
83     {
84        Shapes application = new Shapes();
85        application.setDefaultCloseOperation(
86           JFrame.EXIT_ON_CLOSE );
87
88        application.setSize( 425, 160 );
89        application.setVisible( true );
90     }
91  }
```

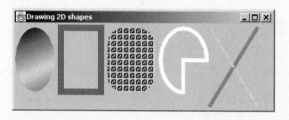

Fig. 4.4   Demonstrating some Java 2D shapes (part 3 of 3).

Line 28 casts the **Graphics** reference received by **paint** to a **Graphics2D** reference to allow access to Java 2D features. The first shape we draw is an oval filled with gradually changing colors. Lines 31–32 invoke method **setPaint** of class **Graphics2D** to set the *Paint* object that determines the color for the shape to display. A **Paint** object is an object of any class that implements interface **java.awt.Paint**. The **Paint** object can be something as simple as one of the predefined **Color** objects (class **Color** implements **Paint**), or the **Paint** object can be an instance of the Java 2D API's *Gradient-Paint*, *SystemColor* or *TexturePaint* classes. In this case, we use a **GradientPaint** object.

Class **GradientPaint** paints a shape in gradually changing colors—a *gradient*. The **GradientPaint** constructor used here requires seven arguments. The first two arguments specify the starting coordinate for the gradient. The third argument specifies the starting **Color** for the gradient. The fourth and fifth arguments specify the ending coordinate for the gradient. The sixth argument specifies the ending **Color** for the gradient. The last argument specifies whether the gradient is *cyclic* (**true**) or *acyclic* (**false**). The two coordinates determine the direction of the gradient. The second coordinate (*35, 100*) is down and to the right of the first coordinate (*5, 30*); therefore, the gradient goes down and to the right at an angle. Since this gradient is cyclic (**true**), the color starts with blue, gradually becomes yellow, then gradually returns to blue. If the gradient is acyclic, the color transitions from the first color specified (e.g., blue) to the second color (e.g., yellow).

Line 33 uses method *fill* of class **Graphics2D** to draw a filled *Shape* object. The **Shape** object is an instance of any class that implements interface **Shape** (package **java.awt**)—in this case, an instance of class **Ellipse2D.Double**. The **Ellipse2D.Double** constructor receives four arguments that specify the bounding rectangle for the ellipse to display.

Next we draw a red rectangle with a thick border. Line 36 uses method **setPaint** to set the **Paint** object to **Color.red**. Line 37 uses method *setStroke* of class **Graphics2D** to set the characteristics of the rectangle's border. Method **setStroke** requires a *Stroke* object as its argument. The **Stroke** object is an instance of any class that implements interface **Stroke** (package **java.awt**)—in this case, an instance of class *BasicStroke*. Class **BasicStroke** provides a variety of constructors to specify the line width, how the line ends (called the *end caps*), how lines join together (called *line joins*) and the dash attributes of the line (if it is a dashed line). The constructor here specifies that the line should be 10 pixels wide.

Lines 38–39 invoke method *draw* of **Graphics2D** to draw a *Shape* object—in this case, an instance of class **Rectangle2D.Double**. The **Rectangle2D.Double** constructor receives four arguments specifying the upper left *x*-coordinate, upper left *y*-coordinate, width and height of the rectangle measured in pixels.

Next we draw a rounded rectangle filled with a pattern created in a *BufferedImage* (package **java.awt.image**) object. Lines 42–43 create the **BufferedImage** object. Class **BufferedImage** can produce images in color and gray scale. This particular **BufferedImage** is 10 pixels wide and 10 pixels tall. The third constructor argument **BufferedImage.TYPE_INT_RGB** specifies that the image is stored in color using the Red Green Blue (RGB) color scheme.

To create the fill pattern for the rounded rectangle, we must first draw into the **BufferedImage**. Line 45 creates a **Graphics2D** object for drawing on the **BufferedImage**. Lines 46–53 use methods **setColor**, **fillRect** and **drawRect** (discussed earlier in this chapter) to create the pattern.

Lines 56–57 set the **Paint** object to a new **TexturePaint** (package **java.awt**) object. A **TexturePaint** object uses the image stored in its associated **BufferedImage** as the fill texture for a filled-in shape. The second argument specifies the **Rectangle** area from the **BufferedImage** that will be replicated through the texture. In this case, the **Rectangle** is the same size as the **BufferedImage**. However, a smaller portion of the **BufferedImage** can be used.

Lines 58–59 invoke method **fill** of **Graphics2D** to draw a filled **Shape** object— *RoundRectangle2D.Double*. The **RoundRectangle2D.Double** constructor receives six arguments specifying the rectangle dimensions and the arc width and arc height—measured in pixels—used to determine the rounding of the corners.

Next we draw a oblong arc with a thick white line. Line 62 sets the **Paint** object to **Color.white**. Line 63 sets the **Stroke** object to a new **BasicStroke** for a line 6 pixels wide. Lines 64–65 use method **draw** of class **Graphics2D** to draw a **Shape** object—in this case, an **Arc2D.Double**. The **Arc2D.Double** constructor's first four arguments specifying the upper left *x*-coordinate, upper left *y*-coordinate, width and height of the bounding rectangle for the arc. The fifth argument specifies the start angle measured in degrees. The sixth argument specifies the arc angle. The start angle and arc angles are measured relative to the shape's bounding rectangle. The last argument specifies how the arc is closed. Constant **Arc2D.PIE** indicates that the arc is closed by drawing two lines. One line from the arc's starting point to the center of the bounding rectangle and one line from the center of the bounding rectangle to the ending point. Class **Arc2D** provides two other **static** constants for specifying how the arc is closed. Constant **Arc2D.CHORD** draws a line from the starting point to the ending point. Constant **Arc2D.OPEN** specifies that the arc is not closed.

Finally, we draw two lines using *Line2D* objects—one solid and one dashed. Line 68 sets the **Paint** object to **Color.green**. Line 69 uses method **draw** of class **Graphics2D** to draw a **Shape** object—in this case, an instance of class **Line2D.Double**. The **Line2D.Double** constructor's arguments specify starting coordinates and ending coordinates of the line.

Line 71 defines a two-element **float** array. This array describes the length—in pixels—of the dashes and spaces in the dashed line. In this case, each dash will be 10 pixels long and each space will be two pixels long. To create dashes of different lengths in a pattern, simply provide the lengths of each dash as an element in the array. Line 73 sets the **Paint** object to **Color.yellow**. Lines 74–76 set the **Stroke** object to a new **BasicStroke**. The line will be **4** pixels wide and will have rounded ends (**BasicStroke.CAP_ROUND**). If lines join together (as in a rectangle at the corners), the joining of the lines will be rounded (**BasicStroke.JOIN_ROUND**). The **dashes** argument specifies the dash lengths for the line. The last argument indicates the starting subscript in the **dashes** array for the first dash in the pattern. Line 77 then draws a line with the current **Stroke**.

Next we present a general path—a shape constructed from lines and complex curves. A general path is represented with an object of class *GeneralPath* (package **java.awt.geom**). Class **Shapes2** (Fig. 4.5) demonstrates drawing a general path in the shape of a five-pointed star.

```
1   // Shapes2.java
2   // Shapes2 demonstrates a general path.
3
4   // Java core packages
5   import java.awt.*;
6   import java.awt.event.*;
7   import java.awt.geom.*;
8
9   // Java extension packages
10  import javax.swing.*;
11
12  public class Shapes2 extends JFrame {
13
14     // set window's title bar String and background color
15
16     public Shapes2()
17     {
18        super( "Drawing 2D Shapes" );
19
20        getContentPane().setBackground( Color.gray );
21     }
22
```

Fig. 4.5 Demonstrating Java 2D paths (part 1 of 3).

```
23      // draw general paths
24      public void paint( Graphics g )
25      {
26         // call superclass' paint method
27         super.paint( g );
28
29         int xPoints[] =
30            { 55, 67, 109, 73, 83, 55, 27, 37, 1, 43 };
31         int yPoints[] =
32            { 0, 36, 36, 54, 96, 72, 96, 54, 36, 36 };
33
34         Graphics2D graphics2D = ( Graphics2D ) g;
35
36         // create a star from a series of points
37         GeneralPath star = new GeneralPath();
38
39         // set the initial coordinate of the General Path
40         star.moveTo( xPoints[ 0 ], yPoints[ 0 ] );
41
42         // create the star--this does not draw the star
43         for ( int count = 1; count < xPoints.length; count++ )
44            star.lineTo( xPoints[ count ], yPoints[ count ] );
45
46         // close the shape
47         star.closePath();
48
49         // translate the origin to (200, 200)
50         graphics2D.translate( 200, 200 );
51
52         // rotate around origin and draw stars in random colors
53         for ( int count = 1; count <= 20; count++ ) {
54
55            // rotate coordinate system
56            graphics2D.rotate( Math.PI / 10.0 );
57
58            // set random drawing color
59            graphics2D.setColor( new Color(
60               ( int ) ( Math.random() * 256 ),
61               ( int ) ( Math.random() * 256 ),
62               ( int ) ( Math.random() * 256 ) ) );
63
64            // draw filled star
65            graphics2D.fill( star );
66         }
67
68      }  // end method paint
69
70      // execute application
71      public static void main( String args[] )
72      {
73         Shapes2 application = new Shapes2();
74         application.setDefaultCloseOperation(
75            JFrame.EXIT_ON_CLOSE );
```

Fig. 4.5   Demonstrating Java 2D paths (part 2 of 3).

```
76           application.setSize( 400, 400 );
77           application.setVisible( true );
78        }
79    }
```

Fig. 4.5   Demonstrating Java 2D paths (part 3 of 3).

Lines 29–32 define two **int** arrays representing the *x*- and *y*-coordinates of the points in the star. Line 37 defines **GeneralPath** object **star**. Line 40 uses method *moveTo* of class **GeneralPath** to specify the first point in the **star**. The **for** structure at lines 43–44 uses method *lineTo* of class **GeneralPath** to draw a line to the next point in the **star**. Each new call to **lineTo** draws a line from the previous point to the current point. Line 47 uses method *closePath* of class **GeneralPath** to draw a line from the last point to the point specified in the last call to **moveTo**. This completes the general path.

Line 50 uses method *translate* of class **Graphics2D** to move the drawing origin to location (*200, 200*). All drawing operations now use location (*200, 200*) as (*0, 0*). The **for** structure at lines 53–65 draws the **star** 20 times by rotating it around the new origin point. Line 56 uses method *rotate* of class **Graphics2D** to rotate the next displayed shape. The argument specifies the rotation angle in radians (360° = 2π radians). Line 65 uses **Graphics2D** method **fill** to draw a filled version of the **star**.

4.3.2 Java 2D Image Processing

Image processing is the manipulation of digital images by applying *filters*—mathematical operations that change images. Java 2D provides an image-processing API to shield developers from the mathematics behind filters. *Compression filters*, *measurement filters* and *enhancement filters* constitute the three major image-processing categories. Compression filters reduce a digital image's memory usage, resulting in reduced storage size and faster transmission of complex digital images. Some common applications of compression filters include high-definition television (HDTV), video phones and virtual reality. Measurement filters collect data from digital images. Measurement filters play a crucial role in the field of image recognition and *machine vision* (e.g., for printed circuit board inspection and assembly-line welding robots). Enhancement filters—filters that alter certain physical aspects of an image—often restore corrupted images to their original form. Sometimes, the processes of creating, storing or transmitting a digital image introduces data corruption such as noise, motion blurring and color loss. Enhancement filters can remove noise, sharpen edges and brighten colors to recover the original image. For example, satellite images use enhancement filters to remove noise created from capturing images at such lengthy distances.

Java 2D image-processing filters operate on objects of class **BufferedImage**, which separates image data into two components—a *Raster* and a *ColorModel*. A **Raster**—composed of a *DataBuffer* and a *SampleModel*—organizes and stores the data that determine a pixel's color. Each pixel is composed of *samples*—number values that represent the pixel's color components. The **DataBuffer** stores the raw sample data for an image. The **SampleModel** accesses the sample values in the **DataBuffer** for any given pixel. The **ColorModel** is an interpreter for the **Raster**, taking the sample values for each pixel in the **Raster** and converting them to the appropriate color. The **ColorModel** converts the sample data to different colors depending on the *color scale* of the image. Two common color scales are *grayscale* and *RGB*. In grayscale, every pixel is represented by one sample interpreted as a color between black and white. In *RGB*, each pixel is represented by three samples that correspond to the red, green and blue color components of the pixel.

This section presents an application that demonstrates how to create and filter **BufferedImage**s. We build filters that blur, sharpen, invert and change the color scale of a **BufferedImage**. These are "fundamental" filters found in mass graphics programs, such as Paint Shop Pro. Our application allows the user to apply a series of filters to a **BufferedImage** to demonstrate the effects of multiple filters. Sample filter results appear in the screen captures of Fig. 4.13. The application consists of three distinct parts:

1. **ImagePanel**—a **JPanel** extended to provide image-processing capabilities.

2. **Java2DImageFilter**—an interface for image-processing filters that will alter the image in an **ImagePanel**. The classes that implement interface **Java2D-ImageFilter** include **BlurFilter**, **SharpenFilter**, **InvertFilter** and **ColorChangeFilter**.

3. **Java2DExample**—a GUI that displays the filtered image and presents the user with a menu for selecting image filters.

Class **ImagePanel** (Fig. 4.6) allows a user to experiment with applying various filters to an image. **ImagePanel** contains an image and methods for filtering that image. Lines 18–19 declare two **BufferedImage** references—**displayImage** and **originalImage**. The image filters manipulate **displayImage**, and **originalImage** stores a copy of the original image so the user can view the original image.

```
1   // ImagePanel.java
2   // ImagePanel contains an image for display. The image is
3   // converted to a BufferedImage for filtering purposes.
4   package com.deitel.advjhtp1.java2d;
```

Fig. 4.6   Class **ImagePanel** allows for displaying and filtering **BufferedImage**s (part 1 of 3).

```
5
6      // Java core packages
7      import java.awt.*;
8      import java.awt.event.*;
9      import java.awt.image.*;
10     import java.net.*;
11
12     // Java extension packages
13     import javax.swing.*;
14     import javax.swing.event.*;
15
16     public class ImagePanel extends JPanel {
17
18        private BufferedImage displayImage; // filtered image
19        private BufferedImage originalImage; // original image
20        private Image image; // image to load
21
22        // ImagePanel constructor
23        public ImagePanel( URL imageURL )
24        {
25           image =
26              Toolkit.getDefaultToolkit().createImage( imageURL );
27
28           // create MediaTracker for image
29           MediaTracker mediaTracker = new MediaTracker( this );
30           mediaTracker.addImage( image, 0 );
31
32           // wait for Image to load
33           try {
34              mediaTracker.waitForAll();
35           }
36
37           // exit program on error
38           catch ( InterruptedException interruptedException ) {
39              interruptedException.printStackTrace();
40           }
41
42           // create BufferedImages from Image
43           originalImage = new BufferedImage( image.getWidth( null ),
44              image.getHeight( null ), BufferedImage.TYPE_INT_RGB );
45
46           displayImage = originalImage;
47
48           // get BufferedImage's graphics context
49           Graphics2D graphics = displayImage.createGraphics();
50           graphics.drawImage( image, null, null );
51
52        } // end ImagePanel constructor
53
54        // apply Java2DImageFilter to Image
55        public void applyFilter( Java2DImageFilter filter )
56        {
```

Fig. 4.6   Class **ImagePanel** allows for displaying and filtering **BufferedImage**s
(part 2 of 3).

```
57          // process Image using Java2DImageFilter
58          displayImage = filter.processImage( displayImage );
59          repaint();
60       }
61
62       // set Image to originalImage
63       public void displayOriginalImage()
64       {
65          displayImage = new BufferedImage( image.getWidth( null ),
66             image.getHeight( null ), BufferedImage.TYPE_INT_RGB );
67
68          Graphics2D graphics = displayImage.createGraphics();
69          graphics.drawImage( originalImage, null, null );
70          repaint();
71       }
72
73       // draw ImagePanel
74       public void paintComponent( Graphics g )
75       {
76          super.paintComponent( g );
77          Graphics2D graphics = ( Graphics2D ) g;
78          graphics.drawImage( displayImage, 0, 0, null );
79       }
80
81       // get preferred ImagePanel size
82       public Dimension getPreferredSize()
83       {
84          return new Dimension( displayImage.getWidth(),
85             displayImage.getHeight() );
86       }
87
88       // get minimum ImagePanel size
89       public Dimension getMinimumSize()
90       {
91          return getPreferredSize();
92       }
93    }
```

Fig. 4.6   Class **ImagePanel** allows for displaying and filtering **BufferedImage**s
(part 3 of 3).

The **ImagePanel** constructor (lines 23–52) accepts as an argument a **URL** that specifies the file containing the image to filter. Lines 25–26 create an **Image** object—**image**—from this file. Lines 29–30 instantiate a **MediaTracker** for **image** loading. Method **waitForAll** (line 34) of class **MediaTracker** ensures that **image** is loaded into memory before we filter this image.

Lines 43–46 create **BufferedImage**s **displayImage** and **originalImage**. The **BufferedImage** constructor accepts three arguments—the image's width, height and type. We use predefined type **TYPE_INT_RGB**, which defines three 8-bit segments each representing a red, green and blue color components. Line 49 creates a **Graphics2D** object for rendering **displayImage**. Line 50 renders the loaded **image** on **ImagePanel** using method **drawImage** of class **Graphics2D**.

Method **applyFilter** (lines 55–60) applies an **Java2DImageFilter** to **displayImage**. Line 58 invokes method **processImage** of class **Java2DImageFilter**, which passes **displayImage** as a parameter. Method **processImage** applies an image filter to **displayImage**. Line 59 calls method **repaint**, which indicates that **ImagePanel** needs to be redrawn. In turn, a system call is made to method **paintComponent** of class **ImagePanel**. Method **paintComponent** (lines 74–79) draws **displayImage** onto **ImagePanel**. Line 77 casts the **Graphics** object to a **Graphics2D** object to access **Graphics2D** methods. The **Graphics2D**'s method **drawImage** (line 78) renders **displayImage** in the **ImagePanel**.

We provide a means to reconstruct the original image after the program applies filters to **displayImage**. Method **displayOriginal** (lines 63–71) creates a new **BufferedImage** that contains a copy of **originalImage** so the user can apply a new set of filters to **displayImage**. Lines 65–66 recreate **displayImage** as a new **BufferedImage**. Line 68 creates a **Graphics2D** for **displayImage**. Line 69 calls method **drawImage** of class **Graphics2D**, which draws **originalImage** into **displayImage**.

We now implement our image-processing filters—**BlurFilter**, **SharpenFilter**, **InvertFilter** and **ColorFilter**. Our filters implement interface **Java2DImageFilter** (Fig. 4.7). Classes that implement **Java2DImageFilter** must implement method **processImage** (line 13). Method **processImage** accepts a **BufferedImage** to filter and returns the filtered **BufferedImage**.

The **Java2DImageFilter**s in this application use well-known Java 2D image-processing operations. Java 2D has several image filters that operate on **BufferedImage**s. Interfaces *BufferedImageOp* and *RasterOp* serve as the base classes for Java 2D image filters. Method **filter** of interfaces **BufferedImageOp** and **RasterOp** takes as arguments two images—the *source* image and the *destination* image. All classes that implement **BufferedImageOp** and **RasterOp** apply a filter to the source image to produce the destination image. A **BufferedImageOp** processes a **BufferedImage**, while a **RasterOp** processes only the **Raster** associated with a **BufferedImage**. Several Java 2D image filters implement **BufferedImageOp** and/or **RasterOp** (Fig. 4.8).

```
1   // Java2DImageFilter.java
2   // Java2DImageFilter is an interface that defines method
3   // processImage for applying a filter to an Image.
4   package com.deitel.advjhtp1.java2d;
5
6   // Java core packages
7   import java.awt.*;
8   import java.awt.image.*;
9
10  public interface ImageFilter {
11
12      // apply filter to Image
13      public BufferedImage processImage( BufferedImage image );
14  }
```

Fig. 4.7   Java2DImageFilter interface for creating Java 2D image filters.

Class	Implements Interfaces	Description
`AffineTransformOp`	`BufferedImageOp` `RasterOp`	Performs linear mapping from 2D coordinates in the source image to 2D coordinates in the destination image. (Example: Rotate an image about a point in the image.)
`BandCombineOp`	`RasterOp`	Performs a linear combination of the bands in a **Raster**. (Example: Change the color palette in an image.)
`ColorConvertOp`	`BufferedImageOp` `RasterOp`	Performs color conversion on each pixel in the source image. (Example: Convert from RGB color to gray scale.)
`ConvolveOp`	`BufferedImageOp` `RasterOp`	Combines source pixel values with surrounding pixel values to derive destination pixel values. (Example: Sharpen edges in an image.)
`LookupOp`	`BufferedImageOp` `RasterOp`	Performs a lookup operation on the source image to create the destination image. (Example: Invert the RGB colors in an image.)
`RescaleOp`	`BufferedImageOp` `RescaleOp`	Rescale the data in the source image by a scalar plus offset. (Example: Darken the coloring of an image.)

Fig. 4.8   Classes that implement `BufferedImageOp` and `RasterOp`.

We now present each **Java2DImageFilter** in our application. Class **Invert-Filter** (Fig. 4.9), which implements interface **Java2DImageFilter**, inverts the color of the pixels in a **BufferedImage**. Each pixel consists of three samples—8-bit R, G and B integers. An 8-bit color sample takes on an integer in the range 0–255. By inverting the numerical value of the pixel sample, we can invert the color of the pixel. Line 15 creates an array to hold the inverted integers. Lines 17–18 invert the array values.

InvertFilter uses a *LookupOp*—a subclass of **BufferedImageOp**—to invert the colors. Class **BufferedImageOp**—the base class for most Java 2D filters—operates on two images (the source image and the destination image). All classes that implement **BufferedImageOp** filter the source image to produce the destination image. A **LookupOp** is an array indexed by source pixel color values and contains destination pixel color values. Lines 21–22 create a new **LookupOp**—**invertFilter**. The **LookupOp** constructor takes as arguments a *ByteLookUpTable* that contains the lookup array table—**invertArray**—and a *RenderingHints*. The **Rendering-Hints** object describes optimizations for the rendering engine. In this application, no optimizations are needed, so **RenderingHints** is **null**. Line 25 invokes method **filter** of class **LookupOp**, which processes **image** with **invertFilter** and returns the filtered image.

```
1   // InvertFilter.java
2   // InvertFilter, which implements Java2DImageFilter, inverts a
3   // BufferedImage's RGB color values.
4   package com.deitel.advjhtp1.java2d;
5
6   // Java core packages
7   import java.awt.image.*;
8
9   public class InvertFilter implements Java2DImageFilter {
10
11      // apply color inversion filter to BufferedImage
12      public BufferedImage processImage( BufferedImage image )
13      {
14          // create 256 color array and invert colors
15          byte[] invertArray = new byte[ 256 ];
16
17          for ( int counter = 0; counter < 256; counter++ )
18              invertArray[ counter ] = ( byte )( 255 - counter );
19
20          // create filter to invert colors
21          BufferedImageOp invertFilter = new LookupOp(
22              new ByteLookupTable( 0, invertArray ), null );
23
24          // apply filter to displayImage
25          return invertFilter.filter( image, null );
26
27      } // end method processImage
28  }
```

Fig. 4.9   **InvertFilter** inverts colors in a **BufferedImage**.

Class **SharpenFilter** (Fig. 4.10) is a filter that detects and enhances *edges*—differences in the sample values of neighboring pixels—in an image. A sharpening filter first detects edges by determining differences in neighboring pixel sample values, then enhances the edge by increasing the difference between the sample values. **Sharpen-Filter** uses a *ConvolveOp*—another subclass of **BufferedImageOp**—to create the sharpening filter. A **ConvolveOp** combines the colors of a source pixel and its surrounding neighbors to determine the color of the corresponding destination pixel. Lines 15–18 create **sharpenMatrix**—the values used in the **ConvolveOp**. Lines 21–23 create the **ConvolveOp**—**sharpenFilter**—passing three parameters (a *Kernel*, an integer edge hint and a **RenderingHints** object). The **Kernel**—a 2D array—specifies how a **ConvolveOp** filter should combine neighboring pixel values. Every **ConvolveOp** is built from a **Kernel**. The **Kernel** constructor takes as arguments a width, height and an array of values. Using these arguments, a two-dimensional array is constructed from the array values. Edge hints instruct the filter how to alter pixels at the perimeter of the image. **EDGE_NO_OP** (line 23) instructs **sharpenFilter** to copy the source pixels at the perimeter of **image** directly to the destination image without modification. Line 26 invokes method **filter** of class **ConvolveOp**, which takes as an argument a **BufferedImage**. Method **filter** returns the filtered image.

```
1   // SharpenFilter.java
2   // SharpenFilter, which implements Java2DImageFilter, sharpens
3   // the edges in a BufferedImage.
4   package com.deitel.advjhtp1.java2d;
5
6   // Java core packages
7   import java.awt.image.*;
8
9   public class SharpenFilter implements Java2DImageFilter {
10
11      // apply edge-sharpening filter to BufferedImage
12      public BufferedImage processImage( BufferedImage image )
13      {
14          // array used to detect edges in image
15          float[] sharpenMatrix = {
16              0.0f, -1.0f, 0.0f,
17              -1.0f, 5.0f, -1.0f,
18              0.0f, -1.0f, 0.0f };
19
20          // create filter to sharpen edges
21          BufferedImageOp sharpenFilter =
22              new ConvolveOp( new Kernel( 3, 3, sharpenMatrix ),
23                  ConvolveOp.EDGE_NO_OP, null );
24
25          // apply sharpenFilter to displayImage
26          return sharpenFilter.filter( image, null );
27
28      } // end method processImage
29  }
```

Fig. 4.10 `SharpenFilter` sharpens edges in a `BufferedImage`.

Class **BlurFilter** (Fig. 4.11) uses a **ConvolveOp** to blur a **BufferedImage**. A blurring filter smooths distinct edges by averaging each pixel value with that of its eight neighboring pixels. Lines 14–17 create **blurMatrix**—an array of values for constructing the **Kernel**. Lines 20–21 create **ConvolveOp blurFilter** using the default constructor, which takes as an argument a **Kernel** constructed from **blurMatrix**. The default constructor uses **EDGE_ZERO_FILL** for the edge hint and a **null RenderingHints**. *EDGE_ZERO_FILL* specifies that pixels at the outer edge of the destination **BufferedImage** be set to **0**—this is the default. Line 24 invokes **blurFilter**'s method **filter** on **image**.

```
1   // BlurFilter.java
2   // Blurfilter blurs a BufferedImage.
3   package com.deitel.advjhtp1.java2d;
4
5   // Java core packages
6   import java.awt.image.*;
7
8   public class BlurFilter implements Java2DImageFilter {
```

Fig. 4.11 `BlurFilter` blurs the colors in a `BufferedImage` (part 1 of 2).

```
9
10        // apply blurring filter to BufferedImage
11        public BufferedImage processImage( BufferedImage image )
12        {
13           // array used to blur BufferedImage
14           float[] blurMatrix = {
15              1.0f / 9.0f, 1.0f / 9.0f, 1.0f / 9.0f,
16              1.0f / 9.0f, 1.0f / 9.0f, 1.0f / 9.0f,
17              1.0f / 9.0f, 1.0f / 9.0f, 1.0f / 9.0f };
18
19           // create ConvolveOp for blurring BufferedImage
20           BufferedImageOp blurFilter = new ConvolveOp(
21              new Kernel( 3, 3, blurMatrix ) );
22
23           // apply blurFilter to BufferedImage
24           return blurFilter.filter( image, null );
25
26        } // end method processImage
27     }
```

Fig. 4.11 **BlurFilter** blurs the colors in a **BufferedImage** (part 2 of 2).

Class **ColorFilter** (Fig. 4.12) alters the *color bands* in a **BufferedImage**. There are three color bands in a **TYPE_INT_RGB BufferedImage**—red, green and blue. Each color band is defined by three coefficients that represent the R, G and B components in the band. The standard red color band consists of **1.0f** R, **0.0f** G and **0.0f** B color components—i.e. the standard red band consists entirely of red. Likewise, the standard green color band consists of **0.0f** R, **1.0f** G and **0.0f** B, while the standard blue color band consists of **0.0f** R, **0.0f** G and **1.0f** B. We can change image colors by altering the values of the R, G and B coefficients in a color band.

```
1     // ColorFilter.java
2     // ColorFilter is an Java2DImageFilter that alters the RGB
3     // color bands in a BufferedImage.
4     package com.deitel.advjhtp1.java2d;
5
6     // Java core packages
7     import java.awt.image.*;
8
9     public class ColorFilter implements Java2DImageFilter {
10
11        // apply color-change filter to BufferedImage
12        public BufferedImage processImage( BufferedImage image )
13        {
14           // create array used to change RGB color bands
15           float[][] colorMatrix = {
16              { 1.0f, 0.0f, 0.0f },
17              { 0.5f, 1.0f, 0.5f },
18              { 0.2f, 0.4f, 0.6f } };
19
```

Fig. 4.12 **ColorFilter** changes the colors in a **BufferedImage** (part 1 of 2).

```
20        // create filter to change colors
21        BandCombineOp changeColors =
22            new BandCombineOp( colorMatrix, null );
23
24        // create source and display Rasters
25        Raster sourceRaster = image.getRaster();
26
27        WritableRaster displayRaster =
28            sourceRaster.createCompatibleWritableRaster();
29
30        // filter Rasters with changeColors filter
31        changeColors.filter( sourceRaster, displayRaster );
32
33        // create new BufferedImage from display Raster
34        return new BufferedImage( image.getColorModel(),
35            displayRaster, true, null );
36
37     } // end method processImage
38 }
```

Fig. 4.12 ColorFilter changes the colors in a **BufferedImage** (part 2 of 2).

Lines 15–18 create **colorMatrix**—a 2D array that represents a nonstandard *color space*—the aggregation of red, green and blue color bands. The red band (line 16) is the same as in the standard space. The green and blue bands (lines 17–18) assume color values from all three color components—green and blue will contain elements of R, G and B. Lines 21–22 create a ***BandCombineOp***—a subclass of **RasterOp**. Class **RasterOp** is the base class for filters that operate on **Raster**s. A **BandCombineOp** operates on the color bands of a **Raster**. Every **BufferedImage** contains a **Raster**. The **Raster** organizes and stores the samples that determine the pixel colors in the **BufferedImage**.

Line 25 calls method **getRaster** of class **BufferedImage**, which returns the **Raster** associated with **image**—**sourceRaster**. Lines 27–28 call method **create-CompatibleWriteableRaster** of class **Raster**, which returns **dis-playRaster**—a *WriteableRaster* compatible with **sourceRaster**. Compatible **Raster**s contain the same number of bands. A **WriteableRaster** allows sample data to be written while a **Raster** is read-only. Line 31 invokes method **filter** of class **BandCombineOp**, which takes as arguments a source **Raster** and a destination **WriteableRaster**. The source **Raster** is filtered and written into the destination **WriteableRaster**.

Lines 34–35 construct a **BufferedImage**. This **BufferedImage** constructor takes four arguments—a **ColorModel**, a **Raster**, a **boolean** and a **Hashtable**. We use the **ColorModel** of the original image, accessed through method **getColorModel** of class **Image** (line 34). Class **ColorModel** converts **Raster** data to colors depending on the *color scale* of the image. The **Raster** argument to the **BufferedImage** constructor is our **displayRaster**. The **boolean** value indicates whether the **Raster** has been premultiplied with *alpha values*. Each pixel is a small square. A curve in an image may require that only a portion of a pixel be colored—the alpha values tell the **Raster** how much of the pixel to cover. The **Hashtable** contains **String**/object properties and is **null** in this case. **BufferedImage**'s constructor will throw a **RasterFormatEx-**

ception if the number and types of bands in the **Raster** do not match the number and types of bands required by the **ColorModel**.

Class **Java2DExample** (Fig. 4.13) provides a user interface for applying **Java2D-ImageFilter**s to **ImagePanel**s. Lines 23–26 declare the **Java2DImageFilter**s. Lines 34–37 initialize the **Java2DImageFilter**s. Lines 40–41 create **imagePanel**—the **ImagePanel** to be filtered. Lines 44–45 create **filterMenu**—the menu of **Java2DImageFilter**s. Lines 52–54 create the first **JMenuItem** for **filterMenu**—**originalMenuItem**. An **ItemListener** invokes **imagePanel**'s **display-Original** method when **originalMenuItem** is selected (lines 56–66). Lines 69–76 call method **createMenuItem** (lines 93–116) for each of the four **Java2DImage-Filters**. This method creates a **JMenuItem** for the filter with the appropriate title and mnemonic. **ImagePanel** invokes method **applyFilter** when the **JMenuItem** is selected (line 108). **Java2DExample** contains method **main** (lines 119–125), for starting the application.

```
1   // Java2DExample.java
2   // Java2DExample is an application that applies filters to an
3   // image using Java 2D.
4   package com.deitel.advjhtp1.java2d;
5
6   // Java core packages
7   import java.awt.*;
8   import java.awt.event.*;
9   import java.awt.image.*;
10  import java.lang.*;
11  import java.net.*;
12
13  // Java extension packages
14  import javax.swing.*;
15  import javax.swing.event.*;
16
17  public class Java2DExample extends JFrame {
18
19      private JMenu filterMenu;
20      private ImagePanel imagePanel;
21
22      // image filters
23      private Java2DImageFilter invertFilter;
24      private Java2DImageFilter sharpenFilter;
25      private Java2DImageFilter blurFilter;
26      private Java2DImageFilter colorFilter;
27
28      // initialize JMenuItems
29      public Java2DExample()
30      {
31          super( "Java 2D Image Processing Demo" );
32
33          // create Java2DImageFilters
34          blurFilter = new BlurFilter();
```

Fig. 4.13   Java 2D image-processing application GUI (part 1 of 4).

```
35        sharpenFilter = new SharpenFilter();
36        invertFilter = new InvertFilter();
37        colorFilter = new ColorFilter();
38
39        // initialize ImagePanel
40        imagePanel = new ImagePanel(
41           Java2DExample.class.getResource( "images/ajhtp.png" ) );
42
43        // create JMenuBar
44        JMenuBar menuBar = new JMenuBar();
45        setJMenuBar( menuBar );
46
47        // create JMenu
48        filterMenu = new JMenu( "Image Filters" );
49        filterMenu.setMnemonic( 'I' );
50
51        // create JMenuItem for displaying original Image
52        JMenuItem originalMenuItem =
53           new JMenuItem( "Display Original" );
54        originalMenuItem.setMnemonic( 'O' );
55
56        originalMenuItem.addActionListener(
57           new ActionListener() {
58
59              // show original Image
60              public void actionPerformed( ActionEvent action )
61              {
62                 imagePanel.displayOriginalImage();
63              }
64
65           } // end anonymous inner class
66        );
67
68        // create JMenuItems for Java2DImageFilters
69        JMenuItem invertMenuItem = createMenuItem(
70           "Invert", 'I', invertFilter );
71        JMenuItem sharpenMenuItem = createMenuItem(
72           "Sharpen", 'S', sharpenFilter );
73        JMenuItem blurMenuItem = createMenuItem(
74           "Blur", 'B', blurFilter );
75        JMenuItem changeColorsMenuItem = createMenuItem(
76           "Change Colors", 'C', colorFilter );
77
78        // add JMenuItems to JMenu
79        filterMenu.add( originalMenuItem );
80        filterMenu.add( invertMenuItem );
81        filterMenu.add( sharpenMenuItem );
82        filterMenu.add( blurMenuItem );
83        filterMenu.add( changeColorsMenuItem );
84
85        // add JMenu to JMenuBar
86        menuBar.add( filterMenu );
87
```

Fig. 4.13   Java 2D image-processing application GUI (part 2 of 4).

```
88            getContentPane().add( imagePanel, BorderLayout.CENTER );
89
90      } // end Java2DExample constructor
91
92      // create JMenuItem and ActionListener for given filter
93      public JMenuItem createMenuItem( String menuItemName,
94         char mnemonic, final Java2DImageFilter filter )
95      {
96         // create JMenuItem
97         JMenuItem menuItem = new JMenuItem( menuItemName );
98
99         // set Mnemonic
100        menuItem.setMnemonic( mnemonic );
101
102        menuItem.addActionListener(
103           new ActionListener() {
104
105              // apply Java2DImageFilter when MenuItem accessed
106              public void actionPerformed( ActionEvent action )
107              {
108                 imagePanel.applyFilter( filter );
109              }
110
111           } // end anonymous inner class
112        );
113
114        return menuItem;
115
116     } // end method createMenuItem
117
118     // start program
119     public static void main( String args[] )
120     {
121        Java2DExample application = new Java2DExample();
122        application.setDefaultCloseOperation( EXIT_ON_CLOSE );
123        application.pack();
124        application.setVisible( true );
125     }
126  }
```

Fig. 4.13   Java 2D image-processing application GUI (part 3 of 4).

Fig. 4.13   Java 2D image-processing application GUI (part 4 of 4).

This concludes our discussion of the Java 2D API. This section has presented several of the features that make Java 2D a powerful 2D graphics API. We discussed geometrical shape-rendering processes, including how to create and fill shapes with different colors and patterns, how to draw a **GeneralPath** and how to apply transforms to Java 2D shapes. We also introduced and discussed Java 2D image processing, including how to create and apply filters to **BufferedImage**s.

4.4 Java 3D API

We live in a 3D world. Our vision enables us to see in three dimensions—*x*, *y*, and *z* coordinates. Many of the surfaces onto which graphics are displayed—for example, monitors and printed pages—are flat. 3D-graphics programming enables us to render realistic models of our 3D world onto a 2D-viewing surface. 3D graphics have advanced to the point that nearly anything you can see around you can be *modeled*—represented numerically by shape and size—and *rendered*—drawn on your computer screen.

There now exists an increasing number of 3D-computer-graphics applications—from flight simulators and medical-imaging equipment to 3D games and screen savers. Rapid advances in computer hardware have resulted in tremendous growth in the 3D-graphics industry. Developments in high-performance hardware led to developments in high-performance 3D graphics APIs—beginning in the 1970s with Siggraph's CORE API, continuing in the 1980s with SGI's *OpenGL* and on through today with Microsoft's *Direct3D* and *Java 3D*™.[1]

Sophisticated 3D graphics require sophisticated graphics algorithms that often involve complex math. However, the *Java 3D API* provides robust and advanced 3D-graphics capabilities to Java developers while hiding the mathematics behind graphics algorithms. Java 3D is a high-level graphics-programming API. Java 3D handles all the necessary low-level graphics calls, so developers can create high-performance 3D-graphics scenes without having to understand any underlying hardware. Like Java, Java 3D is *write once run anywhere*™. Java 3D applications will run in the same way across different 3D graphics platforms.

Sun Microsystems designed the Java 3D API with four major goals in mind—application portability, hardware independence, performance scalability and the ability to produce 3D graphics over a network.[2] Simplifying of complex graphics operations played a key role in developing the Java 3D API. Some of the markets and applications for the Java 3D API include[3]

- 3D-data visualization

- collaborative applications

- gaming (especially network-based multiplayer systems)

- business graphics

- interactive educational systems

- molecular modeling and viewing (MCAD)

- 3D-Web development

- 3D-GUI development

---

1. Sun Microsystems, Inc., "The Fourth Generation of 3D Graphics API's has arrived!" 25 January 2000. **<java.sun.com/products/java-media/3D/collateral/wp_mktg/ j3d_wp.pdf>**.
2. Sun Microsystems, Inc., "The Java 3D API: For Developers and End Users," 1 December 1998. **<http://java.sun.com/products/java-media/3D/collateral/presentation/sld004.html>**.
3. Sun Microsystems, Inc., "The Java 3D API: For Developers and End Users," 1 December 1998. **<http://java.sun.com/products/java-media/3D/collateral/presentation/sld015.html>**.

Java 3D offers several features that these markets use to develop their 3D-applications:

- *Behavior*—Java 3D supports multiple types of behavior including animation and motion, *collision detection* (detecting when two objects collide) and *morphing* (transforming an image into another *image*).

- *Fog*—Java 3D supports fog content that restricts viewers ability to see certain objects in the scene. For example, fog helps to create a realistic model of a rainstorm in a 3D game.

- *Geometry*—Java 3D has built-in 3D-geometric primitives for creating geometric shapes. Java 3D can render scenes generated by existing 3D authoring tools, such as 3DStudioMax, VRML and Lightwave3D.

- *Light*—Lights allow you to illuminate objects in a 3D scene. Java 3D supports different forms of light and control over color, direction and intensity.

- *Sound*—A unique feature of Java 3D is support for 3D sound.

- *Texture*—Java 3D supports *texture mapping* for attaching images over 3D-geometric models.

Next, we present an overview of the Java 3D API—we examine the structure of a Java 3D scene by presenting an application that incorporates 3D geometry, lights and interactive animation. In the next section, we explain how to obtain and install the Java 3D API so you can run the examples in this chapter and create your own 3D content.

4.4.1 Obtaining and Installing the Java 3D API

The Java 3D API requires that you have the *Java 2 Platform, Standard Edition* and either OpenGL or Direct3D installed on your computer—Java 3D uses OpenGL or Direct3D graphics libraries to render 3D scenes. You can obtain OpenGL from **www.opengl.org**. You can obtain Direct3D—part of Microsoft's *DirectX API*—from **www.microsoft.com/directx/**.

The Java 3D API is not integrated in the core Java 2 Platform. To use the Java 3D API, you must install the appropriate Java extension and utility packages. The Java 3D API packages differ slightly depending on which low-level graphics libraries are installed on your computer. The version of Java 3D used in this chapter requires the OpenGL graphics library and *Windows 2000* Operating System. The version of Java 3D packages you install depends on your operating system and graphics API. You can obtain the Java 3D packages and installation instructions from **java.sun.com/products/java-media/3D/download.html**.

4.4.2 Java 3D Scenes

Pictures rendered with Java3D are called *scenes*. A scene—also called a *virtual universe*—is 3D space that contains a set of shapes. The root of the Java 3D scene is a **VirtualUniverse** object. The **VirtualUniverse** has a *coordinate system* for describing the location of *scene graphs* it contains. Each Java 3D scene is described by a number of scene graphs—hierarchical structures that specify attributes of a 3D environment. Each scene graph attaches to the **VirtualUniverse** at a specified point in the **VirtualUniverse**'s coordinate system. A scene graph is composed of an internal coordinate system and a number of *branch graphs*. Each scene graph has an internal coordinate system, so developers can attach scene graphs with different coordinate systems in the same **VirtualUniverse**. Class *Locale* is the root node in a scene graph, which contains the attachment coordinate for the **VirtualUniverse** and a number of branch graphs. There are two types of branch graphs in Java 3D—*content-branch graphs* and *view-branch graphs*. Content-branch graphs specify content in 3D scenes, such as geometry, lighting, textures, fog and behaviors. View-branch graphs contain *viewing platforms*—collections of objects that specify the perspective, position, orientation and scale in 3D scenes. The viewing platform is also called the *viewpoint*.

The Java 3D class *SceneGraphObject* is the base class for all objects in a branch graph. A **SceneGraphObject** may contain a **Group**, which represents a node that contains multiple children. The children of a **Group** may be other **Group**s, **Leaf**s or **NodeComponents**. **Leaf**s specify geometry, lights and sound in content-branch graphs and the viewing-platform components in the view-branch graph. **NodeComponent** objects specify the various *components* of **Group**s and **Leaf**s such as texture and coloring attributes. Figure 4.14 lists some Java 3D **Group**, **Leaf** and **NodeComponent** subclasses.

Class	Description
*Partial list of Java3D **Group** classes*	
BranchGroup	A scene-graph's root **Node** that attaches to a **Locale**.
Switch	Can render either a single child or a mask of children.
TransformGroup	Contains a single transformation (e.g., translation, rotation or scaling).
*Partial list of Java3D **Leaf** classes*	
Behavior	Contains methods for gathering user input (e.g., key presses and mouse clicks) and describing objects' behavior upon certain events (e.g., collisions).
Light	Describes a set of parameters for Java 3D light sources.
Shape3D	Describes 3D-geometric objects.
ViewPlatform	Controls the viewpoint for a 3D scene.
*Partial list of Java3D **NodeComponent** classes*	
Appearance	Specifies **Shape3D** attributes, such as *coloring* and *texture*.
Material	Describes an illuminated object's properties (e.g., *reflective color* and *shininess*).
Texture	Specifies properties for *texture mapping*—a technique for drawing 2D images over 3D geometric models.

Fig. 4.14   Java 3D **Group**, **Leaf** and **NodeComponent** subclasses.

4.4.3 A Java 3D Example

This section creates an interactive Java 3D scene. The application demonstrates how to create and use Java 3D **Geometry** and **Light**s. A Java Swing GUI enables the user to change the properties of the shapes and lights in the 3D scene. The application demonstrates *mouse behaviors*—i.e., using the mouse to rotate, scale and translate the 3D-shapes. The application consists of three classes—**Java3DWorld** (Fig. 4.15), **ControlPanel** (Fig. 4.21) and **Java3DExample** (Fig. 4.22). Figure 4.16–Fig. 4.20 show sample screen captures demonstrating the features of this application.

Class **Java3DWorld** (Fig. 4.15) creates the Java 3D environment using geometry, transforms and lighting. Lines 19–22 import the Java 3D utility packages which simplify the scene-content creation. Class **Java3DWorld** extends class *Canvas3D* (line 24), a **java.awt.Canvas** subclass for 3D rendering. We use a **Canvas3D** as the drawing surface for our 3D graphics application. Lines 26–38 declare the Java 3D objects we use in the application. We discuss each object's function momentarily.

```
1   // Java3DWorld.java
2   // Java3DWorld is a Java 3D Graphics display environment
3   // that creates a SimpleUniverse and provides capabilities for
4   // allowing a user to control lighting, motion, and texture
5   // of the 3D scene.
6   package com.deitel.advjhtp1.java3d;
7
8   // Java core packages
9   import java.awt.event.*;
10  import java.awt.*;
11  import java.net.*;
12
13  // Java extension packages
14  import javax.swing.event.*;
15  import javax.media.j3d.*;
16  import javax.vecmath.*;
17
18  // Java 3D utility packages
19  import com.sun.j3d.utils.universe.*;
20  import com.sun.j3d.utils.image.*;
21  import com.sun.j3d.utils.geometry.*;
22  import com.sun.j3d.utils.behaviors.mouse.*;
23
24  public class Java3DWorld extends Canvas3D {
25
26      private Appearance appearance; // 3D object's appearance
27      private Box shape; // 3D object to manipulate
28      private Color3f lightColor; // Light color
29      private Light ambientLight; // ambient scene lighting
30      private Light directionalLight; //directional light
31      private Material material; // 3D objects color object
32      private SimpleUniverse simpleUniverse; // 3D scene environment
33      private TextureLoader textureLoader; // 3D object's texture
34
```

Fig. 4.15   Creating a Java 3D **SimpleUniverse** with content (part 1 of 5).

```
35        // holds 3D transformation information
36        private TransformGroup transformGroup;
37
38        private String imageName; // texture image file name
39
40        // Java3DWorld constructor
41        public Java3DWorld( String imageFileName )
42        {
43           super( SimpleUniverse.getPreferredConfiguration() );
44
45           imageName = imageFileName;
46
47           // create SimpleUniverse (3D Graphics environment)
48           simpleUniverse = new SimpleUniverse( this );
49
50           // set default view point and direction
51           ViewingPlatform viewPlatform =
52              simpleUniverse.getViewingPlatform();
53
54           viewPlatform.setNominalViewingTransform();
55
56           // create 3D scene
57           BranchGroup branchGroup = createScene();
58
59           // attach BranchGroup to SimpleUniverse
60           simpleUniverse.addBranchGraph( branchGroup );
61
62        } // end Java3DWorld constructor
63
64        // create 3D scene
65        public BranchGroup createScene()
66        {
67           BranchGroup scene = new BranchGroup();
68
69           // initialize TransformGroup
70           transformGroup = new TransformGroup();
71
72           // set TransformGroup's READ and WRITE permission
73           transformGroup.setCapability(
74              TransformGroup.ALLOW_TRANSFORM_READ );
75
76           transformGroup.setCapability(
77              TransformGroup.ALLOW_TRANSFORM_WRITE );
78
79           // add TransformGroup to BranchGroup
80           scene.addChild( transformGroup );
81
82           // create BoundingSphere
83           BoundingSphere bounds = new BoundingSphere(
84              new Point3d( 0.0f, 0.0f, 0.0f ), 100.0 );
85
86           appearance = new Appearance(); // create object appearance
87           material = new Material(); // create texture matieral
```

Fig. 4.15   Creating a Java 3D **SimpleUniverse** with content (part 2 of 5).

```
88          appearance.setMaterial( material );
89
90          String rgb = new String( "RGB" );
91
92          // load texture for scene object
93          textureLoader = new TextureLoader(
94             Java3DWorld.class.getResource( imageName ), rgb, this );
95
96          // set capability bits for enabling texture
97          textureLoader.getTexture().setCapability(
98             Texture.ALLOW_ENABLE_WRITE );
99
100         // initial texture will not show
101         textureLoader.getTexture().setEnable( false );
102
103         // set object's texture
104         appearance.setTexture( textureLoader.getTexture() );
105
106         // create object geometry
107         Box shape = new Box( 0.3f, 0.3f, 0.3f,
108            Box.GENERATE_NORMALS | Box.GENERATE_TEXTURE_COORDS,
109            appearance );
110
111         // add geometry to TransformGroup
112         transformGroup.addChild( shape );
113
114         // initialize Ambient lighting
115         ambientLight = new AmbientLight();
116         ambientLight.setInfluencingBounds( bounds );
117
118         // initialize directionalLight
119         directionalLight = new DirectionalLight();
120
121         lightColor = new Color3f(); // initialize light color
122
123         // set initial DirectionalLight color
124         directionalLight.setColor( lightColor );
125
126         // set capability bits to allow DirectionalLight's
127         // Color and Direction to be changed
128         directionalLight.setCapability(
129            DirectionalLight.ALLOW_DIRECTION_WRITE );
130
131         directionalLight.setCapability(
132            DirectionalLight.ALLOW_DIRECTION_READ );
133
134         directionalLight.setCapability(
135            DirectionalLight.ALLOW_COLOR_WRITE );
136
137         directionalLight.setCapability(
138            DirectionalLight.ALLOW_COLOR_READ );
139
140         directionalLight.setInfluencingBounds( bounds );
```

Fig. 4.15 Creating a Java 3D **SimpleUniverse** with content (part 3 of 5).

```
141
142        // add light nodes to BranchGroup
143        scene.addChild( ambientLight );
144        scene.addChild( directionalLight );
145
146        // initialize rotation behavior
147        MouseRotate rotateBehavior = new MouseRotate();
148        rotateBehavior.setTransformGroup( transformGroup );
149        rotateBehavior.setSchedulingBounds( bounds );
150
151        // initialize translation behavior
152        MouseTranslate translateBehavior = new MouseTranslate();
153        translateBehavior.setTransformGroup( transformGroup );
154        translateBehavior.setSchedulingBounds(
155           new BoundingBox( new Point3d( -1.0f, -1.0f, -1.0f ),
156           new Point3d( 1.0f, 1.0f, 1.0f ) ) );
157
158        // initialize scaling behavior
159        MouseZoom scaleBehavior = new MouseZoom();
160        scaleBehavior.setTransformGroup( transformGroup );
161        scaleBehavior.setSchedulingBounds( bounds );
162
163        // add behaviors to BranchGroup
164        scene.addChild( scaleBehavior );
165        scene.addChild( rotateBehavior );
166        scene.addChild( translateBehavior );
167
168        scene.compile();
169
170        return scene;
171
172     } // end method createScene
173
174     // change DirectionLight color
175     public void changeColor( Color color )
176     {
177        lightColor.set( color );
178        directionalLight.setColor( lightColor );
179     }
180
181     // change geometry surface to textured image or material color
182     public void updateTexture( boolean textureValue )
183     {
184        textureLoader.getTexture().setEnable( textureValue );
185     }
186
187     // change image used for texture
188     public void setImageName( String imageFileName )
189     {
190        imageName = imageFileName;
191     }
192
```

Fig. 4.15   Creating a Java 3D **SimpleUniverse** with content (part 4 of 5).

```
193      // get image file name
194      public String getImageName()
195      {
196         return imageName;
197      }
198
199      // return preferred dimensions of Container
200      public Dimension getPreferredSize()
201      {
202         return new Dimension( 500, 500 );
203      }
204
205      // return minimum size of Container
206      public Dimension getMinimumSize()
207      {
208         return getPreferredSize();
209      }
210   }
```

Fig. 4.15   Creating a Java 3D **SimpleUniverse** with content (part 5 of 5).

The **Java3DWorld** constructor (lines 41–62) accepts as a **String** argument the image file for texture mapping. Class **SimpleUniverse**, which creates a Java 3D scene, encapsulates all the objects in the virtual universe and viewing platform. By using a **SimpleUniverse**, developers create and attach content-branch graphs—the **SimpleUniverse** uses this information to construct the 3D scene.

The first step in creating a Java 3D scene is to initialize the **Canvas3D** (line 43). The **Canvas3D** constructor takes as an argument a **java.awt.GraphicsConfiguration** (line 43). Method **getPreferredConfiguration** of class **SimpleUniverse** returns the system's **java.awt.GraphicsConfiguration**, which specifies a graphics device, such as a computer monitor. Line 48 invokes the **SimpleUniverse** constructor, passing the **Canvas3D** as an argument. This constructor creates a Java 3D **SimpleUniverse** with the **Canvas3D** as the drawing surface. Class **SimpleUniverse** creates and configures the objects in the view branch graph. Lines 51–54 configure the *viewing distance*—the length between the viewer and the canvas—for our 3D scene. All objects in the view branch graph are members of class *ViewingPlatform*. Method **getViewingPlatform** of class **SimpleUniverse** returns a reference to the **ViewingPlatform** created inside the **SimpleUniverse** (lines 51–52). Method **setNominalViewingTransform** of class **ViewPlatform** sets the viewing distance for our 3D scene to the *nominal* (i.e., default) distance of **PI/4.0**. We now create content for our Java 3D scene.

In this application, we add one content branch-graph to the **SimpleUniverse**. Line 57 calls method **createScene** (lines 65–172), which returns a content *BranchGroup*. Class **BranchGroup** is the root node of a scene graph in a Java 3D scene. The **BranchGroup** contains the children **Group**s, **Leaf**s and **NodeComponent**s that describe the Java 3D scene. Line 60 attaches the content **BranchGroup** to the **SimpleUniverse** using method **addBranchGraph** of class **SimpleUniverse**.

Method **createScene** creates, constructs and compiles the **BranchGroup** content. Line 67 creates an instance of class **BranchGroup**. Line 70 creates a *TransformGroup*.

Class **TransformGroup**—a subclass of **Group**—specifies *transformational behavior* such as rotation, scaling and translation. Lines 73–77 set the **READ** and **WRITE** *capability bits* for the **TransformGroup** using method **setCapabilityBits** of the **Transform-Group**. Capability bits are integer flags that specify whether a given object should allow its properties to be read or written during execution. Line 80 calls method **addChild** of class **BranchGroup**, which adds the **TransformGroup** to the **BranchGroup**.

Performance Tip 4.1

By default, Java 3D sets an object's properties so they cannot be changed during run-time. Java 3D does this to increase run-time performance.

Lines 83–84 create a ***BoundingSphere***. Class **BoundingSphere** creates a spherical *bounding volume*, which specifies the volume of space in which **Light**s and **Behavior**s affect geometry in the scene. Outside the bounding volume, the **Light**s and **Behavior**s have no impact on the scene's geometry. Lines 83–84 create a **Bounding-Sphere** that is centered at the origin and has a **100** meter radius.

Line 86 creates the ***Appearance*** that describes the visual attributes of shapes. Lines 87 creates a default **Material** object. Class ***Material*** specifies the properties of an *illuminated* object—any object defined within the bounds of a **Light**. The default **Material** constructor specifies that objects in ambient white light will appear grey. The default **Material** constructor also enables any objects with the associated **Material** to be illuminated in the 3D scene. Line 88 calls method **setMaterial** of class **Appearance** to set the **Material** to the default material, although we could have created a **Material** object that would make the shape's surface reflect like a mirror or shine like metal.

Lines 93–104 create and load the image for texture mapping. Class **com.sun.j3d.utils.image.TextureLoader** loads an **Image** for texturing. The ***TextureLoader*** constructor takes as arguments the image file (**imageName**), the image format (**rgb**) and an ***ImageObserver***. Lines 97–98 invoke method **setCapability** of class **TextureLoader** with argument **ALLOW_ENABLE_WRITE** so the user can apply textures to the **Texture** object during execution. Every **TextureLoader** has an associated **Texture** object that contains the texturing attributes. Line 101 disables texture mapping using method **setEnable** of class **Texture**, although the user can enable it in runtime. Method **setTexture** of class **Appearance** sets the **Texture** object in **Appearance** to our **Texture** (line 104).

Lines 107–109 create a 3D ***Box***—the shape that appears in our scene. The **Box** constructor takes as arguments three **float**s for the length, width and height, a set of integer flags that indicate the *position information* to generate and an **Appearance** object. Position information is generated when geometry is created—by default only spatial coordinates are generated. To ensure proper lighting and texture mapping for geometry, line 108 instructs the compiler to generate additional position information. Line 112 uses method **addChild** of class **TransformGroup** to add the **Box** to the **TransformGroup** so the user can perform transformations on the **Box**.

Line 115 creates an ***AmbientLight*** for the scene. Class **AmbientLight** is a uniform light source that illuminates all objects within its boundary. **AmbientLight** will not illuminate those objects outside its boundary. Line 116 calls method **setInfluencing-Bounds** to set the **AmbientLight** boundary using the **BoundingSphere** we created in line 86. Lines 119–140 create a ***DirectionalLight*** for the scene. Class **Direc-**

tionalLight describes a light source that travels between two points—the *source* and *destination*. Line 119 creates a **DirectionalLight** using the default constructor. Line 121 creates a **Color3f** object—a color defined by three **float**s that represent the RGB color components. Line 124 calls method **setColor** of **DirectionalLight** to set the light source color. Lines 128–138 set the capability bits to allow the user to alter the color and direction of the **DirectionalLight**. Lines 143–144 add the two light sources to the **BranchGroup**. All objects in the **BranchGroup** will be illuminated—as long as these objects are enabled for illumination.

Lines 147–161 create different behaviors for the **Box**. We use *MouseBehavior* class in utility package **com.sun.j3d.utils.behavior.mouse**. Lines 147–149 create an instance of class *MouseRotate*, which stores a rotational transformation for an object controlled with the left mouse button. By moving the mouse while pressing the left mouse button, the user controls the rotation of the **Box**. Line 148 calls method **setTransformGroup** of class **MouseRotate** to gather the rotation information from the **TransformGroup**. Line 149 calls method **setSchedulingBounds** of **MouseRotate** to set **MouseRotate**'s bounding volume. Figure 4.16 shows the output when the user rotates the **Box**.

Class *MouseTranslate*—another subclass of **MouseBehavior** creates a behavior that controls the *translation* (i.e., the displacement) of shapes when the user presses the right mouse button, then drags the mouse. Line 152 creates an instance of **MouseTranslate**. Line 153 calls method **setTransformGroup** of class **Mouse-Translate** to gather the translational information from the **TransformGroup**. Lines 154–156 call method **setSchedulingBounds**, passing as an argument a **Bound-ingBox**. Class **BoundingBox** creates a cubic boundary. **BoundingBox**'s constructors takes as arguments two **Point3d** objects, which represent the upper-right and lower-left vertices of the cube. Outside this **BoundingBox**, the **MouseTranslate** behavior does not work. Figure 4.17 shows the output when the user translates the **Box**.

Class *MouseZoom*—another subclass of **MouseBehavior**—controls the shape's size when the user presses either the middle mouse button (on a three-button mouse) or the Alt key and left button (on a two-button mouse), then drags the mouse. Line 159 creates an instance of class **mouseZoom**. Line 160 calls method **setTransformGroup** of class **MouseZoom** to gather the scaling information from the **TransformGroup**. Line 161 calls method **setSchedulingBounds**, passing the **BoundingSphere** we created earlier in method **createScene**. Figure 4.18 demonstrates the output when the user scales the **Box**.

Lines 164–166 add the three **MouseBehaviors** to the **BranchGroup**. Line 168 calls method **compile** of class **BranchGroup**. Compiling a **BranchGroup** informs the Java 3D engine to optimize rendering the scene using the capability bits set by the developer.

To toggle texture mapping and lighting during execution, we implement methods that update the **Appearance** and **DirectionalLight**. Method **changeColor** (lines 175–179) uses a **Color** object to set the **DirectionalLight** color. Line 177 creates a **Color3D** object from the **Color** argument and passes it to method **setColor** of the **DirectionalLight**. Figure 4.19 shows the output as the user alters the color for **DirectionalLight**.

Method **updateTexture** (lines 182–185) toggles texture mapping of the shapes in the scene. This method takes a **boolean** argument that specifies whether to enable texture mapping for the 3D shape. Figure 4.20 shows the output when the user enables texture mapping.

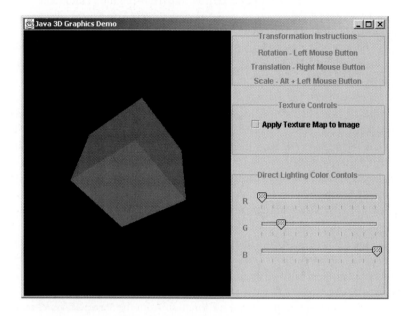

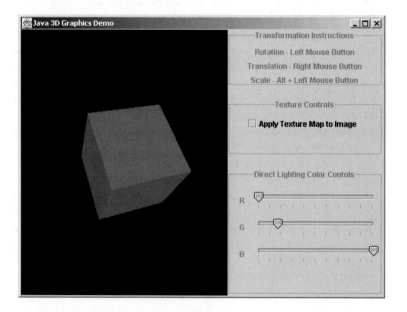

Fig. 4.16   Demonstrating **MouseRotate** behavior.

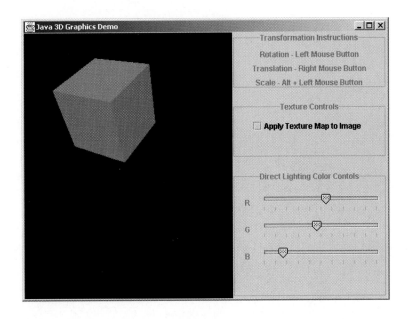

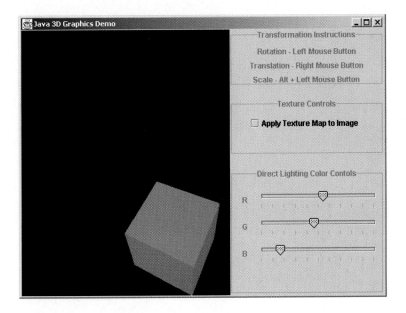

Fig. 4.17   Demonstrating **MouseTranslate** behavior.

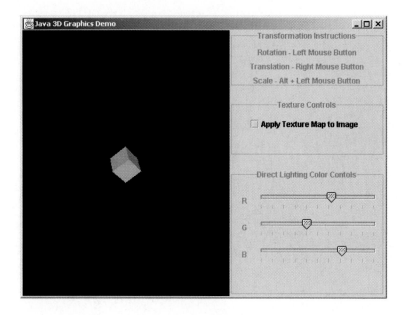

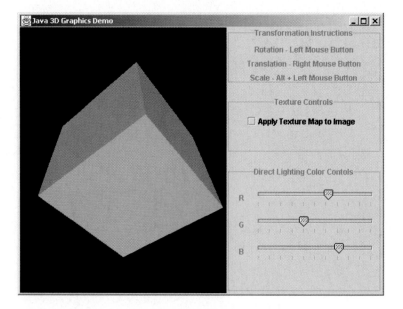

Fig. 4.18   Demonstrating **MouseZoom** behavior.

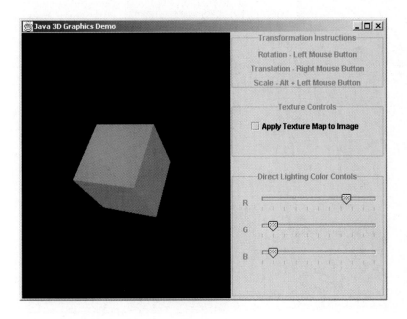

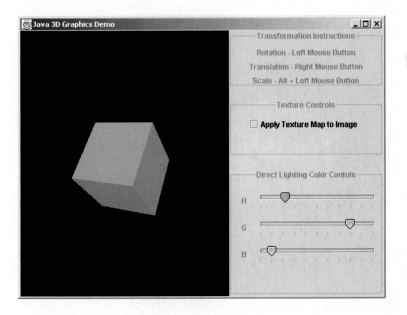

Fig. 4.19   Demonstrating changing color in Java 3D.

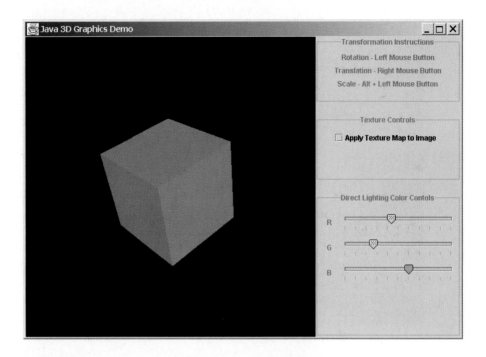

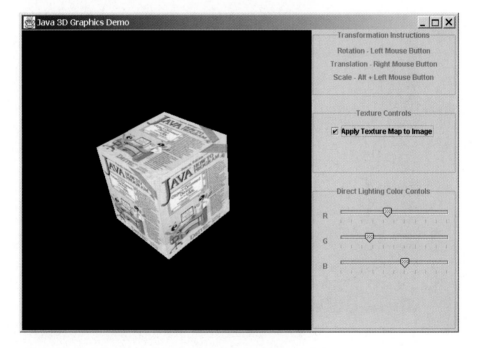

Fig. 4.20   Demonstrating texture mapping in Java 3D.

The user controls the **DirectionalLight** properties and texture mapping in the **Java3DWorld** using class **ControlPanel** (Fig. 4.21). Lines 18–21 declare three **JSlider**s and one **JCheckbox** for the user to interact with the 3D application. Line 24 declares a reference to a **Java3DWorld** object to access its **updateTexture** and **changeColor** methods.

```
1   // ControlPanel.java
2   // ControlPanel is a JPanel that contains Swing controls
3   // for manipulating a Java3DWorld.
4   package com.deitel.advjhtp1.java3d;
5
6   // Java core packages
7   import java.awt.*;
8   import java.awt.event.*;
9
10  // Java extension packages
11  import javax.swing.*;
12  import javax.swing.border.*;
13  import javax.swing.event.*;
14
15  public class ControlPanel extends JPanel {
16
17     // JSliders control lighting color
18     private JSlider redSlider, greenSlider, blueSlider;
19
20     // JCheckbox turns on texture mapping
21     private JCheckBox textureCheckBox;
22
23     // graphics display environment
24     private Java3DWorld java3DWorld;
25
26     // ControlPanel constructor
27     public ControlPanel( Java3DWorld tempJ3DWorld )
28     {
29        java3DWorld = tempJ3DWorld;
30
31         // assemble instruction panel
32        JPanel instructionPanel = new JPanel();
33
34        TitledBorder titledBorder =
35           new TitledBorder( "Transformation Instructions" );
36
37        titledBorder.setTitleJustification( TitledBorder.CENTER );
38        instructionPanel.setBorder( titledBorder );
39
40        JLabel rotationInstructions =
41           new JLabel( "Rotation - Left Mouse Button",
42           SwingConstants.CENTER );
43
44        JLabel translationInstructions =
45           new JLabel( "Translation - Right Mouse Button",
46           SwingConstants.CENTER );
```

Fig. 4.21 **ControlPanel** provides Swing controls for **Java3DWorld** (part 1 of 4).

```
47
48          JLabel scalingInstructions =
49             new JLabel( "Scale - Alt + Left Mouse Button",
50             SwingConstants.CENTER );
51
52          // add instruction JLabels to JPanel
53          instructionPanel.add( rotationInstructions );
54          instructionPanel.add( translationInstructions );
55          instructionPanel.add( scalingInstructions );
56
57          // assemble texture mapping control panel
58          JPanel texturePanel = new JPanel();
59
60          TitledBorder textureBorder =
61             new TitledBorder( "Texture Controls" );
62
63          textureBorder.setTitleJustification( TitledBorder.CENTER );
64          texturePanel.setBorder( textureBorder );
65
66          textureCheckBox = new JCheckBox(
67             "Apply Texture Map to Image" );
68
69          texturePanel.add( textureCheckBox );
70
71          // create ItemListener for JCheckBox
72          textureCheckBox.addItemListener(
73             new ItemListener() {
74
75                // invoked when checkbox selected/deselected
76                public void itemStateChanged( ItemEvent event )
77                {
78                   if( event.getStateChange() == ItemEvent.SELECTED )
79                      Java3DWorld.updateTexture( true );
80                   else
81                      Java3DWorld.updateTexture( false );
82                }
83
84             } // end anonymous inner class
85          );
86
87          // create JPanel with instructionPanel and texturePanel
88          JPanel topPanel = new JPanel(
89             new GridLayout( 2, 1, 0, 20 ) );
90
91          topPanel.add( instructionPanel );
92          topPanel.add( texturePanel );
93
94          // assemble lighting color control panel
95          JPanel colorPanel = new JPanel(
96             new FlowLayout( FlowLayout.LEFT, 15, 15 ) );
97
98          TitledBorder colorBorder =
99             new TitledBorder( "Direct Lighting Color Controls" );
```

Fig. 4.21 ControlPanel provides Swing controls for **Java3DWorld** (part 2 of 4).

```
100
101        colorBorder.setTitleJustification( TitledBorder.CENTER );
102        colorPanel.setBorder( colorBorder );
103
104        JLabel redLabel = new JLabel( "R" );
105        JLabel greenLabel = new JLabel( "G" );
106        JLabel blueLabel = new JLabel( "B" );
107
108        // create JSlider for adjusting red light component
109        redSlider = new JSlider(
110           SwingConstants.HORIZONTAL, 0, 255, 25 );
111
112        redSlider.setMajorTickSpacing( 25 );
113        redSlider.setPaintTicks( true );
114
115        // create JSlider for adjusting green light component
116        greenSlider = new JSlider(
117           SwingConstants.HORIZONTAL, 0, 255, 25 );
118
119        greenSlider.setMajorTickSpacing( 25 );
120        greenSlider.setPaintTicks( true );
121
122        // create JSlider for adjusting blue light component
123        blueSlider = new JSlider(
124           SwingConstants.HORIZONTAL, 0, 255, 25 );
125
126        blueSlider.setMajorTickSpacing( 25 );
127        blueSlider.setPaintTicks( true );
128
129        // create ChangeListener for JSliders
130        ChangeListener slideListener = new ChangeListener() {
131
132           // invoked when slider has been accessed
133           public void stateChanged( ChangeEvent event )
134           {
135              Color color = new Color(
136                 redSlider.getValue(), greenSlider.getValue(),
137                 blueSlider.getValue() );
138
139              Java3DWorld.changeColor( color );
140           }
141
142        }; // end anonymous inner class
143
144        // add listener to sliders
145        redSlider.addChangeListener( slideListener );
146        greenSlider.addChangeListener( slideListener );
147        blueSlider.addChangeListener( slideListener );
148
149        // add lighting color control components to colorPanel
150        colorPanel.add( redLabel );
151        colorPanel.add( redSlider );
152        colorPanel.add( greenLabel );
```

Fig. 4.21   **ControlPanel** provides Swing controls for **Java3DWorld** (part 3 of 4).

```
153        colorPanel.add( greenSlider );
154        colorPanel.add( blueLabel );
155        colorPanel.add( blueSlider );
156
157        // set Java3DWorld object default RGB slider values
158        Java3DWorld.changeColor(
159           new Color( redSlider.getValue(),
160              greenSlider.getValue(), blueSlider.getValue() ) );
161
162        // set GridLayout
163        setLayout( new GridLayout( 2, 1, 0, 20 ) );
164
165        // add JPanels to ControlPanel
166        add( topPanel );
167        add( colorPanel );
168
169     } // end ControlPanel constructor method
170
171     // return preferred dimensions of container
172     public Dimension getPreferredSize()
173     {
174        return new Dimension( 250, 150 );
175     }
176
177     // return minimum size of container
178     public Dimension getMinimumSize()
179     {
180        return getPreferredSize();
181     }
182  }
```

Fig. 4.21   `ControlPanel` provides Swing controls for `Java3DWorld` (part 4 of 4).

There are three sets of controls for the **Java3DWorld**—transformation, texture mapping and lighting controls. The translations are controlled using **MouseTranslate**, **MouseRotate** and **MouseZoom**—no Swing components are needed to control the **Java3DWorld** transforms. Lines 32–55 create a **JPanel** that contains **JLabel**s with instructions for applying transforms to the scene using the mouse.

Lines 58–69 create a **JPanel** with texture-mapping controls. The **JCheckBox** regulates the texture mapping in the application. Lines 72–85 attach an **ItemListener** to **textureCheckBox**. When the user selects this **JCheckBox**, line 79 calls method **updateTexture** of **Java3DWorld** to enable texture mapping. If the user deselects the **JCheckBox**, line 81 disables texture mapping.

Lines 104–127 create three **JSlider**s that can assume an integer 0–255, inclusive. Lines 130–142 create a **ChangeListener** for the **JSlider**s. When the user accesses a **JSlider**, line 139 calls method **changeColor** of **Java3DWorld** to change the shape's color in the 3D scene.

Class **Java3DExample** (Fig. 4.22) contains the **Java3DWorld** and **Control-Panel**. The **Java3DExample** constructor (lines 21–32) creates the **Java3DWorld** object by passing a **String** argument that specifies the image used for texture mapping (line 25). Line 26 creates **controlPanel**, passing the **Java3DWorld** as an argument. Method **main** (lines 35–41) executes the application.

```
1   // Java3DExample.java
2   // Java3DExample is an application that demonstrates Java 3D
3   // and provides an interface for a user to control the
4   // transformation, lighting color, and texture of a 3D scene.
5   package com.deitel.advjhtp1.java3d;
6
7   // Java core packages
8   import java.awt.*;
9   import java.awt.event.*;
10
11  // Java extension packages
12  import javax.swing.*;
13  import javax.swing.event.*;
14
15  public class Java3DExample extends JFrame {
16
17     private Java3DWorld java3DWorld; // 3D scene panel
18     private JPanel controlPanel; // 3D scene control panel
19
20     // initialize Java3DWorld and ControlPanel
21     public Java3DExample()
22     {
23        super( "Java 3D Graphics Demo" );
24
25        java3DWorld = new Java3DWorld( "images/ajhtp.png" );
26        controlPanel = new ControlPanel( java3DWorld );
27
28        // add Components to JFrame
29        getContentPane().add( java3DWorld, BorderLayout.CENTER );
30        getContentPane().add( controlPanel, BorderLayout.EAST );
31
32     } // end Java3DExample constructor
33
34     // start program
35     public static void main( String args[] )
36     {
37        Java3DExample application = new Java3DExample();
38        application.setDefaultCloseOperation( EXIT_ON_CLOSE );
39        application.pack();
40        application.setVisible( true );
41     }
42  }
```

Fig. 4.22   GUI for **Java3DWorld** and **ControlPanel**.

4.5 A Java 3D Case Study: A 3D Game with Custom Behaviors

In Section 4.4.3, we demonstrated how the Java 3D **MouseBehavior** utility classes add interactive behavior to a 3D scene. The *utility behavior classes* provide a simple and convenient way to add interaction to our 3D applications. However, some applications—such as computer games—require custom behaviors (e.g., *collision detection*, *navigation* and *position checking*). In this section, we demonstrate how to implement custom behaviors using the **javax.media.j3d.Behavior** class. We demonstrate collision detection among scene obstacles, navigation through a 3D scene and position checking of a user-navigated shape to determine when it has reached its target. We also introduce how to animate shapes using *Interpolators*. We examine how to use additional **Node** and **Group** subclasses, such as **Switch**es and **Text3D**s. The final product is a 3D game in which the user navigates a shape through a 3D scene full of "flying" obstacles. The goal of the game is to move this shape to a specific target point without having the shape collide with any of the moving obstacles.

Class **Java3DWorld1** (Fig. 4.23) creates the 3D game's objects, behaviors and animation. Class **Java3DWorld1** extends class **Canvas3D** (line 22). Lines 25–54 declare constants for setting various parameters in our 3D scene. Line 56 declares the *Switch* that contains the flying shapes. Class **Switch** extends Java 3D class **Group**. A **Switch** object specifies which of its children to render. Line 57 declares the **BoundingSphere** for scheduling bounds for the scene graph. Line 59 declares the **SimpleUniverse** that contains the **Locale** and view branch graph for our application. Line 61 declares the **String** that describes the image file for texturing shapes.

The **Java3DWorld1** constructor (lines 64–85) accepts as an argument a **String** that represents the image file for texturing the target shape. Line 66 initializes the **Canvas3D** by invoking the superclass constructor with a **GraphicsConfiguration** argument. Method **getPreferredConfiguration** of class **SimpleUniverse** returns the system's **java.awt.GraphicsConfiguration**, which specifies a graphics-output device. Line 71 creates a **SimpleUniverse** with the **Canvas3D** as the drawing surface. Class **SimpleUniverse** creates the Java 3D scene that encapsulates all the shapes in the virtual universe and viewing platform. Lines 74–77 configure the scene's viewing distance to the default value (**PI/4.0**). Line 80 calls method **createScene** (lines 65–248) to create a **BranchGroup** that line 60 attaches to the **SimpleUniverse**.

Method **createScene** constructs the **BranchGroup** content. Line 93 creates the **Switch** object that contains the scenes in our 3D game by calling method **initializeSwitch** (lines 285–297). This method takes an **int** argument (**DEFAULT_SCENE**) that specifies the default scene to display upon creation. Lines 288–294 set the **Switch** group's capability bits to allow the **Switch** (and its children) to be read and written at run time. In this application, we implement collision detection—lines 293–294 set the capability bit that allows collision reporting. Upon collision—i.e., when two shapes intersect—the Java 3D engine compiles the scene-graph path to the object that triggered the collision. When method **initializeSwitch** returns the **Switch** to method **createScene**, line 96 calls method **initializeSwitch** again to create a **Switch** that contains various shapes in the scene. Line 100 creates a **BranchGroup** that aggregates the shapes in **Switch** (line 103). Line 106 attaches the **BranchGroup** to the **Switch** of scenes. Line 109 attaches the **Switch** of scenes to the root **sceneBranchGraph**. Lines 112–113 create the **BoundingSphere** for setting the bounds for the **sceneBranchGraph**.

The 3D game features a scene with several 3D obstacles that "fly" across the screen. These obstacles rotate and translate at random. Rotation and translation are types of transformations. We discussed in the previous section that a **TransformGroup** holds the information about a spatial transformation and applies transformations to its children. The rotation and translation transformations animate the 3D shapes in our scene. Each shape needs two **TransformGroup**s—one for rotation information and one for translation information. Lines 116–121 call method **createTransformGroupArray** (lines 294–

322) to create **TransformGroup** arrays **spinTransform** and **pathTransform**, which store the rotational and translation information, respectively. Method **createTransformGroupArray** takes an **int** argument (**NUMBER_OF_SHAPES**) that specifies the array size. Line 305 initializes each **TransformGroup** in the array, and lines 308–317 set the capability bits of each **TransformGroup** to enable collision reporting and allow reading and writing during run time.

```
1   // Class Java3DWorld1 is a Java 3D game.
2   // The goal is to navigate the small red ball in the bottom right
3   // corner to the screen's top-left corner without colliding with
4   // any of the flying objects. The user can specify the number of
5   // flying objects to make the game more difficult.
6   package com.deitel.advjhtp1.java3dgame;
7
8   // Java core packages
9   import java.awt.*;
10  import java.net.*;
11  import java.util.BitSet;
12
13  // Java extension packages
14  import javax.media.j3d.*;
15  import javax.vecmath.*;
16
17  // Java3D utility packages
18  import com.sun.j3d.utils.geometry.*;
19  import com.sun.j3d.utils.image.*;
20  import com.sun.j3d.utils.universe.*;
21
22  public class Java3DWorld1 extends Canvas3D {
23
24     // container dimensions
25     private static final int CONTAINER_WIDTH = 600;
26     private static final int CONTAINER_HEIGHT = 600;
27
28     // constants that specify number of shapes
29     private static final int NUMBER_OF_SHAPES = 20;
30     private static final int NUMBER_OF_PRIMITIVES = 4;
31
32     // initial scene to display in Switch
33     private static final int DEFAULT_SCENE = 0;
34
35     // constants for animating rotation
36     private static final int MAX_ROTATION_SPEED = 25000;
37     private static final int MIN_ROTATION_SPEED = 20000;
38     private static final float MIN_ROTATION_ANGLE = 0.0f;
39     private static final float MAX_ROTATION_ANGLE =
40        ( float ) Math.PI * 8.0f;
41
42     // constants for animating translation
43     private static final int MAX_TRANSLATION_SPEED = 7500;
44     private static final int MIN_TRANSLATION_SPEED = 2500;
45
```

Fig. 4.23 Class **Java3DWorld1** creates the 3D-game environment (part 1 of 13).

```
46      // maximum time until animations begins
47      public static final int MAX_PHASE_DELAY = 20000;
48
49      // 3D shape information
50      private static final float MAX_RADIUS = 0.15f;
51      private static final float MAX_LENGTH = 0.2f;
52      private static final float MAX_SHININESS = 128.0f;
53      private static final float SPHERE_RADIUS = 0.15f;
54      private static final float BOUNDING_RADIUS = 100.0f;
55
56      private Switch shapeSwitch; // contains flying shapes
57      private BoundingSphere bounds; // bounds for nodes and groups
58
59      private SimpleUniverse simpleUniverse; // 3D environment
60
61      private String imageName; // texture image file name
62
63      // Java3DWorld1 constructor
64      public Java3DWorld1( String imageFileName ) {
65
66         super( SimpleUniverse.getPreferredConfiguration() );
67
68         imageName = imageFileName;
69
70         // create SimpleUniverse ( 3D Graphics environment )
71         simpleUniverse = new SimpleUniverse( this );
72
73         // set viewing distance for 3D scene
74         ViewingPlatform viewPlatform =
75            simpleUniverse.getViewingPlatform();
76
77         viewPlatform.setNominalViewingTransform();
78
79         // create 3D scene
80         BranchGroup branchGroup = createScene();
81
82         // attach BranchGroup to SimpleUniverse
83         simpleUniverse.addBranchGraph( branchGroup );
84
85      } // end Java3DWorld1 constructor
86
87      // create 3D scene
88      public BranchGroup createScene()
89      {
90         BranchGroup sceneBranchGroup = new BranchGroup();
91
92         // create scene Switch group
93         Switch sceneSwitch = initializeSwitch( DEFAULT_SCENE );
94
95         // create Switch group containing shapes
96         shapeSwitch = initializeSwitch( DEFAULT_SCENE );
97
```

Fig. 4.23   Class **Java3DWorld1** creates the 3D-game environment (part 2 of 13).

```
98      // initialize BranchGroup that contains only elements
99      // in game scene
100     BranchGroup gameBranchGroup = new BranchGroup();
101
102     // add shapeSwitch to gameBranchGroup
103     gameBranchGroup.addChild( shapeSwitch );
104
105     // add gameBranchGroup to sceneSwitch
106     sceneSwitch.addChild( gameBranchGroup );
107
108     // add sceneSwitch to sceneBranchGroup
109     sceneBranchGroup.addChild( sceneSwitch );
110
111     // create BoundingSphere for 3D objects and behaviors
112     bounds = new BoundingSphere(
113         new Point3d( 0.0f, 0.0f, 0.0f ), BOUNDING_RADIUS );
114
115     // create rotation TransformGroup array
116     TransformGroup[] spinTransform =
117         createTransformGroupArray( NUMBER_OF_SHAPES );
118
119     // create translation TransformGroup array
120     TransformGroup[] pathTransform =
121         createTransformGroupArray( NUMBER_OF_SHAPES );
122
123     // create RotationInterpolators
124     createRotationInterpolators( spinTransform,
125         NUMBER_OF_SHAPES );
126
127     // create PositonInterpolators
128     createPositionInterpolators( pathTransform,
129         NUMBER_OF_SHAPES );
130
131     // create Appearance objects for Primitives
132     Appearance[] shapeAppearance =
133         createAppearance( NUMBER_OF_SHAPES );
134
135     // create shapes
136     Primitive[] shapes =
137         createShapes( shapeAppearance, NUMBER_OF_SHAPES );
138
139     // add shapes to scene structure
140     for ( int x = 0; x < NUMBER_OF_SHAPES; x++ ) {
141
142         // add primitive to spinTransform group
143         spinTransform[ x ].addChild( shapes[ x ] );
144
145         // add spinTransform group to pathTransform group
146         pathTransform[ x ].addChild( spinTransform[ x ] );
147
148         // add pathTransform group to shapeSwitch group
149         shapeSwitch.addChild( pathTransform[ x ] );
150     }
```

Fig. 4.23   Class **Java3DWorld1** creates the 3D-game environment (part 3 of 13).

```
151
152     // create and set scene lighting
153     setLighting( sceneBranchGroup, bounds );
154
155     // create scene to display if user loses
156     TransformGroup loserTransformGroup =
157        createEndScene( "You Lose!" );
158
159     // add loser scene to sceneSwitch
160     sceneSwitch.addChild( loserTransformGroup );
161
162     // create scene to display if user winss
163     TransformGroup winnerTransformGroup =
164        createEndScene( "You Win!" );
165
166     // add winner scene to sceneSwitch
167     sceneSwitch.addChild( winnerTransformGroup );
168
169     // create shiny red Appearance for navigating shape
170     Appearance flyingAppearance = createAppearance(
171        new Color3f( 1.0f, 0.0f, 0.0f ) );
172
173     // initialize navigable sphere
174     Primitive flyingBall = new Sphere(
175        0.03f,   Sphere.GENERATE_NORMALS, flyingAppearance );
176
177     // set capability bits to enable collision detection and
178     // allow for read/write of bounds
179     flyingBall.setCollidable( true );
180     flyingBall.setCapability( Node.ENABLE_COLLISION_REPORTING );
181     flyingBall.setCapability( Node.ALLOW_BOUNDS_READ );
182     flyingBall.setCapability( Node.ALLOW_BOUNDS_WRITE );
183
184     // create TransformGroup to translate shape position
185     TransformGroup startTransform = createTransform(
186        new Vector3f( 0.9f, -0.9f, 0.0f ) );
187
188     startTransform.addChild( flyingBall );
189     gameBranchGroup.addChild( startTransform );
190
191     // create Material for Appearance for target sphere
192     Appearance targetAppearance = createAppearance(
193        new Color3f( 0.0f, 1.0f, 0.0f ) );
194
195     // obtain textured image for target sphere
196     String rgb = new String( "RGB" );
197     TextureLoader textureLoader = new TextureLoader(
198        Java3DWorld1.class.getResource( imageName ), rgb, this );
199     textureLoader.getTexture().setEnable( true );
200     targetAppearance.setTexture( textureLoader.getTexture() );
201
```

Fig. 4.23 Class **Java3DWorld1** creates the 3D-game environment (part 4 of 13).

```
202        // initialize target sphere
203        Primitive targetSphere = new Sphere( SPHERE_RADIUS,
204           Sphere.GENERATE_TEXTURE_COORDS | Sphere.GENERATE_NORMALS,
205           targetAppearance );
206
207        // disable collision detection for sphere
208        targetSphere.setCollidable( false );
209
210        // create vector to target point
211        Vector3f target = new Vector3f( -1.0f, 1.0f, -1.0f );
212
213        // create TransformGroup that translates sphere position
214        TransformGroup targetTransform = createTransform( target );
215        targetTransform.addChild( targetSphere );
216        gameBranchGroup.addChild( targetTransform );
217
218        // create Navigator behavior
219        Navigator navigator = new Navigator( startTransform );
220        navigator.setSchedulingBounds( bounds );
221
222        // create Collide behavior
223        Collide collider = new Collide(
224           simpleUniverse, flyingBall, sceneSwitch );
225        collider.setSchedulingBounds( bounds );
226
227        // create GoalDetector behavior
228        GoalDetector goalDetector = new GoalDetector(
229           simpleUniverse, startTransform, sceneSwitch,
230           target, SPHERE_RADIUS );
231        goalDetector.setSchedulingBounds( bounds );
232
233        // add Behaviors to scene
234        sceneBranchGroup.addChild( goalDetector );
235        sceneBranchGroup.addChild( collider );
236        sceneBranchGroup.addChild( navigator );
237
238        // create Background for scene
239        Background background = new Background();
240        background.setColor( 0.4f, 0.4f, 1.0f );
241        background.setApplicationBounds( bounds );
242        sceneBranchGroup.addChild( background );
243
244        sceneBranchGroup.compile();
245
246        return sceneBranchGroup;
247
248     } // end method createScene
249
250     // create Appearance object for Primitive in scene
251     private Appearance createAppearance( Color3f diffuseColor )
252     {
253        Appearance appearance = new Appearance();
254        Material material = new Material();
```

Fig. 4.23   Class **Java3DWorld1** creates the 3D-game environment (part 5 of 13).

```
255       material.setShininess( MAX_SHININESS );
256       material.setDiffuseColor( diffuseColor );
257       material.setAmbientColor( 0.0f, 0.0f, 0.0f );
258       appearance.setMaterial( material );
259       return appearance;
260
261    } // end method createAppearance
262
263
264    // create TransformGroup for placing an object in scene
265    private TransformGroup createTransform(
266       Vector3f positionVector )
267    {
268       // initialize a TransformGroup and set capability bits
269       TransformGroup transformGroup = new TransformGroup();
270       transformGroup.setCapability(
271          TransformGroup.ALLOW_TRANSFORM_READ );
272       transformGroup.setCapability(
273          TransformGroup.ALLOW_TRANSFORM_WRITE );
274
275       // translate starting position to bottom right of scene
276       Transform3D location = new Transform3D();
277       location.setTranslation( positionVector );
278       transformGroup.setTransform( location );
279
280       return transformGroup;
281
282    } // end method createTransform
283
284    // initialize Switch group and set capability bits
285    private Switch initializeSwitch( int sceneNumber )
286    {
287       Switch switchGroup = new Switch( sceneNumber );
288       switchGroup.setCollidable( true );
289       switchGroup.setCapability( Switch.ALLOW_SWITCH_WRITE );
290       switchGroup.setCapability( Switch.ALLOW_SWITCH_READ );
291       switchGroup.setCapability( Group.ALLOW_CHILDREN_WRITE );
292       switchGroup.setCapability( Group.ALLOW_CHILDREN_READ );
293       switchGroup.setCapability(
294          Group.ENABLE_COLLISION_REPORTING );
295       return switchGroup;
296
297    } // end method initializeSwitch
298
299    private TransformGroup[] createTransformGroupArray(
300       int size )
301    {
302       TransformGroup[] transformGroup =
303          new TransformGroup[ size ];
304
305       // set TransformGroup's WRITE and READ permissions
306       // and enable collision reporting
```

Fig. 4.23 Class **Java3DWorld1** creates the 3D-game environment (part 6 of 13).

```
307          for ( int i = 0; i < size; i++ ) {
308
309             // create TransformGroups
310             transformGroup[ i ] = new TransformGroup();
311
312             // enable collision reporting
313             transformGroup[ i ].setCapability(
314                Group.ENABLE_COLLISION_REPORTING );
315
316             // enable WRITE permission
317             transformGroup[ i ].setCapability(
318                TransformGroup.ALLOW_TRANSFORM_WRITE );
319
320             // enable READ permission
321             transformGroup[ i ].setCapability(
322                TransformGroup.ALLOW_TRANSFORM_READ );
323          }
324
325          return transformGroup;
326
327       } // end method createTransformGroupArray
328
329       // create RotationInterpolators for scene
330       private void createRotationInterpolators(
331          TransformGroup[] transformGroup, int size )
332       {
333          // declare structures for creating RotationInterpolators
334          Alpha[] alphaSpin = new Alpha[ size ];
335
336          Transform3D[] spinAxis =
337             new Transform3D[ size ];
338
339          RotationInterpolator[] spinner =
340             new RotationInterpolator[ size ];
341
342          // create RotationInterpolator for each shape
343          for ( int x = 0; x < size; x++ ) {
344
345             // initialize Alpha
346             alphaSpin[ x ] = new Alpha();
347
348             // set increasing time for Alpha to random number
349             alphaSpin[ x ].setIncreasingAlphaDuration(
350                MIN_ROTATION_SPEED + ( ( int ) ( Math.random() *
351                   MAX_ROTATION_SPEED ) ) );
352
353             // initialize RotationInterpolator using appropriate
354             // Alpha and TransformGroup
355             spinner[ x ] = new RotationInterpolator(
356                alphaSpin[ x ], transformGroup[ x ] );
357
358             spinAxis[ x ] = new Transform3D();
359
```

Fig. 4.23   Class **Java3DWorld1** creates the 3D-game environment (part 7 of 13).

```
360            // set random X-axis rotation
361            spinAxis[ x ].rotX(
362               ( float ) ( Math.PI * ( Math.random() * 2 ) ) );
363            spinner[ x ].setAxisOfRotation( spinAxis[ x ] );
364
365            // set minimum and maximum rotation angles
366            spinner[ x ].setMinimumAngle( MIN_ROTATION_ANGLE );
367            spinner[ x ].setMaximumAngle( MAX_ROTATION_ANGLE );
368
369            spinner[ x ].setSchedulingBounds( bounds );
370
371            // add RotationInterpolator to appropriate TransformGroup
372            transformGroup[ x ].addChild( spinner[ x ] );
373         }
374
375      } // end method createRotationInterpolators
376
377      // create PositionInterpolators
378      private void createPositionInterpolators(
379         TransformGroup[] transformGroup, int size )
380      {
381         // create structures for PositionInterpolators
382         Alpha[] alphaPath = new Alpha[ size ];
383
384         PositionInterpolator[] mover =
385            new PositionInterpolator[ size ];
386
387         Transform3D[] pathAxis =
388            new Transform3D[ size ];
389
390         // create PositionInterpolator for each shape
391         for ( int x = 0; x < size; x++ ) {
392
393            // initialize Alpha
394            alphaPath[ x ] = new Alpha();
395
396            // set mode to increase and decrease interpolation
397            alphaPath[ x ].setMode(
398               Alpha.INCREASING_ENABLE | Alpha.DECREASING_ENABLE );
399
400            // set random phase delay
401            alphaPath[ x ].setPhaseDelayDuration(
402               ( ( int ) ( Math.random() * MAX_PHASE_DELAY ) ) );
403
404            // randomize translation speed
405            int speed = MIN_TRANSLATION_SPEED +
406               ( int ) ( Math.random() * MAX_TRANSLATION_SPEED );
407
408            // set increasing and decreasing durations
409            alphaPath[ x ].setIncreasingAlphaDuration( speed );
410            alphaPath[ x ].setDecreasingAlphaDuration( speed );
411
```

Fig. 4.23 Class **Java3DWorld1** creates the 3D-game environment (part 8 of 13).

```
412              // randomize translation axis
413              pathAxis[ x ] = new Transform3D();
414              pathAxis[ x ].rotX(
415                  ( float ) ( Math.PI * ( Math.random() * 2 ) ) );
416              pathAxis[ x ].rotY(
417                  ( float ) ( Math.PI * ( Math.random() * 2 ) ) );
418              pathAxis[ x ].rotZ(
419                  ( float ) ( Math.PI * ( Math.random() * 2 ) ) );
420
421              // initialize PositionInterpolator
422              mover[ x ] = new PositionInterpolator( alphaPath[ x ],
423                  transformGroup[ x ], pathAxis[ x ], 1.0f, -1.0f );
424
425              mover[ x ].setSchedulingBounds( bounds );
426
427              // add PostionInterpolator to appropriate TransformGroup
428              transformGroup[ x ].addChild( mover[ x ] );
429           }
430
431      } // end method createPositionInterpolators
432
433      // create appearance and material arrays for Primitives
434      private Appearance[] createAppearance( int size )
435      {
436          // create Appearance objects for each shape
437          Appearance[] appearance =
438              new Appearance[ size ];
439
440          Material[] material = new Material[ size ];
441
442          // set material and appearance properties for each shape
443          for( int i = 0; i < size; i++ ) {
444              appearance[ i ] = new Appearance();
445              material[ i ] = new Material();
446
447              // set material ambient color
448              material[ i ].setAmbientColor(
449                  new Color3f( 0.0f, 0.0f, 0.0f ) );
450
451              // set material Diffuse color
452              material[ i ].setDiffuseColor( new Color3f(
453                  ( float ) Math.random(), ( float ) Math.random(),
454                  ( float ) Math.random() ) );
455
456              // set Material for appropriate Appearance object
457              appearance[ i ].setMaterial( material[ i ] );
458          }
459          return appearance;
460
461      } // end method createAppearance
462
```

Fig. 4.23 Class **Java3DWorld1** creates the 3D-game environment (part 9 of 13).

```
463     // create Primitives shapes
464     private Primitive[] createShapes( Appearance[] appearance,
465        int size )
466     {
467        Primitive[] shapes = new Primitive[ size ];
468
469        // random loop to get index
470        for ( int x = 0; x < size; x++ ) {
471
472           // generate random shape index
473         int index = ( int ) ( Math.random() * NUMBER_OF_PRIMITIVES );
474
475           // create shape based on random index
476         switch( index ) {
477
478            case 0: // create Box
479               shapes[ x ] = new Box(
480                  ( ( float ) Math.random() * MAX_LENGTH ),
481                  ( ( float ) Math.random() * MAX_LENGTH ),
482                  ( ( float ) Math.random() * MAX_LENGTH ),
483                  Box.GENERATE_NORMALS, appearance[ x ] );
484               break;
485
486            case 1: // create Cone
487               shapes[ x ] = new Cone(
488                  ( ( float ) Math.random() * MAX_RADIUS ),
489                  ( ( float ) Math.random() * MAX_LENGTH ),
490                  Cone.GENERATE_NORMALS, appearance[ x ] );
491               break;
492
493            case 2: // create Cylinder
494               shapes[ x ] = new Cylinder(
495                  ( ( float ) Math.random() * MAX_RADIUS ),
496                  ( ( float ) Math.random() * MAX_LENGTH ),
497                  Cylinder.GENERATE_NORMALS, appearance[ x ] );
498               break;
499
500            case 3: // create Sphere
501               shapes[ x ] =  new Sphere(
502                  ( ( float ) Math.random() * MAX_RADIUS ),
503                  Sphere.GENERATE_NORMALS, appearance[ x ] );
504               break;
505
506         } // end switch statement
507
508        // set capability bits to enable collisions and to set
509        // read/write permissions of bounds
510        shapes[ x ].setCapability(
511           Node.ENABLE_COLLISION_REPORTING );
512        shapes[ x ].setCapability(
513           Node.ALLOW_BOUNDS_READ );
514        shapes[ x ].setCapability(
515           Node.ALLOW_BOUNDS_WRITE );
```

Fig. 4.23   Class **Java3DWorld1** creates the 3D-game environment (part 10 of 13).

```
516              shapes[ x ].setCollidable( true );
517
518          }
519
520          return shapes;
521
522      } // end method createShapes
523
524      // initialize ambient and directional lighting
525      private void setLighting( BranchGroup scene,
526          BoundingSphere bounds )
527      {
528          // initialize ambient lighting
529          AmbientLight ambientLight = new AmbientLight();
530          ambientLight.setInfluencingBounds( bounds );
531
532          // initialize directional lighting
533          DirectionalLight directionalLight = new DirectionalLight();
534          directionalLight.setColor(
535              new Color3f( 1.0f, 1.0f, 1.0f ) );
536          directionalLight.setInfluencingBounds( bounds );
537
538          // add lights to scene
539          scene.addChild( ambientLight );
540          scene.addChild( directionalLight );
541
542      } // end method setLighting
543
544      // update scene by rendering different shapes in shapeSwitch
545      public void switchScene( int numberChildren, int size )
546      {
547          // create a new BitSet of size NUMBER_OF_SHAPES
548          BitSet bitSet = new BitSet( size );
549
550          // set BitSet values
551          for ( int i = 0; i < numberChildren; i++ )
552              bitSet.set( i );
553
554          // instruct switchShape to render Mask of objects
555          shapeSwitch.setWhichChild( Switch.CHILD_MASK );
556          shapeSwitch.setChildMask( bitSet );
557
558      } // end method switchScene
559
560      // create end scene when user wins or loses
561      private TransformGroup createEndScene( String text )
562      {
563          TransformGroup transformGroup = new TransformGroup();
564          transformGroup.setCapability(
565              TransformGroup.ALLOW_TRANSFORM_WRITE );
566
567          // disable scene collision detection
568          transformGroup.setCollidable( false );
```

Fig. 4.23   Class **Java3DWorld1** creates the 3D-game environment (part 11 of 13).

```
569
570        // create Alpha object
571        Alpha alpha = new Alpha();
572           alpha.setIncreasingAlphaDuration( MAX_ROTATION_SPEED );
573
574        // create RotationInterpolator for scene
575        RotationInterpolator rotation =
576        new RotationInterpolator( alpha, transformGroup );
577
578        // set axis of rotation
579        Transform3D axis = new Transform3D();
580        axis.rotY( ( float ) ( Math.PI / 2.0 ) );
581        rotation.setAxisOfRotation( axis );
582
583        // set minimum and maximum rotation angles
584        rotation.setMinimumAngle( 0.0f );
585        rotation.setMaximumAngle( ( float ) ( Math.PI * 8.0 ) );
586
587        rotation.setSchedulingBounds( bounds );
588        transformGroup.addChild( rotation );
589
590        // create scene geometry
591        Appearance appearance = new Appearance();
592        Material material = new Material();
593        appearance.setMaterial( material );
594
595        // set diffuse color of material
596        material.setDiffuseColor(
597           new Color3f( 0.0f, 0.8f, 1.0f ) );
598
599        // create Font3D object
600        Font3D font3d = new Font3D(
601           new Font( "Helvetica", Font.ITALIC, 1 ),
602           new FontExtrusion() );
603
604        // create Text3D object from Font3D object
605        Text3D text3d = new Text3D( font3d, text,
606           new Point3f( -2.0f, 0.0f, 0.0f ) );
607
608        // create Shape3D object from Text3D object
609        Shape3D textShape = new Shape3D( text3d );
610
611        textShape.setAppearance( appearance );
612
613        // disable collision detection
614        textShape.setCollidable( false );
615
616        transformGroup.addChild( textShape );
617
618        return transformGroup;
619
620     } // end method createEndScene
621
```

Fig. 4.23   Class **Java3DWorld1** creates the 3D-game environment (part 12 of 13).

```
622
623        // return preferred dimensions of Container
624        public Dimension getPreferredSize()
625        {
626           return new Dimension( CONTAINER_WIDTH, CONTAINER_HEIGHT );
627        }
628
629        // return minimum size of Container
630        public Dimension getMinimumSize()
631        {
632           return getPreferredSize();
633        }
634     }
```

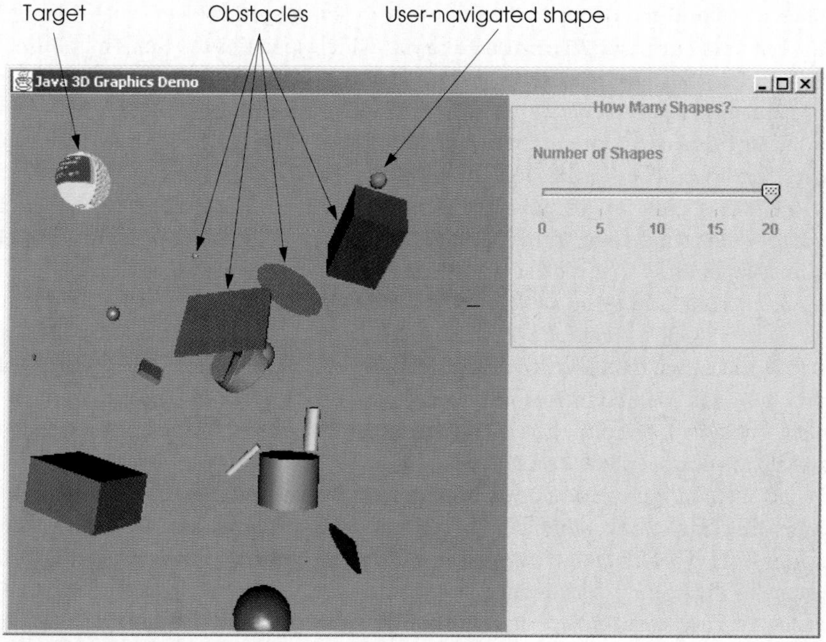

Fig. 4.23   Class **Java3DWorld1** creates the 3D-game environment (part 13 of 13).

When method **createTransformGroupArray** returns the array, method **createScene** creates the **Interpolator**s, which help animate the transformations. Class **Interpolator** is a subclass of **Behavior**—later, we discuss how to implement custom behaviors. Now, we discuss how to use some well-known **Behavior** subclasses provided by Java 3D. To animate shapes smoothly in a scene, Java 3D provides **Interpolator**s and **Alpha**s. **Interpolator**s use **Alpha**s to specify certain characteristics of animation, such as the speed of transformations (e.g., rotation speed), or how fast a shape changes color (e.g., lighting effects). **Interpolator** objects convert time values to transformations of 3D shapes—**Alpha** objects generate these time values. For example, when a shape "flies" across the screen in one second, the **Interpolator** converts **Alpha**-generated time values (from 0 to 1) to translation operations that move the shape in the one-second period. An **Interpolator** operates in conjunction with a **Trans-**

formGroup—each **TransformGroup** has an associated **Interpolator**. The **Interpolator** describes how to animate shapes in the **TransformGroup**. Java 3D provides several **Interpolator** subclasses. In this game, we use **RotationInterpolator** for rotating objects and **PositionInterpolator** for translating objects.

Lines 124–125 pass the **spinTransform** array of **TransformGroup**s to method **createRotationInterpolators** (lines 330–375), which initializes the **RotationInterpolator**s for **spinTransform**. An **Alpha** object and a **Transform3D** object compose a **RotationInterpolator** object. **Alpha** objects contain a series of phases that either *increase* or *decrease*. Increasing **Alpha** objects generate values in a sequence from 0 to 1, whereas decreasing **Alpha** objects generate values in a sequence from 1 to 0. An **Alpha** object's default constructor sets that **Alpha** to generate increasing values, which result in a shape spinning in one specific direction (decreasing values enable the shape to spin in the opposite direction). For each **Alpha** object, lines 349–351 call method **setIncreasingAlphaDuration**, which specifies the time (in milliseconds) for that **Alpha** object to increase from 0 to 1. A random-number generation sets the time value between **MIN_ROTATION_SPEED** and **MAX_ROTATION_SPEED**. Lines 355–356 create the **RotationInterpolator** array that use the **Alpha** array and the **spinTransform** array. The **Alpha** object controls the **Interpolator**, which in turn transforms the 3D shapes in the **TransformGroup**. The **RotationInterpolator** constructor creates a default **Transform3D** for the rotation. Class **Transform3D** is a two-dimensional array that represents a general transform—in this case, a rotation. Each **Transform3D** has an associated integer type that determines the transformation to represent. Lines 358–369 create the **Transform3D** for the **RotationInterpolator**. Lines 361–363 assign the **Transform3D** a random axis of rotation. Lines 366–367 assign the minimum and maximum rotation angles (i.e., the starting and stopping angles for a complete rotational period). Line 372 adds the **RotationInterpolator**s to the **TransformGroup spinTransform**.

When method **createRotationInterpolators** returns, lines 128–129 pass **pathTransform** as an argument to method **createPositionInterpolators** (lines 378–431). This method creates a set of **PositionInterpolator**s that translate the shapes in the scene—specifically, the method creates **PositionInterpolator**s for each **TransformGroup** in **pathTransform**. **PositionInterpolator**s operate similarly to **RotationInterpolator**s, except **PositionInterpolator**s translate a 3D shape's position on a given axis, whereas **RotationInterpolator**s rotate a 3D shape on a given axis. Line 382 creates the **Alpha** objects associated with the **PositionInterpolator**s—these values provide the time values that help to determine the shapes' position. Lines 397–398 set the **Alpha** object as increasing and decreasing to ensure that the 3D shapes move back and forth across the screen. If the **Alpha** object was only decreasing or increasing, the shapes would move in only one direction. We chose to delay the initial movement of each shape to ensure that the 3D obstacle will not collide with the user-navigated shape immediately after the player starts the game. Lines 401–402 accomplish this by setting a randomized *phase delay* on each **Alpha** object. To make the game more interesting, we chose to set the increasing and decreasing durations to random speeds. Lines 413–419 assign random translation axes to the **Transform3D** objects that hold translation information to give obstacles different directions. Lines 422–423 pass five arguments to the **PositionInterpolator** constructor. The first three arguments are the array of **Alpha** values, the array of **TransformGroup** values (**path-Transform**) and the array of **Transform3D** values. The last two arguments specify the starting and ending positions in the 3D scene for the **PositionInterpolator** translation. Line 428 adds each **PositionInterpolator** to each **TransformGroup** in **pathTransform**.

At this point, **Java3DWorld1** has created the **TransformGroup**s and **Inter-polator**s for each 3D shape. Now **Java3DWorld1** must create the actual shapes. Lines 132–133 invoke method **createAppearance** (lines 434–461), which creates an array of randomly colored **Appearance** objects. Line 440 creates an array of **Material** objects, because every **Appearance** object has an associated **Material** object. Lines 448–449 sets each **Material**'s *ambient color*—the **Material**'s color when illuminated by reflected light. Lines 452–454 randomly set each **Material**'s *diffuse color*—the **Material**'s color when illuminated by some light source. Line 457 sets each **Material** in the **Material** array to an associated **Appearance** in the **Appearance** array. Line 459 then returns the **Appearance** array.

Lines 136–137 pass the **Appearance** array to method **createShapes** (lines 464–522) to create an array of *Primitives* that represent the shapes of the obstacles. The Java 3D **com.sun.j3d.utils.geometry** package provides four types of 3D-geometric **Primitive** types: **Box**, **Cone**, **Cylinder** and **Sphere**. Line 473 randomly generates a number between 0 and 3—each number is associated with one of these **Primitive** object. Lines 476–506 implement a **switch** statement—each case creates a unique type. The constructor of each **Primitive** subclass specifies that **Primitive**'s dimensions, lighting and appearance. Consider the **Box** constructor—lines 479–483 pass the **Box**'s length, width and height, the **GENERATE_NORMALS** constant (for the direction of the lighting), and an **Appearance** object. Lines 510–515 set the capability bits for each **Primitive** to enable collision reporting and read/write access during execution. Line 516 invokes method **setCollidable** of each **Primitive**'s **Node** superclass, so each **Primitive** can collide with other "collidable" **Primitive**s. Line 520 returns the array of 3D shapes.

Lines 140–150 set up the **sceneBranchGraph**. Line 143 adds each 3D shape to each **TransformGroup** in **spinTransform**, line 146 adds each **TransformGroup** in **spinTransform** to each **TransformGroup** in **pathTransform**. Line 149 adds each **TransformGroup** in **pathTransform** to **shapeSwitch**. Line 153 calls method **setLighting** (lines 525–542) to create the **AmbientLight** and **Directional-Light** that illuminate the shapes in the scene. Lines 156–157 call method **createEnd-Scene** (lines 561–620) to create a **TransformGroup** associated with the player losing the game. Method **createEndScene** uses its **String** argument to create a rotating object of class *Text3D*—a **Geometry** subclass for representing 3D text. Lines 563–568 create the **TransformGroup** to hold the **Text3D**. Lines 571–587 create the **Rota-tionInterpolator** for rotating the **Text3D**. Lines 591–594 create an **Appearance** object for the **Text3D**. Lines 600–602 create a **Font3D** object, which uses both a **java.awt.Font** object and a Java 3D **FontExtrusion** object. A **FontExtrusion** describes the adding of a third dimension to the **Font**'s 2D text. Using the **Font3D** object, the **String** argument that holds the text and a **Point3f** object—*x-y-z* coordinates that specify a location in a **SimpleUniverse**, lines 605–606 create the **Text3D** object. Line 609 creates a **Shape3D**—a **Node** that describes a 3D shape—from the **Text3D**. Line 611 sets the **Shape3D**'s **Appearance**. Line 614 specifies that the **Shape3D** objects in this scene should not collide with other **Shape3D** objects. Line 616 adds each **Shape3D** to the **TransformGroup**, and line 619 returns the **TransformGroup**. Line 160 adds this **TransformGroup** (for the losing scene) to the **Switch** group. When the user-navigated shape collides with an obstacle, the application displays a scene with the rotating 3D text "**You Lose**." Lines 163–164 call method **createEndScene** to create the scene that displays "**You Win**" when the player navigates the shape to the destination without collision. Line 167 adds this scene (**TransformGroup**) to the **Switch**.

The two missing pieces in our game are the navigable shape and the target (destination) shape. Lines 170–189 create a shiny red **Sphere** as the shape that the user navigates to the target shape. Lines 192–193 call method **createAppearance** (lines 251–261) to set this shape's **Appearance**. This method takes as an argument a **Color3f** object and initializes an **Appearance** object based on a **Material** object that uses the **Color3f** object. Lines 174–175 instantiate the navigable shape as a **Sphere**. Lines 179–182 enable this **Sphere** to collide with the other **Primitive**s in the scene. Lines 185–186 call method **createTransform** to create a **TransformGroup** to translate the **Sphere**'s starting position to the bottom-right corner of the scene. Lines 188–189 add the **Sphere** to this **TransformGroup**, then add the **TransformGroup** to the **gameBranch-Group**. Lines 192–216 create the game's target shape: a **Sphere** that contains an image texture. Lines 196–200 load an image in a **Texture** object, then create an **Appearance** object with this **Texture** object. Lines 203–205 instantiate the target **Sphere**, and line 208 ensures that the **Sphere** cannot collide with the other **Primitive**s in the game. We discuss later how the user-navigated shape interacts with the target **Sphere** (i.e., how the user-navigated shape determines that it has reached its goal). Line 214 calls method **createTransform** to create a **TransformGroup** that places the target **Sphere** in the upper-right corner of the scene. Line 215 adds the **Sphere** to this **Transform-Group**, and line 216 adds the **TransformGroup** to the **gameBranchGroup**.

We designed the game so the user can control the game difficulty. Using a **JSlider** in class **ControlPanel**, the user can specify the number of obstacles in the game. Method **switchScene** (lines 545–558) accepts an **int** argument that represents the number of shapes to display. Lines 548–552 create a **BitMask** from the **int** argument, then lines 555–556 renders each shape associated with the **BitMask**.

The last step in creating **Java3DWorld1** involves implementing a set of custom behaviors—that is, collision detection, navigation and goal detection. Lines 219–231 create these three behaviors. Class **Collide** enables shapes to detect collision, class **Navigator** enables the user (using the keyboard) to navigate the shiny red **Sphere** through the scene and class **GoalDetector** helps determine when this **Sphere** has reached the target **Sphere**. We discuss each class in detail momentarily. We add these behaviors to the **sceneBranchGraph**. Line 244 compiles **sceneBranchGraph** to create the displayable 3D scene.

Custom Behaviors

The previous section demonstrated **Interpolator**s—a set of **Behavior** subclasses that specify certain animation characteristics. Developers often need more specialized behaviors for 3D applications (e.g., collision detection, navigation and position checking). The Java 3D API provides the abstract **Behavior** class to create these custom behaviors. A **Behavior** object has an associated *behavior scheduler* responsible for registering *wake-up conditions*—criteria that determines when the behavior scheduler should trigger a behavior. The behavior scheduler is a Java 3D subsystem that shields developers from implementation details. The behavior scheduler registers the wake-up conditions and handles the logic for when these conditions are satisfied. All classes that extend **Behavior** must implement methods **initialize** and **processStimulus**. Method **initialize** registers a set of wake-up conditions with the behavior scheduler. Method **process-Stimulus** handles the logic when the wake-up conditions are satisfied. The developer must implement method **processStimulus**, although typically, **processStimulus** determines the wake-up conditions that caused the event, handle the event (e.g., modify the scene-graph, etc.) and then reregister the wake-up conditions with the behavior scheduler.

The application in this section demonstrates three types of custom behavior: *collision detection*, *navigation* and *position checking*. We begin with the collision-detection behavior.

Collision detection determines when a shape's bounding volume—the volume enclosing either a shape or the bounds of a shape—intersects another. Class **Collide** (Fig. 4.24), which extends superclass **Behavior**, implements collision-detection behavior for our Java 3D application. In Java 3D, shapes are either *armed nodes* or *triggering nodes*. A collision occurs when an armed node's bounding volume intersects a triggering node's bounding volume. Line 21 declares the armed node for collision detection. Line 24 declares the **WakeupCondition** object for our **Behavior** class. A Java 3D **Behavior** object passes the **WakeupCondition** to the behavior scheduler. When the **WakeupCondition** is satisfied (i.e., upon collision), the behavior scheduler returns an enumeration of the **WakeupCriterion** that triggered the behavior. Line 26 declares the **Switch** that contains scenes for the **SimpleUniverse** to display. Line 27 declares a reference to the Java 3D **SimpleUniverse** for displaying scenes in the **Switch**.

The **Collide** constructor (lines 33–52) takes a **SimpleUniverse**, a **Node** and a **Switch** as arguments. The reference to the **SimpleUniverse** adjusts the **ViewPlatform** when displaying different scenes in the **Switch**. The **Node** is the arming node for the collision-detection behavior. Lines 41–43 initialize **WakeupOnCollisionEntry**— the specific **WakeupCriterion** for our **Behavior** class. Class **WakeupOnCollisionEntry** takes as arguments an arming **Node** and integer **USE_GEOMETRY**, which specifies the **Node**'s geometric volume as the bounding surface for collision detection. Line 46 initializes the array of **WakeupCriterion** for our behavior class. This array contains only one element—**WakeupOnCollisionEntry**. Line 50 initializes the **WakeupCondition** as a **WakeupOr** that contains the **WakeupCriterion**. The objects in **WakeupOr** generate events when a **WakeupCriterion** is satisfied (when a collision occurs). Method **initialize** (lines 55–59) registers the **WakeupCondition** with the behavior scheduler by calling method **wakeupOn** of superclass **Behavior**. Method **wakeupOn** takes as an argument the **WakeupCondition** object, which registers with the behavior scheduler.

Upon collision, the behavior scheduler calls method **processStimulus** (lines 62–81), passing as an argument an **Enumeration** of the **WakeupCriterion**s that triggered the event. Lines 65–79 handle each **WakeupCriterion** in the **Enumeration**. Line 72 handles only those **WakeupCriterion**s that are **WakeupOnCollisionEntry** events. Line 73 invokes method **processCollision** (lines 85–106) for those **WakeupCriterion**s that satisfy this condition. Line 77 reregisters the **WakeupCriterion** with the behavior scheduler.

Method **processCollision** handles the logic in response to the collision. In this application, a collision implies that the armed node (i.e., the user-navigated shape) has collided with an obstacle—the user then loses the game. Lines 87–100 set the translation component of the **ViewPlatform**'s **Transform3D**—the camera shifts back to expand the view. Line 104 switches to the scene associated with a collision—rotating 3D text that reads "**You Lose.**" Figure 4.24 demonstrates the 3D application display after the user-navigated shape collides with an obstacle.

```
1   // Class Collide implements collision-detection behavior
2   // for a Java 3D application. Collide switches scenes
3   // when the armed object collides with another object.
4   package com.deitel.advjhtp1.java3dgame;
5
6   // Core Java packages
7   import java.lang.*;
8   import java.util.*;
9
10  // Java extension packages
11  import javax.media.j3d.*;
12  import javax.vecmath.*;
13
14  // Java 3D utility packages
15  import com.sun.j3d.utils.geometry.*;
16  import com.sun.j3d.utils.universe.*;
17
18  public class Collide extends Behavior {
19
20     // armed node generates WakeupOnCollisionEntry upon collision
21     private Node armingNode;
22
23     // specifies to what WakeupEvents to react
24     private WakeupCondition wakeupCondition;
25
26     private Switch switchScene; // Switch group contains 3D scenes
27     private SimpleUniverse simpleUniverse;
28
29     // index of scene to switch to upon collision
30     private static final int LOSER_SCENE = 1;
31
32     // constructor method initializes members
33     public Collide( SimpleUniverse universe, Node node,
34        Switch tempSwitch )
35     {
36        armingNode = node;
37        switchScene = tempSwitch;
38        simpleUniverse = universe;
39
40        // create WakeupOnCollisionEntry
41        WakeupOnCollisionEntry wakeupEvent =
42           new WakeupOnCollisionEntry( armingNode,
43           WakeupOnCollisionEntry.USE_GEOMETRY );
```

Fig. 4.24   Implementing collision detection in a Java 3D application (part 1 of 3).

```
44
45          // set of WakeupEvents to which Behavior reponds
46          WakeupCriterion[] wakeupCriteria = { wakeupEvent };
47
48          // Behavior responds when any WakeupEvent in
49          // WakeupCriterion occurs
50          wakeupCondition = new WakeupOr( wakeupCriteria );
51
52       } // end constructor
53
54       // initialize Behavior's wakeup conditions
55       public void initialize()
56       {
57          // register WakeupCriterion to respond to collision events
58          wakeupOn( wakeupCondition );
59       }
60
61       // handle WakeupEvents
62       public void processStimulus( Enumeration detected )
63       {
64          // loop to handle events
65          while( detected.hasMoreElements() ) {
66
67             // get next sequential element
68             WakeupCriterion criterion =
69                ( WakeupCriterion ) detected.nextElement();
70
71             // process event if WakeupOnCollisionEntry
72             if ( criterion instanceof WakeupOnCollisionEntry ) {
73                processCollision();
74
75                // re-register WakeupCriterion to respond to new
76                // WakeonOnCollisionEntry event
77                wakeupOn( wakeupCondition );
78             }
79          }
80
81       } // end method processStimulus
82
83       // process collision by moving camera view back and
84       // switching scenes in Switch group
85       private void processCollision()
86       {
87          Transform3D shiftViewBack = new Transform3D();
88
89          // set Transform3D's Translation
90          shiftViewBack.setTranslation(
91             new Vector3f( 0.0f, 0.0f, 8.0f ) );
92
93          // set Transform3D that determines View
94          ViewingPlatform viewPlatform =
95                         simpleUniverse.getViewingPlatform();
96
```

Fig. 4.24   Implementing collision detection in a Java 3D application (part 2 of 3).

```
97              TransformGroup platformTransform =
98                      viewPlatform.getViewPlatformTransform();
99
100         platformTransform.setTransform( shiftViewBack );
101
102
103         // render scene in Switch group
104         switchScene.setWhichChild( LOSER_SCENE );
105
106     } // end method processCollision
107 }
```

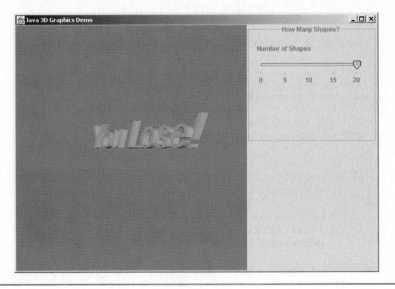

Fig. 4.24 Implementing collision detection in a Java 3D application (part 3 of 3).

We provide class **Navigator** (Fig. 4.25) so the user can navigate the shape in our 3D scene. Class **Navigator** responds to certain key presses by translating a **Node** in a 3D scene. **Navigator** moves the **Node** by updating that **Node**'s **TransformGroup**. Line 22 declares the **TransformGroup**. Lines 25–30 declare **float** constants that represent the amount by which **Navigator** translates the shape upon each keypress. Line 33 declares the **WakeupCondition** for activating the navigational behavior.

```
1  // Class Navigator is a subclass of Behavior that implements a
2  // keyboard translation navigator. Navigator responds to certain
3  // key presses by translating an object in a 3D scene.
4  package com.deitel.advjhtp1.java3dgame;
5
6  // Core Java packages
7  import java.awt.*;
8  import java.awt.event.*;
9  import java.util.*;
```

Fig. 4.25 Behavior that enables the user to navigate a 3D shape (part 1 of 4).

```
10
11   // Java extension packages
12   import javax.media.j3d.*;
13   import javax.vecmath.*;
14
15   // Java 3D utility packages
16   import com.sun.j3d.utils.universe.*;
17
18   public class Navigator extends Behavior {
19
20      // TransformGroup associated with object controlled
21      // by keyboard navigator
22      private TransformGroup objectTransform;
23
24      // translation amounts
25      private static final float LEFT = -0.02f;
26      private static final float RIGHT = 0.02f;
27      private static final float UP = 0.02f;
28      private static final float DOWN = -0.02f;
29      private static final float FORWARD = 0.02f;
30      private static final float BACKWARD = -0.02f;
31
32      // waking conditions for Behavior
33      private WakeupCondition wakeupCondition;
34
35      // constructor method
36      public Navigator( TransformGroup transform )
37      {
38         objectTransform = transform;
39
40         // initialize WakeupOnAWTEvent to repond to
41         // AWT KeyEvent.KEY_PRESSED events
42         WakeupOnAWTEvent wakeupEvent =
43            new WakeupOnAWTEvent( KeyEvent.KEY_PRESSED );
44
45         // set of WakeupEvents to which Behavior responds
46         WakeupCriterion[] wakeupCriteria = { wakeupEvent };
47
48         // Behavior responds when WakeupEvent in the
49         // WakeupCriterion occurs
50         wakeupCondition = new WakeupOr( wakeupCriteria );
51
52      } // end constructor
53
54      // initialize Behavior's wakeup conditions
55      public void initialize()
56      {
57         // register WakeupCriterion to generate WakeupEvents
58         // when AWT events occur
59         wakeupOn( wakeupCondition );
60      }
61
```

Fig. 4.25 Behavior that enables the user to navigate a 3D shape (part 2 of 4).

```
62    // handle WakeupEvents
63    public void processStimulus( Enumeration detected )
64    {
65       // loop to handle events
66       while ( detected.hasMoreElements() ) {
67
68          // get next WakeupCriterion
69          WakeupCriterion wakeupCriterion =
70             ( WakeupCriterion ) detected.nextElement();
71
72          // handle WakeupCriterion if WakeupOnAWTEvent
73          if ( wakeupCriterion instanceof WakeupOnAWTEvent ) {
74             WakeupOnAWTEvent awtEvent =
75                (WakeupOnAWTEvent) wakeupCriterion;
76             AWTEvent[] events = awtEvent.getAWTEvent();
77
78             // invoke method moveObject with AWTEvent
79             moveShape( events );
80          }
81       }
82
83       // re-register wakeupCondition to respond to next key press
84       wakeupOn( wakeupCondition );
85
86    } // end method processStimulus
87
88    // handle AWT KeyEvents by translating an object in 3D scene
89    private void moveShape( AWTEvent[] awtEvents )
90    {
91       // handle all events in AWTEvent array
92       for ( int x = 0; x < awtEvents.length; x++)
93       {
94          // handle if AWTEvent is KeyEvent
95          if ( awtEvents[ x ] instanceof KeyEvent ) {
96
97             // get cooresponding KeyEvent
98             KeyEvent keyEvent = ( KeyEvent ) awtEvents[ x ];
99
100            // respond only if KeyEvent is of type KEY_PRESSED
101            if ( keyEvent.getID() == KeyEvent.KEY_PRESSED ) {
102
103               // get KeyCode associated with KeyEvent
104               int keyCode = keyEvent.getKeyCode();
105
106               Transform3D transform3D = new Transform3D();
107
108               // get Transform3D from TransformGroup of
109               // navigable object
110               objectTransform.getTransform( transform3D );
111
112               Vector3f translateVector = new Vector3f();
113
```

Fig. 4.25   Behavior that enables the user to navigate a 3D shape (part 3 of 4).

```
114                      // retrieve translation vector associated with
115                      // Transform3D
116                      transform3D.get( translateVector );
117
118                      // update x, y, or z component of translation
119                      // vector based on keypress
120                      switch ( keyCode ) {
121
122                         case KeyEvent.VK_A:  // move left
123                            translateVector.x += LEFT;
124                            break;
125
126                         case KeyEvent.VK_D: // move right
127                            translateVector.x += RIGHT;
128                            break;
129
130                         case KeyEvent.VK_W: // move up
131                            translateVector.y += UP;
132                            break;
133
134                         case KeyEvent.VK_S: // move down
135                            translateVector.y += DOWN;
136                            break;
137
138                         case KeyEvent.VK_UP: // move backwards
139                            translateVector.z += BACKWARD;
140                            break;
141
142                         case KeyEvent.VK_DOWN: // move forwards
143                            translateVector.z += FORWARD;
144                            break;
145
146                      } // end switch
147
148                      // set translational component of Transform3D
149                      // with updated translation Vector3f
150                      transform3D.setTranslation( translateVector );
151
152                      // set TransformGroup's Transform3D
153                      objectTransform.setTransform( transform3D );
154
155                   } // end if KeyEvent.KEY_PRESSED
156                }
157
158             } // end for loop that handles key presses
159
160       } // end method moveShape
161 }
```

Fig. 4.25   Behavior that enables the user to navigate a 3D shape (part 4 of 4).

The **Navigator** constructor (lines 36–52) accepts as an argument a **Transform-Group** that contains the navigable 3D shape. Lines 42–43 initialize a **WakeupOnAWT-Event** that triggers a **Behavior** upon an **AWTEvent** (such as a keypress). The

WakeupOnAWTEvent constructor takes as an argument the specific **AWTEvent** satisfies the wake-up conditions. In this case, **KeyEvent.KEY_PRESSED** events activate **Behavior**. Line 46 creates the **WakeupCriterion**s from the **WakeupOnAWTEvent**. Line 50 creates the **WakeupOr** that contains the **WakeupCriterion**s.

Method **initialize** (lines 55–60) registers the **WakeupOr** with the behavior scheduler by passing the **WakeupOr** to method **wakeupOn** of superclass **Behavior**. Method **processStimulus** (lines 63–86) handles the logic for the triggered **Behavior** (i.e., a keypress). This method takes as an argument an **Enumeration** of the **WakeupCriterion** objects associated with the **Behavior**. Lines 69–70 retrieve each **WakeupCriterion** from the **Enumeration**. If the **WakeupCriterion** is a **WakeupOnAWTEvent**, line 76 invokes method **getAWTEvent** of class **WakeupOnAWTEvent**, which returns the array of **AWTEvent**s that triggered the **Behavior**. Line 79 passes this array to method **moveShape** (lines 89–160), which translates the user-navigated shape, depending on which key the user pressed. Lines 95–101 test if each **AWTEvent** in the array is associated with a key press—line 104 determines the specific key pressed. Lines 106–116 declare a **Transform3D** and a **Vector3f** for updating the 3D shape's position. The **Vector3f** holds the coordinates that represent the *translational component* of the 3D shape's **Transform3D**. The translational component of a 3D shape specifies the shape's position on the *x*, *y* and *z*-axis. Lines 120–146 use a **switch** statement to update the 3D shape's position according to the key the user pressed. Figure 4.26 lists the keys and corresponding translations that are valid for **Navigator**. The **Vector3f**'s *x*-component corresponds to the left and right position (*X*-axis) of a shape. The **Vector3f**'s *y*-component corresponds to the up and down position (*Y*-axis) of a shape. The **Vector3f**'s *z*-component corresponds to the back and forward position (*Z*-axis) of a shape. The **switch** statement modifies the appropriate component of the **Vector3f**. Lines 150–153 call method **setTranslation** of class **Transform3D** and method **setTransform** of class **TransformGroup** to make the translation. The Java 3D engine then updates the 3D scene with the modified **TransformGroup** information.

We have implemented **Behavior** for detecting **Node** collision (which causes the user to lose the game) and the **Behavior** for enabling the user to navigate the scene. We now implement class **GoalDetector** (Fig. 4.27)—the **Behavior** for checking the position of a 3D shape (which allows the user to win the game). Line 25 declares the **TransformGroup** for the 3D-shape's position to check. Line 27 declares a **Switch** of scenes to display in the **SimpleUniverse**. The **SimpleUniverse** reference (line 28) adjusts the **ViewPlatform** when displaying different scenes in the **Switch**. We implement the target shape as a sphere with coordinates **goalX**, **goalY** and **goalZ** (line 30) and radius **sphereRadius** (line 33). The user wins the game when the user-navigated shape reaches the target sphere. Line 36 declares the **WakeupCondition** for the position-checking behavior.

Key	Translation
A	move left
D	move right

Fig. 4.26   Keys for navigating the 3D scene in **Navigator** (part 1 of 2).

Key	Translation
W	move up
S	move down
Up Arrow	move forward
Down Arrow	move backward

Fig. 4.26   Keys for navigating the 3D scene in **Navigator** (part 2 of 2).

```
1   // Class GoalDetector defines a position-checking behavior that
2   // checks to see if the position of a Node is equal to the target
3   // position. If the positions are equal, the game is over and
4   // a Java 3D Switch displays a different scene.
5   package com.deitel.advjhtp1.java3dgame;
6
7   // Core Java packages
8   import java.awt.*;
9   import java.awt.event.*;
10  import java.util.*;
11
12  // Java extension packages
13  import javax.media.j3d.*;
14  import javax.vecmath.*;
15
16  // Java 3D utility packages
17  import com.sun.j3d.utils.universe.*;
18
19  public class GoalDetector extends Behavior {
20
21      // index of scene to display if goal detected
22      private static final int WINNER_SCENE = 2;
23
24      // TransformGroup associated with object
25      private TransformGroup objectTransform;
26
27      private Switch switchScene; // Switch group that contains scenes
28      private SimpleUniverse simpleUniverse;
29
30      private float goalX, goalY, goalZ; // goal coordinates
31
32      // radius of sphere at goal coordinates
33      private float sphereRadius;
34
35      // Behavior's waking conditions
36      private WakeupCondition wakeupCondition;
37
```

Fig. 4.27   Implementing a position-checking **Behavior** (part 1 of 5).

```
38     // constructor method initializes members
39     // and creates WakeupCriterion
40     public GoalDetector( SimpleUniverse universe,
41        TransformGroup transform, Switch switchGroup,
42        Vector3f goalVector, float radius )
43     {
44        objectTransform = transform;
45        switchScene = switchGroup;
46        simpleUniverse = universe;
47
48        // set goal coordinates to goalVector coordinates
49        goalX = goalVector.x;
50        goalY = goalVector.y;
51        goalZ = goalVector.z;
52
53        // set radius of sphere at goal coordinates
54        sphereRadius = radius;
55
56        // initialize WakeupOnAWTEvent to respond to
57        // AWT KeyEvent.KEY_PRESSED events
58        WakeupOnAWTEvent wakeupEvent =
59           new WakeupOnAWTEvent( KeyEvent.KEY_PRESSED );
60
61        // set of WakeupEvents to which Behavior responds
62        WakeupCriterion[] wakeupArray = { wakeupEvent };
63
64        // Behavior responds when WakeupEvent in
65        // WakeupCriterion occurs
66        wakeupCondition = new WakeupOr( wakeupArray );
67
68     } // end constructor method
69
70     // register Behavior's wakeup conditions
71     public void initialize()
72     {
73        // register WakeupCriterion to respond to AWTEvents
74        wakeupOn( wakeupCondition );
75     }
76
77     // handle WakeupEvents
78     public void processStimulus( Enumeration detected )
79     {
80        // loop to handle events
81        while ( detected.hasMoreElements() ) {
82
83           // get next sequential WakeupCriterion
84           WakeupCriterion wakeupCriterion =
85              ( WakeupCriterion ) detected.nextElement();
86
87           // handle if WakeupOnAWTEvent
88           if ( wakeupCriterion instanceof WakeupOnAWTEvent ) {
89
```

Fig. 4.27   Implementing a position-checking **Behavior** (part 2 of 5).

```
90              // ensure WakeupOnAWTEvent is KeyEvent.KEY_PRESSED
91              WakeupOnAWTEvent awtEvent =
92                 ( WakeupOnAWTEvent ) wakeupCriterion;
93              AWTEvent[] event = awtEvent.getAWTEvent();
94
95              // check object position
96              checkPosition( event );
97
98              // re-register WakeupCriterion to respond to next
99              // key press
100             wakeupOn( wakeupCondition );
101          }
102       }
103
104    } // end method processStimulus
105
106    // check position of object in objectTransform TransformGroup
107    private void checkPosition( AWTEvent[] awtEvents )
108    {
109       Vector3f translate = new Vector3f();
110       Transform3D transform3d = new Transform3D();
111
112       // get Transform3D associated with objectTransform
113       objectTransform.getTransform( transform3d );
114
115       // get Transform3D's translation vector
116       transform3d.get( translate );
117
118       // handle all key presses in awtEvents
119       for ( int x = 0; x < awtEvents.length; x++ ) {
120
121          // handle if AWTEvent is KeyEvent
122          if ( awtEvents[ x ] instanceof KeyEvent ) {
123             KeyEvent keyEvent = (KeyEvent) awtEvents[ x ];
124
125             // handle if KeyEvent.KEY_PRESSED
126             if ( keyEvent.getID() == KeyEvent.KEY_PRESSED ) {
127
128                // if object position == goal coordinates
129                if ( atGoal( translate ) ) {
130                   Transform3D shiftBack = new Transform3D();
131
132                   // set translation to 8.0 on +z-axis
133                   shiftBack.setTranslation(
134                      new Vector3f( 0.0f, 0.0f, 8.0f ) );
135
136                   // set Transform3D that determines view
137                   // in SimpleUniverse
138                   ViewingPlatform viewPlatform =
139                      simpleUniverse.getViewingPlatform();
140
141                   TransformGroup platformTransform =
142                      viewPlatform.getViewPlatformTransform();
```

Fig. 4.27   Implementing a position-checking **Behavior** (part 3 of 5).

```
143
144                     platformTransform.setTransform( shiftBack );
145
146                     // render winner scene in SimpleUniverse
147                     switchScene.setWhichChild( WINNER_SCENE );
148                 }
149             }
150
151         } // end if KeyEvent
152
153     } // end for loop that handles key presses
154
155 } // end method checkPosition
156
157 // helper method returns true if current position is within
158 // goal boundry
159 private boolean atGoal( Vector3f currentPosition )
160 {
161     // calculate difference between current location and goal
162     float x = Math.abs( currentPosition.x - goalX );
163     float y = Math.abs( currentPosition.y - goalY );
164     float z = Math.abs( currentPosition.z - goalZ );
165
166     // return true if current position within sphereRadius of
167     // goal coordinates
168     return ( ( x < sphereRadius ) && ( y < sphereRadius ) &&
169         ( z < sphereRadius ) );
170 }
171 }
```

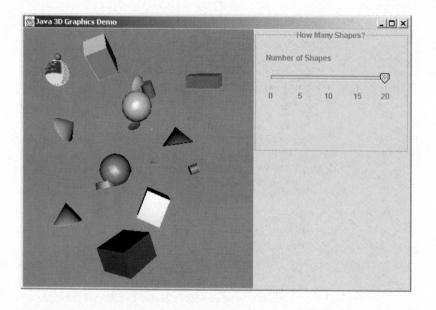

Fig. 4.27 Implementing a position-checking **Behavior** (part 4 of 5).

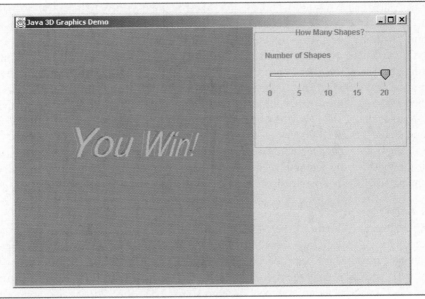

Fig. 4.27 Implementing a position-checking **Behavior** (part 5 of 5).

The constructor method (lines 40–68) takes five arguments. The first three arguments are the **SimpleUniverse**, **TransformGroup** and **Switch**. The fourth argument is a **Vector3f** that contains the target shape's location. Lines 49–51 set the target-point coordinates by extracting the *x*, *y* and *z* coordinates from the **Vector3f**. The final argument is the target-sphere radius. Lines 58–59 create a **WakeupOnAWTEvent** that responds when the user presses a key. **GoalDetector** then checks the user-navigated shape's position to see if that shape has reached the target sphere. Line 62 creates a **WakeupCriterion** from the **WakeupOnAWTEvent**, and line 66 creates a **WakeupOr** from the **WakeupCriterion**. Method **initialize** (lines 71–75) registers the **WakeupOr** with the behavior scheduler by calling method **wakeupOn** of superclass **Behavior**.

Method **processStimulus** (lines 78–104) handles the logic for the triggered **Behavior**. This method takes as an argument an **Enumeration** of the **WakeupCriterion**s that generated the behavioral event. Lines 84–85 retrieve each **WakeupCriterion** from the **Enumeration**. If the **WakeupCriterion** is a **WakeupOnAWTEvent**, line 93 invokes method **getAWTEvent** of class **WakeupOnAWTEvent**, which returns the array of the **AWTEvent**s that triggered the **Behavior**. Line 96 passes this array to method **checkPostion** (lines 107–155), which implements the position-checking algorithm.

Method **checkPosition** (lines 107–155) checks the position of the 3D shape. This method determines the 3D shape's position by checking the **Vector3f**, which represents that shape's translational component. Line 113 calls method **getTransform** of class **TransformGroup** to retrieve the **Transform3D** associated with the **TransformGroup**. Line 116 calls method **get** of class **Transform3D**, which retrieves the **Vector3f** that represents the translational component of the 3D shape. Lines 119–126 check if each **AWTEvent** in the array is a **KeyEvent.KEY_PRESSED** event—line 129 then calls method **atGoal**, which returns a **boolean** variable that represents whether the user-navigated shape has reached the target shape. Method **atGoal** (lines 159–170) takes as an argument the **Vector3f** that contains the coordinates of the user-navigated shape's current position. Lines 162–164 determine the absolute difference between the target shape's coordinates (**goalX**, **goalY** and **goalZ**) and the user-navigated shape's current coordinates. Lines 168–169 return **true** if the absolute difference for each coordinate is within the **sphereRadius**, indicating that the shape has reached the target sphere. If method **atGoal** returns **true**, the user has won the game. Lines 130–144 set the translation component of the **ViewPlatform**'s **Transform3D**; the camera shifts back to expand the view. Line 147 switches to the winning scene: rotating 3D text that reads "**You Win.**" Line 147 invokes method **setWhichChild** of class **Switch** passing as an argument the index of the winning scene. Figure 4.27 illustrates the game both immediately before and after the navigable object has reached the target shape.

User Interface

Using the **ControlPanel1** (Fig. 4.21), the user can specify the number of flying obstacles to control the game difficulty. Line 23 declares the **JSlider** that the player uses to specify the number of obstacles. Line 24 declares a **Java3DWorld1** reference through which **ControlPanel1** can set the user-specified number. The **ControlPanel1** constructor (lines 27–75) accepts as an argument a **Java3DWorld1**—line 29 sets this argument as **ControlPanel1**'s **Java3DWorld1** reference. Lines 44–50 create a **JSlider** that assumes any integer value from 1 to 20, inclusive. Lines 53–62 create a **ChangeListener** for the **JSlider**. When the player uses this **JSlider**, method **stateChanged** (lines 56–60) passes the number of obstacles to method **switchScene** of **Java3DWorld1**. The display then reveals a new scene with the specified number of obstacles.

```
1   // ControlPanel1.java
2   // ControlPanel1 is a JPanel that contains Swing controls
3   // for manipulating a Java3DWorld1.
4   package com.deitel.advjhtp1.java3dgame;
5
6   // Java core packages
7   import java.awt.*;
8   import java.awt.event.*;
9
10  // Java extension packages
11  import javax.swing.*;
12  import javax.swing.border.*;
13  import javax.swing.event.*;
14
15  public class ControlPanel1 extends JPanel {
16
17     private static final int CONTAINER_WIDTH = 250;
18     private static final int CONTAINER_HEIGHT = 150;
19
20     private static final int NUMBER_OF_SHAPES = 20;
21
22     // JSliders control lighting color
23     private JSlider numberSlider;
```

Fig. 4.28   Implementing Swing controls for the **Java3DWorld1** (part 1 of 3).

```
24        private Java3DWorld1 java3DWorld1;
25
26        // ControlPanel constructor
27        public ControlPanel1( Java3DWorld1 tempJ3DWorld )
28        {
29           java3DWorld1 = tempJ3DWorld;
30
31           // assemble lighting color control panel
32           JPanel colorPanel = new JPanel(
33              new FlowLayout( FlowLayout.LEFT, 15, 15 ) );
34
35           TitledBorder colorBorder =
36              new TitledBorder( "How Many Shapes?" );
37
38           colorBorder.setTitleJustification( TitledBorder.CENTER );
39           colorPanel.setBorder( colorBorder );
40
41           JLabel numberLabel = new JLabel( "Number of Shapes" );
42
43           // create JSlider for adjusting number of flying shapes
44           numberSlider = new JSlider(
45              SwingConstants.HORIZONTAL, 1, NUMBER_OF_SHAPES, 1 );
46
47           numberSlider.setMajorTickSpacing( 4 );
48           numberSlider.setPaintTicks( true );
49           numberSlider.setPaintTrack( true );
50           numberSlider.setPaintLabels( true );
51
52           // create ChangeListener for JSliders
53           ChangeListener slideListener = new ChangeListener() {
54
55              // invoked when slider has been accessed
56              public void stateChanged( ChangeEvent event )
57              {
58                 java3DWorld1.switchScene( numberSlider.getValue(),
59                    NUMBER_OF_SHAPES );
60              }
61
62           }; // end anonymous inner class
63
64           // add listener to sliders
65           numberSlider.addChangeListener( slideListener );
66
67           // add lighting color control components to colorPanel
68           colorPanel.add( numberLabel );
69           colorPanel.add( numberSlider );
70           add( colorPanel );
71
72           // set GridLayout
73           setLayout( new GridLayout( 2, 1, 0, 20 ) );
74
75        } // end ControlPanel1 constructor method
76
```

Fig. 4.28   Implementing Swing controls for the **Java3DWorld1** (part 2 of 3).

```
77        // return preferred dimensions of container
78        public Dimension getPreferredSize()
79        {
80           return new Dimension( CONTAINER_WIDTH, CONTAINER_HEIGHT );
81        }
82
83        // return minimum size of container
84        public Dimension getMinimumSize()
85        {
86           return getPreferredSize();
87        }
88     }
```

Fig. 4.28 Implementing Swing controls for the **Java3DWorld1** (part 3 of 3).

This concludes our discussion of the Java 3D API. In this section, we presented a brief overview of Java 3D graphics programming. We have explained how the performance, scalability and simplicity of Java 3D make it an excellent choice for developers to incorporate 3D graphics into applications. We presented two applications that demonstrated Java 3D geometry, textures, lighting and behaviors.

We have discussed several of Java's graphics capabilities. We began with a brief introduction to fundamental graphics topics, including coordinate systems and graphics contexts. We then discussed several Java 2D capabilities, such as controlling how to fill shapes with colors and patterns. We also introduced how to blur, invert, sharpen and change the color of an image using Java 2D's image-processing capabilities. The second half of our graphics discussion presented the Java 3D API. Using the Java 3D utility classes, we built an application that allows the user to change properties of a Java 3D scene, including manipulating (rotate, scale and translate) 3D objects with a mouse and changing a scene's lighting. In Chapter 5, we use Java 2D in the Deitel drawing application. We also introduce design patterns—proven strategies for creating reusable and extensible software—and use them to build this program.

SUMMARY

- A coordinate system is a scheme for identifying every point on the screen.
- The upper-left corner of a GUI component has the coordinates (0, 0).
- A graphics context enables drawing on the screen. A **Graphics** object manages a graphics context by controlling how information is drawn.
- **Graphics** objects contain methods for drawing, font manipulation, color manipulation, etc.
- Method **paint** is called in response to an event such as uncovering a window.
- Method **repaint** requests a call to method **update** of class **Component** as soon as possible to clear the **Component**'s background of any previous drawing. Method **update** then calls **paint** directly.
- The Swing painting mechanism calls method **paintComponent** of class **JComponent** when the contents of the **JComponent** should be painted.
- The Java 2D provides advanced two-dimensional graphics capabilities for processing line art, text and images.
- Class **java.awt.Graphics2D** enables drawing with the Java 2D API.

- To access the **Graphics2D** capabilities, we cast the **Graphics** reference passed to **paint** to a **Graphics2D** reference.

- There are seven **Graphics2D** attributes that determine how graphics primitives are rendered—clipping, compositing, font, paint, rendering hints, stroke and transforms.

- Method **setPaint** of class **Graphics2D** sets the **Paint** object that determines the color for the shape to display. A **Paint** object is an object of any class that implements interface **java.awt.Paint**. The **Paint** object can be a **Color** or an instance of the Java 2D API's **GradientPaint**, **SystemColor** or **TexturePaint** classes.

- Class **GradientPaint** paints a shape in gradually changing colors—known as a gradient.

- Method **fill** of class **Graphics2D** draws a filled **Shape** object. The **Shape** object is an instance of any class that implements interface **Shape**.

- A general path is a shape constructed from lines and complex curves represented with an object of class **GeneralPath** (package **java.awt.geom**).

- Method **moveTo** of class **GeneralPath** specifies the first point in a general path. Method **lineTo** of class **GeneralPath** draws a line to the next point in the general path. Each new call to **lineTo** draws a line from the previous point to the current point. Method **closePath** of class **GeneralPath** draws a line from the last point to the point specified in the last call to **moveTo**.

- Method **translate** of class **Graphics2D** moves the drawing to a new location. All drawing operations now use that location as (0, 0).

- Image processing is the manipulation of digital images by applying filters.

- There are three main types of image-processing filters. Compression filters reduce a digital image's memory usage. Measurement filters collect data from digital images. Enhancement filters appropriate and interpolate missing parts of corrupted images from the existing information.

- A **BufferedImage** separates image data into a **Raster** and a **ColorModel**. A **Raster** organizes and stores the numerical data that determine a pixel's color. The **ColorModel** is an interpreter that takes the sample values in the **Raster** and converts them to different colors depending on color scale the image.

- Java 2D image-processing filters operate on objects of class **BufferedImage**.

- Interfaces **BufferedImageOp** and **RasterOp** serve as the base classes for Java 2D image filters. A **BufferedImageOp** processes a **BufferedImage**, while a **RasterOp** only processes the **Raster** associated with a **BufferedImage**.

- Method **filter** takes as arguments a source image and a destination image. The source image is filtered to produce the destination image.

- A **LookupOp** is an array indexed by source pixel color values that contains destination pixel color values.

- A sharpening filter detects edges by looking for differences in neighboring pixel sample values and enhances the edge by enlarging the difference between the sample values and is created with a **ConvolveOp**.

- A **ConvolveOp** combines the colors of a source pixel and its surrounding neighbors to determine the color of the corresponding destination pixel.

- A **Kernel** is a 2D array that specifies how a **ConvolveOp** filter should combine neighboring pixel values.

- Edge hints instruct the filter on how to alter pixels at the perimeter of the image. **EDGE_NO_OP** instructs the filter to copy the pixels at the source perimeter directly to the destination image without modification. **EDGE_ZERO_FILL** instructs the filter to fill the pixels at the perimeter of the destination with the value **0**.

- A blurring filter averages each pixel value with that of its eight neighboring pixels, smoothing distinct edges and is created using a **ConvolveOp**.
- Each color band in a **TYPE_INT_RGB BufferedImage** is defined by three coefficients that represent the R, G and B components in the band.
- We can change the colors in an image by altering the values of the R, G and B coefficients in a color band using a **BandCombineOp**. A **BandCombineOp** operates on the color bands of a **Raster**.
- The Java 3D API requires that you have either OpenGL or Direct3D installed on your computer. The Java 3D API also requires you to install the appropriate Java extension and utility packages found at **java.sun.com/products/java-media/3D/download.html**.
- The root node of the Java 3D scene is a **VirtualUniverse** that has a coordinate-system, which describes the location of scene graphs.
- A scene graph is a tree-like structure that contains nodes, which describe all attributes of the 3D environment. Each scene graph attaches to the **VirtualUniverse** at a specified point in the **VirtualUniverse's** coordinate-system.
- Class **Locale** is the root node in a scene graph, which contains the attachment coordinate for the **VirtualUniverse** and a number of branch graphs.
- There are two types of branch graphs—content-branch graphs and view-branch graphs. View-branch graphs contain collections of objects that specify the perspective, position, orientation and scale of 3D scenes. Content-branch graphs describe the geometry, lighting, textures, fog, sound and behaviors in the 3D scenes.
- Class **SceneGraphObject** is the base class for all objects in a Java 3D branch graph. **SceneGraphObject** has two subclasses—**Node** and **NodeComponent**.
- Class **Group** serves as the general-purpose grouping **Node**.
- **Leaf** subclasses include **Behavior**, **Light** and **Shape3D**.
- **NodeComponent** objects describe the attributes of **Group**s and **Leaf**s.
- **Canvas3D** is a **Canvas** subclass that supports 3D rendering.
- Class **SimpleUniverse** encapsulates all objects in the virtual universe and viewing platform.
- Class **BranchGroup** is the root node of a scene graph.
- Class **TransformGroup** specifies transformations including rotation, scaling and translation.
- To modify an object in a scene in run time, the developer must set that object's capability bits using method **setCapability**.
- All content **Leaf**s in Java 3D are bounded by a volume that defines the space in which the **Leaf**s are rendered.
- Class **Appearance** describes the attributes of the 3D geometry and has associated attribute objects, such as **Material** and **Texture**.
- Class **Material** defines the properties of any object that falls under illumination.
- Class **com.sun.j3d.utils.image.TextureLoader** loads an **Image** for texturing geometry.
- Class **AmbientLight** is a light source that illuminates all shapes evenly within its bounds.
- Class **DirectionalLight** is a light source that travels from a source point to a destination point.
- When a **Light** source is added to a **Group**, all objects in that **Group** are illuminated.
- The **MouseBehavior** classes in utility package **com.sun.j3d.utils.behavior.mouse** help developers integrate mouse interaction into applications.
- Classes **MouseRotate**, **MouseTranslate** and **MouseZoom** allow the user to use a mouse to rotate, translate and scale a 3D shape, respectively.

- Method **compile** of class **BranchGroup** causes the **BranchGroup** and all its children to be compiled.
- A **Switch** group specifies which of its children to render. A **Switch** can render either one child at a time or several children at once.
- **Interpolator**s use **Alpha**s to specify certain characteristics of animation, such as the speed of transformations (e.g., rotation speed), or how fast a shape changes color (e.g., lighting effects).
- **Interpolators** operates in conjunction with a **TransformGroup**: each **Transform-Group** has an associated **Interpolator**. The **Interpolator** describes how to animate shapes in the **TransformGroup**.
- An **Alpha** object generates the time values to the **Interpolator**. **Alpha** objects consist of a series of phases that can be either increasing or decreasing.
- Class **Transform3D** is a two-dimensional array that represents a general transform. Each **Transform3D** has an associated integer type that determines the transformation to represent.
- A **Material**'s ambient color is the **Material**'s color when illuminated by reflected light. A **Material**'s diffuse color is the **Material**'s color when illuminated by some light source.
- The Java 3D **com.sun.j3d.utils.geometry** package provides four types of 3D geometric **Primitive** objects: **Box**, **Cone**, **Cylinder** and **Sphere**.
- Class **Text3D** is a **Geometry** subclass for representing three-dimensional text.
- A **Font3D** object is constructed from a **java.awt.Font** object and a Java 3D **FontExtrusion** object. A **FontExtrusion** describes process of adding a third dimension to the **Font**'s 2D text.
- A **Point3f** specifies x-y-z coordinates in a 3D **SimpleUniverse**.
- The Java 3D API provides the abstract **Behavior** class to create a variety of custom behaviors.
- A **Behavior** object has an associated behavior scheduler responsible for registering wake-up conditions.
- All classes that extend **Behavior** must implement methods **initialize** and **process-Stimulus**.
- Collision detection determines when a shape's bounding volume—the volume enclosing either a shape or the bounds of a shape—intersects another.
- A collision occurs when an armed node's bounding volume intersects a triggering node's bounding volume.
- When a **WakeupCondition** is satisfied, the behavior scheduler calls method **process-Stimulus**, passing as an argument an **Enumeration** of the **WakeupCriterion**s that triggered the event.

TERMINOLOGY

addChild method
alpha values
AmbientLight class
Appearance class
arc angle
Arc2D.Double class
BandCombineOp class
BasicStroke class
Behavior class
bounding rectangle

bounding volume
BoundingBox class
BoundingSphere class
Box class
branch graph
BranchGroup class
BufferedImage class
BufferedImageOp interface
ByteLookUpTable class
Canvas3D class

setNominalViewingTransform method	**TextureLoader** class
setPaint method	**TexturePaint** class
setStroke method	**TransformGroup** class
setTransformGroup method	transforms
Shape interface	translate
SimpleUniverse class	**update** method
Stroke interface	viewing distance
SystemColor class	**ViewingPlatform** class
Texture class	**VirtualUniverse** class
texture mapping	**WriteableRaster** class

SELF-REVIEW EXERCISES

4.1   Fill in the blanks in each of the following statements:
   a) In Java 2D, class _____ defines the fill for a shape such that the fill gradually changes from one color to another.
   b) In Java 2D, an image-processing filter that operates on both a pixel and its neighboring pixels is implemented using class _____.
   c) Class _____ stores pixel sample data in a **BufferedImage**, while class _____ contains instructions for translating the pixel sample to a color.
   d) Rotation, scaling and translation are all examples of _____.
   e) Method _____ of class **DirectionalLight** sets a flag that alerts the compiler that the **DirectionalLight**'s attributes should be writable during execution.
   f) In Java 3D, class _____ contains **NodeComponent**s that describe the attributes of a shape, including **Material** and **Texture**.

4.2   State whether each of the following is *true* or *false*. If *false*, explain why.
   a) The **LookupOp** constructor takes as arguments a **Kernel** and a **RenderingHints** object.
   b) Method **closePath** of class **GeneralPath** to draw a line from the last point to the point specified in the first call to **moveTo**.
   c) The source and destination **Raster** arguments to the **BandCombineOp** constructor can be the same **Raster**s.
   d) In Java 3D, **Behavior**s do not affect objects outside the **Behavior**'s bounding volume.
   e) Class **SimpleUniverse** creates a Java 3D scene that contains a **VirtualUniverse**, **Locale** and view branch graph.
   f) All children in a **BranchGroup** will be affected behaviors defined in **TransformGroup** objects that are part of that **BranchGroup**.

ANSWERS TO SELF-REVIEW EXERCISES

4.1   a) **GradientPaint**.   b) **ConvolveOp**.   c) **DataBuffer**,   **ColorModel**.
d) transformations. e) **setCapability**. f) **Appearance**.

4.2   a) False. The arguments to the LookupOp constructor are a **LookupTable** that contains the color sample lookup array and a RenderingHints object. b) False. Method **closePath** draws a line from the last point to the point specified in the *last* call to **moveTo**. c) True. d) True. e) True. f) False. Only those **Node**s that are children of the **TransformGroup** will be affected by the **TransformGroup**'s behavior. Any **Node**s outside the **TransformGroup** are not affected by the **TransformGroup**'s behavior.

EXERCISES

4.3   Write a program that draws a pyramid. Use class **GeneralPath** and method **draw** of class **Graphics2D**.

4.4   Write a program that draws a series of eight concentric circles that are separated by 10 pixels using class **Ellipse2D.Double**. The outer seven circles should be filled with randomly generated solid colors. The innermost circle should be filled with a gradient. Use method **draw** of class **Graphics2D**.

4.5   Modify the image-processing program presented in this chapter to include an **Java2DImageFilter** that removes the green color band from a **BufferedImage**. Add this option to the menu created in Fig. 4.13.

4.6   Modify the program of Fig. 4.15 and Fig. 4.21 so that the set of **JSlider** controls affect the direction of the **DirectionalLight** source as opposed to the color. Use method **setDirection** of class **DirectionalLight**.

4.7   For the program of Fig. 4.23, create a **Behavior** that temporarily "shields" the user-navigated sphere from a collision with an obstacle. When the user presses the space-bar, the user-navigated sphere turns blue to indicate that it is "shielded"—the sphere is "invincible" and should not collide with any obstacles for three seconds (i.e., during this time, the sphere can pass through obstacles without the "**You Lose**" screen appearing). The user can use the "shield" feature three times per game—after that, pressing the space-bar has no effect. When the shield "wears off," the user-navigated shape should turn red to indicate that it can collide with obstacles.

5

Case Study: Java 2D GUI Application with Design Patterns

Objectives

- To understand the model-view-controller architecture in a GUI application.
- To understand drag-and-drop techniques for transferring data in and among applications
- To understand the Factory Method design pattern for creating objects based on runtime criteria.
- To understand the integration of multiple Java technologies to build applications.
- To understand the use of multiple design patterns in a single application.
- To understand the implementation of multiple-document-interface applications.

All my life I have struggled to make one authentic gesture.
Isadora Duncan

Whatever is in any way beautiful has its source of beauty in itself, and is complete in itself; praise forms no part of it.
Marcus Aurelius Antoninus

The source of genius is imagination alone, …the refinement of the senses that sees what others do not see, or sees them differently.
Eugene Delacroix

That is a transformation in which imagination collaborates with memory.
Edgar Degas

5.1 Introduction

In this chapter, we implement a Java application case study as a capstone for the many Java features and techniques presented in previous chapters, including Swing GUI components and Java 2D graphics. This case study is a substantial application with almost 4,000 lines of code, so we use several design patterns to facilitate proper object-oriented design and extensibility. These design patterns include some we introduced in previous chapters (e.g., the Command design pattern and the MVC architecture), and some that we introduce in this case study.

5.2 Application Overview

The Deitel Drawing application is a painting program that enables users to create drawings that contain lines, shapes, text and images. Deitel Drawing includes the following features:

1. Colors, filled shapes and gradients

2. Multiple-document interface

3. Drag-and-drop support for moving shapes between drawings

4. Drag-and-drop support for JPEG images

5. Saving drawings as XML documents

6. Scaling drawings to different sizes and aspect ratios

7. Multiple drawing tools (controllers)

8. Modifying shape properties such as line width, fill and gradient

Deitel Drawing uses the model-view-controller architecture to make the application modular and extensible. The model consists of a collection of objects that extend abstract base class **MyShape**. Using polymorphism, views create graphical presentations of the **MyShape** collections. Multiple controllers handle input for drawing **MyShape** subclasses and for processing drag-and-drop operations.

Deitel Drawing uses the Java2D graphics APIs to create high-quality graphical presentations of drawing models. Lines, shapes and fonts are drawn using anti-aliasing to smooth jagged edges. Deitel Drawing takes advantage of Java 2D's **GradientPaint** class to draw shapes using multicolor gradients. Java 2D also provides transformation capabilities that enable the application to display scaled views of drawings. Using Java's event-handling mechanism, Deitel Drawing allows users to scale drawings dynamically by resizing a **ZoomDialog** window. The model-view-controller architecture ensures that each view is consistent with the drawing stored in the model. As a user draws new shapes, those shapes are immediately shown in each view.

Enabling drag-and-drop functionality in applications is nontrivial. The Deitel Drawing application uses Java's sophisticated drag-and-drop API to implement drag-and-drop functionality that allows users to move objects between drawings easily. Users also can drag and drop JPEG images from other applications (such as the host operating system's file manager) into drawings. Once the JPEG image is part of the drawing, the user can drag and drop the image between drawings just as with other shapes.

Figure 5.1 shows the Deitel Drawing application with a sample drawing. The shapes in this drawing were generated randomly by the solution to Exercise 5.8. Figure 5.2 shows the same drawing scaled to approximately twice the original size in a **ZoomDialog**.

5.3 **MyShape** Class Hierarchy

Deitel Drawing represents each shape in a drawing as a separate object that extends class **MyShape**. **MyShape** is an **abstract** base class that defines the basic interface for shapes and default implementations for methods common to all shapes.

Class **MyShape** (Fig. 5.3) is the root of the shape-class hierarchy. Implementing interface **Serializable** enables the Deitel Drawing application to serialize **MyShape** objects to disk, so drawings can be saved.

Lines 17–24 define several properties common to all **MyShape**s, such as the *x*- and *y*-coordinates and the **MyShape**'s colors. Some **MyShape**s can be **filled** (e.g., a filled square) or drawn with a gradient (lines 20–21). Line 22 declares property **strokeSize**, which specifies the thickness of the shape's lines. Methods **getLeftX** (lines 26–29) and **getLeftY** (lines 32–35) return the *x*- and *y*-coordinates of the **MyShape**'s left-most point. Methods **getRightX** (lines 38–41) and **getRightY** (lines 44–47) return the *x*- and *y*-coordinates of the **MyShape**'s right-most point. Methods **getWidth** (lines 50–53) and **getHeight** (lines 56–59) return the **MyShape**'s width and height as calculated from the shape's coordinates. Methods **setPoint1** (lines 62–66) and **setPoint2** (lines 69–73) modify the shape's *x*- and *y*-coordinates. Methods **setStartPoint** (lines 76–80) and **setEndPoint** (lines 83–87) set the points at which drawing began and drawing ended. The **MyShape** uses the start and end points to determine how to draw its gradient. Lines 90–136 provide *get* methods for each individual *x*- and *y*-coordinate. Method **moveByOffset** (lines 139–145) moves the **MyShape** by the given x and y offset values.

Lines 148–181 provide *set* and *get* methods for each of the **MyShape**'s colors. **MyShape**s can be drawn either in their primary color (**startColor**) or with a gradient that starts with **startColor** and ends with **endColor**. Lines 184–193 provide *set* and *get* methods for the **useGradient** property, which, if **true**, draws the shape using a color gradient.

Lines 196–206 provide *set* and *get* methods for property **strokeSize**. The Java2D API uses strokes to draw objects on a graphics context. The **strokeSize** property determines the thickness of the line that strokes the shape. Lines 209–218 provide *set* and *get* methods for property **filled**, which specifies whether the shape should be filled or drawn as an outline.

Line 222 declares **abstract** method **draw**, which takes as a **Graphics2D** argument the graphics context on which to draw the shape. Method draw is **abstract** because a generic **MyShape** object cannot be drawn; only specific subclasses of class **MyShape** (e.g., **MyOval**) can be drawn. Method **contains** (line 225) returns **true** if the given **Point2D** falls within the **MyShape**'s area. Method **contains** also is declared **abstract** to require each subclass to define an appropriate implementation. The drag-and-drop implementation in this example uses method **contains** when beginning a drag operation.

Method **configureGraphicsContext** (lines 228–247) configures the given **Graphics2D** object for drawing this **MyShape**. If there does not exist a **Stroke** for drawing the shape, line 233 creates a **BasicStroke** object using **MyShape**'s **strokeSize** property. Line 234 sets the **Graphics2D** object's **stroke** property. If the **gradient** property is **true**, lines 239–242 create a **GradientPaint** object that begins with **startColor** and ends with **endColor**. The gradient extends from the point (**startX**, **startY**) to the point (**endX**, **endY**). If the **gradient** property is **false**, line 246 invokes method **setPaint** of class **Graphics2D** to use the **MyShape**'s default **Color**.

Method **getXML** (lines 250–337) produces an XML representation of a **MyShape** object. Method **getXML** uses the **Document** argument only to create **Element**s— method **getXML** does not modify this **Document**. Line 252 creates a **shape Element**. Lines 255–293 create **Element**s for the *x*- and *y*-coordinates and add them as children of **Element shape**. Lines 296–299 create a **useGradient Element**, and lines 302–321 create **Element**s for each **MyShape** color. Lines 324–327 create **Element strokeSize** and lines 330–333 create **Element fill**. Line 336 returns the newly created **shape Element** to the caller.

Class **MyLine** (Fig. 5.4) is a **MyShape** subclass that represents a line in the drawing. Lines 15–26 implement method **draw**, which was declared **abstract** in class **MyShape**. Line 18 invokes method **configureGraphicsContext** to configure the given **Graphics2D** object with the **MyLine** object's color, **strokeSize** and other properties. Lines 21–22 create a Java2D **Line2D.Float** object for the **MyLine** object's *x*- and *y*-coordinates. Class **Line2D.Float** represents a line using **float**s for its *x*- and *y*-coordinates. Line 25 invokes method **draw** of class **Graphics2D** to draw the line on the **Graphics2D** context.

Method **contains** (lines 29–32) calculates the line's slope to determine if the given **Point2D** is on the line. Method **getXML** (lines 49–55) invokes method **getXML** of class **MyShape** (line 37) to get the default **shape Element**. Line 38 sets **Attribute type** of **Element shape** to the value **MyLine** to indicate that this **MyShape** object is an instance of class **MyLine**.

DrawingInternalFrames
in multiple-document interface.

JToolBar with
Actions for modifying
MyShape properties.

Title showing file name to
which drawing was saved.

ZoomDialog showing
scaled drawing.

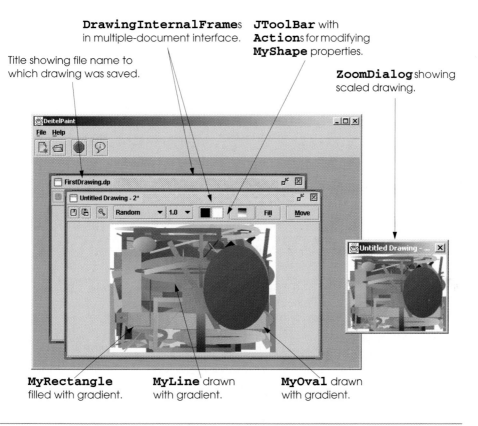

MyRectangle
filled with gradient.

MyLine drawn
with gradient.

MyOval drawn
with gradient.

Fig. 5.1   Deitel Drawing application showing randomly drawn shapes
(Exercise 5.8) and a **ZoomDrawingView** (Fig. 5.13).

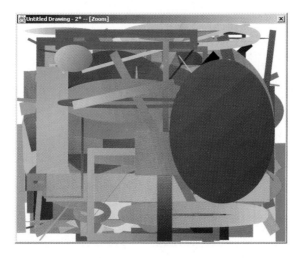

Fig. 5.2   Large-scale view of drawing from Fig. 5.1.

```
1   // MyShape.java
2   // MyShape is an abstract base class that represents a shape
3   // to be drawn in the DeitelDrawing application.
4   package com.deitel.advjhtp1.drawing.model.shapes;
5
6   // Java core packages
7   import java.awt.*;
8   import java.awt.geom.Point2D;
9
10  // third-party packages
11  import org.w3c.dom.*;
12
13  public abstract class MyShape {
14
15     // MyShape properties (coordinates, colors, etc.)
16     private int x1, y1, x2, y2;
17     private int startX, startY, endX, endY;
18     private Color startColor = Color.black;
19     private Color endColor = Color.white;
20     private boolean filled = false;
21     private boolean gradient = false;
22     private float strokeSize = 1.0f;
23     private Stroke currentStroke;
24
25     // get x coordinate of left corner
26     public int getLeftX()
27     {
28        return x1;
29     }
30
31     // get y coordinate of left corner
32     public int getLeftY()
33     {
34        return y1;
35     }
36
37     // get x coordinate of right corner
38     public int getRightX()
39     {
40        return x2;
41     }
42
43     // get y coordinate of right corner
44     public int getRightY()
45     {
46        return y2;
47     }
48
49     // get MyShape width
50     public int getWidth()
51     {
52        return Math.abs( getX1() - getX2() );
53     }
```

Fig. 5.3   **MyShape abstract** base class for drawing objects (part 1 of 7).

```
54
55      // get MyShape height
56      public int getHeight()
57      {
58          return Math.abs( getY1() - getY2() );
59      }
60
61      // set Point1's  x and y coordinates
62      public void setPoint1( int x, int y )
63      {
64          x1 = x;
65          y1 = y;
66      }
67
68      // set Point2's x and y coordinates
69      public final void setPoint2( int x, int y )
70      {
71          x2 = x;
72          y2 = y;
73      }
74
75      // set start Point's x and y coordinates
76      public final void setStartPoint( int x, int y )
77      {
78          startX = x;
79          startY = y;
80      }
81
82      // set end Point's x and y coordinates
83      public final void setEndPoint( int x, int y )
84      {
85          endX = x;
86          endY = y;
87      }
88
89      // get x1 coordinate
90      public final int getX1()
91      {
92          return x1;
93      }
94
95      // get x2 coordinate
96      public final int getX2()
97      {
98          return x2;
99      }
100
101     // get y1 coordinate
102     public final int getY1()
103     {
104         return y1;
105     }
106
```

Fig. 5.3   **MyShape abstract** base class for drawing objects (part 2 of 7).

```
107      // get y2 coordinate
108      public final int getY2()
109      {
110         return y2;
111      }
112
113
114      // get startX coordinate
115      public final int getStartX()
116      {
117         return startX;
118      }
119
120      // get startY coordinate
121      public final int getStartY()
122      {
123         return startY;
124      }
125
126      // get endX coordinate
127      public final int getEndX()
128      {
129         return endX;
130      }
131
132      // get endY coordinate
133      public final int getEndY()
134      {
135         return endY;
136      }
137
138      // move MyShape by given offset
139      public void moveByOffSet( int x, int y )
140      {
141         setPoint1( getX1() + x, getY1() + y );
142         setPoint2( getX2() + x, getY2() + y );
143         setStartPoint( getStartX() + x, getStartY() + y );
144         setEndPoint( getEndX() + x, getEndY() + y );
145      }
146
147      // set default drawing color
148      public void setColor( Color color )
149      {
150         setStartColor( color );
151      }
152
153      // get default drawing color
154      public Color getColor()
155      {
156         return getStartColor();
157      }
158
159      // set primary drawing color
```

Fig. 5.3   **MyShape abstract** base class for drawing objects (part 3 of 7).

```java
160     public void setStartColor( Color color )
161     {
162         startColor = color;
163     }
164
165     // get primary drawing color
166     public Color getStartColor()
167     {
168         return startColor;
169     }
170
171     // set secondary drawing color (for gradients)
172     public void setEndColor( Color color )
173     {
174         endColor = color;
175     }
176
177     // get secondary drawing color
178     public Color getEndColor()
179     {
180         return endColor;
181     }
182
183     // enable/disable gradient drawing
184     public void setUseGradient( boolean useGradient )
185     {
186         gradient = useGradient;
187     }
188
189     // get gradient enabled/disabled property
190     public boolean useGradient()
191     {
192         return gradient;
193     }
194
195     // set stroke size
196     public void setStrokeSize( float size )
197     {
198         strokeSize = size;
199         currentStroke = new BasicStroke( strokeSize );
200     }
201
202     // get stroke size
203     public float getStrokeSize()
204     {
205         return strokeSize;
206     }
207
208     // set filled property
209     public void setFilled ( boolean fill )
210     {
211         filled = fill;
212     }
```

Fig. 5.3   **MyShape abstract** base class for drawing objects (part 4 of 7).

```
213
214    // get filled property
215    public boolean isFilled()
216    {
217       return filled;
218    }
219
220    // abstract draw method to be implemented by subclasses
221    // to draw actual shapes
222    public abstract void draw( Graphics2D g2D );
223
224    // return true if the Point2D falls within this shape
225    public abstract boolean contains( Point2D point );
226
227    // configure Graphics2D context for known drawing properties
228    protected void configureGraphicsContext( Graphics2D g2D )
229    {
230       // set Stroke for drawing shape
231       if ( currentStroke == null )
232          currentStroke = new BasicStroke( getStrokeSize() );
233
234       g2D.setStroke( currentStroke );
235
236       // if gradient selected, create new GradientPaint starting
237       // at x1, y1 with color1 and ending at x2, y2 with color2
238       if ( useGradient() )
239          g2D.setPaint ( new GradientPaint(
240             ( int ) getStartX(), ( int ) getStartY(),
241             getStartColor(), ( int ) getEndX(), ( int ) getEndY(),
242             getEndColor() ) );
243
244       // if no gradient selected, use primary color
245       else
246          g2D.setPaint( getColor() );
247    }
248
249    // get MyShape XML representation
250    public Element getXML( Document document )
251    {
252       Element shapeElement = document.createElement( "shape" );
253
254       // create Elements for x and y coordinates
255       Element temp = document.createElement( "x1" );
256       temp.appendChild( document.createTextNode(
257          String.valueOf( getX1() ) ) );
258       shapeElement.appendChild( temp );
259
260       temp = document.createElement( "y1" );
261       temp.appendChild( document.createTextNode(
262          String.valueOf( getY1() ) ) );
263       shapeElement.appendChild( temp );
264
265       temp = document.createElement( "x2" );
```

Fig. 5.3   **MyShape abstract** base class for drawing objects (part 5 of 7).

```
266        temp.appendChild( document.createTextNode(
267           String.valueOf( getX2() ) ) );
268        shapeElement.appendChild( temp );
269
270        temp = document.createElement( "y2" );
271        temp.appendChild( document.createTextNode(
272           String.valueOf( getY2() ) ) );
273        shapeElement.appendChild( temp );
274
275        temp = document.createElement( "startX" );
276        temp.appendChild( document.createTextNode(
277           String.valueOf( getStartX() ) ) );
278        shapeElement.appendChild( temp );
279
280        temp = document.createElement( "startY" );
281        temp.appendChild( document.createTextNode(
282           String.valueOf( getStartY() ) ) );
283        shapeElement.appendChild( temp );
284
285        temp = document.createElement( "endX" );
286        temp.appendChild( document.createTextNode(
287           String.valueOf( getEndX() ) ) );
288        shapeElement.appendChild( temp );
289
290        temp = document.createElement( "endY" );
291        temp.appendChild( document.createTextNode(
292           String.valueOf( getEndY() ) ) );
293        shapeElement.appendChild( temp );
294
295        // create Element for gradient property
296        temp = document.createElement( "useGradient" );
297        temp.appendChild( document.createTextNode(
298           String.valueOf( useGradient() ) ) );
299        shapeElement.appendChild( temp );
300
301        // create XML element for startColor
302        Color color = getStartColor();
303        temp = document.createElement( "startColor" );
304        temp.setAttribute( "red",
305           String.valueOf( color.getRed() ) );
306        temp.setAttribute( "green",
307           String.valueOf( color.getGreen() ) );
308        temp.setAttribute( "blue",
309           String.valueOf( color.getBlue() ) );
310        shapeElement.appendChild( temp );
311
312        // create XML element for endColor
313        color = getEndColor();
314        temp = document.createElement( "endColor" );
315        temp.setAttribute( "red",
316           String.valueOf( color.getRed() ) );
317        temp.setAttribute( "green",
318           String.valueOf( color.getGreen() ) );
```

Fig. 5.3   **MyShape abstract** base class for drawing objects (part 6 of 7).

```
319            temp.setAttribute( "blue",
320               String.valueOf( color.getBlue() ) );
321            shapeElement.appendChild( temp );
322
323            // add strokeSize element
324            temp = document.createElement( "strokeSize" );
325            temp.appendChild( document.createTextNode(
326               String.valueOf( getStrokeSize() ) ) );
327            shapeElement.appendChild( temp );
328
329            // add fill element
330            temp = document.createElement( "fill" );
331            temp.appendChild( document.createTextNode(
332               String.valueOf( isFilled() ) ) );
333            shapeElement.appendChild( temp );
334
335            return shapeElement;
336
337      } // end method getXML
338 }
```

Fig. 5.3   **MyShape abstract** base class for drawing objects (part 7 of 7).

```
1   // MyLine.java
2   // MyLine is a MyShape subclass that represents a line.
3   package com.deitel.advjhtp1.drawing.model.shapes;
4
5   // Java core packages
6   import java.awt.*;
7   import java.awt.geom.*;
8
9   // third-party packages
10  import org.w3c.dom.*;
11
12  public class MyLine extends MyShape {
13
14     // draw MyLine object on given Graphics2D context
15     public void draw( Graphics2D g2D )
16     {
17        // configure Graphics2D (gradient, color, etc.)
18        configureGraphicsContext( g2D );
19
20        // create new Line2D.Float
21        Shape line = new Line2D.Float( getX1(), getY1(), getX2(),
22           getY2() );
23
24        // draw shape
25        g2D.draw( line );
26     }
27
```

Fig. 5.4   **MyLine** subclass of class **MyShape** that represents a line (part 1 of 2).

```
28        // determine if MyLine contains given Point2D
29        public boolean contains( Point2D point )
30        {
31           // get Point1 and Point2 coordinates
32           float x1 = getX1();
33           float x2 = getX2();
34           float y1 = getY1();
35           float y2 = getY2();
36
37           // determines slope of line
38           float slope = ( y2 - y1 ) / ( x2 - x1 );
39
40           // determines slope from point argument and Point1
41           float realSlope = ( float )
42              ( ( point.getY() - y1 ) / ( point.getX() - x1 ) );
43
44           // return true if slope and realSlope are close in value
45           return Math.abs( realSlope - slope ) < 0.1;
46        }
47
48        // get MyLine XML representation
49        public Element getXML( Document document )
50        {
51           Element shapeElement = super.getXML( document );
52           shapeElement.setAttribute( "type", "MyLine" );
53
54           return shapeElement;
55        }
56     }
```

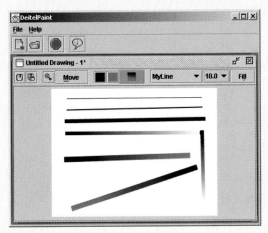

Fig. 5.4   **MyLine** subclass of class **MyShape** that represents a line (part 2 of 2).

Class **MyRectangle** (Fig. 5.5) is a **MyShape** subclass that represents a rectangle.
Lines 17–31 implement method **draw**, which takes as a **Graphics2D** argument the

graphics context on which to draw the **MyRectangle**. Line 20 invokes method **configureGraphicsContext** to set the appropriate **strokeSize**, color and other drawing properties. Lines 23–24 create a new **Rectangle2D.Float** instance. The **Rectangle2D.Float** constructor takes as arguments the *x*- and *y*-coordinates of the rectangle's upper left hand corner and the rectangle's width and height. If **MyRectangle**'s **filled** property is set, line 28 draws a filled rectangle by invoking method **fill** of class **Graphics2D**. If **MyRectangle**'s **filled** property is false, line 30 invokes method **draw** of class **Graphics2D** to draw the rectangle's outline.

```
1   // MyRectangle.java
2   // MyRectangle is a MyShape subclass that represents a
3   // rectangle, including an implementation of the draw method
4   // for drawing the rectangle on a Graphics2D context.
5   package com.deitel.advjhtp1.drawing.model.shapes;
6
7   // Java core packages
8   import java.awt.*;
9   import java.awt.geom.*;
10
11  // third-party packages
12  import org.w3c.dom.*;
13
14  public class MyRectangle extends MyShape {
15
16     // draw MyRectangle on given Graphics2D context
17     public void draw( Graphics2D g2D )
18     {
19        // configure Graphics2D (gradient, color, etc.)
20        configureGraphicsContext( g2D );
21
22        // create Rectangle2D for drawing MyRectangle
23        Shape shape = new Rectangle2D.Float( getLeftX(),
24           getLeftY(), getWidth(), getHeight() );
25
26        // if shape is filled, draw filled shape
27        if ( isFilled() )
28           g2D.fill( shape );
29        else
30           g2D.draw( shape );
31     }
32
33     // return true if point falls within MyRectangle
34     public boolean contains( Point2D point )
35     {
36        Rectangle2D.Float rectangle = new Rectangle2D.Float(
37           getLeftX(), getLeftY(), getWidth(), getHeight() );
38
39        return rectangle.contains( point );
40     }
41
```

Fig. 5.5   **MyRectangle** subclass of class **MyShape** that represents a rectangle (part 1 of 2).

```
42      // get XML representation of MyRectangle
43      public Element getXML( Document document )
44      {
45          Element shapeElement = super.getXML( document );
46          shapeElement.setAttribute( "type", "MyRectangle" );
47
48          return shapeElement;
49      }
50  }
```

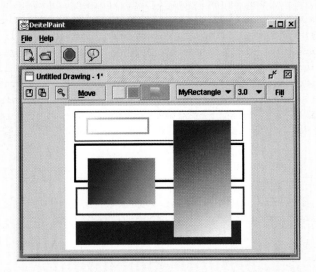

Fig. 5.5   **MyRectangle** subclass of class **MyShape** that represents a rectangle (part 2 of 2).

Method **contains** (lines 34–40) creates a **Rectangle2D.Float** object (line 36–37) and invokes method **contains** of class **Rectangle2D.Float** to determine whether the given **Point2D** falls within the **MyRectangle**. Method **getXML** (lines 43–49) creates an XML **Element** to represent the **MyRectangle** object. Line 45 invokes method **getXML** of class **MyShape** to get the default **shape Element**. Line 46 invokes method **setAttribute** of interface **Element** to add **Attribute type** with the value **MyRectangle** to **Element shape**.

Class **MyOval** (Fig. 5.6) is a **MyShape** subclass that represents an oval. Lines 15–29 implement method **draw** for drawing the **MyOval** object on the given **Graphics2D** context. Line 18 invokes method **configureGraphicsContext** to set the color, **strokeSize** and other properties for drawing the **MyOval**. Lines 21–22 create an **Ellipse2D.Float** instance for drawing the **MyOval**. The **Ellipse2D.Float** constructor takes as arguments the *x*- and *y*-coordinates and the width and height of the oval's bounding rectangle. If the **MyOval** is **filled**, line 26 invokes method **fill** of class **Graphics2D** to draw a filled oval. If the **MyOval** is not **filled**, line 28 invokes method **draw** of class **Graphics2D** to draw the oval's outline.

Method **contains** (lines 32–38) creates an **Ellipse2D.Float** object and invokes method contains of class **Ellipse2D.Float** to determine whether the given **Point2D** falls within the oval. Method **getXML** (lines 41–47) creates an XML **Element** to represent the **MyOval** object. Line 43 invokes method **getXML** of class **MyShape** to get the default **shape Element**. Line 44 invokes method **setAttribute** of interface **Element** to add **Attribute type** with value **MyOval** to **Element shape**.

Class **MyText** (Fig. 5.7) is a **MyShape** subclass that represents styled text in a drawing. A **MyText** object contains a **String** of text (line 18), in a particular font (line 20), of a particular size (line 21) that optionally may be bold, underlined and/or italic (lines 22–24). Method **draw** (lines 27–66) draws the **MyText** object using a *java.text.AttributedString*. An **AttributedString** contains text and attributes of that text, such as its font. Line 30 invokes method **configureGraphicsContext** to initialize the **Graphics2D** object for drawing the **MyText** object. Line 33 creates an **AttributedString**, and lines 36–58 set that **AttributedString**'s attributes, including the font, size, bold, italic, etc. Line 65 invokes method **drawString** of class **Graphics2D** to draw the **AttributedString** on the graphics context. Method **contains** (lines 69–72) always returns **false**, which disallows dragging of **MyText** objects.

```
1   // MyOval.java
2   // MyOval is a MyShape subclass that represents an oval.
3   package com.deitel.advjhtp1.drawing.model.shapes;
4
5   // Java core packages
6   import java.awt.*;
7   import java.awt.geom.*;
8
9   // third-party packages
10  import org.w3c.dom.*;
11
12  public class MyOval extends MyShape {
13
14     // draw MyOval on given Graphics2D context
15     public void draw( Graphics2D g2D )
16     {
17        // configure Graphics2D (gradient, color, etc.)
18        configureGraphicsContext( g2D );
19
20        // create Ellipse2D for drawing oval
21        Shape shape = new Ellipse2D.Float( getLeftX(),
22           getLeftY(), getWidth(), getHeight() );
23
24        // if shape is filled, draw filled shape
25        if ( isFilled() )
26           g2D.fill( shape );
27        else
28           g2D.draw( shape );
29     }
30
```

Fig. 5.6   **MyOval** subclass of class **MyShape** that represents an oval (part 1 of 2).

```
31      // return true if point falls inside MyOval
32      public boolean contains( Point2D point )
33      {
34         Ellipse2D.Float ellipse = new Ellipse2D.Float(
35            getLeftX(), getLeftY(), getWidth(), getHeight() );
36
37         return ellipse.contains( point );
38      }
39
40      // get MyOval XML representation
41      public Element getXML( Document document )
42      {
43         Element shapeElement = super.getXML( document );
44         shapeElement.setAttribute( "type", "MyOval" );
45
46         return shapeElement;
47      }
48   }
```

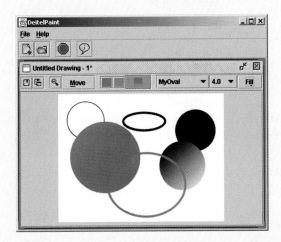

Fig. 5.6   **MyOval** subclass of class **MyShape** that represents an oval (part 2 of 2).

```
1   // MyText.java
2   // MyText is a MyShape subclass that represents styled text
3   // in a drawing.
4   package com.deitel.advjhtp1.drawing.model.shapes;
5
6   // Java core packages
7   import java.awt.*;
8   import java.text.*;
```

Fig. 5.7   **MyText** subclass of class **MyShape** that represents a string of text
            (part 1 of 5).

```
 9   import java.awt.font.*;
10   import java.awt.geom.*;
11
12   // third-party packages
13   import org.w3c.dom.*;
14
15   public class MyText extends MyShape {
16
17      // MyText properties (font, font size, text, etc.)
18      private String text;
19      private AttributedString attributedString;
20      private String fontName = "Serif";
21      private int fontSize = 12;
22      private boolean underlined = false;
23      private boolean boldSelected = false;
24      private boolean italicSelected = false;
25
26      // draw MyText on given Graphics2D context
27      public void draw( Graphics2D g2D )
28      {
29         // configure Graphics2D (gradient, color, etc.)
30         configureGraphicsContext( g2D );
31
32         // create AttributedString for drawing text
33         attributedString = new AttributedString( text );
34
35         // set AttributedString Font
36         attributedString.addAttribute( TextAttribute.FAMILY,
37            fontName );
38
39         // set AttributedString Font size
40         attributedString.addAttribute( TextAttribute.SIZE,
41            new Float( fontSize ) );
42
43         // if selected, set bold, italic and underlined
44         if ( boldSelected )
45            attributedString.addAttribute( TextAttribute.WEIGHT,
46               TextAttribute.WEIGHT_BOLD );
47
48         if ( italicSelected )
49            attributedString.addAttribute( TextAttribute.POSTURE,
50               TextAttribute.POSTURE_OBLIQUE );
51
52         if ( underlined )
53            attributedString.addAttribute( TextAttribute.UNDERLINE,
54               TextAttribute.UNDERLINE_ON );
55
56         // set AttributedString Color
57         attributedString.addAttribute( TextAttribute.FOREGROUND,
58            getColor() );
59
60         // create AttributedCharacterIterator for AttributedString
```

Fig. 5.7   **MyText** subclass of class **MyShape** that represents a string of text (part 2 of 5).

```
61        AttributedCharacterIterator characterIterator =
62           attributedString.getIterator();
63
64        // draw string using AttributedCharacterIterator
65        g2D.drawString( characterIterator, getX1(), getY1() );
66     }
67
68     // return false because MyText objects contain no area
69     public boolean contains( Point2D point )
70     {
71        return false;
72     }
73
74     // set MyText text
75     public void setText( String myText )
76     {
77        text = myText;
78     }
79
80     // get text contained in MyText
81     public String getText()
82     {
83        return text;
84     }
85
86     // set MyText Font size
87     public void setFontSize( int size )
88     {
89        fontSize = size;
90     }
91
92     // get MyText Font size
93     public int getFontSize()
94     {
95        return fontSize;
96     }
97
98     // set MyText Font name
99     public void setFontName( String name )
100    {
101        fontName = name;
102    }
103
104    // get MyText Font name
105    public String getFontName()
106    {
107        return fontName;
108    }
109
110    // set MyText underlined property
111    public void setUnderlineSelected( boolean textUnderlined )
112    {
```

Fig. 5.7   **MyText** subclass of class **MyShape** that represents a string of text (part 3 of 5).

```
113          underlined = textUnderlined;
114       }
115
116       // get MyText underlined property
117       public boolean isUnderlineSelected()
118       {
119          return underlined;
120       }
121
122       // set MyText bold property
123       public void setBoldSelected( boolean textBold )
124       {
125          boldSelected = textBold;
126       }
127
128       // get MyText bold property
129       public boolean isBoldSelected()
130       {
131          return boldSelected;
132       }
133
134       // set MyText italic property
135       public void setItalicSelected( boolean textItalic )
136       {
137          italicSelected = textItalic;
138       }
139
140       // get MyText italic property
141       public boolean isItalicSelected()
142       {
143          return italicSelected;
144       }
145
146       // get MyText XML representation
147       public Element getXML( Document document )
148       {
149          Element shapeElement = super.getXML( document );
150          shapeElement.setAttribute( "type", "MyText" );
151
152          // create text Element
153          Element temp = document.createElement( "text" );
154          temp.appendChild( document.createTextNode( getText() ) );
155          shapeElement.appendChild( temp );
156
157          // create fontSize Element
158          temp = document.createElement( "fontSize" );
159          temp.appendChild( document.createTextNode(
160             String.valueOf( fontSize ) ) );
161          shapeElement.appendChild( temp );
162
163          // create fontName Element
164          temp = document.createElement( "fontName" );
```

Fig. 5.7   **MyText** subclass of class **MyShape** that represents a string of text (part 4 of 5).

```
165          temp.appendChild( document.createTextNode(
166             String.valueOf( fontName ) ) );
167          shapeElement.appendChild( temp );
168
169          // create underlined Element
170          temp = document.createElement( "underlined" );
171          temp.appendChild( document.createTextNode(
172             String.valueOf( underlined ) ) );
173          shapeElement.appendChild( temp );
174
175          // create bold Element
176          temp = document.createElement( "bold" );
177          temp.appendChild( document.createTextNode(
178             String.valueOf( boldSelected ) ) );
179          shapeElement.appendChild( temp );
180
181          // create italic Element
182          temp = document.createElement( "italic" );
183          temp.appendChild( document.createTextNode(
184             String.valueOf( italicSelected ) ) );
185          shapeElement.appendChild( temp );
186
187          return shapeElement;
188
189       } // end method getXML
190    }
```

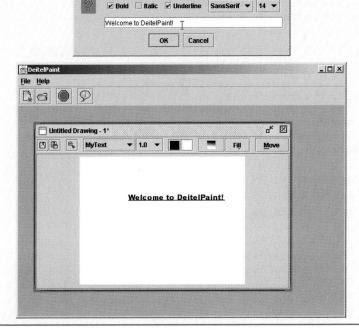

Fig. 5.7   **MyText** subclass of class **MyShape** that represents a string of text
        (part 5 of 5).

Lines 75–144 provide *set* and *get* methods for **MyText** properties, including its text, font, size, bold, italic and underline properties. Method **getXML** (lines 147–189) creates an XML representation of a **MyText** object. Lines 149–150 obtain the default **shape Element** and set its **type** attribute to the value **"MyText"**. Lines 153–185 create **Element**s that represent each **MyText**-specific property.

Class **MyImage** (Fig. 5.8) is a **MyShape** subclass that represents a JPEG image in a drawing. As we will see in Section 5.6.3, Deitel Drawing enables users to add JPEG images to a drawing using drag and drop. Line 17 declares **BufferedImage** member variable **image** for storing the **MyImage** object's image.

```
1   // MyImage.java
2   // MyImage is a MyShape subclass that contains a JPEG image.
3   package com.deitel.advjhtp1.drawing.model.shapes;
4
5   // Java core packages
6   import java.io.*;
7   import java.awt.*;
8   import java.awt.image.*;
9   import java.awt.geom.*;
10
11  // third-party packages
12  import org.w3c.dom.*;
13  import com.sun.image.codec.jpeg.*;
14
15  public class MyImage extends MyShape {
16
17     private BufferedImage image;
18     private String fileName;
19
20     // draw image on given Graphics2D context
21     public void draw( Graphics2D g2D )
22     {
23        // draw image on Graphics2D context
24        g2D.drawImage( getImage(), getX1(), getY1(), null );
25     }
26
27     // return true if Point falls within MyImage
28     public boolean contains( Point2D point )
29     {
30        Rectangle2D.Float rectangle = new Rectangle2D.Float(
31           getX1(), getY1(), getWidth(), getHeight() );
32
33        return rectangle.contains( point );
34     }
35
36     // get MyImage image
37     public BufferedImage getImage()
38     {
39        return image;
40     }
```

Fig. 5.8   **MyImage** subclass of class **MyShape** that represents a JPEG image in a drawing (part 1 of 3).

```
41
42     // set filename for loading image
43     public void setFileName( String name )
44     {
45        // load image from file
46        try {
47           File file = new File( name );
48
49           FileInputStream inputStream =
50              new FileInputStream( file );
51
52           // decode JPEG image
53           JPEGImageDecoder decoder =
54              JPEGCodec.createJPEGDecoder( inputStream );
55
56           image = decoder.decodeAsBufferedImage();
57
58           setPoint2( getX1() + image.getWidth(),
59              getY1() + image.getHeight() );
60        }
61
62        // handle exception reading image from file
63        catch ( IOException ioException ) {
64           ioException.printStackTrace();
65        }
66
67        // set fileName if try is successful
68        fileName = name;
69     }
70
71     // get image filename
72     public String getFileName()
73     {
74        return fileName;
75     }
76
77     // get MyImage XML Element
78     public Element getXML( Document document )
79     {
80        Element shapeElement = super.getXML( document );
81        shapeElement.setAttribute( "type", "MyImage" );
82
83        // create filename Element
84        Element temp = document.createElement( "fileName" );
85        temp.appendChild( document.createTextNode(
86           getFileName() ) );
87        shapeElement.appendChild( temp );
88
89        return shapeElement;
90
91     } // end method getXML
92  }
```

Fig. 5.8 **MyImage** subclass of class **MyShape** that represents a JPEG image in a drawing (part 2 of 3).

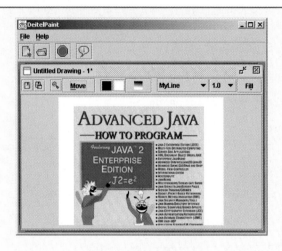

Fig. 5.8   **MyImage** subclass of class **MyShape** that represents a JPEG image in a drawing (part 3 of 3).

Lines 21–25 implement method **draw** to draw the **MyImage** object. Line 24 invokes method **drawImage** of class **Graphics2D** to draw the **MyImage** object's **Buffered-Image**. Method **contains** (lines 28–34) creates a **Rectangle2D.Float** object of the same dimensions as the **MyImage** object. Line 33 invokes method **contains** of class **Rectangle2D.Float** to determine whether the given **Point2D** object falls within the **MyImage** object's area.

Method **getImage** (lines 46–49) gets the **BufferedImage** for the **MyImage** object. Method **setFileName** (lines 43–69) takes as a **String** argument the name of the **File** that contains the **MyImage** object's image. Lines 49–56 open a **FileInput-Stream** for the **File** and decode the **File** as a JPEG image using method **decodeAs-BufferedImage** of class **JPEGImageDecoder**. Line 56 invokes method **setImage** of class **MyImage** to set the **image** property to the newly loaded **BufferedImage**. Method **getFileName** (lines 72–75) returns a **String** that contains the name of the **File** from which the JPEG image was loaded.

Method **getXML** (lines 78–91) creates an XML representation of a **MyImage** object. Line 80 invokes method **getXML** of class **MyShape** to retrieve the default **shape Element**. Line 81 adds **Attribute type** with the value **MyImage** to **Element shape**. Lines 84–87 create a **fileName Element** that contains the name of the **File** from which the JPEG image was loaded, and appends this **Element** as a child of **Element shape**.

5.4 Deitel **DrawingModel**

The Deitel Drawing application employs the model-view-controller architecture to enhance the application's modularity and extensibility. Deitel Drawing represents each drawing as a **Collection** of **MyShape** objects stored in a **DrawingModel** (Fig. 5.9). Class

DrawingModel extends **Observable** (line 13) to allow **Observer**s to register as listeners for changes in the **DrawingModel**.

```
1   // DrawingModel.java
2   // DrawingModel is the model for a DeitelDrawing painting. It
3   // provides methods for adding and removing shapes from a
4   // drawing.
5   package com.deitel.advjhtp1.drawing.model;
6
7   // Java core packages
8   import java.util.*;
9
10  // Deitel packages
11  import com.deitel.advjhtp1.drawing.model.shapes.*;
12
13  public class DrawingModel extends Observable {
14
15     // shapes contained in model
16     private Collection shapes;
17
18     // no-argument constructor
19     public DrawingModel()
20     {
21        shapes = new ArrayList();
22     }
23
24     // add shape to model
25     public void addShape( MyShape shape )
26     {
27        // add new shape to list of shapes
28        shapes.add( shape );
29
30        // send model changed notification
31        fireModelChanged();
32     }
33
34     // remove shape from model
35     public void removeShape( MyShape shape )
36     {
37        // remove shape from list
38        shapes.remove( shape );
39
40        // send model changed notification
41        fireModelChanged();
42     }
43
44     // get Collection of shapes in model
45     public Collection getShapes()
46     {
47        return Collections.unmodifiableCollection( shapes );
48     }
```

Fig. 5.9   **DrawingModel Observable** class that represents a drawing containing multiple **MyShape**s (part 1 of 2).

```
49
50      // set Collection of shapes in model
51      public void setShapes( Collection newShapes )
52      {
53          // copy Collection into new ArrayList
54          shapes = new ArrayList( newShapes );
55
56          // send model changed notification
57          fireModelChanged();
58      }
59
60      // empty the current ArrayList of shapes
61      public void clear()
62      {
63          shapes = new ArrayList();
64
65          // send model changed notification
66          fireModelChanged();
67      }
68
69      // send model changed notification
70      private void fireModelChanged()
71      {
72          // set model changed flag
73          setChanged();
74
75          // notify Observers that model changed
76          notifyObservers();
77      }
78  }
```

Fig. 5.9   **DrawingModel Observable** class that represents a drawing containing multiple **MyShape**s (part 2 of 2).

The **DrawingModel** consists of a **Collection** of **MyShape** objects and methods for adding and removing shapes. Lines 31 and 41 invoke **private** method **fireModelChanged** to notify **Observer**s of additions to, and deletions from, the **Drawing-Model**. Method **fireModelChanged** (lines 72–79) invokes method **setChanged** of class **Observable** to mark the **DrawingModel** as changed (line 75). Line 78 invokes method **notifyObservers** to send a notification to each registered **Observer** that the **DrawingModel** has changed.

Method **getShapes** (lines 51–54) invokes **static** method **unmodifiableCollection** of class **Collections** to obtain an unmodifiable reference to the **shapes Collection**. Returning an unmodifiable **Collection** prevents the caller from changing the model through that **Collection** reference.

Class **DrawingFileReaderWriter** (Fig. 5.10) provides methods **writeFile** and **readFile** for saving and loading drawings. Class **DrawingFileReaderWriter** enables the application to save and load drawings as XML documents. Static method **writeFile** (lines 28–89) takes as arguments a **DrawingModel** and the file name to which the **DrawingModel** should be saved. Lines 34–40 create a new XML DOM object in memory. Lines 43–44 create the **shapes Element**, which is the root of the XML document. Lines 47–55 iterate through the **DrawingModel**'s shapes, and invoke method **getXML** on each **MyShape** to obtain its XML **Element** representation. Line 54 adds each **shape Element** to the XML document. Lines 58–70 use a **Transformer** to output the XML document to the given **fileName**. [*Note*: If you are not familiar with XML and the Java API for XML Processing, please see Appendices A–D.]

```java
1   // DrawingFileReaderWriter.java
2   // DrawingFileReaderWriter defines static methods for reading
3   // and writing DeitelDrawing files on disk.
4   package com.deitel.advjhtp1.drawing;
5
6   // Java core packages
7   import java.io.*;
8   import java.util.*;
9   import java.awt.Color;
10
11  // Java extension packages
12  import javax.xml.parsers.*;
13  import javax.xml.transform.*;
14  import javax.xml.transform.dom.*;
15  import javax.xml.transform.stream.*;
16
17  // third-party packages
18  import org.w3c.dom.*;
19  import org.xml.sax.*;
20
21  // Deitel packages
22  import com.deitel.advjhtp1.drawing.model.*;
23  import com.deitel.advjhtp1.drawing.model.shapes.*;
24
25  public class DrawingFileReaderWriter {
26
27     // write drawing to file with given fileName
28     public static void writeFile( DrawingModel drawingModel,
29        String fileName )
30     {
31        // open file for writing and save drawing data
32        try {
33
34           DocumentBuilderFactory builderFactory =
35              DocumentBuilderFactory.newInstance();
36
37           DocumentBuilder builder =
38              builderFactory.newDocumentBuilder();
39
40           Document document = builder.newDocument();
41
42           // create shapes element to contain all MyShapes
43           Element shapesElement =
44              document.createElement( "shapes" );
45           document.appendChild( shapesElement );
```

Fig. 5.10   **DrawingFileReaderWriter** utility class for saving drawings to files and loading drawings from files (part 1 of 8).

```
46
47              Iterator iterator = drawingModel.getShapes().iterator();
48
49              // populate shapes element with shape element for each
50              // MyShape in DrawingModel
51              while ( iterator.hasNext() ) {
52                 MyShape shape = ( MyShape ) iterator.next();
53
54                 shapesElement.appendChild( shape.getXML( document ) );
55              }
56
57              // use Transformer to write shapes XML document to a file
58              TransformerFactory transformerFactory =
59                 TransformerFactory.newInstance();
60
61              Transformer transformer =
62                 transformerFactory.newTransformer();
63
64              // specify the shapes.dtd Document Type Definition
65              transformer.setOutputProperty(
66                 OutputKeys.DOCTYPE_SYSTEM, "shapes.dtd" );
67
68              transformer.transform( new DOMSource( document ),
69                 new StreamResult( new FileOutputStream(
70                    fileName ) ) );
71
72           } // end try
73
74           // handle exception building XML Document
75           catch ( ParserConfigurationException parserException ) {
76              parserException.printStackTrace();
77           }
78
79           // handle exception transforming XML Document
80           catch ( TransformerException transformerException ) {
81              transformerException.printStackTrace();
82           }
83
84           // handle exception opening FileOutputStream
85           catch ( FileNotFoundException fileException ) {
86              fileException.printStackTrace();
87           }
88
89        } // end method writeFile
90
91        // open existing drawing from file
92        public static Collection readFile( String fileName )
93        {
94           // load shapes from file
95           try {
96
97              // Collection of MyShapes read from XML Document
```

Fig. 5.10   **DrawingFileReaderWriter** utility class for saving drawings to files and loading drawings from files (part 2 of 8).

```
98              Collection shapes = new ArrayList();
99
100             DocumentBuilderFactory builderFactory =
101                DocumentBuilderFactory.newInstance();
102
103             builderFactory.setValidating( true );
104
105             DocumentBuilder builder =
106                builderFactory.newDocumentBuilder();
107
108             Document document = builder.parse(
109                new File( fileName ) );
110
111             // get all shape elements in XML Document
112             NodeList list = document.getElementsByTagName( "shape" );
113
114             // get MyShape from each shape element in XML Document
115             for ( int i = 0; i < list.getLength(); i++ ) {
116                Element element = ( Element ) list.item( i );
117                MyShape shape = getShapeFromElement( element );
118                shapes.add( shape );
119             }
120
121             return shapes;
122
123          } // end try
124
125          // handle exception creating DocumentBuilder
126          catch ( ParserConfigurationException parserException ) {
127             parserException.printStackTrace();
128          }
129
130          // handle exception parsing Document
131          catch ( SAXException saxException ) {
132             saxException.printStackTrace();
133          }
134
135          // handle exception reading Document from file
136          catch ( IOException ioException ) {
137             ioException.printStackTrace();
138          }
139
140          return null;
141
142       } // end method readFile
143
144       // create MyShape using properties specified in given Element
145       private static MyShape getShapeFromElement( Element element )
146       {
147          MyShape shape = null;
148
149          // get MyShape type (e.g., MyLine, MyRectangle, etc.)
```

Fig. 5.10 **DrawingFileReaderWriter** utility class for saving drawings to files and loading drawings from files (part 3 of 8).

```
150         String type = element.getAttribute( "type" );
151
152         // create appropriate MyShape subclass instance
153         if ( type.equals( "MyLine" ) ) {
154            shape = new MyLine();
155         }
156
157         else if ( type.equals( "MyRectangle" ) ) {
158            shape = new MyRectangle();
159         }
160
161         else if ( type.equals( "MyOval" ) ) {
162            shape = new MyOval();
163         }
164
165         else if ( type.equals( "MyText" ) ) {
166            shape = new MyText();
167
168            // create MyText reference for setting MyText-specific
169            // properties, including fontSize, text, etc.
170            MyText textShape  = ( MyText ) shape;
171
172            // set text property
173            String text =
174               getStringValueFromChildElement( element, "text" );
175
176            textShape.setText( text );
177
178            // set fontSize property
179            int fontSize =
180               getIntValueFromChildElement( element, "fontSize" );
181
182            textShape.setFontSize( fontSize );
183
184            // set fontName property
185            String fontName =
186               getStringValueFromChildElement( element, "fontName" );
187
188            textShape.setFontName( fontName );
189
190            // set underlined property
191            boolean underlined = getBooleanValueFromChildElement(
192               element, "underlined" );
193
194            textShape.setUnderlineSelected( underlined );
195
196            // set bold property
197            boolean bold =
198               getBooleanValueFromChildElement( element, "bold" );
199
200            textShape.setBoldSelected( bold );
201
```

Fig. 5.10   **DrawingFileReaderWriter** utility class for saving drawings to files and loading drawings from files (part 4 of 8).

```
202               // set italic property
203               boolean italic =
204                  getBooleanValueFromChildElement( element, "italic" );
205
206               textShape.setItalicSelected( italic );
207            }
208
209            else if ( type.equals( "MyImage" ) ) {
210               shape = new MyImage();
211
212               // create MyImage reference for setting MyImage-specific
213               // fileName property
214               MyImage imageShape = ( MyImage ) shape;
215
216               String fileName = getStringValueFromChildElement(
217                  element, "fileName" );
218
219               imageShape.setFileName( fileName );
220            }
221
222            // set properties common to all MyShapes, including x1, y1,
223            // x2, y2, startColor, endColor, etc.
224
225            // set x1 and y1 properties
226            int x1 = getIntValueFromChildElement( element, "x1" );
227            int y1 = getIntValueFromChildElement( element, "y1" );
228
229            shape.setPoint1( x1, y1 );
230
231            // set x2 and y2 properties
232            int x2 = getIntValueFromChildElement( element, "x2" );
233            int y2 = getIntValueFromChildElement( element, "y2" );
234
235            shape.setPoint2( x2, y2 );
236
237            // set startX and startY properties
238            int startX =
239               getIntValueFromChildElement( element, "startX" );
240            int startY =
241               getIntValueFromChildElement( element, "startY" );
242
243            shape.setStartPoint( startX, startY );
244
245            // set endX and endY properties
246            int endX = getIntValueFromChildElement( element, "endX" );
247            int endY = getIntValueFromChildElement( element, "endY" );
248
249            shape.setEndPoint( endX, endY );
250
251            // set startColor and endColor properties
252            Color startColor =
253               getColorValueFromChildElement( element, "startColor" );
```

Fig. 5.10   **DrawingFileReaderWriter** utility class for saving drawings to files and loading drawings from files (part 5 of 8).

```
254
255        shape.setStartColor( startColor );
256
257        Color endColor =
258           getColorValueFromChildElement( element, "endColor" );
259
260        shape.setEndColor( endColor );
261
262        // set useGradient property
263        boolean useGradient = getBooleanValueFromChildElement(
264           element, "useGradient" );
265
266        shape.setUseGradient( useGradient );
267
268        // set strokeSize property
269        float strokeSize = getFloatValueFromChildElement(
270           element, "strokeSize" );
271
272        shape.setStrokeSize( strokeSize );
273
274        // set filled property
275        boolean fill =
276           getBooleanValueFromChildElement( element, "fill" );
277
278        shape.setFilled( fill );
279
280        return shape;
281
282     } // end method getShapeFromElement
283
284     // get int value from child element with given name
285     private static int getIntValueFromChildElement( Element parent,
286        String childElementName )
287     {
288        // get NodeList for Elements of given childElementName
289        NodeList childNodes = parent.getElementsByTagName(
290           childElementName );
291
292        // get Text Node from zeroth child Element
293        Node childTextNode = childNodes.item( 0 ).getFirstChild();
294
295        // parse int value from Text Node
296        return Integer.parseInt( childTextNode.getNodeValue() );
297
298     } // end method getIntValueFromChildElement
299
300     // get float value from child element with given name
301     private static float getFloatValueFromChildElement(
302        Element parent, String childElementName )
303     {
304        // get NodeList for Elements of given childElementName
305        NodeList childNodes = parent.getElementsByTagName(
```

Fig. 5.10   **DrawingFileReaderWriter** utility class for saving drawings to files and loading drawings from files (part 6 of 8).

```
306            childElementName );
307
308        // get Text Node from zeroth child Element
309        Node childTextNode = childNodes.item( 0 ).getFirstChild();
310
311        // parse float value from Text Node
312        return Float.parseFloat( childTextNode.getNodeValue() );
313
314    } // end method getFloatValueFromChildElement
315
316    // get boolean value from child element with given name
317    private static boolean getBooleanValueFromChildElement(
318        Element parent, String childElementName )
319    {
320        // get NodeList for Elements of given childElementName
321        NodeList childNodes = parent.getElementsByTagName(
322            childElementName );
323
324        Node childTextNode = childNodes.item( 0 ).getFirstChild();
325
326        // parse boolean value from Text Node
327        return Boolean.valueOf(
328            childTextNode.getNodeValue() ).booleanValue();
329
330    } // end method getBooleanValueFromChildElement
331
332    // get String value from child element with given name
333    private static String getStringValueFromChildElement(
334        Element parent, String childElementName )
335    {
336        // get NodeList for Elements of given childElementName
337        NodeList childNodes = parent.getElementsByTagName(
338            childElementName );
339
340        // get Text Node from zeroth child Element
341        Node childTextNode = childNodes.item( 0 ).getFirstChild();
342
343        // return String value of Text Node
344        return childTextNode.getNodeValue();
345
346    }  // end method getStringValueFromChildElement
347
348    // get Color value from child element with given name
349    private static Color getColorValueFromChildElement(
350        Element parent, String childElementName )
351    {
352        // get NodeList for Elements of given childElementName
353        NodeList childNodes = parent.getElementsByTagName(
354            childElementName );
355
356        // get zeroth child Element
357        Element childElement = ( Element ) childNodes.item( 0 );
```

Fig. 5.10 **DrawingFileReaderWriter** utility class for saving drawings to files and loading drawings from files (part 7 of 8).

```
358
359        // get red, green and blue attribute values
360        int red = Integer.parseInt(
361            childElement.getAttribute( "red" ) );
362
363        int green = Integer.parseInt(
364            childElement.getAttribute( "green" ) );
365
366        int blue = Integer.parseInt(
367            childElement.getAttribute( "blue" ) );
368
369        // return Color for given red, green and blue values
370        return new Color( red, green, blue );
371
372     } // end method getColorValueFromChildElement
373 }
```

Fig. 5.10   **DrawingFileReaderWriter** utility class for saving drawings to files and loading drawings from files (part 8 of 8).

Method **readFile** (lines 92–142) loads a drawing from an XML document. Lines 100–109 create a **DocumentBuilder** and parse the XML document with the given **fileName**. Line 112 invokes method **getElementsByTagName** of interface **Document** to retrieve all **shape Element**s in the document. Lines 115–119 process each **shape Element** by invoking method **getShapeFromElement** (line 117), which returns a **MyShape** object for each **Element**. Line 120 adds each **MyShape** to the **shapes Collection**.

Method **getShapeFromElement** (lines 145–282) builds an appropriate **MyShape** subclass instance for the given **shape Element**. Line 150 retrieves the value of the **type Attribute** to determine the appropriate **MyShape** subclass to instantiate. Lines 170–206 obtain values specific to **MyText** objects. Lines 216–219 obtain values specific to **MyImage** objects. Lines 226–278 obtain values that apply to all **MyShape**s.

Method **getIntValueFromChildElement** (lines 285–298) is a utility method for obtaining an **int** value from a particular child **Element**. Lines 289–290 obtain a **NodeList** of **Element**s with the given **childElementName**. Line 293 obtains the **Text Node** child of the **Element** and line 298 parses the **Text Node** to produce an **int** value. Methods **getFloatValueFromChildElement** (lines 301–314), **getBooleanValueFromChildElement** (lines 317–330), **getStringValueFromChildElement** (lines 333–346) and **getColorValueFromChildElement** perform similar processing to retrieve values of other data types.

Figure 5.11 shows a sample XML document produced by **DrawingFileReader-Writer**. Note that the **MyText shape** element (lines 49–69) has child elements **text**, **fontSize**, **fontName**, **underline**, **bold** and **italic**, whereas the other shape elements have only the basic **MyShape**-related elements.

```
1   <?xml version="1.0" encoding="UTF-8"?>
2   <!DOCTYPE shapes SYSTEM "shapes.dtd">
```

Fig. 5.11   Sample XML document generated by **DrawingFileReaderWriter** (part 1 of 3).

```
 3   <shapes>
 4      <shape type="MyLine">
 5         <x1>122</x1>
 6         <y1>36</y1>
 7         <x2>43</x2>
 8         <y2>120</y2>
 9         <startX>43</startX>
10         <startY>120</startY>
11         <endX>122</endX>
12         <endY>36</endY>
13         <useGradient>false</useGradient>
14         <startColor red="0" green="0" blue="0"/>
15         <endColor red="255" green="255" blue="255"/>
16         <strokeSize>1.0</strokeSize>
17         <fill>false</fill>
18      </shape>
19      <shape type="MyRectangle">
20         <x1>62</x1>
21         <y1>71</y1>
22         <x2>124</x2>
23         <y2>132</y2>
24         <startX>62</startX>
25         <startY>71</startY>
26         <endX>124</endX>
27         <endY>132</endY>
28         <useGradient>false</useGradient>
29         <startColor red="0" green="0" blue="0"/>
30         <endColor red="255" green="255" blue="255"/>
31         <strokeSize>1.0</strokeSize>
32         <fill>false</fill>
33      </shape>
34      <shape type="MyOval">
35         <x1>18</x1>
36         <y1>11</y1>
37         <x2>107</x2>
38         <y2>123</y2>
39         <startX>18</startX>
40         <startY>11</startY>
41         <endX>107</endX>
42         <endY>123</endY>
43         <useGradient>false</useGradient>
44         <startColor red="0" green="0" blue="0"/>
45         <endColor red="255" green="255" blue="255"/>
46         <strokeSize>1.0</strokeSize>
47         <fill>false</fill>
48      </shape>
49      <shape type="MyText">
50         <x1>38</x1>
51         <y1>167</y1>
52         <x2>0</x2>
53         <y2>0</y2>
54         <startX>0</startX>
```

Fig. 5.11   Sample XML document generated by **DrawingFileReaderWriter** (part 2 of 3).

```
55              <startY>0</startY>
56              <endX>0</endX>
57              <endY>0</endY>
58              <useGradient>false</useGradient>
59              <startColor red="0" green="0" blue="0"/>
60              <endColor red="255" green="255" blue="255"/>
61              <strokeSize>1.0</strokeSize>
62              <fill>false</fill>
63              <text>Welcome to Deitel Drawing!</text>
64              <fontSize>10</fontSize>
65              <fontName>SansSerif</fontName>
66              <underlined>false</underlined>
67              <bold>true</bold>
68              <italic>false</italic>
69          </shape>
70          <shape type="MyOval">
71              <x1>84</x1>
72              <y1>63</y1>
73              <x2>169</x2>
74              <y2>148</y2>
75              <startX>169</startX>
76              <startY>63</startY>
77              <endX>84</endX>
78              <endY>148</endY>
79              <useGradient>true</useGradient>
80              <startColor red="51" green="51" blue="255"/>
81              <endColor red="255" green="255" blue="255"/>
82              <strokeSize>1.0</strokeSize>
83              <fill>true</fill>
84          </shape>
85      </shapes>
```

Fig. 5.11   Sample XML document generated by **DrawingFileReaderWriter** (part 3 of 3).

5.5 Deitel Drawing Views

The Deitel Drawing application provides two views of user drawings. Class **Drawing-View** (Fig. 5.12) is the primary view and extends **JPanel** to provide a surface onto which the user can draw **MyShape**s. Class **DrawingView** also implements interface **Observer** (line 20), so it can listen for **DrawingModel** changes.

```
1   // DrawingView.java
2   // DrawingView is a view of a DrawingModel that draws shapes using
3   // the Java2D API.
4   package com.deitel.advjhtp1.drawing.view;
5
6   // Java core packages
7   import java.awt.*;
```

Fig. 5.12   **DrawingView** class for displaying **MyShape**s in a **DrawingModel** (part 1 of 4).

```
 8   import java.awt.geom.*;
 9   import java.awt.event.*;
10   import java.util.*;
11   import java.util.List;
12
13   // Java extension packages
14   import javax.swing.*;
15
16   // Deitel packages
17   import com.deitel.advjhtp1.drawing.model.*;
18   import com.deitel.advjhtp1.drawing.model.shapes.*;
19
20   public class DrawingView extends JPanel implements Observer {
21
22      // model for which this is a view
23      private DrawingModel drawingModel;
24
25      // construct DrawingView for given model
26      public DrawingView( DrawingModel model )
27      {
28         // set DrawingModel
29         drawingModel = model;
30
31         // set background color
32         setBackground( Color.white );
33
34         // enable double buffering to reduce screen flicker
35         setDoubleBuffered( true );
36      }
37
38      // set DrawingModel for view to given model
39      public void setModel( DrawingModel model )
40      {
41         if ( drawingModel != null )
42            drawingModel.deleteObserver( this );
43
44         drawingModel = model;
45
46         // register view as observer of model
47         if ( model != null ) {
48            model.addObserver( this );
49            repaint();
50         }
51      }
52
53      // get DrawingModel associated with this view
54      public DrawingModel getModel()
55      {
56         return drawingModel;
57      }
58
59      // repaint view when update received from model
```

Fig. 5.12   **DrawingView** class for displaying **MyShape**s in a **DrawingModel**
(part 2 of 4).

```
60      public void update( Observable observable, Object object )
61      {
62         repaint();
63      }
64
65      // overridden paintComponent method for drawing shapes
66      public void paintComponent( Graphics g )
67      {
68         // call superclass paintComponent
69         super.paintComponent( g );
70
71         // create Graphics2D object for given Graphics object
72         Graphics2D g2D = ( Graphics2D ) g;
73
74         // enable anti-aliasing to smooth jagged lines
75         g2D.setRenderingHint( RenderingHints.KEY_ANTIALIASING,
76            RenderingHints.VALUE_ANTIALIAS_ON );
77
78         // enable high-quality rendering in Graphics2D object
79         g2D.setRenderingHint( RenderingHints.KEY_RENDERING,
80            RenderingHints.VALUE_RENDER_QUALITY );
81
82         // draw all shapes in model
83         drawShapes( g2D );
84      }
85
86      // draw shapes in model
87      public void drawShapes( Graphics2D g2D )
88      {
89         // get Iterator for shapes in model
90         Iterator iterator = drawingModel.getShapes().iterator();
91
92         // draw each MyShape in DrawingModel
93         while ( iterator.hasNext() ) {
94            MyShape shape = ( MyShape ) iterator.next();
95            shape.draw( g2D );
96         }
97      }
98
99      // get preferred size for this component
100     public Dimension getPreferredSize()
101     {
102        return new Dimension( 320, 240 );
103     }
104
105     // insist on preferred size for this component
106     public Dimension getMinimumSize()
107     {
108        return getPreferredSize();
109     }
110
111     // insist on preferred size for this component
```

Fig. 5.12   **DrawingView** class for displaying **MyShape**s in a **DrawingModel** (part 3 of 4).

```
112     public Dimension getMaximumSize()
113     {
114         return getPreferredSize();
115     }
116
117     // add DrawingView as Observer of DrawingModel when
118     // DrawingView obtains screen resources
119     public void addNotify()
120     {
121         super.addNotify();
122         drawingModel.addObserver( this );
123     }
124
125     // remove DrawingView as Observer of DrawingModel when
126     // DrawingView loses screen resources
127     public void removeNotify()
128     {
129         super.removeNotify();
130         drawingModel.deleteObserver( this );
131     }
132 }
```

Fig. 5.12   **DrawingView** class for displaying **MyShape**s in a **DrawingModel** (part 4 of 4).

Method **setModel** (lines 39–51) first removes the **DrawingView** as an **Observer** of the existing **DrawingModel** (line 42), then registers the **DrawingView** as an **Observer** for the new **DrawingModel** (line 48). The **Observable Drawing-Model** invokes method **update** of class **DrawingView** (lines 60–63) each time the **DrawingModel** changes. Method **update** invokes method **repaint** of class **JPanel** (line 62) each time the **DrawingView** receives an update from the **DrawingModel**. Methods **addNotify** (lines 119–123) and **removeNotify** (lines 127–131) add and delete the **DrawingView** as an **Observer** of the **DrawingModel** when the **Draw-ingView** obtains and discards its screen resources, respectively.

Method **paintComponent** (lines 66–84) configures the **Graphics2D** context for high-quality, anti-aliased drawing (lines 75–80) and invokes method **drawShapes** (line 83) to draw the **DrawingModel**'s shapes. Method **drawShapes** (lines 87–101) gets an **Iterator** for the **Collection** of **MyShapes** obtained from the **DrawingModel** (line 90). Lines 93–96 draw each **MyShape** on the given **Graphics2D** context.

Class **ZoomDrawingView** (Fig. 5.13) extends class **DrawingView** to provide a scaled view of a **DrawingModel**. Line 21 declares an **AffineTransform** reference that **ZoomDrawingView** uses to scale its rendering of the **DrawingModel**. The primary **ZoomDrawingView** constructor (lines 38–67) takes as arguments a **DrawingModel** and the factors by which the **AffineTransform** should scale points along the *x*- and *y*-axes.

Lines 48–65 add a **ComponentListener** anonymous inner class for the **Zoom-DrawingView**. This **ComponentListener** adjusts the scale factors when the **Zoom-DrawingView** component changes size. This allows the user to resize a window that contains a **ZoomDrawingView** to change its scale. For example, if the user resizes the window to **640x480**—twice the size of a default **DrawingView**—the **AffineTrans-form** magnifies the drawing view by a scale factor of **2**. If the user resizes the window to

160x120—half the size of a default **DrawingView**—the **AffineTransform** shrinks the drawing view by a scale factor of **0.5**. The *x*- and *y*-axes also scale independently. The user can stretch the window horizontally to produce a short, wide drawing view or vertically to produce a tall, narrow drawing view.

```
1    // ZoomDrawingView.java
2    // ZoomDrawingView is a subclass of DrawingView that scales
3    // the view of the drawing using the given scale factor.
4    package com.deitel.advjhtp1.drawing.view;
5
6    // Java core packages
7    import java.awt.*;
8    import java.awt.geom.*;
9    import java.awt.event.*;
10
11   // Deitel packages
12   import com.deitel.advjhtp1.drawing.model.*;
13
14   public class ZoomDrawingView extends DrawingView {
15
16      // factor for scaling view
17      private double scaleFactorX;
18      private double scaleFactorY;
19
20      // transform for scaling view
21      private AffineTransform scaleTransform;
22
23      // construct ZoomDrawingView with given model and default
24      // scale factor
25      public ZoomDrawingView( DrawingModel model )
26      {
27         this( model, 1.0 );
28      }
29
30      // construct ZoomDrawingView with given model and scale factor
31      public ZoomDrawingView( DrawingModel model, double scale )
32      {
33         this( model, scale, scale );
34      }
35
36      // construct ZoomDrawingView with given model and separate
37      // x and y scale factors
38      public ZoomDrawingView( DrawingModel model, double scaleX,
39         double scaleY )
40      {
41         // call DrawingView constructor
42         super( model );
43
44         // set scale factor for this view
45         setScaleFactors( scaleX, scaleY );
46
```

Fig. 5.13   **ZoomDrawingView** subclass of **DrawingView** for displaying scaled **MyShape**s (part 1 of 3).

```
47          // listen for component resize events to adjust scale
48          addComponentListener(
49            new ComponentAdapter() {
50
51                // when view is resized, update scale factors
52                public void componentResized( ComponentEvent event )
53                {
54                    double width = ( double ) getSize().width;
55                    double height = ( double ) getSize().height;
56
57                    // calculate new scale factors
58                    double factorX = width / 320.0;
59
60                    double factorY = height / 240.0;
61
62                    setScaleFactors( factorX, factorY );
63                }
64            }
65          );
66
67      } // end ZoomDrawingView constructor
68
69      // draw shapes using scaled Graphics2D object
70      public void drawShapes( Graphics2D g2D )
71      {
72          // set Graphics2D object transform
73          g2D.setTransform( scaleTransform );
74
75          // draw shapes on scaled Graphics2D object
76          super.drawShapes( g2D );
77      }
78
79      // set scale factors for view
80      public void setScaleFactors( double scaleX, double scaleY )
81      {
82          // set scale factors
83          scaleFactorX = scaleX;
84          scaleFactorY = scaleY;
85
86          // create AffineTransform with given scale factors
87          scaleTransform = AffineTransform.getScaleInstance(
88            scaleFactorX, scaleFactorY );
89      }
90
91      // get preferred size for this component
92      public Dimension getPreferredSize()
93      {
94          // default size is 320 x 240; scale using scaleFactors
95          return new Dimension( ( int ) ( 320 * scaleFactorX ),
96            ( int ) ( 240 * scaleFactorY ) );
97      }
98  }
```

Fig. 5.13   **ZoomDrawingView** subclass of **DrawingView** for displaying scaled
MyShapes (part 2 of 3).

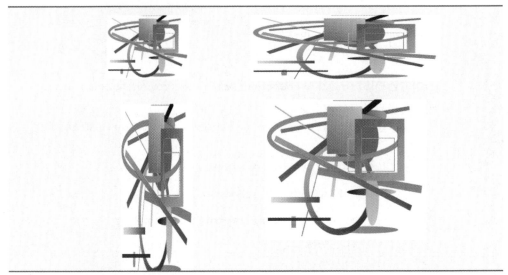

Fig. 5.13   **ZoomDrawingView** subclass of **DrawingView** for displaying scaled **MyShape**s (part 3 of 3).

Method **drawShapes** (lines 70–77) overrides method **drawShapes** from class **DrawingView**. Line 73 invokes method **setTransform** of class **Graphics2D** to cause the **Graphics2D** object to use the provided **AffineTransform** to scale the drawing. Method **setScaleFactors** (lines 80–89) takes as **double** arguments the scale factors to use for the *x*- and *y*-axes. Lines 87–88 create the **AffineTransform** that method **drawShapes** uses to scale the drawing. Static method **getScaleInstance** of class **AffineTransform** returns an **AffineTransform** object that scales drawings based on the provided *x*- and *y*-axis scale factors. For example, scale factors of **0.5** and **0.5** would produce a view that is one quarter the original size.

5.6 Deitel Drawing Controller Logic

The model-view-controller architecture separates logic for processing user input into objects that are separate from the views and the model. The Deitel Drawing application uses two types of controllers to handle user input—**MyShapeController**s and a **DragAndDropController**.

5.6.1 MyShapeControllers for Processing User Input

The primary user-input device for creating drawings is the mouse. A user can create and manipulate new shapes in a drawing by pressing the mouse button, dragging the mouse then releasing the mouse button. For each type of **MyShape**, however, there are different requirements for handling mouse events. For example, drawing a **MyText** shape requires the application to obtain from the user the text to be drawn and that text's properties, such as its font size. Class **MyShapeController** (Fig. 5.14) is an abstract base class that defines the basic functionality required by all **MyShapeController**s. Subclasses of **MyShapeController** provide the implementation details for adding instances of each particular **MyShape** subclass to a drawing.

```
1   // MyShapeController.java
2   // MyShapeController is an abstract base class that represents
3   // a controller for painting shapes.
4   package com.deitel.advjhtp1.drawing.controller;
5
6   // Java core packages
7   import java.awt.*;
8   import java.awt.event.*;
9
10  // Deitel packages
11  import com.deitel.advjhtp1.drawing.model.*;
12  import com.deitel.advjhtp1.drawing.model.shapes.*;
13
14  public abstract class MyShapeController {
15
16     private DrawingModel drawingModel;
17
18     // primary and secondary Colors for drawing and gradients
19     private Color primaryColor = Color.black;
20     private Color secondaryColor = Color.white;
21
22     // Class object for creating new MyShape-subclass instances
23     private Class shapeClass;
24
25     // common MyShape properties
26     private boolean fillShape = false;
27     private boolean useGradient = false;
28     private float strokeSize = 1.0f;
29
30     // indicates whether the user has specified drag mode; if
31     // true, MyShapeController should ignore mouse events
32     private boolean dragMode = false;
33
34     private MouseListener mouseListener;
35     private MouseMotionListener mouseMotionListener;
36
37     // MyShapeController constructor
38     public MyShapeController( DrawingModel model, Class
39        myShapeClass )
40     {
41        // set DrawingModel to control
42        drawingModel = model;
43
44        // set MyShape subclass
45        shapeClass = myShapeClass;
46
47        // listen for mouse events
48        mouseListener = new MouseAdapter() {
49
50           // when mouse button pressed, create new shape
51           public void mousePressed( MouseEvent event )
52           {
```

Fig. 5.14 **MyShapeController** abstract base class for controllers that handle mouse input (part 1 of 5).

```
53                    // if not in dragMode, start new shape at
54                    // given coordinates
55                    if ( !dragMode )
56                        startShape( event.getX(), event.getY() );
57                }
58
59                // when mouse button released, set shape's final
60                // coordinates
61                public void mouseReleased( MouseEvent event )
62                {
63                    // if not in dragMode, finish drawing current shape
64                    if ( !dragMode )
65                        endShape( event.getX(), event.getY() );
66                }
67            };
68
69            // listen for mouse motion events
70            mouseMotionListener = new MouseMotionAdapter() {
71
72                // when mouse is dragged, set coordinates for current
73                // shape's Point2
74                public void mouseDragged( MouseEvent event )
75                {
76                    // if not in dragMode, modify current shape
77                    if ( !dragMode )
78                        modifyShape( event.getX(), event.getY() );
79                }
80            };
81
82        } // end MyShapeController constructor
83
84        // set primary color (start color for gradient)
85        public void setPrimaryColor( Color color )
86        {
87            primaryColor = color;
88        }
89
90        // get primary color
91        public Color getPrimaryColor()
92        {
93            return primaryColor;
94        }
95
96        // set secondary color (end color for gradients)
97        public void setSecondaryColor( Color color )
98        {
99            secondaryColor = color;
100       }
101
102       // get secondary color
103       public Color getSecondaryColor()
104       {
```

Fig. 5.14   **MyShapeController** abstract base class for controllers that handle mouse input (part 2 of 5).

```
105            return secondaryColor;
106        }
107
108        // fill shape
109        public void setShapeFilled( boolean fill )
110        {
111            fillShape = fill;
112        }
113
114        // get shape filled
115        public boolean getShapeFilled()
116        {
117            return fillShape;
118        }
119
120        // use gradient when painting shape
121        public void setUseGradient( boolean gradient )
122        {
123            useGradient = gradient;
124        }
125
126        // get use gradient
127        public boolean getUseGradient()
128        {
129            return useGradient;
130        }
131
132        // set dragMode
133        public void setDragMode( boolean drag )
134        {
135            dragMode = drag;
136        }
137
138        // set stroke size for lines
139        public void setStrokeSize( float stroke )
140        {
141            strokeSize = stroke;
142        }
143
144        // get stroke size
145        public float getStrokeSize()
146        {
147            return strokeSize;
148        }
149
150        // create new instance of current MyShape subclass
151        protected MyShape createNewShape()
152        {
153            // create new instance of current MyShape subclass
154            try {
155                MyShape shape = ( MyShape ) shapeClass.newInstance();
156
```

Fig. 5.14   **MyShapeController** abstract base class for controllers that handle mouse input (part 3 of 5).

```
157          // set MyShape properties
158          shape.setFilled( fillShape );
159          shape.setUseGradient( useGradient );
160          shape.setStrokeSize( getStrokeSize() );
161          shape.setStartColor( getPrimaryColor() );
162          shape.setEndColor( getSecondaryColor() );
163
164          // return reference to newly created shape
165          return shape;
166       }
167
168       // handle exception instantiating shape
169       catch ( InstantiationException instanceException ) {
170          instanceException.printStackTrace();
171          return null;
172       }
173
174       // handle access exception instantiating shape
175       catch ( IllegalAccessException accessException ) {
176          accessException.printStackTrace();
177          return null;
178       }
179
180    } // end method createNewShape
181
182    // get MyShapeController's MouseListener
183    public MouseListener getMouseListener()
184    {
185       return mouseListener;
186    }
187
188    // get MyShapeController's MouseMotionListener
189    public MouseMotionListener getMouseMotionListener()
190    {
191       return mouseMotionListener;
192    }
193
194    // add given shape to DrawingModel
195    protected void addShapeToModel( MyShape shape )
196    {
197       drawingModel.addShape( shape );
198    }
199
200    // remove given shape from DrawingModel
201    protected void removeShapeFromModel( MyShape shape )
202    {
203       drawingModel.removeShape( shape );
204    }
205
206    // start new shape
207    public abstract void startShape( int x, int y );
208
```

Fig. 5.14   **MyShapeController** abstract base class for controllers that handle mouse input (part 4 of 5).

```
209    // modify current shape
210    public abstract void modifyShape( int x, int y );
211
212    // finish shape
213    public abstract void endShape( int x, int y );
214  }
```

Fig. 5.14   MyShapeController abstract base class for controllers that handle mouse input (part 5 of 5).

Each **MyShapeController** is responsible for responding to mouse events to allow users to add shapes to drawings. Lines 48–67 create a **MouseListener** that listens for **mousePressed** and **mouseReleased** events. When the user presses the mouse button, line 56 starts drawing a new shape at the location where the mouse press occurred by invoking method **startShape**. When the user releases the mouse button, line 65 invokes method **endShape** to complete the currently drawn shape. As the user drags the mouse, the **MouseMotionListener** on lines 70–80 invokes method **modifyShape** to modify the shape currently being drawn.

Note that class **MyShapeController** uses instances of **MouseAdapter** and **MouseMotionAdapter** to respond to **MouseEvent**s. Objects of the classes **Mouse-Adapter** and **MouseMotionAdapter** act as adapters between objects that generate **MouseEvent**s and those objects that handle these events. In this case study, **MyShape-Controller**'s **MouseAdapter** (lines 46–65) and **MouseMotionAdapter** (lines 68–79) adapts a **MyShapeController** to a **MouseListener** and **MouseMotion-Listener**, respectively. These adapter classes are examples of the *Adapter design pattern*, which provides an object with a new interface that *adapts* to another object's interface, allowing both objects to collaborate with one another. The adapter in this pattern is similar to an adapter for a plug on an electrical device—electrical sockets in Europe are different from those in the United States, so an adapter is needed to plug an American device into a European electrical socket and vice versa.

Methods **startShape**, **endShape** and **modifyShape** are abstract methods that each **MyShapeController** subclass must implement. This enables the developer to provide custom controllers for different shape types. The developer simply overrides these methods to perform the necessary input processing logic.

Method **createNewShape** (lines 151–180) uses Java's *reflection mechanism* to create new instances of **MyShape** subclasses as the user adds new shapes to a drawing. Reflection enables Java programs to determine information about classes and objects at runtime. In this example, we use reflection to enable our application to create instances of arbitrary **MyShape** subclasses dynamically. Each **MyShapeController** maintains a **Class** reference to the **Class** object for the **MyShape** subclass that the **MyShapeCon-troller** controls. For example, when the application creates a **MyShapeController** for drawing **MyLine**s, the **MyShapeController** stores a reference to the **Class** object for class **MyLine**. Line 155 invokes method **newInstance** of class **Class** to create a new instance of the specified **MyShape** subclass. Lines 158–162 initialize this new instance with the currently selected fill, gradient, stroke size and color properties.

Class **BoundedShapeController** (Fig. 5.15) provides a basic implementation of abstract base class **MyShapeController** for drawing rectangle-bounded shapes (in this application, **MyRectangle**s and **MyOval**s). Method **startShape** (lines 22–37) creates a new instance of the appropriate **MyShape** subclass (line 25), sets the **MyShape**'s position on the drawing (lines 30–32) and adds the **MyShape** to the **DrawingModel** (line 35). The **MouseListener** in class **MyShapeController** invokes method **startShape** when the user presses the mouse button to begin drawing a shape.

```
1   // BoundedShapeController.java
2   // BoundedShapeController is a MyShapeController subclass for
3   // rectangle-bounded shapes, such as MyOvals and MyRectangles.
4   package com.deitel.advjhtp1.drawing.controller;
5
6   // Deitel packages
7   import com.deitel.advjhtp1.drawing.model.*;
8   import com.deitel.advjhtp1.drawing.model.shapes.*;
9
10  public class BoundedShapeController extends MyShapeController {
11
12      private MyShape currentShape;
13
14      // BoundedShapeController constructor
15      public BoundedShapeController(
16         DrawingModel model, Class shapeClass )
17      {
18         super( model, shapeClass );
19      }
20
21      // start drawing shape
22      public void startShape( int x, int y )
23      {
24         // get new shape
25         currentShape = createNewShape();
26
27         if ( currentShape != null ) {
28
29            // set location of shape in drawing
30            currentShape.setPoint1( x, y );
31            currentShape.setPoint2( x, y );
32            currentShape.setStartPoint( x, y );
33
34            // add newly created shape to DrawingModel
35            addShapeToModel( currentShape );
36         }
37      }
38
39      // modify shape currently being drawn
40      public void modifyShape( int x, int y )
41      {
42         // remove shape from DrawingModel
43         removeShapeFromModel( currentShape );
44         currentShape.setEndPoint( x, y );
45
```

Fig. 5.15   **BoundedShapeController MyShapeController** subclass for controlling **MyLine**s, **MyOval**s and **MyRectangle**s (part 1 of 2).

```
46          int startX = currentShape.getStartX();
47          int startY = currentShape.getStartY();
48
49          // set Point1 to upper-left coordinates of shape
50          currentShape.setPoint1(
51             Math.min( x, startX ), Math.min( y, startY ) );
52
53          // set Point2 to lower right coordinates of shape
54          currentShape.setPoint2(
55             Math.max( x, startX ), Math.max( y, startY ) );
56
57          // add shape back into model
58          addShapeToModel( currentShape );
59       }
60
61       // finish drawing shape
62       public void endShape( int x, int y )
63       {
64          modifyShape( x, y );
65       }
66    }
```

Fig. 5.15   **BoundedShapeController MyShapeController** subclass for controlling **MyLine**s, **MyOval**s and **MyRectangle**s (part 2 of 2).

When the user drags the mouse, the **MouseMotionListener** inherited from class **MyShapeController** invokes method **modifyShape** (lines 40–59) and passes the *x*- and *y*-coordinates of the **MouseEvent**. Method **modifyShape** removes **current-Shape** from the **DrawingModel** (line 43), updates the **currentShape**'s various point properties with new coordinates (lines 46–55) and adds **currentShape** to the **DrawingModel**.

When the user releases the mouse button, the mouse handler invokes method **endShape** to complete the addition of the **MyShape** to the drawing. Method **endShape** invokes method **modifyShape** (line 52) to set the final values for **currentShape**'s coordinates.

Class **MyLineController** (Fig. 5.16) is a **MyShapeController** subclass for drawing **MyLine** objects. Method **startShape** (lines 20–36) is similar to method **startShape** in class **BoundedShapeController**. Method **modifyShape** (lines 39–56) removes the **MyLine** from the **DrawingModel** (line 42) and sets the **MyLine**'s **endPoint** to the current *x*, *y* coordinate. Lines 49–52 update the **MyLine**'s **Point1** and **Point2** coordinates.

```
1   // MyLineController.java
2   // MyLineController is a MyShapeController subclass for MyLines.
3   package com.deitel.advjhtp1.drawing.controller;
4
5   // Deitel packages
6   import com.deitel.advjhtp1.drawing.model.*;
```

Fig. 5.16   **MyLineController MyShapeController** subclass for drawing **MyLine**s (part 1 of 3).

```
 7   import com.deitel.advjhtp1.drawing.model.shapes.*;
 8
 9   public class MyLineController extends MyShapeController {
10
11      private MyShape currentShape;
12
13      // MyLineController constructor
14      public MyLineController( DrawingModel model, Class shapeClass )
15      {
16         super( model, shapeClass );
17      }
18
19      // start drawing new shape
20      public void startShape( int x, int y )
21      {
22         // create new shape
23         currentShape = createNewShape();
24
25         if ( currentShape != null ) {
26
27            // set location of shape in drawing
28            currentShape.setPoint1( x, y );
29            currentShape.setPoint2( x, y );
30            currentShape.setStartPoint( x, y );
31
32            // add newly created shape to DrawingModel
33            addShapeToModel( currentShape );
34         }
35
36      } // end method startShape
37
38      // modify shape currently being drawn
39      public void modifyShape( int x, int y )
40      {
41         // remove shape from DrawingModel
42         removeShapeFromModel( currentShape );
43         currentShape.setEndPoint( x, y );
44
45         int startX = currentShape.getStartX();
46         int startY = currentShape.getStartY();
47
48         // set current ( x, y ) to Point1
49         currentShape.setPoint1( x, y );
50
51         // set Point2 to StartPoint
52         currentShape.setPoint2( startX, startY );
53
54         // add shape back into model
55         addShapeToModel( currentShape );
56      }
57
58      // finish drawing shape
```

Fig. 5.16   **MyLineController MyShapeController** subclass for drawing **MyLine**s (part 2 of 3).

```
59      public void endShape( int x, int y )
60      {
61          modifyShape( x, y );
62      }
63   }
```

Fig. 5.16   **MyLineController MyShapeController** subclass for drawing
MyLines (part 3 of 3).

Instances of class **MyText** are drawn quite differently from instances of classes
MyLine, **MyOval** and **MyRectangle** and therefore require a custom implementation of
class **MyShapeController**. Class **MyTextController** (Fig. 5.17) presents a dialog
box that prompts the user for the text to be drawn as well as **MyText** properties (e.g., bold,
italic, font, etc.).

```
1    // MyTextController.java
2    // MyTextController is a MyShapeController subclass for drawing
3    // MyText objects.
4    package com.deitel.advjhtp1.drawing.controller;
5
6    // Java core packages
7    import java.awt.*;
8    import java.awt.event.*;
9
10   // Java extension packages
11   import javax.swing.*;
12
13   // Deitel packages
14   import com.deitel.advjhtp1.drawing.model.*;
15   import com.deitel.advjhtp1.drawing.model.shapes.*;
16
17   public class MyTextController extends MyShapeController {
18
19       // MyTextController constructor
20       public MyTextController( DrawingModel model, Class shapeClass )
21       {
22           // invoke superclass constructor; always use MyText class
23           super( model, MyText.class );
24       }
25
26       // start drawing MyText object
27       public void startShape( int x, int y ) {
28
29           // create MyText shape
30           MyText currentText = new MyText();
31
32           // set MyText's Point1
33           currentText.setPoint1( x, y );
34
```

Fig. 5.17   **MyTextController MyShapeController** subclass for adding
MyText instances to a drawing (part 1 of 4).

```
35          // create TextInputPanel to get text and properties
36          TextInputPanel inputPanel = new TextInputPanel();
37
38          // display TextInputPanel in JOptionPane
39          String text = JOptionPane.showInputDialog( null,
40             inputPanel );
41
42          // ensure provided text is not null or empty
43          if ( text == null || text.equals( "" ) )
44             return;
45
46          // set MyText properties (bold, italic, etc.)
47          currentText.setBoldSelected(
48             inputPanel.boldSelected() );
49
50          currentText.setItalicSelected(
51             inputPanel.italicSelected() );
52
53          currentText.setUnderlineSelected(
54             inputPanel.underlineSelected() );
55
56          currentText.setFontName(
57             inputPanel.getSelectedFontName() );
58
59          currentText.setFontSize(
60             inputPanel.getSelectedFontSize() );
61
62          currentText.setColor( getPrimaryColor() );
63
64          // set MyText's text
65          currentText.setText( text );
66
67          // add MyText object to model
68          addShapeToModel( currentText );
69       }
70
71       // modify shape currently being drawn
72       public void modifyShape( int x, int y ) {}
73
74       // finish drawing shape
75       public void endShape( int x, int y ) {}
76
77       // JPanel with components for inputting MyText properties
78       private static class TextInputPanel extends JPanel {
79
80          private JCheckBox boldCheckBox;
81          private JCheckBox italicCheckBox;
82          private JCheckBox underlineCheckBox;
83          private JComboBox fontComboBox;
84          private JComboBox fontSizeComboBox;
85
86          // TextInputPanel constructor
```

Fig. 5.17   **MyTextController MyShapeController** subclass for adding **MyText** instances to a drawing (part 2 of 4).

```
87          public TextInputPanel()
88          {
89              boldCheckBox = new JCheckBox( "Bold" );
90              italicCheckBox = new JCheckBox( "Italic" );
91              underlineCheckBox = new JCheckBox( "Underline" );
92
93              // create JComboBox for selecting Font
94              fontComboBox = new JComboBox();
95              fontComboBox.addItem( "SansSerif" );
96              fontComboBox.addItem( "Serif" );
97
98              // create JComboBox for selecting Font size
99              fontSizeComboBox = new JComboBox();
100             fontSizeComboBox.addItem( "10" );
101             fontSizeComboBox.addItem( "12" );
102             fontSizeComboBox.addItem( "14" );
103             fontSizeComboBox.addItem( "18" );
104             fontSizeComboBox.addItem( "22" );
105             fontSizeComboBox.addItem( "36" );
106             fontSizeComboBox.addItem( "48" );
107             fontSizeComboBox.addItem( "72" );
108
109             setLayout( new FlowLayout() );
110
111             add( boldCheckBox );
112             add( italicCheckBox );
113             add( underlineCheckBox );
114             add( fontComboBox );
115             add( fontSizeComboBox );
116         }
117
118         // get bold property
119         public boolean boldSelected()
120         {
121             return boldCheckBox.isSelected();
122         }
123
124         // get italic property
125         public boolean italicSelected()
126         {
127             return italicCheckBox.isSelected();
128         }
129
130         // get underline property
131         public boolean underlineSelected()
132         {
133             return underlineCheckBox.isSelected();
134         }
135
136         // get font name property
137         public String getSelectedFontName()
138         {
```

Fig. 5.17   **MyTextController MyShapeController** subclass for adding
MyText instances to a drawing (part 3 of 4).

```
139              return fontComboBox.getSelectedItem().toString();
140          }
141
142          // get font size property
143          public int getSelectedFontSize()
144          {
145              return Integer.parseInt(
146                  fontSizeComboBox.getSelectedItem().toString() );
147          }
148      }
149  }
```

Fig. 5.17 **MyTextController MyShapeController** subclass for adding **MyText** instances to a drawing (part 4 of 4).

Method **startShape** (lines 27–69) creates a new **MyText** object (line 30) and sets its coordinates to the given *x, y* coordinate. Line 36 creates a new **TextInputPanel** and lines 39–40 display the **TextInputPanel** in a **JOptionPane**. After the user enters the text and its properties, lines 47–68 set the **MyText** object's properties and add the **MyText** object to the **DrawingModel**. **MyTextController** uses static class **TextInput-Panel** (lines 78–148) to present a GUI for setting **MyText** object properties. Class **TextInputPanel** includes **JCheckBox**es for selecting bold, italic and underline, and **JComboBox**es for selecting the font and font size.

Class **MyShapeController** uses the *Template Method design pattern* to ensure that all **MyShapeController**s follow the same three-step algorithm for creating shapes—the user clicks on the drawing area to specify a shape's position, drags the mouse cursor across the area to specify its size, then releases the mouse button to create the shape. These steps correspond to the abstract methods **startShape**, **modifyShape** and **endShape**, respectively. Each **MyShapeController** subclass uses this algorithm but implements each step differently from the other implementations. For example, method **startShape** of class **MyTextController** presents a dialog box that obtains font information and text from the user. However, neither class **MyLineController** nor class **BoundedShapeController** needs to set fonts, so their implementations of method **startShape** differ from that of class **MyTextController**. Because the Template Method design pattern encapsulates a step-by-step algorithm that several objects can use, this pattern becomes beneficial when we add new **MyShapeController** subclasses (e.g., **RandomShapeController** in Exercise 5.8) to our system—we need implement only those methods that comprise the algorithm.

5.6.2 MyShapeControllers and Factory Method Design Pattern

The model-view-controller architecture makes the Deitel Drawing application easily extensible through the addition of new **MyShape** subclasses and new views. Creating a new **MyShape** subclass also could require a new **MyShapeController** subclass (as class **MyText** does). To eliminate the need to change existing code when adding a new **MyShapeController** to the application, Deitel Drawing uses a combination of two popular design patterns—the Factory Method design pattern and the Singleton design pattern.

The Deitel Drawing application uses the *Factory Method design pattern* to enable the user to select an appropriate **MyShapeController** at runtime. As its name implies, a Factory method creates objects. Factory methods can create objects based on criteria that are known only at runtime. These criteria could be in the form of user input, system properties, etc. In the Deitel Drawing application, the criterion is the user-selected **MyShape** type. The particular **MyShape** subclass the user selects is known only at run time, so at compile time we cannot determine what type of **MyShapeController** to use for controlling user input. We use a Factory Method in class **MyShapeControllerFactory** (Fig. 5.18) to construct the appropriate **MyShapeController** for the user-selected **MyShape**.

Method **newMyShapeController** (lines 75–106) is a Factory Method that takes as a **DrawingModel** argument the model to be controlled and as a **String** argument the name of the **MyShape** subclass for which to create a **MyShapeController** instance. Lines 83–85 invoke **static** method **forName** of class **Class** to get the **Class** object for the given **MyShape** subclass. If the given **MyShape** subclass is **MyLine**, line 89 returns a **MyLineController**. If the given **MyShape** subclass is **MyText**, line 92 returns a new instance of class **MyTextController**. Otherwise, lines 95–96 return a new instance of class **BoundedShapeController**.

```
1   // MyShapeControllerFactory.java
2   // MyShapeControllerFactory uses the Factory Method design
3   // pattern to create an appropriate instance of MyShapeController
4   // for the given MyShape subclass.
5   package com.deitel.advjhtp1.drawing.controller;
6
7   // Deitel packages
8   import com.deitel.advjhtp1.drawing.model.*;
9   import com.deitel.advjhtp1.drawing.model.shapes.*;
10
11  public class MyShapeControllerFactory {
12
13     private static final String FACTORY_PROPERTY_KEY =
14        "MyShapeControllerFactory";
15
16     private static final String[] supportedShapes =
17        { "MyLine", "MyRectangle", "MyOval", "MyText" };
18
19     // reference to Singleton MyShapeControllerFactory
20     private static MyShapeControllerFactory factory;
21
22     // MyShapeControllerFactory constructor
23     protected MyShapeControllerFactory() {}
24
25     // return Singleton instance of MyShapeControllerFactory
26     public static final MyShapeControllerFactory getInstance()
27     {
28        // if factory is null, create new MyShapeControllerFactory
29        if ( factory == null ) {
```

Fig. 5.18   **MyShapeControllerFactory** class for creating appropriate **MyShapeController** for given **MyShape** type (part 1 of 3).

```
30
31          // get System property that contains the factory
32          // class name
33          String factoryClassName =
34             System.getProperty( FACTORY_PROPERTY_KEY );
35
36          // if the System property is not set, create a new
37          // instance of the default MyShapeControllerFactory
38          if ( factoryClassName == null )
39             factory = new MyShapeControllerFactory();
40
41          // create a new MyShapeControllerFactory using the
42          // class name provided in the System property
43          else {
44
45             // create MyShapeControllerFactory subclass instance
46             try {
47                factory = ( MyShapeControllerFactory )
48                Class.forName( factoryClassName ).newInstance();
49             }
50
51             // handle exception loading instantiating
52             catch ( ClassNotFoundException classException ) {
53                classException.printStackTrace();
54             }
55
56             // handle exception instantiating factory
57             catch ( InstantiationException exception ) {
58                exception.printStackTrace();
59             }
60
61             // handle exception if no access to specified Class
62             catch ( IllegalAccessException accessException ) {
63                accessException.printStackTrace();
64             }
65          }
66
67       } // end if
68
69       return factory;
70
71    } // end method getInstance
72
73    // create new MyShapeController subclass instance for given
74    // suitable for controlling given MyShape subclass type
75    public MyShapeController newMyShapeController(
76       DrawingModel model, String shapeClassName )
77    {
78       // create Class instance for given class name and
79       // construct appropriate MyShapeController
80       try {
81
```

Fig. 5.18   **MyShapeControllerFactory** class for creating appropriate **MyShapeController** for given **MyShape** type (part 2 of 3).

```
82          // get Class object for selected MyShape subclass
83          Class shapeClass = Class.forName(
84             MyShape.class.getPackage().getName() + "." +
85             shapeClassName );
86
87          // return appropriate controller for MyShape subclass
88          if ( shapeClassName.equals( "MyLine" ) )
89             return new MyLineController( model, shapeClass );
90
91          else if ( shapeClassName.equals( "MyText" ) )
92             return new MyTextController( model, shapeClass );
93
94          else
95             return new BoundedShapeController( model,
96                shapeClass );
97       }
98
99       // handle exception if MyShape derived class not found
100      catch ( ClassNotFoundException classException ) {
101         classException.printStackTrace();
102      }
103
104      return null;
105
106   }  // end method newMyShapeController
107
108   // get String array of MyShape subclass names for which this
109   // factory can create MyShapeControllers
110   public String[] getSupportedShapes()
111   {
112      return supportedShapes;
113   }
114 }
```

Fig. 5.18   **MyShapeControllerFactory** class for creating appropriate **MyShapeController** for given **MyShape** type (part 3 of 3).

Class **MyShapeControllerFactory** also uses the *Singleton design pattern* to control how other objects obtain instances of **MyShapeControllerFactory**. Specifically, the Singleton design pattern ensures that only one instance of a particular object can exist in a particular application. Class **MyShapeControllerFactory** declares a **protected**, no-argument constructor to prevent other objects from instantiating **MyShapeControllerFactory** objects directly. Other objects that require an instance of class **MyShapeControllerFactory** can invoke method **getInstance** (lines 26–71) to obtain the Singleton instance. If a **MyShapeControllerFactory** has not been created yet, lines 29–65 create a **MyShapeControllerFactory**. Line 69 returns the Singleton **MyShapeControllerFactory** instance to the caller.

In this example, our implementation provides the benefit of allowing the **MyShapeControllerFactory** to determine at runtime the particular subclass of **MyShapeControllerFactory** to instantiate. Lines 33–34 read a system property whose value specifies from which particular **MyShapeControllerFactory** subclass method **getInstance** should instantiate a new **MyShapeControllerFactory**. By specifying a value for this system property at the command line, a user can "install" a new **MyShapeControllerFactory** subclass without requiring changes to existing application code. For example, Exercise 5.8 asks you to create a **RandomMyShapeController** that draws random shapes in the drawing. To add this new **MyShapeController** to the application, you also must create a **MyShapeControllerFactory** subclass (e.g., **RandomMyShapeControllerFactory**) that creates **RandomMyShapeController**s. From the command line, the user can specify that the program should use this new factory by specifying the system property as follows

```
java -DMyShapeControllerFactory=RandomMyShapeControllerFac-
tory com.deitel.advjhtp1.drawing.DeitelDrawing
```

If the user does not specify a class name in the **MyShapeControllerFactory** system property, the application uses the default **MyShapeControllerFactory** (line 39).

5.6.3 Drag-and-Drop Controller

The Deitel Drawing application supports two types of drag-and-drop operations. First, users can drag and drop certain **MyShape**s within drawings and between drawings in the multiple-document interface. Second, users can drag JPEG images from the host operating system's file manager and drop them on drawings to add those images to drawings.

There are several objects required to enable drag and drop in a Java application. A drag-and-drop operation begins in a **DragSource**. Static method **getDefaultDragSource** of class **DragSource** returns the **DragSource** for the host platform. A **DragGestureRecognizer** recognizes user gestures that begin drag-and-drop operations, such as pressing the mouse button over an object and dragging that object. When a user makes a drag gesture, the **DragGestureRecognizer** notifies its registered **DragGestureListener**s. The **DragGestureListener** then begins the drag-and-drop operation. The user continues the drag gesture until reaching the **DropTarget**, which is the destination for the drag-and-drop operation. When the user makes a gesture to complete the drag-and-drop operation (e.g., by releasing the mouse button), both the **DropTarget** and **DragSource** are notified that the drag-and-drop operation has completed. The event associated with the drag-and-drop operation's completion includes information about the success or failure of the drag-and-drop operation and a **Transferable** object containing the data that was transferred.

In the Deitel Drawing application, an instance of class **DragAndDropController** (Fig. 5.19) controls each drag-and-drop operation. Class **DragAndDropController** implements three interfaces to handle drag-and-drop operations—**DragGestureListener**, **DragSourceListener** and **DropTargetListener**. These interfaces enable **DragAndDropController** to recognize drag gestures, **DragSource** events and **DropTarget** events.

```
1   // DragAndDropController.java
2   // DragAndDropController is a controller for handling drag and
3   // drop in DeitelDrawing. DragAndDropController implements
```

Fig. 5.19 **DragAndDropController** for moving **MyShape**s between drawings and adding JPEG images to drawings using drag and drop (part 1 of 8).

```
4    // DragGestureListener and DragSourceListener to handle drag
5    // events and DropTargetListener to handle drop events.
6    package com.deitel.advjhtp1.drawing.controller;
7
8    // Java core packages
9    import java.util.*;
10   import java.io.*;
11   import java.awt.Point;
12   import java.awt.dnd.*;
13   import java.awt.datatransfer.*;
14
15   // Deitel packages
16   import com.deitel.advjhtp1.drawing.model.*;
17   import com.deitel.advjhtp1.drawing.model.shapes.*;
18
19   public class DragAndDropController implements DragGestureListener,
20      DragSourceListener, DropTargetListener {
21
22      // model to control
23      private DrawingModel drawingModel;
24
25      private boolean dragMode = false;
26
27      // DragAndDropController constructor
28      public DragAndDropController( DrawingModel model )
29      {
30         drawingModel = model;
31      }
32
33      // set drag mode
34      public void setDragMode( boolean drag )
35      {
36         dragMode = drag;
37      }
38
39      // recognize drag operation beginning (method of interface
40      // DragGestureListener)
41      public void dragGestureRecognized( DragGestureEvent event )
42      {
43         // if not in dragMode, ignore drag gesture
44         if ( !dragMode )
45            return;
46
47         // get Point at which drag began
48         Point origin = event.getDragOrigin();
49
50         // get MyShapes from DrawingModel
51         List shapes = new ArrayList( drawingModel.getShapes() );
52
53         // find top-most shape that contains drag origin (i.e.,
54         // start at end of ListIterator and work backwards)
```

Fig. 5.19   **DragAndDropController** for moving **MyShape**s between drawings and adding JPEG images to drawings using drag and drop (part 2 of 8).

```
55          ListIterator shapeIterator =
56             shapes.listIterator( shapes.size() );
57
58          while ( shapeIterator.hasPrevious() ) {
59
60             MyShape shape = ( MyShape ) shapeIterator.previous();
61
62             if ( shape.contains( origin ) ) {
63
64                // create TransferableShape for dragging shape
65                // from Point origin
66                TransferableShape transfer =
67                   new TransferableShape( shape, origin );
68
69                // start drag operation
70                event.startDrag( null, transfer, this );
71
72                break;
73             }
74
75          } // end while
76
77       } // end method dragGestureRecognized
78
79       // handle drop events (method of interface DropTargetListener)
80       public void drop( DropTargetDropEvent event )
81       {
82          // get dropped object
83          Transferable transferable = event.getTransferable();
84
85          // get dropped object's DataFlavors
86          DataFlavor[] dataFlavors =
87             transferable.getTransferDataFlavors();
88
89          // get DropTargetDropEvent location
90          Point location = event.getLocation();
91
92          // process drops for supported types
93          for ( int i = 0; i < dataFlavors.length; i++ ) {
94             DataFlavor dataFlavor = dataFlavors[ i ];
95
96             // handle drop of JPEG images
97             if ( dataFlavor.equals(
98                DataFlavor.javaFileListFlavor ) ) {
99
100                // accept the drop operation
101                event.acceptDrop( DnDConstants.ACTION_COPY );
102
103                // attempt to drop the images and indicate whether
104                // drop is complete
105                event.dropComplete(
106                   dropImages( transferable, location ) );
```

Fig. 5.19   **DragAndDropController** for moving **MyShape**s between drawings and adding JPEG images to drawings using drag and drop (part 3 of 8).

```
107              }
108
109              // handle drop of TransferableShape objects
110              else if ( dataFlavor.isMimeTypeEqual(
111                 TransferableShape.MIME_TYPE ) ) {
112
113                 // accept drop of TransferableShape
114                 event.acceptDrop( DnDConstants.ACTION_MOVE );
115
116                 // drop TransferableShape into drawing
117                 dropShape( transferable, location );
118
119                 // complete drop operation
120                 event.dropComplete( true );
121              }
122
123              // reject all other DataFlavors
124              else
125                 event.rejectDrop();
126
127        } // end for
128
129     } // end method drop
130
131     // drop JPEG images onto drawing
132     private boolean dropImages( Transferable transferable,
133        Point location )
134     {
135        // boolean indicating successful drop
136        boolean success = true;
137
138        // attempt to drop images onto drawing
139        try {
140
141           // get list of dropped files
142           List fileList =
143              ( List ) transferable.getTransferData(
144                 DataFlavor.javaFileListFlavor );
145
146           Iterator iterator = fileList.iterator();
147
148           // search for JPEG images
149           for ( int i = 1; iterator.hasNext(); i++ ) {
150              File file = ( File ) iterator.next();
151
152              // if dropped file is a JPEG image, decode and
153              // add MyImage to drawingModel
154              if ( fileIsJPEG( file ) ) {
155
156                 // create MyImage for given JPEG file
157                 MyImage image = new MyImage();
158                 image.setFileName( file.getPath() );
```

Fig. 5.19 **DragAndDropController** for moving **MyShape**s between drawings and adding JPEG images to drawings using drag and drop (part 4 of 8).

```
159                    image.setPoint1( location.x, location.y );
160
161                    // add to DrawingModel
162                    drawingModel.addShape( image );
163                 }
164
165              else
166                 success = false;
167
168           } // end for
169
170        } // end try
171
172        // handle exception if DataFlavor not supported
173        catch ( UnsupportedFlavorException flavorException ) {
174           success = false;
175           flavorException.printStackTrace();
176        }
177
178        // handle exception reading File
179        catch ( IOException ioException ) {
180           success = false;
181           ioException.printStackTrace();
182        }
183
184        return success;
185
186     } // end method dropImages
187
188     // return true if File has .jpg or .jpeg extension
189     private boolean fileIsJPEG( File file )
190     {
191        String fileName = file.getName().toLowerCase();
192
193        return fileName.endsWith( ".jpg" ) ||
194           fileName.endsWith( ".jpeg" );
195     }
196
197     // drop MyShape object onto drawing
198     private void dropShape( Transferable transferable,
199        Point location )
200     {
201        try {
202
203           DataFlavor flavor = new DataFlavor(
204              TransferableShape.MIME_TYPE, "Shape" );
205
206           // get TransferableShape object
207           TransferableShape transferableShape =
208              ( TransferableShape ) transferable.getTransferData(
209                 flavor );
210
```

Fig. 5.19   **DragAndDropController** for moving **MyShape**s between drawings and adding JPEG images to drawings using drag and drop (part 5 of 8).

```
211            // get MyShape and origin Point from TransferableShape
212            MyShape shape = transferableShape.getShape();
213            Point origin = transferableShape.getOrigin();
214
215            // calculate offset for dropping MyShape
216            int xOffSet = location.x - origin.x;
217            int yOffSet = location.y - origin.y;
218
219            shape.moveByOffSet( xOffSet, yOffSet );
220
221            // add MyShape to target DrawingModel
222            drawingModel.addShape( shape );
223
224         } // end try
225
226         // handle exception if DataFlavor not supported
227         catch ( UnsupportedFlavorException flavorException ) {
228            flavorException.printStackTrace();
229         }
230
231         // handle exception getting Transferable data
232         catch ( IOException ioException ) {
233            ioException.printStackTrace();
234         }
235
236      } // end method dropShape
237
238      // check for success when drag-and-drop operation ends
239      // (method of interface DragSourceListener)
240      public void dragDropEnd( DragSourceDropEvent event )
241      {
242         // if drop successful, remove MyShape from source
243         // DrawingModel
244         if ( event.getDropSuccess() ) {
245
246            // get Transferable object from DragSourceContext
247            Transferable transferable =
248               event.getDragSourceContext().getTransferable();
249
250            // get TransferableShape object from Transferable
251            try {
252
253               // get TransferableShape object
254               TransferableShape transferableShape =
255                  ( TransferableShape ) transferable.getTransferData(
256                     new DataFlavor( TransferableShape.MIME_TYPE,
257                        "Shape" ) );
258
259               // get MyShape from TransferableShape object
260               // and remove from source DrawingModel
261               drawingModel.removeShape(
262                  transferableShape.getShape() );
```

Fig. 5.19   **DragAndDropController** for moving **MyShape**s between drawings and adding JPEG images to drawings using drag and drop (part 6 of 8).

```
263          }
264
265          // handle exception if DataFlavor not supported
266          catch ( UnsupportedFlavorException flavorException ) {
267             flavorException.printStackTrace();
268          }
269
270          // handle exception getting transfer data
271          catch ( IOException ioException ) {
272             ioException.printStackTrace();
273          }
274
275       } // end if
276
277    } // end method dragDropEnd
278
279    // required methods of interface DropTargetListener
280    public void dragEnter( DropTargetDragEvent event ) {}
281    public void dragExit( DropTargetEvent event ) {}
282    public void dragOver( DropTargetDragEvent event ) {}
283    public void dropActionChanged( DropTargetDragEvent event ) {}
284
285    // required methods of interface DragSourceListener
286    public void dragEnter( DragSourceDragEvent event ) {}
287    public void dragExit( DragSourceEvent event ) {}
288    public void dragOver( DragSourceDragEvent event ) {}
289    public void dropActionChanged( DragSourceDragEvent event ) {}
290 }
```

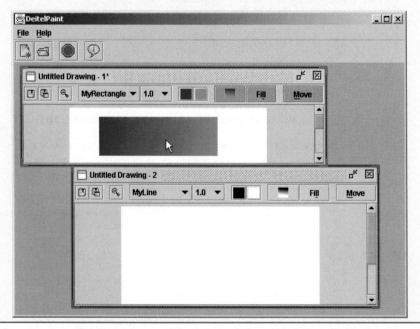

Fig. 5.19   DragAndDropController for moving **MyShape**s between drawings and adding JPEG images to drawings using drag and drop (part 7 of 8).

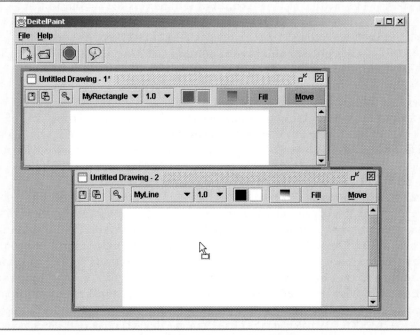

Fig. 5.19   **DragAndDropController** for moving **MyShape**s between drawings and adding JPEG images to drawings using drag and drop (part 8 of 8).

The drag-and-drop subsystem invokes method **dragGestureRecognized** (lines 41–77) when the user makes a drag gesture, such as pressing the mouse button and dragging the mouse on a draggable object. If the user has not selected drag mode in the Deitel Drawing application, line 45 returns to ignore the drag gesture. Lines 58–75 search through the **Collection** of **MyShape**s in the **DrawingModel** for the topmost shape that intersects **Point origin**, which is where the drag gesture occurred. Note that lines 58–75 go through the **Collection** in reverse order, since the topmost shape is at the end of the **Collection**. Lines 66–67 create a **TransferableShape** (Fig. 5.22) that contains the **MyShape** to be dragged and the **Point** at which the drag began. Line 70 invokes method **startDrag** of class **DragGestureEvent** to begin the drag-and-drop operation.

When the user drops a dragged object, the **DropTarget** notifies its **DropTargetListener**s by invoking method **drop** (lines 80–129). Line 83 gets the **Transferable** object from the **DropTargetEvent**. Each **Transferable** object contains an array of **DataFlavor**s that describe the type of data contained in the **Transferable** object. Lines 93–127 process the array of **DataFlavor**s to determine the type of object that the user dropped. If the **DataFlavor** is **DataFlavor.javaFileListFlavor** (lines 97–98), the user dropped a **List** of **File**s from the host operating system's file manager. Line 101 accepts the drop, and line 106 invokes method **dropImages** to process the **File List**. The Deitel Drawing application allows the user to drop only JPEG images, not other file types. If method **dropImages** returns **true**, the files were all JPEG images and the drag-and-drop operation completes successfully. If the **DataFlavor**'s MIME type matches class **TransferableShape**'s MIME type (lines 110–111), line 114 invokes method **acceptDrop** of class **DropTargetDropEvent** to accept the drop and line 117 invokes method **dropShape** to process the **MyShape** that the user dropped. Line 120 invokes method **dropComplete** of class **DropTargetDropEvent** to indicate that the drop completed successfully. If the **DataFlavor** was neither a file list from the file manager nor a **TransferableShape**, line 125 rejects the drop by invoking method **rejectDrop** of class **DropTargetDropEvent**.

Method **dropImages** (lines 132–186) takes as arguments a **Transferable** object containing a **File List** and the **Point** at which the drop occurred. Lines 142–144 get the **File List**, and line 146 obtains an **Iterator** to process the **List**. Lines 149–168 check each **File** to determine whether it contains a JPEG image. If the **File** does contain a JPEG image (line 154), lines 157–162 create a new **MyImage** object for the JPEG image and add it to the **DrawingModel**. Method **fileIsJPEG** (lines 189–195) returns **true** if the given **File**'s name ends with the **.jpg** or **.jpeg** extension.

Method **dropShape** (lines 198–253) takes as a **Transferable** argument the object that the user dropped and a **Point** argument for the drop location. Lines 207–209 get the **TransferableShape** object by invoking method **getTransferData** of interface **Transferable**. If the **Transferable** object does not support the **DataFlavor** passed on line 209, method **getTransferData** throws an **UnsupportedFlavorException**. If there is an error reading the data, method **getTransferData** could throw an **IOException**. Line 212 gets the **MyShape** object from the **TransferableShape**, and line 213 gets the **Point** from which the **MyShape** was dragged. Lines 216–219 calculate the offset from the dragged point to the drop point and invoke **MyShape** method **moveByOffSet** to position the **MyShape**. Line 222 adds the **MyShape** to the **DropTarget**'s **DrawingModel**.

The drag-and-drop subsystem invokes method **dragDropEnd** (lines 240–277) when the drag-and-drop operation completes. If the drag-and-drop operation succeeded (line 244), lines 261–262 remove the dragged **MyShape** object from the source **DrawingModel**. The remaining empty methods (lines 280–289) satisfy interfaces **DropTargetListener** and **DragSourceListener**. Figure 5.20 and Fig. 5.21 describe the methods of interfaces **DragSourceListener** and **DropTargetListener**.

Method	Description
public void **dragEnter(DragSourceDragEvent event)**	
	Invoked when drag-and-drop operation enters the **DragSource**.
public void **dragExit(DragSourceDragEvent event)**	
	Invoked when drag-and-drop operation exits the **DragSource**.
public void **dragOver(DragSourceDragEvent event)**	
	Invoked when drag-and-drop operation moves over **DragSource**.
public void **dragDropEnd(DragSourceDragEvent event)**	
	Invoked when drag-and-drop operation ends.
public void **dragDropActionChanged(DragSourceDragEvent event)**	
	Invoked if user changes drag-and-drop operation (e.g., from copy to move).

Fig. 5.20 **DragSourceListener** interface methods and their descriptions.

Method	Description
`public void` **`dragEnter( DropTargetDragEvent event )`**	
	Invoked when drag-and-drop operation enters the **DropTarget**.
`public void` **`dragExit( DropTargetEvent event )`**	
	Invoked when drag-and-drop operation exits the **DropTarget**.
`public void` **`dragOver( DropTargetDragEvent event )`**	
	Invoked when drag-and-drop operation moves over **DropTarget**.
`public void` **`drop( DragTargetDropEvent event )`**	
	Invoked when user drops dragged object on **DropTarget**.
`public void` **`dragDropActionChanged( DragSourceDragEvent event )`**	
	Invoked if user changes drag-and-drop operation (e.g., from copy to move).

Fig. 5.21   **`DropTargetListener`** interface methods and their descriptions.

Class **TransferableShape** (Fig. 5.22) implements interface **Transferable** to provide a means by which to transfer **MyShape**s using drag and drop. Interface **Transferable** is part of Java's data transfer API, which enables clipboard and drag-and-drop functionality in Java applications. Deitel Drawing enables users to drag and drop **TransferableShape** objects between drawings in the multiple-document interface. Lines 24–25 define **static String** variable **MIME_TYPE**, which the data transfer API uses to determine the type of data being transferred. *MIME types* (*Multipurpose Internet Mail Extension types*) are text strings that were originally created to describe data contained in e-mail attachments sent over the Internet. Many applications and operating systems now use MIME types for the more general purpose of describing objects that contain data, such as files, items on the system clipboard and drag-and-drop objects. Lines 28–29 declare an array of **DataFlavor** objects that class **TransferableShape** supports.

```
1   // TransferableShape.java
2   // TransferableShape is a Transferable object that contains a
3   // MyShape and the point from which the user dragged that MyShape.
4   package com.deitel.advjhtp1.drawing.controller;
5
6   // Java core packages
7   import java.util.*;
8   import java.io.*;
9   import java.awt.Point;
10  import java.awt.dnd.*;
11  import java.awt.datatransfer.*;
12
13  // Deitel packages
14  import com.deitel.advjhtp1.drawing.model.*;
15  import com.deitel.advjhtp1.drawing.model.shapes.*;
16
```

Fig. 5.22   **TransferableShape** enables **DragAndDropController** to transfer MyShape objects through drag-and-drop operations (part 1 of 3).

```
17   public class TransferableShape implements Transferable {
18
19      // the MyShape to transfer from Point origin
20      private MyShape shape;
21      private Point origin;
22
23      // MIME type that identifies dragged MyShapes
24      public static final String MIME_TYPE =
25         "application/x-deitel-shape";
26
27      // DataFlavors that MyShape supports for drag and drop
28      private static final DataFlavor[] flavors = new DataFlavor[] {
29         new DataFlavor( MIME_TYPE, "Shape" ) };
30
31      // TransferableShape constructor
32      public TransferableShape( MyShape myShape, Point originPoint )
33      {
34         shape = myShape;
35         origin = originPoint;
36
37      } // end TransferableShape constructor
38
39      // get Point from which user dragged MyShape
40      public Point getOrigin()
41      {
42         return origin;
43      }
44
45      // get MyShape
46      public MyShape getShape()
47      {
48         return shape;
49      }
50
51      // get data flavors MyShape supports
52      public DataFlavor[] getTransferDataFlavors()
53      {
54         return flavors;
55      }
56
57      // determine if MyShape supports given data flavor
58      public boolean isDataFlavorSupported( DataFlavor flavor )
59      {
60         // search for given DataFlavor in flavors array
61         for ( int i = 0; i < flavors.length; i++)
62
63            if ( flavor.equals( flavors[ i ] ) )
64               return true;
65
66         return false;
67      }
68
```

Fig. 5.22   TransferableShape enables **DragAndDropController** to transfer MyShape objects through drag-and-drop operations (part 2 of 3).

```
69    // get data to be transferred for given DataFlavor
70    public Object getTransferData( DataFlavor flavor )
71       throws UnsupportedFlavorException, IOException
72    {
73       if ( !isDataFlavorSupported( flavor ) )
74          throw new UnsupportedFlavorException( flavor );
75
76       // return TransferableShape object for transfer
77       return this;
78    }
79 }
```

Fig. 5.22   **TransferableShape** enables **DragAndDropController** to transfer MyShape objects through drag-and-drop operations (part 3 of 3).

Method **getTransferDataFlavors** (lines 52–55) returns the **TransferableShape**'s array of **DataFlavor**s. Method **getTransferDataFlavors** returns a **DataFlavor** array because it is possible that some objects support many **DataFlavor**s. Method **isDataFlavorSupported** (lines 58–67) takes a **DataFlavor** argument that lines 61–64 compare to each **DataFlavor** that class **TransferableShape** supports. If the given **DataFlavor** matches a supported **DataFlavor**, line 64 returns **true**.

Method **getTransferData** (lines 70–78) returns an **Object** containing the data to be transferred by the drag-and-drop operation. The **DataFlavor** argument specifies the particular type of data to be transferred. If the **DataFlavor** argument specifies an invalid **DataFlavor** for class **TransferableShape**, line 74 throws an **UnsupportedFlavorException**. If the **DataFlavor** matches a supported **DataFlavor** for class **MyShape**, line 77 returns a reference to the current **TransferableShape** instance to be transferred.

5.7 **DrawingInternalFrame** Component

DrawingInternalFrame (Fig. 5.23) is a **JInternalFrame** subclass that provides a user interface for viewing and modifying drawings. The Deitel Drawing application uses a multiple-document interface to allow the user to view and modify several drawings in a single application window. When the user creates a new drawing or opens a saved drawing, the drawing is displayed in a **DrawingInternalFrame**.

```
1    // DrawingInternalFrame.java
2    // DrawingInternalFrame is a JInternalFrame subclass for
3    // DeitelDrawing drawings.
4    package com.deitel.advjhtp1.drawing;
5
6    // Java core packages
7    import java.awt.*;
8    import java.awt.event.*;
```

Fig. 5.23   **DrawingInternalFrame** class that provides a user interface for creating drawings (part 1 of 15).

```
 9   import java.awt.dnd.*;
10   import java.io.*;
11   import java.util.*;
12   import java.util.List;
13
14   // Java extension packages
15   import javax.swing.*;
16   import javax.swing.event.*;
17   import javax.swing.border.*;
18
19   // Deitel packages
20   import com.deitel.advjhtp1.drawing.model.*;
21   import com.deitel.advjhtp1.drawing.model.shapes.*;
22   import com.deitel.advjhtp1.drawing.view.*;
23   import com.deitel.advjhtp1.drawing.controller.*;
24
25   public class DrawingInternalFrame extends JInternalFrame
26      implements Observer {
27
28      // offsets to stagger new windows
29      private static final int xOffset = 30;
30      private static final int yOffset = 30;
31      private static int openFrameCount = 0;
32
33      // MVC components
34      private DrawingModel drawingModel;
35      private DrawingView drawingView;
36      private MyShapeController myShapeController;
37      private DragAndDropController dragAndDropController;
38      private MyShapeControllerFactory shapeControllerFactory;
39
40      // file management properties
41      private JFileChooser fileChooser;
42      private String fileName;
43      private String absoluteFilePath;
44      private boolean saved = true;
45
46      private DrawingToolBar toolBar;
47      private ZoomDialog zoomDialog;
48
49      // Actions for save, zoom, move, etc.
50      private Action saveAction, saveAsAction, zoomAction,
51         moveAction, fillAction, gradientAction;
52
53      // DrawingInternalFrame constructor
54      public DrawingInternalFrame( String title )
55      {
56         super( title + " - " + ( ++openFrameCount ), true, true,
57            false, true );
58
59         setDefaultCloseOperation(
60            WindowConstants.DO_NOTHING_ON_CLOSE );
```

Fig. 5.23   **DrawingInternalFrame** class that provides a user interface for creating drawings (part 2 of 15).

```
61
62      // create new DrawingModel
63      drawingModel = new DrawingModel();
64
65      // create new DrawingView for DrawingModel
66      drawingView = new DrawingView( drawingModel );
67
68      // register DrawingInternalFrame as a DrawingModel Observer
69      drawingModel.addObserver( this );
70
71      // MyShapeControllerFactory for creating MyShapeControllers
72      shapeControllerFactory =
73         MyShapeControllerFactory.getInstance();
74
75      // create DragAndDropController for drag and drop operations
76      dragAndDropController =
77         new DragAndDropController( drawingModel );
78
79      // get default DragSource for current platform
80      DragSource dragSource = DragSource.getDefaultDragSource();
81
82      // create DragGestureRecognizer to register
83      // DragAndDropController as DragGestureListener
84      dragSource.createDefaultDragGestureRecognizer( drawingView,
85         DnDConstants.ACTION_COPY_OR_MOVE,
86         dragAndDropController );
87
88      // enable drawingView to accept drop operations, using
89      // dragAndDropController as DropTargetListener
90      drawingView.setDropTarget( new DropTarget( drawingView,
91         DnDConstants.ACTION_COPY_OR_MOVE,
92         dragAndDropController ) );
93
94      // add drawingView to viewPanel, put viewPanel in
95      // JScrollPane and add JScrollPane to DrawingInternalFrame
96      JPanel viewPanel = new JPanel();
97      viewPanel.add( drawingView );
98      getContentPane().add( new JScrollPane( viewPanel ),
99         BorderLayout.CENTER );
100
101     // create fileChooser and set its FileFilter
102     fileChooser = new JFileChooser();
103     fileChooser.setFileFilter( new DrawingFileFilter() );
104
105     // show/hide ZoomDialog when frame activated/deactivated
106     addInternalFrameListener(
107        new InternalFrameAdapter() {
108
109           // when DrawingInternalFrame activated, make
110           // associated zoomDialog visible
111           public void internalFrameActivated(
112              InternalFrameEvent event )
```

Fig. 5.23   **DrawingInternalFrame** class that provides a user interface for creating drawings (part 3 of 15).

```
113                 {
114                     if ( zoomDialog != null )
115                         zoomDialog.setVisible( true );
116                 }
117
118                 // when DrawingInternalFrame is deactivated, make
119                 // associated zoomDialog invisible
120                 public void internalFrameDeactivated(
121                     InternalFrameEvent event )
122                 {
123                     if ( zoomDialog != null )
124                         zoomDialog.setVisible( false );
125                 }
126             }
127
128         ); // end call to addInternalFrameListener
129
130         // stagger each DrawingInternalFrame to prevent it from
131         // obscuring other InternalFrames
132         setLocation( xOffset * openFrameCount,
133             yOffset * openFrameCount );
134
135         // add new DrawingToolBar to NORTH area
136         toolBar = new DrawingToolBar();
137         getContentPane().add( toolBar, BorderLayout.NORTH );
138
139         // get name of first MyShape that shapeControllerFactory
140         // supports and create MyShapeController
141         String shapeName =
142             shapeControllerFactory.getSupportedShapes()[ 0 ];
143
144         setMyShapeController(
145             shapeControllerFactory.newMyShapeController(
146                 drawingModel, shapeName ) );
147
148         // set DrawingInternalFrame size
149         setSize( 500, 320 );
150
151     } // end DrawingInternalFrame constructor
152
153     // get DrawingInternalFrame Save Action
154     public Action getSaveAction()
155     {
156         return saveAction;
157     }
158
159     // get DrawingInternalFrame Save As Action
160     public Action getSaveAsAction()
161     {
162         return saveAsAction;
163     }
164
```

Fig. 5.23   DrawingInternalFrame class that provides a user interface for creating drawings (part 4 of 15).

```
165     // set Saved flag for current drawing and update frame
166     // title to indicate saved state to user
167     public void setSaved( boolean drawingSaved )
168     {
169        // set Saved property
170        saved = drawingSaved;
171
172        // get current DrawingInternalFrame title
173        String title = getTitle();
174
175        // if drawing is not saved and title does not end with
176        // an asterisk, add asterisk to title
177        if ( !title.endsWith( " *" ) && !isSaved() )
178           setTitle( title + " *" );
179
180        // if title ends with * and drawing has been saved,
181        // remove * from title
182        else
183
184           if ( title.endsWith( " *" ) && isSaved() )
185              setTitle( title.substring( 0,
186                 title.length() - 2 ) );
187
188        // enable save actions if drawing not saved
189        getSaveAction().setEnabled( !isSaved() );
190     }
191
192     // return value of saved property
193     public boolean isSaved()
194     {
195        return saved;
196     }
197
198     // handle updates from DrawingModel
199     public void update( Observable observable, Object object )
200     {
201        // set saved property to false to indicate that
202        // DrawingModel has changed
203        setSaved( false );
204     }
205
206     // set fileName for current drawing
207     public void setFileName( String file )
208     {
209        fileName = file;
210
211        // update DrawingInternalFrame title
212        setTitle( fileName );
213     }
214
215     // get fileName for current drawing
```

Fig. 5.23   **DrawingInternalFrame** class that provides a user interface for creating drawings (part 5 of 15).

```
216    public String getFileName()
217    {
218       return fileName;
219    }
220
221    // get full path (absoluteFilePath) for current drawing
222    public String getAbsoluteFilePath()
223    {
224       return absoluteFilePath;
225    }
226
227    // set full path (absoluteFilePath) for current drawing
228    public void setAbsoluteFilePath( String path )
229    {
230       absoluteFilePath = path;
231    }
232
233    // get DrawingModel for current drawing
234    public DrawingModel getModel()
235    {
236       return drawingModel;
237    }
238
239    // set JInternalFrame and ZoomDialog titles
240    public void setTitle( String title )
241    {
242       super.setTitle( title );
243
244       if ( zoomDialog != null )
245          zoomDialog.setTitle( title );
246    }
247
248    // set MyShapeController for handling user input
249    public void setMyShapeController(
250       MyShapeController controller )
251    {
252       // remove old MyShapeController
253       if ( myShapeController != null ) {
254
255          // remove mouse listeners
256          drawingView.removeMouseListener(
257             myShapeController.getMouseListener() );
258
259          drawingView.removeMouseMotionListener(
260             myShapeController.getMouseMotionListener() );
261       }
262
263       // set MyShapeController property
264       myShapeController = controller;
265
266       // register MyShapeController to handle mouse events
267       drawingView.addMouseListener(
```

Fig. 5.23   **DrawingInternalFrame** class that provides a user interface for creating drawings (part 6 of 15).

```
268                myShapeController.getMouseListener() );
269
270       drawingView.addMouseMotionListener(
271          myShapeController.getMouseMotionListener() );
272
273       // update new MyShapeController with currently selected
274       // drawing properties (stroke size, color, fill, etc.)
275       myShapeController.setStrokeSize( toolBar.getStrokeSize() );
276
277       myShapeController.setPrimaryColor(
278          toolBar.getPrimaryColor() );
279
280       myShapeController.setSecondaryColor(
281          toolBar.getSecondaryColor() );
282
283       myShapeController.setDragMode( toolBar.getDragMode() );
284
285       myShapeController.setShapeFilled(
286          toolBar.getShapeFilled() );
287
288       myShapeController.setUseGradient(
289          toolBar.getUseGradient() );
290
291    } // end method setMyShapeController
292
293    // close DrawingInternalFrame; return false if drawing
294    // was not saved and user canceled the close operation
295    public boolean close()
296    {
297       // if drawing not saved, prompt user to save
298       if ( !isSaved() ) {
299
300          // display JOptionPane confirmation dialog to allow
301          // user to save drawing
302          int response = JOptionPane.showInternalConfirmDialog(
303             this, "The drawing in this window has been " +
304             "modified.  Would you like to save changes?",
305             "Save Changes", JOptionPane.YES_NO_CANCEL_OPTION,
306             JOptionPane.QUESTION_MESSAGE );
307
308          // if user selects Yes, save drawing and close
309          if ( response == JOptionPane.YES_OPTION ) {
310             saveDrawing();
311             dispose();
312
313             // return true to indicate frame closed
314             return true;
315          }
316
317          // if user selects No, close frame without saving
318          else if ( response == JOptionPane.NO_OPTION ) {
319             dispose();
```

Fig. 5.23   **DrawingInternalFrame** class that provides a user interface for creating drawings (part 7 of 15).

```
320              return true;
321          }
322
323          // if user selects Cancel, do not save or close
324          else
325              return false; // indicate frame was not closed
326      }
327
328      // if drawing has been saved, close frame
329      else {
330          dispose();
331          return true;
332      }
333
334  } // end method close
335
336  // open existing drawing from file
337  public boolean openDrawing()
338  {
339      // open JFileChooser Open dialog
340      int response = fileChooser.showOpenDialog( this );
341
342      // if user selected valid file, open an InputStream
343      // and retrieve the saved shapes
344      if ( response == fileChooser.APPROVE_OPTION ) {
345
346          // get selecte file name
347          String fileName =
348              fileChooser.getSelectedFile().getAbsolutePath();
349
350          // get shapes List from file
351          Collection shapes =
352              DrawingFileReaderWriter.readFile( fileName );
353
354          // set shapes in DrawingModel
355          drawingModel.setShapes( shapes );
356
357          // set fileName property
358          setFileName( fileChooser.getSelectedFile().getName() );
359
360          // set absoluteFilePath property
361          setAbsoluteFilePath( fileName );
362
363          // set saved property
364          setSaved( true );
365
366          // return true to indicate successful file open
367          return true;
368      }
369
370      // return false to indicate file open failed
371      else
```

Fig. 5.23   **DrawingInternalFrame** class that provides a user interface for creating drawings (part 8 of 15).

```
372          return false;
373
374    } // end method openDrawing
375
376    // save current drawing to file
377    public void saveDrawing()
378    {
379       // get absolute path to which file should be saved
380       String fileName = getAbsoluteFilePath();
381
382       // if fileName is null or empty, call saveDrawingAs
383       if ( fileName == null || fileName.equals( "" ) )
384          saveDrawingAs();
385
386       // write drawing to given fileName
387       else {
388          DrawingFileReaderWriter.writeFile( drawingModel,
389             fileName );
390
391          // update saved property
392          setSaved( true );
393       }
394
395    } // end method saveDrawing
396
397    // prompt user for file name and save drawing
398    public void saveDrawingAs()
399    {
400       // display JFileChooser Save dialog
401       int response = fileChooser.showSaveDialog( this );
402
403       // if user selected a file, save drawing
404       if ( response == fileChooser.APPROVE_OPTION )
405       {
406          // set absoluteFilePath property
407          setAbsoluteFilePath(
408             fileChooser.getSelectedFile().getAbsolutePath() );
409
410          // set fileName property
411          setFileName( fileChooser.getSelectedFile().getName() );
412
413          // write drawing to file
414          DrawingFileReaderWriter.writeFile( drawingModel,
415             getAbsoluteFilePath() );
416
417          // update saved property
418          setSaved( true );
419       }
420
421    } // end method saveDrawingAs
422
423    // display zoomDialog
```

Fig. 5.23   DrawingInternalFrame class that provides a user interface for creating drawings (part 9 of 15).

```
424    public void showZoomDialog()
425    {
426       // if zoomDialog is null, create one
427       if ( zoomDialog == null )
428          zoomDialog = new ZoomDialog( getModel(), getTitle() );
429
430       // make extant zoomDialog visible
431       else
432          zoomDialog.setVisible( true );
433    }
434
435    // dispose DrawingInternalFrame
436    public void dispose()
437    {
438       // dispose associated zoomDialog
439       if ( zoomDialog != null )
440          zoomDialog.dispose();
441
442       super.dispose();
443    }
444
445    // JToolBar subclass for DrawingInternalFrame
446    private class DrawingToolBar extends JToolBar {
447
448       // user interface components
449       private GradientIcon gradientIcon;
450       private JPanel primaryColorPanel, secondaryColorPanel;
451       private JButton primaryColorButton;
452       private JButton secondaryColorButton;
453       private JComboBox shapeChoice, strokeSizeChoice;
454       private JToggleButton gradientButton, fillButton;
455       private JToggleButton moveButton;
456
457       // DrawingToolBar constructor
458       public DrawingToolBar()
459       {
460          // create JComboBox for choosing current shape type
461          shapeChoice = new JComboBox(
462             shapeControllerFactory.getSupportedShapes() );
463          shapeChoice.setToolTipText( "Choose Shape" );
464
465          // when shapeChoice changes, get new MyShapeController
466          // from MyShapeControllerFactory
467          shapeChoice.addActionListener(
468             new ActionListener() {
469
470                public void actionPerformed( ActionEvent event )
471                {
472                   // get selected shape type
473                   String className =
474                      shapeChoice.getSelectedItem().toString();
475
```

Fig. 5.23   DrawingInternalFrame class that provides a user interface for creating drawings (part 10 of 15).

```
476              setMyShapeController(
477                 shapeControllerFactory.newMyShapeController(
478                    drawingModel, className ) );
479           }
480        }
481
482   ); // end call to addActionListener
483
484   // create JComboBox for selecting stroke size
485   strokeSizeChoice = new JComboBox(
486      new String[] { "1.0", "2.0", "3.0", "4.0", "5.0",
487         "6.0", "7.0", "8.0", "9.0", "10.0" } );
488
489   strokeSizeChoice.setToolTipText( "Choose Line Width" );
490
491   // set stroke size property to selected value
492   strokeSizeChoice.addActionListener(
493      new ActionListener() {
494
495         public void actionPerformed( ActionEvent event )
496         {
497            myShapeController.setStrokeSize(
498               getStrokeSize() );
499         }
500      }
501   );
502
503   // create JToggleButton for filling shapes
504   fillButton = new JToggleButton( "Fill" );
505
506   fillAction = new AbstractDrawingAction( "Fill", null,
507      "Fill Shape", new Integer( 'L' ) ) {
508
509      public void actionPerformed( ActionEvent event )
510      {
511         myShapeController.setShapeFilled(
512            getShapeFilled() );
513      }
514   };
515
516   fillButton.setAction( fillAction );
517
518   // create GradientIcon to display gradient settings
519   gradientIcon = new GradientIcon( Color.black,
520      Color.white );
521
522   // create JToggleButton to enable/disable gradients
523   gradientButton = new JToggleButton( gradientIcon );
524
525   gradientAction = new AbstractDrawingAction( "",
526      gradientIcon, "Use Gradient", new Integer( 'G' ) ) {
527
```

Fig. 5.23 **DrawingInternalFrame** class that provides a user interface for creating drawings (part 11 of 15).

```
528            public void actionPerformed( ActionEvent event )
529            {
530               myShapeController.setUseGradient(
531                  getUseGradient() );
532            }
533         };
534
535         gradientButton.setAction( gradientAction );
536
537         // create JPanel to display primary drawing color
538         primaryColorPanel = new JPanel();
539         primaryColorPanel.setPreferredSize(
540            new Dimension( 16, 16 ) );
541         primaryColorPanel.setOpaque( true );
542         primaryColorPanel.setBackground( Color.black );
543
544         // create JButton for changing color1
545         primaryColorButton = new JButton();
546         primaryColorButton.add( primaryColorPanel );
547
548         // display JColorChooser for selecting startColor value
549         primaryColorButton.addActionListener(
550            new ActionListener() {
551
552               public void actionPerformed( ActionEvent event )
553               {
554                  Color color = JColorChooser.showDialog(
555                     DrawingInternalFrame.this, "Select Color",
556                     primaryColorPanel.getBackground() );
557
558                  if ( color != null ) {
559                     primaryColorPanel.setBackground( color );
560                     gradientIcon.setStartColor( color );
561                     myShapeController.setPrimaryColor( color );
562                  }
563               }
564
565            } // end ActionListener inner class
566
567         ); // end call to addActionListener
568
569         // create JPanel to display secondary drawing color
570         secondaryColorPanel = new JPanel();
571         secondaryColorPanel.setPreferredSize(
572            new Dimension( 16, 16 ) );
573         secondaryColorPanel.setOpaque( true );
574         secondaryColorPanel.setBackground( Color.white );
575
576         // create JButton for changing secondary color
577         secondaryColorButton = new JButton();
578         secondaryColorButton.add( secondaryColorPanel );
579
```

Fig. 5.23   **DrawingInternalFrame** class that provides a user interface for creating drawings (part 12 of 15).

```
580        // display JColorChooser for selecting endColor value
581   secondaryColorButton.addActionListener(
582      new ActionListener() {
583
584         public void actionPerformed( ActionEvent event )
585         {
586            Color color = JColorChooser.showDialog(
587               DrawingInternalFrame.this, "Select Color",
588               secondaryColorPanel.getBackground() );
589
590            if ( color != null ) {
591               secondaryColorPanel.setBackground( color );
592               gradientIcon.setEndColor( color );
593               myShapeController.setSecondaryColor(
594                  color );
595            }
596         }
597
598      } // end ActionListener inner class
599
600   ); // end call to addActionListener
601
602   // create Action for saving drawings
603   Icon saveIcon = new ImageIcon(
604      DrawingInternalFrame.class.getResource(
605         "images/save.gif" ) );
606
607   saveAction = new AbstractDrawingAction( "Save", saveIcon,
608      "Save Drawing", new Integer( 'S' ) ) {
609
610      public void actionPerformed( ActionEvent event )
611      {
612         saveDrawing();
613      }
614   };
615
616   // create action for saving drawings as given file name
617   Icon saveAsIcon = new ImageIcon(
618      DrawingInternalFrame.class.getResource(
619         "images/saveAs.gif" ) );
620
621   saveAsAction = new AbstractDrawingAction( "Save As",
622      saveAsIcon, "Save Drawing As", new Integer( 'A' ) ) {
623
624      public void actionPerformed( ActionEvent event )
625      {
626         saveDrawingAs();
627      }
628   };
629
630   // create action for displaying zoomDialog
631   Icon zoomIcon = new ImageIcon(
```

Fig. 5.23   **DrawingInternalFrame** class that provides a user interface for creating drawings (part 13 of 15).

```
632            DrawingInternalFrame.class.getResource(
633            "images/zoom.gif" ) );
634
635         zoomAction = new AbstractDrawingAction( "Zoom", zoomIcon,
636            "Show Zoom Window", new Integer( 'Z' ) ) {
637
638            public void actionPerformed( ActionEvent event )
639            {
640               showZoomDialog();
641            }
642         };
643
644         // create JToggleButton for setting drag and drop mode
645         moveButton = new JToggleButton();
646
647         Icon moveIcon = new ImageIcon(
648            DrawingInternalFrame.class.getResource(
649               "images/move.gif" ) );
650
651         moveAction = new AbstractDrawingAction( "Move", null,
652            "Move Shape", new Integer( 'M' ) ) {
653
654            public void actionPerformed( ActionEvent event )
655            {
656               myShapeController.setDragMode(
657                  getDragMode() );
658
659               dragAndDropController.setDragMode(
660                  getDragMode() );
661            }
662         };
663
664         moveButton.setAction( moveAction );
665
666         // add Actions, buttons, etc. to JToolBar
667         add( saveAction );
668         add( saveAsAction );
669         addSeparator();
670         add( zoomAction );
671         addSeparator();
672         add( shapeChoice );
673         add( strokeSizeChoice );
674         addSeparator();
675         add( primaryColorButton );
676         add( secondaryColorButton );
677         addSeparator();
678         add( gradientButton );
679         add( fillButton );
680         addSeparator();
681         add( moveButton );
682
683         // disable floating
```

Fig. 5.23   **DrawingInternalFrame** class that provides a user interface for creating drawings (part 14 of 15).

```
684              setFloatable( false );
685
686          } // end DrawingToolBar constructor
687
688          // get currently selected stroke size
689          public float getStrokeSize()
690          {
691              Object selectedItem = strokeSizeChoice.getSelectedItem();
692
693              return Float.parseFloat( selectedItem.toString() );
694          }
695
696          // get current shape filled value
697          public boolean getShapeFilled()
698          {
699              return fillButton.isSelected();
700          }
701
702          // get current use gradient property
703          public boolean getUseGradient()
704          {
705              return gradientButton.isSelected();
706          }
707
708          // get primary drawing Color
709          public Color getPrimaryColor()
710          {
711              return primaryColorPanel.getBackground();
712          }
713
714          // get secondary drawing Color
715          public Color getSecondaryColor()
716          {
717              return secondaryColorPanel.getBackground();
718          }
719
720          // get current drag mode
721          public boolean getDragMode()
722          {
723              return moveButton.isSelected();
724          }
725
726      } // end DrawingToolBar inner class
727 }
```

Fig. 5.23   **DrawingInternalFrame** class that provides a user interface for creating drawings (part 15 of 15).

Each **DrawingInternalFrame** has a **DrawingModel**, **DrawingView**, **MyShapeController** and **DragAndDropController** (lines 36–39). These objects implement the model-view-controller architecture in the Deitel Drawing application. The **DrawingInternalFrame**'s **DrawingView** displays the drawing contained in the associated **DrawingModel**.

Lines 76–92 enable drag and drop in the **DrawingInternalFrame**. Lines 76–77 create a **DragAndDropController**, which controls drag-and-drop operations. Line 80 invokes static method **getDefaultDragSource** of class **DragSource** to get the host platform's default **DragSource** object. Lines 84–86 invoke method **createDefault-DragGestureRecognizer** of class **DragSource** to register the **DragAndDrop-Controller** as the listener for drag gestures that occur inside the **DrawingView**. This enables the **DragAndDropController** to recognize user gestures to drag **MyShapes** in a drawing. Lines 90–92 invoke method **setDropTarget** of class **DrawingView** to enable the **DrawingView** to accept dropped objects, such as **TransferableShape**s from other drawings or JPEG images from the host operating system's file manager.

Each **DrawingInternalFrame** has an associated **ZoomDialog** that displays a scaled view of the **DrawingModel**. Lines 106–128 create an **InternalFrameListener** that makes the **ZoomDialog** visible when the **DrawingInternalFrame** is activated (lines 111–116) and hides the **ZoomDialog** when the **DrawingInternalFrame** is deactivated (lines 120–125). This ensures that the proper **ZoomDialog** will be displayed when the user switches between **DrawingInternalFrame**s in the multiple-document interface.

Recall that the Deitel Drawing application uses a **MyShapeControllerFactory** to create **MyShapeController**s that handle user input. Lines 141–146 set a **MyShapeController** for the **DrawingInternalFrame**. Line 142 invokes method **getSupportedShapes** of class **MyShapeControllerFactory** to determine for which types of shapes the **MyShapeControllerFactory** can provide **MyShapeController**s. Lines 141–142 assign the zeroth supported shape to reference **shapeName**. Lines 144–146 invoke **MyShapeControllerFactory** method **newMyShapeController** to obtain an appropriate **MyShapeController** for **shapeName**, and set the **DrawingInternalFrame**'s **MyShapeController**.

Class **DrawingInternalFrame** implements interface **Observer**, so the **DrawingModel** can notify the **DrawingInternalFrame** of changes. When **DrawingInternalFrame** receives an update indicating the **DrawingModel** has changed, method **update** (lines 199–204) invokes method **setSaved** (lines 167–190) with argument **false**. If property **saved** is **false**, method **setSaved** adds an asterisk to the **DrawingInternalFrame**'s title to give the user a visual cue that indicates that the drawing has been modified. If property **saved** is **true**—which indicates that the drawing has not been modified since it was last saved—lines 185–186 remove the asterisk from the **DrawingInternalFrame**'s title. If the drawing has been saved, line 189 disables the **saveAction**. When the drawing is modified, line 189 enables the **saveAction**, which allows the user to save the drawing.

Method **setMyShapeController** (lines 249–291) sets the **MyShapeController** object for controlling mouse input. Lines 253–261 remove the previous **MouseListener** and **MouseMotionListener** from the **DrawingView**. Lines 264–289 register the new **MyShapeController**'s **MouseListener** and **MouseMotionListener** and configure the **MyShapeController** with the currently selected stroke size, colors, drag mode, fill and gradient.

Method **close** (lines 295–334) closes the **DrawingInternalFrame** and prompts the user to save the drawing if the **DrawingModel** has been modified since the last save. Lines 302–306 prompt the user to save an unsaved drawing. If the user selects **Yes**, lines

310–314 save the drawing, invoke method **dispose** to close the **DrawingInternal-Frame** and return **true** to indicate that the frame closed successfully. If the user selects **No**, line 319 invokes method **dispose** without saving the drawing, and returns **true** to indicate that the frame closed successfully. If the user selects **Cancel**, the drawing is not saved and line 325 returns **false** to indicate that the **DrawingInternalFrame** was not closed. If the drawing has not been modified since the last save, lines 330–331 invoke method **dispose** and return **true**.

Method **openDrawing** (lines 337–374) opens an existing drawing from the file system. Line 340 displays a **JFileChooser** open dialog. Lines 347–352 get the selected file name and invoke static method **readFile** of class **DrawingFileReaderWriter** to read the **Collection** of shapes from the file.

Method **saveDrawing** (lines 377–395) saves the current drawing. If the drawing does not have an associated file name, line 384 invokes method **saveDrawingAs**. If the drawing does have an associated file name, lines 388–389 invoke static method **writeFile** of class **DrawingFileReaderWriter** to save the drawing. Method **saveDrawingAs** (lines 398–421) displays a **JFileChooser** save dialog to prompt the user for a file in which to save the drawing. Lines 414–415 invoke static method **writeFile** of class **DrawingFileReaderWriter** to save the drawing.

Inner class **DrawingToolBar** (lines 446–726) provides GUI components for saving drawings, selecting the **MyShape** type to draw, and modifying the current **MyShapeController**'s properties, including the stroke size, colors, drag mode, fill mode and gradient. Lines 461–462 populate the **shapeChoice JComboBox** with the array of shape types that the **MyShapeControllerFactory** supports. When the user selects a shape type from **shapeChoice**, lines 477–478 invoke **MyShapeControllerFactory** method **newMyShapeController** to obtain an appropriate **MyShapeController** for the specified shape type. Lines 476–478 invoke method **setMyShapeController** to specify the **MyShapeController** with which the **DrawingInternalFrame** should process user input.

When the user changes the **DrawingInternalFrame**'s state by selecting a new type of shape to draw, that change in state also causes a change in the **DrawingInternalFrame**'s behavior. For example, if the user changes the **MyShapeController** reference from an instance of class **MyTextController** to and instance of class **MyLineController**, the **DrawingInternalFrame** no longer behaves in the same way. Now when the user presses the mouse button and drags the mouse, the **DrawingInternalFrame** draws lines instead of text. This is an example of the *State design pattern*, which enables an object to change its behavior when that object's state changes. Using the State design pattern becomes beneficial when we add new states (i.e., **MyShapeController** subclasses) to our system—we create an additional **MyShapeController** subclass (e.g., **RandomMyShapeController** in Exercise 5.8) that encapsulates **DrawingInternalFrame**'s behavior when occupying that state.

Lines 485–501 create a **JComboBox** for selecting the stroke size for shapes. Lines 504–516 create a **JToggleButton** and **Action** for creating filled shapes. Lines 519–535 create a **JToggleButton** and **Action** for creating shapes that use gradients. Lines 538–600 create **JButton**s for selecting the **startColor** and **endColor** for shapes. Each **JButton** contains a **JPanel** that displays the currently selected color. When clicked, the **ActionListener** for each **JButton** displays a **JColorChooser** dialog that enables the user to select a new color. Lines 603–642 create **Action**s for saving drawings and displaying a **DrawingInternalFrame**'s associated **ZoomDialog** (Fig. 5.25). Lines 645–662 create a **JToggleButton** and **Action** for enabling drag mode, which allows users to drag shapes from this **DrawingInternalFrame**'s **DrawingView**.

Class **DrawingFileFilter** (Fig. 5.24) is a **FileFilter** implementation that enables a **JFileChooser** dialog to show only those files appropriate for our application. Line 15 specifies a description for Deitel Drawing files. Line 8 specifies the filename extension for Deitel Drawing files. Method **accept** (lines 27–31) returns true only if the given **File** matches the filename extension for Deitel Drawing files.

5.8 ZoomDialog, Action and Icon Components

Class **ZoomDialog** (Fig. 5.25) is a **JDialog** subclass that uses class **ZoomDrawingView** (Fig. 5.13) to present a scalable **DrawingModel** view. As the user resizes the **ZoomDialog**, the **ZoomDrawingView** adjusts its scale factors to scale to the appropriate size. Note that **ZoomDialog** is a *non-modal dialog* (i.e., the user does not need to close the dialog to continue working with the main portion of the application).

```java
1   // DrawingFileFilter.java
2   // DrawingFileFilter is a FileFilter subclass for selecting
3   // DeitelDrawing files in a JFileChooser dialog.
4   package com.deitel.advjhtp1.drawing;
5
6   // Java core packages
7   import java.io.File;
8
9   // Java extension packages
10  import javax.swing.filechooser.*;
11
12  public class DrawingFileFilter extends FileFilter {
13
14     // String to use in JFileChooser description
15     private String DESCRIPTION = "DeitelDrawing Files (*.dd)";
16
17     // file extensions for DeitelDrawing files
18     private String EXTENSION = ".dd";
19
20     // get description for DeitelDrawing files
21     public String getDescription()
22     {
23        return DESCRIPTION;
24     }
25
26     // return true if given File has proper extension
27     public boolean accept( File file )
28     {
29        return ( file.getName().toLowerCase().endsWith(
30           EXTENSION ) );
```

Fig. 5.24   **DrawingFileFilter** is a **FileFilter** subclass that enables users to select Deitel Drawing files from **JFileChooser** dialogs (part 1 of 2).

```
31        }
32  }
```

Fig. 5.24   **DrawingFileFilter** is a **FileFilter** subclass that enables users to select Deitel Drawing files from **JFileChooser** dialogs (part 2 of 2).

```
1   // ZoomDialog.java
2   // ZoomDialog is a JDialog subclass that shows a zoomed view
3   // of a DrawingModel.
4   package com.deitel.advjhtp1.drawing;
5
6   // Java core packages
7   import java.awt.*;
8   import java.awt.event.*;
9
10  // Java extension packages
11  import javax.swing.*;
12
13  // Deitel packages
14  import com.deitel.advjhtp1.drawing.model.*;
15  import com.deitel.advjhtp1.drawing.view.*;
16
17  public class ZoomDialog extends JDialog {
18
19     private ZoomDrawingView drawingView;
20     private double zoomFactor = 0.5;
21
22     // ZoomDialog constructor
23     public ZoomDialog( DrawingModel model, String title )
24     {
25        // set ZoomDialog title
26        setTitle( title );
27
28        // create ZoomDrawingView for using default zoomFactor
29        drawingView = new ZoomDrawingView( model, zoomFactor );
30
31        // add ZoomDrawingView to ContentPane
32        getContentPane().add( drawingView );
33
34        // size ZoomDialog to fit ZoomDrawingView's preferred size
35        pack();
36
37        // make ZoomDialog visible
38        setVisible( true );
39     }
40
41     // set JDialog title
42     public void setTitle( String title )
43     {
44        super.setTitle( title + " [Zoom]" );
45     }
46  }
```

Fig. 5.25   **ZoomDialog** for displaying **DrawingModel**s in a scalable view.

Class **AbstractDrawingAction** (Fig. 5.26) is an abstract base class that extends class **AbstractAction** to provide a more convenient way to create Swing **Action**s. The **AbstractDrawingAction** constructor (lines 16–24) takes as arguments the name, **Icon**, description and mnemonic for the **Action**. Lines 27–48 define *set* methods for each **Action** property. Method **actionPerformed** (line 52) is marked **abstract** to require an implementation in each subclass.

```
1   // AbstractDrawingAction.java
2   // AbstractDrawingAction is an Action implementation that
3   // provides set and get methods for common Action properties.
4   package com.deitel.advjhtp1.drawing;
5
6   // Java core packages
7   import java.awt.event.*;
8
9   // Java extension packages
10  import javax.swing.*;
11
12  public abstract class AbstractDrawingAction
13     extends AbstractAction {
14
15     // construct AbstractDrawingAction with given name, icon
16     // description and mnemonic key
17     public AbstractDrawingAction( String name, Icon icon,
18        String description, Integer mnemonic )
19     {
20        setName( name );
21        setSmallIcon( icon );
22        setShortDescription( description );
23        setMnemonic( mnemonic );
24     }
25
26     // set Action name
27     public void setName( String name )
28     {
29        putValue( Action.NAME, name );
30     }
31
32     // set Action Icon
33     public void setSmallIcon( Icon icon )
34     {
35        putValue( Action.SMALL_ICON, icon );
36     }
37
38     // set Action short description
39     public void setShortDescription( String description )
40     {
41        putValue( Action.SHORT_DESCRIPTION, description );
42     }
43
```

Fig. 5.26   AbstractDrawingAction abstract base class for **Action**s (part 1 of 2).

```
44      // set Action mnemonic key
45      public void setMnemonic( Integer mnemonic )
46      {
47         putValue( Action.MNEMONIC_KEY, mnemonic );
48      }
49
50      // abstract actionPerformed method to be implemented
51      // by concrete subclasses
52      public abstract void actionPerformed( ActionEvent event );
53   }
```

Fig. 5.26   **AbstractDrawingAction** abstract base class for **Action**s
(part 2 of 2).

Class **GradientIcon** (Fig. 5.27) implements interface **Icon** and draws a gradient from **startColor** (line 15) to **endColor** (line 16). The Deitel Drawing application uses a **GradientIcon** to show a preview of the currently selected colors drawn as a gradient. Method **paintIcon** (lines 62–75) draws a filled rectangle, using a Java2D **GradientPaint** and the **GradientIcon**'s **startColor** and **endColor**.

```
1    // GradientIcon.java
2    // GradientIcon is an Icon implementation that draws a 16 x 16
3    // gradientfrom startColor to endColor.
4    package com.deitel.advjhtp1.painting;
5
6    // Java core packages
7    import java.awt.*;
8
9    // Java extension packages
10   import javax.swing.*;
11
12   public class GradientIcon implements Icon {
13
14      // Colors to use for gradient
15      private Color startColor;
16      private Color endColor;
17
18      // GradientIcon constructor
19      public GradientIcon( Color start, Color end )
20      {
21         setStartColor( start );
22         setEndColor( end );
23      }
24
25      // set gradient start color
26      public void setStartColor( Color start )
27      {
28         startColor = start;
29      }
30
```

Fig. 5.27   **GradientIcon** implementation of interface **Icon** that draws a gradient (part 1 of 2).

```
31        // get gradient start color
32        public Color getStartColor()
33        {
34            return startColor;
35        }
36
37        // set gradient end color
38        public void setEndColor( Color end )
39        {
40            endColor = end;
41        }
42
43        // get gradient end color
44        public Color getEndColor()
45        {
46            return endColor;
47        }
48
49        // get icon width
50        public int getIconWidth()
51        {
52            return 16;
53        }
54
55        // get icon height
56        public int getIconHeight()
57        {
58            return 16;
59        }
60
61        // draw icon at given location on given component
62        public void paintIcon( Component component, Graphics g,
63            int x, int y )
64        {
65            // get Graphics2D object
66            Graphics2D g2D = ( Graphics2D ) g;
67
68            // set GradientPaint
69            g2D.setPaint ( new GradientPaint( x, y,
70                getStartColor(), 16, 16,
71                getEndColor() ) );
72
73            // fill rectangle with gradient
74            g2D.fillRect( x, y, 16, 16 );
75        }
76  }
```

GradientIcon in a
JToggleButton.

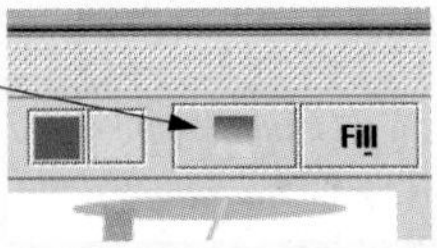

Fig. 5.27   **GradientIcon** implementation of interface **Icon** that draws a gradient (part 2 of 2).

5.9 `DeitelDrawing` Application

Class **DeitelDrawing** (Fig. 5.28) integrates the components we have discussed in this chapter into a multiple-document-interface application. The Deitel Drawing application displays the Deitel logo in a **SplashScreen** (Fig. 5.29) while the application loads (line 44). Lines 60–111 create **AbstractDrawingAction**s for creating new drawings, opening existing drawings, exiting the application and displaying information about the Deitel Drawing application.

```
1   // DeitelDrawing.java
2   // DeitelDrawing is a drawing program that uses, MVC, a
3   // multiple-document interface and Java2D.
4   package com.deitel.advjhtp1.drawing;
5
6   // Java core packages
7   import java.io.*;
8   import java.util.*;
9   import java.awt.*;
10  import java.awt.event.*;
11  import java.beans.*;
12
13  // Java extension packages
14  import javax.swing.*;
15  import javax.swing.event.*;
16  import javax.swing.border.*;
17
18  public class DeitelDrawing extends JFrame {
19
20     private JMenuBar menuBar;
21     private JMenu fileMenu, helpMenu;
22
23     private Action newAction, openAction,
24        exitAction, aboutAction;
25
26     private JMenuItem saveMenuItem, saveAsMenuItem;
27
28     private JToolBar toolBar;
29     private JPanel toolBarPanel, frameToolBarPanel;
30     private JDesktopPane desktopPane;
31
32     private SplashScreen splashScreen;
33
34     // DeitelDrawing constructor
35     public DeitelDrawing()
36     {
37        super( "DeitelDrawing" );
38
39        // set icon for JFrame's upper-left-hand corner
40        ImageIcon icon = new ImageIcon(
41          DeitelDrawing.class.getResource( "images/icon.png" ) );
42        setIconImage( icon.getImage() );
```

Fig. 5.28   **DeitelDrawing** application that uses a multiple-document interface for displaying and modifying **DeitelDrawing** drawings (part 1 of 8).

```
43
44          showSplashScreen();
45
46          // do not hide window when close button clicked
47          setDefaultCloseOperation(
48             WindowConstants.DO_NOTHING_ON_CLOSE );
49
50          // create JDesktopPane for MDI
51          desktopPane = new JDesktopPane();
52
53          // show contents when dragging JInternalFrames
54          desktopPane.setDragMode( JDesktopPane.LIVE_DRAG_MODE );
55
56          // create Action for creating new drawings
57          Icon newIcon = new ImageIcon(
58             DeitelDrawing.class.getResource( "images/new.gif" ) );
59
60          newAction = new AbstractDrawingAction( "New", newIcon,
61             "Create New Drawing", new Integer( 'N' ) ) {
62
63             public void actionPerformed( ActionEvent event )
64             {
65                createNewWindow();
66             }
67          };
68
69          // create Action for opening existing drawings
70          Icon openIcon = new ImageIcon(
71             DeitelDrawing.class.getResource( "images/open.gif" ) );
72
73          openAction = new AbstractDrawingAction( "Open", openIcon,
74             "Open Existing Drawing", new Integer( 'O' ) ) {
75
76             public void actionPerformed( ActionEvent event )
77             {
78                DrawingInternalFrame frame = createNewWindow();
79
80                if ( !frame.openDrawing() )
81                   frame.close();
82             }
83          };
84
85          // create Action for exiting application
86          Icon exitIcon = new ImageIcon(
87             DeitelDrawing.class.getResource( "images/exit.gif" ) );
88
89          exitAction = new AbstractDrawingAction( "Exit", exitIcon,
90             "Exit Application", new Integer( 'X' ) ) {
91
92             public void actionPerformed( ActionEvent event )
93             {
94                exitApplication();
```

Fig. 5.28   **DeitelDrawing** application that uses a multiple-document interface for displaying and modifying **DeitelDrawing** drawings (part 2 of 8).

```
95              }
96          };
97
98          // create Action for opening About dialog
99          Icon aboutIcon = new ImageIcon(
100             DeitelDrawing.class.getResource( "images/about.gif" ) );
101
102         aboutAction = new AbstractDrawingAction( "About",
103             aboutIcon, "About Application", new Integer( 'b' ) ) {
104
105             public void actionPerformed( ActionEvent event )
106             {
107                 JOptionPane.showMessageDialog( DeitelDrawing.this,
108                     "DeitelDrawing v1.0.\n Copyright " +
109                     "2002. Deitel & Associates, Inc." );
110             }
111         };
112
113         // create File menu and set its mnemonic
114         fileMenu = new JMenu( "File" );
115         fileMenu.setMnemonic( 'F' );
116
117         // create Help menu and set its mnemonic
118         helpMenu = new JMenu( "Help" );
119         helpMenu.setMnemonic( 'H' );
120
121         menuBar = new JMenuBar();
122
123         // add New Drawing and Open Drawing actions to
124         // File menu and remove their icons
125         fileMenu.add( newAction ).setIcon( null );
126         fileMenu.add( openAction ).setIcon( null );
127
128         // create JMenuItems for saving drawings; these
129         // JMenuItems will invoke the save Actions for the
130         // current DrawingInternalFrame
131         saveMenuItem = new JMenuItem( "Save" );
132         saveAsMenuItem = new JMenuItem( "Save As" );
133
134         // add Save, Save As and Close JMenuItems to File menu
135         fileMenu.add( saveMenuItem );
136         fileMenu.add( saveAsMenuItem );
137
138         fileMenu.addSeparator();
139
140         // add Exit action to File menu and remove its icon
141         fileMenu.add( exitAction ).setIcon( null );
142
143         // add About action to Help menu and remove its icon
144         helpMenu.add ( aboutAction ).setIcon( null );
145
146         // add File and Help menus to JMenuBar
```

Fig. 5.28   **DeitelDrawing** application that uses a multiple-document interface for displaying and modifying **DeitelDrawing** drawings (part 3 of 8).

```
147        menuBar.add( fileMenu );
148        menuBar.add( helpMenu );
149
150        // set Frame's JMenuBar
151        setJMenuBar( menuBar );
152
153        // create application JToolBar
154        toolBar = new JToolBar();
155
156        // disable JToolBar floating
157        toolBar.setFloatable( false );
158
159        // add New Drawing and Open Drawing actions to JToolBar
160        toolBar.add( newAction );
161        toolBar.add( openAction );
162
163        toolBar.addSeparator();
164
165        // add Exit action to JToolBar
166        toolBar.add( exitAction );
167
168        toolBar.addSeparator();
169
170        // add About action to JToolBar
171        toolBar.add( aboutAction );
172
173        // add toolBar and desktopPane to ContentPane
174        getContentPane().add( toolBar, BorderLayout.NORTH );
175        getContentPane().add( desktopPane, BorderLayout.CENTER );
176
177        // add WindowListener for windowClosing event
178        addWindowListener(
179           new WindowAdapter() {
180
181              public void windowClosing( WindowEvent event )
182              {
183                 exitApplication();
184              }
185           }
186        );
187
188        // wait for SplashScreen to go away
189        while ( splashScreen.isVisible() ) {
190
191           try {
192              Thread.sleep( 10 );
193           }
194
195           // handle exception
196           catch ( InterruptedException interruptedException ) {
197              interruptedException.printStackTrace();
198           }
```

Fig. 5.28   **DeitelDrawing** application that uses a multiple-document interface for displaying and modifying **DeitelDrawing** drawings (part 4 of 8).

```
199          }
200
201          // set initial JFrame size
202          setSize( 640, 480 );
203
204          // position application window
205          centerWindowOnScreen();
206
207          // make application visible
208          setVisible( true );
209
210          // create new, empty drawing window
211          createNewWindow();
212
213      } // end DeitelDrawing constructor
214
215      // create new DrawingInternalFrame
216      private DrawingInternalFrame createNewWindow()
217      {
218          // create new DrawingInternalFrame
219          DrawingInternalFrame frame =
220              new DrawingInternalFrame( "Untitled Drawing" );
221
222          // add listener for InternalFrame events
223          frame.addInternalFrameListener(
224              new DrawingInternalFrameListener() );
225
226          // make DrawingInternalFrame opaque
227          frame.setOpaque( true );
228
229          // add DrawingInternalFrame to desktopPane
230          desktopPane.add( frame );
231
232          // make DrawingInternalFrame visible
233          frame.setVisible( true );
234
235          // select new DrawingInternalFrame
236          try {
237              frame.setSelected( true );
238          }
239
240          // handle exception selecting DrawingInternalFrame
241          catch ( PropertyVetoException vetoException ) {
242              vetoException.printStackTrace();
243          }
244
245          // return reference to newly created DrawingInternalFrame
246          return frame;
247      }
248
249      // InternalFrameAdapter to listen for InternalFrame events
```

Fig. 5.28   **DeitelDrawing** application that uses a multiple-document interface for displaying and modifying **DeitelDrawing** drawings (part 5 of 8).

```
250    private class DrawingInternalFrameListener
251       extends InternalFrameAdapter {
252
253       // when DrawingInternalFrame is closing disable
254       // appropriate Actions
255       public void internalFrameClosing(
256          InternalFrameEvent event )
257       {
258          DrawingInternalFrame frame =
259             ( DrawingInternalFrame ) event.getSource();
260
261          // frame closes successfully, disable Save menu items
262          if ( frame.close() ) {
263             saveMenuItem.setAction( null );
264             saveAsMenuItem.setAction( null );
265          }
266       }
267
268       // when DrawingInternalFrame is activated, make its JToolBar
269       // visible and set JMenuItems to DrawingInternalFrame Actions
270       public void internalFrameActivated(
271          InternalFrameEvent event )
272       {
273          DrawingInternalFrame frame =
274             ( DrawingInternalFrame ) event.getSource();
275
276          // set saveMenuItem to DrawingInternalFrame's saveAction
277          saveMenuItem.setAction( frame.getSaveAction() );
278          saveMenuItem.setIcon( null );
279
280          // set saveAsMenuItem to DrawingInternalFrame's
281          // saveAsAction
282          saveAsMenuItem.setAction( frame.getSaveAsAction() );
283          saveAsMenuItem.setIcon( null );
284       }
285    }
286
287    // close each DrawingInternalFrame to let user save drawings
288    // then exit application
289    private void exitApplication()
290    {
291       // get array of JInternalFrames from desktopPane
292       JInternalFrame frames[] = desktopPane.getAllFrames();
293
294       // keep track of DrawingInternalFrames that do not close
295       boolean allFramesClosed = true;
296
297       // select and close each DrawingInternalFrame
298       for ( int i = 0; i < frames.length; i++ ) {
299          DrawingInternalFrame nextFrame =
300             ( DrawingInternalFrame ) frames[ i ];
301
```

Fig. 5.28   **DeitelDrawing** application that uses a multiple-document interface for displaying and modifying **DeitelDrawing** drawings (part 6 of 8).

```
302              // select current DrawingInternalFrame
303              try {
304                 nextFrame.setSelected( true );
305              }
306
307              // handle exception when selecting DrawingInternalFrame
308              catch ( PropertyVetoException vetoException ) {
309                 vetoException.printStackTrace();
310              }
311
312              // close DrawingInternalFrame and update allFramesClosed
313              allFramesClosed = allFramesClosed && nextFrame.close();
314           }
315
316        // exit application only if all frames were closed
317        if ( allFramesClosed )
318           System.exit( 0 );
319
320     } // end method exitApplication
321
322     // display application's splash screen
323     public void showSplashScreen()
324     {
325        // create ImageIcon for logo
326        Icon logoIcon = new ImageIcon(
327           getClass().getResource( "images/deitellogo.png" ) );
328
329        // create new JLabel for logo
330        JLabel logoLabel = new JLabel( logoIcon );
331
332        // set JLabel background color
333        logoLabel.setBackground( Color.white );
334
335        // set splash screen border
336        logoLabel.setBorder(
337           new MatteBorder( 5, 5, 5, 5, Color.black ) );
338
339        // make logoLabel opaque
340        logoLabel.setOpaque( true );
341
342        // create SplashScreen for logo
343        splashScreen = new SplashScreen( logoLabel );
344
345        // show SplashScreen for 3 seconds
346        splashScreen.showSplash( 3000 );
347
348     } // end method showSplashScreen
349
350     // center application window on user's screen
351     private void centerWindowOnScreen()
352     {
353        // get Dimension of user's screen
```

Fig. 5.28   **DeitelDrawing** application that uses a multiple-document interface for displaying and modifying **DeitelDrawing** drawings (part 7 of 8).

```
354          Dimension screenDimension =
355             Toolkit.getDefaultToolkit().getScreenSize();
356
357          // use screen width and height and application width
358          // and height to center application on user's screen
359          int width = getSize().width;
360          int height = getSize().height;
361          int x = ( screenDimension.width - width ) / 2 ;
362          int y = ( screenDimension.height - height ) / 2 ;
363
364          // place application window at screen's center
365          setBounds( x, y, width, height );
366       }
367
368       // execute application
369       public static void main( String args[] )
370       {
371          new DeitelDrawing();
372       }
373    }
```

Fig. 5.28 **DeitelDrawing** application that uses a multiple-document interface for displaying and modifying **DeitelDrawing** drawings (part 8 of 8).

Method **createNewWindow** (lines 216–247) creates a new **DrawingInternal-Frame**. Inner class **DrawingInternalFrameListener** (lines 250–285) listens for **internalFrameClosing** and **internalFrameActivated** messages. The Deitel Drawing application's **File** menu contains **JMenuItem**s for saving the currently active drawing. When a **DrawingInternalFrame** closes, lines 263–264 remove that **DrawingInternalFrame**'s **saveAction** and **saveAsAction** from **saveMenuItem** and **saveAsMenuItem**. When a **DrawingInternalFrame** is activated, lines 277–283 invoke method **setAction** of class **JMenuItem** to set the **Action**s for **saveMenuItem** and **saveAsMenuItem**.

Method **exitApplication** (lines 289–320) prompts the user to save any unsaved drawings before the application exits. Line 292 invokes method **getAllFrames** of class **JDesktopPane** to retrieve an array of **JInternalFrame**s in the application. Line 313 invokes method **close** of class **DrawingInternalFrame** to attempt to close each **DrawingInternalFrame** in the array. Method **close** returns **true** if the **DrawingInternalFrame** closed successfully, **false** otherwise. Line 313 accumulates the results of closing each **DrawingInternalFrame** in **boolean allFramesClosed**. If all **DrawingInternalFrame**s close successfully, line 318 exits the application. If any **DrawingInternalFrame** did not close, the application assumes that the user cancelled the request to close the application.

The Deitel Drawing application displays the Deitel logo in a **SplashScreen** (Fig. 5.29) while the application loads. The **SplashScreen** constructor (lines 19–58) takes as an argument the **Component** to display. Line 22 creates **JWindow** (a borderless window) in which to display the given component. Lines 46–56 center the **SplashScreen**'s **JWindow** on the user's screen.

```java
1   // SplashScreen.java
2   // SplashScreen implements static method showSplash for
3   // displaying a splash screen.
4   package com.deitel.advjhtp1.drawing;
5
6   // Java core packages
7   import java.awt.*;
8   import java.awt.event.*;
9
10  // Java extension packages
11  import javax.swing.*;
12
13  public class SplashScreen {
14
15     private JWindow window;
16     private Timer timer;
17
18     // SplashScreen constructor
19     public SplashScreen( Component component )
20     {
21        // create new JWindow for splash screen
22        window = new JWindow();
23
24        // add provided component to JWindow
25        window.getContentPane().add( component );
26
27        // allow user to dismiss SplashScreen by clicking mouse
28        window.addMouseListener(
29
30           new MouseAdapter() {
31
32              // when user presses mouse in SplashScreen,
33              // hide and dispose JWindow
34              public void mousePressed( MouseEvent event ) {
35                 window.setVisible( false );
36                 window.dispose();
37              }
38           }
39
40        ); // end call to addMouseListener
41
42        // size JWindow for given Component
43        window.pack();
44
45        // get user's screen size
46        Dimension screenDimension =
47           Toolkit.getDefaultToolkit().getScreenSize();
48
49        // calculate x and y coordinates to center splash screen
50        int width = window.getSize().width;
51        int height = window.getSize().height;
52        int x = ( screenDimension.width - width ) / 2 ;
```

Fig. 5.29   **SplashScreen** class for displaying a logo while the application loads (part 1 of 2).

```
53          int y = ( screenDimension.height - height ) / 2 ;
54
55          // set the bounds of the window to center it on screen
56          window.setBounds( x, y, width, height );
57
58       } // end SplashScreen constructor
59
60       // show splash screen for given delay
61       public void showSplash( int delay ) {
62
63          // display the window
64          window.setVisible( true );
65
66          // crate and start a new Timer to remove SplashScreen
67          // after specified delay
68          timer = new Timer( delay,
69             new ActionListener() {
70
71                public void actionPerformed( ActionEvent event )
72                {
73                   // hide and dispose of window
74                   window.setVisible( false );
75                   window.dispose();
76                   timer.stop();
77                }
78             }
79          );
80
81          timer.start();
82
83       } // end method showSplash
84
85       // return true if SplashScreen window is visible
86       public boolean isVisible()
87       {
88          return window.isVisible();
89       }
90    }
```

Fig. 5.29   **SplashScreen** class for displaying a logo while the application loads
(part 2 of 2).

Method **showSplash** (lines 61–83) takes as an integer argument the number of milliseconds for which to display the **SplashScreen**. Line 64 makes the **JWindow** visible, and line 51 causes the current **Thread** to sleep for the given **delay**. After the **delay** expires, lines 60–61 hide and **dispose** of the **JWindow**.

In this chapter, we presented a substantial application that used the MVC architecture and many popular design patterns, including Observer, Factory Method, Template Method, State and Command. We also demonstrated how applications can store and retrieve information in XML documents. Our drawing application takes advantage of the rich set of GUI components offered by Swing and the powerful drawing capabilities offered by Java 2D. Drag-and-drop functionality enables users to transfer shapes between drawings and add their own images.

Throughout the rest of the book, we use design patterns and the MVC architecture to build substantial examples and case studies. For example, the Enterprise Java case study of Chapters 17–20 presents an online bookstore that uses the MVC architecture.

SELF-REVIEW EXERCISES

5.1   Which part of the model-view-controller architecture processes user input? Which Deitel Drawing classes implement this part of MVC?

5.2   What interface must a class implement to enable data transfer using drag and drop for instances of that class?

5.3   In general, how does a user begin a drag-and-drop operation? Give an example.

5.4   What type of object notifies a **DragGestureListener** that the user made a drag gesture?

5.5   How can a **DropTargetListener** or **DragSourceListener** determine what type of data a **Transferable** object contains?

ANSWERS TO SELF-REVIEW EXERCISES

5.1   The controller in MVC processes user input. In the Deitel Drawing application, **MyShapeController** subclasses process user input via the mouse. Class **DragAndDropController** processes user input via drag-and-drop operations.

5.2   A class that supports drag and drop must implement interface **Transferable**.

5.3   A user begins a drag-and-drop operation by making a drag gesture. For example, on the Windows platform, a user makes a drag gesture by pressing the mouse button on a draggable object and dragging the mouse.

5.4   A **DragGestureRecognizer** issues a **DragGestureEvent** to notify a **DragGestureListener** that the user made a drag gesture.

5.5   Method **getTransferDataFlavors** of interface **Transferable** returns an array of **DataFlavor** objects. Each **DataFlavor** has a MIME type that describes the type of data the **Transferable** object supports.

EXERCISES

5.6   Create class **RotatingDrawingView** that extends class **DrawingView** and uses Java 2D transformations (Chapter 4) to display the drawing rotated by ninety degrees.

5.7   Modify your solution to Exercise 5.6 to use a and a **java.awt.Timer** to continually rotate the drawing in five-degree increments.

5.8   Create class **RandomMyShapeController** that extends class **MyShapeController** and adds random **MyShape** subclasses with random sizes, colors and other properties to the **DrawingModel**. In method **startShape**, class **RandomMyShapeController** should prompt the user for the number of random shapes to add to the drawing. Create a new **MyShapeController-Factory** subclass (Fig. 5.18) named **RandomMyShapeControllerFactory** that constructs a **RandomMyShapeController** when the **String "Random"** is passed to method **newMyShapeController**. [*Hint*: Be sure to override method **getSupportedShapes** of class **MyShapeControllerFactory** to return a **String** array that includes the **String "Random"**.]

6

JavaBeans Component Model

Objectives

- To understand JavaBeans and how they facilitate component-oriented software construction.
- To be able to use Forte for Java Community Edition to build JavaBeans-based applications.
- To be able to wrap class definitions as JAR files for use as JavaBeans and stand-alone applications.
- To be able to define JavaBean properties and events.

Mirrors should reflect a little before throwing back images.
Jean Cocteau

Television is like the invention of indoor plumbing. It didn't change people's habits. It just kept them inside the house.
Alfred Hitchcock

The power of the visible is the invisible.
Marianne Moore

The sun has a right to "set" where it wants to, and so, I may add, has a hen.
Charles Farrar Browne

The causes of events are ever more interesting than the events themselves.
Marcus Tullius Cicero

…the mechanic that would perfect his work must first sharpen his tools.
Confucius

Outline

6.1 Introduction

This chapter presents Java's reusable software component model: *JavaBeans*. JavaBeans (often called *beans)* allow developers to reap the benefits of rapid application development in Java by assembling predefined software components to create powerful applications and applets. *Graphical programming and design environments* (often called *builder tools, IDEs* or *integrated development environments*) that support beans provide programmers with tremendous flexibility by allowing programmers to reuse and integrate existing disparate components that, in many cases, were never intended to be used together. These components can be linked together to create applets, applications or even new beans for reuse by others.

JavaBeans and other component-based technologies have led to a new type of programmer, the *component assembler*, who uses well-defined components to create more robust functionality. Component assemblers do not need to know the implementation details of components. Rather, they need to know what services the components provide, so they can have other components interact with them.

As an example of the concept of beans, assume that a component assembler has an animation bean that has methods to **startAnimation** and **stopAnimation**. The component assembler may want to provide two buttons, one that will start the animation and one that will stop the animation (an example you will see later in this chapter). With beans, we can simply "connect" one button to the animation's **startAnimation** method and connect another button to the animation's **stopAnimation** method, such that when the user clicks a button, the appropriate method of the animation bean is called. The builder tool does all the work of associating the button-click event with the appropriate method to call on the animation bean. All the programmer needs to do is tell the builder tool which two components to "connect."

The benefit of beans in this example is that the animation bean and the button beans do not need to know about each other before they are assembled in a builder tool. Someone else can be responsible for defining the concept of a button in a reusable manner (e.g., `javax.swing.JButton`). A button is not specific to our example. Rather, it is a component used in many applications and applets. When the user of a program clicks a button, the user expects an action specific to that program to occur. (Some buttons, such as **OK** buttons, typically have the same meaning in all programs.) However, the basic concept of a button—how it is displayed, how it works and how it notifies other components that it was clicked—is the same in every application (although we typically customize the button's label). The component assembler's job is not to create the concept of a button, but rather to use the preexisting button component to provide functionality to the user of the program.

Component assemblers can make beans communicate through the beans' well-defined services (i.e., methods), typically without writing any code (the builder tool often generates the code, which is sometimes hidden from the component assembler—depending on the tool). Indeed, a component assembler often can create complex applications literally by "connecting the dots."

In this chapter, we show you how to use existing beans and how to create your own basic beans. After studying this chapter, you will have a foundation in JavaBeans programming that will enable you to develop applications and applets rapidly using the more advanced features of integrated development environments that support beans. You will also have a solid foundation for further study of JavaBeans.

For more JavaBeans information, visit the Sun Microsystems Web site for JavaBeans:

> `java.sun.com/beans/`

This site provides a complete set of resources for learning about and using JavaBeans.

6.2 Using Beans in Forte for Java Community Edition

Sun Microsystem's *Forte for Java Community Edition* (Fig. 6.1) is an integrated development environment that provides a builder tool for assembling JavaBeans. Forte provides visual access to a variety of JavaBeans and allows you to install and manipulate additional beans. In this section, we demonstrate how to use existing beans in Forte. Later in the chapter, we rely on your knowledge of this section to use the beans created in this chapter. We assume you are already familiar with the basic operation of *Forte*. For details on getting started with *Forte*, visit the resources for this book on our Web site, **www.deitel.com**. There, we have a "Getting Started with *Forte for Java Community Edition 2.0*" tutorial.

Software Engineering Observation 6.1

A benefit of working in a bean-ready development environment is that the environment visually presents the properties of the bean to the programmer for easy modification and customization of the bean at design time.

A bean must be installed before it is manipulated in Forte. Click the **Tools** menu and select **Install New JavaBean...** (Fig. 6.2). A file dialog box labelled **Install JavaBean** appears (Fig. 6.3). Copy **LogoAnimator.jar** from the CD-ROM that accompanies this book. The next dialog box lists the JavaBeans within the selected JAR file (Fig. 6.4). Select **LogoAnimator** and click the **OK** button (Fig. 6.4). Select **Beans** in the **Palette Category** dialog box that appears next and click **OK** (Fig. 6.4). Clicking the **Beans** tab in the **Component Palette** shows a question mark icon (Fig. 6.5). Moving the mouse over the icon in the **Component Palette** displays a tool tips showing that the icon represents the **LogoAnimator** JavaBean (Fig. 6.5).

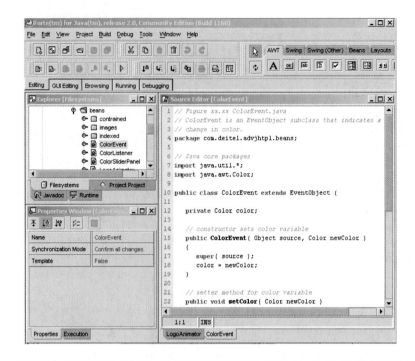

Fig. 6.1   Forte for Java Community Edition 2.0.

Fig. 6.2   **Install New JavaBean...** menu item.

Fig. 6.3   **Install JavaBean** dialog.

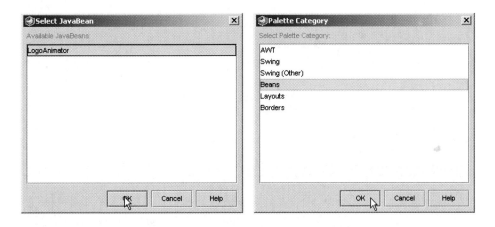

Fig. 6.4   **Select JavaBean** and **Palette Category** dialogs.

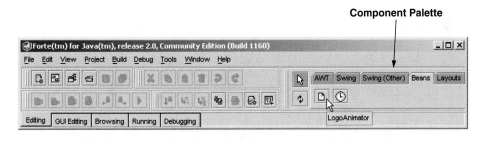

Fig. 6.5   **Beans** tab in the **Component Palette** and tooltip for **LogoAnimator** JavaBean.

GUI JavaBeans must be added to a Java **Container** to be able to use the builder tool to edit the bean properties or to link the beans to other components. To demonstrate adding and manipulating JavaBeans, we open a **JFrame**. Select the **Filesystems** tab in the **Explorer** window (Fig. 6.6). Select the **Development** directory (Fig. 6.7). Select **New...** from the **File** menu (Fig. 6.8). In the **Template Chooser** (Fig. 6.9), expand the **Swing Forms** option and select **JFrame**. Enter "**AnimationWindow**" in the **Name:** field (Fig. 6.9). Click **Finish** to create the new **JFrame**.

Fig. 6.6   **Filesystems** tab in the **Explorer** window.

Fig. 6.7   **Development** directory selected in **Explorer** window.

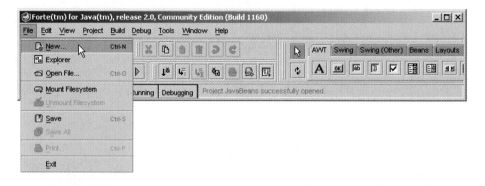

Fig. 6.8   **New...** menu item.

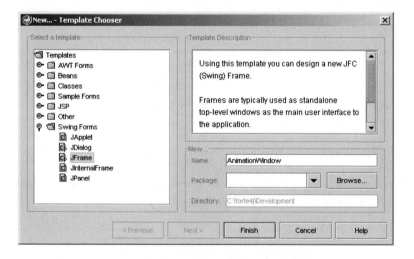

Fig. 6.9   **New...- Template Chooser** dialog.

The new **AnimationWindow** class appears inside the **Filesystems** field of the **Explorer**. The **Component Inspector**, **Form** and **Source Editor** windows should all appear (Fig. 6.10). The **Component Inspector** (Fig. 6.11) lists all the visual and nonvisual components within **AnimationWindow** and also shows the property sheet for selected components (we will discuss the property sheet later). The **Form** window (Fig. 6.11) shows the **JFrame** with its current layout and components. The **Source**

Editor (Fig. 6.12) shows the Java source code Forte generates. Forte updates this code as components and events are added, deleted and changed.

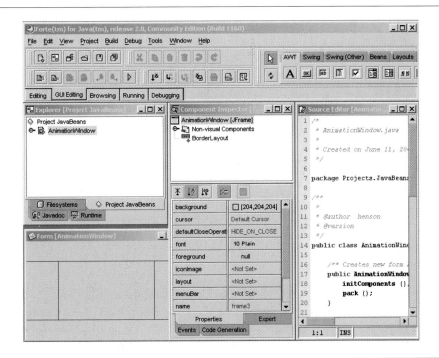

Fig. 6.10   **GUI Editing** tab of Forte.

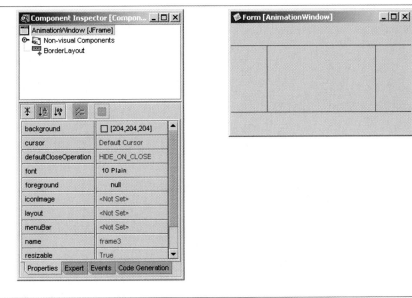

Fig. 6.11   **Component Inspector** and **Form** windows.

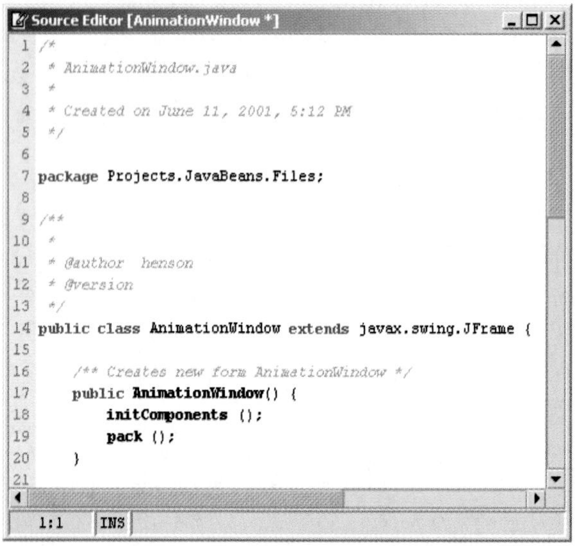

```
Source Editor [AnimationWindow *]                              _ □ ×
 1  /*
 2   * AnimationWindow.java
 3   *
 4   * Created on June 11, 2001, 5:12 PM
 5   */
 6
 7  package Projects.JavaBeans.Files;
 8
 9  /**
10   *
11   * @author  henson
12   * @version
13   */
14  public class AnimationWindow extends javax.swing.JFrame {
15
16      /** Creates new form AnimationWindow */
17      public AnimationWindow() {
18          initComponents ();
19          pack ();
20      }
21
                                                                 ▲
 1:1    INS
```

Fig. 6.12   Source Editor window.

We now begin building the application by placing the **LogoAnimator** JavaBean we just imported into the **AnimationWindow**. Click the **Beans** tab of the **Component Palette** (Fig. 6.13). Next, click the **LogoAnimator** icon (Fig. 6.14). Then, click in the **Form** window in the center of the **JFrame**. A spinning animation of the Deitel and Associates, Inc., logo will appear in the window (Fig. 6.15).

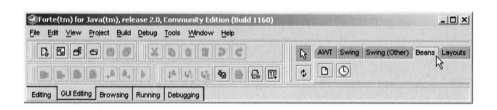

Fig. 6.13   Beans tab of the **Component Palette**.

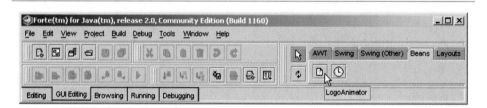

Fig. 6.14   LogoAnimator icon.

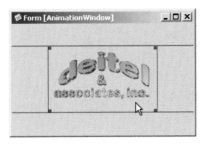

Fig. 6.15 `LogoAnimator` animation in the **Form** window.

The property sheet in the **Component Inspector** displays a component's properties and allows them to be edited. Click the **LogoAnimator** in the **Form** window. Blue squares appear at the corners of the animation to show it is selected (Fig. 6.15). The **Component Inspector** shows all the **LogoAnimator** properties (Fig. 6.16). Many of the properties are inherited from **JPanel**, the superclass of **LogoAnimator**. The **background** property shows a swatch of color and a name indicating the **LogoAnimator** background color. Click the color, and a drop-down menu appears (Fig. 6.17). It lists some of the predefined colors in Java. Select the first color listed in the drop-down menu to change the **LogoAnimator**'s background to white (Fig. 6.18). Try selecting other colors to get used to changing JavaBean properties.

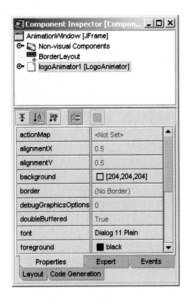

Fig. 6.16 Component Inspector with **LogoAnimator** Properties sheet.

Fig. 6.17   **Component Inspector** drop down-menu for the **background** property.

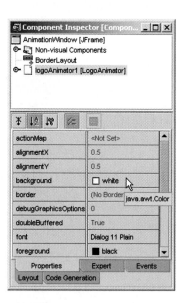

Fig. 6.18   Changing **background** color of **LogoAnimator**.

In addition to changing JavaBean properties with the builder tool, component assemblers can connect JavaBeans with events. For instance, a button can control the function of another component. We demonstrate this with buttons that start and stop the **LogoAnimator**'s animation.

Before adding other components to our example, we change the window's layout to a **FlowLayout**. In the **Explorer** window, expand the **AnimationWindow** node (Fig. 6.19). Right click the **JFrame** node, select **Set Layout** and click **FlowLayout** (Fig. 6.20).

Select the **Swing** tab in the **Component Palette** (Fig. 6.21). This tab contains the most common Swing components. The second component in the list is the **JButton** (Fig. 6.22). Click the **JButton** icon, then click an empty spot in the **Form** that contains the **LogoAnimator**. A new **JButton** appears in the window next to the **LogoAnimator** (Fig. 6.23). Select the **JButton** and locate the **text** property in the **Component Inspector**. Click the text field, type **Start Animation** (Fig. 6.24), then press *Enter*. The button text in the **Form** will change to the new value (Fig. 6.24). Repeat this procedure to add another **JButton** with the text **Stop Animation**.

Fig. 6.19 **AnimationWindow** selected in **Explorer**.

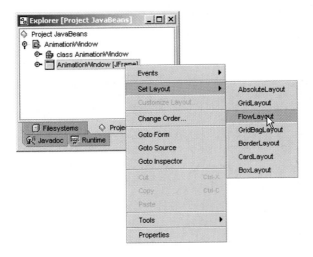

Fig. 6.20 Selecting **FlowLayout** in the **Explorer** menu.

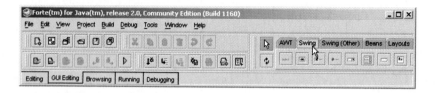

Fig. 6.21 **Swing** tab of the **Component Palette**.

Fig. 6.22 **JButton** icon in the **Component Palette**.

Fig. 6.23 Adding a **JButton** to **AnimationWindow**.

Fig. 6.24 Editing **text** property of **JButton**.

Next, we connect the **Start Animation** and **Stop Animation** buttons to the **Logo-Animator** so the user can start and stop the animation. The button with the mouse pointer icon to the left of the **Component Palette** enables **Selection Mode** (Fig. 6.25). This mode enables Forte users to select components in a **Form** window. The button with the double-arrows icon below the **Selection Mode** icon enables **Connection Mode** (Fig. 6.26), which allows Forte users to connect components with a wizard that generates code in the **Source Editor**. Click the **Connection Mode** icon to enter **Connection Mode** (Fig. 6.27). Click the **Start Animation JButton** (Fig. 6.28), which will be the source of the event (i.e., the source component) that starts the animation. Red squares appear at the corners of the **JButton**. Next, click the **LogoAnimator**. Red squares also appear at the corners of **LogoAnimator** and the **Connection Wizard** dialog appears (Fig. 6.29). Step 1 of the **Connection Wizard** lists all the events that the source component supports. In this application, we want the button click event to call the animator's **startAnimation** method, so we need to connect the button's action event to **LogoAnimator**'s **start-Animation** method. Expand the **action** node, highlight **actionPerformed** and click the **Next** button at the bottom of the **Connection Wizard** (Fig. 6.30). Step 2 (Fig. 6.31) lists the methods or properties that can be set on the target component (**LogoAnimator**). Click the **Method Call** radio button to show a list of **LogoAnimator**'s methods. Many of the methods that appear in the list are inherited from **LogoAnimator**'s superclass—**JPanel**. Select method **startAnimation** from the list and click the **Finish** button at the bottom of the **Connection Wizard** (Fig. 6.31). Repeat the above procedure for the **Stop Animation** button, but select method **stopAnimation** in Step 2 of the **Connection Wizard**

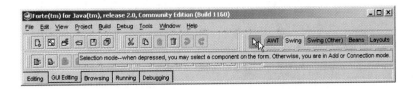

Fig. 6.25   **Component Palette Selection mode.**

Fig. 6.26   **Component Palette Connection mode.**

Fig. 6.27   Select **Connection mode.**

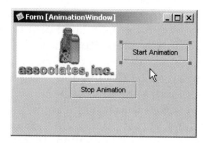

Fig. 6.28 Connecting **JButton** and **LogoAnimator**.

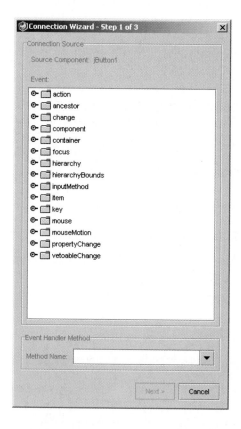

Fig. 6.29 **Connection Wizard** dialog.

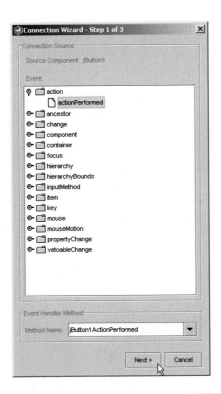

Fig. 6.30 Select `actionPerformed` event.

Fig. 6.31 Selecting method `startAnimation` for the target component.

To test that the connections between the buttons and the LogoAnimator work correctly, execute the **AnimationWindow** application by right clicking **Animation-Window** in the **Explorer** window and selecting **Execute** from the menu (Fig. 6.32). Forte switches to the **Running** tab and displays **AnimationWindow** (Fig. 6.33). **AnimationWindow** contains the **LogoAnimator** and the two **JButton**s. Click the **Stop Animation** button. The Deitel logo in **LogoAnimator** stops. Clicking the **Start Animation** button starts the animation from the point it stopped.

Testing and Debugging Tip 6.1

A benefit of working in a bean-ready development environment is that the beans typically execute live in the development environment. This allows you to view your program immediately in the design environment, rather than using the standard edit, compile and execute cycle.

Fig. 6.32 Select **Execute** from **Explorer** menu.

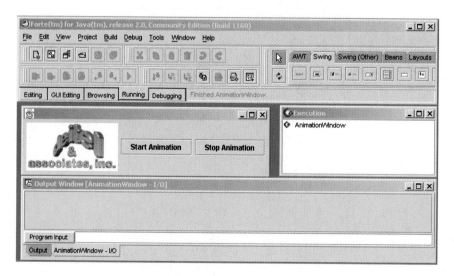

Fig. 6.33 **AnimationWindow** running in **Forte**.

6.3 Preparing a Class to be a JavaBean

In the previous section, we introduced the **LogoAnimator** JavaBean to demonstrate the basics of using JavaBeans within the Forte integrated development environment. This section presents the Java code for **LogoAnimator** (Fig. 6.34).

```java
1   // Fig. 6.34: LogoAnimator.java
2   // LogoAnimator is a JavaBean containing an animated logo.
3   package com.deitel.advjhtp1.beans;
4
5   // Java core packages
6   import java.awt.*;
7   import java.awt.event.*;
8   import java.io.*;
9   import java.net.*;
10
11  // Java extension packages
12  import javax.swing.*;
13
14  public class LogoAnimator extends JPanel
15     implements ActionListener, Serializable {
16
17     protected ImageIcon images[];
18     protected int totalImages = 30, currentImage;
19     protected Timer animationTimer;
20
21     // load images and start animation
22     public LogoAnimator()
23     {
24        images = new ImageIcon[ totalImages ];
25
26        URL url;
27
28        // load animation frames
29        for ( int i = 0; i < images.length; ++i ) {
30           url = LogoAnimator.class.getResource(
31              "images/deitel" + i + ".png" );
32           images[ i ] = new ImageIcon( url );
33        }
34
35        startAnimation();
36     }
37
38     // render one frame of the animation
39     public void paintComponent( Graphics g )
40     {
41        super.paintComponent( g );
42
43        // draw current animation frame
44        images[ currentImage ].paintIcon( this, g, 0, 0 );
45        currentImage = ( currentImage + 1 ) % totalImages;
46     }
```

Fig. 6.34 Definition of class **LogoAnimator** (part 1 of 3).

```
47
48    // start Timer that drives animation
49    public void startAnimation()
50    {
51       // if animationTimer is null, restart animation
52       if ( animationTimer == null ) {
53          currentImage = 0;
54          animationTimer = new Timer( 50, this );
55          animationTimer.start();
56       }
57
58       else   // continue from last image displayed
59
60          if ( !animationTimer.isRunning() )
61             animationTimer.restart();
62    }
63
64    // repaint when Timer event occurs
65    public void actionPerformed( ActionEvent actionEvent )
66    {
67       repaint();
68    }
69
70    // stop Timer that drives animation
71    public void stopAnimation()
72    {
73       animationTimer.stop();
74    }
75
76    // get animation preferred width and height
77    public Dimension getPreferredSize()
78    {
79       return new Dimension( 160, 80 );
80    }
81
82    // get animation minimum width and height
83    public Dimension getMinimumSize()
84    {
85       return getPreferredSize();
86    }
87
88    // execute bean as standalone application
89    public static void main( String args[] )
90    {
91       // create new LogoAnimator
92       LogoAnimator animation = new LogoAnimator();
93
94       // create new JFrame with title "Animation test"
95       JFrame application = new JFrame( "Animator test" );
96       application.setDefaultCloseOperation(
97          JFrame.EXIT_ON_CLOSE );
98
```

Fig. 6.34 Definition of class **LogoAnimator** (part 2 of 3).

```
99          // add LogoAnimator to JFrame
100         application.getContentPane().add( animation,
101            BorderLayout.CENTER );
102
103         // set the window size and validate layout
104         application.pack();
105         application.setVisible( true );
106      }
107
108  }  // end class LogoAnimator
```

Fig. 6.34 Definition of class **LogoAnimator** (part 3 of 3).

Class **LogoAnimator** (Fig. 6.34) implements the **LogoAnimator** JavaBean. **LogoAnimator** extends **JPanel** (line 14), making it a GUI component. Many Java-Beans are GUI components intended to be manipulated visually in a builder tool, such as Forte. In fact, most Java **Swing** components are JavaBeans, such as the **JButton**s we manipulated visually in Forte in the previous section. GUIs using **Swing** components can be developed quickly in Forte and other JavaBean-enabled builder tools.

Class **LogoAnimator** implements interface **Serializable** (line 15). The **Serializable** interface allows an instance of **LogoAnimator** to be saved as a file. By implementing **Serializable**, a customized JavaBean can be saved and reloaded in a builder tool or in a Java application. Forte can save an instance of **LogoAnimator** with the **Serialize As...** option in the **Customize Bean** dialog. **Serializable** objects can be serialized in Java programs with the **ObjectOutputStream** and **ObjectInputStream** classes.

Software Engineering Observation 6.2

*JavaBeans must all implement interface **Serializable** to support persistence using standard Java serialization.*

Line 17 declares **ImageIcon** array **images**, which contains the 30 PNG images that comprise the animated logo in **LogoAnimator**. Line 18 declares two integer variables, **totalImages** and **currentImage**. Line 19 declares **animationTimer**, a **Timer** object that controls the animation speed.

Lines 22–36 define **LogoAnimator**'s no-argument constructor. Line 24 initializes array **images** with length **totalImages**. Lines 29–33 load the PNG images into the array. Line 35 invokes method **startAnimation** to start the **LogoAnimator** animation.

LogoAnimator overrides method **paintComponent** (lines 39–46), inherited from class **JPanel**. Method **paintComponent** draws **LogoAnimator** whenever it is called. Line 44 calls method **paintIcon** on an **ImageIcon** in array **images**. The **ImageIcon** is at index **currentImage**. This paints one of the animation frames. Line 45 advances the variable **currentImage** to the next animation frame.

Method **startAnimation** (lines 49–62) initializes **animationTimer**, the **Timer** object that controls the delay between animation frames. If **animationTimer** is null, lines 52–56 create a new **Timer** object with a delay of 50 milliseconds. Otherwise, **startAnimation** restarts **animationTimer** on lines 58–61.

LogoAnimator implements method **actionPerformed** of interface **ActionListener** on lines 65–68. The **animationTimer** generates an **ActionEvent** at a rate specified in its constructor argument. When **animationTimer** generates an **ActionEvent**, line 67 calls method **repaint**. Method **repaint**, in turn, calls **paintComponent**, which draws the next animation frame.

Method **stopAnimation** (lines 71–74) calls method **stop** on **animationTimer** (line 73). This stops **animationTimer** from generating **ActionEvent**s, which stops the animation.

Method **getPreferredSize** (lines 77–80) returns a **Dimension** object with the preferred size of **LogoAnimator**. Method **getMinimumSize** (line 83–86) simply calls **getPreferredSize**. The **LayoutManager** calls these two methods to determine how to size **LogoAnimator** within the runtime environment.

Method **main** (lines 89–106) allows **LogoAnimator** to be executed as an application. Method **main** creates a new **JFrame** and adds an instance of **LogoAnimator** to the **JFrame**. JavaBeans do not need a **main** method, but the **main** method is needed to execute a JavaBean independently.

LogoAnimator can be compiled either from the command line or in Forte. **Logo-Animator** declares a package, so use the **-d** option of the Java compiler to create the proper directory structure. The command line

```
javac -d . LogoAnimator.java
```

compiles **LogoAnimator** and places the package directory in the current directory. The full directory structure for the package is **com\deitel\advjhtp1\beans** (substitute forward slashes, **/**, in UNIX/Linux). For **LogoAnimator** to execute properly, the directory **images** with the PNG files used by **LogoAnimator** must be placed in the same directory as class **LogoAnimator** (e.g. **com\deitel\advjhtp1\beans**). The **images** directory and the **PNG** files for **LogoAnimator** are on the CD-ROM that accompanies this book.

To compile in Forte, open the **LogoAnimator.java** file in Forte, right click in the **Source Editor** window and select **Compile** (Fig. 6.35). Forte compiles the source code and reports any errors in a separate window. Be sure to place the **images** directory in the same directory as **LogoAnimator.class**. **LogoAnimator** will not execute properly without the images.

6.4 Creating a JavaBean: Java Archive Files

JavaBeans normally are stored and distributed in a *Java Archive files (JAR files)*. A JAR file for a JavaBean must contain a *manifest file*, which describes the JAR file contents. Manifest files contain attributes (called *headers*) that describe the individual components in the JAR. This is important for integrated development environments that support JavaBeans. When a JAR file containing a JavaBean (or a set of JavaBeans) is loaded into an IDE, the IDE reads at the manifest file to determine which of the classes in the JAR represent JavaBeans. IDEs typically make these classes available to the programmer in a visual manner, as shown in the Forte overview earlier in this chapter. We create file **manifest.tmp**, which the **jar** utility uses to create the file as **MANIFEST.MF** and places in the **META-INF** directory of the JAR file. [*Note:* The file **manifest.tmp** can have any name—**jar** simply uses the file's contents to create **MANIFEST.MF** in the JAR file.] All JavaBean-aware development environments know to read the **MANIFEST.MF**

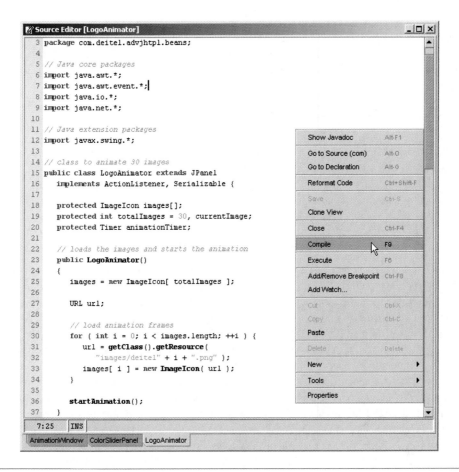

Fig. 6.35 **Compile** option in the **Source Editor** menu.

file in the **META-INF** directory of the JAR file. The Java interpreter can execute an application directly from a JAR file if the manifest file specifies which class in the JAR contains method **main**. Figure 6.36 shows the manifest file (**manifest.tmp**) for the **LogoAnimator** JavaBean.

 **Software Engineering Observation 6.3**

You must define a manifest file that describes the contents of a JAR file if you intend either to use the bean in a bean-aware integrated development environment or execute an application directly from a JAR file.

```
1   Main-Class: com.deitel.advjhtp1.beans.LogoAnimator
2
3   Name: com/deitel/advjhtp1/beans/LogoAnimator.class
4   Java-Bean: True
```

Fig. 6.36 Method file **manifest.tmp** for the **LogoAnimator** bean.

Class **com.deitel.advjhtp1.beans.LogoAnimator** contains method **main**. This is specified by the **Main-Class** header (line 1). This header enables the virtual machine to execute the application in the JAR file directly. To execute **LogoAnimator** from its JAR file, launch the Java virtual machine with the **-jar** command-line option as follows:

```
java -jar LogoAnimator.jar
```

The interpreter looks at the manifest file to determine which class to execute. On many platforms, you can execute an application in a JAR file by double clicking the JAR file in your system's file manager. This executes the **jar** command with the **-jar** option for the JAR file the user clicks. The application can also be executed from a JAR file that does not contain a manifest with the command

```
java -classpath LogoAnimator.jar
     com.deitel.advjhtp1.beans.LogoAnimator
```

where **-classpath** indicates the *class path* (i.e., the directories and JAR files in which the interpreter should search for classes). The **-classpath** option is followed by the JAR file containing the application class. The last command-line argument is the full class name (including the package name) for the application class.

Line 3 of the manifest file specifies the **Name** header of the file containing the bean class (including the **.class** file name extension), using its package and class name. Notice that the dots (**.**) typically used in package names are replaced with forward slashes (**/**) for the **Name** header in the manifest file. Line 4 use the **Java-Bean** header to specify that the class named on line 3 is a JavaBean. It is possible to have classes that are not Java-Beans in a JAR file. Such classes typically support the JavaBeans in the archive. For example, a linked-list bean might have a supporting linked-list-node class, objects of which represent each node in the list. Each class listed in the manifest file should be separated from other classes by a blank line. If the class is a bean, its **Name** header should be followed immediately by its **Java-Bean** header.

In the manifest file, a bean's name is specified with the **Name** header followed by the fully qualified name of the bean (i.e., the complete package name and class name). The dots (**.**) normally used to separate package names and class names are replaced with forward slash (**/**) in this line of the manifest file.

Common Programming Error 6.1

*If a class represents a bean, the **Java-Bean** header must follow the **Name** header immediately with a value of **True**. Otherwise, IDEs will not recognize the class as a bean.*

Software Engineering Observation 6.4

*If a class containing **main** is included in a JAR file, that class can be used by the interpreter to execute the application directly from the JAR file by specifying the **Main-Class** header at the beginning of the manifest file. The full package name and class name of the class should be specified with periods (**.**) separating the package components and class name.*

Common Programming Error 6.2

Not specifying a manifest file or specifying a manifest file with incorrect syntax when creating a JAR file is an error—builder tools will not recognize the beans in the JAR file.

Common Programming Error 6.3

*If a JAR file manifest does not specify the **Main-Class** header, there must be a blank line at the top of the manifest file before listing any **Name** headers. Some JAR utilities will report an error and not create a JAR without a blank line at the top of the manifest.*

Next, we create the JAR file for the **LogoAnimator** bean. This is accomplished with the **jar** utility at the command line (such as the MS-DOS prompt or UNIX shell). The command

```
jar cfm LogoAnimator.jar manifest.tmp
  com\deitel\advjhtp1\beans\*.*
```

creates the JAR file. [*Note*: This command uses the backslash (****) as the directory separator from the Windows Command Prompt. UNIX would use the forward slash (**/**) as the directory separator.] In the preceding command, **jar** is the Java archive utility used to create JAR files. The options for the **jar** utility—*cfm* are provided next. The letter *c* indicates that we are creating a JAR file. The letter *f* indicates that the next argument in the command line (**LogoAnimator.jar**) is the name of the JAR file to create. The letter *m* indicates that the next argument in the command line (**manifest.tmp**) is the manifest file that **jar** uses to create the file **META-INF/MANIFEST.MF** in the JAR. Following the options, the JAR file name and the manifest file name are the actual files to include in the JAR file. We specified **com\deitel\advjhtp1\beans*.*,** indicating that all the files in the **beans** directory should be included in the JAR file. The **com.deitel.advjhtp1.beans** package directory contains the **.class** files for the **LogoAnimator** and its supporting classes, as well as the images used in the animation. [*Note*: You can include particular files by specifying the path and file name for each individual file.] It is important that the directory structure in the JAR file match the class' package structure. Therefore, we executed the **jar** command from the directory on our system in which the **com** directory that begins the package name reside.

To confirm that the files were archived correctly, issue the command

```
jar tvf LogoAnimator.jar
```

In this command, the letter *t* indicates that **jar** should list the table of contents for the JAR file. The letter *v* indicates that the output should be verbose (the *verbose output* includes the file size in bytes and the date and time each file was created, in addition to the directory structure and file name). The letter *f* specifies that the next argument on the command line is the JAR file for which **jar** should display information.

Try executing the **LogoAnimator** application with the command

```
java -jar LogoAnimator.jar
```

You will see that the animation appears in its own window on your screen.

JAR files also can be created inside Forte's integrated development environment. Right click **LogoAnimator** in the **Explorer** window and select **Add to JAR** from the **Tools** menu, as described in Section 6.2. This displays the **JAR Packager** dialog. Our class **LogoAnimator** already is selected to be included in the JAR file. At the top of the dialog, type **LogoAnimator.jar** in the JAR Archive textfield and specify the directory in which the JAR will appear. Add the **images** directory to the JAR (Fig. 6.37). Next, click the **Manifest** tab and select the **Generate File List** check box. This creates a list of all files in the JAR, including **LogoAnimator.class** and the PNG files. The **Java-Bean** and **Main-Class** headers are not generated by Forte and must be typed into the manifest (Fig. 6.38). Click **Create JAR** to create **LogoAnimator.jar**. Now the Logo-Animator can be loaded into the **Component Palette** as described in Section 6.2.

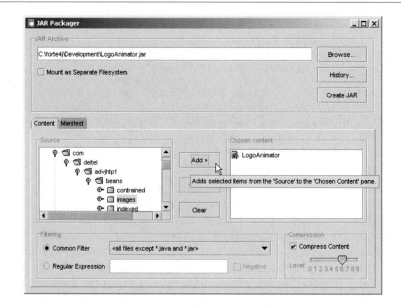

Fig. 6.37   Add **images** directory to **LogoAnimator.jar**.

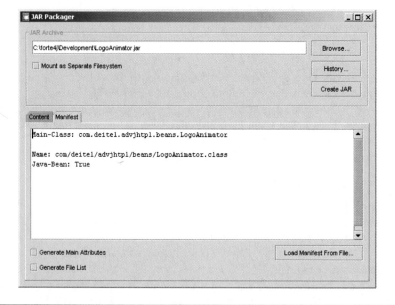

Fig. 6.38   **Manifest** tab of **JAR Packager** dialog.

6.5　JavaBean Properties

In this section, we demonstrate adding an **animationDelay** property to **LogoAnima-tor**, to control the animation's speed. For this purpose, we extend class **LogoAnimator** to create class **LogoAnimator2**. The new code for our property is defined by methods **setAnimationDelay** (lines 16–19) and **getAnimationDelay** (lines 22–25) in Fig. 6.39.

```java
1    // Fig. 6.39: LogoAnimator2.java
2    // LogoAnimator2 extends LogoAnimator to include
3    // animationDelay property and implements ColorListener
4    package com.deitel.advjhtp1.beans;
5
6    // Java core packages
7    import java.awt.*;
8    import java.awt.event.*;
9
10   // Java extension packages
11   import javax.swing.*;
12
13   public class LogoAnimator2 extends LogoAnimator {
14
15      // set animationDelay property
16      public void setAnimationDelay( int delay )
17      {
18         animationTimer.setDelay( delay );
19      }
20
21      // get animationDelay property
22      public int getAnimationDelay()
23      {
24         return animationTimer.getDelay();
25      }
26
27      // launch LogoAnimator in JFrame for testing
28      public static void main( String args[] )
29      {
30         // create new LogoAnimator2
31         LogoAnimator2 animation = new LogoAnimator2();
32
33         // create new JFrame and add LogoAnimator2 to it
34         JFrame application = new JFrame( "Animator test" );
35         application.getContentPane().add( animation,
36            BorderLayout.CENTER );
37
38         application.setDefaultCloseOperation(
39            JFrame.EXIT_ON_CLOSE );
40         application.pack();
41         application.setVisible( true );
42      }
43
44   }  // end class LogoAnimator2
```

Fig. 6.39　**LogoAnimator2** with property **animationDelay**.

To create the **animationDelay** property, we defined methods **setAnimation-Delay** and **getAnimationDelay**. A *read/write* property of a bean is defined as a *set/get* method pair of the form

```
public void setPropertyName( DataType value )
public DataType getPropertyName()
```

where **PropertyName** is replaced in each case by the actual property name. These methods often are referred to as a "property *set* method" and "property *get* method," respectively.

Software Engineering Observation 6.5

A JavaBean read/write property is defined by a set/get *method pair in which the* set *method returns* **void** *and takes one argument and the* get *method returns the same type as the corresponding* set *method's argument and takes no arguments. It is also possible to have read-only properties (defined with only a* get *method) and write-only properties (defined with only a* set *method).*

Software Engineering Observation 6.6

For a property with the name propertyName, *the corresponding* set/get *method pair would be* **set**PropertyName/**get**PropertyName *by default. Note that the first letter of* property-Name *is capitalized in the* set/get *method names.*

If the property is a **boolean** data type, the *set/get* method pair is sometimes defined as

```
public void setPropertyName( boolean value )
public boolean isPropertyName()
```

where the *get* method name begins with the word **is** rather than **get**.

When a builder tool examines a bean, it inspects the bean methods for pairs of *set/get* methods that represent properties (some builder tools also expose read-only and write-only properties). This process is known as *introspection*. If the builder tool finds an appropriate *set/get* method pair during the introspection process, the builder tool exposes that pair of methods as a property in the builder tool's user interface. In the first **LogoAnimator**, the pair of methods

```
public void setBackground( Color c )
public Color getBackground()
```

that were inherited from class **JPanel** allowed Forte to expose the **background** property in the **Component Inspector** for customization. Notice that the naming convention for the *set/get* method pair used a capital letter for the first letter of the property name, but the exposed property in the **Component Inspector** is shown with a lowercase first letter.

Software Engineering Observation 6.7

When a builder tool examines a bean, if it locates a set/get *method pair that matches the JavaBean's property pattern, it exposes that pair of methods as a property in the bean.*

Remember that class **LogoAnimator2** must be wrapped as a JavaBean to load it into Forte and other builder tools. Compile **LogoAnimator2**, and then place it in a JAR file as described in the previous section. Now import **LogoAnimator2** into the **Component Palette**, and drop an instance of **LogoAnimator2** into a **JFrame** as in Section 6.2. Select **LogoAnimator2** in the **Form** window or **Component Inspector**. The **animationDelay** property is now exposed in the **Component Inspector** (Fig. 6.40). Try

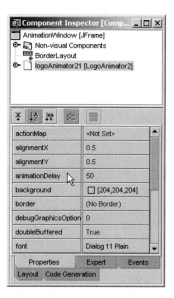

Fig. 6.40 LogoAnimator2 bean with property **animationDelay** exposed in Forte's **Component Inspector**.

changing the value of the property to see its effect on the speed of the animation (you must press *Enter* after changing the value to effect the change). Smaller values cause the animation to spin faster, larger values cause it to spin slower. Try typing **1000** to see one frame of the animation per second.

6.6 Bound Properties

A *bound property* causes the JavaBean that owns the property to notify other objects when the bound property's value changes. This notification is accomplished with standard Java event-handling features—the bean notifies its registered ***PropertyChangeListener***s when the bound property's value changes. To support this feature, the ***java.beans*** *package* provides interface **PropertyChangeListener** so listeners can be configured to receive property-change notifications, class ***PropertyChangeEvent*** to provide information to a **PropertyChangeListener** about the change in a property's value and class ***PropertyChangeSupport*** to provide the listener registration and notification services (i.e., to maintain the list of listeners and notify them when an event occurs).

Software Engineering Observation 6.8

A bound property causes the object that owns the property to notify other objects that there has been a change in the value of that property.

The next example creates a new GUI component (**SliderFieldPanel**) that extends **JPanel** and includes one **JSlider** object and one **JTextField** object. When the **JSlider** value changes, our new GUI component automatically updates the **JTextField** with the new value. Also, when a new value is entered in the **JTextField** and the user presses the *Enter* key, the **JSlider** is automatically repositioned to the appropriate location. Our purpose in defining this new component is to link one of these to the **LogoAnimator2** animation to control the speed of the animation. When the **Slider-FieldPanel** value changes, we want the animation speed to change. Figure 6.41 presents the code for class **SliderFieldPanel**.

```
1   // Fig. 6.41: SliderFieldPanel.java
2   // SliderFieldPanel provides a slider to adjust the animation
3   // speed of LogoAnimator2.
4   package com.deitel.advjhtp1.beans;
5
6   // Java core packages
7   import java.io.*;
8   import java.awt.*;
9   import java.awt.event.*;
10  import java.beans.*;
11
12  // Java extension packages
13  import javax.swing.*;
14  import javax.swing.event.*;
15
16  public class SliderFieldPanel extends JPanel
17     implements Serializable {
18
19     private JSlider slider;
20     private JTextField field;
21     private Box boxContainer;
22     private int currentValue;
23
24     // object to support bound property changes
25     private PropertyChangeSupport changeSupport;
26
27     // SliderFieldPanel constructor
28     public SliderFieldPanel()
29     {
30        // create PropertyChangeSupport for bound properties
31        changeSupport = new PropertyChangeSupport( this );
32
33        // initialize slider and text field
34        slider = new JSlider(
35           SwingConstants.HORIZONTAL, 1, 100, 1 );
36        field = new JTextField(
37           String.valueOf( slider.getValue() ), 5 );
38
39        // set box layout and add slider and text field
40        boxContainer = new Box( BoxLayout.X_AXIS );
41        boxContainer.add( slider );
42        boxContainer.add( Box.createHorizontalStrut( 5 ) );
43        boxContainer.add( field );
44
45        setLayout( new BorderLayout() );
46        add( boxContainer );
47
```

Fig. 6.41   Definition for class **SliderFieldPanel** (part 1 of 4).

```
48          // add ChangeListener for JSlider
49          slider.addChangeListener(
50
51             new ChangeListener() {
52
53                // handle state change for JSlider
54                public void stateChanged( ChangeEvent changeEvent )
55                {
56                   setCurrentValue( slider.getValue() );
57                }
58
59             } // end anonymous inner class
60
61          ); // end call to addChangeListener
62
63          // add ActionListener for JTextField
64          field.addActionListener(
65
66             new ActionListener() {
67
68                // handle action for JTextField
69                public void actionPerformed( ActionEvent
70                   actionEvent )
71                {
72                   setCurrentValue(
73                      Integer.parseInt( field.getText() ) );
74                }
75
76             } // end anonymous inner class
77
78          ); // end call to addActionListener
79
80       } // end SliderFieldPanel constructor
81
82       // add PropertyChangeListener
83       public void addPropertyChangeListener(
84          PropertyChangeListener listener )
85       {
86          changeSupport.addPropertyChangeListener( listener );
87       }
88
89       //  remove PropertyChangeListener
90       public void removePropertyChangeListener(
91          PropertyChangeListener listener )
92       {
93          changeSupport.removePropertyChangeListener( listener );
94       }
95
96       // set minimumValue property
97       public void setMinimumValue( int minimum )
98       {
99          slider.setMinimum( minimum );
```

Fig. 6.41   Definition for class **SliderFieldPanel** (part 2 of 4).

```
100
101        if ( slider.getValue() < slider.getMinimum() ) {
102           slider.setValue( slider.getMinimum() );
103           field.setText( String.valueOf( slider.getValue() ) );
104        }
105     }
106
107     // get minimumValue property
108     public int getMinimumValue()
109     {
110        return slider.getMinimum();
111     }
112
113     // set maximumValue property
114     public void setMaximumValue( int maximum )
115     {
116        slider.setMaximum( maximum );
117
118        if ( slider.getValue() > slider.getMaximum() ) {
119           slider.setValue( slider.getMaximum() );
120           field.setText( String.valueOf( slider.getValue() ) );
121        }
122     }
123
124     // get maximumValue property
125     public int getMaximumValue()
126     {
127        return slider.getMaximum();
128     }
129
130     // set currentValue property
131     public void setCurrentValue( int current )
132        throws IllegalArgumentException
133     {
134        if ( current < 0 )
135           throw new IllegalArgumentException();
136
137        int oldValue = currentValue;
138
139        // set currentValue property
140        currentValue = current;
141
142        // change slider and textfield values
143        slider.setValue( currentValue );
144        field.setText( String.valueOf( currentValue ) );
145
146        // fire PropertyChange
147        changeSupport.firePropertyChange(
148           "currentValue", new Integer( oldValue ),
149           new Integer( currentValue ) );
150     }
151
```

Fig. 6.41   Definition for class **SliderFieldPanel** (part 3 of 4).

```
152     // get currentValue property
153     public int getCurrentValue()
154     {
155         return slider.getValue();
156     }
157
158     // set fieldWidth property
159     public void setFieldWidth( int columns )
160     {
161         field.setColumns( columns );
162         boxContainer.validate();
163     }
164
165     // get fieldWidth property
166     public int getFieldWidth()
167     {
168         return field.getColumns();
169     }
170
171     // get minimum panel size
172     public Dimension getMinimumSize()
173     {
174         return boxContainer.getMinimumSize();
175     }
176
177     // get preferred panel size
178     public Dimension getPreferredSize()
179     {
180         return boxContainer.getPreferredSize();
181     }
182
183 }   // end class SliderFieldPanel
```

Fig. 6.41   Definition for class **SliderFieldPanel** (part 4 of 4).

Class **SliderFieldPanel** (Fig. 6.41) begins by specifying that it will be part of the **com.deitel.advjhtp1.beans** package (line 4). The class is a subclass of **JPanel**, so we can add a **JSlider** and a **JTextField** to it. Objects of class **SliderFieldPanel** can then be added to other containers.

Lines 19–25 declare instance variables of type **JSlider** (**slider**) and **JTextField** (**field**) that represent the subcomponents the user will use to set the **SliderFieldPanel** value, a **Box** (**boxContainer**) that will manage the layout, an **int** (**currentValue**) that stores the current value of the **SliderFieldPanel** and a **PropertyChangeSupport** (**changeSupport**) that will provide the listener registration and notification services.

Line 31 creates the **PropertyChangeSupport** object. The argument **this** specifies that an object of this class (**SliderFieldPanel**) is the source of the **PropertyChangeEvent**. Lines 49–61 of the constructor register the **ChangeListener** for **slider**. When **slider**'s value changes, line 56 calls **setCurrentValue** to update **field** and notify registered **PropertyChangeListener**s of the change in value. Similarly, lines 64–78 register the **ActionListener** for **field**. When **field**'s value changes, lines 72–73 call **setCurrentValue** to update **slider** and notify registered **PropertyChangeListeners** of the change in value.

To support registration of listeners for changes to our **SliderFieldPanel**'s bound property, we define methods **addPropertyChangeListener** (lines 83–87) and **removePropertyChangeListener** (lines 90–94). Each of these methods calls the corresponding method in the **PropertyChangeSupport** object **changeSupport**. This object provides the event notification services when the property value changes.

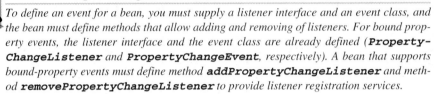

Software Engineering Observation 6.9

*To define an event for a bean, you must supply a listener interface and an event class, and the bean must define methods that allow adding and removing of listeners. For bound property events, the listener interface and the event class are already defined (**Property-ChangeListener** and **PropertyChangeEvent**, respectively). A bean that supports bound-property events must define method **addPropertyChangeListener** and method **removePropertyChangeListener** to provide listener registration services.*

Class **SliderFieldPanel** provides several properties. Methods **setMinimum-Value** (lines 97–105) and **getMinimumValue** (lines 108–111) define property **minimumValue**. Property **maximumValue** is defined by methods **setMaximumValue** (lines 114–122) and **getMaximumValue** (lines 125–128). Methods **setFieldWidth** (lines 159–163) and **getFieldWidth** (lines 166–169) define property **fieldWidth**. Methods **getMinimumSize** (lines 172–175) and **getPreferredSize** (line 178–181) return the minimum size and preferred size of the **Box** object **boxContainer**, which manages the layout of the **JSlider** and **JTextField**.

Look-and-Feel Observation 6.1

*If a bean will appear as part of a user interface, the bean should define method **getPreferredSize**, which takes no arguments and returns a **Dimension** object containing the preferred width and height of the bean. This helps the layout manager size the bean.*

Methods **setCurrentValue** (lines 131–150) and **getCurrentValue** (lines 153–156) define the bound property **currentValue**. When the bound property changes, the registered **PropertyChangeListener**s must be notified of the change. The JavaBeans specification (**java.sun.com/products/javabeans/docs/spec.html**) requires that each bound-property listener be presented with the old and new property values when notified of the change (the values can be **null** if they are not needed). For this reason, line 137 saves the previous property value. Line 140 sets the new property value. Lines 143–144 ensure that the **JSlider** and **JTextField** show the appropriate new values. Lines 147–149 invoke the **PropertyChangeSupport** object's **firePropertyChange** method to notify each registered **Property-ChangeListener**. The first argument is a **String** containing the property name that changed—**currentValue**. The second argument is the old property value. The third argument is the new property value.

Software Engineering Observation 6.10

***PropertyChangeListener**s are notified of a property-change event with both the old and the new value of the property. If these values are not needed, they can be **null**.*

Software Engineering Observation 6.11

*Class **PropertyChangeSupport** is provided as a convenience to implement the listener registration and notification support for property-change events.*

Remember that you should package the **SliderFieldPanel** class as a JavaBean to load it into a builder tool. Archive the class in a JAR file. The manifest file for this example is shown in Fig. 6.42. Line 2 specifies the name of the class file (**com\deitel\advjhtp1\beans\SliderFieldPanel.class**) that represents the bean. Line 3 specifies that the class named in line 1 is a JavaBean. There is no **Main-Class** header in this file, because the **SliderFieldPanel** is not an application. Finally, install **SliderFieldPanel.jar** into the builder tool.

To demonstrate the functionality of the bound property, place a **SliderField-Panel** bean and a **LogoAnimator2** bean into a **JFrame**. Select the **SliderField-Panel** bean (Fig. 6.43), set its **maximumValue** property to 1000 and set its **currentValue** to 50 (the default animation speed for the **LogoAnimator2**). In Forte, select **Connection Mode** from the **Component Palette**. Click the **SliderField-Panel**; then click **LogoAnimator2**. Red squares appear at the corners of each component and the **Connection Wizard** opens.

In Step 1 of the **Connection Wizard**, select **propertyChange** as the event for the source component and click the **Next** button (Fig. 6.44). Select **LogoAnimator2**'s **animationDelay** property in Step 2 of the **Connection Wizard** (Fig. 6.45) and click **Next**. Finally, select **SliderFieldPanel**'s **currentValue** property in Step 3 (Fig. 6.46) and click **Finish**. The **animationDelay** property is now bound to the **SliderFieldPanel**'s **currentValue** property. Execute the **JFrame** to see the connected **LogoAnimator2** and **SliderFieldPanel** (Fig. 6.47).

Try adjusting the slider to see the animation speed change. Move the slider left to see the speed of the animation increase; move the slider right to see the animation speed decrease.

```
1
2   Name: com/deitel/advjhtp1/beans/SliderFieldPanel.class
3   Java-Bean: True
```

Fig. 6.42   Manifest file for the **SliderFieldPanel** JavaBean.

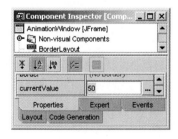 

Fig. 6.43   Change properties **currentValue** and **maximumValue**.

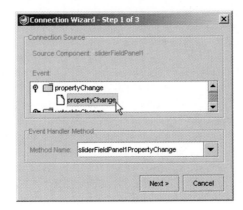

Fig. 6.44   Select **propertyChange** event.

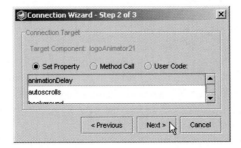

Fig. 6.45   Select **animationDelay** property of **LogoAnimator2**.

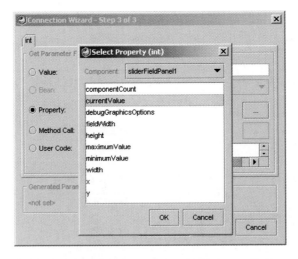

Fig. 6.46   Select **currentValue** Bound Property.

Fig. 6.47 JFrame with **LogoAnimator2** and **SliderFieldPanel**.

6.7 Indexed Properties and Custom Events

Although standard properties, bound properties and standard Java events provide a great deal of functionality, JavaBeans can be further customized with other types of properties and programmer-defined events. An *indexed property* is like a standard property, except that the indexed property is an array of primitives or objects. Two *get* and two *set* methods define an indexed property. The *get* methods are of the form

```
public Datatype[] getPropertyName()
public Datatype getPropertyName( int index )
```

The first *get* method returns the entire array of an indexed property. The second *get* method returns the item at the array index indicated by the *get* method's parameter. The *set* methods are of the form

```
public void setPropertyName( Datatype[] data)
public void setPropertyName( int index, Datatype data )
```

The first *set* method sets the indexed property to the value of the argument. The second *set* method sets the item at the indicated array index to the value of the second parameter.

 Software Engineering Observation 6.12

An indexed property functions like a regular property and is exposed in the property sheet like normal properties.

A JavaBean can generate programmer-defined events. A programmer-defined event, or *custom event*, provides functionality that standard Java events do not provide. An event class extends **java.util.EventObject** and the listener interface extends **java.util.EventListener**.

Our next example demonstrates an indexed property and a custom event. In the example we create a **ColorSliderPanel** that enables a user to choose values for the red, green and blue parts of a color. The **ColorSliderPanel** maintains these three integer values in an indexed property and uses them to create **Color** objects. This custom GUI component also generates custom **ColorEvent**s, so that it can notify its registered listeners when the user changes the color.

We begin by defining an **EventObject** class and an **EventListener** interface for the custom event **ColorEvent**. Figure 6.48 shows the **ColorEvent** class and Fig. 6.49 shows the **ColorListener** interface. Class **ColorEvent** is a custom event that extends class **EventObject**. Parameter **color** in the constructor (lines 15–19) represents the value of the **ColorEvent**'s **color** property. Method **setColor** (lines 22–25) sets the **color** instance variable. Method **getColor** (lines 28–31) returns the **color** property.

```
1   // Fig. 6.48 ColorEvent.java
2   // ColorEvent is an EventObject subclass that indicates a
3   // change in color.
4   package com.deitel.advjhtp1.beans;
5
6   // Java core packages
7   import java.util.*;
8   import java.awt.Color;
9
10  public class ColorEvent extends EventObject {
11
12     private Color color;
13
14     // constructor sets color property
15     public ColorEvent( Object source, Color color )
16     {
17        super( source );
18        setColor( color );
19     }
20
21     // set method for color property
22     public void setColor( Color newColor )
23     {
24        color = newColor;
25     }
26
27     // get method for color property
28     public Color getColor()
29     {
30        return color;
31     }
32
33  }  // end class ColorEvent
```

Fig. 6.48   **ColorEvent** custom-event class indicating a color change.

Interface **ColorListener** (Fig. 6.49) is a custom listener interface that extends class **EventListener**. Classes that implement **ColorListener** listen for **Color-Event**s. The **ColorEvent** event source calls its registered listeners' **colorChanged** method (declared at line 11) with a **ColorEvent** object describing the change. All listeners for **ColorEvent**s must implement the **ColorListener** interface.

```
1   // Fig. 6.49 ColorListener.java
2   // Color listener is the interface for custom event ColorEvent.
3   package com.deitel.advjhtp1.beans;
4
5   // Java core packages
6   import java.util.*;
7
8   public interface ColorListener extends EventListener {
```

Fig. 6.49   **ColorListener** interface for receiving **colorChanged** notifications (part 1 of 2).

```
9
10      // send colorChanged ColorEvent to listener
11      public void colorChanged( ColorEvent colorEvent );
12
13   } // end interface ColorListener
```

Fig. 6.49 **ColorListener** interface for receiving **colorChanged** notifications (part 2 of 2).

Class **ColorSliderPanel** (Fig. 6.50) is a JavaBean that issues **colorChanged** **ColorEvent**s when the sliders change the color value. **ColorSliderPanel** consists of three **SliderFieldPanel**s marked with **JLabel**s as **Red**, **Green** and **Blue**. Three **JTextField**s, one in each **SliderFieldPanel**, display integers from zero through 255. The three values are stored in an indexed property called **redGreenBlue**. Moving a **JSlider** changes the number displayed in its **JTextField** and changes the value of **redGreenBlue**. Changing **redGreenBlue**'s value causes **ColorSliderPanel** to fire a **ColorEvent**. The **ColorEvent** contains a **Color** object initialized to the three values of **redGreenBlue**. Our purpose in defining **ColorSliderPanel** is to link one of these to the **LogoAnimator2** animation, to change the background color of **LogoAnimator2**.

```
1    // Fig. 6.50 ColorSliderPanel.java
2    // ColorSliderPanel contains 3 SliderFieldPanels connected to
3    // indexed property redGreenBlue that adjusts the red, green
4    // and blue colors of an object.
5    package com.deitel.advjhtp1.beans;
6
7    // Java core packages
8    import java.io.*;
9    import java.awt.*;
10   import java.awt.event.*;
11   import java.beans.*;
12   import java.util.*;
13
14   // Java extension packages
15   import javax.swing.*;
16   import javax.swing.event.*;
17
18   public class ColorSliderPanel extends JPanel
19      implements Serializable {
20
21      private JLabel redLabel, greenLabel, blueLabel;
22      private SliderFieldPanel redSlider, greenSlider, blueSlider;
23      private JPanel labelPanel, sliderPanel;
24      private int[] redGreenBlue;
25      public int RED_INDEX = 0;
26      public int GREEN_INDEX = 1;
27      public int BLUE_INDEX = 2;
28      private Set listeners = new HashSet();
29
```

Fig. 6.50 Definition of class **ColorSliderPanel** (part 1 of 5).

```
30    // constructor for ColorSliderPanel
31    public ColorSliderPanel()
32    {
33       // initialize redGreenBlue property
34       redGreenBlue = new int[] { 0, 0, 0 };
35
36       // initialize gui components for red slider
37       redLabel = new JLabel( "Red:" );
38       redSlider = new SliderFieldPanel();
39       redSlider.setMinimumValue( 0 );
40       redSlider.setMaximumValue( 255 );
41
42       // initialize gui components for green slider
43       greenLabel = new JLabel( "Green: " );
44       greenSlider = new SliderFieldPanel();
45       greenSlider.setMinimumValue( 0 );
46       greenSlider.setMaximumValue( 255 );
47
48       // initialize gui components for blue slider
49       blueLabel = new JLabel( "Blue:" );
50       blueSlider = new SliderFieldPanel();
51       blueSlider.setMinimumValue( 0 );
52       blueSlider.setMaximumValue( 255 );
53
54       // set layout and add components
55       setLayout( new BorderLayout() );
56
57       labelPanel = new JPanel( new GridLayout( 3, 1 ) );
58       labelPanel.add( redLabel );
59       labelPanel.add( greenLabel );
60       labelPanel.add( blueLabel );
61
62       sliderPanel = new JPanel( new GridLayout( 3, 1 ) );
63       sliderPanel.add( redSlider );
64       sliderPanel.add( greenSlider );
65       sliderPanel.add( blueSlider );
66
67       add( labelPanel, BorderLayout.WEST );
68       add( sliderPanel, BorderLayout.CENTER );
69
70       // add PropertyChangeListener for redSlider
71       redSlider.addPropertyChangeListener(
72
73          new PropertyChangeListener() {
74
75             // handle propertyChange for redSlider
76             public void propertyChange( PropertyChangeEvent
77                propertyChangeEvent )
78             {
79                setRedGreenBlue( RED_INDEX,
80                   redSlider.getCurrentValue() );
81             }
82
```

Fig. 6.50   Definition of class **ColorSliderPanel** (part 2 of 5).

```
83                } // end anonymous inner class
84
85        ); // end call to addPropertyChangeListener
86
87        // add PropertyChangeListener for greenSlider
88        greenSlider.addPropertyChangeListener(
89
90            new PropertyChangeListener() {
91
92                // handle propertyChange for greenSlider
93                public void propertyChange( PropertyChangeEvent
94                    propertyChangeEvent )
95                {
96                    setRedGreenBlue( GREEN_INDEX,
97                        greenSlider.getCurrentValue() );
98                }
99
100               } // end anonymous inner class
101
102       ); // end call to addPropertyChangeListener
103
104       // add PropertyChangeListener for blueSlider
105       blueSlider.addPropertyChangeListener(
106
107           new PropertyChangeListener() {
108
109               // handle propertyChange for blueSlider
110               public void propertyChange( PropertyChangeEvent
111                   propertyChangeEvent )
112               {
113                   setRedGreenBlue( BLUE_INDEX,
114                       blueSlider.getCurrentValue() );
115               }
116
117               } // end anonymous inner class
118
119       ); // end call to addPropertyChangeListener
120
121   } // end ColorSliderPanel constructor
122
123   // add ColorListener
124   public void addColorListener(
125       ColorListener colorListener )
126   {
127       // listeners must be accessed atomically
128       synchronized ( listeners ) {
129           listeners.add( colorListener );
130       }
131   }
132
```

Fig. 6.50   Definition of class **ColorSliderPanel** (part 3 of 5).

```
133      // remove ColorListener
134      public void removeColorListener(
135         ColorListener colorListener )
136      {
137         // listeners must be accessed by one thread only
138         synchronized ( listeners ) {
139            listeners.remove( colorListener );
140         }
141      }
142
143      // fire ColorEvent
144      public void fireColorChanged()
145      {
146         Iterator iterator;
147
148         // listeners must be accessed atomically
149         synchronized ( listeners ) {
150            iterator = new HashSet( listeners ).iterator();
151         }
152
153         // create new Color with values of redGreenBlue
154         // create new ColorEvent with color variable
155         Color color = new Color( redGreenBlue[ RED_INDEX ],
156            redGreenBlue[ GREEN_INDEX ],
157               redGreenBlue[ BLUE_INDEX ] );
158         ColorEvent colorEvent = new ColorEvent( this, color );
159
160         // notify all registered ColorListeners of ColorChange
161         while ( iterator.hasNext() ) {
162            ColorListener colorListener = ( ColorListener )
163               iterator.next();
164            colorListener.colorChanged( colorEvent );
165         }
166      }
167
168      // get redGreenBlue property
169      public int[] getRedGreenBlue()
170      {
171         return redGreenBlue;
172      }
173
174      // get redGreenBlue indexed property
175      public int getRedGreenBlue( int index )
176      {
177         return redGreenBlue[ index ];
178      }
179
180      // set redGreenBlue property
181      public void setRedGreenBlue( int[] array )
182      {
183         redGreenBlue = array;
184      }
185
```

Fig. 6.50   Definition of class **ColorSliderPanel** (part 4 of 5).

```
186        // set redGreenBlue indexed property
187        public void setRedGreenBlue( int index, int value )
188        {
189            redGreenBlue[ index ] = value;
190            fireColorChanged();
191        }
192
193    }  // end class ColorSliderPanel
```

Fig. 6.50   Definition of class **ColorSliderPanel** (part 5 of 5).

Lines 31–121 contain the constructor for **ColorSliderPanel**. Line 34 initializes the **redGreenBlue** indexed property. Lines 37–52 initialize the **JLabel**s' components and **SliderFieldPanel**s. Each part of property **redGreenBlue** has a **JLabel** and a **SliderFieldPanel** associated with it. The **SliderFieldPanel**s' **JSlider**s are set to a range of 0 through 255, and the **JTextField**s are set with the initial value of the **JSlider**s. Line 55 sets the layout to **BorderLayout**. Lines 57–60 add the **JLabel**s to a new **JPanel** with a three-by-one **GridLayout**. Lines 62–65 add the **Slider-FieldPanel**s to a new **JPanel** with a three-by-one **GridLayout**. Lines 67–68 add the **JPanel**s to **ColorSliderPanel**. Lines 71–119 add **PropertyChangeListener**s to the **SliderFieldPanel**s. Each call to **addPropertyChangeListener** creates an instance of a **PropertyChangeListener** anonymous inner class. When a **SliderFieldPanel** fires a **PropertyChangeEvent**, the **propertyChanged** method of the appropriate **PropertyChangeListener** updates the value of indexed property **redGreenBlue**.

Methods **addColorListener** (lines 124–131) and **removeColorListener** (lines 134–141) contain **synchronized** blocks in which the **Set listeners** (line 28) is modified. **Set listeners** contains all the registered listeners of type **ColorListener**. Method **fireColorChanged** (lines 144–166) uses method **iterator** to create an **Iterator** from **listeners**. Lines 155–158 create a **ColorEvent** object with a **Color** attribute matching the values of the **redGreenBlue** property. Method **fireColorChanged** then sends the event to all registered listeners by calling method **colorChanged** on every listener.

Lines 169–191 contain methods to manipulate the **redGreenBlue** property. Method **getRedGreenBlue** (lines 169–172) with no parameters returns the **integer** array **redGreenBlue**. Method **getRedGreenBlue** (lines 175–178) with an **integer** parameter returns the value of **redGreenBlue** at the index of the parameter. Property **redGreenBlue** can be set with two versions of method **setRedGreenBlue**. Method **setRedGreenBlue** (lines 181–184) with an **integer** array parameter sets **redGreenBlue** to the parameter. Method **setRedGreenBlue** (lines 187–191) with **integer** parameters **index** and **value** sets the **value** of **redGreenBlue** at **index**. This version of the method also calls **fireColorChanged** to generate a **ColorEvent**.

Classes **ColorEvent**, **ColorListener** and **ColorSliderPanel** should be packaged in a JAR file so **ColorSliderPanel** can be used as a JavaBean. Figure 6.51 shows the manifest file for this example. Line 2 specifies the name of the class file (**com\deitel\advjhtp1\beans\ColorSliderPanel.class**) that represents the bean. Line 3 specifies that the class named in line 2 is a JavaBean. There is no **Main-Class** header line in this file, because **ColorSliderPanel** is not an application. No entries are listed for **ColorEvent** and **ColorListener**, because they are only supporting classes.

Install **ColorSliderPanel** into the **Component Palette** and drop instances of **LogoAnimator2** and **ColorSliderPanel** into a **JFrame**. Switch to **Connection Mode** and click **ColorSliderPanel** then **LogoAnimator2**. The **Connection Wizard** opens with a list of events from which to choose. Select **colorChanged** from the menu and click the **Next** button (Fig. 6.52). In Step 2, click the **Method** radio button and select method **setBackground** (Fig. 6.53). This method of **LogoAnimator2** will be called with the **ColorEvent**'s **Color** property as the argument. In Step 3, click the **User Code:** radio button and type **evt.getColor()** into the text area then click **Finish** (Fig. 6.54). This line calls **ColorEvent**'s **getColor** method, which returns a **Color** object. **LogoAnimator2** now listens for **ColorEvent**s generated by **Color-SliderPanel**.

Execute the **JFrame** to see **LogoAnimator2** and **ColorSliderPanel**. Try adjusting the three different sliders. Each slider changes one of the elements of the **Color** object of the **background** of **LogoAnimator2**. Try moving the sliders to change the **background** color and try entering a new value as text. Figure 6.55 shows several of the possible colors.

```
1
2    Name: com/deitel/advjhtp1/beans/ColorSliderPanel.class
3    Java-Bean: True
```

Fig. 6.51   Manifest file for the **ColorSliderPanel** JavaBean.

Fig. 6.52   Selecting **colorChanged** method in **Connection Wizard**.

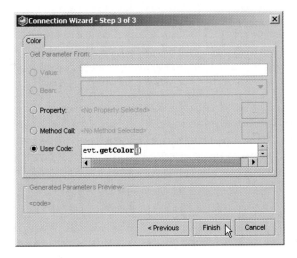

Fig. 6.53 Selecting **setBackground** method for target **LogoAnimator2**.

Fig. 6.54 Entering user code in **Connection Wizard**.

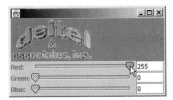 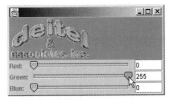

Fig. 6.55 Using the **ColorSliderPanel** to change the **background** color of **LogoAnimator2**.

6.8 Customizing JavaBeans for Builder Tools

As mentioned previously, builder tools use Java's introspection mechanism to expose a
JavaBean's properties, methods and events if the programmer follows the proper JavaBean
design patterns (such as the special naming conventions discussed for *set/get* method pairs
that define bean properties). Builder tools use the classes and interfaces of package
java.lang.reflect to perform introspection. For JavaBeans that do not follow the
JavaBean design patterns, or for JavaBeans in which the programmer wants to customize
the exposed set of properties, methods and events, the programmer can supply a class that
implements interface **BeanInfo** (package **java.beans**). The **BeanInfo** class describes to the builder tool how to present the features of the bean to the programmer.

Software Engineering Observation 6.13

*A JavaBean's properties, methods and events can be exposed by a builder tool if the pro-
grammer follows the proper JavaBean design patterns.*

Software Engineering Observation 6.14

*Every **BeanInfo** class must implement interface **BeanInfo**. This interface describes the
methods used by a builder tool to determine the features of a bean.*

Class **SliderFieldPanel** (Fig. 6.41) exposes many properties and events when
it is selected in the **Component Inspector** or connected with the **Connection Wizard**.
For this bean, we want the programmer to see only properties **fieldWidth**, **current-
Value**, **minimumValue** and **maximumValue** (the other properties were inherited from
class **JPanel** and are not truly relevant to our bean). Also, the only event we want the programmer to use for our component is the bound-property event.

Software Engineering Observation 6.15

*By convention, the **BeanInfo** class has the same name as the bean and ends with **Bean-
Info** and is placed in the same **package** as the bean it describes or else it will not be found
automatically.*

Software Engineering Observation 6.16

*By convention, the **BeanInfo** class is included in the same JAR as the **SliderField-
Panel** JavaBean. When the bean is loaded, the builder tool determines whether the JAR file
contains a **BeanInfo** class for a bean. If a **BeanInfo** class is found, it is used to determine
the exposed features of the bean. Otherwise, standard introspection is used to determine the
exposed features of the bean.*

Figure 6.56 presents class **SliderFieldPanelBeanInfo** to customize the properties and events exposed in builder tools for our **SliderFieldPanel** bean. The screen
captures in Fig. 6.57 show the exposed features of the **SliderFieldPanel** JavaBean.

```
1   // Fig. 6.56 SliderFieldPanelBeanInfo.java
2   // SliderFieldPanelBeanInfo is the BeanInfo class for
3   // SliderFieldPanel
4   package com.deitel.advjhtp1.beans;
```

Fig. 6.56   **SliderFieldPanelBeanInfo** exposes properties and events for
SliderFieldPanel (part 1 of 5).

```
5
6    // Java core packages
7    import java.beans.*;
8    import java.awt.Image;
9
10   // Java extension packages
11   import javax.swing.*;
12
13   public class SliderFieldPanelBeanInfo extends SimpleBeanInfo {
14
15      public static final Class beanClass =
16         SliderFieldPanel.class;
17
18      // return general description of bean
19      public BeanDescriptor getBeanDescriptor()
20      {
21         BeanDescriptor descriptor = new BeanDescriptor(
22            beanClass, SliderFieldPanelCustomizer.class );
23         descriptor.setDisplayName( "Slider Field" );
24         descriptor.setShortDescription(
25            "A slider bar to change a numerical property." );
26
27         return descriptor;
28      }
29
30      // return bean icon
31      public Image getIcon( int iconKind )
32      {
33         Image image = null;
34
35         switch( iconKind ) {
36
37            case ICON_COLOR_16x16:
38               image = loadImage( "icon1.gif" );
39               break;
40
41            case ICON_COLOR_32x32:
42               image = loadImage( "icon2.gif" );
43               break;
44
45            case ICON_MONO_16x16:
46               image = loadImage( "icon3.gif" );
47               break;
48
49            case ICON_MONO_32x32:
50               image = loadImage( "icon4.gif" );
51               break;
52
53            default:
54               break;
55         }
```

Fig. 6.56 SliderFieldPanelBeanInfo exposes properties and events for SliderFieldPanel (part 2 of 5).

```
56
57          return image;
58      }
59
60      // return array of MethodDescriptors for public get methods
61      // of class SliderFieldPanel
62      public MethodDescriptor[] getMethodDescriptors()
63      {
64         // create array of MethodDescriptors
65         try {
66            MethodDescriptor getMinimumValue = new
67               MethodDescriptor( beanClass.getMethod(
68                  "getMinimumValue", null ) );
69
70            MethodDescriptor getMaximumValue = new
71               MethodDescriptor( beanClass.getMethod(
72                  "getMaximumValue", null ) );
73
74            MethodDescriptor getCurrentValue = new
75               MethodDescriptor( beanClass.getMethod(
76                  "getCurrentValue", null ) );
77
78            MethodDescriptor getFieldWidth = new
79               MethodDescriptor( beanClass.getMethod(
80                  "getFieldWidth", null ) );
81            MethodDescriptor[] descriptors = { getMinimumValue,
82               getMaximumValue, getCurrentValue, getFieldWidth };
83
84            return descriptors;
85         }
86
87         // printStackTrace if NoSuchMethodException thrown
88         catch ( NoSuchMethodException methodException ) {
89            methodException.printStackTrace();
90         }
91
92         // printStackTrace if SecurityException thrown
93         catch ( SecurityException securityException ) {
94            securityException.printStackTrace();
95         }
96
97         return null;
98      }
99
100     // return PropertyDescriptor array
101     public PropertyDescriptor[] getPropertyDescriptors()
102        throws RuntimeException
103     {
104        // create array of PropertyDescriptors
105        try {
106
```

Fig. 6.56   `SliderFieldPanelBeanInfo` exposes properties and events for
`SliderFieldPanel` (part 3 of 5).

```
107          // fieldWidth property
108          PropertyDescriptor fieldWidth = new
109             PropertyDescriptor( "fieldWidth", beanClass );
110          fieldWidth.setShortDescription(
111             "Width of the text field." );
112
113          // currentValue property
114          PropertyDescriptor currentValue = new
115             PropertyDescriptor( "currentValue", beanClass );
116          currentValue.setShortDescription(
117             "Current value of slider." );
118
119          // maximumValue property
120          PropertyDescriptor maximumValue = new
121             PropertyDescriptor( "maximumValue", beanClass );
122          maximumValue.setPropertyEditorClass(
123             MaximumValueEditor.class );
124          maximumValue.setShortDescription(
125             "Maximum value of slider." );
126
127          // minimumValue property
128          PropertyDescriptor minimumValue = new
129             PropertyDescriptor( "minimumValue", beanClass );
130          minimumValue.setShortDescription(
131             "Minimum value of slider." );
132          minimumValue.setPropertyEditorClass(
133             MinimumValueEditor.class );
134
135          // ensure PropertyChangeEvent occurs for this property
136          currentValue.setBound( true );
137
138          PropertyDescriptor descriptors[] = { fieldWidth,
139             currentValue, maximumValue, minimumValue };
140
141          return descriptors;
142       }
143
144       // throw RuntimeException if IntrospectionException
145       // thrown
146       catch ( IntrospectionException exception ) {
147          throw new RuntimeException( exception.getMessage() );
148       }
149    }
150
151    // get currentValue property index
152    public int getDefaultPropertyIndex()
153    {
154       return 1;
155    }
156
```

Fig. 6.56 `SliderFieldPanelBeanInfo` exposes properties and events for `SliderFieldPanel` (part 4 of 5).

```
157    // return EventSetDescriptors array
158    public EventSetDescriptor[] getEventSetDescriptors()
159       throws RuntimeException
160    {
161       // create array of EventSetDescriptors
162       try {
163          EventSetDescriptor changed = new
164             EventSetDescriptor( beanClass, "propertyChange",
165                java.beans.PropertyChangeListener.class,
166                "propertyChange" );
167
168          // set event description and name
169          changed.setShortDescription(
170             "Property change event for currentValue." );
171          changed.setDisplayName(
172             "SliderFieldPanel value changed" );
173
174          EventSetDescriptor[] descriptors = { changed };
175
176          return descriptors;
177       }
178
179       // throw RuntimeException if IntrospectionException
180       // thrown
181       catch ( IntrospectionException exception ) {
182          throw new RuntimeException( exception.getMessage() );
183       }
184    }
185
186    // get PropertyChange event index
187    public int getDefaultEventIndex()
188    {
189       return 0;
190    }
191
192 }   // end class SliderFieldPanelBeanInfo
```

Fig. 6.56 `SliderFieldPanelBeanInfo` exposes properties and events for `SliderFieldPanel` (part 5 of 5).

Fig. 6.57 Properties and events exposed by `SliderFieldPanelBeanInfo`.

Every **BeanInfo** class must implement interface **BeanInfo**. This interface describes the methods used by builder tools to determine the exposed features of the bean described by its corresponding **BeanInfo** class. As a convenience, the **java.beans** package includes class *SimpleBeanInfo*, which provides a default implementation of every method in interface **BeanInfo**. The programmer can extend this class and selectively override its methods to implement a proper **BeanInfo** class. Class **Slider-FieldPanelBeanInfo** extends class **SimpleBeanInfo** (line 13). In Fig. 6.56, we override **BeanInfo** methods *getBeanDescriptor*, *getIcon*, *getMethodDescriptors*, *getPropertyDescriptors*, *getDefaultPropertyIndex*, *getEventSetDescriptors* and *getDefaultEventIndex*.

Software Engineering Observation 6.17

*Class **SimpleBeanInfo** provides a default implementation of every method in interface **BeanInfo**. The programmer can selectively override methods of this class to implement a proper **BeanInfo** class.*

Lines 19–28 override method **getBeanDescriptor**, to return a **BeanDescriptor** object. The constructor for **BeanDescriptor** takes as arguments the JavaBean customizer **Class** object. A customizer provides a specialized user interface for customizing a bean. We discuss customizers and specifically the **SliderFieldPanelCustomizer** in Section 6.8.2. Methods **setDisplayName** (line 23) and **setShortDescription** (line 24) set the JavaBean's name and a short description, respectively. The builder tool extracts this information and displays it when selecting the bean.

Lines 31–58 override method **getIcon**. Interface **BeanInfo** defines the constants used by the **switch** statement. The **switch** (lines 35–55) loads the appropriate **Image**. The builder tool uses this **Image** as an icon in the **Component Palette**.

Software Engineering Observation 6.18

*Method **getIcon** allows a programmer to customize the look of a JavaBean within a builder tool. Common icons are company logos and descriptive graphics.*

Lines 62–98 override method **getMethodDescriptors** to return an array of **MethodDescriptor** objects for the **SliderFieldPanel** bean. Each **MethodDescriptor** represents a specific method exposed to the builder tool. Method **getMethodDescriptors** describes the *get* methods for properties **maximumValue**, **minimumValue**, **currentValue** and **fieldWidth**. The method calls in lines 66–80 may throw **NoSuchMethodException** and **SecurityException** exceptions.

Lines 101–149 override method **getPropertyDescriptors**, to return an array of *PropertyDescriptor* objects for **SliderFieldPanel** properties. Each **PropertyDescriptor** indicates a specific property that should be exposed by a builder tool. There are several ways to construct a **PropertyDescriptor**. In this example, each **PropertyDescriptor** constructor call has the form

```
new PropertyDescriptor( "propertyName", beanClass );
```

where *propertyName* is a **String** that specifies the name of a property defined by the pair of methods **set***PropertyName* and **get***PropertyName*. Note that the *propertyName* begins with a lowercase letter and the *get/set* property methods begin the property name with an uppercase letter. We defined **PropertyDescriptor**s for **fieldWidth**, **currentValue**, **minimumValue** and **maximumValue** in class **SliderFieldPanel**.

Method **setShortDescription** sets a short text description of the property. For the **maximumValue** and **minimumValue** properties, we also specify **PropertyEditor**s with method **setPropertyEditorClass**. A **PropertyEditor** defines a custom user interface for editing a bean property. We discuss **PropertyEditor**s—and specifically **MinimumValueEditor** and **MaximumValueEditor**—in Section 6.8.1. Line 136 specifies that property **currentValue** is a bound property. Some builder tools visually treat bound-property events separately from other events.

Software Engineering Observation 6.19

If the set/get *methods for a property do not use the JavaBean's naming convention for properties, there are two other* **PropertyDescriptor** *constructors in which the actual method names are passed. This allows the builder tools to use nonstandard property methods to expose a property for manipulation by the programmer at design time. This is particularly useful in retrofitting a class as a JavaBean when that class was not originally designed and implemented using JavaBeans design patterns.*

Lines 138–139 create the **PropertyDescriptor** array that method **getPropertyDescriptors** returns (line 141). Note the exception handler for **IntrospectionException**s. If a **PropertyDescriptor** constructor is unable to confirm the property in the corresponding **Class** object that represents the class definition, the constructor throws an **IntrospectionException**. Because the **BeanInfo** class and its methods are actually used by the builder tool at design time (i.e., during the development of the program in the IDE), the **RuntimeException** thrown in the **catch** handler would normally be caught by the builder tool.

Lines 152–155 define method **getDefaultPropertyIndex** to return the value **1**, indicating that the property at position 1 in the **PropertyDescriptor** array returned from **getPropertyDescriptors** is the *default property* for developers to customize in a builder tool. Typically, the default property is selected when you click a bean. In this example, property **currentValue** is the default property.

Lines 158–184 override method **getEventSetDescriptors** to return an array of **EventSetDescriptor** objects that describes to a builder tool the events supported by this bean. Lines 163–166 define an **EventSetDescriptor** object for the **PropertyChangeEvent** associated with the bound property **currentValue**. The four arguments to the constructor describe the event that should be exposed by the builder tool. The first argument is the **Class** object (**beanClass**) representing the *event source* (i.e., the bean that generates the event). The second argument is a **String** representing the *event set* name (e.g., the **mouse** event set includes **mousePressed**, **mouseClicked**, **mouseReleased**, **mouseEntered** and **mouseExited**). In this example, the event set name is *propertyChange*. The third argument is the **Class** object representing the event listener interface implemented by listeners for this event. Finally, the last argument is a **String** representing the name of the listener method to call (**propertyChange**) when this event occurs.

When using the standard JavaBeans design patterns, the event set name is part of all the data type names and method names used to process the event. For example, the types and methods for the **propertyChange** event set are: **PropertyChangeListener** (the interface an object must implement to be notified of an event in this event set), **PropertyChangeEvent** (the type passed to a listener method for an event in this event set), **addPropertyChangeListener** (the method called to add a listener for an event in this event set), **removePropertyChangeListener** (the method called to remove a listener for an event in this event set) and **firePropertyChange** (the method called to notify listeners when an event in this event set occurs—this method is named as such by convention).

Software Engineering Observation 6.20

EventSetDescriptors can be constructed with other arguments to expose events that do not follow the standard JavaBeans design patterns.

A benefit of an **EventSetDescriptor** is customizing the name for the event set for display in the builder tool. Lines 171–172 call method *setDisplayName* on the **EventSetDescriptor** to indicate that its display name should be "**SliderField-Panel value changed**."

Good Programming Practice 6.1

Customizing the event set name displayed by a builder tool can make the purpose of that event set more understandable to the component assembler using the bean.

Lines 174–176 create the **EventSetDescriptor** array and return it. Note the exception handler for **IntrospectionException**s at line 182. If an **EventSetDescriptor** constructor is unable to confirm the event in the corresponding **Class** object that represents the class definition, the constructor **throws** an **IntrospectionException**.

Lines 187–190 define method *getDefaultEventIndex* to return the value 0, indicating that the property at position 0 in the **EventSetDescriptor** array returned from **getEventSetDescriptors** is the *default event* for developers to customize in a builder tool. Typically, the default event is automatically selected when you click a bean. In this example, event **propertyChange** is the default event.

6.8.1 PropertyEditors

JavaBeans can be customized further by implementing other support classes in addition to **BeanInfo**. A **PropertyEditor** determines how a particular property is edited inside a builder tool. The **PropertyEditor** constrains the property to a particular range of values determined by the programmer. This prevents illegal values that would cause undesired operation in the JavaBean. A **PropertyEditor** appears often in the property sheet as a pull-down menu with a list of values. A class implementing interface **PropertyEditor** is written for every property of a JavaBean that will have a **PropertyEditor**.

Software Engineering Observation 6.21

By convention, a PropertyEditor class has the same name as the property or type and ends with Editor.

The **PropertyEditors MaximumValueEditor** (Fig. 6.58) and **Minimum-ValueEditor** (Fig. 6.59) edit the **maximumValue** and **minimumValue** properties of class **SliderFieldPanel**. Both **PropertyEditors** extend class **PropertyEditorSupport**. **PropertyEditorSupport** is a simple implementation of interface **PropertyEditor**. The **PropertyEditors** each use a combo box with values from 50 through 500, in increments of 50. These values provide a wide range of animation speeds and prevent an illegal value from being entered for the properties.

```
1   // Fig. 6.58 MaximumValueEditor.java
2   // MaximumValueEditor is the PropertyEditor for the
3   // maximumValue property of the SliderFieldPanel bean.
4   package com.deitel.advjhtp1.beans;
5
6   // Java core packages
7   import java.beans.*;
8
9   public class MaximumValueEditor extends PropertyEditorSupport {
10
11     private Integer maximumValue;
12
13     // set maximumValue property
14     public void setValue( Object value )
15     {
16        maximumValue = ( Integer ) value;
17        firePropertyChange();
18     }
19
20     // get maximumValue property
21     public Object getValue()
22     {
23        return maximumValue;
24     }
25
26     // set maximumValue property from text string
27     public void setAsText( String string )
28     {
29        // decode may throw NumberFormatException
30        try {
31           maximumValue = Integer.decode( string );
32           firePropertyChange();
33        }
34
35        // throw IllegalArgumentException if decode throws
36        // NumberFormatException
37        catch ( NumberFormatException numberFormatException ) {
38           throw new IllegalArgumentException();
39        }
40
41     } // end method setAsText
42
43     // get String array for pull-down menu
44     public String[] getTags()
45     {
46        return new String[] { "50", "100", "150", "200", "250",
47           "300", "350", "400", "450", "500" };
48     }
49
50     // get maximumValue property as string
51     public String getAsText()
52     {
```

Fig. 6.58   **MaximumValueEditor** is a **PropertyEditor** for
   SliderFieldPanel's **maximumValue** property (part 1 of 2).

```
53            return getValue().toString();
54        }
55
56        // get initialization string for Java code
57        public String getJavaInitializationString()
58        {
59            return getValue().toString();
60        }
61
62    }  // end class MaximumValueEditor
```

Fig. 6.58   **MaximumValueEditor** is a **PropertyEditor** for
SliderFieldPanel's **maximumValue** property (part 2 of 2).

Integer maximumValue (line 11) stores the value selected in the combo box.
Method **setValue** (lines 14–18) takes an **Object value** as a parameter, sets **maximumValue** to **value** and calls method **firePropertyChange**. Method **getValue**
(lines 21–24) returns **maximumValue**. Method **setAsText** (lines 27–41) takes a
parameter **string** and decodes **string** into a new **Integer** value for **maximumValue**. Method **getTags** (lines 44–48) returns a **String** array of all of the tags that
appear in the combo box. Method **getAsText** (lines 51–54) returns **maximumValue** as
a **String**. Method **getJavaInitializationString** (lines 57–60) returns **maximumValue** as a **String** for use as a method parameter in generated source code.

   MinimumValueEditor's source code (Fig. 6.59) follows the exact same structure as **MaximumValueEditor**, but edits the **minimumValue** property of bean
SliderFieldPanel.

```
1    // Fig. 6.59 MinimumValueEditor.java
2    // MinimumValueEditor is the PropertyEditor for the
3    // minimumValue property of the SliderFieldPanel bean.
4    package com.deitel.advjhtp1.beans;
5
6    // Java core packages
7    import java.beans.*;
8
9    public class MinimumValueEditor extends PropertyEditorSupport {
10
11       protected Integer minimumValue;
12
13       // set minimumValue property
14       public void setValue( Object value )
15       {
16           minimumValue = ( Integer ) value;
17           firePropertyChange();
18       }
19
20       // get value of property minimum
21       public Object getValue()
22       {
```

Fig. 6.59   **MinimumValueEditor** is a **PropertyEditor** for
SliderFieldPanel's **minimumValue** property (part 1 of 2).

```
23            return minimumValue;
24        }
25
26        // set maximumValue property from text string
27        public void setAsText( String string )
28        {
29            // decode may throw NumberFormatException
30            try {
31               minimumValue = Integer.decode( string );
32               firePropertyChange();
33            }
34
35            // throw IllegalArgumentException if decode throws
36            // NumberFormatException
37            catch ( NumberFormatException numberFormatException ) {
38               throw new IllegalArgumentException();
39            }
40        }
41
42        // string array for pull-down menu
43        public String[] getTags()
44        {
45            return new String[] { "50", "100", "150", "200", "250",
46               "300", "350", "400", "450", "500" };
47        }
48
49        // get minimumValue property as string
50        public String getAsText()
51        {
52            return getValue().toString();
53        }
54
55        // get initialization string for Java code
56        public String getJavaInitializationString()
57        {
58            return getValue().toString();
59        }
60
61    }  // end class MinimumValueEditor
```

Fig. 6.59 **MinimumValueEditor** is a **PropertyEditor** for
     SliderFieldPanel's minimumValue property (part 2 of 2).

MaximumValueEditor and MinimumValueEditor must be compiled and
packaged in the same JAR file as SliderFieldPanel and SliderFieldPanel-
BeanInfo. When SliderFieldPanel is installed, the builder tool instantiates the
PropertyEditors. MaximumValueEditor and MinimumValueEditor are presented as pull-down menus with values from 50–500 (Fig. 6.60). Try changing the values
of maximumValue and minimumValue with the pull-down menus. When the
SliderFieldPanel is linked to LogoAnimator2 and executed, the selected values
of minimumValue and maximumValue constrain the animation speed within the range
50–500 (Fig. 6.61).

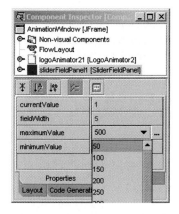 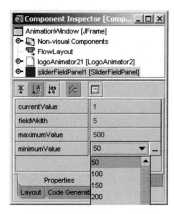

Fig. 6.60 **MaximumValueEditor** and **MinimumValueEditor** pull-down menus in Forte.

Fig. 6.61 **SliderFieldPanel** values constrained by **PropertyEditor**s.

6.8.2 Customizers[1]

The final option for customizing a JavaBean is a **Customizer** class. A class that implements interface **Customizer** creates a customized interface for setting the properties of a JavaBean. This interface is separate from the builder-tool style sheet. A **Customizer** is useful for manipulating JavaBean properties that cannot be edited in the standard property sheet, such as instance fields in objects that are themselves properties.

　　SliderFieldPanelCustomizer (Fig. 6.62) implements the **Customizer** interface. A **Customizer** must extend a **Component** and provide a no-argument constructor so the builder tool can instantiate it. The constructor (lines 26–75) initializes the components of the customizer. Object **changeSupport** (line 29) registers **Property-ChangeListener**s with class **PropertyChangeSupport**. **SliderFieldPanelCustomizer** consists of two **JLabel**s and two **JComboBox**es. The **JLabel**s label

---

1. Due to a problem in Forte that prevents bean **Customizer**s from working properly, we use Net-Beans 3.2 to demonstrate the example in this section. NetBeans is the open-source development environment project on which Forte is based. NetBeans can be downloaded free of charge from **www.netbeans.org**.

the **JComboBox**es for the **minimumValue** and **maximumValue** properties (lines 32–33). Properties **minimumValue** and **maximumValue** can be set from 50 through 500, in increments of 50 (lines 36–39). Lines 42–69 add **ActionListeners** to the **JCombo-Boxes**. Selecting a value causes the **actionPerformed** method of the listener to call the right method to change either **maximumValue** or **minimumValue**.

```
1   // Fig. 6.62 SliderFieldPanelCustomizer.java
2   // SliderFieldPanelCustomizer is the Customizer class for
3   // SliderFieldPanel.
4   package com.deitel.advjhtp1.beans;
5
6   // Java core packages
7   import java.awt.*;
8   import java.awt.event.*;
9   import java.beans.*;
10  import java.util.*;
11
12  // Java extension packages
13  import javax.swing.*;
14
15  public class SliderFieldPanelCustomizer extends JPanel
16     implements Customizer {
17
18     private JComboBox maximumCombo, minimumCombo;
19     private JLabel minimumLabel, maximumLabel;
20     protected SliderFieldPanel slider;
21     private PropertyChangeSupport changeSupport;
22     private static final String[] VALUES = { "50", "100",
23        "150", "200", "250", "300", "350", "400", "450", "500" };
24
25     // initialize GUI components
26     public SliderFieldPanelCustomizer()
27     {
28        // create PropertyChangeSupport to handle PropertyChange
29        changeSupport = new PropertyChangeSupport( this );
30
31        // labels for maximum and minimum properties
32        minimumLabel = new JLabel( "Minimum Slider Value:" );
33        maximumLabel = new JLabel( "Maximum Slider Value:" );
34
35        // combo boxes adjust maximum and minimum properties
36        minimumCombo = new JComboBox( VALUES );
37        minimumCombo.setSelectedIndex( 0 );
38        maximumCombo = new JComboBox( VALUES );
39        maximumCombo.setSelectedIndex( 9 );
40
41        // add ActionListener to minimumValue combo box
42        minimumCombo.addActionListener(
43
```

Fig. 6.62 **SliderFieldPanelCustomizer** custom GUI for modifying **SliderFieldPanel** beans (part 1 of 3).

```
44              new ActionListener() {
45
46                  // handle action of minimum combo box
47                  public void actionPerformed( ActionEvent event )
48                  {
49                      setMinimum( minimumCombo.getSelectedIndex() );
50                  }
51
52              } // end anonymous inner class
53
54          ); // end addActionListener
55
56          // add ActionListener to maximumValue combo box
57          maximumCombo.addActionListener(
58
59              new ActionListener() {
60
61                  // handle action of maximum combo box
62                  public void actionPerformed( ActionEvent event )
63                  {
64                      setMaximum( maximumCombo.getSelectedIndex() );
65                  }
66
67              } // end anonymous inner class
68
69          ); // end addActionListener
70
71          add( minimumLabel );
72          add( minimumCombo );
73          add( maximumLabel );
74          add( maximumCombo );
75      }
76
77      // set the customized object
78      public void setObject( Object bean )
79      {
80          slider = ( SliderFieldPanel ) bean;
81      }
82
83      // add PropertyChangeListener with PropertyChangeSupport
84      public void addPropertyChangeListener(
85          PropertyChangeListener listener )
86      {
87          changeSupport.addPropertyChangeListener( listener );
88      }
89
90      // remove PropertyChangeListener with PropertyChangeSupport
91      public void removePropertyChangeListener(
92          PropertyChangeListener listener )
93      {
94          changeSupport.removePropertyChangeListener( listener );
95      }
```

Fig. 6.62 SliderFieldPanelCustomizer custom GUI for modifying
SliderFieldPanel beans (part 2 of 3).

```
96
97      // set minimumValue property
98      public void setMinimum( int index )
99      {
100        int oldValue = slider.getMinimumValue();
101        int newValue = Integer.parseInt( VALUES[ index ] );
102
103        slider.setMinimumValue( newValue );
104        changeSupport.firePropertyChange( "minimumValue",
105           new Integer( oldValue ), new Integer( newValue ) );
106     }
107
108     // set maximumValue property
109     public void setMaximum( int index )
110     {
111        int oldValue = slider.getMaximumValue();
112        int newValue = Integer.parseInt( VALUES[ index ] );
113
114        slider.setMaximumValue( newValue );
115        changeSupport.firePropertyChange( "maximumValue",
116           new Integer( oldValue ), new Integer( newValue ) );
117     }
118
119 }   // end class SliderFieldPanelCustomizer
```

Fig. 6.62 **SliderFieldPanelCustomizer** custom GUI for modifying **SliderFieldPanel** beans (part 3 of 3).

Method **setObject** (lines 78–81) takes as an object argument an instance of the JavaBean being customized. Line 80 casts the object reference to **SliderField-Panel** and assigns it to instance variable **slider**.

Class **SliderFieldPanelCustomizer** provides methods for adding (lines 84–88) and removing (lines 91–95) **PropertyChangeListener**s. The builder tool registers with **SliderFieldPanelCustomizer** when the customizer is instantiated. A **PropertyChangeSupport** object (line 21) maintains the list of active listeners. Methods **setMinimum** (lines 98–106) and **setMaximum** (lines 109–117) call **firePropertyChangeEvent** to change the **minimumValue** and **maximumValue** properties of the JavaBean. Method **firePropertyChangeEvent** creates a new **PropertyChangeEvent** object with the new and old values of the changing property and sends the event to all registered listeners through **changeSupport**.

SliderFieldPanelCustomizer must be packaged in the same JAR file as **SliderFieldPanel** and **SliderFieldPanelBeanInfo**. Once it is installed, right click an instance of **SliderFieldPanel** and select **Customize** (Fig. 6.63). The **Customizer Dialog** opens and contains the **SliderFieldPanelCustomizer** (Fig. 6.64). Select the desired values for **minimumValue** and **maximumValue** and click the **Close** button. The new values take effect when you execute the application.

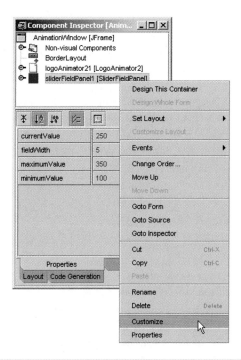

Fig. 6.63   Select **Customize** from **Component Inspector** menu.

Fig. 6.64   `SliderFieldPanel`'s Customizer Dialog.

6.9 Internet and World Wide Web Resources

java.sun.com/beans

The JavaBeans Home Page at the Sun Microsystems, Inc., Web site. Here, you can download *the Beans Development Kit (BDK)* and other bean-related software. Other features of the site include JavaBeans documentation and specifications, a frequently asked questions list, an overview of integrated development environments that support JavaBeans development, training and support, upcoming JavaBeans events, a searchable directory of JavaBeans components, a support area for marketing your JavaBeans and a variety of on-line resources for communicating with other programmers regarding JavaBeans.

java.sun.com/beans/spec.html

Visit this site to download the JavaBeans specification.

java.sun.com/beans/tools.html

Visit this site for information about JavaBeans-enabled development tools.

java.sun.com/beans/directory

Visit this site for a searchable directory of available beans.

SUMMARY

- A JavaBean is a reusable software component that can be manipulated visually in a builder tool.

- JavaBeans (often called beans) allow developers to reap the benefits of rapid application development in Java by assembling predefined software components to create powerful applications and applets.

- Graphical programming and design environments (often called builder tools) that support beans provide programmers with tremendous flexibility by allowing programmers to reuse and integrate existing disparate components that in many cases, were never intended to be used together.

- The component assembler uses well-defined components to create more robust functionality.

- Sun Microsystem's Forte for Java Community Edition is an integrated development environment that provides a builder tool for assembling JavaBeans.

- A bean must be installed before it can be manipulated in Forte.

- GUI JavaBeans must be added to a Java **Container**.

- The property sheet in a builder tool displays a component's properties and allows them to be edited.

- JavaBeans can be connected with events.

- JavaBeans can be saved to disk as serialized objects or as Java Archive files (JAR). Saving a JavaBean in either of these methods allows other builder tools and code to use the JavaBean.

- Most JavaBeans are GUI components intended to be visually manipulated within a builder tool, such as Forte.

- Most Java **Swing** components, such as **JButton**s, are JavaBeans.

- By implementing **Serializable**, a customized JavaBean can be saved and reloaded in a builder tool or a Java application.

- To use a class as a JavaBean, one must first place it in a Java Archive file (JAR file). A JAR file for a JavaBean must contain a manifest file, which describes the JAR file contents. Manifest files contain attributes (called headers) that describe the individual contents of the JAR.

- When a JAR file containing a JavaBean (or a set of JavaBeans) is loaded into an IDE, the IDE looks at the manifest file to determine which of the classes in the JAR represent JavaBeans. These classes are made available to the programmer in a visual manner

- All JavaBean-aware development environments know to look for the **MANIFEST.MF** file in the **META-INF** directory of the JAR file.

- The Java interpreter can execute an application directly from a JAR file if the manifest file specifies which class in the JAR contains method **main**.

- To execute a JavaBean from its JAR file, launch the Java interpreter with the **-jar** command-line option as follows:

  java -jar *JARFileName*.**jar**

- The command

  jar cfm *JARFileName*.**jar manifest.tmp** *files*

  creates a JAR file.

- A read/write property of a bean is defined as a *set/get* method pair of the form

  public void set*PropertyName***(** *DataType* **value)**
  public *DataType* **get***PropertyName***()**

  where *PropertyName* is replaced in each case by the actual property name. These methods are often referred to as a "property *set* method" and "property *get* method," respectively.

- If the property is a **boolean** data type, the *set/get* method pair is normally defined as

      public void set*PropertyName*(boolean value)
      public boolean is*PropertyName*()

  where the *get* method name begins with the word **is** rather than **get**.

- When a builder tool examines a bean, it inspects the bean methods for pairs of *set/get* methods that represent properties (some builder tools also expose read-only and write-only properties). This is a process known as introspection. If an appropriate *set/get* method pair is found during the introspection process, the builder tool exposes that pair of methods as a property in the builder tool's user interface.

- A bound property causes the JavaBean that owns the property to notify other objects when there is a change in the bound property's value. This is accomplished using standard Java event-handling features—registered **PropertyChangeListener**s are notified when the property's value changes. To support this feature, the **java.beans** package provides interface **PropertyChangeListener** so listeners can be configured to receive property-change notifications, class **PropertyChangeEvent** to provide information to a **PropertyChangeListener** about the change in a property's value and class **PropertyChangeSupport** to provide the listener registration and notification services (i.e., to maintain the list of listeners and notify them when an event occurs).

- To support registration of listeners for changes to a bound property, a bean defines methods **addPropertyChangeListener** and **removePropertyChangeListener**. Each of these methods calls the corresponding method in the **PropertyChangeSupport** object **changeSupport**. This object provides the event notification services when the property value changes.

- When the bound property changes, the registered **PropertyChangeListener**s must be notified of the change. Each bound-property listener is presented with the old and new property values when notified of the change (the values can be **null** if they are not needed). The **PropertyChangeSupport** object's **firePropertyChange** method notifies each registered **PropertyChangeListener**.

- An indexed property is like a standard property except that the indexed property is an array of primitives or objects. Two *get* and two *set* methods define an indexed property. The *get* methods are of the form

      public *Datatype*[] get*PropertyName*()
      public *Datatype* get*PropertyName*(int index)

  The first *get* method returns the entire array of an indexed property. The second *get* method returns the item at the array index indicated by the *get* method's parameter.

- The *set* methods are of the form

      public void set*PropertyName*(*Datatype*[] data)
      public void set*PropertyName*(int index, *Datatype* data)

  The first *set* method sets the indexed property to the value of the argument. The second *set* method sets the item at the indicated array index to the value of the second parameter.

- A JavaBean can generate programmer-defined events. A programmer-defined event, or custom event, provides functionality that standard Java events do not provide. An event class extends **java.util.EventObject** and the listener class extends **java.util.EventListener**.

- Builder tools use Java's introspection mechanism to expose a JavaBean's properties, methods and events if the programmer follows the proper JavaBean design patterns (such as the special naming conventions discussed for *set/get* method pairs that define bean properties). Builder tools use the classes and interfaces of package **java.lang.reflect** to perform introspection. For Java-

Beans that do not follow the JavaBean design patterns or for JavaBeans in which the programmer wants to customize the exposed set of properties, methods and events, the programmer can supply a class that implements interface **BeanInfo** (package **java.beans**). The **BeanInfo** class describes to the builder tool how to present the features of the bean to the programmer.

- Every **BeanInfo** class must implement interface **BeanInfo**. This interface describes the methods used by builder tools to determine the exposed features of the bean described by its corresponding **BeanInfo** class. As a convenience, the **java.beans** package includes class **SimpleBeanInfo**, which provides a default implementation of every method in interface **BeanInfo**. The programmer can extend this class and selectively override its methods to implement a proper **BeanInfo** class.

- Override method **getBeanDescriptor** to return a **BeanDescriptor** object. A **BeanDescriptor** specifies a **Customizer** class and information about the JavaBean.

- Override method **getIcon** to specify an icon to represent the bean in a builder tool.

- Override method **getMethodDescriptors** to return an array of **MethodDescriptor** objects. Each **MethodDescriptor** represents a specific method exposed to the builder tool.

- Override method **getPropertyDescriptors** to return an array of **PropertyDescriptor** objects. Each **PropertyDescriptor** indicates a specific property that should be exposed by a builder tool.

- Override method **getEventSetDescriptors** to return an array of **EventSetDescriptor** objects that describes to a builder tool the events supported by a bean.

- A **PropertyEditor** determines how a particular property is edited inside a builder tool. The **PropertyEditor** constrains the property to a particular range of values determined by the programmer. This prevents illegal values that would cause undesired operation in the JavaBean. A **PropertyEditor** may appear in the property sheet as a pull-down menu with a list of values. A class implementing interface **PropertyEditor** is written for every property of a JavaBean that will have a special **PropertyEditor**.

- A class that implements interface **Customizer** creates a customized interface for setting the properties of a JavaBean. This interface is separate from the builder-tool style sheet. A **Customizer** is useful for manipulating JavaBean properties that cannot be edited in the standard property sheet, such as instance fields in objects that are themselves properties.

TERMINOLOGY

actionPerformed method of interface
    ActionListener
adapter class
Add to Jar menu item of **Tools** menu
addPropertyChangeListener method of
    class **PropertyChangeSupport**
bean
BeanDescriptor class
BeanInfo interface
Beans tab of the **Component Palette** toolbar
bound property of a bean
builder tool
Compile menu item
component assembler
Component Inspector window
Component Palette toolbar

connecting beans
Connection mode button
Connection Wizard dialog
"connect-the-dots" programming
creating a JAR file
custom event
customize a JavaBean
Customize menu item
Customizer interface
default property
deserialize an object
design pattern
event
event adapter class
event hookup
event listener

Swing Forms option of **Template Chooser** dialog
Swing tab of the **Component Palette** toolbar
target of an event

Template Chooser dialog
Timer class
Tools menu

SELF-REVIEW EXERCISES

6.1 State whether each of the following is *true* or *false*. If *false*, explain why.
   a) A JavaBean is a reusable software component.
   b) Forte for Java is a builder tool.
   c) JavaBeans cannot generate events.
   d) A **Customizer** modifies an individual property of a JavaBean.
   e) An indexed property represents an array variable.

6.2   Fill in the blanks in each of the following statements:
   a) The four windows of the Forte **GUI Editing** tab are _____, _____, _____ and _____.
   b) A _____ allows the programmer to customize a property's value.
   c) In Forte, the _____ provides access to the events supported by a bean that is an event source.
   d) JavaBeans should all implement the _____ interface so they can be saved from a builder tool after being customized by the programmer.
   e) All registered _____ are notified when a bound property's value changes.
   f) A builder tool uses _____ to expose a JavaBean's properties, methods and events.
   g) An _____ consists of an event class and a listener class.
   h) For JavaBeans that do not follow the JavaBean design pattern, or for JavaBeans in which the programmer wants to customize the exposed set of properties, methods and events, the programmer can supply a _____ class that describes to the builder tool how to present the features of the bean.
   i) A _____ object describes a property that a builder tool should expose.
   j) A _____ object describes an event set that a builder tool should expose.
   k) A _____ is a custom editor for a bean property that appears in a property sheet.

ANSWERS TO SELF-REVIEW EXERCISES

6.1 a) True. b) True. c) False. A JavaBean can generate Java events. d) False. A **Customizer** can modify any number of JavaBean properties. e) True.

6.2   a) **Explorer**, **Component Inspector**, **Form**, **Source Editor**.   b) property sheet.
c) **Component Inspector**. d) **Serializable**. e) **PropertyChangeListener**s. f) introspection. g) event set. h) **BeanInfo**. i) **PropertyDescriptor**. j) **EventSetDescriptor**.
k) **PropertyEditor**.

EXERCISES

6.3   Try some of the **Swing** components provided with Forte. Every **Swing** component is a JavaBean. While using each bean, try the following:
   a) Inspect the properties of each bean and try modifying them.
   b) Inspect the events supported by each bean and try using those events to hook various beans together.

6.4   Modify **ColorSliderPanel** to provide a mechanism for viewing the selected color. For this purpose, add a **JPanel** object to the bean. Test your bean in Forte by changing the background color of a **JFrame** or other **Swing** component.

6.5   Create a **BeanInfo** class for the **LogoAnimator2** bean that exposes only the **background** and **animationDelay** properties. Test your bean in Forte.

6.6   Modify **ColorSliderPanel** to use a bound property **color** instead of indexed property **redGreenBlue** and custom event **ColorEvent**. Bound property **color** is an instance of class **Color**. Test the bean in Forte by changing the **background** color of **LogoAnimator2**.

6.7   Create a **Customizer** class for **ColorSliderPanel** that can set a narrower range of values than 0–255 for the red, green and blue sliders. A **BeanInfo** class must also be created to use this **Customizer**.

6.8   Modify **MaximumValueEditor** and **MinimumValueEditor** to accept the values 1–1000 as a **String** instead of using a pull-down menu.

7

Security

Objectives

- To understand the basic concepts of security.
- To understand public-key/private-key cryptography.
- To learn about popular security protocols, such as SSL.
- To understand digital signatures, digital certificates and certification authorities.
- To learn how Java provides solutions to security problems.
- To learn how to produce secure code with Java technology.

Three may keep a secret, if two of them are dead.
Benjamin Franklin

Attack—Repeat—Attack.
William Frederick Halsey, Jr.

Private information is practically the source of every large modern fortune.
Oscar Wilde

There must be security for all—or not one is safe.
The Day the Earth Stood Still, screenplay by Edmund H. North

No government can be long secure without formidable opposition.
Benjamin Disraeli

Outline

7.1 Introduction

The explosion of e-business and e-commerce is forcing businesses and consumers to focus on Internet and network security. Consumers are buying products, trading stocks and banking online. They are submitting their credit-card numbers, social-security numbers and other highly confidential information to vendors through Web sites. Businesses are sending confidential information to clients and vendors over the Internet. At the same time, e-businesses are experiencing an increasing number of security attacks. Individuals and organizations are vulnerable to data theft and hacker attacks that can corrupt files and shut down systems, effectively halting business. Hence, security is fundamental.

Modern computer security addresses the various problems and concerns of protecting electronic communications and maintaining network security. There are five fundamental requirements of a successful, secure transaction: *privacy, integrity, authentication, authorization* and *nonrepudiation. The privacy issue is*: How do you ensure that the information you transmit over the Internet has not been captured or passed on to a third party without your knowledge? *The integrity issue is*: How do you ensure that the information you send or receive has not been compromised or altered? *The authentication issue is*: How do the sender and receiver of a message prove their identities to each other? *The authorization issue is*: How do we ensure that users can access certain necessary resources, while valuable information is protected? *The nonrepudiation issue is*: How do you legally prove that a message was sent or received?

In this chapter, we will explore computer and Java security, from secure electronic transactions to secure coding. The Java programming language provides prevention of and solutions for many of today's security problems. The *Java Sandbox architecture* and *policy files* protect users and systems from malicious programs that would otherwise crash computers or steal valuable information. Several APIs, such as the *Java Cryptography Extension (JCE), Java Secure Sockets Extension (JSSE)* and the *Java Authentication and Authorization Service (JAAS)*, provide additional security to Java applications.

We encourage you to visit the Web resources provided in Section 7.16 to learn more about the latest developments in e-commerce and Java security. These resources include many informative and entertaining demonstrations.

7.2 Ancient Ciphers to Modern Cryptosystems

The channels through which data pass are inherently unsecure; therefore, any private information passed through these channels must somehow be protected. To secure information, data can be encrypted. *Cryptography* transforms data by using a *cipher*, or *cryptosystem*—a mathematical algorithm for encrypting messages. A *key*—a string of alpha-numeric characters that acts as a password—is input to the cipher. The cipher uses the key to make data incomprehensible to all but the sender and intended receivers. Unencrypted data is called *plaintext*; encrypted data is called *ciphertext*. The algorithm is responsible for encrypting data, while the key acts as a variable—using different keys results in different ciphertext. Only the intended receivers should have the corresponding key to decrypt the ciphertext into plaintext.

Cryptographic ciphers have been used throughout history, first recorded by the ancient Egyptians, to conceal and protect valuable information. In ancient cryptography, messages were encrypted by hand, usually with a method based on the alphabetic characters of the message. The two main types of ciphers were *substitution ciphers* and *transposition ciphers*. In a substitution cipher, every occurrence of a given letter is replaced by a different letter; for example, if every "a" is replaced by "b," every "b" by "c," etc., the word "security" would encrypt to "tfdvsjuz." The first prominent substitution cipher was credited to Julius Caesar and is referred to today as the *Caesar Cipher*. Using the Caesar Cipher, we replace every instance of a letter with the alphabetical letter three positions to the right. For example, according to the Caesar Cipher, the word "security" would encrypt to "vhfxulwb." In a transposition cipher, the ordering of the letters is shifted; for example, if every other letter, starting with "s," in the word "security" creates the first word in the ciphertext and the remaining letters create the second word in the ciphertext, the word "security" would encrypt to "scrt euiy." Complicated ciphers are created by combining substitution and transposition ciphers. For example, with the substitution cipher first, then the transposition cipher, the word "security" would encrypt to "tdsu fvjz." The problem with many historical ciphers is that their security relied on the sender and receiver to remember the encryption algorithm and keep it secret. Such algorithms are called *restricted algorithms*. Restricted algorithms are not feasible to implement among a large group of people. Imagine if the security of U.S. government communications relied on every U.S. government employee to keep a secret; the encryption algorithm could be compromised easily.

Modern cryptosystems are digital. Their algorithms are based on the individual *bits* or *blocks* (a group of bits) of a message, rather than letters of the alphabet. Encryption and decryption keys are binary strings with a given *key length*. For example, 128-bit encryption systems have a key length of 128 bits. Longer keys have stronger encryption; it takes more time and computing power to crack messages encrypted with longer keys.

Until January 2000, the U.S. government placed restrictions on the strength of cryptosystems that could be exported from the United States. Federal regulations limited the key length of encryption algorithms. Today, the regulations on exporting products that employ cryptography are less stringent. Any cryptography product may be exported, as long as the end user is not a foreign government or from a country with embargo restrictions on it.[1]

7.3 Secret-key Cryptography

In the past, organizations wishing to maintain a secure computing environment used *symmetric cryptography*, also known as *secret-key cryptography*. Secret-key cryptography utilizes the same secret key to encrypt and decrypt messages (Fig. 7.1). The sender encrypts a message using the secret key, then sends the encrypted message to the intended recipient. A fundamental problem with secret-key cryptography is that before two people can communicate securely, they must find a secure way to exchange the secret key. One approach is to have the key delivered by a courier, such as a mail service or FedEx. While this approach may be feasible when two individuals communicate, it is not efficient for securing communication in a large network, nor can it be considered completely secure. The privacy and the integrity of the message could be compromised if the key is intercepted as it is passed between the sender and the receiver over unsecure channels. Also, since both parties in the transaction use the same key to encipher and decipher a message, one cannot authenticate which party created the message. Finally, to keep communications with each receiver private, a sender needs a different secret key for each receiver. As a result, organizations may have huge numbers of secret keys to maintain.

An alternative approach to the key-exchange problem is to have a central authority, called a *key distribution center* (*KDC*). The key distribution center shares a (different) secret key with every user in the network. In this system, the key distribution center generates a *session key* to be used for a transaction (Fig. 7.2). Next, the key distribution center distributes the session key to the sender and receiver, encrypting the session key itself with the secret key they each share with the key distribution center. For example, suppose a merchant and a customer want to conduct a secure transaction. The merchant and the customer each have unique secret keys they share with the key distribution center. The key distribution center generates a session key for the merchant and customer to use in the transaction. The key distribution center then sends the session key for the transaction to the merchant, encrypted using the secret key the merchant already shares with the center. The key distribution center sends the same session key for the transaction to the customer, encrypted using the secret key the customer already shares with the key distribution center. Once the merchant and the customer have the session key for the transaction, they can communicate with each other, encrypting their messages using the shared session key.

Using a key distribution center reduces the number of courier deliveries (again, by means such as mail) of secret keys to each user in the network. In addition, users can have a new secret key for each communication with other users in the network, which greatly increases the overall security of the network. However, if the security of the key distribution center is compromised, then so is the security of the entire network.

One of the most commonly used symmetric encryption algorithms is the *Data Encryption Standard (DES)*. Horst Feistel of IBM created the *Lucifer* algorithm, which the United States government and the National Security Agency (NSA) chose as the DES in the 1970s.[2] DES has a key length of 56 bits and encrypts data in 64-bit blocks, a type of encryption known as a *block cipher*. A block cipher is an encryption method that creates groups of bits from an original message, then applies an encryption algorithm to the block as a whole, rather than as individual bits. This method reduces the amount of computer processing power and time required, while maintaining a fair level of security. For many years, DES was the encryption standard set by the U.S. government and the *American National Standards Institute (ANSI)*. However, due to advances in technology and computing speed, DES is no longer considered secure. In the late 1990s, specialized *DES cracker machines* were built that recovered DES keys after just several hours.[3] As a result, the old standard of symmetric encryption has been replaced by *Triple DES*, or *3DES*, a variant of DES that is essentially three DES systems in series, each having its own secret key. 3DES is more secure, however the three passes through the DES algorithm result in slower performance. The United States government recently selected a new, more secure standard for symmetric encryption to replace DES. The new standard is called the *Advanced Encryption Standard (AES)*. The *National Institute of Standards and Technology (NIST)*, which sets the cryptographic standards for the U.S. government, is evaluating *Rijndael* as the encryption method for AES. Rijndael is a block cipher developed by Dr. Joan Daemen and Dr. Vincent Rijmen of Belgium.[4] Rijndael can be used with key sizes and block sizes of 128, 192 or 256 bits. Rijndael was chosen over four other finalists as the AES candidate because of its high security, performance, efficiency, flexibility and low-memory requirement for computing systems. For more information about AES, visit `csrc.nist.gov/encryption/aes`.

7.4 Public-key Cryptography

In 1976, Whitfield Diffie and Martin Hellman, researchers at Stanford University, developed *public-key cryptography* to solve the problem of exchanging keys securely. Public-key cryptography is asymmetric. It uses two inversely related keys: A *public key* and a *private key*. The private key is kept secret by its owner, while the public key is freely distributed. If the public key is used to encrypt a message, only the corresponding private key can decrypt it, and vice versa (Fig. 7.3). Each party in a transaction has both a public key and a private key. To transmit a message securely, the sender uses the receiver's public key to encrypt the message. The receiver then decrypts the message using his or her unique private key. Assuming that the private key has been kept secret, the message cannot be read by anyone other than the intended receiver; the system ensures the privacy of the message. The defining property of a secure public-key algorithm is that it is computationally infeasible to deduce the private key from the public key. Although the two keys are mathematically related, deriving one from the other would take enormous amounts of computing power and time, enough to discourage attempts to deduce the private key. An outside party cannot participate in communication without the correct keys. The security of the entire process is based on the secrecy of the private keys. Therefore, if a third party does obtain the decryption key, the security of the whole system is compromised. If a system's integrity is compromised, the user can simply change the key, instead of changing the entire encryption or decryption algorithm.

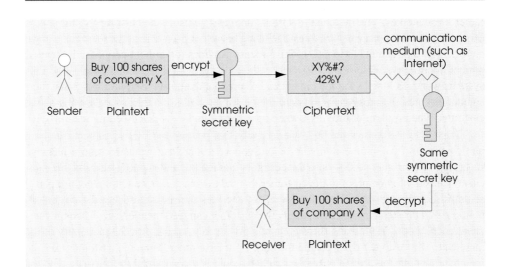

Fig. 7.1   Encrypting and decrypting a message using a symmetric secret key.

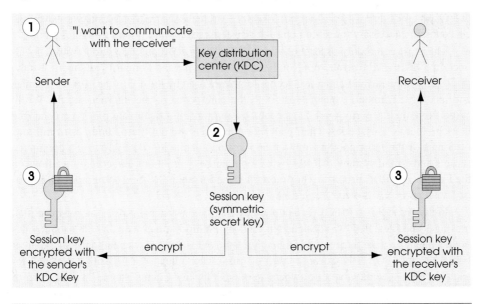

Fig. 7.2   Distributing a session key with a key distribution center.

Either the public key or the private key can be used to encrypt or decrypt messages. For example, if a customer uses a merchant's public key to encrypt a message, only the merchant can decrypt the message, using the merchant's private key. Thus, the merchant's identity can be authenticated, since only the merchant knows the private key. However, the merchant has no way of validating the customer's identity, since the encryption key the customer used is publicly available. If the encryption key is the sender's private key and the decryption key is the sender's public key, the sender of the message can be authenticated. For example, suppose a customer sends a merchant a message encrypted using the customer's private key. The merchant decrypts the message using the customer's public key. Since the customer encrypted the message using his or her private key, the merchant can be confident of the customer's identity. This process provides for authentication of the sender, not confidentiality, as anyone could decrypt the message with the sender's public key. This systems works as long as the merchant can be sure that the public key with which the merchant decrypted the message belongs to the customer, and not a third party posing as the customer. The problem of proving ownership of a public key is discussed in Section 7.10.

These two methods of public-key encryption can be used together to authenticate both participants in a communication (Fig. 7.4). Suppose a merchant wants to send a message securely to a customer so that only the customer can read it, and suppose also that the merchant wants to provide proof to the customer that the merchant (not an unknown third party) actually sent the message. First, the merchant encrypts the message using the customer's public key. This step guarantees that only the customer can read the message. Then the merchant encrypts the result using the merchant's private key, which proves the identity of the merchant. The customer decrypts the message in reverse order. First, the customer uses the merchant's public key. Since only the merchant could have encrypted the message with the inversely related private key, this step authenticates the merchant. Then the customer uses the customer's private key to decrypt the next level of encryption. This step ensures that the message content was kept private in the transmission, since only the customer has the key to decrypt the message. This system provides for extremely secure transactions; however, the cost and time necessary for setting up such a system prevent this system from present use.

The most commonly used public-key algorithm is *RSA*, an encryption system developed in 1977 by MIT professors Ron Rivest, Adi Shamir and Leonard Adleman.[5] Today, their encryption and authentication technologies are used by most Fortune 1000 companies and leading e-commerce businesses. With the emergence of the Internet and the World Wide Web, their security work has become even more significant and plays a crucial role in e-commerce transactions. Their encryption products are built into hundreds of millions of copies of the most popular Internet applications, including Web browsers, commerce servers and e-mail systems. Most secure e-commerce transactions and communications on the Internet use RSA products. (For more information about RSA, cryptography and security, visit **www.rsasecurity.com**).

Pretty Good Privacy (PGP) is a public-key encryption system used for encrypting e-mail messages and files. PGP was designed in 1991 by Phillip Zimmermann.[6] PGP also provides digital signatures (see Section 7.9, Digital Signatures) that confirm the author of an e-mail or public posting. PGP is based on a "web of trust"; each client in a network can vouch for another client's identity to prove ownership of a public key. Clients use the "web of trust" to authenticate one another. To learn more about PGP and to download a free copy of the software, go to the MIT distribution center for PGP at **web.mit.edu/network/pgp.html**.

7.5 Cryptanalysis

Even if keys are kept secret, it may be possible to compromise the security of a system. Trying to decrypt ciphertext without knowledge of the decryption key is known as *cryptanalysis*. Commercial encryption systems are constantly being researched by cryptologists to ensure that the systems are not vulnerable to a *cryptanalytic attack*. The most common form of cryptanalytic attacks are those in which the encryption algorithm is analyzed to find relations between bits of the encryption key and bits of the ciphertext. Often, these relations are only statistical in nature and incorporate an analyzer's outside knowledge about the plaintext. The goal of such an attack is to determine the key from the ciphertext.

Weak statistical trends between ciphertext and keys can be exploited to gain knowledge about the key if enough ciphertext is known. Proper key management and expiration dates on keys help prevent cryptanalytic attacks. When a key is used for long periods of time, more ciphertext is generated that can be beneficial to an attacker trying to derive a key. If a key is unknowingly recovered by an attacker, it can be used to decrypt every message for the life of that key. Using public-key cryptography to exchange secret keys securely allows a new secret key to encrypt every message.

7.6 Key Agreement Protocols

A drawback of public-key algorithms is that they are not efficient for sending large amounts of data. They require significant computer power, which slows down communication. Public-key algorithms should not be thought of as a replacement for secret-key algorithms. Instead, public-key algorithms can be used to allow two parties to agree upon a key to be used for secret-key encryption over an unsecure medium. The process by which two parties can exchange keys over an unsecure medium is called a *key agreement protocol*. A *protocol* sets the rules for communication: Exactly what encryption algorithm(s) is (are) going to be used?

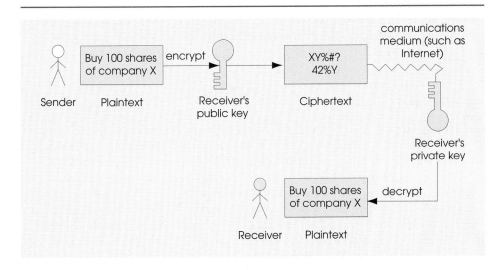

Fig. 7.3   Encrypting and decrypting a message using public-key cryptography.

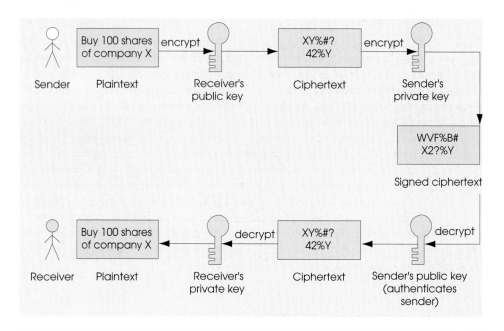

Fig. 7.4   Authentication with a public-key algorithm

The most common key agreement protocol is a *digital envelope* (Fig. 7.5). With a digital envelope, the message is encrypted using a secret key (Step 1), and the secret key is encrypted using public-key encryption (Step 2). The sender attaches the encrypted secret key to the encrypted message and sends the receiver the entire package. The sender could also digitally sign the package before sending it to prove the sender's identity to the receiver (Section 7.9). To decrypt the package, the receiver first decrypts the secret key, using the receiver's private key. Then the receiver uses the secret key to decrypt the actual message. Since only the receiver can decrypt the encrypted secret key, the sender can be sure that only the intended receiver is reading the message.

7.7 Key Management

Maintaining the secrecy of private keys is crucial to keeping cryptographic systems secure. Most compromises in security result from poor *key management* (e.g., the mishandling of private keys, resulting in key theft) rather than attacks that attempt to guess the keys.[7]

A main component of key management is *key generation*—the process by which keys are created. A malicious third party could try to decrypt a message by using every possible decryption key, a process known as *brute-force cracking*. Key-generation algorithms are sometimes unintentionally constructed to choose from only a small subset of possible keys. If the subset is too small, then the encrypted data is more susceptible to brute-force attacks. Therefore, it is important to have a key-generation program that can generate a large number of keys as randomly as possible. Keys are made more secure by choosing a key length so large that it is computationally infeasible to try all combinations.

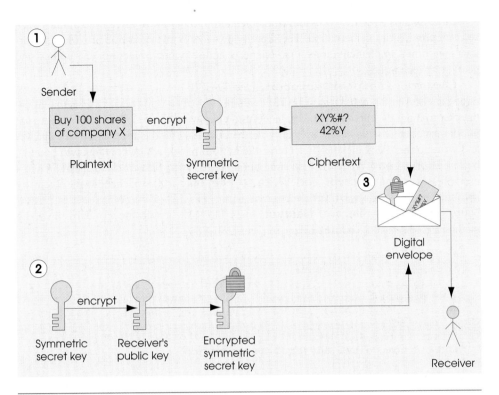

Fig. 7.5   Creating a digital envelope.

7.8 Java Cryptography Extension (JCE)

The *Java Cryptography Extension* (*JCE*) provides Java applications with several security facilities. JCE supports secret-key encryption, such as 3DES, and public-key algorithms, such as Diffie-Hellman and RSA. Customizable levels of security are available through multiple encryption algorithms and various key sizes. The JCE architecture is *provider-based*—developers can add new algorithms to their programs by adding new algorithm providers. Each provider may support many different algorithms. This feature allows developers to use their own algorithms from trusted sources with the JCE API (the API is located at **<java.sun.com/products/jce/doc/guide/API_users_guide.html>**).

7.8.1 Password-Based Encoding with JCE

Class **EncipherDecipher** (Fig. 7.6) uses JCE to demonstrate Password-Based Encryption (PBE). Class **EncipherDecipher** provides users with a graphical user interface that allows them to specify the file name of a file that the application will use to write to and read from, the contents of the file to encrypt/decrypt, and the password used to encrypt/decrypt the file. The password-based encryption algorithm implementation uses an array of bytes (lines 28–31)—called a *salt*— and an integer (line 34) to randomize the sets of generated keys.

Line 45 adds a security provider implementation to the JVM. Each system must set a security provider implementation. The security provider implementation provides the various algorithm implementations that clients can use when selecting encrypting and decrypting techniques.

Constructor **EncipherDecipher** (lines 42–130) creates a **JFrame** that contains three panels. The top panel (lines 52–73) contains two labels and two textfields that allow the user to input the file name and the encryption password to use. Lines 76–88 create the middle panel which allows the user to write the contents that the application will encrypt and write to the file. Lines 91–121 create the bottom panel, which contains two buttons, button **Encrypt and Write to File** and button **Read from File and Decrypt**. When a user presses button **Encrypt and Write to File**, lines 100–103 handle the event by invoking method **encryptAndWriteToFile** (lines 131–277). When a user presses button **Read from File and Decrypt**, lines 115–118 handle the event by invoking method **readFromFileAndDecrypt** (lines 280–384).

```
1   // EncipherDecipher.java
2   // Displays a frame that allows users to specify
3   // a password and a file name. Contents written
4   // to an Editor Pane can be encrypted and written
5   // to a file, or encrypted contents can be read from
6   // a file and decrypted
7   package com.deitel.advjhtp1.security.jce;
8
9   // Java core package
10  import java.awt.*;
11  import java.awt.event.*;
12  import java.io.*;
13  import java.util.*;
14  import java.security.*;
15  import java.security.spec.*;
16
17  // third-party packages
18  import com.sun.crypto.provider.SunJCE;
19
20  // Java extension package
21  import javax.swing.*;
22  import javax.crypto.*;
23  import javax.crypto.spec.*;
24
25  public class EncipherDecipher extends JFrame {
26
27     // salt for password-based encryption-decryption algorithm
28     private static final byte[] salt = {
29        ( byte )0xf5, ( byte )0x33, ( byte )0x01, ( byte )0x2a,
30        ( byte )0xb2, ( byte )0xcc, ( byte )0xe4, ( byte )0x7f
31     };
32
33     // iteration count
34     private int iterationCount = 100;
```

Fig. 7.6   **EncipherDecipher** application for demonstrating Password-Based Encryption (part 1 of 8).

```
35
36        // user input components.
37        private JTextField passwordTextField;
38        private JTextField fileNameTextField;
39        private JEditorPane fileContentsEditorPane;
40
41        // frame constructor
42        public EncipherDecipher() {
43
44            // set security provider
45            Security.addProvider( new SunJCE() );
46
47            // initialize main frame
48            setSize( new Dimension( 400, 400 ) );
49            setTitle( "Encryption and Decryption Example" );
50
51            // construct top panel
52            JPanel topPanel = new JPanel();
53            topPanel.setBorder( BorderFactory.createLineBorder(
54                Color.black ) );
55            topPanel.setLayout( new BorderLayout() );
56
57            // panel where password and file name labels will be placed
58            JPanel labelsPanel = new JPanel();
59            labelsPanel.setLayout( new GridLayout( 2, 1 ) );
60            JLabel passwordLabel = new JLabel( " Password: " );
61            JLabel fileNameLabel = new JLabel( " File Name: " );
62            labelsPanel.add( fileNameLabel );
63            labelsPanel.add( passwordLabel );
64            topPanel.add( labelsPanel, BorderLayout.WEST );
65
66            // panel where password and file name textfields will be placed
67            JPanel textFieldsPanel = new JPanel();
68            textFieldsPanel.setLayout( new GridLayout( 2, 1 ) );
69            passwordTextField = new JPasswordField();
70            fileNameTextField = new JTextField();
71            textFieldsPanel.add( fileNameTextField );
72            textFieldsPanel.add( passwordTextField );
73            topPanel.add( textFieldsPanel, BorderLayout.CENTER );
74
75            // construct middle panel
76            JPanel middlePanel = new JPanel();
77            middlePanel.setLayout( new BorderLayout() );
78
79            // construct and place title label for contents pane
80            JLabel fileContentsLabel = new JLabel();
81            fileContentsLabel.setText( " File Contents" );
82            middlePanel.add( fileContentsLabel, BorderLayout.NORTH );
83
84            // initialize and place editor pane within scroll panel
85            fileContentsEditorPane = new JEditorPane();
```

Fig. 7.6   **EncipherDecipher** application for demonstrating Password-Based Encryption (part 2 of 8).

```
86          middlePanel.add(
87             new JScrollPane( fileContentsEditorPane ),
88                BorderLayout.CENTER );
89
90          // construct bottom panel
91          JPanel bottomPanel = new JPanel();
92
93          // create encrypt button
94          JButton encryptButton =
95             new JButton( "Encrypt and Write to File" );
96          encryptButton.addActionListener(
97
98             new ActionListener() {
99
100               public void actionPerformed( ActionEvent event )
101               {
102                  encryptAndWriteToFile();
103               }
104            }
105         );
106         bottomPanel.add( encryptButton );
107
108         // create decrypt button
109         JButton decryptButton =
110            new JButton( "Read from File and Decrypt" );
111         decryptButton.addActionListener(
112
113            new ActionListener() {
114
115               public void actionPerformed( ActionEvent event )
116               {
117                  readFromFileAndDecrypt();
118               }
119            }
120         );
121         bottomPanel.add( decryptButton );
122
123         // initialize main frame window
124         JPanel contentPane = ( JPanel ) this.getContentPane();
125         contentPane.setLayout( new BorderLayout() );
126         contentPane.add( topPanel, BorderLayout.NORTH );
127         contentPane.add( middlePanel, BorderLayout.CENTER );
128         contentPane.add( bottomPanel, BorderLayout.SOUTH );
129
130      } // end constructor
131
132      // obtain contents from editor pane and encrypt
133      private void encryptAndWriteToFile()
134      {
135
136         // obtain user input
137         String originalText = fileContentsEditorPane.getText();
```

Fig. 7.6   **EncipherDecipher** application for demonstrating Password-Based Encryption (part 3 of 8).

```
138        String password = passwordTextField.getText();
139        String fileName = fileNameTextField.getText();
140
141        // create secret key and get cipher instance
142        Cipher cipher = null;
143
144        try {
145
146           // create password based encryption key object
147           PBEKeySpec keySpec =
148              new PBEKeySpec( password.toCharArray() );
149
150           // obtain instance for secret key factory
151           SecretKeyFactory keyFactory =
152              SecretKeyFactory.getInstance( "PBEWithMD5AndDES" );
153
154           // generate secret key for encryption
155           SecretKey secretKey = keyFactory.generateSecret( keySpec );
156
157           // specifies parameters used with password based encryption
158           PBEParameterSpec parameterSpec =
159              new PBEParameterSpec( salt, iterationCount );
160
161           // obtain cipher instance reference
162           cipher = Cipher.getInstance( "PBEWithMD5AndDES" );
163
164           // initialize cipher in encrypt mode
165           cipher.init( Cipher.ENCRYPT_MODE, secretKey,
166              parameterSpec );
167        }
168
169        // handle NoSuchAlgorithmException
170        catch ( NoSuchAlgorithmException exception ) {
171           exception.printStackTrace();
172           System.exit( 1 );
173        }
174
175        // handle InvalidKeySpecException
176        catch ( InvalidKeySpecException exception ) {
177           exception.printStackTrace();
178           System.exit( 1 );
179        }
180
181        // handle InvalidKeyException
182        catch ( InvalidKeyException exception ) {
183           exception.printStackTrace();
184           System.exit( 1 );
185        }
186
187        // handle NoSuchPaddingException
188        catch ( NoSuchPaddingException exception ) {
189           exception.printStackTrace();
```

Fig. 7.6   **EncipherDecipher** application for demonstrating Password-Based Encryption (part 4 of 8).

```
190                 System.exit( 1 );
191             }
192
193             // handle InvalidAlgorithmParameterException
194             catch ( InvalidAlgorithmParameterException exception ) {
195                 exception.printStackTrace();
196                 System.exit( 1 );
197             }
198
199             // create array of bytes
200             byte[] outputArray = null;
201
202             try {
203                 outputArray = originalText.getBytes( "ISO-8859-1" );
204             }
205
206             // handle UnsupportedEncodingException
207             catch ( UnsupportedEncodingException exception ) {
208                 exception.printStackTrace();
209                 System.exit( 1 );
210             }
211
212             // create FileOutputStream
213             File file = new File( fileName );
214             FileOutputStream fileOutputStream = null;
215
216             try {
217                 fileOutputStream = new FileOutputStream( file );
218             }
219
220             // handle IOException
221             catch ( IOException exception ) {
222                 exception.printStackTrace();
223                 System.exit( 1 );
224             }
225
226             // create CipherOutputStream
227             CipherOutputStream out =
228                 new CipherOutputStream( fileOutputStream, cipher );
229
230             // write contents to file and close
231             try {
232                 out.write( outputArray );
233                 out.flush();
234                 out.close();
235             }
236
237             // handle IOException
238             catch ( IOException exception ) {
239                 exception.printStackTrace();
240                 System.exit( 1 );
241             }
```

Fig. 7.6   **EncipherDecipher** application for demonstrating Password-Based Encryption (part 5 of 8).

```
242
243        // contain bytes read from file
244        Vector fileBytes = new Vector();
245
246        // read contents from file to show user encrypted text
247        try {
248           FileInputStream in = new FileInputStream( file );
249
250           // read bytes from stream.
251           byte contents;
252
253           while ( in.available() > 0 ) {
254              contents = ( byte )in.read();
255              fileBytes.add( new Byte( contents ) );
256           }
257
258           in.close();
259        }
260
261        // handle IOException
262        catch ( IOException exception ) {
263           exception.printStackTrace();
264           System.exit( 1 );
265        }
266
267        // create byte array from contents in Vector fileBytes
268        byte[] encryptedText = new byte[ fileBytes.size() ];
269
270        for ( int i = 0; i < fileBytes.size(); i++ ) {
271           encryptedText[ i ] =
272              ( ( Byte ) fileBytes.elementAt( i ) ).byteValue();
273        }
274
275        // update Editor Pane contents
276     fileContentsEditorPane.setText( new String( encryptedText ) );
277     }
278
279  // obtain contents from file and decrypt
280  private void readFromFileAndDecrypt()
281  {
282
283        // used to rebuild byte list
284        Vector fileBytes = new Vector();
285
286        // obtain user input
287        String password = passwordTextField.getText();
288        String fileName = fileNameTextField.getText();
289
290        // create secret key
291        Cipher cipher = null;
292
```

Fig. 7.6 **EncipherDecipher** application for demonstrating Password-Based Encryption (part 6 of 8).

```
293        try {
294           // create password based encryption key object
295           PBEKeySpec keySpec =
296              new PBEKeySpec( password.toCharArray() );
297
298           // obtain instance for secret key factory
299           SecretKeyFactory keyFactory =
300              SecretKeyFactory.getInstance( "PBEWithMD5AndDES" );
301
302           // generate secret key for encryption
303         SecretKey secretKey = keyFactory.generateSecret( keySpec );
304
305         // specifies parameters used with password based encryption
306           PBEParameterSpec parameterSpec =
307              new PBEParameterSpec( salt, iterationCount );
308
309         // obtain cipher instance reference.
310           cipher = Cipher.getInstance( "PBEWithMD5AndDES" );
311
312         // initialize cipher in decrypt mode
313           cipher.init( Cipher.DECRYPT_MODE, secretKey,
314              parameterSpec );
315        }
316
317        // handle NoSuchAlgorithmException
318        catch ( NoSuchAlgorithmException exception ) {
319           exception.printStackTrace();
320           System.exit( 1 );
321        }
322
323        // handle InvalidKeySpecException
324        catch ( InvalidKeySpecException exception ) {
325           exception.printStackTrace();
326           System.exit( 1 );
327        }
328
329        // handle InvalidKeyException
330        catch ( InvalidKeyException exception ) {
331           exception.printStackTrace();
332           System.exit( 1 );
333        }
334
335        // handle NoSuchPaddingException
336        catch ( NoSuchPaddingException exception ) {
337           exception.printStackTrace();
338           System.exit( 1 );
339        }
340
341        // handle InvalidAlgorithmParameterException
342        catch ( InvalidAlgorithmParameterException exception ) {
343           exception.printStackTrace();
```

Fig. 7.6   **EncipherDecipher** application for demonstrating Password-Based Encryption (part 7 of 8).

```
344              System.exit( 1 );
345        }
346
347
348        // read and decrypt contents from file
349        try {
350           File file = new File( fileName );
351           FileInputStream fileInputStream =
352              new FileInputStream( file );
353
354           CipherInputStream in =
355              new CipherInputStream( fileInputStream, cipher );
356
357           // read bytes from stream.
358           byte contents = ( byte ) in.read();
359
360           while ( contents != -1 ) {
361              fileBytes.add( new Byte( contents ) );
362              contents = ( byte ) in.read();
363           }
364           in.close();
365
366        }
367
368        // handle IOException
369        catch ( IOException exception ) {
370           exception.printStackTrace();
371           System.exit( 1 );
372        }
373
374        // create byte array from contents in Vector fileBytes
375        byte[] decryptedText = new byte[ fileBytes.size() ];
376
377        for ( int i = 0; i < fileBytes.size(); i++ ) {
378           decryptedText[ i ] =
379              ( ( Byte )fileBytes.elementAt( i ) ).byteValue();
380        }
381
382        // update Editor Pane contents.
383        fileContentsEditorPane.setText( new String( decryptedText ) );
384     }
385
386     // create frame and display
387     public static void main( String[] args )
388     {
389        EncipherDecipher crypto =
390           new EncipherDecipher();
391        crypto.validate();
392        crypto.setVisible( true );
393     }
394  }
```

Fig. 7.6   **EncipherDecipher** application for demonstrating Password-Based Encryption (part 8 of 8).

Method **encryptAndWriteToFile** (lines 131–277) obtains the user's input from the both **JTextField**s and the **JEditorPane**. Lines 147–148 create a **PBEKeySpec** instance. The **PBEKeySpec** instance acts as a wrapper for the array of characters that represents the password for encrypting and decrypting an array of bytes. Class *Cipher* is the fundamental building block for applications that use JCE. A **Cipher** performs encryption and decryption using a specified algorithm (e.g., DES, 3DES, Blowfish, etc.). Lines 151–152 obtain a reference to a **SecretKeyFactory**, which generates secret keys. Line 155 generates a **SecretKey** using the **PBEKeySpec** instance from lines 147–148. Lines 158–159 create a **PBEParameterSpec** instance, which contains randomization information such as the **salt** and the **iterationCount**. Line 162 obtains an instance of a **PBEWithMD5AndDES** algorithm **Cipher**. Line 165–166 initializes **Cipher** to encryption mode using the **SecretKey** and the **PBEParameterSpec** instances.

Lines 170–173 handle **NoSuchAlgorithmException**s, which occur when the program specifies a non-existent algorithm. Lines 176–179 handle **InvalidKeySpecException**s, which occur when an invalid key specification is handed to method **generateSecret** from **SecretKeyFactory**. Lines 182–185 handle all **InvalidKeyException**s which occur when an invalid key is handed to method **init** from **Cipher**. Lines 188–191 handle **NoSuchPaddingException**s, which occur when an application specifies an invalid padding scheme. Lines 194–197 handle **InvalidAlgorithmParameterException**s, which method **init** of class **Cipher** throws if an application specifies invalid algorithm parameters.

Line 203 converts the **String** obtained from **JEditorPanel** into an array of bytes. Method **getBytes** ensures that the conversion of a **String** to an array of bytes conforms to the ISO-8859-1 standard. Lines 207–210 catch an **UnsupportedEncodingException** if the application specifies an invalid character encoding standard.

Lines 213–218 instantiate a **FileOutputStream**. **CipherOutputStream** (lines 227–228) acts as the *decorator* in the *Decorator design pattern* (Section 7.8.2) to add encryption capability to the **FileOutputStream** instance. The **CipherOutputStream** encodes bytes using the specified **Cipher** object before writing those bytes to the **FileOutputStream**. Lines 232–234 write the contents to the file, and finalize the operation by closing the file. Lines 244–276 read the newly encoded file contents and display them in the **JEditorPane** so the user can see the encrypted text.

Method **readFromFileAndDecrypt** decrypts the message from the file using the specified password. Lines 291–314 create an instance of class **Cipher** and initialize the **Cipher** to decrypt data (lines 313–314). Lines 350–352 create a **FileInputStream** for the encrypted file. Lines 354–355 create a **CipherInputStream** to decrypt data from the **FileInputStream**. Lines 358–364 read the file contents from the **CipherInputStream**. Lines 375–383 create an array of bytes that contains the decrypted text and display the text in the **JEditorPane**.

Figure 7.7 displays the contents that application **EncipherDecipher** will encrypt and write to file **TestFile.txt** using password "I am a BIG secret!". The image on the right displays the contents of the file after pressing button **Encrypt and Write to File**.

For more information on JCE, please visit the JCE Web site at **java.sun.com/jce**. Refer to the included documentation for download and installation instructions.

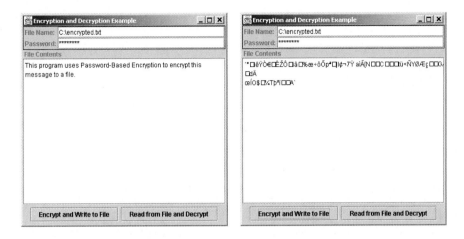

Fig. 7.7   `EncipherDecipher` before and after encrypting contents.

7.8.2 Decorator Design Pattern

The preceding program uses an important design pattern—the *Decorator design pattern.* Method **encryptAndWriteToFile** writes encrypted data to a file. However, neither the **CipherOutputStream** nor the **FileOutputStream**, by itself, can encrypt data and write those data to a file. By "chaining" these two objects together—i.e., by passing a **FileOutputStream** reference to the **CipherOutputStream** constructor—the method can encrypt data and write those data to a file. This "chaining" is an example of the Decorator design pattern, which allows an object to gain additional capabilities dynamically. In this example, the **CipherOutputStream** *decorates* the **FileOutputStream**—the **CipherOutputStream** provides the **FileOutputStream** with the capability to encrypt data before writing those data to a file. One benefit to this pattern is that designers need not create additional classes (e.g., using inheritance) to extend the functionality of a particular class. For example, because a **FileOutputStream** object can gain the behavior of a **CipherOutputStream** dynamically, we need not create a separate class called **CipherFileOutputStream**, which would implement the behaviors of both classes. Lines 227–228 accomplish the same result simply by chaining the streams together.

If necessary, we could extend this principle further and decorate a **CipherOutputStream** (which decorates a **FileOutputStream**) with an **ObjectOutputStream**. The resulting **ObjectOutputStream** instance would enable us to write encrypted objects to a file. Using the Decorator design pattern, we would write

```
ObjectOutputStream objectStream = new ObjectOutputStream(
    new CipherOutputStream(
        new FileOutputStream( filename ), cipher ) );
```

We can chain objects in this manner because **CipherOutputStream**, **ObjectOutputStream** and **FileOutputStream** extend abstract superclass **OutputStream**, and each subclass constructor takes an **OutputStream** reference as a parameter. If Java's stream objects did not use the Decorator pattern (i.e., did not satisfy these two requirements), we would have to design classes **CipherFileOutputStream**, **CipherObjectOut-**

putStream, **CipherObjectFileOutputStream** and **ObjectFileOutput-
Stream** to achieve the same functionality. If we were to chain more objects without using
the Decorator pattern, the number of classes would grow exponentially.

7.9 Digital Signatures

Digital signatures—the electronic equivalent of written signatures—were developed for
use in public-key cryptography to solve the problems of authentication and integrity (see
Microsoft Authenticode feature). A digital signature authenticates the sender's identity
and, like a written signature, is difficult to forge. To create a digital signature, a sender first
takes the original plaintext message and runs it through a *hash function*, which is a mathematical calculation that gives the message a *hash value*. The Secure Hash Algorithm (SHA-
1) is the standard for hash functions. Running a message through the SHA-1 algorithm produces a 160-bit hash value. For example, using SHA-1, the phrase "Buy 100 shares of company X" produces the hash value D8 A9 B6 9F 72 65 0B D5 6D 0C 47 00 95 0D FD 31 96
0A FD B5. MD5 is another popular hash function, which was developed by Ronald Rivest
to verify data integrity through a 128-bit hash value of the input file.[8] Examples of SHA-1
and MD5 are available at **home.istar.ca/~neutron/messagedigest**. At this
site, users can input text or files into a program to generate the hash value. The hash value
is also known as a *message digest*. The chance that two different messages will have the
same message digest is statistically insignificant. *Collision* occurs when multiple messages
have the same hash value. It is computationally infeasible to compute a message from its
hash value or to find two different messages with the same hash value.

Next, the sender uses the its private key to encrypt the message digest. This step creates
a digital signature and authenticates the sender, since only the owner of that private key could
encrypt the message. The sender encrypts the original message with the receiver's public key
and sends the encrypted message and the digital signature to the receiver. The receiver uses
the sender's public key to decipher the original digital signature and reveal the message
digest. The receiver then uses his or her own private key to decipher the original message.
Finally, the receiver applies the agreed upon hash function (e.g. SHA-1 or MD5) to the original message. If the hash value of the original message matches the message digest included
in the signature, there is *message integrity*—the message has not been altered in transmission.

There is a fundamental difference between digital signatures and handwritten signatures. A handwritten signature is independent of the document being signed. Thus, if
someone can forge a handwritten signature, he or she can use that signature to forge multiple documents. A digital signature is created using the contents of the document. Therefore, your digital signature is different for each document you sign.

Digital signatures do not provide proof that a message has been sent. Consider the following situation: A contractor sends a company a digitally signed contract, which the contractor later would like to revoke. The contractor could do so by releasing the private key
and claiming that the digitally signed contract came from an intruder who stole the contractor's private key. *Timestamping*, which binds a time and date to a digital document, can
help solve the problem of non-repudiation. For example, suppose the company and the contractor are negotiating a contract. The company requires the contractor to digitally sign the
contract, and have the document digitally time-stamped by a third party called a *timestamping agency*. The contractor sends the digitally signed contract to the time-stamping
agency. The privacy of the message is maintained, since the timestamping agency sees only

the encrypted, digitally signed message (as opposed to the original plaintext message). The timestamping agency affixes the time and date of receipt to the encrypted, signed message and digitally signs the whole package with the timestamping agency's private key. The timestamp cannot be altered by anyone except the timestamping agency, since no one else possesses the timestamping agency's private key. Unless the contractor reports the private key to have been compromised before the document was timestamped, the contractor cannot legally prove that the document was signed by an unauthorized third party. The sender could also require the receiver to sign and timestamp the message digitally as proof of receipt. To learn more about timestamping, visit **AuthentiDate.com**.

The U.S. government's digital-authentication standard is called the *Digital Signature Algorithm (DSA)*. The U.S. government recently passed legislation that makes digital signatures as legally binding as handwritten signatures. This legislation will result in an increase in e-business. For the latest news about U.S. government legislation in information security, visit **www.itaa.org/infosec**. For more information about the bills, visit the following government sites:

```
thomas.loc.gov/cgi-bin/bdquery/z?d106:hr.01714:
thomas.loc.gov/cgi-bin/bdquery/z?d106:s.00761:
```

7.10 Public-key Infrastructure, Certificates and Certification Authorities

One problem with public-key cryptography is that anyone with a set of keys could assume another party's identity. For example, say a customer wants to place an order with an online merchant. How does the customer know that the Web site indeed belongs to that merchant and not to a third party that posted a site and is masquerading as a merchant to steal credit-card information? *Public-Key Infrastructure (PKI)* integrates public-key cryptography with *digital certificates* and *certificate authorities* to authenticate parties in a transaction.

A digital certificate is a digital document that identifies a user and is issued by a *certificate authority (CA)*. A digital certificate includes the name of the subject (the company or individual being certified), the subject's public key, a serial number, an expiration date, the signature of the trusted certificate authority and any other relevant information (Fig. 7.8). A CA is a financial institution or other trusted third party, such as *VeriSign*. Once issued, digital certificates are publicly available and are held by the certificate authority in *certificate repositories*.

The CA signs the certificate by encrypting either the subject's public key or a hash value of the public key using the CA's own private key. The CA has to verify every subject's public key. Thus, users must trust the public key of a CA. Usually, each CA is part of a *certificate-authority hierarchy*. A certificate authority hierarchy is a chain of certificate authorities, starting with the *root-certificate authority*, which is the Internet Policy Registration Authority (IPRA). The IPRA signs certificates using the *root key*. The root key signs certificates only for *policy-creation authorities*, which are organizations that set policies for obtaining digital certificates. In turn, policy-creation authorities sign digital certificates for CAs. CAs then sign digital certificates for individuals and organizations. The CA takes responsibility for authentication, so it must check information carefully before issuing a digital certificate. In one case, human error caused VeriSign to issue two digital certificates to an imposter posing as a Microsoft employee.[9] Such an error is significant: The inappropriately issued certificates can cause users to unknowingly download malicious code onto their machines.

Fig. 7.8   A portion of the VeriSign digital certificate. (Courtesy of VeriSign, Inc.)

VeriSign, Inc., is a leading certificate authority. For more information about VeriSign, visit **www.verisign.com**. For a listing of other digital-certificate vendors, see Section 7.16.

Periodically, changing key pairs is necessary to maintain a secure system, as a private key may be compromised without a user's knowledge. The longer a key pair is used, the more vulnerable the keys are to attack and cryptanalysis. As a result, digital certificates contain an expiration date to force users to switch key pairs. If a private key is compromised before its expiration date, the digital certificate can be canceled, and the user can get a new key pair and digital certificate. Canceled and revoked certificates are placed on a *certificate revocation list* *(CRL)*. CRLs are stored with the certificate authority that issued the certificates. It is essential for users to report immediately if they suspect that their private keys have been compromised, as the issue of non-repudiation makes certificate owners responsible for anything appearing with their digital signatures. In states with laws dealing with digital signatures, certificates legally bind certificate owners to any transactions involving their certificates.

One problem with CRLs is that they are similar to old paper lists of revoked credit card numbers that were used at the points of sale in stores.[10] This makes for a great inconvenience when checking the validity of a certificate. An alternative to CRLs is the *Online Cer-*

tificate Status Protocol (*OCSP*), which validates certificates in real-time. OCSP technology is currently under development. For an overview of OCSP, read "X.509 Internet Public Key Infrastructure Online Certificate Status Protocol—OCSP" located at `ftp.isi.edu/in-notes/rfc2560.txt`.

Many people still consider e-commerce unsecure. However, transactions using PKI and digital certificates can be more secure than exchanging private information over phone lines or through the mail. They are even more secure than paying by credit card in person! After all, when you go to a restaurant and the waiter takes your credit card in back to process your bill, how do you know the waiter did not write down your credit-card information? In contrast, the key algorithms used in most secure online transactions are nearly impossible to compromise. By some estimates, the key algorithms used in public-key cryptography are so secure that even millions of today's computers working in parallel could not break the codes in a century. However, as computing increases, key algorithms that are considered strong today could be broken in the future.

Digital-certificate capabilities are built into many e-mail packages. For example, in Microsoft Outlook, you can go to the **Tools** menu and select **Options**. Then click on the **Security** tab. At the bottom of the dialog box, you will see the option to obtain a digital ID. Selecting the option will take you to a Microsoft Web site with links to several worldwide certificate authorities. Once you have a digital certificate, you can digitally sign your e-mail messages.

To obtain a digital certificate for your personal e-mail messages, visit **www.verisign.com** or **www.thawte.com**. VeriSign offers a free 60-day trial, or you can purchase the service for a yearly fee. Thawte offers free digital certificates for personal e-mail. Web server certificates may also be purchased through VeriSign and Thawte; however, they are more expensive than e-mail certificates.

7.10.1 Java Keystores and `keytool`

Java provides the **keytool** *utility* for managing and generating keys, certificates and digital signatures. The **keytool** utility enables users to generate and import keys in a *keystore*; you can use the stored keys for functions such as identification verification, encryption and decryption. A keystore is a repository for storing public and private keys. Modifying the set of keys that a keystore contains requires entering that keystore's password. Note that if no keystore exists, the **keytool** will create one; the password is set when creating the keystore. The default keystore is in the user's home directory (e.g., **/home/**user**/.keystore**). The **-genkey** command-line argument produces a public and private key pair and stores that key pair in the keystore. The user can export a certificate based on that key pair using the **-export** command-line option. To import a trusted certificate from a CA, the **-import** command is used. To list all of the contents of the keystore, use the **-list** command.[11] For example, to create a public and private key pair, enter the following at a command prompt:

```
keytool -genkey -alias MyCertificate
```

MyCertificate is an *alias* for the public and private key pair. The alias simply identifies a particular public and private key pair for later use. Keystores contain aliases for each public and private key pair. Certificates generated with **keytool** allow for identification through *commonName (CN)*, *organizationUnit (OU)*, *organizationName (O)*, *locality-*

Name (L), *stateName (S)* and *country (C)*. When executing the above command line, **keytool** prompts the user for this information. You then can generate a certificate request to obtain a verified digital certificate from a certificate authority, such as Verisign or Thawte, using the command:

```
keytool -certreq -alias MyCertificate -file myRequest.cer
```

This creates a file called **myRequest.cer** that contains your digital certificate. Follow the instructions on the certificate authority's Web site to submit your certificate request and obtain your verified certificate.

To create a certificate that others may use to validate your signature, use the command

```
keytool -export -alias MyCertificate -file myCertificate.cer
```

This generates an X.509 certificate that other users can import into their *trusted keystores*—keystores that contain certificates that the user knows to be correct, such as those from certificate authorities—to validate information with the signature. For more information on the keytool utility, please refer to the documentation at **java.sun.com/j2se/1.3/docs/tooldocs/win32/keytool.html** or **java.sun.com/j2se/1.3/docs/tooldocs/solaris/keytool.html**.

7.11 Java Policy Files

The basis of Java security is the *Java Sandbox*—the protected environment in which Java applications and applets run. This model is similar to placing a child in a sandbox to play; it is a safe environment where certain objects are placed out of reach and can be used only with permission. On a computer, the user must grant an application or applet specific permissions to access certain system resources outside the sandbox. The Java Sandbox security model is comprised of three individual security checks: the *bytecode verifier*, the *class loader* and *security manager*.[12]

If a developer would like to allow certain operations that the security manager would deem potentially dangerous, *permissions* may be granted on the basis of *security policy files*. Permissions are comprised of varying levels of access to specific resources. Reading and writing to a file or directory or connecting to an identified port on a host's machine are two common permissions granted by a policy file.

Permissions may be granted on the basis of the code signer (using **signedBy**) and the source of the code (using **codeBase**). Any permission that is not declared explicitly in the policy file is not granted; therefore, it is necessary to have a policy file with at least some content for the JVM to run any applet. All of the parameters for permission granting are defined in the security policy files, which enable the Java Virtual Machine to offer a great level of access control. The security policy files are external text files with certain syntax and class names; note that, as an alternative to learning this syntax, tools such as *policytool* are available for use with JDK 1.3. Figure 7.9 describes a few of the permissions available for the Java 2 security model.[13]

A system-wide security policy file is responsible for granting code the permission to access files and ports on the entire system. The virtual machine loads this policy file as part of the virtual machine's initialization. The system-wide policy file (**java.policy**) is in the **lib/security** directory of the Java Runtime Environment (e.g., **C:\Program Files\JavaSoft\JRE\1.3.1\lib\security**). Particular applications can

Permission	Description

`java.security.AllPermission`

    Grants all possible permissions. Developers should use this permission only for testing purposes as this permission disables all security checks.

`java.io.FilePermission`

    Grants access to particular sets of files for reading, writing and deleting those files.

`java.lang.RuntimePermission`

    Grants permissions for modifying runtime behavior, such as the allowing a program to exit the virtual machine, change the source of **System.in** and queue print jobs.

`java.net.SocketPermission`

    Grants permission to create socket connections for connecting to other computers over the network. This permission allows fine-grained control over particular ports, host names and connection types.

`java.net.NetPermission`

    Grants permission to modify to network properties, such as the host with which to validate usernames and passwords.

Fig. 7.9 Some permissions available in the Java 2 security model.

specify custom security policy files on the command line. Loading other security policy files does not compromise the original system-wide configuration, any modifications are made in addition to the current policy files in use.[14]

    Figure 7.10 presents class **AuthorizedFileWriter**, which accepts a file path and file body from the command line. Using a **SecurityManager** to protect against unauthorized access (line 16), lines 26–39 write the specified **fileBody** to **file**.

```
1   // AuthorizedFileWriter.java
2   // AuthorizedFileWriter writes to file using a security manager.
3   // Permissions must be given via policy files.
4   package com.deitel.advjhtp1.security.policyfile;
5
6   // Java core package
7   import java.io.*;
8
9   public class AuthorizedFileWriter {
10
11     // launch application
12     public static void main( String[] args )
13     {
14        // create and set security manager
15        System.setSecurityManager( new SecurityManager() );
```

Fig. 7.10 **AuthorizedFileWriter** writes to file using a security manager (part 1 of 2).

```
16
17          // check command-line arguments for proper usage
18          if ( args.length != 2 )
19              System.err.println( "Usage: java com.deitel.advjhtp1." +
20                  "security.policyfile.AuthorizedFileWriter file " +
21                  "filebody" );
22
23          // write fileBody to file
24          else {
25
26              String file = args[ 0 ];
27              String fileBody = args[ 1 ];
28
29              // write fileBody to file
30              try {
31
32                  // create FileWriter
33                  FileWriter fileWriter = new FileWriter( file );
34
35                  fileWriter.write( fileBody );
36
37                  fileWriter.close();
38
39                  System.exit( 0 );
40              }
41
42              // handle IO exception
43              catch ( IOException ioException ) {
44                  ioException.printStackTrace();
45                  System.exit( 1 );
46              }
47          }
48      }
49  }
```

Fig. 7.10 **AuthorizedFileWriter** writes to file using a security manager (part 2 of 2).

Policy file **authorized.policy** (Fig. 7.11) grants write **FilePermission** for file **authorized.txt**. Should the command line specify a different file, the **SecurityManager** will deny permission to write to it. The following command executes the **AuthorizedFileWriter** application with the **authorized.policy** policy file:

```
java -Djava.security.policy=authorized.policy com.dei-
tel.advjhtp1.security.policyfile.AuthorizedFileWriter "autho-
rized.txt" "Policy file authorized.policy granted file write
permission for file authorized.txt."
```

Policy file **codebase_authorized.policy** (Fig. 7.12) grants the **C:/myclasses** codebase write **FilePermission** for file **codebase_authorized.txt**. If the code is executing from a different codebase, or the command line specifies a different file, the **SecurityManager** will deny permission to write to that file. The following executes the **AuthorizedFileWriter** application with the **codebase_authorized.policy** policy file:

```
1   // authorized.policy
2   // Policy file that grants file write permission
3   // only to file "authorized.txt"
4
5   grant {
6      permission java.io.FilePermission
7         "authorized.txt", "write";
8   };
```

Fig. 7.11   Policy file grants permission to write to file **authorized.txt**.

```
1   // codebase_authorized.policy
2   // Policy file that grants write permission to
3   // file "codebase_authorized.txt" for codebase "C:/myclasses"
4
5   grant codebase "file:/C:/myclasses" {
6      permission java.io.FilePermission
7         "codebase_authorized.txt", "write";
8   };
```

Fig. 7.12   Policy file grants permission to the specified codebase.

```
java -Djava.security.policy=codebase_authorized.policy
com.deitel.advjhtp1.security.policyfile.AuthorizedFileWriter
"codebase_authorized.txt" "Policy file
codebase_authorized.policy granted file write permission for
file codebase_authorized.txt to codebase C:/myclasses."
```

For more information on current and upcoming uses of policy files and permissions in Java, visit the Web sites **java.sun.com/j2se/1.3/docs/guide/security/ PolicyFiles.html** and **java.sun.com/j2se/1.3/docs/guide/security/ permissions.html**.

7.12 Digital Signatures for Java Code

Java applets run under strict security restrictions due to the unreliability of code downloaded over public networks. Unlike Java applications, Java applets run in the sandbox by default—an applet developer need not specify a security manager for an applet. Developers who wish to distribute applets with special permissions (e.g., the ability to read or write files on the user's computer) must sign those applets with digital signatures. This enables users to verify that a signed applet came from a particular company. If the user trusts that company, the user can grant that applet special permissions.

The applet of Fig. 7.13 uses class **FileTreePanel** (similar to class **FileTree-Frame** in Chapter 3) to display a tree of files on the user's hard drive. The Java sandbox does not allow applets to read or write files on the user's hard drive, so we must sign the **FileTreeApplet** with a digital signature. When the user's Web browser downloads the applet and runs it in the Java Plug-in, the plug-in prompts the user with the digital signature of the applet and allows the user to grant permission to the applet.

Signing an applet with a digital signature requires that the signing party stores the applet and its supporting classes in a JAR file. Figure 7.14 lists the contents of the JAR file

```
1   // FileTreeApplet.java
2   // A JApplet that browses files on the local file system
3   // using a FileTreePanel.
4   package com.deitel.advjhtp1.security.signatures;
5
6   // Java extension packages
7   import javax.swing.*;
8
9   // Deitel packages
10  import com.deitel.advjhtp1.security.signatures.FileTreePanel;
11
12  public class FileTreeApplet extends JApplet {
13
14     // initialize JApplet
15     public void init()
16     {
17        // get rootDirectory from user
18        String rootDirectory = JOptionPane.showInputDialog( this,
19           "Please enter a directory name:" );
20
21        // create FileTreePanel for browsing user's hard drive
22        FileTreePanel panel = new FileTreePanel( rootDirectory );
23
24        getContentPane().add( panel );
25     }
26  }
```

Fig. 7.13   Applet that browses a user's local filesystem.

Directory Name	File Name

```
com\deitel\advjhtp1\security\signatures\
              FileTreeApplet.class
              FileTreePanel.class
              FileTreePanel$1.class
com\deitel\advjhtp1\mvc\tree\filesystem\
              FileSystemModel.class
              FileSystemModel$TreeFile.class
```

Fig. 7.14   File listing for **FileTreeApplet.jar**.

FileTreeApplet.jar. For instructions on creating JAR files, please refer to Chapter 6, JavaBeans.

The **keytool** utility enables developers to generate public and private key pairs suitable for signing applets. The Java Plug-in supports applets signed with RSA digital signatures. To generate an RSA key pair, type the following at a command prompt:

```
keytool -genkey -keyalg RSA -alias MyCertificate
```

The **keytool** utility prompts you for your name, organization name and location. To export your digital signature into a certificate file, use the command:

```
keytool -export -alias MyCertificate -file myCertificate.cer
```

The Java Plug-in maintains a keystore for trusted certificates in its **lib/security** folder (e.g., **C:\Program Files\JavaSoft\JRE\1.3.1\lib\security**) named **cacerts**. This keystore contains certificates from certificate authorities such as Verisign and Thawte. The plug-in uses these certificates to verify digital signatures through a certificate chain. Adding a new certificate to this keystore allows the Java Plug-in to verify applets signed with that new certificate. (If your certificate has been signed by a Certificate Authority such as Verisign or Thawte, you need not add this certificate to the **cacerts** trusted keystore.) Add **myCertificate.cer** to the **cacerts** keystore using the command

```
keytool -import -alias MyTrustedCertificate -keystore
     cacerts -file myCertificate.cer
```

where **cacerts** is the complete path to the **cacerts** keystore in the Java Plug-in's **lib/security** folder. When prompted for a password, enter **changeit**, which is the **cacert** keystore's default password.

Next, sign the applet's JAR file with your digital signature using the ***jarsigner*** utility. The **jarsigner** utility updates the manifest file in the JAR with the appropriate security information and signs each class in the JAR file. To sign the JAR, enter the following at a command prompt:

```
jarsigner FileTreeApplet.jar MyCertificate
```

Next, create an HTML file that contains an **applet** element for the **FileTreeApplet**. Figure 7.15 contains a basic HTML file for this purpose.

```
1   <html>
2
3   <head>
4      <title>FileTreeApplet Signed Applet</title>
5   </head>
6
7   <body>
8
9   <h1>File Browser</h1>
10
11  <applet
12     code = "com.deitel.advjhtp1.security.signatures.FileTreeApplet"
13     archive = "FileTreeApplet.jar" width = "400" height = "200">
14  </applet>
15
16  </body>
17
18  </html>
```

Fig. 7.15   HTML file for **FileTreeApplet**.

To enable the Web browser to load the Java Plug-in instead of the Web browser's own Java Virtual Machine, use the **htmlconverter** utility to convert the **applet** element into appropriate object and embed elements using the command

    htmlconverter signedApplet.html

and load the resulting Web page in a Web browser. When the Java Plug-in loads the applet, the plug-in displays the **Java Plug-in Security Warning** dialog (Fig. 7.16). This dialog displays information about the signing certificate and enables the user to grant special permission to the applet. The user can click **Grant this Session** to allow the applet **AllPermission** for the current browsing session, **Deny** to deny special permission to the applet, **Grant Always** to allow the applet **AllPermission** for this and future browsing sessions, or **More Info** to display detailed information about the applet's signature.

Figure 7.17 shows the applet running with **AllPermission**. The applet prompts the user to enter a directory to use as the root of the **JTree**. The user then can browse through the filesystem and click on individual files or folders to view information about those files and folders in the right-hand pane. The user also can rename files in the **JTree**.

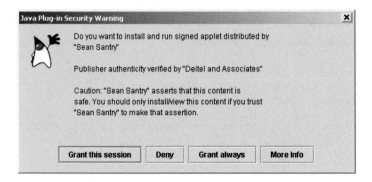

Fig. 7.16   Java Plug-in security warning when loading a signed applet.

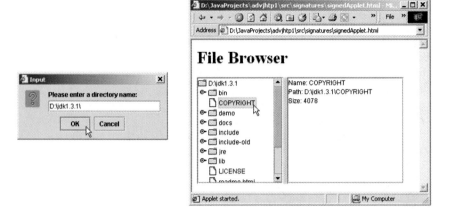

Fig. 7.17   FileTreeApplet browsing the **D:\jdk1.3.1** directory.

7.13 Authentication

Ensuring that users actually are who they claim to be is a large part of computer security, known as authentication. Current authentication models restrict access to certain aspects of a program, allow users to connect to a network and regulate the resources available to users on the network. Java uses the *Java Authentication and Authorization Service (JAAS)* for authenticating and authorizing users. JAAS is based on a plug-in framework, which allows *Kerberos* and *single sign-on* to be implemented for authentication and authorization.

7.13.1 Kerberos

Kerberos is a freely available open-source protocol developed at MIT. It employs secret-key cryptography to authenticate users in a network and to maintain the integrity and privacy of network communications.

Authentication in a Kerberos system is handled by the main Kerberos system and a secondary *Ticket Granting Service (TGS)*. The latter system is similar to key distribution centers, which were described in Section 7.3. The main Kerberos system authenticates a client's identity to the TGS, which in turn authenticates client's rights to access specific network services.

Each client in the network shares a secret key with the Kerberos system. This secret key may be used by multiple TGSs in the Kerberos system. The client starts by entering a login name and password into the Kerberos authentication server, which maintains a database of all clients in the network. The authentication server returns a *Ticket-Granting Ticket (TGT)* encrypted with the client's secret key that it shared with the authentication server. Since the secret key is known only by the authentication server and the client, only the client can decrypt the TGT, thus authenticating the client's identity. Next, the client sends the decrypted TGT to the Ticket Granting Service to request a *service ticket*, which authorizes the client's access to specific network services. Service tickets have a set expiration time. Tickets may be renewed by the TGS.

7.13.2 Single Sign-On

To access multiple applications on different servers, users must provide a separate password for authentication on each. Remembering multiple passwords is cumbersome. People tend to write their passwords down, creating security threats.

Single sign-on systems allow users to log in once with a single password. Users can access multiple applications. It is important to secure single sign-on passwords, because if the password becomes available to hackers, all applications can be accessed and attacked.

There are three types of single sign-on services: *workstation logon scripts*, *authentication server scripts* and *tokens*. Workstation logon scripts are the simplest form of single sign-on. Users log in at their workstations, then choose applications from a menu. The workstation logon script sends the user's password to the application servers, and the user is authenticated for future access to those applications. Workstation logon scripts do not provide a sufficient amount of security since user passwords are stored on the workstation in plaintext. Anyone who can access the workstation can obtain the user's password. Authentication server scripts authenticate users with a central server. The central server controls connections between the user and the applications the user wishes to access. Authentication server scripts are more secure than workstation logon scripts because passwords are kept on the server, which is more secure than the individual PC.

The most advanced single sign-on systems use token-based authentication. Once a user is authenticated, a non-reusable token is issued to the user to access specific applications. The logon for creating the token is secured with encryption or with a single password, which is the only password the user needs to remember or change. The only problem with token authentication is that all applications must be built to accept tokens instead of traditional logon passwords.[15]

7.13.3 Java Authentication and Authorization Service (JAAS)

Java addresses the problems often associated with authenticating users and controlling access with the *Java Authentication and Authorization Service (JAAS)* API. Whereas policy files and permissions protect a user from running malicious programs, JAAS protects applications from unauthorized users.[16]

The *Pluggable Authentication Module (PAM)* architecture is the standard method for authentication on which JAAS is based.[17] The PAM framework supports multiple authentication systems, including Kerberos tickets and smart cards. Additionally, PAM allows different systems to be combined to create even greater levels of security. Developers determine what forms of authentication will be used in the associated security policy. PAM also supports single sign-on systems. Java's implementation of PAM in JAAS enables Java programs to identify users, allowing developers to establish access controls to protect those programs from unauthorized access.

After a user has been authenticated, JAAS can grant or restrict access to certain resources of an application. JAAS can control access by group, user or role-based security policies.[18] User-based access control governs access to resources on an individual user basis. After providing a password, Kerberos ticket or other means of identification to the Java application, the privileges of the individual user are determined and applied. Group-based authorization identifies a user as a part of a group and grants access to certain resources based on the identifying group. For example, a member of the group "doctors" would be able to access patient databases, connect to remote hospitals and write prescriptions that are sent electronically to a pharmacy. *Role-based access control (RBAC)* is used in addition to group-access control, allowing for more control over resources. Users request specific roles, each of which have corresponding privileges, based on what tasks the user would need to access. Roles and the corresponding permissions are based on the makeup of an organization. What separates roles from groups is the fact that by default, roles are not enabled. This feature increases security by allowing users to access only necessary applications. Using the "doctors" example, it would be risky for an application to allow the doctor to delete a patient's profile by default. Deleting patient files should be an available option only when it is necessary. Therefore, in order to gain access to a deletion resource, the doctor would have to present additional identification.[19]

Class **AuthenticateNT** (Fig. 7.18) uses a sample login module available for JAAS that authenticates the current user with the Windows NT authentication system. Lines 20–21 create a new **LoginContext** with the name **AuthenticateNT**. This **LoginContext** is associated with a specific login module in the configuration file of Fig. 7.20. Line 24 invokes method **login** of class **LoginContext**. This begins the authentication process. The Windows NT sample login module does not prompt the user for login information, it simply obtains the credentials for the currently logged-in user. Other login modules may use a **CallbackHandler** to prompt the user to enter a username, password and

other authentication information. If the login is successful (i.e., invoking method **login**
does not generate any exceptions), line 28 prints a message indicating so.

```
1   // AuthenticateNT.java
2   // Authenticates a user using the NTLoginModule and performs
3   // a WriteFileAction PrivilegedAction.
4   package com.deitel.advjhtp1.security.jaas;
5
6   // Java extension packages
7   import javax.swing.*;
8   import javax.security.auth.*;
9   import javax.security.auth.login.*;
10
11  public class AuthenticateNT {
12
13     // launch application
14     public static void main( String[] args )
15     {
16        // authenticate user and perform PrivilegedAction
17        try {
18
19           // create LoginContext for AuthenticateNT context
20           LoginContext loginContext =
21              new LoginContext( "AuthenticateNT" );
22
23           // perform login
24           loginContext.login();
25
26           // if login executes without exceptions, login
27           // was successful
28           System.out.println( "Login Successful" );
29
30           // get Subject now associated with LoginContext
31           Subject subject = loginContext.getSubject();
32
33           // display Subject details
34           System.out.println( subject );
35
36           // perform the WriteFileAction as current Subject
37           Subject.doAs( subject, new WriteFileAction() );
38
39           // log out current Subject
40           loginContext.logout();
41
42           System.exit( 0 );
43
44        } // end try
45
46        // handle exception loggin in
47        catch ( LoginException loginException ) {
48           loginException.printStackTrace();
```

Fig. 7.18 AuthenticateNT uses the **NTLoginModule** to authenticate a user
and invoke a **PrivilegedAction** (part 1 of 2).

```
49            System.exit( -1 );
50        }
51
52    } // end method main
53  }
```

```
Login Successful
Subject:
        Principal: NTUserPrincipal:
        userName: santry

        Principal: NTDomainPrincipal:
        domainName DEITEL

        Principal: NTSidUserPrincipal:
        NTSid:  S-1-5-21-1275210071-1682526488-1343024091-1000

        Principal: NTSidPrimaryGroupPrincipal:
        NTSid:  S-1-5-21-1275210071-1682526488-1343024091-513

        Principal: NTSidGroupPrincipal:
        NTSid:  S-1-5-21-1275210071-1682526488-1343024091-513

        Principal: NTSidGroupPrincipal:
        NTSid:  S-1-1-0

        Principal: NTSidGroupPrincipal:
        NTSid:  S-1-5-32-544

        Principal: NTSidGroupPrincipal:
        NTSid:  S-1-5-32-545

        Principal: NTSidGroupPrincipal:
        NTSid:  S-1-5-5-0-39645

        Principal: NTSidGroupPrincipal:
        NTSid:  S-1-2-0

        Principal: NTSidGroupPrincipal:
        NTSid:  S-1-5-4

        Principal: NTSidGroupPrincipal:
        NTSid:  S-1-5-11

        Public Credential: NTNumericCredential:
        value: 896
```

Fig. 7.18 **AuthenticateNT** uses the **NTLoginModule** to authenticate a user and invoke a **PrivilegedAction** (part 2 of 2).

Line 31 obtains a **Subject** from the current **LoginContext**. A **Subject** represents a particular user or other entity (e.g., an automated service) that requests an action. Each **Subject** has associated **Principal**s. These **Principal**s represent the different roles or identities that a user can assume during a particular login session. The security restrictions in place for a particular application can grant permissions for **Principal**s to make certain requests (e.g., read from a particular file). Line 34 prints the **Subject**'s information, including a list of the **Subject**'s **Principal**s.

Line 37 invokes method **doAs** of class **Subject** to make a request using the given **Subject**. Method **doAs** takes as arguments the **Subject** for the request and a **PrivilegedAction** that contains the request. For this example, line 37 passes a new **WriteFileAction** (Fig. 7.19), which writes a simple message to a text file. Line 40 logs out from the current **LoginContext**.

Class **WriteFileAction** (Fig. 7.19) implements interface **Privileged-Action**. **PrivilegedAction**s execute in the context of an **AccessController**, which verifies that the **Subject** invoking the **PrivilegedAction** has the appropriate permissions. Interface **PrivilegedAction** requires that implementations define method **run** (lines 13–32). Method **run** of class **WriteFileAction** creates a text file and writes a message to that text file.

```
1   // WriteFileAction.java
2   // WriteFileAction is a PrivilegedAction implementation that
3   // simply writes a file to the local file system.
4   package com.deitel.advjhtp1.security.jaas;
5
6   // Java core packages
7   import java.io.*;
8   import java.security.PrivilegedAction;
9
10  public class WriteFileAction implements PrivilegedAction {
11
12     // perform the PrivilegedAction
13     public Object run()
14     {
15        // attempt to write a message to the specified file
16        try {
17           File file = new File( "D:/", "privilegedFile.txt" );
18           FileWriter fileWriter = new FileWriter( file );
19
20           // write message to File and close FileWriter
21           fileWriter.write( "Welcome to JAAS!" );
22           fileWriter.close();
23        }
24
25        // handle exception writing file
26        catch ( IOException ioException ) {
27           ioException.printStackTrace();
28        }
29
30        return null;
31
32     } // end method run
33  }
```

Fig. 7.19 **WriteFileAction** is a **PrivilegedAction** for writing a simple text file.

The configuration file of Fig. 7.20 specifies the **LoginModule**s to use for the **AuthenticateNT LoginContext**. Line 5 specifies that the **Subject** must authenticate with the **NTLoginModule** for a successful login. **LoginContext**s can require a sequence of several **LoginModule**s for proper authentication. For more information on JAAS configuration files, please refer to the JAAS documentation at **java.sun.com/security/jaas/doc/api.html**.

The policy file of Fig. 7.21 grants permissions to the specified **Principal** when executing code in the specified **codeBase**. JAAS offers fine-grained permissions control. This example grants read and write **FilePermission** to the **Principal "santry"** when executing code in the **file:d:/JavaProjects/advjhtp1/src/-** codebase.

The policy file of Fig. 7.22 specifies permissions for JAAS itself and for the **AuthenticateNT** class codebase. Lines 5–7 grant **AllPermission** to the JAAS standard extension. This permission enables JAAS to perform authentication on behalf of this application. Line 13 grants permission to execute **PrivilegedAction**s using method **doAs**. Lines 15–19 grant permission to read and write the text file **D:\privileged-File.txt**.

```
1   // jaas.config
2   // Configures JAAS to use NTLoginModule
3   // for authentication.
4   AuthenticateNT {
5       com.sun.security.auth.module.NTLoginModule required debug=false;
6   };
```

Fig. 7.20 Configuration file for authentication using **NTLoginModule**.

```
1    // jaas.policy
2    // Policy file defining the permissions for the named Principal
3    grant codeBase "file:D:/JavaProjects/advjhtp1/src/-",
4        Principal com.sun.security.auth.NTUserPrincipal "santry" {
5
6        permission java.io.FilePermission "D:/privilegedFile.txt",
7            "write";
8
9        permission java.io.FilePermission "D:/privilegedFile.txt",
10           "read";
11   };
```

Fig. 7.21 JAAS policy file for granting permissions to a **Principal** and codebase.

```
1    // java.policy
2    // Policy file that grants AllPermission
3    // to JAAS modules and specific permissions
4    // to the D:\Projects\Java codebase.
5    grant codebase "file:/D:/jdk1.3.1/jre/lib/ext/jaas.jar" {
6        permission java.security.AllPermission;
7    };
8
```

Fig. 7.22 Policy file for JAAS application (part 1 of 2).

```
 9   grant codebase "file:/D:/JavaProjects/advjhtp1/src/-" {
10       permission javax.security.auth.AuthPermission
11          "createLoginContext";
12
13       permission javax.security.auth.AuthPermission "doAs";
14
15       permission java.io.FilePermission "D:/privilegedFile.txt",
16          "write";
17
18       permission java.io.FilePermission "D:/privilegedFile.txt",
19          "read";
20   };
```

Fig. 7.22   Policy file for JAAS application (part 2 of 2).

Executing the **AuthenticateNT** example requires several command-line options to the Java virtual machine. Enter the following at a command prompt:

```
java -Djava.security.policy==java.policy
    -Djava.security.auth.policy==jaas.policy
    -Djava.security.auth.login.config==jaas.config
    com.deitel.advjhtp1.security.jaas.AuthenticateNT
```

where **java.policy** is the policy file of Fig. 7.22, **jaas.policy** is the policy file of Fig. 7.21 and **jaas.config** is the configuration file of Fig. 7.20.

7.14 Secure Sockets Layer (SSL)

Currently, most e-businesses use SSL for secure online transactions, although SSL is not designed specifically for securing transactions. Rather, SSL secures World Wide Web connections. The Secure Sockets Layer (SSL) protocol, developed by Netscape Communications, is a nonproprietary protocol commonly used to secure communication between two computers on the Internet and the Web.[20] SSL is built into many Web browsers, including Netscape *Communicator* and Microsoft *Internet Explorer*, as well as numerous other software products. It operates between the Internet's TCP/IP communications protocol and the application software.[21]

SSL implements public-key technology using the RSA algorithm and digital certificates to authenticate the server in a transaction and to protect private information as it passes from one party to another over the Internet. SSL transactions do not require client authentication; many servers consider a valid credit-card number to be sufficient for authentication in secure purchases. To begin, a client sends a message to a server. The server responds and sends its digital certificate to the client for authentication. Using public-key cryptography to communicate securely, the client and server negotiate *session keys* to continue the transaction. Session keys are secret keys used for the duration of that transaction. Once the keys are established, the communication proceeds between the client and the server using the session keys and digital certificates. Encrypted data are passed through TCP/IP, just as regular packets travel over the Internet. However, before sending a message with TCP/IP, the SSL protocol breaks the information into blocks and compresses and encrypts those blocks. Conversely, after the data reach the receiver through

TCP/IP, the SSL protocol decrypts the packets, then decompresses and assembles the data. These extra processes provide an extra layer of security between TCP/IP and applications. SSL is used primarily to secure *point-to-point connections*—transmissions of data from one computer to another.[22] SSL allows for the authentication of the server, the client, both or neither; in most Internet SSL sessions, only the server is authenticated. The Transport Layer Security (TLS) protocol, designed by the Internet Engineering Task Force, is similar to SSL. For more information on TLS, visit: **www.ietf.org/rfc/rfc2246.txt**.

Although SSL protects information as it is passed over the Internet, it does not protect private information, such as credit-card numbers, once the information is stored on the merchant's server. When a merchant receives credit-card information with an order, the information is often decrypted and stored on the merchant's server until the order is placed. If the server is not secure and the data are not encrypted, an unauthorized party can access the information. For more information about the SSL protocol, check out the Netscape SSL tutorial at **developer.netscape.com/tech/security/ssl/protocol.html** and the Netscape Security Center site at **www.netscape.com/security/index.html**.

7.14.1 Java Secure Socket Extension (JSSE)

The strength of SSL encryption has been integrated into Java technology through Sun's *Java Secure Socket Extension (JSSE)*. Java applications that use JSSE can secure a passage between a client and a server over TCP/IP. JSSE provides encryption, message integrity checks and authentication of the server and client.[23] JSSE uses keystores to secure storage of key pairs and certificates used in PKI. A *truststore* is a keystore containing keys and certificates used to validate the identities of servers and clients.[24][25]

The algorithms used in JSSE for encryption, key agreement and authentication include DES, 3DES, Diffie-Hellman and DSA. Like JCE, JSSE uses a provider-based model that enables third parties to provide additional cryptographic algorithms. JSSE is free for commercial use and is available for free download at **java.sun.com/products/jsse**.

Class **LoginServer** (Fig. 7.23) uses an **SSLServerSocket** to listen for SSL connections on port **7070**. JSSE uses the Factory design pattern for constructing **SSLServerSocket**s and **SSLSocket**s. Line 25 invokes **static** method **getDefault** of class **SSLServerSocketFactory** to obtain the default **SSLServerSocketFactory**. Line 29 invokes method **createServerSocket** of class **SSLServerSocketFactory** to create the **SSLServerSocket**. This method takes as an argument the port number on which the **SSLServerSocket** will listen.

Method **runServer** (lines 34–84) starts **LoginServer**. Line 46 invokes method **accept** of class **SSLServerSocket** to accept a new client connection. Method **accept** is a blocking call that returns an **SSLSocket** when a client connects. Lines 49–55 obtain the **InputStream** and **OutputStream** for the **SSLSocket** and lines 57–58 read two lines of text. Lines 60–61 validate the client's user name and password against constants **CORRECT_USER_NAME** and **CORRECT_PASSWORD**. If the user name and password are correct, line 63 sends a welcome message to the client. If the user name and password are incorrect, line 67 notifies the client that the login failed. Lines 71–73 close the **InputStream**, **OutputStream** and **SSLSocket**.

Note that using **SSLServerSocket**s and **SSLSocket**s is identical to using standard **ServerSocket**s and **Socket**s. JSSE hides the details of the SSL protocol and encryption from the programmer entirely.

```
1   // LoginServer.java
2   // LoginServer uses an SSLServerSocket to demonstrate JSSE's
3   // SSL implementation.
4   package com.deitel.advjhtp1.security.jsse;
5
6   // Java core packages
7   import java.io.*;
8
9   // Java extension packages
10  import javax.net.ssl.*;
11
12  public class LoginServer {
13
14     private static final String CORRECT_USER_NAME = "Java";
15     private static final String CORRECT_PASSWORD = "HowToProgram";
16
17     private SSLServerSocket serverSocket;
18
19     // LoginServer constructor
20     public LoginServer() throws Exception
21     {
22        // SSLServerSocketFactory for building SSLServerSockets
23        SSLServerSocketFactory socketFactory =
24           ( SSLServerSocketFactory )
25              SSLServerSocketFactory.getDefault();
26
27        // create SSLServerSocket on specified port
28        serverSocket = ( SSLServerSocket )
29           socketFactory.createServerSocket( 7070 );
30
31     } // end LoginServer constructor
32
33     // start server and listen for clients
34     private void runServer()
35     {
36        // perpetually listen for clients
37        while ( true ) {
38
39           // wait for client connection and check login information
40           try {
41
42              System.err.println( "Waiting for connection..." );
43
44              // create new SSLSocket for client
45              SSLSocket socket =
46                 ( SSLSocket ) serverSocket.accept();
47
48              // open BufferedReader for reading data from client
49              BufferedReader input = new BufferedReader(
50                 new InputStreamReader( socket.getInputStream() ) );
51
```

Fig. 7.23 `LoginServer` uses an `SSLServerSocket` for secure communication (part 1 of 2).

```
52              // open PrintWriter for writing data to client
53              PrintWriter output = new PrintWriter(
54                 new OutputStreamWriter(
55                    socket.getOutputStream() ) );
56
57              String userName = input.readLine();
58              String password = input.readLine();
59
60              if ( userName.equals( CORRECT_USER_NAME ) &&
61                 password.equals( CORRECT_PASSWORD ) ) {
62
63                 output.println( "Welcome, " + userName );
64              }
65
66              else {
67                 output.println( "Login Failed." );
68              }
69
70              // clean up streams and SSLSocket
71              output.close();
72              input.close();
73              socket.close();
74
75           } // end try
76
77           // handle exception communicating with client
78           catch ( IOException ioException ) {
79              ioException.printStackTrace();
80           }
81
82        } // end while
83
84     } // end method runServer
85
86     // execute application
87     public static void main( String args[] ) throws Exception
88     {
89        LoginServer server = new LoginServer();
90        server.runServer();
91     }
92  }
```

Fig. 7.23 **LoginServer** uses an **SSLServerSocket** for secure communication (part 2 of 2).

Class **LoginClient** (Fig. 7.24) uses an **SSLSocket** to communicate with the **LoginServer**. Lines 22–23 invoke method **getDefault** of class **SSLSocketFactory** to obtain the default **SSLSocketFactory**. Lines 26–28 invoke method **createSocket** of class **SSLSocketFactory** to create a new **SSLSocket** that connects to **localhost** on port **7070**. Lines 31–32 create a new **PrintWriter** for the **SSLSocket**'s **OutputStream** to facilitate sending data to the server. Lines 35–48 prompt the user for a username and password and send them to the server. Lines 51–58 then read the response from the server and display this response in a **JOptionPane** message dialog. Note that once the client establishes the connection with the **SSLSocket**, the fact that SSL encrypts the communication between the client and server is transparent to the programmer.

```
1   // LoginClient.java
2   // LoginClient uses an SSLSocket to transmit fake login
3   // information to LoginServer.
4   package com.deitel.advjhtp1.security.jsse;
5
6   // Java core packages
7   import java.io.*;
8
9   // Java extension packages
10  import javax.swing.*;
11  import javax.net.ssl.*;
12
13  public class LoginClient {
14
15     // LoginClient constructor
16     public LoginClient()
17     {
18        // open SSLSocket connection to server and send login
19        try {
20
21           // obtain SSLSocketFactory for creating SSLSockets
22           SSLSocketFactory socketFactory =
23              ( SSLSocketFactory ) SSLSocketFactory.getDefault();
24
25           // create SSLSocket from factory
26           SSLSocket socket =
27              ( SSLSocket ) socketFactory.createSocket(
28                 "localhost", 7070 );
29
30           // create PrintWriter for sending login to server
31           PrintWriter output = new PrintWriter(
32              new OutputStreamWriter( socket.getOutputStream() ) );
33
34           // prompt user for user name
35           String userName = JOptionPane.showInputDialog( null,
36              "Enter User Name:" );
37
38           // send user name to server
39           output.println( userName );
40
41           // prompt user for password
42           String password = JOptionPane.showInputDialog( null,
43              "Enter Password:" );
44
45           // send password to server
46           output.println( password );
47
48           output.flush();
```

Fig. 7.24 LoginClient communicates with **LoginServer** via SSL (part 1 of 2).

```
49
50          // create BufferedReader for reading server response
51          BufferedReader input = new BufferedReader(
52             new InputStreamReader( socket.getInputStream () ) );
53
54          // read response from server
55          String response = input.readLine();
56
57          // display response to user
58          JOptionPane.showMessageDialog( null, response );
59
60          // clean up streams and SSLSocket
61          output.close();
62          input.close();
63          socket.close();
64
65       } // end try
66
67       // handle exception communicating with server
68       catch ( IOException ioException ) {
69          ioException.printStackTrace();
70       }
71
72       // exit application
73       finally {
74          System.exit( 0 );
75       }
76
77    } // end LoginClient constructor
78
79    // execute application
80    public static void main( String args[] )
81    {
82       new LoginClient();
83    }
84 }
```

Fig. 7.24 `LoginClient` communicates with `LoginServer` via SSL (part 2 of 2).

Enabling SSL requires that **LoginServer** uses a certificate that **LoginClient** trusts. Use the **keytool** to generate a new certificate and keystore for this purpose:

```
keytool -genkey -keystore SSLStore -alias SSLCertificate
```

Next, launch **LoginServer** and specify the keystore that contains the **Login-Server**'s certificate:

```
java -Djavax.net.ssl.keyStore=SSLStore
   -Djavax.net.ssl.keyStorePassword=password
   com.deitel.advjhtp1.security.jsse.LoginServer
```

where password is the password you specified for the **SSLStore** keystore. Finally, launch the **LoginClient** and specify the truststore for that client. The truststore contains certificates that the client trusts for the purposes of digital-signature validation. For simplicity in this example, we use the same keystore as both the **LoginServer**'s keystore and the **Login-**

Client's truststore. In real-world applications, the client's truststore should contain trusted certificates, such as those from certificate authorities. Execute the client using the command

```
java -Djavax.net.ssl.trustStore=SSLStore
    -Djavax.net.ssl.trustStorePassword=password
    com.deitel.advjhtp1.security.jsse.LoginClient
```

Figure 7.25 shows two executions of class **LoginClient**. The first execution (the left column) shows a successful login. The second execution shows a failed login. For each execution, the **LoginServer** and **LoginClient** used SSL to encrypt all data transfer.

7.15 Java Language Security and Secure Coding

The Java language provides programmers with a security advantage that other languages do not. Java code goes through several stages before and during execution that help to ensure that the Java code is not malicious. Each stage prevents many exploitations that other programming languages allow. For example, the Java Virtual Machine ensures that programs cannot read memory beyond the end of an array. This prevents programs from reading data from arbitrary locations in memory.

The Java compiler performs several security checks in the normal process of compiling Java source code into bytecode. The compiler ensures that the program does not read from uninitialized variables—a common technique for reading data from arbitrary memory locations. Also, the compiler checks the access modifiers for each method invocation and variable to ensure that the program accesses private data only from the proper classes. The compiler also can detect certain illegal casts between data types. These simple steps help prevent many types of security attacks.

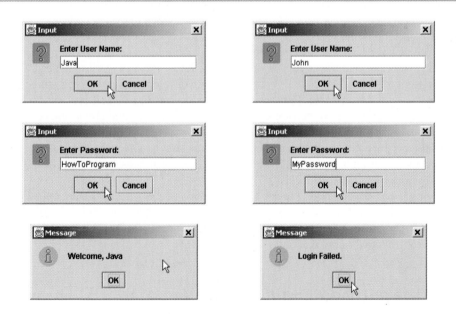

Fig. 7.25 Two sample executions of class **LoginClient**.

Before the Java Virtual Machine executes a Java program, the bytecodes for that program must pass through the *bytecode verifier*. The bytecode verifier ensures that the bytecodes are valid Java bytecodes that do not perform certain illegal operations (according to the rules of the Java language). For example, the bytecode verifier checks that no class has more than one superclass and that final classes do not have subclasses. The bytecode verifier also checks that classes have the proper format. This second stage helps eliminate security risks that the compiler could not detect.

The Java Virtual Machine performs the remaining integrity checks on Java programs. The virtual machine checks any remaining cast operations to ensure their validity and performs array-bounds checking to prevent programs from reading arbitrary memory locations. The Java Virtual Machine uses *class loaders* to read class definitions from **.class** files and produce class representations in memory. The class loader uses separate *namespaces* to prevent malicious code from interacting with safe code.[26] Every class that the JVM loads is assigned a corresponding set of unique names, known as a namespace. Namespaces in Java act as barriers between classes. The JVM allows classes within the same namespace to interact, but requires explicit permission for classes from separate namespaces to operate together. To protect trusted classes, developers can use different class loaders for trusted and untrusted packages. This allows for trusted code to belong to the same *runtime package*. A runtime package is code that was loaded by the same class loader and belong to the same package. The *bootstrap* class loader loads all of the trusted core Java classes, so that additional, potentially unsecure classes will belong to a separate runtime package and can not interfere with the core classes.

The Java security manager is the module that performs security checks while code is running. If, during run-time, code attempts to execute a dangerous operation, a *security exception* is generated. Class operations that the security manager considers dangerous include: deleting a file, reading from a file, appending or editing a file, adding or loading a class to a package, and opening a socket connection.[27] When untrusted code attempts one of these operations, the security manager throws an **AccessControlException**.

Although the Java language and the associated compiler, bytecode verifier and virtual machine enforce a number of security constraints, Java developers still may need to take certain steps to secure their code. For example, when developing classes, programmers can declare those classes as final. Final classes cannot be subclassed, and can help make an application more secure by preventing attackers from creating malicious subclasses that can cause damage to an application or gain access to protected information. A hacker would generally exploit an ordinary class by creating a subclass to replace the original. This new class could expose the same public interface as the original class, and would deceive the compiler into using the hostile class.[28]

Fortunately, the compiler will not compile a class that attempts to extent a final class. The bytecode verifier also checks to ensure that classes are not subclasses of a final class. If declaring an entire class as final is excessive for a program's needs, final methods prevent subclasses from overriding particular methods.

7.16 Internet and World Wide Web Resources

The notation **<www.domain-name.com>** indicates that the citation is for information found at that Web site.

Security Resource Sites

www.securitysearch.com

This is a comprehensive resource for computer security. The site has thousands of links to products, security companies, tools and more. The site also offers a free weekly newsletter with information about vulnerabilities.

www.securityfocus.com

A site covering all aspects of computer security, with special sections in the basics, numerous operating systems, intrusion detection and viruses. This site is also responsible for maintaining the BugTraq list.

www.esecurityonline.com

This site is a great resource for information on online security. The site has links to news, tools, events, training and other valuable security information and resources.

www.epic.org

The *Electronic Privacy Information Center* deals with protecting privacy and civil liberties. Visit this site to learn more about the organization and its latest initiatives.

theory.lcs.mit.edu/~rivest/crypto-security.html

The *Ronald L. Rivest: Cryptography and Security* site has an extensive list of links to security resources, including newsgroups, government agencies, FAQs, tutorials and more.

www.w3.org/Security/Overview.html

The *W3C Security Resources* site has FAQs, information about W3C security and e-commerce initiatives and links to other security related Web sites.

web.mit.edu/network/ietf/sa

The Internet Engineering Task Force (IETF), which is an organization concerned with the architecture of the Internet, has working groups dedicated to Internet Security. Visit the *IETF Security Area* to learn about the working groups, join the mailing list or check out the latest drafts of the IETF's work.

dir.yahoo.com/Computers_and_Internet/Security_and_Encryption

The *Yahoo Security and Encryption* page is a great resource for links to Web sites security and encryption.

www.counterpane.com/hotlist.html

The Counterpane Internet Security, Inc., site includes links to downloads, source code, FAQs, tutorials, alert groups, news and more.

www.rsasecurity.com/rsalabs/faq

This site is an excellent set of FAQs about cryptography from RSA Laboratories, one of the leading makers of public key cryptosystems.

www.nsi.org/compsec.html

Visit the National Security Institute's *Security Resource Net* for the latest security alerts, government standards, and legislation, as well as security FAQs links and other helpful resources.

www.itaa.org/infosec

The Information Technology Association of America (ITAA) *InfoSec* site has information about the latest U.S. government legislation related to information security.

staff.washington.edu/dittrich/misc/ddos

The *Distributed Denial of Service Attacks* site has links to news articles, tools, advisory organizations and even a section on security humor.

www.infoworld.com/cgi-bin/displayNew.pl?/security/links/security_corner.htm

The Security Watch site on **Infoword.com** has loads of links to security resources.

www.antionline.com
AntiOnline has security-related news and information, a tutorial titled "Fight-back! Against Hackers," information about hackers and an archive of hacked sites.

www.microsoft.com/security/default.asp
The Microsoft security site has links to downloads, security bulletins and tutorials.

www.grc.com
This site offers a service to test the security of your computer's Internet connection.

General Security Sites

www.sans.org/giac.html
Sans Institute presents information on system and security updates, along with new research and discoveries. The site offers current publications, projects, and weekly digests.

www.packetstorm.securify.com
The Packet Storm page describes the twenty latest advisories, tools, and exploits. This site also provides links to the top security news stories.

www.xforce.iss.net
This site allows one to search a virus by name, reported date, expected risk, or affected platforms. Updated news reports can be found on this page.

www.ntbugtraq.com
This site provides a list and description of various Windows NT Security Exploits/Bugs encountered by Windows NT users. One can download updated service applications.

nsi.org/compsec.html
The Security Resource Net page states various warnings, threats, legislation and documents of viruses and security in an organized outline.

www.tno.nl/instit/fel/intern/wkinfsec.html
This site includes numerous links to other security sites.

www.microsoft.com/security
The Microsoft security site offers news, product information and tools.

www.securitystats.com
This computer security site provides statistics on viruses, web defacements and security spending.

Magazines, Newsletters and News sites

www.networkcomputing.com/consensus
The *Security Alert Consensus* is a free weekly newsletter with information about security threats, holes, solutions and more.

www.infosecuritymag.com
Information Security Magazine has the latest Web security news and vendor information.

www.issl.org/cipher.html
Cipher is an electronic newsletter on security and privacy from the Institute of Electrical and Electronics Engineers (IEEE). You can view current and past issues online.

securityportal.com
The *Security Portal* has news and information about security, cryptography and the latest viruses.

www.scmagazine.com
SC Magazine has news, product reviews and a conference schedule for security events.

www.cnn.com/TECH/specials/hackers
Insurgency on the Internet from CNN Interactive has news on hacking, plus a gallery of hacked sites.

rootshell.com/beta/news.html
Visit Rootshell for security-related news and white papers.

Government Sites for Computer Security

www.cit.nih.gov/security.html
This site has links to security organizations, security resources and tutorials on PKI, SSL and other protocols.

cs-www.ncsl.nist.gov
The *Computer Security Resource Clearing House* is a resource for network administrators and others concerned with security. This site has links to incident-reporting centers, information about security standards, events, publications and other resources.

www.cdt.org/crypto
Visit the Center for Democracy and Technology for U. S. legislation and policy news regarding cryptography.

www.epm.ornl.gov/~dunigan/security.html
This site has links to loads of security-related sites. The links are organized by subject and include resources on digital signatures, PKI, smart cards, viruses, commercial providers, intrusion detection and several other topics.

www.alw.nih.gov/Security
The *Computer Security Information* page is an excellent resource, providing links to news, newsgroups, organizations, software, FAQs and an extensive number of Web links.

www.fedcirc.gov
The Federal Computer Incident Response Capability deals with the security of government and civilian agencies. This site has information about incident statistics, advisories, tools, patches and more.

axion.physics.ubc.ca/pgp.html
This site has a list of freely available cryptosystems, along with a discussion of each system and links to FAQs and tutorials.

www.ifccfbi.gov
The Internet Fraud Complaint Center, founded by the Justice Department and the FBI, fields reports of Internet fraud.

www.disa.mil/infosec/iaweb/default.html
The Defense Information Systems Agency's *Information Assurance* page includes links to sites on vulnerability warnings, virus information and incident-reporting instructions, as well as other helpful links.

www.nswc.navy.mil/ISSEC/
The objective of this site is to provide information on protecting your computer systems from security hazards. Contains a page on hoax versus real viruses.

www.cit.nih.gov/security.html
You can report security issues at this site. The site also lists official federal security policies, regulations, and guidelines.

cs-www.ncsl.nist.gov/
The Computer Security Resource Center provides services for vendors and end users. The site includes information on security testing, management, technology, education and applications.

Advanced Encryption Standard (AES)

csrc.nist.gov/encryption/aes
This is the official site for the AES; this site includes press releases and a discussion forum.

`www.esat.kuleuven.ac.be/~rijmen/rijndael/`
Visit this site for information about the Rijndael algorithm, including links to various implementations of the algorithm and a small FAQ.

`home.ecn.ab.ca/~jsavard/crypto/co040801.htm`
This site is dedicated to AES. It includes an explanation of the algorithm with diagrams and examples.

Internet Security Vendors

`www.rsasecurity.com`
RSA is one of the leaders in electronic security. Visit its site for more information about its current products and tools, which are used by companies worldwide.

`www.ca.com/protection`
Computer Associates is a vendor of Internet security software. It has various software packages to help companies set up a firewall, scan files for viruses and protect against viruses.

`www.checkpoint.com`
Check Point™ Software Technologies Ltd. is a leading provider of Internet security products and services.

`www.opsec.com`
The Open Platform for Security (OPSEC) has over 200 partners that develop security products and solutions using the OPSEC to allow for interoperability and increased security over a network.

`www.baltimore.com`
Baltimore Security is an e-commerce security solutions provider. Their UniCERT digital certificate product is used in PKI applications.

`www.ncipher.com`
nCipher is a vendor of hardware and software products, including an SSL accelerator that increases the speed of secure Web server transactions and a secure key management system.

`www.entrust.com`
Entrust Technologies provides e-security products and services.

`www.tenfour.co.uk`
TenFour provides software for secure e-mail.

`www.antivirus.com`
ScanMail® is an e-mail virus detection program for Microsoft Exchange.

`www.contenttechnologies.com/ads`
Content Technologies is a security software provider. Its products include firewall and secure e-mail programs.

`www.zixmail.com`
Zixmail™ is a secure e-mail product that allows you to encrypt and digitally sign your messages using different e-mail programs.

`web.mit.edu/network/pgp.html`
Visit this site to download *Pretty Good Privacy*® freeware. PGP allows you to send messages and files securely.

`www.certicom.com`
Certicom provides security solutions for the wireless Internet.

`www.raytheon.com`
Raytheon Corporation's *SilentRunner* monitors activity on a network to find internal threats, such as data theft or fraud.

SSL

developer.netscape.com/tech/security/ssl/protocol.html
This Netscape page has a brief description of SSL, plus links to an SSL tutorial and FAQs.

www.netscape.com/security/index.html
The Netscape Security Center is an extensive resource for Internet and Web security. You will find news, tutorials, products and services on this site.

psych.psy.uq.oz.au/~ftp/Crypto
This FAQs page has an extensive list of questions and answers about SSL technology.

www.visa.com/nt/ecomm/security/main.html
Visa International's security page includes information on SSL and SET. The page includes a demonstration of an online shopping transaction, which explains how SET works.

www.openssl.org
The *Open SSL Project* provides a free, open source toolkit for SSL.

Public-key Cryptography

www.entrust.com
Entrust produces effective security software products using Public Key Infrastructure (PKI).

www.cse.dnd.ca
The Communication Security Establishment has a short tutorial on Public Key Infrastructure (PKI) that defines PKI, public-key cryptography and digital signatures.

www.magnet.state.ma.us/itd/legal/pki.htm
The Commonwealth of Massachusetts Information Technology page has loads of links to sites related to PKI that contain information about standards, vendors, trade groups and government organizations.

www.ftech.net/~monark/crypto/index.htm
The Beginner's Guide to Cryptography is an online tutorial and includes links to other sites on privacy and cryptography.

www.faqs.org/faqs/cryptography-faq
The *Cryptography FAQ* has an extensive list of questions and answers.

www.pkiforum.org
The PKI Forum promotes the use of PKI.

www.counterpane.com/pki-risks.html
Visit the Counterpane Internet Security, Inc.'s site to read the article "Ten Risks of PKI: What You're Not Being Told About Public Key Infrastructure."

Digital Signatures

www.ietf.org/html.charters/xmldsig-charter.html
The *XML Digital Signatures* site was created by a group working to develop digital signatures using XML. You can view the group's goals and drafts of their work.

www.elock.com
E-Lock Technologies is a vendor of digital-signature products used in Public Key Infrastructure. This site has an FAQs list covering cryptography, keys, certificates and signatures.

www.digsigtrust.com
The Digital Signature Trust Co. is a vendor of Digital Signature and Public Key Infrastructure products. It has a tutorial titled "Digital Signatures and Public Key Infrastructure (PKI) 101."

Digital Certificates

www.verisign.com
VeriSign creates digital IDs for individuals, small businesses and large corporations. Check out its Web site for product information, news and downloads.

www.thawte.com
Thawte Digital Certificate Services offers SSL, developer and personal certificates.

www.silanis.com/index.htm
Silanis Technology is a vendor of digital-certificate software.

www.belsign.be
Belsign issues digital certificates in Europe. It is the European authority for digital certificates.

www.certco.com
Certco issues digital certificates to financial institutions.

www.openca.org
Set up your own CA using open-source software from The OpenCA Project.

Kerberos

www.nrl.navy.mil/CCS/people/kenh/kerberos-faq.html
This site is an extensive list of FAQs on Kerberos from the Naval Research Laboratory.

web.mit.edu/kerberos/www
Kerberos: The Network Authentication Protocol is a list of FAQs provided by MIT.

www.contrib.andrew.cmu.edu/~shadow/kerberos.html
The Kerberos Reference Page has links to several informational sites, technical sites and other helpful resources.

www.pdc.kth.se/kth-krb
Visit this site to download various Kerberos white papers and documentation.

Newsgroups

news://comp.security.firewalls

news://comp.security.unix

news://comp.security.misc

news://comp.protocols.kerberos

SUMMARY

- There are five fundamental requirements of a successful, secure transaction: privacy, integrity, authentication, authorization and nonrepudiation.

- Network security addresses the issue of availability: How do we ensure that the network and the computer systems it connects will stay in operation continuously?

- The Java Sandbox architecture and policy files protect users and systems from malicious programs that would otherwise crash computers or steal valuable information.

- To secure information, data can be encrypted. Cryptography transforms data by using a cipher, or cryptosystem—a mathematical algorithm for encrypting messages. Unencrypted data is called plaintext; encrypted data is called ciphertext.

- A key—a string of alpha-numeric characters that acts as a password—is input to the cipher. The cipher uses the key to make data incomprehensible to all but the sender and intended receivers.

- Encryption and decryption keys are binary strings with a given key length. Symmetric cryptography, also known as secret-key cryptography, utilizes the same secret key to encrypt and decrypt messages.

- A key distribution center shares a (different) secret key with every user in the network; the key distribution center generates a session key to be used for a transaction.

- One of the most commonly used symmetric encryption algorithms is the Data Encryption Standard (DES).

- A block cipher is an encryption method that creates groups of bits from an original message, then applies an encryption algorithm to the block as a whole, rather than as individual bits.

- Triple DES, or 3DES, is a variant of DES that is essentially three DES systems in a row, each having its own secret key.

- The new standard for encryption is called the Advanced Encryption Standard (AES). Rijndael—a candidate for AES—is an encryption method that can be used with key sizes and block sizes of 128, 192 or 256 bits.

- Public-key cryptography is asymmetric—it uses two inversely related keys: A public key and a private key. The most commonly used public-key algorithm is *RSA*, an encryption system developed in 1977 by MIT professors Ron Rivest, Adi Shamir and Leonard Adleman.

- Pretty Good Privacy (PGP) is a public-key encryption system used for encrypting e-mail messages and files. PGP was designed in 1991 by Phillip Zimmermann.

- Public-key algorithms should not be thought of as a replacement for secret-key algorithms. Instead, public-key algorithms can be used to allow two parties to agree upon a key to be used for secret-key encryption over an unsecure medium.

- The process by which two parties can exchange keys over an unsecure medium is called a key agreement protocol. A protocol sets the rules for communication: Exactly what encryption algorithm(s) is (are) going to be used? The most common key agreement protocol is a digital envelope.

- Maintaining the secrecy of private keys is crucial to keeping cryptographic systems secure. Most compromises in security result from poor key management (e.g., the mishandling of private keys, resulting in key theft) rather than attacks that attempt to guess the keys.

- A main component of key management is key generation—the process by which keys are created. A malicious third party could try to decrypt a message by using every possible decryption key, a process known as brute-force cracking.

- The Java Cryptography Extension (JCE) provides Java applications with secret-key encryption, such as 3DES, and public-key algorithms, such as Diffie-Hellman and RSA.

- The JCE architecture is provider-based—developers can add new algorithms to their programs by adding a new algorithm provider.

- Class **Cipher** is the fundamental building block for applications that use JCE. A **Cipher** performs encryption and decryption using a specified algorithm (e.g., DES, 3DES, Blowfish, etc.).

- The JCE includes the **SunJCE** provider, which has support for several common algorithms.

- A digital signature—the electronic equivalent of written signature—authenticates the sender's identity and, like a written signature, is difficult to forge. To create a digital signature, a sender first takes the original plaintext message and runs it through a hash function, which is a mathematical calculation that gives the message a hash value.

- The Secure Hash Algorithm (SHA-1) is the standard for hash functions. Running a message through the SHA-1 algorithm produces a 160-bit hash value.

- MD5 is another popular hash function, which was developed by Ronald Rivest to verify data integrity through a 128-bit hash value of the input file.

- The hash value is also known as a message digest. The chance that two different messages will have the same message digest is statistically insignificant.

- A digital certificate is a digital document that identifies a user and is issued by a certificate authority (CA). Digital certificates contain an expiration date to force users to switch key pairs. Canceled and revoked certificates are placed on a certificate revocation list (CRL). An alternative to CRLs is the Online Certificate Status Protocol (OCSP), which validates certificates in real-time. OCSP technology is currently under development.

- Java provides the **keytool** utility for managing and generating keys, certificates and digital signatures. A keystore is a repository for storing public and private keys. An alias identifies a particular public and private key pair.

- A trusted keystore is a keystore that contains certificates that the user knows to be correct, such as those from certificate authorities—to validate information with the signature.

- The basis of Java security is the Java Sandbox—the protected environment in which Java applications and applets run. The Java Sandbox security model is comprised of three individual security checks: the bytecode verifier, the class loader and security manager.

- Permissions may be granted on the basis of security policy files. Permissions are comprised of varying levels of access to specific resources. Any permission that is not declared explicitly in the policy file is not granted. The security policy files are external text files with certain syntax and class names.

- A system-wide security policy file is responsible for granting code the permission to access files and ports on the entire system. The virtual machine loads this policy file as part of the virtual machine's initialization. Particular applications can specify custom security policy files on the command line.

- Java applets run under strict security restrictions due to the unreliability of code downloading over public networks. Developers who wish to distribute applets with special permissions must sign those applets with digital signatures.

- Signing an applet with a digital signature requires that the signing party stores the applet and its supporting classes in a JAR file.

- Ensuring that users actually are who they claim to be is a large part of computer security, known as authentication. Java uses the Java Authentication and Authorization Service (JAAS) for authenticating and authorizing users.

- JAAS is based on a plug-in framework, which allows Kerberos and single sign-on to be implemented for authentication and authorization.

- Kerberos is a freely available open-source protocol developed at MIT. It employs secret-key cryptography to authenticate users in a network and to maintain the integrity and privacy of network communications.

- Java addresses the problems often associated with authenticating users and controlling access with the Java Authentication and Authorization Service (JAAS) API.

- The Pluggable Authentication Module (PAM) architecture is the standard method for authentication on which JAAS is based.

- After a user has been authenticated, JAAS can grant or restrict access to certain resources of an application. JAAS can control access by group, user or role-based security policies.

- User-based access control governs access to resources on an individual user basis. Group-based authorization identifies a user as a part of a group and grants access to certain resources based on the identifying group. Role-based access control (RBAC) is used in addition to group-access control, allowing for more control over resources.

- The Secure Sockets Layer (SSL) protocol, developed by Netscape Communications, is a nonproprietary protocol commonly used to secure communication between two computers on the Internet and the Web. SSL operates between the Internet's TCP/IP communications protocol and the application software.

- SSL implements public-key technology using the RSA algorithm and digital certificates to authenticate the server in a transaction and to protect private information.

- SSL is used primarily to secure point-to-point connections—transmissions of data from one computer to another. The Transport Layer Security (TLS) protocol, designed by the Internet Engineering Task Force, is similar to SSL.

- Sun's Java Secure Socket Extension (JSSE) provides encryption, message integrity checks and authentication of the server and client.

- Before the Java Virtual Machine executes a Java program, the bytecodes for that program must pass through the bytecode verifier. The bytecode verifier ensures that the bytecodes are valid Java bytecodes that do not perform certain illegal operations.

- The Java Virtual Machine checks any remaining cast operations to ensure their validity and performs array-bounds checking to prevent programs from reading arbitrary memory locations.

- The Java Virtual Machine uses class loaders to read class definitions from **.class** files and produce class representations in memory.

- The class loader uses separate namespaces to prevent malicious code from interacting with safe code. Every class that the JVM loads is assigned a corresponding set of unique names, known as a namespace. Namespaces in Java act as barriers between classes.

- The bootstrap class loader loads all of the trusted core Java classes.

- The Java security manager is the module that performs security checks while code is running. If, during run-time, code attempts to execute a dangerous operation, a security exception is generated.

- Final classes cannot be subclassed, and can help make an application more secure by preventing attackers from creating malicious subclasses that can cause damage to an application or gain access to protected information.

TERMINOLOGY

Advanced Encryption Standard (AES)
asymmetric algorithms
authentication
block
block-cipher
bootstrap class loader
brute-force
byte-code verifier
Caesar cipher
certificate authority hierarchy
certificate repository
certificate revocation list (CRL)
certification authority (CA)
cipher
Cipher class
ciphertext
class loader
codebase

collision
cryptanalysis
cryptography
cryptosystem
Data Encryption Standard (DES)
Decorator design pattern
decryption
DES cracker machine
Diffie-Hellman Key Agreement Protocol
digital certificate
digital envelope
digital IDs
digital signature
Digital Signature Algorithm (DSA)
encryption
hacker
hash function
hash value

integrity
Internet Engineering Task Force (IETF)
Internet Policy Registration Authority (IPRA)
Internet Protocol (IP)
Internet Security Architecture
Java Authentication and Authorization
    Service (JAAS)
Java Cryptography Extension (JCE)
Java Sandbox
Java Secure Socket Extension (JSSE)
Kerberos
key
key agreement protocol
key distribution center
key generation
key length
key management
keystore
keytool utility
message digest
message integrity
namespace
National Institute of Standards and Technology
network security
nonrepudiation
Password-Based Encryption (PBE)
permissions
plaintext
Pluggable Authentication Module (PAM)
point-to-point connection
policy creation authorities
policy file
policytool
privacy

private key
protocol
provider-based architecture
public key
Public Key Infrastructure (PKI)
public-key algorithms
public-key cryptography
restricted algorithms
Rijndael
Role-Based Access Control (RBAC)
root certification authority
root key
RSA Security, Inc.
runtime package
secret key
SecretKey class
Secure Sockets Layer (SSL)
security manager
service ticket
session keys
single sign-on
socket
strong encryption
substitution cipher
symmetric encryption algorithms
Ticket Granting Service (TGS)
Ticket Granting Ticket (TGT)
timestamping
timestamping agency
token
transposition cipher
Triple DES
VeriSign

SELF-REVIEW EXERCISES

7.1 State whether the following are *true* or *false*. If the answer is *false*, explain why.
  a) In a public-key algorithm, one key is used for both encryption and decryption.
  b) Digital certificates are intended to be used indefinitely.
  c) Secure Sockets Layer protects data stored on a merchant's server.
  d) Transport Layer Security is similar to the Secure Sockets Layer protocol.
  e) Digital signatures can be used to provide undeniable proof of the author of a document.
  f) In a network of 10 users communicating using public-key cryptography, only 10 keys are
     needed in total.
  g) The security of modern cryptosystems lies in the secrecy of the algorithm.
  h) Users should avoid changing keys as much as possible, unless they have reason to believe
     that the security of the key has been compromised.
  i) Increasing the security of a network often decreases its functionality and efficiency.
  j) Kerberos is an authentication protocol that is used over TCP/IP networks.
  k) SSL can be used to connect a network of computers over the Internet.

7.2   Fill in the blanks in each of the following statements:
   a) Cryptographic algorithms in which the message's sender and receiver both hold an identical key are called _____.
   b) A _____ is used to authenticate the sender of a document.
   c) In a _____, a document is encrypted using a symmetric secret key and sent with that symmetric secret key, encrypted using a public-key algorithm.
   d) A certificate that needs to be revoked before its expiration date is placed on a _____.
   e) A digital fingerprint of a document can be created using a _____.
   f) The four main issues addressed by cryptography are _____, _____, _____ and _____.
   g) Trying to decrypt ciphertext without knowing the decryption key is known as _____.
   h) A hacker that tries every possible solution to crack a code is using a method known as _____.

ANSWERS TO SELF-REVIEW EXERCISES

7.1   a) False. The encryption key is different from the decryption key. One is made public, and the other is kept private. b) False. Digital certificates are created with an expiration date to encourage users to periodically change their public/private-key pair. c) False. Secure Sockets Layer is an Internet security protocol, which secures the transfer of information in electronic communication. It does not protect data stored on a merchant's server. d) True. e) False. A user who digitally signed a document could later intentionally give up his or her private key and then claim that the document was written by an imposter. Thus, timestamping a document is necessary, so that users cannot repudiate documents written before the public/private-key pair is reported as invalidated. f) False. Each user needs a public key and a private key. Thus, in a network of 10 users, 20 keys are needed in total. g) False. The security of modern cryptosystems lies in the secrecy of the encryption and decryption keys. h) False. Changing keys often is a good way to maintain the security of a communication system. i) True. j) True. k) False, IPSec can connect a whole network of computers, while SSL can only connect two secure systems.

7.2   a) symmetric key algorithms. b) digital signature. c) digital envelope. d) certificate revocation list. e) hash function. f) privacy, authentication, integrity, nonrepudiation. g) cryptanalysis. h) brute-force hacking.

EXERCISES

7.3   Define each of the following security terms, and give an example of how it is used:
   a) secret-key cryptography
   b) public-key cryptography
   c) digital signature
   d) digital certificate
   e) hash function
   f) SSL
   g) Kerberos

7.4   Write the full name and describe each of the following acronyms:
   a) PKI
   b) CRL
   c) AES
   d) SSL

7.5   List the four problems addressed by cryptography, and give a real-world example of each.

7.6   Compare symmetric-key algorithms with public-key algorithms. What are the benefits and drawbacks of each type of algorithm? How are these differences manifested in the real-world uses of the two types of algorithms?

7.7   Create a simple application that reads a file; the application should accept the file path from the command line. Install a **SecurityManager** to control access and create two policy files—one that grants read permission to a particular directory (e.g., a **C:\readOnly** directory), and another that grants read permission to that directory for a specific codebase (e.g., the **C:/myclasses** codebase). [*Note*: Code always has read permission to the directory in which it is running and any subdirectories.]

7.8   Using your solution to Exercise 7.7, store your application in a JAR file. Sign the JAR file with a digital signature (use the **keytool** to create a public/private key pair); grant read permission to the directory for code signed by this signature in a policy file. [Note: To grant permission for a particular digital signature, use the **signedBy** field in a **grant** statement. The **signedBy** field requires that you specify the keystore in which this public/private key pair is stored using a **keystore "keystore_URL";** statement outside of the **grant** statements in the policy file.]

WORKS CITED

1.   "RSA Laboratories' Frequently Asked Questions About Today's Cryptography, Version 4.1," <**www.rsasecurity.com/rsalabs/faq**>.

2.   "Math 5410 Data Encryption Standard (DES)," <**www-math.cudenver.edu/ ~wcherowi/courses/m5410/m5410des.html**>.

3.   M. Dworkin, "Advanced Encryption Standard (AES) Fact Sheet," 5 March 2001.

4.   "The Block Cipher Rijndael," <**www.esat.kuleuven.ac.be/~rijmen/rijndael**>.

5.   "RSA-Based Cryptographic Schemes," <**www.rsasecurity.com/rsalabs/ rsa_algorithm**>.

6.   "Overview of PGP," <**www.pgpi.org/doc/overview**>.

7.   "RSA Laboratories' Frequency Asked Questions About JAAS," <**www.rsasecurity.com/rsalabs/faq**>.

8.   "MD5 Homepage (Unofficial)," <**userpages.umbc.edu/~mabzug1/cs/md5/ md5.html**>.

9.   G. Hulme, "VeriSign Gave Microsoft Certificates to Imposter," Information Week 3 March 2001.

10.   C. Ellison and B. Schneier, "Ten Risks of PKI: What You're not Being Told about Public Key Infrastructure," Computer Security Journal 2000.

11.   "keytool—Key and Certificate Management Tool," <**java.sun.com/products/jdk/ 1.2/docs/tooldocs/solaris/keytool.html**>.

12.   B. Venners, <**www.javaworld.com/javaworld/jw-08-1997/jw-08- hood_p.html**>.

13.   "Introducing Java 2 Security," <**www.ryerson.ca/~dgrimsha/courses/cps530/ securityFrame.html**>.

14.   R. Baldwin, "Security, Policy Files in JDK 1.2," <**home.att.net/~baldwin.rick/ Advanced/Java715.htm**>.

15.   F. Trickey, "Secure Single Sign-On: Fantasy or Reality," Computer Security Institute, <**www.gocsi.com/sso_ft.htm**>.

16. C. Lai, et al., "User Authentication and Authorization in the Java™ Platform," **<java.sun.com/security/jaas/doc/acsac.html>**.

17. B. Rich, "JAAS Java Authentication and Authorization Services," O'Reilly Conference on Enterprise Java, 26-29 March 2001 **<ftp.oreilly.com/pub/conference/java2001/ Rich_Jaas.pdf>**.

18. "Java Authentication and Authorization Service (JAAS)," **<www.onjava.com/pub/st/7>**.

19. "Role Based Access Control," NIST Web site **<csrc.nist.gov/rbac>**.

20. S. Abbot, "The Debate for Secure E-Commerce," Performance Computing February 1999: 37-42.

21. T. Wilson, "E-Biz Bucks Lost Under the SSL Train," Internet Week 24 May 1999: 1, 3.

22. "Security Protocols Overview," **<www.rsasecurity.com/standards/protocols>**.

23. "Java Secure Socket Extension (JSSE)," **<java.sun.com/products/jsse>**.

24. J. Jaworski, "Secure Your Sockets With JSSE," November 1997 **<www.onjava.com/pub/ a/onjava/2001/05/03/java_security.html>**.

25. K. Angell, "The Java Secure Socket Extensions," February 2001 **<www.ddj.com/arti- cles/2001/0102/0102a/0102a.htm?topic=security>**.

26. B. Venners, "Security," *Inside the Java 2 Virtual Machine* **<www.artima.com/inside- jvm/ed2/ch03Security2.html>**.

27. B. Venners, "Java Security: How to Install the Security Manager and Customize Your Secu- rity Policy," November 1997 **<www.javaworld.com/javaworld/jw-11-1997/jw-11- hood_p.html>**.

28. "Writing Final Classes and Methods," **<java.sun.com/docs/books/tutorial/ java/javaOO/final.html>**.

BIBLIOGRAPHY

Bank, J. "Java Security," (August 1994) **<www.swiss.ai.mit.edu/~jbank/javapaper/ javapaper.html>**.

Bringer, P. "Creating Signed, Persistent Java Applets," *Dr. Dobb's Journal*, February 1999, 82-88.

Garms, J. and D. Somerfield. "Java 2 Cryptography," *Java Pro*, October 1999, 30-37.

Heiser, J. "Java and Cryptography," *Java Developer's Journal*, 2: no. 5 (1997): 36-38.

Heiser, J. "Java Security Mechanisms," *Java Developer's Journal*, 2: no. 5 (1997): 36-38.

Mahmoud, Q. "Implementing a Security Policy," *Java Developer's Journal*, 2: no. 8 (1997): 52-54.

McGraw, G and E. Felten, "New Issues in Java Security," *Enterprise Java Development*, August 1998, 52-56.

Moreh, J. "Protection Domains," *Java Developer's Journal*, 3: no. 5 (1998):16-22.

Neville, P. "Mastering Java Security Policies and Permissions," *Java Developer's Journal*, no. 7 (2000): 22-28.

Sagar, A. "Securing Java Commerce," *Java Developer's Journal*, 4: no. 6 (1999): 40-44.

Java Database Connectivity (JDBC)

Objectives

- To understand the relational-database model.
- To understand basic database queries using Structured Query Language (SQL).
- To use the classes and interfaces of package **java.sql** to manipulate databases.
- To use transaction processing to prevent database updates from modifying the database if an error occurs during a transaction.
- To introduce the JDBC 2.0 optional package **javax.sql**'s capabilities for obtaining database connections, creating connection pools and treating result sets as JavaBeans.

It is a capital mistake to theorize before one has data.
Arthur Conan Doyle

Now go, write it before them in a table, and note it in a book, that it may be for the time to come for ever and ever.
The Holy Bible: The Old Testament

Let's look at the record.
Alfred Emanuel Smith

Get your facts first, and then you can distort them as much as you please.
Mark Twain

I like two kinds of men: domestic and foreign.
Mae West

Outline

8.1 Introduction

A *database* is an integrated collection of data. There are many different strategies for organizing data to facilitate easy access and manipulation of the data. A *database management system* (*DBMS*) provides mechanisms for storing and organizing data in a manner consistent with the database's format. Database management systems allow for the access and storage of data without worrying about the internal representation of databases.

Today's most popular database systems are *relational databases*. A language called *Structured Query Language* (*SQL*—pronounced as its individual letters, or as "sequel") is used almost universally with relational-database systems to perform *queries* (i.e., to request information that satisfies given criteria) and to manipulate data. [*Note*: In this chapter, we assume that SQL is pronounced as its individual letters. For this reason, we often precede SQL with the article "an," as in "an SQL database" or "an SQL statement."]

Some popular enterprise-level relational-database systems are Microsoft SQL Server, Oracle, Sybase, DB2, Informix and MySQL. In this chapter, we present examples using *Cloudscape 3.6.4*—a pure-Java database management system from Informix Software. Cloudscape 3.6.4 is on the CD that accompanies this book and can be downloaded from **www.cloudscape.com**. Later chapters reuse the material presented in this chapter. Chapter 11 introduces the *Java 2 Enterprise Edition reference implementation*, which includes an earlier version of Cloudscape. That chapter discusses how to integrate the latest version of Cloudscape with the Java 2 Enterprise Edition. [*Note*: We discuss basic Cloudscape features required to execute the examples in this chapter. Please refer to the detailed Cloudscape documentation for complete information on using Cloudscape.]

Java programs communicate with databases and manipulate their data using the *Java Database Connectivity* (*JDBC*) *API*. A *JDBC driver* implements the interface to a particular database. This separation of the API from particular drivers enables developers to change the underlying database without modifying Java code that accesses the database. Most popular database management systems now include JDBC drivers. There are also many third-party JDBC drivers available. In this chapter, we introduce JDBC and use it to manipulate a Cloudscape database. The techniques demonstrated here also can be used to manipulate other databases that have JDBC drivers. Check your database management system's documentation to determine whether your DBMS comes with a JDBC driver. Even if your DBMS does not come with a JDBC driver, many third-party vendors provide JDBC drivers for a wide variety of databases. For more information on JDBC, visit

> **java.sun.com/products/jdbc/**

This site contains information concerning JDBC, including the JDBC specifications, FAQs on JDBC, a learning resource center, software downloads and other important information. For a list of available JDBC drivers, visit

> **industry.java.sun.com/products/jdbc/drivers/**

This site provides a search engine to help you locate drivers appropriate to your DBMS.

8.2 Relational-Database Model

The *relational-database model* is a logical representation of data that allows the relationships between the data to be examined without consideration of the physical structure of the data. A relational database is composed of *tables*. Figure 8.1 illustrates a sample table that might be used in a personnel system. The table name is **Employee**, and its primary purpose is to illustrate the attributes of an employee and how they are related to a specific employee. Each row of the table is called a *record*. This table consists of six records. The **Number** *field* (or *column*) of each record in this table is the *primary key* for referencing data in the table. A primary key is a field (or fields) in a table that contain(s) unique data that cannot be duplicated in other records. This guarantees that each record can be identified by a unique value. Good

	Number	Name	Department	Salary	Location
	23603	Jones	413	1100	New Jersey
	24568	Kerwin	413	2000	New Jersey
Row/Record	34589	Larson	642	1800	Los Angeles
	35761	Myers	611	1400	Orlando
	47132	Neumann	413	9000	New Jersey
	78321	Stephens	611	8500	Orlando

Primary key   Column/Field

Fig. 8.1   Relational-database structure of an **Employee** table.

examples of primary key fields are a Social Security number, an employee ID number and a part number in an inventory system. The records of Fig. 8.1 are *ordered* by primary key. In this case, the records are listed in increasing order; we could also use decreasing order.

Each column of the table represents a different *field* (or *column,* or *attribute*). Records are normally unique (by primary key) within a table, but particular field values may be duplicated between records. For example, three different records in the **Employee** table's **Department** field contain number 413.

Different users of a database often are interested in different data and different relationships among those data. Some users require only subsets of the table columns. To obtain table subsets, we use SQL statements to specify the data to *select* from a table. SQL provides a complete set of commands (including *SELECT*) that enable programmers to define complex *queries* that select data from a table. The results of a query are commonly called *result sets* (or *record sets*). For example, we might select data from the table in Fig. 8.1 to create a new result set that shows where departments are located. This result set is shown in Fig. 8.2. SQL queries are discussed in Section 8.4.

8.3 Relational Database Overview: The books Database

This section gives an overview of SQL in the context of a sample **books** database we created for this chapter. Before we discuss SQL, we overview the tables of the **books** database. We use this to introduce various database concepts, including the use of SQL to obtain useful information from the database and to manipulate the database. We provide a script to create the database. You can find the script in the examples directory for this chapter on the CD that accompanies this book. Section 8.5 explains how to use this script.

Department	Location
413	New Jersey
611	Orlando
642	Los Angeles

Fig. 8.2   Result set formed by selecting **Department** and **Location** data from the **Employee** table.

The database consists of four tables: **authors**, **publishers**, **authorISBN** and **titles**. The **authors** table (described in Fig. 8.3) consists of three fields (or columns) that maintain each author's unique ID number, first name and last name. Figure 8.4 contains the data from the **authors** table of the **books** database.

The **publishers** table (described in Fig. 8.5) consists of two fields representing each publisher's unique ID and name. Figure 8.6 contains the data from the **publishers** table of the **books** database.

Field	Description
authorID	Author's ID number in the database. In the **books** database, this integer field is defined as an *autoincremented field*. For each new record inserted in this table, the database automatically increments the **authorID** value to ensure that each record has a unique **authorID**. This field represents the table's primary key.
firstName	Author's first name (a string).
lastName	Author's last name (a string).

Fig. 8.3   **authors** table from **books**.

authorID	firstName	lastName
1	Harvey	Deitel
2	Paul	Deitel
3	Tem	Nieto
4	Sean	Santry

Fig. 8.4   Data from the **authors** table of **books**.

Field	Description
publisherID	The publisher's ID number in the database. This autoincremented integer is the table's primary-key field.
publisherName	The name of the publisher (a string).

Fig. 8.5   **publishers** table from **books**.

publisherID	publisherName
1	Prentice Hall
2	Prentice Hall PTG

Fig. 8.6   Data from the **publishers** table of **books**.

The **authorISBN** table (described in Fig. 8.7) consists of two fields that maintain each ISBN number and its corresponding author's ID number. This table helps associate the names of the authors with the titles of their books. Figure 8.8 contains the data from the **authorISBN** table of the **books** database. ISBN is an abbreviation for "International Standard Book Number"—a numbering scheme that publishers worldwide use to give every book a unique identification number. [*Note*: To save space, we have split the contents of this table into two columns, each containing the **authorID** and **isbn** fields.]

Field	Description
authorID	The author's ID number, which allows the database to associate each book with a specific author. The integer ID number in this field must also appear in the **authors** table.
isbn	The ISBN number for a book (a string).

Fig. 8.7   **authorISBN** table from **books**.

authorID	isbn	authorID	isbn
1	0130895725	2	0139163050
1	0132261197	2	013028419x
1	0130895717	2	0130161438
1	0135289106	2	0130856118
1	0139163050	2	0130125075
1	013028419x	2	0138993947
1	0130161438	2	0130852473
1	0130856118	2	0130829277
1	0130125075	2	0134569555
1	0138993947	2	0130829293
1	0130852473	2	0130284173
1	0130829277	2	0130284181
1	0134569555	2	0130895601
1	0130829293	3	013028419x
1	0130284173	3	0130161438
1	0130284181	3	0130856118
1	0130895601	3	0134569555
2	0130895725	3	0130829293
2	0132261197	3	0130284173
2	0130895717	3	0130284181
2	0135289106	4	0130895601

Fig. 8.8   Data from the **authorISBN** table of **books**.

The **titles** table (described in Fig. 8.9) consists of six fields that maintain general information about each book in the database, including the ISBN number, title, edition number, copyright year, publisher's ID number, name of a file containing an image of the book cover, and finally, the price. Figure 8.10 contains the data from the **titles** table.

Field	Description
isbn	ISBN number of the book (a string).
title	Title of the book (a string).
editionNumber	Edition number of the book (an integer).
copyright	Copyright year of the book (a string).
publisherID	Publisher's ID number (an integer). This value must correspond to an ID number in the **publishers** table.
imageFile	Name of the file containing the book's cover image (a string).
price	Suggested retail price of the book (a real number). [*Note*: The prices shown in this book are for example purposes only.]

Fig. 8.9   **titles** table from **books**.

isbn	title	edition-Number	copy-right	publish-erID	image-File	price
0130895725	C How to Program	3	2001	1	**chtp3.jpg**	69.95
0132261197	C How to Program	2	1994	1	**chtp2.jpg**	49.95
0130895717	C++ How to Program	3	2001	1	**cpphtp3.jpg**	69.95
0135289106	C++ How to Program	2	1998	1	**cpphtp2.jpg**	49.95
0139163050	The Complete C++ Training Course	3	2001	2	**cppctc3.jpg**	109.95
013028419x	e-Business and e-Commerce How to Program	1	2001	1	**ebechtp1.jpg**	69.95
0130161438	Internet and World Wide Web How to Program	1	2000	1	**iw3htp1.jpg**	69.95
0130856118	The Complete Internet and World Wide Web Programming Training Course	1	2000	2	**iw3ctc1.jpg**	109.95
0130125075	Java How to Program (Java 2)	3	2000	1	**jhtp3.jpg**	69.95
0138993947	Java How to Program (Java 1.1)	2	1998	1	**jhtp2.jpg**	49.95

Fig. 8.10   Data from the **titles** table of **books** (part 1 of 2).

isbn	title	edition-Number	copy-right	publish-erID	image-File	price
0130852473	The Complete Java 2 Training Course	3	2000	2	`javactc3.jpg`	109.95
0130829277	The Complete Java Training Course (Java 1.1)	2	1998	2	`javactc2.jpg`	99.95
0134569555	Visual Basic 6 How to Program	1	1999	1	`vbhtp1.jpg`	69.95
0130829293	The Complete Visual Basic 6 Training Course	1	1999	2	`vbctc1.jpg`	109.95
0130284173	XML How to Program	1	2001	1	`xmlhtp1.jpg`	69.95
0130284181	Perl How to Program	1	2001	1	`perlhtp1.jpg`	69.95
0130895601	Advanced Java 2 Platform How to Program	1	2002	1	`advjhtp1.jpg`	69.95

Fig. 8.10 Data from the **titles** table of **books** (part 2 of 2).

Figure 8.11 illustrates the relationships among the tables in the **books** database. The first line in each table is the table's name. The field name in green contains that table's primary key. A table's primary key uniquely identifies each record in the table. Every record must have a value in the primary-key field, and the value must be unique. This is known as the *Rule of Entity Integrity.*

Common Programming Error 8.1

Not providing a value for a primary-key field in every record breaks the Rule of Entity Integrity and causes the DBMS to report an error.

Common Programming Error 8.2

Providing duplicate values for the primary-key field in multiple records causes the DBMS to report an error.

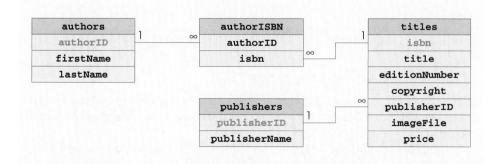

Fig. 8.11 Table relationships in **books**.

The lines connecting the tables in Fig. 8.11 represent the *relationships* between the tables. Consider the line between the **publishers** and **titles** tables. On the **publishers** end of the line, there is a **1**, and on the **titles** end, there is an infinity (∞) symbol, indicating a *one-to-many relationship* in which every publisher in the **publishers** table can have an arbitrarily large number of books in the **titles** table. Note that the relationship line links the **publisherID** field in the table **publishers** to the **publisherID** field in table **titles**. The **publisherID** field in the **titles** table is a *foreign key*—a field for which every entry has a unique value in another table and where the field in the other table is the primary key for that table (e.g., **publisherID** in the **publishers** table). Foreign keys are specified when creating a table. The foreign key helps maintain the *Rule of Referential Integrity*: Every foreign key-field value must appear in another table's primary-key field. Foreign keys enable information from multiple tables to be *joined* together for analysis purposes. There is a one-to-many relationship between a primary key and its corresponding foreign key. This means that a foreign key-field value can appear many times in its own table, but can only appear once as the primary key of another table. The line between the tables represents the link between the foreign key in one table and the primary key in another table.

Common Programming Error 8.3

Providing a foreign-key value that does not appear as a primary-key value in another table breaks the Rule of Referential Integrity and causes the DBMS to report an error.

The line between the **authorISBN** and **authors** tables indicates that for each author in the **authors** table, there can be an arbitrary number of ISBNs for books written by that author in the **authorISBN** table. The **authorID** field in the **authorISBN** table is a foreign key of the **authorID** field (the primary key) of the **authors** table. Note again that the line between the tables links the foreign key of table **authorISBN** to the corresponding primary key in table **authors**. The **authorISBN** table links information in the **titles** and **authors** tables.

Finally, the line between the **titles** and **authorISBN** tables illustrates a one-to-many relationship; a title can be written by any number of authors. In fact, the sole purpose of the **authorISBN** table is to represent a many-to-many relationship between the **authors** and **titles** tables; an author can write any number of books and a book can have any number of authors.

8.4 Structured Query Language (SQL)

In this section, we provide an overview of SQL in the context of our **books** sample database. You will be able to use the SQL queries discussed here in the examples later in the chapter.

The SQL keywords listed in Fig. 8.12 are discussed in the context of complete SQL queries in the next several subsections; other SQL keywords are beyond the scope of this text. [*Note*: For more information on SQL, please refer to the World Wide Web resources in Section 8.13 and the bibliography at the end of this chapter.]

SQL keyword	Description
SELECT	Select (retrieve) fields from one or more tables.
FROM	Tables from which to get fields. Required in every **SELECT**.
WHERE	Criteria for selection that determine the rows to be retrieved.
GROUP BY	Criteria for grouping records.
ORDER BY	Criteria for ordering records.
INSERT INTO	Insert data into a specified table.
UPDATE	Update data in a specified table.
DELETE FROM	Delete data from a specified table.

Fig. 8.12   SQL query keywords.

8.4.1 Basic SELECT Query

Let us consider several SQL queries that extract information from database **books**. A typical SQL query "selects" information from one or more tables in a database. Such selections are performed by **SELECT** *queries*. The simplest format of a **SELECT** query is

> SELECT * FROM *tableName*

In this query, the asterisk (*****) indicates that all rows and columns from the *tableName* table of the database should be selected. For example, to select the entire contents of the **authors** table (i.e., all the data in Fig. 8.4), use the query

> SELECT * FROM authors

To select specific fields from a table, replace the asterisk (*****) with a comma-separated list of the field names to select. For example, to select only the fields **authorID** and **lastName** for all rows in the **authors** table, use the query

> SELECT authorID, lastName FROM authors

This query returns the data listed in Fig. 8.13. [*Note*: If a field name contains spaces, it must be enclosed in square brackets (**[]**) in the query. For example, if the field name is **first name**, the field name would appear in the query as **[first name]**.]

authorID	lastName
1	Deitel
2	Deitel
3	Nieto
4	Santry

Fig. 8.13   **authorID** and **lastName** from the **authors** table.

Software Engineering Observation 8.1

*For most SQL statements, the asterisk (***** *) should not be used to specify field names to select from a table (or several tables). In general, programmers process result sets by knowing in advance the order of the fields in the result set. For example, selecting **authorID** and **lastName** from table **authors** guarantees that the fields will appear in the result set with **authorID** as the first field and **lastName** as the second field. As you will see, programs typically process result set fields by specifying the column number in the result set (column numbers start at 1 for the first field in the result set).*

Software Engineering Observation 8.2

Specifying the field names to select from a table (or several tables) guarantees that the fields are always returned in the specified order and also avoid returning unused fields, even if the actual order of the fields in the database table(s) changes.

Common Programming Error 8.4

*If a programmer assumes that the fields in a result set are always returned in the same order from an SQL statement that uses the asterisk (***** *) to select fields, the program may process the result set incorrectly. If the field order in the database table(s) changes, the order of the fields in the result set would change accordingly.*

Performance Tip 8.1

If the order of fields in a result set is unknown to a program, the program must process the fields by name. This can require a linear search of the field names in the result set. Specifying the field names to select from a table (or several tables) enables the application receiving the result set to know the order of the fields in advance. In this case, the program can process the data more efficiently, because fields can be accessed directly by column number.

8.4.2 WHERE Clause

In most cases, it is necessary to locate records in a database that satisfy certain *selection criteria*. Only records that match the selection criteria are selected. SQL uses the optional **WHERE** *clause* in a **SELECT** query to specify the selection criteria for the query. The simplest format of a **SELECT** query with selection criteria is

> **SELECT** *fieldName1*, *fieldName2*, … **FROM** *tableName* **WHERE** *criteria*

For example, to select the **title**, **editionNumber** and **copyright** fields from table **titles** for which the **copyright** date is greater than **1999**, use the query

```
SELECT title, editionNumber, copyright
   FROM titles
   WHERE copyright > 1999
```

Figure 8.14 shows the results of the preceding query. [*Note*: When we construct a query for use in Java, we simply create a **String** containing the entire query. When we display queries in the text, we often use multiple lines and indentation for readability.]

Performance Tip 8.2

Using selection criteria improves performance by selecting a portion of the database that is normally smaller than the entire database. Working with a smaller portion of the data is more efficient than working with the entire set of data stored in the database.

title	editionNumber	copyright
C How to Program	3	2001
C++ How to Program	3	2001
The Complete C++ Training Course	3	2001
e-Business and e-Commerce How to Program	1	2001
Internet and World Wide Web How to Program	1	2000
The Complete Internet and World Wide Web Programming Training Course	1	2000
Java How to Program (Java 2)	3	2000
The Complete Java 2 Training Course	3	2000
XML How to Program	1	2001
Perl How to Program	1	2001
Advanced Java 2 Platform How to Program	1	2002

Fig. 8.14 Titles with copyrights after 1999 from table **titles**.

The **WHERE** clause condition can contain operators **<**, **>**, **<=**, **>=**, **=**, **<>** and **LIKE**. Operator **LIKE** is used for *pattern matching* with wildcard characters *percent* (**%**) and *underscore* (**_**). Pattern matching allows SQL to search for similar strings that match a given pattern.

A pattern that contains a percent character (**%**) searches for strings that have zero or more characters at the percent character's position in the pattern. For example, the following query locates the records of all the authors whose last name starts with the letter **D**:

```
SELECT authorID, firstName, lastName
    FROM authors
    WHERE lastName LIKE 'D%'
```

The preceding query selects the two records shown in Fig. 8.15, because two of the four authors in our database have a last name starting with the letter **D** (followed by zero or more characters). The **%** in the **WHERE** clause's **LIKE** pattern indicates that any number of characters can appear after the letter **D** in the **lastName** field. Notice that the pattern string is surrounded by single-quote characters.

authorID	firstName	lastName
1	Harvey	Deitel
2	Paul	Deitel

Fig. 8.15 Authors whose last name starts with **D** from the **authors** table.

Portability Tip 8.1

See the documentation for your database system to determine whether SQL is case sensitive on your system and to determine the syntax for SQL keywords (i.e., should they be all uppercase letters, all lowercase letters or some combination of the two?).

Portability Tip 8.2

*Not all database systems support the **LIKE** operator, so be sure to read your database system's documentation carefully.*

Portability Tip 8.3

*Some databases use the * character in place of the % character in a **LIKE** expression.*

Portability Tip 8.4

In some databases (including Cloudscape), string data is case sensitive.

Good Programming Practice 8.1

By convention, SQL keywords should use all uppercase letters on systems that are not case sensitive, to emphasize the SQL keywords in an SQL statement.

An underscore (_) in the pattern string indicates a single character at that position in the pattern. For example, the following query locates the records of all the authors whose last name starts with any character (specified by _), followed by the letter **i**, followed by any number of additional characters (specified by **%**):

```
SELECT authorID, firstName, lastName
    FROM authors
    WHERE lastName LIKE '_i%'
```

The preceding query produces the record shown in Fig. 8.16, because only one author in our database has a last name that contains the letter **i** as its second letter.

Portability Tip 8.5

*Some databases use the **?** character in place of the _ character in a **LIKE** expression.*

8.4.3 ORDER BY Clause

The results of a query can be arranged in ascending or descending order by using the optional ***ORDER BY*** *clause*. The simplest form of an **ORDER BY** clause is

```
SELECT fieldName1, fieldName2, ... FROM tableName ORDER BY field ASC
SELECT fieldName1, fieldName2, ... FROM tableName ORDER BY field DESC
```

authorID	firstName	lastName
3	Tem	Nieto

Fig. 8.16 The only author from the **authors** table whose last name contains **i** as the second letter.

where **ASC** specifies ascending order (lowest to highest), **DESC** specifies descending order (highest to lowest) and *field* specifies the field on which the sort is based.

For example, to obtain the list of authors in ascending order by last name (Fig. 8.17), use the query

```
SELECT authorID, firstName, lastName
    FROM authors
    ORDER BY lastName ASC
```

Note that the default sorting order is ascending, so **ASC** is optional. To obtain the same list of authors in descending order by last name (Fig. 8.18), use the query

```
SELECT authorID, firstName, lastName
    FROM authors
    ORDER BY lastName DESC
```

Multiple fields can be used for ordering purposes with an **ORDER BY** clause of the form

```
ORDER BY field1 sortingOrder, field2 sortingOrder, ...
```

where *sortingOrder* is either **ASC** or **DESC**. Note that the *sortingOrder* does not have to be identical for each field. The query

```
SELECT authorID, firstName, lastName
    FROM authors
    ORDER BY lastName, firstName
```

sorts in ascending order all the authors by last name, then by first name. If any authors have the same last name, their records are returned in sorted order by their first name (Fig. 8.19).

authorID	firstName	lastName
2	Paul	Deitel
1	Harvey	Deitel
3	Tem	Nieto
4	Sean	Santry

Fig. 8.17 Authors from table **authors** in ascending order by **lastName**.

authorID	firstName	lastName
4	Sean	Santry
3	Tem	Nieto
2	Paul	Deitel
1	Harvey	Deitel

Fig. 8.18 Authors from table **authors** in descending order by **lastName**.

authorID	firstName	lastName
1	Harvey	Deitel
2	Paul	Deitel
3	Tem	Nieto
4	Sean	Santry

Fig. 8.19 Authors from table **authors** in ascending order by **lastName** and by **firstName**.

The **WHERE** and **ORDER BY** clauses can be combined in one query. For example, the query

```
SELECT isbn, title, editionNumber, copyright, price
   FROM titles
   WHERE title
   LIKE '%How to Program' ORDER BY title ASC
```

returns the **isbn**, **title**, **editionNumber**, **copyright** and **price** of each book in the **titles** table that has a **title** ending with "**How to Program**" and orders them in ascending order by **title**. The results of the query are shown in Fig. 8.20. Note that the title "e-Business and e-Commerce How to Program" appears at the end of the list, because Cloudscape uses the Unicode numeric values of the characters for comparison purposes. Remember that lowercase letters have larger numeric values than uppercase letters.

isbn	title	edition-Number	copy-right	price
0130895601	Advanced Java 2 Platform How to Program	1	2002	69.95
0132261197	C How to Program	2	1994	49.95
0130895725	C How to Program	3	2001	69.95
0135289106	C++ How to Program	2	1998	49.95
0130895717	C++ How to Program	3	2001	69.95
0130161438	Internet and World Wide Web How to Program	1	2000	69.95
0130284181	Perl How to Program	1	2001	69.95
0134569555	Visual Basic 6 How to Program	1	1999	69.95
0130284173	XML How to Program	1	2001	69.95
013028419x	e-Business and e-Commerce How to Program	1	2001	69.95

Fig. 8.20 Books from table **titles** whose title ends with **How to Program** in ascending order by **title**.

8.4.4 Merging Data from Multiple Tables: Joining

Often, it is necessary to merge data from multiple tables into a single view for analysis purposes. This is referred to as *joining* the tables and is accomplished by using a comma-separated list of tables in the **FROM** clause of a **SELECT** query. A join merges records from two or more tables by testing for matching values in a field that is common to both tables. The simplest format of a join is

```
SELECT fieldName1, fieldName2, ...
    FROM table1, table2
    WHERE table1.fieldName = table2.fieldName
```

The query's **WHERE** clause specifies the fields from each table that should be compared to determine which records will be selected. These fields normally represent the primary key in one table and the corresponding foreign key in the other table. For example, the following query produces a list of authors and the ISBN numbers for the books that each author wrote:

```
SELECT firstName, lastName, isbn
    FROM authors, authorISBN
    WHERE authors.authorID = authorISBN.authorID
    ORDER BY lastName, firstName
```

The query merges the **firstName** and **lastName** fields from table **authors** and the **isbn** field from table **authorISBN** and sorts the results in ascending order by **lastName** and **firstName**. Notice the use of the syntax *tableName.fieldName* in the **WHERE** clause of the query. This syntax (called a *fully qualified name*) specifies the fields from each table that should be compared to join the tables. The "*tableName.*" syntax is required if the fields have the same name in both tables.

Software Engineering Observation 8.3

If an SQL statement uses fields with the same name from multiple tables, the field name must be fully qualified with its table name and a dot operator (.), as in **authors.authorID***.*

Common Programming Error 8.5

In a query, not providing fully qualified names for fields with the same name from two or more tables is an error.

As always, the **FROM** clause can be followed by an **ORDER BY** clause. Figure 8.21 shows the results of the preceding query. [*Note*: To save space, we split the results of the query into two columns, each containing the **firstName**, **lastName** and **isbn** fields.]

firstName	lastName	isbn	firstName	lastName	isbn
Harvey	Deitel	0130895601	Harvey	Deitel	0130284173
Harvey	Deitel	0130284181	Harvey	Deitel	0130829293

Fig. 8.21   Authors and the ISBN numbers for the books they have written in ascending order by **lastName** and **firstName** (part 1 of 2).

firstName	lastName	isbn	firstName	lastName	isbn
Harvey	Deitel	0134569555	Paul	Deitel	0130852473
Harvey	Deitel	0130829277	Paul	Deitel	0138993947
Harvey	Deitel	0130852473	Paul	Deitel	0130125075
Harvey	Deitel	0138993947	Paul	Deitel	0130856118
Harvey	Deitel	0130125075	Paul	Deitel	0130161438
Harvey	Deitel	0130856118	Paul	Deitel	013028419x
Harvey	Deitel	0130161438	Paul	Deitel	0139163050
Harvey	Deitel	013028419x	Paul	Deitel	0135289106
Harvey	Deitel	0139163050	Paul	Deitel	0130895717
Harvey	Deitel	0135289106	Paul	Deitel	0132261197
Harvey	Deitel	0130895717	Paul	Deitel	0130895725
Harvey	Deitel	0132261197	Tem	Nieto	0130284181
Harvey	Deitel	0130895725	Tem	Nieto	0130284173
Paul	Deitel	0130895601	Tem	Nieto	0130829293
Paul	Deitel	0130284181	Tem	Nieto	0134569555
Paul	Deitel	0130284173	Tem	Nieto	0130856118
Paul	Deitel	0130829293	Tem	Nieto	0130161438
Paul	Deitel	0134569555	Tem	Nieto	013028419x
Paul	Deitel	0130829277	Sean	Santry	0130895601

Fig. 8.21   Authors and the ISBN numbers for the books they have written in ascending order by `lastName` and `firstName` (part 2 of 2).

8.4.5 INSERT INTO Statement

The *INSERT INTO* statement inserts a new record into a table. The simplest form of this statement is

```
INSERT INTO tableName ( fieldName1, fieldName2, ..., fieldNameN )
    VALUES ( value1, value2, ..., valueN )
```

where *tableName* is the table in which to insert the record. The *tableName* is followed by a comma-separated list of field names in parentheses (this list is not required if the **INSERT INTO** operation specifies a value for every column of the table in the correct order). The list of field names is followed by the SQL keyword **VALUES** and a comma-separated list of values in parentheses. The values specified here should match the field names specified after the table name in order and type (i.e., if *fieldName1* is supposed to be the **firstName** field, then *value1* should be a string in single quotes representing the first name). Always use the list of field names when inserting new records. If the order of the fields changes in the table, entering only **VALUES** may cause an error. The **INSERT INTO** statement

```
INSERT INTO authors ( firstName, lastName )
    VALUES ( 'Sue', 'Smith' )
```

inserts a record into the **authors** table. The statement indicates that values will be inserted for the **firstName** and **lastName** fields. The corresponding values to insert are **'Sue'** and **'Smith'**. We do not specify an **authorID** in this example, because **authorID** is an *autoincremented field* in the Cloudscape database. For every new record added to this table, Cloudscape assigns a unique **authorID** value that is the next value in the autoincremented sequence (i.e., 1, 2, 3 and so on). In this case, Sue Smith would be assigned **authorID** number 5. Figure 8.22 shows the **authors** table after the **INSERT INTO** operation.

Common Programming Error 8.6

It is an error to specify a value for an autoincrement field.

Common Programming Error 8.7

SQL statements use the single-quote (') character as a delimiter for strings. To specify a string containing a single quote (such as O'Malley) in an SQL statement, the string must have two single quotes in the position where the single-quote character appears in the string (e.g., **'O''Malley'***). The first of the two single-quote characters acts as an escape character for the second. Not escaping single-quote characters in a string that is part of an SQL statement is an SQL syntax error.*

8.4.6 UPDATE Statement

An ***UPDATE*** statement modifies data in a table. The simplest form for an **UPDATE** statement is

```
UPDATE  tableName
    SET  fieldName1 = value1, fieldName2 = value2, ..., fieldNameN = valueN
    WHERE  criteria
```

where *tableName* is the table in which to update a record (or records). The *tableName* is followed by keyword ***SET*** and a comma-separated list of field name/value pairs in the format *fieldName = value*. The **WHERE** clause provides the criteria that specify which record(s) to update. The **UPDATE** statement

```
UPDATE  authors
    SET  lastName = 'Jones'
    WHERE  lastName = 'Smith' AND firstName = 'Sue'
```

authorID	firstName	lastName
1	Harvey	Deitel
2	Paul	Deitel
3	Tem	Nieto
4	Sean	Santry
5	Sue	Smith

Fig. 8.22   Table **Authors** after an **INSERT INTO** operation to add a record.

updates a record in the **authors** table. The statement indicates that the **lastName** will be assigned the value **Jones** for the record in which **lastName** is equal to **Smith** and **firstName** is equal to **Sue**. [*Note:* If there are multiple records with the first name "Sue" and the last name "Smith," this statement will modify all such records to have the last name "Jones."] If we know the **authorID** in advance of the **UPDATE** operation (possibly because we searched for the record previously), the **WHERE** clause could be simplified as follows:

```
WHERE AuthorID = 5
```

Figure 8.23 shows the **authors** table after the **UPDATE** operation has taken place.

8.4.7 DELETE FROM Statement

An SQL *DELETE* statement removes data from a table. The simplest form for a **DELETE** statement is

```
DELETE FROM tableName WHERE criteria
```

where *tableName* is the table from which to delete a record (or records). The **WHERE** clause specifies the criteria used to determine which record(s) to delete. The **DELETE** statement

```
DELETE FROM authors
    WHERE lastName = 'Jones' AND firstName = 'Sue'
```

deletes the record for Sue Jones in the **authors** table. If we know the **authorID** in advance of the **DELETE** operation, the **WHERE** clause could be simplified as follows:

```
WHERE authorID = 5
```

Figure 8.24 shows the **authors** table after the **DELETE** operation has taken place.

authorID	firstName	lastName
1	Harvey	Deitel
2	Paul	Deitel
3	Tem	Nieto
4	Sean	Santry
5	Sue	Jones

Fig. 8.23 Table **authors** after an **UPDATE** operation to change a record.

authorID	firstName	lastName
1	Harvey	Deitel
2	Paul	Deitel
3	Tem	Nieto
4	Sean	Santry

Fig. 8.24 Table **authors** after a **DELETE** operation to remove a record.

8.5 Creating Database books in Cloudscape

The CD that accompanies this book includes *Cloudscape 3.6.4*, a pure-Java database management system from Informix Software. A complete set of information on Cloudscape is available from **www.cloudscape.com**. Follow the provided instructions to install Cloudscape. Cloudscape executes on many platforms, including Windows, Solaris, Linux, Macintosh and others. For a complete list of platforms on which Cloudscape 3.6 has been tested, visit

```
cloudweb1.cloudscape.com/support/servepage.jsp?
    page=fyi_cert36vms.html
```

The Cloudscape server must be executing to create and manipulate databases in Cloudscape. To execute the server, begin by opening a command window. Change directories to the Cloudscape installation directory (**Cloudscape_3.6** by default). In that directory is a **frameworks** directory. Cloudscape comes with two frameworks in which it can execute: **embedded** and **RmiJdbc**. The **embedded** framework enables Cloudscape to execute as part of a Java application. The **RmiJdbc** framework enables Cloudscape to execute as a stand-alone database server, which is how we use Cloudscape in this book. Each framework directory has a **bin** subdirectory containing batch files (Windows) and shell scripts (Linux/UNIX) to set environment variables and execute Cloudscape. Change directories to the **bin** directory in the **RmiJdbc** framework. Execute the batch file or shell script starting with the name **setServerCloudscapeCP** to set the environment variables required by the server. Then execute the batch file or shell script starting with the name **startCS** to launch the Cloudscape database server. Figure 8.25 shows the command-line output when Cloudscape is executed from a Windows 2000 command window. Note that you can shut down the server by executing the script **stopCS** from another command window.

For each Cloudscape database we discuss in this book, we provide an SQL script that will set up the database and its tables. These scripts can be executed with an interactive command line tool, called **ij**, that is part of Cloudscape. We provide a batch file (**createDatabase.bat**) and a shell script (**createDatabase.ksh**) that you can use to start **ij** and execute the SQL scripts. In the examples directory for this chapter on the CD that accompanies this book, you will find the **createDatabase** scripts and the SQL script **books.sql**. To create database **books**, first ensure that the Cloudscape server is executing. Open a new command prompt, then change to Cloudscape's **frameworks\RmiJdbc\bin** directory. In that directory, execute the batch file or shell script starting with the name **setClientCloudscapeCP**. This sets the environment variables required by our **createDatabase** script. Next, change to the directory where you placed our JDBC examples on your computer and type

```
createDatabase books.sql
```

to execute the SQL script. After completing this task, you are ready to proceed to the first JDBC example. [*Note:* We wrote this script such that you can execute the script again at any time to restore the database's original contents. When you run this script the first time, it will generate four error messages as it tries to delete the four tables in the books database. This occurs because the database does not exist, so there are no tables to delete. You can simply ignore these messages.]

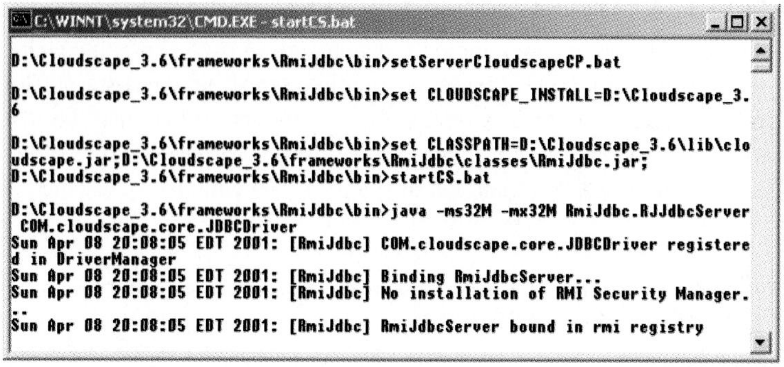

Fig. 8.25   Executing Cloudscape from a command prompt in Windows 2000.

8.6   Manipulating Databases with JDBC

In this section, we present two examples that introduce how to connect to a database, query the database and display the results of the query.

8.6.1 Connecting to and Querying a JDBC Data Source

The first example (Fig. 8.26) performs a simple query on the **books** database that retrieves the entire **authors** table and displays the data in a **JTextArea**. The program illustrates connecting to the database, querying the database and processing the results. The following discussion presents the key JDBC aspects of the program. [*Note*: Section 8.5 demonstrates how to execute the Cloudscape database server and how to create the **books** database. The steps in Section 8.5 must be performed before executing the program of Fig. 8.26.]

```
1   // Fig. 8.26: DisplayAuthors.java
2   // Displaying the contents of table authors in database books.
3   package com.deitel.advjhtp1.jdbc;
4
5   // Java core packages
6   import java.awt.*;
7   import java.sql.*;
8   import java.util.*;
9
10  // Java extension packages
11  import javax.swing.*;
12
13  public class DisplayAuthors extends JFrame {
14
15     // constructor connects to database, queries database,
16     // processes results and displays results in window
17     public DisplayAuthors()
18     {
19        super( "Authors Table of Books Database" );
20
21
```

Fig. 8.26   Displaying the **authors** table from the **books** database (part 1 of 3).

```
22          // connect to database books and query database
23          try {
24
25              // load database driver class
26              Class.forName( "COM.cloudscape.core.RmiJdbcDriver" );
27
28              // connect to database
29              Connection connection = DriverManager.getConnection(
30                  "jdbc:cloudscape:rmi:books" );
31
32              // create Statement to query database
33              Statement statement = connection.createStatement();
34
35              // query database
36              ResultSet resultSet =
37                  statement.executeQuery( "SELECT * FROM authors" );
38
39              // process query results
40              StringBuffer results = new StringBuffer();
41              ResultSetMetaData metaData = resultSet.getMetaData();
42              int numberOfColumns = metaData.getColumnCount();
43
44              for ( int i = 1; i <= numberOfColumns; i++ ) {
45                  results.append( metaData.getColumnName( i )
46                      + "\t" );
47              }
48
49              results.append( "\n" );
50
51              while ( resultSet.next() ) {
52
53                  for ( int i = 1; i <= numberOfColumns; i++ ) {
54                      results.append( resultSet.getObject( i )
55                          + "\t" );
56                  }
57
58                  results += "\n";
59              }
60
61              // close statement and connection
62              statement.close();
63              connection.close();
64
65              // set up GUI and display window
66              JTextArea textArea = new JTextArea(
67                  results.toString() );
68              Container container = getContentPane();
69
70              container.add( new JScrollPane( textArea ) );
71
72              setSize( 300, 100 );  // set window size
73              setVisible( true );   // display window
74          }  // end try
```

Fig. 8.26 Displaying the **authors** table from the **books** database (part 2 of 3).

```
75
76          // detect problems interacting with the database
77          catch ( SQLException sqlException ) {
78             JOptionPane.showMessageDialog( null,
79                sqlException.getMessage(), "Database Error",
80                JOptionPane.ERROR_MESSAGE );
81
82             System.exit( 1 );
83          }
84
85          // detect problems loading database driver
86          catch ( ClassNotFoundException classNotFound ) {
87             JOptionPane.showMessageDialog( null,
88                classNotFound.getMessage(), "Driver Not Found",
89                JOptionPane.ERROR_MESSAGE );
90
91             System.exit( 1 );
92          }
93       }  // end DisplayAuthors constructor definition
94
95       // launch the application
96       public static void main( String args[] )
97       {
98          DisplayAuthors window = new DisplayAuthors();
99
100         window.setDefaultCloseOperation( JFrame.EXIT_ON_CLOSE );
101      }
102   }  // end class DisplayAuthors
```

AUTHORID	FIRSTNAME	LASTNAME
1	Harvey	Deitel
2	Paul	Deitel
3	Tem	Nieto
4	Sean	Santry

Fig. 8.26   Displaying the **authors** table from the **books** database (part 3 of 3).

Line 7 imports package **java.sql**, which contains classes and interfaces for the JDBC API. The **DisplayAuthors** constructor (lines 17–93) connects to the books database, queries the database, displays the results of the query and closes the database connection.

The program must load the database driver class before the program can connect to the database. Line 26 loads the class definition for the database driver. This line throws a checked exception of type *java.lang.ClassNotFoundException* if the class loader cannot locate the driver class. Notice that the statement specifies the complete package name and class name for the Cloudscape driver—**COM.cloudscape.core.RmiJdbcDriver**.

JDBC supports four categories of drivers: *JDBC-to-ODBC bridge driver* (Type 1), *Native-API, partly Java driver* (Type 2); *JDBC-Net pure Java driver* (Type 3) and *Native-Protocol pure Java driver* (Type 4). A description of each driver type is shown in Fig. 8.27.

Type	Description
1	The *JDBC-to-ODBC bridge driver* connects Java to a Microsoft ODBC (Open Database Connectivity) data source. The Java 2 Software Development Kit from Sun Microsystems, Inc. includes the JDBC-to-ODBC bridge driver (**sun.jdbc.odbc.JdbcOdbcDriver**). This driver typically requires the ODBC driver to be installed on the client computer and normally requires configuration of the ODBC data source. The bridge driver was introduced primarily to allow Java programmers to build data-driven Java applications before the database vendors had Type 3 and Type 4 drivers.
2	*Native-API, partly Java drivers* enable JDBC programs to use database-specific APIs (normally written in C or C++) that allow client programs to access databases via the Java Native Interface. This driver type translates JDBC into database-specific code. Type 2 drivers were introduced for reasons similar to the Type 1 ODBC bridge driver.
3	*JDBC-Net pure Java drivers* take JDBC requests and translate them into a network protocol that is not database specific. These requests are sent to a server, which translates the database requests into a database-specific protocol.
4	*Native-protocol pure Java drivers* convert JDBC requests to database-specific network protocols, so that Java programs can connect directly to a database.

Fig. 8.27   JDBC driver types.

Type 3 and 4 drivers are preferred, because they are pure Java solutions. As mentioned in Fig. 8.27, Type 1 and Type 2 drivers were provided primarily to allow Java programmers to create data-driven solutions before the database vendors created pure Java drivers. The Cloudscape driver **COM.cloudscape.core.RmiJdbcDriver** is a Type 4 driver.

Software Engineering Observation 8.4

*Most major database vendors provide their own JDBC database drivers, and many third-party vendors provide JDBC drivers as well. For more information on JDBC drivers, visit the Sun Microsystems JDBC Web site, **java.sun.com/products/jdbc**.*

Software Engineering Observation 8.5

*On the Microsoft Windows platform, most databases support access via Open Database Connectivity (ODBC). ODBC is a technology developed by Microsoft to allow generic access to disparate database systems on the Windows platform (and some UNIX platforms). The Java 2 Software Development Kit (J2SDK) comes with the JDBC-to-ODBC-bridge database driver to allow any Java program to access any ODBC data source. The driver is defined by class **JdbcOdbcDriver** in package **sun.jdbc.odbc**.*

Lines 29–30 of Fig. 8.26 declare and initialize a **Connection** reference (package **java.sql**) called **connection**. An object that implements interface **Connection** manages the connection between the Java program and the database. **Connection** objects enable programs to create SQL statements that manipulate databases and to perform *transaction processing* (discussed later in this chapter). The program initializes **connection** with the result of a call to **static** method **getConnection** of class **DriverManager** (package **java.sql**), which attempts to connect to the database specified by its URL argument. The URL helps the program locate the database (possibly on a network or in the local file system of the computer). The URL **jdbc:cloudscape:rmi:books** specifies the *protocol* for communication (**jdbc**), the *subprotocol* for communication (**cloudscape:rmi**) and the name of the database (**books**). The subprotocol **cloudscape:rmi** indicates that the program uses **jdbc** to connect to a Cloudscape database via *remote method invocation* (*RMI*). [*Note*: Knowledge of the RMI networking technology is not required for this chapter. We discuss RMI in Chapter 13.] If the **DriverManager** cannot connect to the database, method **getConnection** throws an *SQLException* (package **java.sql**).

Software Engineering Observation 8.6

Most database management systems require the user to log in before accessing the database contents. **DriverManager** *method* **getConnection** *is overloaded with versions that enable the program to supply the user name and password to gain access.*

Line 33 invokes **Connection** method *createStatement* to obtain an object that implements interface **Statement** (package **java.sql**). The program uses the **Statement** object to submit SQL statements to the database.

Lines 36–37 use the **Statement** object's *executeQuery* method to execute a query that selects all the author information from table **authors**. This method returns an object that implements interface *ResultSet* and contains the results of the query. The **ResultSet** methods enable the program to manipulate the query results.

Lines 30–59 process the **ResultSet**. Line 41 obtains the *metadata* for the **ResultSet** and assigns it to a *ResultSetMetaData* (package **java.sql**) reference. The metadata describes the **ResultSet**'s contents. Programs can use metadata programmatically to obtain information about the **ResultSet**'s column names and types. Line 42 uses **ResultSetMetaData** method *getColumnCount* to retrieve the number of columns in the **ResultSet**. Lines 44–47 append the column names to the **StringBuffer results**.

Software Engineering Observation 8.7

Metadata enables programs to process **ResultSet** *contents dynamically when detailed information about the* **ResultSet** *is not known in advance of a query.*

Lines 51–59 appends the data in each **ResultSet** row to the **StringBuffer results**. Before processing the **ResultSet**, the program positions the **ResultSet** *cursor* to the first record in the **ResultSet** with method *next* (line 51). The cursor keeps track of the current record (or row). Method **next** returns **boolean** value **true** if it is able to position to the next record; otherwise the method returns **false**.

Common Programming Error 8.8

Initially, a **ResultSet** *cursor is positioned before the first record. Attempting to access a* **ResultSet**'s *contents before positioning the* **ResultSet** *cursor to the first record with method* **next** *causes an SQLException.*

If there are records in the **ResultSet**, lines 53–56 extract the contents of the current row. When processing a **ResultSet**, it is possible to extract each column of the **ResultSet** as a specific Java data type. In fact, **ResultSetMetaData** method *getColumnType* returns a constant integer from class *Types* (package **java.sql**) that indicates the type of the data for a specific column. Programs can use such information in a **switch** structure to invoke a **ResultSet** method that returns the column value as the appropriate Java data type. For example, if the type of a column is **Types.INT**,

ResultSet method ***getInt*** returns the column value as an **int**. **ResultSet** *get* methods typically receive as an argument either a *column number* (as an **int**) or a *column name* (as a **String**) indicating which column's value to obtain. Visit

```
java.sun.com/j2se/1.3/docs/guide/jdbc/getstart/
   GettingStartedTOC.fm.html
```

for detailed mappings of SQL types to Java types and to determine the appropriate **ResultSet** method to call for each SQL type.

Performance Tip 8.3

*If a query specifies the exact fields to select from the database, the **ResultSet** contains the fields in the specified order. In this case, using the column number to obtain the column's value is more efficient than using the column's name. The column number is similar to an array subscript in that the column number provides direct access to the specified column. Using the column's name requires a linear search of the column names to locate the appropriate column.*

For simplicity, this example treats each column's value as an **Object**. The program retrieves each column value with **ResultSet** method ***getObject*** (line 54) and appends the **String** representation of the **Object** to **results**. When **ResultSet** processing completes, the program closes the **Statement** (line 63) and the database **Connection** (line 64). Notice that, unlike array subscripts, which start at 0, **ResultSet** column numbers start at 1.

Common Programming Error 8.9

*Specifying column number 0 when obtaining values from a **ResultSet** causes an **SQLException**.*

Common Programming Error 8.10

*Attempting to manipulate a **ResultSet** after closing the **Statement** that created the **ResultSet** causes an **SQLException**. The program discards the **ResultSet** when the corresponding **Statement** is closed.*

Software Engineering Observation 8.8

*Each **Statement** object can open only one **ResultSet** object at a time. When a **Statement** returns a new **ResultSet**, the **Statement** closes the prior **ResultSet**. To use multiple **ResultSet**s in parallel, separate **Statement** objects must return the **ResultSet**s.*

Lines 66–73 create the GUI that displays the **StringBuffer results**, set the size of the application window and show the application window.

To run this example as well as the others in the Chapter, the **classpath** in the following command line must be used[1]

```
java -classpath f:\Cloudscape_3.6\lib\cloudscape.jar;
   f:\Cloudscape_3.6\frameworks\RmiJdbc\classes\RmiJdbc.jar;.
   com.deitel.advjhtp1.jdbc.DisplayAuthors
```

---

1. You will need to modify this command line to indicate the proper location of your Cloudscape installation and to use directory separators that are appropriate to your operating system (e.g., colons on UNIX/Linux).

These JARs (**cloudscape.jar** and **RmiJdbc.jar**) must be present in the **classpath** or none of the examples in this Chapter will execute. Note that the **classpath** includes **.** for the current directory. When setting the **classpath** at the command line, this ensures that the interpreter can locate classes in the current directory. You can also set the **classpath** using Cloudscape's **setServerCloudscapeCP** batch file or shell script discussed earlier in this section.

8.6.2 Querying the books Database

The next example (Fig. 8.28 and Fig. 8.31) enhances the example of Fig. 8.26 by allowing the user to enter any query into the program. The example displays the results of a query in a **JTable**, using a **TableModel** object to provide the **ResultSet** data to the **JTable**. Class **ResultSetTableModel** (Fig. 8.28) performs the connection to the database and maintains the model. Class **DisplayQueryResults** (Fig. 8.31) creates the GUI and specifies an instance of class **ResultSetTableModel** as the model for the **JTable**.

Class **ResultSetTableModel** (Fig. 8.28) extends class *AbstractTableModel* (package **javax.swing.table**), which implements interface **TableModel**. Class **ResultSetTableModel** overrides **TableModel** methods **getColumnClass**, **getColumnCount**, **getColumnName**, **getRowCount** and **getValueAt**. The default implementations of **TableModel** methods **isCellEditable** and **setValueAt** (provided by **AbstractTableModel**) are not overridden, because this example does not support editing the **JTable** cells. Also, the default implementations of **TableModel** methods **addTableModelListener** and **removeTableModelListener** (provided by **AbstractTableModel**) are not overridden, because the implementations of these methods from **AbstractTableModel** properly add and remove event listeners.

```
1   // Fig. 8.28: ResultSetTableModel.java
2   // A TableModel that supplies ResultSet data to a JTable.
3   package com.deitel.advjhtp1.jdbc;
4
5   // Java core packages
6   import java.sql.*;
7   import java.util.*;
8
9   // Java extension packages
10  import javax.swing.table.*;
11
12  // ResultSet rows and columns are counted from 1 and JTable
13  // rows and columns are counted from 0. When processing
14  // ResultSet rows or columns for use in a JTable, it is
15  // necessary to add 1 to the row or column number to manipulate
16  // the appropriate ResultSet column (i.e., JTable column 0 is
17  // ResultSet column 1 and JTable row 0 is ResultSet row 1).
18  public class ResultSetTableModel extends AbstractTableModel {
19      private Connection connection;
20      private Statement statement;
```

Fig. 8.28   **ResultSetTableModel** enables a **JTable** to display the contents of a **ResultSet** (part 1 of 4).

```
21      private ResultSet resultSet;
22      private ResultSetMetaData metaData;
23      private int numberOfRows;
24
25      // initialize resultSet and obtain its meta data object;
26      // determine number of rows
27      public ResultSetTableModel( String driver, String url,
28          String query ) throws SQLException, ClassNotFoundException
29      {
30          // load database driver class
31          Class.forName( driver );
32
33          // connect to database
34          connection = DriverManager.getConnection( url );
35
36          // create Statement to query database
37          statement = connection.createStatement(
38              ResultSet.TYPE_SCROLL_INSENSITIVE,
39              ResultSet.CONCUR_READ_ONLY );
40
41          // set query and execute it
42          setQuery( query );
43      }
44
45      // get class that represents column type
46      public Class getColumnClass( int column )
47      {
48          // determine Java class of column
49          try {
50              String className =
51                  metaData.getColumnClassName( column + 1 );
52
53              // return Class object that represents className
54              return Class.forName( className );
55          }
56
57          // catch SQLExceptions and ClassNotFoundExceptions
58          catch ( Exception exception ) {
59              exception.printStackTrace();
60          }
61
62          // if problems occur above, assume type Object
63          return Object.class;
64      }
65
66      // get number of columns in ResultSet
67      public int getColumnCount()
68      {
69          // determine number of columns
70          try {
71              return metaData.getColumnCount();
72          }
```

Fig. 8.28   **ResultSetTableModel** enables a **JTable** to display the contents of a **ResultSet** (part 2 of 4).

```
73
74        // catch SQLExceptions and print error message
75        catch ( SQLException sqlException ) {
76           sqlException.printStackTrace();
77        }
78
79        // if problems occur above, return 0 for number of columns
80        return 0;
81     }
82
83     // get name of a particular column in ResultSet
84     public String getColumnName( int column )
85     {
86        // determine column name
87        try {
88           return metaData.getColumnName( column + 1 );
89        }
90
91        // catch SQLExceptions and print error message
92        catch ( SQLException sqlException ) {
93           sqlException.printStackTrace();
94        }
95
96        // if problems, return empty string for column name
97        return "";
98     }
99
100    // return number of rows in ResultSet
101    public int getRowCount()
102    {
103       return numberOfRows;
104    }
105
106    // obtain value in particular row and column
107    public Object getValueAt( int row, int column )
108    {
109       // obtain a value at specified ResultSet row and column
110       try {
111          resultSet.absolute( row + 1 );
112
113          return resultSet.getObject( column + 1 );
114       }
115
116       // catch SQLExceptions and print error message
117       catch ( SQLException sqlException ) {
118          sqlException.printStackTrace();
119       }
120
121       // if problems, return empty string object
122       return "";
123    }
124
```

Fig. 8.28 ResultSetTableModel enables a **JTable** to display the contents of a **ResultSet** (part 3 of 4).

```
125      // close Statement and Connection
126      protected void finalize()
127      {
128         // close Statement and Connection
129         try {
130            statement.close();
131            connection.close();
132         }
133
134         // catch SQLExceptions and print error message
135         catch ( SQLException sqlException ) {
136            sqlException.printStackTrace();
137         }
138      }
139
140      // set new database query string
141      public void setQuery( String query ) throws SQLException
142      {
143         // specify query and execute it
144         resultSet = statement.executeQuery( query );
145
146         // obtain meta data for ResultSet
147         metaData = resultSet.getMetaData();
148
149         // determine number of rows in ResultSet
150         resultSet.last();                        // move to last row
151         numberOfRows = resultSet.getRow();   // get row number
152
153         // notify JTable that model has changed
154         fireTableStructureChanged();
155      }
156   }  // end class ResultSetTableModel
```

Fig. 8.28   **ResultSetTableModel** enables a **JTable** to display the contents of a **ResultSet** (part 4 of 4).

The **ResultSetTableModel** constructor (lines 27–43) receives three **String** arguments—the driver class name, the URL of the database and the default query to perform. The constructor throws any exceptions that occur in its body back to the application that created the **ResultSetTableModel** object, so that the application can determine how to handle the exception (e.g., report an error and terminate the application). Line 31 loads the database driver. Line 34 establishes a connection to the database. Line 37 invokes **Connection** method **createStatement** to create a **Statement** object. This example uses a version of method **createStatement** that takes two arguments—the *result-set type* and the *result-set concurrency*. The result-set type (Fig. 8.29) specifies whether the **ResultSet**'s cursor is able to scroll in both directions or forward only and whether the **ResultSet** is sensitive to changes. **ResultSet**s that are sensitive to changes reflect those changes immediately after they are made with methods of interface **ResultSet**. If a **ResultSet** is insensitive to changes, the query that produced the **ResultSet** must be executed again to reflect any changes made. The result-set concurrency (Fig. 8.30) specifies whether the **ResultSet** can be updated with **ResultSet**'s update methods. This example uses a **ResultSet** that is scrollable, insensitive to changes and read only. Line 42 invokes **ResultSetTableModel** method **setQuery** (lines 141–155) to perform the default query.

Portability Tip 8.6

*Some **ResultSet** implementations do not support scrollable **ResultSet**s. In such cases, typically the driver returns a **ResultSet** in which the cursor can move only forward. For more information, see your database-driver documentation.*

Portability Tip 8.7

*Some **ResultSet** implementations do not support updatable **ResultSet**s. In such cases, typically the driver returns a read-only **ResultSet**. For more information, see your database-driver documentation.*

Common Programming Error 8.11

*Attempting to update a **ResultSet** when the database driver does not support updatable **ResultSet**s causes **SQLException**s.*

Common Programming Error 8.12

*Attempting to move the cursor backwards through a **ResultSet** when the database driver does not support backwards scrolling causes an **SQLException***

Method **getColumnClass** (lines 46–64) returns a **Class** object that represents the superclass of all objects in a particular column. The **JTable** uses this information to configure the default cell renderer and cell editor for that column in the **JTable**. Lines 50–51 use **ResultSetMetaData** method *getColumnClassName* to obtain the fully qualified class name for the specified column. Line 54 loads the class definition for that class and returns the corresponding **Class** object. If an exception occurs, the **catch** at lines 58–60 prints a stack trace and line 63 returns **Object.class**—the **Class** instance that represents class **Object**—as the default type. [*Note*: Line 51 uses the argument **column + 1**. Like arrays, **JTable** row and column numbers are counted from 0. However, **ResultSet** row and column numbers are counted from 1. Thus, when processing **ResultSet** rows or columns for use in a **JTable**, it is necessary to add 1 to the row or column number to manipulate the appropriate **ResultSet** row or column.]

ResultSet static type constant	Description
TYPE_FORWARD_ONLY	Specifies that a **ResultSet**'s cursor can move only in the forward direction (i.e., from the first record to the last record in the **ResultSet**).
TYPE_SCROLL_INSENSITIVE	Specifies that a **ResultSet**'s cursor can scroll in either direction and that the changes made to the **ResultSet** during **ResultSet** processing are not reflected in the **ResultSet** unless the program queries the database again.

Fig. 8.29   **ResultSet** constants for specifying **ResultSet** type (part 1 of 2).

ResultSet static type constant	Description
TYPE_SCROLL_SENSITIVE	Specifies that a **ResultSet**'s cursor can scroll in either direction and that the changes made to the **ResultSet** during **ResultSet** processing are reflected immediately in the **ResultSet**.

Fig. 8.29 **ResultSet** constants for specifying **ResultSet** type (part 2 of 2).

ResultSet static concurrency constant	Description
CONCUR_READ_ONLY	Specifies that a **ResultSet** cannot be updated (i.e., changes to the **ResultSet** contents cannot be reflected in the database with **ResultSet**'s *update* methods).
CONCUR_UPDATABLE	Specifies that a **ResultSet** can be updated (i.e., changes to the **ResultSet** contents can be reflected in the database with **ResultSet**'s *update* methods).

Fig. 8.30 **ResultSet** constants for specifying result set properties.

Method **getColumnCount** (lines 67–81) returns the number of columns in the model's underlying **ResultSet**. Line 71 uses **ResultSetMetaData** method *getColumnCount* to obtain the number of columns in the **ResultSet**. If an exception occurs, the **catch** at lines 75–77 prints a stack trace and line 80 returns 0 as the default number of columns.

Method **getColumnName** (lines 84–98) returns the name of the column in the model's underlying **ResultSet**. Line 88 uses **ResultSetMetaData** method *getColumnName* to obtain the column name from the **ResultSet**. If an exception occurs, the **catch** at lines 92–94 prints a stack trace and line 97 returns the empty string as the default column name.

Method **getRowCount** (lines 101–104) returns the number of rows in the model's underlying **ResultSet**. When method **setQuery** (lines 141–155) performs a query, it stores the number of rows in variable **numberOfRows**.

Method **getValueAt** (lines 107–123) returns the **Object** in a particular row and column of the model's underlying **ResultSet**. Line 111 uses **ResultSet** method *absolute* to position the **ResultSet** cursor at a specific row. Line 113 uses **ResultSet** method **getObject** to obtain the **Object** in a specific column of the current row. If an exception occurs, the **catch** at lines 117–119 prints a stack trace and line 122 returns the empty string object as the default value.

Method **finalize** (lines 126–138) closes the **Statement** and **Connection** objects if a **ResultSetTableModel** object is garbage collected.

Method **setQuery** (lines 141–155) executes the query it receives as an argument to obtain a new **ResultSet** (line 144). Line 147 gets the **ResultSetMetaData** for the new **ResultSet**. Line 150 uses **ResultSet** method *last* to position the **ResultSet** cursor at the last row in the **ResultSet**. Line 151 uses **ResultSet** method *getRow* to obtain the row number for the current row in the **ResultSet**. Line 154 invokes method *fireTableStructureChanged* (inherited from class **AbstractTableModel**) to notify any **JTable** using this **ResultSetTableModel** object as its model that the structure of the model has changed (i.e., the underlying **ResultSet** contains new data or new columns). This causes the **JTable** to repopulate its rows and columns with the new **ResultSet** data. Method **setQuery** throws any exceptions that occur in its body back to the application that invoked **setQuery**.

The **DisplayQueryResults** (Fig. 8.31) constructor (lines 21–121) creates a **ResultSetTableModel** object and defines the GUI for the application. Lines 26, 29 and 32 define the database driver class name, database URL and default query that are passed to the **ResultSetTableModel** constructor to make the initial connection to the database and perform the default query. Line 61 creates the **JTable** object and passes a **ResultSetTableModel** object to the **JTable** constructor, which then registers the **JTable** as a listener for **TableModelEvent**s generated by the **ResultSetTableModel**. Lines 70–94 register an event handler for the **submitButton** that the user clicks to submit a query to the database. When the user clicks the button, method **actionPerformed** (lines 75–90) invokes **ResultSetTableModel** method **setQuery** to execute the new query. The screen captures in Fig. 8.31 show the results of two queries. The first screen capture shows the default query that selects all the authors from table **authors** of database **books**. The second screen capture shows a query that selects each author's first name and last name from the **authors** table and combines that information with the title and edition number from the **titles** table. Try entering your own queries in the text area and clicking the **Submit Query** button to execute the query.

```
1   // Fig. 8.31: DisplayQueryResults.java
2   // Display the contents of the Authors table in the
3   // Books database.
4   package com.deitel.advjhtp1.jdbc;
5
6   // Java core packages
7   import java.awt.*;
8   import java.awt.event.*;
9   import java.sql.*;
10  import java.util.*;
11
12  // Java extension packages
13  import javax.swing.*;
14  import javax.swing.table.*;
15
16  public class DisplayQueryResults extends JFrame {
17     private ResultSetTableModel tableModel;
18     private JTextArea queryArea;
19
```

Fig. 8.31 **DisplayQueryResults** for querying database **books**. (part 1 of 4)

```
20      // create ResultSetTableModel and GUI
21      public DisplayQueryResults()
22      {
23          super( "Displaying Query Results" );
24
25          // Cloudscape database driver class name
26          String driver = "COM.cloudscape.core.RmiJdbcDriver";
27
28          // URL to connect to books database
29          String url = "jdbc:cloudscape:rmi:books";
30
31          // query to select entire authors table
32          String query = "SELECT * FROM authors";
33
34          // create ResultSetTableModel and display database table
35          try {
36
37              // create TableModel for results of query
38              // SELECT * FROM authors
39              tableModel =
40                  new ResultSetTableModel( driver, url, query );
41
42              // set up JTextArea in which user types queries
43              queryArea = new JTextArea( query, 3, 100 );
44              queryArea.setWrapStyleWord( true );
45              queryArea.setLineWrap( true );
46
47              JScrollPane scrollPane = new JScrollPane( queryArea,
48                  ScrollPaneConstants.VERTICAL_SCROLLBAR_AS_NEEDED,
49                  ScrollPaneConstants.HORIZONTAL_SCROLLBAR_NEVER );
50
51              // set up JButton for submitting queries
52              JButton submitButton = new JButton( "Submit Query" );
53
54              // create Box to manage placement of queryArea and
55              // submitButton in GUI
56              Box box = Box.createHorizontalBox();
57              box.add( scrollPane );
58              box.add( submitButton );
59
60              // create JTable delegate for tableModel
61              JTable resultTable = new JTable( tableModel );
62
63              // place GUI components on content pane
64              Container c = getContentPane();
65              c.add( box, BorderLayout.NORTH );
66              c.add( new JScrollPane( resultTable ),
67                      BorderLayout.CENTER );
68
69              // create event listener for submitButton
70              submitButton.addActionListener(
71
72                  new ActionListener() {
```

Fig. 8.31 **DisplayQueryResults** for querying database **books**. (part 2 of 4)

```
73
74                      // pass query to table model
75                      public void actionPerformed( ActionEvent e )
76                      {
77                          // perform a new query
78                          try {
79                              tableModel.setQuery( queryArea.getText() );
80                          }
81
82                          // catch SQLExceptions that occur when
83                          // performing a new query
84                          catch ( SQLException sqlException ) {
85                              JOptionPane.showMessageDialog( null,
86                                  sqlException.toString(),
87                                  "Database error",
88                                  JOptionPane.ERROR_MESSAGE );
89                          }
90                      }  // end actionPerformed
91
92                  }  // end ActionListener inner class
93
94              ); // end call to addActionListener
95
96              // set window size and display window
97              setSize( 500, 250 );
98              setVisible( true );
99          }  // end try
100
101         // catch ClassNotFoundException thrown by
102         // ResultSetTableModel if database driver not found
103         catch ( ClassNotFoundException classNotFound ) {
104             JOptionPane.showMessageDialog( null,
105                 "Cloudscape driver not found", "Driver not found",
106                 JOptionPane.ERROR_MESSAGE );
107
108             System.exit( 1 );   // terminate application
109         }
110
111         // catch SQLException thrown by ResultSetTableModel
112         // if problems occur while setting up database
113         // connection and querying database
114         catch ( SQLException sqlException ) {
115             JOptionPane.showMessageDialog( null,
116                 sqlException.toString(),
117                 "Database error", JOptionPane.ERROR_MESSAGE );
118
119             System.exit( 1 );   // terminate application
120         }
121     }  // end DisplayQueryResults constructor
122
123     // execute application
124     public static void main( String args[] )
125     {
```

Fig. 8.31 `DisplayQueryResults` for querying database **books**. (part 3 of 4)

```
126            DisplayQueryResults app = new DisplayQueryResults();
127
128            app.setDefaultCloseOperation( JFrame.EXIT_ON_CLOSE );
129         }
130    }  // end class DisplayQueryResults
```

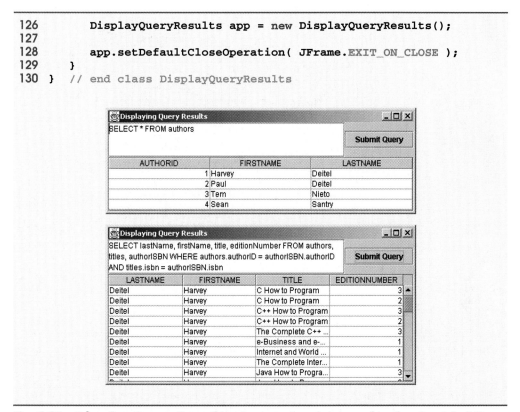

Fig. 8.31 **DisplayQueryResults** for querying database **books**. (part 4 of 4)

8.7 Case Study: Address-Book Application

Our next example uses the SQL and JDBC concepts presented so far to implement a substantial address-book application that enables the user to insert, locate, update and delete address-book entries in the Cloudscape database **addressbook**. [*Note*: An SQL script to create this database is provided with the example code for this chapter. Section 8.5 demonstrates executing an SQL script with Cloudscape.]

Database **addressbook** contains four tables: **names**, **addresses**, **phoneNumbers** and **emailAddresses**. Figure 8.32 shows the relationships between the tables. The first line in each table is the table's name. Each table's primary-key field is highlighted in green. Tables **addresses**, **phoneNumbers** and **emailAddresses** each have **personID** as a foreign key. Thus, a program cannot place records in those tables unless the **personID** is a valid value in table **names**. Although the address-book application currently allows only one address, one phone number and one e-mail address per person, the database was designed to support multiple addresses, phone numbers and e-mail addresses for each person. So there is a one-to-many relationship between a record in the **names** table and records in the other tables. Note that the relationship lines between the tables link the foreign key (**personID**) of tables **phoneNumbers**, **emailAddresses** and **addresses** to the primary key of table **names**. In each of the tables, fields **personID**, **addressID**, **emailID** and **phoneID** are integers. All other fields are strings.

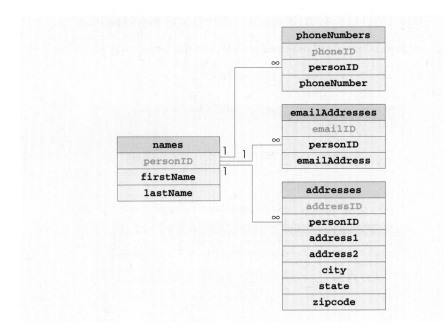

Fig. 8.32   Table relationships in database **addressbook**.

This example introduces two new concepts: **PreparedStatement**s and *transaction processing*. Section 8.7.1 and Section 8.7.2 discuss these new concepts. Then, Section 8.7.3 presents the **AddressBook** application and its supporting classes.

8.7.1 PreparedStatements

Interface **PreparedStatement** enables an application programmer to create SQL statements that are maintained in a compiled form that enables the statements to execute more efficiently than **Statement** objects. **PreparedStatement** objects also are more flexible than **Statement** objects, because they can specify parameters. This allows programs to execute the same query repeatedly with different parameter values. For example, in the **books** database, you might want to locate all book titles for an author with a specific last name and first name, and you might want to execute that query for several authors. With a **PreparedStatement**, that query is defined as follows:

```
PreparedStatement authorBooks = connection.prepareStatement(
   "SELECT lastName, firstName, title " +
   "FROM authors, titles, authorISBN " +
   "WHERE authors.authorID = authorISBN.authorID AND " +
   "   titles.ISBN = authorISBN.isbn AND " +
   "   lastName = ? AND firstName = ?" );
```

Note the two *question marks* (**?**) in the last line of the preceding statement. These characters represent placeholders for values that will be passed as part of the query to the database. Before the program executes a **PreparedStatement**, the program must specify the values of those parameters by using the *set* methods of interface **PreparedStatement**.

For the preceding query, both parameters are strings that can be set with **Prepared-Statement** method *setString* as follows:

```
authorBooks.setString( 1, "Deitel" );
authorBooks.setString( 2, "Paul" );
```

Method **setString**'s first argument represents the number of the parameter being set and the second argument is the value to set for that parameter. Parameter numbers are counted from 1, starting with the first question mark (**?**) in the SQL statement. When the program executes the preceding **PreparedStatement** with the parameter values shown here, the SQL statement passed to the database is

```
SELECT lastName, firstName, title
FROM authors, titles, authorISBN
WHERE authors.authorID = authorISBN.authorID AND
    titles.ISBN = authorISBN.isbn AND
    lastName = 'Deitel' AND firstName = 'Paul'
```

It is important to note that method **setString** escapes **String** parameter values properly. For example, if the last name is O'Brien, the statement

```
authorBooks.setString( 1, "O'Brien" );
```

escapes the **'** character in O'Brien by replacing it with two single-quote characters.

Performance Tip 8.4

*In programs that execute SQL statements multiple times with different parameter values, **PreparedStatement**s are more efficient than **Statement**s, because **Prepared-Statement**s maintain the SQL statement in a compiled format. This is a very important performance enhancement.*

Software Engineering Observation 8.9

***PreparedStatement**s are more flexible than **Statement**s, because **Prepared-Statement**s support customization of a query with parameter values. With a **Statement**, the program must create a new **String** containing an SQL statement for each new query.*

Good Programming Practice 8.2

*Use **PreparedStatement**s with parameters for queries that receive **String** values as arguments to ensure that the **String**s are quoted properly in the SQL statement.*

Interface **PreparedStatement** provides *set* methods for each SQL type supported. It is important to use the *set* method that is appropriate for the SQL type of the parameter in the database; otherwise, **SQLException**s can occur when the program attempts to convert the parameter value to an incorrect type. For a complete list of these *set* methods, see the Java API documentation for interface **PreparedStatement**.

Common Programming Error 8.13

*Using the incorrect **PreparedStatement** set method can cause **SQLException**s if an attempt is made to convert a parameter value to an incorrect data type.*

8.7.2 Transaction Processing

Many database applications require guarantees that a series of database insertions, updates and deletions executes properly before the applications continue processing the next database operation. For example, when you transfer money electronically between bank accounts, several factors determine if the transaction is successful. You begin by specifying the source account and the amount you wish to transfer from that account to a destination account. Next, you specify the destination account. The bank checks the source account to determine if there are sufficient funds in the account to complete the transfer. If so, the bank withdraws the specified amount from the source account and, if all goes well, deposits the money into the destination account to complete the transfer. What happens if the transfer fails after the bank withdraws the money from the source account? In a proper banking system, the bank redeposits the money in the source account. How would you feel if the money was subtracted from your source account and the bank *did not* deposit the money in the destination account?

Transaction processing enables a program that interacts with a database to treat a database operation (or set of operations) as a single operation. Such an operation also is known as an *atomic operation* or a *transaction*. At the end of a transaction, a decision can be made either to *commit the transaction* or *back the transaction*. Committing the transaction finalizes the database operation(s); all insertions, updates and deletions performed as part of the transaction cannot be reversed without performing a new database operation. Rolling back the transaction leaves the database in its state prior to the database operation. This is useful when a portion of a transaction fails to complete properly. In our bank-account-transfer discussion, the transaction would be rolled back if the deposit could not be made into the destination account.

Java provides transaction processing via methods of interface **Connection**. Method **setAutoCommit** specifies whether each SQL statement commits after it completes (a **true** argument) or if several SQL statements should be grouped as a transaction (a **false** argument). If the argument to **setAutoCommit** is **false**, the program must follow the last SQL statement in the transaction with a call to **Connection** method **commit** (to commit the changes to the database) or **Connection** method **rollback** (to return the database to its state prior to the transaction). Interface **Connection** also provides method **getAutoCommit** to determine the autocommit state for the **Connection**.

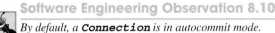

Software Engineering Observation 8.10

*By default, a **Connection** is in autocommit mode.*

Software Engineering Observation 8.11

Most JDBC drivers support transaction processing. Those that do not are not JDBC compliant drivers.

8.7.3 Address-Book Application

The address-book application consists of five classes and interfaces: class **AddressBookEntry** (Fig. 8.33), interface **AddressBookDataAccess** (Fig. 8.34), class **DataAccessException** (Fig. 8.35), class **CloudscapeDataAccess** (Fig. 8.36), class **AddressBookEntryFrame** (Fig. 8.37) and class **AddressBook** (Fig. 8.38).

Class **AddressBookEntry** (Fig. 8.33) represents the data for an entry in the address book. The class contains properties for all the fields in the four tables of database **addressbook**.

```
1   // Fig. 8.33: AddressBookEntry.java
2   // JavaBean to represent one address book entry.
3   package com.deitel.advjhtp1.jdbc.addressbook;
4
5   public class AddressBookEntry {
6      private String firstName = "";
7      private String lastName = "";
8      private String address1 = "";
9      private String address2 = "";
10     private String city = "";
11     private String state = "";
12     private String zipcode = "";
13     private String phoneNumber = "";
14     private String emailAddress = "";
15     private int personID;
16     private int addressID;
17     private int phoneID;
18     private int emailID;
19
20     // empty constructor
21     public AddressBookEntry()
22     {
23     }
24
25     // set person's id
26     public AddressBookEntry( int id )
27     {
28        personID = id;
29     }
30
31     // set person's first name
32     public void setFirstName( String first )
33     {
34        firstName = first;
35     }
36
37     // get person's first name
38     public String getFirstName()
39     {
40        return firstName;
41     }
42
43     // set person's last name
44     public void setLastName( String last )
45     {
46        lastName = last;
47     }
48
```

Fig. 8.33 **AddressBookEntry** bean represents an address book entry (part 1 of 4).

```
49      // get person's last name
50      public String getLastName()
51      {
52          return lastName;
53      }
54
55      // set first line of person's address
56      public void setAddress1( String firstLine )
57      {
58          address1 = firstLine;
59      }
60
61      // get first line of person's address
62      public String getAddress1()
63      {
64          return address1;
65      }
66
67      // set second line of person's address
68      public void setAddress2( String secondLine )
69      {
70          address2 = secondLine;
71      }
72
73      // get second line of person's address
74      public String getAddress2()
75      {
76          return address2;
77      }
78
79      // set city in which person lives
80      public void setCity( String personCity )
81      {
82          city = personCity;
83      }
84
85      // get city in which person lives
86      public String getCity()
87      {
88          return city;
89      }
90
91      // set state in which person lives
92      public void setState( String personState )
93      {
94          state = personState;
95      }
96
97      // get state in which person lives
98      public String getState()
99      {
100         return state;
101     }
```

Fig. 8.33 **AddressBookEntry** bean represents an address book entry (part 2 of 4).

```
102
103      // set person's zip code
104      public void setZipcode( String zip )
105      {
106         zipcode = zip;
107      }
108
109      // get person's zip code
110      public String getZipcode()
111      {
112         return zipcode;
113      }
114
115      // set person's phone number
116      public void setPhoneNumber( String number )
117      {
118         phoneNumber = number;
119      }
120
121      // get person's phone number
122      public String getPhoneNumber()
123      {
124         return phoneNumber;
125      }
126
127      // set person's email address
128      public void setEmailAddress( String email )
129      {
130         emailAddress = email;
131      }
132
133      // get person's email address
134      public String getEmailAddress()
135      {
136         return emailAddress;
137      }
138
139      // get person's ID
140      public int getPersonID()
141      {
142         return personID;
143      }
144
145      // set person's addressID
146      public void setAddressID( int id )
147      {
148         addressID = id;
149      }
150
151      // get person's addressID
152      public int getAddressID()
153      {
154         return addressID;
```

Fig. 8.33 AddressBookEntry bean represents an address book entry (part 3 of 4).

```
155       }
156
157       // set person's phoneID
158       public void setPhoneID( int id )
159       {
160          phoneID = id;
161       }
162
163       // get person's phoneID
164       public int getPhoneID()
165       {
166          return phoneID;
167       }
168
169       // set person's emailID
170       public void setEmailID( int id )
171       {
172          emailID = id;
173       }
174
175       // get person's emailID
176       public int getEmailID()
177       {
178          return emailID;
179       }
180   }   // end class AddressBookEntry
```

Fig. 8.33 **AddressBookEntry** bean represents an address book entry (part 4 of 4).

Interface **AddressBookDataAccess** (Fig. 8.34) describes methods required by the address-book application to perform insertions, updates, deletions and searches with the **addressbook** database. Any class that implements this interface can be used by the **AddressBook** application class to interact with the database. Thus, if you want to modify the application to use a database other than Cloudscape, you can do so by providing your own implementation of class **AddressBookDataAccess**.

```
1    // Fig. 8.34: AddressBookDataAccess.java
2    // Interface that specifies the methods for inserting,
3    // updating, deleting and finding records.
4    package com.deitel.advjhtp1.jdbc.addressbook;
5
6    // Java core packages
7    import java.sql.*;
8
9    public interface AddressBookDataAccess {
10
11       // Locate specified person by last name. Return
12       // AddressBookEntry containing information.
13       public AddressBookEntry findPerson( String lastName );
14
```

Fig. 8.34 **AddressBookDataAccess** interface describes the methods for accessing the **addressbook** database (part 1 of 2).

```
15      // Update information for specified person.
16      // Return boolean indicating success or failure.
17      public boolean savePerson(
18         AddressBookEntry person ) throws DataAccessException;
19
20      // Insert a new person. Return boolean indicating
21      // success or failure.
22      public boolean newPerson( AddressBookEntry person )
23         throws DataAccessException;
24
25      // Delete specified person. Return boolean indicating if
26      // success or failure.
27      public boolean deletePerson(
28         AddressBookEntry person ) throws DataAccessException;
29
30      // close database connection
31      public void close();
32   }  // end interface AddressBookDataAccess
```

Fig. 8.34 **AddressBookDataAccess** interface describes the methods for accessing the **addressbook** database (part 2 of 2).

Interface **AddressBookDataAccess** contains five methods. Method **find-Person** (line 13) receives an **String** argument containing the last name of the person for which to search. The method returns the **AddressBookEntry** containing the person's complete information if the person was found in the database; otherwise, the method returns **false**. Method **savePerson** (lines 17–18) receives an **Address-BookEntry** argument containing the data to save and updates the corresponding record in the database. Method **newPerson** (lines 22–23) receives an **AddressBookEntry** argument containing the information for a new person and inserts the person's information in the database. Method **deletePerson** (lines 27–28) receives an **Address-BookEntry** argument containing the person to delete from the database and uses the **personID** to remove the records that represent the person from all four tables in the database. Method **close** (line 31) closes the statements and the connection to the database.

Class **DataAccessException** (Fig. 8.35) extends class **Exception**. Some of the methods of interface **AddressBookDataAccess** throw **DataAccessException**s when there is a problem with the data source connection.

```
1   // Fig. 8.35 DataAccessException.java
2   // Class AddressBookDataAccess throws DataAccessExceptions
3   // when there is a problem accessing the data source.
4   package com.deitel.advjhtp1.jdbc.addressbook;
5
6   public class DataAccessException extends Exception {
7
8      private Exception exception;
9
```

Fig. 8.35 **DataAccessException** is thrown when there is a problem accessing the data source (part 1 of 2).

```
10        // constructor with String argument
11        public DataAccessException( String message )
12        {
13           super( message );
14        }
15
16        // constructor with Exception argument
17        public DataAccessException( Exception exception )
18        {
19           exception = this.exception;
20        }
21
22        // printStackTrace of exception from constructor
23        public void printStackTrace()
24        {
25           exception.printStackTrace();
26        }
27     }
```

Fig. 8.35   **DataAccessException** is thrown when there is a problem accessing the data source (part 2 of 2).

Class **CloudscapeDataAccess** (Fig. 8.36) implements interface **AddressBookDataAccess** to interact with our **addressbook** database in Cloudscape. An object of this class contains a reference to a **Connection** object (line 13) that maintains the connection to the database and several references to **PreparedStatement** objects (lines 16–37) that represent the interactions with the database for inserting, updating, deleting and finding records.

```
1     // Fig. 8.36: CloudscapeDataAccess.java
2     // An implementation of interface AddressBookDataAccess that
3     // performs database operations with PreparedStatements.
4     package com.deitel.advjhtp1.jdbc.addressbook;
5
6     // Java core packages
7     import java.sql.*;
8
9     public class CloudscapeDataAccess
10        implements AddressBookDataAccess {
11
12        // reference to database connection
13        private Connection connection;
14
15        // reference to prepared statement for locating entry
16        private PreparedStatement sqlFind;
17
18        // reference to prepared statement for determining personID
19        private PreparedStatement sqlPersonID;
20
```

Fig. 8.36   **CloudscapeDataAccess** implements interface **AddressBookDataAccess** to perform the connection to the database and the database interactions (part 1 of 10).

```
21      // references to prepared statements for inserting entry
22      private PreparedStatement sqlInsertName;
23      private PreparedStatement sqlInsertAddress;
24      private PreparedStatement sqlInsertPhone;
25      private PreparedStatement sqlInsertEmail;
26
27      // references to prepared statements for updating entry
28      private PreparedStatement sqlUpdateName;
29      private PreparedStatement sqlUpdateAddress;
30      private PreparedStatement sqlUpdatePhone;
31      private PreparedStatement sqlUpdateEmail;
32
33      // references to prepared statements for updating entry
34      private PreparedStatement sqlDeleteName;
35      private PreparedStatement sqlDeleteAddress;
36      private PreparedStatement sqlDeletePhone;
37      private PreparedStatement sqlDeleteEmail;
38
39      // set up PreparedStatements to access database
40      public CloudscapeDataAccess() throws Exception
41      {
42         // connect to addressbook database
43         connect();
44
45         // locate person
46         sqlFind = connection.prepareStatement(
47            "SELECT names.personID, firstName, lastName, " +
48               "addressID, address1, address2, city, state, " +
49               "zipcode, phoneID, phoneNumber, emailID, " +
50               "emailAddress " +
51            "FROM names, addresses, phoneNumbers, emailAddresses " +
52            "WHERE lastName = ? AND " +
53               "names.personID = addresses.personID AND " +
54               "names.personID = phoneNumbers.personID AND " +
55               "names.personID = emailAddresses.personID" );
56
57         // Obtain personID for last person inserted in database.
58         // [This is a Cloudscape-specific database operation.]
59         sqlPersonID = connection.prepareStatement(
60            "VALUES ConnectionInfo.lastAutoincrementValue( " +
61               "'APP', 'NAMES', 'PERSONID')" );
62
63         // Insert first and last names in table names.
64         // For referential integrity, this must be performed
65         // before sqlInsertAddress, sqlInsertPhone and
66         // sqlInsertEmail.
67         sqlInsertName = connection.prepareStatement(
68            "INSERT INTO names ( firstName, lastName ) " +
69            "VALUES ( ? , ? )" );
70
```

Fig. 8.36   CloudscapeDataAccess implements interface
AddressBookDataAccess to perform the connection to the
database and the database interactions (part 2 of 10).

```
71          // insert address in table addresses
72          sqlInsertAddress = connection.prepareStatement(
73             "INSERT INTO addresses ( personID, address1, " +
74                "address2, city, state, zipcode ) " +
75             "VALUES ( ? , ? , ? , ? , ? , ? )" );
76
77          // insert phone number in table phoneNumbers
78          sqlInsertPhone = connection.prepareStatement(
79             "INSERT INTO phoneNumbers " +
80                "( personID, phoneNumber) " +
81             "VALUES ( ? , ? )" );
82
83          // insert email in table emailAddresses
84          sqlInsertEmail = connection.prepareStatement(
85             "INSERT INTO emailAddresses " +
86                "( personID, emailAddress ) " +
87             "VALUES ( ? , ? )" );
88
89          // update first and last names in table names
90          sqlUpdateName = connection.prepareStatement(
91             "UPDATE names SET firstName = ?, lastName = ? " +
92             "WHERE personID = ?" );
93
94          // update address in table addresses
95          sqlUpdateAddress = connection.prepareStatement(
96             "UPDATE addresses SET address1 = ?, address2 = ?, " +
97                "city = ?, state = ?, zipcode = ? " +
98             "WHERE addressID = ?" );
99
100         // update phone number in table phoneNumbers
101         sqlUpdatePhone = connection.prepareStatement(
102            "UPDATE phoneNumbers SET phoneNumber = ? " +
103            "WHERE phoneID = ?" );
104
105         // update email in table emailAddresses
106         sqlUpdateEmail = connection.prepareStatement(
107            "UPDATE emailAddresses SET emailAddress = ? " +
108            "WHERE emailID = ?" );
109
110         // Delete row from table names. This must be executed
111         // after sqlDeleteAddress, sqlDeletePhone and
112         // sqlDeleteEmail, because of referential integrity.
113         sqlDeleteName = connection.prepareStatement(
114            "DELETE FROM names WHERE personID = ?" );
115
116         // delete address from table addresses
117         sqlDeleteAddress = connection.prepareStatement(
118            "DELETE FROM addresses WHERE personID = ?" );
119
```

Fig. 8.36 CloudscapeDataAccess implements interface
AddressBookDataAccess to perform the connection to the
database and the database interactions (part 3 of 10).

```
120          // delete phone number from table phoneNumbers
121          sqlDeletePhone = connection.prepareStatement(
122             "DELETE FROM phoneNumbers WHERE personID = ?" );
123
124          // delete email address from table emailAddresses
125          sqlDeleteEmail = connection.prepareStatement(
126             "DELETE FROM emailAddresses WHERE personID = ?" );
127       }  // end CloudscapeDataAccess constructor
128
129       // Obtain a connection to addressbook database. Method may
130       // may throw ClassNotFoundException or SQLException. If so,
131       // exception is passed via this class's constructor back to
132       // the AddressBook application so the application can display
133       // an error message and terminate.
134       private void connect() throws Exception
135       {
136          // Cloudscape database driver class name
137          String driver = "COM.cloudscape.core.RmiJdbcDriver";
138
139          // URL to connect to addressbook database
140          String url = "jdbc:cloudscape:rmi:addressbook";
141
142          // load database driver class
143          Class.forName( driver );
144
145          // connect to database
146          connection = DriverManager.getConnection( url );
147
148          // Require manual commit for transactions. This enables
149          // the program to rollback transactions that do not
150          // complete and commit transactions that complete properly.
151          connection.setAutoCommit( false );
152       }
153
154       // Locate specified person. Method returns AddressBookEntry
155       // containing information.
156       public AddressBookEntry findPerson( String lastName )
157       {
158          try {
159             // set query parameter and execute query
160             sqlFind.setString( 1, lastName );
161             ResultSet resultSet = sqlFind.executeQuery();
162
163             // if no records found, return immediately
164             if ( !resultSet.next() )
165                return null;
166
167             // create new AddressBookEntry
168             AddressBookEntry person = new AddressBookEntry(
169                resultSet.getInt( 1 ) );
170
```

Fig. 8.36 **CloudscapeDataAccess** implements interface
AddressBookDataAccess to perform the connection to the
database and the database interactions (part 4 of 10).

```
171              // set AddressBookEntry properties
172              person.setFirstName( resultSet.getString( 2 ) );
173              person.setLastName( resultSet.getString( 3 ) );
174
175              person.setAddressID( resultSet.getInt( 4 ) );
176              person.setAddress1( resultSet.getString( 5 ) );
177              person.setAddress2( resultSet.getString( 6 ) );
178              person.setCity( resultSet.getString( 7 ) );
179              person.setState( resultSet.getString( 8 ) );
180              person.setZipcode( resultSet.getString( 9 ) );
181
182              person.setPhoneID( resultSet.getInt( 10 ) );
183              person.setPhoneNumber( resultSet.getString( 11 ) );
184
185              person.setEmailID( resultSet.getInt( 12 ) );
186              person.setEmailAddress( resultSet.getString( 13 ) );
187
188              // return AddressBookEntry
189              return person;
190           }
191
192        // catch SQLException
193        catch ( SQLException sqlException ) {
194           return null;
195        }
196     }  // end method findPerson
197
198     // Update an entry. Method returns boolean indicating
199     // success or failure.
200     public boolean savePerson( AddressBookEntry person )
201        throws DataAccessException
202     {
203        // update person in database
204        try {
205           int result;
206
207           // update names table
208           sqlUpdateName.setString( 1, person.getFirstName() );
209           sqlUpdateName.setString( 2, person.getLastName() );
210           sqlUpdateName.setInt( 3, person.getPersonID() );
211           result = sqlUpdateName.executeUpdate();
212
213           // if update fails, rollback and discontinue
214           if ( result == 0 ) {
215              connection.rollback(); // rollback update
216              return false;          // update unsuccessful
217           }
218
219           // update addresses table
220           sqlUpdateAddress.setString( 1, person.getAddress1() );
221           sqlUpdateAddress.setString( 2, person.getAddress2() );
```

Fig. 8.36 `CloudscapeDataAccess` implements interface
`AddressBookDataAccess` to perform the connection to the
database and the database interactions (part 5 of 10).

```
222          sqlUpdateAddress.setString( 3, person.getCity() );
223          sqlUpdateAddress.setString( 4, person.getState() );
224          sqlUpdateAddress.setString( 5, person.getZipcode() );
225          sqlUpdateAddress.setInt( 6, person.getAddressID() );
226          result = sqlUpdateAddress.executeUpdate();
227
228          // if update fails, rollback and discontinue
229          if ( result == 0 ) {
230             connection.rollback(); // rollback update
231             return false;          // update unsuccessful
232          }
233
234          // update phoneNumbers table
235          sqlUpdatePhone.setString( 1, person.getPhoneNumber() );
236          sqlUpdatePhone.setInt( 2, person.getPhoneID() );
237          result = sqlUpdatePhone.executeUpdate();
238
239          // if update fails, rollback and discontinue
240          if ( result == 0 ) {
241             connection.rollback(); // rollback update
242             return false;          // update unsuccessful
243          }
244
245          // update emailAddresses table
246          sqlUpdateEmail.setString( 1, person.getEmailAddress() );
247          sqlUpdateEmail.setInt( 2, person.getEmailID() );
248          result = sqlUpdateEmail.executeUpdate();
249
250          // if update fails, rollback and discontinue
251          if ( result == 0 ) {
252             connection.rollback(); // rollback update
253             return false;          // update unsuccessful
254          }
255
256          connection.commit();   // commit update
257          return true;           // update successful
258       } // end try
259
260       // detect problems updating database
261       catch ( SQLException sqlException ) {
262
263          // rollback transaction
264          try {
265             connection.rollback(); // rollback update
266             return false;          // update unsuccessful
267          }
268
269          // handle exception rolling back transaction
270          catch ( SQLException exception ) {
271             throw new DataAccessException( exception );
272          }
```

Fig. 8.36 CloudscapeDataAccess implements interface
AddressBookDataAccess to perform the connection to the
database and the database interactions (part 6 of 10).

```
273         }
274    }   // end method savePerson
275
276    // Insert new entry. Method returns boolean indicating
277    // success or failure.
278    public boolean newPerson( AddressBookEntry person )
279        throws DataAccessException
280    {
281        // insert person in database
282        try {
283            int result;
284
285            // insert first and last name in names table
286            sqlInsertName.setString( 1, person.getFirstName() );
287            sqlInsertName.setString( 2, person.getLastName() );
288            result = sqlInsertName.executeUpdate();
289
290            // if insert fails, rollback and discontinue
291            if ( result == 0 ) {
292                connection.rollback(); // rollback insert
293                return false;          // insert unsuccessful
294            }
295
296            // determine new personID
297            ResultSet resultPersonID = sqlPersonID.executeQuery();
298
299            if ( resultPersonID.next() ) {
300                int personID =  resultPersonID.getInt( 1 );
301
302                // insert address in addresses table
303                sqlInsertAddress.setInt( 1, personID );
304                sqlInsertAddress.setString( 2,
305                    person.getAddress1() );
306                sqlInsertAddress.setString( 3,
307                    person.getAddress2() );
308                sqlInsertAddress.setString( 4,
309                    person.getCity() );
310                sqlInsertAddress.setString( 5,
311                    person.getState() );
312                sqlInsertAddress.setString( 6,
313                    person.getZipcode() );
314                result = sqlInsertAddress.executeUpdate();
315
316                // if insert fails, rollback and discontinue
317                if ( result == 0 ) {
318                    connection.rollback(); // rollback insert
319                    return false;          // insert unsuccessful
320                }
321
322                // insert phone number in phoneNumbers table
323                sqlInsertPhone.setInt( 1, personID );
```

Fig. 8.36 **CloudscapeDataAccess** implements interface
AddressBookDataAccess to perform the connection to the
database and the database interactions (part 7 of 10).

```
324              sqlInsertPhone.setString( 2,
325                 person.getPhoneNumber() );
326              result = sqlInsertPhone.executeUpdate();
327
328              // if insert fails, rollback and discontinue
329              if ( result == 0 ) {
330                 connection.rollback(); // rollback insert
331                 return false;          // insert unsuccessful
332              }
333
334              // insert email address in emailAddresses table
335              sqlInsertEmail.setInt( 1, personID );
336              sqlInsertEmail.setString( 2,
337                 person.getEmailAddress() );
338              result = sqlInsertEmail.executeUpdate();
339
340              // if insert fails, rollback and discontinue
341              if ( result == 0 ) {
342                 connection.rollback(); // rollback insert
343                 return false;          // insert unsuccessful
344              }
345
346              connection.commit();   // commit insert
347              return true;           // insert successful
348           }
349
350        else
351           return false;
352     }  // end try
353
354     // detect problems updating database
355     catch ( SQLException sqlException ) {
356        // rollback transaction
357        try {
358           connection.rollback(); // rollback update
359           return false;          // update unsuccessful
360        }
361
362        // handle exception rolling back transaction
363        catch ( SQLException exception ) {
364           throw new DataAccessException( exception );
365        }
366     }
367  } // end method newPerson
368
369  // Delete an entry. Method returns boolean indicating
370  // success or failure.
371  public boolean deletePerson( AddressBookEntry person )
372     throws DataAccessException
373  {
```

Fig. 8.36 CloudscapeDataAccess implements interface
AddressBookDataAccess to perform the connection to the
database and the database interactions (part 8 of 10).

```
374          // delete a person from database
375          try {
376             int result;
377
378             // delete address from addresses table
379             sqlDeleteAddress.setInt( 1, person.getPersonID() );
380             result = sqlDeleteAddress.executeUpdate();
381
382             // if delete fails, rollback and discontinue
383             if ( result == 0 ) {
384                connection.rollback(); // rollback delete
385                return false;          // delete unsuccessful
386             }
387
388             // delete phone number from phoneNumbers table
389             sqlDeletePhone.setInt( 1, person.getPersonID() );
390             result = sqlDeletePhone.executeUpdate();
391
392             // if delete fails, rollback and discontinue
393             if ( result == 0 ) {
394                connection.rollback(); // rollback delete
395                return false;          // delete unsuccessful
396             }
397
398             // delete email address from emailAddresses table
399             sqlDeleteEmail.setInt( 1, person.getPersonID() );
400             result = sqlDeleteEmail.executeUpdate();
401
402             // if delete fails, rollback and discontinue
403             if ( result == 0 ) {
404                connection.rollback(); // rollback delete
405                return false;          // delete unsuccessful
406             }
407
408             // delete name from names table
409             sqlDeleteName.setInt( 1, person.getPersonID() );
410             result = sqlDeleteName.executeUpdate();
411
412             // if delete fails, rollback and discontinue
413             if ( result == 0 ) {
414                connection.rollback(); // rollback delete
415                return false;          // delete unsuccessful
416             }
417
418             connection.commit();   // commit delete
419             return true;           // delete successful
420          } // end try
421
422          // detect problems updating database
423          catch ( SQLException sqlException ) {
424             // rollback transaction
```

Fig. 8.36 CloudscapeDataAccess implements interface
AddressBookDataAccess to perform the connection to the
database and the database interactions (part 9 of 10).

```
425                try {
426                    connection.rollback(); // rollback update
427                    return false;          // update unsuccessful
428                }
429
430                // handle exception rolling back transaction
431                catch ( SQLException exception ) {
432                    throw new DataAccessException( exception );
433                }
434            }
435        } // end method deletePerson
436
437        // method to close statements and database connection
438        public void close()
439        {
440            // close database connection
441            try {
442                sqlFind.close();
443                sqlPersonID.close();
444                sqlInsertName.close();
445                sqlInsertAddress.close();
446                sqlInsertPhone.close();
447                sqlInsertEmail.close();
448                sqlUpdateName.close();
449                sqlUpdateAddress.close();
450                sqlUpdatePhone.close();
451                sqlUpdateEmail.close();
452                sqlDeleteName.close();
453                sqlDeleteAddress.close();
454                sqlDeletePhone.close();
455                sqlDeleteEmail.close();
456                connection.close();
457            } // end try
458
459            // detect problems closing statements and connection
460            catch ( SQLException sqlException ) {
461                sqlException.printStackTrace();
462            }
463        } // end method close
464
465        // Method to clean up database connection. Provided in case
466        // CloudscapeDataAccess object is garbage collected.
467        protected void finalize()
468        {
469            close();
470        }
471    } // end class CloudscapeDataAccess
```

Fig. 8.36   **CloudscapeDataAccess** implements interface
AddressBookDataAccess to perform the connection to the
database and the database interactions (part 10 of 10).

Line 43 of the **CloudscapeDataAccess** constructor (lines 40–127) invokes utility method **connect** (defined at lines 134–152) to perform the connection to the database.

Any exceptions that occur in method **connect** are thrown back to class **AddressBook**, so the application can determine an appropriate course of action to take for a failed connection. If the connection is successful, lines 46–126 invoke **Connection** method **prepareStatement** to create each of the SQL statements that manipulate database **addressbook**. These **PreparedStatement**s perform standard **SELECT**, **INSERT**, **UPDATE** and **DELETE** operations, as discussed in Section 8.4. The question marks (**?**) in each **PreparedStatement** represent the parameters that must be set before the program executes each statement.

PreparedStatement sqlFind (lines 46–55) selects all the data for a person with a specific **lastName** from the four tables in database **addressbook**. Note that the **WHERE** clause uses **AND**ed conditions to ensure that the query retrieves the appropriate data from each table. These conditions compare the **personID** fields in each table. The only records this query returns are those with the specified last name where the **personID** field in table **names** matches the **personID** field in tables **addresses**, **phoneNumbers** and **emailAddresses**. [*Note*: As implemented, this application assumes that all last names are unique.]

PreparedStatement sqlPersonID (lines 59–61) is a Cloudscape-specific operation to determine the last autoincrement value for the **names** table's **personID** field. **ConnectionInfo.lastAutoincrementValue** is a **static** Java method built into Cloudscape. The method receives three SQL string arguments that represent the name of the database *schema* (**'APP'**) containing the table, the name of the table containing the autoincrement field (**'NAMES'**) and the name of the autoincrement field (**'PERSONID'**). Cloudscape *requires* each of these names to be in all uppercase letters. In a database, it is possible to group tables into sets of tables with a specific schema name. SQL statements can qualify table names with schema names to interact with tables from different schemas in the same SQL statement. Cloudscape places database tables in schema **APP** by default.

The remaining **PreparedStatement**s are straightforward. For more detail on the SQL used in those statements, refer back to Section 8.4.

CloudscapeDataAccess method **connect** (lines 134–152) establishes the connection to database **addressbook** with the techniques shown earlier in this chapter. Any exceptions that occur while attempting to load the database driver and connect to the database are thrown from this method back to the called method (the constructor). The database connection in this example differs from those in prior examples in that line 151 disables automatic commitment of transactions. Thus, the program must indicate when a transaction should be committed to the database or rolled back to maintain the database's state before the transaction. This enables **CloudscapeDataAccess** to execute a series of SQL statements and commit the results only if all the statements in the series are successful.

CloudscapeDataAccess method **findPerson** (lines 156–196) receives a **String** containing the last name of the person to locate in the database and uses that last name to set the parameter in **PreparedStatement sqlFind** (line 160). Line 161 executes **sqlFind**. If a record is found, lines 168–186 set the properties of the **Address-BookEntry**, and line 189 returns the **AddressBookEntry**. If no records are found for the specified last name, the method returns **null**.

CloudscapeDataAccess method **savePerson** (lines 200–274) receives an **AddressBookEntry** containing the complete information for a person to update in the database and uses that information to set the parameters of **PreparedStatement**s **sqlUpdateName** (lines 208–210), **sqlUpdateAddress** (lines 220–225), **sqlUpdatePhone** (lines 235–236) and **sqlUpdateEmail** (lines 246–247). Note that parameter values are set by invoking **PreparedStatement** *set* methods for the appropriate data type. In this example, the ID parameters are all integers and the remaining data are all strings, so the program uses methods **setInt** and **setString** to specify parameters. After setting the parameters for a particular **PreparedStatement**, the method calls that statement's **executeUpdate** method (lines 211, 226, 237 and 248), which returns an integer indicating the number of rows modified by the update. The execution of each **PreparedStatement** is followed by an **if** structure that tests the return value of **executeUpdate**. If **executeUpdate** returns 0, the **PreparedStatement** did not update any records. Therefore, **savePerson** invokes **Connection** method **rollback** to restore the database to its state before the **PreparedStatement** executed and returns **false** to indicate to the **AddressBook** application that the update failed. If **savePerson** reaches line 256, it commits the transaction in the database and returns **true** to indicate that the update was successful.

    CloudscapeDataAccess method **newPerson** (lines 278–367) is similar to method **savePerson**. Method **newPerson** receives an **AddressBookEntry** containing the complete information for a person to insert in the database and uses that information to set the parameters of **PreparedStatement**s **sqlInsertName** (lines 286–287), **sqlInsertAddress** (lines 303–313), **sqlInsertPhone** (lines 323–325) and **sqlInsertEmail** (lines 335–337). The primary difference between **newPerson** and **savePerson** is that the entry does not exist in the database yet. To insert rows in tables **addresses**, **phoneNumbers** and **emailAddresses**, the **personID** foreign-key field for each new record must correspond to the **personID** primary-key field in the **names** table. The new **personID** in table **names** is not known until the program inserts the new record in the table. So, after inserting a new record into table **names**, line 297 executes **PreparedStatement sqlPersonID** to obtain the **personID** number for the last new person added to table **names**. Line 300 places this value in the local variable **personID**. Then, the program inserts records in tables **addresses**, **phoneNumbers** and **emailAddresses**, using the new **personID** as the value of the foreign-key field in each table. As in method **savePerson**, if no records are inserted after a given **PreparedStatement** executes, method **newPerson** rolls back the transaction and returns **false** to indicate that the insertion failed. Otherwise, method **newPerson** commits the transaction and returns **true** to indicate that the insertion succeeded.

    CloudscapeDataAccess method **deletePerson** (lines 371–435) receives an **AddressBookEntry** containing the **personID** of the person to remove from the database and uses that ID as the parameter value for the **PreparedStatement**s **sqlDeleteName**, **sqlDeleteAddress**, **sqlDeletePhone** and **sqlDeleteEmail**. When each **PreparedStatement** executes, it deletes all records with the specified **personID** in the appropriate table. If any part of the delete fails, method **deletePerson** rolls back the transaction and returns **false** to indicate that the deletion failed. Otherwise, method **deletePerson** commits the transaction and returns **true** to indicate that the deletion succeeded. In the future, if this program supports multiple addresses, phone numbers and e-mail addresses for each person, this **deletePerson** method will delete all the information for a particular entry properly.

CloudscapeDataAccess methods **close** (lines 438–463) and **finalize** (lines 467–470) close the **PreparedStatement**s and database connection. Method **finalize** is provided in case an object of class **CloudscapeDataAccess** gets garbage collected and the client forgot to call **close** explicitly.

Class **AddressBookEntryFrame** (Fig. 8.37) is a subclass of **JInternalFrame** that enables address-book application users to view or edit the details of an **AddressBookEntry**. The **AddressBook** application class (Fig. 8.38) creates a new **AddressBookEntryFrame** to display the results of a search for an entry and to enable the user to input information for a new entry. **AddressBookEntryFrame** maintains a reference to the currently displayed **AddressBookEntry** and provides *set* and *get* methods to specify an **AddressBookEntry** to display and to return the currently displayed **AddressBookEntry**, respectively. The class also has several **private** utility methods for setting up the GUI and accessing the individual **JTextField**s in the GUI. Objects of class **AddressBookEntryFrame** are managed by class **AddressBook**, which contains a **JDesktopPane**.

```
1    // Fig. 8.37: AddressBookEntryFrame.java
2    // A subclass of JInternalFrame customized to display and
3    // an AddressBookEntry or set an AddressBookEntry's properties
4    // based on the current data in the UI.
5    package com.deitel.advjhtp1.jdbc.addressbook;
6
7    // Java core packages
8    import java.util.*;
9    import java.awt.*;
10
11   // Java extension packages
12   import javax.swing.*;
13
14   public class AddressBookEntryFrame extends JInternalFrame {
15
16       // HashMap to store JTextField references for quick access
17       private HashMap fields;
18
19       // current AddressBookEntry set by AddressBook application
20       private AddressBookEntry person;
21
22       // panels to organize GUI
23       private JPanel leftPanel, rightPanel;
24
25       // static integers used to determine new window positions
26       // for cascading windows
27       private static int xOffset = 0, yOffset = 0;
28
29       // static Strings that represent name of each text field.
30       // These are placed on JLabels and used as keys in
31       // HashMap fields.
32       private static final String FIRST_NAME = "First Name",
```

Fig. 8.37 **AddressBookEntryFrame** for viewing and editing an **AddressBookEntry** (part 1 of 3).

```
33            LAST_NAME = "Last Name", ADDRESS1 = "Address 1",
34            ADDRESS2 = "Address 2", CITY = "City", STATE = "State",
35            ZIPCODE = "Zipcode", PHONE = "Phone", EMAIL = "Email";
36
37      // construct GUI
38      public AddressBookEntryFrame()
39      {
40         super( "Address Book Entry", true, true );
41
42         fields = new HashMap();
43
44         leftPanel = new JPanel();
45         leftPanel.setLayout( new GridLayout( 9, 1, 0, 5 ) );
46         rightPanel = new JPanel();
47         rightPanel.setLayout( new GridLayout( 9, 1, 0, 5 ) );
48
49         createRow( FIRST_NAME );
50         createRow( LAST_NAME );
51         createRow( ADDRESS1 );
52         createRow( ADDRESS2 );
53         createRow( CITY );
54         createRow( STATE );
55         createRow( ZIPCODE );
56         createRow( PHONE );
57         createRow( EMAIL );
58
59         Container container = getContentPane();
60         container.add( leftPanel, BorderLayout.WEST );
61         container.add( rightPanel, BorderLayout.CENTER );
62
63         setBounds( xOffset, yOffset, 300, 300 );
64         xOffset = ( xOffset + 30 ) % 300;
65         yOffset = ( yOffset + 30 ) % 300;
66      }
67
68      // set AddressBookEntry then use its properties to
69      // place data in each JTextField
70      public void setAddressBookEntry( AddressBookEntry entry )
71      {
72         person = entry;
73
74         setField( FIRST_NAME, person.getFirstName() );
75         setField( LAST_NAME, person.getLastName() );
76         setField( ADDRESS1, person.getAddress1() );
77         setField( ADDRESS2, person.getAddress2() );
78         setField( CITY, person.getCity() );
79         setField( STATE, person.getState() );
80         setField( ZIPCODE, person.getZipcode() );
81         setField( PHONE, person.getPhoneNumber() );
82         setField( EMAIL, person.getEmailAddress() );
83      }
84
```

Fig. 8.37 `AddressBookEntryFrame` for viewing and editing an
`AddressBookEntry` (part 2 of 3).

```
85        // store AddressBookEntry data from GUI and return
86        // AddressBookEntry
87        public AddressBookEntry getAddressBookEntry()
88        {
89           person.setFirstName( getField( FIRST_NAME ) );
90           person.setLastName( getField( LAST_NAME ) );
91           person.setAddress1( getField( ADDRESS1 ) );
92           person.setAddress2( getField( ADDRESS2 ) );
93           person.setCity( getField( CITY ) );
94           person.setState( getField( STATE ) );
95           person.setZipcode( getField( ZIPCODE ) );
96           person.setPhoneNumber( getField( PHONE ) );
97           person.setEmailAddress( getField( EMAIL ) );
98
99           return person;
100       }
101
102       // set text in JTextField by specifying field's
103       // name and value
104       private void setField( String fieldName, String value )
105       {
106          JTextField field =
107             ( JTextField ) fields.get( fieldName );
108
109          field.setText( value );
110       }
111
112       // get text in JTextField by specifying field's name
113       private String getField( String fieldName )
114       {
115          JTextField field =
116             ( JTextField ) fields.get( fieldName );
117
118          return field.getText();
119       }
120
121       // utility method used by constructor to create one row in
122       // GUI containing JLabel and JTextField
123       private void createRow( String name )
124       {
125          JLabel label = new JLabel( name, SwingConstants.RIGHT );
126          label.setBorder(
127             BorderFactory.createEmptyBorder( 5, 5, 5, 5 ) );
128          leftPanel.add( label );
129
130          JTextField field = new JTextField( 30 );
131          rightPanel.add( field );
132
133          fields.put( name, field );
134       }
135 }   // end class AddressBookEntryFrame
```

Fig. 8.37 **AddressBookEntryFrame** for viewing and editing an **AddressBookEntry** (part 3 of 3).

Class **AddressBook** (Fig. 8.38) is the main application class for the address-book application. **AddressBook** uses several of the GUI techniques presented in Chapter 2, including tool bars, menus, actions and multiple-document interfaces. The discussion of class **AddressBook** concentrates on the functionality, rather than on the GUI details. Screen captures demonstrating the program's execution appear in Fig. 8.39.

```java
1    // Fig. 8.38: AddressBook.java
2    // An address book database example that allows information to
3    // be inserted, updated and deleted. The example uses
4    // transactions to ensure that the operations complete
5    // successfully.
6    package com.deitel.advjhtp1.jdbc.addressbook;
7
8    // Java core packages
9    import java.awt.*;
10   import java.awt.event.*;
11   import java.sql.*;
12
13   // Java extension packages
14   import javax.swing.*;
15   import javax.swing.event.*;
16
17   public class AddressBook extends JFrame {
18
19      // reference for manipulating multiple document interface
20      private JDesktopPane desktop;
21
22      // reference to database access object
23      private AddressBookDataAccess database;
24
25      // references to Actions
26      Action newAction, saveAction, deleteAction,
27         searchAction, exitAction;
28
29      // set up database connection and GUI
30      public AddressBook()
31      {
32         super( "Address Book" );
33
34         // create database connection
35         try {
36            database = new CloudscapeDataAccess();
37         }
38
39         // detect problems with database connection
40         catch ( Exception exception ) {
41            exception.printStackTrace();
42            System.exit( 1 );
43         }
44
```

Fig. 8.38 **AddressBook** application class that enables the user to interact with the **addressbook** database (part 1 of 8).

```
45          // database connection successful, create GUI
46          JToolBar toolBar = new JToolBar();
47          JMenu fileMenu = new JMenu( "File" );
48          fileMenu.setMnemonic( 'F' );
49
50          // Set up actions for common operations. Private inner
51          // classes encapsulate the processing of each action.
52          newAction = new NewAction();
53          saveAction = new SaveAction();
54          saveAction.setEnabled( false );    // disabled by default
55          deleteAction = new DeleteAction();
56          deleteAction.setEnabled( false );  // disabled by default
57          searchAction = new SearchAction();
58          exitAction = new ExitAction();
59
60          // add actions to tool bar
61          toolBar.add( newAction );
62          toolBar.add( saveAction );
63          toolBar.add( deleteAction );
64          toolBar.add( new JToolBar.Separator() );
65          toolBar.add( searchAction );
66
67          // add actions to File menu
68          fileMenu.add( newAction );
69          fileMenu.add( saveAction );
70          fileMenu.add( deleteAction );
71          fileMenu.addSeparator();
72          fileMenu.add( searchAction );
73          fileMenu.addSeparator();
74          fileMenu.add( exitAction );
75
76          // set up menu bar
77          JMenuBar menuBar = new JMenuBar();
78          menuBar.add( fileMenu );
79          setJMenuBar( menuBar );
80
81          // set up desktop
82          desktop = new JDesktopPane();
83
84          // get the content pane to set up GUI
85          Container c = getContentPane();
86          c.add( toolBar, BorderLayout.NORTH );
87          c.add( desktop, BorderLayout.CENTER );
88
89          // register for windowClosing event in case user
90          // does not select Exit from File menu to terminate
91          // application
92          addWindowListener(
93             new WindowAdapter() {
94                public void windowClosing( WindowEvent event )
95                {
96                   shutDown();
```

Fig. 8.38 **AddressBook** application class that enables the user to interact with the **addressbook** database (part 2 of 8).

```
 97                }
 98             }
 99          );
100
101          // set window size and display window
102          Toolkit toolkit = getToolkit();
103          Dimension dimension = toolkit.getScreenSize();
104
105          // center window on screen
106          setBounds( 100, 100, dimension.width - 200,
107             dimension.height - 200 );
108
109          setVisible( true );
110       }  // end AddressBook constructor
111
112       // close database connection and terminate program
113       private void shutDown()
114       {
115          database.close();    // close database connection
116          System.exit( 0 );    // terminate program
117       }
118
119       // create a new AddressBookEntryFrame and register listener
120       private AddressBookEntryFrame createAddressBookEntryFrame()
121       {
122          AddressBookEntryFrame frame = new AddressBookEntryFrame();
123          setDefaultCloseOperation( DISPOSE_ON_CLOSE );
124          frame.addInternalFrameListener(
125             new InternalFrameAdapter() {
126
127                // internal frame becomes active frame on desktop
128                public void internalFrameActivated(
129                   InternalFrameEvent event )
130                {
131                   saveAction.setEnabled( true );
132                   deleteAction.setEnabled( true );
133                }
134
135                // internal frame becomes inactive frame on desktop
136                public void internalFrameDeactivated(
137                   InternalFrameEvent event )
138                {
139                   saveAction.setEnabled( false );
140                   deleteAction.setEnabled( false );
141                }
142             }  // end InternalFrameAdapter anonymous inner class
143          ); // end call to addInternalFrameListener
144
145          return frame;
146       }  // end method createAddressBookEntryFrame
147
```

Fig. 8.38 **AddressBook** application class that enables the user to interact with the **addressbook** database (part 3 of 8).

```
148    // method to launch program execution
149    public static void main( String args[] )
150    {
151       new AddressBook();
152    }
153
154    // Private inner class defines action that enables
155    // user to input new entry. User must "Save" entry
156    // after inputting data.
157    private class NewAction extends AbstractAction {
158
159       // set up action's name, icon, descriptions and mnemonic
160       public NewAction()
161       {
162          putValue( NAME, "New" );
163          putValue( SMALL_ICON, new ImageIcon(
164             getClass().getResource( "images/New24.png" ) ) );
165          putValue( SHORT_DESCRIPTION, "New" );
166          putValue( LONG_DESCRIPTION,
167             "Add a new address book entry" );
168          putValue( MNEMONIC_KEY, new Integer( 'N' ) );
169       }
170
171       // display window in which user can input entry
172       public void actionPerformed( ActionEvent e )
173       {
174          // create new internal window
175          AddressBookEntryFrame entryFrame =
176             createAddressBookEntryFrame();
177
178          // set new AddressBookEntry in window
179          entryFrame.setAddressBookEntry(
180             new AddressBookEntry() );
181
182          // display window
183          desktop.add( entryFrame );
184          entryFrame.setVisible( true );
185       }
186
187    }  // end inner class NewAction
188
189    // inner class defines an action that can save new or
190    // updated entry
191    private class SaveAction extends AbstractAction {
192
193       // set up action's name, icon, descriptions and mnemonic
194       public SaveAction()
195       {
196          putValue( NAME, "Save" );
197          putValue( SMALL_ICON, new ImageIcon(
198             getClass().getResource( "images/Save24.png" ) ) );
199          putValue( SHORT_DESCRIPTION, "Save" );
```

Fig. 8.38 **AddressBook** application class that enables the user to interact with the **addressbook** database (part 4 of 8).

```
200            putValue( LONG_DESCRIPTION,
201               "Save an address book entry" );
202            putValue( MNEMONIC_KEY, new Integer( 'S' ) );
203         }
204
205      // save new entry or update existing entry
206      public void actionPerformed( ActionEvent e )
207      {
208         // get currently active window
209         AddressBookEntryFrame currentFrame =
210            ( AddressBookEntryFrame ) desktop.getSelectedFrame();
211
212         // obtain AddressBookEntry from window
213         AddressBookEntry person =
214            currentFrame.getAddressBookEntry();
215
216         // insert person in address book
217         try {
218
219            // Get personID. If 0, this is a new entry;
220            // otherwise an update must be performed.
221            int personID = person.getPersonID();
222
223            // determine string for message dialogs
224            String operation =
225               ( personID == 0 ) ? "Insertion" : "Update";
226
227            // insert or update entry
228            if ( personID == 0 )
229               database.newPerson( person );
230            else
231               database.savePerson( person );
232
233            // display success or failure message
234            JOptionPane.showMessageDialog( desktop,
235               operation + " successful" );
236         } // end try
237
238         // detect database errors
239         catch ( DataAccessException exception ) {
240            JOptionPane.showMessageDialog( desktop, exception,
241               "DataAccessException",
242                  JOptionPane.ERROR_MESSAGE );
243            exception.printStackTrace();
244         }
245
246         // close current window and dispose of resources
247         currentFrame.dispose();
248
249      } // end method actionPerformed
250
251   } // end inner class SaveAction
```

Fig. 8.38 **AddressBook** application class that enables the user to interact with the **addressbook** database (part 5 of 8).

```
252
253    // inner class defines action that deletes entry
254    private class DeleteAction extends AbstractAction {
255
256       // set up action's name, icon, descriptions and mnemonic
257       public DeleteAction()
258       {
259          putValue( NAME, "Delete" );
260          putValue( SMALL_ICON, new ImageIcon(
261             getClass().getResource( "images/Delete24.png" ) ) );
262          putValue( SHORT_DESCRIPTION, "Delete" );
263          putValue( LONG_DESCRIPTION,
264             "Delete an address book entry" );
265          putValue( MNEMONIC_KEY, new Integer( 'D' ) );
266       }
267
268       // delete entry
269       public void actionPerformed( ActionEvent e )
270       {
271          // get currently active window
272          AddressBookEntryFrame currentFrame =
273             ( AddressBookEntryFrame ) desktop.getSelectedFrame();
274
275          // get AddressBookEntry from window
276          AddressBookEntry person =
277             currentFrame.getAddressBookEntry();
278
279          // If personID is 0, this is new entry that has not
280          // been inserted. Therefore, delete is not necessary.
281          // Display message and return.
282          if ( person.getPersonID() == 0 ) {
283             JOptionPane.showMessageDialog( desktop,
284                "New entries must be saved before they can be " +
285                "deleted. \nTo cancel a new entry, simply " +
286                "close the window containing the entry" );
287             return;
288          }
289
290          // delete person
291          try {
292             database.deletePerson( person );
293
294             // display message indicating success
295             JOptionPane.showMessageDialog( desktop,
296                "Deletion successful" );
297          }
298
299          // detect problems deleting person
300          catch ( DataAccessException exception ) {
301             JOptionPane.showMessageDialog( desktop, exception,
302                "Deletion failed", JOptionPane.ERROR_MESSAGE );
```

Fig. 8.38 **AddressBook** application class that enables the user to interact with the **addressbook** database (part 6 of 8).

```
303                        exception.printStackTrace();
304                    }
305
306               // close current window and dispose of resources
307               currentFrame.dispose();
308
309          }  // end method actionPerformed
310
311     }  // end inner class DeleteAction
312
313     // inner class defines action that locates entry
314     private class SearchAction extends AbstractAction {
315
316          // set up action's name, icon, descriptions and mnemonic
317          public SearchAction()
318          {
319               putValue( NAME, "Search" );
320               putValue( SMALL_ICON, new ImageIcon(
321                    getClass().getResource( "images/Find24.png" ) ) );
322               putValue( SHORT_DESCRIPTION, "Search" );
323               putValue( LONG_DESCRIPTION,
324                    "Search for an address book entry" );
325               putValue( MNEMONIC_KEY, new Integer( 'r' ) );
326          }
327
328          // locate existing entry
329          public void actionPerformed( ActionEvent e )
330          {
331               String lastName =
332                    JOptionPane.showInputDialog( desktop,
333                         "Enter last name" );
334
335               // if last name was input, search for it; otherwise,
336               // do nothing
337               if ( lastName != null ) {
338
339                    // Execute search. If found, AddressBookEntry
340                    // is returned containing data.
341                    AddressBookEntry person = database.findPerson(
342                         lastName );
343
344                    if ( person != null ) {
345
346                         // create window to display AddressBookEntry
347                         AddressBookEntryFrame entryFrame =
348                              createAddressBookEntryFrame();
349
350                         // set AddressBookEntry to display
351                         entryFrame.setAddressBookEntry( person );
352
353                         // display window
354                         desktop.add( entryFrame );
```

Fig. 8.38 **AddressBook** application class that enables the user to interact with the **addressbook** database (part 7 of 8).

```
355                     entryFrame.setVisible( true );
356                  }
357               else
358                  JOptionPane.showMessageDialog( desktop,
359                     "Entry with last name \"" + lastName +
360                     "\" not found in address book" );
361
362            }  // end "if ( lastName == null )"
363
364         }  // end method actionPerformed
365
366      }  // end inner class SearchAction
367
368      // inner class defines action that closes connection to
369      // database and terminates program
370      private class ExitAction extends AbstractAction {
371
372         // set up action's name, descriptions and mnemonic
373         public ExitAction()
374         {
375            putValue( NAME, "Exit" );
376            putValue( SHORT_DESCRIPTION, "Exit" );
377            putValue( LONG_DESCRIPTION, "Terminate the program" );
378            putValue( MNEMONIC_KEY, new Integer( 'x' ) );
379         }
380
381         // terminate program
382         public void actionPerformed( ActionEvent e )
383         {
384            shutDown();  // close database connection and terminate
385         }
386
387      }  // end inner class ExitAction
388   }
```

Fig. 8.38   **AddressBook** application class that enables the user to interact with the
addressbook database (part 8 of 8).

Class **AddressBook**'s constructor (lines 30–110) creates a **Cloudscape-
DataAccess** object to interact with the database (line 36), builds the GUI (lines 46–87),
registers an event handler for the window-closing event (lines 92–99) and displays the
application window (lines 102–109). As part of building the tool bar and menu for the
application, lines 52–58 of the constructor create instances of five **private** inner classes
that implement the actions for the GUI—**NewAction** (lines 157–187), **SaveAction**
(lines 191–251), **DeleteAction** (lines 254–311), **SearchAction** (lines 314–366)
and **ExitAction** (lines 370–387). Note that the program disables the **SaveAction** and
DeleteAction by default. These are enabled only if there is an active internal frame on
the desktop.

Each action (except **ExitAction**) uses a standard icon from the Sun Microsystems
Java Look and Feel Graphics Repository, located at **developer.java.sun.com/
developer/techDocs/hi/repository**. The first screen capture of Fig. 8.39
describes each of the icons in the GUI.

New   Save   Delete   Search

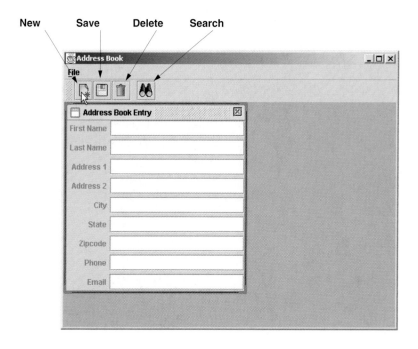

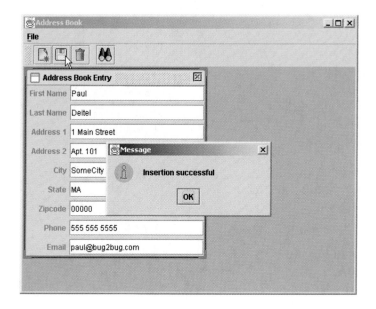

Fig. 8.39   Screen captures of the **AddressBook** application (part 1 of 3).

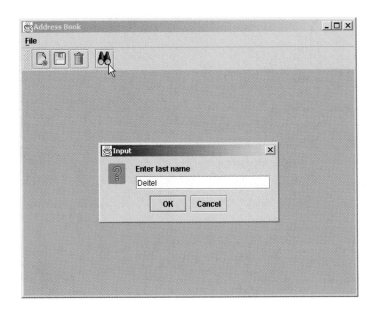

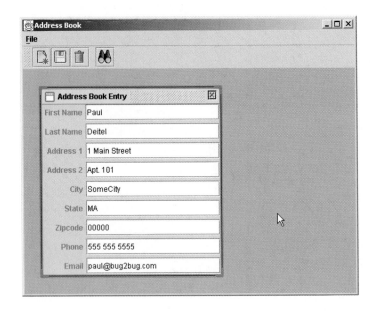

Fig. 8.39   Screen captures of the **AddressBook** application (part 2 of 3).

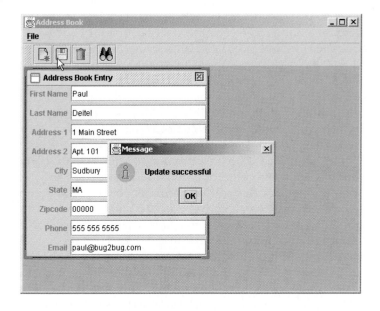

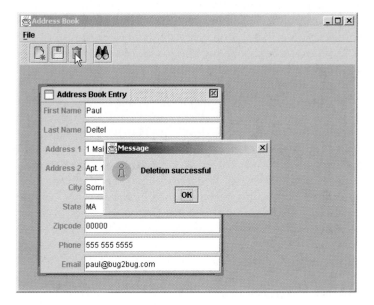

Fig. 8.39 Screen captures of the **AddressBook** application (part 3 of 3).

NewAction (lines 157–187) does not perform any database manipulations. It simply displays an **AddressBookEntryFrame** in which the user inputs the information for a new address book entry. To perform the actual insert into the database, the user must click the **Save** button or select **Save** from the **File** menu, which invokes the **SaveAction**. Class **NewAction**'s **actionPerformed** method (lines 172–185) creates a new **AddressBookEntryFrame** (lines 175–176), sets a new **AddressBookEntry** for the frame (lines 179–180), attaches the frame to the **JDesktopPane** (line 183) and displays the frame (line 184).

SaveAction (lines 191–251) determines whether to save a new entry or update an existing entry based on the **personID** for the **AddressBookEntry** in the currently active internal frame. Method **actionPerformed** (lines 206–249) obtains a reference to the active internal frame (lines 209–210) and gets the **AddressBookEntry** currently displayed (lines 213–214). Line 221 gets the **personID** from the **AddressBookEntry**. If the **personID** is 0, the **AddressBookEntry** represents a new address book entry, and line 229 invokes the **CloudscapeDataAccess** object's **newPerson** method to insert a new record in the database. If the **personID** is not 0, the **AddressBookEntry** represents an existing address book entry to update, and line 231 invokes the **CloudscapeDataAccess** object's **savePerson** method to update the record in the database. Methods **newPerson** and **savePerson** each receive an **AddressBookEntry** as an argument. Line 247 disposes of the active internal frame after the save operation completes.

DeleteAction (lines 254–311) uses the **AddressBookEntry** in the currently active internal frame to remove an entry from the database. Method **actionPerformed** (lines 269–309) obtains a reference to the active internal frame (lines 272–273) and gets the currently displayed **AddressBookEntry** (lines 276–277). If the **personID** in the **AddressBookEntry** is 0, the entry has not been stored in the database, so **actionPerformed** displays a message to the user and terminates (lines 282–288). Line 292 invokes the **CloudscapeDataAccess** object's **deletePerson** method, passing the **AddressBookEntry** to delete as an argument. Line 307 disposes of the active internal frame after the delete operation completes.

SearchAction (lines 314–366) searches for an address book entry based on the last name of the person input by the user. Method **actionPerformed** (lines 329–364) obtains the last name for which to search (lines 331–333). If the last name is not **null** (i.e., the user did not click the **Cancel** button in the input dialog), lines 341–342 create a new **AddressBookEntry** reference and invokes **database**'s **findPerson** method to locate the person in the database. If the person exists, **findPerson** returns the **AddressBookEntry** containing the information for that person. Then, **actionPerformed** creates a new **AddressBookEntryFrame** (lines 347–348), sets the **AddressBookEntry** for the frame (line 351), attaches the frame to the **JDesktopPane** (line 354) and displays the frame (line 355). Otherwise, **actionPerformed** displays a message dialog indicating that the record was not found.

In Fig. 8.39, the first screen capture shows the address-book application after the user clicks the **New** button to create a new entry. The second screen capture shows the results after the user inputs the information for the new entry and clicks the **Save** button to insert the data in the database. The third and fourth screen captures demonstrate searching for an entry in the database. The fifth screen capture demonstrates updating the person's city information. The sixth screen capture demonstrates deleting the record for the currently displayed entry. [*Note*: The screen captures do not show that after completing a **Save** or **Delete** operation, the internal frame that displays the entry is removed from the screen.]

8.8 Stored Procedures

Many database management systems can store individual SQL statements or sets of SQL statements in a database, so that programs accessing that database can invoke them. Such SQL statements are called *stored procedures*. JDBC enables programs to invoke stored procedures using objects that implement interface **CallableStatement**. Like **PreparedStatement**s, **CallableStatement**s can receive arguments specified with the methods inherited from interface **PreparedStatement**. In addition, **CallableStatement**s can specify *output parameters* in which a stored procedure can place return values. Interface **CallableStatement** includes methods to specify which parameters in a stored procedure are output parameters. The interface also includes methods to obtain the values of output parameters returned from a stored procedure.

Portability Tip 8.8

*Although the syntax for creating stored procedures differs across database management systems, interface **CallableStatement** provides a uniform interface for specifying input and output parameters for stored procedures and for invoking stored procedures.*

Portability Tip 8.9

*According to the Java API documentation for interface **CallableStatement**, for maximum portability between database systems, programs should process the update counts or **ResultSet**s returned from a **CallableStatement** before obtaining the values of any output parameters.*

8.9 Batch Processing

A series of database updates (e.g., inserts, updates, deletes) can be performed in a *batch update* to the database. JDBC **Statement**s, **PreparedStatement**s and **CallableStatement**s provide an *addBatch* method that enables the program to add SQL statements to a batch for future execution. Each **Statement**, **PreparedStatement** or **CallableStatement** object maintains its own list of SQL statements to perform in a batch update. Figure 8.40 describes the batch-processing methods of interfaces **Statement** and **PreparedStatement**. (**CallableStatement**s inherit the methods of interface **PreparedStatement**.)

Method	Description
public void addBatch(String sql)	
	Method of interface **Statement** that receives a **String** argument specifying an SQL statement to add to the **Statement**'s batch for future execution. This method should not be used with **PreparedStatement**s and **CallableStatement**s.

Fig. 8.40 **Statement** and **PreparedStatement** methods for batch updates (part 1 of 2).

Method	Description

public void addBatch()

Method of interface **PreparedStatement** that adds the statement to a batch for future execution. This method should be called after setting the parameters for the **PreparedStatement**. This version of **addBatch** also can be used with **CallableStatement**s.

public void clearBatch()

Method of interface **Statement** that clears the statement's batch.

public int[] executeBatch()

Method of interface **Statement** that executes the statement's batch. The method returns an array of **int** values indicating the status of each SQL statement in the batch. The order of the values in the array corresponds to the order in which the SQL statements are added to the batch.

Fig. 8.40 **Statement** and **PreparedStatement** methods for batch updates (part 2 of 2).

Each method in Fig. 8.40 throws a **BatchUpdateException** (a subclass of **SQLException**) if database errors occur while executing any of the SQL statements or if the particular database management system does not support batch update processing. Method **executeBatch** also throws **BatchUpdateException**s if the batch update contains any SQL statements that return **ResultSet**s.

Common Programming Error 8.14

*Batch updates are for use only with SQL statements that do not return **ResultSet**s. Executing an SQL statement that returns a **ResultSet** as part of a batch update causes a **BatchUpdateException***

After adding statements to a batch update, a program invokes **Statement** method **executeBatch** to execute the SQL statements in the batch. This method performs each SQL statement and returns an array of **int** values containing the status of each SQL statement. If the database connection is in autocommit mode, the database commits each statement as it completes execution. Otherwise, the program can determine whether or not to commit the transaction by inspecting the array of return values and then invoke the **Connection**'s **commit** or **rollback** method as appropriate. Figure 8.41 summarizes the return values of method **executeBatch**.

Return value	Description
a value greater than or equal to **0**	Indicates successful execution of the SQL statements in the batch update. The value specifies the actual number of rows updated in the database.
-2	Indicates successful execution of the SQL statements in the batch update and that the affected number of rows is unknown.

Fig. 8.41 Return values of method **executeBatch** (part 1 of 2).

Return value	Description
-3	Indicates an SQL statement that failed to execute properly during a batch update. When the batch update is allowed to complete its processing, the array returned by **getUpdateCounts** contains the value **-3** for any SQL statement that failed. When the batch update is not allowed to continue after an exception, the array returned by **getUpdateCounts** contains elements for only the SQL statements that executed successfully before the exception occurred. When a failure occurs, **executeUpdate** throws a **BatchUpdateException**. In such cases, the program can catch the exception and invoke **BatchUpdateException** method **getUpdateCounts** to obtain the array of update counts. Some databases allow a batch update to continue executing when an exception occurs, while others do not.

Fig. 8.41   Return values of method **executeBatch** (part 2 of 2).

Software Engineering Observation 8.12

*Normally, programs disable autocommit mode for a **Connection** before executing a batch update. Otherwise, each SQL statement in the batch update is committed individually, which prevents programs from deciding whether groups of SQL statements should be committed or rolled back, based on logic in the program.*

8.10 Processing Multiple **ResultSet**s or Update Counts

Some **Statement**s, **PreparedStatement**s and **CallableStatement**s return multiple **ResultSet**s or update counts. In such cases, programs should use **Statement** method *execute* to execute the SQL statements. After executing SQL statements, method **execute** returns a **boolean** indicating whether the first result is a **ResultSet** (**true**) or an update count (**false**). Based on **execute**'s return value, the program invokes method *getResultSet* or method *getUpdateCount* to obtain the first result. The program can obtain subsequent results by calling method *getMoreResults*. Figure 8.42 summarizes the methods for processing multiple results. [*Note*: Each of the methods in Fig. 8.42 is defined in interface **Statement** and inherited into interfaces **PreparedStatement** and **CallableStatement**.]

Method	Description
public boolean execute()	
	Programs use this method to execute SQL statements that can return multiple **ResultSet**s or update counts. This method returns a **boolean** indicating whether the first result is a **ResultSet** (**true**) or an update count (**false**). Based on the value returned, the program can call **getResultSet** or **getUpdateCount** to obtain the first result.

Fig. 8.42   **Statement** methods that enable processing of multiple results returned by method **execute** (part 1 of 2).

Method	Description

public boolean getMoreResults()

> After obtaining the first result returned from method **execute**, a program invokes this method to move to the next result. This method returns a **boolean** indicating whether the next result is a **ResultSet** (**true**) or an update count (**false**). Based on the value returned, the program can call **getResultSet** or **getUpdateCount** to obtain the next result.

public ResultSet getResultSet()

> Obtains a **ResultSet** from the results returned by method **execute**. This method returns **null** if the result is not a **ResultSet** or if there are no more results.

public int getUpdateCount()

> Obtains an update count from the results returned by method **execute**. This method returns **-1** if the result is not an update count or if there are no more results.

Fig. 8.42 **Statement** methods that enable processing of multiple results returned by method **execute** (part 2 of 2).

Software Engineering Observation 8.13

*A program has completed processing the results returned by method **execute** when method **getMoreResults** returns **false** and method **getUpdateCount** returns **-1**.*

8.11 Updatable ResultSets

Some JDBC drivers support *updatable* **ResultSet**s. Such **ResultSet**s enable a program to insert, update and delete records using methods of interface **ResultSet**. If the JDBC driver supports updatable **ResultSet**s, the program can invoke **Connection** method **createStatement**, **prepareStatement** or **prepareCall** and specify the constant *ResultSet.CONCUR_UPDATABLE* as the second argument (the first argument specifies the type of scrolling supported by the **ResultSet**).

Software Engineering Observation 8.14

*Normally, a query that produces an updatable **ResultSet** must select a table's primary key, so that updates can determine the proper records to manipulate in the database. Otherwise, the query returns a read-only **ResultSet**.*

Interface **ResultSet** provides update methods that enable the program to specify new values for particular columns in the current **ResultSet** row. In addition, interface **ResultSet** provides methods *deleteRow*, *insertRow* and *updateRow* to manipulate the **ResultSet** and the underlying database. Method **deleteRow** deletes the current **ResultSet** row from the **ResultSet** and the database. Method **updateRow** updates the current row in the **ResultSet** and the database. Method **insertRow** inserts a new row in the **ResultSet** and the database. Every updatable **ResultSet** maintains an insert row where the program can build a new record before inserting it in the **ResultSet** and the database. Before invoking **ResultSet**'s update methods to build the new record, the program must invoke **ResultSet** method *moveToInsertRow*. The **ResultSet** keeps track of the cursor's location before that operation. The program can return to the cursor location to continue processing the **ResultSet** by invoking **ResultSet** method *moveToCurrentRow*.

8.12 JDBC 2.0 Optional Package `javax.sql`

In addition to the classes and interfaces of package **java.sql**, many database vendors now support the JDBC 2.0 optional package *javax.sql*. Typically, this package is included with the implementation of the Java 2 Enterprise Edition. Some of the key interfaces in package **javax.sql** include *DataSource*, *ConnectionPoolDataSource*, *PooledConnection* and *RowSet*. Each of these interfaces is explained briefly in the next several subsections.

8.12.1 DataSource

A **DataSource** is new way for programs to obtain database connections. Enterprise Java applications often access information and resources (such as databases) that are external to those applications. In some cases, resources are distributed across a network. Enterprise application components must be able to locate the resources they use. An Enterprise Java application container must provide a *naming service* that implements the *Java Naming and Directory Interface* (*JNDI*) and enables the components executing in that container to perform name lookups to locate resources. Typically, **DataSource**s are registered with a JNDI service that enables a program to locate the **DataSource**. Chapter 11 demonstrates our first Enterprise Java application that uses a JNDI service to look up a **DataSource** and connect to a database.

8.12.2 Connection Pooling

The process of connecting to a database requires substantial overhead in both time and resources. In a program that performs many separate database connections (such as a server in a Web-based shopping-cart application), such overhead can become a burden on the program. Applications can establish *connection pools* that maintain many database connections to eliminate the overhead of connecting to the database while many clients are waiting for responses in distributed applications. These connection objects can be shared between the application clients.

Databases that provide full support for the JDBC optional package include implementations of interfaces *ConnectionPoolDataSource* and *PooledConnection*. Like **DataSource**s **ConnectionPoolDataSource**s typically are registered with a JNDI service, so that a program can locate them dynamically. After obtaining a reference to a **ConnectionPoolDataSource**, a program can invoke its *getPooledConnection* method to obtain a **PooledConnection** object that represents the connection to the database. **PooledConnection** method *getConnection* returns the underlying **Connection** object that the program uses to create **Statement**s, **PreparedStatement**s and **CallableStatement**s for executing SQL statements.

8.12.3 RowSets

The JDBC optional package introduces a new interface, **RowSet**, for manipulating tabular data sources such as **ResultSet**s. **RowSet**s are not implemented as part of the database driver. Instead, they are implemented as JavaBeans that encapsulate a tabular data source.

Interface **RowSet** extends interface **ResultSet**. Thus, a **RowSet** object has all the functionality of a **ResultSet**, including the ability to scroll through the records, insert new records, update existing records and delete existing records. What makes a **RowSet** interesting is that all of these features are supported regardless of whether the **ResultSet** implementation provided by a particular database driver supports these features. For example, a program can create a **RowSet** based on a **ResultSet**, disconnect from the database and allow the program to update the data in the **RowSet**. Then the **RowSet** can connect to the database and update it, based on the changes made to the data in the **RowSet**. All of this can be accomplished even if the database driver does not support updatable **ResultSet**s. **RowSet**s that disconnect from the database and then reconnect to perform updates are called *disconnected RowSets*.

Unlike **ResultSet**s, **RowSet**s implementations can be serializable, so they can be saved locally or transmitted across a network. **RowSet**s also support JavaBean events (with interface *RowSetListener* and class *RowSetEvent*) that enable an application using a **RowSet** to be notified when the **RowSet** cursor moves, a record is inserted, a record is updated, a record is deleted or the entire set of data in the **RowSet** changes. **RowSet**s also allow a program to set parameters to the **RowSet**'s *command string*—normally, the SQL statement that obtains the data.

If you are interested in experimenting with **RowSet**s, Sun Microsystems has three early access **RowSet** implementations available at

```
developer.java.sun.com/developer/earlyAccess/crs
```

These implementations are *CachedRowSet*, *WebRowSet* and *JDBCRowSet*.

Class **CachedRowSet** defines a disconnected **RowSet** that can be serialized. **CachedRowSet** provides full support for scrolling through data and updating data—both particularly useful in applications that require these capabilities even if the database driver's **ResultSet** implementation does not support scrolling through and updating data. The fact that **CachedRowSet**s are serializable enables them to be sent across a network in a distributed network application.

Class **WebRowSet** is a subclass of **CachedRowSet** that enables **RowSet** data to be output as an XML document. Class **JDBCRowSet** defines a connected **RowSet** that encapsulates a **ResultSet** to make the **ResultSet** appear like a JavaBean to the program.

For a tutorial on using the Sun Microsystems, Inc., **RowSet** implementations, visit

```
developer.java.sun.com/developer/Books/JDBCTutorial/
    chapter5.html
```

Also, check your database management system's documentation to determine whether your database provides any **RowSet** implementations.

8.13 Internet and World Wide Web Resources

```
java.sun.com/products/jdbc
```
Sun Microsystems, Inc.'s JDBC home page.

java.sun.com/docs/books/tutorial/jdbc/index.html
The Sun Microsystems, Inc., Java Tutorial's JDBC track.

www.sql.org
This SQL portal provides links to many resources, including SQL syntax, tips, tutorials, books, magazines, discussion groups, companies with SQL services, SQL consultants and free software.

industry.java.sun.com/products/jdbc/drivers
Sun Microsystems, Inc., search engine for locating JDBC drivers.

java.sun.com/j2se/1.3/docs/guide/jdbc/index.html
Sun Microsystems, Inc.'s JDBC API documentation.

java.sun.com/products/jdbc/faq.html
Sun Microsystems, Inc.'s frequently asked questions on JDBC.

www.jguru.com/jguru/faq/faqpage.jsp?name=JDBC
The JGuru JDBC FAQs.

www.cloudscape.com
This site is Informix's Cloudscape database home page. Here, you can download the latest version of Cloudscape and access all of its documentation on line.

java.sun.com/products/jdbc/articles/package2.html
An overview of the JDBC 2.0 optional package API.

developer.java.sun.com/developer/earlyAccess/crs
Early access to the Sun **RowSet** implementations. [*Note*: You may need to register at the Java Developer Connection (**developer.java.sun.com/developer/index.html**) before downloading from this site.]

developer.java.sun.com/developer/Books/JDBCTutorial/chapter5.html
Chapter 5 (**RowSet** Tutorial) of the book *The JDBC 2.0 API Tutorial and Reference, Second Edition*.

SUMMARY

- A database is an integrated collection of data. A database management system (DBMS) provides mechanisms for storing and organizing data.

- Today's most popular database systems are relational databases.

- A language called Structured Query Language (SQL) is used almost universally with relational database systems to perform queries and manipulate data.

- A programming language connects to, and interacts with, relational databases via an interface— software that facilitates communications between a database management system and a program.

- Java programmers communicate with databases and manipulate their data using the Java Database Connectivity (JDBC) API. A JDBC driver implements the interface to a particular database.

- A relational database is composed of tables. A row of a table is called a record (or row).

- A primary key is a field that contains unique data that cannot be duplicated in other records.

- Each column of the table represents a different field (or column or attribute).

- The primary key can be composed of more than one column (or field) in the database.

- SQL provides a complete set of commands that enable programmers to define complex queries that select data from a table. The results of a query are commonly called result sets (or record sets).

- Every record must have a value in the primary-key field, and that value must be unique. This is known as the Rule of Entity Integrity.

- A one-to-many relationship between tables indicates that a record in one table can have many records in a separate table.

- A foreign key is a field for which every entry in one table has a unique value in another table and where the field in the other table is the primary key for that table.

- The foreign key helps maintain the Rule of Referential Integrity: Every foreign key field value must appear in another table's primary key field. Foreign keys enable information from multiple tables to be joined together for analysis purposes. There is a one-to-many relationship between a primary key and its corresponding foreign key.

- The simplest format of a **SELECT** query is

      SELECT * FROM *tableName*

  where the asterisk (*****) indicates that all rows and columns from *tableName* should be selected and *tableName* specifies the table in the database from which the data will be selected.

- To select specific fields from a table, replace the asterisk (*****) with a comma-separated list of the field names to select.

- Programmers process result sets by knowing in advance the order of the fields in the result set. Specifying the field names to select guarantees that the fields are always returned in the specified order, even if the actual order of the fields in the database table(s) changes.

- The optional **WHERE** clause in a **SELECT** query specifies the selection criteria for the query. The simplest format of a **SELECT** query with selection criteria is

      SELECT *fieldName1*, *fieldName2*, ... FROM *tableName* WHERE *criteria*

- The **WHERE** clause condition can contain operators **<, >, <=, >=, =, <>** and **LIKE**. Operator **LIKE** is used for pattern matching with wildcard characters percent (**%**) and underscore (**_**).

- A percent character (**%**) in a pattern indicates that a string matching the pattern can have zero or more characters at the percent character's location in the pattern.

- An underscore (**_**) in the pattern string indicates a single character at that position in the pattern.

- The results of a query can be arranged in ascending or descending order using the optional **ORDER BY** clause. The simplest form of an **ORDER BY** clause is

      SELECT *fieldName1*, *fieldName2*, ... FROM *tableName* ORDER BY *field* ASC
      SELECT *fieldName1*, *fieldName2*, ... FROM *tableName* ORDER BY *field* DESC

  where **ASC** specifies ascending order, **DESC** specifies descending order and *field* specifies the field on which the sort is based. The default sorting order is ascending, so **ASC** is optional.

- Multiple fields can be used for ordering purposes with an **ORDER BY** clause of the form

      ORDER BY *field1* *sortingOrder*, *field2* *sortingOrder*, ...

- The **WHERE** and **ORDER BY** clauses can be combined in one query.

- A join merges records from two or more tables by testing for matching values in a field that is common to both tables. The simplest format of a join is

      SELECT *fieldName1*, *fieldName2*, ...
          FROM *table1*, *table2*
          WHERE *table1*.*fieldName* = *table2*.*fieldName*

  The query's **WHERE** clause specifies the fields from each table that should be compared to determine which records will be selected. These fields normally represent the primary key in one table and the corresponding foreign key in the other table.

- If an SQL statement uses fields with the same name from multiple tables, the field names must be fully qualified with its table name and a dot operator (**.**).
- An **INSERT INTO** statement inserts a new record in a table. The simplest form of this statement is

      INSERT INTO *tableName* **(** *fieldName1, fieldName2, ..., fieldNameN* **)**
             VALUES (*value1, value2, ..., valueN* **)**

  where *tableName* is the table in which to insert the record. The *tableName* is followed by a comma-separated list of field names in parentheses. The list of field names is followed by the SQL keyword **VALUES** and a comma-separated list of values in parentheses.
- SQL statements use single quote (**'**) as a delimiter for strings. To specify a string containing a single quote in an SQL statement, the single quote must be escaped with another single quote.
- An **UPDATE** statement modifies data in a table. The simplest form for an **UPDATE** statement is

      UPDATE *tableName*
             SET *fieldName1* **=** *value1, fieldName2* **=** *value2, ..., fieldNameN* **=** *valueN*
             WHERE *criteria*

  where *tableName* is the table in which to update a record (or records). The *tableName* is followed by keyword **SET** and a comma-separated list of field name/value pairs in the format *fieldName* **=** *value*. The **WHERE** clause *criteria* determines the record(s) to update.
- A **DELETE** statement removes data from a table. The simplest form for a **DELETE** statement is

      DELETE FROM *tableName* **WHERE** *criteria*

  where *tableName* is the table from which to delete a record (or records). The **WHERE** *criteria* determines which record(s) to delete.
- Package **java.sql** contains classes and interfaces for manipulating relational databases in Java.
- A program must load the database driver class before the program can connect to the database.
- JDBC supports four categories of drivers: JDBC-to-ODBC bridge driver (Type 1); Native-API, partly Java driver (Type 2); JDBC-Net pure Java driver (Type 3) and Native-Protocol pure Java driver (Type 4). Type 3 and 4 drivers are preferred, because they are pure Java solutions.
- An object that implements interface **Connection** manages the connection between the Java program and the database. **Connection** objects enable programs to create SQL statements that manipulate databases and to perform transaction processing.
- Method **getConnection** of class **DriverManager** attempts to connect to a database specified by its URL argument. The URL helps the program locate the database. The URL includes the protocol for communication, the subprotocol for communication and the name of the database.
- **Connection** method **createStatement** creates an object of type **Statement**. The program uses the **Statement** object to submit SQL statements to the database.
- **Statement** method **executeQuery** executes a query that selects information from a table or set of tables and returns an object that implements interface **ResultSet** containing the query results. **ResultSet** methods enable a program to manipulate query results.
- A **ResultSetMetaData** object describes a **ResultSet**'s contents. Programs can use metadata programmatically to obtain information about the **ResultSet** column names and types.
- **ResultSetMetaData** method **getColumnCount** retrieves the number of columns in the **ResultSet**.
- **ResultSet** method **next** positions the **ResultSet** cursor to the next record in the **ResultSet**. The cursor keeps track of the current record. Method **next** returns **boolean** value **true**

if it is able to position to the next record; otherwise, the method returns **false**. This method must be called to begin processing a **ResultSet**.

- When processing **ResultSet**s, it is possible to extract each column of the **ResultSet** as a specific Java data type. **ResultSetMetaData** method **getColumnType** returns a constant integer from class **Types** (package **java.sql**) indicating the type of the data for a specific column.

- **ResultSet** *get* methods typically receive as an argument either a column number (as an **int**) or a column name (as a **String**) indicating which column's value to obtain.

- **ResultSet** column numbers start at 1.

- Each **Statement** object can open only one **ResultSet** object at a time. When a **Statement** returns a new **ResultSet**, the **Statement** closes the prior **ResultSet**.

- **Connection** method **createStatement** has an overloaded version that takes two arguments: the result set type and the result set concurrency. The result set type specifies whether the **ResultSet**'s cursor is able to scroll in both directions or forward only and whether the **ResultSet** is sensitive to changes. The result set concurrency specifies whether the **ResultSet** can be updated with **ResultSet**'s update methods.

- Some **ResultSet** implementations do not support scrollable and/or updatable **ResultSet**s.

- **TableModel** method **getColumnClass** returns a **Class** object that represents the superclass of all objects in a particular column. **JTable** uses this information to set up the default cell renderer and cell editor for that column in a **JTable**.

- **ResultSetMetaData** method **getColumnClassName** obtains the fully qualified class name of the specified column.

- **TableModel** method **getColumnCount** returns the number of columns in the model's underlying **ResultSet**.

- **ResultSetMetaData** method **getColumnCount** obtains the number of columns in the **ResultSet**.

- **TableModel** method **getColumnName** returns the name of the column in the model's underlying **ResultSet**.

- **ResultSetMetaData** method **getColumnName** obtains the column name from the **ResultSet**.

- **TableModel** method **getRowCount** returns the number of rows in the model's underlying **ResultSet**.

- **TableModel** method **getValueAt** returns the **Object** in a particular row and column of the model's underlying **ResultSet**.

- **ResultSet** method **absolute** positions the **ResultSet** cursor at a specific row.

- **AbstractTableModel** method **fireTableStructureChanged** notifies any **JTable** using a particular **TableModel** object as its model that the data in the model has changed.

- Interface **PreparedStatement** enables an application programmer to create SQL statements that are maintained in a compiled form that enables the statements to execute more efficiently than **Statement** objects. **PreparedStatement** objects are more flexible than **Statement** objects, because they can specify parameters.

- Question marks (**?**) in the SQL of a **PreparedStatement** represent placeholders for values that will be passed as part of the SQL statement to the database. Before the program executes a **PreparedStatement**, the program must specify the values of those parameters by using interface **PreparedStatement**'s *set* methods.

- Transaction processing enables a program that interacts with a database to treat a database operation (or set of operations) as a transaction. When the transaction completes, a decision can be made to either commit the transaction or roll back the transaction. Java provides transaction processing via methods of interface **Connection**.

- Method **setAutoCommit** specifies whether each SQL statement commits after it completes (a **true** argument) or if SQL statements should be grouped as a transaction (a **false** argument).

- If autocommit is disabled the program must follow the last SQL statement in the transaction with a call to **Connection** method **commit** or **rollback**.

- JDBC enables programs to invoke stored procedures using objects that implement interface **CallableStatement**.

- **CallableStatement**s can receive arguments specified with the methods inherited from interface **PreparedStatement**. In addition, **CallableStatement**s can specify output parameters in which a stored procedure can place return values.

- A series of database updates can be performed in a batch update to the database. JDBC **Statement**s, **PreparedStatement**s and **CallableStatement**s provide an **addBatch** method that enables the program to add SQL statements to a batch for future execution. Each **Statement**, **PreparedStatement** or **CallableStatement** object maintains its own list of SQL statements to perform in a batch update.

- **Statement** method **executeBatch** executes the SQL statements in a batch and returns an array of **int** values containing the status of each SQL statement. If the database connection is in autocommit mode, the database commits each statement as it completes execution. Otherwise, **Connection** methods **commit** or **rollback** must be called as appropriate.

- Programs use **Statement** method **execute** to execute **Statement**s, **PreparedStatement**s and **CallableStatement**s that return multiple **ResultSet**s or update counts. Method **execute** returns a **boolean** indicating whether the first result is a **ResultSet** (**true**) or an update count (**false**). The program invokes method **getResultSet** or method **getUpdateCount** to obtain the first result and obtains subsequent results with **getMoreResults**.

- Some JDBC drivers support updatable **ResultSet**s. Such **ResultSet**s enable a program to insert, update and delete records using methods of interface **ResultSet**.

- Interface **ResultSet** provides *update* methods that enable the program to specify new values for particular columns in the current **ResultSet** row.

- Interface **ResultSet** provides methods **deleteRow**, **insertRow** and **updateRow** to manipulate the **ResultSet** and the underlying database.

- Every updatable **ResultSet** maintains an insert row where the program can build a new record before inserting it into the **ResultSet** and the database. Before invoking **ResultSet**'s *update* methods to build the new record, the program must invoke **ResultSet** method **moveToInsertRow**. The **ResultSet** keeps track of the cursor's location before that operation and can return to the cursor location to continue processing the **ResultSet** by invoking **ResultSet** method **moveToCurrentRow**.

- A **DataSource** is new way for programs to obtain database connections that access databases which are external to those applications.

- Applications can establish connection pools that maintain many database connections. Databases that provide full support for the JDBC optional package include implementations of interfaces **ConnectionPoolDataSource** and **PooledConnection** for this purpose.

- The JDBC optional package introduces a new interface, **RowSet**, for manipulating tabular data sources such as **ResultSet**s. **RowSet**s are not implemented as part of the database driver. Instead, they are implemented as JavaBeans that encapsulate a tabular data source.

- Interface **RowSet** extends interface **ResultSet**. Thus, a **RowSet** object has all the functionality of a **ResultSet**, including the ability to scroll through the records, insert new records, update existing records and delete existing records.

- Unlike **ResultSet**s, **RowSet**s implementations can be serializable so they can be saved locally or transmitted across a network.

- **RowSet**s support JavaBean events that enable an application using a **RowSet** to be notified when the **RowSet** cursor is moved, a record is inserted, a record is updated, a record is deleted or the entire set of data in the **RowSet** changes.

- Class **CachedRowSet** defines a disconnected **RowSet** that can be serialized. **CachedRowSet** provides full support for scrolling through data and updating data.

- Class **WebRowSet** is a subclass of **CachedRowSet** that enables **RowSet** data to be output as an XML document.

- Class **JDBCRowSet** defines a connected **RowSet** that encapsulates a **ResultSet** to make the **ResultSet** appear like a JavaBean to the program.

TERMINOLOGY

% SQL wildcard character
_ SQL wildcard character
absolute method of **ResultSet**
AbstractTableModel class
addBatch method of **PreparedStatement**
addBatch method of **Statement**
addTableModelListener method of
    TableModel
autocommit state
batch processing
BatchUpdateException class
CachedRowSet class
CallableStatement interface
clearBatch method of **Statement**
close method of **Connection**
close method of **Statement**
Cloudscape database
COM.cloudscape.core.RmiJdbcDriver
commit a transaction
commit method of **Connection**
connect to a database
Connection interface
connection pool
ConnectionPoolDataSource interface
createStatement method of **Connection**
database
database driver
DataSource interface
DELETE FROM SQL statement
deleteRow method of **ResultSet**
disconnected **RowSet**
DriverManager class
execute method of **Statement**

executeBatch method of **Statement**
executeQuery method of **Statement**
executeUpdate method of **Statement**
field
fireTableStructureChanged method of
    AbstractTableModel
foreign key
getAutoCommit method of **Connection**
getColumnClass method of **TableModel**
getColumnClassName method of
    ResultSetMetaData
getColumnCount method of
    ResultSetMetaData
getColumnCount method of **TableModel**
getColumnName method of
    ResultSetMetaData
getColumnName method of **TableModel**
getColumnType method of
    ResultSetMetaData
getConnection method of **DriverManager**
getConnection method of
    PooledConnection
getMetaData method of **ResultSet**
getMoreResults method of **Statement**
getObject method of **ResultSet**
getPooledConnection method of
    ConnectionPoolDataSource
getResultSet method of **Statement**
getRow method of **ResultSet**
getRowCount method of **TableModel**
getUpdateCount method of **Statement**
getUpdateCounts method of
    BatchUpdateException

getValueAt method of **TableModel**

INSERT INTO SQL statement

insertRow method of **ResultSet**

Java Database Connectivity (JDBC)

Java Look and Feel Graphics Repository

Java Naming and Directory Interface (JNDI)

java.sql package

javax.sql package

javax.swing.table package

JDBC driver

jdbc:cloudscape:rmi:books

JdbcOdbcDriver

JDBCRowSet class

last method of **ResultSet**

metadata

moveToCurrentRow method of **ResultSet**

moveToInsertRow method of **ResultSet**

next method of **ResultSet**

one-to-many relationship

ORDER BY clause of an SQL statement

ordering records

pattern matching

PooledConnection interface

PreparedStatement interface

prepareStatement method of **Connection**

primary key

query a database

record

record set

relational database

removeTableModelListener method of
  TableModel

result set

ResultSet interface

ResultSet types

ResultSetMetaData interface

roll back a transaction

rollBack method of **Connection**

RowSet command string

RowSet interface

RowSetEvent class

RowSetListener interface

Rule of Entity Integrity

Rule of Referential Integrity

SELECT SQL statement

selection criteria

setAutoCommit method of **Connection**

setString method of **PreparedStatement**

SQL (Structured Query Language)

SQL script

SQLException class

Statement interface

stored procedure

table column

table row

TableModel interface

TableModelEvent class

transaction processing

Type 1 (JDBC-to-ODBC bridge) driver

Type 2 (Native-API, partly Java) driver

Type 3 (JDBC-Net pure Java) driver

Type 4 (Native-Protocol pure Java) driver

Types class

updatable **ResultSet**

UPDATE operation

updateRow method of **ResultSet**

WebRowSet class

WHERE clause of an SQL statement

SELF-REVIEW EXERCISES

8.1 Fill in the blanks in each of the following statements:

    a) The most popular database query language is _____.

    b) A table in a database consists of _____ and _____.

    c) Tables are manipulated in Java as _____ objects.

    d) The _____ uniquely identifies each record in a table.

    e) SQL keyword _____ is followed by the selection criteria that specify the records to
       select in a query.

    f) SQL keywords _____ specify the order in which records are sorted in a query.

    g) Selecting data from multiple database tables is called _____ the data.

    h) A _____ is an integrated collection of data that is centrally controlled.

    i) A _____ is a field in a table for which every entry has a unique value in another
       table and where the field in the other table is the primary key for that table.

    j) Package _____ contains classes and interfaces for manipulating relational databas-
       es in Java.

k) Interface _____ helps manage the connection between the Java program and the database.

l) A _____ object is used to submit a query to a database.

ANSWERS TO SELF-REVIEW EXERCISES

8.1 a) SQL. b) rows, columns. c) **ResultSet**. d) primary key. e) **WHERE**. f) **ORDER BY**. g) joining. h) database. i) foreign key. j) **java.sql**. k) **Connection**. l) **Statement**.

EXERCISES

8.2   Using the techniques shown in this chapter, define a complete query application for the **books** database. Provide a series of predefined queries, with an appropriate name for each query, displayed in a **JComboBox**. Also allow users to supply their own queries and add them to the **JComboBox**. Provide the following predefined queries:

a) Select all authors from the **Authors** table.

b) Select all publishers from the **Publishers** table.

c) Select a specific author and list all books for that author. Include the title, year and ISBN number. Order the information alphabetically by the author's last name and first name.

d) Select a specific publisher and list all books published by that publisher. Include the title, year and ISBN number. Order the information alphabetically by title.

e) Provide any other queries you feel are appropriate.

8.3   Modify Exercise 8.2 to define a complete database manipulation application for the **books** database. In addition to the querying, the user should be able to edit existing data and add new data to the database (obeying referential and entity integrity constraints). Allow the user to edit the database in the following ways:

a) Add a new author.

b) Edit the existing information for an author.

c) Add a new title for an author. (Remember that the book must have an entry in the **AuthorISBN** table.) Be sure to specify the publisher of the title.

d) Add a new publisher.

e) Edit the existing information for a publisher.

f) For each of the preceding database manipulations, design an appropriate GUI to allow the user to perform the data manipulation.

8.4   Modify the **Search** capability in the address book example of Fig. 8.33–Fig. 8.38 to allow the user to scroll through the **ResultSet** in case there is more than one person with the specified last name in the **addressbook** database. Provide an appropriate GUI.

8.5   Modify the address book example of Fig. 8.33–Fig. 8.38 to enable each address book entry to have multiple addresses, phone numbers and e-mail addresses. The user of the program should be able to view multiple addresses, phone numbers and e-mail addresses. The user also should be able to add, update or delete individual addresses, phone numbers and e-mail addresses. [*Note*: This exercise is large and requires substantial modifications to the original classes in the address book example.]

BIBLIOGRAPHY

Ashmore, D. C. "Best Practices for JDBC Programming." *Java Developers Journal*, 5: no. 4 (2000): 42–54.

Blaha, M. R., W. J. Premerlani and J. E. Rumbaugh. "Relational Database Design Using an Object-Oriented Methodology." *Communications of the ACM*, 31: no. 4 (1988): 414–427.

Brunner, R. J. "The Evolution of Connecting." *Java Developers Journal*, 5: no. 10 (2000): 24–26.

Brunner, R. J. "After the Connection." *Java Developers Journal*, 5: no. 11 (2000): 42–46.

Callahan, T. "So You Want a Stand-Alone Database for Java." *Java Developers Journal*, 3: no. 12 (1998): 28–36.

Codd, E. F. "A Relational Model of Data for Large Shared Data Banks." *Communications of the ACM*, June 1970.

Codd, E. F. "Further Normalization of the Data Base Relational Model." *Courant Computer Science Symposia*, Vol. 6, *Data Base Systems*. Upper Saddle River, NJ: Prentice Hall, 1972.

Codd, E. F. "Fatal Flaws in SQL." *Datamation*, 34: no. 16 (1988): 45–48.

Cooper, J. W. "Making Databases Easier for Your Users." *Java Pro*, 4: no. 10 (2000): 47–54.

Date, C. J. *An Introduction to Database Systems, Seventh Edition*. Reading, MA: Addison Wesley, 2000.

Deitel, H. M. *Operating Systems, Second Edition*. Reading, MA: Addison Wesley, 1990.

Duguay, C. "Electronic Mail Merge." *Java Pro*, Winter 1999/2000, 22–32.

Ergul, S. "Transaction Processing with Java." *Java Report*, January 2001, 30–36.

Fisher, M. "JDBC Database Access," (a trail in *The Java Tutorial*), <**java.sun.com/docs/ books/tutorial/jdbc/index.html**>.

Harrison, G., "Browsing the JDBC API," *Java Developers Journal*, 3: no. 2 (1998): 44–52.

Jasnowski, M. "Persistence Frameworks," *Java Developers Journal*, 5: no. 11 (2000): 82–86.

"JDBC API Documentation," <**java.sun.com/j2se/1.3/docs/guide/jdbc/ index.html**>.

Jordan, D. "An Overview of Sun's Java Data Objects Specification," *Java Pro*, 4: no. 6 (2000): 102–108.

Khanna, P. "Managing Object Persistence with JDBC," *Java Pro*, 4: no. 5 (2000): 28–33.

Reese, G. *Database Programming with JDBC and Java, Second Edition*. Cambridge, MA: O'Reilly, 2001.

Spell, B. "Create Enterprise Applications with JDBC 2.0," *Java Pro*, 4: no. 4 (2000): 40–44.

Stonebraker, M. "Operating System Support for Database Management," *Communications of the ACM*, 24: no. 7 (1981): 412–418.

Taylor, A. *JDBC Developer's Resource: Database Programming on the Internet*. Upper Saddle River, NJ: Prentice Hall, 1999.

Thilmany, C. "Applying Patterns to JDBC Development," *Java Developers Journal*, 5: no. 6 (2000): 80–90.

Venugopal, S. 2000. "Cross-Database Portability with JDBC, *Java Developers Journal*, 5: no. 1 (2000): 58–62.

White, S., M. Fisher, R. Cattell, G. Hamilton and M. Hapner. *JDBC API Tutorial and Reference, Second Edition*. Boston, MA: Addison Wesley, 1999.

Winston, A. "A Distributed Database Primer," *UNIX World*, April 1988, 54–63.

Servlets

Objectives

- To execute servlets with the Apache Tomcat server.
- To be able to respond to HTTP requests from an **HttpServlet**.
- To be able to redirect requests to static and dynamic Web resources.
- To be able to maintain session information with cookies and **HttpSession** objects.
- To be able to access a database from a servlet.

A fair request should be followed by the deed in silence.
Dante Alighieri

The longest part of the journey is said to be the passing of the gate.
Marcus Terentius Varro

If nominated, I will not accept; if elected, I will not serve.
General William T. Sherman

Me want cookie!
The Cookie Monster, *Sesame Street*

When to the sessions of sweet silent thought
I summon up remembrance of things past, …
William Shakespeare

Friends share all things.
Pythagorus

If at first you don't succeed, destroy all evidence that you tried.
Newt Heilscher

Outline

9.1 Introduction

There is much excitement over the Internet and the World Wide Web. The Internet ties the "information world" together. The World Wide Web makes the Internet easy to use and gives it the flair and sizzle of multimedia. Organizations see the Internet and the Web as crucial to their information systems strategies. Java provides a number of built-in networking capabilities that make it easy to develop Internet-based and Web-based applications. Not only can Java specify parallelism through multithreading, but it can enable programs to search the world for information and to collaborate with programs running on other computers internationally, nationally or just within an organization. Java can even enable applets and applications running on the same computer to communicate with one another, subject to security constraints.

Networking is a massive and complex topic. Computer science and computer engineering students typically take a full-semester, upper-level course in computer networking and continue with further study at the graduate level. Java provides a rich complement of networking capabilities and will likely be used as an implementation vehicle in computer networking courses. In *Advanced Java 2 Platform How to Program* we introduce several Java networking concepts and capabilities.

Java's networking capabilities are grouped into several packages. The fundamental networking capabilities are defined by classes and interfaces of package ***java.net***, through which Java offers *socket-based communications* that enable applications to view networking as streams of data—a program can read from a *socket* or write to a socket as simply as reading from a file or writing to a file. The classes and interfaces of package **java.net** also offer *packet-based communications* that enable individual *packets* of information to be transmitted—commonly used to transmit audio and video over the Internet. Our book *Java How to Program, Fourth Edition* shows how to create and manipulate sockets and how to communicate with packets of data.

Higher-level views of networking are provided by classes and interfaces in the **java.rmi** packages (five packages) for *Remote Method Invocation (RMI)* and **org.omg** packages (seven packages) for *Common Object Request Broker Architecture (CORBA)* that are part of the Java 2 API. The RMI packages allow Java objects running on separate Java Virtual Machines (normally on separate computers) to communicate via remote method calls. Such method calls appear to be to an object in the same program, but actually have built-in networking (based on the capabilities of package **java.net**) that communicates the method calls to another object on a separate computer. The CORBA packages provide similar functionality to the RMI packages. A key difference between RMI and CORBA is that RMI can only be used between Java objects, whereas CORBA can be used between any two applications that understand CORBA—including applications written in other programming languages. In Chapter 13 of *Advanced Java 2 Platform How to Program*, we present Java's RMI capabilities. Chapters 26–27 of *Advanced Java 2 Platform How to Program* discuss the basic CORBA concepts and present a case study that implements a distributed system in CORBA.

Our discussion of networking over the next two chapters focuses on both sides of a *client-server relationship*. The *client* requests that some action be performed and the *server* performs the action and responds to the client. This request-response model of communication is the foundation for the highest-level views of networking in Java—*servlets* and *JavaServer Pages (JSP)*. A servlet extends the functionality of a server. Packages **javax.servlet** and **javax.servlet.http** provide the classes and interfaces to define servlets. Packages **javax.servlet.jsp** and **javax.servlet.jsp.tagext** provide the classes and interfaces that extend the servlet capabilities for JavaServer Pages. Using special syntax, JSP allows Web-page implementors to create pages that use encapsulated Java functionality and even to write *scriptlets* of actual Java code directly in the page.

A common implementation of the request-response model is between World Wide Web browsers and World Wide Web servers. When a user selects a Web site to browse through their browser (the client application), a request is sent to the appropriate Web server (the server application). The server normally responds to the client by sending the appropriate XHTML Web page. Servlets are effective for developing Web-based solutions that help provide secure access to a Web site, interact with databases on behalf of a client, dynamically generate custom XHTML documents to be displayed by browsers and maintain unique session information for each client.

Software Engineering Observation 9.1

Although servlets typically are used in distributed Web applications, not all servlets are required to enhance the functionality of a Web server.

This chapter begins our networking discussions with servlets that enhance the functionality of World Wide Web servers—the most common form of servlet today. Chapter 10 discusses JSPs, which are translated into servlets. JSPs are a convenient and powerful way to implement the request/response mechanism of the Web without getting into the lower-level details of servlets. Together, servlets and JSPs form the Web tier of the Java 2 Enterprise Edition (J2EE).

Many developers feel that servlets are the right solution for database-intensive applications that communicate with so-called *thin clients*—applications that require minimal client-side support. The server is responsible for database access. Clients connect to the server using standard protocols available on most client platforms. Thus, the presentation-logic code for generating dynamic content can be written once and reside on the server for access by clients, to allow programmers to create efficient thin clients.

In this chapter, our servlet examples demonstrate the Web's request/response mechanism (primarily with **get** and **post** requests), session-tracking capabilities, redirecting requests to other resources and interacting with databases through JDBC. We placed this chapter after our discussion of JDBC and databases intentionally, so that we can build multi-tier, client–server applications that access databases. In Chapter 11, we build a bookstore Web application, using XML technologies (Appendices A-D), JDBC technology from Chapter 8, the servlet technology from this chapter and the JSP technology from Chapter 10. We present additional servlet capabilities in the case study.

Sun Microsystems, through the *Java Community Process*, is responsible for the development of the servlet and JavaServer Pages specifications. The reference implementation of both these standards is under development by the *Apache Software Foundation* (**www.apache.org**) as part of the *Jakarta Project* (**jakarta.apache.org**). As stated on the Jakarta Project's home page, "The goal of the Jakarta Project is to provide commercial-quality server solutions based on the Java Platform that are developed in an open and cooperative fashion." There are many subprojects under the Jakarta project to help commercial server-side developers. The servlet and JSP part of the Jakarta Project is called *Tomcat*. This is the official reference implementation of the JSP and servlet standards. We use Tomcat to demonstrate the servlets in this chapter. The most recent implementation of Tomcat at the time of this writing was version 3.2.3. For your convenience, Tomcat 3.2.3 is included on the CD that accompanies *Advanced Java 2 Platform How to Program*. However, the most recent version always can be downloaded from the Apache Group's Web site. To execute the servlets in this chapter, you must install Tomcat or an equivalent servlet and JavaServer Pages implementation. We discuss the set up and configuration of Tomcat in Section 9.3.1 and Section 9.3.2 after we introduce our first example.

In our directions for testing each of the examples in this chapter, we indicate that you should copy files into specific Tomcat directories. All the example files for this chapter are located on the CD that accompanies this book and on our Web site **www.deitel.com**.

[*Note*: At the end of Section 9.10, we provide a list of Internet specifications (as discussed in the Servlet 2.2 Specification) for technologies related to servlet development. Each is listed with its RFC (Request for Comments) number. We provide the URL of a Web site that allows you to locate each specification for your review.]

9.2 Servlet Overview and Architecture

In this section, we overview Java servlet technology. We discuss at a high level the servlet-related classes, methods and exceptions. The next several sections present live-code examples in which we build multi-tier client–server systems using servlet and JDBC technology.

The Internet offers many protocols. The *HTTP* (*Hypertext Transfer Protocol*) that forms the basis of the World Wide Web uses *URIs* (*Uniform Resource Identifiers*— sometimes called *Universal Resource Locators* or *URLs*) to locate resources on the Internet. Common URIs represent files or directories and can represent complex tasks such as database lookups and Internet searches. For more information on URL formats, visit

> **www.w3.org/Addressing**

For more information on the HTTP protocol, visit

> **www.w3.org/Protocols/HTTP**

For information on a variety of World Wide Web topics, visit

> **www.w3.org**

JavaServer Pages technology is an extension of servlet technology. Normally, JSPs are used primarily when most of the content sent to the client is static text and markup, and only a small portion of the content is generated dynamically with Java code. Normally, servlets are used when a small portion of the content sent to the client is static text or markup. In fact, some servlets do not produce content. Rather, they perform a task on behalf of the client, then invoke other servlets or JSPs to provide a response. Note that in most cases servlet and JSP technologies are interchangeable. The server that executes a servlet often is referred to as the *servlet container* or *servlet engine*.

Servlets and JavaServer Pages have become so popular that they are now supported directly or with third-party plug-ins by most major Web servers and application servers, including the Netscape iPlanet Application Server, Microsoft's Internet Information Server (IIS), the Apache HTTP Server, BEA's WebLogic application server, IBM's Web-Sphere application server, the World Wide Web Consortium's Jigsaw Web server, and many more.

The servlets in this chapter demonstrate communication between clients and servers via the HTTP protocol. A client sends an HTTP request to the server or servlet container. The server or servlet container receives the request and directs it to be processed by the appropriate servlet. The servlet does its processing, which may include interacting with a database or other server-side components such as other servlets, JSPs or Enterprise Java-Beans (Chapter 16). The servlet returns its results to the client—normally in the form of an HTML, XHTML or XML document to display in a browser, but other data formats, such as images and binary data, can be returned.

9.2.1 Interface **Servlet** and the Servlet Life Cycle

Architecturally, all servlets must implement the **Servlet** interface. As with many key applet methods, the methods of interface **Servlet** are invoked automatically (by the server on which the servlet is installed, also known as the servlet container). This interface defines five methods described in Fig. 9.1.

Software Engineering Observation 9.2

*All servlets must implement the **Servlet** interface of package **javax.servlet**.*

Method	Description

void init(ServletConfig config)

> This method is automatically called once during a servlet's execution cycle to initialize the servlet. The **ServletConfig** argument is supplied by the servlet container that executes the servlet.

ServletConfig getServletConfig()

> This method returns a reference to an object that implements interface **ServletConfig**. This object provides access to the servlet's configuration information such as servlet initialization parameters and the servlet's **ServletContext**, which provides the servlet with access to its environment (i.e., the servlet container in which the servlet executes).

String getServletInfo()

> This method is defined by a servlet programmer to return a **String** containing servlet information such as the servlet's author and version.

void service(ServletRequest request, ServletResponse response)

> The servlet container calls this method to respond to a client request to the servlet.

void destroy()

> This "cleanup" method is called when a servlet is terminated by its servlet container. Resources used by the servlet, such as an open file or an open database connection, should be deallocated here.

Fig. 9.1 Methods of interface **Servlet** (package **javax.servlet**).

A servlet's life cycle begins when the servlet container loads the servlet into memory—normally, in response to the first request that the servlet receives. Before the servlet can handle that request, the servlet container invokes the servlet's *init* method. After **init** completes execution, the servlet can respond to its first request. All requests are handled by a servlet's *service* method, which receives the request, processes the request and sends a response to the client. During a servlet's life cycle, method **service** is called once per request. Each new request typically results in a new thread of execution (created by the servlet container) in which method **service** executes. When the servlet container terminates the servlet, the servlet's **destroy** method is called to release servlet resources.

Performance Tip 9.1

> *Starting a new thread for each request is more efficient than starting an entirely new process, as is the case in some other server-side technologies such as CGI. [Note: Like servlets, Fast CGI eliminates the overhead of starting a new process for each request.]*

The servlet packages define two **abstract** classes that implement the interface **Servlet**—class *GenericServlet* (from the package **javax.servlet**) and class *HttpServlet* (from the package **javax.servlet.http**). These classes provide default implementations of all the **Servlet** methods. Most servlets extend either **GenericServlet** or **HttpServlet** and override some or all of their methods.

The examples in this chapter all extend class **HttpServlet**, which defines enhanced processing capabilities for servlets that extend the functionality of a Web server. The key method in every servlet is **service**, which receives both a *ServletRequest* object and a *ServletResponse* object. These objects provide access to input and output streams that allow the servlet to read data from the client and send data to the client. These streams can be either byte based or character based. If problems occur during the execution of a servlet, either **ServletException**s or **IOException**s are thrown to indicate the problem.

Software Engineering Observation 9.3

*Servlets can implement tagging interface **javax.servlet.SingleThreadModel** to indicate that only one thread of execution may enter method **service** on a particular servlet instance at a time. When a servlet implements **SingleThreadModel**, the servlet container can create multiple instances of the servlet to handle multiple requests to the servlet in parallel. In this case, you may need to provide synchronized access to shared resources used by method **service**.*

9.2.2 **HttpServlet** Class

Web-based servlets typically extend class **HttpServlet**. Class **HttpServlet** overrides method **service** to distinguish between the typical requests received from a client Web browser. The two most common *HTTP request types* (also known as *request methods*) are *get* and *post*. A *get* request *gets* (or *retrieves*) information from a server. Common uses of *get* requests are to retrieve an HTML document or an image. A *post* request *posts* (or *sends*) data to a server. Common uses of *post* requests typically send information, such as authentication information or data from a *form* that obtains user input, to a server.

Class **HttpServlet** defines methods *doGet* and *doPost* to respond to *get* and *post* requests from a client, respectively. These methods are called by the **service** method, which is called when a request arrives at the server. Method **service** first determines the request type, then calls the appropriate method for handling such a request. Other less common request types are beyond the scope of this book. Methods of class **HttpServlet** that respond to the other request types are shown in Fig. 9.2. They all receive parameters of type **HttpServletRequest** and **HttpServletResponse** and return **void**. The methods of Fig. 9.2 are not frequently used. For more information on the HTTP protocol, visit

www.w3.org/Protocols.

Software Engineering Observation 9.4

*Do not override method service in an **HttpServlet** subclass. Doing so prevents the servlet from distinguishing between request types.*

Methods **doGet** and **doPost** receive as arguments an **HttpServletRequest** object and an **HttpServletResponse** object that enable interaction between the client and the server. The methods of **HttpServletRequest** make it easy to access the data supplied as part of the request. The **HttpServletResponse** methods make it easy to return the servlet's results to the Web client. Interfaces **HttpServletRequest** and **HttpServletResponse** are discussed in the next two sections.

Method	Description
doDelete	Called in response to an HTTP **delete** request. Such a request is normally used to delete a file from a server. This may not be available on some servers, because of its inherent security risks (i.e., the client could delete a file that is critical to the execution of the server or an application).
doOptions	Called in response to an HTTP **options** request. This returns information to the client indicating the HTTP options supported by the server, such as the version of HTTP (1.0 or 1.1) and the request methods the server supports.
doPut	Called in response to an HTTP **put** request. Such a request is normally used to store a file on the server. This may not be available on some servers, because of its inherent security risks (i.e., the client could place an executable application on the server, which, if executed, could damage the server—perhaps by deleting critical files or occupying resources).
doTrace	Called in response to an HTTP **trace** request. Such a request is normally used for debugging. The implementation of this method automatically returns a\n HTML document to the client containing the request header information (data sent by the browser as part of the request).

Fig. 9.2   Other methods of class **HttpServlet**.

9.2.3 **HttpServletRequest** Interface

Every call to **doGet** or **doPost** for an **HttpServlet** receives an object that implements interface **HttpServletRequest**. The Web server that executes the servlet creates an **HttpServletRequest** object and passes this to the servlet's **service** method (which, in turn, passes it to **doGet** or **doPost**). This object contains the request from the client. A variety of methods are provided to enable the servlet to process the client's request. Some of these methods are from interface *ServletRequest*—the interface that **HttpServletRequest** extends. A few key methods used in this chapter are presented in Fig. 9.3. You can view a complete list of **HttpServletRequest** methods online at

> **java.sun.com/j2ee/j2sdkee/techdocs/api/javax/servlet/http/
> HttpServletRequest.html**

or you can download and install Tomcat (discussed in Section 9.3.1) and view the documentation on your local computer.

Method	Description
String getParameter(String name)	Obtains the value of a parameter sent to the servlet as part of a **get** or **post** request. The **name** argument represents the parameter name.

Fig. 9.3   Some methods of interface **HttpServletRequest** (part 1 of 2).

Method	Description

Enumeration getParameterNames()

Returns the names of all the parameters sent to the servlet as part of a **post** request.

String[] getParameterValues(String name)

For a parameter with multiple values, this method returns an array of **String**s containing the values for a specified servlet parameter.

Cookie[] getCookies()

Returns an array of **Cookie** objects stored on the client by the server. **Cookie**s can be used to uniquely identify clients to the servlet.

HttpSession getSession(boolean create)

Returns an **HttpSession** object associated with the client's current browsing session. An **HttpSession** object can be created by this method (**true** argument) if an **HttpSession** object does not already exist for the client. **HttpSession** objects can be used in similar ways to **Cookie**s for uniquely identifying clients.

Fig. 9.3   Some methods of interface **HttpServletRequest** (part 2 of 2).

9.2.4 **HttpServletResponse** Interface

Every call to **doGet** or **doPost** for an **HttpServlet** receives an object that implements interface **HttpServletResponse**. The Web server that executes the servlet creates an **HttpServletResponse** object and passes it to the servlet's **service** method (which, in turn, passes it to **doGet** or **doPost**). This object provides a variety of methods that enable the servlet to formulate the response to the client. Some of these methods are from interface *ServletResponse*—the interface that **HttpServletResponse** extends. A few key methods used in this chapter are presented in Fig. 9.4. You can view a complete list of **HttpServletResponse** methods online at

> **java.sun.com/j2ee/j2sdkee/techdocs/api/javax/servlet/http/**
> **HttpServletResponse.html**

or you can download and install Tomcat (discussed in Section 9.3.1) and view the documentation on your local computer..

Method	Description

void addCookie(Cookie cookie)

Used to add a **Cookie** to the header of the response to the client. The **Cookie**'s maximum age and whether **Cookie**s are enabled on the client determine if **Cookie**s are stored on the client.

Fig. 9.4   Some methods of interface **HttpServletResponse** (part 1 of 2).

Method	Description

`ServletOutputStream getOutputStream()`

Obtains a byte-based output stream for sending binary data to the client.

`PrintWriter getWriter()`

Obtains a character-based output stream for sending text data to the client.

`void setContentType( String type )`

Specifies the MIME type of the response to the browser. The MIME type helps the browser determine how to display the data (or possibly what other application to execute to process the data). For example, MIME type `"text/html"` indicates that the response is an HTML document, so the browser displays the HTML page. For more information on

Fig. 9.4   Some methods of interface `HttpServletResponse` (part 2 of 2).

9.3 Handling HTTP get Requests

The primary purpose of an HTTP **get** request is to retrieve the content of a specified URL—normally the content is an HTML or XHTML document (i.e., a Web page). The servlet of Fig. 9.5 and the XHTML document of Fig. 9.6 demonstrate a servlet that handles HTTP **get** requests. When the user clicks the **Get HTML Document** button (Fig. 9.6), a **get** request is sent to the servlet **WelcomeServlet** (Fig. 9.5). The servlet responds to the request by generating dynamically an XHTML document for the client that displays "**Welcome to Servlets!**". Figure 9.5 shows the **WelcomeServlet** source code. Figure 9.6 shows the XHTML document the client loads to access the servlet and shows screen captures of the client's browser window before and after the interaction with the servlet. [*Note*: Section 9.3.1 discusses how to set up and configure Tomcat to execute this example.]

Lines 5 and 6 import the **javax.servlet** and **javax.servlet.http** packages. We use several data types from these packages in the example.

Package **javax.servlet.http** provides superclass **HttpServlet** for servlets that handle HTTP **get** requests and HTTP **post** requests. This class implements interface **javax.servlet.Servlet** and adds methods that support HTTP protocol requests. Class **WelcomeServlet** extends **HttpServlet** (line 9) for this reason.

Superclass **HttpServlet** provides method *doGet* to respond to **get** requests. Its default functionality is to indicate a "Method not allowed" error. Typically, this error is indicated in Internet Explorer with a Web page that states "This page cannot be displayed" and in Netscape Navigator with a Web page that states "Error: 405." Lines 12–44 override method **doGet** to provide custom **get** request processing. Method **doGet** receives two arguments—an **HttpServletRequest** object and an **HttpServletResponse** object (both from package **javax.servlet.http**). The **HttpServletRequest** object represents the client's request, and the **HttpServletResponse** object represents the server's response to the client. If method **doGet** is unable to handle a client's request, it throws an exception of type *javax.servlet.ServletException*. If **doGet** encounters an error during stream processing (reading from the client or writing to the client), it throws a *java.io.IOException*.

```
1   // Fig. 9.5: WelcomeServlet.java
2   // A simple servlet to process get requests.
3   package com.deitel.advjhtp1.servlets;
4
5   import javax.servlet.*;
6   import javax.servlet.http.*;
7   import java.io.*;
8
9   public class WelcomeServlet extends HttpServlet {
10
11      // process "get" requests from clients
12      protected void doGet( HttpServletRequest request,
13         HttpServletResponse response )
14            throws ServletException, IOException
15      {
16         response.setContentType( "text/html" );
17         PrintWriter out = response.getWriter();
18
19         // send XHTML page to client
20
21         // start XHTML document
22         out.println( "<?xml version = \"1.0\"?>" );
23
24         out.println( "<!DOCTYPE html PUBLIC \"-//W3C//DTD " +
25            "XHTML 1.0 Strict//EN\" \"http://www.w3.org" +
26            "/TR/xhtml1/DTD/xhtml1-strict.dtd\">" );
27
28         out.println(
29            "<html xmlns = \"http://www.w3.org/1999/xhtml\">" );
30
31         // head section of document
32         out.println( "<head>" );
33         out.println( "<title>A Simple Servlet Example</title>" );
34         out.println( "</head>" );
35
36         // body section of document
37         out.println( "<body>" );
38         out.println( "<h1>Welcome to Servlets!</h1>" );
39         out.println( "</body>" );
40
41         // end XHTML document
42         out.println( "</html>" );
43         out.close();  // close stream to complete the page
44      }
45   }
```

Fig. 9.5   `WelcomeServlet` that responds to a simple HTTP **get** request.

To demonstrate a response to a **get** request, our servlet creates an XHTML document containing the text "**Welcome to Servlets!**". The text of the XHTML document is the response to the client. The response is sent to the client through the **PrintWriter** object obtained from the **HttpServletResponse** object.

Line 16 uses the **response** object's *setContentType* method to specify the content type of the data to be sent as the response to the client. This enables the client browser to understand and handle the content. The content type also is known as the *MIME* type (*Multipurpose Internet Mail Extension*) of the data. In this example, the content type is *text/html* to indicate to the browser that the response is an XHTML document. The browser knows that it must read the XHTML tags in the document, format the document according to the tags and display the document in the browser window. For more information on MIME types visit **www.irvine.com/~mime**.

Line 17 uses the **response** object's *getWriter* method to obtain a reference to the **PrintWriter** object that enables the servlet to send content to the client. [*Note*: If the response is binary data, such as an image, method *getOutputStream* is used to obtain a reference to a **ServletOutputStream** object.]

Lines 22–42 create the XHTML document by writing strings with the **out** object's *println* method. This method outputs a newline character after its **String** argument. When rendering the Web page, the browser does not use the newline character. Rather, the newline character appears in the XHTML source that you can see by selecting **Source** from the **View** menu in Internet Explorer or **Page Source** from the **View** menu in Netscape Navigator. Line 43 closes the output stream, flushes the output buffer and sends the information to the client. This commits the response to the client.

The XHTML document in Fig. 9.6 provides a **form** that invokes the servlet defined in Fig. 9.5. The **form**'s **action** (**/advjhtp1/welcome**) specifies the URL path that invokes the servlet, and the **form**'s **method** indicates that the browser sends a **get** request to the server, which results in a call to the servlet's **doGet** method. The URL specified as the **action** in this example is discussed in detail in Section 9.3.2 after we show how to set up and configure the *Apache Tomcat server* to execute the servlet in Fig. 9.5.

```
1   <?xml version = "1.0"?>
2   <!DOCTYPE html PUBLIC "-//W3C//DTD XHTML 1.0 Strict//EN"
3      "http://www.w3.org/TR/xhtml11/DTD/xhtml1-strict.dtd">
4
5   <!-- Fig. 9.6: WelcomeServlet.html -->
6
7   <html xmlns = "http://www.w3.org/1999/xhtml">
8   <head>
9      <title>Handling an HTTP Get Request</title>
10  </head>
11
12  <body>
13     <form action = "/advjhtp1/welcome1" method = "get">
14
15        <p><label>Click the button to invoke the servlet
16           <input type = "submit" value = "Get HTML Document" />
17        </label></p>
18
19     </form>
20  </body>
21  </html>
```

Fig. 9.6   HTML document in which the **form**'s **action** invokes **WelcomeServlet** through the alias **welcome1** specified in **web.xml** (part 1 of 2).

Fig. 9.6   HTML document in which the **form**'s **action** invokes **WelcomeServlet**
through the alias **welcome1** specified in **web.xml** (part 2 of 2).

Note that the sample screen captures show a URL containing the server name **local-host**—a well-known server *host name* on most computers that support TCP/IP-based networking protocols such as HTTP. We often use **localhost** to demonstrate networking programs on the local computer, so that readers without a network connection can still learn network programming concepts. In this example, **localhost** indicates that the server on which the servlet is installed is running on the local machine. The server host name is followed by **:8080**, specifying the TCP port number at which the Tomcat server awaits requests from clients. Web browsers assume TCP port 80 by default as the server port at which clients make requests, but the Tomcat server awaits client requests at TCP port 8080. This allows Tomcat to execute on the same computer as a standard Web server application without affecting the Web server application's ability to handle requests. If we do not explicitly specify the port number in the URL, the servlet never will receive our request and an error message will be displayed in the browser.

Software Engineering Observation 9.5

The Tomcat documentation specifies how to integrate Tomcat with popular Web server applications such as the Apache HTTP Server and Microsoft's IIS.

Ports in this case are not physical hardware ports to which you attach cables; rather, they are logical locations named with integer values that allow clients to request different services on the same server. The port number specifies the logical location where a server waits for and receives connections from clients—this is also called the *handshake point*. When a client connects to a server to request a service, the client must specify the port number for that service; otherwise, the client request cannot be processed. Port numbers are positive integers with values up to 65,535, and there are separate sets of these port numbers for both the TCP and UDP protocols. Many operating systems reserve port numbers below

1024 for system services (such as email and World Wide Web servers). Generally, these ports should not be specified as connection ports in your own server programs. In fact, some operating systems require special access privileges to use port numbers below 1024.

With so many ports from which to choose, how does a client know which port to use when requesting a service? The term *well-known port number* often is used when describing popular services on the Internet such as Web servers and email servers. For example, a Web server waits for clients to make requests at port 80 by default. All Web browsers know this number as the well-known port on a Web server where requests for HTML documents are made. So when you type a URL into a Web browser, the browser normally connects to port 80 on the server. Similarly, the Tomcat server uses port 8080 as its port number. Thus, requests to Tomcat for Web pages or to invoke servlets and Java-Server Pages must specify that the Tomcat server waiting for requests on port 8080.

The client can access the servlet only if the servlet is installed on a server that can respond to servlet requests. In some cases, servlet support is built directly into the Web server, and no special configuration is required to handle servlet requests. In other cases, it is necessary to integrate a servlet container with a Web server (as can be done with Tomcat and the Apache or IIS Web servers). Web servers that support servlets normally have an installation procedure for servlets. If you intend to execute your servlet as part of a Web server, please refer to your Web server's documentation on how to install a servlet. For our examples, we demonstrate servlets with the Apache Tomcat server. Section 9.3.1 discusses the setup and configuration of Tomcat for use with this chapter. Section 9.3.2 discusses the deployment of the servlet in Fig. 9.5.

9.3.1 Setting Up the Apache Tomcat Server

Tomcat is a fully functional implementation of the JSP and servlet standards. It includes a Web server, so it can be used as a standalone test container for JSPs and servlets. Tomcat also can be specified as the handler for JSP and servlet requests received by popular Web servers such as the Apache Software Foundation's Apache Web server or Microsoft's Internet Information Server (IIS). Tomcat is integrated into the Java 2 Enterprise Edition reference implementation from Sun Microsystems.

The most recent release of Tomcat (version 3.2.3) can be downloaded from

jakarta.apache.org/builds/jakarta-tomcat/release/v3.2.3/bin/

where there are a number of archive files. The complete Tomcat implementation is contained in the files that begin with the name **jakarta-tomcat-3.2.3**. Zip, tar and compressed tar files are provided for Windows, Linux and Solaris.

Extract the contents of the archive file to a directory on your hard disk. By default, the name of the directory containing Tomcat is **jakarta-tomcat-3.2.3**. For Tomcat to work correctly, you must define environment variables **JAVA_HOME** and **TOMCAT_HOME**. **JAVA_HOME** should point to the directory containing your Java installation (ours is **d:\jdk1.3.1**), and **TOMCAT_HOME** should point to the directory that contains Tomcat (ours is **d:\jakarta-tomcat-3.2.3**).

Testing and Debugging Tip 9.1

On some platforms you may need to restart your computer for the new environment variables to take effect.

After setting the environment variables, you can start the Tomcat server. Open a command prompt (or shell) and change directories to **bin** in **jakarta-tomcat-3.2.3**. In this directory are the files ***tomcat.bat*** and ***tomcat.sh***, for starting the Tomcat server on Windows and UNIX (Linux or Solaris), respectively. To start the server, type

tomcat start

This launches the Tomcat server. The Tomcat server executes on TCP port 8080 to prevent conflicts with standard Web servers that typically execute on TCP port 80. To prove that Tomcat is executing and can respond to requests, open your Web browser and enter the URL

http://localhost:8080/

This should display the Tomcat documentation home page (Fig. 9.7). The host **local-host** indicates to the Web browser that it should request the home page from the Tomcat server on the local computer.

If the Tomcat documentation home page does not display, try the URL

http://127.0.0.1:8080/

The host **localhost** translates to the IP address **127.0.0.1**.

Testing and Debugging Tip 9.2

*If the host name **localhost** does not work on your computer, substitute the IP address **127.0.0.1** instead.*

To shut down the Tomcat server, issue the command

tomcat stop

from a command prompt (or shell).

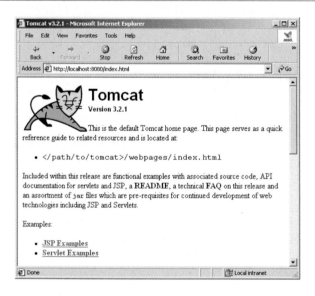

Fig. 9.7   Tomcat documentation home page. (Courtesy of The Apache Software Foundation.)

9.3.2 Deploying a Web Application

JSPs, servlets and their supporting files are deployed as part of *Web applications*. Normally, Web applications are deployed in the **webapps** subdirectory of **jakarta-tomcat-3.2.3**. A Web application has a well-known directory structure in which all the files that are part of the application reside. This directory structure can be created by the server administrator in the **webapps** directory, or the entire directory structure can be archived in a *Web application archive file*. Such an archive is known as a *WAR file* and ends with the **.war** file extension. If a WAR file is placed in the **webapps** directory, then, when the Tomcat server begins execution, it extracts the contents of the WAR file into the appropriate **webapps** subdirectory structure. For simplicity as we teach servlets and JavaServer Pages, we create the already expanded directory structure for all the examples in this chapter and Chapter 10.

The Web application directory structure contains a *context root*—the top-level directory for an entire Web application—and several subdirectories. These are described in Fig. 9.8.

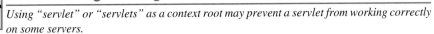

Common Programming Error 9.1

Using "servlet" or "servlets" as a context root may prevent a servlet from working correctly on some servers.

Configuring the context root for a Web application in Tomcat simply requires creating a subdirectory in the **webapps** directory. When Tomcat begins execution, it creates a context root for each subdirectory of **webapps**, using each subdirectory's name as a context root name. To test the examples in this chapter and Chapter 10, create the directory **advjhtp1** in Tomcat's **webapps** directory.

Directory	Description
context root	This is the root directory for the Web application. The name of this directory is chosen by the Web application developer. All the JSPs, HTML documents, servlets and supporting files such as images and class files reside in this directory or its subdirectories. The name of this directory is specified by the Web application creator. To provide structure in a Web application, subdirectories can be placed in the context root. For example, if your application uses many images, you might place an images subdirectory in this directory. The examples of this chapter and Chapter 10 use **advjhtp1** as the context root.
WEB-INF	This directory contains the Web application *deployment descriptor* (**web.xml**).
WEB-INF/classes	This directory contains the servlet class files and other supporting class files used in a Web application. If the classes are part of a package, the complete package directory structure would begin here.
WEB-INF/lib	This directory contains Java archive (JAR) files. The JAR files can contain servlet class files and other supporting class files used in a Web application.

Fig. 9.8   Web application standard directories.

After configuring the context root, we must configure our Web application to handle the requests. This configuration occurs in a *deployment descriptor*, which is stored in a file called **web.xml**. The deployment descriptor specifies various configuration parameters such as the name used to invoke the servlet (i.e., its *alias*), a description of the servlet, the servlet's fully qualified class name and a *servlet mapping* (i.e., the path or paths that cause the servlet container to invoke the servlet). You must create the **web.xml** file for this example. Many Java Web-application deployment tools create the **web.xml** file for you. The **web.xml** file for the first example in this chapter is shown in Fig. 9.9. We enhance this file as we add other servlets to the Web application throughout this chapter.

```
1    <!DOCTYPE web-app PUBLIC
2       "-//Sun Microsystems, Inc.//DTD Web Application 2.2//EN"
3       "http://java.sun.com/j2ee/dtds/web-app_2_2.dtd">
4
5    <web-app>
6
7       <!-- General description of your Web application -->
8       <display-name>
9          Advanced Java How to Program JSP
10         and Servlet Chapter Examples
11      </display-name>
12
13      <description>
14         This is the Web application in which we
15         demonstrate our JSP and Servlet examples.
16      </description>
17
18      <!-- Servlet definitions -->
19      <servlet>
20         <servlet-name>welcome1</servlet-name>
21
22         <description>
23            A simple servlet that handles an HTTP get request.
24         </description>
25
26         <servlet-class>
27            com.deitel.advjhtp1.servlets.WelcomeServlet
28         </servlet-class>
29      </servlet>
30
31      <!-- Servlet mappings -->
32      <servlet-mapping>
33         <servlet-name>welcome1</servlet-name>
34         <url-pattern>/welcome1</url-pattern>
35      </servlet-mapping>
36
37   </web-app>
```

Fig. 9.9   Deployment descriptor (**web.xml**) for the **advjhtp1** Web application.

Lines 1–3 specify the document type for the Web application deployment descriptor and the location of the DTD for this XML file. Element **web-app** (lines 5–37) defines the configuration of each servlet in the Web application and the servlet mapping for each servlet. Element **display-name** (lines 8–11) specifies a name that can be displayed to the administrator of the server on which the Web application is installed. Element **description** (lines 13–16) specifies a description of the Web application that might be displayed to the administrator of the server.

Element **servlet** (lines 19–29) describes a servlet. Element **servlet-name** (line 20) is the name we chose for the servlet (**welcome1**). Element **description** (lines 22–24) specifies a description for this particular servlet. Again, this can be displayed to the administrator of the Web server. Element **servlet-class** (lines 26–28) specifies compiled servlet's fully qualified class name. Thus, the servlet **welcome1** is defined by class **com.deitel.advjhtp1.servlets.WelcomeServlet**.

Element **servlet-mapping** (lines 32–35) specifies **servlet-name** and **url-pattern** elements. The *URL pattern* helps the server determine which requests are sent to the servlet (**welcome1**). Our Web application will be installed as part of the **advjhtp1** context root discussed in Section 9.3.2. Thus, the URL we supply to the browser to invoke the servlet in this example is

> **/advjhtp1/welcome1**

where **/advjhtp1** specifies the context root that helps the server determine which Web application handles the request and **/welcome1** specifies the URL pattern that is mapped to servlet **welcome1** to handle the request. Note that the server on which the servlet resides is not specified here, although it is possible to do so as follows:

> **http://localhost:8080/advjhtp1/welcome1**

If the explicit server and port number are not specified as part of the URL, the browser assumes that the form handler (i.e., the servlet specified in the **action** property of the **form** element) resides at the same server and port number from which the browser downloaded the Web page containing the **form**.

There are several URL pattern formats that can be used. The **/welcome1** URL pattern requires an exact match of the pattern. You can also specify *path mappings*, extension mappings and a *default servlet* for a Web application. A path mapping begins with a **/** and ends with a **/***. For example, the URL pattern

> **/advjhtp1/example/***

indicates that any URL path beginning with **/advjhtp1/example/** will be sent to the servlet that has the preceding URL pattern. An extension mapping begins with ***.** and ends with a file name extension. For example, the URL pattern

> ***.jsp**

indicates that any request for a file with the extension **.jsp** will be sent to the servlet that handles JSP requests. In fact, servers with JSP containers have an implicit mapping of the **.jsp** extension to a servlet that handles JSP requests. The URL pattern **/** represents the default servlet for the Web application. This is similar to the default document of a Web server. For example, if you type the URL **www.deitel.com** into your Web browser, the document you receive from our Web server is the default document **index.html**. If the URL pattern matches the default servlet for a Web application, that servlet is invoked to return a default response to the client. This can be useful for personalizing Web content to specific users. We discuss personalization in Section 9.7, Session Tracking.

   Finally, we are ready to place our files into the appropriate directories to complete the deployment of our first servlet, so we can test it. There are three files we must place in the appropriate directories—**WelcomeServlet.html**, **WelcomeServlet.class** and **web.xml**. In the **webapps** subdirectory of your **jakarta-tomcat-3.2.3** directory, create the **advjhtp1** subdirectory that represents the context root for our Web application. In this directory, create subdirectories named **servlets** and **WEB-INF**. We place our HTML files for this servlets chapter in the **servlets** directory. Copy the **WelcomeServlet.html** file into the **servlets** directory. In the **WEB-INF** directory, create the subdirectory **classes**, then copy the **web.xml** file into the **WEB-INF** directory, and copy the **WelcomeServlet.class** file, including all its package name directories, into the **classes** directory. Thus, the directory and file structure under the **webapps** directory should be as shown in Fig. 9.10 (file names are in italics).

Testing and Debugging Tip 9.3

Restart the Tomcat server after modifying the **web.xml** *deployment descriptor file. Otherwise, Tomcat will not recognize your new Web application.*

   After the files are placed in the proper directories, start the Tomcat server, open your browser and type the following URL—

```
http://localhost:8080/advjhtp1/servlets/WelcomeServlet.html
```

—to load **WelcomeServlet.html** into the Web browser. Then, click the **Get HTML Document** button to invoke the servlet. You should see the results shown in Fig. 9.6. You can try this servlet from several different Web browsers to demonstrate that the results are the same across Web browsers.

WelcomeServlet Web application directory and file structure

```
advjhtp1
   servlets
      WelcomeServlet.html
   WEB-INF
      web.xml
      classes
         com
            deitel
               advjhtp1
                  servlets
                     WelcomeServlet.class
```

Fig. 9.10   Web application directory and file structure for **WelcomeServlet**.

Common Programming Error 9.2

Not placing servlet or other class files in the appropriate package directory structure prevents the server from locating those classes properly. This, in turn, results in an error response to the client Web browser. This error response normally is "Not Found (404)" in Netscape Navigator and "The page cannot be found" plus an explanation in Microsoft Internet Explorer.

Actually, the HTML file in Fig. 9.6 was not necessary to invoke this servlet. A **get** request can be sent to a server simply by typing the URL in the Web browser. In fact, that is exactly what you are doing when you request a Web page in the browser. In this example, you can type

    http://localhost:8080/advjhtp1/welcome1

in the **Address** or **Location** field of your browser to invoke the servlet directly.

Testing and Debugging Tip 9.4

*You can test a servlet that handles HTTP **get** requests by typing the URL that invokes the servlet directly into your browser's **Address** or **Location** field.*

9.4 Handling HTTP get Requests Containing Data

When requesting a document or resource from a Web server, it is possible to supply data as part of the request. The servlet **WelcomeServlet2** of Fig. 9.11 responds to an HTTP **get** request that contains a name supplied by the user. The servlet uses the name as part of the response to the client.

```
1   // Fig. 9.11: WelcomeServlet2.java
2   // Processing HTTP get requests containing data.
3   package com.deitel.advjhtp1.servlets;
4
5   import javax.servlet.*;
6   import javax.servlet.http.*;
7   import java.io.*;
8
9   public class WelcomeServlet2 extends HttpServlet {
10
11      // process "get" request from client
12      protected void doGet( HttpServletRequest request,
13         HttpServletResponse response )
14            throws ServletException, IOException
15      {
16         String firstName = request.getParameter( "firstname" );
17
18         response.setContentType( "text/html" );
19         PrintWriter out = response.getWriter();
20
```

Fig. 9.11 **WelcomeServlet2** responds to a **get** request that contains data (part 1 of 2).

```
21        // send XHTML document to client
22
23        // start XHTML document
24        out.println( "<?xml version = \"1.0\"?>" );
25
26        out.println( "<!DOCTYPE html PUBLIC \"-//W3C//DTD " +
27           "XHTML 1.0 Strict//EN\" \"http://www.w3.org" +
28           "/TR/xhtml1/DTD/xhtml1-strict.dtd\">" );
29
30        out.println(
31           "<html xmlns = \"http://www.w3.org/1999/xhtml\">" );
32
33        // head section of document
34        out.println( "<head>" );
35        out.println(
36           "<title>Processing get requests with data</title>" );
37        out.println( "</head>" );
38
39        // body section of document
40        out.println( "<body>" );
41        out.println( "<h1>Hello " + firstName + ",<br />" );
42        out.println( "Welcome to Servlets!</h1>" );
43        out.println( "</body>" );
44
45        // end XHTML document
46        out.println( "</html>" );
47        out.close();  // close stream to complete the page
48     }
49  }
```

Fig. 9.11 **WelcomeServlet2** responds to a **get** request that contains data (part 2 of 2).

Parameters are passed as name/value pairs in a **get** request. Line 16 demonstrates how to obtain information that was passed to the servlet as part of the client request. The **request** object's **getParameter** method receives the parameter name as an argument and returns the corresponding **String** value, or **null** if the parameter is not part of the request. Line 41 uses the result of line 16 as part of the response to the client.

The **WelcomeServlet2.html** document (Fig. 9.12) provides a **form** in which the user can input a name in the text **input** element **firstname** (line 17) and click the **Submit** button to invoke **WelcomeServlet2**. When the user presses the **Submit** button, the values of the **input** elements are placed in name/value pairs as part of the request to the server. In the second screen capture of Fig. 9.12, notice that the browser appended

   ?firstname=Paul

to the end of the **action** URL. The **?** separates the *query string* (i.e., the data passed as part of the **get** request) from the rest of the URL in a **get** request. The name/value pairs are passed with the name and the value separated by **=**. If there is more than one name/value pair, each name/value pair is separated by **&**.

```
1   <?xml version = "1.0"?>
2   <!DOCTYPE html PUBLIC "-//W3C//DTD XHTML 1.0 Strict//EN"
3      "http://www.w3.org/TR/xhtml1/DTD/xhtml1-strict.dtd">
4
5   <!-- Fig. 9.12: WelcomeServlet2.html -->
6
7   <html xmlns = "http://www.w3.org/1999/xhtml">
8   <head>
9      <title>Processing get requests with data</title>
10  </head>
11
12  <body>
13     <form action = "/advjhtp1/welcome2" method = "get">
14
15        <p><label>
16           Type your first name and press the Submit button
17           <br /><input type = "text" name = "firstname" />
18           <input type = "submit" value = "Submit" />
19        </p></label>
20
21     </form>
22  </body>
23  </html>
```

Processing get requests with data - Microsoft Internet Explorer

File Edit View Favorites Tools Help

Back   Forward   Stop   Refresh   Home   Search

Address http://localhost:8080/advjhtp1/servlets/WelcomeServlet2.html   Go

Type your first name and press the Submit button
Paul   Submit

Done   Local intranet

Processing get requests with data - Microsoft Internet Explorer

File Edit View Favorites Tools Help

Back   Forward   Stop   Refresh   Home   Search

Address http://localhost:8080/advjhtp1/welcome2?firstname=Paul   Go

form data
specified in
URL's query
string as
part of a
get

Hello Paul,
Welcome to Servlets!

Done   Local intranet

Fig. 9.12 HTML document in which the **form**'s **action** invokes
WelcomeServlet2 through the alias **welcome2** specified in
web.xml.

Once again, we use our **advjhtp1** context root to demonstrate the servlet of Fig. 9.11.
Place **WelcomeServlet2.html** in the **servlets** directory created in Section 9.3.2.
Place **WelcomeServlet2.class** in the **classes** subdirectory of **WEB-INF** in the

advjhtp1 context root. Remember that classes in a package must be placed in the appropriate package directory structure. Then, edit the **web.xml** deployment descriptor in the **WEB-INF** directory to include the information specified in Fig. 9.13. This table contains the information for the **servlet** and **servlet-mapping** elements that you will add to the **web.xml** deployment descriptor. You should not type the italic text into the deployment descriptor. Restart Tomcat and type the following URL in your Web browser:

```
http://localhost:8080/advjhtp1/servlets/WelcomeServlet2.html
```

Type your name in the text field of the Web page, then click **Submit** to invoke the servlet.

Once again, note that the **get** request could have been typed directly into the browser's **Address** or **Location** field as follows:

```
http://localhost:8080/advjhtp1/welcome2?firstname=Paul
```

Try it with your own name.

9.5 Handling HTTP post Requests

An HTTP **post** request is often used to post data from an HTML form to a server-side form handler that processes the data. For example, when you respond to a Web-based survey, a **post** request normally supplies the information you specify in the HTML form to the Web server.

Browsers often *cache* (save on disk) Web pages so they can quickly reload the pages. If there are no changes between the last version stored in the cache and the current version on the Web, this helps speed up your browsing experience. The browser first asks the server if the document has changed or expired since the date the file was cached. If not, the browser loads the document from the cache. Thus, the browser minimizes the amount of data that must be downloaded for you to view a Web page. Browsers typically do not cache the server's response to a **post** request, because the next **post** might not return the same result. For example, in a survey, many users could visit the same Web page and respond to a question. The survey results could then be displayed for the user. Each new response changes the overall results of the survey.

Descriptor element	Value
servlet element	
servlet-name	welcome2
description	Handling HTTP get requests with data.
servlet-class	com.deitel.advjhtp1.servlets.WelcomeServlet2
servlet-mapping element	
servlet-name	welcome2
url-pattern	/welcome2

Fig. 9.13 Deployment descriptor information for servlet **WelcomeServlet2**.

When you use a Web-based search engine, the browser normally supplies the information you specify in an HTML form to the search engine with a **get** request. The search engine performs the search, then returns the results to you as a Web page. Such pages are often cached by the browser in case you perform the same search again. As with **post** requests, **get** requests can supply parameters as part of the request to the Web server.

The **WelcomeServlet3** servlet of Fig. 9.14 is identical to the servlet of Fig. 9.11, except that it defines a **doPost** method (line 12) to respond to **post** requests rather than a **doGet** method. The default functionality of **doPost** is to indicate a "Method not allowed" error. We override this method to provide custom **post** request processing. Method **doPost** receives the same two arguments as **doGet**—an object that implements interface **HttpServletRequest** to represent the client's request and an object that implements interface **HttpServletResponse** to represent the servlet's response. As with **doGet**, method **doPost** throws a **ServletException** if it is unable to handle a client's request and throws an **IOException** if a problem occurs during stream processing.

```java
1   // Fig. 9.14: WelcomeServlet3.java
2   // Processing post requests containing data.
3   package com.deitel.advjhtp1.servlets;
4
5   import javax.servlet.*;
6   import javax.servlet.http.*;
7   import java.io.*;
8
9   public class WelcomeServlet3 extends HttpServlet {
10
11      // process "post" request from client
12      protected void doPost( HttpServletRequest request,
13         HttpServletResponse response )
14            throws ServletException, IOException
15      {
16         String firstName = request.getParameter( "firstname" );
17
18         response.setContentType( "text/html" );
19         PrintWriter out = response.getWriter();
20
21         // send XHTML page to client
22
23         // start XHTML document
24         out.println( "<?xml version = \"1.0\"?>" );
25
26         out.println( "<!DOCTYPE html PUBLIC \"-//W3C//DTD " +
27            "XHTML 1.0 Strict//EN\" \"http://www.w3.org" +
28            "/TR/xhtml11/DTD/xhtml11-strict.dtd\">" );
29
30         out.println(
31            "<html xmlns = \"http://www.w3.org/1999/xhtml\">" );
32
33         // head section of document
34         out.println( "<head>" );
```

Fig. 9.14 **WelcomeServlet3** responds to a **post** request that contains data (part 1 of 2).

```
35          out.println(
36             "<title>Processing post requests with data</title>" );
37          out.println( "</head>" );
38
39          // body section of document
40          out.println( "<body>" );
41          out.println( "<h1>Hello " + firstName + ",<br />" );
42          out.println( "Welcome to Servlets!</h1>" );
43          out.println( "</body>" );
44
45          // end XHTML document
46          out.println( "</html>" );
47          out.close();  // close stream to complete the page
48       }
49    }
```

Fig. 9.14   `WelcomeServlet3` responds to a **post** request that contains data (part 2 of 2).

WelcomeServlet3.html (Fig. 9.15) provides a **form** (lines 13–21) in which the user can input a name in the text **input** element **firstname** (line 17), then click the **Submit** button to invoke **WelcomeServlet3**. When the user presses the **Submit** button, the values of the **input** elements are sent to the server as part of the request. However, note that the values are not appended to the request URL. Note that the form's **method** in this example is **post**. Also, note that a **post** request cannot be typed into the browser's **Address** or **Location** field and users cannot bookmark **post** requests in their browsers.

```
1   <?xml version = "1.0"?>
2   <!DOCTYPE html PUBLIC "-//W3C//DTD XHTML 1.0 Strict//EN"
3      "http://www.w3.org/TR/xhtml1/DTD/xhtml1-strict.dtd">
4
5   <!-- Fig. 9.15: WelcomeServlet3.html -->
6
7   <html xmlns = "http://www.w3.org/1999/xhtml">
8   <head>
9      <title>Handling an HTTP Post Request with Data</title>
10  </head>
11
12  <body>
13     <form action = "/advjhtp1/welcome3" method = "post">
14
15        <p><label>
16           Type your first name and press the Submit button
17           <br /><input type = "text" name = "firstname" />
18           <input type = "submit" value = "Submit" />
19        </label></p>
20
21     </form>
22  </body>
23  </html>
```

Fig. 9.15   HTML document in which the **form**'s **action** invokes **WelcomeServlet3** through the alias **welcome3** specified in **web.xml** (part 1 of 2).

Fig. 9.15 HTML document in which the **form**'s **action** invokes **WelcomeServlet3** through the alias **welcome3** specified in **web.xml** (part 2 of 2).

We use our **advjhtp1** context root to demonstrate the servlet of Fig. 9.14. Place **WelcomeServlet3.html** in the **servlets** directory created in Section 9.3.2. Place **WelcomeServlet3.class** in the **classes** subdirectory of **WEB-INF** in the **advjhtp1** context root. Then, edit the **web.xml** deployment descriptor in the **WEB-INF** directory to include the information specified in Fig. 9.16. Restart Tomcat and type the following URL in your Web browser:

http://localhost:8080/advjhtp1/servlets/WelcomeServlet3.html

Type your name in the text field of the Web page, then click **Submit** to invoke the servlet.

Descriptor element	Value
servlet *element*	
servlet-name	welcome3
description	Handling HTTP post requests with data.
servlet-class	com.deitel.advjhtp1.servlets.WelcomeServlet3
servlet-mapping *element*	
servlet-name	welcome3
url-pattern	/welcome3

Fig. 9.16 Deployment descriptor information for servlet **WelcomeServlet3**.

9.6 Redirecting Requests to Other Resources

Sometimes it is useful to redirect a request to a different resource. For example, a servlet could determine the type of the client browser and redirect the request to a Web page that was designed specifically for that browser. The **RedirectServlet** of Fig. 9.17 receives a page parameter as part of a **get** request, then uses that parameter to redirect the request to a different resource.

```
1   // Fig. 9.17: RedirectServlet.java
2   // Redirecting a user to a different Web page.
3   package com.deitel.advjhtp1.servlets;
4
5   import javax.servlet.*;
6   import javax.servlet.http.*;
7   import java.io.*;
8
9   public class RedirectServlet extends HttpServlet {
10
11      // process "get" request from client
12      protected void doGet( HttpServletRequest request,
13         HttpServletResponse response )
14            throws ServletException, IOException
15      {
16         String location = request.getParameter( "page" );
17
18         if ( location != null )
19
20            if ( location.equals( "deitel" ) )
21               response.sendRedirect( "http://www.deitel.com" );
22            else
23               if ( location.equals( "welcome1" ) )
24                  response.sendRedirect( "welcome1" );
25
26         // code that executes only if this servlet
27         // does not redirect the user to another page
28
29         response.setContentType( "text/html" );
30         PrintWriter out = response.getWriter();
31
32         // start XHTML document
33         out.println( "<?xml version = \"1.0\"?>" );
34
35         out.println( "<!DOCTYPE html PUBLIC \"-//W3C//DTD " +
36            "XHTML 1.0 Strict//EN\" \"http://www.w3.org" +
37            "/TR/xhtml1/DTD/xhtml1-strict.dtd\">" );
38
39         out.println(
40            "<html xmlns = \"http://www.w3.org/1999/xhtml\">" );
41
42         // head section of document
43         out.println( "<head>" );
44         out.println( "<title>Invalid page</title>" );
```

Fig. 9.17   Redirecting requests to other resources (part 1 of 2).

```
45          out.println( "</head>" );
46
47          // body section of document
48          out.println( "<body>" );
49          out.println( "<h1>Invalid page requested</h1>" );
50          out.println( "<p><a href = " +
51             "\"servlets/RedirectServlet.html\">" );
52          out.println( "Click here to choose again</a></p>" );
53          out.println( "</body>" );
54
55          // end XHTML document
56          out.println( "</html>" );
57          out.close();  // close stream to complete the page
58       }
59    }
```

Fig. 9.17   Redirecting requests to other resources (part 2 of 2).

Line 16 obtains the **page** parameter from the request. If the value returned is not **null**, the **if/else** structure at lines 20–24 determines if the value is either "**deitel**" or "**welcome1**." If the value is "**deitel**," the **response** object's *sendRedirect* method (line 21) redirects the request to **www.deitel.com**. If the value is "**welcome1**," line 24 redirect the request to the servlet of Fig. 9.5. Note that line 24 does not explicitly specify the **advjhtp1** context root for our Web application. When a servlet uses a relative path to reference another static or dynamic resource, the servlet assumes the same base URL and context root as the one that invoked the servlet—unless a complete URL is specified for the resource. So, line 24 actually is requesting the resource located at

> **http://localhost:8080/advjhtp1/welcome1**

Similarly, line 51 actually is requesting the resource located at

> **http://localhost:8080/advjhtp1/servlets/RedirectServlet.html**

Software Engineering Observation 9.6

Using relative paths to reference resources in the same context root makes your Web application more flexible. For example, you can change the context root without making changes to the static and dynamic resources in the application.

Once method **sendRedirect** executes, processing of the original request by the **RedirectServlet** terminates. If method **sendRedirect** is not called, the remainder of method **doPost** outputs a Web page indicating that an invalid request was made. The page allows the user to try again by returning to the XHTML document of Fig. 9.18. Note that one of the redirects is sent to a static XHTML Web page and the other is sent to a servlet.

The **RedirectServlet.html** document (Fig. 9.18) provides two hyperlinks (lines 15–16 and 17–18) that allow the user to invoke the servlet **RedirectServlet**. Note that each hyperlink specifies a **page** parameter as part of the URL. To demonstrate passing an invalid page, you can type the URL into your browser with no value for the **page** parameter.

```
1    <?xml version = "1.0"?>
2    <!DOCTYPE html PUBLIC "-//W3C//DTD XHTML 1.0 Strict//EN"
3        "http://www.w3.org/TR/xhtml1/DTD/xhtml1-strict.dtd">
4
5    <!-- Fig. 9.18: RedirectServlet.html -->
6
7    <html xmlns = "http://www.w3.org/1999/xhtml">
8    <head>
9        <title>Redirecting a Request to Another Site</title>
10   </head>
11
12   <body>
13       <p>Click a link to be redirected to the appropriate page</p>
14       <p>
15       <a href = "/advjhtp1/redirect?page=deitel">
16           www.deitel.com</a><br />
17       <a href = "/advjhtp1/redirect?page=welcome1">
18           Welcome servlet</a>
19       </p>
20   </body>
21   </html>
```

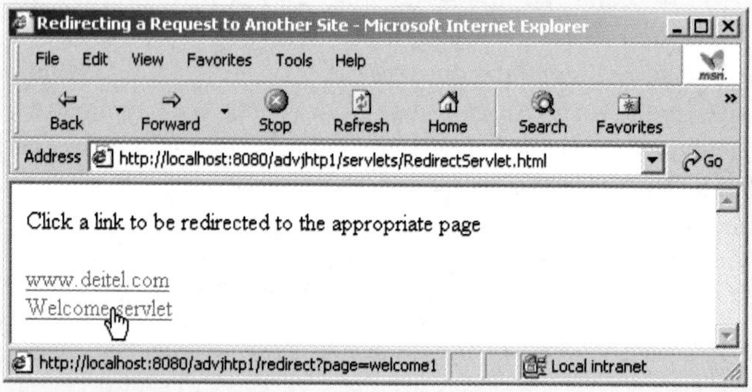

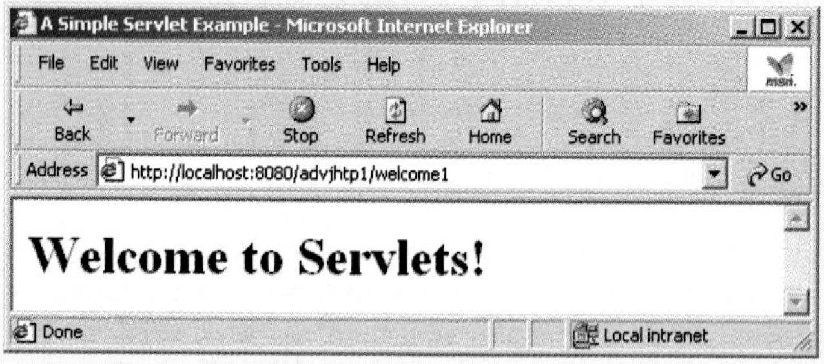

Fig. 9.18   `RedirectServlet.html` document to demonstrate redirecting
requests to other resources.

We use our **advjhtp1** context root to demonstrate the servlet of Fig. 9.17. Place
RedirectServlet.html in the **servlets** directory created in Section 9.3.2. Place
RedirectServlet.class in the **classes** subdirectory of **WEB-INF** in the
advjhtp1 context root. Then, edit the **web.xml** deployment descriptor in the **WEB-INF**

directory to include the information specified in Fig. 9.19. Restart Tomcat, and type the following URL in your Web browser:

```
http://localhost:8080/advjhtp1/servlets/RedirectServlet.html
```

Click a hyperlink in the Web page to invoke the servlet.

When redirecting requests, the request parameters from the original request are passed as parameters to the new request. Additional request parameters also can be passed. For example, the URL passed to **sendRedirect** could contain name/value pairs. Any new parameters are added to the existing parameters. If a new parameter has the same name as an existing parameter, the new parameter value takes precedence over the original value. However, all the values are still passed. In this case, the complete set of values for a given parameter name can be obtained by calling method ***getParameterValues*** from interface **HttpServletRequest**. This method receives the parameter name as an argument and returns an array of **String**s containing the parameter values in order from most recent to least recent.

9.7 Session Tracking

Many e-businesses can personalize users' browsing experiences, tailoring Web pages to their users' individual preferences and letting users bypass irrelevant content. This is done by tracking the consumer's movement through the Internet and combining that data with information provided by the consumer, which could include billing information, interests and hobbies, among other things. *Personalization* is making it easier and more pleasant for many people to surf the Internet and find what they want. Consumers and companies can benefit from the unique treatment resulting from personalization. Providing content of special interest to your visitor can help establish a relationship that you can build upon each time that person returns to your site. Targeting consumers with personal offers, advertisements, promotions and services may lead to more customer loyalty—many customers enjoy the individual attention that a customized site provides. Originally, the Internet lacked personal assistance when compared with the individual service often experienced in bricks-and-mortar stores. Sophisticated technology helps many Web sites offer a personal touch

Descriptor element	Value
servlet *element*	
servlet-name	redirect
description	Redirecting to static Web pages and other servlets.
servlet-class	com.deitel.advjhtp1.servlets.RedirectServlet
servlet-mapping *element*	
servlet-name	redirect
url-pattern	/redirect

Fig. 9.19 Deployment descriptor information for servlet **RedirectServlet**.

to their visitors. For example, Web sites such as MSN.com and CNN.com allow you to customize their home page to suit your needs. Online shopping sites often customize their Web pages to individuals, and such sites must distinguish between clients so the company can determine the proper items and charge the proper amount for each client. Personalization is important for Internet marketing and for managing customer relationships to increase customer loyalty.

Hand in hand with the promise of personalization, however, comes the problem of *privacy invasion*. What if the e-business to which you give your personal data sells or gives those data to another organization without your knowledge? What if you do not want your movements on the Internet to be tracked by unknown parties? What if an unauthorized party gains access to your private data, such as credit-card numbers or medical history? These are some of the many questions that must be addressed by consumers, e-businesses and lawmakers alike.

As we have discussed, the request/response mechanism of the Web is based on HTTP. Unfortunately, HTTP is a *stateless protocol*—it does not support persistent information that could help a Web server determine that a request is from a particular client. As far as a Web server is concerned, every request could be from the same client or every request could be from a different client. Thus, sites like MSN.com and CNN.com need a mechanism to identify individual clients. To help the server distinguish between clients, each client must identify itself to the server. There are a number of popular techniques for distinguishing between clients. We introduce two techniques to track clients individually—*cookies* (Section 9.7.1) and *session tracking* (Section 9.7.2). Two other techniques not discussed in this chapter are using **input** form elements of type **"hidden"** and *URL rewriting*. With "hidden" form elements, the servlet can write session-tracking data into a **form** in the Web page it returns to the client to satisfy a prior request. When the user submits the form in the new Web page, all the form data, including the "hidden" fields, are sent to the form handler on the server. With URL rewriting, the servlet embeds session-tracking information as **get** parameters directly in the URLs of hyperlinks that the user might click to make the next request to the Web server.

9.7.1 Cookies

A popular way to customize Web pages is via *cookies*. Browsers can store cookies on the user's computer for retrieval later in the same browsing session or in future browsing sessions. For example, cookies could be used in a shopping application to store unique identifiers for the users. When users add items to their online shopping carts or perform other tasks resulting in a request to the Web server, the server receives cookies containing unique identifiers for each user. The server then uses the unique identifier to locate the shopping carts and perform the necessary processing. Cookies could also be used to indicate the client's shopping preferences. When the servlet receives the client's next communication, the servlet can examine the cookie(s) it sent to the client in a previous communication, identify the client's preferences and immediately display products of interest to the client.

Cookies are text-based data that are sent by servlets (or other similar server-side technologies) as part of responses to clients. Every HTTP-based interaction between a client and a server includes a *header* containing information about the request (when the communication is from the client to the server) or information about the response (when the communication is from the server to the client). When an **HttpServlet** receives a request, the header includes information such as the request type (e.g., **get** or **post**) and the cookies that are sent by the server to be stored on the client machine. When the server formulates its response, the header information includes any cookies the server wants to store on the client computer and other information such as the MIME type of the response.

Testing and Debugging Tip 9.5

Some clients do not accept cookies. When a client declines a cookie, the Web site or the browser application can inform the client that the site may not function correctly without cookies enabled.

Depending on the *maximum age* of a cookie, the Web browser either maintains the cookie for the duration of the browsing session (i.e., until the user closes the Web browser) or stores the cookie on the client computer for future use. When the browser requests a resource from a server, cookies previously sent to the client by that server are returned to the server as part of the request formulated by the browser. Cookies are deleted automatically when they *expire* (i.e., reach their maximum age).

Figure 9.20 demonstrates cookies. The example allows the user to select a favorite programming language and **post** the choice to the server. The response is a Web page in which the user can select another favorite language or click a link to view a list of book recommendations. When the user selects the list of book recommendations, a **get** request is sent to the server. The cookies previously stored on the client are read by the servlet and used to form a Web page containing the book recommendations.

CookieServlet (Fig. 9.20) handles both the **get** and the **post** requests. The **CookieSelectLanguage.html** document of Fig. 9.21 contains four radio buttons (**C**, **C++**, **Java** and **VB 6**) and a **Submit** button. When the user presses **Submit**, the **CookieServlet** is invoked with a **post** request. The servlet adds a cookie containing the selected language to the response header and sends an XHTML document to the client. Each time the user clicks **Submit**, a cookie is sent to the client.

Line 11 defines **Map books** as a **HashMap** (package **java.util**) in which we store key/value pairs that use the programming language as the key and the ISBN number of the recommended book as the value. The **CookieServlet init** method (line 14–20) populates books with four key/value pairs of books. Method **doPost** (lines 24–69) is invoked in response to the **post** request from the XHTML document of Fig. 9.21. Line 28 uses method **getParameter** to obtain the user's **language** selection (the value of the selected radio button on the Web page). Line 29 obtains the ISBN number for the selected language from **books**.

```
1   // Fig. 9.20: CookieServlet.java
2   // Using cookies to store data on the client computer.
3   package com.deitel.advjhtp1.servlets;
4
5   import javax.servlet.*;
6   import javax.servlet.http.*;
7   import java.io.*;
8   import java.util.*;
9
```

Fig. 9.20   Storing user data on the client computer with cookies (part 1 of 4).

```
10   public class CookieServlet extends HttpServlet {
11      private final Map books = new HashMap();
12
13      // initialize Map books
14      public void init()
15      {
16         books.put( "C", "0130895725" );
17         books.put( "C++", "0130895717" );
18         books.put( "Java", "0130125075" );
19         books.put( "VB6", "0134569555" );
20      }
21
22      // receive language selection and send cookie containing
23      // recommended book to the client
24      protected void doPost( HttpServletRequest request,
25         HttpServletResponse response )
26            throws ServletException, IOException
27      {
28         String language = request.getParameter( "language" );
29         String isbn = books.get( language ).toString();
30         Cookie cookie = new Cookie( language, isbn );
31
32         response.addCookie( cookie );   // must precede getWriter
33         response.setContentType( "text/html" );
34         PrintWriter out = response.getWriter();
35
36         // send XHTML page to client
37
38         // start XHTML document
39         out.println( "<?xml version = \"1.0\"?>" );
40
41         out.println( "<!DOCTYPE html PUBLIC \"-//W3C//DTD " +
42            "XHTML 1.0 Strict//EN\" \"http://www.w3.org" +
43            "/TR/xhtml1/DTD/xhtml1-strict.dtd\">" );
44
45         out.println(
46            "<html xmlns = \"http://www.w3.org/1999/xhtml\">" );
47
48         // head section of document
49         out.println( "<head>" );
50         out.println( "<title>Welcome to Cookies</title>" );
51         out.println( "</head>" );
52
53         // body section of document
54         out.println( "<body>" );
55         out.println( "<p>Welcome to Cookies! You selected " +
56            language + "</p>" );
57
58         out.println( "<p><a href = " +
59            "\"/advjhtp1/servlets/CookieSelectLanguage.html\">" +
60            "Click here to choose another language</a></p>" );
61
```

Fig. 9.20 Storing user data on the client computer with cookies (part 2 of 4).

```
62          out.println( "<p><a href = \"/advjhtp1/cookies\">" +
63              "Click here to get book recommendations</a></p>" );
64          out.println( "</body>" );
65
66          // end XHTML document
67          out.println( "</html>" );
68          out.close();      // close stream
69       }
70
71       // read cookies from client and create XHTML document
72       // containing recommended books
73       protected void doGet( HttpServletRequest request,
74          HttpServletResponse response )
75             throws ServletException, IOException
76       {
77          Cookie cookies[] = request.getCookies();   // get cookies
78
79          response.setContentType( "text/html" );
80          PrintWriter out = response.getWriter();
81
82          // start XHTML document
83          out.println( "<?xml version = \"1.0\"?>" );
84
85          out.println( "<!DOCTYPE html PUBLIC \"-//W3C//DTD " +
86              "XHTML 1.0 Strict//EN\" \"http://www.w3.org" +
87              "/TR/xhtml1/DTD/xhtml1-strict.dtd\">" );
88
89          out.println(
90              "<html xmlns = \"http://www.w3.org/1999/xhtml\">" );
91
92          // head section of document
93          out.println( "<head>" );
94          out.println( "<title>Recommendations</title>" );
95          out.println( "</head>" );
96
97          // body section of document
98          out.println( "<body>" );
99
100         // if there are any cookies, recommend a book for each ISBN
101         if ( cookies != null && cookies.length != 0 ) {
102             out.println( "<h1>Recommendations</h1>" );
103             out.println( "<p>" );
104
105             // get the name of each cookie
106             for ( int i = 0; i < cookies.length; i++ )
107                 out.println( cookies[ i ].getName() +
108                     " How to Program. ISBN#: " +
109                     cookies[ i ].getValue() + "<br />" );
110
111             out.println( "</p>" );
112         }
113         else {   // there were no cookies
114             out.println( "<h1>No Recommendations</h1>" );
```

Fig. 9.20   Storing user data on the client computer with cookies (part 3 of 4).

```
115              out.println( "<p>You did not select a language.</p>" );
116          }
117
118          out.println( "</body>" );
119
120          // end XHTML document
121          out.println( "</html>" );
122          out.close();      // close stream
123      }
124  }
```

Fig. 9.20   Storing user data on the client computer with cookies (part 4 of 4).

Line 30 creates a new *Cookie* object (package *javax.servlet.http*), using the **language** and **isbn** values as the *cookie name* and *cookie value*, respectively. The cookie name identifies the cookie; the cookie value is the information associated with the cookie. Browsers that support cookies must be able to store a minimum of 20 cookies per Web site and 300 cookies per user. Browsers may limit the cookie size to 4K (4096 bytes). Each cookie stored on the client includes a domain. The browser sends a cookie only to the domain stored in the cookie.

Software Engineering Observation 9.7

Browser users can disable cookies, so Web applications that use cookies may not function properly for clients with cookies disabled.

Software Engineering Observation 9.8

By default, cookies exist only for the current browsing session (until the user closes the browser). To make cookies persist beyond the current session, call **Cookie** *method* **set-MaxAge** *to indicate the number of seconds until the cookie expires.*

Line 32 adds the cookie to the **response** with method *addCookie* of interface **HttpServletResponse**. Cookies are sent to the client as part of the HTTP header. The header information is always provided to the client first, so the cookies should be added to the **response** with **addCookie** before any data is written as part of the response. After the cookie is added, the servlet sends an XHTML document to the client (see the second screen capture of Fig. 9.21).

Common Programming Error 9.3

Writing response data to the client before calling method **addCookie** *to add a cookie to the response is a logic error. Cookies must be added to the header first.*

The XHTML document sent to the client in response to a **post** request includes a hyperlink that invokes method **doGet** (lines 73–123). The method reads any **Cookie**s that were written to the client in **doPost**. For each **Cookie** written, the servlet recommends a Deitel book on the subject. Up to four books are displayed on the Web page created by the servlet.

Line 77 retrieves the cookies from the client using **HttpServletRequest** method *getCookies*, which returns an array of **Cookie** objects. When a **get** or **post** operation is performed to invoke a servlet, the cookies associated with that server's domain are automatically sent to the servlet.

If method **getCookies** does not return **null** (i.e., there were no cookies), lines 106–109 retrieve the name of each **Cookie** using **Cookie** method *getName*, retrieve the value of each **Cookie** using **Cookie** method *getValue* and write a line to the client indicating the name of a recommended book and its ISBN number.

Software Engineering Observation 9.9

Normally, each servlet class handles one request type (e.g., get or post, but not both).

Figure 9.21 shows the XHTML document the user loads to select a language. When the user presses **Submit**, the value of the currently selected radio button is sent to the server as part of the **post** request to the **CookieServlet**, which we refer to as **cookies** in this example.

```
1   <?xml version = "1.0"?>
2   <!DOCTYPE html PUBLIC "-//W3C//DTD XHTML 1.0 Strict//EN"
3      "http://www.w3.org/TR/xhtml1/DTD/xhtml1-strict.dtd">
4
5   <!-- Fig. 9.21: CookieSelectLanguage.html -->
6
7   <html xmlns = "http://www.w3.org/1999/xhtml">
8   <head>
9      <title>Using Cookies</title>
10  </head>
11
12  <body>
13     <form action = "/advjhtp1/cookies" method = "post">
14
15        <p>Select a programming language:</p>
16        <p>
17           <input type = "radio" name = "language"
18              value = "C" />C <br />
19
20           <input type = "radio" name = "language"
21              value = "C++" />C++ <br />
22
23           <!-- this radio button checked by default -->
24           <input type = "radio" name = "language"
25              value = "Java" checked = "checked" />Java<br />
26
27           <input type = "radio" name = "language"
28              value = "VB6" />VB 6
29        </p>
30
31        <p><input type = "submit" value = "Submit" /></p>
32
33     </form>
34  </body>
35  </html>
```

Fig. 9.21 **CookieSelectLanguage.html** document for selecting a programming language and posting the data to the **CookieServlet** (part 1 of 3).

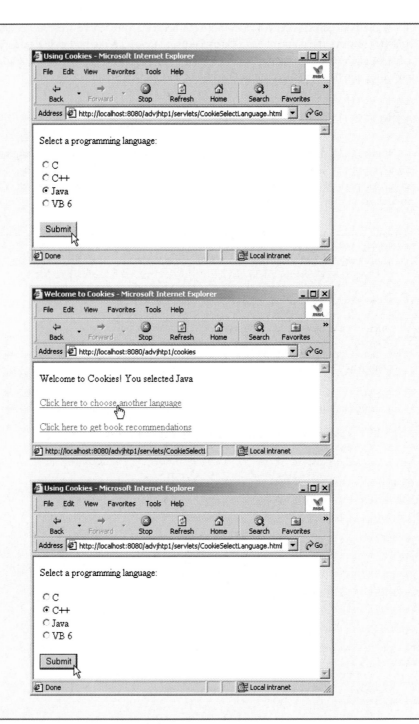

Fig. 9.21   `CookieSelectLanguage.html` document for selecting a
programming language and posting the data to the `CookieServlet`
(part 2 of 3).

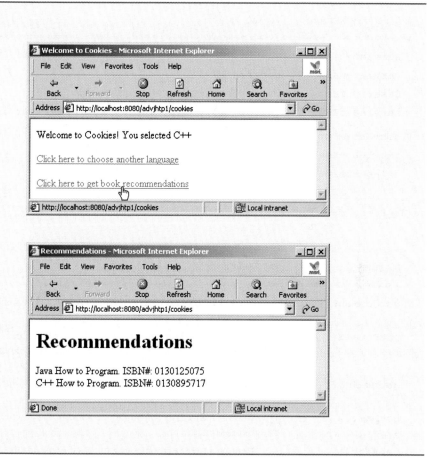

Fig. 9.21 `CookieSelectLanguage.html` document for selecting a programming language and posting the data to the `CookieServlet` (part 3 of 3).

We use our **advjhtp1** context root to demonstrate the servlet of Fig. 9.20. Place **CookieSelectLanguage.html** in the **servlets** directory created previously. Place **CookieServlet.class** in the **classes** subdirectory of **WEB-INF** in the **advjhtp1** context root. Then, edit the **web.xml** deployment descriptor in the **WEB-INF** directory to include the information specified in Fig. 9.22. Restart Tomcat and type the following URL in your Web browser:

```
http://localhost:8080/advjhtp1/servlets/
CookieSelectLanguage.html
```

Select a language, and press the **Submit** button in the Web page to invoke the servlet.

Various **Cookie** methods are provided to manipulate the members of a **Cookie**. Some of these methods are listed in Fig. 9.23.

Descriptor element	Value
servlet element	
servlet-name	cookies
description	Using cookies to maintain state information.
servlet-class	com.deitel.advjhtp1.servlets.CookieServlet
servlet-mapping element	
servlet-name	cookies
url-pattern	/cookies

Fig. 9.22 Deployment descriptor information for servlet **CookieServlet**.

Method	Description
getComment()	Returns a **String** describing the purpose of the cookie (**null** if no comment has been set with **setComment**).
getDomain()	Returns a **String** containing the cookie's domain. This determines which servers can receive the cookie. By default, cookies are sent to the server that originally sent the cookie to the client.
getMaxAge()	Returns an **int** representing the maximum age of the cookie in seconds.
getName()	Returns a **String** containing the name of the cookie as set by the constructor.
getPath()	Returns a **String** containing the URL prefix for the cookie. Cookies can be "targeted" to specific URLs that include directories on the Web server. By default, a cookie is returned to services operating in the same directory as the service that sent the cookie or a subdirectory of that directory.
getSecure()	Returns a **boolean** value indicating if the cookie should be transmitted using a secure protocol (**true**).
getValue()	Returns a **String** containing the value of the cookie as set with **setValue** or the constructor.
getVersion()	Returns an **int** containing the version of the cookie protocol used to create the cookie. A value of 0 (the default) indicates the original cookie protocol as defined by Netscape. A value of 1 indicates the current version, which is based on *Request for Comments (RFC) 2109*.
setComment(String)	The comment describing the purpose of the cookie that is presented by the browser to the user. (Some browsers allow the user to accept cookies on a per-cookie basis.)

Fig. 9.23 Important methods of class **Cookie** (part 1 of 2).

Method	Description
`setDomain( String )`	This determines which servers can receive the cookie. By default, cookies are sent to the server that originally sent the cookie to the client. The domain is specified in the form `".deitel.com"`, indicating that all servers ending with `.deitel.com` can receive this cookie.
`setMaxAge( int )`	Sets the maximum age of the cookie in seconds.
`setPath( String )`	Sets the "target" URL prefix indicating the directories on the server that lead to the services that can receive this cookie.
`setSecure( boolean )`	A `true` value indicates that the cookie should only be sent using a secure protocol.
`setValue( String )`	Sets the value of a cookie.
`setVersion( int )`	Sets the cookie protocol for this cookie.

Fig. 9.23   Important methods of class **Cookie** (part 2 of 2).

9.7.2 Session Tracking with `HttpSession`

Java provides enhanced session tracking support with the servlet API's *HttpSession* interface. To demonstrate basic session-tracking techniques, we modified the servlet from Fig. 9.20 to use *HttpSession* objects (Fig. 9.24). Once again, the servlet handles both **get** and **post** requests. The document **SessionSelectLanguage.html** of Fig. 9.25 contains four radio buttons (**C**, **C++**, **Java** and **VB 6**) and a **Submit** button. When the user presses **Submit**, **SessionServlet** is invoked with a **post** request. The servlet responds by creating an object of type **HttpSession** for the client (or using an existing session for the client) and adds the selected language and an ISBN number for the recommended book to the **HttpSession** object. Then, the servlet sends an XHTML page to the client. Each time the user clicks **Submit**, a new language/ISBN pair is added to the **HttpSession** object.

Software Engineering Observation 9.10

*A servlet should not use instance variables to maintain client state information, because clients accessing that servlet in parallel might overwrite the shared instance variables. Servlets should maintain client state information in **HttpSession** objects.*

```
1  // Fig. 9.24: SessionServlet.java
2  // Using HttpSession to maintain client state information.
3  package com.deitel.advjhtp1.servlets;
4
5  import javax.servlet.*;
6  import javax.servlet.http.*;
7  import java.io.*;
8  import java.util.*;
```

Fig. 9.24   Maintaining state information with **HttpSession** objects (part 1 of 4).

```
9
10  public class SessionServlet extends HttpServlet {
11      private final Map books = new HashMap();
12
13      // initialize Map books
14      public void init()
15      {
16          books.put( "C", "0130895725" );
17          books.put( "C++", "0130895717" );
18          books.put( "Java", "0130125075" );
19          books.put( "VB6", "0134569555" );
20      }
21
22      // receive language selection and create HttpSession object
23      // containing recommended book for the client
24      protected void doPost( HttpServletRequest request,
25          HttpServletResponse response )
26              throws ServletException, IOException
27      {
28          String language = request.getParameter( "language" );
29
30          // Get the user's session object.
31          // Create a session (true) if one does not exist.
32          HttpSession session = request.getSession( true );
33
34          // add a value for user's choice to session
35          session.setAttribute( language, books.get( language ) );
36
37          response.setContentType( "text/html" );
38          PrintWriter out = response.getWriter();
39
40          // send XHTML page to client
41
42          // start XHTML document
43          out.println( "<?xml version = \"1.0\"?>" );
44
45          out.println( "<!DOCTYPE html PUBLIC \"-//W3C//DTD " +
46              "XHTML 1.0 Strict//EN\" \"http://www.w3.org" +
47              "/TR/xhtml1/DTD/xhtml1-strict.dtd\">" );
48
49          out.println(
50              "<html xmlns = \"http://www.w3.org/1999/xhtml\">" );
51
52          // head section of document
53          out.println( "<head>" );
54          out.println( "<title>Welcome to Sessions</title>" );
55          out.println( "</head>" );
56
57          // body section of document
58          out.println( "<body>" );
59          out.println( "<p>Welcome to Sessions! You selected " +
60              language + ".</p>" );
61
```

Fig. 9.24   Maintaining state information with **HttpSession** objects (part 2 of 4).

```
62          // display information about the session
63          out.println( "<p>Your unique session ID is: " +
64             session.getId() + "<br />" );
65
66          out.println(
67             "This " + ( session.isNew() ? "is" : "is not" ) +
68             " a new session<br />" );
69
70          out.println( "The session was created at: " +
71             new Date( session.getCreationTime() ) + "<br />" );
72
73          out.println( "You last accessed the session at: " +
74             new Date( session.getLastAccessedTime() ) + "<br />" );
75
76          out.println( "The maximum inactive interval is: " +
77             session.getMaxInactiveInterval() + " seconds</p>" );
78
79          out.println( "<p><a href = " +
80             "\"servlets/SessionSelectLanguage.html\">" +
81             "Click here to choose another language</a></p>" );
82
83          out.println( "<p><a href = \"sessions\">" +
84             "Click here to get book recommendations</a></p>" );
85          out.println( "</body>" );
86
87          // end XHTML document
88          out.println( "</html>" );
89          out.close();    // close stream
90       }
91
92       // read session attributes and create XHTML document
93       // containing recommended books
94       protected void doGet( HttpServletRequest request,
95          HttpServletResponse response )
96             throws ServletException, IOException
97       {
98          // Get the user's session object.
99          // Do not create a session (false) if one does not exist.
100         HttpSession session = request.getSession( false );
101
102         // get names of session object's values
103         Enumeration valueNames;
104
105         if ( session != null )
106            valueNames = session.getAttributeNames();
107         else
108            valueNames = null;
109
110         PrintWriter out = response.getWriter();
111         response.setContentType( "text/html" );
112
113         // start XHTML document
114         out.println( "<?xml version = \"1.0\"?>" );
```

Fig. 9.24   Maintaining state information with **HttpSession** objects (part 3 of 4).

```
115
116     out.println( "<!DOCTYPE html PUBLIC \"-//W3C//DTD " +
117        "XHTML 1.0 Strict//EN\" \"http://www.w3.org" +
118        "/TR/xhtml1/DTD/xhtml1-strict.dtd\">" );
119
120     out.println(
121        "<html xmlns = \"http://www.w3.org/1999/xhtml\">" );
122
123     // head section of document
124     out.println( "<head>" );
125     out.println( "<title>Recommendations</title>" );
126     out.println( "</head>" );
127
128     // body section of document
129     out.println( "<body>" );
130
131     if ( valueNames != null &&
132          valueNames.hasMoreElements() ) {
133        out.println( "<h1>Recommendations</h1>" );
134        out.println( "<p>" );
135
136        String name, value;
137
138        // get value for each name in valueNames
139        while ( valueNames.hasMoreElements() ) {
140           name = valueNames.nextElement().toString();
141           value = session.getAttribute( name ).toString();
142
143           out.println( name + " How to Program. " +
144              "ISBN#: " + value + "<br />" );
145        }
146
147        out.println( "</p>" );
148     }
149     else {
150        out.println( "<h1>No Recommendations</h1>" );
151        out.println( "<p>You did not select a language.</p>" );
152     }
153
154     out.println( "</body>" );
155
156     // end XHTML document
157     out.println( "</html>" );
158     out.close();    // close stream
159     }
160  }
```

Fig. 9.24 Maintaining state information with **HttpSession** objects (part 4 of 4).

Most of class **SessionServlet** is identical to **CookieServlet** (Fig. 9.20), so we concentrate on only the new features here. When the user selects a language from the document **SessionSelectLanguage.html** (Fig. 9.25) and presses **Submit**, method **doPost** (lines 24–90) is invoked. Line 28 gets the user's **language** selection. Then, line 32 uses method *getSession* of interface **HttpServletRequest** to obtain the

HttpSession object for the client. If the server has an existing **HttpSession** object for the client from a previous request, method **getSession** returns that **HttpSession** object. Otherwise, the **true** argument to method **getSession** indicates that the servlet should create a unique new **HttpSession** object for the client. A **false** argument would cause method **getSession** to return **null** if the **HttpSession** object for the client did not already exist. Using a **false** argument could help determine whether a client has logged into a Web application.

Like a cookie, an **HttpSession** object can store name/value pairs. In session terminology, these are called *attributes*, and they are placed into an **HttpSession** object with method *setAttribute*. Line 35 uses **setAttribute** to put the language and the corresponding recommended book's ISBN number into the **HttpSession** object. One of the primary benefits of using **HttpSession** objects rather than cookies is that **HttpSession** objects can store any object (not just **String**s) as the value of an attribute. This allows Java programmers flexibility in determining the type of state information they wish to maintain for clients of their Web applications. If an attribute with a particular name already exists when **setAttribute** is called, the object associated with that attribute name is replaced.

> ### Software Engineering Observation 9.11
>
> *Name/value pairs added to an **HttpSession** object with **setAttribute** remain available until the client's current browsing session ends or until the session is invalidated explicitly by a call to the **HttpSession** object's **invalidate** method. Also, if the servlet container is restarted, these attributes may be lost.*

After the values are added to the **HttpSession** object, the servlet sends an XHTML document to the client (see the second screen capture of Fig. 9.25). In this example, the document contains various information about the **HttpSession** object for the current client. Line 64 uses **HttpSession** method *getID* to obtain the session's unique ID number. Line 67 determines whether the session is new or already exists with method *isNew*, which returns **true** or **false**. Line 71 obtains the time at which the session was created with method *getCreationTime*. Line 74 obtains the time at which the session was last accessed with method *getLastAccessedTime*. Line 77 uses method *getMaxInactiveInterval* to obtain the maximum amount of time that an **HttpSession** object can be inactive before the servlet container discards it.

The XHTML document sent to the client in response to a **post** request includes a hyperlink that invokes method **doGet** (lines 94–159). The method obtains the **HttpSession** object for the client with method **getSession** (line 100). We do not want to make any recommendations if the client does not have an existing **HttpSession** object. So, this call to **getSession** uses a **false** argument. Thus, **getSession** returns an **HttpSession** object only if one already exists for the client.

If method **getSession** does not return **null**, line 106 uses **HttpSession** method *getAttributeNames* to retrieve an **Enumeration** of the attribute names (i.e., the names used as the first argument to **HttpSession** method **setAttribute**). Each name is passed as an argument to **HttpSession** method *getAttribute* (line 141) to retrieve the ISBN of a book from the **HttpSession** object. Method **getAttribute** receives the name and returns an **Object** reference to the corresponding value. Next, a line is written in the response to the client containing the title and ISBN number of the recommended book.

Figure 9.25 shows the XHTML document the user loads to select a language. When the user presses **Submit**, the value of the currently selected radio button is sent to the server as part of the **post** request to the **SessionServlet**, which we refer to as **sessions** in this example.

We use our **advjhtp1** context root to demonstrate the servlet of Fig. 9.24. Place **SessionSelectLanguage.html** in the **servlets** directory created previously. Place **SessionServlet.class** in the **classes** subdirectory of **WEB-INF** in the **advjhtp1** context root. Then, edit the **web.xml** deployment descriptor in the **WEB-INF** directory to include the information specified in Fig. 9.26. Restart Tomcat and type the following URL in your Web browser:

```
http://localhost:8080/advjhtp1/servlets/
SessionSelectLanguage.html
```

Select a language, and press the **Submit** button in the Web page to invoke the servlet.

```
1   <?xml version = "1.0"?>
2   <!DOCTYPE html PUBLIC "-//W3C//DTD XHTML 1.0 Strict//EN"
3      "http://www.w3.org/TR/xhtml11/DTD/xhtml11-strict.dtd">
4
5   <!-- Fig. 9.25: SessionSelectLanguage.html -->
6
7   <html xmlns = "http://www.w3.org/1999/xhtml">
8   <head>
9      <title>Using Sessions</title>
10  </head>
11
12  <body>
13     <form action = "/advjhtp1/sessions" method = "post">
14
15        <p>Select a programming language:</p>
16        <p>
17           <input type = "radio" name = "language"
18              value = "C" />C <br />
19
20           <input type = "radio" name = "language"
21              value = "C++" />C++ <br />
22
23           <!-- this radio button checked by default -->
24           <input type = "radio" name = "language"
25              value = "Java" checked = "checked" />Java<br />
26
27           <input type = "radio" name = "language"
28              value = "VB6" />VB 6
29        </p>
30
31        <p><input type = "submit" value = "Submit" /></p>
32
33     </form>
34  </body>
35  </html>
```

Fig. 9.25 **SessionSelectLanguage.html** document for selecting a programming language and posting the data to the **SessionServlet** (part 1 of 4).

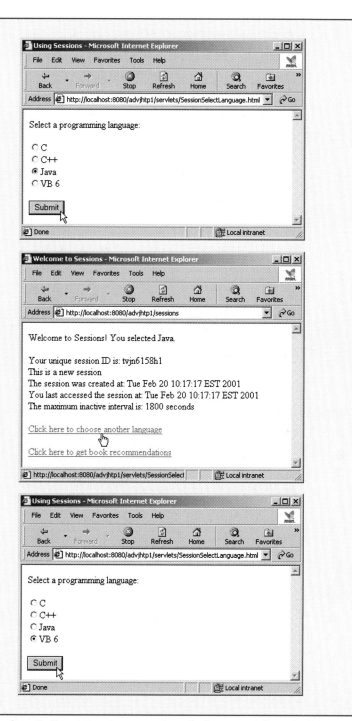

Fig. 9.25 `SessionSelectLanguage.html` document for selecting a programming language and posting the data to the `SessionServlet` (part 2 of 4).

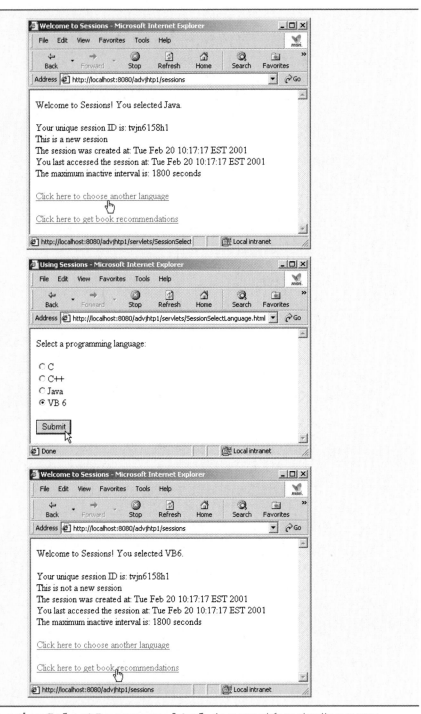

Fig. 9.25 `SessionSelectLanguage.html` document for selecting a programming language and posting the data to the **SessionServlet**
(part 3 of 4).

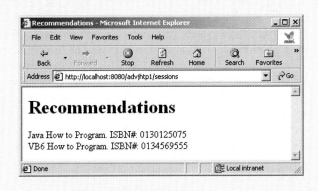

Fig. 9.25 `SessionSelectLanguage.html` document for selecting a programming language and posting the data to the `SessionServlet` (part 4 of 4).

Descriptor element	Value
servlet element	
servlet-name	sessions
description	Using sessions to maintain state information.
servlet-class	com.deitel.advjhtp1.servlets.SessionServlet
servlet-mapping element	
servlet-name	sessions
url-pattern	/sessions

Fig. 9.26 Deployment descriptor information for servlet `WelcomeServlet2`.

9.8 Multi-Tier Applications: Using JDBC from a Servlet

Servlets can communicate with databases via JDBC (Java Database Connectivity). As we discussed in Chapter 8, JDBC provides a uniform way for a Java program to connect with a variety of databases in a general manner without having to deal with the specifics of those database systems.

Many of today's applications are *three-tier distributed applications*, consisting of a *user interface*, *business logic* and *database access*. The user interface in such an application is often created using HTML, XHTML (as shown in this chapter) or Dynamic HTML. In some cases, Java applets are also used for this tier. HTML and XHTML are the preferred mechanisms for representing the user interface in systems where portability is a concern. Because HTML is supported by all browsers, designing the user interface to be accessed through a Web browser guarantees portability across all platforms that have browsers. Using the networking provided automatically by the browser, the user interface can communicate with the middle-tier business logic. The middle tier can then access the database to manipulate the data. The three tiers can reside on separate computers that are connected to a network.

In multi-tier architectures, Web servers often represent the middle tier. They provide the business logic that manipulates data from databases and that communicates with client Web browsers. Servlets, through JDBC, can interact with popular database systems. Developers do not need to be familiar with the specifics of each database system. Rather, developers use SQL-based queries and the JDBC driver handles the specifics of interacting with each database system.

The **SurveyServlet** of Fig. 9.27 and the **Survey.html** document of Fig. 9.28 demonstrate a three-tier distributed application that displays the user interface in a browser using XHTML. The middle tier is a Java servlet that handles requests from the client browser and provides access to the third tier—a Cloudscape database accessed via JDBC. The servlet in this example is a survey servlet that allows users to vote for their favorite animal. When the servlet receives a **post** request from the **Survey.html** document, the servlet updates the total number of votes for that animal in the database and returns a dynamically generated XHTML document containing the survey results to the client.

```
1   // Fig. 9.27: SurveyServlet.java
2   // A Web-based survey that uses JDBC from a servlet.
3   package com.deitel.advjhtp1.servlets;
4
5   import java.io.*;
6   import java.text.*;
7   import java.sql.*;
8   import javax.servlet.*;
9   import javax.servlet.http.*;
10
11  public class SurveyServlet extends HttpServlet {
12     private Connection connection;
13     private PreparedStatement updateVotes, totalVotes, results;
14
15     // set up database connection and prepare SQL statements
16     public void init( ServletConfig config )
17        throws ServletException
18     {
19        // attempt database connection and create PreparedStatements
20        try {
21           Class.forName( "COM.cloudscape.core.RmiJdbcDriver" );
22           connection = DriverManager.getConnection(
23              "jdbc:rmi:jdbc:cloudscape:animalsurvey" );
24
25           // PreparedStatement to add one to vote total for a
26           // specific animal
27           updateVotes =
28              connection.prepareStatement(
29                 "UPDATE surveyresults SET votes = votes + 1 " +
30                 "WHERE id = ?"
31              );
32
```

Fig. 9.27   Multi-tier Web-based survey using XHTML, servlets and JDBC (part 1 of 4).

```
33              // PreparedStatement to sum the votes
34              totalVotes =
35                 connection.prepareStatement(
36                    "SELECT sum( votes ) FROM surveyresults"
37                 );
38
39              // PreparedStatement to obtain surveyoption table's data
40              results =
41                 connection.prepareStatement(
42                    "SELECT surveyoption, votes, id " +
43                    "FROM surveyresults ORDER BY id"
44                 );
45           }
46
47           // for any exception throw an UnavailableException to
48           // indicate that the servlet is not currently available
49           catch ( Exception exception ) {
50              exception.printStackTrace();
51              throw new UnavailableException(exception.getMessage());
52           }
53
54        }  // end of init method
55
56        // process survey response
57        protected void doPost( HttpServletRequest request,
58           HttpServletResponse response )
59              throws ServletException, IOException
60        {
61           // set up response to client
62           response.setContentType( "text/html" );
63           PrintWriter out = response.getWriter();
64           DecimalFormat twoDigits = new DecimalFormat( "0.00" );
65
66           // start XHTML document
67           out.println( "<?xml version = \"1.0\"?>" );
68
69           out.println( "<!DOCTYPE html PUBLIC \"-//W3C//DTD " +
70              "XHTML 1.0 Strict//EN\" \"http://www.w3.org" +
71              "/TR/xhtml1/DTD/xhtml1-strict.dtd\">" );
72
73           out.println(
74              "<html xmlns = \"http://www.w3.org/1999/xhtml\">" );
75
76           // head section of document
77           out.println( "<head>" );
78
79           // read current survey response
80           int value =
81              Integer.parseInt( request.getParameter( "animal" ) );
82
83           // attempt to process a vote and display current results
84           try {
85
```

Fig. 9.27 Multi-tier Web-based survey using XHTML, servlets and JDBC (part 2 of 4).

```
86              // update total for current surevy response
87              updateVotes.setInt( 1, value );
88              updateVotes.executeUpdate();
89
90              // get total of all survey responses
91              ResultSet totalRS = totalVotes.executeQuery();
92              totalRS.next();
93              int total = totalRS.getInt( 1 );
94
95              // get results
96              ResultSet resultsRS = results.executeQuery();
97              out.println( "<title>Thank you!</title>" );
98              out.println( "</head>" );
99
100             out.println( "<body>" );
101             out.println( "<p>Thank you for participating." );
102             out.println( "<br />Results:</p><pre>" );
103
104             // process results
105             int votes;
106
107             while ( resultsRS.next() ) {
108                out.print( resultsRS.getString( 1 ) );
109                out.print( ": " );
110                votes = resultsRS.getInt( 2 );
111                out.print( twoDigits.format(
112                   ( double ) votes / total * 100 ) );
113                out.print( "%  responses: " );
114                out.println( votes );
115             }
116
117             resultsRS.close();
118
119             out.print( "Total responses: " );
120             out.print( total );
121
122             // end XHTML document
123             out.println( "</pre></body></html>" );
124             out.close();
125          }
126
127          // if database exception occurs, return error page
128          catch ( SQLException sqlException ) {
129             sqlException.printStackTrace();
130             out.println( "<title>Error</title>" );
131             out.println( "</head>" );
132             out.println( "<body><p>Database error occurred. " );
133             out.println( "Try again later.</p></body></html>" );
134             out.close();
135          }
136
137       }  // end of doPost method
138
```

Fig. 9.27   Multi-tier Web-based survey using XHTML, servlets and JDBC (part 3 of 4).

```
139    // close SQL statements and database when servlet terminates
140    public void destroy()
141    {
142       // attempt to close statements and database connection
143       try {
144          updateVotes.close();
145          totalVotes.close();
146          results.close();
147          connection.close();
148       }
149
150       // handle database exceptions by returning error to client
151       catch( SQLException sqlException ) {
152          sqlException.printStackTrace();
153       }
154    } // end of destroy method
155 }
```

Fig. 9.27   Multi-tier Web-based survey using XHTML, servlets and JDBC (part 4 of 4).

Lines 12 and 13 begin by declaring a **Connection** reference to manage the database connection and three **PreparedStatement** references for updating the vote count for an animal, totalling all the votes and obtaining the complete survey results.

Servlets are initialized by overriding method **init** (lines 16–54). Method **init** is called exactly once in a servlet's lifetime, before any client requests are accepted. Method **init** takes a **ServletConfig** argument and throws a **ServletException**. The argument provides the servlet with information about its *initialization parameters* (i.e., parameters not associated with a request, but passed to the servlet for initializing servlet variables). These parameters are specified in the **web.xml** deployment descriptor file as part of a **servlet** element. Each parameter appears in an **init-param** element of the following form:

```
<init-param>
    <param-name>parameter name goes here</param-name>
    <param-value>parameter value goes here</param-value>
</init-param>
```

Servlets can obtain initialization parameter values by invoking **ServletConfig** method **getInitParameter**, which receives a string representing the name of the parameter.

In this example, the servlet's **init** method (lines 16–54) performs the connection to the Cloudscape database. Line 21 loads the driver (**COM.cloudscape.core.RmiJdbcDriver**). Lines 22–23 attempt to open a connection to the **animalsurvey** database. The database contains one table (**surveyresults**) that consists of three fields—a unique integer to identify each record called **id**, a string representing the survey option called **surveyoption** and an integer representing the number of votes for a survey option called **votes**. [*Note*: The examples folder for this chapter contains an SQL script (**animalsurvey.sql**) that you can use to create the **animalsurvey** database for this example. For information on starting the Cloudscape server and executing the SQL script, please refer back to Chapter 8.]

Lines 27–44 create **PreparedStatement** objects called **updateVotes**, **totalVotes** and **results**. The **updateVotes** statement adds one to the **votes** value for the record with the specified ID. The **totalVotes** statement uses SQL's built-in *sum* capability to total all the **votes** in the **surveyresults** table. The results statement returns all the data in the **surveyresults** table.

When a user submits a survey response, method **doPost** (lines 57–137) handles the request. Lines 80–81 obtain the survey response, then the **try** block (lines 84–125) attempts to process the response. Lines 87–88 set the first parameter of **Prepared-Statement updateVotes** to the survey response and update the database. Lines 91–93 execute **PreparedStatement totalVotes** to retrieve the total number of votes received. Then, lines 96–123 execute **PreparedStatement results** and process the **ResultSet** to create the survey summary for the client. When the servlet container terminates the servlet, method *destroy* (lines 140–154) closes each **PreparedStatement**, then closes the database connection. Figure 9.28 shoes survey.html, which invokes **SurveyServlet** with the alias **animalsurvey** when the user submits the form.

```
1   <?xml version = "1.0"?>
2   <!DOCTYPE html PUBLIC "-//W3C//DTD XHTML 1.0 Strict//EN"
3       "http://www.w3.org/TR/xhtml1/DTD/xhtml1-strict.dtd">
4
5   <!-- Fig. 9.28: Survey.html -->
6
7   <html xmlns = "http://www.w3.org/1999/xhtml">
8   <head>
9       <title>Survey</title>
10  </head>
11
12  <body>
13  <form method = "post" action = "/advjhtp1/animalsurvey">
14
15      <p>What is your favorite pet?</p>
16
17      <p>
18          <input type = "radio" name = "animal"
19              value = "1" />Dog<br />
20          <input type = "radio" name = "animal"
21              value = "2" />Cat<br />
22          <input type = "radio" name = "animal"
23              value = "3" />Bird<br />
24          <input type = "radio" name = "animal"
25              value = "4" />Snake<br />
26          <input type = "radio" name = "animal"
27              value = "5" checked = "checked" />None
28      </p>
29
30      <p><input type = "submit" value = "Submit" /></p>
31
32  </form>
33  </body>
34  </html>
```

Fig. 9.28 Survey.html document that allows users to submit survey responses to **SurveyServlet** (part 1 of 2).

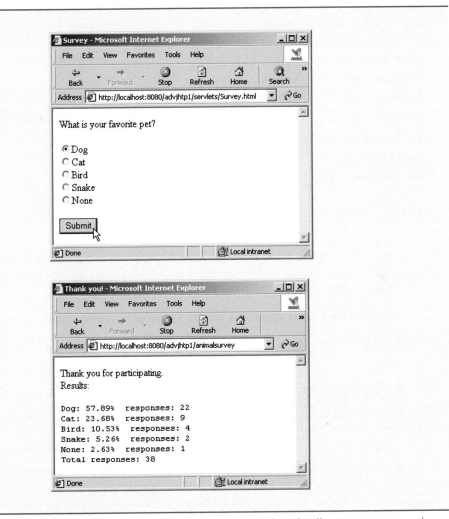

Fig. 9.28 `Survey.html` document that allows users to submit survey responses to `SurveyServlet` (part 2 of 2).

We use our **advjhtp1** context root to demonstrate the servlet of Fig. 9.27. Place **Survey.html** in the **servlets** directory created previously. Place **SurveyServlet.class** in the **classes** subdirectory of **WEB-INF** in the **advjhtp1** context root. Then, edit the **web.xml** deployment descriptor in the **WEB-INF** directory to include the information specified in Fig. 9.29. Also, this program cannot execute in Tomcat unless the Web application is aware of the JAR files **cloudscape.jar** and **RmiJdbc.jar** that contain the Cloudscape database driver and its supporting classes. The **cloudscape.jar** file is located in your Cloudscape installation's **lib** directory. The **RmiJdbc.jar** file is located in your Cloudsape installation's **frameworks\RmiJdbc\classes** directory. Place *copies* of these files in the **WEB-INF** subdirectory **lib** to make them available to the Web application. Please refer back to Chapter 8 for more information on the set up and configuration of Cloudscape.

Descriptor element	Value
servlet element	
servlet-name	animalsurvey
description	Connecting to a database from a servlet.
servlet-class	com.deitel.advjhtp1.servlets.SurveyServlet
servlet-mapping element	
servlet-name	animalsurvey
url-pattern	/animalsurvey

Fig. 9.29   Deployment descriptor information for servlet **SurveyServlet**.

A copy of these files should be placed in the **advjhtp1** context root's **WEB-INF** sub-directory called **lib**. After copying these files, restart Tomcat and type the following URL in your Web browser:

> **http://localhost:8080/advjhtp1/servlets/Survey.html**

Select a survey response, and press the **Submit** button in the Web page to invoke the servlet.

9.9 HttpUtils Class

Class *HttpUtils* provides three **static** utility methods to simplify servlet programming. These methods are discussed in Fig. 9.30.

Method	Description
getRequestURL	This method takes the **HttpServletRequest** object as an argument and returns a **StringBuffer** containing the original URL that initiated the request.
parsePostData	This method receives an integer and **ServletInputStream** as arguments. The integer represents the number of bytes in the **ServletInputStream**. The **ServletInputStream** contains the key/value pairs **post**ed to the servlet from a **form**. The method returns a **Hashtable** containing the key/value pairs.
parseQueryString	This method receives a **String** representing the query string in a **get** request as an argument and returns a **Hashtable** containing the key/value pairs in the query string. The value of each key is an array of **String**s. The query string can be obtained with **HttpServletRequest** method **getQueryString**.

Fig. 9.30   **HttpUtils** class methods.

9.10 Internet and World Wide Web Resources

This section lists a variety of servlet resources available on the Internet and provides a brief description of each.

java.sun.com/products/servlet/index.html
The servlet page at the Sun Microsystems, Inc., Java Web site provides access to the latest servlet information and servlet resources.

jakarta.apache.org
This is the Apache Project's home page for the *Jakarta Project*. *Tomcat*—the servlets and JavaServer Pages reference implementation— is one of many subprojects of the Jakarta Project.

jakarta.apache.org/tomcat/index.html
Home page for the Tomcat servlets and JavaServer Pages reference implementation.

java.apache.org
This is the Apache Project's home page for all Java-related technologies. This site provides access to many Java packages useful to servlet and JSP developers.

www.servlets.com
This is the Web site for the book *Java Servlet Programming* published by O'Reilly. The book provides a variety of resources. This book is an excellent resource for programmers who are learning servlets.

theserverside.com
TheServerSide.com is dedicated to information and resources for Enterprise Java.

www.servletsource.com
ServletSource.com is a general servlet resource site containing code, tips, tutorials and links to many other Web sites with information on servlets.

www.cookiecentral.com
A good all-around resource site for cookies.

developer.netscape.com/docs/manuals/communicator/jsguide4/cookies.htm
A description of Netscape cookies.

www.javacorporate.com
Home of the open-source *Expresso Framework*, which includes a library of extensible servlet components to help speed Web application development.

www.servlet.com/srvdev.jhtml
ServletInc's Servlet Developers Forum provides resources for server-side Java developers and information about Web servers that support servlet technologies.

www.servletforum.com
ServletForum.com is a newsgroup where you can post questions and have them answered by your peers.

www.coolservlets.com
Provides free open-source Java servlets.

www.cetus-links.org/oo_java_servlets.html
Provides a list of links to resources on servlets and other technologies.

www.javaskyline.com
Java Skyline is an online magazine for servlet developers.

www.rfc-editor.org
The RFC Editor provides a search engine for RFCs (Request for Comments). Many of these RFCs provide details of Web-related technologies. RFCs of interest to servlet developers include *URIs* (RFC

1630), *URLs* (RFC 1738)URL, *Relative URLs* (RFC 1808), *HTTP/1.0* (RFC 1945), *MIME* (RFCs 2045–2049), *HTTP State Management Mechanism* (RFC 2109), *Use and Interpretation of HTTP Version Numbers* (RFC 2145), *Hypertext Coffee Pot Control Protocol* (RFC 2324), HTTP/1.1 (RFC 2616) and *HTTP Authentication: Basic and Digest Authentication* (RFC 2617).

www.irvine.com/~mime
The *Multipurpose Internet Mail Extensions FAQ* provides information on MIME and a list of many registered MIME types, as well as links to other MIME resources.

SUMMARY

- The classes and interfaces used to define servlets are found in packages **javax.servlet** and **javax.servlet.http**.

- The Internet offers many protocols. The HTTP protocol (Hypertext Transfer Protocol) that forms the basis of the World Wide Web uses URIs (Uniform Resource Identifiers) to locate resources on the Internet.

- Common URLs represent files or directories and can represent complex tasks such as database lookups and Internet searches.

- JavaServer Pages technology is an extension of servlet technology.

- Servlets are normally executed as part of a Web server (also known as the servlet container).

- Servlets and JavaServer Pages have become so popular that they are now supported by most major Web servers and application servers.

- All servlets must implement the **Servlet** interface. The methods of interface **Servlet** are invoked automatically by the servlet container.

- A servlet's life cycle begins when the servlet container loads the servlet into memory—normally in response to the first request to that servlet. Before the servlet can handle the first request, the servlet container invokes the servlet's **init** method. After **init** completes execution, the servlet can respond to its first request. All requests are handled by a servlet's **service** method, which may be called many times during the life cycle of a servlet. When the servlet container terminates the servlet, the servlet's **destroy** method is called to release servlet resources.

- The servlet packages define two **abstract** classes that implement the interface **Servlet**— class **GenericServlet** and class **HttpServlet**. Most servlets extend one of these classes and override some or all of their methods with appropriate customized behaviors.

- The key method in every servlet is method **service**, which receives both a **ServletRequest** object and a **ServletResponse** object. These objects provide access to input and output streams that allow the servlet to read data from the client and send data to the client.

- Web-based servlets typically extend class **HttpServlet**. Class **HttpServlet** overrides method **service** to distinguish between the typical requests received from a client Web browser. The two most common HTTP request types (also known as request methods) are **get** and **post**.

- Class **HttpServlet** defines methods **doGet** and **doPost** to respond to **get** and **post** requests from a client, respectively. These methods are called by the **HttpServlet** class's **service** method, which is called when a request arrives at the server.

- Methods **doGet** and **doPost** receive as arguments an **HttpServletRequest** object and an **HttpServletResponse** object that enable interaction between the client and the server.

- A response is sent to the client through a **PrintWriter** object returned by the **getWriter** method of the **HttpServletResponse** object.

- The **HttpServletResponse** object's **setContentType** method specifies the MIME type of the response to the client. This enables the client browser to understand and handle the content.

- The server **localhost** (IP address **127.0.0.1**) is a well-known server host name on most computers that support TCP/IP-based networking protocols such as HTTP. This host name can be used to test TCP/IP applications on the local computer.
- The Tomcat server awaits requests from clients on port 8080. This port number must be specified as part of the URL to request a servlet running in Tomcat.
- The client can access a servlet only if that servlet is installed on a server that can respond to servlet requests. Web servers that support servlets normally have an installation procedure for servlets.
- Tomcat is a fully functional implementation of the JSP and servlet standards. It includes a Web server, so it can be used as a stand-alone test container for JSPs and servlets.
- Tomcat can be specified as the handler for JSP and servlet requests received by popular Web servers such as Apache and IIS. Tomcat also is integrated into the Java 2 Enterprise Edition reference implementation from Sun Microsystems.
- JSPs, servlets and their supporting files are deployed as part of Web applications. In Tomcat, Web applications are deployed in the **webapps** subdirectory of the Tomcat installation.
- A Web application has a well-known directory structure in which all the files that are part of the application reside. This directory structure can be set up by the Tomcat server administrator in the **webapps** directory, or the entire directory structure can be archived in a Web application archive file. Such an archive is known as a WAR file and ends with the **.war** file extension.
- If a WAR file is placed in the **webapps** directory, when the Tomcat server starts up it extracts the contents of the WAR file into the appropriate **webapps** subdirectory structure.
- The Web application directory structure is separated into a context root—the top-level directory for an entire Web application—and several subdirectories. The context root is the root directory for the Web application. All the JSPs, HTML documents, servlets and supporting files such as images and class files reside in this directory or its subdirectories. The **WEB-INF** directory contains the Web application deployment descriptor (**web.xml**). The **WEB-INF/classes** directory contains the servlet class files and other supporting class files used in a Web application. The **WEB-INF/lib** directory contains Java archive (JAR) files that may include servlet class files and other supporting class files used in a Web application.
- Before deploying a Web application, the servlet container must be made aware of the context root for the Web application. In Tomcat, this can be done simply by placing a directory in the **webapps** subdirectory. Tomcat uses the directory name as the context name.
- Deploying a Web application requires the creation of a deployment descriptor (**web.xml**).
- HTTP **get** requests can be typed directly into your browser's **Address** or **Location** field.
- Parameters are passed as name/value pairs in a **get** request. A **?** separates the URL from the data passed as part of a **get** request. Name/value pairs are passed with the name and the value separated by **=**. If there is more than one name/value pair, each name/value pair is separated by **&**.
- Method **getParameter** of interface **HttpServletRequest** receives the parameter name as an argument and returns the corresponding **String** value, or **null** if the parameter is not part of the request.
- An HTTP **post** request is often used to post data from an Web-page form to a server-side form handler that processes the data.
- Browsers often cache (save on disk) Web pages so they can quickly reload the pages. Browsers do not cache the server's response to a **post** request.
- Method **doPost** receives the same two arguments as **doGet**—an object that implements interface **HttpServletRequest** to represent the client's request and an object that implements interface **HttpServletResponse** to represent the servlet's response.

- Method **sendRedirect** of **HttpServletResponse** redirects a request to the specified URL.

- When a servlet uses a relative path to reference another static or dynamic resource, the servlet assumes the same context root unless a complete URL is specified for the resource.

- Once method **sendRedirect** executes, processing of the request by the servlet that called **sendRedirect** terminates.

- When redirecting requests, the request parameters from the original request are passed as parameters to the new request. Additional request parameters also can be passed.

- New parameters are added to the existing request parameters. If a new parameter has the same name as an existing parameter, the new parameter value takes precedence over the original value. However, all the values are still passed.

- The complete set of values for a given request-parameter name can be obtained by calling method **getParameterValues** from interface **HttpServletRequest**, which receives the parameter name as an argument and returns an array of **String**s containing the parameter values in order from the most recently added value for that parameter to the least recently added.

- Many Web sites today provide custom Web pages and/or functionality on a client-by-client basis.

- HTTP is a stateless protocol—it does not support persistent information that could help a Web server determine that a request is from a particular client.

- Cookies can store information on the user's computer for retrieval later in the same or in future browsing sessions.

- Cookies are text-based data that are sent by servlets (or other similar technologies) as part of responses to clients.

- Every HTTP-based interaction between a client and a server includes a header containing information about the request (when the communication is from the client to the server) or information about the response (when the communication is from the server to the client).

- When the server receives a request, the header includes information such as the request type (e.g., **get** or **post**) and the cookies stored on the client machine by the server.

- When the server formulates its response, the header information includes any cookies the server wants to store on the client computer and other information such as the MIME type of the response.

- Depending on the maximum age of a cookie, the Web browser either maintains the cookie for the duration of the browsing session or stores the cookie on the client computer for future use. When the browser requests a resource from a server, cookies previously sent to the client by that server are returned to the server as part of the request formulated by the browser. Cookies are deleted automatically when they expire.

- By default, cookies only exist for the current browsing session (until the user closes the browser). To make cookies persist beyond the current session, call **Cookie** method **setMaxAge** to indicate the number of seconds until the cookie expires.

- Method **addCookie** of interface **HttpServletResponse** adds a cookie to the response. Cookies are sent to the client as part of the HTTP header. The header information is always provided to the client first, so the cookies should be added before the response is output.

- **HttpServletRequest** method **getCookies** returns an array of **Cookie** objects. Method **getCookies** returns **null** if there are no cookies in the request.

- **Cookie** method **getName** retrieves the name of a cookie. **Cookie** method **getValue** retrieves the value of a cookie.

- Java provides enhanced session An alternative approach to cookies is to track a session with **HttpSession**s, which eliminate the problems associated with clients disabling cookies in their browsers by making the session-tracking mechanism transparent to the programmer.

- Method **getSession** of interface **HttpServletRequest** obtains an **HttpSession** object for the client.
- Like a cookie, an **HttpSession** object can store name/value pairs. In sessions, these are called attributes, and they are stored with **setAttribute** and retrieved with **getAttribute**.
- Name/value pairs added to an **HttpSession** object with **setAttribute** remain available until the client's current browsing session ends or until the session is explicitly invalidated by a call to the **HttpSession** object's **invalidate** method.
- **HttpSession** method **getID** obtains the session's unique ID number.
- **HttpSession** method **isNew** determines whether a session is new or already exists. Method **getCreationTime** obtains the time at which the session was created.
- **HttpSession** method **getLastAccessedTime** obtains the time at which the session was last accessed.
- **HttpSession** method **getMaxInactiveInterval** obtains the maximum amount of time that an **HttpSession** object can be inactive before the servlet container discards it.
- Many of today's applications are three-tier distributed applications, consisting of a user interface, business logic and database access.
- In multi-tier architectures, Web servers often represent the middle tier. They provide the business logic that manipulates data from databases and that communicates with client Web browsers.
- **Servlet** method **init** takes a **ServletConfig** argument and throws a **ServletException**. The argument provides the servlet with information about its initialization parameters that are specified in a **servlet** element in the deployment descriptor. Each parameter appears in an **init-param** element with child elements **param-name** and **param-value**.

TERMINOLOGY

addCookie method of
   HttpServletResponse
Apache Tomcat server
cache a Web page
commit a response
context root
Cookie class
delete request
deploy a Web application
deployment descriptor
destroy method of **Servlet**
doGet method of **HttpServlet**
doPost method of **HttpServlet**
GenericServlet class from
   javax.servlet
get request
getAttribute method of **HttpSession**
getAttributeNames method of
   HttpSession
getCookies method of
   HttpServletRequest
getCreationTime method of **HttpSession**
getID method of **HttpSession**

getLastAccessedTime method of
   HttpSession
getMaxInactiveInterval method of
   HttpSession
getName method of **Cookie**
getOutputStream method of
   HTTPServletResponse
getParameter method of
   HttpServletRequest
getParameterNames method of
   HttpServletRequest
getParameterValues method of
   HttpServletRequest
getServletConfig method of **Servlet**
getServletInfo method of **Servlet**
getSession method of
   HttpServletRequest
getValue method of **Cookie**
getWriter method of
   HTTPServletResponse
host name
HTTP (Hypertext Transfer Protocol)
HTTP header

HTTP request
HttpServlet interface
HttpServletRequest interface
HttpServletResponse interface
HttpSession interface
init method of **Servlet**
initialization parameter
invalidate method of **HttpSession**
isNew method of **HttpSession**
Jakarta project
JAVA_HOME environment variable
javax.servlet package
javax.servlet.http package
Jigsaw Web server
localhost (127.0.0.1)
maximum age of a cookie
MIME type
options request
path attribute
port
post request
put request
redirect a request
request method
request parameter
sendRedirect method of
   HttpServletResponse
service method of **Servlet**
servlet

servlet container
Servlet interface
servlet life cycle
servlet mapping
ServletConfig interface
ServletContext interface
ServletException class
ServletOutputStream class
ServletRequest interface
ServletResponse interface
session tracking
setAttribute method of **HttpSession**
setContentType method of
   HttpServletResponse
shopping cart
text/html MIME type
thin client
TOMCAT_HOME environment variable
trace request
URL pattern
WAR (Web application archive) file
Web application
Web application deployment
   descriptor (**web.xml**)
webapps directory
WEB-INF directory
WEB-INF/classes directory
WEB-INF/lib directory
well-known port number

SELF-REVIEW EXERCISES

9.1   Fill in the blanks in each of the following statements:
  a) Classes **HttpServlet** and **GenericServlet** implement the _____ interface.
  b) Class **HttpServlet** defines the methods _____ and _____ to respond to **get** and **post** requests from a client.
  c) **HttpServletResponse** method _____ obtains a character-based output stream that enables text data to be sent to the client.
  d) The **form** attribute _____ specifies the server-side *form handler,* i.e., the program that handles the request.
  e) _____ is the well-known host name that refers to your own computer.
  f) **Cookie** method _____ returns a **String** the name of the cookie as set with _____ or the constructor.
  g) **HttpServletRequest** method **getSession** returns an _____ object for the client.

9.2   State whether each of the following is *true* or *false.* If *false,* explain why.
  a) Servlets usually are used on the client side of a networking application.
  b) Servlet methods are executed automatically.
  c) The two most common HTTP requests are **get** and **put**.
  d) The well-known port number for Web requests is 55.

e) **Cookie**s never expire.

f) **HttpSession**s expire only when the browsing session ends or when the **invali-date** method is called.

g) The **HttpSession** method **getAttribute** returns the object associated with a particular name.

ANSWERS TO SELF-REVIEW EXERCISES

9.1 a) **Servlet**. b) **doGet**, **doPost**. c) **getWriter**. d) **action**. e) **localhost**. f) **getName**, **setName**. g) **HttpSession**.

9.2 a) False. Servlets are usually used on the server side.
   b) True.
   c) False. The two most common HTTP request types are **get** and **post**.
   d) False. The well-known port number for Web requests is 80.
   e) False. **Cookie**s expire when they reach their maximum age.
   f) True.
   g) True.

EXERCISES

9.3 Modify the **Cookie** example of Fig. 9.20 to list prices for each book in the book recommendations. Also, allow the user to select some or all of the recommended books and "order" them. Deploy your Web application on the Tomcat server.

9.4 Modify the **HttpSession** example of Fig. 9.24 to list prices for each book in the book recommendations. Also, allow the user to select some or all of the recommended books and "order" them. Deploy your Web application on the Tomcat server.

9.5 Create a Web application for dynamic FAQs. The application should obtain the information to create the dynamic FAQ Web page from a database that consists of a **Topics** table and an **FAQ** table. The **Topics** table should have two fields—a unique integer ID for each topic (**topicID**) and a name for each topic (**topicName**). The **FAQ** table should have three fields—the **topicID** (a foreign key), a string representing the question (**question**) and the answer to the question (**answer**). When the servlet is invoked, it should read the data from the database and return a dynamically created Web page containing each question and answer, sorted by topic.

9.6 Modify the Web application of Exercise 9.5 so that the initial request to the servlet returns a Web page of topics in the FAQ database. Then, the user can hyperlink to another servlet that returns only the frequently asked questions for a particular topic.

9.7 Modify the Web application of Fig. 9.27 to allow the user to see the survey results without responding to the survey.

9.8 Fig. 9.27 would allow users to vote as many times as they want by simply returning to the survey Web page and submitting additional votes. Modify your solution to Exercise 9.7 such that it uses cookies that last for one day to prevent users from voting more than once a day. When a user returns to the site, the cookie previously stored on their system is sent to the server. The servlet should check for the cookie and, if it exists, indicate that the client already voted in the last 24 hours. The servlet should also return the current survey results.

9.9 Modify the Web application of Fig. 9.27 to make it generic for use with any survey of the appropriate form. Use servlet parameters (as discussed in Section 9.8) to specify the survey options. When the user requests the survey, dynamically generate a **form** containing the survey options. Deploy this Web application twice using different context roots. *Note*: You may need to modify the database in this example so that it can store multiple surveys at once.

9.10   Write a Web application that consists of a servlet (**DirectoryServlet**) and several Web documents. Document **index.html** should be the first document the user sees. In that document, you should have a series of hyperlinks for other Web pages in your site. When clicked, each hyperlink should invoke the servlet with a **get** request that contains a **page** parameter. The servlet should obtain parameter **page** and redirect the request to the appropriate document.

9.11   Modify the Web application of Exercise 9.10 so that the first document the user sees in the browser is dynamically generated from servlet initialization parameters (as discussed in Section 9.8) by servlet **HomePageServlet**. There should be a separate initialization parameter for each page in the Web site. The **HomePageServlet** reads each parameter name and value and creates a **Hash-Map** of the parameter name/value pairs. This information should be used to create the initial home page dynamically. The **HashMap** also should be placed in the **ServletContext** with method **setAttribute**, so that the **HashMap** can be used in the **DirectoryServlet** to determine where to direct each request. The dynamic home page should have hyperlinks to each document in the Web site. As in Exercise 9.10, when the user clicks a link, servlet **DirectoryServlet** should be invoked and passed a page parameter. Then, the **DirectoryServlet** should obtain the **Hash-Map** from the **ServletContext**, look up the corresponding document and redirect the user to that document.

10

JavaServer Pages (JSP)

Objectives

- To be able to create and deploy JavaServer Pages.
- To use JSP's implicit objects and Java to create dynamic Web pages.
- To specify global JSP information with directives.
- To use actions to manipulate JavaBeans in a JSP, to include resources dynamically and to forward requests to other JSPs.
- To create custom tag libraries that encapsulate complex functionality in new tags that can be reused by JSP programmers and Web-page designers.

A tomato does not communicate with a tomato, we believe. We could be wrong.
Gustav Eckstein

A donkey appears to me like a horse translated into Dutch.
Georg Christoph Licthtenberg

Talent is a question of quantity. Talent does not write one page: it writes three hundred.
Jules Renard

Every action must be due to one or other of seven causes: chance, nature, compulsion, habit, reasoning, anger, or appetite.
Aristotle

10.1 Introduction

Our discussion of client–server networking continues in this chapter with *JavaServer Pages (JSP)*—an extension of servlet technology. JavaServer Pages simplify the delivery of dynamic Web content. They enable Web application programmers to create dynamic content by reusing predefined components and by interacting with components using server-side scripting. JavaServer Page programmers can reuse JavaBeans and create custom tag libraries that encapsulate complex, dynamic functionality. Custom-tag libraries even enable Web-page designers who are not familiar with Java to enhance Web pages with powerful dynamic content and processing capabilities.

In addition to the classes and interfaces for programming servlets (from packages **javax.servlet** and **javax.servlet.http**), classes and interfaces specific to JavaServer Pages programming are located in packages ***javax.servlet.jsp*** and ***javax.servlet.jsp.tagext***. We discuss many of these classes and interfaces throughout this chapter as we present JavaServer Pages fundamentals. For a complete description of JavaServer Pages, see the JavaServer Pages 1.1 specification, which can be downloaded from **java.sun.com/products/jsp/download.html**. We also include other JSP resources in Section 10.9. [*Note:* The source code and images for all the examples in this chapter can be found on the CD that accompanies this book and on our Web site **www.deitel.com**.]

10.2 JavaServer Pages Overview

There are four key components to JSPs: *directives, actions, scriptlets* and *tag libraries.* Directives are messages to the JSP container that enable the programmer to specify page settings, to include content from other resources and to specify custom tag libraries for use in a JSP. Actions encapsulate functionality in predefined tags that programmers can embed in a JSP. Actions often are performed based on the information sent to the server as part of a particular client request. They also can create Java objects for use in JSP scriptlets. Scriptlets, or *scripting elements*, enable programmers to insert Java code that interacts with components in a JSP (and possibly other Web application components) to perform request processing. Tag libraries are part of the *tag extension mechanism* that enables programmers to create custom tags. Such tags enable programmers to manipulate JSP content. These JSP component types are discussed in detail in subsequent sections.

In many ways, Java Server Pages look like standard XHTML or XML documents. In fact, JSPs normally include XHTML or XML markup. Such markup is known as *fixed-template data* or *fixed-template text.* Fixed-template data often help a programmer decide whether to use a servlet or a JSP. Programmers tend to use JSPs when most of the content sent to the client is fixed template data and only a small portion of the content is generated dynamically with Java code. Programmers use servlets when only a small portion of the content sent to the client is fixed-template data. In fact, some servlets do not produce content. Rather, they perform a task on behalf of the client, then invoke other servlets or JSPs to provide a response. Note that in most cases, servlet and JSP technologies are interchangeable. As with servlets, JSPs normally execute as part of a Web server. The server often is referred to as the *JSP container.*

Software Engineering Observation 10.1

Literal text in a JSP becomes string literals in the servlet that represents the translated JSP.

When a JSP-enabled server receives the first request for a JSP, the JSP container translates that JSP into a Java servlet that handles the current request and future requests to the JSP. If there are any errors compiling the new servlet, these errors result in *translation-time errors.* The JSP container places the Java statements that implement the JSP's response in method **_jspService** at translation time. If the new servlet compiles properly, the JSP container invokes method **_jspService** to process the request. The JSP may respond directly to the request or may invoke other Web application components to assist in processing the request. Any errors that occur during request processing are known as *request-time errors.*

Performance Tip 10.1

Some JSP containers translate JSPs to servlets at installation time. This eliminates the translation overhead for the first client that requests each JSP.

Overall, the request/response mechanism and life cycle of a JSP is the same as that of a servlet. JSPs can define methods **jspInit** and **jspDestroy** (similar to servlet methods **init** and **destroy**), which the JSP container invokes when initializing a JSP and terminating a JSP, respectively. JSP programmers can define these methods using JSP *declarations*—part of the JSP scripting mechanism.

10.3 A First JavaServer Page Example

We begin our introduction to JavaServer Pages with a simple example (Fig. 10.1) in which the current date and time are inserted into a Web page using a JSP expression.

As you can see, most of **clock.jsp** consists of XHTML markup. In cases like this, JSPs are easier to implement than servlets. In a servlet that performs the same task as this JSP, each line of XHTML markup typically is a separate Java statement that outputs the string representing the markup as part of the response to the client. Writing code to output markup can often lead to errors. Most JSP editors provide syntax coloring to help programmers check that their markup follows proper syntax.

```
1   <?xml version = "1.0"?>
2   <!DOCTYPE html PUBLIC "-//W3C//DTD XHTML 1.0 Strict//EN"
3      "http://www.w3.org/TR/xhtml1/DTD/xhtml1-strict.dtd">
4
5   <!-- Fig. 10.1: clock.jsp -->
6
7   <html xmlns = "http://www.w3.org/1999/xhtml">
8
9      <head>
10        <meta http-equiv = "refresh" content = "60" />
11
12        <title>A Simple JSP Example</title>
13
14        <style type = "text/css">
15           .big { font-family: helvetica, arial, sans-serif;
16                  font-weight: bold;
17                  font-size: 2em; }
18        </style>
19     </head>
20
21     <body>
22        <p class = "big">Simple JSP Example</p>
23
24        <table style = "border: 6px outset;">
25           <tr>
26              <td style = "background-color: black;">
27                 <p class = "big" style = "color: cyan;">
28
29                    <!-- JSP expression to insert date/time -->
30                    <%= new java.util.Date() %>
31
32                 </p>
33              </td>
34           </tr>
35        </table>
36     </body>
```

Fig. 10.1   Using a JSP expression to insert the date and time in a Web page (part 1 of 2).

```
37
38    </html>
```

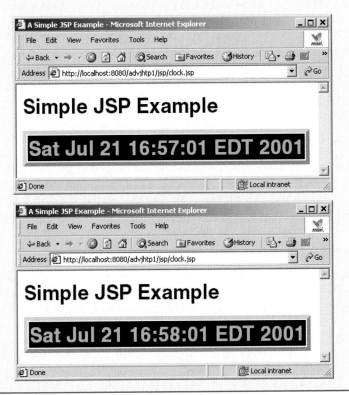

Fig. 10.1   Using a JSP expression to insert the date and time in a Web page (part 2 of 2).

 Software Engineering Observation 10.2

JavaServer Pages are easier to implement than servlets when the response to a client request consists primarily of markup that remains constant between requests.

The JSP of Fig. 10.1 generates an XHTML document that displays the current date and time. The key line in this JSP (line 30) is the expression

```
<%= new java.util.Date() %>
```

JSP expressions are delimited by **<%=** and **%>**. This particular expression creates a new instance of class **Date** from package **java.util**. When the client requests this JSP, the preceding expression inserts the **String** representation of the date and time in the response to the client. [Note: Proper internationalization requires that the JSP return the date in the client locale's format. In this example, the server's local determines the **String** representation of the **Date**. In Fig. 10.9, **clock2.jsp** demonstrates how to determine the client's locale and uses a **DateFormat** (package **java.text**) object to format the date using that locale.]

 **Software Engineering Observation 10.3**

*The JSP container converts the result of every JSP expression into a **String** that is output as part of the response to the client.*

Note that we use the XHTML *meta* element on line 10 to set a *refresh interval* of 60 seconds for the document. This causes the browser to request **clock.jsp** every 60 seconds. For each request to **clock.jsp**, the JSP container reevaluates the expression on line 30, creating a new **Date** object with the server's current date and time.

As in Chapter 9, we use Apache Tomcat to test our JSPs in the **advjhtp1** Web application we created previously. For details on creating and configuring the **advjhtp1** Web application, review Section 9.3.1 and Section 9.3.2. To test **clock.jsp**, create a new directory called **jsp** in the **advjhtp1** subdirectory of Tomcat's **webapps** directory. Next, copy **clock.jsp** into the **jsp** directory. Open your Web browser and enter the following URL to test **clock.jsp**:

```
http://localhost:8080/advjhtp1/jsp/clock.jsp
```

When you first invoke the JSP, notice the delay as Tomcat translates the JSP into a servlet and invokes the servlet to respond to your request. [*Note:* It is not necessary to create a directory named **jsp** in a Web application. We use this directory to separate the examples in this chapter from the servlet examples in Chapter 9.]

10.4 Implicit Objects

Implicit objects provide programmers with access to many servlet capabilities in the context of a JavaServer Page. Implicit objects have four scopes: *application*, *page*, *request* and *session*. The JSP and servlet container application owns objects with *application scope*. Any servlet or JSP can manipulate such objects. Objects with *page scope* exist only in the page that defines them. Each page has its own instances of the page-scope implicit objects. Objects with *request scope* exist for the duration of the request. For example, a JSP can partially process a request, then forward the request to another servlet or JSP for further processing. Request-scope objects go out of scope when request processing completes with a response to the client. Objects with *session scope* exist for the client's entire browsing session. Figure 10.2 describes the JSP implicit objects and their scopes. This chapter demonstrates several of these objects.

Implicit Object	Description
Application Scope	
application	This **javax.servlet.ServletContext** object represents the container in which the JSP executes.
Page Scope	
config	This **javax.servlet.ServletConfig** object represents the JSP configuration options. As with servlets, configuration options can be specified in a Web application descriptor.
exception	This **java.lang.Throwable** object represents the exception that is passed to the JSP error page. This object is available only in a JSP error page.

Fig. 10.2 JSP implicit objects (part 1 of 2).

Implicit Object	Description
out	This **javax.servlet.jsp.JspWriter** object writes text as part of the response to a request. This object is used implicitly with JSP expressions and actions that insert string content in a response.
page	This **java.lang.Object** object represents the **this** reference for the current JSP instance.
pageContext	This **javax.servlet.jsp.PageContext** object hides the implementation details of the underlying servlet and JSP container and provides JSP programmers with access to the implicit objects discussed in this table.
response	This object represents the response to the client. The object normally is an instance of a class that implements **HttpServletResponse** (package **javax.servlet.http**). If a protocol other than HTTP is used, this object is an instance of a class that implements **javax.servlet.ServletResponse**.
Request Scope	
request	This object represents the client request. The object normally is an instance of a class that implements **HttpServletRequest** (package **javax.servlet.http**). If a protocol other than HTTP is used, this object is an instance of a subclass of **javax.servlet.ServletRequest**.
Session Scope	
session	This **javax.servlet.http.HttpSession** object represents the client session information if such a session has been created. This object is available only in pages that participate in a session.

Fig. 10.2 JSP implicit objects (part 2 of 2).

Note that many of the implicit objects extend classes or implement interfaces discussed in Chapter 9. Thus, JSPs can use the same methods that servlets use to interact with such objects, as described in Chapter 9. Most of the examples in this chapter use one or more of the implicit objects in Fig. 10.2.

10.5 Scripting

JavaServer Pages often present dynamically generated content as part of an XHTML document sent to the client in response to a request. In some cases, the content is static, but is output only if certain conditions are met during a request (such as providing values in a **form** that submits a request). JSP programmers can insert Java code and logic in a JSP using scripting.

Software Engineering Observation 10.4

JavaServer Pages currently support scripting only with Java. Future JSP versions may support other scripting languages.

10.5.1 Scripting Components

JSP scripting components include scriptlets, comments, expressions, declarations and escape sequences. This section describes each of these scripting components. Many of these scripting components are demonstrated in Fig. 10.4 at the end of Section 10.5.2.

Scriptlets are blocks of code delimited by **<%** and **%>**. They contain Java statements that the container places in method **_jspService** at translation time.

JSPs support three comment styles: JSP comments, XHTML comments and comments from the scripting language. *JSP comments* are delimited by **<%--** and **--%>**. Such comments can be placed throughout a JSP, but not inside scriptlets. *XHTML comments* are delimited with **<!--** and **-->**. These comments can be placed throughout a JSP, but not inside scriptlets. Scripting language comments are currently Java comments, because Java is the only JSP scripting language at the present time. Scriptlets can use Java's single-line comments (delimited by **/** and **/**) and multiline comments (delimited by **/*** and ***/**).

Common Programming Error 10.1

Placing a JSP comment or XHTML comment inside a scriptlet is a translation-time syntax error that prevents the JSP from being translated properly.

JSP comments and scripting-language comments are ignored and do not appear in the response to a client. When clients view the source code of a JSP response, they will see only the XHTML comments in the source code. The different comment styles are useful for separating comments that the user should be able to see from comments that document logic processed on the server.

A JSP expression, delimited by **<%=** and **%>**, contains a Java expression that is evaluated when a client requests the JSP containing the expression. The container converts the result of a JSP expression to a **String** object, then outputs the **String** as part of the response to the client.

Declarations (delimited by **<%!** and **%>**) enable a JSP programmer to define variables and methods. Variables become instance variables of the servlet class that represents the translated JSP. Similarly, methods become members of the class that represents the translated JSP. Declarations of variables and methods in a JSP use Java syntax. Thus, a variable declaration must end in a semicolon, as in

```
<%! int counter = 0; %>
```

Common Programming Error 10.2

Declaring a variable without using a terminating semicolon is a syntax error.

Software Engineering Observation 10.5

Variables and methods declared in JSP declarations are initialized when the JSP is initialized and are available for use in all scriptlets and expressions in that JSP. Variables declared in this manner become instance variables of the servlet class that represents the translated JSP.

Software Engineering Observation 10.6

*As with servlets, JSPs should not store client state information in instance variables. Rather, JSPs should use the JSP implicit **session** object.*

Special characters or character sequences that the JSP container normally uses to delimit JSP code can be included in a JSP as literal characters in scripting elements, fixed template data and attribute values using *escape sequences*. Figure 10.3 shows the literal character or characters and the corresponding escape sequences and discusses where to use the escape sequences.

10.5.2 Scripting Example

The JSP of Fig. 10.4 demonstrates basic scripting capabilities by responding to **get** requests. The JSP enables the user to input a first name, then outputs that name as part of the response. Using scripting, the JSP determines whether a **firstName** parameter was passed to the JSP as part of the request; if not, the JSP returns an XHTML document containing a **form** through which the user can input a first name. Otherwise, the JSP obtains the **firstName** value and uses it as part of an XHTML document that welcomes the user to JavaServer Pages.

Literal	Escape sequence	Description
<%	**<\%**	The character sequence **<%** normally indicates the beginning of a scriptlet. The **<\%** escape sequence places the literal characters **<%** in the response to the client.
%>	**%\>**	The character sequence **%>** normally indicates the end of a scriptlet. The **%\>** escape sequence places the literal characters **%>** in the response to the client.
'	**\'**	As with string literals in a Java program, the escape sequences for characters **'**, **"** and **** allow these characters to appear in attribute values. Remember that the literal text in a JSP becomes string literals in the servlet that represents the translated JSP.
"	**\"**	
****	****	

Fig. 10.3 JSP escape sequences.

```
1   <?xml version = "1.0"?>
2   <!DOCTYPE html PUBLIC "-//W3C//DTD XHTML 1.0 Strict//EN"
3      "http://www.w3.org/TR/xhtml1/DTD/xhtml1-strict.dtd">
4
5   <!-- Fig. 10.4: welcome.jsp -->
6   <!-- JSP that processes a "get" request containing data. -->
7
8   <html xmlns = "http://www.w3.org/1999/xhtml">
9
10     <!-- head section of document -->
11     <head>
12        <title>Processing "get" requests with data</title>
13     </head>
14
```

Fig. 10.4 Scripting a JavaServer Page—**welcome.jsp** (part 1 of 3).

```
15      <!-- body section of document -->
16      <body>
17         <% // begin scriptlet
18
19             String name = request.getParameter( "firstName" );
20
21             if ( name != null ) {
22
23         %> <%-- end scriptlet to insert fixed template data --%>
24
25             <h1>
26                 Hello <%= name %>, <br />
27                 Welcome to JavaServer Pages!
28             </h1>
29
30         <% // continue scriptlet
31
32             }  // end if
33             else {
34
35         %> <%-- end scriptlet to insert fixed template data --%>
36
37             <form action = "welcome.jsp" method = "get">
38                 <p>Type your first name and press Submit</p>
39
40                 <p><input type = "text" name = "firstName" />
41                     <input type = "submit" value = "Submit" />
42                 </p>
43             </form>
44
45         <% // continue scriptlet
46
47             }  // end else
48
49         %> <%-- end scriptlet --%>
50      </body>
51
52   </html>   <!-- end XHTML document -->
```

Fig. 10.4   Scripting a JavaServer Page—**welcome.jsp** (part 2 of 3).

Fig. 10.4   Scripting a JavaServer Page—**welcome.jsp** (part 3 of 3).

Notice that the majority of the code in Fig. 10.4 is XHTML markup (i.e., fixed template data). Throughout the **body** element are several scriptlets (lines 17–23, 30–35 and 45–49) and a JSP expression (line 26). Note that three comment styles appear in this JSP.

The scriptlets define an **if/else** structure that determines whether the JSP received a value for the first name as part of the request. Line 19 uses method **getParameter** of JSP implicit object **request** (an **HttpServletRequest** object) to obtain the value for parameter **firstName** and assigns the result to variable **name**. Line 21 determines if **name** is not **null**, (i.e., a value for the first name was passed to the JSP as part of the request). If this condition is **true**, the scriptlet terminates temporarily so the fixed template data at lines 25–28 can be output. The JSP expression in line 26 outputs the value of variable **name** (i.e., the first name passed to the JSP as a request parameter). The scriptlet continues at lines 30–35 with the closing curly brace of the **if** structure's body and the beginning of the **else** part of the **if/else** structure. If the condition at line 21 is **false**, lines 25–28 are not output. Instead, lines 37–43 output a **form** element. The user can type a first name in the **form** and press the **Submit** button to request the JSP again and execute the **if** structure's body (lines 25–28).

Software Engineering Observation 10.7

Scriptlets, expressions and fixed template data can be intermixed in a JSP to create different responses based on information in a request to a JSP.

Testing and Debugging Tip 10.1

It is sometimes difficult to debug errors in a JSP, because the line numbers reported by a JSP container normally refer to the servlet that represents the translated JSP, not the original JSP line numbers. Program development environments such as Sun Microsystems, Inc.'s Forte for Java Community Edition enable JSPs to be compiled in the environment, so you can see syntax error messages. These messages include the statement in the servlet that represents the translated JSP, which can be helpful in determining the error.

Testing and Debugging Tip 10.2

*Many JSP containers store the servlets representing the translated JSPs. For example, the Tomcat installation directory contains a subdirectory called **work** in which you can find the source code for the servlets translated by Tomcat.*

To test Fig. 10.4 in Tomcat, copy **welcome.jsp** into the **jsp** directory created in Section 10.3. Open your Web browser and enter the following URL to test **welcome.jsp**:

http://localhost:8080/advjhtp1/jsp/welcome.jsp

When you first execute the JSP, it displays the **form** in which you can enter your first name, because the preceding URL does not pass a **firstName** parameter to the JSP. After you submit your first name, your browser should appear as shown in the second screen capture of Fig. 10.4. *Note*: As with servlets, it is possible to pass **get** request arguments as part of the URL. The following URL supplies the **firstName** parameter to **welcome.jsp**:

http://localhost:8080/advjhtp1/jsp/welcome.jsp?firstName=Paul

10.6 Standard Actions

We continue our JSP discussion with the *JSP standard actions* (Fig. 10.5). These actions provide JSP implementors with access to several of the most common tasks performed in a JSP, such as including content from other resources, forwarding requests to other resources and interacting with JavaBeans. JSP containers process actions at request time. Actions are delimited by **<jsp:***action***>** and **</jsp:***action***>**, where *action* is the standard action name. In cases where nothing appears between the starting and ending tags, the XML empty element syntax **<jsp:***action* **/>** can be used. Figure 10.5 summarizes the JSP standard actions. We use the actions in the next several subsections.

Action	Description
<jsp:include>	Dynamically includes another resource in a JSP. As the JSP executes, the referenced resource is included and processed.
<jsp:forward>	Forwards request processing to another JSP, servlet or static page. This action terminates the current JSP's execution.
<jsp:plugin>	Allows a plug-in component to be added to a page in the form of a browser-specific **object** or **embed** HTML element. In the case of a Java applet, this action enables the downloading and installation of the *Java Plug-in*, if it is not already installed on the client computer.
<jsp:param>	Used with the **include**, **forward** and **plugin** actions to specify additional name/value pairs of information for use by these actions.
JavaBean Manipulation	
<jsp:useBean>	Specifies that the JSP uses a JavaBean instance. This action specifies the scope of the bean and assigns it an ID that scripting components can use to manipulate the bean.

Fig. 10.5 JSP standard actions (part 1 of 2).

Action	Description
`<jsp:setProperty>`	Sets a property in the specified JavaBean instance. A special feature of this action is automatic matching of request parameters to bean properties of the same name.
`<jsp:getProperty>`	Gets a property in the specified JavaBean instance and converts the result to a string for output in the response.

Fig. 10.5 JSP standard actions (part 2 of 2).

10.6.1 `<jsp:include>` Action

JavaServer Pages support two include mechanisms—the `<jsp:include>` *action* and the *include directive*. Action `<jsp:include>` enables dynamic content to be included in a JavaServer Page. If the included resource changes between requests, the next request to the JSP containing the `<jsp:include>` action includes the new content of the resource. On the other hand, the `include` directive copies the content into the JSP once, at JSP translation time. If the included resource changes, the new content will not be reflected in the JSP that used the `include` directive unless that JSP is recompiled. Figure 10.6 describes the attributes of action `<jsp:include>`.

Software Engineering Observation 10.8

According to the JavaServer Pages 1.1 specification, a JSP container is allowed to determine whether a resource included with the `include` *directive has changed. If so, the container can recompile the JSP that included the resource. However, the specification does not provide a mechanism to indicate a change in an included resource to the container.*

Performance Tip 10.2

The `<jsp:include>` *action is more flexible than the* `include` *directive, but requires more overhead when page contents change frequently. Use the* `<jsp:include>` *action only when dynamic content is necessary.*

Common Programming Error 10.3

Setting the `<jsp:include>` *action's* `flush` *attribute to* `false` *is a translation-time error. Currently, the* `flush` *attribute supports only* `true` *values.*

Attribute	Description
`page`	Specifies the relative URI path of the resource to include. The resource must be part of the same Web application.
`flush`	Specifies whether the buffer should be flushed after the `include` is performed. In JSP 1.1, this attribute is required to be `true`.

Fig. 10.6 Action `<jsp:include>` attributes.

Common Programming Error 10.4

Not specifying the **<jsp:include>** *action's* **flush** *attribute is a translation-time error. Specifying this attribute is mandatory.*

Common Programming Error 10.5

Specifying in a **<jsp:include>** *action a page that is not part of the same Web application is a request-time error. In such a case, the* **<jsp:include>** *action does not include any content.*

The next example demonstrates action **<jsp:include>** using four XHTML and JSP resources that represent both static and dynamic content. JavaServer Page **include.jsp** (Fig. 10.10) includes three other resources: **banner.html** (Fig. 10.7), **toc.html** (Fig. 10.8) and **clock2.jsp** (Fig. 10.9). JavaServer Page **include.jsp** creates an XHTML document containing a **table** in which **banner.html** spans two columns across the top of the **table**, **toc.html** is the left column of the second row and **clock2.jsp** (a simplified version of Fig. 10.1) is the right column of the second row. Figure 10.10 uses three **<jsp:include>** actions (lines 38–39, 48 and 55–56) as the content in **td** elements of the **table**. Using two XHTML documents and a JSP in Fig. 10.10 demonstrates that JSPs can include both static and dynamic content. The output windows in Fig. 10.10 demonstrate the results of two separate requests to **include.jsp**.

Figure 10.9 (**clock2.jsp**) demonstrates how to determine the client's **Locale** (package **java.util**) and uses that **Locale** to format a **Date** with a *DateFormat* (package **java.text**) object. Line 14 invokes the **request** object's **getLocale** method, which returns the client's **Locale**. Lines 17–20 invoke **DateFormat static** method **getDateTimeInstance** to obtain a **DateFormat** object. The first two arguments indicate that the date and time formats should each be **LONG** format (other options are **FULL**, **MEDIUM**, **SHORT** and **DEFAULT**). The third argument specifies the **Locale** for which the **DateFormat** object should format the date. Line 25 invokes the **DateFormat** object's **format** method to produce a **String** representation of the **Date**. The **DateFormat** object formats this **String** for the **Locale** specified on lines 17–20. [*Note*: This example works for Western languages that use the ISO-8859-1 character set. However, for languages that do not use this character set, the JSP must specify the proper character set using the JSP **page** directive (Section 10.7.1). At the site **java.sun.com/ j2se/1.3/docs/guide/intl/encoding.doc.html**, Sun provides a list of character encodings. The response's content type defines the character set to use in the response. The content type has the form: **"***mimeType***;charset=***enconding***"** (e.g., **"text/html;charset=ISO-8859-1"**.]

To test Fig. 10.10 in Tomcat, copy **banner.html**, **toc.html**, **clock2.jsp**, **include.jsp** and the **images** directory into the **jsp** directory created in Section 10.3. Open your Web browser and enter the following URL to test **welcome.jsp**:

```
http://localhost:8080/advjhtp1/jsp/include.jsp
```

```
1   <!-- Fig. 10.7: banner.html                      -->
2   <!-- banner to include in another document -->
```

Fig. 10.7   Banner (**banner.html**) to include across the top of the XHTML document created by Fig. 10.10 (part 1 of 2).

```
3   <div style = "width: 580px">
4      <p>
5         Java(TM), C, C++, Visual Basic(R),
6         Object Technology, and <br /> Internet and
7         World Wide Web Programming Training <br />
8         On-Site Seminars Delivered Worldwide
9      </p>
10
11      <p>
12         <a href = "mailto:deitel@deitel.com">
13            deitel@deitel.com</a><br />
14
15         978.579.9911<br />
16         490B Boston Post Road, Suite 200,
17         Sudbury, MA 01776
18      </p>
19   </div>
```

Fig. 10.7   Banner (**banner.html**) to include across the top of the XHTML document created by Fig. 10.10 (part 2 of 2).

```
1   <!-- Fig. 10.8: toc.html                    -->
2   <!-- contents to include in another document -->
3
4   <p><a href = "http://www.deitel.com/books/index.html">
5      Publications/BookStore
6   </a></p>
7
8   <p><a href = "http://www.deitel.com/whatsnew.html">
9      What's New
10   </a></p>
11
12   <p><a href = "http://www.deitel.com/books/downloads.html">
13      Downloads/Resources
14   </a></p>
15
16   <p><a href = "http://www.deitel.com/faq/index.html">
17      FAQ (Frequently Asked Questions)
18   </a></p>
19
20   <p><a href = "http://www.deitel.com/intro.html">
21      Who we are
22   </a></p>
23
24   <p><a href = "http://www.deitel.com/index.html">
25      Home Page
26   </a></p>
27
28   <p>Send questions or comments about this site to
29      <a href = "mailto:deitel@deitel.com">
30         deitel@deitel.com
```

Fig. 10.8   Table of contents (**toc.html**) to include down the left side of the XHTML document created by Fig. 10.10 (part 1 of 2).

```
31      </a><br />
32      Copyright 1995-2002 by Deitel &amp; Associates, Inc.
33      All Rights Reserved.
34   </p>
```

Fig. 10.8 Table of contents (`toc.html`) to include down the left side of the XHTML document created by Fig. 10.10 (part 2 of 2).

```
1    <!-- Fig. 10.9: clock2.jsp                        -->
2    <!-- date and time to include in another document -->
3
4    <table>
5       <tr>
6          <td style = "background-color: black;">
7             <p class = "big" style = "color: cyan; font-size: 3em;
8                font-weight: bold;">
9
10               <%-- script to determine client local and --%>
11               <%-- format date accordingly              --%>
12               <%
13                   // get client locale
14                   java.util.Locale locale = request.getLocale();
15
16                   // get DateFormat for client's Locale
17                   java.text.DateFormat dateFormat =
18                       java.text.DateFormat.getDateTimeInstance(
19                           java.text.DateFormat.LONG,
20                           java.text.DateFormat.LONG, locale );
21
22               %>  <%-- end script --%>
23
24               <%-- output date --%>
25               <%= dateFormat.format( new java.util.Date() ) %>
26            </p>
27         </td>
28      </tr>
29   </table>
```

Fig. 10.9 JSP `clock2.jsp` to include as the main content in the XHTML document created by Fig. 10.10.

```
1    <?xml version = "1.0"?>
2    <!DOCTYPE html PUBLIC "-//W3C//DTD XHTML 1.0 Strict//EN"
3       "http://www.w3.org/TR/xhtml1/DTD/xhtml1-strict.dtd">
4
5    <!-- Fig. 10.7: include.jsp -->
6
7    <html xmlns = "http://www.w3.org/1999/xhtml">
8
9       <head>
10         <title>Using jsp:include</title>
```

Fig. 10.10 JSP `include.jsp` Includes resources with `<jsp:include>` (part 1 of 3).

```
11
12          <style type = "text/css">
13              body {
14                  font-family: tahoma, helvetica, arial, sans-serif;
15              }
16
17              table, tr, td {
18                  font-size: .9em;
19                  border: 3px groove;
20                  padding: 5px;
21                  background-color: #dddddd;
22              }
23          </style>
24      </head>
25
26      <body>
27          <table>
28              <tr>
29                  <td style = "width: 160px; text-align: center">
30                      <img src = "images/logotiny.png"
31                          width = "140" height = "93"
32                          alt = "Deitel & Associates, Inc. Logo" />
33                  </td>
34
35                  <td>
36
37                      <%-- include banner.html in this JSP --%>
38                      <jsp:include page = "banner.html"
39                          flush = "true" />
40
41                  </td>
42              </tr>
43
44              <tr>
45                  <td style = "width: 160px">
46
47                      <%-- include toc.html in this JSP --%>
48                      <jsp:include page = "toc.html" flush = "true" />
49
50                  </td>
51
52                  <td style = "vertical-align: top">
53
54                      <%-- include clock2.jsp in this JSP --%>
55                      <jsp:include page = "clock2.jsp"
56                          flush = "true" />
57
58                  </td>
59              </tr>
60          </table>
61      </body>
62  </html>
```

Fig. 10.10 JSP `include.jsp` Includes resources with `<jsp:include>` (part 2 of 3).

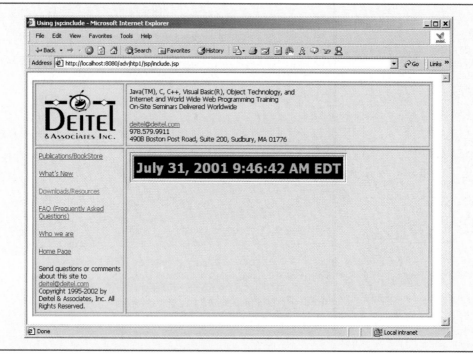

Fig. 10.10 JSP `include.jsp` Includes resources with `<jsp:include>` (part 3 of 3).

10.6.2 `<jsp:forward>` Action

Action **`<jsp:forward>`** enables a JSP to forward request processing to a different resource. Request processing by the original JSP terminates as soon as the JSP forwards the request. Action **`<jsp:forward>`** has only a **page** attribute that specifies the relative URI of the resource (in the same Web application) to which the request should be forwarded.

Software Engineering Observation 10.9

When using the `<jsp:forward>` action, the resource to which the request will be forwarded must be in the same context (Web application) as the JSP that originally received the request.

JavaServer Page **forward1.jsp** (Fig. 10.11) is a modified version of **welcome.jsp** (Fig. 10.4). The primary difference is in lines 22–25 in which JavaServer Page **forward1.jsp** forwards the request to JavaServer Page **forward2.jsp** (Fig. 10.12). Notice the **`<jsp:param>`** action in lines 23–24. This action adds a request parameter representing the date and time at which the initial request was received to the request object that is forwarded to **forward2.jsp**.

The **`<jsp:param>`** action specifies name/value pairs of information that are passed to the **`<jsp:include>`**, **`<jsp:forward>`** and **`<jsp:plugin>`** actions. Every **`<jsp:param>`** action has two required attributes: **name** and **value**. If a **`<jsp:param>`** action specifies a parameter that already exists in the request, the new value for the parameter takes precedence over the original value. All values for that parameter can be obtained by using the JSP implicit object **request**'s **getParameterValues** method, which returns an array of **String**s.

JSP **forward2.jsp** uses the **name** specified in the **<jsp:param>** action (**"date"**) to obtain the date and time. It also uses the **firstName** parameter originally passed to **forward1.jsp** to obtain the user's first name. JSP expressions in Fig. 10.12 (lines 23 and 31) insert the request parameter values in the response to the client. The screen capture in Fig. 10.11 shows the initial interaction with the client. The screen capture in Fig. 10.12 shows the results returned to the client after the request was forwarded to **forward2.jsp**.

To test Fig. 10.11 and Fig. 10.12 in Tomcat, copy **forward1.jsp** and **forward2.jsp** into the **jsp** directory created in Section 10.3. Open your Web browser and enter the following URL to test **welcome.jsp**:

```
http://localhost:8080/advjhtp1/jsp/forward1.jsp
```

```
1   <?xml version = "1.0"?>
2   <!DOCTYPE html PUBLIC "-//W3C//DTD XHTML 1.0 Strict//EN"
3      "http://www.w3.org/TR/xhtml1/DTD/xhtml1-strict.dtd">
4
5   <!-- Fig. 10.11: forward1.jsp -->
6
7   <html xmlns = "http://www.w3.org/1999/xhtml">
8
9   <head>
10     <title>Forward request to another JSP</title>
11  </head>
12
13  <body>
14     <% // begin scriptlet
15
16        String name = request.getParameter( "firstName" );
17
18        if ( name != null ) {
19
20     %> <%-- end scriptlet to insert fixed template data --%>
21
22           <jsp:forward page = "forward2.jsp">
23              <jsp:param name = "date"
24                 value = "<%= new java.util.Date() %>" />
25           </jsp:forward>
26
27     <% // continue scriptlet
28
29        }  // end if
30        else {
31
32     %> <%-- end scriptlet to insert fixed template data --%>
33
34           <form action = "forward1.jsp" method = "get">
35              <p>Type your first name and press Submit</p>
36
```

Fig. 10.11 JSP **forward1.jsp** receives a **firstName** parameter, adds a date to the request parameters and forwards the request to **forward2.jsp** for further processing (part 1 of 2).

```
37                    <p><input type = "text" name = "firstName" />
38                       <input type = "submit" value = "Submit" />
39                    </p>
40              </form>
41
42     <%  // continue scriptlet
43
44        }  // end else
45
46     %> <%-- end scriptlet --%>
47 </body>
48
49 </html>  <!-- end XHTML document -->
```

Fig. 10.11 JSP `forward1.jsp` receives a `firstName` parameter, adds a date to the request parameters and forwards the request to `forward2.jsp` for further processing (part 2 of 2).

```
1  <?xml version = "1.0"?>
2  <!DOCTYPE html PUBLIC "-//W3C//DTD XHTML 1.0 Strict//EN"
3     "http://www.w3.org/TR/xhtml11/DTD/xhtml1-strict.dtd">
4
5  <!-- forward2.jsp -->
6
7  <html xmlns = "http://www.w3.org/1999/xhtml"v
8
9  <head>
10     <title>Processing a forwarded request</title>
11
12     <style type = "text/css">
13        .big {
14           font-family: tahoma, helvetica, arial, sans-serif;
15           font-weight: bold;
16           font-size: 2em;
17        }
18     </style>
19 </head>
20
```

Fig. 10.12 JSP `forward2.jsp` receives a request (from `forward1.jsp` in this example) and uses the request parameters as part of the response to the client (part 1 of 2).

```
21   <body>
22      <p class = "big">
23         Hello <%= request.getParameter( "firstName" ) %>, <br />
24         Your request was received <br /> and forwarded at
25      </p>
26
27      <table style = "border: 6px outset;">
28         <tr>
29            <td style = "background-color: black;">
30               <p class = "big" style = "color: cyan;">
31                  <%= request.getParameter( "date" ) %>
32               </p>
33            </td>
34         </tr>
35      </table>
36   </body>
37
38   </html>
```

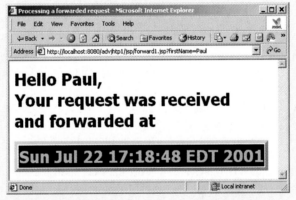

Fig. 10.12 JSP `forward2.jsp` receives a request (from `forward1.jsp` in this example) and uses the request parameters as part of the response to the client (part 2 of 2).

10.6.3 `<jsp:plugin>` Action

Action `<jsp:plugin>` adds an applet or JavaBean to a Web page in the form of a browser-specific **object** or **embed** XHTML element. This action also enables the client to download and install the *Java Plug-in* if it is not already installed. Figure 10.13 describes the attributes of action `<jsp:plugin>`.

Attribute	Description
`type`	Component type—bean or applet.
`code`	Class that represents the component.

Fig. 10.13 Attributes of the `<jsp:plugin>` action (part 1 of 2).

Attribute	Description
codebase	Location of the class specified in the **code** attribute and the archives specified in the **archive** attribute.
align	Alignment of the component.
archive	A space-separated list of archive files that contain resources used by the component. Such an archive may include the class specified by the **code** attribute.
height	Component height in the page specified in pixels or percentage.
hspace	Number of pixels of space that appear to the left and to the right of the component.
jreversion	Version of the Java Runtime Environment and plug-in required to execute the component. The default value is 1.1.
name	Name of the component.
vspace	Number of pixels of space that appear above and below the component.
title	Text that describes the component.
width	Component width in the page specified in pixels or percentage.
nspluginurl	Location for download of the Java Plug-in for Netscape Navigator.
iepluginurl	Location for download of the Java Plug-in for Internet Explorer.

Fig. 10.13 Attributes of the **<jsp:plugin>** action (part 2 of 2).

Figure 10.14 defines an applet that draws a picture using the Java2D API. The applet has three parameters that enable the JSP implementor to specify the background color for the drawing. The parameters represent the **red**, **green** and **blue** portions of an RGB color with values in the range 0–255. The applet obtains the parameter values in lines 21–23. If any exceptions occur while processing the parameters, the exceptions are caught at line 32 and ignored, leaving the applet with its default white background color.

```
1   // Fig. 10.14: ShapesApplet.java
2   // Applet that demonstrates a Java2D GeneralPath.
3   package com.deitel.advjhtp1.jsp.applet;
4
5   // Java core packages
6   import java.applet.*;
7   import java.awt.event.*;
8   import java.awt.*;
9   import java.awt.geom.*;
10
11  // Java extension packages
12  import javax.swing.*;
13
14  public class ShapesApplet extends JApplet {
15
```

Fig. 10.14 An applet to demonstrate **<jsp:plugin>** in Fig. 10.15 (part 1 of 3).

```
16      // initialize the applet
17      public void init()
18      {
19         // obtain color parameters from XHTML file
20         try {
21            int red = Integer.parseInt( getParameter( "red" ) );
22            int green = Integer.parseInt( getParameter( "green" ) );
23            int blue = Integer.parseInt( getParameter( "blue" ) );
24
25            Color backgroundColor = new Color( red, green, blue );
26
27            setBackground( backgroundColor );
28         }
29
30         // if there is an exception while processing the color
31         // parameters, catch it and ignore it
32         catch ( Exception exception ) {
33            // do nothing
34         }
35      }
36
37      public void paint( Graphics g )
38      {
39         // create arrays of x and y coordinates
40         int xPoints[] =
41            { 55, 67, 109, 73, 83, 55, 27, 37, 1, 43 };
42         int yPoints[] =
43            { 0, 36, 36, 54, 96, 72, 96, 54, 36, 36 };
44
45         // obtain reference to a Graphics2D object
46         Graphics2D g2d = ( Graphics2D ) g;
47
48         // create a star from a series of points
49         GeneralPath star = new GeneralPath();
50
51         // set the initial coordinate of the GeneralPath
52         star.moveTo( xPoints[ 0 ], yPoints[ 0 ] );
53
54         // create the star--this does not draw the star
55         for ( int k = 1; k < xPoints.length; k++ )
56            star.lineTo( xPoints[ k ], yPoints[ k ] );
57
58         // close the shape
59         star.closePath();
60
61         // translate the origin to (200, 200)
62         g2d.translate( 200, 200 );
63
64         // rotate around origin and draw stars in random colors
65         for ( int j = 1; j <= 20; j++ ) {
66            g2d.rotate( Math.PI / 10.0 );
67
```

Fig. 10.14 An applet to demonstrate `<jsp:plugin>` in Fig. 10.15 (part 2 of 3).

```
68            g2d.setColor(
69                new Color( ( int ) ( Math.random() * 256 ),
70                           ( int ) ( Math.random() * 256 ),
71                           ( int ) ( Math.random() * 256 ) ) );
72
73            g2d.fill( star );    // draw a filled star
74        }
75    }
76 }
```

Fig. 10.14 An applet to demonstrate **<jsp:plugin>** in Fig. 10.15 (part 3 of 3).

Most Web browsers in use today do not support applets written for the Java 2 platform. Executing such applets in most of today's browsers requires the Java Plug-in. Figure 10.15 uses the **<jsp:plugin>** action (lines 10–22) to embed the Java Plug-in. Line 11 indicates the package name and class name of the applet class. Line 12 indicates the **code-base** from which the applet should be downloaded. Line 13 indicates that the applet should be 400 pixels wide and line 14 indicates that the applet should be 400 pixels tall. Lines 16–20 specify the applet parameters. You can change the background color in the applet by changing the red, green and blue values. Note that the **<jsp:plugin>** action requires any **<jsp:param>** actions to appear in a **<jsp:params>** action.

To test the **<jsp:plugin>** action in Tomcat, copy **plugin.jsp** and **ShapesApplet.class** into the **jsp** directory created in Section 10.3. [*Note:* **ShapesApplet** is defined in package **com.deitel.advjhtp1.jsp.applet**. This example will work only if the proper package directory structure is defined in the **classes** directory.] Open your Web browser and enter the following URL to test **plugin.jsp**:

> **http://localhost:8080/advjhtp1/jsp/plugin.jsp**

The screen captures in Fig. 10.15 show the applet executing in Microsoft Internet Explorer 5.5 and Netscape Navigator 6.0.

```
1  <!-- Fig. 10.15: plugin.jsp -->
2
3  <html>
4
5     <head>
6        <title>Using jsp:plugin to load an applet</title>
7     </head>
8
9     <body>
10       <jsp:plugin type = "applet"
11          code = "com.deitel.advjhtp1.jsp.applet.ShapesApplet"
12          codebase = "/advjhtp1/jsp"
13          width = "400"
14          height = "400">
15
16          <jsp:params>
17             <jsp:param name = "red" value = "255" />
```

Fig. 10.15 Using **<jsp:plugin>** to embed a Java 2 applet in a JSP (part 1 of 2).

```
18                    <jsp:param name = "green" value = "255" />
19                    <jsp:param name = "blue" value = "0" />
20            </jsp:params>
21
22        </jsp:plugin>
23      </body>
24    </html>
```

Fig. 10.15 Using `<jsp:plugin>` to embed a Java 2 applet in a JSP (part 2 of 2).

10.6.4 `<jsp:useBean>` Action

Action `<jsp:useBean>` enables a JSP to manipulate a Java object. This action creates a Java object or locates an existing object for use in the JSP. Figure 10.16 summarizes action `<jsp:useBean>`'s attributes. If attributes `class` and `beanName` are not specified, the JSP container attempts to locate an existing object of the type specified in attribute `type`. Like JSP implicit objects, objects specified with action `<jsp:useBean>` have `page`, `request`, `session` or `application` scope that indicates where they can be used in a Web application. Objects with `page` scope are accessible only to the page in which they are defined. Multiple JSP pages potentially can access objects with other scopes. For example, all JSPs that process a single request can access an object with `request` scope.

Common Programming Error 10.6

One or both of the **<jsp:useBean>** *attributes* **class** *and* **type** *must be specified; otherwise, a translation-time error occurs.*

Many Web sites today place rotating advertisements on their Web pages. Each visit to one of these pages typically results in a different advertisement being displayed in the user's Web browser. Typically, clicking an advertisement takes you to the Web site of the company that placed the advertisement. Our first example of **<jsp:useBean>** demonstrates a simple advertisement rotator bean that cycles through a list of five advertisements. In this example, the advertisements are covers for some of our books. Clicking a cover takes you to the Amazon.com Web site where you can read about and possibly order the book.

The **Rotator** bean (Fig. 10.17) has three methods: **getImage**, **getLink** and **nextAd**. Method **getImage** returns the image file name for the book cover image. Method **getLink** returns the hyperlink to the book at Amazon.com. Method **nextAd** updates the **Rotator** so the next calls to **getImage** and **getLink** return information for a different advertisement. Methods **getImage** and **getLink** each represent a read-only JavaBean property—**image** and **link**, respectively. **Rotator** keeps track of the current advertisement with its **selectedIndex** variable, which is updated by invoking method **nextAd**.

Attribute	Description
id	The name used to manipulate the Java object with actions **<jsp:setProperty>** and **<jsp:getProperty>**. A variable of this name is also declared for use in JSP scripting elements. The name specified here is case sensitive.
scope	The scope in which the Java object is accessible—**page**, **request**, **session** or **application**. The default scope is **page**.
class	The fully qualified class name of the Java object.
beanName	The name of a bean that can be used with method **instantiate** of class **java.beans.Beans** to load a JavaBean into memory.
type	The type of the JavaBean. This can be the same type as the **class** attribute, a superclass of that type or an interface implemented by that type. The default value is the same as for attribute **class**. A **ClassCastException** occurs if the Java object is not of the type specified with attribute **type**.

Fig. 10.16 Attributes of the **<jsp:useBean>** action.

```
1   // Fig. 10.17: Rotator.java
2   // A JavaBean that rotates advertisements.
3   package com.deitel.advjhtp1.jsp.beans;
4
5   public class Rotator {
6      private String images[] = { "images/jhtp3.jpg",
7         "images/xmlhtp1.jpg", "images/ebechtp1.jpg",
8         "images/iw3htp1.jpg", "images/cpphtp3.jpg" };
9
```

Fig. 10.17 Rotator bean that maintains a set of advertisements (part 1 of 2).

```
10    private String links[] = {
11        "http://www.amazon.com/exec/obidos/ASIN/0130125075/" +
12            "deitelassociatin",
13        "http://www.amazon.com/exec/obidos/ASIN/0130284173/" +
14            "deitelassociatin",
15        "http://www.amazon.com/exec/obidos/ASIN/013028419X/" +
16            "deitelassociatin",
17        "http://www.amazon.com/exec/obidos/ASIN/0130161438/" +
18            "deitelassociatin",
19        "http://www.amazon.com/exec/obidos/ASIN/0130895717/" +
20            "deitelassociatin" };
21
22    private int selectedIndex = 0;
23
24    // returns image file name for current ad
25    public String getImage()
26    {
27        return images[ selectedIndex ];
28    }
29
30    // returns the URL for ad's corresponding Web site
31    public String getLink()
32    {
33        return links[ selectedIndex ];
34    }
35
36    // update selectedIndex so next calls to getImage and
37    // getLink return a different advertisement
38    public void nextAd()
39    {
40        selectedIndex = ( selectedIndex + 1 ) % images.length;
41    }
42 }
```

Fig. 10.17 `Rotator` bean that maintains a set of advertisements (part 2 of 2).

Lines 7–8 of JavaServer Page **adrotator.jsp** (Fig. 10.18) obtain a reference to an instance of class **Rotator**. The **id** for the bean is **rotator**. The JSP uses this name to manipulate the bean. The scope of the object is **session**, so that each individual client will see the same sequence of ads during their browsing session. When **adrotator.jsp** receives a request from a new client, the JSP container creates the bean and stores it in JSP that client's **session** (an **HttpSession** object). In each request to this JSP, line 22 uses the **rotator** reference created in line 7 to invoke the **Rotator** bean's **nextAd** method. Thus, each request will receive the next advertisement maintained by the **Rotator** bean. Lines 29–34 define a hyperlink to the Amazon.com site for a particular book. Lines 29–30 introduce action **<jsp:getProperty>** to obtain the value of the **Rotator** bean's **link** property. Action **<jsp:getProperty>** has two attributes—**name** and **property**—that specify the bean object to manipulate and the property to get. If the JavaBean object uses standard JavaBean naming conventions, the method used to obtain the **link** property value from the bean should be **getLink**. Action **<jsp:getProperty>** invokes **getLink** on the bean referenced with **rotator**, converts the return value into a **String** and outputs the **String** as part of the response to the client. The **link** property becomes the value of the hyperlink's **href** attribute. The hyperlink is represented in the resulting Web page as the book cover image. Lines 32–33 create an **img** element and use another **<jsp:getProperty>** action to obtain the **Rotator** bean's **image** property value.

Note that the link and image properties also can be obtained with JSP expressions. For example, the **<jsp:getProperty>** action in lines 29–30 can be replaced with the expression

```
<%= rotator.getLink() %>
```

Similarly, the **<jsp:getProperty>** action in lines 32–33 can be replaced with the expression

```
<%= rotator.getImage() %>
```

```
1    <?xml version = "1.0"?>
2    <!DOCTYPE html PUBLIC "-//W3C//DTD XHTML 1.0 Strict//EN"
3       "http://www.w3.org/TR/xhtml1/DTD/xhtml1-strict.dtd">
4
5    <!-- Fig. 10.18: adrotator.jsp -->
6
7    <jsp:useBean id = "rotator" scope = "application"
8       class = "com.deitel.advjhtp1.jsp.beans.Rotator" />
9
10   <html xmlns = "http://www.w3.org/1999/xhtml">
11
12      <head>
13         <title>AdRotator Example</title>
14
15         <style type = "text/css">
16            .big { font-family: helvetica, arial, sans-serif;
17                  font-weight: bold;
18                  font-size: 2em }
19         </style>
20
21         <%-- update advertisement --%>
22         <% rotator.nextAd(); %>
23      </head>
24
25      <body>
26         <p class = "big">AdRotator Example</p>
27
28         <p>
29            <a href = "<jsp:getProperty name = "rotator"
30               property = "link" />">
31
32               <img src = "<jsp:getProperty name = "rotator"
33                  property = "image" />" alt = "advertisement" />
34            </a>
35         </p>
36      </body>
37   </html>
```

Fig. 10.18 JSP **adrotator.jsp** uses a **Rotator** bean to display a different advertisement on each request to the page (part 1 of 2).

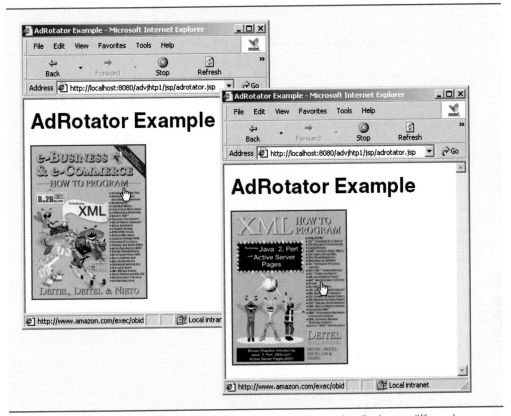

Fig. 10.18 JSP **adrotator.jsp** uses a **Rotator** bean to display a different advertisement on each request to the page (part 2 of 2).

To test **adrotator.jsp** in Tomcat, copy **adrotator.jsp** into the **jsp** directory created in Section 10.3. You should have copied the **images** directory into the **jsp** directory when you tested Fig. 10.10. If not, you must copy the **images** directory there now. Copy **Rotator.class** into the **advjhtp1** Web application's **WEB-INF\classes** directory in Tomcat. [*Note:* This example will work only if the proper package directory structure for **Rotator** is defined in the **classes** directory. **Rotator** is defined in package **com.deitel.advjhtp1.jsp.beans**.] Open your Web browser and enter the following URL to test **adrotator.jsp**:

> **http://localhost:8080/advjhtp1/jsp/adrotator.jsp**

Try reloading this JSP several times in your browser to see the advertisement change with each request.

　　　Action **<jsp:setProperty>** can set JavaBean property values. This action is particularly useful for mapping request parameter values to JavaBean properties. Request parameters can be used to set properties of primitive types **boolean**, **byte**, **char**, **int**, **long**, **float** and **double** and **java.lang** types **String**, **Boolean**, **Byte**, **Character**, **Integer**, **Long**, **Float** and **Double**. Figure 10.19 summarizes the **<jsp:setProperty>** attributes.

Attribute	Description
name	The ID of the JavaBean for which a property (or properties) will be set.
property	The name of the property to set. Specifying **"*"** for this attribute causes the JSP to match the request parameters to the properties of the bean. For each request parameter that matches (i.e., the name of the request parameter is identical to the bean's property name), the corresponding property in the bean is set to the value of the parameter. If the value of the request parameter is **""**, the property value in the bean remains unchanged.
param	If request parameter names do not match bean property names, this attribute can be used to specify which request parameter should be used to obtain the value for a specific bean property. This attribute is optional. If this attribute is omitted, the request parameter names must match bean property names.
value	The value to assign to a bean property. The value typically is the result of a JSP expression. This attribute is particularly useful for setting bean properties that cannot be set using request parameters. This attribute is optional. If this attribute is omitted, the JavaBean property must be of a data type that can be set using request parameters.

Fig. 10.19 Attributes of the **<jsp:setProperty>** action.

Common Programming Error 10.7

Use action **<jsp:setProperty>**'s **value** *attribute to set JavaBean property types that cannot be set with request parameters; otherwise, conversion errors occur.*

Software Engineering Observation 10.10

Action **<jsp:setProperty>** *can use request-parameter values to set JavaBean properties only for properties of the following types:* **String**s, *primitive types (***boolean**, **byte**, **char**, **short**, **int**, **long**, **float** *and* **double***) and type wrapper classes (***Boolean**, **Byte**, **Character**, **Short**, **Integer**, **Long**, **Float** *and* **Double***).*

Our next example is a guest book that enables users to place their first name, last name and e-mail address into a guest book database. After submitting their information, users see a Web page containing all the users in the guest book. Each person's e-mail address is displayed as a hyperlink that allows the user to send an e-mail message to the person. The example demonstrates action **<jsp:setProperty>**. In addition, the example introduces the JSP *page directive* and *JSP error pages*.

The guest book example consists of JavaBeans **GuestBean** (Fig. 10.20) and **GuestDataBean** (Fig. 10.21), and JSPs **guestBookLogin.jsp** (Fig. 10.22), **guestBookView.jsp** (Fig. 10.23) and **guestBookErrorPage.jsp** (Fig. 10.24). Sample outputs from this example are shown in Fig. 10.25.

JavaBean **GuestBean** (Fig. 10.20) defines three guest properties: **firstName**, **lastName** and **email**. Each is a read/write property with *set* and *get* methods to manipulate the property.

```
1   // Fig. 10.20: GuestBean.java
2   // JavaBean to store data for a guest in the guest book.
3   package com.deitel.advjhtp1.jsp.beans;
4
5   public class GuestBean {
6      private String firstName, lastName, email;
7
8      // set the guest's first name
9      public void setFirstName( String name )
10     {
11        firstName = name;
12     }
13
14     // get the guest's first name
15     public String getFirstName()
16     {
17        return firstName;
18     }
19
20     // set the guest's last name
21     public void setLastName( String name )
22     {
23        lastName = name;
24     }
25
26     // get the guest's last name
27     public String getLastName()
28     {
29        return lastName;
30     }
31
32     // set the guest's email address
33     public void setEmail( String address )
34     {
35        email = address;
36     }
37
38     // get the guest's email address
39     public String getEmail()
40     {
41        return email;
42     }
43  }
```

Fig. 10.20 GuestBean stores information for one guest.

JavaBean **GuestDataBean** (Fig. 10.21) connects to the **guestbook** database and provides methods **getGuestList** and **addGuest** to manipulate the database. The guestbook database has a single table (**guests**) containing three columns (**firstName**, **lastName** and **email**). We provide an SQL script (**guestbook.sql**) with this example that can be used with the Cloudscape DBMS to create the **guestbook** database. For further details on creating a database with Cloudscape, refer back to Chapter 8.

```
1   // Fig. 10.21: GuestDataBean.java
2   // Class GuestDataBean makes a database connection and supports
3   // inserting and retrieving data from the database.
4   package com.deitel.advjhtp1.jsp.beans;
5
6   // Java core packages
7   import java.io.*;
8   import java.sql.*;
9   import java.util.*;
10
11  public class GuestDataBean {
12     private Connection connection;
13     private PreparedStatement addRecord, getRecords;
14
15     // construct TitlesBean object
16     public GuestDataBean() throws Exception
17     {
18        // load the Cloudscape driver
19        Class.forName( "COM.cloudscape.core.RmiJdbcDriver" );
20
21        // connect to the database
22        connection = DriverManager.getConnection(
23           "jdbc:rmi:jdbc:cloudscape:guestbook" );
24
25        getRecords =
26           connection.prepareStatement(
27              "SELECT firstName, lastName, email FROM guests"
28           );
29
30        addRecord =
31           connection.prepareStatement(
32              "INSERT INTO guests ( " +
33                 "firstName, lastName, email ) " +
34              "VALUES ( ?, ?, ? )"
35           );
36     }
37
38     // return an ArrayList of GuestBeans
39     public ArrayList getGuestList() throws SQLException
40     {
41        ArrayList guestList = new ArrayList();
42
43        // obtain list of titles
44        ResultSet results = getRecords.executeQuery();
45
46        // get row data
47        while ( results.next() ) {
48           GuestBean guest = new GuestBean();
49
50           guest.setFirstName( results.getString( 1 ) );
51           guest.setLastName( results.getString( 2 ) );
52           guest.setEmail( results.getString( 3 ) );
```

Fig. 10.21 GuestDataBean performs database access on behalf of guestBookLogin.jsp (part 1 of 2).

```
53
54              guestList.add( guest );
55         }
56
57         return guestList;
58    }
59
60    // insert a guest in guestbook database
61    public void addGuest( GuestBean guest ) throws SQLException
62    {
63        addRecord.setString( 1, guest.getFirstName() );
64        addRecord.setString( 2, guest.getLastName() );
65        addRecord.setString( 3, guest.getEmail() );
66
67        addRecord.executeUpdate();
68    }
69
70    // close statements and terminate database connection
71    protected void finalize()
72    {
73        // attempt to close database connection
74        try {
75           getRecords.close();
76           addRecord.close();
77           connection.close();
78        }
79
80        // process SQLException on close operation
81        catch ( SQLException sqlException ) {
82           sqlException.printStackTrace();
83        }
84    }
85 }
```

Fig. 10.21 GuestDataBean performs database access on behalf of
guestBookLogin.jsp (part 2 of 2).

GuestDataBean method getGuestList (lines 39–58) returns an ArrayList
of GuestBean objects representing the guests in the database. Method getGuestList
creates the GuestBean objects from the ResultSet returned by PreparedStatement getRecords (defined at lines 25–28 and executed at line 44).

GuestDataBean method addGuest (lines 61–68) receives a GuestBean as an
argument and uses the GuestBean's properties as the arguments to PreparedStatement addRecord (defined at lines 30–35). This PreparedStatement (executed at
line 67) inserts a new guest in the database.

Note that the GuestDataBean's constructor, getGuestList and addGuest
methods do not process potential exceptions. In the constructor, line 19 can throw a
ClassNotFoundException, and the other statements can throw SQLExceptions.
Similarly, SQLExceptions can be thrown from the bodies of methods getGuestList
and addGuest. In this example, we purposely let any exceptions that occur get passed

back to the JSP that invokes the **GuestDataBean**'s constructor or methods. This enables us to demonstrate JSP error pages. When a JSP performs an operation that causes an exception, the JSP can include scriptlets that catch the exception and process it. Exceptions that are not caught can be forwarded to a JSP error page for handling.

JavaServer Page **guestBookLogin.jsp** (Fig. 10.22) is a modified version of **forward1.jsp** (Fig. 10.11) that displays a **form** in which users can enter their first name, last name and e-mail address. When the user submits the **form**, **guestBook-Login.jsp** is requested again, so it can ensure that all the data values were entered. If not, the **guestBookLogin.jsp** responds with the **form** again, so the user can fill in missing field(s). If the user supplies all three pieces of information, **guestBook-Login.jsp** forwards the request to **guestBookView.jsp**, which displays the guest book contents.

```
1   <?xml version = "1.0"?>
2   <!DOCTYPE html PUBLIC "-//W3C//DTD XHTML 1.0 Strict//EN"
3      "http://www.w3.org/TR/xhtml1/DTD/xhtml1-strict.dtd">
4
5   <!-- Fig. 10.22: guestBookLogin.jsp -->
6
7   <%-- page settings --%>
8   <%@ page errorPage = "guestBookErrorPage.jsp" %>
9
10  <%-- beans used in this JSP --%>
11  <jsp:useBean id = "guest" scope = "page"
12     class = "com.deitel.advjhtp1.jsp.beans.GuestBean" />
13  <jsp:useBean id = "guestData" scope = "request"
14     class = "com.deitel.advjhtp1.jsp.beans.GuestDataBean" />
15
16  <html xmlns = "http://www.w3.org/1999/xhtml">
17
18  <head>
19     <title>Guest Book Login</title>
20
21     <style type = "text/css">
22        body {
23           font-family: tahoma, helvetica, arial, sans-serif;
24        }
25
26        table, tr, td {
27           font-size: .9em;
28           border: 3px groove;
29           padding: 5px;
30           background-color: #dddddd;
31        }
32     </style>
33  </head>
34
```

Fig. 10.22 JavaServer page **guestBookLogin.jsp** enables the user to submit a first name, a last name and an e-mail address to be placed in the guest book (part 1 of 3).

```
35   <body>
36      <jsp:setProperty name = "guest" property = "*" />
37
38      <% // start scriptlet
39
40         if ( guest.getFirstName() == null ||
41               guest.getLastName() == null ||
42               guest.getEmail() == null ) {
43
44      %> <%-- end scriptlet to insert fixed template data --%>
45
46            <form method = "post" action = "guestBookLogin.jsp">
47               <p>Enter your first name, last name and email
48                  address to register in our guest book.</p>
49
50            <table>
51               <tr>
52                  <td>First name</td>
53
54                  <td>
55                     <input type = "text" name = "firstName" />
56                  </td>
57               </tr>
58
59               <tr>
60                  <td>Last name</td>
61
62                  <td>
63                     <input type = "text" name = "lastName" />
64                  </td>
65               </tr>
66
67               <tr>
68                  <td>Email</td>
69
70                  <td>
71                     <input type = "text" name = "email" />
72                  </td>
73               </tr>
74
75               <tr>
76                  <td colspan = "2">
77                     <input type = "submit"
78                        value = "Submit" />
79                  </td>
80               </tr>
81            </table>
82         </form>
83
```

Fig. 10.22 JavaServer page **guestBookLogin.jsp** enables the user to submit a first name, a last name and an e-mail address to be placed in the guest book (part 2 of 3).

```
84      <% // continue scriptlet
85
86         }  // end if
87         else {
88            guestData.addGuest( guest );
89
90      %> <%-- end scriptlet to insert jsp:forward action --%>
91
92            <%-- forward to display guest book contents --%>
93            <jsp:forward page = "guestBookView.jsp" />
94
95      <% // continue scriptlet
96
97         }  // end else
98
99      %> <%-- end scriptlet --%>
100 </body>
101
102 </html>
```

Fig. 10.22 JavaServer page **guestBookLogin.jsp** enables the user to submit a first name, a last name and an e-mail address to be placed in the guest book (part 3 of 3).

Line 8 of **guestBookLogin.jsp** introduces the **page** *directive*, which defines information that is globally available in a JSP. Directives are delimited by **<%@** and **%>**. In this case, the **page** directive's ***errorPage*** *attribute* is set to **guestBookErrorPage.jsp** (Fig. 10.24), indicating that all uncaught exceptions are forwarded to **guestBookErrorPage.jsp** for processing. A complete description of the **page** directive appears in Section 10.7.

Lines 11–14 define two **<jsp:useBean>** actions. Lines 11–12 create an instance of **GuestBean** called **guest**. This bean has **page** scope—it exists for use only in this page. Lines 14–14 create an instance of **GuestDataBean** called **guestData**. This bean has **request** scope—it exists for use in this page and any other page that helps process a single client request. Thus, when **guestBookLogin.jsp** forwards a request to **guestBookView.jsp**, the **GuestDataBean** is still available for use in **guestBookView.jsp**.

Line 36 demonstrates setting properties of the **GuestBean** called **guest** with request parameter values. The **input** elements on lines 55, 63 and 71 have the same names as the **GuestBean** properties. So, we use action **<jsp:setProperty>**'s ability to match request parameters to properties by specifying **"*"** for attribute **property**. Line 36 also can set the properties individually with the following lines:

```
<jsp:setProperty name = "guest" property = "firstName"
    param = "firstName" />

<jsp:setProperty name = "guest" property = "lastName"
    param = "lastName" />

<jsp:setProperty name = "guest" property = "email"
    param = "email" />
```

If the request parameters had names that differed from **GuestBean**'s properties, the **param** attribute in each of the preceding **<jsp:setProperty>** actions could be changed to the appropriate request parameter name.

JavaServer Page **guestBookView.jsp** (Fig. 10.23) outputs an XHTML document containing the guest book entries in tabular format. Lines 8–10 define three **page** directives. Line 8 specifies that the error page for this JSP is **guestBookErrorPage.jsp**. Lines 9–10 introduce attribute **import** of the **page** directive. Attribute **import** enables programmers to specify Java classes and packages that are used in the context of the JSP. Line 9 indicates that classes from package **java.util** are used in this JSP, and line 10 indicates that classes from our package **com.deitel.advjhtp1.jsp.beans** also are used.

Lines 13–14 specify a **<jsp:useBean>** action that obtains a reference to a **GuestDataBean** object. If a **GuestDataBean** object already exists, the action returns a reference to the existing object. Otherwise, the action creates a **GuestDataBean** for use in this JSP. Lines 50–59 define a scriptlet that gets the guest list from the **GuestDataBean** and begin a loop to output the entries. Lines 61–70 combine fixed template text with JSP expressions to create rows in the table of guest book data that will be displayed on the client. The scriptlet at lines 72–76 terminates the loop.

```
1   <?xml version = "1.0"?>
2   <!DOCTYPE html PUBLIC "-//W3C//DTD XHTML 1.0 Strict//EN"
3       "http://www.w3.org/TR/xhtml1/DTD/xhtml1-strict.dtd">
4
5   <!-- Fig. 10.23: guestBookView.jsp -->
6
7   <%-- page settings --%>
8   <%@ page errorPage = "guestBookErrorPage.jsp" %>
9   <%@ page import = "java.util.*" %>
10  <%@ page import = "com.deitel.advjhtp1.jsp.beans.*" %>
11
12  <%-- GuestDataBean to obtain guest list --%>
13  <jsp:useBean id = "guestData" scope = "request"
14      class = "com.deitel.advjhtp1.jsp.beans.GuestDataBean" />
15
16  <html xmlns = "http://www.w3.org/1999/xhtml">
17
18      <head>
19          <title>Guest List</title>
20
21          <style type = "text/css">
22              body {
23                  font-family: tahoma, helvetica, arial, sans-serif;
24              }
25
26              table, tr, td, th {
27                  text-align: center;
28                  font-size: .9em;
29                  border: 3px groove;
30                  padding: 5px;
```

Fig. 10.23 JavaServer page **guestBookView.jsp** displays the contents of the guest book (part 1 of 2).

```
31                    background-color: #dddddd;
32                }
33          </style>
34     </head>
35
36     <body>
37          <p style = "font-size: 2em;">Guest List</p>
38
39          <table>
40              <thead>
41                  <tr>
42                      <th style = "width: 100px;">Last name</th>
43                      <th style = "width: 100px;">First name</th>
44                      <th style = "width: 200px;">Email</th>
45                  </tr>
46              </thead>
47
48              <tbody>
49
50          <% // start scriptlet
51
52              List guestList = guestData.getGuestList();
53              Iterator guestListIterator = guestList.iterator();
54              GuestBean guest;
55
56              while ( guestListIterator.hasNext() ) {
57                  guest = ( GuestBean ) guestListIterator.next();
58
59          %> <%-- end scriptlet; insert fixed template data --%>
60
61                  <tr>
62                      <td><%= guest.getLastName() %></td>
63
64                      <td><%= guest.getFirstName() %></td>
65
66                      <td>
67                          <a href = "mailto:<%= guest.getEmail() %>">
68                              <%= guest.getEmail() %></a>
69                      </td>
70                  </tr>
71
72          <% // continue scriptlet
73
74              } // end while
75
76          %> <%-- end scriptlet --%>
77
78              </tbody>
79          </table>
80     </body>
81
82  </html>
```

Fig. 10.23 JavaServer page `guestBookView.jsp` displays the contents of the guest book (part 2 of 2).

JavaServer Page **guestBookErrorPage.jsp** (Fig. 10.24) outputs an XHTML document containing an error message based on the type of exception that causes this error page to be invoked. Lines 8–10 define several **page** directives. Line 8 introduces **page** directive attribute **isErrorPage**. Setting this attribute to **true** makes the JSP an error page and enables access to the JSP implicit object **exception** that refers to an exception object indicating the problem that occurred.

Common Programming Error 10.8

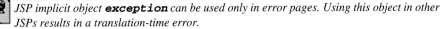

*JSP implicit object **exception** can be used only in error pages. Using this object in other JSPs results in a translation-time error.*

Lines 29–46 define scriptlets that determine the type of exception that occurred and begin outputting an appropriate error message with fixed template data. The actual error message from the exception is output at line 56.

```
 1   <?xml version = "1.0"?>
 2   <!DOCTYPE html PUBLIC "-//W3C//DTD XHTML 1.0 Strict//EN"
 3       "http://www.w3.org/TR/xhtml1/DTD/xhtml1-strict.dtd">
 4
 5   <!-- Fig. 10.24: guestBookErrorPage.jsp -->
 6
 7   <%-- page settings --%>
 8   <%@ page isErrorPage = "true" %>
 9   <%@ page import = "java.util.*" %>
10   <%@ page import = "java.sql.*" %>
11
12   <html xmlns = "http://www.w3.org/1999/xhtml">
13
14      <head>
15         <title>Error!</title>
16
17         <style type = "text/css">
18            .bigRed {
19               font-size: 2em;
20               color: red;
21               font-weight: bold;
22            }
23         </style>
24      </head>
25
26      <body>
27         <p class = "bigRed">
28
29            <% // scriptlet to determine exception type
30               // and output beginning of error message
31               if ( exception instanceof SQLException )
32            %>
33
34               An SQLException
35
```

Fig. 10.24 JavaServer page **guestBookErrorPage.jsp** responds to exceptions in **guestBookLogin.jsp** and **guestBookView.jsp** (part 1 of 2).

```
36        <%
37            else if ( exception instanceof ClassNotFoundException )
38        %>
39
40            A ClassNotFoundException
41
42        <%
43            else
44        %>
45
46            An exception
47
48    <%-- end scriptlet to insert fixed template data --%>
49
50        <%-- continue error message output --%>
51        occurred while interacting with the guestbook database.
52    </p>
53
54    <p class = "bigRed">
55        The error message was:<br />
56        <%= exception.getMessage() %>
57    </p>
58
59    <p class = "bigRed">Please try again later</p>
60    </body>
61
62  </html>
```

Fig. 10.24 JavaServer page `guestBookErrorPage.jsp` responds to exceptions in `guestBookLogin.jsp` and `guestBookView.jsp` (part 2 of 2).

Figure 10.25 shows sample interactions between the user and the JSPs in the guest book example. In the first two rows of output, separate users entered their first name, last name and e-mail. In each case, the current contents of the guest book are returned and displayed for the user. In the final interaction, a third user specified an e-mail address that already existed in the database. The e-mail address is the primary key in the **guests** table of the **guestbook** database, so its values must be unique. Thus, the database prevents the new record from being inserted, and an exception occurs. The exception is forwarded to **guestBookErrorPage.jsp** for processing, which results in the last screen capture.

To test the guest book in Tomcat, copy **guestBookLogin.jsp**, **guestBook-View.jsp** and **guestBookErrorPage.jsp** into the **jsp** directory created in Section 10.3. Copy **GuestBean.class** and **GuestDataBean.class** into the **advjhtp1** Web application's **WEB-INF\classes** directory in Tomcat. [*Note:* This example will work only if the proper package directory structure for **GuestBean** and **GuestDataBean** is defined in the **classes** directory. These classes are defined in package **com.deitel.advjhtp1.jsp.beans**.] Open your Web browser and enter the following URL to test **guestBookLogin.jsp**:

```
http://localhost:8080/advjhtp1/jsp/guestBookLogin.jsp
```

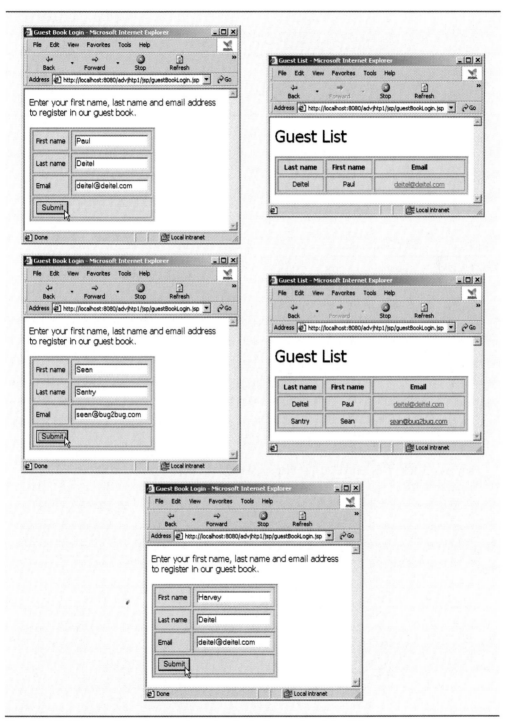

Fig. 10.25 JSP guest book sample output windows. (part 1 of 2)

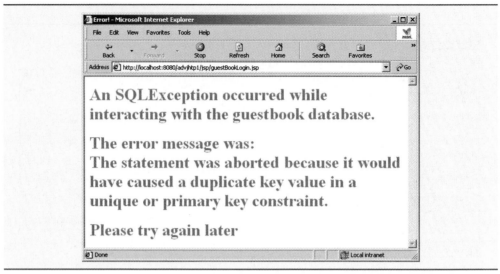

Fig. 10.25 JSP guest book sample output windows. (part 2 of 2)

10.7 Directives

Directives are messages to the JSP container that enable the programmer to specify page settings (such as the error page), to include content from other resources and to specify custom-tag libraries for use in a JSP. Directives (delimited by **<%@** and **%>**) are processed at translation time. Thus, directives do not produce any immediate output, because they are processed before the JSP accepts any requests. Figure 10.26 summarizes the three directive types. These directives are discussed in the next several subsections.

10.7.1 **page** Directive

The **page** *directive* specifies global settings for the JSP in the JSP container. There can be many **page** directives, provided that there is only one occurrence of each attribute. The only exception to this rule is the **import** attribute, which can be used repeatedly to import Java packages used in the JSP. Figure 10.27 summarizes the attributes of the **page** directive.

Directive	Description
page	Defines page settings for the JSP container to process.
include	Causes the JSP container to perform a translation-time insertion of another resource's content. As the JSP is translated into a servlet and compiled, the referenced file replaces the **include** directive and is translated as if it were originally part of the JSP.
taglib	Allows programmers to include their own new tags in the form of *tag libraries*. These libraries can be used to encapsulate functionality and simplify the coding of a JSP.

Fig. 10.26 JSP directives.

Common Programming Error 10.9

*Providing multiple **page** directives with one or more attributes in common is a JSP translation-time error.*

Common Programming Error 10.10

*Providing a **page** directive with an attribute or value that is not recognized is a JSP translation-time error.*

Attribute	Description
language	The scripting language used in the JSP. Currently, the only valid value for this attribute is **java**.
extends	Specifies the class from which the translated JSP will be inherited. This attribute must be a fully qualified package and class name.
import	Specifies a comma-separated list of fully qualified class names and/or packages that will be used in the current JSP. When the scripting language is **java**, the default import list is **java.lang.***, **javax.servlet.***, **javax.serv-let.jsp.*** and **javax.servlet.http.***. If multiple **import** properties are specified, the package names are placed in a list by the container.
session	Specifies whether the page participates in a session. The values for this attribute are **true** (participates in a session—the default) or **false** (does not participate in a session). When the page is part of a session, the JSP implicit object **session** is available for use in the page. Otherwise, **session** is not available. In the latter case, using **session** in the scripting code results in a translation-time error.
buffer	Specifies the size of the output buffer used with the implicit object **out**. The value of this attribute can be **none** for no buffering, or a value such as **8kb** (the default buffer size). The JSP specification indicates that the buffer used must be at least the size specified.
autoFlush	When set to **true** (the default value), this attribute indicates that the output buffer used with implicit object **out** should be flushed automatically when the buffer fills. If set to **false**, an exception occurs if the buffer overflows. This attribute's value must be **true** if the buffer attribute is set to **none**.
isThreadSafe	Specifies if the page is thread safe. If **true** (the default), the page is considered to be thread safe, and it can process multiple requests at the same time. If **false**, the servlet that represents the page implements interface **java.lang.SingleThreadModel** and only one request can be processed by that JSP at a time. The JSP standard allows multiple instances of a JSP to exists for JSPs that are not thread safe. This enables the container to handle requests more efficiently. However, this does not guarantee that resources shared across JSP instances are accessed in a thread-safe manner.
info	Specifies an information string that describes the page. This string is returned by the **getServletInfo** method of the servlet that represents the translated JSP. This method can be invoked through the JSP's implicit **page** object.

Fig. 10.27 Attributes of the **page** directive (part 1 of 2).

Attribute	Description
errorPage	Any exceptions in the current page that are not caught are sent to the error page for processing. The error page implicit object **exception** references the original exception.
isErrorPage	Specifies if the current page is an error page that will be invoked in response to an error on another page. If the attribute value is **true**, the implicit object **exception** is created and references the original exception that occurred. If **false** (the default), any use of the **exception** object in the page results in a translation-time error.
contentType	Specifies the MIME type of the data in the response to the client. The default type is **text/html**.

Fig. 10.27 Attributes of the **page** directive (part 2 of 2).

Software Engineering Observation 10.11

*According to the JSP specification section 2.7.1, the **extends** attribute "should not be used without careful consideration as it restricts the ability of the JSP container to provide specialized superclasses that may improve on the quality of rendered service." Rememeber that a Java class can extend exactly one other class. If your JSP specifies an explicit superclass, the JSP container cannot translate your JSP into a sublcass of one of the container application's own enhanced servlet classes.*

Common Programming Error 10.11

*Using JSP implicit object **session** in a JSP that does not have its **page** directive attribute **session** set to **true** is a translation-time error.*

10.7.2 include Directive

The **include** *directive* includes the content of another resource once, at JSP translation time. The **include** directive has only one attribute—**file**—that specifies the URL of the page to include. The difference between directive **include** and action **<jsp:include>** is noticeable only if the included content changes. For example, if the definition of an XHTML document changes after it is included with directive **include**, future invocations of the JSP will show the original content of the XHTML document, not the new content. In contrast, action **<jsp:include>** is processed in each request to the JSP. Therefore, changes to included content would be apparent in the next request to the JSP that uses action **<jsp:include>**.

Software Engineering Observation 10.12

*The JavaServer Pages 1.1 specification does not provide a mechanism for updating text included in a JSP with the **include** directive. Version 1.2 of the JSP specification allows the container to provide such a mechanism, but the specification does not provide for this directly.*

JavaServer Page **includeDirective.jsp** (Fig. 10.28) reimplements JavaServer Page **include.jsp** (Fig. 10.10) using **include** directives. To test **includeDirective.jsp** in Tomcat, copy **includeDirective.jsp** into the **jsp** directory created in Section 10.3. Open your Web browser and enter the following URL to test **include-Directive.jsp**:

http://localhost:8080/advjhtp1/jsp/includeDirective.jsp

```
1   <?xml version = "1.0"?>
2   <!DOCTYPE html PUBLIC "-//W3C//DTD XHTML 1.0 Strict//EN"
3      "http://www.w3.org/TR/xhtml1/DTD/xhtml1-strict.dtd">
4
5   <!-- Fig. 10.28: includeDirective.jsp -->
6
7   <html xmlns = "http://www.w3.org/1999/xhtml">
8
9      <head>
10        <title>Using the include directive</title>
11
12        <style type = "text/css">
13           body {
14              font-family: tahoma, helvetica, arial, sans-serif;
15           }
16
17           table, tr, td {
18              font-size: .9em;
19              border: 3px groove;
20              padding: 5px;
21              background-color: #dddddd;
22           }
23        </style>
24     </head>
25
26     <body>
27        <table>
28           <tr>
29              <td style = "width: 160px; text-align: center">
30                 <img src = "images/logotiny.png"
31                    width = "140" height = "93"
32                    alt = "Deitel & Associates, Inc. Logo" />
33              </td>
34
35              <td>
36
37                 <%-- include banner.html in this JSP --%>
38                 <%@ include file = "banner.html" %>
39
40              </td>
41           </tr>
42
43           <tr>
44              <td style = "width: 160px">
45
46                 <%-- include toc.html in this JSP --%>
47                 <%@ include file = "toc.html" %>
```

Fig. 10.28 JSP **includeDirective.jsp** demonstrates including content at translation-time with directive **include** (part 1 of 2).

```
48
49                    </td>
50
51                    <td style = "vertical-align: top">
52
53                        <%-- include clock2.jsp in this JSP --%>
54                        <%@ include file = "clock2.jsp" %>
55
56                    </td>
57                </tr>
58            </table>
59        </body>
60    </html>
```

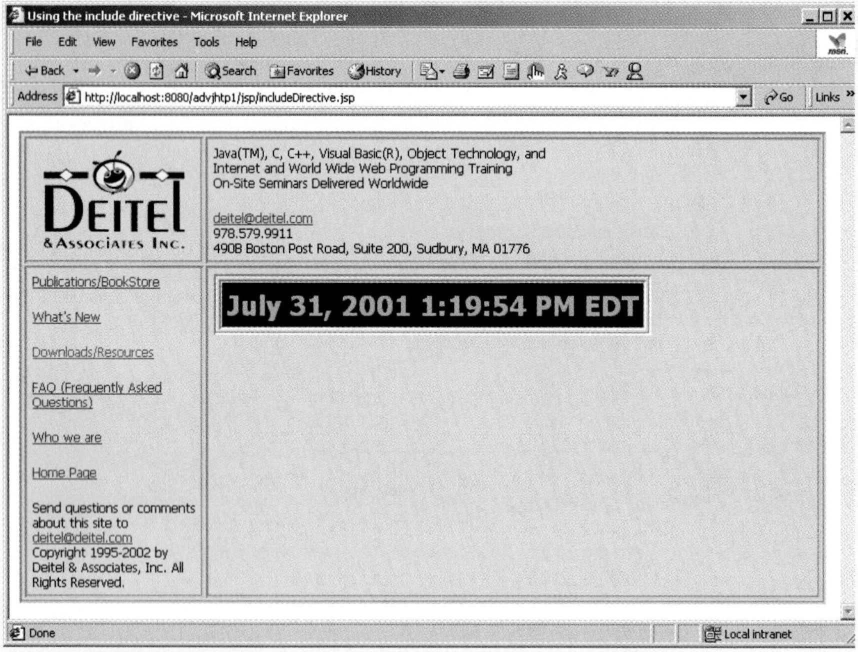

Fig. 10.28 JSP `includeDirective.jsp` demonstrates including content at translation-time with directive `include` (part 2 of 2).

10.8 Custom Tag Libraries

Throughout this chapter, you have seen how JavaServer Pages can simplify the delivery of dynamic Web content. Our discussion continues with JSP *custom tag libraries*, which provide another mechanism for encapsulating complex functionality for use in JSPs. Custom tag libraries define one or more *custom tags* that JSP implementors can use to create dynamic content. The functionality of these custom tags is defined in Java classes that implement interface **Tag** (package **javax.servlet.jsp.tagext**), normally by extending class **TagSupport** or **BodyTagSupport**. This mechanism enables Java programmers to create complex functionality for Web page designers who have no Java programming knowledge.

Previously, we introduced action **<jsp:useBean>** and JavaBeans to incorporate complex, encapsulated functionality in a JSP. In many cases, action **<jsp:useBean>** and JavaBeans can perform the same tasks as custom tags can. However, action **<jsp:useBean>** and JavaBeans have disadvantages—JavaBeans cannot manipulate JSP content and Web page designers must have some Java knowledge to use JavaBeans in a page. With custom tags, it is possible for Web page designers to use complex functionality without knowing any Java.

In this section, we present three examples of custom tags. Each tag is part of a single custom tag library that we refer to as **advjhtp1**. A JSP includes a custom tag library with the *taglib* directive. Figure 10.29 summarizes the **taglib** directive's attributes.

Each of the examples in this section uses directive **taglib**. There are several types of custom tags that have different levels of complexity. We demonstrate simple tags, simple tags with attributes and tags that can process their body elements. For complete details on custom tag libraries, see the resources in Section 10.9.

10.8.1 Simple Custom Tag

Our first custom tag example implements a simple custom tag that inserts the string "**Welcome to JSP Tag Libraries**" in a JSP. When implementing custom tags, you must define a tag-handler class for each tag that implements the tag's functionality, a *tag library descriptor* that provides information about the tag library and its custom tags to the JSP container and a JSP that uses the custom tag. Figure 10.30 (**customTagWelcome.jsp**) demonstrates our first custom tag. At the end of this section, we discuss how to configure this example for testing on Tomcat.

Attribute	Description
uri	Specifies the relative or absolute URI of the tag library descriptor.
tagPrefix	Specifies the required prefix that distinguishes custom tags from built-in tags. The prefix names **jsp**, **jspx**, **java**, **javax**, **servlet**, **sun** and **sunw** are reserved.

Fig. 10.29 Attributes of the **taglib** directive.

```
1   <?xml version = "1.0"?>
2   <!DOCTYPE html PUBLIC "-//W3C//DTD XHTML 1.0 Strict//EN"
3       "http://www.w3.org/TR/xhtml1/DTD/xhtml1-strict.dtd">
4
5   <!-- Fig. 10.30: customTagWelcome.jsp            -->
6   <!-- JSP that uses a custom tag to output content. -->
7
8   <%-- taglib directive --%>
9   <%@ taglib uri = "advjhtp1-taglib.tld" prefix = "advjhtp1" %>
10
11  <html xmlns = "http://www.w3.org/1999/xhtml">
```

Fig. 10.30 JSP **customTagWelcome.jsp** uses a simple custom tag (part 1 of 2).

```
12
13       <head>
14          <title>Simple Custom Tag Example</title>
15       </head>
16
17       <body>
18          <p>The following text demonstrates a custom tag:</p>
19          <h1>
20             <advjhtp1:welcome />
21          </h1>
22       </body>
23
24    </html>
```

```
Simple Custom Tag Example - Microsoft Internet Explorer          _ □ ×
 File   Edit   View   Favorites   Tools   Help                     msn.
   ←          →          ⊗          ↻          ⌂              »
  Back      Forward      Stop      Refresh      Home
 Address  http://localhost:8080/advjhtp1/jsp/customTagWelcome.jsp   ↓   Go

 The following text demonstrates a custom tag:

 Welcome to JSP Tag Libraries!

  Done                                        Local intranet
```

Fig. 10.30 JSP `customTagWelcome.jsp` uses a simple custom tag (part 2 of 2).

The **taglib** directive at line 9 enables the JSP to use the tags in our tag library. The directive specifies the *uri* of the tag library descriptor file (**advjhtp1-taglib.tld**; Fig. 10.32) that provides information about our tag library to the JSP container and the *prefix* for each tag (**advjhtp1**). JSP programmers use the tag library **prefix** when referring to tags in a specific tag library. Line 20 uses a custom tag called **welcome** to insert text in the JSP. Note that the prefix **advjhtp1:** precedes the tag name. This enables the JSP container to interpret the meaning of the tag and invoke the appropriate *tag handler*. Also note that line 20 can be written with start and end tags as follows:

```
<advjhtp1:welcome> </advjhtp1:welcome>
```

Figure 10.31 defines class **WelcomeTagHandler**—the tag handler that implements the functionality of our custom tag **welcome**. Every tag handler must implement interface **Tag**, which defines the methods a JSP container invokes to incorporate a tag's functionality in a JSP. Most tag handler classes implement interface **Tag** by extending either class *TagSupport* or class *BodyTagSupport*.

Software Engineering Observation 10.13

*Classes that define custom tag handlers must implement interface **Tag** from package **javax.servlet.jsp.tagext**.*

Software Engineering Observation 10.14

*A custom tag handler class should extend class **TagSupport** if the body of the tag is ignored or simply output during custom tag processing.*

Software Engineering Observation 10.15

*A custom tag handler class should extend class **BodyTagSupport** if the handler interacts with the tag's body content.*

Software Engineering Observation 10.16

Custom tag handlers must be defined in Java packages.

Class **WelcomeTagHandler** implements interface **Tag** by extending class **TagSupport** (both from package **java.servlet.jsp.tagext**). The most important methods of interface **Tag** are *doStartTag* and *doEndTag*. The JSP container invokes these methods when it encounters the starting custom tag and the ending custom tag, respectively. These methods throw **JspException**s if problems are encountered during custom-tag processing.

```
1   // Fig. 10.31: WelcomeTagHandler.java
2   // Custom tag handler that handles a simple tag.
3   package com.deitel.advjhtp1.jsp.taglibrary;
4
5   // Java core packages
6   import java.io.*;
7
8   // Java extension packages
9   import javax.servlet.jsp.*;
10  import javax.servlet.jsp.tagext.*;
11
12  public class WelcomeTagHandler extends TagSupport {
13
14     // Method called to begin tag processing
15     public int doStartTag() throws JspException
16     {
17        // attempt tag processing
18        try {
19           // obtain JspWriter to output content
20           JspWriter out = pageContext.getOut();
21
22           // output content
23           out.print( "Welcome to JSP Tag Libraries!" );
24        }
25
26        // rethrow IOException to JSP container as JspException
27        catch( IOException ioException ) {
28           throw new JspException( ioException.getMessage() );
29        }
30
31        return SKIP_BODY;  // ignore the tag's body
32     }
33  }
```

Fig. 10.31 **WelcomeTagHandler** custom tag handler.

Software Engineering Observation 10.17

If exceptions other than **JspException***s occur in a custom tag handler class, the exceptions should be caught and processed. If such exceptions would prevent proper tag processing, the exceptions should be rethrown as* **JspException***s.*

In this example, class **WelcomeTagHandler** overrides method **doStartTag** to output text that becomes part of the JSP's response. Line 20 uses the custom tag handler's **pageContext** object (inherited from class **TagSupport**) to obtain the JSP's **Jsp-Writer** object that method **doStartTag** uses to output text. Line 23 uses the **Jsp-Writer** to output a string. Line 31 returns the **static** integer constant **SKIP_BODY** (defined in interface **Tag**) to indicate that the JSP container should ignore any text or other elements that appear in the tag's body. To include the body content as part of the response, specify **static** integer constant **EVAL_BODY_INCLUDE** as the return value. This example does not require any processing when the ending tag is encountered by the JSP container, so we did not override **doEndTag**.

Figure 10.32 defines the custom tag library descriptor file. This XML document specifies information required by the JSP container such as the version number of the tag library (element **tlibversion**), the JSP version number (element **jspversion**), information about the library (element **info**) and information about the tags in the library (one **tag** element for each tag). In this tag library descriptor, the **tag** element at lines 18–30 describes our **welcome** tag. Line 19 specifies the tag's **name**—used by JSP programmers to access the custom functionality in a JSP. Lines 21–23 specify the **tagclass**—the custom tag handler class. This element associates the tag name with a specific tag handler class. Element **bodycontent** (line 25) specifies that our custom tag has an **empty** body. This value can also be **tagdependent** or **JSP**. Lines 27–29 specify information about the tag with an **info** element. [*Note:* We introduce other elements of the tag library descriptor as necessary. For a complete description of the tag library descriptor, see the JavaServer Pages 1.1 specification, which can be downloaded from **java.sun.com/products/jsp/download.html**.]

Software Engineering Observation 10.18

The custom tag handler class must be specified with its full package name in the **tagclass** *element of the tag library descriptor.*

```
1   <?xml version = "1.0" encoding = "ISO-8859-1" ?>
2   <!DOCTYPE taglib PUBLIC
3      "-//Sun Microsystems, Inc.//DTD JSP Tag Library 1.1//EN"
4      "http://java.sun.com/j2ee/dtds/web-jsptaglibrary_1_1.dtd">
5
6   <!-- a tag library descriptor -->
7
8   <taglib>
9      <tlibversion>1.0</tlibversion>
10     <jspversion>1.1</jspversion>
11     <shortname>advjhtp1</shortname>
12
```

Fig. 10.32 Custom tag library descriptor file **advjhtp1-taglib.tld** (part 1 of 2).

```
13      <info>
14         A simple tab library for the examples
15      </info>
16
17      <!-- A simple tag that outputs content -->
18      <tag>
19         <name>welcome</name>
20
21         <tagclass>
22            com.deitel.advjhtp1.jsp.taglibrary.WelcomeTagHandler
23         </tagclass>
24
25         <bodycontent>empty</bodycontent>
26
27         <info>
28            Inserts content welcoming user to tag libraries
29         </info>
30      </tag>
31   </taglib>
```

Fig. 10.32 Custom tag library descriptor file `advjhtp1-taglib.tld` (part 2 of 2).

To test **customTagWelcome.jsp** in Tomcat, copy **customTagWelcome.jsp** and **advjhtp1-taglib.tld** into the **jsp** directory created in Section 10.3. Copy **WelcomeTagHandler.class** into the **advjhtp1** Web application's **WEB-INF\classes** directory in Tomcat. [*Note*: Class **WelcomeTagHandler** must appear in its proper package director structure in **classes** directory. **WelcomeTagHandler** is defined in package **com.deitel.advjhtp1.jsp.taglibrary**.] Open your Web browser and enter the following URL to test **customTagWelcome.jsp**:

> `http://localhost:8080/advjhtp1/jsp/customTagWelcome.jsp`

10.8.2 Custom Tag with Attributes

Many XHTML and JSP elements use attributes to customize functionality. For example, an XHTML element can specify a **style** attribute that indicates how the element should be formatted in a client's Web browser. Similarly, the JSP action elements have attributes that help customize their behavior in a JSP. Our next example demonstrates how to specify attributes for your custom tags.

Figure 10.33 (**customTagAttribute.jsp**) is similar to Fig. 10.30. This example uses a new tag called, **welcome2**, to insert text in the JSP that is customized based on the value of attribute **firstName**. The screen capture shows the results of the **welcome2** tags on lines 20 and 30. The tag at line 20 specifies the value **"Paul"** for attribute **first-Name**. Lines 26–28 define a scriptlet that obtains the value of request parameter **name** and assign it to **String** reference **name**. Line 30 uses the **name** in a JSP expression as the value for the **firstName** attribute. In the sample screen capture, this JSP was invoked with the following URL:

> `http://localhost:8080/advjhtp1/jsp/`
> `customTagAttribute.jsp?firstName=Sean`

```
1   <?xml version = "1.0"?>
2   <!DOCTYPE html PUBLIC "-//W3C//DTD XHTML 1.0 Strict//EN"
3       "http://www.w3.org/TR/xhtml1/DTD/xhtml1-strict.dtd">
4
5   <!-- Fig. 10.33: customTagAttribute.jsp                -->
6   <!-- JSP that uses a custom tag to output content. -->
7
8   <%-- taglib directive --%>
9   <%@ taglib uri = "advjhtp1-taglib.tld" prefix = "advjhtp1" %>
10
11  <html xmlns = "http://www.w3.org/1999/xhtml">
12
13     <head>
14        <title>Specifying Custom Tag Attributes</title>
15     </head>
16
17     <body>
18        <p>Demonstrating an attribute with a string value</p>
19        <h1>
20           <advjhtp1:welcome2 firstName = "Paul" />
21        </h1>
22
23        <p>Demonstrating an attribute with an expression value</p>
24        <h1>
25           <%-- scriptlet to obtain "name" request parameter --%>
26           <%
27              String name = request.getParameter( "name" );
28           %>
29
30           <advjhtp1:welcome2 firstName = "<%= name %>" />
31        </h1>
32     </body>
33
34  </html>
```

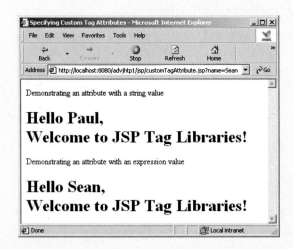

Fig. 10.33 Specifying attributes for a custom tag.

When defining the custom tag handler for a tag with attributes, you must provide methods that enable the JSP container to set the attribute values in the tag handler. Methods that manipulate attributes follow the same *set-* and *get-*method naming conventions as do JavaBean properties. Thus, the custom tag's **firstName** attribute is set with method **setFirstName**. Similarly, the method to obtain the **firstName** attribute's value would be **getFirstName** (we did not define this method for this example). Class **Welcome2TagHandler** (Fig. 10.34) defines its **firstName** variable at line 13 and a corresponding *set* method **setFirstName** (lines 37–40). When the JSP container encounters a **welcome2** tag in a JSP, it creates a new **Welcome2TagHandler** object to process the tag and sets the tag's attributes. Next, the container invokes method **doStartTag** (lines 16–34) to perform the custom tag processing. Lines 24–25 use the **firstName** attribute value as part of the text output by the custom tag.

```java
1   // Fig. 10.34: Welcome2TagHandler.java
2   // Custom tag handler that handles a simple tag.
3   package com.deitel.advjhtp1.jsp.taglibrary;
4
5   // Java core packages
6   import java.io.*;
7
8   // Java extension packages
9   import javax.servlet.jsp.*;
10  import javax.servlet.jsp.tagext.*;
11
12  public class Welcome2TagHandler extends TagSupport {
13     private String firstName = "";
14
15     // Method called to begin tag processing
16     public int doStartTag() throws JspException
17     {
18        // attempt tag processing
19        try {
20           // obtain JspWriter to output content
21           JspWriter out = pageContext.getOut();
22
23           // output content
24           out.print( "Hello " + firstName +
25              ", <br />Welcome to JSP Tag Libraries!" );
26        }
27
28        // rethrow IOException to JSP container as JspException
29        catch( IOException ioException ) {
30           throw new JspException( ioException.getMessage() );
31        }
32
33        return SKIP_BODY;   // ignore the tag's body
34     }
35
```

Fig. 10.34 **Welcome2TagHandler** custom tag handler for a tag with an attribute (part 1 of 2).

```
36        // set firstName attribute to the users first name
37        public void setFirstName( String username )
38        {
39            firstName = username;
40        }
41    }
```

Fig. 10.34 `Welcome2TagHandler` custom tag handler for a tag with an attribute (part 2 of 2).

Before the **welcome2** tag can be used in a JSP, we must make the JSP container aware of the tag by adding it to a tag library. To do this, add the tag element of Fig. 10.35 as a child of element **taglib** in the tag library descriptor **advjhtp1-taglib.tld**. As in the previous example, element **tag** contains elements **name**, **tagclass**, **bodycontent** and **info**. Lines 16–20 introduce element *attribute* for specifying the characteristics of a tag's attributes. Each attribute must have a separate attribute element that contains the **name**, *required* and *rtexprvalue* elements. Element **name** (line 17) specifies the attribute's name. Element **required** specifies whether the attribute is required (**true**) or optional (**false**). Element **rtexprvalue** specifies whether the value of the attribute can be the result of a JSP expression evaluated at runtime (**true**) or whether it must be a string literal (**false**).

To test **customTagAttribute.jsp** in Tomcat, copy **customTagAttribute.jsp** and the updated **advjhtp1-taglib.tld** into the **jsp** directory created in Section 10.3. Copy **Welcome2TagHandler.class** into the **advjhtp1** Web application's **WEB-INF\classes** directory in Tomcat. [*Note:* This example will work only if the proper package-directory structure for **Welcome2TagHandler** is defined in the **classes** directory.] Open your Web browser and enter the following URL to test **customTagAttribute.jsp**:

```
http://localhost:8080/advjhtp1/jsp/
customTagAttribute.jsp?firstName=Sean
```

The text **?firstName=Sean** in the preceding URL specifies the value for request parameter **name** that is used by the custom tag **welcome2** at line 30 in Fig. 10.33.

```
1    <!-- A tag with an attribute -->
2    <tag>
3        <name>welcome2</name>
4
5        <tagclass>
6            com.deitel.advjhtp1.jsp.taglibrary.Welcome2TagHandler
7        </tagclass>
8
9        <bodycontent>empty</bodycontent>
10
11       <info>
12           Inserts content welcoming user to tag libraries. Uses
13           attribute "name" to insert the user's name.
14       </info>
```

Fig. 10.35 Element **tag** for the **welcome2** custom tag (part 1 of 2).

```
15
16      <attribute>
17         <name>firstName</name>
18         <required>true</required>
19         <rtexprvalue>true</rtexprvalue>
20      </attribute>
21   </tag>
```

Fig. 10.35 Element **tag** for the **welcome2** custom tag (part 2 of 2).

10.8.3 Evaluating the Body of a Custom Tag

Custom tags are particularly powerful for processing the element body. When a custom tag interacts with the element body, additional methods are required to perform those interactions. The methods are defined in class **BodyTagSupport**. In our next example, we re-implement **guestBookView.jsp** (Fig. 10.23) and replace the JavaBean processing performed in the JSP with a custom **guestlist** tag.

Figure 10.36 (**customTagBody.jsp**) uses the custom **guestlist** tag at lines 41–52. Note that the JSP expressions in the body of element **guestlist** use variable names that are not defined in the JSP. These variables are defined by the custom tag handler when the custom tag is encountered. The custom tag handler places the variables in the JSP's **PageContext**, so the variables can be used throughout the page. Although no repetition is defined in the JSP, the custom tag handler is defined to iterate over all the guests in the **guestbook** database. This action results in the creation of a table row in the resulting Web page for each guest in the database.

```
1   <?xml version = "1.0"?>
2   <!DOCTYPE html PUBLIC "-//W3C//DTD XHTML 1.0 Strict//EN"
3      "http://www.w3.org/TR/xhtml1/DTD/xhtml1-strict.dtd">
4
5   <!-- customTagBody.jsp -->
6
7   <%-- taglib directive --%>
8   <%@ taglib uri = "advjhtp1-taglib.tld" prefix = "advjhtp1" %>
9
10  <html xmlns = "http://www.w3.org/1999/xhtml">
11
12     <head>
13        <title>Guest List</title>
14
15        <style type = "text/css">
16           body {
17              font-family: tahoma, helvetica, arial, sans-serif
18           }
19
20           table, tr, td, th {
21              text-align: center;
22              font-size: .9em;
23              border: 3px groove;
```

Fig. 10.36 Using a custom tag that interacts with its body (part 1 of 2).

```
24                    padding: 5px;
25                    background-color: #dddddd
26            }
27        </style>
28    </head>
29
30    <body>
31        <p style = "font-size: 2em">Guest List</p>
32
33        <table>
34            <thead>
35                <th style = "width: 100px">Last name</th>
36                <th style = "width: 100px">First name</th>
37                <th style = "width: 200px">Email</th>
38            </thead>
39
40            <%-- guestlist custom tag --%>
41            <advjhtp1:guestlist>
42                <tr>
43                    <td><%= lastName %></td>
44
45                    <td><%= firstName %></td>
46
47                    <td>
48                        <a href = "mailto:<%= email %>">
49                            <%= email %></a>
50                    </td>
51                </tr>
52            </advjhtp1:guestlist>
53        </table>
54    </body>
55
56 </html>
```

Fig. 10.36 Using a custom tag that interacts with its body (part 2 of 2).

As in **guestBookView.jsp**, the custom tag handler **GuestBookTag** (Fig. 10.37) creates a **GuestDataBean** to access the **guestbook** database. Class **GuestBookTag** extends **BodyTagSupport**, which contains several new methods including *doInit-*

Body and ***doAfterBody*** (from interface ***BodyTag***). Method ***doInitBody*** is called once, after ***doStartTag*** and before ***doAfterBody***. Method ***doAfterBody*** can be called many times to process the body of a custom tag.

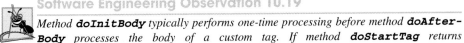

Software Engineering Observation 10.19

*Method **doInitBody** typically performs one-time processing before method **doAfter-Body** processes the body of a custom tag. If method **doStartTag** returns **Tag.SKIP_BODY**, method **doInitBody** will not be called.*

```java
1   // Fig. 10.37: GuestBookTag.java
2   // Custom tag handler that reads information from the guestbook
3   // database and makes that data available in a JSP.
4   package com.deitel.advjhtp1.jsp.taglibrary;
5
6   // Java core packages
7   import java.io.*;
8   import java.util.*;
9
10  // Java extension packages
11  import javax.servlet.jsp.*;
12  import javax.servlet.jsp.tagext.*;
13
14  // Deitel packages
15  import com.deitel.advjhtp1.jsp.beans.*;
16
17  public class GuestBookTag extends BodyTagSupport {
18     private String firstName;
19     private String lastName;
20     private String email;
21
22     private GuestDataBean guestData;
23     private GuestBean guest;
24     private Iterator iterator;
25
26     // Method called to begin tag processing
27     public int doStartTag() throws JspException
28     {
29        // attempt tag processing
30        try {
31           guestData = new GuestDataBean();
32
33           List list = guestData.getGuestList();
34           iterator = list.iterator();
35
36           if ( iterator.hasNext() ) {
37              processNextGuest();
38
39              return EVAL_BODY_TAG;      // continue body processing
40           }
41           else
42              return SKIP_BODY;          // terminate body processing
43        }
```

Fig. 10.37 GuestBookTag custom tag handler (part 1 of 2).

```
44
45        // if any exceptions occur, do not continue processing
46        // tag's body
47        catch( Exception exception ) {
48           exception.printStackTrace();
49           return SKIP_BODY;    // ignore the tag's body
50        }
51     }
52
53     // process body and determine if body processing
54     // should continue
55     public int doAfterBody()
56     {
57        // attempt to output body data
58        try {
59           bodyContent.writeOut( getPreviousOut() );
60        }
61
62        // if exception occurs, terminate body processing
63        catch ( IOException ioException ) {
64           ioException.printStackTrace();
65           return SKIP_BODY;          // terminate body processing
66        }
67
68        bodyContent.clearBody();
69
70        if ( iterator.hasNext() ) {
71           processNextGuest();
72
73           return EVAL_BODY_TAG;     // continue body processing
74        }
75        else
76           return SKIP_BODY;          // terminate body processing
77     }
78
79     // obtains the next GuestBean and extracts its data
80     private void processNextGuest()
81     {
82        // get next guest
83        guest = ( GuestBean ) iterator.next();
84
85        pageContext.setAttribute(
86           "firstName", guest.getFirstName() );
87
88        pageContext.setAttribute(
89           "lastName", guest.getLastName() );
90
91        pageContext.setAttribute(
92           "email", guest.getEmail() );
93     }
94  }
```

Fig. 10.37 GuestBookTag custom tag handler (part 2 of 2).

The JSP container invokes method **doStartTag** (lines 27–51) when it encounters the custom **guestlist** tag in a JSP. Lines 31–34 create a new **GuestDataBean**, obtain a **List** of **GuestBean**s from the **GuestDataBean** and create an **Iterator** for manipulating the **ArrayList** contents. If there are no elements in the list (tested at line 36), line 42 returns **SKIP_BODY** to indicate that the container should perform no further processing of the **guestlist** tag's body. Otherwise, line 37 invokes **private** method **processNextGuest** (lines 80–93) to extract the information for the first guest and create variables containing that information in the JSP's **PageContext** (represented with variable **pageContext** that was inherited from **BodyTagSupport**). Method **processNextGuest** uses **PageContext** method *setAttribute* to specify each variable's name and value. The container is responsible for creating the actual variables used in the JSP. This is accomplished with the help of class **GuestBookTagExtraInfo** (Fig. 10.38).

Method **doAfterBody** (lines 55–77)performs the repetitive processing of the **guestlist** tag's body. The JSP container determines whether method **doAfterBody** should be called again, based on the method's return value. If **doAfterBody** returns **EVAL_BODY_TAG**, the container calls method **doAfterBody** again. If **doAfterBody** returns **SKIP_BODY**, the container stops processing the body and invokes the custom tag handler's **doEndTag** method to complete the custom processing. Line 59 invokes **writeOut** on variable **bodyContent** (inherited from **BodyTagSupport**) to process the first client's data (stored when **doStartTag** was called). Variable **bodyContent** refers to an object of class **BodyContent** from package **javax.servlet.jsp.tagext**. The argument to method **writeOut** is the result of method **getPreviousOut** (inherited from class **BodyTagSupport**), which returns the **JspWriter** object for the JSP that invokes the custom tag. This enables the custom tag to continue building the response to the client using the same output stream as the JSP. Next, line 68 invokes **bodyContent**'s method **clearBody** to ensure that the body content that was just output does not get processed as part of the next call to **doAfterBody**. Lines 70–76 determine whether there are more guests to process. If so, **doAfterBody** invokes **private** method **processNextGuest** to obtain the data for the next guest and returns **EVAL_BODY_TAG** to indicate that the container should call **doAfterBody** again. Otherwise, **doAfterBody** returns **SKIP_BODY** to terminate processing of the body.

The JSP container cannot create variables in the **PageContext** unless the container knows the names and types of those variables. This information is specified by a class with the same name as the custom tag handler and that ends with **ExtraInfo** (**GuestBookTagExtraInfo** in Fig. 10.38). **ExtraInfo** classes extend class *TagExtraInfo* (package **javax.servlet.jsp.tagext**). The container uses the information specified by a subclass of **TagExtraInfo** to determine what variables it should create (or use) in the **PageContext**. To specify variable information, override method *getVariableInfo*. This method returns an array of **VariableInfo** objects that the container uses either to create new variables in the **PageContext** or to enable a custom tag to use existing variables in the **PageContext**. The **VariableInfo** constructor receives four arguments—a **String** representing the name of the variable, a **String** representing the variable's class name, a **boolean** indicating whether or not the variable should be created by the container (**true** if so) and a **static** integer constant representing the variable's scope in the JSP. The constants in class **VariableInfo** are **NESTED**, **AT_BEGIN** and

AT_END. **NESTED** indicates that the variable can be used only in the custom tag's body. **AT_BEGIN** indicates that the variable can be used anywhere in the JSP after the starting tag of the custom tag is encountered. **AT_END** indicates that the variable can be used anywhere in the JSP after the ending tag of the custom tag.

Before the **guestlist** tag can be used in a JSP, we must make the JSP container aware of the tag by adding it to a tag library. To do this, add the **tag** element of Fig. 10.39 as a child of element **taglib** in the tag library descriptor **advjhtp1-taglib.tld**. As in the previous example, element **tag** contains elements **name**, **tagclass**, **bodycontent** and **info**. Lines 10–12 introduce element **teiclass** for specifying the custom tag's **ExtraInfo** class.

To test **customTagBody.jsp** in Tomcat, copy **customTagBody.jsp** and the updated **advjhtp1-taglib.tld** into the **jsp** directory created in Section 10.3. Copy **GuestBookTag.class** and **GuestBookTagExtraInfo.class** into the **advjhtp1** Web application's **WEB-INF\classes** directory in Tomcat. [*Note*: This example will work only if the proper package directory structure for **GuestBookTag** and **GuestBookTagExtraInfo** is defined in the **classes** directory.] Open your Web browser and enter the following URL to test **customTagBody.jsp**:

    http://localhost:8080/advjhtp1/jsp/customTagBody.jsp

```
1   // Fig. 10.38: GuestBookTagExtraInfo.java
2   // Class that defines the variable names and types created by
3   // custom tag handler GuestBookTag.
4   package com.deitel.advjhtp1.jsp.taglibrary;
5
6   // Java core packages
7   import javax.servlet.jsp.tagext.*;
8
9   public class GuestBookTagExtraInfo extends TagExtraInfo {
10
11     // method that returns information about the variables
12     // GuestBookTag creates for use in a JSP
13     public VariableInfo [] getVariableInfo( TagData tagData )
14     {
15        VariableInfo firstName = new VariableInfo( "firstName",
16           "String", true, VariableInfo.NESTED );
17
18        VariableInfo lastName = new VariableInfo( "lastName",
19           "String", true, VariableInfo.NESTED );
20
21        VariableInfo email = new VariableInfo( "email",
22           "String", true, VariableInfo.NESTED );
23
24        VariableInfo varableInfo [] =
25           { firstName, lastName, email };
26
27        return varableInfo;
28     }
29  }
```

Fig. 10.38 GuestBookTagExtraInfo used by the container to define scripting variables in a JSP that uses the **guestlist** custom tag.

```
 1   <!-- A tag that iterates over an ArrayList of GuestBean -->
 2   <!-- objects, so they can be output in a JSP            -->
 3   <tag>
 4      <name>guestlist</name>
 5
 6      <tagclass>
 7         com.deitel.advjhtp1.jsp.taglibrary.GuestBookTag
 8      </tagclass>
 9
10      <teiclass>
11         com.deitel.advjhtp1.jsp.taglibrary.GuestBookTagExtraInfo
12      </teiclass>
13
14      <bodycontent>JSP</bodycontent>
15
16      <info>
17         Iterates over a list of GuestBean objects
18      </info>
19   </tag>
```

Fig. 10.39 Element **tag** for the **guestlist** custom tag.

This chapter has presented many JSP capabilities. However, there are additional features that are beyond the scope of this book. For a complete description of JavaServer Pages, see the JavaServer Pages 1.1 specification, which can be downloaded from **java.sun.com/products/jsp/download.html**. Other JSP resources are listed in Section 10.9. The next chapter continues our JSP and servlet discussion by presenting a substantial e-business case study in which we build an online bookstore. The case study integrates many topics discussed up to this point in the text, including JDBC, servlets, JSP and XML. Also, we discuss several additional servlet features as part of the case study. The techniques shown in the case study provide a foundation for the capstone e-business case study presented in Chapters 16 through 19.

10.9 Internet and World Wide Web Resources

java.sun.com/products/jsp
The home page for information about JavaServer Pages at the Sun Microsystems Java site.

java.sun.com/products/servlet
The home page for information about servlets at the Sun Microsystems Java site.

java.sun.com/j2ee
The home page for the Java 2 Enterprise Edition at the Sun Microsystems Java site.

www.w3.org
The World Wide Web Consortium home page. This site provides information about current and developing Internet and Web standards, such as XHTML, XML and CSS.

jsptags.com
This site includes tutorials, tag libraries, software and other resources for JSP programmers.

jspinsider.com
This Web programming site concentrates on resources for JSP programmers. It includes software, tutorials, articles, sample code, references and links to other JSP and Web programming resources.

SUMMARY

- JavaServer Pages (JSPs) are an extension of servlet technology.

- JavaServer Pages enable Web application programmers to create dynamic content by reusing predefined components and by interacting with components using server-side scripting.

- JSP programmers can create custom tag libraries that enable Web-page designers who are not familiar with Java programming to enhance their Web pages with powerful dynamic content and processing capabilities.

- Classes and interfaces specific to JavaServer Pages programming are located in packages **javax.servlet.jsp** and **javax.servlet.jsp.tagext**.

- The JavaServer Pages 1.1 specification can be downloaded from **java.sun.com/products/jsp/download.html**.

- There are four key components to JSPs—directives, actions, scriptlets and tag libraries.

- Directives specify global information that is not associated with a particular JSP request.

- Actions encapsulate functionality in predefined tags that programmers can embed in a JSP.

- Scriptlets, or scripting elements, enable programmers to insert Java code that interacts with components in a JSP (and possibly other Web application components) to perform request processing.

- Tag libraries are part of the tag extension mechanism that enables programmers to create new tags that encapsulate complex Java functionality.

- JSPs normally include XHTML or XML markup. Such markup is known as fixed template data or fixed template text.

- Programmers tend to use JSPs when most of the content sent to the client is fixed template data and only a small portion of the content is generated dynamically with Java code.

- Programmers use servlets when a small portion of the content is fixed template data.

- JSPs normally execute as part of a Web server. The server often is referred to as the JSP container.

- When a JSP-enabled server receives the first request for a JSP, the JSP container translates that JSP into a Java servlet that handles the current request and future requests to the JSP.

- The JSP container places the Java statements that implement a JSP's response in method **_jspService** at translation time.

- The request/response mechanism and life cycle of a JSP are the same as those of a servlet.

- JSPs can define methods **jspInit** and **jspDestroy** that are invoked when the container initializes a JSP and when the container terminates a JSP, respectively.

- JSP expressions are delimited by **<%=** and **%>**. Such expressions are converted to **String**s by the JSP container and are output as part of the response.

- The XHTML *meta element* can set a refresh interval for a document that is loaded into a browser. This causes the browser to request the document repeatedly at the specified interval in seconds.

- When you first invoke a JSP in Tomcat, there is a delay as Tomcat translates the JSP into a servlet and invokes the servlet to respond to your request.

- Implicit objects provide programmers with servlet capabilities in the context of a JavaServer Page.

- Implicit objects have four scopes—application, page, request and session.

- Objects with application scope are part of the JSP and servlet container application.

- Objects with page scope exist only as part of the page in which they are used. Each page has its own instances of the page-scope implicit objects.

- Objects with request scope exist for the duration of the request. Request-scope objects go out of scope when request processing completes with a response to the client.

- Objects with session scope exist for the client's entire browsing session.

- JSP scripting components include scriptlets, comments, expressions, declarations and escape sequences.

- Scriptlets are blocks of code delimited by **<%** and **%>**. They contain Java statements that are placed in method **_jspService** when the container translates a JSP into a servlet.

- JSP comments are delimited by **<%--** and **--%>**. XHTML comments are delimited by **<!--** and **-->**. Java's single-line comments (**//**) and multiline comments (delimited by **/*** and ***/**) can be used inside scriptlets.

- JSP comments and scripting language comments are ignored and do not appear in the response.

- A JSP expression, delimited by **<%=** and **%>**, contains a Java expression that is evaluated when a client requests the JSP containing the expression. The container converts the result of a JSP expression to a **String** object, then outputs the **String** as part of the response to the client.

- Declarations, delimited by **<%!** and **%>**, enable a JSP programmer to define variables and methods. Variables become instance variables of the class that represents the translated JSP. Similarly, methods become members of the class that represents the translated JSP.

- Special characters or character sequences that the JSP container normally uses to delimit JSP code can be included in a JSP as literal characters in scripting elements, fixed template data and attribute values by using escape sequences.

- JSP standard actions provide JSP implementors with access to several of the most common tasks performed in a JSP. JSP containers process actions at request time.

- JavaServer Pages support two include mechanisms—the **<jsp:include>** action and the **include** directive.

- Action **<jsp:include>** enables dynamic content to be included in a JavaServer Page. If the included resource changes between requests, the next request to the JSP containing the **<jsp:include>** action includes the new content of the resource.

- The **include** directive is processed once, at JSP translation time, and causes the content to be copied into the JSP. If the included resource changes, the new content will not be reflected in the JSP that used the include directive unless that JSP is recompiled.

- Action **<jsp:forward>** enables a JSP to forward the processing of a request to a different resource. Processing of the request by the original JSP terminates as soon as the request is forwarded.

- Action **<jsp:param>** specifies name/value pairs of information that are passed to the **include**, **forward** and **plugin** actions. Every **<jsp:param>** action has two required attributes—**name** and **value**. If a **param** action specifies a parameter that already exists in the request, the new value for the parameter takes precedence over the original value. All values for that parameter can be obtained with the JSP implicit object **request**'s **getParameterValues** method, which returns an array of **String**s.

- JSP action **<jsp:plugin>** enables an applet or JavaBean to be added to a Web page in the form of a browser-specific **object** or **embed** XHTML element. This action also enables the downloading and installation of the Java Plug-in if it is not already installed on the client computer.

- Action **<jsp:useBean>** enables a JSP to manipulate a Java object. This action can be used to create a Java object for use in the JSP or to locate an existing object.

- Like JSP implicit objects, objects specified with action **<jsp:useBean>** have **page**, **request**, **session** or **application** scope that indicates where they can be used in a Web application.

- Action **<jsp:getProperty>** obtains the value of JavaBean's property. Action **<jsp:getProperty>** has two attributes—**name** and **property**—that specify the bean object to manipulate and the property to get.

- JavaBean property values can be set with action **<jsp:setProperty>**. This action is particularly useful for mapping request parameter values to JavaBean properties. Request parameters can be used to set properties of primitive types **boolean**, **byte**, **char**, **int**, **long**, **float** and **double** and **java.lang** types **String**, **Boolean**, **Byte**, **Character**, **Integer**, **Long**, **Float** and **Double**.

- The **page** directive defines information that is globally available in a JSP. Directives are delimited by **<%@** and **%>**. The **page** directive's **errorPage** attribute indicates where all uncaught exceptions are forwarded for processing.

- Action **<jsp:setProperty>** has the ability to match request parameters to properties of the same name in a bean by specifying **"*"** for attribute **property**.

- Attribute **import** of the **page** directive enables programmers to specify Java classes and packages that are used in the context of a JSP.

- If the attribute **isErrorPage** of the **page** directive is set to **true**, the JSP is an error page. This condition enables access to the JSP implicit object **exception** that refers to an exception object indicating the problem that occurred.

- Directives are messages to the JSP container that enable the programmer to specify page settings (such as the error page), to include content from other resources and to specify custom tag libraries that can be used in a JSP. Directives are processed at the time a JSP is translated into a servlet and compiled. Thus, directives do not produce any immediate output.

- The **page** directive specifies global settings for a JSP in the JSP container. There can be many **page** directives, provided that there is only one occurrence of each attribute. The exception to this rule is the **import** attribute, which can be used repeatedly to import Java packages.

- Custom tag libraries define one or more custom tags that JSP implementors can use to create dynamic content. The functionality of these custom tags is defined in Java classes that implement interface **Tag** (package **javax.servlet.jsp.tagext**), normally by extending class **TagSupport** or **BodyTagSupport**.

- A JSP can include a custom tag library with the **taglib** directive.

- When implementing custom tags, you must define a tag handler class for each tag that provides the tag's functionality, a tag library descriptor that provides information about the tag library and its custom tags to the JSP container and a JSP that uses the custom tag.

- The most important methods of interface **Tag** are **doStartTag** and **doEndTag**. The JSP container invokes these methods when it encounters the starting custom tag and the ending custom tag, respectively.

- A custom tag library descriptor file is an XML document that specifies information about the tag library that is required by the JSP container.

- Class **BodyTagSupport** contains several methods for interacting with the body of a custom tag, including **doInitBody** and **doAfterBody** (from interface **BodyTag**). Method **doInitBody** is called once after **doStartTag** and once before **doAfterBody**. Method **doAfterBody** can be called many times to process the body of a custom tag.

TERMINOLOGY

%\> escape sequence for %>
<!-- and --> XHTML comment delimiters
<%-- and --%> JSP comment delimiters
<% and %> scriptlet delimiters
<%! and %> declaration delimiters
<%= and %> JSP expression delimiters

<%@ and %> directive delimiters
<\% escape sequence for <%
action
align attribute of **<jsp:plugin>** action
application implicit object
application scope

request implicit object
request scope
request-time error
required element of tag library descriptor
response implicit object
rtexprvalue element of tag library descriptor
scope attribute of **<jsp:useBean>**
scope of a bean
scripting element
scriptlet
session attribute of **page** directive
session implicit object
session scope
setAttribute method of **PageContext**
simple custom tag
SKIP_BODY constant
specify attributes of a custom tag
standard actions
tag element of tag library descriptor
tag extension mechanism
tag handler

Tag interface
tag library
tag library descriptor
tagclass element of tag library descriptor
TagExtraInfo class
taglib directive
tagPrefix attribute of **taglib** directive
TagSupport class
teiclass element of tag library descriptor
title attribute of **<jsp:plugin>**
tlibversion element of tag library descriptor
translation-time error
translation-time include
type attribute of **<jsp:plugin>**
type attribute of **<jsp:useBean>**
uri attribute of **taglib** directive
value attribute of **<jsp:param>**
value attribute of **<jsp:setProperty>**
vspace attribute of **<jsp:plugin>**
width attribute of **<jsp:plugin>**

SELF-REVIEW EXERCISES

10.1 Fill in the blanks in each of the following statements:
  a) JSP action _____ enables an applet or JavaBean to be added to a Web page in the form of a browser-specific **object** or **embed** XHTML element.
  b) Action _____ has the ability to match request parameters to properties of the same name in a bean by specifying **"*"** for attribute **property**.
  c) There are four key components to JSPs: _____, _____, _____ and _____.
  d) A JSP can include a custom tag library with the _____ directive.
  e) The implicit objects have four scopes: _____, _____, _____ and _____.
  f) The _____ directive is processed once, at JSP translation time and causes content to be copied into the JSP.
  g) Classes and interfaces specific to JavaServer Pages programming are located in packages _____ and _____.
  h) JSPs normally execute as part of a Web server that is referred to as the _____.
  i) Method _____ can be called repeatedly to process the body of a custom tag.
  j) JSP scripting components include _____, _____, _____, _____ and _____.

10.2 State whether each of the following is *true* or *false*. If *false*, explain why.
  a) An object with page scope exists in every JSP of a particular Web application.
  b) Directives specify global information that is not associated with a particular JSP request.
  c) The JSP container invokes methods **doInitBody** and **doAfterBody** when it encounters the starting custom tag and the ending custom tag, respectively.
  d) Tag libraries are part of the tag extension mechanism that enables programmers to create new tags that encapsulate complex Java functionality.
  e) Action **<jsp:include>** is evaluated once at page translation time.

f) Like XHTML comments, JSP comments and script language comments appear in the response to the client.

g) Objects with application scope are part of a particular Web application.

h) Each page has its own instances of the page-scope implicit objects.

i) Action **`<jsp:setProperty>`** has the ability to match request parameters to properties of the same name in a bean by specifying **`"*"`** for attribute **`property`**.

j) Objects with session scope exist for the client's entire browsing session.

ANSWERS TO SELF-REVIEW EXERCISES

10.1 a) **`<jsp:plugin>`**. b) **`<jsp:setProperty>`**. c) directives, actions, scriptlets, tag libraries. d) **`taglib`**. e) application, page, request and session. f) **`include`**. g) **`javax.servlet.jsp`**, **`javax.servlet.jsp.tagext`**. h) JSP container. i) **`doAfterBody`**. j) scriptlets, comments, expressions, declarations, escape sequences.

10.2 a) False. Objects with page scope exist only as part of the page in which they are used. b) True. c) False. The JSP container invokes methods **`doStartTag`** and **`doEndTag`** when it encounters the starting custom tag and the ending custom tag, respectively. d) True. e) False. Action **`<jsp:include>`** enables dynamic content to be included in a JavaServer Page. f) False. JSP comments and script language comments are ignored and do not appear in the response. g) False. Objects with application scope are part of the JSP and servlet container application. h) True. i) True. j) True.

EXERCISES

10.3 Create class **`ResultSetTag`** (a custom tag handler) that can display information from any **`ResultSet`**. Use class **`GuestBookTag`** of Fig. 10.37 as a guide. The **`pageContext`** attribute names should be the column names in the **`ResultSet`**. The column names can be obtained through the **`ResultSetMetaData`** associated with the **`ResultSet`**. Create the tag library descriptor for the custom tag in this exercise and test the custom tag in a JSP.

10.4 Create a JSP and JDBC-based address book. Use the guest book example of Fig. 10.20 through Fig. 10.24 as a guide. Your address book should allow one to insert entries, delete entries and search for entries.

10.5 Incorporate the **`ResultSetTag`** of Exercise 10.3 into the address book example in Exercise 10.4.

10.6 Reimplement your solution to Exercise 9.5 (Dynamic Web FAQs) using JSPs rather than servlets. Create a custom tag handler similar to the one you created in Exercise 10.3 to help display the FAQs information.

10.7 Modify your solution to Exercise 10.6 so that the first JSP invoked by the user returns a list of FAQs topics from which to choose. Each topic should be a hyperlink that invokes another JSP with an argument indicating which topic the user would like to view. The JSP should query the FAQs database and return an XHTML document containing only FAQs for that topic.

10.8 Reimplement the Web application of Fig. 9.27 (favorite animal survey) using JSPs.

10.9 Modify your solution to Exercise 10.8 to allow the user to see the survey results without responding to the survey.

10.10 Reimplement Fig. 9.24 (book recommendations) using JSPs. Use the JSP implicit object **`session`** to track the user's selections and determine appropriate book recommendations. Remember to use the **`page`** directive to indicate that each JSP participates in a session.

11

Case Study: Servlet and JSP Bookstore

Objectives

- To build a three-tier, client/server, distributed Web application using Java servlet and JavaServer Pages technology.
- To be able to perform servlet/JSP interactions.
- To be able to use a **RequestDispatcher** to forward requests to another resource for further processing.
- To be able to create XML from a servlet and XSL transformations to convert the XML into a format the client can display.
- To introduce the Java 2 Enterprise Edition reference implementation server.
- To be able to deploy a Web application using the Java 2 Enterprise Edition.

The world is a book, and those who do not travel, read only a page.
Saint Augustine

If we do not lay out ourselves in the service of mankind, whom should we serve?
John Adams

We must take the current when it serves, or lose our ventures.
William Shakespeare

11.1 Introduction

This chapter serves as a capstone for our presentation of JSP and servlets. Here, we implement a bookstore Web application that integrates JDBC, XML, JSP and servlet technologies. The case study introduces additional servlet features that are discussed as they are encountered in the case study.

This chapter also serves as an introduction to the *Java 2 Enterprise Edition 1.2.1 reference implementation* used in Chapters 14–18. Unlike the JSP and servlet chapters, which demonstrated examples using Apache's Tomcat JSP and servlet container, this chapter deploys the bookstore application on the J2EE 1.2.1 reference implementation application server software, which is downloadable from **java.sun.com/j2ee/download.html** (see Appendix E for installation and configuration instructions). The J2EE 1.2.1 reference implementation includes the Apache Tomcat JSP and servlet container. After reading this chapter, you will be able to implement a substantial distributed Web application with many components, and you will be able to deploy that application on the J2EE 1.2.1 application server.

11.2 Bookstore Architecture

This section overviews the architecture of the **Bug2Bug.com** bookstore application. We present a diagram of the basic interactions between XHTML documents, JSPs and servlets. Also, we present a table of all the documents and classes used in the case study. Our sample outputs demonstrate how the XHTML documents sent to the client are rendered.

Our **Bug2Bug.com** shopping-cart case study consists of a series of XHTML documents, JSPs and servlets that interact to simulate a bookstore selling Deitel publications. This case study is implemented as a distributed, three-tier, Web-based application. The client tier is represented by the user's Web browser. The browser displays static XHTML documents and dynamically created XHTML documents that allow the user to interact with the server tier. The server tier consists of several JSPs and servlets that act on behalf of the client. These JSPs and servlets perform tasks such as creating a list of publications, creating documents containing the details about a publication, adding items to the shopping cart, viewing the shopping cart and processing the final order. Some of the JSPs and servlets perform database interactions on behalf of the client.

The database tier uses the **books** database introduced in Chapter 8, Java Database Connectivity. In this case study, we use only the **titles** table from the database (see Chapter 8).

Figure 11.1 illustrates the interactions between the bookstore's application components. In the diagram, names without file extensions (**displayBook** and **addToCart**) represent servlet aliases (i.e., the names used to invoke the servlets). As you will see when we deploy the case study in Section 11.10, the Java 2 Enterprise Edition 1.2.1 reference implementation includes an *Application Deployment Tool*. Among its many features, this tool enables us to specify the alias used to invoke a servlet. For example, **addToCart** is the alias for servlet **AddToCartServlet**. The Application Deployment Tool creates the deployment descriptor for a servlet as part of deploying an application.

After the application is deployed, users can visit the bookstore by entering the following URL in a browser:

```
http://localhost:8000/advjhtp1/store/
```

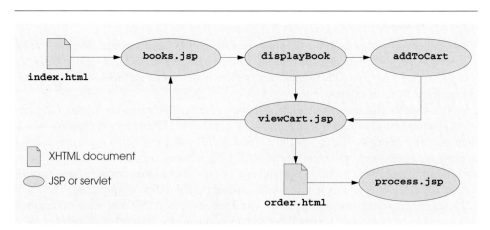

Fig. 11.1   Bug2Bug.com bookstore component interactions.

This URL requests the default home page for the store (**index.html**). The user can view the list of products by clicking a button on the home page. This invokes **books.jsp**, which interacts with a database to create the list of books dynamically. The result is an XHTML document containing links to the servlet with alias **displayBook**. This servlet receives as a parameter the ISBN number for the selected book and returns an XHTML document containing the information for that book. From this document, the user can click buttons to place the current book in the shopping cart or view the shopping cart. Adding a book to a shopping cart invokes the servlet with alias **addToCart**. Viewing the contents of the cart invokes **viewCart.jsp** to return an XHTML document containing the contents of the cart, subtotals the dollar cost of each item and a total dollar cost of all the items in the cart. When the user adds an item to the shopping cart, the **addToCart** servlet processes the user's request, then forwards it to **viewCart.jsp** to create the document that displays the current cart. At this point, the user can either continue shopping (**books.jsp**) or proceed to checkout (**order.html**). In the latter case, the user is presented with a form to input name, address and credit-card information. Then, the user submits the form to invoke **process.jsp**, which completes the transaction by sending a confirmation document to the user.

Figure 11.2 overviews the XHTML documents, JSPs, servlets, JavaBeans and other files used in this case study.

File	Description
index.html	This is the default home page for the bookstore, which is displayed by entering the following URL in the client's Web browser: **http://localhost:8000/advjhtp1/store**
styles.css	This Cascading Style Sheet (CSS) file is linked to all XHTML documents rendered on the client. The CSS file allows us to apply uniform formatting across all the XHTML static and dynamic documents rendered.
books.jsp	This JSP uses **BookBean** objects and a **TitlesBean** object to create an XHTML document containing the product list. The **TitlesBean** object queries the **books** database to obtain the list of titles in the database. The results are processed and placed in an **ArrayList** of **BookBean** objects. The list is stored as a session attribute for the client.
BookBean.java	An instance of this JavaBean represents the data for one book. The bean's **getXML** method returns an XML **Element** representing the book.
TitlesBean.java	JSP **books.jsp** uses an instance of this JavaBean to obtain an **ArrayList** containing a **BookBean** for every product in the database.

Fig. 11.2 Servlet and JSP components for bookstore case study (part 1 of 2).

File	Description
BookServlet.java	This servlet (aliased as **displayBook** in Fig. 11.1) obtains the XML representation of a book selected by the user, then applies an XSL transformation to the XML to produce an XHTML document that can be rendered by the client. In this example, the client is assumed to be a browser that supports Cascading Style Sheets (CSS). Later examples in this book apply different XSL transformations for different client types.
book.xsl	This XSL style sheet specifies how to transform the XML representation of a book into an XHTML document that the client browser can render.
CartItemBean.java	An instance of this JavaBean maintains a **BookBean** and the current quantity for that book in the shopping cart. These beans are stored in a **HashMap** that represents the contents of the shopping cart.
AddToCartServlet.java	This servlet (aliased as **addToCart** in Fig. 11.1) updates the shopping cart. If the cart does not exist, the servlet creates a cart (a **HashMap** in this example). If a **CartItemBean** for the item is already in the cart, the servlet updates the quantity of that item in the bean. Otherwise, the servlet creates a new **CartItemBean** with a quantity of 1. After updating the cart, the user is forwarded to **viewCart.jsp** to view the current cart contents.
viewCart.jsp	This JSP extracts the **CartItemBean**s from the shopping cart, subtotals each item in the cart, totals all the items in the cart and creates an XHTML document that allows the client to view the cart in tabular form.
order.html	When viewing the cart, the user can click a **Check Out** button to view this order form. In this example, the form has no functionality. However, it is provided to help complete the application.
process.jsp	This final JSP pretends to process the user's credit-card information and creates an XHTML document indicating that the order was processed and the total order value.

Fig. 11.2   Servlet and JSP components for bookstore case study (part 2 of 2).

11.3 Entering the Bookstore

Figure 11.3 (**index.html**) is the default home page for the **Bug2Bug.com** bookstore. This file is also known as the *welcome file*—an option specified at application deployment time (see Section 11.10). When the bookstore application is running on your computer in the Java 2 Enterprise Edition 1.2.1 reference implementation, you can enter the following URL in your Web browser to display the home page:

```
http://localhost:8000/advjhtp1/store
```

```
1   <?xml version = "1.0"?>
2   <!DOCTYPE html PUBLIC "-//W3C//DTD XHTML 1.0 Strict//EN"
3       "http://www.w3.org/TR/xhtml1/DTD/xhtml1-strict.dtd">
4   <!-- index.html -->
5
6   <html xmlns = "http://www.w3.org/1999/xhtml">
7
8   <head>
9       <title>Shopping Cart Case Study</title>
10
11      <link rel = "stylesheet" href = "styles.css"
12          type = "text/css" />
13  </head>
14
15  <body>
16      <p class = "bigFont">Bug2Bug.com</p>
17
18      <p class = "bigFont italic">
19          Deitel & Associates, Inc.<br />
20          Shopping Cart Case Study
21      </p>
22
23      <!-- form to request books.jsp -->
24      <form method = "get" action = "books.jsp">
25          <p><input type = "submit" name = "enterButton"
26              value = "Click here to enter store" /></p>
27      </form>
28  </body>
29
30  </html>
```

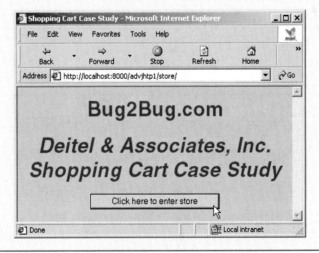

Fig. 11.3   Bookstore home page (`index.html`).

Lines 11–12 specify a linked style sheet **styles.css** (Fig. 11.4). All XHTML documents sent to the client use this style sheet, so that uniform formatting can be applied to the documents. The **form** at lines 24–27 provides a **submit** button that enables you to enter the store. Clicking this button invokes **books.jsp** (Fig. 11.7), which creates and returns an XHTML document containing the product list.

Figure 11.4 (**styles.css**) defines the common styles for rendering XHTML documents in this case study. Lines 1–2 indicate that all text in the **body** element should be centered and that the background color of the body should be steel blue. The background color is represented by the hexadecimal number **#b0c4de**. Line 3 defines class **.bold** to apply bold font weight to text. Lines 4–7 define class **.bigFont** with four CSS attributes. Elements to which this class is applied appear in bold, Helvetica font, which is double the size of the base-text font. The color of the font is dark blue (represented by the hexadecimal number **#00008b**). If the Helvetica font is not available, the browser will attempt to use Arial, and then the generic font **sans-serif** as a last resort. Line 8 defines class **.italic** to apply italic font style to text. Line 9 defines class **.right** to right justify text. Lines 10–11 indicate that all **table**, **th** (table head data) and **td** (table data) elements should have a three-pixel, grooved border with five pixels of internal padding between the text in a table cell and the border of that cell. Lines 12–14 indicate that all **table** elements should have a bright-blue background color (represented by the hexadecimal number **#6495ed**) and that all **table** elements should use automatically determined margins on both their left and right sides. This causes the table to be centered on the page. Not all of these styles are used in every XHTML document. However, using a single linked style sheet allows us to change the look and feel of our store quickly and easily by modifying the CSS file. For more information on CSS visit

> **www.w3.org/Style/CSS**

At this Web site, you will find the CSS specifications. Each specification includes an index of all the current CSS attributes and their permitted values.

Portability Tip 11.1

Different browsers have different levels of support for Cascading Style Sheets.

```
1   body               { text-align: center;
2                        background-color: #B0C4DE; }
3   .bold              { font-weight: bold; }
4   .bigFont           { font-family: helvetica, arial, sans-serif;
5                        font-weight: bold;
6                        font-size: 2em;
7                        color: #00008B; }
8   .italic            { font-style: italic; }
9   .right             { text-align: right; }
10  table, th, td      { border: 3px groove;
11                       padding: 5px; }
12  table              { background-color: #6495ed;
13                       margin-left: auto;
14                       margin-right: auto }
```

Fig. 11.4   Shared cascading style sheet (**styles.css**) used to apply common formatting across XHTML documents rendered on the client.

11.4 Obtaining the Book List from the Database

JavaServer Pages often generate XHTML that is sent to the client for rendering. JSP **books.jsp** (Fig. 11.7) generates an XHTML document containing a list of hyperlinks to information about each book in the **titles** table of the **books** database. From this list, the user can view information about a particular book by clicking the hyperlink for that book. This JSP uses a **TitlesBean** (Fig. 11.5) object and **BookBean** (Fig. 11.6) objects to create the product list. Each of the JavaBeans and **books.jsp** are discussed in this section. Figure 11.7 shows the rendering of the XHTML document sent to the browser by **books.jsp**.

The **TitlesBean** (Fig. 11.5) JavaBean performs a database query to obtain the list of titles in the database. Then, the results are processed and placed in an **ArrayList** of **BookBean** objects. As we will see in Fig. 11.7, the **ArrayList** is stored by **books.jsp** as a session attribute for the client.

```java
1   // TitlesBean.java
2   // Class TitlesBean makes a database connection and retrieves
3   // the books from the database.
4   package com.deitel.advjhtp1.store;
5
6   // Java core packages
7   import java.io.*;
8   import java.sql.*;
9   import java.util.*;
10
11  // Java extension packages
12  import javax.naming.*;
13  import javax.sql.*;
14
15  public class TitlesBean implements Serializable {
16     private Connection connection;
17     private PreparedStatement titlesQuery;
18
19     // construct TitlesBean object
20     public TitlesBean()
21     {
22        // attempt database connection and setup SQL statements
23        try {
24           InitialContext ic = new InitialContext();
25
26           DataSource source =
27              ( DataSource ) ic.lookup(
28                 "java:comp/env/jdbc/books" );
29
30           connection = source.getConnection();
31
```

Fig. 11.5 TitlesBean for obtaining book information from the **books** database and creating an **ArrayList** of **BookBean** objects (part 1 of 3).

```
32              titlesQuery =
33                  connection.prepareStatement(
34                      "SELECT isbn, title, editionNumber, " +
35                      "copyright, publisherID, imageFile, price " +
36                      "FROM titles ORDER BY title"
37                  );
38          }
39
40          // process exceptions during database setup
41          catch ( SQLException sqlException ) {
42              sqlException.printStackTrace();
43          }
44
45          // process problems locating data source
46          catch ( NamingException namingException ) {
47              namingException.printStackTrace();
48          }
49      }
50
51      // return a List of BookBeans
52      public List getTitles()
53      {
54          List titlesList = new ArrayList();
55
56          // obtain list of titles
57          try {
58              ResultSet results = titlesQuery.executeQuery();
59
60              // get row data
61              while ( results.next() ) {
62                  BookBean book = new BookBean();
63
64                  book.setISBN( results.getString( "isbn" ) );
65                  book.setTitle( results.getString( "title" ) );
66                  book.setEditionNumber(
67                      results.getInt( "editionNumber" ) );
68                  book.setCopyright( results.getString( "copyright" ) );
69                  book.setPublisherID(
70                      results.getInt( "publisherID" ) );
71                  book.setImageFile( results.getString( "imageFile" ) );
72                  book.setPrice( results.getDouble( "price" ) );
73
74                  titlesList.add( book );
75              }
76          }
77
78          // process exceptions during database query
79          catch ( SQLException exception ) {
80              exception.printStackTrace();
81          }
82
```

Fig. 11.5 `TitlesBean` for obtaining book information from the **books** database and creating an **ArrayList** of **BookBean** objects (part 2 of 3).

```
83          // return the list of titles
84          finally {
85             return titlesList;
86          }
87       }
88
89       // close statements and terminate database connection
90       protected void finalize()
91       {
92          // attempt to close database connection
93          try {
94             connection.close();
95          }
96
97          // process SQLException on close operation
98          catch ( SQLException sqlException ) {
99             sqlException.printStackTrace();
100          }
101       }
102 }
```

Fig. 11.5 **TitlesBean** for obtaining book information from the **books** database and creating an **ArrayList** of **BookBean** objects (part 3 of 3).

The JavaBean **TitlesBean** requires us to introduce the *Java Naming and Directory Interface (JNDI)*. Enterprise Java applications often access information and resources (such as databases) that are external to those applications. In some cases, those resources are distributed across a network. Just as an RMI client uses the RMI registry to locate a server object so the client can request a server, Enterprise application components must be able to locate the resources they use. An Enterprise Java application container must provide a *naming service* that implements JNDI and enables the components executing in that container to perform name lookups to locate resources. The J2EE 1.2.1 reference implementation server includes such a naming service that we use to locate our **books** database at execution time.

The **TitlesBean** uses JNDI to interact with the naming service and locate the data source (i.e., the **books** database). The **TitlesBean** constructor (lines 20–49) attempts the connection to the database using class **InitialContext** from package **javax.naming** and interface *DataSource* from package **javax.sql**. [These packages must be available to your compiler to compile this example.] When you deploy an Enterprise Java application (see Section 11.10), you specify the resources (such as databases) used by the application and the JNDI names for those resources. Using an **InitialContext**, an Enterprise application component can look up a resource. The **InitialContext** provides access to the application's *naming environment*.

Line 24 creates a new **InitialContext**. The **InitialContext** constructor throws a **NamingException** if it cannot locate a naming service. Lines 26–28 invoke **InitialContext** method **lookup** to locate our **books** data source. In the argument, the text **java:comp/env** indicates that method **lookup** should search for the resource in the application's component environment entries (i.e., the resource names specified at deployment time). The text **jdbc/books** indicates that the resource is a JDBC data source called **books**. Method **lookup** returns a **DataSource** object and throws a

NamingException if it cannot resolve the name it receives as an argument. Line 25 uses the **DataSource** to connect to the database. Lines 32–37 create a **PreparedStatement** that, when executed, returns the information about each title from the **titles** table of the **books** database.

Method **getTitles** (lines 52–87) returns a **List** (**titlesList**) containing a **BookBean** JavaBean for each title in the database. Line 58 executes **titlesQuery**. Lines 57–76 process the **ResultSet** (**results**). For each row in **results**, line 62 creates a new **BookBean**, and lines 64–72 set the attributes of the **BookBean** to columns in that **ResultSet** row. **ResultSet** methods **getString**, **getInt** and **getDouble** return the column data in the appropriate formats. Line 74 adds the new **BookBean** to **titlesList**. In the **finally** block, **titlesList** is returned. If there is an exception while performing the database interactions or if there are no records in the database, the **List** will be empty.

An instance of the **BookBean** (Fig. 11.6) JavaBean represents the properties for one book, including the book's ISBN number, title, copyright, cover image file name, edition number, publisher ID number and price. Each of these properties is a read/write property. Some of this information is not used in this example. **BookBean** method **getXML** returns an XML **Element** representing the book.

```
1    // BookBean.java
2    // A BookBean object contains the data for one book.
3    package com.deitel.advjhtp1.store;
4
5    // Java core packages
6    import java.io.*;
7    import java.text.*;
8    import java.util.*;
9
10   // third-party packages
11   import org.w3c.dom.*;
12
13   public class BookBean implements Serializable {
14      private String ISBN, title, copyright, imageFile;
15      private int editionNumber, publisherID;
16      private double price;
17
18      // set ISBN number
19      public void setISBN( String isbn )
20      {
21         ISBN = isbn;
22      }
23
24      // return ISBN number
25      public String getISBN()
26      {
27         return ISBN;
28      }
```

Fig. 11.6   **BookBean** that represents a single book's information and defines the XML format of that information (part 1 of 4).

```
29
30      // set book title
31      public void setTitle( String bookTitle )
32      {
33         title = bookTitle;
34      }
35
36      // return book title
37      public String getTitle()
38      {
39         return title;
40      }
41
42      // set copyright year
43      public void setCopyright( String year )
44      {
45         copyright = year;
46      }
47
48      // return copyright year
49      public String getCopyright()
50      {
51         return copyright;
52      }
53
54      // set file name of image representing product cover
55      public void setImageFile( String fileName )
56      {
57         imageFile = fileName;
58      }
59
60      // return file name of image representing product cover
61      public String getImageFile()
62      {
63         return imageFile;
64      }
65
66      // set edition number
67      public void setEditionNumber( int edition )
68      {
69         editionNumber = edition;
70      }
71
72      // return edition number
73      public int getEditionNumber()
74      {
75         return editionNumber;
76      }
77
78      // set publisher ID number
79      public void setPublisherID( int id )
80      {
```

Fig. 11.6 BookBean that represents a single book's information and defines the XML format of that information (part 2 of 4).

```
81          publisherID = id;
82       }
83
84       // return publisher ID number
85       public int getPublisherID()
86       {
87          return publisherID;
88       }
89
90       // set price
91       public void setPrice( double amount )
92       {
93          price = amount;
94       }
95
96       // return price
97       public double getPrice()
98       {
99          return price;
100      }
101
102      // get an XML representation of the Product
103      public Element getXML( Document document )
104      {
105         // create product root element
106         Element product = document.createElement( "product" );
107
108         // create isbn element, append as child of product
109         Element temp = document.createElement( "isbn" );
110         temp.appendChild( document.createTextNode( getISBN() ) );
111         product.appendChild( temp );
112
113         // create title element, append as child of product
114         temp = document.createElement( "title" );
115         temp.appendChild( document.createTextNode( getTitle() ) );
116         product.appendChild( temp );
117
118         // create a currency formatting object for US dollars
119         NumberFormat priceFormatter =
120            NumberFormat.getCurrencyInstance( Locale.US );
121
122         // create price element, append as child of product
123         temp = document.createElement( "price" );
124         temp.appendChild( document.createTextNode(
125            priceFormatter.format( getPrice() ) ) );
126         product.appendChild( temp );
127
128         // create imageFile element, append as child of product
129         temp = document.createElement( "imageFile" );
130         temp.appendChild(
131            document.createTextNode( getImageFile() ) );
132         product.appendChild( temp );
```

Fig. 11.6   BookBean that represents a single book's information and defines the XML format of that information (part 3 of 4).

```
133
134        // create copyright element, append as child of product
135        temp = document.createElement( "copyright" );
136        temp.appendChild(
137           document.createTextNode( getCopyright() ) );
138        product.appendChild( temp );
139
140        // create publisherID element, append as child of product
141        temp = document.createElement( "publisherID" );
142        temp.appendChild( document.createTextNode(
143           String.valueOf( getPublisherID() ) ) );
144        product.appendChild( temp );
145
146        // create editionNumber element, append as child of product
147        temp = document.createElement( "editionNumber" );
148        temp.appendChild( document.createTextNode(
149           String.valueOf( getEditionNumber() ) ) );
150        product.appendChild( temp );
151
152        // return product element
153        return product;
154     }
155  }
```

Fig. 11.6 **BookBean** that represents a single book's information and defines the XML format of that information (part 4 of 4).

Method **getXML** (lines 103–154) uses the **org.w3c.dom** package's **Document** and **Element** interfaces to create an XML representation of the book data as part of the **Document** that is passed to the method as an argument. The complete information for one book is placed in a **product** element (created at line 106). The elements for the individual properties of a book are appended to the **product** element as children. For example, line 109 uses **Document** method **createElement** to create element **isbn**. Line 110 uses **Document** method **createTextNode** to specify the text in the **isbn** element, and **Element** method **appendChild** to append the text to element **isbn**. Then, line 111 appends element **isbn** as a child of element **product** with **Element** method **append-Child**. Similar operations are performed for the other book properties. Lines 119–120 obtain a **NumberFormat** object that formats currency for the U. S. locale to format the book price in US dollars (line 125). Line 150 returns element **product** to the caller. We revisit method **getXML** in our **BookServlet** discussion (Fig. 11.8). For more information about XML and Java, refer to Appendices A–F.

JavaServer Page **books.jsp** dynamically generates the list of titles as an XHTML document to be rendered on the client. Lines 7–11 specify the JSP page settings. This JSP uses classes from our store package (**com.deitel.advjhtp1.store**) and package **java.util**. Also, this JSP uses session-tracking features. The dynamic parts of this JSP are defined in lines 31–64 with JSP scriptlets and expressions.

```
1   <?xml version = "1.0"?>
2   <!DOCTYPE html PUBLIC "-//W3C//DTD XHTML 1.0 Strict//EN"
3       "http://www.w3.org/TR/xhtml1/DTD/xhtml1-strict.dtd">
4   <!-- books.jsp -->
5
6   <%-- JSP page settings --%>
7   <%@
8       page language = "java"
9       import = "com.deitel.advjhtp1.store.*, java.util.*"
10      session = "true"
11  %>
12
13  <!-- begin document -->
14  <html xmlns = "http://www.w3.org/1999/xhtml">
15
16  <head>
17      <title>Book List</title>
18
19      <link rel = "stylesheet" href = "styles.css"
20          type = "text/css" />
21  </head>
22
23  <body>
24      <p class = "bigFont">Available Books</p>
25
26      <p class = "bold">Click a link to view book information</p>
27
28      <p>
29
30      <%-- begin JSP scriptlet to create list of books --%>
31      <%
32          TitlesBean titlesBean = new TitlesBean();
33          List titles = titlesBean.getTitles();
34          BookBean currentBook;
35
36          // store titles in session for further use
37          session.setAttribute( "titles", titles );
38
39          // obtain an Iterator to the set of keys in the List
40          Iterator iterator = titles.iterator();
41
42          // use the Iterator to get each BookBean and create
43          // a link to each book
44          while ( iterator.hasNext() ) {
45              currentBook = ( BookBean ) iterator.next();
46
47      %> <%-- end scriptlet to insert literal XHTML and --%>
48          <%-- JSP expressions output from this loop      --%>
49
50              <%-- link to a book's information --%>
51              <span class = "bold">
```

Fig. 11.7   JSP **books.jsp** returns to the client an XHTML document containing the book list (part 1 of 2).

```
52                      <a href =
53                         "displayBook?isbn=<%= currentBook.getISBN() %>">
54
55                         <%= currentBook.getTitle() + ", " +
56                            currentBook.getEditionNumber() + "e" %>
57                      </a>
58                   </span><br />
59
60        <% // continue scriptlet
61
62           }    // end while loop
63
64        %> <%-- end scriptlet --%>
65
66        </p>
67   </body>
68
69   </html>
```

Fig. 11.7   JSP **books.jsp** returns to the client an XHTML document containing the book list (part 2 of 2).

The scriptlet begins at line 31. Line 32 creates a **TitlesBean**, and line 33 invokes its **getTitles** method to obtain the **List** of **BookBean** objects. Line 37 sets a **titles** session attribute to store the **List** for use later in the client's session. Line 40 obtains an

Iterator for the **List**. Lines 44–45 begin a loop that uses the **Iterator** to output each hyperlink. The scriptlet temporarily terminates here so that lines 51–58 can insert XHTML markup. In this markup, line 53 uses a JSP expression to insert the book's ISBN number as the value in a name/value pair that is passed to the **displayBook** servlet (**BookServlet**) as an argument. Lines 55–56 use another JSP expression to insert the book's title and edition number as the text displayed for the hyperlink. Lines 60–64 continue the scriptlet with the closing curly brace of the **while** loop that started at line 44.

11.5 Viewing a Book's Details

Like many companies, **Bug2Bug.com** is beginning to use XML on its Web site. When the user selects a book in **books.jsp**, **Bug2Bug.com** converts the book's information to XML. **BookServlet** (Fig. 11.8) transforms the XML representation of the book into an XHTML document using XSL style sheet **book.xsl** (Fig. 11.9).

There are two major parts in **BookServlet**'s **doGet** method (lines 24–103). Lines 28–62 locate the **BookBean** for the book selected by the user in **books.jsp**. Lines 65–102 process the XML representation of a book and apply an XSL transformation to that XML.

```
1  // BookServlet.java
2  // Servlet to return one book's information to the client.
3  // The servlet produces XML which is transformed with XSL to
4  // produce the client XHTML page.
5  package com.deitel.advjhtp1.store;
6
7  // Java core packages
8  import java.io.*;
9  import java.util.*;
10
11 // Java extension packages
12 import javax.servlet.*;
13 import javax.servlet.http.*;
14 import javax.xml.parsers.*;
15 import javax.xml.transform.*;
16 import javax.xml.transform.dom.*;
17 import javax.xml.transform.stream.*;
18
19 // third-party packages
20 import org.w3c.dom.*;
21 import org.xml.sax.*;
22
23 public class BookServlet extends HttpServlet {
24    protected void doGet( HttpServletRequest request,
25       HttpServletResponse response )
26       throws ServletException, IOException
27    {
28       HttpSession session = request.getSession( false );
29
```

Fig. 11.8   **BookServlet** obtains the XML representation of a book and applies an XSL transformation to output an XHTML document as the response to the client (part 1 of 4).

```
30          // RequestDispatcher to forward client to bookstore home
31          // page if no session exists or no books are selected
32          RequestDispatcher dispatcher =
33             request.getRequestDispatcher( "/index.html" );
34
35          // if session does not exist, forward to index.html
36          if ( session == null )
37             dispatcher.forward( request, response );
38
39          // get books from session object
40          List titles =
41             ( List ) session.getAttribute( "titles" );
42
43          // locate BookBean object for selected book
44          Iterator iterator = titles.iterator();
45          BookBean book = null;
46
47          String isbn = request.getParameter( "isbn" );
48
49          while ( iterator.hasNext() ) {
50             book = ( BookBean ) iterator.next();
51
52             if ( isbn.equals( book.getISBN() ) ) {
53
54                // save the book in a session attribute
55                session.setAttribute( "bookToAdd", book );
56                break;  // isbn matches current book
57             }
58          }
59
60          // if book is not in list, forward to index.html
61          if ( book == null )
62             dispatcher.forward( request, response );
63
64          // get XML document and transform for browser client
65          try {
66             // get a DocumentBuilderFactory for creating
67             // a DocumentBuilder (i.e., an XML parser)
68             DocumentBuilderFactory factory =
69                DocumentBuilderFactory.newInstance();
70
71             // get a DocumentBuilder for building the DOM tree
72             DocumentBuilder builder =
73                factory.newDocumentBuilder();
74
75             // create a new Document (empty DOM tree)
76             Document messageDocument = builder.newDocument();
77
78             // get XML from BookBean and append to Document
79             Element bookElement = book.getXML( messageDocument );
80             messageDocument.appendChild( bookElement );
```

Fig. 11.8　BookServlet obtains the XML representation of a book and applies
an XSL transformation to output an XHTML document as the response to
the client (part 2 of 4).

```
81
82            // get PrintWriter for writing data to client
83            response.setContentType( "text/html" );
84            PrintWriter out = response.getWriter();
85
86            // open InputStream for XSL document
87            InputStream xslStream =
88               getServletContext().getResourceAsStream(
89                  "/book.xsl" );
90
91            // transform XML document using XSLT
92            transform( messageDocument, xslStream, out );
93
94            // flush and close PrintWriter
95            out.flush();
96            out.close();
97         }
98
99         // catch XML parser exceptions
100        catch ( ParserConfigurationException pcException ) {
101           pcException.printStackTrace();
102        }
103     }
104
105     // transform XML document using provided XSLT InputStream
106     // and write resulting document to provided PrintWriter
107     private void transform( Document document,
108        InputStream xslStream, PrintWriter output )
109     {
110        try {
111           // create DOMSource for source XML document
112           Source xmlSource = new DOMSource( document );
113
114           // create StreamSource for XSLT document
115           Source xslSource =
116              new StreamSource( xslStream );
117
118           // create StreamResult for transformation result
119           Result result = new StreamResult( output );
120
121           // create TransformerFactory to obtain a Transformer
122           TransformerFactory transformerFactory =
123              TransformerFactory.newInstance();
124
125           // create Transformer for performing XSL transformation
126           Transformer transformer =
127              transformerFactory.newTransformer( xslSource );
128
129           // perform transformation and deliver content to client
130           transformer.transform( xmlSource, result );
131        }
```

Fig. 11.8 BookServlet obtains the XML representation of a book and applies an XSL transformation to output an XHTML document as the response to the client (part 3 of 4).

```
132
133          // handle exception when transforming XML document
134          catch ( TransformerException transformerException ) {
135             transformerException.printStackTrace( System.err );
136          }
137       }
138 }
```

Fig. 11.8 BookServlet obtains the XML representation of a book and applies an XSL transformation to output an XHTML document as the response to the client (part 4 of 4).

Line 28 obtains the **HttpSession** object for the current client. This object contains a session attribute indicating the book selected by the user in **books.jsp**. Lines 32–33 obtain a *RequestDispatcher* for the **"/index.html"** document by calling **ServletRequest** method **getRequestDispatcher**. A **RequestDispatcher** (package **javax.servlet**) provides two methods—*forward* and *include*—that enable a servlet to forward a client request to another resource or include content from another resource in a servlet's response. In this example, if there is no session object for the current client (lines 36–37) or if there is no book selected (lines 61–62), the request is forwarded back to the **index.html** home page of our bookstore. Methods **forward** and **include** each take two arguments—the **HttpServletRequest** and **HttpServletResponse** objects for the current request.

Note that **RequestDispatcher** objects can be obtained with method **getRequestDispatcher** from an object that implements interface **ServletRequest** or from the **ServletContext** with methods **getRequestDispatcher** or **getNamedDispatcher**. **ServletContext** method **getNamedDispatcher** receives the name of a servlet as an argument, then searches the **ServletContext** for a servlet by that name. If no such servlet is found, the method returns **null**. Both the **ServletRequest** and the **ServletContext getRequestDispatcher** methods simply return to the client browser the content of the specified path if the path does not represent a servlet.

Lines 40–41 get the **List** of **BookBean**s from the session object. Lines 44–58 perform a linear search to locate the **BookBean** for the selected book. (Note: For larger databases, it would be more appropriate to use a **Map** rather than a **List**.) The ISBN number for that book is stored in an **isbn** parameter passed to the servlet (retrieved at line 47). If the **BookBean** is found, line 55 sets session attribute **bookToAdd** with that **BookBean** as the attribute's value. **AddToCartServlet** (Fig. 11.10) uses this attribute to update the shopping cart.

The **try** block (lines 65–97) performs the XML and XSL processing that result in an XHTML document containing a single book's information. Before the XML and XSL capabilities can be used, you must download and install Sun's *Java API for XML Parsing* (*JAXP*) version 1.1 from **java.sun.com/xml/download.htm**. The root directory of JAXP (**jaxp-1.1**) contains three JAR files—**crimson.jar**, **jaxp.jar** and **xalan.jar**—that are required for compiling and running programs that use JAXP. These files must be added to the Java extension mechanism for your Java 2 Standard Edition installation. Place a *copy* of these files in your Java installation's extensions directory (**jre/lib/ext** on Linux/UNIX, and **jre\lib\ext** on Windows).

Software Engineering Observation 11.1

JAXP 1.1 is part of the J2EE 1.3 reference implementation.

Creating a Document Object Model (DOM) tree from an XML document requires a **DocumentBuilder** parser object. **DocumentBuilder** objects are obtained from a **DocumentBuilderFactory**. Lines 68–69 obtain a **DocumentBuilderFactory**. Lines 72–73 obtain a **DocumentBuilder** parser object that enables the program to create a **Document** object tree in which the XML document elements are represented as **Element** objects. Line 76 uses the **DocumentBuilder** object to create a new **Document**. Line 79 invokes the **BookBean**'s **getXML** method to obtain an **Element** representation of the book. Line 80 appends this **Element** to **messageDocument** (the **Document** object). Classes **DocumentBuilderFactory** and **DocumentBuilder** are located in package **javax.xml.parsers**. Classes **Document** and **Element** are located in package **org.w3c.dom**. [*Note*: For detailed information on XML, see Appendices A–D.]

Next, line 83 specifies the response content type, and line 84 obtains a **PrintWriter** to output the response to the client. Lines 87–89 create an **InputStream** that will be used by the XSL transformation processor to read the XSL file. The response is created by the XSL transformation performed in method **transform** (lines 107–137). We pass three arguments to this method—the XML **Document** to which the XSL transformation will be applied (**messageDocument**), the **InputStream** that reads the XSL file (**xslStream**) and the target stream to which the results should be written (**out**). The output target can be one of several types, including a character stream (i.e., the **response** object's **PrintWriter** in this example).

Line 112 creates a **DOMSource** that represents the XML document. This serves as the source of the XML to transform. Lines 115–116 create a **StreamSource** for the XSL file. This serves as the source of the XSL that transforms the **DOMSource**. Line 119 creates a **StreamResult** for the **PrintWriter** to which the results of the XSL transformation are written. Lines 122–123 create a **TransformerFactory** with **static** method **newInstance**. This object enables the program to obtain a **Transformer** object that applies the XSL transformation. Lines 126–127 create a **Transformer** using **TransformerFactory** method **newTransformer**, which receives a **StreamSource** argument representing the XSL (**xslSource** in this example). Line 130 invokes **Transformer** method **transform** to perform the XSL transformation on the given **DOMSource** object (**xmlSource**) and writes the result to the given **StreamResult** object (**result**). Lines 134–136 catch a **TransformerException** if a problem occurs when creating the **TransformerFactory**, creating the **Transformer** or performing the transformation.

Figure 11.9 contains the **book.xsl** style sheet file used in the XSL transformation. The values of six elements in the XML document are placed in the resulting XHTML document. Lines 23 and 30 place the book's **title** in the document's **title** element and in a paragraph at the beginning of the document's **body** element, respectively. Line 36 specifies an **img** element in which the value of the **imageFile** element of an XML document specifies the name of the file representing the book's cover image. Line 37 specifies the **alt** attribute of the **img** element using the book's **title**. Lines 43, 51, 59 and 67 place the book's **price**, **isbn**, **editionNumber** and **copyright** in table cells. The resulting XHTML document is shown in the screen capture at the end of Fig. 11.9. For more details on XSL, refer to Appendix D.

```
1   <?xml version = "1.0"?>
2
3   <xsl:stylesheet xmlns:xsl = "http://www.w3.org/1999/XSL/Transform"
4      version = "1.0">
5
6   <xsl:output method = "xml" omit-xml-declaration = "no"
7      indent = "yes" doctype-system =
8      "http://www.w3.org/TR/xhtml11/DTD/xhtml1-strict.dtd"
9      doctype-public = "-//W3C//DTD XHTML 1.0 Strict//EN"/>
10
11  <!-- book.xsl                                          -->
12  <!-- XSL document that transforms XML into XHTML -->
13
14  <!-- specify the root of the XML document -->
15  <!-- that references this stylesheet       -->
16  <xsl:template match = "product">
17
18     <html xmlns = "http://www.w3.org/1999/xhtml">
19
20     <head>
21
22        <!-- obtain book title from JSP to place in title -->
23        <title><xsl:value-of select = "title"/></title>
24
25        <link rel = "stylesheet" href = "styles.css"
26           type = "text/css" />
27     </head>
28
29     <body>
30        <p class = "bigFont"><xsl:value-of select = "title"/></p>
31
32        <table>
33           <tr>
34              <!-- create table cell for product image -->
35              <td rowspan = "5">  <!-- cell spans 5 rows -->
36                 <img border = "thin solid black" src =
37                    "images/{ imageFile }" alt = "{ title }" />
38              </td>
39
40              <!-- create table cells for price in row 1 -->
41              <td class = "bold">Price:</td>
42
43              <td><xsl:value-of select = "price"/></td>
44           </tr>
```

Fig. 11.9 XSL style sheet (**books.xsl**) that transforms a book's XML representation into an XHTML document (part 1 of 3).

```
45
46             <tr>
47
48                 <!-- create table cells for ISBN in row 2 -->
49                 <td class = "bold">ISBN #:</td>
50
51                 <td><xsl:value-of select = "isbn"/></td>
52             </tr>
53
54             <tr>
55
56                 <!-- create table cells for edition in row 3 -->
57                 <td class = "bold">Edition:</td>
58
59                 <td><xsl:value-of select = "editionNumber"/></td>
60             </tr>
61
62             <tr>
63
64                 <!-- create table cells for copyright in row 4 -->
65                 <td class = "bold">Copyright:</td>
66
67                 <td><xsl:value-of select = "copyright"/></td>
68             </tr>
69
70             <tr>
71
72                 <!-- create Add to Cart button in row 5 -->
73                 <td>
74                     <form method = "post" action = "addToCart">
75                         <input type = "submit" value = "Add to Cart" />
76                     </form>
77                 </td>
78
79                 <!-- create View Cart button in row 5 -->
80                 <td>
81                     <form method = "get" action = "viewCart.jsp">
82                         <input type = "submit" value = "View Cart" />
83                     </form>
84                 </td>
85             </tr>
86         </table>
87
88     </body>
89
90     </html>
91
92 </xsl:template>
93
94 </xsl:stylesheet>
```

Fig. 11.9   XSL style sheet (**books.xsl**) that transforms a book's XML representation into an XHTML document (part 2 of 3).

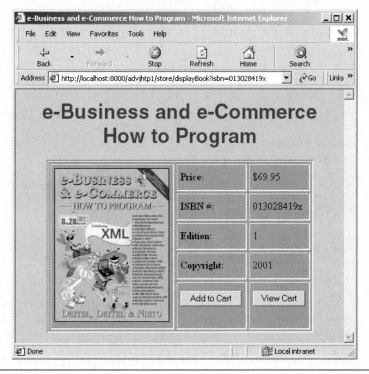

Fig. 11.9 XSL style sheet (**books.xsl**) that transforms a book's XML representation into an XHTML document (part 3 of 3).

11.6 Adding an Item to the Shopping Cart

When the user clicks the **Add to Cart** button in the XHTML document produced in the last section, the **AddToCartServlet** (aliased as **addToCart**) updates the shopping cart. If the cart does not exist, the servlet creates a shopping cart (a **HashMap** in this example). Items in the shopping cart are represented with **CartItemBean** objects. An instance of this JavaBean maintains a **BookBean** and the current quantity for that book in the shopping cart. When the user adds an item to the cart, if that item already is represented in the cart with a **CartItemBean**, the quantity of that item is updated in the bean. Otherwise, the servlet creates a new **CartItemBean** with a quantity of 1. After updating the cart, the user is forwarded to **viewCart.jsp** to view the current cart contents.

Class **CartItemBean** (Fig. 11.10) stores a **BookBean** and a quantity for that book. It maintains the **BookBean** as a read-only property of the bean and the **quantity** as a read–write property of the bean.

```
1   // CartItemBean.java
2   // Class that maintains a book and its quantity.
3   package com.deitel.advjhtp1.store;
```

Fig. 11.10 CartItemBeans contain a **BookBean** and the **quantity** of a book in the shopping cart (part 1 of 2).

```
4
5    import java.io.*;
6
7    public class CartItemBean implements Serializable {
8        private BookBean book;
9        private int quantity;
10
11       // initialize a CartItemBean
12       public CartItemBean( BookBean bookToAdd, int number )
13       {
14           book = bookToAdd;
15           quantity = number;
16       }
17
18       // get the book (this is a read-only property)
19       public BookBean getBook()
20       {
21           return book;
22       }
23
24       // set the quantity
25       public void setQuantity( int number )
26       {
27           quantity = number;
28       }
29
30       // get the quantity
31       public int getQuantity()
32       {
33           return quantity;
34       }
35   }
```

Fig. 11.10 CartItemBeans contain a BookBean and the quantity of a book in the shopping cart (part 2 of 2).

Class **AddToCartServlet** is shown in Fig. 11.11. The **AddToCartServlet**'s **doPost** method obtains the **HttpSession** object for the current client (line 18). If a session does not exist for this client, a **RequestDispatcher** forwards the request to the bookstore home page **index.html** (lines 22–26). Otherwise, line 29 obtains the value of session attribute **cart**—the **Map** that represents the shopping cart. Lines 30–31 obtain the value of session attribute **bookToAdd**—the **BookBean** representing the book to add to the shopping cart. If the shopping cart does not exist, lines 34–39 create a new **HashMap** to store the cart contents, then place the **HashMap** in the **"cart"** attribute of the **session** object. Lines 42–43 attempt to locate the **CartItemBean** for the book being added to the cart. If one exists, line 48 increments the quantity for that **CartItemBean**. Otherwise, line 50 creates a new **CartItemBean** with a quantity of 1 and puts it into the shopping cart (**Map cart**). Then lines 53–55 create a **RequestDispatcher** for JSP **viewCart.jsp** and **forward** the processing of the request to that JSP, so it can display the cart contents.

```
1   // AddToCartServlet.java
2   // Servlet to add a book to the shopping cart.
3   package com.deitel.advjhtp1.store;
4
5   // Java core packages
6   import java.io.*;
7   import java.util.*;
8
9   // Java extension packages
10  import javax.servlet.*;
11  import javax.servlet.http.*;
12
13  public class AddToCartServlet extends HttpServlet {
14     protected void doPost( HttpServletRequest request,
15        HttpServletResponse response )
16        throws ServletException, IOException
17     {
18        HttpSession session = request.getSession( false );
19        RequestDispatcher dispatcher;
20
21        // if session does not exist, forward to index.html
22        if ( session == null ) {
23           dispatcher =
24              request.getRequestDispatcher( "/index.html" );
25           dispatcher.forward( request, response );
26        }
27
28        // session exists, get cart Map and book to add
29        Map cart = ( Map ) session.getAttribute( "cart" );
30        BookBean book =
31           ( BookBean ) session.getAttribute( "bookToAdd" );
32
33        // if cart does not exist, create it
34        if ( cart == null ) {
35           cart = new HashMap();
36
37           // update the cart attribute
38           session.setAttribute( "cart", cart );
39        }
40
41        // determine if book is in cart
42        CartItemBean cartItem =
43           ( CartItemBean ) cart.get( book.getISBN() );
44
45        // If book is already in cart, update its quantity.
46        // Otherwise, create an entry in the cart.
47        if ( cartItem != null )
48           cartItem.setQuantity( cartItem.getQuantity() + 1 );
49        else
50           cart.put( book.getISBN(), new CartItemBean( book, 1 ) );
51
```

Fig. 11.11 `AddToCartServlet` places an item in the shopping cart and invokes `viewCart.jsp` to display the cart contents (part 1 of 2).

```
52          // send the user to viewCart.jsp
53          dispatcher =
54             request.getRequestDispatcher( "/viewCart.jsp" );
55          dispatcher.forward( request, response );
56       }
57    }
```

Fig. 11.11 **AddToCartServlet** places an item in the shopping cart and invokes **viewCart.jsp** to display the cart contents (part 2 of 2).

11.7 Viewing the Shopping Cart

JSP **viewCart.jsp** (Fi. 11.12) extracts the **CartItemBean**s from the shopping cart, subtotals each item in the cart, totals all the items in the cart and creates an XHTML document that allows the client to view the cart in tabular format. This JSP uses classes from our bookstore package (**com.deitel.advjhtp1.store**) and from packages **java.util** and **java.text**.

The scriptlet at lines 25–43 begins by retrieving the session attribute for the shopping cart **Map** (line 26). If there is no shopping cart, the JSP simply outputs a message indicating that the cart is empty. Otherwise, lines 34–41 create the variables used to obtain the information that is displayed in the resulting XHTML document. In particular, line 34 obtains the **Set** of keys in **Map cart**. These keys are used to retrieve the **CartItemBean**'s that represent each book in the cart.

Lines 45–51 output the literal XHTML markup that begins the table that appears in the document. Lines 55–63 continue the scriptlet with a loop that uses each key in the **Map** to obtain the corresponding **CartItemBean**, extracts the data from that bean, calculates the dollar subtotal for that product and calculates the dollar total of all products so far. The last part of the loop body appears outside the scriptlet at lines 70–86, in which the preceding data is formatted into a row in the XHTML table. JSP expressions are used to place each data value into the appropriate table cell. After the loop completes (line 90), lines 95–100 output the dollar total of all items in the cart and line 105 sets a session attribute containing the total. This value is used by **process.jsp** (Fig. 11.14) to display the dollar total as part of the order-processing confirmation. Line 101 outputs the dollar total of all items in the cart as the last row in the XHTML table.

```
1    <?xml version = "1.0"?>
2    <!DOCTYPE html PUBLIC "-//W3C//DTD XHTML 1.0 Strict//EN"
3       "http://www.w3.org/TR/xhtml1/DTD/xhtml1-strict.dtd">
4    <!-- viewCart.jsp -->
5
6    <%-- JSP page settings --%>
7    <%@ page language = "java" session = "true" %>
8    <%@ page import = "com.deitel.advjhtp1.store.*" %>
9    <%@ page import = "java.util.*" %>
10   <%@ page import = "java.text.*" %>
11
```

Fig. 11.12 JSP **viewCart.jsp** obtains the shopping cart and outputs an XHTML document with the cart contents in tabular format (part 1 of 4).

```
12   <html xmlns = "http://www.w3.org/1999/xhtml">
13
14   <head>
15      <title>Shopping Cart</title>
16
17      <link rel = "stylesheet" href = "styles.css"
18         type = "text/css" />
19   </head>
20
21   <body>
22      <p class = "bigFont">Shopping Cart</p>
23
24   <%-- start scriptlet to display shopping cart contents --%>
25   <%
26      Map cart = ( Map ) session.getAttribute( "cart" );
27      double total = 0;
28
29      if ( cart == null || cart.size() == 0 )
30         out.println( "<p>Shopping cart is currently empty.</p>" );
31      else {
32
33         // create variables used in display of cart
34         Set cartItems = cart.keySet();
35         Iterator iterator = cartItems.iterator();
36
37         BookBean book;
38         CartItemBean cartItem;
39
40         int quantity;
41         double price, subtotal;
42
43   %> <%-- end scriptlet for literal XHTML output --%>
44
45      <table>
46         <thead><tr>
47            <th>Product</th>
48            <th>Quantity</th>
49            <th>Price</th>
50            <th>Total</th>
51         </tr></thead>
52
53   <% // continue scriptlet
54
55         while ( iterator.hasNext() ) {
56
57            // get book data; calculate subtotal and total
58            cartItem = ( CartItemBean ) cart.get( iterator.next() );
59            book = cartItem.getBook();
60            quantity = cartItem.getQuantity();
61            price = book.getPrice();
62            subtotal = quantity * price;
63            total += subtotal;
```

Fig. 11.12 JSP **viewCart.jsp** obtains the shopping cart and outputs an XHTML
document with the cart contents in tabular format (part 2 of 4).

```
64
65   %> <%-- end scriptlet for literal XHTML and    --%>
66      <%-- JSP expressions output from this loop --%>
67
68            <%-- display table row of book title, quantity, --%>
69            <%-- price and subtotal --%>
70            <tr>
71               <td><%= book.getTitle() %></td>
72
73               <td><%= quantity %></td>
74
75               <td class = "right">
76                  <%=
77                     new DecimalFormat( "0.00" ).format( price )
78                  %>
79               </td>
80
81               <td class = "bold right">
82                  <%=
83                     new DecimalFormat( "0.00" ).format( subtotal )
84                  %>
85               </td>
86            </tr>
87
88   <% // continue scriptlet
89
90         } // end of while loop
91
92   %> <%-- end scriptlet for literal XHTML and    --%>
93
94      <%-- display table row containing shopping cart total --%>
95      <tr>
96         <td colspan = "4" class = "bold right">Total:
97            <%= new DecimalFormat( "0.00" ).format( total ) %>
98         </td>
99      </tr>
100   </table>
101
102  <% // continue scriptlet
103
104      // make current total a session attribute
105      session.setAttribute( "total", new Double( total ) );
106   } // end of else
107
108  %> <%-- end scriptlet --%>
109
110   <!-- link back to books.jsp to continue shopping -->
111   <p class = "bold green">
112      <a href = "books.jsp">Continue Shopping</a>
113   </p>
114
```

Fig. 11.12 JSP **viewCart.jsp** obtains the shopping cart and outputs an XHTML document with the cart contents in tabular format (part 3 of 4).

```
115     <!-- form to proceed to checkout -->
116     <form method = "get" action = "order.html">
117         <p><input type = "submit" value = "Check Out" /></p>
118     </form>
119 </body>
120
121 </html>
```

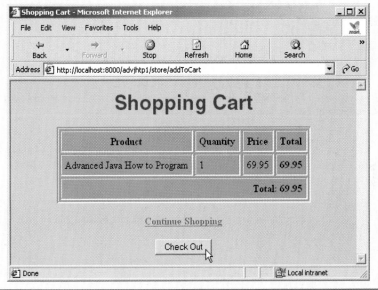

Fig. 11.12 JSP `viewCart.jsp` obtains the shopping cart and outputs an XHTML document with the cart contents in tabular format (part 4 of 4).

From the XHTML document produced in this JSP, the user can either continue shopping or click the **Check Out** button to proceed to the `order.html` ordering page (Fig. 11.13).

11.8 Checking Out

When viewing the cart, the user can click a **Check Out** button to view `order.html` (Fig. 11.13). In this example, the form has no functionality. However, it is provided to help complete the application. Normally, there would be some client-side validation of the form elements, some server-side validation of form elements or a combination of both. When the user clicks the **Submit** button, the browser requests `process.jsp` to finalize the order.

```
1   <?xml version = "1.0"?>
2   <!DOCTYPE html PUBLIC "-//W3C//DTD XHTML 1.0 Strict//EN"
3       "http://www.w3.org/TR/xhtml1/DTD/xhtml1-strict.dtd">
4   <!-- order.html -->
```

Fig. 11.13 Order form (`order.html`) in which the user inputs name, address and credit-card information to complete an order (part 1 of 4).

```
5
6   <html xmlns = "http://www.w3.org/1999/xhtml">
7
8   <head>
9      <title>Order</title>
10
11     <link rel = "stylesheet" href = "styles.css"
12        type = "text/css" />
13  </head>
14
15  <body>
16     <p class = "bigFont">Shopping Cart Check Out</p>
17
18     <!-- Form to input user information and credit card.    -->
19     <!-- Note: No need to input real data in this example. -->
20     <form method = "post" action = "process.jsp">
21
22        <p style = "font-weight: bold">
23           Please input the following information.</p>
24
25        <!-- table of form elements -->
26        <table>
27           <tr>
28              <td class = "right bold">First name:</td>
29
30              <td>
31                 <input type = "text" name = "firstname"
32                    size = "25" />
33              </td>
34           </tr>
35
36           <tr>
37              <td class = "right bold">Last name:</td>
38
39              <td>
40                 <input type = "text" name = "lastname"
41                    size = "25" />
42              </td>
43           </tr>
44
45           <tr>
46              <td class = "right bold">Street:</td>
47
48              <td>
49                 <input type = "text" name = "street" size = "25" />
50              </td>
51           </tr>
52
53           <tr>
54              <td class = "right bold">City:</td>
55
```

Fig. 11.13 Order form (`order.html`) in which the user inputs name, address and credit-card information to complete an order (part 2 of 4).

```
56                     <td>
57                        <input type = "text" name = "city" size = "25" />
58                     </td>
59                  </tr>
60
61                  <tr>
62                     <td class = "right bold">State:</td>
63
64                     <td>
65                        <input type = "text" name = "state" size = "2" />
66                     </td>
67                  </tr>
68
69                  <tr>
70                     <td class = "right bold">Zip code:</td>
71
72                     <td>
73                        <input type = "text" name = "zipcode"
74                           size = "10" />
75                     </td>
76                  </tr>
77
78                  <tr>
79                     <td class = "right bold">Phone #:</td>
80
81                     <td>
82                        (
83                           <input type = "text" name = "phone" size = "3" />
84                        )
85
86                        <input type = "text" name = "phone2"
87                              size = "3" /> -
88
89                        <input type = "text" name = "phone3" size = "4" />
90                     </td>
91                  </tr>
92
93                  <tr>
94                     <td class = "right bold">Credit Card #:</td>
95
96                     <td>
97                        <input type = "text" name = "creditcard"
98                           size = "25" />
99                     </td>
100                 </tr>
101
102                 <tr>
103                    <td class = "right bold">Expiration (mm/yy):</td>
104
105                    <td>
106                       <input type = "text" name = "expires"
107                          size = "2" /> /
```

Fig. 11.13 Order form (`order.html`) in which the user inputs name, address and credit-card information to complete an order (part 3 of 4).

```
108
109                     <input type = "text" name = "expires2"
110                        size = "2" />
111                 </td>
112             </tr>
113         </table>
114
115         <!-- enable user to submit the form   -->
116         <p><input type = "submit" value = "Submit" /></p>
117     </form>
118 </body>
119
120 </html>
```

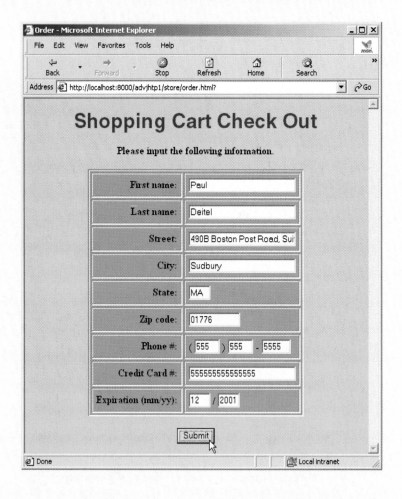

Fig. 11.13 Order form (`order.html`) in which the user inputs name, address and credit-card information to complete an order (part 4 of 4).

11.9 Processing the Order

JSP **process.jsp** (Fig. 11.14) pretends to process the user's credit-card information and creates an XHTML document containing a message that the order was processed and the final order dollar total. The scriptlet at lines 19–28 obtains the session attribute **total**. The **Double** object returned is converted to a **double** and stored in Java variable **total**. Our simulation of a bookstore does not perform real credit-card processing, so the transaction is now complete. Therefore, line 26 invokes **HttpSession** method **invalidate** to discard the session object for the current client. In a real store, the session would not be invalidated until the purchase is confirmed by the credit-card company. Lines 30–40 define the body of the XHTML document sent to the client. Line 37 uses a JSP expression to insert the dollar total of all items purchased.

```
1   <?xml version = "1.0"?>
2   <!DOCTYPE html PUBLIC "-//W3C//DTD XHTML 1.0 Strict//EN"
3      "http://www.w3.org/TR/xhtml1/DTD/xhtml1-strict.dtd">
4   <!-- process.jsp -->
5
6   <%-- JSP page settings --%>
7   <%@ page language = "java" session = "true" %>
8   <%@ page import = "java.text.*" %>
9
10  <html xmlns = "http://www.w3.org/1999/xhtml">
11
12  <head>
13     <title>Thank You!</title>
14
15     <link rel = "stylesheet" href = "styles.css"
16        type = "text/css" />
17  </head>
18
19  <% // start scriptlet
20
21     // get total order amount
22     Double d = ( Double ) session.getAttribute( "total" );
23     double total = d.doubleValue();
24
25     // invalidate session because processing is complete
26     session.invalidate();
27
28  %> <%-- end scriptlet --%>
29
30  <body>
31     <p class = "bigFont">Thank You</p>
32
33     <p>Your order has been processed.</p>
34
35     <p>Your credit card has been billed:
36        <span class = "bold">
37           $<%= new DecimalFormat( "0.00" ).format( total ) %>
38        </span>
```

Fig. 11.14 JSP **process.jsp** performs the final order processing (part 1 of 2).

```
39        </p>
40    </body>
41
42    </html>
```

Fig. 11.14 JSP `process.jsp` performs the final order processing (part 2 of 2).

11.10 Deploying the Bookstore Application in J2EE 1.2.1

Next, we deploy the bookstore application in the Java 2 Enterprise Edition 1.2.1 reference implementation. This section assumes that you have downloaded and installed J2EE 1.2.1. If not, please refer to Appendix E for installation and configuration instructions. Note that the files for this entire bookstore application can be found on the CD that accompanies this book and at **www.deitel.com**.

In Section 11.10.1 through Section 11.10.8, we demonstrate the steps needed to deploy this application:

1. Configure the **books** data source for use with the J2EE 1.2.1 reference implementation server.

2. Launch the Cloudscape database server and the J2EE 1.2.1 reference implementation server for deployment and execution of the application.

3. Launch the **Application Deployment Tool**. This tool provides a graphical user interface for deploying applications on the J2EE 1.2.1 server.

4. Create a new application in the **Application Deployment Tool**.

5. Add library JAR files to the application. These files are available to all application components.

6. Create a new Web component in the application for the **BookServlet**.

7. Create a new Web component in the application for the **AddToCartServlet**.

8. Add the nonservlet components to the application. These include XHTML documents, JSPs, images, CSS files, XSL files and JavaBeans used in the application.

9. Specify the Web context that causes this J2EE application to execute. This determines the URL that will be used to invoke the application.

10. Specify the database resource (i.e., **books**) used by our application.

11. Set up the JNDI name for the database in the application. This is used to register the name with the Java Naming and Directory Service so the database can be located at execution time.

12. Set up the *welcome file* for the application. This is the initial file that is returned when the user invokes the bookstore application.

13. Deploy the application.

14. Run the application.

At the end of Section 11.10.8, you will be able to deploy and test the bookstore application.

11.10.1 Configuring the **books** Data Source

Before deploying the bookstore application, you must configure the **books** data source so the J2EE server registers the data source with the naming server. This enables the application to use JNDI to locate the data source at execution time. J2EE comes with Cloudscape—a pure-Java database application from Informix Software. We use Cloudscape to perform our database manipulations in this case study.

To configure the Cloudscape data source, you must modify the J2EE default configuration file **default.properties** in the J2EE installation's **config** directory. Below the comment **JDBC URL Examples** is a line that begins with **jdbc.datasources**. Append the following text to this line

> **|jdbc/books|jdbc:cloudscape:rmi:books;create=true**

The vertical bar, **|**, at the beginning of the text separates the new data source we are registering from a data source that is registered by default when you install J2EE. The text **jdbc/books** is the JNDI name for the database. After the second **|** character in the preceding text is the JDBC URL **jdbc:cloudscape:rmi:books**. The URL indicates that the J2EE will use the JDBC protocol to interact with the Cloudscape subprotocol, which, in turn, uses RMI to communicate with the database (**books** in this case). Finally, **create=true** specifies that J2EE should create a database if the database does not already exist. [Remember, that the **books** database was created in Chapter 8.] After configuring the database, save the **default.properties** file. This completes *Step 1* of Section 11.10.

Portability Tip 11.2

Each database driver typically has its own URL format that enables an application to interact with databases hosted on that database server. See your database server's documentation for more information.

11.10.2 Launching the Cloudscape Database and J2EE Servers

Step 2 of Section 11.10 specifies that you must launch the Cloudscape database server and the J2EE server, so you can deploy and execute the application. First, open a command prompt (or shell) and launch the Cloudscape server as discussed in Section 8.5. Next, open a command prompt (or shell) and change directories to the **bin** subdirectory of your J2EE installation. Then, issue the following command:

```
j2ee -verbose
```

to start the J2EE server. Note that the J2EE server includes the Tomcat JSP and servlet container discussed in Chapter 9.

Portability Tip 11.3

On some UNIX/Linux systems, you may need to precede the commands that launch the Cloudscape server and the J2EE server with ./, to indicate that the command is located in the current directory.

Testing and Debugging Tip 11.1

Use separate command prompts (or shells) to execute the commands that launch the Cloudscape database server and the J2EE 1.2.1 server, so you can see any error messages generated by these programs.

Testing and Debugging Tip 11.2

To ensure that the J2EE server communicates properly with the Cloudscape server (or any other database server), always launch the database server before the J2EE server. Otherwise, exceptions will occur when the J2EE server attempts to configure its data sources.

To shut down the J2EE server, use a command prompt (or shell) to execute the following command from the **bin** subdirectory of your J2EE installation:

```
j2ee -stop
```

Testing and Debugging Tip 11.3

Always shut down the J2EE server before the Cloudscape database server to ensure that the J2EE server does not attempt to communicate with the Cloudscape database server after the database server has been shut down. If Cloudscape is terminated first, it is possible that the J2EE server will receive another request and attempt to access the database again. This will result in exceptions.

11.10.3 Launching the J2EE Application Deployment Tool

Step 3 of Section 11.10 begins the process of deploying our bookstore application. The J2EE reference implementation comes with a graphical application, called the **Application Deployment Tool**, that helps you deploy Enterprise Java applications. In Chapter 9, we created an XML deployment descriptor by hand to deploy our servlets. The **Application Deployment Tool** is nice in that it writes the deployment descriptor files for you and automatically archives the Web application's components. The tool places all Web application components and auxiliary files for a particular application into a single *Enterprise Application Archive (EAR) file*. This file contains deployment descriptor information, WAR files with Web application components and additional information that is discussed later in the book.

Execute the deployment tool by opening a command prompt (or shell) and changing directories to the **bin** subdirectory of your J2EE installation. Then, type the following command:

```
deploytool
```

The **Application Deployment Tool** window (Fig. 11.15) appears. [*Note:* In our deployment discussion, we cover only those aspects of the deployment tool required to deploy this bookstore application. Later in the book, we discuss other aspects of this tool in detail.]

11.10.4 Creating the Bookstore Application

The **Application Deployment Tool** simplifies the task of deploying Enterprise applications. Next (*Step 4* of Section 11.10), we create the new application. Click the ***New Application*** *button* to display the ***New Application*** *window* (Fig. 11.16).

In the ***Application File Name*** *field*, you can type the name of the EAR file in which the **Application Deployment Tool** stores the application components, or you can click **Browse** to specify both the name and location of the file. In the ***Application Display Name*** *field*, you can specify the name for your application. This name will appear in the **Local Applications** area of the deployment tool's main window (Fig. 11.15). Click **OK** to create the application. The main **Application Deployment Tool** window now appears as shown in Fig. 11.17.

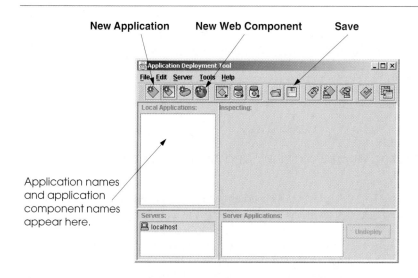

Fig. 11.15 Application Deployment Tool main window.

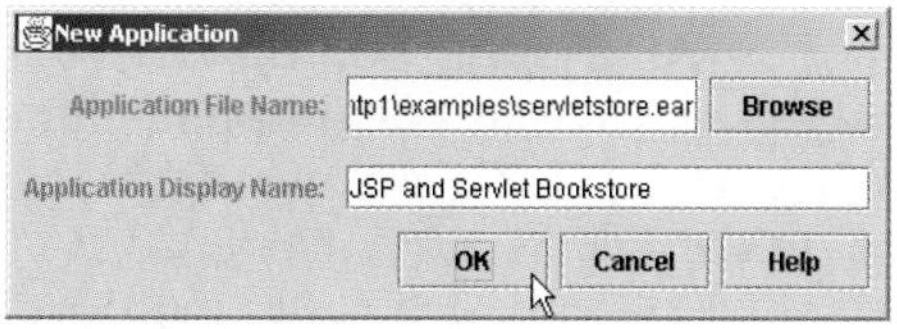

Fig. 11.16 New Application window.

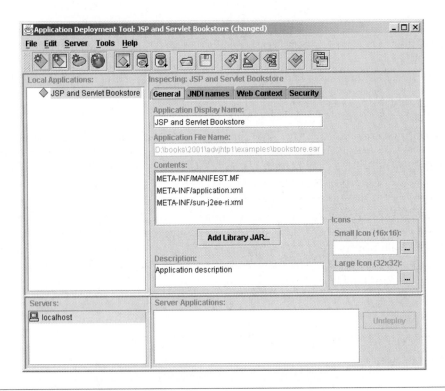

Fig. 11.17 Application Deployment Tool main window after creating a new application.

11.10.5 Creating `BookServlet` and `AddToCartServlet` Web Components

Step 6 of Section 11.10 is to create Web components for the **BookServlet** and the **AddToCartServlet**. This will enable us to specify the alias that is used to invoke each servlet. We will show the details of creating the **BookServlet** Web component. Then, you can repeat the steps to create the **AddToCartServlet** Web component.

To begin, click the **New Web Component** *button* (see Fig. 11.15) to display the **Introduction** *window* of the **New Web Component Wizard** (Fig. 11.18).

Click the **Next >** *button* to display the **WAR File General Properties** (Fig. 11.19) window of the **New Web Component Wizard**.

Ensure that **JSP and Servlet Bookstore** is selected in the **Web Component will Go In:** drop-down list. In the **WAR Display Name** *field*, type a name (**Store Components**) for the WAR that will appear in the **Local Applications** area of the deployment tool's main window (see Fig. 11.15). Then, click the **Add...** *button* to display the **Add Files to .WAR - Add Content Files** *window* (Fig. 11.20). Content files are nonservlet files such as images, XHTML documents, style sheets and JSPs. We will be adding these in another step later, so click **Next >** to proceed to the **Add Files to .WAR - Add Class Files** *window* (Fig. 11.21)

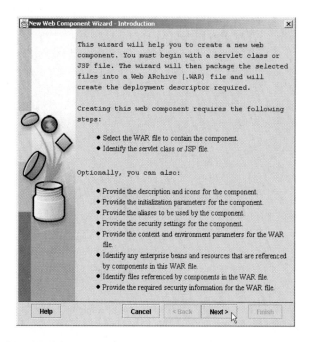

Fig. 11.18 **New Web Component Wizard - Introduction** window.

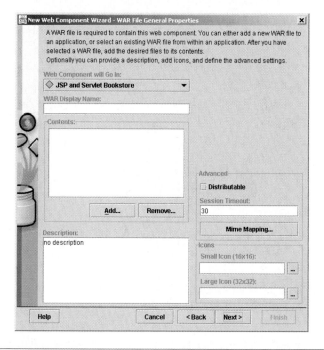

Fig. 11.19 **New Web Component Wizard - WAR File General Properties** window.

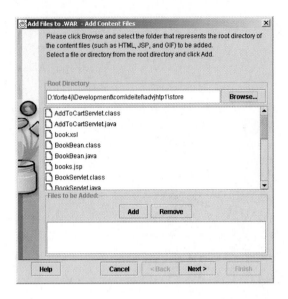

Fig. 11.20 Add Files to .WAR - Add Content Files window.

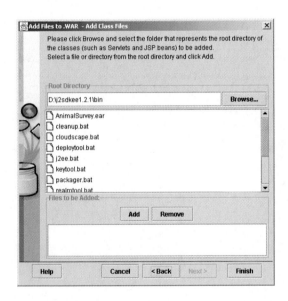

Fig. 11.21 Add Files to .WAR - Add Class Files window.

To add the **BookServlet.class** file, click the ***Browse...*** *button* to display the ***Choose Root Directory*** *window* (Fig. 11.22).

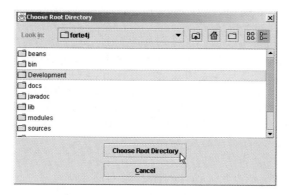

Fig. 11.22 Choose Root Directory window.

When adding a class file for a class in a package (as all classes are in this example), it is imperative that the files be added and maintained in their full package directory structure or as part of a JAR file that contains the full package directory structure. In this example, we did not create a JAR file containing the entire **com.deitel.advjhtp1.store** package. Therefore, we need to locate the directory in which the first package directory name is found.

On our system, the **com** directory that starts the package name is located in a directory called **Development**. When you click the **Choose Root Directory** *button*, you are returned to the **Add Files to .WAR - Add Class Files** window. In that window, you should be able to locate the **com** directory (Fig. 11.23).

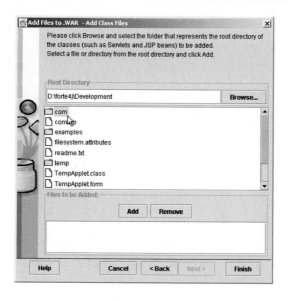

Fig. 11.23 Add Files to .WAR - Add Class Files window after selecting the root directory in which the files are located.

Double click the **com** directory name to expand its contents in the window. Do the same for the subdirectory **deitel**, then the subdirectory **advjhtp1** and finally, for the directory **store**. In the **store** directory, select the **.class** file for **BookServlet**, then click the **Add** button. At the bottom of the **Add Files to .WAR - Add Class Files** window, the **.class** file should be displayed with its full package directory structure. After doing this, click the **Finish** button to return to the **New Web Component Wizard - WAR File General Properties** window. Note that the files selected with the **Add Files to .WAR** window now appear in the **Contents** text area of the window (Fig. 11.24).

Common Programming Error 11.1

Not including the full package directory structure for a class in a package will prevent the application from loading the class and from executing properly.

Click **Next >** to proceed to the **New Web Component Wizard - Choose Component Type** *window* and select **Servlet** (Fig. 11.25).

Click **Next >** to proceed to the **New Web Component Wizard - Component General Properties** *window* (Fig. 11.26). Select the **BookServlet** class in the **Servlet Class** *drop-down list* and type **Book Servlet** in the **Web Component Display Name** *field*.

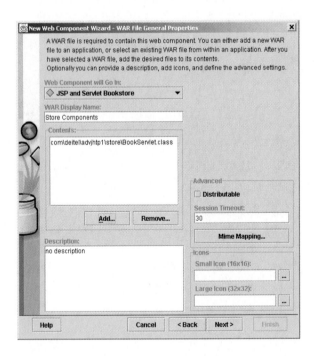

Fig. 11.24 **New Web Component Wizard - WAR File General Properties** window after selecting the file **BookServlet.class**.

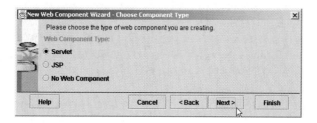

Fig. 11.25 New Web Component Wizard - **Choose Component Type** window.

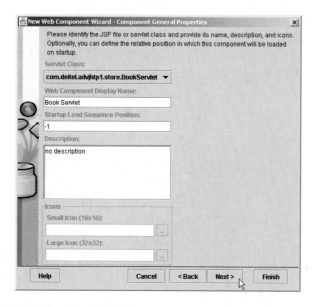

Fig. 11.26 New Web Component Wizard - **Component General Properties** window.

Click **Next >** twice to display the ***New Web Component Wizard - Component Aliases*** *window* (Fig. 11.27). Click **Add** to specify an alias for the **BookServlet**. Click the white box that appears in the window, type **displayBook** as the alias for the servlet and press *Enter*. Next, click **_Finish_** to complete the setup of the **BookServlet**.

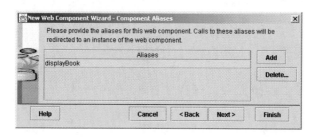

Fig. 11.27 New Web Component Wizard - **Component Aliases** window.

Now, create a Web component for **AddToCartServlet** (*Step 7* of Section 11.10), by repeating the steps shown in this section. For this Web component, specify **Add to Cart Servlet** as the **Web Component Display Name** and **addToCart** as the alias for the servlet. After adding the two servlet Web components, the **Application Deployment Tool** window should appear as shown in Fig. 11.28.

11.10.6 Adding Non-Servlet Components to the Application

Next, we will add our non-servlet components to the application (*Step 8* of Section 11.10). These files include JSPs, XHTML documents, style sheets, images and JavaBeans used in the application.

Begin by expanding the application component tree and clicking **Store Components** in the *Local Applications* area of the **Application Deployment Tool** window (see Fig. 11.28). In the contents area of the **Application Deployment Tool** window, click the **Add...** button to display the **Add Files to .WAR - Add Content Files** window (Fig. 11.29).

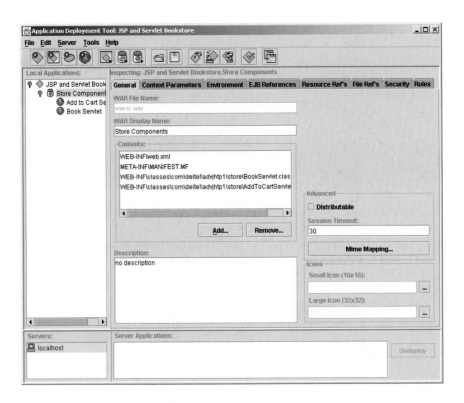

Fig. 11.28 Application Deployment Tool window after deploying **BookServlet** and **AddToCartServlet**.

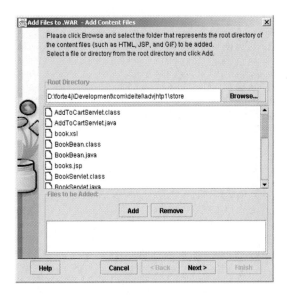

Fig. 11.29 Add Files to .WAR - Add Content Files window.

Navigate to the directory on your system that contains the files for the bookstore application. In the list box that appears in the window, locate each of the following files and directories: **book.xsl**, **books.jsp**, **images**, **index.html**, **order.html**, **process.jsp**, **styles.css** and **viewCart.jsp**. For each file or directory, click the **Add** button. You can select multiple items at one time by holding down the *<Ctrl>* key and clicking each item. All the items you add should appear in the text area at the bottom of the window. When you are done, click **Next >** to display the **Add Files to .WAR - Add Class Files** window (Fig. 11.30).

We will use this window to add the **.class** files for the non-servlet classes (i.e., our JavaBeans) to our application. Remember that the JavaBeans used in the bookstore are in a package, so their **.class** files must be added and maintained in their full package directory structure. Once again, click the **Browse...** button to display the **Choose Root Directory** window and locate the directory in which the first package directory name is found. Select that directory as the root directory. Double click the **com** directory name to expand its contents in the window. Do the same for the subdirectory **deitel**, then the subdirectory **advjhtp1** and finally, for the directory **store**. In the **store** directory, select the **.class** files for each of the JavaBeans in this bookstore example (**Book-Bean.class**, **CartItemBean.class** and **TitlesBean.class**), then click the **Add** button. At the bottom of the **Add Files to .WAR - Add Class Files** window, each **.class** file should be displayed with its full package directory structure. After doing this, click the **Finish** button to return to the **Application Deployment Tool** window. Note that the files selected with the **Add Files to .WAR** windows now appear in the **Contents** text area of the window. Click the **Save** button to save your work.

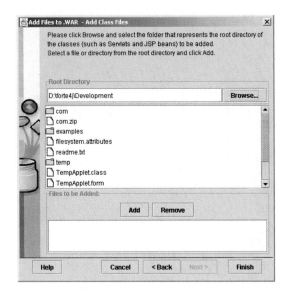

Fig. 11.30 Add Files to .WAR - Add Class Files window.

11.10.7 Specifying the Web Context, Resource References, JNDI Names and Welcome Files

Steps 9 through 13 of Section 11.10 perform the final configuration and deployment of the bookstore application. After performing the steps in this section, you will be able to execute the bookstore application.

We begin by specifying the Web context for our application (*Step 9* of Section 11.10). At the beginning of this chapter, we indicated that the user would enter the URL

```
http://localhost:8000/advjhtp1/store
```

in a browser to access the bookstore application. The Web context is the part of the preceding URL that enables the server to determine which application to execute when the server receives a request from a client. In this case, the Web context is **advjhtp1/store**. Once again, note that the J2EE server uses port 8000, rather than port 8080, used by Tomcat.

 Common Programming Error 11.2

Specifying the wrong port number in a URL that is supposed to access the J2EE server causes your Web browser to indicate that the server was not found.

 Testing and Debugging Tip 11.4

When deploying an Enterprise Java application on a production application server (the J2EE server is for testing only), it is typically not necessary to specify a port number in the URL when accessing the application. See your application server's documentation for further details.

To specify the Web context, click the **JSP and Servlet Bookstore** node in the **Local Applications** area of the **Application Deployment Tool** window. Then, click the **Web Context** *tab* (Fig. 11.31). Click the white box in the **Context Root** *column* and type `advjhtp1/store`; then click *Enter*.

Next, we must specify the database resource referenced by the bookstore application (*Step 10* of Section 11.10). Click the **Store Components** node in the **Local Applications** area of the **Application Deployment Tool** window. Then, click the **Resource Ref's** *tab* (Fig. 11.32). Click the **Add** button. Under the **Coded Name** *column* click the white box and type `jdbc/books` (the JNDI name of our data source). Figure 11.32 shows the **Application Deployment Tool** window after creating the resource reference.

Next, we specify the JNDI name for the database in the application (*Step 11* of Section 11.10). This is used to register the name with the Java Naming and Directory Service, so the database can be located by the application at execution time.

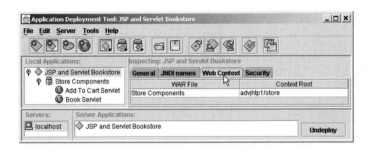

Fig. 11.31 Specifying the **Web Context** in the **Application Deployment Tool**.

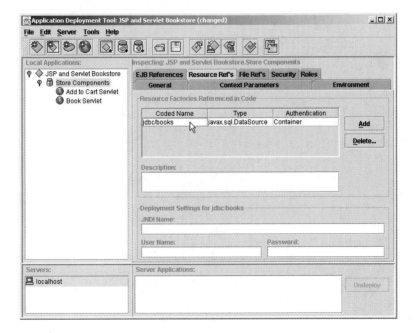

Fig. 11.32 Specifying the **Resource Ref's** in the **Application Deployment Tool**.

To specify the JNDI name for the database, click the **JSP and Servlet Bookstore** node in the **Local Applications** area of the **Application Deployment Tool** window. Then, click the ***JNDI names*** *tab* (Fig. 11.33). In the ***JNDI Name*** *column*, click the white box and type `jdbc/books`; then click *Enter*.

The last task to perform before deploying the application is specifying the welcome file that is displayed when the user first visits the bookstore. Click the **Store Components** node in the **Local Applications** area of the **Application Deployment Tool** window. Then, click the ***File Ref's*** *tab* (Fig. 11.34). Click the **Add** button. In the ***Welcome Files*** area click the white box and type `index.html`. Figure 11.34 shows the **Application Deployment Tool** window after specifying the welcome file. Click the **Save** button to save the application settings.

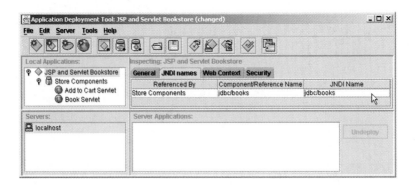

Fig. 11.33 Specifying the **Resource Ref's** in the **Application Deployment Tool**.

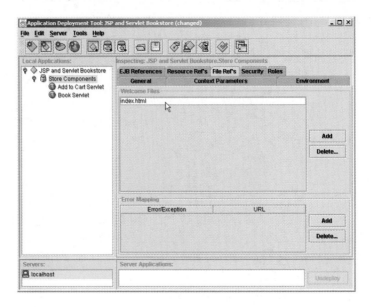

Fig. 11.34 Specifying the welcome file in the **File Ref's** tab of the **Application Deployment Tool**.

11.10.8 Deploying and Executing the Application

Now, you are ready to deploy the bookstore application so you can test it. Figure 11.35 shows **Application Deployment Tool** toolbar buttons for updating application files and deploying applications. The **Update Application Files** *button* updates the application's EAR file after changes are made to any of the files, such as recompiling classes or modifying files. The **Deploy Application** *button* causes the **Application Deployment Tool** to communicate with the J2EE server and deploy the application. The functionality of both these buttons is combined in the **Update and Redeploy Application** *button*.

Click the **Deploy Application** button to display the **Deploy JSP and Servlet Bookstore - Introduction** window (Fig. 11.36). Click the **Next >** button three times, then click the **Finish** button. A **Deployment Progress** *window* appears. This window will indicate when the deployment is complete. When that occurs, open a Web browser and enter the following URL to test the bookstore application:

```
http://localhost:8000/advjhtp1/store
```

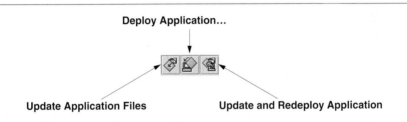

Deploy Application...

Update Application Files   **Update and Redeploy Application**

Fig. 11.35 **Application Deployment Tool** toolbar buttons for updating application files and deploying applications.

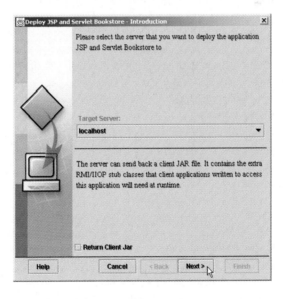

Fig. 11.36 Deploy JSP and Servlet Bookstore - Introduction window.

In this chapter, we have presented our first substantial Enterprise Java application. The steps presented in this section for deploying the bookstore application are just some of the steps required in a typical Enterprise application. For example, there were no security requirements in the bookstore application. In real Enterprise Java applications, some or all of the application components have security restrictions, such as "the user must enter a valid username and password before access is granted to a component." Such restrictions are specified at deployment time with the **Application Deployment Tool** or some similar tool in an Enterprise Java development environment. These security restrictions are enforced by the application server. In our bookstore example, if the JSPs had security restrictions, it would be necessary to deploy each one individually, as we did with the **BookServlet** and the **AddToCartServlet**. In later chapters, we discuss more of the deployment options for application components. The *Java 2 Enterprise Edition Specification* (available at **java.sun.com/j2ee/download.html**) discusses the complete set of deployment options that are required in J2EE-compliant application servers.

The next chapter continues our client/server discussions. In that chapter, we use servlets and XML to create content for wireless devices, such as pagers, cell phones and personal digital assistants.

SUMMARY

- The Java 2 Enterprise Edition 1.2.1 reference implementation includes the Apache Tomcat JSP and servlet container.
- A three-tier, distributed Web application consists of client, server and database tiers.
- The client tier in a Web application often is represented by the user's Web browser.
- The server tier in a Web application often consists of JSPs and servlets that act on behalf of the client to perform tasks.
- The database tier maintains the database accessed from the server tier.
- The Java 2 Enterprise Edition 1.2.1 reference implementation comes with an **Application Deployment Tool**. Among its many features, this tool enables us to specify the alias used to invoke a servlet.
- The **Application Deployment Tool** creates the deployment descriptor for a servlet as part of deploying an application.
- The welcome file is the default document sent as the response to a client when the client initially interacts with a J2EE application.
- Different browsers have different levels of support for Cascading Style Sheets.
- JavaServer Pages often generate XHTML that is sent to the client for rendering.
- The Java Naming and Directory Interface (JNDI) enables Enterprise Java application components to access information and resources (such as databases) that are external to an application. In some cases, those resources are distributed across a network.
- An Enterprise Java application container must provide a naming service that implements JNDI and enables the components executing in that container to perform name lookups to locate resources. The J2EE 1.2.1 reference implementation server includes such a naming service.
- When you deploy an Enterprise Java application, you specify the resources used by the application (such as databases) and the JNDI names for those resources.
- Using an **InitialContext**, an Enterprise application component can look up a resource. The **InitialContext** provides access to the application's naming environment.

- **InitialContext** method **lookup** locates a resource with a JNDI name. Method **lookup** returns an **Object** object and throws a **NamingException** if it cannot resolve the name it receives as an argument.

- A **DataSource** is used to connect to a database.

- The **org.w3c.dom** package's **Document** and **Element** interfaces are used to create an XML document tree.

- **Document** method **createElement** creates an element for an XML document.

- **Document** method **createTextNode** specifies the text for an **Element**.

- **Element** method **appendChild** appends a node to an **Element** as a child of that **Element**.

- An XML document can be transformed into an XHTML document using an XSL style sheet.

- **ServletRequest** method **getRequestDispatcher** returns a **RequestDispatcher** object that can **forward** requests to other resources or **include** other resources as part of the current servlet's response.

- When **RequestDispatcher** method **forward** is called, processing of the request by the current servlet terminates.

- **RequestDispatcher** objects can be obtained with method **getRequestDispatcher** from an object that implements interface **ServletRequest**, or from the **ServletContext** with methods **getRequestDispatcher** or **getNamedDispatcher**.

- **ServletContext** method **getNamedDispatcher** receives the name of a servlet as an argument, then searches the **ServletContext** for a servlet by that name. If no such servlet is found, the method returns **null**.

- Both the **ServletRequest** and the **ServletContext getRequestDispatcher** methods simply return the content of the specified path if the path does not represent a servlet.

- Before the XML and XSL capabilities can be used, you must download and install Sun's Java API for XML Parsing (JAXP) version 1.1 from **java.sun.com/xml/download.htm**.

- The root directory of JAXP (normally called **jaxp-1.1**) contains three JAR files that are required for compiling and running programs that use JAXP—**crimson.jar**, **jaxp.jar** and **xalan.jar**. These files must be added to the Java extension mechanism for your Java 2 Standard Edition installation.

- JAXP 1.1 is part of the forthcoming J2EE 1.3 reference implementation.

- Creating a Document Object Model (DOM) tree from an XML document requires a **DocumentBuilder** parser object. **DocumentBuilder** objects are obtained from a **DocumentBuilderFactory**.

- Classes **Document** and **Element** are located in package **org.w3c.dom**.

- A **DOMSource** represents an XML document in an XSL transformation. A **StreamSource** can be used to read a stream of bytes that represent an XSL file.

- A **StreamResult** specifies the **PrintWriter** to which the results of the XSL transformation are written.

- **TransformerFactory** **static** method **newInstance** creates a **TransformerFactory** object. This object enables the program to obtain a **Transformer** object that applies the XSL transformation.

- **TransformerFactory** method **newTransformer** receives a **StreamSource** argument representing the XSL that will be applied to an XML document.

- **Transformer** method **transform** performs an XSL transformation on the given **DOMSource** object and writes the result to the given **StreamResult** object.

- A **TransformerException** is thrown if a problem occurs when creating the **Transform-erFactory**, creating the **Transformer** or performing the transformation.

- **HttpSession** method **invalidate** discards the session object for the current client.

- Before deploying an Enterprise Java application, you must configure your data sources and other resources, so the J2EE server can register those resources with the naming server. This enables the application to use JNDI to locate the resources at execution time.

- J2EE comes with Cloudscape—a pure-Java database application from Informix Software.

- To configure a Cloudscape data source, you must modify the J2EE default configuration file **de-fault.properties** in the J2EE installation's **config** directory. Below the comment **JDBC URL Examples** is a line that begins with **jdbc.datasources**. Append the following text (in which *dataSource* represents your data source name) to this line:

  |**jdbc/***dataSource***|jdbc:cloudscape:rmi:***dataSource***;create=true**

- Each database server typically has its own URL format that enables an application to interact with databases hosted on that database server.

- You must launch the Cloudscape database server and the J2EE server before you can deploy and execute an application.

- To ensure that the J2EE server communicates properly with the Cloudscape server (or any other database server), always launch the database server before the J2EE server.

- Always shut down the J2EE server before the Cloudscape database server, to ensure that the J2EE server does not attempt to communicate with the Cloudscape database server after the database server has been shut down.

- The J2EE reference implementation comes with a graphical application, called the **Application Deployment Tool**, that helps you deploy Enterprise Java applications.

- The **Application Deployment Tool** is nice in that it writes the deployment descriptor files for you and automatically archives the Web application's components. The tool places all Web application components and auxiliary files for a particular application into a single Enterprise Application Archive (EAR) file. This file contains deployment descriptor information, WAR files with Web application components and additional information that is discussed later in the book.

- When adding a class file for a class in a package to an application with the **Application Deployment Tool**, it is imperative that the files be added and maintained in their full package directory structure or as part of a JAR file that contains the full package directory structure.

- Not including the full package directory structure for a class in a package will prevent the application from loading the class and from executing properly.

- The Web context for an application is the part of the URL that enables the server to determine which application to execute when the server receives a request from a client.

- The J2EE server uses port 8000, rather than port 8080, used by Tomcat.

- When deploying an Enterprise Java application on a production application server, it is typically not necessary to specify a port number in the URL when accessing the application.

- Part of deploying an application is to specify the resource references for the components in the application.

- Each resource reference has a corresponding JNDI name that is used by the deployment tool to register the resource with the Java Naming and Directory Service. This enables the resource to be located by the application at execution time.

TERMINOLOGY

Application Deployment Tool
Cascading Style Sheets (CSS)
component environment entries
configure a data source
create a Web component
database resource
DataSource interface
default.properties
deploy an application
dynamic XHTML document
Enterprise Application Archive (EAR) file
external resource
forward method of **RequestDispatcher**
getRequestDispatcher method of
    ServletRequest
include content from a resource
include method of **RequestDispatcher**
InitialContext class
invalidate method of **HttpSession**
J2EE **config** directory
Java 2 Enterprise Edition 1.2.1
    reference implementation
Java API for XML Parsing (JAXP)

Java Naming and Directory Interface (JNDI)
javax.naming package
jdbc.datasources J2EE
    configuration property
jdbc:cloudscape:rmi:books JDBC URL
JNDI name
locate a naming service
lookup method of **InitialContext**
name lookup
name resolution
naming service
register a data source with a naming server
RequestDispatcher interface
server tier
ServletContext interface
shopping cart
style sheet
Web component
Web context
welcome file
XML
XSL transformation

SELF-REVIEW EXERCISES

11.1 Fill in the blanks in each of the following statements:
   a) A three-tier, distributed Web application consists of _____, _____ and _____ tiers.
   b) The _____ is the default document sent as the response to a client when the client initially interacts with a J2EE application.
   c) The _____ enables Enterprise Java application components to access information and resources (such as databases) that are external to an application.
   d) An _____ object provides access to the application's naming environment.
   e) A **RequestDispatcher** object can _____ requests to other resources or _____ other resources as part of the current servlet's response.
   f) Sun's _____ provides XML and XSL capabilities in a Java program.
   g) Method _____ of interface _____ discards the session object for the current client.
   h) The _____ for an application is the part of the URL that enables the server to determine which application to execute when the server receives a request from a client.
   i) An Enterprise Java application container must provide a _____ that implements JNDI and enables the components executing in that container to perform name lookups to locate resources.
   j) The J2EE reference implementation comes with a graphical application, called the _____, that helps you deploy Enterprise Java applications.

11.2 State whether each of the following is *true* or *false*. If *false*, explain why.
   a) The J2EE server uses port 8080 to await client requests.

b) When deploying applications with the J2EE server, you can launch the Cloudscape and J2EE servers in any order.

c) **InitialContext** method **lookup** locates a resource with a JNDI name.

d) Method **lookup** returns a **Connection** object representing the connection to the database.

e) The Java 2 Enterprise Edition 1.2.1 reference implementation includes the Apache Tomcat JSP and servlet container.

f) When **RequestDispatcher** method **forward** is called, processing of the request by the current servlet is temporarily suspended to wait for a response from the resource to which the request is forwarded.

g) Both the **ServletRequest** and the **ServletContext getRequestDispatcher** methods throw exceptions if the argument to **getRequestDispatcher** is not a servlet.

h) Each resource reference has a corresponding JNDI name that is used by the deployment tool to register the resource with the Java Naming and Directory Service.

i) If you do not configure your data sources and other resources before deploying an Enterprise Java application, the J2EE server will search the application to determine the resources used and register those resources with the naming server.

j) Not including the full package directory structure for a class in a package will prevent the application from loading the class and from executing properly.

ANSWERS TO SELF-REVIEW EXERCISES

11.1 a) client, server, database. b) welcome file. c) Java Naming and Directory Interface (JNDI). d) **InitialContext**. e) **forward, include**. f) Java API for XML Parsing (JAXP). g) **invalidate, HttpSession**. h) Web context. i) naming service. j) **Application Deployment Tool**.

11.2   a) False. Port 8080 is the default port for the Tomcat server. The J2EE server uses port 8000.

b) False. To ensure that the J2EE server communicates properly with the Cloudscape server (or any other database server), the database server must be launched before the J2EE server.

c) True.

d) False. Method **lookup** returns a **DataSource** object that can be used to obtain a **Connection**.

e) True.

f) False. When **RequestDispatcher** method **forward** is called, processing of the request by the current servlet terminates.

g) False. Both the **ServletRequest** and the **ServletContext getRequestDispatcher** methods simply return the contents of the specified path if the path does not represent a servlet.

h) True.

i) False. Before deploying an Enterprise Java application, you must configure your data sources and other resources, so the J2EE server can register those resources with the naming server. Otherwise, exceptions will occur when the application attempts to access the resources.

j) True.

EXERCISES

11.3   Modify the bookstore case study to enable the client to change the quantity of an item currently in the shopping cart. In **viewCart.jsp**, display the quantity in an **input** element of type

text in a **form**. Provide the user with a **submit** button with the value **Update Cart** that enables the user to submit the form to a servlet that updates the quantity of the items in the cart. The servlet should forward the request to **viewCart.jsp**, so the user can see the updated cart contents. Redeploy the bookstore application, and test the update capability.

11.4   Enhance the bookstore case study's **TitlesBean** to obtain author information from the **books** database. Incorporate that author data into the **BookBean** class, and display the author information as part of the Web page users see when they select a book and view that book's information.

11.5   Add server-side form validation to the order form in the bookstore case study. Check that the credit-card expiration date is after today's date. Make all the fields in the form required fields. When the user does not supply data for all fields, return an XHTML document containing the order form. Any fields in which the user previously entered data should contain that data. For this exercise, replace the **order.html** document with a JSP that generates the form dynamically.

11.6   Create an **order** table and an **orderItems** table in the **books** database to store orders placed by customers. The **order** table should store an **orderID**, an **orderDate** and the **email** address of the customer who placed the order. [*Note*: You will need to modify the **form** in Exercise 11.6 to include the customer's e-mail address]. The **orderItems** table should store the **orderID**, **ISBN**, **price** and **quantity** of each book in the order. Modify **process.jsp** so that it stores the order information in the **order** and **orderItems** tables.

11.7   Create a JSP that enables client to view their order history. Integrate this JSP into the bookstore case study.

11.8   Create and deploy a single application that allows a user to test all the JSP examples in Chapter 10. The application should have a welcome file that is an XHTML document containing links to each of the examples in Chapter 10.

11.9   Create and deploy a single application that allows a user to test all the servlets in Chapter 9. The application should have a welcome file that is an XHTML document containing links to each of the examples in Chapter 9.

12

Java-Based Wireless Applications Development and J2ME

Objectives

- To construct a three-tier, client/server application.
- To use XML and XSLT to present content for several client types.
- To understand the Java 2 Micro Edition (J2ME) Platform.
- To understand the MIDlet lifecycle.
- To be able to use J2ME CLDC and MIDP.
- To understand how our case study incorporates J2ME technology.

One thing I know: the only ones among you who will be really happy are those who will have sought and found how to serve.
Albert Schweitzer

It was a miracle of rare device, ...
Samuel Taylor Coleridge

Knowledge is of two kinds. We know a subject ourselves, or we know where we can find information upon it.
Samuel Johnson

... all the light I can command must be concentrated on this particular web ...
George Elliot

When you can do the common things of life in an uncommon way, you will command the attention of the world.
George Washington Carver

Outline

12.1 Introduction

In this chapter, present a case study of a multiple-choice test (*Tip Test*) for users to test their knowledge of Deitel programming tips. Each question consists of a tip image and a list of four possible answers. A client downloads the test from a server. The user then selects an answer and submits it to the server, which responds with content that describes if the answer is correct or incorrect. The client then can download another question and continue playing indefinitely.

The Tip-Test application is a three-tier architecture, as shown in Fig. 12.1. The information tier consists of a database that contains a table (defined in the SQL script **tips.sql**) with seven rows and five columns. Each row contains information about a Deitel programming tip—Good Programming Practice, Software-Engineering Observation, Performance Tip, Portability Tip, Look-And-Feel Observation, Testing and Debugging Tip and Common Programming Error. The first database column stores integers that represent unique identifiers for each tip. The second column stores the names of the tips. The third column stores the tips' descriptions—i.e., definitions of each tip and explanations of why each tip is important. The fourth column stores the image names for each tip. The fifth column stores the tips' abbreviated names—e.g., the abbreviation for Good Programming Practice is GPP. Figure 12.2 shows the contents of **tips.sql**.

The middle tier consists of two servlets—**WelcomeServlet** and **TipTestServlet**. **WelcomeServlet** delivers a "welcome screen" that introduces the game to the user. **WelcomeServlet** then redirects the client to **TipTestServlet**. Using the database, **TipTestServlet** randomly selects a tip image and four possible answers (in the form of abbreviated tip names) and marks up this information as an XML document. **TipTestServlet** then applies an XSL transformation to the XML document and sends the resulting content to the client.

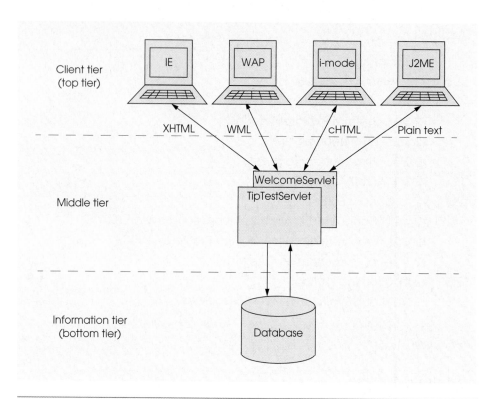

Fig. 12.1   Three-tier architecture for Tip Test.

tipID	tipName	tipDescription	tipImage	shortName
1	Good Programming Practice	Good Programming Practice call the student's attention to techniques that...	goodProgramming	GPP
2	Common Programming Error	Students learning a language tend to make certain kinds of errors...	programmingError	CPE
3	Look-and-Feel Observation	We provide Look-And-Feel Observations to highlight graphical user...	lookAndFeel	LAF
4	Performance Tip	Performance Tips highlight opportunities for improving program performance.	perf	PERF
5	Portability Tip	Organizations that develop software must often produce versions customized...	portability	PORT

Fig. 12.2   Database contents of **tips.sql** (part 1 of 2).

tipID	tipName	tipDescription	tipImage	shortName
6	Software Engineering Observation	The Software Engineering Observations highlight techniques, architectural...	softwareEngineering	SEO
7	Testing and Debugging Tip	Most of these tips tend to be observations about capabilities and features...	testingDebugging	TAD

Fig. 12.2   Database contents of `tips.sql` (part 2 of 2).

The client tier consists of four client types—Internet Explorer, WAP (Wireless Application Protocol), i-mode and J2ME. Each client can render a different content type. **TipTestServlet** handles all game logic—i.e., selecting the Tip-Test question at random and determining if the user's answer is correct—and sends the content to each client. Microsoft Internet Explorer receives XHTML (Extensible HyperText Markup Language) content. The Openwave UP simulator is the WAP client that receives WML (Wireless Markup Language) content. WAP is a protocol that enables wireless devices to transfer information over the Internet. WML marks up content rendered on the wireless device. The Pixo Internet Microbrowser is the i-mode client that receives cHTML content—i-mode provides a popular Japanese-based wireless Internet service, and cHTML (compact HTML) is an HTML subset for resource-limited devices. The Sun MIDP-device emulator acts as the J2ME client that receives content in plain-text format. J2ME™ (Java™ 2 Micro Edition) is Sun's newest Java platform for developing applications for various consumer devices, such as set-top boxes, Web terminals, embedded systems, mobile phones and cell pagers. MIDP (Mobile Information Device Profile) is a set of APIs that allows developers to handle mobile-device-specific issues, such as creating user interfaces, storing information locally and networking. Devices that run applications for MIDP are called *MIDP devices* (e.g., cell phones or pagers). We discuss J2ME and MIDP in much greater detail in Section 12.4.

We present this case study by discussing how each servlet sends content to each client type, then how each client type renders that content. Section 12.2 and Section 12.3 discuss how **WelcomeServlet** and **TipTestServlet** handle client requests. Sections 27.3.1–27.3.4 discuss how **TipTestServlet** responds to each client request and how each client renders the servlet-generated content. Lastly, Section 12.4 discusses Java 2 Micro Edition. Our treatment of J2ME focuses on only the client (i.e., our serlvets do not use J2ME technology), so we discuss J2ME after we discuss the application's servlets. Until we discuss Section 12.4, we recommend that you regard the J2ME client as "just another client" that receives servlet-generated content (i.e., you need not know J2ME-related topics to understand servlet behavior). In Section 12.4, we discuss how the J2ME client receives and interprets this content—e.g., how the J2ME client presents this data in a user interface. We also recommend that you follow the instructions in Section 12.5 for installing and configuring the software in this case study.

12.2 WelcomeServlet Overview

We begin by discussing class **WelcomeServlet** (Fig. 12.1), which redirects a client request to a static page that displays Tip-Test game instructions—this static page contains a link to the **TipTestServlet**, which enables the user to play the game.

Clients interact with servlets by making **get** or **post** requests to the servlets. Clients send **get** requests to **WelcomeServlet** to get the "welcome screen." When a client sends a **get** request to **WelcomeServlet**, method **doGet** (lines 15–39) handles the request.

Each client type receives a different welcome screen from the servlet, because each client type supports a different content type. For example, Internet Explorer receives **index.html** as a welcome screen, because Internet Explorer can render XHTML documents. On the other hand, the Openwave UP simulator receives **index.wml**, because a WAP browser can render only WML documents. The Sun MIDP-device emulator can render only plain text, so **WelcomeServlet** sends **index.txt** to this device.[1] The Pixo browser for i-mode can render cHTML (compact-HTML), so the servlet sends a different **index.html** than the one for Internet Explorer.

```
1   // WelcomeServlet.java
2   // Delivers appropriate "Welcome" screen to client
3   package com.deitel.advjhtp1.wireless;
4
5   // Java core package
6   import java.io.*;
7
8   // Java extension packages
9   import javax.servlet.*;
10  import javax.servlet.http.*;
11
12  public class WelcomeServlet extends HttpServlet {
13
14     // respond to get request
15     protected void doGet( HttpServletRequest request,
16        HttpServletResponse response )
17        throws ServletException, IOException
18     {
19        // determine User-Agent header
20        String userAgent = request.getHeader( "User-Agent" );
21
22        // send welcome screen to appropriate client
23        if ( userAgent.indexOf (
24           ClientUserAgentHeaders.IE ) != -1 )
25           sendIEClientResponse( request, response );
26
27        else if ( userAgent.indexOf( // WAP
28              ClientUserAgentHeaders.WAP ) != -1 )
29              sendWAPClientResponse( request, response );
```

Fig. 12.3   Class **WelcomeServlet** sends an introductory screen that provides game directions to a client (part 1 of 3).

1. At the time of this writing, J2ME clients can interpret XML documents only by using proprietary software—i.e., there does not exist a standard for J2ME clients to integrate XML.

```
30
31          else if ( userAgent.indexOf( // i-mode
32              ClientUserAgentHeaders.IMODE ) != -1 )
33              sendIModeClientResponse( request, response );
34
35          else if ( userAgent.indexOf( // J2ME
36              ClientUserAgentHeaders.J2ME ) != -1 )
37              sendJ2MEClientResponse( request, response );
38
39       } // end method doGet
40
41       // send welcome screen to IE client
42       private void sendIEClientResponse(
43          HttpServletRequest request, HttpServletResponse response )
44          throws IOException, ServletException
45       {
46          redirect( "text/html", "/XHTML/index.html", request,
47             response );
48       }
49
50       // send welcome screen to Nokia WAP client
51       private void sendWAPClientResponse(
52          HttpServletRequest request, HttpServletResponse response )
53          throws IOException, ServletException
54       {
55          redirect( "text/vnd.wap.wml", "/WAP/index.wml", request,
56             response );
57       }
58
59       // send welcome screen to i-mode client
60       private void sendIModeClientResponse(
61          HttpServletRequest request, HttpServletResponse response )
62          throws IOException, ServletException
63       {
64          redirect( "text/html", "/iMode/index.html", request,
65             response );
66       }
67
68       // send welcome screen to J2ME client
69       private void sendJ2MEClientResponse(
70          HttpServletRequest request, HttpServletResponse response )
71          throws IOException
72       {
73          // send J2ME client text data
74          response.setContentType( "text/plain" );
75          PrintWriter out = response.getWriter();
76
77          // open file to send J2ME client
78          BufferedReader bufferedReader =
79             new BufferedReader( new FileReader(
80                getServletContext().getRealPath(
81                   "j2me/index.txt" ) ) );
```

Fig. 12.3 Class **WelcomeServlet** sends an introductory screen that provides
game directions to a client (part 2 of 3).

```
82
83         String inputString = bufferedReader.readLine();
84
85         // send each line in file to J2ME client
86         while ( inputString != null ) {
87            out.println( inputString );
88            inputString = bufferedReader.readLine();
89         }
90
91         out.close(); // done sending data
92
93      } // end method sendJ2MEClientResponse
94
95      // redirects client request to another page
96      private void redirect( String contentType, String redirectPage,
97         HttpServletRequest request, HttpServletResponse response )
98         throws IOException, ServletException
99      {
100        // set new content type
101        response.setContentType( contentType );
102        RequestDispatcher dispatcher =
103           getServletContext().getRequestDispatcher(
104              redirectPage );
105
106        // forward user to redirectPage
107        dispatcher.forward( request, response );
108     }
109  }
```

Fig. 12.3   Class **WelcomeServlet** sends an introductory screen that provides game directions to a client (part 3 of 3).

Before responding to a client, method **doGet** must determine what type of client made the request. Each client includes a ***User-Agent*** *header* with each request. This header contains information on the type of client requesting data from the server. Interface **ClientUserAgentHeaders** (Fig. 12.4) lists a unique **User-Agent** header substring for each client in our application. For example, a **User-Agent** header for Microsoft Internet Explorer running on Windows 2000 might be

```
Mozilla/4.0 (compatible; MSIE 5.0; Windows NT 5.0)
```

We search for the substring **"MSIE 5"** in the **User-Agent** header to recognize Internet Explorer requests from different platforms. Also, **WelcomeServlet** will recognize variance among other versions of Internet Explorer 5 (e.g., v.5.0, v.5.5, etc.). For example, the **User-Agent** header for a Windows 98 client might not be identical to the one shown, but the header will contain the **"MSIE 5"** substring.

Line 20 of class **WelcomeServlet** extracts the **User-Agent** header from the **HttpServletRequest**. Lines 23–37 determine which client made the request by matching the **User-Agent** header with the ones in interface **ClientUserAgent-Headers**. If an Internet Explorer browser made the request, line 25 invokes method **sendIEClientResponse** (lines 42–48). Lines 46–47 calls method **redirect** (lines 96–108), which redirects the request to a static page. For Internet Explorer, line 101 calls

```
1   // ClientUserAgentHeaders.java
2   // Contains all User-Agent header for clients
3   package com.deitel.advjhtp1.wirless;
4
5   public interface ClientUserAgentHeaders {
6
7      // User-Agent header for Internet Explorer browser
8      public static final String IE = "MSIE 5";
9
10     // User-Agent header for WAP browser
11     public static final String WAP = "UP";
12
13     // User-Agent header for i-mode browser
14     public static final String IMODE = "Pixo";
15
16     // User-Agent header for J2ME device
17     public static final String J2ME = "MIDP-1.0";
18  }
```

Fig. 12.4   Interface **ClientUserAgentHeaders** contains unique User-Agent header substrings for all clients.

method **setContentType** of the **HttpServletResponse** object to set the *MIME* type to **text/html**—the MIME type for XHTML clients. The *MIME type* (*Multipurpose Internet Mail Extensions*) helps browsers determine how to interpret data. Lines 102–107 redirect the request to **index.html** by creating a **RequestDispatcher** object with the name of the static page and invoking method **forward** of the **RequestDispatcher**. The IE browser then displays **index.html** (Fig. 12.5).

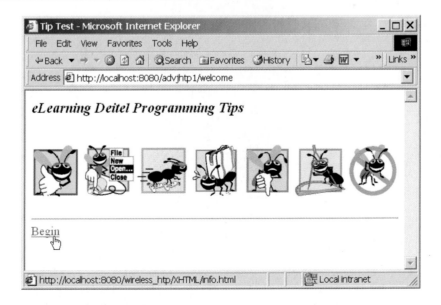

Fig. 12.5   WelcomeServlet output (**index.html**) for XHTML client.

If the Openwave UP simulator made the request, line 29 invokes method **sendWAP-ClientResponse** (lines 51–57), which invokes method **redirect** with the MIME type to **text/vnd.wap.wml**—the MIME type for WML clients—and redirects the request to **index.wml**. At this point, the simulator displays **index.wml**, as shown in Fig. 12.6.

If the Pixo i-mode browser made the request, line 33 invokes method **sendIMode-ClientResponse** (lines 60–66). This method also invokes method **redirect**, but sets the MIME type to **text/html**—the MIME type for cHTML clients—and redirects the request to a cHTML version of **index.html**. At this point, the Pixo browser displays **index.html**, as shown in Fig. 12.7.

If the Sun MIDP-device emulator made the request, line 37 invokes method **sendJ2MEClientResponse** (lines 69–93). To transfer **index.txt** to the J2ME client, the servlet must send **index.txt** through a stream between the servlet and the J2ME client. Line 74 sets the MIME type to **text/plain**. Line 75 invokes method **getWriter** of class **HttpServletResponse** to obtain a **PrintWriter** for sending data to the client. Lines 78–81 create a **BufferedReader** that reads **index.txt** from the **j2me** directory located in the servlet context. Lines 86–89 send each line from **BufferedReader** to the client. At this point, Sun's emulator displays **index.txt**, as shown in Fig. 12.8.

Fig. 12.6 **WelcomeServlet** output (**index.wml**) for WAP client. (Image of UP.SDK courtesy Openwave Systems Inc. Openwave, the Openwave logo, and UP.SDK are trademarks of Openwave Systems Inc. All rights reserved.)

Fig. 12.7   **WelcomeServlet** output (**index.html**) for i-mode client.
(Courtesy of Pixo, Inc.)

Fig. 12.8   **WelcomeServlet** output (**index.txt**) for J2ME client. (Courtesy of
Sun Microsystems, Inc.)

12.3 `TipTestServlet` Overview

In this section, we discuss how the **`TipTestServlet`** (Fig. 12.9) generates and sends Tip-Test questions and answers to each client. Each welcome screen contains a link to an "instructions" screen—**`info.html`**, **`info.wml`** or **`info.txt`**, depending on the client—that provides game information. The instructions screen contains a link to **`TipTestServlet`**.[2]

If the user accesses **`TipTestServlet`** and the servlet has not received a previous request from a client, the servlet container calls method **`init`** (lines 30–67) to initialize **`TipTestServlet`**. This method performs operations that **`TipTestServlet`** need only perform once, such as loading the JDBC driver, connecting to the database and instantiating objects for creating XML documents. Lines 36–38 retrieve the class name for the JDBC-database driver from the servlet-initialization parameter in **`web.xml`** (which we discussed when we installed Tomcat), and line 40 loads this driver.

```
1   // TipTestServlet.java
2   // TipTestServlet sends Tip Test to clients.
3   package com.deitel.advjhtp1.wireless;
4
5   // Java core packages
6   import java.io.*;
7   import java.sql.*;
8   import java.util.*;
9
10  // Java extension packages
11  import javax.servlet.*;
12  import javax.servlet.http.*;
13  import javax.xml.parsers.*;
14  import javax.xml.transform.*;
15  import javax.xml.transform.dom.*;
16  import javax.xml.transform.stream.*;
17
18  // import third-party packages
19  import org.w3c.dom.*;
20  import org.xml.sax.SAXException;
21
22  public class TipTestServlet extends HttpServlet {
23
24      private Connection connection; // database connection
25
26      private DocumentBuilderFactory factory;
27      private TransformerFactory transformerFactory;
28
29      // initialize servlet
30      public void init() throws ServletException
31      {
```

Fig. 12.9   **`TipTestServlet`** handles game logic and sends Tip Test to clients (part 1 of 13).

---

2. The client is not required to access **`TipTestServlet`** through **`WelcomeServlet`**. The user can type the **`TipTestServlet`** URL in the browser to access **`TipTestServlet`** and bypass the "welcome screen" that **`WelcomeServlet`** generates.

```
32              // load database driver and instantiate XML factories
33              try {
34
35                 // get JDBC driver from servlet container
36                 String jdbcDriver =
37                    getServletConfig().getInitParameter(
38                       "JDBC_DRIVER" );
39
40                 Class.forName( jdbcDriver ); // load JDBC driver
41
42                 // get database URL from servlet container
43                 String databaseUrl =
44                    getServletConfig().getInitParameter(
45                       "DATABASE_URL" );
46
47                 connection = DriverManager.getConnection( databaseUrl );
48
49                 // create a Factory to build XML Documents
50                 factory = DocumentBuilderFactory.newInstance();
51
52                 // create new TransformerFactory
53                 transformerFactory = TransformerFactory.newInstance();
54
55              } // end try
56
57              // handle exception database driver class does not exist
58              catch ( ClassNotFoundException classNotFoundException ) {
59                 classNotFoundException.printStackTrace();
60              }
61
62              // handle exception in making Connection
63              catch ( SQLException sqlException ) {
64                 sqlException.printStackTrace();
65              }
66
67           } // end method init
68
69           // respond to get requests
70           protected void doGet( HttpServletRequest request,
71              HttpServletResponse response )
72              throws ServletException, IOException
73           {
74              // get Statement from database, then send Tip-Test Question
75              try {
76
77                 // SQL query to database
78                 Statement statement = connection.createStatement();
79
80                 // get database information using SQL query
81                 ResultSet resultSet =
82                    statement.executeQuery( "SELECT * FROM tipInfo" );
83
```

Fig. 12.9 **TipTestServlet** handles game logic and sends Tip Test to clients (part 2 of 13).

```
84                   // parse and send ResultSet to client
85                   if ( resultSet != null ) {
86
87                      // ensure that client does not cache questions
88                      response.setHeader( "Cache-Control",
89                         "no-cache, must-revalidate" );
90                      response.setHeader( "Pragma", "no-cache" );
91
92                      sendTipTestQuestion( request, response, resultSet );
93                   }
94
95                   statement.close(); // close Statement
96                }
97
98                // handle exception in exectuting Statement
99                catch ( SQLException sqlException ) {
100                  sqlException.printStackTrace();
101               }
102
103           } // end method doGet
104
105           // respond to post requests
106           protected void doPost( HttpServletRequest request,
107              HttpServletResponse response )
108              throws ServletException, IOException
109           {
110              // send ResultSet to appropriate client
111              try {
112
113                 // determine User-Agent header
114                 String userAgent = request.getHeader( "User-Agent" );
115
116                 // if Internet Explorer is requesting client
117                 if ( userAgent.indexOf(
118                    ClientUserAgentHeaders.IE ) != -1 ) {
119
120                    Document document =
121                       createXMLTipTestAnswer( request );
122
123                    // set appropriate Content-Type for client
124                    response.setContentType( "text/html" );
125
126                    // send XML content to client after XSLT
127                    applyXSLT( "XHTML/XHTMLTipAnswer.xsl", document,
128                       response );
129                 }
130
131                 // if WAP client is requesting client
132                 else if ( userAgent.indexOf(
133                    ClientUserAgentHeaders.WAP ) != -1 ) {
134
```

Fig. 12.9 TipTestServlet handles game logic and sends Tip Test to clients (part 3 of 13).

```
135                 Document document =
136                     createXMLTipTestAnswer( request );
137
138                 // set appropriate Content-Type for client
139                 response.setContentType( "text/vnd.wap.wml" );
140
141                 // send XML content to client after XSLT
142                 applyXSLT( "WAP/WAPTipAnswer.xsl", document,
143                     response );
144             }
145
146             // if i-mode client is requesting client
147             else if ( userAgent.indexOf(
148                 ClientUserAgentHeaders.IMODE ) != -1 ) {
149
150                 Document document =
151                     createXMLTipTestAnswer( request );
152
153                 // set appropriate Content-Type for client
154                 response.setContentType( "text/html" );
155
156                 // send XML content to client after XSLT
157                 applyXSLT( "iMode/IMODETipAnswer.xsl", document,
158                     response );
159             }
160
161             // if J2ME client is requesting client
162             else if ( userAgent.indexOf(
163                 ClientUserAgentHeaders.J2ME ) != -1 )
164                 sendJ2MEAnswer( request, response );
165
166         } // end try
167
168         // handle exception if Document is null
169         catch ( NullPointerException nullPointerException ) {
170             nullPointerException.printStackTrace();
171         }
172
173     } // end method doPost
174
175     // send Tip-Test data to client
176     private void sendTipTestQuestion(
177         HttpServletRequest request, HttpServletResponse response,
178         ResultSet resultSet ) throws IOException
179     {
180         // send ResultSet to appropriate client
181         try {
182
183             // determine User-Agent header
184             String userAgent = request.getHeader( "User-Agent" );
185
```

Fig. 12.9 TipTestServlet handles game logic and sends Tip Test to clients (part 4 of 13).

```
186            // if Internet Explorer is requesting client
187            if ( userAgent.indexOf(
188               ClientUserAgentHeaders.IE ) != -1 ) {
189
190               Document document =
191                  createXMLTipTestQuestion( resultSet, request,
192                     request.getContextPath() + "/XHTML/images/",
193                        ".gif" );
194
195               // set appropriate Content-Type for client
196               response.setContentType( "text/html" );
197               applyXSLT( "XHTML/XHTMLTipQuestion.xsl", document,
198                  response );
199            }
200
201            // if WAP client is requesting client
202            else if ( userAgent.indexOf(
203               ClientUserAgentHeaders.WAP ) != -1 ) {
204
205               Document document =
206                  createXMLTipTestQuestion( resultSet, request,
207                     request.getContextPath() + "/WAP/images/",
208                        ".wbmp" );
209
210               // set appropriate Content-Type for client
211               response.setContentType( "text/vnd.wap.wml" );
212               applyXSLT( "WAP/WAPTipQuestion.xsl", document,
213                  response );
214            }
215
216            // if i-mode client is requesting client
217            else if ( userAgent.indexOf(
218               ClientUserAgentHeaders.IMODE ) != -1 ) {
219
220               Document document =
221                  createXMLTipTestQuestion( resultSet, request,
222                     request.getContextPath() + "/iMode/images/",
223                        ".gif" );
224
225               // set appropriate Content-Type for client
226               response.setContentType( "text/html" );
227               applyXSLT( "iMode/IMODETipQuestion.xsl", document,
228                  response );
229            }
230
231            // if J2ME client is requesting client
232            else if ( userAgent.indexOf(
233               ClientUserAgentHeaders.J2ME ) != -1 )
234               sendJ2MEClientResponse( resultSet, request,
235                  response );
236
237         } // end try
```

Fig. 12.9   TipTestServlet handles game logic and sends Tip Test to clients (part 5 of 13).

```
238
239          // handle exception if Document is null
240          catch ( NullPointerException nullPointerException ) {
241             nullPointerException.printStackTrace();
242          }
243
244       } // end method sendTipTestQuestion
245
246       // send Tip Test to Internet Explorer client
247       private Document createXMLTipTestQuestion(
248          ResultSet resultSet, HttpServletRequest request,
249          String imagePrefix, String imageSuffix )
250          throws IOException
251       {
252          // convert ResultSet to two-dimensional String array
253          String resultTable[][] = getResultTable( resultSet );
254
255          // create random-number generator
256          Random random = new Random( System.currentTimeMillis() );
257
258          // create 4 random tips
259          int randomRow[] = getRandomIndices( random );
260
261          // randomly determine correct index from 4 random indices
262          int correctAnswer = Math.abs( random.nextInt() ) %
263             randomRow.length;
264
265          int correctRow = randomRow[ correctAnswer ];
266
267          // open new session
268          HttpSession session = request.getSession();
269
270          // store correct answer in session
271          session.setAttribute( "correctAnswer",
272             new Integer( correctAnswer ) );
273
274          // store correct tip name
275          session.setAttribute( "correctTipName", new String(
276             resultTable[ correctRow ][ 1 ] ) );
277
278          // store correct tip description
279          session.setAttribute( "correctTipDescription", new String(
280             resultTable[ correctRow ][ 2 ] ) );
281
282          // determine image to send client
283          String imageName = imagePrefix +
284             resultTable[ correctRow ][ 3 ] + imageSuffix;
285
286          // create XML document based on randomly determined info
287          try {
288
```

Fig. 12.9 TipTestServlet handles game logic and sends Tip Test to clients (part 6 of 13).

```
289          // create document
290          DocumentBuilder builder = factory.newDocumentBuilder();
291          Document document = builder.newDocument();
292
293          // create question root Element
294          Element root = document.createElement( "question" );
295          document.appendChild( root );
296
297          // append Element image, which references image name
298          Element image = document.createElement( "image" );
299          image.appendChild(
300             document.createTextNode( imageName ) );
301          root.appendChild( image );
302
303          // create choices Element to hold 4 choice Elements
304          Element choices = document.createElement( "choices" );
305
306          // append 4 choice Elements that represent user choices
307          for ( int i = 0; i < randomRow.length; i++ )
308          {
309             // determine choice Elements from resultTable
310             Element choice = document.createElement( "choice" );
311             choice.appendChild( document.createTextNode(
312                resultTable[ randomRow[ i ] ][ 4 ] ) );
313
314             // set choice Element as correct or incorrect
315             Attr attribute =
316                document.createAttribute( "correct" );
317
318             if ( i == correctAnswer )
319                attribute.setValue( "true" );
320             else
321                attribute.setValue( "false" );
322
323             // append choice Element to choices Element
324             choice.setAttributeNode( attribute );
325             choices.appendChild( choice );
326          }
327
328          root.appendChild( choices );
329
330          return document;
331
332       } // end try
333
334       // handle exception building Document
335       catch ( ParserConfigurationException parserException ) {
336          parserException.printStackTrace();
337       }
338
339       return null;
340
```

Fig. 12.9 TipTestServlet handles game logic and sends Tip Test to clients (part 7 of 13).

```
341    } // end method createXMLTipTestQuestion
342
343    // send tip test to J2ME client
344    private void sendJ2MEClientResponse( ResultSet resultSet,
345       HttpServletRequest request,
346       HttpServletResponse response ) throws IOException
347    {
348       // convert ResultSet to two-dimensional String array
349       String resultTable[][] = getResultTable( resultSet );
350
351       // create random-number generator
352       Random random = new Random( System.currentTimeMillis() );
353
354       // create 4 random tips
355       int randomRow[] = getRandomIndices( random );
356
357       // randomly determine correct index from 4 random indices
358       int correctAnswer = Math.abs( random.nextInt() ) %
359          randomRow.length;
360
361       int correctRow = randomRow[ correctAnswer ];
362
363       // open old session
364       HttpSession session = request.getSession();
365
366       // store correct answer in session
367       session.setAttribute( "correctAnswer",
368          new Integer( correctAnswer ) );
369
370       // store correct tip name in session
371       session.setAttribute( "correctTipName", new String(
372          resultTable[ correctRow ][ 1 ] ) );
373
374       // store correct tip description in session
375       session.setAttribute( "correctTipDescription", new String(
376          resultTable[ correctRow ][ 2 ] ) );
377
378       // send J2ME client image name
379       String imageName = "/j2me/images/"  +
380          resultTable[ correctRow ][ 3 ] + ".png";
381
382       response.setContentType( "text/plain" );
383       PrintWriter out = response.getWriter();
384       out.println( imageName );
385
386       // send J2ME client test
387       for ( int i = 0; i < randomRow.length; i++ )
388          out.println( resultTable[ randomRow[ i ] ][ 4 ] );
389
390    } // end method sendJ2MEClientResponse
391
```

Fig. 12.9 TipTestServlet handles game logic and sends Tip Test to clients (part 8 of 13).

```
392    // convert ResultSet to two-dimensional String array
393    private String[][] getResultTable( ResultSet resultSet )
394    {
395       // create table of Strings to store ResultSet
396       String resultTable[][] = new String[ 7 ][ 5 ];
397
398       for ( int i = 0; i < 7; i++ ) {
399
400          for ( int j = 0; j < 5; j++ )
401             resultTable[ i ][ j ] = "";
402       }
403
404       // store all columns in table
405       try {
406
407          // for each row in resultSet
408          for ( int row = 0; resultSet.next(); row++ ) {
409
410             // for each column in resultSet
411             for ( int column = 0; column < 5; column++ ) {
412
413                // store resultSet element in resultTable
414                resultTable[ row ][ column ] +=
415                   resultSet.getObject( column + 1 );
416             }
417          }
418       }
419
420       // handle exception if servlet cannot get ResultSet Object
421       catch ( SQLException sqlException ) {
422          sqlException.printStackTrace();
423          return null;
424       }
425
426       return resultTable;
427
428    } // end method getResultTable
429
430    // get 4 randomly generated indices from resultTable
431    private int[] getRandomIndices( Random random )
432    {
433       // create list containing row indices for resultTable
434       int list[] = new int[ 7 ];
435
436       for ( int i = 0; i < list.length; i++ )
437          list[ i ] = i;
438
439       int randomRow[] = new int[ 4 ];
440
441       // select 4 randomly generated indices from list
442       for ( int i = 0; i < randomRow.length; i++ )
443          randomRow[ i ] = getRandomRow( list, random );
```

Fig. 12.9   TipTestServlet handles game logic and sends Tip Test to clients (part 9 of 13).

```
444
445         return randomRow; // return these indices
446
447     } // end method getRandomIndices
448
449     // get random element from list, then nullify element
450     private int getRandomRow( int list[], Random random )
451     {
452         // get random element from list
453         int randomRow = Math.abs( random.nextInt() ) % list.length;
454
455         while ( list[ randomRow ] < 0 )
456             randomRow = Math.abs( random.nextInt() ) % list.length;
457
458         list[ randomRow ] = -1; // nullify element
459
460         return randomRow;
461
462     } // end method getRandomRow
463
464     // apply XSLT style sheet to XML document
465     private void applyXSLT( String xslFile,
466         Document xmlDocument, HttpServletResponse response )
467         throws IOException
468     {
469         // apply XSLT
470         try {
471
472             // open InputStream for XSL document
473             InputStream xslStream =
474                 getServletContext().getResourceAsStream( xslFile );
475
476             // create StreamSource for XSLT document
477             Source xslSource = new StreamSource( xslStream );
478
479             // create DOMSource for source XML document
480             Source xmlSource = new DOMSource( xmlDocument );
481
482             // get PrintWriter for writing data to client
483             PrintWriter output = response.getWriter();
484
485             // create StreamResult for transformation result
486             Result result = new StreamResult( output );
487
488             // create Transformer for XSL transformation
489             Transformer transformer =
490                 transformerFactory.newTransformer( xslSource );
491
492             // transform and deliver content to client
493             transformer.transform( xmlSource, result );
494
495         } // end try
```

Fig. 12.9 `TipTestServlet` handles game logic and sends Tip Test to clients (part 10 of 13).

```
496
497        // handle exception transforming content
498        catch ( TransformerException exception ) {
499           exception.printStackTrace();
500        }
501
502     } // end method applyXSLT
503
504     // create XML Document that stores Tip Test answer
505     private Document createXMLTipTestAnswer(
506        HttpServletRequest request ) throws IOException
507     {
508        // get session
509        HttpSession session = request.getSession();
510
511        // match correct answer with session answer
512        Integer integer =
513           ( Integer ) session.getAttribute( "correctAnswer" );
514        int correctAnswer = integer.intValue();
515
516        // give client correct tip name and description
517        String correctTipName =
518           ( String ) session.getAttribute( "correctTipName" );
519
520        String correctTipDescription =
521           ( String ) session.getAttribute(
522              "correctTipDescription" );
523
524        // get user selection
525        int selection = Integer.parseInt(
526           request.getParameter( "userAnswer" ) );
527
528        String answer;
529
530        // determine if user answer is correct
531        if ( correctAnswer == selection )
532           answer = "Correct";
533        else
534           answer = "Incorrect";
535
536        // get link to TipTestServlet
537        String servletName = request.getContextPath() + "/" +
538           getServletConfig().getServletName();
539
540        // create XML document based on randomly determined info
541        try {
542
543           // create document
544           DocumentBuilder builder = factory.newDocumentBuilder();
545           Document document = builder.newDocument();
546
```

Fig. 12.9 **TipTestServlet** handles game logic and sends Tip Test to clients (part 11 of 13).

```
547              // create question root Element
548              Element root = document.createElement( "answer" );
549              document.appendChild( root );
550
551              // append Element that informs client of correct answer
552              Element correct = document.createElement( "correct" );
553              correct.appendChild(
554                 document.createTextNode( answer ) );
555              root.appendChild( correct );
556
557              // append Element that describes tip name
558              Element name =
559                 document.createElement( "correctTipName" );
560              name.appendChild(
561                 document.createTextNode( correctTipName ) );
562              root.appendChild( name );
563
564              // append Element that describes tip description
565              Element description =
566                 document.createElement( "correctTipDescription" );
567              description.appendChild(
568                 document.createTextNode( correctTipDescription ) );
569              root.appendChild( description );
570
571              // append Element that links to TipTestServlet
572              Element servletLink =
573                 document.createElement( "servletName" );
574              servletLink.appendChild(
575                 document.createTextNode( servletName ) );
576              root.appendChild( servletLink );
577
578              return document;
579
580           } // end try
581
582           // handle exception building Document
583           catch ( ParserConfigurationException parserException ) {
584              parserException.printStackTrace();
585           }
586
587           return null;
588
589        } // end method createXMLTipTestAnswer
590
591        // send answer to J2ME client
592        private void sendJ2MEAnswer( HttpServletRequest request,
593           HttpServletResponse response ) throws IOException
594        {
595           // get client test response
596           BufferedReader in = request.getReader();
597           int selection = Integer.parseInt( in.readLine().trim() );
598
```

Fig. 12.9   `TipTestServlet` handles game logic and sends Tip Test to clients (part 12 of 13).

```
599            // send J2ME client text data
600            response.setContentType( "text/plain" );
601            PrintWriter out = response.getWriter();
602
603            // inform client whether client is correct or incorrect
604            HttpSession session = request.getSession();
605
606            // match correct answer with session answer
607            Integer integer =
608               ( Integer ) session.getAttribute( "correctAnswer" );
609            int correctAnswer = integer.intValue();
610
611            // send correct tip name and description
612            String correctTipName =
613               ( String ) session.getAttribute( "correctTipName" );
614
615            String correctTipDescription =
616               ( String ) session.getAttribute(
617                  "correctTipDescription" );
618
619            // determine whether answer is correct
620            if ( selection == correctAnswer )
621               out.println( "Correct" );
622            else
623               out.println( "Incorrect" );
624
625            // give client correct tip name and description
626            out.println( correctTipName );
627            out.println( correctTipDescription );
628
629         } // end method sendJ2MEAnswer
630
631         // invoked when servlet is destroyed
632         public void destroy()
633         {
634            // close database connection
635            try {
636               connection.close();
637            }
638
639            // handle if connection cannot be closed
640            catch ( SQLException sqlException ) {
641               sqlException.printStackTrace();
642            }
643
644         } // end method destroy
645      }
```

Fig. 12.9   **TipTestServlet** handles game logic and sends Tip Test to clients (part 13 of 13).

Using method **getInitParameter** in line 37 allows us to specify the database out-side the servlet—we can change the database (e.g., change from Cloudscape to mySQL) by modifying the **<param-value>** element in the **<init-param>** element in **web.xml**, without having to recompile the servlet. For this case study, this element contains

```
<init-param>
   <param-name>JDBC_DRIVER</param-name>
   <param-value>
      COM.cloudscape.core.RmiJdbcDriver
   </param-value>
</init-param>
```

Lines 43–45 retrieve the database URL from **web.xml**, and line 47 makes the connection to this URL—note that method **destroy** (lines 632–644) closes this connection. If we decide to change the location of the database, we need only to modify the **<param-value>** element in a separate **<init-param>** element in **web.xml**. For this case study, this element contains

```
<init-param>
   <param-name>DATABASE_URL</param-name>
   <param-value>jdbc:cloudscape:rmi:tips</param-value>
</init-param>
```

Lines 50–53 create objects that we use later to build XML **Document**s and use **Transformer**s to apply XSLTs. We discuss XML-related Java packages later in this section.

TipTestServlet calls method **doGet** (lines 70–103) to handle the **get** request. Line 78 creates a **Statement** from the **Connection** instantiated in method init. Lines 81–82 obtain a **ResultSet** of all database elements from this **Statement**. As discussed in the introduction, our database (the **ResultSet**) contains seven rows and five columns—resulting in 35 **String** objects. Lines 88–90 set the **HttpServletResponse**'s header so the client will not cache the information that **TipTestServlet** sends. Line 92 calls method **sendTipTestQuestion** (lines 176–244) to perform the game logic and send the client the Tip-Test question. Line 184 extracts the **User-Agent** header from the **HttpServletRequest**. Lines 187–235 determine which client made the request by matching the **User-Agent** header with those in interface **ClientUserAgentHeaders**. This client-determination process is identical to the one in **WelcomeServlet**.

Until this point in execution, the servlet has behaved identically for all client requests. Now, **TipTestServlet** performs different operations based on the type of client making the request. These operations are almost identical among the Internet Explorer, Openwave UP simulator and the Pixo i-mode browser. The servlet's operations for the J2ME client differ from that of the other three clients, because the J2ME client cannot interpret XML documents without using non-standard software (although this is likely to change in the future). We now trace the servlet's behavior for each client type's request. We begin discussing **TipTestServlet**'s behavior for an Internet Explorer request. Next, we discuss the servlet's behavior for a Openwave UP simulator request. We then discuss the servlet's behavior for a Pixo i-mode browser request. Finally, we discuss the servlet's behavior for a Sun MIDP-device client request.

12.3.1 Internet Explorer Request

If Internet Explorer sent the request, lines 190–193 invoke method **createXML-TipTestQuestion** (lines 247–341), which creates and returns an XML **Document** that contains the Tip-Test question. Interface **Document** of package **org.w3c.dom** represents an XML document's top-level node, which provides access to all the document's nodes. Line 253 calls method **getResultTable** (lines 393–428), which converts the **ResultSet** into a two-dimensional array of **String**s. We use this method so we have an easier time accessing individual elements of the **ResultSet** through an array. Lines 396–402 instantiate this array, and lines 408–417 transfer the **ResultSet** content to the array.

When method **getResultTable** returns the **String** array, line 256 creates a **Random** object that enables **TipTestServlet** to select the tip image and possible answers randomly. Line 259 passes a reference to the **Random** object to method **getRandomIndices** (lines 431–447), which returns an array of four integers. Each integer is a distinct, random index that corresponds to a tip in the two-dimensional **String** array that method **getResultTable** generated. Lines 434–437 create an array of seven integers called **list**—each integer represents that integer's index in the array (i.e., **list[0] = 0**, **list[1] = 1**, etc.). Line 439 creates an empty array of four integers that correspond to the four possible tip answers. Lines 442–443 invoke method **getRandomRow** (lines 450–462) for each element in the four-integer array. Line 453 select an integer at random from the seven-integer array. If the integer has been selected previously—indicated by a **-1** value—lines 455–456 select an integer that has not been selected. If the integer has not been selected previously, line 458 nullifies this array element by setting that element to **-1**. Nullifying this element ensures that method **getRandomRow** will not return duplicate integers. Line 460 returns the integer.

Array **randomRow** contains four distinct integers that correspond to tips in **resultTable**. Lines 262–263 randomly select an integer from **randomRow**. This integer indicates the "correct" answer in the game—specifically, this integer represents the **resultTable** row that holds the information for the correct tip (line 265). **TipTestServlet** stores this information in an **HttpSession** object (line 268), so when the client sends the user's selection back to **TipTestServlet**, **TipTestServlet** can check this selection against the correct answer stored in the **HttpSession** object. An **HttpSession** object acts like a cookie—both can store name/value pairs. In session terminology, these pairs are called *attributes*. We may store attributes in an **HttpSession** object with method **setAttribute**. Lines 271–280 store the correct answer, tip name and tip description in the **HttpSession** object. Using the correct answer and parameters **imagePrefix** and **imageSuffix** of method **createXMLTipTestQuestion**, lines 283–284 determine the proper image to send to the client.

At this point, **TipTestServlet** has determined the Tip-Test question (the image and four possible answers) to send the client. We now explain how **TipTestServlet** marks up this data as an XML **Document**, applies an XSL transformation to this **Document**, then sends the resulting document to the client.

Lines 290–328 mark up the Tip-Test question as an XML **Document**, which represents an XML document and provides a means for creating and retrieving its nodes. Line 290 creates a **DocumentBuilder** using the **DocumentBuilderFactory** instantiated in method **init**. Line 291 creates an XML **Document** using the **DocumentBuilder**.

Class **Element** represents an element node in an XML document. A **Document** creates an **Element** with method **createElement**. Lines 294–295 create **Element** **question** and assign it as the root **Element** in the **Document**. Lines 298–301 create **Element image** from the correct tip's image and assign **Element image** as a child of

Element question. Line 304 creates **Element choices**, which hold the four **choice Element**s created on lines 307–326. Each **choice Element** represents a possible answer for the question. Lines 315–324 include an attribute that specifies whether the choice is **correct** or **incorrect**—obviously, only one attribute specifies a value of **correct**. Line 325 appends the **choice Element**s to **Element choices**, and line 328 appends **choices** to root **Element question**.

When method **createXMLTipTestQuestion** returns the XML **Document**, **TipTestServlet** must apply an XSLT to this **Document** and send the result of the transformation to the client. Line 124 sets the **HttpServletResponse**'s MIME type to **text/html**, because the XSL transformation generates an XHTML document. Lines 127–128 call method **applyXSLT** (465–502) to apply **XHTMLTipQuestion.xsl** (Fig. 12.10) to the XML **Document**. Lines 473–474 open an **InputStream** for **XHTMLTipQuestion.xsl**. Line 477 creates a **StreamSource** from this **InputStream** for the XSL document. Line 480 creates a **DOMSource** for the XML **Document**. Line 486 creates a **Result** for the resulting transformation—in this case, an XHTML document. **TipTestServlet** uses a **PrintWriter** to create the **Result**, so **TipTestServlet** will send the resulting transformation directly to the client. Lines 489–490 create a **Transformer** using the XSL **StreamSource** and the **TranformerFactory** (instantiated in method **init**). The **Transformer** is the object that applies the XSLT to the XML document. Line 493 invokes method **transform** of class **Transformer** to apply the transformation to produce the XHTML document.

In Fig. 12.10, lines 9–11 specify the DTD and other output options using the **xsl:output** element. Line 15 specifies that **Element question** is the root **Element** in the XML **Document** that **XHTMLTipQuestion.xsl** will transform. Line 16 begins the XHTML document with the element **html**. Lines 22–86 contain the **body** element, which contains the tip image and the four possible answers. Lines 27–29 display the image associated with the image **Element** in the XML **Document**. Lines 40–83 create a form with four possible answers. Lines 47–77 create four radio buttons associated with these answers. Line 82 creates a **Submit** button so the user can submit the selection. Figure 12.11 shows Tip Test in action after the servlet applies the XSLT to the XML **Document**. The image on the left shows the user selecting the answer, and the image on the right shows the user about to submit the answer.

```
1   <?xml version="1.0"?>
2
3   <!-- XHTMLTipQuestion.xsl -->
4   <!-- XHTML stylesheet      -->
5
6   <xsl:stylesheet version = "1.0"
7      xmlns:xsl = "http://www.w3.org/1999/XSL/Transform">
8
9      <xsl:output method = "xml" omit-xml-declaration = "no"
10        doctype-system = "DTD/xhtml1-strict.dtd"
11        doctype-public = "-//W3C//DTD XHTML 1.0 Strict//EN"/>
```

Fig. 12.10 **XHTMLTipQuestion.xsl** transforms XML Tip-Test question to XHTML document (part 1 of 3).

```
12
13      <!-- specify the root of the XML document -->
14      <!-- that references this stylesheet      -->
15      <xsl:template match = "question">
16         <html xmlns="http://www.w3.org/1999/xhtml">
17
18            <head>
19               <title>Tip Test</title>
20            </head>
21
22            <body>
23
24               <p>
25
26                  <!-- display image -->
27                  <img name = "image" alt = "Tip Image"
28                     src = "{image}">
29                  </img>
30
31               </p>
32
33               <p>
34                  What is the name of the icon shown?
35               </p>
36
37               <p>
38
39                  <!-- create a form with four checkboxes -->
40                  <form method = "post"
41                     action = "/advjhtp1/tiptest">
42
43                     <!-- build a table for the options -->
44                     <table>
45                        <tr>
46                           <td>
47                              <input type = "radio"
48                                 name = "userAnswer" value = "0">
49                              </input>
50                              <xsl:value-of select =
51                                 "choices/choice[1]"/>
52                           </td>
53
54                           <td>
55                              <input type = "radio"
56                                 name = "userAnswer" value = "1">
57                              </input>
58                              <xsl:value-of select =
59                                 "choices/choice[2]"/>
60                           </td>
61                        </tr>
62
```

Fig. 12.10 `XHTMLTipQuestion.xsl` transforms XML Tip-Test question to XHTML document (part 2 of 3).

```
63                            <tr>
64                                <td>
65                                    <input type = "radio"
66                                        name = "userAnswer" value = "2">
67                                    </input>
68                                    <xsl:value-of select =
69                                        "choices/choice[3]"/>
70                                </td>
71
72                                <td>
73                                    <input type = "radio"
74                                        name = "userAnswer" value = "3">
75                                    </input>
76                                    <xsl:value-of select =
77                                        "choices/choice[4]"/>
78                                </td>
79                            </tr>
80                        </table>
81
82                        <input type = "submit" value = "Submit"/>
83                    </form>
84                </p>
85
86            </body>
87        </html>
88    </xsl:template>
89 </xsl:stylesheet>
```

Fig. 12.10 **`XHTMLTipQuestion.xsl`** transforms XML Tip-Test question to XHTML
document (part 3 of 3).

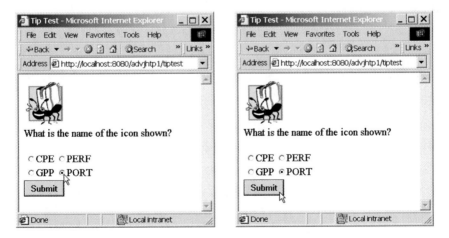

Fig. 12.11 Internet Explorer Tip-Test question output screen.

Each radio button in the XHTML document contains a unique value, so when the user
presses the **Submit** button, Internet Explorer sends the selected value to **TipTest-**
Servlet (as **post** data). **TipTestServlet** (Fig. 12.9) invokes method **doPost**

(lines 106–173) upon receiving **post** data. Lines 117–129 recognize that the request is from the Internet Explorer and call method **createXMLTipTestAnswer** (lines 505–589) to determine if the user's answer is correct.

Line 509 retrieves the **HttpSession**, and lines 512–522 extract the correct tip answer, name and description from the **HttpSession**. Lines 525–526 retrieve the user's selection from the **HttpServletRequest**. Lines 531–534 match the user's selection with the tip answer to determine if the user is correct. Lines 537–538 determine the **TipTestServlet**'s URL so clients can reconnect to **TipTestServlet** to receive another Tip-Test question.

Lines 544–576 mark up the **HttpSession** contents and **TipTestServlet**'s URL as an XML **Document** from the **DocumentBuilder**. Line 544 creates a **Document-Builder**, and line 545 creates an XML **Document**. Lines 548–549 create **Element answer** and assign it as the root **Element** in the **Document**. Lines 552–554 create **Element correct**, which stores whether the user is correct or incorrect. Line 555 assigns **Element correct** as a child of **Element answer**. Lines 558–561 and lines 565–568 create **Elements correctTipName** and **correctTipDescription**, which hold the name and description of the correct tip, respectively. Lines 562 and 569 assign these **Elements** as children of **Element answer**. Lines 572–575 create **Element servletName**, which holds **TipTestServlet**'s URL. Line 576 assigns this **Element** as a child of **Element answer**.

When method **createXMLTipTestAnswer** returns the XML **Document** (line 578), **TipTestServlet** must apply an XSLT to this **Document** and send the resulting transformation to the client. Line 124 sets the MIME type to **text/html**, and lines 127–128 call method **applyXSLT** to apply **XHTMLTipAnswer.xsl** (Fig. 12.12) to the XML **Document**.

```
1    <?xml version="1.0"?>
2
3    <!-- XHTMLTipAnswer.xsl -->
4    <!-- XHTML stylesheet -->
5
6    <xsl:stylesheet version = "1.0"
7       xmlns:xsl = "http://www.w3.org/1999/XSL/Transform">
8
9       <xsl:output method = "xml" omit-xml-declaration = "no"
10         doctype-system = "DTD/xhtml1-strict.dtd"
11         doctype-public = "-//W3C//DTD XHTML 1.0 Strict//EN"/>
12
13      <!-- specify the root of the XML document -->
14      <!-- that references this stylesheet       -->
15      <xsl:template match = "answer">
16         <html xmlns="http://www.w3.org/1999/xhtml">
17
18            <head>
19               <title>Tip Test Answer</title>
20            </head>
21
```

Fig. 12.12 XHTMLTipAnswer.xsl transforms XML Tip-Test answer to XHTML document (part 1 of 2).

```
22              <body>
23
24                 <p>
25                    <h1>
26                       <xsl:value-of select = "correct"/>
27                    </h1>
28                 </p>
29
30                 <p>
31                    <h2>Tip Name</h2>
32                 </p>
33
34                 <p>
35                    <h3>
36                       <xsl:value-of select = "correctTipName"/>
37                    </h3>
38                 </p>
39
40                 <p>
41                    <h2>Tip Description</h2>
42                 </p>
43
44                 <p>
45                    <h3>
46                       <xsl:value-of
47                          select = "correctTipDescription"/>
48                    </h3>
49                 </p>
50
51                 <p>
52                    <h2>
53                       <a href="{servletName}">Next Tip</a>
54                    </h2>
55                 </p>
56
57              </body>
58           </html>
59        </xsl:template>
60     </xsl:stylesheet>
```

Fig. 12.12 XHTMLTipAnswer.xsl transforms XML Tip-Test answer to XHTML
document (part 2 of 2).

In Fig. 12.12, lines 9–11 specify the DTD using the **xsl:output** element. Line 15
specifies that **Element answer** is the root **Element** in the XML **Document** that
XHTMLTipAnswer.xsl will transform. Line 16 begins the XHTML document. Line 26
uses **Element correct** from the XML **Document** to display whether the user's selection is the correct answer. Lines 36 and 47 use **Element**s **correctTipName** and **correctTipDescription** to display the name and description of the correct tip,
respectively. Line 53 uses **Element servletName** to provide a link to **TipTest-
Servlet** so the user can receive another Tip-Test question. Figure 12.21 shows the Tip-
Test answer in Internet Explorer.

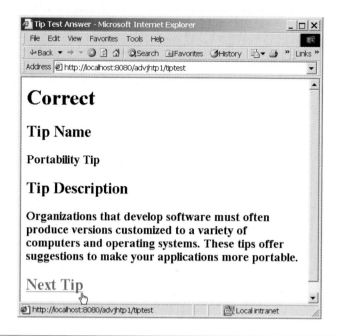

Fig. 12.13 Internet Explorer Tip-Test answer output screen.

12.3.2 WAP Request

If the Openwave UP simulator made the original **get** request to **TipTestServlet** (Fig. 12.9), lines 202–214 determine that the requesting client is a WAP client. Lines 205–208 invoke method **createXMLTipTestQuestion** to create an XML **Document** that contains the Tip-Test question. Using the arguments for this method, we specify that the tip images are in **wbmp** format and are located in the **WAP/images** directory of the servlet-context path. Line 211 sets the MIME type to **text/vnd.wap.wml** to produce WML content. Lines 212–213 call method **applyXSLT** to apply **WAPTipQuestion.xsl** (Fig. 12.14) to the XML **Document**.

```
1    <?xml version="1.0"?>
2
3    <!-- WAPTipQuestion.xsl -->
4    <!-- WAP stylesheet       -->
5
6    <xsl:stylesheet
7       xmlns:xsl="http://www.w3.org/1999/XSL/Transform"
8          version="1.0">
9
10      <xsl:output method = "xml" omit-xml-declaration = "no"
11         doctype-system = "http://www.wapforum.org/DTD/wml_1.1.xml"
12         doctype-public = "-//WAPFORUM//DTD WML 1.1//EN"/>
```

Fig. 12.14 **WAPTipQuestion.xsl** transforms XML Tip-Test question to WML document (part 1 of 2).

```
13
14      <!-- specify the root of the XML document -->
15      <!-- that references this stylesheet      -->
16      <xsl:template match = "question">
17
18         <wml>
19            <card id = "card1" title = "Tip Test">
20
21               <do type = "accept" label = "OK">
22                  <go href = "#card2"/>
23               </do>
24
25               <p>
26                  <img src = "{image}" height = "55" width = "55"
27                     alt = "Tip Image"/>
28               </p>
29
30            </card>
31
32            <card id = "card2" title = "Tip Test">
33               <do type = "accept" label = "Submit">
34                  <go method = "post" href = "/advjhtp1/tiptest">
35                     <postfield name = "userAnswer"
36                        value = "$(question)"/>
37                  </go>
38               </do>
39
40               <p>
41                  The tip shown on the previous screen is called:
42               </p>
43
44               <p>
45                  <select name = "question"
46                     iname = "iquestion" ivalue = "1">
47
48                     <option value = "0"><xsl:value-of
49                        select = "choices/choice[1]"/></option>
50
51                     <option value = "1"><xsl:value-of
52                        select = "choices/choice[2]"/></option>
53
54                     <option value = "2"><xsl:value-of
55                        select = "choices/choice[3]"/></option>
56
57                     <option value = "3"><xsl:value-of
58                        select = "choices/choice[4]"/></option>
59                  </select>
60               </p>
61            </card>
62         </wml>
63      </xsl:template>
64   </xsl:stylesheet>
```

Fig. 12.14 WAPTipQuestion.xsl transforms XML Tip-Test question to WML
document (part 2 of 2).

In Fig. 12.14, lines 10–12 specify the DTD using the **xsl:output** element. Line 16 specifies that **Element question** is the root **Element** in the XML **Document** that **WAPTipQuestion.xsl** will transform. Line 18 begins the WML document with the **wml** element. Lines 19–30 declare the first *card*—or the page that displays WML content—that the browser will display. Lines 26–27 display the image associated with the **image Element** in the XML **Document**. The **do** element (lines 21–23) informs the simulator to show the second card when the user presses the **OK** button on the simulator. Lines 32–61 declare the second card onto which the UP simulator places the four possible answers. Using the **choice Element**s in the **choices Element**, lines 45–59 create a selection list that contains the possible answers. The **do** element (lines 33–38) informs the simulator to send the user's selection to **TipTestServlet** when the user presses the **Submit** button.

Figure 12.15 shows Tip Test after **TipTestServlet** applies the XSLT to the XML **Document**. The image on the left shows the tip image, and the image on the right shows the user selecting the answer.

Fig. 12.15 Openwave UP simulator Tip-Test question screen. (Image of UP.SDK courtesy Openwave Systems Inc. Openwave, the Openwave logo, and UP.SDK are trademarks of Openwave Systems Inc. All rights reserved.)

Each selection list item contains a unique value. When the user presses **Submit**, the UP simulator **post**s the selected value to **TipTestServlet**. **TipTestServlet** (Fig. 12.9) invokes method **doPost** when receiving **post** data. Lines 132–144 determine that the request is from the Openwave UP simulator. Lines 135–136 call method **createXMLTipTestAnswer** to create an XML **Document** that stores whether the user is correct, the name and description of the correct tip and **TipTestServlet**'s URL. Line 139 sets the MIME type to **text/vnd.wap.wml** to produce WML content and lines 157–158 call **applyXSLT** to apply **WAPTipAnswer.xsl** (Fig. 12.16) to the XML **Document**.

In Fig. 12.16, lines 10–12 specify the DTD using the **xsl:output** element. Line 16 specifies that **Element answer** is the root **Element** in the XML **Document** that **WAPTipAnswer.xsl** will transform. Line 18 begins the WML document with the **wml** element. Lines 20–48 declare the card (the answer screen) in this WML document. Line 29 uses **Element correct** from the XML **Document** to display whether the user's selection is the correct answer. Lines 37 and 45 use **Element**s **correctTipName** and **correctTipDescription** to display the name and description of the correct tip, respectively. Using **Element servletName** in the XML **Document**, the **do** element (lines 22–26) provides a link to **TipTestServlet**, so the user can receive another Tip-Test question. Figure 12.17 shows the Tip-Test answer in the Openwave UP simulator.

```
1    <?xml version="1.0"?>
2
3    <!-- WAPTipAnswer.xsl -->
4    <!-- WAP stylesheet    -->
5
6    <xsl:stylesheet
7       xmlns:xsl="http://www.w3.org/1999/XSL/Transform"
8          version="1.0">
9
10       <xsl:output method = "xml" omit-xml-declaration = "no"
11          doctype-system = "http://www.wapforum.org/DTD/wml_1.1.xml"
12          doctype-public = "-//WAPFORUM//DTD WML 1.1//EN"/>
13
14       <!-- specify the root of the XML document -->
15       <!-- that references this stylesheet      -->
16       <xsl:template match = "answer">
17
18          <wml>
19
20             <card id = "card1" title = "Tip Test Answer">
21
22                <do type = "accept" label = "OK">
23                   <go method = "get"
24                      href = "/advjhtp1/tiptest">
25                   </go>
26                </do>
27
28                <p>
29                   <xsl:value-of select = "correct"/>
30                </p>
```

Fig. 12.16 WAPTipAnswer.xsl transforms answer to WML document (part 1 of 2).

```
31
32              <p>
33                 Tip Name
34              </p>
35
36              <p>
37                 <xsl:value-of select = "correctTipName"/>
38              </p>
39
40              <p>
41                 Tip Description
42              </p>
43
44              <p>
45                 <xsl:value-of select = "correctTipDescription"/>
46              </p>
47
48           </card>
49
50        </wml>
51     </xsl:template>
52  </xsl:stylesheet>
```

Fig. 12.16 `WAPTipAnswer.xsl` transforms answer to WML document (part 2 of 2).

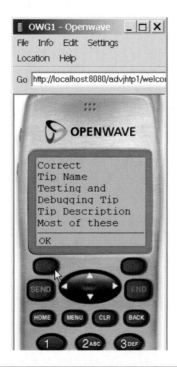

Fig. 12.17 Openwave UP simulator Tip-Test answer screen. (Image of UP.SDK courtesy Openwave Systems Inc. Openwave, the Openwave logo, and UP.SDK are trademarks of Openwave Systems Inc. All rights reserved.)

12.3.3 Pixo i-mode Request

If the Pixo browser made the original **get** request to **TipTestServlet** (Fig. 12.9), lines 217–229 determine that the requesting client is an i-mode client. Lines 220–223 invoke method **createXMLTipTestQuestion** to create the XML **Document** that contains the Tip Test question. Using the arguments for this method, we specify that the tip images are in **gif** format and are located in the **iMode/images** directory of the servlet-context path. Line 226 sets the MIME type to **text/html** to produce cHTML content. Lines 227–228 call method **applyXSLT** to apply **IMODETipQuestion.xsl** (Fig. 12.18) to the XML **Document**.

```
1    <?xml version="1.0"?>
2
3    <!-- IMODETipQuestion.xsl -->
4    <!-- i-mode stylesheet      -->
5
6    <xsl:stylesheet version = "1.0"
7       xmlns:xsl = "http://www.w3.org/1999/XSL/Transform">
8
9       <xsl:output method = "html" omit-xml-declaration = "yes"
10         doctype-public = "-//W3C//DTD Compact HTML 1.0 Draft//EN"/>
11
12      <!-- specify the root of the XML document -->
13      <!-- that references this stylesheet       -->
14      <xsl:template match = "question">
15         <html>
16
17            <head>
18               <title>Tip Test</title>
19            </head>
20
21            <body>
22
23               <p>
24
25                  <!-- display image -->
26                  <img name = "image" height = "40"
27                     width = "40" alt = "Tip Image"
28                        src = "{image}">
29                  </img>
30               </p>
31
32               <p>
33                  What is the name of the icon shown?
34               </p>
35
36               <p>
37
38                  <!-- create a form with four checkboxes -->
39                  <form method = "post"
40                     action = "/advjhtp1/tiptest">
```

Fig. 12.18 **IMODETipQuestion.xsl** transforms XML Tip-Test question to cHTML document (part 1 of 2).

```
41
42                    <!-- build a table for the options -->
43                    <table>
44                       <tr>
45                          <td>
46                             <input type = "radio"
47                                name = "userAnswer" value = "0">
48                             </input>
49                             <xsl:value-of select =
50                                "choices/choice[1]"/>
51                          </td>
52
53                          <td>
54                             <input type = "radio"
55                                name = "userAnswer" value = "1">
56                             </input>
57                             <xsl:value-of select =
58                                "choices/choice[2]"/>
59                          </td>
60                       </tr>
61
62                       <tr>
63                          <td>
64                             <input type = "radio"
65                                name = "userAnswer" value = "2">
66                             </input>
67                             <xsl:value-of select =
68                                "choices/choice[3]"/>
69                          </td>
70
71                          <td>
72                             <input type = "radio"
73                                name = "userAnswer" value = "3">
74                             </input>
75                             <xsl:value-of select =
76                                "choices/choice[4]"/>
77                          </td>
78                       </tr>
79                    </table>
80
81                    <input type = "submit" value = "Submit"/>
82                 </form>
83              </p>
84
85           </body>
86        </html>
87     </xsl:template>
88  </xsl:stylesheet>
```

Fig. 12.18 `IMODETipQuestion.xsl` transforms XML Tip-Test question to cHTML document (part 2 of 2).

In Fig. 12.18, lines 9–10 specify the DTD using the **xsl:output** element. Line 14 specifies that **Element question** is the root **Element** in the XML **Document** that

IMODETipQuestion.xsl will transform. Line 15 begins the cHTML document with the **html** element. Lines 21–85 contain the **body** element that stores the tip image and the four possible answers. Lines 26–29 display the image associated with the image **Element** in the XML **Document**. Lines 39–82 create a form for the four possible answers. Lines 46–76 create four radio buttons associated with these answers. Line 81 creates a **Submit** button so the user can submit the choice.

Figure 12.19 shows Tip Test in action after **TipTestServlet** applies the XSLT to the XML **Document**. The image on the left shows the user selecting the answer, and the image on the right shows the user about to submit the answer.

Each radio button in the cHTML document contains a unique value, so when the user presses **Submit**, the Pixo browser **post**s the selected value to **TipTestServlet**. **TipTestServlet** invokes method **doPost** upon receiving **post** data. Lines 147–159 determine that the request is from the Pixo browser. Lines 150–151 call method **createXM-LTipTestAnswer** to create an XML **Document** that stores whether the user is correct, the name and description of the correct tip, and **TipTestServlet**'s URL. Line 154 sets the MIME type to **text/html** to produce cHTML content, and lines 157–158 call method **applyXSLT** to apply **IMODETipAnswer.xsl** (Fig. 12.20) to the XML **Document**.

In Fig. 12.20, lines 9–10 specify the DTD using the **xsl:output** element. Line 14 specifies that **Element answer** is the root **Element** in the XML **Document** that **IMODETipAnswer.xsl** will transform. Line 15 begins the cHTML document with the **html** element. Line 25 uses **Element correct** from the XML **Document** to display whether the user's selection is correct. Lines 35 and 45–46 use **Element**s **correctTipName** and **correctTipDescription** to display the name and description of the correct tip, respectively. Using **Element servletName**, line 52 provides a link to **TipTestServlet**, so the user can receive another Tip-Test question. Figure 12.21 shows the Tip-Test answer on the Pixo i-mode browser.

Fig. 12.19 Pixo i-mode browser Tip-Test question screen. (Courtesy of Pixo, Inc.)

```
1   <?xml version="1.0"?>
2
3   <!-- IMODETipAnswer.xsl -->
4   <!-- i-mode stylesheet   -->
5
6   <xsl:stylesheet version = "1.0"
7      xmlns:xsl = "http://www.w3.org/1999/XSL/Transform">
8
9      <xsl:output method = "html" omit-xml-declaration = "yes"
10        doctype-public = "-//W3C//DTD Compact HTML 1.0 Draft//EN"/>
11
12     <!-- specify the root of the XML document -->
13     <!-- that references this stylesheet        -->
14     <xsl:template match = "answer">
15        <html>
16
17           <head>
18              <title>Tip Test Answer</title>
19           </head>
20
21           <body>
22
23              <p>
24                 <h1>
25                    <xsl:value-of select = "correct"/>
26                 </h1>
27              </p>
28
29              <p>
30                 <h2>Tip Name</h2>
31              </p>
32
33              <p>
34                 <h3>
35                    <xsl:value-of select = "correctTipName"/>
36                 </h3>
37              </p>
38
39              <p>
40                 <h2>Tip Description</h2>
41              </p>
42
43              <p>
44                 <h3>
45                    <xsl:value-of
46                       select = "correctTipDescription"/>
47                 </h3>
48              </p>
49
50              <p>
51                 <h2>
52                    <a href="{servletName}">Next Tip</a>
```

Fig. 12.20 IMODETipAnswer.xsl transforms XML Tip-Test answer to cHTML document (part 1 of 2).

```
53                    </h2>
54                </p>
55
56            </body>
57         </html>
58      </xsl:template>
59   </xsl:stylesheet>
```

Fig. 12.20 `IMODETipAnswer.xsl` transforms XML Tip-Test answer to cHTML document (part 2 of 2).

Fig. 12.21 Pixo i-mode browser Tip-Test answer screen. (Courtesy of Pixo, Inc.)

12.3.4 J2ME Client Request

TipTestServlet behaves differently if a J2ME client made the **get** request. **TipTestServlet** does not use XML for the J2ME client, because currently, a J2ME client cannot interpret XML data without using proprietary software. Sun Microsystems claims that "it is not yet clear how far in the future this Java-XML nirvana is, but we can say that WAP 2.0 will use XHTML as its markup... We will see thousands, then millions, of devices using XHTML in consumers' hands in the not too distant future."[3]

---

3. Day, B., "Developing Wireless Applications using Java™ 2 Platform, Micro Edition (J2ME™)," developer.java.sun.com/developer/products/wireless/getstart/articles/wirelessdev/wireless-dev.pdf, June 2001.

We do not use XML for the J2ME client, so **TipTestServlet** does not send marked up data to our J2ME client. We could have used an XSLT to generate the plain text, but we chose not to for two reasons. Firstly, plain text is not well-formed and defeats the purpose of using XSLT, which should create well-formed documents. Secondly, the **ResultSet** in **TipTestServlet** already contains plain text, so converting the text to an XML **Document**, then converting the **Document** back to text, is convoluted.

In **TipTestServlet** (Fig. 12.9), lines 232–235 determine that a J2ME client made the request and invoke method **sendJ2MEClientResponse** (lines 344–390). Line 349 calls method **getResultTable** to convert the **ResultSet** into a two-dimensional array of **String**s—**resultTable**, so we have instant access to database contents. Line 352 creates a **Random** object, which allows **TipTestServlet** to generate randomly the tip image and tip questions to display. Line 355 passes the **Random** object to method **getRandomIndices**, which returns an array of four integers—each integer is a distinct, randomly generated index that corresponds to a tip in **result-Table**.

Lines 358–359 randomly select an integer from **randomRow**—this integer is the "correct" answer in the game—specifically, this integer represents the row in **result-Table** that holds the information for the correct tip. Using the correct answer, line 361 determines the row in **resultTable** that contains the name and description of the correct tip. **TipTestServlet** stores this information in an **HttpSession** object (line 364), so when the J2ME client sends the user's selection back to the server, **TipTest-Servlet** can check the user's selection against the correct answer stored in the **HttpSession** object. Lines 367–376 store the correct answer and the tip name and description in the **HttpSession** object. Using the correct answer, lines 379–380 determine the proper image to send to the J2ME client. Line 382 sets the MIME type to **text/plain**, because J2ME clients interprets plain text. Line 383 creates a **Print-Writer** object through which **TipTestServlet** sends the data to the J2ME client. Line 384 sends the name of the tip image, and lines 387–388 send the four tip abbreviations to the client. Section 12.4.3 discusses in detail how the J2ME client displays the Tip Test and exchanges data between itself and **TipTestServlet**. Figure 12.22 shows a sample output after **TipTestServlet** sends the Tip-Test question to the J2ME client. The image on the left shows the tip image, and the image on the right shows the user selecting an answer.

When the client sends the user's selection, **TipTestServlet** invokes method **doPost**. Lines 162–164 determine that the request is from the J2ME client and call method **sendJ2MEAnswer** (lines 592–629). Lines 596–597 use a **BufferedReader** object to read the user's selection from the client. Line 600 sets the MIME type to **text/plain**, and line 601 gets a **PrintWriter** object through which **TipTestServlet** sends content. Line 604 retrieves the **HttpSession** that stores the correct tip answer, name and description—lines 607–617 extract this information from this **HttpSes-sion**. Lines 620–623 match the user's selection with the correct tip answer and determine if the user is correct. Using the **PrintWriter** object, lines 626–627 send the correct tip name and description to the client. Figure 12.23 shows the answer screen on the Sun MIDP-device emulator. The picture on the left shows the screen that contains the correct tip name and description. When the user scrolls down on this screen, the user will see the picture on the right, which shows the remainder of the tip description.

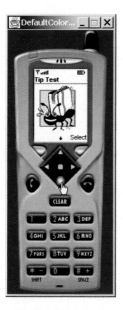 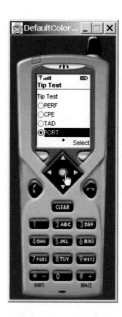

Fig. 12.22 J2ME client Tip-Test question screen. (Courtesy of Sun Microsystems, Inc.)

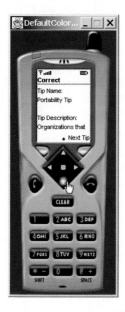 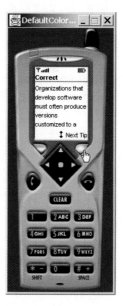

Fig. 12.23 J2ME client Tip-Test answer screen. (Courtesy of Sun Microsystems, Inc.)

12.4 Java 2 Micro Edition

This section introduces *Java 2 Micro Edition* (*J2ME*™)—a platform that enables developers to write applications for various consumer devices, such as set-top boxes, Web terminals, embedded systems, mobile phones and cell pagers. We discuss the Connected Limited Device Configuration (CLDC) and the Mobile Information Device Profile (MIDP), which offer developers a set of APIs to write J2ME applications—called *MIDlets*—and deploy them across several mobile devices. We then discuss the lifecycle of a MIDlet and explain how we use J2ME in our case study.

12.4.1 Connected Limited Device Configuration (CLDC)

The *Connected Limited Device Configuration (CLDC)* is a set of APIs that allow developers to create applications for devices that have limited resources—i.e., limited screen size, memory, power and bandwidth. The J2ME CLDC contains both a *virtual machine*—an interpreter that runs applications—and a set of classes that developers can use to develop and run programs on resource-limited devices. The *KVM*—the virtual machine offered by the CLDC—runs J2ME applications (as the JVM runs J2SE applications). The "K" in KVM represents the word "kilo," because J2ME applications are small enough to be measured in kilobytes.

The J2ME CLDC contains packages **java.io**, **java.lang**, **java.util** that developers use to perform such common operations as creating primitive data types, using simple data structures and sending and receiving data from networks. These packages are subsets of the J2SE packages **java.io**, **java.lang** and **java.util**—that is, the J2ME CLDC packages do not contain every class from the J2SE packages. Figure 12.24 lists the J2ME **java.io**, **java.lang** and **java.util** packages. To conserve space, we did not include exception or error classes. For the complete J2ME CLDC class list, visit **java.sun.com/j2me/docs/pdf/cldcapi.pdf**.

Classes	java.io	java.lang	java.util
Interfaces	`DataInput` `DataOutput`	`Runnable`	`Enumeration`

Classes	`ByteArrayInputStream`
	`ByteArrayOutputStream`
	`DataInputStream`
	`DataOutputStream`
	`InputStream`
	`InputStreamReader`
	`OutputStream`
	`OutputStreamReader`
	`PrintStream`
	`Reader`
	`Writer`
		`Boolean`
		`Byte`
		`Character`
		`Class`
		`Integer`
		`Long`
		`Math`
		`Object`
		`Runtime`
		`Short`
		`String`
		`StringBuffer`
		`System`
		`Thread`
		`Throwable`
			`Calendar`
			`Data`
			`Hashtable`
			`Random`
			`Stack`
			`Timer`
			`TimerTask`
			`TimeZone`
			`Vector`

Fig. 12.24 J2ME **java.io**, **java.lang** and **java.util** packages.

Common Programming Error 12.1

Attempting to use J2SE packages in the KVM will result in a compilation error—the KVM cannot handle the volume of classes due to KVM's limited resources.

One challenge of J2ME programming is that the API does not contain certain data types and classes that developers often "take for granted" in other Java platforms. For example, J2ME does not include floating-point operations, serializable objects, thread groups or JNI (Java Native Interface). As wireless-device technology advances, it is possible that future versions of J2ME will support those features.

12.4.2 Mobile Information Device Profile (MIDP)

The *Mobile Information Device Profile* (*MIDP*) is a set of APIs that allow developers to handle mobile-device-specific issues, such as creating user interfaces, permitting local storage and defining the lifecycles of MIDP client applications (MIDlets). Devices that run applications using the MIDP are called *MIDP devices*. Such devices include cell phones or pagers.

MIDP contains packages `javax.microedition.lcdui`, `javax.microedition.io`, `javax.microedition.rms` and `javax.microedition.midlet`. Package `javax.microedition.lcdui` contains classes that allow developers to construct user-interfaces for MIDlets, package `javax.microedition.io` enables networking between MIDlets and other systems, package `javax.microedition.rms` contains classes that permit local storage, and package `javax.microedition.midlet` defines the MIDlet lifecycle. Figure 12.26 lists the MIDP `javax.microedition.lcdui` and `javax.microedition.io` packages. Figure 12.26 lists the MIDP `javax.microedition.rms` and `javax.microedition.midlet` packages. To conserve space, we did not include exception or error classes. For the complete J2ME MIDP class list, visit

`java.sun.com/products/midp/midp-wirelessapps-wp.pdf`

Classes	javax.microedition.lcdui	javax.microedition.io
Interfaces	`Choice`	`Connection`
	`CommandListener`	`ContentConnection`
	`ItemListener`	`Datagram`
		`DatagramConnection`
		`HttpConnection`
		`InputConnection`
		`OutputConnection`
		`StreamConnection`
		`StreamConnectionNotifier`

Fig. 12.25 MIDP `javax.microedition.lcdui` and `javax.microedition.io` packages (part 1 of 2).

Classes	javax.microedition.lcdui	javax.microedition.io
Classes	Alert AlertType Canvas ChoiceGroup Command DateField Display Displayable Font Form Gauge Graphics Image ImageItem Item List Screen ScreenItem TextBox TextField Ticker	Connector

Fig. 12.25 MIDP `javax.microedition.lcdui` and `javax.microedition.io` packages (part 2 of 2).

Classes	javax.microedition.rms	javax.microedition.midlet
Interfaces	RecordComparator RecordEnumeration RecordFilter RecordListener	
Classes	RecordStore	MIDlet

Fig. 12.26 MIDP `javax.microedition.rms` and `javax.microedition.midlet` packages.

To run a MIDP application, a MIDP device requires a monochrome display of at least 96 pixels x 54 pixels, a two-way wireless network, some input device (such as a one-handed keypad or touch screen), at least 128 kilobytes for CLDC/MIDP classes and at least 32 kilobytes for the KVM. A MIDlet will run on any device that meets these requirements.

12.4.3 **TipTestMIDlet** Overview

In Section 12.3.4, we discussed how a servlet sends data to a J2ME client called a MIDlet. We discussed that MIDlets cannot interpret XML documents without proprietary software packages and must receive all information through streams or **PrintReader** objects. This section defines a MIDlet more specifically, discusses the MIDlet lifecycle and introduces **TipTestMIDlet**—the MIDlet in our case study.

A MIDlet is a Mobile Information Device application that runs on a MIDP device. The name is similar to the terms "applet" and "servlet," because these applications share similar characteristics—for example, each has a lifecycle and occupies various states during program execution. Also, the developer does not invoke a constructor for objects of these classes (**Applet**, **HttpServlet** and **MIDlet**) explicitly to instantiate these objects. We discussed in Section 9.2.1 that a servlet container loads the servlet into memory—normally in response to the first request that servlet receives. MIDlets are loaded in a similar manner. MIDP developers store several MIDlets in a jar file—called a *MIDlet suite*—on a server. The MIDP device contains a program called the *application management software* (AMS), which downloads the MIDlet suite from the server, opens the MIDlet suite, then launches the user-specified MIDlet on the MIDP device.

The AMS uses an *application descriptor file* to load the MIDlet application. This file, which has a **.jad** extension, contains information such as the MIDlets in the MIDlet suite, the MIDlet suite's size and URL, each MIDlet's name, vendor and version, and the MIDP device's profile and configuration. The AMS uses this information to ensure that the MIDlet application will run on the given MIDP device. Both the J2ME Wireless Toolkit and Forte create this file when creating a new MIDlet suite (see Section 12.5). The code below shows the structure of **TipTestMIDlet**'s application descriptor file.

```
MIDlet-1: TipTestMIDlet, TipTestMIDlet.png,
          com.deitel.advjhtp1.wireless.TipTestMIDlet
MIDlet-Jar-Size: 9577
MIDlet-Jar-URL: TipTestMIDlet.jar
MIDlet-Name: TipTestMIDlet
MIDlet-Vendor: Sun Microsystems
MIDlet-Version: 1.0
MicroEdition-Configuration:CLDC-1.0
MicroEdition-Profile:MIDP-1.0
```

Figure 12.27 shows the **TipTestMIDlet**. Before we discuss how **TipTest-MIDlet** retrieves information from the server, we must discuss the lifecycle of a MIDlet. Every MIDlet must extend class **MIDlet** (line 13) from package **javax.microedition.midlet** (line 9). The lifecycle begins when the AMS calls the MIDlet's constructor (lines 43–75) to launch the MIDlet. The MIDlet then enters a paused state, so it cannot accept user input or display screens created by the developer. When the constructor finishes, the AMS calls method **startApp** (lines 78–82), which places the MIDlet in the active state, allowing the MIDlet to display content and accept user input. The MIDlet then waits for user input or another notification from the AMS. If the AMS calls method **pauseApp** (line 85), the MIDlet returns to the "paused state." When the MIDlet is paused, the AMS must call method **startApp** to enable the MIDlet to reenter the active state. If the AMS calls method **destroyApp** (line 88) to clear the device's memory for another application, the MIDlet's execution terminates. Methods **startApp**, **pauseApp** and

destroyApp are abstract methods of class **MIDlet**, so every **MIDlet** subclass must override these methods.

Line 6 imports the J2ME CLDC I/O package that enable **TipTestMIDlet** to send and receive data from the servlets. Lines 9–11 import the MIDP packages for defining the MIDlet lifecycle, creating user interfaces and networking. J2ME divides the user-interface API between low-level and high-level APIs. The low-level API allows developers to incorporate graphics and shapes at precise pixel locations and to provide animation for applications such as games. The high-level user-interface API allows developers to incorporate text-fields, lists, forms and images for programs such as e-commerce applications and basic user interfaces.

```
1   // TipTestMIDlet.java
2   // Receives TipTest from Servlet
3   package com.deitel.advjhtp1.wireless;
4
5   // J2ME Java package subset
6   import java.io.*;
7
8   // J2ME packages
9   import javax.microedition.midlet.*;
10  import javax.microedition.lcdui.*;
11  import javax.microedition.io.*;
12
13  public class TipTestMIDlet extends MIDlet {
14
15      private Display display; // display manager
16
17      // Screens displayed to user
18      private List mainScreen;
19      private List welcomeScreen;
20      private Form infoScreen;
21      private Form tipScreen;
22      private Form answerScreen;
23
24      // actions for soft-buttons
25      private Command selectCommand;
26      private Command nextCommand;
27      private Command backCommand;
28
29      private static final String servletBaseURL =
30          "http://localhost:8080/advjhtp1/";
31
32      private static final String welcomeServletName = "welcome";
33
34      // welcome servlet determines tip test servlet name
35      private String tipTestServletName;
36
37      private static final String welcomeServletURL =
38          servletBaseURL + welcomeServletName;
```

Fig. 12.27 **TipTestMIDlet** downloads Tip Test from **TipTestServlet** (part 1 of 11).

```
39
40      private String sessionID;
41
42      // constructor initializes display and main Screen
43      public TipTestMIDlet()
44      {
45         // create soft button commands
46         selectCommand = new Command( "Select", Command.OK, 0 );
47         nextCommand = new Command( "Next Tip", Command.OK, 0 );
48         backCommand = new Command( "Back", Command.BACK, 1 );
49
50         // create main screen allowing welcome servlet connection
51         mainScreen = new List( "TipTestMIDlet", List.IMPLICIT );
52         mainScreen.addCommand( selectCommand );
53
54         // allow soft button access for mainScreen
55         mainScreen.setCommandListener(
56            new CommandListener() {
57
58               // invoked when user presses soft button
59               public void commandAction(
60                  Command command, Displayable displayable )
61               {
62                  // get data from welcome servlet
63                  String data = getServerData( welcomeServletURL );
64
65                  // create welcome Screen using servlet data
66                  display.setCurrent( createWelcomeScreen( data ) );
67               }
68
69            } // end anonymous inner class
70         );
71
72         // get appropriate Display for device
73         display = Display.getDisplay( this );
74
75      } // end TipTestMIDlet constructor
76
77      // start MIDlet
78      public void startApp()
79      {
80         // set display to main Screen
81         display.setCurrent( mainScreen );
82      }
83
84      // pause MIDlet
85      public void pauseApp() {}
86
87      // destroy MIDlet
88      public void destroyApp( boolean unconditional ) {}
```

Fig. 12.27 TipTestMIDlet downloads Tip Test from **TipTestServlet** (part 2 of 11).

```
89
90        // create "welcome" Screen introducing tip test
91        private Screen createWelcomeScreen( String data )
92        {
93           String list[] = parseData( data, ';' );
94
95           // create Screen welcoming user to tip test
96           welcomeScreen = new List( list[ 0 ], List.IMPLICIT );
97
98           welcomeScreen.append( "Take TipTest", null );
99           welcomeScreen.addCommand( selectCommand );
100          welcomeScreen.addCommand( backCommand );
101
102          // get URL of information page
103          final String url = new String( list[ 1 ].toCharArray() );
104
105          // allow soft button access for welcomeScreen
106          welcomeScreen.setCommandListener(
107             new CommandListener() {
108
109                // invoked when user presses soft button
110                public void commandAction(
111                   Command command, Displayable displayable )
112                {
113                   // soft button pressed is SELECT button
114                   if ( command.getCommandType() == Command.OK ) {
115
116                      // get data from static page
117                      String data =
118                         getServerData( servletBaseURL + url );
119
120                      // display this data
121                      display.setCurrent(
122                         createInformationScreen( data ) );
123                   }
124
125                   // soft button pressed is BACK button
126                   else if ( command.getCommandType() ==
127                      Command.BACK ) {
128                      display.setCurrent( mainScreen );
129                   }
130
131                } // end method commandAction
132
133             } // end anonymous inner class
134          );
135
136          return welcomeScreen;
137
138       } // end method createWelcomeScreen
```

Fig. 12.27 **TipTestMIDlet** downloads Tip Test from **TipTestServlet** (part 3 of 11).

```
139
140      // create Screen showing servlets to which client can connect
141      private Screen createInformationScreen( String data )
142      {
143         String list[] = parseData( data, ';' );
144
145         // create Form showing available servlets
146         infoScreen = new Form( "Information" );
147
148         // create StringItem that provides directions
149         StringItem infoTitle = new StringItem( list[ 0 ], null );
150         infoScreen.append( infoTitle );
151
152         // create ChoiceGroup allowing user to select servlet
153         final ChoiceGroup choices = new ChoiceGroup( "",
154            ChoiceGroup.EXCLUSIVE );
155         choices.append( list[ 1 ], null );
156
157         // append ChoiceGroup to Form
158         infoScreen.append( choices );
159
160         infoScreen.addCommand( selectCommand );
161         infoScreen.addCommand( backCommand );
162
163         // allow soft button access for this Screen
164         infoScreen.setCommandListener(
165            new CommandListener() {
166
167               // invoked when user presses soft button
168               public void commandAction(
169                  Command command, Displayable displayable )
170               {
171                  // soft button pressed is SELECT button
172                  if ( command.getCommandType() == Command.OK ) {
173
174                     // user chooses which servlet to connect
175                     int selectedIndex = choices.getSelectedIndex();
176
177                     tipTestServletName =
178                        choices.getString( selectedIndex );
179
180                     // connect to servlet and receive data
181                     String data = getServerData( servletBaseURL +
182                        tipTestServletName );
183
184                     // display next Screen according to data
185                     display.setCurrent( createTipTestScreen(
186                        servletBaseURL + data ) );
187                  }
188
```

Fig. 12.27 TipTestMIDlet downloads Tip Test from **TipTestServlet** (part 4 of 11).

```
189                    // soft button pressed is BACK button
190                    else if ( command.getCommandType() == Command.BACK )
191                        display.setCurrent( welcomeScreen );
192
193                } // end method commandAction
194
195            } // end anonymous inner class
196        );
197
198        return infoScreen;
199
200    } // end method createInformationScreen
201
202    // create Screen to display Tip Test
203    private Screen createTipTestScreen( String data )
204    {
205        // parse server data
206        String list[] = parseData( data, '\n' );
207
208        // create new Form to display test
209        tipScreen = new Form( "Tip Test" );
210
211        // create image from server data
212        Image serverImage = getServerImage( list[ 0 ] );
213
214        // append image to Form
215        if ( serverImage != null )
216            tipScreen.append( serverImage );
217
218        String choiceList[] = new String[ 4 ];
219
220        // construct list for ChoiceGroup from data
221        for ( int i = 0; i < choiceList.length; i++ )
222            choiceList[ i ] = list[ i + 1 ];
223
224        // create ChoiceGroup allowing user to input choice
225        final ChoiceGroup choices = new ChoiceGroup( "Tip Test",
226            ChoiceGroup.EXCLUSIVE, choiceList, null );
227
228        // append ChoiceGroup to Form
229        tipScreen.append( choices );
230
231        tipScreen.addCommand( selectCommand );
232
233        // allow soft button access for this Screen
234        tipScreen.setCommandListener(
235            new CommandListener() {
236
237                // invoked when user presses soft button
238                public void commandAction(
239                    Command command, Displayable displayable )
240                {
```

Fig. 12.27 TipTestMIDlet downloads Tip Test from **TipTestServlet** (part 5 of 11).

```
241              // send user selection to servlet
242              int selection = choices.getSelectedIndex();
243
244              String result = postData( selection );
245
246              // display results
247              display.setCurrent(
248                 createAnswerScreen( result ) );
249           }
250
251        } // end anonymous inner class
252     );
253
254     return tipScreen;
255
256  } // end method createTipTestScreen
257
258  // create Screen to display Tip Test answer and results
259  private Screen createAnswerScreen( String data )
260  {
261     // parse server data
262     String list[] = parseData( data, '\n' );
263
264     // create new Form to display test answers
265     answerScreen = new Form( list[ 0 ] );
266
267     // create StringItem showing tip name
268     StringItem tipNameItem =
269        new StringItem( "Tip Name:\n", list[ 1 ] );
270
271     // create StringItem showing tip description
272     StringItem tipDescriptionItem =
273        new StringItem( "\nTip Description:\n", list[ 2 ] );
274
275     // append StringItems to Form
276     answerScreen.append( tipNameItem );
277     answerScreen.append( tipDescriptionItem );
278
279     answerScreen.addCommand( nextCommand );
280
281     // allow soft button access for this Screen
282     answerScreen.setCommandListener(
283        new CommandListener() {
284
285           // invoked when user presses soft button
286           public void commandAction(
287              Command command, Displayable displayable )
288           {
289              // get next question
290              String data = getServerData( servletBaseURL +
291                 tipTestServletName );
292
```

Fig. 12.27 `TipTestMIDlet` downloads Tip Test from `TipTestServlet` (part 6 of 11).

```
293                     // display next question
294                     display.setCurrent( createTipTestScreen(
295                        servletBaseURL + data ) );
296                  }
297
298               } // end anonymous inner class
299            );
300
301         return answerScreen;
302
303      } // end method createAnswerScreen
304
305      // sends user's test selection to servlet
306      private String postData( int selection )
307      {
308         // connect to server, then post data
309         try {
310
311            // connect to server sending User-Agent header
312            HttpConnection httpConnection =
313               ( HttpConnection ) Connector.open(
314                  servletBaseURL + tipTestServletName,
315                  Connector.READ_WRITE );
316
317            setUserAgentHeader( httpConnection );
318
319            // send sessionID, if one exists
320            if ( sessionID != null )
321               httpConnection.setRequestProperty(
322                  "cookie", sessionID );
323
324            // inform servlet of post request
325            httpConnection.setRequestMethod( HttpConnection.POST );
326
327            // open output stream to servlet
328            DataOutputStream out =
329               httpConnection.openDataOutputStream();
330
331            // send selection
332            out.writeUTF( Integer.toString( selection ) );
333            out.flush();
334
335            // get result from servlet
336            String data = getData( httpConnection );
337
338            httpConnection.close(); // close connection
339
340            return data;
341
342         } // end try
343
```

Fig. 12.27 TipTestMIDlet downloads Tip Test from **TipTestServlet** (part 7 of 11).

```
344          // handle if MIDlet cannot open HTTP connection
345          catch ( IOException ioException ) {
346             ioException.printStackTrace();
347          }
348
349          return null;
350
351       } // end method postData
352
353       // string tokenizer parses String into sub-string array
354       private String[] parseData( String data, char delimiter )
355       {
356          int newLines = 0;
357
358          // determine number of delimiter characters in String
359          for ( int i = 0; i < data.length(); i++ )
360
361             // increase number of delimiters by one
362             if ( data.charAt( i ) == delimiter )
363                newLines++;
364
365          // create new String array
366          String list[] = new String[ newLines ];
367
368          int oldNewLineIndex = 0;
369          int currentNewLineIndex;
370
371          // store Strings into array based on demiliter
372          for ( int i = 0; i < newLines; i++ ) {
373
374             // determine index where delimiter occurs
375             currentNewLineIndex =
376                data.indexOf( delimiter, oldNewLineIndex );
377
378             // extract String within delimiter characters
379             list[ i ] = data.substring( oldNewLineIndex,
380                currentNewLineIndex - 1 );
381
382             oldNewLineIndex = currentNewLineIndex + 1;
383          }
384
385          return list;
386
387       } // end method parseData
388
389       // connect to server and receive data
390       private String getServerData( String serverUrl )
391       {
392          // connect to server, then get data
393          try {
394
```

Fig. 12.27 `TipTestMIDlet` downloads Tip Test from `TipTestServlet` (part 8 of 11).

```
395            // connect to server sending User-Agent header
396            HttpConnection httpConnection =
397               ( HttpConnection ) Connector.open( serverUrl );
398            setUserAgentHeader( httpConnection );
399
400            // send sessionID to server
401            if ( sessionID != null )
402               httpConnection.setRequestProperty(
403                  "cookie", sessionID );
404
405            // get sessionID from server
406            String sessionIDHeaderField =
407               httpConnection.getHeaderField( "Set-cookie" );
408
409            // store sessionID from cookie
410            if ( sessionIDHeaderField != null ) {
411               int index = sessionIDHeaderField.indexOf( ';' );
412               sessionID =
413                  sessionIDHeaderField.substring( 0, index );
414            }
415
416            // receive server data
417            String data = getData( httpConnection );
418
419            httpConnection.close(); // close connection
420
421            return data;
422
423         } // end try
424
425         // handle exception communicating with HTTP server
426         catch ( IOException ioException ) {
427            ioException.printStackTrace();
428         }
429
430         return null;
431
432      } // end method getServerData
433
434      // downloads an image from a server
435      private Image getServerImage( String imageUrl )
436      {
437         // download image
438         try {
439
440            // open connection to server
441            HttpConnection httpConnection =
442               ( HttpConnection ) Connector.open( imageUrl );
443
444            int connectionSize = ( int ) httpConnection.getLength();
445            byte imageBytes[] = new byte[ connectionSize ];
446
```

Fig. 12.27 **TipTestMIDlet** downloads Tip Test from **TipTestServlet** (part 9 of 11).

```
447          // read image from server
448          InputStream input = httpConnection.openInputStream();
449          input.read( imageBytes );
450
451          // create image from imageBytes
452          return
453             Image.createImage( imageBytes, 0, connectionSize );
454       }
455
456       // handle exception if InputStream cannot input bytes
457       catch ( IOException ioException   ) {
458          ioException.printStackTrace();
459       }
460
461       return null;
462
463    } // end method getServerImage
464
465    // set User-Agent header to identify client to servlet
466    private void setUserAgentHeader(
467       HttpConnection httpConnection )
468    {
469       // set User-Agent header
470       try {
471
472          // use profile/configuration properties for User-Agent
473          String userAgentHeader = "Profile=" +
474             System.getProperty( "microedition.profiles" ) +
475             " Configuration=" +
476             System.getProperty( "microedition.configuration" );
477
478          // set header
479          httpConnection.setRequestProperty(
480             "User-Agent", userAgentHeader );
481       }
482
483       // handle exception getting request property
484       catch ( IOException ioException ) {
485          ioException.printStackTrace();
486       }
487
488    } // end method setUserAgentHeader
489
490    // open DataInputStream to receive data
491    private String getData( HttpConnection httpConnection )
492       throws IOException
493    {
494       String data = ""; // stores data
495
```

Fig. 12.27 TipTestMIDlet downloads Tip Test from **TipTestServlet** (part 10 of 11).

```
496        // open input stream from connection
497        DataInputStream dataInputStream =
498          new DataInputStream(
499            httpConnection.openInputStream() );
500
501        int inputCharacter = dataInputStream.read();
502
503        // read all data
504        while ( inputCharacter != -1 ) {
505          data = data + ( char ) inputCharacter;
506          inputCharacter = dataInputStream.read();
507        }
508
509        dataInputStream.close(); // close stream
510
511        return data;
512
513      } // end method getData
514 }
```

Fig. 12.27 TipTestMIDlet downloads Tip Test from **TipTestServlet** (part 11 of 11).

Figure 12.28 shows a portion of the J2ME user-interface API. Each rectangle represents a class in the API. Each class with its name placed in italics is abstract, and the arrows represent inheritance relationships (an arrow points to the superclass). In the J2ME user-interface API, abstract superclass **Displayable** represents content that a MIDP-device can display on screen. The abstract superclasses **Screen** and **Canvas** both inherit from class **Displayable** and represent the high-level and low-level displayable content, respectively. Classes **Alert**, **Form**, **TextBox** and **List** are concrete subclasses of class **Screen**. An **Alert** is a **Screen** that the MIDlet displays for a brief period before displaying another **Screen**. A **Form** aggregates text-fields, images and group of selectable items for the user. A **TextBox** enables the user to input and edit text. A **List** is a list of **String**s from which the user can select using the MIDP device's keypad. Our case study uses classes **Form** and **List** to display information on screen. Class **Canvas** does not contain any subclasses. To use a **Canvas**, first create a concrete class that extends class **Canvas**, then override its **paint** method to draw graphics to the **Canvas**. Our case study incorporates only high-level user-interface classes, so we do not discuss how to use class **Canvas**.

Portability Tip 12.1

The J2ME low-level user-interface API helps developers create more visually appealing screens than does the high-level API. However, the low-level API does not guarantee layout congruity among several devices with different screen sizes. The high-level API provides a more consistent layout among devices.

Line 15 of class **TipTestMIDlet** declares an instance of class **Display**, which acts as a display manager for a MIDlet. A MIDlet must contain exactly one **Display** to display any **Displayable** object. Class **Display** is an example of the *Singleton design pattern*, which guarantees that a system instantiates a maximum of one object of a class. Occasionally, a system should contain exactly one object of a class—that is, once the system instantiates that object, the program should not be allowed to create additional

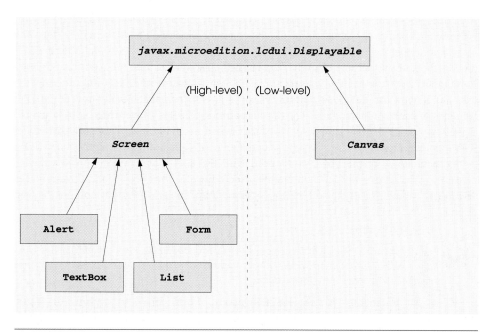

Fig. 12.28 J2ME user-interface API class hierarchy.

objects of that class. Because a MIDP device has only one screen, a MIDlet should contain only one display manager to display the contents on that screen—therefore, only one **Display** object can exist in each MIDlet. The **static** method **getDisplay** of class **Display** returns a reference to the only **Display** object in the system—this **Display** object is also referred to as the *singleton object*. If the **Display** object has been created, subsequent calls to method **getDisplay** merely return the same reference to the singleton **Display** object.

The **Display** object ensures that only one of the **Screen**s (**Displayable** subclasses) in **TipTestMIDlet** displays at a time. Lines 18–22 declare five **Screen**s for **TipTestMIDlet**. **TipTestMIDlet** contains a **List** (line 18) to represent the main screen that contains a link to **WelcomeServlet**, a **List** (line 19) to show **index.txt**, a **Form** (line 20) to show **info.txt** (which provides the link to **TipTestServlet**), a **Form** (line 21) to show Tip-Test questions and a **Form** (line 22) to show Tip-Test answers.

Screens also have support for *soft-buttons*—buttons that are usually located below the display (but above the keypad) on wireless devices. In Fig. 12.8, the mouse cursor is hovering over the right soft button, which is highlighted. The word **Select** on the screen above the right soft button indicates that the user will select the highlighted **List** item when the user presses this soft button—the **Display** will then show a different **Screen**. J2ME provides this functionality to MIDlets through **Command** objects, which encapsulates an action to be executed by the object that receives the **Command** object. Lines 25–27 of **TipTestMIDlet** declare three **Command** objects—**selectCommand**, **nextCommand** and **backCommand**. The **selectCommand** object—as we will see momentarily—allows the user to select **List** items on the screen. The **nextCommand** object allows the user to receive the next tip from **TipTestServlet** when playing Tip Test. The **backCommand** object enables the user to view the previous **Screen**.

Lines 46–48 instantiate these objects. The first argument to the **Command** constructor is the desired name—or label—to be displayed on the **Screen** above the soft button. The second argument is a constant that specifies how the MIDlet should respond after the user presses the soft button. For example, **Command.OK** indicates that the user has provided some input (via a text-field or via selecting a list item). **Command.BACK** indicates that the user should view the previous **Screen**. We program the logic that handles how the MIDlet behaves for each command type. The third argument indicates above which soft button the device will place the label. In a series of **Command** instantiations, the **Command** object with the lowest number has its label situated above the right soft button in the Sun MIDP-device emulator. For the object associated with the next lowest number, Sun's device places its label above the left soft button. According to lines 46–48, the device places "**Select**" above the right soft button, "**Next Tip**" above the right soft button and "**Back**" above the left soft button.

Portability Tip 12.2

*The **Command** numbering scheme varies from device-to-device. For example, the Sun emulator's default location for **Command** text is above the right soft button. Other devices may situate the text above the left soft button.*

Line 51 instantiates **List mainScreen**, which provides a link to **WelcomeServlet**. The first argument to the **List** represents the **List** name—this text appears at the top of the MIDP-device screen. The second argument is a constant that indicates the type of **List** instantiated. The **List** type determines how the user navigates the **List** with the keypad. This argument can assume one of three constant values—**List.IMPLICIT**, **List.EXCLUSIVE** and **List.MULTIPLE**. **List.IMPLICIT** indicates that the current focused item in the **List** is the user's selection—i.e., the user changes the selection when scrolling among **List** items. **List.EXCLUSIVE** requires the user to press the center soft button to indicate a selection among **List** items, then press the right soft button to finalize the selection—however, before finalizing the selection (but after having marked the selection), the user can scroll among **List** items. **List.MULTIPLE** enables the user to select several items in the **List**.

Line 52 adds **selectCommand** to **mainScreen**, so the user will see "**Select**" above the right soft button. Lines 55–69 allow **mainScreen** to listen for events from **selectCommand** by creating a new **CommandListener** object. When the user presses a soft button, **selectCommand** invokes method **commandAction** (lines 59–67). This method takes as arguments the **Command** object associated with the recently pressed soft button and the **Displayable** object on which this action occurred. We explain method **commandAction**'s logic momentarily.

Line 73 gets the display manager for the device. When the constructor returns, the AMS invokes method **startApp**, which informs **TipTestMIDlet** to accept user input and to display screens. Using the display manager, line 81 sets the current display to the **mainScreen**. Figure 12.29 shows the output of this operation.

TipTestMIDlet now waits for user input. The only events registered to **TipTestMIDlet** originate from the right soft button—when the user presses this button, **selectCommand** calls method **commandAction** of any registered **CommandListener**. Line 63 passes **WelcomeServlet**'s URL to method **getServerData** (lines 390–432), which connects to a server and receives data. Lines 396–397 open an **HttpConnection** using the URL parameter. Line 398 calls method **setUserAgentHeader** (lines 466–488), so the

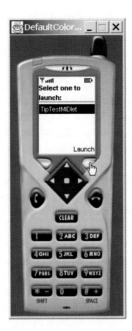

Fig. 12.29 TipTestMIDlet main screen. (Courtesy of Sun Microsystems, Inc.)

server can identify which client is making the request. Unlike the Internet Explorer, Openwave UP browser and Pixo clients, a J2ME client does not have a well-known **User-Agent** header, so we must define our own header and store it in interface **ClientUserAgent-Headers**, so our servlets can distinguish **TipTestMIDlet** as a J2ME client. Lines 473–476 create a **User-Agent** header using **TipTestMIDlet**'s profile and configuration information. Lines 479–480 assign this header to the **HttpConnection** request.

We also require a means to track this session so the servlet can maintain state information—such as the correct answer—between sessions. Lines 406–407 store the **HttpConnection**'s **Set-cookie** header field, which provides information on this session, in **String sessionID** (line 40). The **Set-cookie** header contains information delimited by semicolons. A server stores a session identifier before the first semicolon—lines 410–413 extract the session identifier. The next time **TipTestMIDlet** connects to the server, lines 401–403 send this information to identify the session.

Line 417 calls method **getData** (lines 491–513) to receive data from the server. Lines 497–499 open a **DataInputStream** to read the server-generated data. Lines 501–507 read this data into a **String**, then return the **String**.

At this point, **TipTestMIDlet** has connected to **WelcomeServlet** and received data—which is **index.txt**—that represents the "welcome screen." The data is

```
eLearning Deitel Programming Tips ;j2me/info.txt ;
```

Line 66 passes this **String** as an argument to method **createWelcomeScreen** (lines 91–138). Line 93 calls method **parseData** (lines 354–387), which parses the data into an array of **String**s, so we can access individual **String**s. Method **parseData** acts like the J2SE class **java.util.StringTokenizer**, which the J2ME **java.util** package does not contain (due to limited resources specified by MIDP requirements). We use a semicolon as the delimiter to parse the data, so method **parseData** returns a two-element **String** array that contains "**eLearning Deitel Programming Tips**" (the screen name) and "**j2me/info.txt**" (the link to Tip-Test directions). Line 96 creates **welcomeScreen** using the first element in the **String** array as the **List** name. Line 98 appends the **String** "**Take TipTest**" to the **List**, informing the user to download the Tip Test. Figure 12.30 shows **TipTestMIDlet**'s welcome screen.

Lines 99–134 register **welcomeScreen** as a **CommandListener** for events from **selectCommand** and **backCommand**. When the user presses a soft button, either **selectCommand** or **backCommand** calls method **commandAction** (lines 110–131), depending on which button the user pressed. The **Command** is an example of the Command Design Pattern, which we discussed in Section 2.3 when we presented Swing **Action**s. In J2ME, a **Command** object can contain various commands, or instructions, such as "show the next **Screen**," "show the previous **Screen**," or "exit the application." Several **Displayable** objects in the system can listen for these commands—MIDP-application developers write the operations that each **Displayable** object performs when receiving **Command**s. For example, we register **welcomeScreen** as a listener for the **selectCommand** and **backCommand** object. When each **Screen** receives a **Command** event, method **commandAction** uses the **Command** event's method **getCommandType** to determine if the command type is **Command.OK** ("show the next **Screen**") or **Command.BACK** ("show the previous **Screen**"). We design **TipTestMIDlet** to act according to the command type received. If the user pressed the left soft button (**Back**), line 128 sets the **Display** to display **mainScreen**. If the user pressed the right soft button (**Select**), lines 117–122 draw the "information" **Screen**. Lines 117–118 call method **getServerData**, which connects to the server and receives **j2me/info.txt** as the **String**:

```
In this exercise, we will test your knowledge of the Deitel
programming tips ;tiptest ;
```

Lines 121–122 pass this **String** as an argument to method **createInformationScreen** (lines 141–200), which constructs a screen that provides more information on Tip Test. Line 143 calls method **parseData** to parse the server-generated data into a two-element **String** array. **String** array's first element represents the title of the **Screen** we will create, and the second element represents the link to **TipTestServlet**. Line 146 creates **infoScreen** as a **Form**. A **Form** uses **StringItem**s—components that contain **String**s—to display several lines of text. A **List** is able to display only one line of text and therefore would display only part of the **String** array's first element. We use a **Form** to display the **String** array's first element in its entirety. Lines 149–150 append a **StringItem** to **infoScreen** using the **String** array's first element. Lines 153–158 create a **ChoiceGroup**—a group of items that the user can select in a **Form**—using the **String** array's second element, so **TipTestMIDlet** can link to **TipTestServlet**. Note that line 154 declares the **ChoiceGroup** as **EXCLUSIVE**, so the user must specify which item to select—in our example, there exists only one choice (**tiptest**), so this item is selected by default. Figure 12.31 shows **TipTestMIDlet**'s information screen.

Fig. 12.30 `TipTestMIDlet` welcome screen. (Courtesy of Sun Microsystems, Inc.)

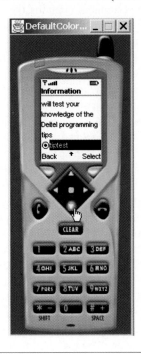

Fig. 12.31 `TipTestMIDlet` information screen. (Courtesy of Sun Microsystems, Inc.)

Common Programming Error 12.2

*ChoiceGroup*s *can be declared only as either* ***EXCLUSIVE*** *or* ***MULTIPLE***. *Declaring a* ***ChoiceGroup*** *as* ***INCLUSIVE*** *results in an* **IllegalArgumentException**

Lines 160–196 register **infoScreen** as a **CommandListener** for events from **selectCommand** and **backCommand**. When the user presses a soft button, either **selectCommand** or **backCommand** calls method **commandAction** (lines 168–193), depending on which button the user pressed. If the user pressed the left soft button (**Back**), line 191 sets the **Display** to display **welcomeScreen**. If the user pressed the right soft button (**Select**), lines 175–186 display the "question" **Screen**. Line 175 determines which item in **ChoiceGroup** is selected—lines 177–178 assign this item to the **TipTestServlet** link. Lines 181–182 call method **getServerData**, which connects to **TipTestServlet** and receives Tip Test. **TipTestServlet** generates random information each time **TipTestMIDlet** establishes a connection; the data that **TipTestServlet** generates appears in the following format:

```
http://localhost:8080/advjhtp1/j2me/png/portability.png
PERF
CPE
TAD
PORT
```

Lines 185–186 call method **createTipTestScreen** (lines 203–256) to display the Tip-Test question. Line 206 calls method **parseData** to parse the Tip Test into a five-element **String** array. The first element contains the image file name located on the server. The remaining four elements contain the four tip abbreviations from which the user must choose the correct answer. We create a **Form**, so we can show an **Image** and a **ChoiceGroup**—no other **Displayable** subclass offers this functionality. Line 209 creates a new **Form**—**tipScreen**—to show Tip Test.

Line 212 passes the **String** array's first element to method **getServerImage** (lines 435–463), which creates an **Image** object from the image file on the server. Lines 441–442 create an **HttpConnection** to the server, lines 448–449 read the data into an **InputStream** and lines 452–453 return an **Image** from the **InputStream** data.

Lines 215–216 append the **Image** to **tipScreen**. We now represent the four possible answers associated with this **Image** as a **ChoiceGroup**. Lines 218–222 create a **String** array to hold each of the four **String** answers. Lines 225–226 instantiate the **ChoiceGroup**, and line 229 appends this **ChoiceGroup** to **tipScreen**. Note that the **ChoiceGroup**'s constructor takes four arguments (unlike the **ChoiceGroup** constructor in method **createInformationScreen**, which took two arguments). The first argument represents the **ChoiceGroup**s name, which we title "**Tip Test**." The second argument declares this **ChoiceGroup** as **EXCLUSIVE**, so the user must indicate the selection before proceeding. The third argument is the **String** array that contains each possible **String** answer. The fourth argument represents an array of **Image**s associated with the **String** array—the device places each **Image** in the **Image** array next to the respective **String** in the **String** array. We pass a **null** value for this argument, because we do not need to display any **Image**s next to the four possible answers.

Figure 12.32 shows **tipScreen**. The picture on the left shows the **Image** for which the user must guess the correct name. When the user scrolls down on this screen (picture

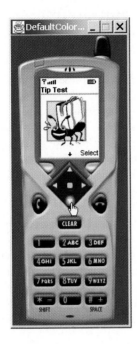

Fig. 12.32 `TipTestMIDlet` Tip-Test question screen. (Courtesy of Sun Microsystems, Inc.)

on the right), the user will see the four possible answers. The user must press the center soft button to indicate the selection.

Lines 231–251 register **`tipScreen`** as a **`CommandListener`** for events from **`selectCommand`**. When the user presses the **Select** button, **`selectCommand`** calls method **`commandAction`** (lines 238–249). Line 242 determines which item in the **`ChoiceGroup`** has been selected—this item represents the user's selection. Line 244 passes the selection to method **`postData`** (lines 306–351), which sends the selection to **`TipTestServlet`**. Lines 312–315 connect to **`TipTestServlet`** and specify that the connection is bidirectional, so **`TipTestMIDlet`** can send data to, and receive data from, **`TipTestServlet`**. Line 317 sets the **User-Agent** header so **`TipTestServlet`** can distinguish **`TipTestMIDlet`** as a J2ME client. Lines 320–322 send the session identifier that method **`getServerData`** stored to identify the session. Line 325 specifies that **`TipTestServlet`** will receive **post** data from **`TipTestMIDlet`**. Lines 328–329 open a **`DataOutputStream`**, through which line 332 sends the user selection to **`TipTest-Servlet`**. As we discussed in Section 12.3.4, **`TipTestServlet`** sends the correct answer to the J2ME client upon receiving this data. Line 336 calls method **`getData`** to receive this **`String`** data from the servlet. This data will have the following format:

```
Correct
Portability Tip
Organizations that develop software must often produce ver-
sions customized to a variety of computers and operating sys-
tems. These tips offer suggestions to make your applications
more portable.
```

Line 338 closes the connection between **TipTestMIDlet** and **TipTest-Servlet**, and line 340 returns the data that contains the correct answer. Lines 247–248 pass this **String** data to method **createAnswerScreen** (lines 259–303), which creates the **Screen** that displays the answer. Line 262 calls method **parseData** to parse the data into a three-element **String** array. The first element represents whether the user was correct or incorrect. The second and third elements hold the correct tip name and description, respectively. Line 265 instantiates **Form answerScreen** by passing the **String** array's first element to the constructor—we use a **Form** to show the tip description in its entirety. Lines 268–273 instantiate two **StringItem**s to hold the tip name and description. Lines 276–277 append these **StringItem**s to **answerScreen**. Figure 12.33 shows **answerScreen**. The picture on the left shows the screen that contains the correct tip name and description. When the user scrolls down on this screen, the user will see the right picture, which shows the remainder of the tip description.

Lines 279–299 register **tipScreen** as a **CommandListener** for events from **nextCommand**. The **nextCommand** object's behavior is identical to that of the **selectCommand** object; however, because we cannot alter **selectCommand**'s label to hold "**Next Tip**" as a value, we had to instantiate another **Command** object to ensure that the "**Next Tip**" text appears above the right soft button. When the user presses the right soft button, **nextCommand** calls method **commandAction** (lines 286–296), which calls method **createTipTestScreen** to generate another Tip-Test question—users can play Tip Test for as long as they desire.

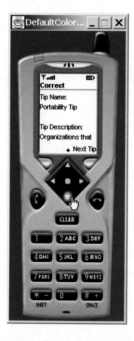
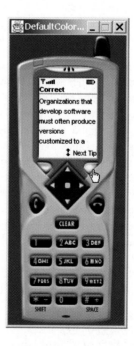

Fig. 12.33 TipTestMIDlet Tip-Test answer screen. (Courtesy of Sun Microsystems, Inc.)

This concludes our case study of Java-based wireless application development and Java 2 Micro Edition. In this section, we created a three-tier architecture in which **TipTestServlet** (middle tier) marked up a randomly generated Tip-Test question as XML, applied an XSLT to the XML document, then sent the resulting document to clients. We then introduced J2ME by discussing the CLDC and MIDP—the fundamental J2ME APIs for building applications to run on mobile devices. We studied a MIDlet's lifecycle and examined how to create a new MIDlet from class **MIDlet**. We created a MIDP application—**TipTestMIDlet**—then discussed how it retrieves data from **WelcomeServlet** and **TipTestServlet**. We also discussed how **TipTestMIDlet** uses this data to construct user interfaces and how, by using **Command** objects, a **TipTestMIDlet** enables the user to navigate through various **Screen**s.

In Chapter 13, we continue our discussion by presenting Remote Method Invocation (RMI), which enables client objects to call methods of objects on other systems. In Chapter 14, we begin discussing Enterprise JavaBeans (EJBs), which provide a model for building business logic in enterprise Java applications.

12.5 Installation Instructions

This section provides installation instructions for the software in this case study.

Web Server Configuration

This case study requires a web server that can run servlets. We recommend the Apache Tomcat Server. We provided directions to install Tomcat in Section 9.3.1. When you have installed Tomcat, copy the contents of the **advjhtp1** directory on the CD to the **advjhtp1** directory in the Tomcat directory on your system. The **advjhtp1** directory on the CD contains four directories—**iMode**, **j2me**, **XHTML**, **WAP**—that contain content that the servlets distribute to each client.

Next, you must copy the contents of Fig. 12.34, which we provide on the CD, in **web.xml**'s **web-app** element. The **web.xml** file should exist in the **WEB-INF** Tomcat directory. For example, on our system, **web.xml** is located in

```
C:\jakarta-tomcat-3.2.2\webapps\advjhtp1\WEB-INF\
```

```
1   <!-- Servlet definitions -->
2   <servlet>
3      <servlet-name>welcome</servlet-name>
4
5      <description>
6         A servlet that returns a "Welcome" screen through
7         an HTTP get request
8      </description>
9
10     <servlet-class>
11        com.deitel.advjhtp1.wireless.WelcomeServlet
12     </servlet-class>
13  </servlet>
14
```

Fig. 12.34 Deployment descriptor to run **WelcomeServlet** and **TipTestServlet** (part 1 of 2).

```
15   <servlet>
16      <servlet-name>tiptest</servlet-name>
17
18      <description>
19         A servlet that accesses a database to generate tests for
20         Deitel programming tips
21      </description>
22
23      <init-param>
24         <param-name>DATABASE_URL</param-name>
25         <param-value>jdbc:cloudscape:rmi:tips</param-value>
26      </init-param>
27
28      <init-param>
29         <param-name>JDBC_DRIVER</param-name>
30         <param-value>
31            COM.cloudscape.core.RmiJdbcDriver
32         </param-value>
33      </init-param>
34
35      <servlet-class>
36         com.deitel.advjhtp1.wireless.TipTestServlet
37      </servlet-class>
38   </servlet>
39
40   <!-- Servlet mappings -->
41   <servlet-mapping>
42      <servlet-name>welcome</servlet-name>
43      <url-pattern>/welcome</url-pattern>
44   </servlet-mapping>
45
46   <servlet-mapping>
47      <servlet-name>tiptest</servlet-name>
48      <url-pattern>/tiptest</url-pattern>
49   </servlet-mapping>
50
51   <mime-mapping> <!-- WML Source -->
52      <extension>wml</extension>
53      <mime-type>text/vnd.wap.wml</mime-type>
54   </mime-mapping>
55
56   <mime-mapping> <!-- Wireless Bitmap -->
57      <extension>wbmp</extension>
58      <mime-type>image/vnd.wap.wbmp</mime-type>
59   </mime-mapping>
```

Fig. 12.34 Deployment descriptor to run **WelcomeServlet** and
TipTestServlet (part 2 of 2).

In Fig. 12.34, lines 2–13 describe **WelcomeServlet**, and line 15–38 describe
TipTestServlet. Lines 23–33 declare two **init-param** elements that enable us to
change the database that **TipTestServlet** uses, without having to modify **TipTest-
Servlet.java**. Lines 41–49 map the two servlets to specified URLs. Lines 51–59 con-

figure Tomcat to serve WML content with correct MIME types—if we do not specify these MIME types, the WAP clients will not receive content.

The last step for configuring Tomcat to run the case study involves specifying those classes that Tomcat uses to run the servlets. Create the directory structure **com/deitel/ advjhtp1/wireless** in the **WEB-INF/classes** directory. For example, on our system, the directory structure is

```
C:\jakarta-tomcat-3.2.2\webapps\advjhtp1\WEB-INF\classes\com\
deitel\advjhtp1\wireless\
```

Copy **WelcomeServlet.class** and **TipTestServlet.class** into this directory.

Database Configuration

This case study also requires a database from which the servlet can extract tip information. We recommend the Cloudscape database, which we provide installation instructions in Sections 8.1 and 8.5. Copy the **tips.sql** file and the **tips** directory from our CD to the **frameworks/RmiJdbc/bin** directory where you have installed Cloudscape on your system. For example, **c:\cloudscape_3.6** is the directory that contains Cloudscape on our system, so

```
C:\cloudscape_3.6\frameworks\RmiJdbc\bin\
```

should contain **tips.sql** and the **tips** directory. Next, copy **cloudscape.jar** and **RmiJdbc.jar** (located on the CD) into the **WEB-INF/lib** Tomcat directory. For example, on our system, this directory is

```
C:\jakarta-tomcat-3.2.2\webapps\advjhtp1\WEB-INF\lib\
```

Placing **cloudscape.jar** and **RmiJdbc.jar** in this directory enable **TipTest-Servlet** to connect to, and extract from, a Cloudscape database.

J2ME Wireless Toolkit Installation and Configuration

To use the Sun MIDP-device emulator and develop MIDP applications, you must use the J2ME Wireless Toolkit. We include this toolkit on the CD, or you may download the toolkit from

```
java.sun.com/products/j2mewtoolkit/
```

At the time of this writing, Release 1.0.2 is available for download. In the installation procedure, you can specify whether you want to integrate the J2ME Wireless Toolkit with Forte—which facilitates developing MIDP applications in Forte—or to run the toolkit as a "stand-alone" application. We recommend that you integrate the toolkit in Forte.

If you integrate the toolkit in Forte, create the directory structure **com/deitel/ advjhtp1/wireless** in your system's Forte development directory. For example, **c:\forte4j\Development** is the Forte development directory on our system, so we create the directory structure

```
C:\forte4j\Development\com\deitel\advjhtp1\wireless\
```

Next, copy **TipTestMIDlet.java** and **TipTestMIDlet.jar** from our CD to this directory. When you expand this directory structure in Forte, you should see

```
TipTestMIDlet.java
TipTestMIDlet.jar
```

TipTestMIDlet.jar is the MIDlet suite that contains class **TipTestMIDlet**. To run class **TipTestMIDlet**, right-click on the **TipTestMIDlet.jar** icon, then select execute.

If you prefer to use the Wireless Toolkit (or if you had installed the toolkit as a stand-alone application), first open the Wireless Toolkit by selecting **KToolbar** in the directory where you installed the toolkit. Next, press the **New Project** button. In the **Project Name** text field, type

```
TipTestMIDlet
```

In the **MIDlet Class Name** text field, type

```
com.deitel.advjhtp1.wireless.TipTestMIDlet
```

then press the **Create Project** button. When the **Settings** frame appears, press the **OK** button. Next, copy **TipTestMIDlet.java** from our CD to the **apps/TipTest-MIDlet/src** directory in the directory where you installed the toolkit. For example, **C:\J2mewtk** is the directory where we installed the toolkit on our system, so we copy **TipTestMIDlet.java** to

```
C:\J2mewtk\apps\TipTestMIDlet\src\
```

Return to the Wireless toolkit, and press the **Build** button. When **TipTestMIDlet** has finished compiling and preverifying, press the **Run** button to execute **TipTest-MIDlet**. The **Device** menu—located on the toolkit's right side—enables you to select from among several devices to run **TipTestMIDlet**. Although the default device is the Sun grayscale MIDP-device emulator, you can specify to run **TipTestMIDlet** on other devices, such as RIM's Blackberry-957™ and the Motorola i85s™.

Other clients
Figure 12.35 lists the URLs to download the browsers used in this case study.

Browser	URL
Microsoft Internet Explorer	**www.microsoft.com/downloads/search.asp?**
Openwave UP simulator	**developer.openwave.com/download/license_41.html**
Pixo Internet Microbrowser	**www.pixo.com/products/products001.htm**

Fig. 12.35 Case-study browser URLs.

12.6 Internet and World Wide Web Resources

www.java.sun.com/j2me
This site contains Sun's Java 2 Micro Edition available for download.

www.onjava.com/pub/a/onjava/2001/03/08/J2ME.html
This site contains a J2ME article.

www.jguru.com/faq/home.jsp?topic=J2ME
This site presents the J2ME FAQ.

www.wirelessdevnet.com/channels/java/features/j2me_http.phtml
This site discusses network programming with J2ME devices.

www.ericgiguere.com/microjava/fallacies.html
This site lists some common misconceptions of J2ME.

www.motorola.com/java
This site discusses J2ME integration in new Motorola's wireless devices.

www.internetnews.com/wd-news/article/0,,10_533091,00.html
This site discusses J2ME integration in the Palm devices.

www.mot.com/java/devices.html
This site lists several wireless devices that use J2ME technology in the market.

www.nttdocomo.com/i/index.html
This is the Web site of NTT DoCoMo—the creators of i-mode.

www.anywhereyougo.com/imode/Index.po
This site presents news about i-mode development.

www.i-modesales.com
This site offers information on i-mode phones and services.

www.wap.com
This site offers news about WAP development.

www.wapforum.org/
This site discusses advancements in the WAP field.

SUMMARY

- This case study is a three-tier architecture of a multiple choice test (Tip Test) that allows users to test their knowledge of Deitel programming tips.

- Developers can use Java technology to develop wireless and server-side applications that developers can also develop with ASP.

- The information tier consists of a database. The middle tier consists of two servlets—**WelcomeServlet** and **TipTestServlet**—that generate content to clients of various types. The client tier consists of four client types—Internet Explorer, WAP, i-mode and J2ME. Each client type renders content differently.

- Microsoft Internet Explorer receives XHTML content.

- The Openwave UP simulator is the WAP client that receives WML content.

- The Pixo Internet Microbrowser is the i-mode client that receives cHTML content.

- The Sun MIDP-device emulator displays a J2ME client that receives content in plain-text format.

- J2ME™ (Java™ 2 Micro Edition) is Sun's newest Java platform for developing applications for various consumer devices, such as set-top boxes, Web terminals, embedded systems, mobile phones and cell pagers.

- MIDP (Mobile Information Device Profile) is a set of APIs that allow developers to handle mobile-device-specific issues, such as creating user interfaces, storing information locally and networking.)
- Devices that run applications for MIDP are called MIDP devices (e.g., cell phones or pagers).
- Clients interact with servlets by making a series of **get** and **post** request to the servlets. When a client sends a **get** request to an **HttpServlet**, method **doGet** handles the request. When a client sends a **post** request to an **HttpServlet**, method **doPost** handles the request.
- All clients contain a unique **User-Agent** header, which contains information on what type of client is requesting data from the server.
- Method **getInitParameter** of **HttpServlet** allows us to specify information (such as database locations or drivers) declared in **web.xml**. We need only to modify the **<param-value>** element in the **<init-param>** element in **web.xml** to change this information.
- **org.w3c.dom.Element** objects element nodes in XML documents.
- We can apply an XSLT to an XML **Document** to produce different content for each different client type. Each client type renders this content accordingly.
- We did not use XML for our J2ME client, because at the time of this writing, J2ME cannot support XML without using non-standard XML-based software.
- J2ME uses the Connected Limited Device Configuration (CLDC) and the Mobile Information Device Profile (MIDP), which offer developers a set of APIs to write J2ME applications and deploy them across several mobile devices.
- The CLDC is a set of APIs that allow developers to create applications for devices that have limited resources—i.e., limited screen size, memory, power and bandwidth.
- Currently, the CLDC does not contain certain features that developers often "take for granted" in other Java platforms—e.g., floating-point operations, serializable objects and thread groups.
- The MIDP is a set of APIs that allow developers to handle mobile-device-specific issues, such as creating user interfaces, permitting local storage and defining the lifecycles of MIDP-client applications.
- A MIDlet is a type of MIDP-client application. All MIDlets must extend class **javax.microedition.midlet.MIDlet**.
- MIDP developers store several MIDlets in a jar file—called a MIDlet suite—on a server.
- The application management software (AMS) on the MIDP device downloads the MIDlet suite from the server, opens the MIDlet suite, then launches the user-specified MIDlet on the MIDP device.
- The AMS uses an application descriptor file to load the MIDlet application. This file contains various information on the MIDlet suite and the MIDP device.
- The MIDlet lifecycle consists of methods **startApp**, **pauseApp** and **destroyApp**.
- J2ME divides the user-interface API between low-level and high-level APIs. The low-level API allows developers to incorporate graphics and provide animation, whereas the high-level user-interface API allows developers to incorporate text fields, lists and forms.
- Class **Displayable** represents content that a MIDP-device can display on screen. Classes **Screen** (high-level) and **Canvas** (low-level) extend class **Displayable**.
- Class **Display** acts as a display manager for a MIDlet. Exactly one **Display** object can exist in a MIDlet.
- J2ME provides "soft-button support" in MIDlets through **Command** objects, which encapsulates an action to be executed by the object that receives the **Command** object.
- **List**s and **Form**s are two high-level user-interface classes that extend class **Screen**.
- A **Form** can include **ChoiceGroup**s—groups of items the user can select in a **Form**.

TERMINOLOGY

application management software (AMS)
cHTML (compact HTML)
class **Alert**
class **Canvas**
class **ChoiceGroup**
class **Command**
class **CommandListener**
class **Display**
class **Displayable**
class **DocumentBuilder**
class **DocumentBuilderFactory**
class **DOMSource**
class **Element**
class **Form**
class **HttpServletResponse**
class **HttpServletRequest**
class **HttpSession**
class **InputStream**
class **List**
class **Screen**
class **StreamSource**
class **StringItem**
class **TextBox**
class **Transformer**
class **TransformerFactory**
client
CLDC packages **java.io**, **java.lang**
  and **java.util**
Connected Limited Device
  Configuration (CLDC)
database
Extensible HyperText Markup)
  Language (XHTML)
get and **post** data
i-mode
information tier
Java 2 Micro Edition (J2ME)
J2ME high-level user-interface API

J2ME low-level user-interface API
Java application descriptor file
KVM
Openwave UP simulator
method **commandAction** of class
  CommandListener
method **doGet** of class **HttpServlet**
method **doPost** of class **HttpServlet**
method **destroyApp** of class MIDlet
method **pauseApp** of class MIDlet
method **startApp** of class MIDlet
middle tier
MIDlet
MIDlet lifecycle
MIDlet suite
MIDP application
MIDP devices
MIDP package **javax.microedition.io**
MIDP package
  javax.microedition.lcdui
MIDP package
  javax.microedition.midlet
MIDP package **javax.microedition.rms**
mobile device
Mobile Information Device Profile (MIDP)
namespace
Pixo Internet Microbrowser
server
Sun MIDP-device emulator
three-tier architecture
User-Agent header
servlet
Wireless Application Protocol (WAP)
Wireless Markup Language (WML)
XML
XML **Document**
XSLT

SELF-REVIEW EXERCISES

12.1   Fill in the blanks in each of the following statements:
  a) Typically, a three-tier architecture contains a _____ layer, a _____ layer and
      a _____ layer.
  b) The servlets in our case study generated _____ content to Internet Explorer,
      _____ content to the WAP client, _____ content to the i-mode client and
      _____ content to the J2ME client.
  c) **TipTestServlet** used a _____ object to store the correct tip name and de-
      scription.

    d) CLDC stands for _____.

    e) MIDP stands for _____.

    f) Developers can package several MIDlets in a jar file called a _____.

    g) The application descriptor file contains the _____ extension.

    h) The MIDlet lifecycle consists of methods _____, _____ and _____.

    i) In package **javax.microedition.lcdui**, class _____ represents content that a MIDP device can display on screen.

    j) Class **javax.microedition.Display** is an example of the _____ design pattern.

12.2 State whether each of the following statements is *true* or *false*. If *false*, explain why.

    a) An **HttpServlet**'s calls method **doGet** upon receiving a **get** request and method **doPost** upon receiving a **post** request. (true/false).

    b) A User-Agent header contains information about the server. (true/false).

    c) **DocumentBuilder**'s **static** method **newDocumentBuilder** creates a new **DocumentBuilder**. (true/false).

    d) In this case study, **TipTestServlet** uses XSLT to transform XML Tip Test **Document**s to well formed content for all clients. (true/false).

    e) The J2ME CLDC package consist of **java.io**, **java.lang** and **java.net**. (true/false).

    f) The application management software loads a MIDlet on a MIDP device. (true/false).

    g) The application description file specifies such information as the MIDP device's configuration and the MIDlet's name. (true/false).

    h) Classes **Alert**, **Form**, **Screen**, and **List** are the concrete classes of the MIDP high-level user-interface package. (true/false).

    i) A **javax.microedition.lcdui.Command** object encapsulates an action to be executed by the object that received the **Command**. (true/false).

    j) An **HttpSession**'s **Set-Cookie** header field contains session information. (true/false).

ANSWERS TO SELF-REVIEW EXERCISES

12.1 a) client (top), middle, information (bottom). b) XHTML, WAP, cHTML, plain text. c) **HttpSession**. d) Connected Limited Device Configuration. e) Mobile Information Device Profile. f) MIDlet suite. g) **.jad**. h) **startApp, pauseApp, destroyApp**. i) **Displayable**. j) Singleton.

12.2 a) True. b) False. A User-Agent header contains information on what client type is requesting data from a server. c) False. **DocumentBuilderFactory**'s **static** method **newDocumentBuilder** creates a new **DocumentBuilder**. Class **DocumentBuilder** creates new **Document**s. d) False. **TipTestServlet** uses XSLT to transform XML Tip Test **Document**s to well- formed content for only Internet-Explorer, WAP and i-mode clients. e) False. The J2ME CLDC package consist of **java.io**, **java.lang** and **java.util**. f) True. g) True. h) Classes **Alert**, **Form**, **TextBox**, and **List** are the concrete classes of the MIDP high-level user-interface package. Class **Screen** is an abstract class these classes extend. i) True. j) True.

EXERCISES

12.3 To make **TipTestServlet** more manageable and extendable, we stored the database driver name and URL in the **<init-param>** element in **web.xml**. List 3 other constants that we could have stored from **WelcomeServlet** and **TipTestServlet** in the **<init-param>** element.

12.4 Extend the list of possible answers in the Tip-Test question from four to five.

12.5   Method **getResultTable** of **TipTestServlet** creates a two-dimensional **String**-array **ResultSet** representation. However, because these dimensions are pre-defined (seven rows by five columns), the **String** array cannot store additional rows if we append another tip to the database. Modify **TipTestServlet** so that it can handle any number of tips from the database. Use techniques shown in Chapter 8, Java Database Connectivity (JDBC), to create a scrollable **Result-Set** so that you can determine the number of rows in the **ResultSet** and size the **String** array accordingly.

12.6   Lines 29–38 of class **TipTestMIDlet** specify the servlet URL and the **WelcomeServ-let** URL. This approach can be problematic if a network administrator changes either URL. In practice, we would like the application descriptor file to contain the servlet URL and the MIDP-device user to specify the **WelcomeServlet** URL with the MIDP-device keypad.

   a) Encode the servlet URL—**http://localhost:8080/advjhtp1/**—in the **TipTestMIDlet** application descriptor file by typing

   Servlet-URL:http://localhost:8080/advjhtp1/

   at the end of **TipTestMIDlet**'s **.jad** file. In **TipTestMIDlet**, use method **getAppProperty** of class **MIDlet** to return the servlet URL. (Method **getApp-Property** takes a property-tag **String**—e.g., **"Servlet-URL"**—as an argument and returns the **String** associated with that property.)

   b) Enable the user to specify the **WelcomeServlet** URL. Modify the class **TipTest-MIDlet** constructor to create **mainScreen** (line 51) as a **TextBox**—a **Screen** subclass that enables the user to input text. A **TextBox** constructor takes four arguments: 1) a **String** that represents the **TextBox**'s title; 2) a **String** that represents the **TextBox**'s initial contents; 3) an **int** that represents the maximum number of characters allowed in the **TextBox**; 4) an input constraint **int** that specifies the required input format—e.g., if you want the user to enter a phone number, the constraint is **Text-Field.PHONENUMBER**. We want the user to enter a URL, so the constraint is **Text-Field.URL**. Use method **getString** of class **TextBox** to return the **TextBox**'s contents (user input) to store the **WelcomeServlet** URL when the user presses the Select soft button.

12.7   Modify **TipTestMIDlet** to enable the user to exit the application in the Tip-Test answer screen in addition to receiving the next Tip-Test question. Create a new **Command** object that uses **Command.EXIT** and register **answerScreen** as a listener for this **Command**. (Hint: override method **destroyApp** to call method **notifyDestroy** of class **javax.microedi-tion.midlet.MIDlet**.

BIBLIOGRAPHY

Feng, Y. and Zhu, J., *Wireless Java™ Programming with J2ME*. SAMS. Indiana; 2001.

Giguere, E., *Java 2 Micro Edition: Professional Developer's Guide*. John Wiley & Sons. 2000.

Knudsen, J. *Wireless Java: Developing with Java 2, Micro Edition*. Apress. California; 2001.

Kroll, M. and Haustein, S., *Java 2 Micro Edition (J2ME) Application Development*. SAMS. Indiana; 2001.

Morrison, M. *Sams Teach Yourself Wireless Java with J2ME in 21 Days*. SAMS. Indiana; 2001.

Riggs, R, Taivalsaari, A., and VandenBrink, M., *Programming Wireless Devices with Java™ 2 Platform, Micro Edition*. Addison-Wesley. Boston; 2001.

13

Remote Method Invocation

Objectives

- To understand the distributed computing concepts.
- To understand the architecture of RMI.
- To be able to use activatable RMI objects to build resilient distributed systems.
- To understand how to use RMI callbacks.
- To be able to build RMI clients that download necessary classes dynamically.
- To be able to build activatable RMI objects.

Dealing with more than one client at a time is the business world's equivalent of bigamy. It's so awkward to tell one client that you're working on someone else's business that you inevitably start lying.
Andrew Frothingham

They also serve who only stand and wait.
John Milton

Rule 1: The client is always right.
Rule 2: If you think the client is wrong, see Rule 1.
Sign seen in shops

I love being a writer. What I can't stand is the paperwork.
Peter De Vries

Outline

13.1 Introduction

In this chapter, we introduce Java's distributed computing capabilities with *Remote Method Invocation (RMI)*. RMI allows Java objects running on separate computers or in separate processes to communicate with one another via *remote method calls*. Such method calls appear to the programmer the same as those operating on objects in the same program.

RMI is based on a similar, earlier technology for procedural programming called *remote procedure calls (RPCs)* developed in the 1980s. RPC allows a procedural program (i.e., a program written in C or another procedural programming language) to call a function residing on another computer as conveniently as if that function were part of the same program running on the same computer. A goal of RPC was to allow programmers to concentrate on the required tasks of an application by calling functions, while making the mechanism that allows the application's parts to communicate over a network transparent to the programmer. RPC performs all the networking and *marshaling of data* (i.e., packaging of function arguments and return values for transmission over a network). A disadvantage of RPC is that it supports a limited set of simple data types. Therefore, RPC is not suitable for passing and returning Java objects. Another disadvantage of RPC is that it requires the programmer to learn a special *interface definition language (IDL)* to describe the functions that can be invoked remotely.

RMI is Java's implementation of RPC for Java-object-to-Java-object distributed communication. Once a Java object registers as being remotely accessible (i.e., it is a *remote object*), a client can obtain a remote reference to that object, which allows the client to use that object remotely. The method call syntax is identical to the syntax for calling methods of other objects in the same program. As with RPC, RMI handles the marshaling of data across the network. However, RMI also enables Java programs to transfer complete Java objects using Java's object-serialization mechanism. The programmer need not be concerned with the transmission of the data over the network. RMI does not require the programmer to learn an IDL, because the J2SE SDK includes tools for generating all the networking code from the program's interface definitions. Also, because RMI supports only Java, no language-neutral IDL is required; Java's own interfaces are sufficient.

We present two substantial RMI examples and discuss the key concepts of RMI as we encounter them throughout the examples. After studying these examples, you should have an understanding of the RMI networking model and should be able to take advantage of advanced RMI features for building Java-to-Java distributed applications.

[*Note*: For Java-to-non-Java communication, you can use Java IDL (introduced in Java 1.2) or RMI-IIOP. Java IDL and RMI-IIOP enable applications and applets written in Java to communicate with objects written in any language that supports CORBA (Common Object Request Broker Architecture). Please see Chapter 26, CORBA: Part 1 and Chapter 27, CORBA: Part 2 for our discussion of CORBA and RMI-IIOP.]

13.2 Case Study: Creating a Distributed System with RMI

In the next several sections, we present an RMI example that downloads the *Traveler's Forecast* weather information from the National Weather Service Web site:

http://iwin.nws.noaa.gov/iwin/us/traveler.html

[*Note*: As we developed this example, the format of the *Traveler's Forecast* Web page changed several times (a common occurrence with today's dynamic Web pages). The information we use in this example depends directly on the format of the *Traveler's Forecast* Web page. If you have trouble running this example, please refer to the FAQ page on our Web site, **www.deitel.com**.]

We store the *Traveler's Forecast* information in an RMI remote object that accepts requests for weather information through remote method calls.

The four major steps in this example include:

1. Defining a *remote interface* that declares methods that clients can invoke on the remote object.

2. Defining the *remote object implementation* for the remote interface. [*Note*: By convention, the remote object implementation class has the same name as the remote interface and ends with **Impl**.]

3. Defining the client application that uses a *remote reference* to interact with the interface implementation (i.e., an object of the class that implements the remote interface).

4. Compiling and executing the remote object and the client.

13.3 Defining the Remote Interface

The first step in creating a distributed application with RMI is to define the remote interface that describes the *remote methods* through which the client interacts with the remote object using RMI. To create a remote interface, define an interface that extends interface **java.rmi.Remote**. Interface **Remote** is a *tagging interface*—it does not declare any methods, and therefore places no burden on the implementing class. An object of a class that implements interface **Remote** directly or indirectly is a *remote object* and can be accessed—with appropriate security permissions—from any Java virtual machine that has a connection to the computer on which the remote object executes.

Software Engineering Observation 13.1

Every remote method must be declared in an interface that extends `java.rmi.Remote`.

Software Engineering Observation 13.2

An RMI distributed application must export an object of a class that implements the **Remote** *interface to make that remote object available to receive remote method calls.*

Interface **WeatherService** (Fig. 13.1)—which extends interface **Remote** (line 10)—is the remote interface for our remote object. Line 13 declares method **getWeatherInformation**, which clients can invoke to retrieve weather information from the remote object. Note that although the **WeatherService** remote interface defines only one method, remote interfaces can declare multiple methods. A remote object must implement all methods declared in its remote interface.

When computers communicate over networks, there exists the potential for communication problems. For example, a server computer could malfunction, or a network resource could malfunction. If a communication problem occurs during a remote method call, the remote method throws a ***RemoteException***, which is a checked exception.

Software Engineering Observation 13.3

Each method in a **Remote** *interfaces must have a* **throws** *clause that indicates that the method can throw* ***RemoteException****s.*

Software Engineering Observation 13.4

RMI uses Java's default serialization mechanism to transfer method arguments and return values across the network. Therefore, all method arguments and return values must be ***Serializable*** *or primitive types.*

13.4 Implementing the Remote Interface

The next step is to define the remote object implementation. Class **WeatherServiceImpl** (Fig. 13.2) is the remote object class that implements the **WeatherService** remote interface. The client interacts with an object of class **WeatherServiceImpl** by invoking

```
1   // WeatherService.java
2   // WeatherService interface declares a method for obtaining
3   // wether information.
4   package com.deitel.advjhtp1.rmi.weather;
5
6   // Java core packages
7   import java.rmi.*;
8   import java.util.*;
9
10  public interface WeatherService extends Remote {
11
12      // obtain List of WeatherBean objects from server
13      public List getWeatherInformation() throws RemoteException;
14
15  }
```

Fig. 13.1   **WeatherService** interface.

method **getWeatherInformation** of interface **WeatherService** to obtain weather information. Class **WeatherServiceImpl** stores weather data in a **List** of **WeatherBean** (Fig. 13.3) objects. When a client invokes remote method **getWeatherInformation**, the **WeatherServiceImpl** returns a reference to the **List** of **WeatherBean**s. The RMI system returns a serialized copy of the **List** to the client. The RMI system then de-serializes the **List** on the receiving end and provides the caller with a reference to the **List**.

The National Weather Service updates the Web page from which we retrieve information twice a day. However, class **WeatherServiceImpl** downloads this information only once, when the server starts. The exercises ask you to modify the server to update the data twice a day. [*Note*: **WeatherServiceImpl** is the class affected if the National Weather Service changes the format of the *Traveler's Forecast* Web page. If you encounter problems with this example, visit the FAQ page at our Web site **www.deitel.com**.]

```
1   // WeatherServiceImpl.java
2   // WeatherServiceImpl implements the WeatherService remote
3   // interface to provide a WeatherService remote object.
4   package com.deitel.advjhtp1.rmi.weather;
5
6   // Java core packages
7   import java.io.*;
8   import java.net.URL;
9   import java.rmi.*;
10  import java.rmi.server.*;
11  import java.util.*;
12
13  public class WeatherServiceImpl extends UnicastRemoteObject
14     implements WeatherService {
15
16     private List weatherInformation;  // WeatherBean object List
17
18     // initialize server
19     public WeatherServiceImpl() throws RemoteException
20     {
21        super();
22        updateWeatherConditions();
23     }
24
25     // get weather information from NWS
26     private void updateWeatherConditions()
27     {
28        try {
29           System.out.println( "Update weather information..." );
30
31           // National Weather Service Traveler's Forecast page
32           URL url = new URL(
33              "http://iwin.nws.noaa.gov/iwin/us/traveler.html" );
34
```

Fig. 13.2 **WeatherServiceImpl** class implements remote interface **WeatherService** (part 1 of 3).

```
35              // create BufferedReader for reading Web page contents
36              BufferedReader in = new BufferedReader(
37                 new InputStreamReader( url.openStream() ) );
38
39              // separator for starting point of data on Web page
40              String separator = "TAV12";
41
42              // locate separator string in Web page
43              while ( !in.readLine().startsWith( separator ) )
44                 ;      // do nothing
45
46              // strings representing headers on Traveler's Forecast
47              // Web page for daytime and nighttime weather
48              String dayHeader =
49                 "CITY            WEA     HI/LO   WEA     HI/LO";
50              String nightHeader =
51                 "CITY            WEA     LO/HI   WEA     LO/HI";
52
53              String inputLine = "";
54
55              // locate header that begins weather information
56              do {
57                 inputLine = in.readLine();
58              } while ( !inputLine.equals( dayHeader ) &&
59                        !inputLine.equals( nightHeader ) );
60
61              weatherInformation = new ArrayList(); // create List
62
63              // create WeatherBeans containing weather data and
64              // store in weatherInformation List
65              inputLine = in.readLine();  // get first city's info
66
67              // The portion of inputLine containing relevant data is
68              // 28 characters long. If the line length is not at
69              // least 28 characters long, done processing data.
70              while ( inputLine.length() > 28 ) {
71
72                 // Create WeatherBean object for city. First 16
73                 // characters are city name. Next, six characters
74                 // are weather description. Next six characters
75                 // are HI/LO or LO/HI temperature.
76                 WeatherBean weather = new WeatherBean(
77                    inputLine.substring( 0, 16 ),
78                    inputLine.substring( 16, 22 ),
79                    inputLine.substring( 23, 29 ) );
80
81                 // add WeatherBean to List
82                 weatherInformation.add( weather );
83
84                 inputLine = in.readLine();  // get next city's info
85              }
86
```

Fig. 13.2 WeatherServiceImpl class implements remote interface
WeatherService (part 2 of 3).

```
87            in.close();  // close connection to NWS Web server
88
89            System.out.println( "Weather information updated." );
90
91         } // end method updateWeatherConditions
92
93         // handle exception connecting to National Weather Service
94         catch( java.net.ConnectException connectException ) {
95            connectException.printStackTrace();
96            System.exit( 1 );
97         }
98
99         // process other exceptions
100        catch( Exception exception ) {
101           exception.printStackTrace();
102           System.exit( 1 );
103        }
104     }
105
106     // implementation for WeatherService interface remote method
107     public List getWeatherInformation() throws RemoteException
108     {
109        return weatherInformation;
110     }
111
112     // launch WeatherService remote object
113     public static void main( String args[] ) throws Exception
114     {
115        System.out.println( "Initializing WeatherService..." );
116
117        // create remote object
118        WeatherService service = new WeatherServiceImpl();
119
120        // specify remote object name
121        String serverObjectName = "rmi://localhost/WeatherService";
122
123        // bind WeatherService remote object in RMI registry
124        Naming.rebind( serverObjectName, service );
125
126        System.out.println( "WeatherService running." );
127     }
128 }
```

Fig. 13.2 **WeatherServiceImpl** class implements remote interface
WeatherService (part 3 of 3).

Class **WeatherServiceImpl** extends class *UnicastRemoteObject* (package
java.rmi.server) and implements **Remote** interface **WeatherService** (lines 13–
14). Class **UnicastRemoteObject** provides the basic functionality required for all
remote objects. In particular, its constructor *exports* the object to make it available to
receive remote calls. Exporting the object enables the remote object to wait for client connections on an *anonymous port number* (i.e., one chosen by the computer on which the
remote object executes). This enables the object to perform *unicast communication* (point-

to-point communication between two objects via method calls) using standard streams-based socket connections. RMI abstracts away these communication details so the programmer can work with simple method calls. The **WeatherServiceImpl** constructor (lines 19–23) invokes the default constructor for class **UnicastRemoteObject** (line 21) and calls **private** method **updateWeatherConditions** (line 22). Overloaded constructors for class **UnicastRemoteObject** allow the programmer to specify additional information, such as an explicit port number on which to export the remote object. All **UnicastRemoteObject** constructors throw **RemoteException**s.

Software Engineering Observation 13.5

*Class **UnicastRemoteObject** constructors and methods throw checked **RemoteExceptions**, so **UnicastRemoteObject** subclasses must define constructors that also throw **RemoteExceptions**.*

Software Engineering Observation 13.6

*Class **UnicastRemoteObject** provides basic functionality that remote objects require to handle remote requests. Remote object classes need not extend this class if those remote object classes use **static** method **exportObject** of class **UnicastRemoteObject** to export remote objects.*

Method **updateWeatherConditions** (lines 26–91) reads weather information from the *Traveler's Forecast* Web page and stores this information in a **List** of **WeatherBean** objects. Lines 32–33 create a **URL** object for the *Traveler's Forecast* Web page. Lines 36–37 invoke method **openStream** of class **URL** to open a connection to the specified **URL** and wrap that connection with a **BufferedReader**.

Lines 40–87 perform *HTML scraping* (i.e., extracting data from a Web page) to retrieve the weather forecast information. Line 40 defines a separator **String**—**"TAV12"**—that determines the starting point from which to locate the appropriate weather information. Lines 43–44 read through the *Traveler's Forecast* Web page until reaching the sentinel. This process skips over information not needed for this application.

Lines 48–51 define two **String**s that represent the column heads for the weather information. Depending on the time of day, the column headers are either

```
     "CITY                WEA      HI/LO    WEA      HI/LO"
```

after the morning update (normally around 10:30 AM Eastern Standard Time) or

```
     "CITY                WEA      LO/HI    WEA      LO/HI"
```

after the evening update (normally around 10:30 PM Eastern Standard Time).

Lines 65–85 read each city's weather information and place this information in **WeatherBean** objects. Each **WeatherBean** contains the city's name, the temperature and a description of the weather. Line 61 creates a **List** for storing the **WeatherBean** objects. Lines 76–79 construct a **WeatherBean** object for the current city. The first 16 characters of **inputLine** are the city name, the next 6 characters of **inputLine** are the description (i.e., weather forecast) and the next 6 characters of **inputLine** are the high and low temperatures. The last two columns of data represent the next day's weather forecast, which we ignore in this example. Line 82 adds the **WeatherBean** object to the **List**. Line 87 closes the **BufferedReader** and its associated **InputStream**.

Method **getWeatherInformation** (lines 107–110) is the method from interface **WeatherService** that **WeatherServiceImpl** must implement to respond to remote requests. The method returns a serialized copy of the **weatherInformation List**. Clients invoke this remote method to obtain the weather information.

Method **main** (lines 113–127) creates the **WeatherServiceImpl** remote object. When the constructor executes, it exports the remote object so the object can listen for remote requests. Line 106 defines the URL that a client can use to obtain a *remote reference* to the server object. The client uses this remote reference to invoke methods on the remote object. The URL normally is of the form

rmi://*host***:***port***/***remoteObjectName*

where *host* represents the computer that is running the *registry for remote objects* (this also is the computer on which the remote object executes), *port* represents the port number on which the registry is running on the *host* and *remoteObjectName* is the name the client will supply when it attempts to locate the remote object in the registry. The **rmiregistry** utility program manages the registry for remote objects and is part of the J2SE SDK. The default port number for the RMI registry is **1099**.

Software Engineering Observation 13.7

*RMI clients assume that they should connect to port **1099** when attempting to locate a remote object through the RMI registry (unless specified otherwise with an explicit port number in the URL for the remote object).*

Software Engineering Observation 13.8

*A client must specify a port number only if the RMI registry is running on a port other than the default port, **1099**.*

In this program, the remote object URL is

rmi://localhost/WeatherService

indicating that the RMI registry is running on the **localhost** (i.e., the local computer) and that the name the client must use to locate the service is **WeatherService**. The name **localhost** is synonymous with the IP address **127.0.0.1**, so the preceding URL is equivalent to

rmi://127.0.0.1/WeatherService

Line 124 invokes **static** method *rebind* of class *Naming* (package **java.rmi**) to bind the remote **WeatherServiceImpl** object **service** to the RMI registry with the URL **rmi://localhost/WeatherService**. There also is a *bind* method for binding a remote object to the registry. Programmers use method **rebind** more commonly, because method **rebind** guarantees that if an object already has registered under the given name, the new remote object will replace the previously registered object. This could be important when registering a new version of an existing remote object.

Class **WeatherBean** (Fig. 13.3) stores data that class **WeatherServiceImpl** retrieves from the National Weather Service Web site. This class stores the city, temperature and weather descriptions as **String**s. Lines 64–85 provide *get* methods for each piece of information. Lines 25–45 load a property file that contains image names for displaying the weather information. This **static** block ensures that the image names are available as soon as the virtual machine loads the **WeatherBean** class into memory.

```
1    // WeatherBean.java
2    // WeatherBean maintains weather information for one city.
3    package com.deitel.advjhtp1.rmi.weather;
4
5    // Java core packages
6    import java.awt.*;
7    import java.io.*;
8    import java.net.*;
9    import java.util.*;
10
11   // Java extension packages
12   import javax.swing.*;
13
14   public class WeatherBean implements Serializable {
15
16      private String cityName;          // name of city
17      private String temperature;       // city's temperature
18      private String description;       // weather description
19      private ImageIcon image;          // weather image
20
21      private static Properties imageNames;
22
23      // initialize imageNames when class WeatherBean
24      // is loaded into memory
25      static {
26         imageNames = new Properties();  // create properties table
27
28         // load weather descriptions and image names from
29         // properties file
30         try {
31
32            // obtain URL for properties file
33            URL url = WeatherBean.class.getResource(
34               "imagenames.properties" );
35
36            // load properties file contents
37            imageNames.load( new FileInputStream( url.getFile() ) );
38         }
39
40         // process exceptions from opening file
41         catch ( IOException ioException ) {
42            ioException.printStackTrace();
43         }
44
45      } // end static block
46
47      // WeatherBean constructor
48      public WeatherBean( String city, String weatherDescription,
49         String cityTemperature )
50      {
51         cityName = city;
52         temperature = cityTemperature;
53         description = weatherDescription.trim();
```

Fig. 13.3   WeatherBean stores weather forecast for one city (part 1 of 2).

```
54
55          URL url = WeatherBean.class.getResource( "images/" +
56            imageNames.getProperty( description, "noinfo.jpg" ) );
57
58          // get weather image name or noinfo.jpg if weather
59          // description not found
60          image = new ImageIcon( url );
61       }
62
63       // get city name
64       public String getCityName()
65       {
66          return cityName;
67       }
68
69       // get temperature
70       public String getTemperature()
71       {
72          return temperature;
73       }
74
75       // get weather description
76       public String getDescription()
77       {
78          return description;
79       }
80
81       // get weather image
82       public ImageIcon getImage()
83       {
84          return image;
85       }
86    }
```

Fig. 13.3   WeatherBean stores weather forecast for one city (part 2 of 2).

Next, we define the client application that will obtain weather information from the **WeatherServiceImpl**. Class **WeatherServiceClient** (Fig. 13.4) is the client application that invokes remote method **getWeatherInformation** of interface **WeatherService** to obtain weather information through RMI. Class **WeatherServiceClient** uses a **JList** with a custom **ListCellRenderer** to display the weather information for each city.

The **WeatherServiceClient** constructor (lines 16–58) takes as an argument the name of computer on which the **WeatherService** remote object is running. Line 24 creates a **String** that contains the URL for this remote object. Lines 27–28 invoke **Naming**'s **static** method *lookup* to obtain a remote reference to the **WeatherService** remote object at the specified URL. Method **lookup** connects to the RMI registry and returns a **Remote** reference to the remote object, so line 28 casts this reference to type **WeatherService**. Note that the **WeatherServiceClient** refers to the remote object only through interface **WeatherService**—the remote interface for the **WeatherServiceImpl** remote object implementation. The client can use this remote reference as if it referred to a local object running in the same virtual machine. This remote reference refers to a *stub* object on the client. Stubs allow clients to invoke remote objects' methods. Stub objects receive each remote method call and pass those calls to the RMI system, which performs the networking that allows clients to interact with the remote object. In this case, the **WeatherServiceImpl** stub will handle the communication between **WeatherServiceClient** and **WeatherServiceImpl**. The RMI layer is responsible for network connections to the remote object, so referencing remote objects is transparent to the client. RMI handles the underlying communication with the remote object and the transfer of arguments and return values between the objects.

Lines 31–32 invoke remote method **getWeatherInformation** on the **weatherService** remote reference. This method call returns a copy of the **List** of **WeatherBean**s, which contains information from the *Traveler's Forecast* Web page. It is important to note that RMI returns a copy of the **List**, because returning a reference from a remote method call is different from returning a reference from a local method call. RMI uses object serialization to send the **List** of **WeatherBean** objects to the client. Therefore, the argument and return types for remote methods must be **Serializable**.

```java
1   // WeatherServiceClient.java
2   // WeatherServiceClient uses the WeatherService remote object
3   // to retrieve weather information.
4   package com.deitel.advjhtp1.rmi.weather;
5
6   // Java core packages
7   import java.rmi.*;
8   import java.util.*;
9
10  // Java extension packages
11  import javax.swing.*;
12
13  public class WeatherServiceClient extends JFrame
14  {
15     // WeatherServiceClient constructor
16     public WeatherServiceClient( String server )
17     {
18        super( "RMI WeatherService Client" );
19
20        // connect to server and get weather information
21        try {
22
23           // name of remote server object bound to rmi registry
24           String remoteName = "rmi://" + server + "/WeatherService";
25
26           // lookup WeatherServiceImpl remote object
27           WeatherService weatherService =
28              ( WeatherService ) Naming.lookup( remoteName );
29
30           // get weather information from server
31           List weatherInformation =
32              weatherService.getWeatherInformation();
33
```

Fig. 13.4 **WeatherServiceClient** client for **WeatherService** remote object (part 1 of 2).

```
34            // create WeatherListModel for weather information
35            ListModel weatherListModel =
36                new WeatherListModel( weatherInformation );
37
38            // create JList, set ListCellRenderer and add to layout
39            JList weatherJList = new JList( weatherListModel );
40            weatherJList.setCellRenderer( new WeatherCellRenderer());
41            getContentPane().add( new JScrollPane( weatherJList ) );
42
43         } // end try
44
45         // handle exception connecting to remote server
46         catch ( ConnectException connectionException ) {
47            System.err.println( "Connection to server failed. " +
48               "Server may be temporarily unavailable." );
49
50            connectionException.printStackTrace();
51         }
52
53         // handle exceptions communicating with remote object
54         catch ( Exception exception ) {
55            exception.printStackTrace();
56         }
57
58      } // end WeatherServiceClient constructor
59
60      // execute WeatherServiceClient
61      public static void main( String args[] )
62      {
63         WeatherServiceClient client = null;
64
65         // if no sever IP address or host name specified,
66         // use "localhost"; otherwise use specified host
67         if ( args.length == 0 )
68            client = new WeatherServiceClient( "localhost" );
69         else
70            client = new WeatherServiceClient( args[ 0 ] );
71
72         // configure and display application window
73         client.setDefaultCloseOperation( JFrame.EXIT_ON_CLOSE );
74         client.pack();
75         client.setResizable( false );
76         client.setVisible( true );
77      }
78   }
```

Fig. 13.4 WeatherServiceClient client for **WeatherService** remote
object (part 2 of 2).

Lines 35–36 create a **WeatherListModel** (Fig. 13.5) to facilitate displaying the
weather information in a **JList** (line 39). Line 40 sets a **ListCellRenderer** for the
JList. Class **WeatherCellRenderer** (Fig. 13.6) is a **ListCellRenderer** that
uses **WeatherItem** objects to display weather information stored in **WeatherBean**s.

Method **main** (lines 61–77) checks the command-line arguments for a user-provided hostname. If the user did not provide a hostname, line 68 creates a new **WeatherService-Client** that connects to an RMI registry running on **localhost**. If the user did provide a hostname, line 70 creates a **WeatherServiceClient** using the given hostname.

Class **WeatherListModel** (Fig. 13.5) is a **ListModel** that contains **Weather-Bean**s to be displayed in a **JList**. This example continues our design patterns discussion by introducing the *Adapter design pattern*, which enables two objects with incompatible interfaces to communicate with each other.[1] The Adapter design pattern has many parallels in the real world. For example, the electrical plugs on appliances in the United States are not compatible with European electrical sockets. Using an American electrical appliance in Europe requires the user to place an adapter between the electrical plug and the electrical socket. On one side, this adapter provides an interface compatible with the American electrical plug. On the other side, this adapter provides an interface compatible with the European electrical socket. Class **WeatherListModel** plays the role of the *Adapter* in the Adapter design pattern. In Java, interface **List** is not compatible with class **JList**'s interface—a **JList** can retrieve elements only from a **ListModel**. Therefore, we provide class **WeatherListModel**, which adapts interface **List** to make it compatible with **JList**'s interface. When the **JList** invokes **WeatherListModel** method **getSize**, **WeatherListModel** invokes method **size** of interface **List**. When the **JList** invokes **WeatherListModel** method **getElementAt**, **WeatherListModel** invokes **JList** method **get**, etc. Class **WeatherListModel** also plays the role of the model in Swing's delegate-model architecture, as we discussed in Chapter 3, Model-View-Controller.

```
1   // WeatherListModel.java
2   // WeatherListModel extends AbstractListModel to provide a
3   // ListModel for storing a List of WeatherBeans.
4   package com.deitel.advjhtp1.rmi.weather;
5
6   // Java core packages
7   import java.util.*;
8
9   // Java extension packages
10  import javax.swing.AbstractListModel;
11
12  public class WeatherListModel extends AbstractListModel {
13
14     // List of elements in ListModel
15     private List list;
16
17     // no-argument WeatherListModel constructor
18     public WeatherListModel()
19     {
20        // create new List for WeatherBeans
21        list = new ArrayList();
22     }
```

Fig. 13.5   **WeatherListModel** is a **ListModel** implementation for storing weather information (part 1 of 2).

1. Gamma, Erich, Richard Helm, Ralph Johnson, and John Vlissides. *Design Patterns; Elements of Reusable Object-Oriented Software*. (Reading, MA: Addison-Wesley, 1995): p. 139.

```
23
24      // WeatherListModel constructor
25      public WeatherListModel( List elementList )
26      {
27         list = elementList;
28      }
29
30      // get size of List
31      public int getSize()
32      {
33         return list.size();
34      }
35
36      // get Object reference to element at given index
37      public Object getElementAt( int index )
38      {
39         return list.get( index );
40      }
41
42      // add element to WeatherListModel
43      public void add( Object element )
44      {
45         list.add( element );
46         fireIntervalAdded( this, list.size(), list.size() );
47      }
48
49      // remove element from WeatherListModel
50      public void remove( Object element )
51      {
52         int index = list.indexOf( element );
53
54         if ( index != -1 ) {
55            list.remove( element );
56            fireIntervalRemoved( this, index, index );
57         }
58
59      } // end method remove
60
61      // remove all elements from WeatherListModel
62      public void clear()
63      {
64         // get original size of List
65         int size = list.size();
66
67         // clear all elements from List
68         list.clear();
69
70         // notify listeners that content changed
71         fireContentsChanged( this, 0, size );
72      }
73   }
```

Fig. 13.5   **WeatherListModel** is a **ListModel** implementation for storing weather information (part 2 of 2).

Class **JList** uses a **ListCellRenderer** to render each element in that **JList**'s **ListModel**. Class **WeatherCellRenderer** (Fig. 13.6) is a **DefaultListCell-Renderer** subclass for rendering **WeatherBean**s in a **JList**. Method **getList-CellRendererComponent** creates and returns a **WeatherItem** (Fig. 13.7) for the given **WeatherBean**.

Class **WeatherItem** (Fig. 13.7) is a **JPanel** subclass for displaying weather information stored in a **WeatherBean**. Class **WeatherCellRenderer** uses instances of class **WeatherItem** to display weather information in a **JList**. The **static** block (lines 22–29) loads the **ImageIcon backgroundImage** into memory when the virtual machine loads the **WeatherItem** class itself. This ensures that **backgroundImage** is available to all instances of class **WeatherItem**. Method **paintComponent** (lines 38–56) draws the **backgroundImage** (line 43), the city name (line 50), the temperature (line 51) and the **WeatherBean**'s **ImageIcon**, which describes the weather conditions (line 54).

```
1   // WeatherCellRenderer.java
2   // WeatherCellRenderer is a custom ListCellRenderer for
3   // WeatherBeans in a JList.
4   package com.deitel.advjhtp1.rmi.weather;
5
6   // Java core packages
7   import java.awt.*;
8
9   // Java extension packages
10  import javax.swing.*;
11
12  public class WeatherCellRenderer extends DefaultListCellRenderer {
13
14     // returns a WeatherItem object that displays city's weather
15     public Component getListCellRendererComponent( JList list,
16        Object value, int index, boolean isSelected, boolean focus )
17     {
18        return new WeatherItem( ( WeatherBean ) value );
19     }
20  }
```

Fig. 13.6 **WeatherCellRenderer** is a custom **ListCellRenderer** for displaying **WeatherBean**s in a **JList**.

```
1   // WeatherItem.java
2   // WeatherItem displays a city's weather information in a JPanel.
3   package com.deitel.advjhtp1.rmi.weather;
4
5   // Java core packages
6   import java.awt.*;
7   import java.net.*;
8   import java.util.*;
9
10  // Java extension packages
11  import javax.swing.*;
12
```

Fig. 13.7 **WeatherItem** displays weather information for one city (part 1 of 2).

```
13  public class WeatherItem extends JPanel {
14
15     private WeatherBean weatherBean;  // weather information
16
17     // background ImageIcon
18     private static ImageIcon backgroundImage;
19
20     // static initializer block loads background image when class
21     // WeatherItem is loaded into memory
22     static {
23
24        // get URL for background image
25        URL url = WeatherItem.class.getResource( "images/back.jpg" );
26
27        // background image for each city's weather info
28        backgroundImage = new ImageIcon( url );
29     }
30
31     // initialize a WeatherItem
32     public WeatherItem( WeatherBean bean )
33     {
34        weatherBean = bean;
35     }
36
37     // display information for city's weather
38     public void paintComponent( Graphics g )
39     {
40        super.paintComponent( g );
41
42        // draw background
43        backgroundImage.paintIcon( this, g, 0, 0 );
44
45        // set font and drawing color,
46        // then display city name and temperature
47        Font font = new Font( "SansSerif", Font.BOLD, 12 );
48        g.setFont( font );
49        g.setColor( Color.white );
50        g.drawString( weatherBean.getCityName(), 10, 19 );
51        g.drawString( weatherBean.getTemperature(), 130, 19 );
52
53        // display weather image
54        weatherBean.getImage().paintIcon( this, g, 253, 1 );
55
56     } // end method paintComponent
57
58     // make WeatherItem's preferred size the width and height of
59     // the background image
60     public Dimension getPreferredSize()
61     {
62        return new Dimension( backgroundImage.getIconWidth(),
63           backgroundImage.getIconHeight() );
64     }
65  }
```

Fig. 13.7 **WeatherItem** displays weather information for one city (part 2 of 2).

The images in this example are available with the example code from this text on the CD that accompanies the text and from our Web site (**www.deitel.com**). Click the **Downloads** link and download the examples for *Advanced Java 2 Platform How to Program.*

13.5 Compiling and Executing the Server and the Client

Now that the pieces are in place, we can build and execute our distributed application; this requires several steps. First, we must compile the classes. Next, we must compile the remote object class (**WeatherServiceImpl**), using the *rmic* compiler (a utility supplied with the J2SE SDK) to produce a *stub class*. As we discussed in Section 13.4, a stub class forwards method invocations to the RMI layer, which performs the network communication necessary to invoke the method call on the remote object. The command line

```
rmic -v1.2 com.deitel.advjhtp1.rmi.weather.WeatherServiceImpl
```

generates the file **WeatherServiceImpl_Stub.class**. This class must be available to the client (either locally or via download) to enable remote communication with the server object. Depending on the command line options passed to **rmic**, this may generate several files. In Java 1.1, **rmic** produced two classes—a stub class and a *skeleton class*. Java 2 no longer requires the skeleton class. The command-line option **-v1.2** indicates that **rmic** should create only the stub class.

The next step is to start the RMI registry with which the **WeatherServiceImpl** object will register. The command line

```
rmiregistry
```

launches the RMI registry on the local machine. The command line window (Fig. 13.8) will not show any text in response to this command.

 Common Programming Error 13.1

*Not starting the RMI registry before attempting to bind the remote object to the registry results in a **java.rmi.ConnectException**, which indicates that the program cannot connect to the registry.*

To make the remote object available to receive remote method calls, we bind the object to a name in the RMI registry. Run the **WeatherServiceImpl** application from the command line as follows:

```
java com.deitel.advjhtp1.rmi.weather.WeatherServiceImpl
```

Figure 13.9 shows the **WeatherServiceImpl** application output. Class **WeatherServiceImpl** retrieves the data from the *Traveler's Forecast* Web page and displays a message indicating that the service is running.

Fig. 13.8 Running the **rmiregistry**.

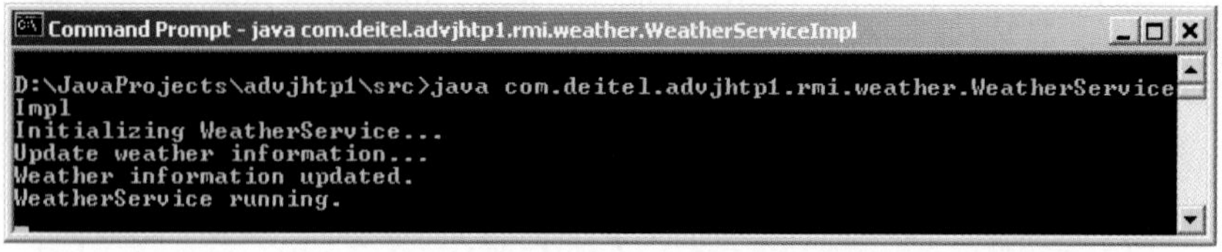

Fig. 13.9 Executing the `WeatherServiceImpl` remote object.

The **WeatherServiceClient** program now can connect with the **Weather-ServiceImpl** running on **localhost** with the command

```
java com.deitel.advjhtp1.rmi.weather.WeatherServiceClient
```

Figure 13.10 shows the **WeatherServiceClient** application window. When the program executes, the **WeatherServiceClient** connects to the remote server object and displays the current weather information.

If the **WeatherServiceImpl** is running on a different machine from the client, you can specify the IP address or host name of the server computer as a command-line argument when executing the client. For example, to access a computer with IP address **192.168.0.150**, enter the command

```
java com.deitel.advjhtp1.rmi.weather.WeatherServiceClient
192.168.0.150
```

In the first part of this chapter, we built a simple distributed system that demonstrated the basics of RMI. In the following case study, we build a more sophisticated RMI distributed system that takes advantage of some advanced RMI features.

Fig. 13.10 `WeatherServiceClient` application window.

13.6 Case Study: Deitel Messenger with `Activatable` Server

In this section, we present a case study that implements an online chat system using RMI and an *activatable* chat server. This case study—the Deitel Messenger—uses several advanced RMI features and a modular architecture that promotes reusability. Figure 13.11 lists the classes and interfaces that make up the case study and brief descriptions of each. Interfaces are shown in italic font.

Standard RMI objects exported as **UnicastRemoteObject**s must run continuously on the server to handle client requests. RMI objects that extend class **java.rmi.activation.Activatable** are able to *activate*, or start running, when a client invokes one of the remote object's methods. This can conserve resources on the server because a remote object's processes are put to sleep and release memory when there are no clients using that particular remote object. The *RMI activation daemon* (**rmid**) is a server process that enables activatable remote objects to become active when clients invoke remote methods on these objects.

Name	Role
ChatServer	Remote interface through which clients register for a chat, leave a chat, and post chat messages.
StoppableChatServer	Administrative remote interface for terminating the chat server.
ChatServerImpl	Implementation of the ChatServer remote interface that provides an RMI-based chat server.
ChatServerAdministrator	Utility program for launching and terminating the activatable **ChatServer**.
ChatClient	Remote interface through which the ChatServer communicates with clients.
ChatMessage	**Serializable** object for sending messages between **ChatServer** and **ChatClient**s.
MessageManager	Interface that defines methods for managing communication between the client's user interface and the **ChatServer**.
RMIMessageManager	**ChatClient** and **MessageManager** implementation for managing communication between the client and the **ChatServer**.
MessageListener	Interface for classes that wish to receive new chat messages.
DisconnectListener	Interface for classes that wish to receive notifications when the server disconnects.
ClientGUI	GUI for sending and receiving chat messages using a **MessageManager**.
DeitelMessenger	Application launcher for Deitel Messenger client.

Fig. 13.11 Participants of DeitelMessenger case study.

Activatable remote objects also are able to recover from server crashes, because remote references to activatable objects are persistent—when the server restarts, the RMI activation daemon maintains the remote reference, so clients can continue to use the remote object. We discuss the details of implementing **Activatable** remote objects when we present the chat server implementation.

13.6.1 **Activatable** Deitel Messenger **ChatServer**

Like every RMI remote object, an **Activatable** remote object must implement a remote interface. Interface **ChatServer** (Fig. 13.12) is the remote interface for the Deitel Messenger server. Clients interact with the Deitel Messenger server through the **ChatServer** remote interface. Remote interfaces for an **Activatable** RMI have the same requirements as standard RMI remote interfaces.

Line 13 declares that interface **ChatServer** extends interface **Remote**, which RMI requires for all remote interfaces. Method **registerClient** (lines 16–17) enables a **ChatClient** (Fig. 13.17) to register with the **ChatServer** and take part in the chat session. Method **registerClient** takes as an argument the **ChatClient** to register. Interface **ChatClient** is itself a remote interface, so both the server and client are remote objects in this application. This enables the server to communicate with clients by invoking remote methods on those clients. We discuss this communication—called an RMI callback—in more detail when we present the **ChatClient** implementation.

```
1   // ChatServer.java
2   // ChatServer is a remote interface that defines how a client
3   // registers for a chat, leaves a chat and posts chat messages.
4   package com.deitel.messenger.rmi.server;
5
6   // Java core packages
7   import java.rmi.*;
8
9   // Deitel packages
10  import com.deitel.messenger.rmi.ChatMessage;
11  import com.deitel.messenger.rmi.client.ChatClient;
12
13  public interface ChatServer extends Remote {
14
15     // register new ChatClient with ChatServer
16     public void registerClient( ChatClient client )
17        throws RemoteException;
18
19     // unregister ChatClient with ChatServer
20     public void unregisterClient( ChatClient client )
21        throws RemoteException;
22
23     // post new message to ChatServer
24     public void postMessage( ChatMessage message )
25        throws RemoteException;
26  }
```

Fig. 13.12 ChatServer remote interface for Deitel Messenger chat server.

Method **unregisterClient** (lines 20–21) enables clients to remove themselves from the chat session. Method **postMessage** enables clients to post new messages to the chat session. Method **postMessage** takes as an argument a reference to a **ChatMessage**. A **ChatMessage** (Fig. 13.18) is a **Serializable** object that contains the name of the sender and the message body. We discuss this class in more detail shortly.

The server side of the Deitel Messenger application includes a program for managing the **Activatable** remote object. Interface **StoppableChatServer** (Fig. 13.13) declares method **stopServer**. The program that manages the Deitel Messenger server invokes method **stopServer** to terminate the server.

Class **ChatServerImpl** (Fig. 13.14) is an **Activatable** RMI object that implements the **ChatServer** and **StoppableChatServer** remote interfaces. Line 23 creates a **Set** for maintaining remote references to registered **ChatClient**s. The **ChatServerImpl** constructor (lines 29–34) takes as arguments an **ActivationID** and a **MarshalledObject**. The RMI activation mechanism requires that **Activatable** objects provide this constructor. When the activation daemon activates a remote object of this class, it invokes this *activation constructor*. The **ActivationID** argument specifies a unique identifier for the remote object. Class **MarshalledObject** is a wrapper class that contains a serialized object for transmission over RMI. In this case, the **MarshalledObject** argument contains application-specific initialization information, such as the name under which the activation daemon registered the remote object. Line 33 invokes the superclass constructor to complete activation. The second argument to the superclass constructor (**0**) specifies that the activation daemon should export the object on an anonymous port.

```
1   // StoppableChatServer.java
2   // StoppableChatServer is a remote interface that provides a
3   // mechansim to terminate the chat server.
4   package com.deitel.messenger.rmi.server;
5
6   // Java core packages
7   import java.rmi.*;
8
9   public interface StoppableChatServer extends Remote {
10
11      // stop ChatServer
12      public void stopServer() throws RemoteException;
13   }
```

Fig. 13.13 **StoppableChatServer** remote interface for stopping a **ChatServer** remote object.

```
1   // ChatServerImpl.java
2   // ChatServerImpl implements the ChatServer remote interface
3   // to provide an RMI-based chat server.
4   package com.deitel.messenger.rmi.server;
5
```

Fig. 13.14 **ChatServerImpl** implementation of remote interfaces **ChatServer** and **StoppableChatServer** as **Activatable** remote objects (part 1 of 5).

```
6    // Java core packages
7    import java.io.*;
8    import java.net.*;
9    import java.rmi.*;
10   import java.rmi.activation.*;
11   import java.rmi.server.*;
12   import java.rmi.registry.*;
13   import java.util.*;
14
15   // Deitel packages
16   import com.deitel.messenger.rmi.ChatMessage;
17   import com.deitel.messenger.rmi.client.ChatClient;
18
19   public class ChatServerImpl extends Activatable
20      implements ChatServer, StoppableChatServer {
21
22      // Set of ChatClient references
23      private Set clients = new HashSet();
24
25      // server object's name
26      private String serverObjectName;
27
28      // ChatServerImpl constructor
29      public ChatServerImpl( ActivationID id, MarshalledObject data )
30         throws RemoteException {
31
32         // register activatable object and export on anonymous port
33         super( id, 0 );
34      }
35
36      // register ChatServerImpl object with RMI registry.
37      public void register( String rmiName ) throws RemoteException,
38         IllegalArgumentException, MalformedURLException
39      {
40         // ensure registration name was provided
41         if ( rmiName == null )
42            throw new IllegalArgumentException(
43               "Registration name cannot be null" );
44
45         serverObjectName = rmiName;
46
47         // bind ChatServerImpl object to RMI registry
48         try {
49
50            // create RMI registry
51            System.out.println( "Creating registry ..." );
52            Registry registry =
53               LocateRegistry.createRegistry( 1099 );
54
55            // bind RMI object to default RMI registry
56            System.out.println( "Binding server to registry ..." );
```

Fig. 13.14 ChatServerImpl implementation of remote interfaces ChatServer and StoppableChatServer as Activatable remote objects (part 2 of 5).

```
57              registry.rebind( serverObjectName, this );
58          }
59
60          // if registry already exists, bind to existing registry
61          catch ( RemoteException remoteException ) {
62              System.err.println( "Registry already exists. " +
63                  "Binding to existing registry ..." );
64              Naming.rebind( serverObjectName, this );
65          }
66
67          System.out.println( "Server bound to registry" );
68
69      } // end method register
70
71      // register new ChatClient with ChatServer
72      public void registerClient( ChatClient client )
73          throws RemoteException
74      {
75          // add client to Set of registered clients
76          synchronized ( clients ) {
77              clients.add( client );
78          }
79
80          System.out.println( "Registered Client: " + client );
81
82      } // end method registerClient
83
84      // unregister client with ChatServer
85      public void unregisterClient( ChatClient client )
86          throws RemoteException
87      {
88          // remove client from Set of registered clients
89          synchronized( clients ) {
90              clients.remove( client );
91          }
92
93          System.out.println( "Unregistered Client: " + client );
94
95      } // end method unregisterClient
96
97      // post new message to chat server
98      public void postMessage( ChatMessage message )
99          throws RemoteException
100      {
101          Iterator iterator = null;
102
103          // get Iterator for Set of registered clients
104          synchronized( clients ) {
105              iterator = new HashSet( clients ).iterator();
106          }
107
```

Fig. 13.14 **ChatServerImpl** implementation of remote interfaces **ChatServer** and **StoppableChatServer** as **Activatable** remote objects (part 3 of 5).

```
108        // send message to every ChatClient
109        while ( iterator.hasNext() ) {
110
111           // attempt to send message to client
112           ChatClient client = ( ChatClient ) iterator.next();
113
114           try {
115              client.deliverMessage( message );
116           }
117
118           // unregister client if exception is thrown
119           catch( Exception exception ) {
120              System.err.println( "Unregistering absent client." );
121              unregisterClient( client );
122           }
123
124        } // end while loop
125
126     } // end method postMessage
127
128     // notify each client that server is shutting down and
129     // terminate server application
130     public void stopServer() throws RemoteException
131     {
132        System.out.println( "Terminating server ..." );
133
134        Iterator iterator = null;
135
136        // get Iterator for Set of registered clients
137        synchronized( clients ) {
138           iterator = new HashSet( clients ).iterator();
139        }
140
141        // send message to every ChatClient
142        while ( iterator.hasNext() ) {
143           ChatClient client = ( ChatClient ) iterator.next();
144           client.serverStopping();
145        }
146
147        // create Thread to terminate application after
148        // stopServer method returns to caller
149        Thread terminator = new Thread(
150           new Runnable() {
151
152              // sleep for 5 seconds, print message and terminate
153              public void run()
154              {
155                 // sleep
156                 try {
157                    Thread.sleep( 5000 );
158                 }
```

Fig. 13.14 ChatServerImpl implementation of remote interfaces **ChatServer** and **StoppableChatServer** as **Activatable** remote objects (part 4 of 5).

```
159
160                          // ignore InterruptedExceptions
161                          catch ( InterruptedException exception ) {
162                          }
163
164                          System.err.println( "Server terminated" );
165                          System.exit( 0 );
166                  }
167              }
168          );
169
170          terminator.start(); // start termination thread
171
172      } // end method stopServer
173 }
```

Fig. 13.14 `ChatServerImpl` implementation of remote interfaces `ChatServer` and `StoppableChatServer` as `Activatable` remote objects (part 5 of 5).

Method **register** (lines 37–69) registers a **ChatServerImpl** remote object with the RMI registry. If the provided name for the remote object is **null**, lines 42–43 throw an **IllegalArgumentException**, indicating that the caller must specify a name for the remote object. Lines 52–53 use **static** method **createRegistry** of class **LocateRegistry** to create a new **Registry** on the local machine at port **1099**, which is the default port. This is equivalent to executing the **rmiregistry** utility to start a new RMI registry. Line 57 invokes method **rebind** of class **Registry** to bind the activatable object to the **Registry**. If creating or binding to the **Registry** fails, we assume that an RMI registry already is running on the local machine. Line 64 invokes **static** method **rebind** of class **Naming** to bind the remote object to the existing RMI registry.

Method **registerClient** (lines 72–82) enables **ChatClient** remote objects to register with the **ChatServer** to participate in the chat session. The **ChatClient** argument to method **registerClient** is a remote reference to the registering client, which is itself a remote object. Line 77 adds the **ChatClient** remote reference to the **Set** of **ChatClient**s participating in the chat session. Method **unregisterClient** (lines 85–95) enables **ChatClient**s to leave the chat session. Line 90 removes the given **ChatClient** remote reference from the **Set** of **ChatClient** references.

ChatClients invoke method **postMessage** (lines 98–124) to post new **ChatMessage**s to the chat session. Each **ChatMessage** (Fig. 13.18) instance is a **Serializable** object that contains as properties the message sender and the message body. Lines 109–123 iterate through the **Set** of **ChatClient** references and invoke remote method **deliverMessage** of interface **ChatClient** to deliver the new **ChatMessage** to each client. If delivering a message to a client throws an exception, we assume that the client is no longer available. Line 121 therefore unregisters the absent client from the server.

Interface **StoppableChatServer** requires that class **ChatServerImpl** implements method **stopServer** (lines 128–170). Lines 140–143 iterate through the **Set** of **ChatClient** references and invoke method **serverStopping** of interface **ChatClient** to notify each **ChatClient** that the server is shutting down. Lines 147–168 create and start a new **Thread** to ensure that the **ChatServerAdministrator** (Fig. 13.15) can unbind the remote object from the RMI **Registry** before the remote object terminates.

Class **ChatServerAdministrator** (Fig. 13.15) is a utility program for registering and unregistering the activatable **ChatServer** remote object. Method **start-Server** (lines 14–52) launches the activatable **ChatServer**. Activatable RMI objects execute as part of an *ActivationGroup* (package **java.rmi.activation**). The RMI activation daemon starts a new virtual machine for each **ActivationGroup**. Lines 21–22 create a **Properties** object and add a property that specifies the policy file under which the **ActivationGroup**'s JVM should run. This policy file (Fig. 13.16) allows **Activatable** objects in this **ActivationGroup** to terminate the virtual machine for this activation group. Recall that **ChatServerImpl** invokes **static** method **exit** of class **System** in method **stopServer**, which terminates the **ActivationGroup**'s virtual machine along with all of its executing remote objects.

```
1   // ChatServerAdministrator.java
2   // ChatServerAdministrator is a utility program for launching
3   // and terminating the Activatable ChatServer.
4   package com.deitel.messenger.rmi.server;
5
6   // Java core packages
7   import java.rmi.*;
8   import java.rmi.activation.*;
9   import java.util.*;
10
11  public class ChatServerAdministrator {
12
13      // set up activatable server object
14      private static void startServer( String policy,
15          String codebase ) throws Exception
16      {
17          // set up RMI security manager
18          System.setSecurityManager( new RMISecurityManager() );
19
20          // set security policy for ActivatableGroup JVM
21          Properties properties = new Properties();
22          properties.put( "java.security.policy", policy );
23
24          // create ActivationGroupDesc for activatable object
25          ActivationGroupDesc groupDesc =
26              new ActivationGroupDesc( properties, null );
27
28          // register activation group with RMI activation system
29          ActivationGroupID groupID =
30              ActivationGroup.getSystem().registerGroup( groupDesc );
31
32          // create activation group
33          ActivationGroup.createGroup( groupID, groupDesc , 0 );
34
```

Fig. 13.15 **ChatServerAdministrator** application for starting and stopping the **ChatServer** remote object (part 1 of 3).

```
35        // activation description for ChatServerImpl
36        ActivationDesc description = new ActivationDesc(
37           "com.deitel.messenger.rmi.server.ChatServerImpl",
38           codebase, null );
39
40        // register description with rmid
41        ChatServer server =
42           ( ChatServer ) Activatable.register( description );
43        System.out.println( "Obtained ChatServerImpl stub" );
44
45        // bind ChatServer in registry
46        Naming.rebind( "ChatServer", server );
47        System.out.println( "Bound object to registry" );
48
49        // terminate setup program
50        System.exit( 0 );
51
52     } // end method startServer
53
54     // terminate server
55     private static void terminateServer( String hostname )
56        throws Exception
57     {
58        // lookup ChatServer in RMI registry
59        System.out.println( "Locating server ..." );
60        StoppableChatServer server = ( StoppableChatServer )
61           Naming.lookup( "rmi://" + hostname + "/ChatServer" );
62
63        // terminate server
64        System.out.println( "Stopping server ..." );
65        server.stopServer();
66
67        // remove ChatServer from RMI registry
68        System.out.println( "Server stopped" );
69        Naming.unbind( "rmi://" + hostname + "/ChatServer" );
70
71     } // end method terminateServer
72
73     // launch ChatServerAdministrator application
74     public static void main( String args[] ) throws Exception
75     {
76        // check for stop server argument
77        if ( args.length == 2 ) {
78
79           if ( args[ 0 ].equals( "stop" ) )
80              terminateServer( args[ 1 ] );
81
82           else printUsageInstructions();
83        }
84
```

Fig. 13.15 **ChatServerAdministrator** application for starting and stopping the **ChatServer** remote object (part 2 of 3).

```
85        // check for start server argument
86        else if ( args.length == 3 ) {
87
88           // start server with user-provided policy, codebase
89           // and Registry hostname
90           if ( args[ 0 ].equals( "start" ) )
91              startServer( args[ 1 ], args[ 2 ] );
92
93           else printUsageInstructions();
94        }
95
96        // wrong number of arguments provided, so print instructions
97        else printUsageInstructions();
98
99     } // end method main
100
101    // print instructions for running ChatServerAdministrator
102    private static void printUsageInstructions()
103    {
104       System.err.println( "\nUsage:\n" +
105          "\tjava com.deitel.messenger.rmi.server." +
106          "ChatServerAdministrator start <policy> <codebase>\n" +
107          "\tjava com.deitel.messenger.rmi.server." +
108          "ChatServerAdministrator stop <registry hostname>" );
109    }
110 }
```

Fig. 13.15 **ChatServerAdministrator** application for starting and stopping the **ChatServer** remote object (part 3 of 3).

```
1  // allow ActivationGroup to terminate the virtual machine
2  grant {
3     permission java.lang.RuntimePermission "exitVM";
4  };
```

Fig. 13.16 Policy file for **ChatServer**'s **ActivationGroup**.

Lines 25–26 create an **ActivationGroupDesc** object, which is an *activation group descriptor*. The activation group descriptor specifies configuration information for the **ActivationGroup**. The first argument to the **ActivationGroupDesc** constructor is a **Properties** reference that contains replacement values for system properties in the **ActivationGroup**'s virtual machine. In this example, we override the **java.security.policy** system property to provide an appropriate security policy for the **ActivationGroup**'s virtual machine. The second argument is a reference to an **ActivationGroupDesc.CommandEnvironment** object. This object enables the **ActivationGroup** to customize the commands that the activation daemon executes when starting the **ActivationGroup**'s virtual machine. This example requires no such customization, so we pass a **null** reference for the second argument.

Lines 29–30 obtain an **ActivationSystem** by invoking **static** method **get-System** of class **ActivationGroup**. Line 30 invokes method **registerGroup** of interface **ActivationSystem** and passes as an argument the **groupDesc** activation group descriptor. Method **registerGroup** returns the **ActivationGroupID** for the newly registered **ActivationGroup**. Line 33 invokes **static** method **create-Group** of class **ActivationGroup** to create the **ActivationGroup**. This method takes as arguments the **ActivationGroupID**, the **ActivationGroupDesc** and the *incarnation number* for the **ActivationGroup**. The incarnation number identifies different instances of the same **ActivationGroup**. Each time the activation daemon activates the **ActivationGroup**, the daemon increments the incarnation number.

Lines 36–38 create an **ActivationDesc** object for the **ChatServer** remote object. This *activation descriptor* specifies configuration information for a particular **Activatable** remote object. The first argument to the **ActivationDesc** constructor specifies the name of the class that implements the **Activatable** remote object. The second argument specifies the codebase that contains the remote object's class files. The final argument is a **MarshalledObject** reference, whose object specifies initialization information for the remote object. Recall that the **ChatServerImpl** activation constructor takes as its second argument a **MarshalledObject** reference. Our **Chat-Server** remote object requires no special initialization information, so line 38 passes a **null** reference for the **MarshalledObject** argument.

Line 42 invokes **static** method **register** of class **Activatable** to register the **Activatable** remote object. Method **register** takes as an argument the **Activa-tionDesc** for the **Activatable** object and returns a reference to the remote object's stub. Line 46 invokes **static** method **rebind** of class **Naming** to bind the **Chat-Server** in the RMI **Registry**.

Method **terminateServer** (lines 55–71) provides a means to shut down the activatable **ChatServer** remote object. Line 61 invokes **static** method **lookup** of class **Naming** to obtain a remote reference to the **ChatServer**. Line 60 casts the reference to type **StoppableChatServer**, which declares method **stopServer**. Line 65 invokes method **stopServer** to notify clients that the **ChatServer** is shutting down. Recall that method **stopServer** of class **ChatServerImpl** starts a **Thread** that waits five seconds before invoking **static** method **exit** of class **System**. This **Thread** keeps the **ChatServer** remote object running after method **stopServer** returns, allowing the **ChatServerAdministrator** to remove the remote object from the RMI **Registry**. Line 69 invokes **static** method **unbind** of class **Naming** to remove the **ChatServer** remote object from the RMI **Registry**. The **Thread** in class **ChatServerImpl** then terminates the virtual machine in which the **Chat-Server** remote object ran.

Method **main** (lines 74–99) checks the command-line arguments to determine whether to start or stop the **ChatServer** remote object. When stopping the server, the user must provide as the second argument the hostname of the computer on which the server is running. When starting the server, the user must provide as arguments the location of the policy file for the **ActivationGroup** and the codebase for the remote object. If the user passes argument **"stop"**, line 80 invokes method **terminateServer** to shut down the **ChatServer** on the specified host. If the user passes argument **"start"**, line 91 invokes method **startServer** with the given policy file location and codebase. If the user provides an invalid number or type of arguments, lines 82, 93 and 97 invoke method **printUsageInstructions** (lines 102–109) to display information about the required command-line arguments.

13.6.2 Deitel Messenger Client Architecture and Implementation

Throughout this book, we present several versions of the Deitel Messenger case study. Each version implements the underlying communications using a different technology. For example, in Chapter 26, Common Object Request Broker Architecture (CORBA): Part 1, we present an implementation that uses CORBA as the underlying communication mechanism. The client for the Deitel Messenger application uses a modularized architecture to optimize code reuse in the several versions of this case study.

Communication Interfaces and Implementation

The client for the Deitel Messenger system separates the application GUI and the network communication into separate objects that interact through a set of interfaces. This enables us to use the same client-side GUI for different versions of the Deitel Messenger application. In this section, we present these interfaces and implementations with RMI.

Interface **ChatClient** (Fig. 13.17) is an RMI remote interface that enables the **ChatServer** to communicate with the **ChatClient** through *RMI callbacks*—remote method calls from the **ChatServer** back to the client. Recall that when a client connects to the **ChatServer**, the client invokes **ChatServer** method **registerClient** and passes as an argument a **ChatClient** remote reference. The server then uses this **ChatClient** remote reference to invoke RMI callbacks on the **ChatClient** (e.g., to deliver **ChatMessage**s to that client). Method **deliverMessage** (lines 16–17) enables the **ChatServer** to send new **ChatMessages** to the **ChatClient**. Method **serverStopping** (line 20) enables the **ChatServer** to notify the **ChatClient** when the **ChatServer** is shutting down.

```
1   // ChatClient.java
2   // ChatClient is a remote interface that defines methods for a
3   // chat client to receive messages and status information from
4   // a ChatServer.
5   package com.deitel.messenger.rmi.client;
6
7   // Java core packages
8   import java.rmi.*;
9
10  // Deitel packages
11  import com.deitel.messenger.rmi.ChatMessage;
12
13  public interface ChatClient extends Remote {
14
15      // method called by server to deliver message to client
16      public void deliverMessage( ChatMessage message )
17          throws RemoteException;
18
19      // method called when server shuting down
20      public void serverStopping() throws RemoteException;
21  }
```

Fig. 13.17 **ChatClient** remote interface to enable RMI callbacks.

Class **ChatMessage** (Fig. 13.18) is a **Serializable** class that represents a message in the Deitel Messenger system. Instance variables **sender** and **message** contain the name of the person who sent the message and the message body, respectively. Class **ChatMessage** provides *set* and *get* methods for the **sender** and **message** and method **toString** for producing a **String** representation of a **ChatMessage**.

Interface **MessageManager** (Fig. 13.19) declares methods for classes that implement communication logic for a **ChatClient**. The methods that this interface declares are not specific to any underlying communication implementation. The chat client GUI uses a **MessageManager** implementation to connect to and disconnect from the **Chat-Server**, and to send messages. Method **connect** (lines 10–11) connects to the **Chat-Server** and takes as an argument the **MessageListener** to which the **MessageManager** should deliver new incoming messages. We discuss interface **MessageListener** in detail when we present the client user interface. Method **disconnect** (lines 15–16) disconnects the **MessageManager** from the **ChatServer** and stops routing messages to the given **MessageListener**. Method **sendMessage** (lines 19–20) takes as **String** arguments a user name (**from**) and a **message** to send to the **ChatServer**. Method **setDisconnectListener** registers a **DisconnectListener** to be notified when the **ChatServer** disconnects the client. We discuss interface **DisconnectListener** in detail when we present the client user interface.

```
1   // ChatMessage.java
2   // ChatMessage is a Serializable object for messages in the RMI
3   // ChatClient and ChatServer.
4   package com.deitel.messenger.rmi;
5
6   // Java core packages
7   import java.io.*;
8
9   public class ChatMessage implements Serializable {
10
11      private String sender;    // person sending message
12      private String message;   // message being sent
13
14      // construct empty ChatMessage
15      public ChatMessage()
16      {
17         this( "", "" );
18      }
19
20      // construct ChatMessage with sender and message values
21      public ChatMessage( String sender, String message )
22      {
23         setSender( sender );
24         setMessage( message );
25      }
26
```

Fig. 13.18 ChatMessage is a serializable class for transmitting messages over RMI (part 1 of 2).

```
27        // set name of person sending message
28        public void setSender( String name )
29        {
30           sender = name;
31        }
32
33        // get name of person sending message
34        public String getSender()
35        {
36           return sender;
37        }
38
39        // set message being sent
40        public void setMessage( String messageBody )
41        {
42           message = messageBody;
43        }
44
45        // get message being sent
46        public String getMessage()
47        {
48           return message;
49        }
50
51        // String representation of ChatMessage
52        public String toString()
53        {
54           return getSender() + "> " + getMessage();
55        }
56    }
```

Fig. 13.18 ChatMessage is a serializable class for transmitting messages over RMI (part 2 of 2).

```
1     // MessageManager.java
2     // MessageManger is an interface for objects capable of managing
3     // communications with a message server.
4     package com.deitel.messenger;
5
6     public interface MessageManager {
7
8        // connect to message server and route incoming messages
9        // to given MessageListener
10       public void connect( MessageListener listener )
11          throws Exception;
12
13       // disconnect from message server and stop routing
14       // incoming messages to given MessageListener
15       public void disconnect( MessageListener listener )
16          throws Exception;
17
```

Fig. 13.19 MessageManager interface for classes that implement communication logic for a **ChatClient** (part 1 of 2).

```
18    // send message to message server
19    public void sendMessage( String from, String message )
20       throws Exception;
21
22    // set listener for disconnect notifications
23    public void setDisconnectListener(
24       DisconnectListener listener );
25 }
```

Fig. 13.19 **MessageManager** interface for classes that implement communication logic for a **ChatClient** (part 2 of 2).

Class **RMIMessageManager** (Fig. 13.20) handles all communication between the client and the **ChatServer**. Class **RMIMessageManager** is an RMI remote object that extends class **UnicastRemoteObject** and implements the **ChatClient** remote interface (lines 18–19). Class **RMIMessageManager** also implements interface **MessageManager**, enabling the client user interface to use an **RMIMessageManager** object to communicate with the **ChatServer**.

The **RMIMessageManager** constructor takes as a **String** argument the hostname of the computer running the RMI registry with which the **ChatServer** has registered. Note that because class **RMIMessenger** is itself an RMI remote object, the **RMIMessageManager** constructor throws **RemoteException**, which RMI requires of all **UnicastRemoteObject** subclasses. Line 31 assigns the given server name to instance variable **serverAddress**.

```
1    // RMIMessageManager.java
2    // RMIMessageManager implements the ChatClient remote interface
3    // and manages incoming and outgoing chat messages using RMI.
4    package com.deitel.messenger.rmi.client;
5
6    // Java core packages
7    import java.awt.*;
8    import java.awt.event.*;
9    import java.rmi.*;
10   import java.rmi.server.*;
11   import java.util.*;
12
13   // Deitel packages
14   import com.deitel.messenger.*;
15   import com.deitel.messenger.rmi.*;
16   import com.deitel.messenger.rmi.server.ChatServer;
17
18   public class RMIMessageManager extends UnicastRemoteObject
19      implements ChatClient, MessageManager {
20
21      // listeners for incoming messages and disconnect notifications
22      private MessageListener messageListener;
23      private DisconnectListener disconnectListener;
24
```

Fig. 13.20 **RMIMessageManager** remote object and **MessageManager** implementation for managing **ChatClient** communication (part 1 of 3).

```
25     private String serverAddress;
26     private ChatServer chatServer;
27
28     // RMIMessageManager constructor
29     public RMIMessageManager( String server ) throws RemoteException
30     {
31        serverAddress = server;
32     }
33
34     // connect to ChatServer
35     public void connect( MessageListener listener )
36        throws Exception
37     {
38        // look up ChatServer remote object
39        chatServer = ( ChatServer ) Naming.lookup(
40           "//" + serverAddress + "/ChatServer" );
41
42        // register with ChatServer to receive messages
43        chatServer.registerClient( this );
44
45        // set listener for incoming messages
46        messageListener = listener;
47
48     } // end method connect
49
50     // disconnect from ChatServer
51     public void disconnect( MessageListener listener )
52        throws Exception
53     {
54        if ( chatServer == null )
55           return;
56
57        // unregister with ChatServer
58        chatServer.unregisterClient( this );
59
60        // remove references to ChatServer and MessageListener
61        chatServer = null;
62        messageListener = null;
63
64     } // end method disconnect
65
66     // send ChatMessage to ChatServer
67     public void sendMessage( String fromUser, String message )
68        throws Exception
69     {
70        if ( chatServer == null )
71           return;
72
73        // create ChatMessage with message text and userName
74        ChatMessage chatMessage =
75           new ChatMessage( fromUser, message );
76
```

Fig. 13.20 RMIMessageManager remote object and MessageManager implementation for managing ChatClient communication (part 2 of 3).

```
77              // post message to ChatServer
78              chatServer.postMessage( chatMessage );
79
80          }  // end method sendMessage
81
82          // process delivery of ChatMessage from ChatServer
83          public void deliverMessage( ChatMessage message )
84              throws RemoteException
85          {
86              if ( messageListener != null )
87                  messageListener.messageReceived( message.getSender(),
88                      message.getMessage() );
89          }
90
91          // method called when server shutting down
92          public void serverStopping() throws RemoteException
93          {
94              chatServer = null;
95              fireServerDisconnected( "Server shut down." );
96          }
97
98          // register listener for disconnect notifications
99          public void setDisconnectListener(
100             DisconnectListener listener )
101         {
102             disconnectListener = listener;
103         }
104
105         // send disconnect notification
106         private void fireServerDisconnected( String message )
107         {
108             if ( disconnectListener != null )
109                 disconnectListener.serverDisconnected( message );
110         }
111     }
```

Fig. 13.20 **RMIMessageManager** remote object and **MessageManager** implementation for managing **ChatClient** communication (part 3 of 3).

Method **connect** (lines 35–48)—declared in interface **MessageManager**—connects the **RMIMessageManager** to the **ChatServer**. Lines 39–40 invoke **static** method **lookup** of class **Naming** to retrieve a remote reference to the **ChatServer**. Line 43 invokes method **registerClient** of interface **ChatServer** to register the **RMIMessageManager** for RMI callbacks from the **ChatServer**. Note that line 43 passes the **this** reference as the argument to method **registerClient**. Recall that class **RMIMessageManager** is a remote object, therefore the **this** reference can serve as a remote **ChatClient** reference to the **RMIMessageManager** remote object.

Method **disconnect** (lines 51–64) disconnects the **RMIMessageManager** from the **ChatServer**. If remote **ChatServer** reference **chatServer** is **null**, line 55 returns immediately, because the **RMIMessageManager** is disconnected already. Line 58 invokes method **unregisterClient** of remote interface **ChatServer** to unregister the **RMIMessageManager** from the **ChatServer**. Line 58 passes the **this** reference as an argument to method **unregisterClient**, specifying that the **ChatServer** should **unregister** this **RMIMessageManager** remote object. Line 62 sets **MessageListener** reference **messageListener** to **null**.

Method **sendMessage** (lines 67–80) delivers a message from the client to the **ChatServer**. Line 71 returns immediately if the **chatServer** remote reference is **null**. Lines 74–75 create a new **ChatMessage** object to contain the user name from whom the message came and the message body. Line 78 invokes method **postMessage** of remote interface **ChatServer** to post the new **ChatMessage** to the **ChatServer**. The **ChatServer** will use RMI callbacks to deliver this message to each registered **ChatClient**.

Method **deliverMessage** (lines 83–89)—defined in remote interface **ChatClient**—enables the **ChatServer** to use RMI callbacks to deliver incoming **ChatMessages** to the **ChatClient**. If there is a **MessageListener** registered with the **RMIMessageManager** (line 86), lines 87–88 invoke method **messageReceived** of interface **MessageListener** to notify the **MessageListener** of the incoming **ChatMessage**. Lines 87–88 invoke methods **getSender** and **getMessage** of class **ChatMessage** to retrieve the message sender and message body, respectively.

Method **serverStopping** (lines 92–96)—defined in remote interface **ChatClient**—enables the **ChatServer** to use RMI callbacks to notify the **ChatClient** that the **ChatServer** is shutting down so the **ChatClient** can disconnect and notify the **DisconnectListener**. Line 95 invokes method **fireServerDisconnected** of class **RMIMessageManager** to notify the registered **DisconnectListener** that the **ChatServer** has disconnected the **ChatClient**.

Method **setDisconnectListener** (lines 99–103)—defined in interface **MessageManager**—enables a **DisconnectListener** to register for notifications when the **ChatServer** disconnects the client. For example, the client user interface could register for these notifications to notify the user that the server has disconnected. Method **fireServerDisconnected** (lines 106–110) is a utility method for sending **serverDisconnected** messages to the **DisconnectListener**. If there is a registered **DisconnectListener**, line 109 invokes method **serverDisconnected** of interface **DisconnectListener** to notify the listener that the server disconnected. We discuss interface **DisconnectListener** in detail when we present the client user interface.

Client GUI Interfaces and Implementation

We uncouple the client user interface from the **MessageManager** implementation through interfaces **MessageListener** and **DisconnectListener** (Fig. 13.19 and 13.20). Class **ClientGUI** uses implementations of interfaces **MessageListener** and **DisconnectListener** to interact with the **MessageManager** and provides a graphical user interface for the client.

Interface **MessageListener** (Fig. 13.21) enables objects of an implementing class to receive incoming messages from a **MessageManager**. Line 9 defines method **messageReceived**, which takes as arguments the user name **from** whom the message came and the **message** body.

Interface **DisconnectListener** (Fig. 13.22) enables implementing objects to receive notifications when the server disconnects the **MessageManager**. Line 9 defines method **serverDisconnected**, which takes as a **String** argument a **message** that indicates why the server disconnected.

```
 1   // MessageListener.java
 2   // MessageListener is an interface for classes that wish to
 3   // receive new chat messages.
 4   package com.deitel.messenger;
 5
 6   public interface MessageListener {
 7
 8      // receive new chat message
 9      public void messageReceived( String from, String message );
10   }
```

Fig. 13.21 MessageListener interface for receiving new messages.

```
 1   // DisconnectListener.java
 2   // DisconnectListener defines method serverDisconnected, which
 3   // indicates that the server has disconnected the client.
 4   package com.deitel.messenger;
 5
 6   public interface DisconnectListener {
 7
 8      // receive notification that server disconnected
 9      public void serverDisconnected( String message );
10   }
```

Fig. 13.22 DisconnectListener interface for receiving server disconnect notifications.

Class **ClientGUI** (Fig. 13.23) provides a user interface for the Deitel Messenger client. The GUI consists of a menu and a toolbar with **Action**s for connecting to and disconnecting from a **ChatServer**, a **JTextArea** for displaying incoming **Chat-Message**s and a **JTextArea** and **JButton** for sending new messages to the **ChatServer**. Lines 27–29 declare **Action** references for connecting to and disconnecting from the **ChatServer** and for sending **ChatMessage**s. Line 35 declares a **MessageManager** reference for the **MessageManager** implementation that provides the network communication. Line 38 declares a **MessageListener** reference for receiving new **ChatMessage**s from the **ChatServer** through the **Message-Manager**.

```
 1   // ClientGUI.java
 2   // ClientGUI provides a GUI for sending and receiving
 3   // chat messages using a MessageManager.
 4   package com.deitel.messenger;
 5
 6   // Java core packages
 7   import java.awt.*;
 8   import java.awt.event.*;
 9   import java.util.*;
```

Fig. 13.23 ClientGUI provides a graphical user interface for the Deitel Messenger client (part 1 of 9).

```
10
11   // Java extension packages
12   import javax.swing.*;
13   import javax.swing.border.*;
14   import javax.swing.text.*;
15
16   public class ClientGUI extends JFrame {
17
18      // JLabel for displaying connection status
19      private JLabel statusBar;
20
21      // JTextAreas for displaying and inputting messages
22      private JTextArea messageArea;
23      private JTextArea inputArea;
24
25      // Actions for connecting and disconnecting MessageManager
26      // and sending messages
27      private Action connectAction;
28      private Action disconnectAction;
29      private Action sendAction;
30
31      // userName to add to outgoing messages
32      private String userName = "";
33
34      // MessageManager for communicating with server
35      MessageManager messageManager;
36
37      // MessageListener for receiving new messages
38      MessageListener messageListener;
39
40      // ClientGUI constructor
41      public ClientGUI( MessageManager manager )
42      {
43         super( "Deitel Messenger" );
44
45         messageManager = manager;
46
47         messageListener = new MyMessageListener();
48
49         // create Actions
50         connectAction = new ConnectAction();
51         disconnectAction = new DisconnectAction();
52         disconnectAction.setEnabled( false );
53         sendAction = new SendAction();
54         sendAction.setEnabled( false );
55
56         // set up File menu
57         JMenu fileMenu = new JMenu ( "File" );
58         fileMenu.setMnemonic( 'F' );
59         fileMenu.add( connectAction );
60         fileMenu.add( disconnectAction );
61
```

Fig. 13.23 ClientGUI provides a graphical user interface for the Deitel Messenger client (part 2 of 9).

```
62              // set up JMenuBar and attach File menu
63              JMenuBar menuBar = new JMenuBar();
64              menuBar.add ( fileMenu );
65              setJMenuBar( menuBar );
66
67              // set up JToolBar
68              JToolBar toolBar = new JToolBar();
69              toolBar.add( connectAction );
70              toolBar.add( disconnectAction );
71
72              // create JTextArea for displaying messages
73              messageArea = new JTextArea( 15, 15 );
74
75              // disable editing and wrap words at end of line
76              messageArea.setEditable( false );
77              messageArea.setLineWrap( true );
78              messageArea.setWrapStyleWord( true );
79
80              JPanel panel = new JPanel();
81              panel.setLayout( new BorderLayout( 5, 5 ) );
82              panel.add( new JScrollPane( messageArea ),
83                 BorderLayout.CENTER );
84
85              // create JTextArea for entering new messages
86              inputArea = new JTextArea( 3, 15 );
87              inputArea.setLineWrap( true );
88              inputArea.setWrapStyleWord( true );
89              inputArea.setEditable( false );
90
91              // map Enter key in inputArea to sendAction
92              Keymap keyMap = inputArea.getKeymap();
93              KeyStroke enterKey = KeyStroke.getKeyStroke(
94                 KeyEvent.VK_ENTER, 0 );
95              keyMap.addActionForKeyStroke( enterKey, sendAction );
96
97              // lay out inputArea and sendAction JButton in BoxLayout
98              // and add Box to messagePanel
99              Box box = new Box( BoxLayout.X_AXIS );
100             box.add( new JScrollPane( inputArea ) );
101             box.add( new JButton( sendAction ) );
102
103             panel.add( box, BorderLayout.SOUTH );
104
105             // create statusBar JLabel with recessed border
106             statusBar = new JLabel( "Not Connected" );
107             statusBar.setBorder(
108                new BevelBorder( BevelBorder.LOWERED ) );
109
110             // lay out components
111             Container container = getContentPane();
112             container.add( toolBar, BorderLayout.NORTH );
113             container.add( panel, BorderLayout.CENTER );
```

Fig. 13.23 **ClientGUI** provides a graphical user interface for the Deitel Messenger client (part 3 of 9).

```
114            container.add( statusBar, BorderLayout.SOUTH );
115
116            // disconnect and exit if user closes window
117            addWindowListener(
118
119               new WindowAdapter() {
120
121                  // disconnect MessageManager when window closes
122                  public void windowClosing( WindowEvent event )
123                  {
124                     // disconnect from chat server
125                     try {
126                        messageManager.disconnect( messageListener );
127                     }
128
129                     // handle exception disconnecting from server
130                     catch ( Exception exception ) {
131                        exception.printStackTrace();
132                     }
133
134                     System.exit( 0 );
135
136                  } // end method windowClosing
137
138               } // end WindowAdapter inner class
139            );
140
141      } // end ClientGUI constructor
142
143      // Action for connecting to server
144      private class ConnectAction extends AbstractAction {
145
146         // configure ConnectAction
147         public ConnectAction()
148         {
149            putValue( Action.NAME, "Connect" );
150            putValue( Action.SMALL_ICON, new ImageIcon(
151               ClientGUI.class.getResource(
152                  "images/Connect.gif" ) ) );
153            putValue( Action.SHORT_DESCRIPTION,
154               "Connect to Server" );
155            putValue( Action.LONG_DESCRIPTION,
156               "Connect to server to send Instant Messages" );
157            putValue( Action.MNEMONIC_KEY, new Integer( 'C' ) );
158         }
159
160         // connect to server
161         public void actionPerformed( ActionEvent event )
162         {
163            // connect MessageManager to server
164            try {
165
```

Fig. 13.23 ClientGUI provides a graphical user interface for the Deitel Messenger client (part 4 of 9).

```
166              // clear messageArea
167              messageArea.setText( "" );
168
169              // connect MessageManager and register MessageListener
170              messageManager.connect( messageListener );
171
172              // listen for disconnect notifications
173              messageManager.setDisconnectListener(
174                 new DisconnectHandler() );
175
176              // get desired userName
177              userName = JOptionPane.showInputDialog(
178                 ClientGUI.this, "Please enter your name: " );
179
180              // update Actions, inputArea and statusBar
181              connectAction.setEnabled( false );
182              disconnectAction.setEnabled( true );
183              sendAction.setEnabled( true );
184              inputArea.setEditable( true );
185              inputArea.requestFocus();
186              statusBar.setText( "Connected: " + userName );
187
188              // send message indicating user connected
189              messageManager.sendMessage( userName, userName +
190                 " joined chat" );
191
192           } // end try
193
194           // handle exception connecting to server
195           catch ( Exception exception ) {
196              JOptionPane.showMessageDialog( ClientGUI.this,
197                 "Unable to connect to server.", "Error Connecting",
198                 JOptionPane.ERROR_MESSAGE );
199
200              exception.printStackTrace();
201           }
202
203        }  // end method actionPerformed
204
205     } // end ConnectAction inner class
206
207     // Action for disconnecting from server
208     private class DisconnectAction extends AbstractAction {
209
210        // configure DisconnectAction
211        public DisconnectAction()
212        {
213           putValue( Action.NAME, "Disconnect" );
214           putValue( Action.SMALL_ICON, new ImageIcon(
215              ClientGUI.class.getResource(
216                 "images/Disconnect.gif" ) ) );
```

Fig. 13.23 **ClientGUI** provides a graphical user interface for the Deitel Messenger client (part 5 of 9).

```
217             putValue( Action.SHORT_DESCRIPTION,
218                "Disconnect from Server" );
219             putValue( Action.LONG_DESCRIPTION,
220                "Disconnect to end Instant Messaging session" );
221             putValue( Action.MNEMONIC_KEY, new Integer( 'D' ) );
222          }
223
224          // disconnect from server
225          public void actionPerformed( ActionEvent event )
226          {
227             // disconnect MessageManager from server
228             try {
229
230                // send message indicating user disconnected
231                messageManager.sendMessage( userName, userName +
232                   " exited chat" );
233
234                // disconnect from server and unregister
235                // MessageListener
236                messageManager.disconnect( messageListener );
237
238                // update Actions, inputArea and statusBar
239                sendAction.setEnabled( false );
240                disconnectAction.setEnabled( false );
241                inputArea.setEditable( false );
242                connectAction.setEnabled( true );
243                statusBar.setText( "Not Connected" );
244
245             } // end try
246
247             // handle exception disconnecting from server
248             catch ( Exception exception ) {
249                JOptionPane.showMessageDialog( ClientGUI.this,
250                   "Unable to disconnect from server.",
251                   "Error Disconnecting", JOptionPane.ERROR_MESSAGE );
252
253                exception.printStackTrace();
254             }
255
256          } // end method actionPerformed
257
258       } // end DisconnectAction inner class
259
260       // Action for sending messages
261       private class SendAction extends AbstractAction {
262
263          // configure SendAction
264          public SendAction()
265          {
266             putValue( Action.NAME, "Send" ) ;
267             putValue( Action.SMALL_ICON, new ImageIcon(
268                ClientGUI.class.getResource( "images/Send.gif" ) ) );
```

Fig. 13.23 ClientGUI provides a graphical user interface for the Deitel Messenger client (part 6 of 9).

```
269                 putValue( Action.SHORT_DESCRIPTION, "Send Message" );
270                 putValue( Action.LONG_DESCRIPTION,
271                    "Send an Instant Message" );
272                 putValue( Action.MNEMONIC_KEY, new Integer( 'S' ) );
273              }
274
275              // send message and clear inputArea
276              public void actionPerformed( ActionEvent event )
277              {
278                 // send message to server
279                 try {
280
281                    // send userName and text in inputArea
282                    messageManager.sendMessage( userName,
283                       inputArea.getText() );
284
285                    inputArea.setText( "" );
286                 }
287
288                 // handle exception sending message
289                 catch ( Exception exception ) {
290                    JOptionPane.showMessageDialog( ClientGUI.this,
291                       "Unable to send message.", "Error Sending Message",
292                       JOptionPane.ERROR_MESSAGE );
293
294                    exception.printStackTrace();
295                 }
296
297              } // end method actionPerformed
298
299           } // end SendAction inner class
300
301           // MyMessageListener listens for new messages from the
302           // MessageManager and displays the messages in messageArea
303           // using a MessageDisplayer.
304           private class MyMessageListener implements MessageListener {
305
306              // when new message received, display in messageArea
307              public void messageReceived( String from, String message )
308              {
309                 // append message using MessageDisplayer and invokeLater
310                 // to ensure thread-safe access to messageArea
311                 SwingUtilities.invokeLater(
312                    new MessageDisplayer( from, message ) );
313              }
314
315           } // end MyMessageListener inner class
316
317           // MessageDisplayer displays a new messaage by appending
318           // the message to the messageArea JTextArea. This Runnable
319           // object should be executed only on the event-dispatch
320           // thread, as it modifies a live Swing component.
```

Fig. 13.23 **ClientGUI** provides a graphical user interface for the Deitel Messenger client (part 7 of 9).

```
321      private class MessageDisplayer implements Runnable {
322
323         private String fromUser;
324         private String messageBody;
325
326         // MessageDisplayer constructor
327         public MessageDisplayer( String from, String body )
328         {
329            fromUser = from;
330            messageBody = body;
331         }
332
333         // display new message in messageArea
334         public void run()
335         {
336            // append new message
337            messageArea.append( "\n" + fromUser + "> " +
338               messageBody );
339
340            // move caret to end of messageArea to ensure new
341            // message is visible on screen
342            messageArea.setCaretPosition(
343               messageArea.getText().length() );
344         }
345
346      } // end MessageDisplayer inner class
347
348      // DisconnectHandler listens for serverDisconnected messages
349      // from the MessageManager and updates the user interface.
350      private class DisconnectHandler implements DisconnectListener {
351
352         // receive disconnect notifcation
353         public void serverDisconnected( final String message )
354         {
355            // update GUI in thread-safe manner
356            SwingUtilities.invokeLater(
357
358               new Runnable() {
359
360                  // update Actions, inputs and status bar
361                  public void run()
362                  {
363                     sendAction.setEnabled( false );
364                     disconnectAction.setEnabled( false );
365                     inputArea.setEditable( false );
366                     connectAction.setEnabled( true );
367                     statusBar.setText( message );
368                  }
369
370               } // end Runnable inner class
371            );
372
```

Fig. 13.23 `ClientGUI` provides a graphical user interface for the Deitel Messenger client (part 8 of 9).

```
373              } // end method serverDisconnected
374
375        } // end DisconnectHandler inner class
376 }
```

Fig. 13.23 **ClientGUI** provides a graphical user interface for the Deitel Messenger client (part 9 of 9).

The **ClientGUI** constructor (lines 41–141) creates and lays out the various user-interface components. The constructor takes as an argument the **MessageManager** that implements the underlying network communications. A **WindowAdapter** inner class (lines 119–138) ensures that the **MessageManager** disconnects from the **ChatServer** (line 126) when the user closes the application window.

The **ConnectAction** inner class (lines 144–205) is an **Action** implementation for connecting to the Deitel Messenger server. Lines 170–174 invoke method **connect** of interface **MessageManager** and register a **DisconnectListener** for receiving **serverDisconnected** notifications. Lines 177–186 prompt the user for a name to use in the chat session and update the user-interface components to allow the user to send messages and disconnect from the Deitel Messenger server. Lines 188–189 invoke method **sendMessage** of interface **MessageManager** to send a **ChatMessage** that announces the user's arrival in the chat session.

The **DisconnectAction** inner class (lines 211–258) is an **Action** implementation for disconnecting the **MessageManager** from the Deitel Messenger server. Lines 231–232 send a **ChatMessage** to announce the user's departure from the chat session. Line 236 invokes method **disconnect** of interface **MessageManager** to disconnect from the server. Lines 239–243 update the user-interface components to disable the message **inputArea** and display a message in the status bar.

The **SendAction** inner class (lines 261–299) is an **Action** implementation for sending messages to the server. Lines 282–283 invoke method **sendMessage** of interface **MessageManager** and pass the contents of **inputArea** and the user's **userName** as arguments.

An instance of inner class **MyMessageListener** (lines 304–315) listens for incoming **ChatMessage**s. When the **MessageManager** receives a new **ChatMessage** from the server, the **MessageManager** invokes method **messageReceived** (lines 307–313). Lines 311–312 invoke **static** method **invokeLater** of class **SwingUtilities** with a **MessageDisplayer** argument to display the new message.

Inner class **MessageDisplayer** (lines 321–346) is a **Runnable** implementation that appends a new message to the **messageArea JTextArea** to display that message to the user. Lines 337–338 append the message text and sender's user name to **messageArea**, and lines 342–343 move the cursor to the end of **messageArea**.

An instance of inner class **DisconnectHandler** (lines 350–375) receives **serverDisconnected** notifications from the **MessageManager** when the server disconnects. Lines 356–371 update the user-interface components to indicate that the server disconnected.

Class **DeitelMessenger** (Fig. 13.24) launches the client application using a **ClientGUI** and **RMIMessageManager**. Line 18 invokes method **setSecurityManager** of class **System** to install an **RMISecurityManager** for the client application.

The client requires this **SecurityManager** for downloading the **ChatServer**'s stub dynamically. We discuss dynamic class downloading in Section 13.6.3. If the user does not specify a hostname for the **ChatServer**, line 24 creates an **RMIMessageManager** that connects to the server running on **localhost**. Line 26 creates an **RMIMessageManager** that connects to the user-provided hostname. Lines 29–32 create a **ClientGUI** for the **RMIMessageManager** and display that GUI to the user.

13.6.3 Running the Deitel Messenger Server and Client Applications

Running the Deitel Messenger case study server and clients requires several steps. In addition to the RMI registry, RMI applications that use **Activatable** objects require the RMI activation daemon (**rmid**). The RMI activation daemon is a server process that manages the registration, activation and deactivation of **Activatable** remote objects.\

```
1   // DeitelMessenger.java
2   // DeitelMessenger uses a ClientGUI and RMIMessageManager to
3   // implement an RMI-based chat client.
4   package com.deitel.messenger.rmi.client;
5
6   // Java core packages
7   import java.rmi.RMISecurityManager;
8
9   // Deitel packages
10  import com.deitel.messenger.*;
11
12  public class DeitelMessenger {
13
14      // launch DeitelMessenger application
15      public static void main ( String args[] ) throws Exception
16      {
17          // install RMISecurityManager
18          System.setSecurityManager( new RMISecurityManager() );
19
20          MessageManager messageManager;
21
22          // create new DeitelMessenger
23          if ( args.length == 0 )
24              messageManager = new RMIMessageManager( "localhost" );
25          else
26              messageManager = new RMIMessageManager( args[ 0 ] );
27
28          // finish configuring window and display it
29          ClientGUI clientGUI = new ClientGUI( messageManager );
30          clientGUI.pack();
31          clientGUI.setResizable( false );
32          clientGUI.setVisible( true );
33      }
34  }
```

Fig. 13.24 DeitelMessenger launches a chat client using classes **ClientGUI** and **RMIMessageManager**.

To begin, start the RMI registry by executing the command

```
rmiregistry
```

at a command prompt. Be sure that the stub file for the **ChatServer** remote object (**ChatServerImpl_Stub.class**) is not in the RMI registry's **CLASSPATH**, as this will disable dynamic class downloading. Next, start the RMI activation daemon by executing the command

```
rmid -J-Djava.security.policy=rmid.policy
```

where **rmid.policy** is the complete path to the policy file of Fig. 13.25. This policy file allows the **ActivationGroup** in which the **ChatServer** runs to specify **C:\activationGroup.policy** as the policy file for the **ActivationGroup**'s virtual machine. If you place **activationGroup.policy** in a location other than the **C:** directory, be sure to modify **rmid.policy** to specify the appropriate location.

Dynamic class downloading enables Java programs to download classes not available in the local **CLASSPATH**. This is particularly useful in RMI applications for enabling clients to download stub files dynamically. When an RMI object specifies the **java.rmi.server.codebase** system property, the RMI registry adds an *annotation* to that object's remote references. This annotation specifies the codebase from which clients can download any necessary classes. These classes might include the stub for the remote object and other classes. These **.class** files must be available for download from an HTTP server. Sun provides a basic HTTP server suitable for testing purposes, which is downloadable from

```
java.sun.com/products/jdk/rmi/class-server.zip
```

Extract the files from **class-server.zip** and read the included instructions for running the HTTP server. Figure 13.26 lists the files to include in the HTTP server's download directory. For example, if the HTTP server's download directory is **C:\classes**, copy the directory structure and **.class** files listed in Fig. 13.26 to **C:\classes**. Be sure to start the HTTP server before continuing.

Next, run the **ChatServerAdministrator** application to launch the **Activatable** remote object by using the command

```
java -Djava.security.policy=administrator.policy
    -Djava.rmi.server.codebase=http://hostname:port/
    com.deitel.messenger.rmi.server.ChatServerAdministrator
    start
```

```
1   // allow ActivationGroup to specify C:\activationGroup.policy
2   // as its VM's security policy
3   grant {
4      permission com.sun.rmi.rmid.ExecOptionPermission
5         "-Djava.security.policy=file:///C:/activationGroup.policy";
6   };
```

Fig. 13.25 Policy file for the RMI activation daemon.

Directory	File Name

```
com\deitel\messenger\rmi\server\
              ChatServer.class
              ChatServerImpl.class
              ChatServerImpl$1.class
              ChatServerImpl_Stub.class
              StoppableChatServer.class
com\deitel\messenger\rmi\client\
              ChatClient.class
              RMIMessageManager_Stub.class
com\deitel\messenger\rmi\
              ChatMessage.class
```

Fig. 13.26 File listing for the HTTP server's download directory.

where **administrator.policy** is the complete path to the policy file of Fig. 13.27, *hostname* is the name of the computer running the HTTP server and *port* is the port number on which that HTTP server is running. The RMI registry will annotate each remote reference it returns with this codebase. The policy file must permit **ChatServerAdminist-rator** to connect to port 1098 on the local machine, which is the port for the RMI activation daemon. The policy file also must allow the **ChatServerAdministrator** to access the port on which the Web server is running. Lines 4–5 of Fig. 13.27 specify that the **ChatServerAdministrator** can access all ports above and including **1024** on *hostname*. Be sure to replace *hostname* with the appropriate name or IP address of the machine running the Web server and RMI activation daemon. The **ChatServerAdministrator** also requires the permission **setFactory** of type **java.lang.RuntimePermission**, which permits the **ActivationGroup** to set a **SecurityManager**.

The **ChatServerAdministrator** application registers the **Activation-Group** for the **Activatable ChatServer**, then exits. Clients then may access the **ChatServer** by obtaining a remote reference to the **ChatServer** from the RMI registry and invoking methods on that remote reference. Note that the **ChatServer** does not begin executing until the first client invokes a method on the **ChatServer** remote object.

```
1   // allow ChatServerAdministrator to connect to
2   // activation daemon
3   grant {
4      permission java.net.SocketPermission "hostname:1024-",
5         "connect, accept, resolve";
6
7      permission java.lang.RuntimePermission "setFactory";
8   };
```

Fig. 13.27 Policy file for **ChatServerAdministrator**.

At that time, the activation system activates the **ChatServer**'s **ActivationGroup**. To launch a client for the **ChatServer**, type the following at a command prompt:

```
java -Djava.security.policy=client.policy
    com.deitel.messenger.rmi.client.DeitelMessenger
```

where **client.policy** is the policy file of Fig. 13.28. This policy file enables the client to connect, accept and resolve connnections to the specified hostname on ports above and including **1024**. Recall that the client is itself a remote object, so the client must be able to accept incoming network connections from the **ChatServer**. Be sure to replace **hostname** with the hostname or IP address of the computer on which the **ChatServer** is running.

Figure 13.29 shows a sample conversation in Deitel Messenger. Notice that the GUI elements properly reflect the current connection state—when the client is disconnected, only the **ConnectAction** is enabled. After the client connects, the **DisconnectAction**, input **JTextArea** and **SendAction** become enabled. Note also that the bottom of each window displays the message **Java Applet Window**. The virtual machine places this message in the windows because the application is running under security restrictions.

```
1   // allow client to connect to network resources on hostname
2   // at ports above 1024
3   grant {
4      permission java.net.SocketPermission "hostname:1024-",
5         "connect, accept, resolve";
6   };
```

Fig. 13.28 Policy file for the **DeitelMessenger** client.

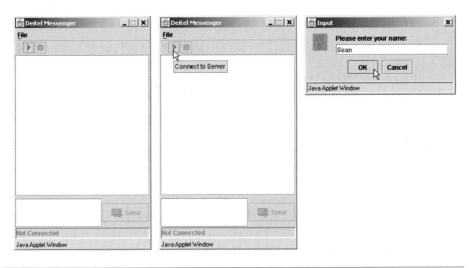

Fig. 13.29 Sample conversation using Deitel Messenger.

Fig. 13.29 Sample conversation using Deitel Messenger.

13.7 Internet and World Wide Web Resources

java.sun.com/products/jdk/rmi/index.html
Sun's Remote Method Invocation (RMI) home page, which provides links to technical articles, documentation and other resources.

java.sun.com/j2se/1.3/docs/guide/rmi/index.html
Sun's RMI guide, which includes links to tutorials on building activatable remote objects and other useful resources.

www.jguru.com/faq/home.jsp?topic=RMI
jGuru's RMI Frequently Asked Questions with answers, which provides tips and answers to many common questions that developer's ask about RMI.

www.javaworld.com/javaworld/topicalindex/jw-ti-rmi.html
JavaWorld's list of articles related to RMI. Articles include discussions of activatable RMI objects, integrating RMI with CORBA and RMI-related technologies, such as Jini.

SUMMARY

- RMI allows Java objects running on separate computers or in separate processes to communicate with one another via remote method calls. Such method calls appear to the programmer the same as those operating on objects in the same program.

- RMI is based on a similar, earlier technology for procedural programming called remote procedure calls (RPCs) developed in the 1980s.

- RMI enables Java programs to transfer complete Java objects using Java's object-serialization mechanism. The programmer need not be concerned with the transmission of the data over the network.

- For Java-to-non-Java communication, you can use Java IDL (introduced in Java 1.2) or RMI-IIOP. Java IDL and RMI-IIOP enable applications and applets written in Java to communicate with objects written in any language that supports CORBA (Common Object Request Broker Architecture).

- The four major steps for building an RMI distributed system are 1) defining the remote interface, 2) defining the remote object implementation, 3) defining the client application that uses the remote object and 4) compiling and executing the remote object and the client.

- To create a remote interface, define an interface that extends interface **_java.rmi.Remote_**. Interface **Remote** is a tagging interface—it does not declare any methods, and therefore places no burden on the implementing class.

- An object of a class that implements interface **Remote** directly or indirectly is a remote object and can be accessed—with appropriate security permissions—from any Java virtual machine that has a connection to the computer on which the remote object executes.

- Every remote method must be declared in an interface that extends **_java.rmi.Remote_**. A remote object must implement all methods declared in its remote interface.

- An RMI distributed application must export an object of a class that implements the **_Remote_** interface to make that remote object available to receive remote method calls.

- Each method in a **Remote** interface must have a **throws** clause that indicates that the method can throw **RemoteException**s. A **RemoteException** indicates a problem communicating with the remote object.

- RMI uses Java's default serialization mechanism to transfer method arguments and return values across the network. Therefore, all method arguments and return values must be **Serializable** or primitive types.

- Class **UnicastRemoteObject** provides the basic functionality required for all remote objects. In particular, its constructor exports the object to make it available to receive remote calls.

- Exporting a remote object enables that object to wait for client connections on an anonymous port number (i.e., one chosen by the computer on which the remote object executes). RMI abstracts away communication details so the programmer can work with simple method calls.

- Constructors for class **UnicastRemoteObject** allow the programmer to specify information about the remote object, such as an explicit port number on which to export the remote object. All **UnicastRemoteObject** constructors throw **RemoteException**s.

- The **rmiregistry** utility program manages the registry for remote objects and is part of the J2SE SDK. The default port number for the RMI registry is **1099**.

- Method **lookup** connects to the RMI registry and returns a **Remote** reference to the remote object. Note that clients refer to remote objects only through those object's remote interfaces.

- A remote reference refers to a stub object on the client. Stubs allow clients to invoke remote objects' methods. Stub objects receive each remote method call and pass those calls to the RMI system, which performs the networking that allows clients to interact with the remote object.

- The RMI layer is responsible for network connections to the remote object, so referencing remote objects is transparent to the client. RMI handles the underlying communication with the remote object and the transfer of arguments and return values between the objects. Argument and return types for remote methods must be **Serializable**.

- The **rmic** utility compiles the remote object class to produce a stub class. A stub class forwards method invocations to the RMI layer, which performs the network communication necessary to invoke the method call on the remote object.

- Standard RMI objects exported as **UnicastRemoteObject**s must run continuously on the server to handle client requests. RMI objects that extend class **java.rmi.activation.Activatable** are able to activate, or start running, when a client invokes one of the remote object's methods.

- The RMI activation daemon (**rmid**) is a server process that enables activatable remote objects to become active when clients invoke remote methods on these objects.

- Activatable remote objects also are able to recover from server crashes, because remote references to activatable objects are persistent—when the server restarts, the RMI activation daemon maintains the remote reference, so clients can continue to use the remote object.

- The RMI activation mechanism requires that **Activatable** objects provide a constructor that takes as arguments an **ActivationID** and a **MarshalledObject**. When the activation daemon activates a remote object of this class, it invokes this activation constructor. The **ActivationID** argument specifies a unique identifier for the remote object.

- Class **MarshalledObject** is a wrapper class that contains a serialized object for transmission over RMI. The **MarshalledObject** passed to the activation constructor can contain application-specific initialization information, such as the name under which the activation daemon registered the remote object.

- Activatable RMI objects execute as part of an *ActivationGroup* (package **java.rmi.activation**). The RMI activation daemon—a server-side process that manages activatable objects—starts a new virtual machine for each **ActivationGroup**.

- Class **ActivationGroupDesc** specifies configuration information for an **ActivationGroup**. The first argument to the **ActivationGroupDesc** constructor is a **Properties** reference that contains replacement values for system properties in the **ActivationGroup**'s virtual machine. The second argument is a reference to an **ActivationGroupDesc.CommandEnvironment** object, which enables the **ActivationGroup** to customize the commands that the activation daemon executes when starting the **ActivationGroup**'s virtual machine.

- The incarnation number of an **ActivationGroup** identifies different instances of the same **ActivationGroup**. Each time the activation daemon activates the **ActivationGroup**, the daemon increments the incarnation number.

- Class **ActivationDesc** specifies configuration information for a particular **Activatable** remote object. The first argument to the **ActivationDesc** constructor specifies the name of the class that implements the **Activatable** remote object. The second argument specifies the codebase that contains the remote object's class files. The final argument is a **MarshalledObject** reference, whose object specifies initialization information for the remote object.

- Method **register** of class **Activatable** takes as an argument the **ActivationDesc** for the **Activatable** object and returns a reference to the remote object's stub.

- Dynamic class downloading enables Java programs to download classes not available in the local **CLASSPATH**. This is particularly useful in RMI applications for enabling clients to download stub files dynamically.

- When an RMI object specifies the **java.rmi.server.codebase** system property, the RMI registry adds an annotation to that object's remote references, which specifies the codebase from which clients can download necessary classes. Downloadable **.class** files must be available from an HTTP server.

TERMINOLOGY

Activatable class (package
    java.rmi.activation)
activatable remote object
activation daemon
activation descriptor
activation group descriptor
ActivationGroup class
ActivationGroupDesc class
ActivationGroupDescd.Command-
    Environment class
ActivationID class
ActivationSystem interface
Adapter design pattern
anonymous port number
bind method of class **Naming**
createRegistry method of class
    LocateRegistry
distributed computing
export
exportObject method of class
    UnicastRemoteObject
HTML scraping
Interface Definition Language (IDL)
ListCellRenderer interface
LocateRegistry class

marshaling of data
MarshalledObject class
rebind method of class **Naming**
Registry class
remote interface
Remote interface (package **java.rmi**)
remote method
remote method call
Remote Method Invocation (RMI)
remote object
remote object implementation
Remote Procedure Call (RPC)
remote reference
RemoteException class (package
    java.rmi)
RMI registry
rmic compiler
rmid utility
rmiregistry utility
RMISecurityManager class
stub class
tagging interface
UnicastRemoteObject class (package
    java.rmi.server)

SELF-REVIEW EXERCISES

13.1 Fill in the blanks in each of the following statements:

    a) The remote object class must be compiled using the _____ to produce a stub class.

    b) RMI is based on a similar technology for procedural programming called _____.

    c) Clients use method _____ of class **Naming** to obtain a remote reference to a remote object.

    d) To create a remote interface, define an interface that extends interface _____ of package _____.

    e) Method _____ or _____ of class *Naming* binds a remote object to the RMI registry.

    f) Remote objects normally extend class _____, which provides the basic functionality required for all remote objects.

    g) Remote objects use the _____ and _____ to locate the RMI registry so they can register themselves as remote services. Clients use these to locate a service.

    h) The default port number for the RMI registry is _____.

    i) Interface **Remote** is a _____.

    j) _____ allows Java objects running on separate computers (or possibly the same computer) to communicate with one another via remote method calls.

13.2   State whether each of the following is true or false. If false, explain why.

 a) Not starting the RMI registry before attempting to bind the remote object to the registry results in a **RuntimeException** refusing connection to the registry.

 b) Every remote method must be part of an interface that extends **java.rmi.Remote**.

 c) The **stubcompiler** creates a stub class that performs the networking which allows the client to connect to the server and use the remote object's methods.

 d) Class **UnicastRemoteObject** provides basic functionality required by remote objects.

 e) An object of a class that implements interface **Serializable** can be registered as a remote object and receive a remote method call.

 f) All methods in a *Remote* interface must have a **throws** clause indicating the potential for a **RemoteException**.

 g) RMI clients assume that they should connect to port 80 on a server computer when attempting to locate a remote object through the RMI registry.

 h) Once a remote object is bound to the RMI registry with method **bind** or **rebind** of class **Naming**, the client can look up the remote object with **Naming** method **lookup**.

 i) Method **find** of class **Naming** interacts with the RMI registry to help the client obtain a reference to a remote object so the client can use the remote object's services.

ANSWERS TO SELF-REVIEW EXERCISES

13.1 a) **rmic** compiler. b) RPC. c) **lookup**. d) **Remote, java.rmi**. e) **bind, rebind**. f) **UnicastRemoteObject**. g) host, port. h) 1099. i) tagging interface. j) RMI.

13.2 a) False. This results in a **java.rmi.ConnectException**.

 b) True.

 c) False. The **rmic** compiler creates a stub class.

 d) True.

 e) False. An object of a class that implements a subinterface of **java.rmi.Remote** can be registered as a remote object and receive remote method calls.

 f) True.

 g) False. RMI clients assume port 1099 by default. Web browser clients assume port 80.

 h) True.

 i) False. Method **lookup** interacts with the RMI registry to help the client obtain a reference to a remote object.

EXERCISES

13.3   The current implementation of class **WeatherServiceImpl** downloads the weather information only once. Modify class **WeatherServiceImpl** to obtain weather information from the National Weather Service twice a day.

13.4   Modify interface **WeatherService** to include support for obtaining the current day's forecast and the next day's forecast. Study the Traveler's Forecast Web page

http://iwin.nws.noaa.gov/iwin/us/traveler.html

13.5   Visit the NWS Web site for the format of each line of information. Next, modify class **WeatherServiceImpl** to implement the new features of the interface. Finally, modify class **WeatherServiceClient** to allow the user to select the weather forecast for either day. Modify the support classes **WeatherBean** and **WeatherItem** as necessary to support the changes to classes **WeatherServiceImpl** and **WeatherServiceClient**.

13.6   (Project: Weather for Your State) There is a wealth of weather information on the National Weather Service Web site. Study the following Web pages:

```
http://iwin.nws.noaa.gov/
http://iwin.nws.noaa.gov/iwin/textversion/main.html
```

and create a complete weather forecast server for your state. Design your classes for reusability.

13.7   (Project: Weather for Your State) Modify the Exercise 13.6 project solution to allow the user to select the weather forecast for any state. [*Note*: For some states, the format of the weather forecast differs from the standard format. Your solution should allow the user to select only from those states whose forecasts are in the standard format.]

13.8   (*For International Readers*) If there is a similar World Wide Web-based weather service in your own country, provide a different **WeatherServiceImpl** implementation with the same remote interface **WeatherService** (Fig. 13.1). The server should return weather information for major cities in your country.

13.9   (*Remote Phone Book Server*) Create a remote phone book server that maintains a file of names and phone numbers. Define interface **PhoneBookServer** with the following methods:

```
public PhoneBookEntry[] getPhoneBook()
public void addEntry( PhoneBookEntry entry )
public void modifyEntry( PhoneBookEntry entry )
public void deleteEntry( PhoneBookEntry entry )
```

Create **Activatable** remote object class **PhoneBookServerImpl**, which implements interface **PhoneBookServer**. Class **PhoneBookEntry** should contain **String** instance variables that represent the first name, last name and phone number for one person. The class should also provide appropriate *set/get* methods and perform validation on the phone number format. Remember that class **PhoneBookEntry** also must implement **Serializable**, so that RMI can serialize objects of this class.

13.10   Class **PhoneBookClient** should provide a user interface that allows the user to scroll through entries, add a new entry, modify an existing entry and delete an existing entry. The client and the server should provide proper error handling (e.g., the client cannot modify an entry that does not exist).

14

Session EJBs and Distributed Transactions

Objectives

- To understand EJBs as business-logic components.
- To understand the advantages and disadvantages of stateful and stateless session EJBs.
- To understand JNDI's role in enterprise Java applications.
- To understand distributed transactions.
- To understand the advantages and disadvantages of container-managed and bean-managed transaction demarcation.

Only the traveling is good which reveals to me the value of home and enables me to enjoy it better.
Henry David Thoreau

Youth would be an ideal state if it came a little later in life.
Herbert Henry Asquith

We cannot make events. Our business is wisely to improve them.
Samuel Adams

14.1 Introduction

In previous chapters, we presented Java servlets and JavaServer Pages for implementing business and presentation logic in multi-tier applications. In this chapter, we introduce *Enterprise JavaBeans* (*EJBs*), which provide a component model for building business logic in enterprise Java applications.

In this chapter, we introduce *session EJBs* in their two forms: *stateful* and *stateless*. We also introduce EJB support for *distributed transactions*, which help to ensure data integrity across databases and across application servers. After reading this chapter, you will be able to develop stateless and stateful session EJBs. You also will be able to build EJBs that take advantage of J2EE's distributed transaction support to update data across multiple databases atomically.

14.2 EJB Overview

Every EJB consists of a *remote interface*, a *home interface* and an *EJB implementation*. The remote interface declares *business methods* that clients of the EJB may invoke. The home interface provides **create** methods for creating new EJB instances, *finder* methods for finding EJB instances and **remove** methods for removing EJB instances. The EJB implementation defines the business methods declared in the remote interface and the **create**, **remove** and *finder* methods of the home interface. An *EJB container* provides the EJB's runtime environment and life-cycle management.

The J2EE specification defines six *roles* for people implementing enterprise systems. Each role is responsible for producing some part of an enterprise application. The *enterprise bean provider* implements the Java classes for EJBs. The *application assembler* constructs application components from EJBs implemented by the enterprise bean provider. The *deployer* takes application components provided by the application assembler and deploys the application to an EJB container, ensuring that all dependencies are met. The *EJB server provider* and *EJB container provider* implement an *application server* suitable for the deployment of J2EE applications. An application server typically includes an EJB container and a servlet container and provides services such as JNDI directories, database connection pooling, integration with distributed systems and resource management. The same developer or team of developers can play more than one role in the construction and deployment of an enterprise application. For more information on the various roles in building J2EE applications, please see the resources listed in Section 14.5.

14.2.1 Remote Interface

The EJB remote interface declares business methods that EJB clients can invoke. The remote interface must extend interface **javax.ejb.EJBObject**. The EJB container generates a class that implements the remote interface. This generated class implements interface **EJBObject** methods and delegates business method invocations to the EJB implementation (Section 14.2.3). Figure 14.1 describes interface **EJBObject** methods.

Each remote-interface method is required to declare that it throws **RemoteException**. Each method also may throw application-specific exceptions—for example, an **IllegalArgumentException** if a provided argument does not meet certain criteria.

14.2.2 Home Interface

The EJB home interface declares methods for creating, removing and finding EJB instances. The home interface must extend interface **javax.ejb.EJBHome**. The EJB container provides an implementation of the home interface. Depending on the type of EJB (i.e., session or entity), the container will invoke EJB implementation methods that correspond to methods **create** and **remove** and *finder* methods of the home interface. These *finder* methods enable clients to locate a particular instance of an EJB. Figure 14.2 describes interface **EJBHome** methods.

Method	Description
getEJBHome	Returns the **EJBHome** interface for the **EJBObject**.
getHandle	Returns a **Handle** for the **EJBObject**. A **Handle** is a persistent, **Serializable** reference to an **EJBObject**.
getPrimaryKey	Returns the **EJBObject**'s primary key if **EJBObject** is an entity bean.
isIdentical	Returns a **boolean** indicating if the **EJBObject** argument is identical to the current **EJBObject**.
remove	Removes the **EJBObject**.

Fig. 14.1   Methods of interface **javax.ejb.EJBObject**.

Method	Description
getEJBMetaData	Returns an **EJBMetaData** object that provides information about the EJB, such as its home interface class and whether it is a session EJB.
getHomeHandle	Returns a **Handle** for the **EJBHome** interface.
remove	Removes the **EJBObject** identified by the given **Handle** or primary key **Object**.

Fig. 14.2 Methods of interface **javax.ejb.EJBHome**.

14.2.3 EJB Implementation

The EJB implementation defines the business methods declared in the EJB remote interface and the **create**, **remove** and *finder* methods declared in the EJB home interface. Session EJBs also must implement interface **javax.ejb.SessionBean**. We discuss interface **SessionBean** in detail in Section 14.3.

14.2.4 EJB Container

The EJB container manages an EJB's client interactions, method invocations, transactions, security, exceptions, etc. Clients of an EJB do not interact directly with the EJB. Clients access the EJB container to obtain remote references to EJB instances. When a client invokes an EJB business method, the invocation goes first to the EJB container, which then delegates the business method invocation to the EJB implementation.

The EJB container also manages the life cycles of its EJBs. EJB containers typically perform *pooling* of EJB instances to enhance performance. By maintaining a pool of inactive EJB instances, the EJB container can increase performance by avoiding the overhead associated with creating new EJB instances for each client request. The EJB container simply activates a pooled instance and performs any necessary initialization. The EJB container also can create new EJB instances and remove existing instances. In addition, the EJB container provides more advanced services for entity EJBs (Chapter 15, Entity EJBs).

14.3 Session Beans

A session EJB instance performs business logic processing for a particular client. Session EJBs can manipulate data in a database, but unlike entity EJBs (Chapter 15), session EJBs are not persistent and do not represent database data directly. Session EJB instances are lost if the EJB container crashes. There are two session EJB types: *stateful* and *stateless*. Section 14.3.1 presents stateful session EJBs and Section 14.3.3 presents stateless session EJBs. Section 14.3.2 discusses deploying session EJBs to the J2EE 1.2.1 reference implementation.

14.3.1 Stateful Session EJBs

Stateful session EJBs maintain state information between business method invocations. For example, a stateful session EJB could maintain information about a customer's shopping cart while the customer browses an on-line store. The stateful session EJB would provide business methods for adding and removing items from the shopping cart. Each time the customer added an item to the shopping cart, information about the item, such as its price and quantity, would be stored in the stateful session EJB. If the customer left the site or otherwise terminated the session, the shopping-cart information would be lost.

InterestCalculator (Fig. 14.3) is the remote interface for a stateful session EJB that calculates simple interest. Methods **setPrincipal** (lines 15–16), **setInterestRate** (lines 19–20) and **setTerm** (lines 23–24) set the principal, rate and term values needed to calculate simple interest. Method **getBalance** (line 27) calculates the total balance after interest accrues for the given term. Method **getInterestEarned** (line 30) calculates the amount of interest earned.

Clients of the **InterestCalculator** EJB can invoke only those methods declared in the **InterestCalculator** remote interface. The EJB container for the **InterestCalculator** EJB will create a class that implements the **InterestCalculator** remote interface, including methods declared in interface **javax.ejb.EJBObject**. When a client invokes an **InterestCalculator** remote-interface method, the EJB container will invoke the corresponding method in EJB implementation **InterestCalculatorEJB** (Fig. 14.5). When a client invokes a method declared in interface **javax.ejb.EJBObject**, the container will invoke the corresponding method in the class generated by the EJB container.

```
1   // InterestCalculator.java
2   // InterestCalculator is the remote interface for the
3   // InterestCalculator EJB.
4   package com.deitel.advjhtp1.ejb.session.stateful.ejb;
5
6   // Java core libraries
7   import java.rmi.RemoteException;
8
9   // Java standard extensions
10  import javax.ejb.EJBObject;
11
12  public interface InterestCalculator extends EJBObject {
13
14     // set principal amount
15     public void setPrincipal( double amount )
16        throws RemoteException;
17
18     // set interest rate
19     public void setInterestRate( double rate )
20        throws RemoteException;
21
22     // set loan length in years
23     public void setTerm( int years )
24        throws RemoteException;
25
26     // get loan balance
27     public double getBalance() throws RemoteException;
28
29     // get amount of interest earned
30     public double getInterestEarned() throws RemoteException;
31  }
```

Fig. 14.3 **InterestCalculator** remote interface for calculating simple interest.

InterestCalculatorHome (Fig. 14.4) is the home interface for the **InterestCalculator** EJB. **InterestCalculatorHome** provides method **create** (lines 15–16) for creating instances of the **InterestCalculator** EJB. When a client invokes **InterestCalculatorHome** method **create**, the EJB container invokes method **ejbCreate** of class **InterestCalculatorEJB** (Fig. 14.5). The home interface may declare zero or more **create** methods. For example, we could declare an additional **create** method that takes a **double** argument that initializes the principal amount to use in the simple interest calculation.

InterestCalculatorEJB (Fig. 14.5) implements the business methods declared in the **InterestCalculator** remote interface. On line 12, **InterestCalculatorEJB** implements interface **SessionBean**. This indicates that the **InterestCalculatorEJB** is a session EJB. Lines 17–19 declare variables that maintain the state of the EJB between business method invocations. The state information consists of the **principal** amount, the **interestRate** and the **term**. Method **setPrincipal** (lines 22–25) sets the **principal** amount and stores the value in the **principal** state variable. Method **setInterestRate** (lines 28–31) sets the **interestRate** state variable for the calculation. Method **setTerm** (lines 34–37) sets the **term** for which interest will accrue. Method **getBalance** (lines 40–44) uses the formula

$$a = p \ (1 + r)^n$$

where

> **p** is the principal amount
> **r** is the annual interest rate (e.g., .05 for 5%)
> **n** is the number of years
> **a** is the amount on deposit at the end of the **n**th year

to calculate the balance (i.e., amount on deposit). Method **getInterestEarned** (lines 47–50) calculates the amount of interest earned by subtracting the **principal** amount from the balance—calculated by method **getBalance**.

```
1   // InterestCalculatorHome.java
2   // InterestCalculatorHome is the home interface for the
3   // InterestCalculator EJB.
4   package com.deitel.advjhtp1.ejb.session.stateful.ejb;
5
6   // Java core libraries
7   import java.rmi.RemoteException;
8
9   // Java standard extensions
10  import javax.ejb.*;
11
12  public interface InterestCalculatorHome extends EJBHome {
13
14      // create InterestCalculator EJB
15      public InterestCalculator create() throws RemoteException,
16          CreateException;
17  }
```

Fig. 14.4   InterestCalculatorHome interface for creating
InterestCalculator EJBs.

```
1   // InterestCalculatorEJB.java
2   // InterestCalculator is a stateful session EJB for calculating
3   // simple interest.
4   package com.deitel.advjhtp1.ejb.session.stateful.ejb;
5
6   // Java core libraries
7   import java.util.*;
8
9   // Java standard extensions
10  import javax.ejb.*;
11
12  public class InterestCalculatorEJB implements SessionBean {
13
14      private SessionContext sessionContext;
15
16      // state variables
17      private double principal;
18      private double interestRate;
19      private int term;
20
21      // set principal amount
22      public void setPrincipal( double amount )
23      {
24          principal = amount;
25      }
26
27      // set interest rate
28      public void setInterestRate( double rate )
29      {
30          interestRate = rate;
31      }
32
33      // set loan length in years
34      public void setTerm( int years )
35      {
36          term = years;
37      }
38
39      // get loan balance
40      public double getBalance()
41      {
42          // calculate simple interest
43          return principal * Math.pow( 1.0 + interestRate, term );
44      }
45
46      // get amount of interest earned
47      public double getInterestEarned()
48      {
49          return getBalance() - principal;
50      }
51
```

Fig. 14.5 `InterestCalculatorEJB` implementation of
`InterestCalculator` remote interface (part 1 of 2).

```
52      // set SessionContext
53      public void setSessionContext( SessionContext context )
54      {
55          sessionContext = context;
56      }
57
58      // create InterestCalculator instance
59      public void ejbCreate() {}
60
61      // remove InterestCalculator instance
62      public void ejbRemove() {}
63
64      // passivate InterestCalculator instance
65      public void ejbPassivate() {}
66
67      // activate InterestCalculator instance
68      public void ejbActivate() {}
69   }
```

Fig. 14.5   **InterestCalculatorEJB** implementation of
InterestCalculator remote interface (part 2 of 2).

Method **setSessionContext** (lines 53–56) is a callback method defined in interface **SessionBean**. The EJB container invokes method **setSessionContext** after creating the EJB instance. Interface **SessionContext** extends interface **EJBContext**, which provides methods for obtaining information about the EJB container.

Common Programming Error 14.1

*Returning the **this** reference from a method or passing the **this** reference as an argument is not allowed in an EJB. Instead, use **SessionContext** or **EntityContext** method **getEJBObject** to obtain a reference to the current **EJBObject**.*

When a client invokes a **create** method in the home interface, the EJB container invokes method **ejbCreate** (line 59). The EJB implementation must provide an **ejbCreate** method for each **create** method declared in the home interface. The **ejbCreate** methods must have the same number and types of arguments as their corresponding **create** methods. The **ejbCreate** methods also must return **void**. For example, if the **InterestCalculatorHome** interface declares a **create** method that takes a **double** argument for the **principal** amount, the EJB implementation must define an **ejbCreate** method that takes a **double** argument. The **InterestCalculator** EJB has an empty implementation of method **ejbCreate**, because no initialization is necessary for this EJB.

The EJB container invokes method **ejbRemove** (line 62) in response to an invocation of method **remove** in the home interface. The EJB container also may invoke method **ejbRemove** if the session expires due to lengthy inactivity. Method **ejbRemove** should free resources the EJB has used.

The EJB container invokes method **ejbPassivate** (line 65) when the container determines that the EJB is no longer needed in memory. The algorithm that the EJB container uses to determine when it should passivate an EJB is application-server dependent. Many application servers enforce a *least recently used policy*, which passivates EJBs that clients have not accessed recently. When the EJB container passivates an EJB, the container serializes the state of the EJB and removes the EJB from memory.

The EJB container invokes method **ejbActivate** (line 68) to restore an EJB instance that the container passivated previously. The EJB container activates an EJB instance if the client associated with the EJB instance invokes a business method of that EJB instance. The EJB container reads the state information that it saved during passivation and restores the EJB instance in memory.

Software Engineering Observation 14.1

*Use the **transient** keyword to mark instance variables that the EJB container should not save and restore during passivation and activation.*

InterestCalculatorClient (Fig. 14.6) is an application that uses the **InterestCalculator** EJB to calculate simple interest. Line 25 declares an **InterestCalculator** reference, which **InterestCalculatorClient** uses to calculate simple interest. Method **createInterestCalculator** (lines 71–108) creates an **InterestCalculator** EJB instance to use throughout the application. A client application must use a JNDI directory to *look up* the home interface for an EJB. Line 77 creates an **InitialContext**, which is an interface into a JNDI directory. The **InitialContext** represents a *naming context*, which maps names (e.g., **"InterestCalculator"**) to objects, such as EJBs. Lines 80–81 use method **lookup** of class **InitialContext** to retrieve an **Object** remote reference to the **InterestCalculatorHome** interface. The **String** argument passed to method **lookup** is the name to which the EJB is mapped in the JNDI directory.

```
1   // InterestCalculatorClient.java
2   // InterestCalculatorClient is a GUI for interacting with the
3   // InterestCalculator EJB.
4   package com.deitel.advjhtp1.ejb.session.stateful.client;
5
6   // Java core libraries
7   import java.awt.*;
8   import java.awt.event.*;
9   import java.rmi.*;
10  import java.text.*;
11  import java.util.*;
12
13  // Java standard extensions
14  import javax.swing.*;
15  import javax.rmi.*;
16  import javax.naming.*;
17  import javax.ejb.*;
18
19  // Deitel libraries
20  import com.deitel.advjhtp1.ejb.session.stateful.ejb.*;
21
22  public class InterestCalculatorClient extends JFrame {
23
```

Fig. 14.6 **InterestCalculatorClient** for interacting with **InterestCalculator** EJB (part 1 of 7).

```
24       // InterestCalculator remote reference
25       private InterestCalculator calculator;
26
27       private JTextField principalTextField;
28       private JTextField rateTextField;
29       private JTextField termTextField;
30       private JTextField balanceTextField;
31       private JTextField interestEarnedTextField;
32
33       // InterestCalculatorClient constructor
34       public InterestCalculatorClient()
35       {
36          super( "Stateful Session EJB Example" );
37
38          // create InterestCalculator for calculating interest
39          createInterestCalculator();
40
41          // create JTextField for entering principal amount
42          createPrincipalTextField();
43
44          // create JTextField for entering interest rate
45          createRateTextField();
46
47          // create JTextField for entering loan term
48          createTermTextField();
49
50          // create uneditable JTextFields for displaying balance
51          // and interest earned
52          balanceTextField = new JTextField( 10 );
53          balanceTextField.setEditable( false );
54
55          interestEarnedTextField = new JTextField( 10 );
56          interestEarnedTextField.setEditable( false );
57
58          // layout components for GUI
59          layoutGUI();
60
61          // add WindowListener to remove EJB instances when user
62          // closes window
63          addWindowListener( getWindowListener() );
64
65          setSize( 425, 200 );
66          setVisible( true );
67
68       } // end InterestCalculatorClient constructor
69
70       // create InterestCalculator EJB instance
71       public void createInterestCalculator()
72       {
73          // lookup InterestCalculatorHome and create
74          // InterestCalculator EJB
75          try {
```

Fig. 14.6   InterestCalculatorClient for interacting with
InterestCalculator EJB (part 2 of 7).

```
76
77            InitialContext initialContext = new InitialContext();
78
79            // lookup InterestCalculator EJB
80            Object homeObject =
81               initialContext.lookup( "InterestCalculator" );
82
83            // get InterestCalculatorHome interface
84            InterestCalculatorHome calculatorHome =
85               ( InterestCalculatorHome )
86                  PortableRemoteObject.narrow( homeObject,
87                     InterestCalculatorHome.class );
88
89            // create InterestCalculator EJB instance
90            calculator = calculatorHome.create();
91
92         } // end try
93
94         // handle exception if InterestCalculator EJB not found
95         catch ( NamingException namingException ) {
96            namingException.printStackTrace();
97         }
98
99         // handle exception when creating InterestCalculator EJB
100        catch ( RemoteException remoteException ) {
101           remoteException.printStackTrace();
102        }
103
104        // handle exception when creating InterestCalculator EJB
105        catch ( CreateException createException ) {
106           createException.printStackTrace();
107        }
108     } // end method createInterestCalculator
109
110     // create JTextField for entering principal amount
111     public void createPrincipalTextField()
112     {
113        principalTextField = new JTextField( 10 );
114
115        principalTextField.addActionListener(
116           new ActionListener() {
117
118              public void actionPerformed( ActionEvent event )
119              {
120                 // set principal amount in InterestCalculator
121                 try {
122                    double principal = Double.parseDouble(
123                       principalTextField.getText() );
124
125                    calculator.setPrincipal( principal );
126                 }
127
```

Fig. 14.6 `InterestCalculatorClient` for interacting with `InterestCalculator` EJB (part 3 of 7).

```
128                    // handle exception setting principal amount
129                    catch ( RemoteException remoteException ) {
130                       remoteException.printStackTrace();
131                    }
132
133                    // handle wrong number format
134                    catch ( NumberFormatException
135                       numberFormatException ) {
136                       numberFormatException.printStackTrace();
137                    }
138                 }
139              }
140       ); // end addActionListener
141    } // end method createPrincipalTextField
142
143    // create JTextField for entering interest rate
144    public void createRateTextField()
145    {
146       rateTextField = new JTextField( 10 );
147
148       rateTextField.addActionListener(
149          new ActionListener() {
150
151             public void actionPerformed( ActionEvent event )
152             {
153                // set interest rate in InterestCalculator
154                try {
155                   double rate = Double.parseDouble(
156                      rateTextField.getText() );
157
158                   // convert from percentage
159                   calculator.setInterestRate( rate / 100.0 );
160                }
161
162                // handle exception when setting interest rate
163                catch ( RemoteException remoteException ) {
164                   remoteException.printStackTrace();
165                }
166             }
167          }
168       ); // end addActionListener
169    } // end method createRateTextField
170
171    // create JTextField for entering loan term
172    public void createTermTextField()
173    {
174       termTextField = new JTextField( 10 );
175
176       termTextField.addActionListener(
177          new ActionListener() {
178
```

Fig. 14.6   `InterestCalculatorClient` for interacting with
`InterestCalculator` EJB (part 4 of 7).

```
179                public void actionPerformed( ActionEvent event )
180                {
181                    // set loan term in InterestCalculator
182                    try {
183                        int term = Integer.parseInt(
184                            termTextField.getText() );
185
186                        calculator.setTerm( term );
187                    }
188
189                    // handle exception when setting loan term
190                    catch ( RemoteException remoteException ) {
191                        remoteException.printStackTrace();
192                    }
193                }
194            }
195        ); // end addActionListener
196    } // end method getTermTextField
197
198    // get JButton for starting calculation
199    public JButton getCalculateButton()
200    {
201        JButton calculateButton = new JButton( "Calculate" );
202
203        calculateButton.addActionListener(
204            new ActionListener() {
205
206                public void actionPerformed( ActionEvent event )
207                {
208                    // use InterestCalculator to calculate interest
209                    try {
210
211                        // get balance and interest earned
212                        double balance = calculator.getBalance();
213                        double interest =
214                            calculator.getInterestEarned();
215
216                        NumberFormat dollarFormatter =
217                            NumberFormat.getCurrencyInstance(
218                                Locale.US );
219
220                        balanceTextField.setText(
221                            dollarFormatter.format( balance ) );
222
223                        interestEarnedTextField.setText(
224                            dollarFormatter.format( interest ) );
225                    }
226
227                    // handle exception when calculating interest
228                    catch ( RemoteException remoteException ) {
229                        remoteException.printStackTrace();
230                    }
```

Fig. 14.6 `InterestCalculatorClient` for interacting with
`InterestCalculator` EJB (part 5 of 7).

```
231                    } // end method actionPerformed
232               }
233          ); // end addActionListener
234
235          return calculateButton;
236
237     } // end method getCalculateButton
238
239     // lay out GUI components in JFrame
240     public void layoutGUI()
241     {
242          Container contentPane = getContentPane();
243
244          // layout user interface components
245          JPanel inputPanel = new JPanel( new GridLayout( 5, 2 ) );
246
247          inputPanel.add( new JLabel( "Principal" ) );
248          inputPanel.add( principalTextField );
249
250          inputPanel.add( new JLabel( "Interest Rate (%)" ) );
251          inputPanel.add( rateTextField );
252
253          inputPanel.add( new JLabel( "Term (years)" ) );
254          inputPanel.add( termTextField );
255
256          inputPanel.add( new JLabel( "Balance" ) );
257          inputPanel.add( balanceTextField );
258
259          inputPanel.add( new JLabel( "Interest Earned" ) );
260          inputPanel.add( interestEarnedTextField );
261
262          // add inputPanel to contentPane
263          contentPane.add( inputPanel, BorderLayout.CENTER );
264
265          // create JPanel for calculateButton
266          JPanel controlPanel = new JPanel( new FlowLayout() );
267          controlPanel.add( getCalculateButton() );
268          contentPane.add( controlPanel, BorderLayout.SOUTH );
269     }
270
271     // get WindowListener for exiting application
272     public WindowListener getWindowListener()
273     {
274          return new WindowAdapter() {
275
276             public void windowClosing( WindowEvent event )
277             {
278                // check to see if calculator is null
279                if ( calculator.equals( null ) ) {
280                   System.exit( -1 );
281                }
282
```

Fig. 14.6 `InterestCalculatorClient` for interacting with
`InterestCalculator` EJB (part 6 of 7).

```
283                    else {
284                        // remove InterestCalculator instance
285                        try {
286                            calculator.remove();
287                        }
288
289                        // handle exception removing InterestCalculator
290                        catch ( RemoveException removeException ) {
291                            removeException.printStackTrace();
292                            System.exit( -1 );
293                        }
294
295                        // handle exception removing InterestCalculator
296                        catch ( RemoteException remoteException ) {
297                            remoteException.printStackTrace();
298                            System.exit( -1 );
299                        }
300
301                        System.exit( 0 );
302                    }
303                }
304            };
305    } // end method getWindowListener
306
307    // execute the application
308    public static void main( String[] args )
309    {
310        new InterestCalculatorClient();
311    }
312 }
```

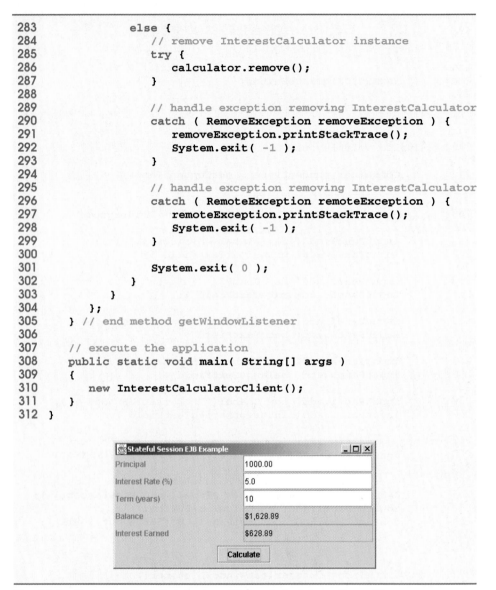

Fig. 14.6 **InterestCalculatorClient** for interacting with
InterestCalculator EJB (part 7 of 7).

Lines 84–87 use class **PortableRemoteObject** method **narrow** to convert the
remote reference to an **InterestCalculatorHome** remote reference. This is the standard method for casting a remote reference to the proper interface type when using *RMI-
IIOP*. RMI-IIOP allows RMI objects to interact with CORBA components, which communicate using the *Internet Inter-Orb Protocol* (IIOP). CORBA is a language-independent
framework for building distributed systems. To enable interoperability among EJBs and
CORBA components, EJBs communicate using RMI-IIOP. We discuss CORBA and RMI-
IIOP in Chapters 26 and 27.

Line 90 invokes method **create** of interface **InterestCalculatorHome** to create a new instance of the **InterestCalculator** EJB. This **InterestCalculator** EJB instance is exclusive to the client that creates it, because it is a session EJB. The **InterestCalculator** EJB instance will maintain state information, because it is a stateful session EJB. Method **create** returns a remote reference to the newly created **InterestCalculator** EJB instance. Line 90 assigns this remote reference to the **calculator** member variable. Instances of class **InterestCalculatorClient** can use this remote reference to invoke the business methods defined in the **Interest-Calculator** remote interface.

Lines 95–97 catch a **NamingException**, which indicates a problem accessing the JNDI directory. If the **InitialContext** cannot be created, the **InitialContext** constructor throws a **NamingException**. Method **lookup** also throws a **NamingException** if the name passed as an argument cannot be found in the JNDI directory.

Lines 100–102 **catch** a **RemoteException**. If there is an error communicating with the EJB container, method **create** throws a **RemoteException**. Lines 105–107 **catch** a **CreateException**. Method **create** throws a **CreateException** if there is an error creating the EJB instance.

Method **createPrincipalTextField** (lines 111–141) creates a **JTextField** for the user to input the **principal** amount. An **ActionListener** anonymous inner class (lines 116–139) uses **static** method **parseDouble** of class **Double** to get the **principal** entered by the user (lines 122–123). Line 125 sets the **principal** in the **InterestCalculator** EJB by invoking method **setPrincipal**. Note that **JTextField**s generate **ActionEvent**s when the user presses the *Enter* key in the **JTextField**. Therefore, the user must press the *Enter* key after entering each piece of data to cause the **ActionListener**'s **actionPerformed** method to invoke the appropriate **InterestCalculator** business method.

Method **createRateTextField** (lines 144–169) creates a **JTextField** for inputting an interest rate for the calculation. Lines 149–167 create an **ActionListener** anonymous inner class to parse the input from the user (lines 155–156) and invoke **InterestCalculator** method **setInterestRate** to set the interest rate (line 159).

Method **createTermTextfield** (lines 172–196) creates a **JTextField** for inputting the number of years for which interest will accrue. An **ActionListener** anonymous inner class (lines 177–194) parses the input from the user (lines 183–184) and sets the term in the **InterestCalculator** by invoking method **setTerm** (line 186) of the **InterestCalculator** remote interface.

Method **getCalculateButton** (lines 199–237) creates a **JButton** that, when clicked, invokes **InterestCalculator** methods **getBalance** and **getInterestEarned**. Lines 220–224 set the text in **balanceTextField** and **interestEarnedTextField** to display the calculation results to the user.

The **InterestCalculatorClient** constructor (lines 34–68) invokes method **createInterestCalculator** to create a new **InterestCalculator** EJB instance (line 39). Lines 42–56 create the application's user-interface components and invoke method **layoutGUI** (line 59), which creates a **JLabel** for each **JTextField** and lays out the components (lines 240–269).

Method **getWindowListener** (lines 272–305) creates a **WindowAdapter** anonymous inner class that provides method **windowClosing** to perform cleanup tasks when the user closes the application window. Line 279 checks to see if **calculator** is **null**. If calculator is **null**, the program exits with an error code (line 280). Otherwise, line 286 invokes method **remove** of the **InterestCalculator** remote interface to remove the EJB instance that the application used. If there is an error when removing the EJB instance, lines 290–293 **catch** a **RemoveException**. If there is an error communicating with the EJB container, lines 296–299 **catch** a **RemoteException**.

14.3.2 Deploying Session EJBs

Enterprise JavaBeans execute in the context of an EJB container, which is a fundamental part of a J2EE-compliant application server. This section details the steps necessary to deploy the **InterestCalculator** session EJB in the Java 2 Enterprise Edition version 1.2.1 reference implementation from Sun Microsystems. If you have not yet installed and configured the J2EE SDK, please see Appendix E for instructions.

Create a new enterprise application by selecting **New Application** from the **File** menu (Fig. 14.7). Specify the file name for the EAR file and the name of the application in the **New Application** dialog box and click **OK** (Fig. 14.8).

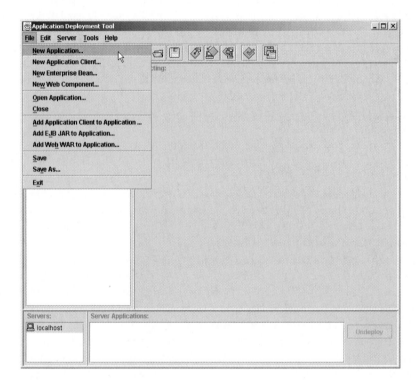

Fig. 14.7 Creating **New Application** in **Application Deployment Tool**.

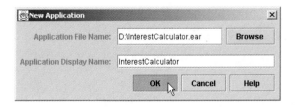

Fig. 14.8   Specifying EAR file for **New Application**.

Select **New Enterprise Bean** from the **File** menu to begin deploying the EJB (Fig. 14.9). Click **Next**, provide a **JAR Display Name** and click **Add** to add the class files for the **InterestCalculator** EJB (Fig. 14.10).

Specify the **Root Directory** for the classes that make up the **InterestCalculator** EJB (Fig. 14.11). The **InterestCalculator** classes are in package **com.deitel.advjhtp1.ejb.session.stateful.ejb**, so select as the **Root Directory** the directory that contains the **com** directory. Select the **InterestCalculator** class files—**InterestCalculator.class**, **InterestCalculatorHome.class** and **InterestCalculatorEJB.class**—and click **Add** and **OK**. After adding the class files, they will appear in the **Contents** of the **EJB JAR** (Fig. 14.12). Click **Next** to begin adding class files to the **EJB JAR**.

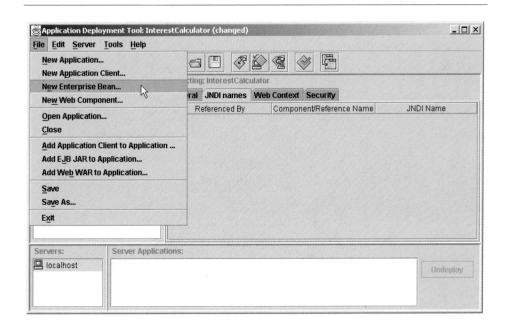

Fig. 14.9   Creating a **New Enterprise Bean**.

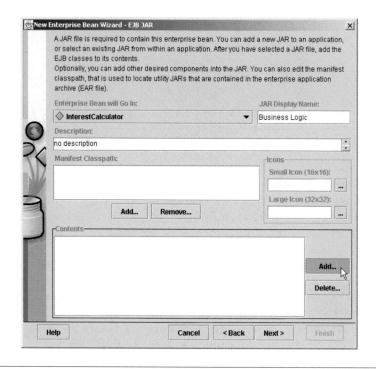

Fig. 14.10 Adding **InterestCalculator** EJB classes.

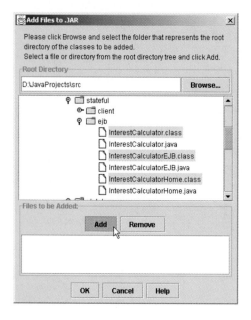

Fig. 14.11 Selecting **InterestCalculator** EJB classes to add.

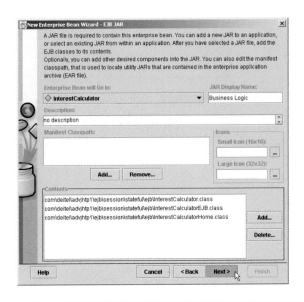

Fig. 14.12 Result of adding `InterestCalculator` EJB classes.

Specify the **Enterprise Bean Class**, **Home Interface** and **Remote Interface** by selecting the appropriate classes from the drop-down lists (Fig. 14.13). Specify an **Enterprise Bean Display Name** to be displayed in the **Application Deployment Tool** and select the **Bean Type**. The `InterestCalculator` EJB is a stateful session bean, so select the **Session** and **Stateful** radio buttons and click **Next** (Fig. 14.14). When deploying the `MathToolEJB`, specify **Stateless** instead of **Stateful** for the **Bean Type**.

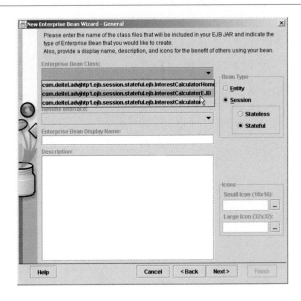

Fig. 14.13 Specifying **Enterprise Bean Class** for `InterestCalculator` EJB.

Fig. 14.14 Specifying **InterestCalculator** EJB classes and **Stateful Session Bean Type**.

Specify **Container-Managed Transactions** in the **Transaction Management** dialog (Fig. 14.15). For each **Method**, specify the **Supports** Transaction Type, and click **Next**. We discuss the details of transactions in Section 14.4.

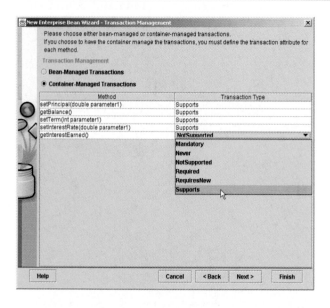

Fig. 14.15 Specifying **Container Managed Transactions** for **InterestCalculator** EJB.

Figure 14.16 shows the XML deployment descriptor generated for the **Interest-Calculator** EJB. The application server uses this XML descriptor to configure the **InterestCalculator** EJB.

You must specify a **JNDI Name** for the **InterestCalculator**, so that clients may obtain references to the EJB. For this example, specify the **JNDI Name Interest-Calculator** (Fig. 14.17). The **JNDI Name** need not be the same as the EJB name.

Good Programming Practice 14.1

Use an EJB's remote interface name as the EJB's JNDI name. This makes your code more readable and makes the JNDI name easier to remember.

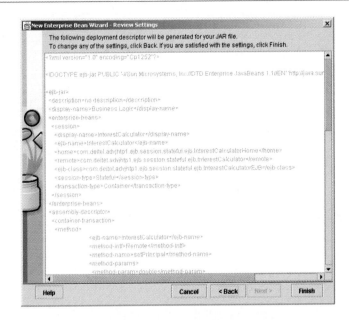

Fig. 14.16 XML deployment descriptor for **InterestCalculator** EJB.

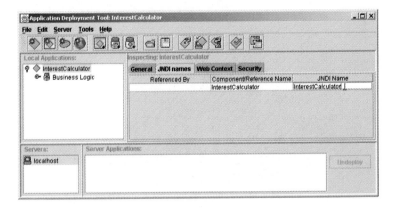

Fig. 14.17 Specifying **JNDI Name** for **InterestCalculator** EJB.

Deploy the application to the J2EE server by selecting **Deploy Application** from the **Tools** menu, or by clicking the **Deploy Application** button on the toolbar (Fig. 14.18).

Specify `localhost` as the **Target Server** and select the checkbox **Return Client Jar** (Fig. 14.19). The client JAR contains the stub classes the client will use to communicate with the EJB.

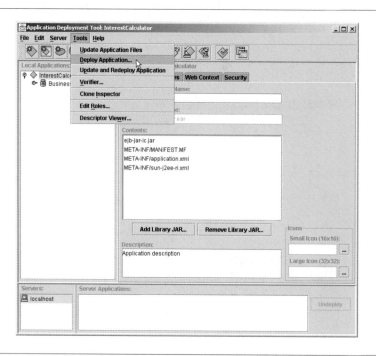

Fig. 14.18 Deploying enterprise application to `localhost`.

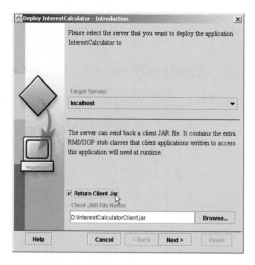

Fig. 14.19 Specifying the **Application Deployment Tool** should **Return Client Jar**.

After deploying the **InterestCalculator** EJB (Fig. 14.20), execute the **InterestCalculatorClient** to test the **InterestCalculator**. The **InterestCalculatorClient.jar** and the **j2ee.jar** must be in the CLASSPATH when executing the **InterestCalculatorClient**. For example, from the command line, type

```
java -classpath D:\j2sdkee1.2.1\lib\j2ee.jar;D:\Interest-
CalculatorClient.jar;. com.deitel.advjhtp1.ejb.session.state-
ful.client.InterestCalculatorClient
```

14.3.3 Stateless Session EJBs

Stateless session EJBs maintain no state information between business method invocations. As a result, the EJB container can use any stateless session EJB instance to respond to any client's request.

Performance Tip 14.1

Stateless session EJBs may perform better than stateful session EJBs, because a single stateless session EJB instance can be shared among many clients, reducing memory, processor and other resource requirements on the server.

Figure 14.21 shows the **MathTool** remote interface. **MathTool** is a stateless session EJB with business methods for generating a Fibonacci series and calculating factorials. Method **getFibonacciSeries** (lines 14–15) generates a Fibonacci series of the length supplied in integer argument **howMany**. Method **getFactorial** (lines 18–19) calculates the factorial of the provided integer.

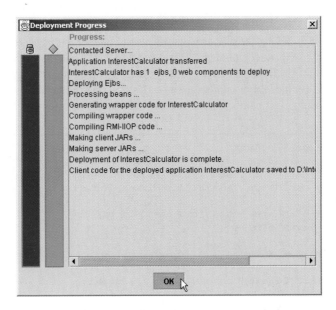

Fig. 14.20 Successful completion of deployment process.

```
1   // MathTool.java
2   // MathTool is the remote interface for the MathTool EJB.
3   package com.deitel.advjhtp1.ejb.session.stateless.ejb;
4
5   // Java core libraries
6   import java.rmi.RemoteException;
7
8   // Java standard extensions
9   import javax.ejb.EJBObject;
10
11  public interface MathTool extends EJBObject
12  {
13     // get Fibonacci series
14     public int[] getFibonacciSeries( int howMany )
15        throws RemoteException, IllegalArgumentException;
16
17     // get factorial of given integer
18     public int getFactorial( int number )
19        throws RemoteException, IllegalArgumentException;
20  }
```

Fig. 14.21 **MathTool** remote interface for calculating factorials and generating Fibonacci series.

MathToolEJB (Fig. 14.22) provides implementations of the business methods declared in the **MathTool** remote interface. **MathToolEJB** implements the **Session-Bean** interface (line 9), indicating **MathTool** is a session EJB. Method **getFibonacciSeries** (lines 14–48) generates a Fibonacci series. The Fibonacci series

0, 1, 1, 2, 3, 5, 8, 13, 21, …

begins with **0** and **1** and has the property that each subsequent Fibonacci number is the sum of the previous two Fibonacci numbers. The **MathTool** EJB calculates the Fibonacci series on lines 25–44. Each number in the series is placed in the integer array **series** (line 29). Lines 32–33 set the zeroth number in the series to **0** and the first number in the series to **1**. Line 39 sets the next number in the series to the sum of the previous two numbers.

```
1    // MathToolEJB.java
2    // MathToolEJB is a stateless session EJB with methods for
3    // calculating Fibonacci series and factorials.
4    package com.deitel.advjhtp1.ejb.session.stateless.ejb;
5
6    // Java standard extensions
7    import javax.ejb.*;
8
9    public class MathToolEJB implements SessionBean {
10
11       private SessionContext sessionContext;
12
```

Fig. 14.22 **MathToolEJB** implementation of **MathTool** remote interface (part 1 of 3).

```
13      // get Fibonacci series
14      public int[] getFibonacciSeries( int howMany )
15         throws IllegalArgumentException
16      {
17         // throw IllegalArgumentException if series length
18         // is less than zero
19         if ( howMany < 2 )
20            throw new IllegalArgumentException(
21               "Cannot generate Fibonacci series of " +
22               "length less than two." );
23
24         // starting points
25         int startPoint1 = 0;
26         int startPoint2 = 1;
27
28         // array to contain Fibonacci sequence
29         int[] series = new int[ howMany ];
30
31         // set base cases
32         series[ 0 ] = 0;
33         series[ 1 ] = 1;
34
35         // generate Fibonacci series
36         for ( int i = 2; i < howMany; i++ ) {
37
38            // calculate next number in series
39            series[ i ] = startPoint1 + startPoint2;
40
41            // set start points for next iteration
42            startPoint1 = startPoint2;
43            startPoint2 = series[ i ];
44         }
45
46         return series;
47
48      } // end method getFibonacciSeries
49
50      // get factorial of given integer
51      public int getFactorial( int number )
52         throws IllegalArgumentException
53      {
54         // throw IllegalArgumentException if number less than zero
55         if ( number < 0 )
56            throw new IllegalArgumentException(
57               "Cannot calculate factorial of negative numbers." );
58
59         // base case for recursion, return 1
60         if ( number == 0 )
61            return 1;
62
```

Fig. 14.22 MathToolEJB implementation of **MathTool** remote interface (part 2 of 3).

```
63          // call getFactorial recursively to calculate factorial
64          else
65             return number * getFactorial( number - 1 );
66
67       } // end method getFactorial
68
69       // set SessionContext
70       public void setSessionContext( SessionContext context )
71       {
72          sessionContext = context;
73       }
74
75       // create new MathTool instance
76       public void ejbCreate() {}
77
78       // remove MathTool instance
79       public void ejbRemove() {}
80
81       // activate MathTool instance
82       public void ejbActivate() {}
83
84       // passivate MathTool instance
85       public void ejbPassivate() {}
86    }
```

Fig. 14.22 **MathToolEJB** implementation of **MathTool** remote interface (part 3 of 3).

Method **getFactorial** (lines 51–67) calculates the factorial of a nonnegative integer, which is defined to be the product

$$n \cdot (n-1) \cdot (n-2) \cdot \ldots \cdot 1$$

Lines 56–57 throw an **IllegalArgumentException** if the integer argument **number** is less than **0**. Lines 60–61 implement the base case for the recursive calculation. Line 65 calculates the factorial with a recursive call to **getFactorial**.

The EJB container invokes method **setSessionContext** (lines 70–73) when the EJB instance is activated and a remote reference is given to a client. The **SessionContext** argument implements method **getEJBObject**, which the EJB can use to retrieve a reference to the current EJB instance.

When a client invokes method **create** of interface **MathToolHome** (Fig. 14.23), the EJB container invokes method **ejbCreate** (line 76). Method **ejbCreate** performs initialization of the EJB. **MathToolEJB** method **ejbCreate** has an empty implementation, because this EJB requires no initialization. The EJB container invokes method **ejbRemove** (line 79) to remove a **MathTool** EJB instance.

The EJB container invokes method **ejbActivate** (line 82) when the EJB instance is taken out of the EJB container's pool and associated with a particular client. The EJB container invokes method **ejbPassivate** (line 85) when the EJB instance is no longer needed and can be returned to the ready pool.

MathToolHome (Fig. 14.23) is the home interface for the **MathTool** EJB. Method **create** (lines 15–16) creates a new **MathTool** EJB. The EJB container invokes **MathToolEJB** method **ejbCreate** when a client invokes **MathToolHome** method **create**.

```
1   // MathToolHome.java
2   // MathToolHome is the home interface for the MathTool EJB.
3   package com.deitel.advjhtp1.ejb.session.stateless.ejb;
4
5   // Java core libraries
6   import java.rmi.RemoteException;
7
8   // Java standard extensions
9   import javax.ejb.EJBHome;
10  import javax.ejb.CreateException;
11
12  public interface MathToolHome extends EJBHome {
13
14      // create new MathTool EJB
15      public MathTool create() throws RemoteException,
16          CreateException;
17  }
```

Fig. 14.23 `MathToolHome` interface for creating `MathTool` EJBs.

Please refer to Section 14.3.2 for deployment instructions. Recall that **MathTool** is a stateless session EJB, so you must specify this in the deployment process. Also, be sure to specify an appropriate JNDI name (e.g., **MathTool**) for the **MathTool** EJB.

MathToolClient (Fig. 14.24) is an application client for the **MathTool** EJB. The user interface consists of a **JTextField** into which the user can enter an integer, a **JButton** to invoke **MathTool** method **getFactorial** and a **JButton** to invoke **MathTool** method **getFibonacciSeries**. The calculation results are displayed in a **JTextArea**.

The **MathToolClient** constructor (lines 29–45) invokes method **createMathTool** (line 35) to create a new instance of the **MathTool** EJB. Line 38 invokes method **createGUI** to create and lay out GUI components for the application's user interface. Method **createMathTool** (lines 48–83) uses an **InitialContext** (line 53) to look up the **MathToolHome** interface in the JNDI Directory (lines 56–57). Line 65 invokes **MathToolHome** method **create** to create a **MathTool** EJB instance.

Method **getFactorialButton** (lines 86–122) creates a **JButton** that, when pressed, invokes **MathTool** EJB method **getFactorial**. Lines 100–104 parse the number entered in **numberTextField** and invoke method **getFactorial** of the **MathTool** remote interface. Lines 107–108 display the factorial in **resultsTextArea**. Lines 113–115 catch a **RemoteException** if there is an error invoking method **getFactorial**.

Method **getFibonacciButton** (lines 125–182) creates a **JButton** that, when clicked, invokes **MathTool** EJB method **getFibonacciSeries**. Lines 140–145 parse the number entered in **numberTextField** and invoke method **getFibonacciSeries** of the **MathTool** remote interface. Method **getFibonacciSeries** returns an array of integers containing a Fibonacci series of the length specified by the integer argument **howMany**. Lines 148–168 build a **StringBuffer** containing the Fibonacci series and display the series in **resultsTextArea**.

```
1    // MathToolClient.java
2    // MathToolClient is a GUI for calculating factorials and
3    // Fibonacci series using the MathTool EJB.
4    package com.deitel.advjhtp1.ejb.session.stateless.client;
5
6    // Java core libraries
7    import java.awt.*;
8    import java.awt.event.*;
9    import java.rmi.*;
10
11   // Java standard extensions
12   import javax.swing.*;
13   import javax.rmi.*;
14   import javax.naming.*;
15   import javax.ejb.*;
16
17   // Deitel libraries
18   import com.deitel.advjhtp1.ejb.session.stateless.ejb.*;
19
20   public class MathToolClient extends JFrame {
21
22      private MathToolHome mathToolHome;
23      private MathTool mathTool;
24
25      private JTextArea resultsTextArea;
26      private JTextField numberTextField;
27
28      // MathToolClient constructor
29      public MathToolClient()
30      {
31         super( "Stateless Session EJB Example" );
32
33         // create MathTool for calculating factorials
34         // and Fibonacci series
35         createMathTool();
36
37         // create and lay out GUI components
38         createGUI();
39
40         addWindowListener( getWindowListener() );
41
42         setSize( 425, 200 );
43         setVisible( true );
44
45      } // end MathToolClient constructor
46
47      // create MathTool EJB instance
48      private void createMathTool()
49      {
50         // lookup MathToolHome and create MathTool EJB
51         try {
52
53            InitialContext initialContext = new InitialContext();
```

Fig. 14.24 MathToolClient for interacting with **MathTool** EJB (part 1 of 6).

```
54
55            // lookup MathTool EJB
56         Object homeObject =
57            initialContext.lookup( "MathTool" );
58
59            // get MathToolHome interface
60         mathToolHome = ( MathToolHome )
61            PortableRemoteObject.narrow( homeObject,
62               MathToolHome.class );
63
64            // create MathTool EJB instance
65         mathTool = mathToolHome.create();
66
67      } // end try
68
69      // handle exception if MathTool EJB is not found
70      catch ( NamingException namingException ) {
71         namingException.printStackTrace();
72      }
73
74      // handle exception when creating MathTool EJB
75      catch ( RemoteException remoteException ) {
76         remoteException.printStackTrace();
77      }
78
79      // handle exception when creating MathTool EJB
80      catch ( CreateException createException ) {
81         createException.printStackTrace();
82      }
83   } // end method createMathTool
84
85   // create JButton for calculating factorial
86   private JButton getFactorialButton()
87   {
88      JButton factorialButton =
89         new JButton( "Calculate Factorial" );
90
91      // add ActionListener for factorial button
92      factorialButton.addActionListener(
93         new ActionListener() {
94
95            public void actionPerformed( ActionEvent event )
96            {
97               // use MathTool EJB to calculate factorial
98               try {
99
100                  int number = Integer.parseInt(
101                     numberTextField.getText() );
102
103                  // get Factorial of number input by user
104                  int result = mathTool.getFactorial( number );
105
```

Fig. 14.24 MathToolClient for interacting with **MathTool** EJB (part 2 of 6).

```
106                    // display results in resultsTextArea
107                    resultsTextArea.setText( number + "! = " +
108                       result );
109
110                 } // end try
111
112                 // handle exception calculating factorial
113                 catch ( RemoteException remoteException ) {
114                    remoteException.printStackTrace();
115                 }
116              } // end method actionPerformed
117           }
118        ); // end addActionListener
119
120        return factorialButton;
121
122     } // end method getFactorialButton
123
124     // create JButton for generating Fibonacci series
125     private JButton getFibonacciButton()
126     {
127        JButton fibonacciButton =
128           new JButton( "Fibonacci Series" );
129
130        // add ActionListener for generating Fibonacci series
131        fibonacciButton.addActionListener(
132           new ActionListener() {
133
134              public void actionPerformed( ActionEvent event )
135              {
136                 // generate Fibonacci series using MathTool EJB
137                 try {
138
139                    // get number entered by user
140                    int number = Integer.parseInt(
141                       numberTextField.getText() );
142
143                    // get Fibonacci series
144                    int[] series = mathTool.getFibonacciSeries(
145                       number );
146
147                    // create StringBuffer to store series
148                    StringBuffer buffer =
149                       new StringBuffer( "The first " );
150
151                    buffer.append( number );
152
153                    buffer.append( " Fibonacci number(s): \n" );
154
155                    // append each number in series to buffer
156                    for ( int i = 0; i < series.length; i++ ) {
157
```

Fig. 14.24 MathToolClient for interacting with **MathTool** EJB (part 3 of 6).

```
158                          // do not add comma before first number
159                          if ( i != 0 )
160                             buffer.append( ", " );
161
162                          // append next number in series to buffer
163                          buffer.append( String.valueOf(
164                             series[ i ] ) );
165                       }
166
167                       // display series in resultsTextArea
168                       resultsTextArea.setText( buffer.toString() );
169
170                    } // end try
171
172                    // handle exception calculating series
173                    catch ( RemoteException remoteException ) {
174                       remoteException.printStackTrace();
175                    }
176                 } // end method actionPerformed
177              }
178           ); // end addActionListener
179
180           return fibonacciButton;
181
182        } // end method getFibonacciButton
183
184        // create lay out GUI components
185        public void createGUI()
186        {
187           // create JTextArea to show results
188           resultsTextArea = new JTextArea();
189           resultsTextArea.setLineWrap( true );
190           resultsTextArea.setWrapStyleWord( true );
191           resultsTextArea.setEditable( false );
192
193           // create JTextField for user input
194           numberTextField = new JTextField( 10 );
195
196           // create JButton for calculating factorial
197           JButton factorialButton = getFactorialButton();
198
199           // create JButton for generating Fibonacci series
200           JButton fibonacciButton = getFibonacciButton();
201
202           Container contentPane = getContentPane();
203
204           // put resultsTextArea in a JScrollPane
205           JScrollPane resultsScrollPane =
206              new JScrollPane( resultsTextArea );
207
208           contentPane.add( resultsScrollPane,
209              BorderLayout.CENTER );
210
```

Fig. 14.24 MathToolClient for interacting with **MathTool** EJB (part 4 of 6).

```
211          // add input components to new JPanel
212          JPanel inputPanel = new JPanel( new FlowLayout() );
213          inputPanel.add( new JLabel( "Enter an integer: " ) );
214          inputPanel.add( numberTextField );
215
216          // add JButton components to new JPanel
217          JPanel buttonPanel = new JPanel( new FlowLayout() );
218          buttonPanel.add( factorialButton );
219          buttonPanel.add( fibonacciButton );
220
221          // add inputPanel and buttonPanel to new JPanel
222          JPanel controlPanel =
223             new JPanel( new GridLayout( 2, 2 ) );
224
225          controlPanel.add( inputPanel );
226          controlPanel.add( buttonPanel );
227
228          contentPane.add( controlPanel, BorderLayout.NORTH );
229
230       } // end method createGUI
231
232       // get WindowListener for exiting application
233       private WindowListener getWindowListener()
234       {
235          return new WindowAdapter() {
236
237             public void windowClosing( WindowEvent event )
238             {
239                // remove MathTool instance
240                try {
241                   mathTool.remove();
242                }
243
244                // handle exception when removing MathTool EJB
245                catch ( RemoveException removeException ) {
246                   removeException.printStackTrace();
247                   System.exit( -1 );
248                }
249
250                // handle exception when removing MathTool EJB
251                catch ( RemoteException remoteException ) {
252                   remoteException.printStackTrace();
253                   System.exit( -1 );
254                }
255
256                System.exit( 0 );
257             } // end method windowClosing
258          };
259       } // end method getWindowListener
260
261       // execute application
262       public static void main( String[] args )
263       {
```

Fig. 14.24 MathToolClient for interacting with **MathTool** EJB (part 5 of 6).

```
264        MathToolClient client = new MathToolClient();
265    }
266 }
```

Fig. 14.24 MathToolClient for interacting with **MathTool** EJB (part 6 of 6).

14.4 EJB Transactions

The Java 2 Enterprise Edition supports *distributed transactions*. A distributed transaction is a transaction that includes multiple databases or multiple application servers. For example, a distributed transaction could transfer funds from an account at one bank into an account at another bank atomically.

J2EE supports two methods for defining transaction boundaries: *bean-managed transaction demarcation* and *container-managed transaction demarcation*. Bean-managed transaction demarcation requires the EJB developer to code the transaction boundaries manually in the EJBs using the *Java Transaction API (JTA)*. Container-managed transaction demarcation allows the EJB deployer to specify transaction boundaries declaratively when deploying EJBs.

Software Engineering Observation 14.2

Entity EJBs may use only container-managed transaction demarcation.

14.4.1 MoneyTransfer EJB Home and Remote Interfaces

The **MoneyTransfer** EJB demonstrates the need for distributed transactions and their implementation using bean-managed and container-managed transaction demarcation. In this example, we transfer money from an account at **BankABC** to an account at **BankXYZ**. We first withdraw money from an account at **BankABC** and then deposit the same amount at **BankXYZ**. Transactions are needed to ensure that the money is "put back" in the **Bank-**

ABC account if the deposit at **BankXYZ** fails. We also need to ensure that if the withdrawal from **BankABC** fails, the money is not deposited at **BankXYZ**.

The **MoneyTransfer** remote interface (Fig. 14.25) provides methods for transferring money between accounts and for getting the balances of accounts at two different banks. Method **transfer** (line 15) transfers the given amount of money from an account at **BankABC** to an account at **BankXYZ**. Method **getBankABCBalance** (line 18) returns the account balance at **BankABC**. Method **getBankXYZBalance** (line 21) returns the account balance at **BankXYZ**. Interface **MoneyTransferHome** (Fig. 14.26) provides method **create** (lines 15–16) for creating **MoneyTransfer** EJB instances.

```
1   // MoneyTransfer.java
2   // MoneyTransfer is the remote interface for the MoneyTransfer
3   // EJB.
4   package com.deitel.advjhtp1.ejb.transactions;
5
6   // Java core libraries
7   import java.rmi.RemoteException;
8
9   // Java standard extensions
10  import javax.ejb.EJBObject;
11
12  public interface MoneyTransfer extends EJBObject {
13
14     // transfer amount from BankABC to BankXYZ
15     public void transfer( double amount ) throws RemoteException;
16
17     // get  BankABC account balance
18     public double getBankABCBalance() throws RemoteException;
19
20     // get BankXYZ account balance
21     public double getBankXYZBalance() throws RemoteException;
22  }
```

Fig. 14.25 MoneyTransfer remote interface for transferring money and getting account balances.

```
1   // MoneyTransferHome.java
2   // MoneyTransferHome is the home interface for the
3   // MoneyTransferHome EJB.
4   package com.deitel.advjhtp1.ejb.transactions;
5
6   // Java core libraries
7   import java.rmi.RemoteException;
8
9   // Java standard extensions
10  import javax.ejb.*;
11
12  public interface MoneyTransferHome extends EJBHome {
13
```

Fig. 14.26 MoneyTransferHome interface for creating **MoneyTransfer** EJBs (part 1 of 2).

```
14      // create MoneyTransfer EJB
15      public MoneyTransfer create() throws RemoteException,
16         CreateException;
17   }
```

Fig. 14.26 **MoneyTransferHome** interface for creating **MoneyTransfer**
EJBs (part 2 of 2).

14.4.2 Bean-Managed Transaction Demarcation

Bean-managed transaction demarcation requires the EJB developer to code the transaction
boundaries manually in the EJBs. Bean-managed transaction demarcation may be used
only with session EJBs.

     MoneyTransferEJB (Fig. 14.27) implements the **MoneyTransfer** remote inter-
face using bean-managed transaction demarcation to ensure atomicity of the database
updates in method **transfer** (lines 26–81). Lines 29–30 create a **UserTransaction**.
Line 34 begins the **transaction** by invoking **UserTransaction** method **begin**.
All statements after the **transaction** begins are part of the **transaction** until the
transaction is committed or rolled back.

```
1    // MoneyTransferEJB.java
2    // MoneyTransferEJB is a stateless session EJB for transferring
3    // funds from an Account at BankABC to an Account at BankXYZ
4    // using bean-managed transaction demarcation.
5    package com.deitel.advjhtp1.ejb.transactions.beanmanaged;
6
7    // Java core libraries
8    import java.util.*;
9    import java.sql.*;
10
11   // Java standard extensions
12   import javax.ejb.*;
13   import javax.naming.*;
14   import javax.transaction.*;
15   import javax.sql.*;
16
17   public class MoneyTransferEJB implements SessionBean {
18
19      private SessionContext sessionContext;
20      private Connection bankOneConnection;
21      private Connection bankTwoConnection;
22      private PreparedStatement withdrawalStatement;
23      private PreparedStatement depositStatement;
24
25      // transfer funds from BankABC to BankXYZ
26      public void transfer( double amount ) throws EJBException
27      {
28         // create transaction for transferring funds
29         UserTransaction transaction =
30            sessionContext.getUserTransaction();
```

Fig. 14.27 **MoneyTransferEJB** implementation of **MoneyTransfer** remote
interface using bean-managed transaction demarcation (part 1 of 6).

```
31
32        // begin bean-managed transaction demarcation
33        try {
34            transaction.begin();
35        }
36
37        // catch exception if method begin fails
38        catch ( Exception exception ) {
39
40            // throw EJBException indicating transaction failed
41            throw new EJBException( exception );
42        }
43
44        // transfer funds from account in BankABC to account
45        // in BankXYZ using bean-managed transaction demarcation
46        try {
47
48            withdrawalStatement.setDouble( 1, amount );
49
50            // withdraw funds from account at BankABC
51            withdrawalStatement.executeUpdate();
52
53            depositStatement.setDouble( 1, amount );
54
55            // deposit funds in account at BankXYZ
56            depositStatement.executeUpdate();
57
58            // commit transaction
59            transaction.commit();
60
61        } // end try
62
63        // handle exceptions when withdrawing, depositing and
64        // committing transaction
65        catch ( Exception exception ) {
66
67            // attempt rollback of transaction
68            try {
69                transaction.rollback();
70            }
71
72            // handle exception when rolling back transaction
73            catch ( SystemException systemException ) {
74                throw new EJBException( systemException );
75            }
76
77            // throw EJBException indicating transaction failed
78            throw new EJBException( exception );
79        }
80
81    } // end method transfer
82
```

Fig. 14.27 **MoneyTransferEJB** implementation of **MoneyTransfer** remote
interface using bean-managed transaction demarcation (part 2 of 6).

```
83      // get balance of Account at BankABC
84      public double getBankABCBalance() throws EJBException
85      {
86         // get balance of Account at BankABC
87         try {
88
89            // select balance for Account # 12345
90            String select = "SELECT balance FROM Account " +
91               "WHERE accountID = 12345";
92
93            PreparedStatement selectStatement =
94               bankOneConnection.prepareStatement( select );
95
96            ResultSet resultSet = selectStatement.executeQuery();
97
98            // get first record in ResultSet and return balance
99            if ( resultSet.next() )
100              return resultSet.getDouble( "balance" );
101           else
102              throw new EJBException( "Account not found" );
103
104        } // end try
105
106        // handle exception when getting Account balance
107        catch ( SQLException sqlException ) {
108           throw new EJBException( sqlException );
109        }
110
111     } // end method getBankABCBalance
112
113     // get balance of Account at BankXYZ
114     public double getBankXYZBalance() throws EJBException
115     {
116        // get balance of Account at BankXYZ
117        try {
118
119           // select balance for Account # 54321
120           String select = "SELECT balance FROM Account " +
121              "WHERE accountID = 54321";
122
123           PreparedStatement selectStatement =
124              bankTwoConnection.prepareStatement( select );
125
126           ResultSet resultSet = selectStatement.executeQuery();
127
128           // get first record in ResultSet and return balance
129           if ( resultSet.next() )
130              return resultSet.getDouble( "balance" );
131           else
132              throw new EJBException( "Account not found" );
133
134        } // end try
```

Fig. 14.27 **MoneyTransferEJB** implementation of **MoneyTransfer** remote interface using bean-managed transaction demarcation (part 3 of 6).

```
135
136        // handle exception when getting Account balance
137        catch ( SQLException sqlException ) {
138           throw new EJBException( sqlException );
139        }
140
141     } // end method getBankXYZBalance
142
143     // set SessionContext
144     public void setSessionContext( SessionContext context )
145        throws EJBException
146     {
147        sessionContext = context;
148
149        openDatabaseResources();
150     }
151
152     // create MoneyTransfer instance
153     public void ejbCreate() {}
154
155     // remove MoneyTransfer instance
156     public void ejbRemove() throws EJBException
157     {
158        closeDatabaseResources();
159     }
160
161     // passivate MoneyTransfer instance
162     public void ejbPassivate() throws EJBException
163     {
164        closeDatabaseResources();
165     }
166
167     // activate MoneyTransfer instance
168     public void ejbActivate() throws EJBException
169     {
170        openDatabaseResources();
171     }
172
173     // close database Connections and PreparedStatements
174     private void closeDatabaseResources() throws EJBException
175     {
176        // close database resources
177        try {
178
179           // close PreparedStatements
180           depositStatement.close();
181           depositStatement = null;
182
183           withdrawalStatement.close();
184           withdrawalStatement = null;
185
```

Fig. 14.27 MoneyTransferEJB implementation of **MoneyTransfer** remote
interface using bean-managed transaction demarcation (part 4 of 6).

```
186              // close database Connections
187              bankOneConnection.close();
188              bankOneConnection = null;
189
190              bankTwoConnection.close();
191              bankTwoConnection = null;
192           }
193
194        // handle exception closing database connections
195        catch ( SQLException sqlException ) {
196           throw new EJBException( sqlException );
197        }
198
199     } // end method closeDatabaseResources
200
201     // open database Connections and create PreparedStatements
202     private void openDatabaseResources() throws EJBException
203     {
204        // look up the BankABC and BankXYZ DataSources and create
205        // Connections for each
206        try {
207           Context initialContext = new InitialContext();
208
209           // get DataSource reference from JNDI directory
210           DataSource dataSource = ( DataSource )
211              initialContext.lookup(
212                 "java:comp/env/jdbc/BankABC" );
213
214           // get Connection from DataSource
215           bankOneConnection = dataSource.getConnection();
216
217           dataSource = ( DataSource) initialContext.lookup(
218              "java:comp/env/jdbc/BankXYZ" );
219
220           bankTwoConnection = dataSource.getConnection();
221
222           // prepare withdraw statement for account #12345 at
223           // BankABC
224           String withdrawal = "UPDATE Account SET balance = " +
225              "balance - ? WHERE accountID = 12345";
226
227           withdrawalStatement =
228              bankOneConnection.prepareStatement( withdrawal );
229
230           // prepare deposit statment for account #54321 at
231           // BankXYZ
232           String deposit = "UPDATE Account SET balance = " +
233              "balance + ? WHERE accountID = 54321";
234
235           depositStatement =
236              bankTwoConnection.prepareStatement( deposit );
237
```

Fig. 14.27 MoneyTransferEJB implementation of **MoneyTransfer** remote interface using bean-managed transaction demarcation (part 5 of 6).

```
238          } // end try
239
240          // handle exception if DataSource not found in directory
241          catch ( NamingException namingException ) {
242             throw new EJBException( namingException );
243          }
244
245          // handle exception getting Connection to DataSource
246          catch ( SQLException sqlException ) {
247             throw new EJBException( sqlException );
248          }
249
250       } // end method openDatabaseResources
251    }
```

Fig. 14.27 **MoneyTransferEJB** implementation of **MoneyTransfer** remote interface using bean-managed transaction demarcation (part 6 of 6).

Lines 48–51 withdraw the given transfer **amount** from an account in the **BankABC** database. Lines 53–56 deposit the given transfer **amount** in an account in the **BankXYZ** database. Both of these updates are part of the **transaction** begun on line 34 even though they are in separate databases. Line 59 commits the **transaction** to save the updates to each database.

Lines 65–79 catch any **Exception**s thrown from lines 46–61. Line 69 invokes **UserTransaction** method **rollback** to undo any updates that were made within the **transaction** boundaries. This **rollback** ensures that if any critical part of method **transfer** failed, all of the changes made in both databases are undone to ensure the integrity of the data. Lines 73–75 catch a **SystemException**, which is thrown by **UserTransaction** method **rollback** if the **rollback** fails. Lines 74 and 78 throw **EJBException**s to aid in debugging the application.

Methods **getBankABCBalance** (lines 84–111) and **getBankXYZBalance** (lines 114–141) execute simple SQL **SELECT** statements to retrieve the balances of the accounts at each bank. Methods **setSessionContext** (lines 144–150) and **ejbActivate** (lines 168–171) invoke method **openDatabaseResources** (lines 202–250) to create **Connection**s and **PreparedStatement**s for each database for use throughout the lifetime of the **MoneyTransfer** EJB instance. Methods **ejbRemove** (lines 156–159) and **ejbPassivate** (lines 162–165) invoke method **closeDatabaseResources** (lines 174–199) to close the **Connection**s and **PreparedStatement**s.

14.4.3 Container-Managed Transaction Demarcation

Container-managed transaction demarcation allows the EJB developer to implement an EJB without specifying transaction boundaries. The EJB deployer provides transaction demarcation semantics declaratively when deploying the application.

MoneyTransferEJB (Fig. 14.28) implements the **MoneyTransfer** remote interface using container-managed transaction demarcation. Method **transfer** (lines 25–51) is similar to method **transfer** in Fig. 14.27. Note, however, that this version of method **transfer** does not declare any transaction boundaries, as this is now the responsibility of the EJB deployer. The EJB deployer specifies the transaction semantics using one of the six transaction types listed in Fig. 14.29.

```
1    // MoneyTransferEJB.java
2    // MoneyTransferEJB is a stateless session EJB for transferring
3    // funds from an Account at BankABC to an Account at BankXYZ
4    // using container-managed transaction demarcation.
5    package com.deitel.advjhtp1.ejb.transactions.containermanaged;
6
7    // Java core libraries
8    import java.util.*;
9    import java.sql.*;
10
11   // Java standard extensions
12   import javax.ejb.*;
13   import javax.naming.*;
14   import javax.sql.*;
15
16   public class MoneyTransferEJB implements SessionBean {
17
18      private SessionContext sessionContext;
19      private Connection bankOneConnection;
20      private Connection bankTwoConnection;
21      private PreparedStatement withdrawalStatement;
22      private PreparedStatement depositStatement;
23
24      // transfer funds from BankABC to BankXYZ
25      public void transfer( double amount ) throws EJBException
26      {
27         // transfer funds from account in BankABC to account in
28         // BankXYZ using container-managed transaction demarcation
29         try {
30
31            withdrawalStatement.setDouble( 1, amount );
32
33            // withdraw funds from account at BankABC
34            withdrawalStatement.executeUpdate();
35
36            depositStatement.setDouble( 1, amount );
37
38            // deposit funds in account at BankXYZ
39            depositStatement.executeUpdate();
40
41         } // end try
42
43         // handle exception withdrawing and depositing
44         catch ( SQLException sqlException ) {
45
```

Fig. 14.28 **MoneyTransferEJB** implementation of **MoneyTransfer** remote interface using container-managed transaction demarcation (part 1 of 5).

```
46              // throw EJBException to indicate transfer failed
47              // and roll back container-managed transaction
48              throw new EJBException( sqlException );
49           }
50
51       } // end method transfer
52
53       // get balance of Account at BankABC
54       public double getBankABCBalance() throws EJBException
55       {
56          // get balance of Account at BankABC
57          try {
58
59             // select balance for Account # 12345
60             String select = "SELECT balance FROM Account " +
61                "WHERE accountID = 12345";
62
63             PreparedStatement selectStatement =
64                bankOneConnection.prepareStatement( select );
65
66             ResultSet resultSet = selectStatement.executeQuery();
67
68             // get first record in ResultSet and return balance
69             if ( resultSet.next() )
70                return resultSet.getDouble( "balance" );
71             else
72                throw new EJBException( "Account not found" );
73
74          } // end try
75
76          // handle exception when getting Account balance
77          catch ( SQLException sqlException ) {
78             throw new EJBException( sqlException );
79          }
80
81       } // end method getBankABCBalance
82
83       // get balance of Account at BankXYZ
84       public double getBankXYZBalance() throws EJBException
85       {
86          // get balance of Account at BankXYZ
87          try {
88
89             // select balance for Account # 54321
90             String select = "SELECT balance FROM Account " +
91                "WHERE accountID = 54321";
92
93             PreparedStatement selectStatement =
94                bankTwoConnection.prepareStatement( select );
95
96             ResultSet resultSet = selectStatement.executeQuery();
97
```

Fig. 14.28 **MoneyTransferEJB** implementation of **MoneyTransfer** remote interface using container-managed transaction demarcation (part 2 of 5).

```
98              // get first record in ResultSet and return balance
99              if ( resultSet.next() )
100                 return resultSet.getDouble( "balance" );
101             else
102                 throw new EJBException( "Account not found" );
103
104         } // end try
105
106         // handle exception when getting Account balance
107         catch ( SQLException sqlException ) {
108             throw new EJBException( sqlException );
109         }
110
111     } // end method getBankXYZBalance
112
113     // set SessionContext
114     public void setSessionContext( SessionContext context )
115         throws EJBException
116     {
117         sessionContext = context;
118
119         openDatabaseResources();
120     }
121
122     // create MoneyTransfer instance
123     public void ejbCreate() {}
124
125     // remove MoneyTransfer instance
126     public void ejbRemove() throws EJBException
127     {
128         closeDatabaseResources();
129     }
130
131     // passivate MoneyTransfer instance
132     public void ejbPassivate() throws EJBException
133     {
134         closeDatabaseResources();
135     }
136
137     // activate MoneyTransfer instance
138     public void ejbActivate() throws EJBException
139     {
140         openDatabaseResources();
141     }
142
143     // close database Connections and PreparedStatements
144     private void closeDatabaseResources() throws EJBException
145     {
146         // close database resources
147         try {
148
```

Fig. 14.28 **MoneyTransferEJB** implementation of **MoneyTransfer** remote interface using container-managed transaction demarcation (part 3 of 5).

```
149            // close PreparedStatements
150            depositStatement.close();
151            depositStatement = null;
152
153            withdrawalStatement.close();
154            withdrawalStatement = null;
155
156            // close database Connections
157            bankOneConnection.close();
158            bankOneConnection = null;
159
160            bankTwoConnection.close();
161            bankTwoConnection = null;
162         }
163
164         // handle exception closing database connections
165         catch ( SQLException sqlException ) {
166            throw new EJBException( sqlException );
167         }
168
169      } // end method closeDatabaseConnections
170
171      // open database Connections and create PreparedStatements
172      private void openDatabaseResources() throws EJBException
173      {
174         // look up the BankABC and BankXYZ DataSources and create
175         // Connections for each
176         try {
177            Context initialContext = new InitialContext();
178
179            // get DataSource reference from JNDI directory
180            DataSource dataSource = ( DataSource )
181               initialContext.lookup(
182                  "java:comp/env/jdbc/BankABC" );
183
184            // get Connection from DataSource
185            bankOneConnection = dataSource.getConnection();
186
187            dataSource = ( DataSource) initialContext.lookup(
188               "java:comp/env/jdbc/BankXYZ" );
189
190            bankTwoConnection = dataSource.getConnection();
191
192            // prepare withdraw statement for account #12345 at
193            // BankABC
194            String withdrawal = "UPDATE Account SET balance = " +
195               "balance - ? WHERE accountID = 12345";
196
197            withdrawalStatement =
198               bankOneConnection.prepareStatement( withdrawal );
199
```

Fig. 14.28 MoneyTransferEJB implementation of **MoneyTransfer** remote
interface using container-managed transaction demarcation (part 4 of 5).

```
200          // prepare deposit statment for account #54321 at
201          // BankXYZ
202          String deposit = "UPDATE Account SET balance = " +
203             "balance + ? WHERE accountID = 54321";
204
205          depositStatement =
206             bankTwoConnection.prepareStatement( deposit );
207
208       } // end try
209
210       // handle exception if DataSource not found in directory
211       catch ( NamingException namingException ) {
212          throw new EJBException( namingException );
213       }
214
215       // handle exception getting Connection to DataSource
216       catch ( SQLException sqlException ) {
217          throw new EJBException( sqlException );
218       }
219
220    } // end method openDatabaseConnections
221 }
```

Fig. 14.28 `MoneyTransferEJB` implementation of `MoneyTransfer` remote interface using container-managed transaction demarcation (part 5 of 5).

Line 66 throws an **EJBException** in response to any **SQLException** thrown from lines 29–41. The **EJBContainer** rolls back the current **transaction** when method **transfer** throws an **EJBException** (line 48).

Figure 14.29 lists the available transaction types for container-managed persistence. The deployer specifies the transaction type for each business method when deploying the application.

Transaction Type	Description
NotSupported	Method does not support transactions. The EJB container suspends the existing transaction context if the method is invoked within a transaction context.
Required	Method requires a transaction. The EJB container creates a new transaction if the method is invoked without an existing transaction context and commits the transaction at the end of the method.
Supports	Method supports transactions. The EJB container will not create a new transaction if the method is invoked without an existing transaction context, but will execute the method as part of an existing transaction context if one is available.
RequiresNew	Method requires a new transaction. The EJB container suspends the existing transaction context and starts a new transaction if the method is invoked as part of another transaction.

Fig. 14.29 Transaction types for container-managed transaction demarcation (part 1 of 2).

Transaction Type	Description
`Mandatory`	The method must execute in an existing transaction context. The EJB container throws a **`TransactionRequiredException`** if the method is invoked without a valid transaction context.
`Never`	The method must not execute in a transaction context. The EJB container throws a **`RemoteException`** if the method is invoked inside a transaction context.

Fig. 14.29 Transaction types for container-managed transaction demarcation (part 2 of 2).

14.4.4 `MoneyTransfer` EJB Client

`MoneyTransferEJBClient` (Fig. 14.30) provides a user interface for interacting with the **`MoneyTransfer`** EJB. Lines 24–26 declare **`JTextField`**s to display the account balances and accept a user-input **`transfer amount`**. Line 34 invokes method **`createMoneyTransfer`** to create a new **`MoneyTransfer`** EJB instance. Line 37 invokes method **`createGUI`** to create and lay out GUI components for the application. The GUI consists of **`JTextField`**s for displaying account balances and inputting the transfer amount and a **`JButton`** for transferring funds. Line 40 invokes method **`displayBalances`** to display the current account balances at **`BankABC`** and **`BankXYZ`**.

Method **`createMoneyTransfer`** (lines 47–80) uses the **`MoneyTransferHome`** interface to create a **`MoneyTransfer`** EJB instance. Line 51 creates an **`InitialContext`** for locating the **`MoneyTransfer`** EJB in the JNDI directory. Lines 54–59 invoke **`InitialContext`** method **`lookup`** to get a remote reference to the **`MoneyTransferHome`** interface. Line 62 creates a new **`MoneyTransfer`** EJB instance by invoking **`MoneyTransferHome`** method **`create`**.

Method **`getTransferButton`** (lines 108–142) creates a **`JButton`** to transfer funds from **`BankABC`** to **`BankXYZ`**. Lines 120–124 read the **`transfer amount`** from the user and invoke **`MoneyTransfer`** method **`transfer`**. Line 127 invokes method **`displayBalances`** to update the display with the new account balances.

```
1   // MoneyTransferEJBClient.java
2   // MoneyTransferEJBClient is a client for interacting with
3   // the MoneyTransfer EJB.
4   package com.deitel.advjhtp1.ejb.transactions.client;
5
6   // Java core libraries
7   import java.awt.*;
8   import java.awt.event.*;
9   import java.rmi.*;
10
11  // Java standard extensions
12  import javax.swing.*;
```

Fig. 14.30 **`MoneyTransferEJBClient`** for interacting with **`MoneyTransfer`** EJB (part 1 of 6).

```
13   import javax.ejb.*;
14   import javax.rmi.*;
15   import javax.naming.*;
16
17   // Deitel libraries
18   import com.deitel.advjhtp1.ejb.transactions.*;
19
20   public class MoneyTransferEJBClient extends JFrame {
21
22      private MoneyTransfer moneyTransfer;
23
24      private JTextField bankABCBalanceTextField;
25      private JTextField bankXYZBalanceTextField;
26      private JTextField transferAmountTextField;
27
28      // MoneyTransferEJBClient constructor
29      public MoneyTransferEJBClient( String JNDIName )
30      {
31         super( "MoneyTransferEJBClient" );
32
33         // create MoneyTransfer EJB for transferring money
34         createMoneyTransfer( JNDIName );
35
36         // create and lay out GUI components
37         createGUI();
38
39         // display current balances at BankABC and BankXYZ
40         displayBalances();
41
42         setSize( 400, 300 );
43         setVisible( true );
44      }
45
46      // create MoneyTransferEJB for transferring money
47      private void createMoneyTransfer( String JNDIName )
48      {
49         // look up MoneyTransfer EJB using given JNDIName
50         try {
51            InitialContext context = new InitialContext();
52
53            // lookup MoneyTransfer EJB
54            Object homeObject = context.lookup( JNDIName );
55
56            // get MoneyTransfer interface
57            MoneyTransferHome moneyTransferHome =
58               ( MoneyTransferHome ) PortableRemoteObject.narrow(
59                  homeObject, MoneyTransferHome.class );
60
61            // create MathTool EJB instance
62            moneyTransfer = moneyTransferHome.create();
63
64         } // end try
```

Fig. 14.30 MoneyTransferEJBClient for interacting with
   MoneyTransfer EJB (part 2 of 6).

```
65
66         // handle exception when looking up MoneyTransfer EJB
67         catch ( NamingException namingException ) {
68            namingException.printStackTrace();
69         }
70
71         // handle exception when looking up MoneyTransfer EJB
72         catch ( CreateException createException ) {
73            createException.printStackTrace();
74         }
75
76         // handle exception when looking up MoneyTransfer EJB
77         catch ( RemoteException remoteException ) {
78            remoteException.printStackTrace();
79         }
80     } // end method createMoneyTransfer
81
82     // display balance in account at BankABC
83     private void displayBalances()
84     {
85         try {
86
87            // get and display BankABC Account balance
88            double balance = moneyTransfer.getBankABCBalance();
89
90            bankABCBalanceTextField.setText(
91               String.valueOf( balance ) );
92
93            // get and display BankXYZ Account balance
94            balance = moneyTransfer.getBankXYZBalance();
95
96            bankXYZBalanceTextField.setText(
97               String.valueOf( balance ) );
98         }
99
100        // handle exception when invoke MoneyTransfer EJB methods
101        catch ( RemoteException remoteException ) {
102           JOptionPane.showMessageDialog( this,
103              remoteException.getMessage() );
104        }
105    } // end method displayBalances
106
107    // create button to transfer funds between accounts
108    private JButton getTransferButton()
109    {
110        JButton transferButton = new JButton( "Transfer" );
111
112        transferButton.addActionListener(
113           new ActionListener() {
114
115              public void actionPerformed( ActionEvent event )
116              {
```

Fig. 14.30 MoneyTransferEJBClient for interacting with
   MoneyTransfer EJB (part 3 of 6).

```
117                  try {
118
119                      // get transfer amount from JTextField
120                      double amount = Double.parseDouble(
121                         transferAmountTextField.getText() );
122
123                      // transfer money
124                      moneyTransfer.transfer( amount );
125
126                      // display new balances
127                      displayBalances();
128                  }
129
130                  // handle exception when transferring money
131                  catch ( RemoteException remoteException ) {
132                      JOptionPane.showMessageDialog(
133                         MoneyTransferEJBClient.this,
134                         remoteException.getMessage() );
135                  }
136             } // end method actionPerformed
137         }
138      ); // end addActionListener
139
140      return transferButton;
141
142  } // end method getTransferButton
143
144  // create and lay out GUI components
145  private void createGUI()
146  {
147      // create JTextFields for user input and display
148      bankABCBalanceTextField = new JTextField( 10 );
149      bankABCBalanceTextField.setEditable( false );
150
151      bankXYZBalanceTextField = new JTextField( 10 );
152      bankXYZBalanceTextField.setEditable( false );
153
154      transferAmountTextField = new JTextField( 10 );
155
156      // create button to transfer between accounts
157      JButton transferButton = getTransferButton();
158
159      // layout user interface
160      Container contentPane = getContentPane();
161      contentPane.setLayout( new GridLayout( 3, 2 ) );
162
163      contentPane.add( transferButton );
164      contentPane.add( transferAmountTextField );
165
166      contentPane.add( new JLabel( "Bank ABC Balance: " ) );
167      contentPane.add( bankABCBalanceTextField );
```

Fig. 14.30 `MoneyTransferEJBClient` for interacting with
`MoneyTransfer` EJB (part 4 of 6).

```
168
169        contentPane.add( new JLabel( "Bank XYZ Balance: " ) );
170        contentPane.add( bankXYZBalanceTextField );
171
172     } // end method createGUI
173
174     // get WindowListener for exiting application
175     private WindowListener getWindowListener()
176     {
177        // remove MoneyTransfer EJB when user exits application
178        return new WindowAdapter() {
179
180           public void windowClosing( WindowEvent event ) {
181
182              // remove MoneyTransfer EJB
183              try {
184                 moneyTransfer.remove();
185              }
186
187              // handle exception removing MoneyTransfer EJB
188              catch ( RemoveException removeException ) {
189                 removeException.printStackTrace();
190                 System.exit( 1 );
191              }
192
193              // handle exception removing MoneyTransfer EJB
194              catch ( RemoteException remoteException ) {
195                 remoteException.printStackTrace();
196                 System.exit( 1 );
197              }
198
199              System.exit( 0 );
200
201           } // end method windowClosing
202        };
203     } // end method getWindowListener
204
205     // execute application
206     public static void main( String[] args )
207     {
208        // ensure user provided JNDI name for MoneyTransfer EJB
209        if ( args.length != 1 )
210           System.err.println(
211              "Usage: java MoneyTransferEJBClient <JNDI Name>" );
212
213        // start application using provided JNDI name
214        else
215           new MoneyTransferEJBClient( args[ 0 ] );
216     }
217 }
```

Fig. 14.30 MoneyTransferEJBClient for interacting with
MoneyTransfer EJB (part 5 of 6).

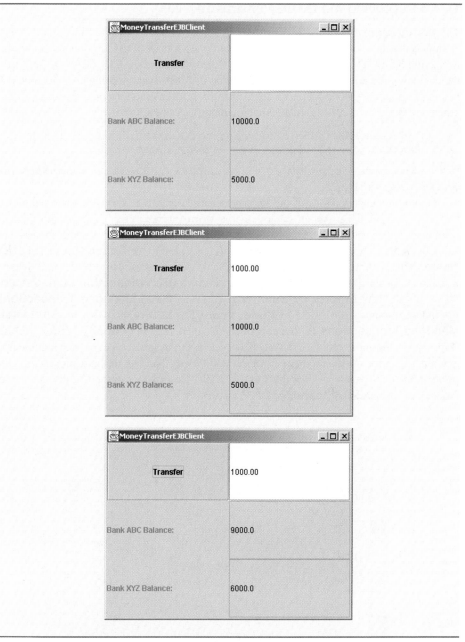

Fig. 14.30 `MoneyTransferEJBClient` for interacting with
`MoneyTransfer` EJB (part 6 of 6).

Figure 14.30 shows three screen captures of **MoneyTransferEJBClient**. Enter
any legal value in the text field and press the **Transfer** button. This causes the EJB to
update the database entries. The client then updates its GUI to reflect the new account balances.

14.4.5 Deploying the `MoneyTransfer` EJB

The **MoneyTransfer** EJB accesses two databases that store account information. The examples use the Cloudscape DBMS introduced in Chapter 8, JDBC. Follow the directions in Section 8.5 to set up the databases for the **MoneyTransfer** EJB. The SQL script for the databases, **transactions.sql**, is on the CD-ROM that accompanies this book. If you have not already done so, please see Appendix E for instructions on integrating Cloudscape with the J2EE 1.2.1 reference implementation. Add the following

```
|jdbc/BankABC|jdbc:cloudscape:rmi:BankABC;create=true;|jdbc/
BankXYZ|jdbc:cloudscape:rmi:BankXYZ;create=true;
```

to the **jdbc.datasources** property in the file **C:\j2sdkee1.2.1\config\default.properties**.

Deploying each versions of the **MoneyTransfer** EJB is very similar to deploying the other session EJBs. When deploying the **MoneyTransfer** EJB, we must create resource references to the two databases in the **New Enterprise Bean Wizard** (Fig. 14.31). Click the **Add** button to add a new resource reference. Fill in the **Coded Name** and **JNDI Name** fields with **jdbc/BankABC** for the BankABC database (Fig. 14.32) and **jdbc/BankXYZ** for the BankXYZ database (Fig. 14.33). In the **Transaction Management** dialog of the **New Enterprise Bean Wizard** select **Bean-Managed Transactions** for the bean-managed version of **MoneyTransferEJB** (Fig. 14.34) or **Container-Managed Transactions** for the container-managed version of **MoneyTransferEJB** (Fig. 14.35). For the container-managed EJB, select a transaction type for each method (see Section 14.4.3 for information about transaction types). The rest of the deployment is the same as the deployment of the other session EJBs. Be sure to run the Cloudscape server before executing **MoneyTransferEJBClient**.

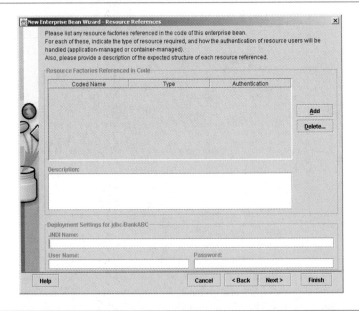

Fig. 14.31 Resource References dialog of New Enterprise Bean Wizard.

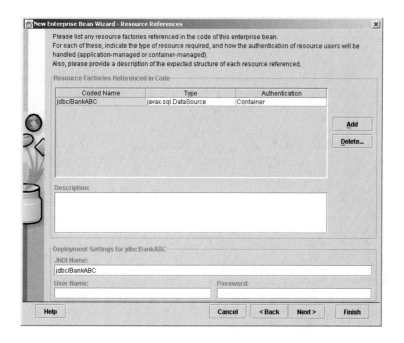

Fig. 14.32 Add **Resource Reference** for BankABC.

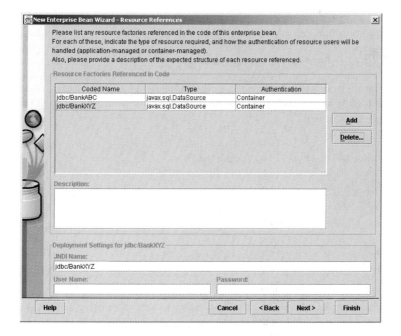

Fig. 14.33 Add **Resource Reference** for BankXYZ.

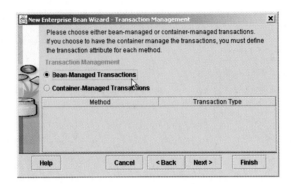

Fig. 14.34 Selecting **Bean-Managed Transactions**.

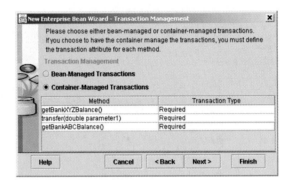

Fig. 14.35 Selecting **Container-Managed Transactions**.

14.5 Internet and World Wide Web Resources

java.sun.com/products/ejb
Sun's Enterprise Java Bean home page. Contains articles, documentation and examples.

www.javaworld.com/javaworld/topicalindex/jw-ti-ejb.html
List of EJB-related articles from JavaWorld.

www.jguru.com/faq/home.jsp?topic=EJB
List of frequently asked questions on EJBs at **jguru.com**.

www.theserverside.com
TheServerSide.com is an online community for J2EE developers. There are forums, articles and other resources for building applications with J2EE.

SUMMARY

- Every EJB consists of a remote interface, a home interface and an EJB implementation.
- The remote interface declares business methods that clients of the EJB may invoke. The home interface provides **create** methods for creating new instances of the EJB, *finder* methods for finding instances of the EJB and **remove** methods for removing instances of the EJB. The EJB implementation defines the business methods declared in the remote interface and the **create**, **remove** and *finder* methods of the home interface.

- EJBs have a complex life cycle that is managed by an EJB container. The EJB container creates classes that implement the home and remote interfaces.

- The J2EE specification defines six roles for implementing enterprise systems. Each role is responsible for producing some part of an enterprise application.

- The remote interface for an EJB declares the business methods that clients of the EJB may invoke. The remote interface must extend interface **javax.ejb.EJBObject**.

- Each method of the remote interface is required to declare that it throws **java.rmi.RemoteException**. Each method also may throw application-specific exceptions—for example, an **IllegalArgumentException** if a provided argument does not meet certain criteria.

- The home interface for an EJB declares methods for creating, removing and finding EJB instances. The home interface must extend interface **javax.ejb.EJBHome**.

- Depending on the EJB type (i.e., session or entity), the container invokes EJB implementation methods that correspond to methods **create** and **remove** and *finder* methods of the home interface.

- The EJB implementation defines the business methods declared in the EJB remote interface and the **create**, **remove** and *finder* methods declared in the EJB home interface. The EJB implementation must also implement the methods of interface **javax.ejb.SessionBean** for session EJBs, or interface **javax.ejb.EntityBean** for entity EJBs.

- The EJB container manages the life cycle, client interactions and method invocations, transactions, security and exceptions of an EJB. Clients of an EJB do not interact directly with the EJB. When a client invokes a business method of the EJB's remote interface, the invocation goes first to the EJB container, which then delegates the business method invocation to the EJB implementation.

- Session EJBs exist for the duration of a client's session. Each session EJB instance is associated with a single client. Session EJBs can manipulate data in a database, but unlike entity EJBs, session EJBs are not persistent and do not represent database data directly.

- Stateful session EJBs maintain state information between business method invocations. For example, a stateful session EJB could maintain information about a customer's shopping cart while the customer browses an on-line store.

- Interface **SessionContext** extends interface **EJBContext**, which provides methods for obtaining information about the EJB container.

- The EJB container invokes method **ejbCreate** when a client invokes a **create** method in the home interface. The EJB implementation must provide an **ejbCreate** method for each **create** method declared in the home interface. The **ejbCreate** methods must have the same number and types of arguments as their corresponding **create** methods.

- The EJB container invokes method **ejbRemove** in response to an invocation of method **remove** in the home interface.

- The EJB container invokes method **ejbPassivate** when it determines that the EJB is no longer needed in memory.

- The EJB container invokes method **ejbActivate** to restore an EJB instance that the container passivated previously. The EJB container activates an EJB instance if a client invokes a business method of that EJB instance.

- RMI-IIOP allows RMI objects to interact with CORBA components, which communicate using the *Internet Inter-Orb Protocol* (IIOP). CORBA is a language-independent framework for building distributed systems. To enable interoperability among EJBs and CORBA components, EJBs communicate using RMI-IIOP. We discuss CORBA and RMI-IIOP in detail in Chapter 22.

- Stateless session EJBs maintain no state information between business method invocations. As a result, any stateless session EJB instance can be used to respond to any client's request. This improves the performance of stateless session EJBs over stateful session EJBs.

- The Java 2 Enterprise Edition supports distributed transactions. A distributed transaction is a transaction that is applied across multiple databases or across multiple EJB servers.

- J2EE supports two methods for defining transaction boundaries: bean-managed transaction demarcation and container-managed transaction demarcation. Bean-managed transaction demarcation requires the EJB developer to code the transaction boundaries manually in the EJBs, using the Java Transaction Services. Container-managed transaction demarcation allows the EJB deployer to specify transaction boundaries declaratively when deploying EJBs.

- Bean-managed transaction demarcation requires the EJB developer to code the transaction boundaries manually in the EJBs. Bean-managed transaction demarcation may be used only with session EJBs.

- Container-managed transaction demarcation allows the EJB developer to implement an EJB without specifying transaction boundaries. The EJB deployer provides transaction demarcation semantics declaratively when deploying the application.

TERMINOLOGY

application server
bean-managed transaction demarcation
business methods
container-managed transaction demarcation
CORBA (Common Object Request
   Broker Architecture)
create methods
distributed transaction
EJB container
EJB implementation
EJB server
ejbActivate method
EJBContext interface
ejbCreate methods
ejbPassivate method
ejbRemove method
Enterprise JavaBeans (EJBs)
entity EJB
home interface
IllegalArgumentException

Internet Inter-Orb Protocol (IIOP)
J2EE (Java 2 Enterprise Edition)
Java Transaction Services (JTS)
java.rmi.RemoteException
java:comp/env naming context
javax.ejb.EJBHome
javax.ejb.EJBObject
javax.ejb.SessionBean
JNDI (Java Naming and Directory
   Interface) directory
least recently used
naming context
remote interface of an EJB
remove methods
RMI-IIOP
session EJB
SessionContext interface
stateful session EJB
stateless session EJB

SELF-REVIEW EXERCISES

14.1   What are the two main types of session EJBs? What is the primary difference between them?

14.2   What three Java objects must the EJB developer provide for each EJB?

14.3   What are the responsibilities of the EJB container?

14.4   How does a client get a remote reference to an EJB instance?

14.5   What types of transaction demarcation can EJBs use? What are the benefits of each type?

ANSWERS TO SELF-REVIEW EXERCISES

14.1   There are stateful session EJBs and stateless session EJBs. Stateful session EJBs maintain state information between business method invocations in a client's session. Stateless session EJBs maintain no state information between business method invocations.

14.2   The EJB developer must provide a remote interface, a home interface and the EJB implementation.

14.3   The EJB container is responsible for managing the life cycle of the EJB. The EJB container creates classes to implement the home and remote interfaces, and delegates business method invocations to the developer-supplied EJB implementation. The EJB container also provides runtime resources, such as database connections and transactions, as well as life-cycle management.

14.4   A client looks up the EJB's home interface in a JNDI directory. For session EJBs, the client then invokes one of the home interface's **create** methods. For entity EJBs, the client can invoke one of the home interface's **create** methods or *finder* methods.

14.5   EJBs can use either bean-managed or container-managed transaction demarcation. Bean-managed transaction demarcation allows the developer to have fine-grained control over transaction boundaries. Container-managed transaction demarcation simplifies the EJB implementation by allowing the EJB deployer to specify transaction boundaries declaratively at deployment time.

EXERCISES

14.6   Stateless session EJBs offer a performance advantage over stateful session beans. Convert the example of Fig. 14.3, Fig. 14.4, Fig. 14.5 and Fig. 14.6 from a stateful session EJB to a stateless session EJB.

14.7   Add a new recursive business method **power(base, exponent)** to the **MathTool** EJB (Fig. 14.21, Fig. 14.22, Fig. 14.23) that, when invoked, returns

$$base^{exponent}$$

For example, **power(3, 4) = 3 * 3 * 3 * 3**. If the **exponent** is not an integer greater than or equal to **1**, **throw** an **IllegalArgumentException**. [*Hint*: The recursion step would use the relationship

$$base^{exponent} = base \cdot base^{exponent - 1}$$

and the terminating condition occurs when exponent is equal to 1 because

$$base^{1} = base$$

Modify the client in Fig. 14.24 to enable the user to enter the **base** and **exponent**.]

15

Entity EJBs

Objectives

- To understand how entity EJBs represent persistent data.
- To understand synchronization issues between EJBs and database data.
- To understand the life-cycle of an entity EJB.
- To understand the advantages and disadvantages of container-managed and bean-managed persistence.

There is nothing more requisite in business than dispatch.
Joseph Addison

All meanings, we know, depend on the key of interpretation.
George Eliot

Events that are predestined require but little management. They manage themselves. They slip into place while we sleep, and suddenly we are aware that the thing we fear to attempt, is already accomplished.
Amelia Barr

Outline

15.1 Introduction

A fundamental part of an enterprise application is the information tier, which maintains data for the application. In this chapter, we introduce *entity EJBs*, which enable developers to build object-based representations of information-tier data, such as data stored in a relational database. EJB containers provide advanced features that simplify developing entity EJBs. For example, based on information provided at deployment time (e.g., SQL queries), an entity EJB's container can generate code automatically for storing and retrieving data represented by the EJB. For entity EJBs that represent more complex data (e.g., data stored in multiple database tables), the programmer can implement code for storing and retrieving the data manually.

In this chapter, we present two versions of an entity EJB that represents a company employee. The first version demonstrates an entity EJB that uses JDBC to persist data to a relational database. The second version takes advantage of the container's ability to manage data storage and retrieval to simplify the EJB implementation. After completing this chapter, you will be able to build and deploy entity EJBs through which business-logic components, such as session EJBs (Chapter 14), can access data in the information tier.

15.2 Entity EJB Overview

Each entity EJB instance represents a particular unit of data, such as a record in a database table. There are two types of entity EJBs—those that use *bean-managed persistence* and those that use *container-managed persistence*. Entity EJBs that use bean-managed persistence must implement code for storing and retrieving data from the persistent data sources they represent. For example, an entity EJB that uses bean-managed persistence might use the JDBC API to store and retrieve data in a relational database. Entity EJBs that use container-managed persistence rely on the EJB container to implement the data-access calls to their persistent data sources. The deployer must supply information about the persistent data source when deploying the EJB.

Entity EJBs provide **create** methods for creating new EJB instances, **remove** methods for removing EJB instances and *finder* methods for finding EJB instances. For entity EJBs that represent information in a database, each **create** method performs **INSERT** operations to create new records in the database, and each **remove** method performs **DELETE** operations to remove records from the database. Each *finder* method locates entity EJB instances that conform to certain search criteria (e.g using **SELECT** operations). We discuss each of these method types throughout the chapter.

15.3 **Employee** Entity EJB

In the following sections, we build an entity EJB that represents an **Employee**. We provide two implementations of the **Employee** EJB. The first implementation (Section 15.5) uses bean-managed persistence to store and retrieve **Employee** information in an underlying database. The second implementation (Section 15.6) uses container-managed persistence. Both of these implementations use the same **Employee** remote interface and **EmployeeHome** interface, which we present in Section 15.4.

We use the Cloudscape database for storing **Employee** data. To create the **Employee** database, run the SQL script **employee.sql** that is on the CD-ROM that accompanies the book. Please see Chapter 8, JDBC, for instructions on running SQL scripts in Cloudscape. To configure the J2EE reference implementation to use the **Employee** database, append the text

```
|jdbc/Employee|jdbc:cloudscape:rmi:Employee;create=true
```

to the end of the **jdbc.datasources** property in the J2EE **default.properties** configuration file.

15.4 **Employee** EJB Home and Remote Interfaces

The **Employee** remote interface (Fig. 15.1) provides methods for setting and getting **Employee** information. Note that interface **Employee** extends interface **EJBObject** (line 11). This is a requirement for all EJB remote interfaces. The **Employee** remote interface provides *set* and *get* methods for each **Employee** property, including the **socialSecurityNumber**, **firstName**, **lastName**, **title** and **salary**. There is no *set* method for property **employeeID** because **employeeID** is the primary key. Each *set* and *get* method throws a **RemoteException**. This is required of all methods in the remote interface.

```
1    // Employee.java
2    // Employee is the remote interface for the Address EJB.
3    package com.deitel.advjhtp1.ejb.entity;
4
5    // Java core libraries
6    import java.rmi.RemoteException;
7
8    // Java standard extensions
9    import javax.ejb.EJBObject;
10
11   public interface Employee extends EJBObject {
```

Fig. 15.1 **Employee** remote interface for setting and getting **Employee** information (part 1 of 2).

```
12
13      // get Employee ID
14      public Integer getEmployeeID() throws RemoteException;
15
16      // set social security number
17      public void setSocialSecurityNumber( String number )
18         throws RemoteException;
19
20      // get social security number
21      public String getSocialSecurityNumber()
22         throws RemoteException;
23
24      // set first name
25      public void setFirstName( String name )
26         throws RemoteException;
27
28      // get first name
29      public String getFirstName() throws RemoteException;
30
31      // set last name
32      public void setLastName( String name )
33         throws RemoteException;
34
35      // get last name
36      public String getLastName() throws RemoteException;
37
38      // set title
39      public void setTitle( String title )
40         throws RemoteException;
41
42      // get title
43      public String getTitle() throws RemoteException;
44
45      // set salary
46      public void setSalary( Double salary ) throws RemoteException;
47
48      // get salary
49      public Double getSalary() throws RemoteException;
50   }
```

Fig. 15.1   **Employee** remote interface for setting and getting **Employee**
information (part 2 of 2).

An EJB instance represents a particular row in the corresponding database table. The
home interface for an entity EJB represents the table as a whole. The home interface provides *finder* methods for locating particular rows in the table and *create* methods for
inserting new records. Interface **EmployeeHome** (Fig. 15.2) provides *finder* method
findByPrimaryKey (lines 15–16) to locate instances of the **Employee** EJB based on
a primary key. The primary key for the **Employee** EJB is the **employeeID**. Method
findByPrimaryKey throws a **FinderException** if the **Employee** with the given
primaryKey cannot be found. Method **create** (lines 19–20) creates new instances of
the **Employee** EJB. Method **create throws** a **CreateException** if there is a
problem with creating the EJB instance.

```
1   // EmployeeHome.java
2   // EmployeeHome is the home interface for the Employee EJB.
3   package com.deitel.advjhtp1.ejb.entity;
4
5   // Java core libraries
6   import java.rmi.*;
7   import java.util.*;
8
9   // Java standard extensions
10  import javax.ejb.*;
11
12  public interface EmployeeHome extends EJBHome {
13
14     // find Employee with given primary key
15     public Employee findByPrimaryKey( Integer primaryKey )
16        throws RemoteException, FinderException;
17
18     // create new Employee EJB
19     public Employee create( Integer primaryKey )
20        throws RemoteException, CreateException;
21  }
```

Fig. 15.2   **EmployeeHome** interface for finding and creating **Employee** EJBs.

Method **findByPrimaryKey** is one type of *finder* method for entity EJBs. Every entity EJB must have a **findByPrimaryKey** method that takes the entity EJB's primary-key class as an argument. Entity EJBs also can define additional *finder* methods. A *finder* method name must begin with **findBy** and should end with the name of property to be used as the search criteria. For example, a *finder* method for finding **Employee**s based on the **title** property would be named **findByTitle**. A *finder* method for finding **Employee**s within a certain salary range would be named **findBySalaryRange**.

15.5 Employee EJB with Bean-Managed Persistence

This section describes the **Employee** EJB with bean-managed persistence and deploying the EJB. This bean-managed implementation uses JDBC to store **Employee** data in an underlying database.

15.5.1 Employee EJB Implementation

Figure 15.3 shows the **Employee** EJB implementation using bean-managed persistence. Class **EmployeeEJB** implements interface **EntityBean** (line 15). All entity EJB implementations must implement interface **EntityBean**. Line 17 declares an **EntityContext** reference for the EJB's **EntityContext**. The **EntityContext** provides the EJB with information about the container in which the EJB is deployed. The **Connection** object (line 18) is the EJB's **Connection** to the **Employee** database. Lines 20–25 declare **private** member variables that cache data retrieved from the database and updates from the client.

```
1    // EmployeeEJB.java
2    // EmployeeEJB is an entity EJB that uses bean-managed
3    // persistence to persist Employee data in a database.
4    package com.deitel.advjhtp1.ejb.entity.bmp;
5
6    // Java core libraries
7    import java.sql.*;
8    import java.rmi.RemoteException;
9
10   // Java standard extensions
11   import javax.ejb.*;
12   import javax.sql.*;
13   import javax.naming.*;
14
15   public class EmployeeEJB implements EntityBean {
16
17       private EntityContext entityContext;
18       private Connection connection;
19
20       private Integer employeeID;
21       private String socialSecurityNumber;
22       private String firstName;
23       private String lastName;
24       private String title;
25       private Double salary;
26
27       // get Employee ID
28       public Integer getEmployeeID()
29       {
30           return employeeID;
31       }
32
33       // set social security number
34       public void setSocialSecurityNumber( String number )
35       {
36           socialSecurityNumber = number;
37       }
38
39       // get social security number
40       public String getSocialSecurityNumber()
41       {
42           return socialSecurityNumber;
43       }
44
45       // set first name
46       public void setFirstName( String name )
47       {
48           firstName = name;
49       }
50
```

Fig. 15.3 **EmployeeEJB** implementation of **Employee** remote interface using bean-managed persistence (part 1 of 8).

```
51        // get first name
52        public String getFirstName()
53        {
54            return firstName;
55        }
56
57        // set last name
58        public void setLastName( String name )
59        {
60            lastName = name;
61        }
62
63        // get last name
64        public String getLastName()
65        {
66            return lastName;
67        }
68
69        // set title
70        public void setTitle( String jobTitle )
71        {ey
72            title = jobTitle;
73        }
74
75        // get title
76        public String getTitle()
77        {
78            return title;
79        }
80
81        // set salary
82        public void setSalary( Double amount )
83        {
84            salary = amount;
85        }
86
87        // get salary
88        public Double getSalary()
89        {
90            return salary;
91        }
92
93        // create new Employee
94        public Integer ejbCreate( Integer primaryKey )
95            throws CreateException
96        {
97            employeeID = primaryKey;
98
99            // INSERT new Employee in database
100           try {
101
```

Fig. 15.3 **EmployeeEJB** implementation of **Employee** remote interface using bean-managed persistence (part 2 of 8).

```
102            // create INSERT statement
103            String insert = "INSERT INTO Employee " +
104               "( employeeID ) VALUES ( ? )";
105
106            // create PreparedStatement to perform INSERT
107            PreparedStatement insertStatement =
108               connection.prepareStatement( insert );
109
110            // set values for PreparedStatement
111            insertStatement.setInt( 1, employeeID.intValue() );
112
113            // execute INSERT and close PreparedStatement
114            insertStatement.executeUpdate();
115            insertStatement.close();
116
117            return employeeID;
118         }
119
120      // throw EJBException if INSERT fails
121      catch ( SQLException sqlException ) {
122         throw new CreateException( sqlException.getMessage() );
123      }
124   } // end method ejbCreate
125
126   // do post-creation tasks when creating new Employee
127   public void ejbPostCreate( Integer primaryKey ) {}
128
129   // remove Employee information from database
130   public void ejbRemove() throws RemoveException
131   {
132      // DELETE Employee record
133      try {
134
135         // get primary key of Employee to be removed
136         Integer primaryKey =
137            ( Integer ) entityContext.getPrimaryKey();
138
139         // create DELETE statement
140         String delete = "DELETE FROM Employee WHERE " +
141            "employeeID = ?";
142
143         // create PreparedStatement to perform DELETE
144         PreparedStatement deleteStatement =
145            connection.prepareStatement( delete );
146
147         // set values for PreparedStatement
148         deleteStatement.setInt( 1, primaryKey.intValue() );
149
150         // execute DELETE and close PreparedStatement
151         deleteStatement.executeUpdate();
152         deleteStatement.close();
153      }
```

Fig. 15.3 **EmployeeEJB** implementation of **Employee** remote interface using bean-managed persistence (part 3 of 8).

```
154
155        // throw new EJBException if DELETE fails
156        catch ( SQLException sqlException ) {
157          throw new RemoveException( sqlException.getMessage() );
158        }
159     } // end method ejbRemove
160
161     // store Employee information in database
162     public void ejbStore() throws EJBException
163     {
164        // UPDATE Employee record
165        try {
166
167           // get primary key for Employee to be updated
168           Integer primaryKey =
169              ( Integer ) entityContext.getPrimaryKey();
170
171           // create UPDATE statement
172           String update = "UPDATE Employee SET " +
173              "socialSecurityNumber = ?, firstName = ?, " +
174              "lastName = ?, title = ?, salary = ? " +
175              "WHERE employeeID = ?";
176
177           // create PreparedStatement to perform UPDATE
178           PreparedStatement updateStatement =
179              connection.prepareStatement( update );
180
181           // set values in PreparedStatement
182           updateStatement.setString( 1,socialSecurityNumber);
183           updateStatement.setString( 2,firstName );
184           updateStatement.setString( 3,lastName );
185           updateStatement.setString( 4,title );
186           updateStatement.setDouble( 5,salary.doubleValue());
187           updateStatement.setInt( 6, primaryKey.intValue() );
188
189           // execute UPDATE and close PreparedStatement
190           updateStatement.executeUpdate();
191           updateStatement.close();
192        }
193
194        // throw EJBException if UPDATE fails
195        catch ( SQLException sqlException ) {
196           throw new EJBException( sqlException );
197        }
198     } // end method ejbStore
199
200     // load Employee information from database
201     public void ejbLoad() throws EJBException
202     {
203        // get Employee record from Employee database table
204        try {
205
```

Fig. 15.3 **EmployeeEJB** implementation of **Employee** remote interface using bean-managed persistence (part 4 of 8).

```
206              // get primary key for Employee to be loaded
207              Integer primaryKey =
208                ( Integer ) entityContext.getPrimaryKey();
209
210              // create SELECT statement
211              String select = "SELECT * FROM Employee WHERE " +
212                "employeeID = ?";
213
214              // create PreparedStatement for SELECT
215              PreparedStatement selectStatement =
216                connection.prepareStatement( select );
217
218              // set employeeID value in PreparedStatement
219              selectStatement.setInt( 1, primaryKey.intValue() );
220
221              // execute selectStatement
222              ResultSet resultSet = selectStatement.executeQuery();
223
224              // get Employee information from ResultSet and update
225              // local member variables to cache data
226              if ( resultSet.next() ) {
227
228                 // get employeeID
229                 employeeID = new Integer( resultSet.getInt(
230                    "employeeID" ) );
231
232                 // get social-security number
233                 socialSecurityNumber = resultSet.getString(
234                    "socialSecurityNumber" );
235
236                 // get first name
237                 firstName = resultSet.getString( "firstName" );
238
239                 // get last name
240                 lastName = resultSet.getString( "lastName" );
241
242                 // get job title
243                 title = resultSet.getString( "title" );
244
245                 // get salary
246                 salary = new Double( resultSet.getDouble(
247                    "salary" ) );
248
249              } // end if
250
251              else
252                 throw new EJBException( "No such employee." );
253
254              // close PreparedStatement
255              selectStatement.close();
256
257           } // end try
```

Fig. 15.3 **EmployeeEJB** implementation of **Employee** remote interface using bean-managed persistence (part 5 of 8).

```
258
259        // throw EJBException if SELECT fails
260        catch ( SQLException sqlException ) {
261           throw new EJBException( sqlException );
262        }
263     } // end method ejbLoad
264
265     // find Employee using its primary key
266     public Integer ejbFindByPrimaryKey( Integer primaryKey )
267        throws FinderException, EJBException
268     {
269        // find Employee in database
270        try {
271
272           // create SELECT statement
273           String select = "SELECT employeeID FROM Employee " +
274              "WHERE employeeID = ?";
275
276           // create PreparedStatement for SELECT
277           PreparedStatement selectStatement =
278              connection.prepareStatement( select );
279
280           // set employeeID value in PreparedStatement
281           selectStatement.setInt( 1, primaryKey.intValue() );
282
283           // execute selectStatement
284           ResultSet resultSet = selectStatement.executeQuery();
285
286           // return primary key if SELECT returns a record
287           if ( resultSet.next() ) {
288
289              // close resultSet and selectStatement
290              resultSet.close();
291              selectStatement.close();
292
293              return primaryKey;
294           }
295
296           // throw ObjectNotFoundException if SELECT produces
297           // no records
298           else
299              throw new ObjectNotFoundException();
300        }
301
302        // throw EJBException if SELECT fails
303        catch ( SQLException sqlException ) {
304           throw new EJBException( sqlException );
305        }
306     } // end method ejbFindByPrimaryKey
307
```

Fig. 15.3 **EmployeeEJB** implementation of **Employee** remote interface using bean-managed persistence (part 6 of 8).

```
308     // set EntityContext and create DataSource Connection
309     public void setEntityContext( EntityContext context )
310        throws EJBException
311     {
312        // set entityContext
313        entityContext = context;
314
315        // look up the Employee DataSource and create Connection
316        try {
317           InitialContext initialContext = new InitialContext();
318
319           // get DataSource reference from JNDI directory
320           DataSource dataSource = ( DataSource )
321              initialContext.lookup(
322                 "java:comp/env/jdbc/Employee" );
323
324           // get Connection from DataSource
325           connection = dataSource.getConnection();
326        }
327
328        // handle exception if DataSource not found in directory
329        catch ( NamingException namingException ) {
330           throw new EJBException( namingException );
331        }
332
333        // handle exception when getting Connection to DataSource
334        catch ( SQLException sqlException ) {
335           throw new EJBException( sqlException );
336        }
337     } // end method setEntityContext
338
339     // unset EntityContext
340     public void unsetEntityContext() throws EJBException
341     {
342        entityContext = null;
343
344        // close DataSource Connection
345        try {
346           connection.close();
347        }
348
349        // throw EJBException if closing Connection fails
350        catch ( SQLException sqlException ) {
351           throw new EJBException( sqlException );
352        }
353
354        // prepare connection for reuse
355        finally {
356           connection = null;
357        }
358     }
359
```

Fig. 15.3   **EmployeeEJB** implementation of **Employee** remote interface using bean-managed persistence (part 7 of 8).

```
360      // set employeeID to null when container passivates EJB
361      public void ejbPassivate()
362      {
363         employeeID = null;
364      }
365
366      // get primary key value when container activates EJB
367      public void ejbActivate()
368      {
369         employeeID = ( Integer ) entityContext.getPrimaryKey();
370      }
371  }
```

Fig. 15.3 **EmployeeEJB** implementation of **Employee** remote interface using bean-managed persistence (part 8 of 8).

Lines 28–91 provide implementations of the *set* and *get* business methods declared in the **Employee** remote interface. When a client invokes interface **EmployeeHome** method **create**, the EJB container invokes method **ejbCreate** (lines 94–126). This EJB uses bean-managed persistence, so method **ejbCreate** must implement the appropriate logic to create a new **Employee** in the underlying database. Line 97 sets the **employeeID** member variable to the value of the **primaryKey** argument. Lines 103–111 create a **PreparedStatement** to **INSERT** the new **Employee** in the database. Line 111 sets the **employeeID** in the **PreparedStatement**, and line 114 inserts the new record by invoking **PreparedStatement** method **executeUpdate**. Line 115 closes the **PreparedStatement**, and line 117 returns the **employeeID** primary key. Lines 121–122 **catch** the **SQLException** that could be thrown when creating, executing or closing the **PreparedStatement**. An **SQLException** would indicate a problem inserting the record, so line 122 throws a **CreateException** to indicate that method **ejbCreate** could not create the **Employee** EJB instance.

Method **ejbCreate** declares an **Integer** return type. All **ejbCreate** methods in entity EJBs are required to return the EJB's *primary-key class*. The primary key for the **Employee** table is an integer, so the primary-key class for the **Employee** EJB is **java.lang.Integer**. Most EJBs use a standard Java class (e.g., **Integer** or **String**) as their primary-key class. If a database table has a *complex primary key* (i.e., a primary key that consists of more than one field), the developer must define a custom primary-key class. For an example of a custom primary-key class, please see the **Order-Product** EJB example in Chapter 19.

The EJB container invokes method **ejbPostCreate** (line 127) after invoking method **ejbCreate** to perform any required tasks after creating the EJB instance. For example, method **ejbPostCreate** could change the format of the **socialSecurityNumber** to include dashes. No additional work is needed in this EJB, so line 127 is an empty implementation of method **ejbPostCreate**.

When a client invokes method **remove** in either the **Employee** remote interface or interface **EmployeeHome**, the EJB container invokes method **ejbRemove** (lines 130–159). To **remove** an entity EJB instance means to **DELETE** the associated database record. Lines 136–137 get the primary key for the current EJB instance from the **entityContext** object associated with the EJB. Lines 140–145 create a **PreparedStatement** to **DELETE** the **Employee** record from the database. Line 148 sets the **employeeID** primary key in the **PreparedStatement**. Lines 151–152 execute and close the **PreparedStatement**. Lines 156–158 catch the **SQLException** that could be thrown when creating, executing or closing the **PreparedStatement**. If an **SQLException** is thrown, line 157 throws a **RemoveException** to indicate that removing the **Employee** EJB failed.

The EJB container invokes method **ejbStore** to save **Employee** data in the database. The EJB container determines the best time to update the database, so method **ejbStore** is only called by the container. Lines 168–169 get the primary key for the current EJB instance from the **entityContext**. Lines 172–187 create a **PreparedStatement** to **UPDATE** the **Employee** record in the database. Lines 190–191 execute and close the **PreparedStatement**. Lines 195–196 catch the **SQLException** that could be thrown when creating, executing or closing the **PreparedStatement**. Line 196 throws an **EJBException** to indicate the **ejbStore** method failed to update the data properly. Line 196 passes the **SQLException** to the **EJBException** constructor to aid in debugging the application.

The EJB container invokes method **ejbLoad** to load **Employee** data from the database and store the data in the EJB instance's member variables. The EJB container determines the best time to load from the database, so method **ejbLoad** is only called by the container. Lines 207–208 get the primary key for the current **Employee** EJB instance from the EJB's **EntityContext**. Lines 211–219 create a **PreparedStatement** to **SELECT** the **Employee** data from the database. Line 226 ensures that the **ResultSet** contains data, and lines 229–247 update the **private** member variables with the data from the **ResultSet**. Line 252 throws a new **EJBException** if the **ResultSet** is empty. Lines 260–262 catch an **SQLException** and throw an **EJBException** to indicate the **ejbLoad** method failed to load the **Employee** information from the database.

When a client invokes **EmployeeHome** method **findByPrimaryKey**, the EJB container invokes method **ejbFindByPrimaryKey** (lines 266–306). Method **findByPrimaryKey** must take a single argument whose type is the EJB's primary-key class. Lines 273–281 create a **PreparedStatement** to **SELECT** data from the database for the **Employee** with the given **employeeID** primary key. Lines 287–294 check on whether the **Employee** was found and return its primary key. If the **Employee** with the given primary key was not found in the database, lines 298–299 **throw** an **ObjectNotFoundException**. If there was an error in searching for the **Employee**, lines 303–305 catch an **SQLException** and throw a new **EJBException**.

The EJB container invokes method **setEntityContext** after the EJB instance is first created, but before the EJB instance is associated with a particular database record. The **EntityContext** argument provides methods for obtaining information about the EJB container in which the EJB instance executes. Line 313 sets the **entityContext** member variable so other methods can use the given **EntityContext** to discover information about the EJB container. There are some restrictions on what can be done in method **setEntityContext**, because when this method is invoked, the EJB instance is not yet associated with a particular database record. For example, the EJB must not invoke **EntityContext** method **getPrimaryKey**, because there is no primary key associated with the current EJB instance. Invoking **EntityContext** method **getPrimaryKey** would cause an **IllegalStateException**.

Method **setEntityContext** should allocate resources the EJB instance will need throughout its lifetime. This **Employee** EJB implementation uses bean-managed persistence and therefore needs a database **Connection** to exchange data with the database throughout the EJB's lifetime. Line 317 creates a new **InitialContext** that the EJB will use to look up the **Employee** database in the JNDI directory. Lines 320–322 invoke **InitialContext** method **lookup** to obtain a **DataSource** reference to the **Employee** database. J2EE applications use a special JNDI naming context called **java:comp/env**, which stands for "component environment." There are subcontexts in the **java:comp/env** naming context for different types of objects. For example, EJBs are found in the **ejb** subcontext and databases are found in the **jdbc** subcontext. Line 322 uses the JNDI name **java:comp/env/jdbc/Employee** to locate the **Employee** database in the JNDI directory. Line 325 sets the **connection** member variable to a newly created database **Connection**. If the database with the given name cannot be found, lines 329–331 catch a **NamingException**, which is thrown by the **Initial-Context** constructor or by method **lookup**.

Common Programming Error 15.1

*The **java:comp/env** naming context is available only within a J2EE application (e.g., in a servlet, JSP or EJB). Using this naming context in a Java application or applet will result in a **javax.naming.NamingException***

The EJB container invokes method **unsetEntityContext** (lines 340–358) when the EJB instance is no longer needed. Method **unsetEntityContext** should deallocate any resources the EJB instance used throughout its lifetime. Line 346 closes the **Connection** to the database. If there was an error closing the database **Connection**, lines 350–352 catch an **SQLException** and throw an **EJBException**. Lines 355–357 set the **Connection** to **null** for later reuse.

The EJB container maintains a pool of inactive EJB instances that the container can associate with particular database records when needed. This pooling prevents the EJB container from incurring the overhead required to create a new EJB instance each time an EJB instance is needed. The EJB container invokes method **ejbPassivate** (lines 361–364) to place an active EJB back in the inactive pool. Line 363 sets the **employeeID** to **null** because a passivated EJB is no longer associated with any particular database record.

The EJB container invokes method **ejbActivate** (lines 367–371) to activate an EJB instance taken from the pool of inactive EJB instances. Line 369 sets the **employeeID** to the **primaryKey** value retrieved from the EJB's **entityContext** to associate the EJB with the appropriate database record.

15.5.2 **Employee** EJB Deployment

Deploying entity EJBs is similar to deploying session EJBs (Chapter 14), but with the following changes. In the **General** dialog of the **New Enterprise Bean Wizard**, select the **Entity** radio button in the **Bean Type** field (Fig. 15.4). Next, select the type of persistence in the **Entity Settings** dialog. Click the **Bean-Managed Persistence** radio button for bean-managed persistence and enter the class name for the primary key in the **Primary Key Class** text field (Fig. 15.5). Finally, in the **Resource References** dialog, add a reference to the **Employee** database. The information for the reference must match that in Fig. 15.6. The rest of the deployment is the same as deploying a session EJB. For the Employee EJB's JNDI name, we recommend you specify **BMPEmployee** for the bean-managed persistence version.

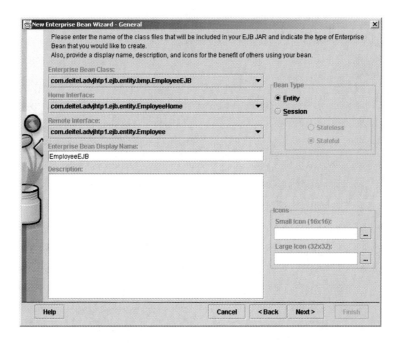

Fig. 15.4 **General** dialog of **New Enterprise Bean Wizard**.

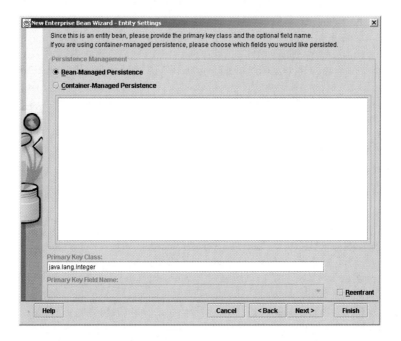

Fig. 15.5 **Bean-Managed Persistence** selected in **Entity Settings dialog**.

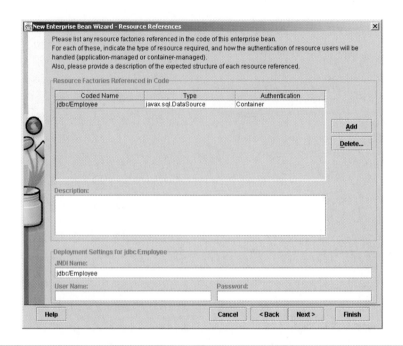

Fig. 15.6   **Resource References** dialog in **New Enterprise Bean Wizard**.

15.6 `Employee` EJB with Container-Managed Persistence

Figure 15.7 shows an **Employee** EJB implementation that uses container-managed persistence to simplify the EJB implementation. Class **EmployeeEJB** implements interface **EntityBean** (line 12), indicating that this is an entity EJB. Line 14 declares an **EntityContext** reference to store the **EntityContext** associated with the EJB instance.

Lines 17–22 declare the *container-managed fields* for the **Employee** EJB. Container-managed fields are member variables that a container-managed persistence EJB instance uses to cache data retrieved from the database. The container-managed fields must have the same names as the fields in the corresponding database table. The container-managed fields also must be marked **public** so the EJB container can access them directly. The EJB container is responsible for synchronizing the container-managed fields with the database. When deploying the EJB, the deployer must provide the SQL statements for updating, inserting, deleting and retrieving data from the database. Lines 25–88 provide implementations of the methods declared in the **Employee** remote interface.

Method **ejbCreate** (lines 91–96) takes an **Integer primaryKey** argument and stores this **primaryKey** in the **employeeID** member variable (line 93). The EJB container executes the SQL **INSERT** statement (supplied by the deployer) after method **ejb-Create** completes. This SQL **INSERT** statement takes the current values of the container-managed fields in the EJB and inserts their values into the database. Note that, although method **ejbCreate** specifies **Integer** as its return type (line 91), line 95 returns **null**. According to the EJB specification, method **ejbCreate** must return the primary-key class type, which for the **Employee** EJB is **Integer**. However, the EJB container ignores the return value from **ejbCreate** when using container-managed persistence, so we return **null**. The EJB specification requires an **ejbPostCreate** method for each **ejbCreate** method. Line 99 provides an empty implementation of method **ejbPostCreate** because this EJB requires no further initialization.

Methods **setEntityContext** (lines 102–105) and **unsetEntityContext** (lines 108–111) manage the **EntityContext** member variable. This EJB implementation does not have any resources it needs throughout the EJB lifetime, so no other work is done in either method.

```java
1   // EmployeeEJB.java
2   // EmployeeEJB is an entity EJB that uses container-managed
3   // persistence to persist Employee data in a database.
4   package com.deitel.advjhtp1.ejb.entity.cmp;
5
6   // Java core libraries
7   import java.rmi.RemoteException;
8
9   // Java standard extensions
10  import javax.ejb.*;
11
12  public class EmployeeEJB implements EntityBean {
13
14      private EntityContext entityContext;
15
16      // container-managed fields
17      public Integer employeeID;
18      public String socialSecurityNumber;
19      public String firstName;
20      public String lastName;
21      public String title;
22      public Double salary;
23
24      // get Employee ID
25      public Integer getEmployeeID()
26      {
27          return employeeID;
28      }
29
30      // set social security number
31      public void setSocialSecurityNumber( String number )
32      {
33          socialSecurityNumber = number;
34      }
35
36      // get social security number
37      public String getSocialSecurityNumber()
38      {
39          return socialSecurityNumber;
40      }
41
```

Fig. 15.7 EmployeeEJB implementation of **Employee** remote interface using container-managed persistence (part 1 of 3).

```
42        // set first name
43        public void setFirstName( String name )
44        {
45            firstName = name;
46        }
47
48        // get first name
49        public String getFirstName()
50        {
51            return firstName;
52        }
53
54        // set last name
55        public void setLastName( String name )
56        {
57            lastName = name;
58        }
59
60        // get last name
61        public String getLastName()
62        {
63            return lastName;
64        }
65
66        // set title
67        public void setTitle( String jobTitle )
68        {
69            title = jobTitle;
70        }
71
72        // get title
73        public String getTitle()
74        {
75            return title;
76        }
77
78        // set salary
79        public void setSalary( Double amount )
80        {
81            salary = amount;
82        }
83
84        // get salary
85        public Double getSalary()
86        {
87            return salary;
88        }
89
90        // create new Employee instance
91        public Integer ejbCreate( Integer primaryKey )
92        {
93            employeeID = primaryKey;
```

Fig. 15.7 **EmployeeEJB** implementation of **Employee** remote interface using container-managed persistence (part 2 of 3).

```
94
95          return null;
96      }
97
98      // do post-creation tasks when creating new Employee
99      public void ejbPostCreate( Integer primaryKey ) {}
100
101     // set EntityContext
102     public void setEntityContext( EntityContext context )
103     {
104         entityContext = context;
105     }
106
107     // unset EntityContext
108     public void unsetEntityContext()
109     {
110         entityContext = null;
111     }
112
113     // activate Employee instance
114     public void ejbActivate()
115     {
116         employeeID = ( Integer ) entityContext.getPrimaryKey();
117     }
118
119     // passivate Employee instance
120     public void ejbPassivate()
121     {
122         employeeID = null;
123     }
124
125     // load Employee instance in database
126     public void ejbLoad() {}
127
128     // store Employee instance in database
129     public void ejbStore() {}
130
131     // remove Employee instance from database
132     public void ejbRemove() {}
133 }
```

Fig. 15.7 **EmployeeEJB** implementation of **Employee** remote interface using container-managed persistence (part 3 of 3).

Methods **ejbActivate** (lines 114–117) and **ejbPassivate** (lines 120–123) perform the same functions they did in the bean-managed persistence version of the **Employee** EJB. Method **ejbActivate** associates an EJB instance taken from the inactive pool with a particular database record, and method **ejbPassivate** disassociates the EJB instance from its database record.

Methods **ejbLoad** (line 126), **ejbStore** (line 129) and **ejbRemove** (line 132) also perform the same functions they did in the bean-managed persistence version of the **Employee** EJB. However with container-managed persistence, the deployer specifies the necessary **SELECT**, **UPDATE** and **DELETE** statements when deploying the application.

The EJB container executes these statements at runtime. These methods could perform further processing on the data if necessary. No further processing is necessary in this **Employee** EJB, so these methods are given empty implementations.

Common Programming Error 15.2

*For entity EJBs using container-managed persistence, the EJB container loads database data and invokes method **ejbLoad** when the client first invokes a business method. However, the business method must be invoked in a transaction context.*

Performance Tip 15.1

*Entity EJBs using container-managed persistence might not perform as well as their bean-managed persistence counterparts, because all database data is loaded before the EJB container invokes method **ejbLoad**. Entity EJBs using bean-managed persistence can defer the loading of data from the database until the data is needed, which may enhance performance for EJBs with large amounts of data.*

To deploy the container-managed persistence version of the Employee EJB, follow the instructions in Section 15.5.2. We recommend you use the JNDI Name **CMPEmployee** for the container-managed persistence version of the **Employee** EJB. In the **Persistence Management** dialog (Fig. 15.8), click the **Container-Managed Persistence** radio button and place check marks next to each container-managed field. Enter the class name of the primary key in the **Primary Key Class** text field and select the primary key field name from the **Primary Key Field Name** drop-down menu.

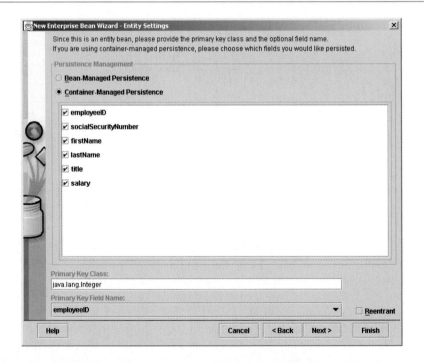

Fig. 15.8   **Container-Managed Persistence** selected in **Entity Settings** dialog.

15.7 `Employee` EJB Client

Figure 15.9 shows class **EmployeeEJBClient** for interacting with entity EJB **Employee**. The GUI provides buttons for finding, adding, updating and deleting **Employee** EJBs, and **JTextField**s for displaying **Employee** information. Lines 26–27 declare an **EmployeeHome** reference and an **Employee** reference for accessing the **Employee** EJB. The **EmployeeEJBClient** constructor takes a **String** argument containing the JNDI Name of the **Employee** EJB to load. This client works with both the bean-managed and container-managed persistence versions of the **Employee** EJB, because both versions use the same home and remote interfaces. The constructor uses the **JNDIName** argument to determine which version of the **Employee** EJB to use.

Line 47 creates a new **InitialContext** to look up the **Employee** EJB using the **JNDIName** argument. Lines 50–51 look up the **EmployeeHome** interface using **InitialContext** method **lookup**. Lines 54–56 use **PortableRemoteObject** method **narrow** to convert the **Object** reference returned by method **lookup** to an **EmployeeHome** reference. We will use this **EmployeeHome** reference throughout the program to create, find and remove **Employee** EJBs. If there is an error creating the **InitialContext** or looking up the **EmployeeHome** interface, lines 60–62 **catch** a **NamingException**.

Method **getEmployeeID** (lines 74–85) displays a **JOptionPane** to prompt the user for an **employeeID**. This **employeeID** can be used to find an existing **Employee** EJB instance or to create a new **Employee** EJB instance.

Method **getEmployee** (lines 88–119) uses method **getEmployeeID** on line 91 to prompt the user for the **employeeID** of the **Employee** the user would like to find. Lines 99–100 use **EmployeeHome** method **findByPrimaryKey** to locate the **Employee** EJB instance for the **Employee** with the given **employeeID**. Method **findByPrimaryKey** returns a remote reference to the **Employee** EJB instance. Line 103 invokes method **setCurrentEmployee** to display the **Employee**'s information to the user. If there was an error communicating with the **Employee** EJB, lines 107–111 **catch** a **RemoteException**. If there is no **Employee** with the given **employeeID**, lines 114–118 catch a **FinderException**.

Method **addEmployee** (lines 122–150) adds a new **Employee** to the database by creating a new **Employee** EJB. Line 126 invokes method **getEmployeeID** to prompt the user for an **employeeID**. Line 133 invokes **EmployeeHome** method **create** to create a new **Employee** EJB instance with the given **employeeID**. Line 136 invokes method **setCurrentEmployee** to display the **Employee**'s information to the user. Lines 140–143 **catch** a **CreateException**, which is thrown if there is an error creating the **Employee** EJB. For example, if the **employeeID** entered by the user is already in use by another **Employee** EJB, the EJB container will throw a **DuplicateKeyException**, which is a subclass of **CreateException**. If there is an error communicating with the **Employee** EJB, lines 146–149 catch a **RemoteException**.

Method **updateEmployee** (lines 153–184) uses the values provided in the **JTextField**s to update the current **Employee**'s information. Lines 159–175 invoke the **Employee** EJB *set* methods with values from each **JTextField**. If there is an error communicating with the **Employee** EJB, lines 180–183 catch a **RemoteException**.

Method **deleteEmployee** (lines 187–214) deletes the current **Employee** from the database by invoking **Employee** EJB method **remove** (line 191). Lines 194–199 set the

JTextFields in the user interface to the empty string. If there is an error communicating with the **Employee** EJB, lines 204–207 **catch** a **RemoteException**. If there is an error removing the **Employee** EJB, lines 210–213 **catch** a **RemoveException**.

Method **setCurrentEmployee** (lines 217–266) takes an **Employee** remote reference argument and updates the user interface with the information from this **Employee** EJB. Lines 224–258 retrieve values for each of the **Employee** EJB properties and update the **JTextField**s in the user interface. If there is an error communicating with the **Employee** EJB, lines 262–265 catch a **RemoteException**.

```
1   // EmployeeEJBClient.java
2   // EmployeeEJBClient is a user interface for interacting with
3   // bean- and container-managed persistence Employee EJBs.
4   package com.deitel.advjhtp1.ejb.entity.client;
5
6   // Java core libraries
7   import java.awt.*;
8   import java.awt.event.*;
9   import java.text.*;
10  import java.util.*;
11  import java.rmi.RemoteException;
12
13  // Java standard extensions
14  import javax.swing.*;
15  import javax.ejb.*;
16  import javax.naming.*;
17  import javax.rmi.*;
18
19  // Deitel libraries
20  import com.deitel.advjhtp1.ejb.entity.*;
21
22  public class EmployeeEJBClient extends JFrame {
23
24     // variables for accessing EJBs
25     private InitialContext initialContext;
26     private EmployeeHome employeeHome;
27     private Employee currentEmployee;
28
29     // JTextFields for user input
30     private JTextField employeeIDTextField;
31     private JTextField socialSecurityTextField;
32     private JTextField firstNameTextField;
33     private JTextField lastNameTextField;
34     private JTextField titleTextField;
35     private JTextField salaryTextField;
36
37     // BMPEmployeeEJBClient constructor
38     public EmployeeEJBClient( String JNDIName )
39     {
40        super( "Employee EJB Client" );
41
```

Fig. 15.9   **EmployeeEJBClient** for interacting with **Employee** EJB (part 1 of 9).

```
42          // create user interface
43          createGUI();
44
45          // get EmployeeHome reference for Employee EJB
46          try {
47             initialContext = new InitialContext();
48
49             // look up Employee EJB using given JNDI name
50             Object homeObject =
51                initialContext.lookup( JNDIName );
52
53             // get EmployeeHome interface
54             employeeHome = ( EmployeeHome )
55                PortableRemoteObject.narrow(
56                   homeObject, EmployeeHome.class );
57          }
58
59          // handle exception when looking up Employee EJB
60          catch ( NamingException namingException ) {
61             namingException.printStackTrace( System.err );
62          }
63
64          // close application when user closes window
65          setDefaultCloseOperation( EXIT_ON_CLOSE );
66
67          // set size of application window and make it visible
68          setSize( 600, 300 );
69          setVisible( true );
70
71       } // end EmployeeEJBClient constructor
72
73       // prompt user for employeeID
74       private Integer getEmployeeID()
75       {
76          String primaryKeyString = JOptionPane.showInputDialog(
77             this, "Please enter an employeeID" );
78
79          // check if primaryKeyString is null, else return
80          // Integer
81          if ( primaryKeyString == null )
82             return null;
83          else
84             return new Integer( primaryKeyString );
85       }
86
87       // get Employee reference for user-supplied employeeID
88       private void getEmployee()
89       {
90          // prompt user for employeeID and get Employee reference
91          Integer employeeID = getEmployeeID();
92
```

Fig. 15.9 **EmployeeEJBClient** for interacting with **Employee** EJB (part 2 of 9).

```
93          // return if employeeID is null
94          if ( employeeID == null )
95             return;
96
97          try {
98             // find Employee with given employeeID
99             Employee employee =
100               employeeHome.findByPrimaryKey( employeeID );
101
102            // update display with current Employee
103            setCurrentEmployee( employee );
104         }
105
106         // handle exception when finding Employee
107         catch ( RemoteException remoteException ) {
108            JOptionPane.showMessageDialog(
109               EmployeeEJBClient.this,
110               remoteException.getMessage() );
111         }
112
113         // handle exception when finding Employee
114         catch ( FinderException finderException ) {
115            JOptionPane.showMessageDialog(
116               EmployeeEJBClient.this, "Employee not " +
117               "found: " + finderException.getMessage() );
118         }
119      } // end method getEmployee
120
121      // add new Employee by creating new Employee EJB instance
122      private void addEmployee()
123      {
124         // prompt user for employeeID and create Employee
125         try {
126            Integer employeeID = getEmployeeID();
127
128            // return if employeeID null
129            if ( employeeID == null )
130               return;
131
132            // create new Employee
133            Employee employee = employeeHome.create( employeeID );
134
135            // update display with new Employee
136            setCurrentEmployee( employee );
137         }
138
139         // handle exception when creating Employee
140         catch ( CreateException createException ) {
141            JOptionPane.showMessageDialog( this,
142               createException.getMessage() );
143         }
144
```

Fig. 15.9   EmployeeEJBClient for interacting with **Employee** EJB (part 3 of 9).

```
145         // handle exception when creating Employee
146         catch ( RemoteException remoteException ) {
147            JOptionPane.showMessageDialog( this,
148               remoteException.getMessage() );
149         }
150      } // end method addEmployee
151
152      // update current Employee with user-supplied information
153      private void updateEmployee()
154      {
155         // get information from JTextFields and update Employee
156         try {
157
158            // set Employee socialSecurityNumber
159            currentEmployee.setSocialSecurityNumber(
160               socialSecurityTextField.getText() );
161
162            // set Employee firstName
163            currentEmployee.setFirstName(
164               firstNameTextField.getText() );
165
166            // set Employee lastName
167            currentEmployee.setLastName(
168               lastNameTextField.getText() );
169
170            // set Employee title
171            currentEmployee.setTitle( titleTextField.getText() );
172
173            // set Employee salary
174          Double salary = new Double( salaryTextField.getText() );
175            currentEmployee.setSalary( salary );
176
177         } // end try
178
179         // handle exception invoking Employee business methods
180         catch ( RemoteException remoteException ) {
181            JOptionPane.showMessageDialog( this,
182               remoteException.getMessage() );
183         }
184      } // end method updateEmployee
185
186      // delete current Employee
187      private void deleteEmployee()
188      {
189         // remove current Employee EJB
190         try {
191            currentEmployee.remove();
192
193            // clear JTextFields
194            employeeIDTextField.setText( "" );
195            socialSecurityTextField.setText( "" );
```

Fig. 15.9   EmployeeEJBClient for interacting with **Employee** EJB (part 4 of 9).

```
196              firstNameTextField.setText( "" );
197              lastNameTextField.setText( "" );
198              titleTextField.setText( "" );
199              salaryTextField.setText( "" );
200
201          } // end try
202
203          // handle exception when removing Employee
204          catch ( RemoteException remoteException ) {
205              JOptionPane.showMessageDialog( this,
206                  remoteException.getMessage() );
207          }
208
209          // handle exception when removing Employee
210          catch ( RemoveException removeException ) {
211              JOptionPane.showMessageDialog( this,
212                  removeException.getMessage() );
213          }
214      } // end method deleteEmployee
215
216      // update display with current Employee information
217      private void setCurrentEmployee( Employee employee )
218      {
219          // get information for currentEmployee and update display
220          try {
221              currentEmployee = employee;
222
223              // get the employeeID
224              Integer employeeID = ( Integer )
225                  currentEmployee.getEmployeeID();
226
227              // update display
228              employeeIDTextField.setText( employeeID.toString() );
229
230              // set socialSecurityNumber in display
231              socialSecurityTextField.setText(
232                currentEmployee.getSocialSecurityNumber() );
233
234              // set firstName in display
235              firstNameTextField.setText(
236                  currentEmployee.getFirstName() );
237
238              // set lastName in display
239              lastNameTextField.setText(
240                  currentEmployee.getLastName() );
241
242              // set title in display
243              titleTextField.setText( currentEmployee.getTitle() );
244
245              // get Employee salary
246              Double salary = (Double) currentEmployee.getSalary();
247
```

Fig. 15.9 **EmployeeEJBClient** for interacting with **Employee** EJB (part 5 of 9).

```
248            // ensure salary is not null and update display
249            if ( salary != null ) {
250               NumberFormat dollarFormatter =
251                  NumberFormat.getCurrencyInstance(
252                     Locale.US );
253
254             salaryTextField.setText( dollarFormatter.format(
255                salary ) );
256            }
257            else
258               salaryTextField.setText( "" );
259        } // end try
260
261        // handle exception invoking Employee business methods
262        catch ( RemoteException remoteException ) {
263           JOptionPane.showMessageDialog( this,
264              remoteException.getMessage() );
265        }
266     } // end method setCurrentEmployee
267
268     // create the application GUI
269     private void createGUI()
270     {
271        // create JPanel for Employee form components
272        JPanel formPanel = new JPanel( new GridLayout( 6, 2 ) );
273
274        // create read-only JTextField for employeeID
275        employeeIDTextField = new JTextField();
276        employeeIDTextField.setEditable( false );
277        formPanel.add( new JLabel( "Employee ID" ) );
278        formPanel.add( employeeIDTextField );
279
280        // create JTextField and JLabel for social security #
281        socialSecurityTextField = new JTextField();
282        formPanel.add( new JLabel( "Social Security #" ) );
283        formPanel.add( socialSecurityTextField );
284
285        // create JTextField and JLabel for first name
286        firstNameTextField = new JTextField();
287        formPanel.add( new JLabel( "First Name" ) );
288        formPanel.add( firstNameTextField );
289
290        // create JTextField and JLabel for last name
291        lastNameTextField = new JTextField();
292        formPanel.add( new JLabel( "Last Name" ) );
293        formPanel.add( lastNameTextField );
294
295        // create JTextField and JLabel for job title
296        titleTextField = new JTextField();
297        formPanel.add( new JLabel( "Title" ) );
298        formPanel.add( titleTextField );
299
```

Fig. 15.9 **EmployeeEJBClient** for interacting with **Employee** EJB (part 6 of 9).

```
300        // create JTextField and JLabel for salary
301        salaryTextField = new JTextField();
302        formPanel.add( new JLabel( "Salary" ) );
303        formPanel.add( salaryTextField );
304
305        // add formPanel to the JFrame's contentPane
306        Container contentPane = getContentPane();
307        contentPane.add( formPanel, BorderLayout.CENTER );
308
309        // create JPanel for JButtons
310        JPanel employeeButtonPanel =
311           new JPanel( new FlowLayout() );
312
313        // create JButton for adding Employees
314        JButton addButton = new JButton( "Add Employee" );
315        addButton.addActionListener(
316           new ActionListener() {
317
318              public void actionPerformed( ActionEvent event )
319              {
320                 addEmployee();
321              }
322           }
323        );
324        employeeButtonPanel.add( addButton );
325
326        // create JButton for saving Employee information
327        JButton saveButton = new JButton( "Save Changes" );
328        saveButton.addActionListener(
329           new ActionListener() {
330
331              public void actionPerformed( ActionEvent event )
332              {
333                 updateEmployee();
334              }
335           }
336        );
337        employeeButtonPanel.add( saveButton );
338
339        // create JButton for deleting Employees
340        JButton deleteButton = new JButton( "Delete Employee" );
341        deleteButton.addActionListener(
342           new ActionListener() {
343
344              public void actionPerformed( ActionEvent event )
345              {
346                 deleteEmployee();
347              }
348           }
349        );
350        employeeButtonPanel.add( deleteButton );
351
```

Fig. 15.9   **EmployeeEJBClient** for interacting with **Employee** EJB (part 7 of 9).

```
352         // create JButton for finding existing Employees
353         JButton findButton = new JButton( "Find Employee" );
354         findButton.addActionListener(
355            new ActionListener() {
356
357               public void actionPerformed( ActionEvent event )
358               {
359                  getEmployee();
360               }
361            }
362         );
363         employeeButtonPanel.add( findButton );
364
365         // add employeeButtonPanel to JFrame's contentPane
366         contentPane.add( employeeButtonPanel,
367            BorderLayout.NORTH );
368
369      } // end method createGUI
370
371      // execute application
372      public static void main( String[] args )
373      {
374         // ensure user provided JNDI name for Employee EJB
375         if ( args.length != 1 ) {
376            System.err.println(
377               "Usage: java EmployeeEJBClient <JNDI Name>" );
378            System.exit( 1 );
379         }
380
381         // start application using provided JNDI name
382         else
383            new EmployeeEJBClient( args[ 0 ] );
384      }
385   }
```

Fig. 15.9   EmployeeEJBClient for interacting with Employee EJB (part 8 of 9).

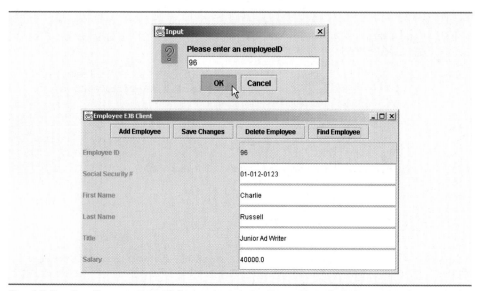

Fig. 15.9   **EmployeeEJBClient** for interacting with **Employee** EJB (part 9 of 9).

Method **createGUI** (lines 269–369) builds the user interface for the **EmployeeE-JBClient**. Lines 275–303 create **JTextField**s and **JLabel**s for each **Employee** property. Lines 314–363 create **JButton**s and associated **ActionListener**s to allow the user to add, update, delete and find **Employee**s.

Method **main** (lines 372–384) requires that the user provide a command-line argument containing the JNDI name of the **Employee** EJB to use in the application. This command-line argument enables the user to specify the JNDI name of either the bean- or container-managed persistence version of the **Employee** EJB (i.e., **BMPEmployee** or **CMPEmployee**). Lines 376–377 print instructions to the user if a JNDI name is not provided. Line 383 creates a new instance of the **EmployeeEJBClient** using the given JNDI name argument. When executing the **EmployeeEJBClient**, be sure that the client JAR for the **Employee** EJB is in the **EmployeeEJBClient**'s **CLASSPATH**.

15.8 Internet and World Wide Web Resources

java.sun.com/products/ejb/news.html
This site provides articles and news related to Enterprise JavaBeans.

www.theserverside.com/resources/pdf/ejbmatrix11.pdf
This document (in PDF format) provides a quick reference for EJB interfaces, classes and methods.

java.sun.com/products/ejb/docs.html
The Enterprise JavaBeans specification home page provides documentation and specifications for EJBs.

developer.java.sun.com/developer/technicalArticles/J2EE/build
This article at the Java Developer Connection (requires free registration) discusses techniques for ensuring J2EE applications are portable across application servers from different vendors.

java.sun.com/j2ee/blueprints
The J2EE Blueprints discuss proven strategies for building enterprise applications with J2EE. Included are technical articles that discuss the blueprints and code examples that implement the blueprints in real systems.

SUMMARY

- Entity EJBs provide an object-oriented representation of persistent data, such as data stored in a relational database.

- Entity EJBs that use bean-managed persistence require the developer to implement code for storing and retrieving data from the persistent data sources the EJB represents.

- Entity EJBs use container-managed persistence rely on the EJB container to implement the data-access calls to their persistent data sources. The deployer must supply information about the persistent data source when deploying the EJB.

- Entity EJBs provide **create** methods for creating new EJB instances, **remove** methods for removing EJB instances and *finder* methods for finding EJB instances. Each **create** method performs **INSERT** operations to create new records in the database. Each **remove** method performs **DELETE** operations to remove records from the database. Each *finder* method locates entity EJB instances that match certain criteria.

- Method **findByPrimaryKey** is one type of *finder* method for entity EJBs. Every entity EJB must have a **findByPrimaryKey** method that takes the entity EJB's primary-key class as an argument. Entity EJBs can also define other *finder* methods. A *finder* method name must begin with **findBy** and should end with the name of property to be used as the search criteria.

- All entity EJB implementations must implement interface **EntityBean**.

- An **EntityContext** provides the EJB with information about the container in which the EJB is deployed.

- All **ejbCreate** methods in entity EJBs are required to return the EJB's primary-key class. Most EJBs use a standard Java class (e.g., **Integer** or **String**) as their primary-key class.

- If a database table has a complex primary key (i.e., a primary key that consists of more than one field), the developer must define a custom primary-key class.

- The EJB container invokes method **ejbPostCreate** after invoking method **ejbCreate** to perform any required tasks after creating the EJB instance.

- To **remove** an entity EJB instance means to **DELETE** the associated database record. A **RemoveException** indicates that removing the EJB instance failed.

- There are some restrictions on what can be done in method **setEntityContext**, because when this method is invoked, the EJB instance is not yet associated with a particular database record. For example, the EJB must not invoke **EntityContext** method **getPrimaryKey**, because there is no primary key associated with the current EJB instance.

- Method **setEntityContext** should allocate resources the EJB instance will need throughout its lifetime (e.g., a database connection).

- J2EE applications use a special JNDI naming context called **java:comp/env**, which stands for "component environment." EJBs are found in the **ejb** subcontext and databases are found in the **jdbc** subcontext.

- Container-managed fields are member variables that a container-managed persistence EJB instance uses to cache data retrieved from the database. The container-managed fields must have the same names as the fields in the corresponding database table. The container-managed fields also must be marked **public** so the EJB container can access them directly.

TERMINOLOGY

application server	complex primary key
bean-managed persistence	container-managed field
business methods	container-managed persistence

EntityBean interface	*finder* methods
EntityContext interface	home interface
findByPrimaryKey method	javax.ejb.EntityBean interface
ejbCreate methods	primary-key class
ejbPassivate method	remove methods
ejbRemove method	setEntityContext method
entity EJB	unsetEntityContext method

SELF-REVIEW EXERCISES

15.1 State which of the following are *true* and which are *false*. If *false*, explain why.
a) Data associated with an entity EJB typically is stored in a relational database.
b) The remote interface for an entity EJB represents the database table with which the EJB is associated.
c) Entity EJBs that use bean-managed persistence require the deployer to specify SQL queries for inserting, updating, deleting and querying data from the database.
d) The *create* methods in the home interface for an entity EJB insert new records into the underlying database.
e) Entity EJBs should obtain necessary resources in method **ejbCreate**.
f) Entity EJBs that use container-managed persistence must implement interface **CMPEntityBean**, whereas those that use bean-managed persistence must implement interface **EntityBean**.

15.2 Fill in the blanks in each of the following:
a) For entity EJBs that use _____ persistence to represent data in a relational database, the _____ must specify SQL queries when deploying the EJB.
b) For entity EJBs that use _____ persistence to represent data in a relational database, the _____ must implement code that synchronizes data with the database.
c) Each create method in the home interface must have a corresponding _____ method in the EJB implementation.
d) If an entity EJB has a complex primary key, the developer must provide a custom _____ that represents the complex primary key.

ANSWERS TO SELF-REVIEW EXERCISES

15.1 a) True. b) False. The remote interface specifies the business methods for the EJB. The home interface represents the database table. c) False. The developer must provide code for managing synchronization with the underlying database. d) True. e) False. Entity EJBs should obtain necessary resources in method **setEntityContext**. f) False. All entity EJBs must implement interface **EntityBean**.

15.2 a) container-managed, deployer. b) bean-managed persistence, developer. c) **ejbCreate**. d) primary-key class.

EXERCISES

15.3 What types of persistence can entity EJBs use? What are the benefits of each?

15.4 Create an entity EJB for the **Titles** table in the **books** database of Chapter 8. The entity EJB should use bean-managed persistence to synchronize its data members with the values in the database. Provide *set* and *get* methods for each field in the **Titles** table. Provide a **create** method that takes the **ISBN** and **Title** as arguments.

15.5 Modify the entity EJB you created in Exercise 15.4 to use container-managed persistence instead of bean-managed persistence.

16

Messaging with JMS

Objectives

- To understand message-oriented middleware.
- To understand the point-to-point messaging model.
- To understand the publish/subscribe messaging model.
- To understand the difference between the two messaging models and when it is appropriate to use each.
- To understand how to use the Java Message Service (JMS) API to build messaging applications in Java.
- To introduce message-driven EJBs.

The next thing most like living one's life over again seems to be a recollection of that life, and to make that recollection as durable as possible by putting it down in writing.
Benjamin Franklin

Sow good services: sweet remembrances will grow from them.
Anne Louise Germaine de Stael

… And many a message from the skies, …
Robert Burns

16.1 Introduction

When creating enterprise applications, it often is useful for ordinarily uncoupled components of the applications to "talk" to each other. For instance, a book supplier's clients need to communicate book orders to the supplier. One solution is to loosely couple the client's buying application with the supplier's ordering application through a *messaging system*, sometimes called *message-oriented middleware* (*MOM*). Messaging systems allow components to post *messages* for other components to read. There are two basic messaging-system models—*point-to-point* and *publish/subscribe*.

The *point-to-point messaging model* allows components to send messages to a *message queue*. In this model, the sender intends the messages for one *message consumer*—a target component that processes the received messages. When this target component connects to the queue to receive messages, the target component receives any messages not yet consumed. A message is consumed once the server sends the message to the target component. Note that in the point-to-point model, exactly one client consumes a message.

The *publish/subscribe messaging model* allows components to *publish* messages to a *topic* on a server. The server maintains various topics to which components can connect. Components interested in messages published to a particular topic can *subscribe* to that topic. When a publisher publishes a message to a given topic, current subscribers receive that message. Note that in the publish/subscribe model, unlike in the point-to-point model, zero or more subscribers consume each published message.

In both messaging models, a message consists of a *header*, *properties* (optional) and a *body* (also optional). The message header contains information, such as the message destination and the sending time. Message properties allow message receivers to select which types of messages they would like to receive; the sender of a message can set these properties. Message receivers use *message selectors* to filter out messages. Filtering is done on the server side; the server does not send those messages to the receiver.

Message-driven beans are Enterprise JavaBeans that support messaging. Like an EJB container can use any instance of a stateless session EJB to handle client requests, the EJB container for message-driven beans can use any instance of a message-driven bean to process incoming messages for a given queue or topic. Since the container may use any instance, message-driven beans cannot maintain state for a specific client. Using message-driven beans, a component can receive messages asynchronously, without tying up resources waiting for a message to arrive.

In this chapter, we explore the *Java Message Service* (*JMS*) API. JMS standardizes the API for enterprise messaging, and supports both the point-to-point and publish/subscribe messaging models. JMS provides five types of messages—**BytesMessage**s, **MapMessage**s, **ObjectMessage**s, **StreamMessage**s and **TextMessage**s. There are several implementations of JMS available from various vendors. For more information on these vendors and JMS, please visit **java.sun.com/jms**.

16.2 Installation and Configuration of J2EE 1.3

The Java 2 Enterprise Edition version 1.3 reference implementation provides support for the Java Message Service API. At the time of this writing, the beta 2 release of the J2EE 1.3 reference implementation was available. Note that J2EE 1.3 beta 2 supports only the Windows 2000, Windows NT 4.0, Solaris SPARC 7, Solaris SPARC 8 and RedHat Linux v. 6.1 operating systems. Also note that J2SE 1.3.1 is required for J2EE 1.3 beta 2. To install the J2EE 1.3 reference implementation, follow these steps:

1. Download and unpack the appropriate software bundle from **java.sun.com/j2ee/j2sdkee-beta/index.html**.

2. Set the environment variables according to the values in Fig. 16.1.

Environment variable	Value
J2EE_HOME	Directory in which J2EE 1.3 is installed (e.g., **C:\j2sdkee1.3**).
JAVA_HOME	Directory in which J2SE 1.3.1 is installed (e.g., **C:\jdk1.3.1**).
PATH	The existing **PATH** plus the J2EE 1.3 **bin** directory (e.g., **C:\j2sdkee1.3\bin**).

Fig. 16.1   Setting environment variables for J2EE 1.3 installation.

16.3 Point-To-Point Messaging

The point-to-point messaging model (Fig. 16.2) allows clients to send messages to a message queue. A receiver connects to the queue to consume messages that have not been consumed. In general, messages in a queue are intended for exactly one client, so only one client connects as the receiver. If there is no receiver, the server maintains messages sent to the queue until a receiver connects and consumes those messages.

16.3.1 Voter Application: Overview

To demonstrate point-to-point messaging, we present an application that tallies votes for the voters' favorite programming language. Class **Voter** (Section 16.3.2) sends votes as messages to the **Votes** queue. These messages are simple **TextMessage** objects (package **javax.jms**). The message body contains the candidate name. Class **VoteCollector** (Section 16.3.3) consumes the messages and tallies the votes. Class **VoteCollector** can connect to the **Votes** queue before or after messages have been sent. As additional votes arrive in the queue, the **VoteCollector** updates the tallies and displays the totals. Figure 16.3 provides a diagram overview of the application.

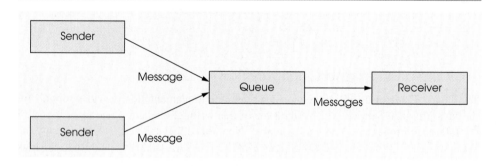

Fig. 16.2 Point-to-point messaging model.

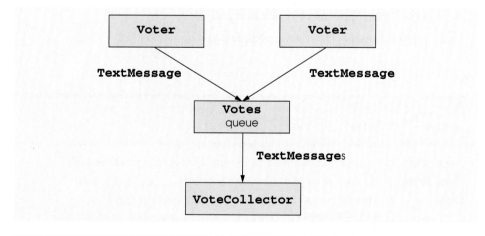

Fig. 16.3 Voter application overview.

16.3.2 Voter Application: Sender Side

The sender side of the application consists of a single class—**Voter** (Fig. 16.4). Class **Voter** allows the user to select a programming language and sends a vote for the selected language to the **Votes** queue as a **TextMessage**.

```
1   // Voter.java
2   // Voter is the GUI that allows the client to vote
3   // for a programming language. Voter sends the vote
4   // to the "Votes" queue as a TextMessage.
5   package com.deitel.advjhtp1.jms.voter;
6
7   // Java core packages
8   import java.awt.*;
9   import java.awt.event.*;
10
11  // Java extension packages
12  import javax.swing.*;
13  import javax.jms.*;
14  import javax.naming.*;
15
16  public class Voter extends JFrame {
17
18     private String selectedLanguage;
19
20     // JMS variables
21     private QueueConnection queueConnection;
22     private QueueSession queueSession;
23     private QueueSender queueSender;
24
25     // Voter constructor
26     public Voter()
27     {
28        // lay out user interface
29        super( "Voter" );
30
31        Container container = getContentPane();
32        container.setLayout( new BorderLayout() );
33
34        JTextArea voteArea =
35           new JTextArea( "Please vote for your\n" +
36              "favorite programming language" );
37        voteArea.setEditable( false );
38        container.add( voteArea, BorderLayout.NORTH );
39
40        JPanel languagesPanel = new JPanel();
41        languagesPanel.setLayout( new GridLayout( 0, 1 ) );
42
43        // add each language as its own JCheckBox
44        // ButtonGroup ensures exactly one language selected
45        ButtonGroup languagesGroup = new ButtonGroup();
46        CheckBoxHandler checkBoxHandler = new CheckBoxHandler();
```

Fig. 16.4   Voter class submits votes as messages to queue (part 1 of 4).

```
47        String languages[] =
48           { "C", "C++", "Java", "Lisp", "Python" };
49        selectedLanguage = "";
50
51        // create JCheckBox for each language
52        // and add to ButtonGroup and JPanel
53        for ( int i = 0; i < languages.length; i++ ) {
54           JCheckBox checkBox = new JCheckBox( languages[ i ] );
55           checkBox.addItemListener( checkBoxHandler );
56           languagesPanel.add( checkBox );
57           languagesGroup.add( checkBox );
58        }
59
60        container.add( languagesPanel, BorderLayout.CENTER );
61
62        // create button to submit vote
63        JButton submitButton = new JButton( "Submit vote!" );
64        container.add( submitButton, BorderLayout.SOUTH );
65
66        // invoke method submitVote when submitButton clicked
67        submitButton.addActionListener (
68
69           new ActionListener() {
70
71              public void actionPerformed ( ActionEvent event ) {
72                 submitVote();
73              }
74           }
75        );
76
77        // invoke method quit when window closed
78        addWindowListener(
79
80           new WindowAdapter() {
81
82              public void windowClosing( WindowEvent event ) {
83                 quit();
84              }
85           }
86        );
87
88        // connect to message queue
89        try {
90
91           // create JNDI context
92           Context jndiContext = new InitialContext();
93
94           // retrieve queue connection factory and
95           // queue from JNDI context
96           QueueConnectionFactory queueConnectionFactory =
97              ( QueueConnectionFactory )
98              jndiContext.lookup( "VOTE_FACTORY" );
99           Queue queue = ( Queue ) jndiContext.lookup( "Votes" );
```

Fig. 16.4 **Voter** class submits votes as messages to queue (part 2 of 4).

```
100
101         // create connection, session and sender
102         queueConnection =
103            queueConnectionFactory.createQueueConnection();
104         queueSession =
105            queueConnection.createQueueSession( false,
106               Session.AUTO_ACKNOWLEDGE );
107         queueSender = queueSession.createSender( queue );
108      }
109
110      // process Naming exception from JNDI context
111      catch ( NamingException namingException ) {
112         namingException.printStackTrace();
113         System.exit( 1 );
114      }
115
116      // process JMS exception from queue connection or session
117      catch ( JMSException jmsException ) {
118         jmsException.printStackTrace();
119         System.exit( 1 );
120      }
121
122   } // end Voter constructor
123
124   // submit selected vote to "Votes" queue as TextMessage
125   public void submitVote()
126   {
127      if ( selectedLanguage != "" ) {
128
129         // create text message containing selected language
130         try {
131            TextMessage voteMessage =
132               queueSession.createTextMessage();
133            voteMessage.setText( selectedLanguage );
134
135            // send the message to the queue
136            queueSender.send( voteMessage );
137         }
138
139         // process JMS exception
140         catch ( JMSException jmsException ) {
141            jmsException.printStackTrace();
142         }
143      }
144
145   } // end method submitVote
146
147   // close client application
148   public void quit()
149   {
150      if ( queueConnection != null ) {
151
```

Fig. 16.4 Voter class submits votes as messages to queue (part 3 of 4).

```
152              // close queue connection if it exists
153              try {
154                  queueConnection.close();
155              }
156
157              // process JMS exception
158              catch ( JMSException jmsException ) {
159                  jmsException.printStackTrace();
160              }
161          }
162
163          System.exit( 0 );
164
165      } // end method quit
166
167      // launch Voter application
168      public static void main( String args[] )
169      {
170          Voter voter = new Voter();
171          voter.pack();
172          voter.setVisible( true );
173      }
174
175      // CheckBoxHandler handles event when checkbox checked
176      private class CheckBoxHandler implements ItemListener {
177
178          // checkbox event
179          public void itemStateChanged( ItemEvent event )
180          {
181              // update selectedLanguage
182              JCheckBox source = ( JCheckBox ) event.getSource();
183              selectedLanguage = source.getText();
184          }
185      }
186  }
```

Fig. 16.4   **Voter** class submits votes as messages to queue (part 4 of 4).

Line 13 imports package **javax.jms**, which contains JMS API classes and interfaces. Lines 29–86 set up the GUI for the **Voter** client. Lines 53–58 create **JCheckBox** objects to allow the client to vote. Note that these are added to a **ButtonGroup** (lines 45–58) so that the user can select only one candidate.

Lines 89–120 set up JMS connections. Line 92 creates the JNDI context, from which the program retrieves a **QueueConnectionFactory** and **Queue**, identified by **VOTE_FACTORY** and **Votes**, respectively. Note that the server administrator must create the queue connection factory and queue (Section 16.3.4). A queue connection factory allows the client to create a **QueueConnection** (lines 102–103). The **QueueConnection** creates a **QueueSession** (lines 104–106). Finally, the **QueueSession** creates either a **QueueSender** or a **QueueReceiver**. Here, the **QueueSession** creates a **QueueSender** for the **Votes** queue (line 107); the **QueueSender** now can post messages to the queue.

When the user selects a language and clicks the **Submit vote** button (Fig. 16.5), method **submitVote** creates a **TextMessage** object and sets the text of the message to **selectedLanguage** (lines 131–133). Line 136 sends the message to the **Votes** queue.

The program invokes method **quit** (lines 148–165) when the user closes the application window. Lines 150–161 close the connection to the queue.

16.3.3 Voter Application: Receiver Side

In the Voter application example, a **VoteCollector** (Fig. 16.6) is the intended receiver of messages sent to the **Votes** queue. Class **VoteCollector** tallies and displays votes it receives from the queue. Note that the **Voter** can send messages to the queue before the **VoteCollector** has connected; once connected, the **VoteCollector** will receive these messages.

Fig. 16.5 Voter application votes for favorite programming language

```
1   // VoteCollector.java
2   // VoteCollector tallies and displays the votes
3   // posted as TextMessages to the "Votes" queue.
4   package com.deitel.advjhtp1.jms.voter;
5
6   // Java core packages
7   import java.awt.*;
8   import java.awt.event.*;
9   import java.util.*;
10
11  // Java extension packages
12  import javax.swing.*;
13  import javax.jms.*;
14  import javax.naming.*;
15
16  public class VoteCollector extends JFrame {
17
18     private JPanel displayPanel;
19     private Map tallies = new HashMap();
20
21     // JMS variables
22     private QueueConnection queueConnection;
```

Fig. 16.6 VoteCollector class retrieves and tallies votes (part 1 of 4).

```
23
24      // VoteCollector constructor
25      public VoteCollector()
26      {
27         super( "Vote Tallies" );
28
29         Container container = getContentPane();
30
31         // displayPanel will display tally results
32         displayPanel = new JPanel();
33         displayPanel.setLayout( new GridLayout( 0, 1 ) );
34         container.add( new JScrollPane( displayPanel ) );
35
36         // invoke method quit when window closed
37         addWindowListener(
38
39            new WindowAdapter() {
40
41               public void windowClosing( WindowEvent event ) {
42                  quit();
43               }
44            }
45         );
46
47         // connect to "Votes" queue
48         try {
49
50            // create JNDI context
51            Context jndiContext = new InitialContext();
52
53            // retrieve queue connection factory
54            // and queue from JNDI context
55            QueueConnectionFactory queueConnectionFactory =
56               ( QueueConnectionFactory )
57               jndiContext.lookup( "VOTE_FACTORY" );
58            Queue queue = ( Queue ) jndiContext.lookup( "Votes" );
59
60            // create connection, session and receiver
61            queueConnection =
62               queueConnectionFactory.createQueueConnection();
63            QueueSession queueSession =
64               queueConnection.createQueueSession( false,
65                  Session.AUTO_ACKNOWLEDGE );
66            QueueReceiver queueReceiver =
67               queueSession.createReceiver( queue );
68
69            // initialize and set message listener
70            queueReceiver.setMessageListener(
71               new VoteListener( this ) );
72
73            // start connection
74            queueConnection.start();
75         }
```

Fig. 16.6 **VoteCollector** class retrieves and tallies votes (part 2 of 4).

```
76
77        // process Naming exception from JNDI context
78        catch ( NamingException namingException ) {
79           namingException.printStackTrace();
80           System.exit( 1 );
81        }
82
83        // process JMS exception from queue connection or session
84        catch ( JMSException jmsException ) {
85           jmsException.printStackTrace();
86           System.exit( 1 );
87        }
88
89     } // end VoteCollector constructor
90
91     // add vote to corresponding tally
92     public void addVote( String vote )
93     {
94        if ( tallies.containsKey( vote ) ) {
95
96           // if vote already has corresponding tally
97           TallyPanel tallyPanel =
98              ( TallyPanel ) tallies.get( vote );
99           tallyPanel.updateTally();
100       }
101
102       // add to GUI and tallies
103       else {
104          TallyPanel tallyPanel = new TallyPanel( vote, 1 );
105          displayPanel.add( tallyPanel );
106          tallies.put( vote, tallyPanel );
107          validate();
108       }
109    }
110
111    // quit application
112    public void quit()
113    {
114       if ( queueConnection != null ) {
115
116          // close the queue connection if it exists
117          try {
118             queueConnection.close();
119          }
120
121          // process JMS exception
122          catch ( JMSException jmsException ) {
123             jmsException.printStackTrace();
124             System.exit( 1 );
125          }
126
127       }
128
```

Fig. 16.6 VoteCollector class retrieves and tallies votes (part 3 of 4).

```
129          System.exit( 0 );
130
131     } // end method quit
132
133     // launch VoteCollector
134     public static void main( String args[] )
135     {
136        VoteCollector voteCollector = new VoteCollector();
137        voteCollector.setSize( 200, 200 );
138        voteCollector.setVisible( true );
139     }
140 }
```

Fig. 16.6   **VoteCollector** class retrieves and tallies votes (part 4 of 4).

Class **VoteCollector** collects and tallies votes retrieved from the **Votes** queue. Variable **tallies** (line 19) is a **Map** from candidate names to corresponding **Tally-Panel** objects (Fig. 16.9); it updates tallies when a new vote is received. Lines 27–45 lay out the GUI. Note that the GUI initially displays nothing as the VoteCollector has received no votes.

Lines 48–87 establish a connection to the **Votes** queue. Line 51 creates a JNDI context for retrieving the **QueueConnectionFactory** and **Queue** (lines 55–58). The **QueueConnectionFactory** allows the program to create the **QueueConnection** (lines 61–62). The **QueueConnection** creates the **QueueSession** (lines 63–65). The **QueueSession**, in turn, creates the **QueueReceiver** (lines 66–67), which recieves votes from the **Queue**. Lines 70–71 create a new **VoteListener** (Fig. 16.8) and set the **VoteListener** as the message listener for the **QueueReceiver**. Line 74 starts the **queueConnection**; at this point, the **VoteListener** will process messages received from the **queue**.

Method **addVote** (lines 92–109) updates the tallies and display (Fig. 16.7). If there is a **TallyPanel** corresponding to the **vote**'s candidate, lines 97–99 increment the tally by invoking method **updateTally**. If there is no corresponding **TallyPanel**, lines 104–106 add a new entry to the **tallies Map**. The program invokes method **quit** (lines 112–131) when the client closes the application window. Lines 114–127 close the **queue-Connection**.

Fig. 16.7   **VoteCollector** tallies and displays votes.

Class **VoteListener** (Fig. 16.8) implements interface **MessageListener**. When the **QueueReceiver** receives a message, the **QueueReceiver**'s *message listener* processes the message. Interface **MessageListener** specifies the single method **onMessage** (lines 22–49), which the program invokes when a new message arrives. Line 29 checks that the message is of type **TextMessage**. If so, lines 30–31 retrieve the text of the message; line 32 then invokes method **addVote** of class **VoteCollector** to update the tallies.

```
1   // VoteListener.java
2   // VoteListener is the message listener for the
3   // receiver of the "Votes" queue. It implements
4   // the specified onMessage method to update the
5   // GUI with the received vote.
6   package com.deitel.advjhtp1.jms.voter;
7
8   // Java extension packages
9   import javax.jms.*;
10
11  public class VoteListener implements MessageListener {
12
13      private VoteCollector voteCollector;
14
15      // VoteListener constructor
16      public VoteListener( VoteCollector collector )
17      {
18          voteCollector = collector;
19      }
20
21      // receive new message
22      public void onMessage( Message message )
23      {
24          TextMessage voteMessage;
25
26          // retrieve and process message
27          try {
28
29              if ( message instanceof TextMessage ) {
30                  voteMessage = ( TextMessage ) message;
31                  String vote = voteMessage.getText();
32                  voteCollector.addVote( vote );
33
34                  System.out.println( "Received vote: " + vote );
35              }
36
37              else {
38                  System.out.println( "Expecting " +
39                      "TextMessage object, received " +
40                      message.getClass().getName() );
41              }
42          }
43
```

Fig. 16.8 **VoteListener** class receives messages from the queue (part 1 of 2).

```
44         // process JMS exception from message
45         catch ( JMSException jmsException ) {
46             jmsException.printStackTrace();
47         }
48
49     } // end method onMessage
50 }
```

Fig. 16.8 VoteListener class receives messages from the queue (part 2 of 2).

Class **TallyPanel** (Fig. 16.9) maintains and displays the **tally** for a vote candidate. Method **updateTally** (lines 37–41) increments the **tally** by one.

```
 1 // TallyPanel.java
 2 // TallPanel is the GUI component which displays
 3 // the name and tally for a vote candidate.
 4 package com.deitel.advjhtp1.jms.voter;
 5
 6 // Java core packages
 7 import java.awt.*;
 8
 9 // Java extension packages
10 import javax.swing.*;
11
12 public class TallyPanel extends JPanel {
13
14     private JLabel nameLabel;
15     private JTextField tallyField;
16     private String name;
17     private int tally;
18
19     // TallyPanel constructor
20     public TallyPanel( String voteName, int voteTally )
21     {
22         name = voteName;
23         tally = voteTally;
24
25         nameLabel = new JLabel( name );
26         tallyField =
27             new JTextField( Integer.toString( tally ), 10 );
28         tallyField.setEditable( false );
29         tallyField.setBackground( Color.white );
30
31         add( nameLabel );
32         add( tallyField );
33
34     } // end TallyPanel constructor
35
36     // update tally by one vote
37     public void updateTally()
38     {
39         tally++;
```

Fig. 16.9 TallyPanel class displays candidate name and tally (part 1 of 2).

```
40          tallyField.setText( Integer.toString( tally ) );
41     }
42   }
```

Fig. 16.9 TallyPanel class displays candidate name and tally (part 2 of 2).

16.3.4 Voter Application: Configuring and Running

To run the application, issue the following commands at a command prompt:

1. Start J2EE server in a command window:

   ```
   j2ee -verbose
   ```

2. In a new command window, create the **Votes** queue:

   ```
   j2eeadmin -addJmsDestination Votes queue
   ```

3. Verify that the queue was created:

   ```
   j2eeadmin -listJmsDestination
   ```

4. Create the connection factory:

   ```
   j2eeadmin -addJmsFactory VOTE_FACTORY queue
   ```

5. Start **VoteCollector**:

   ```
   java -classpath %J2EE_HOME%\lib\j2ee.jar;.
   -Djms.properties=%J2EE_HOME%\config\jms_client.properties
   com.deitel.advjhtp1.jms.voter.VoteCollector
   ```

6. Start **Voter** in a new command window:

   ```
   java -classpath %J2EE_HOME%\lib\j2ee.jar;.
   -Djms.properties=%J2EE_HOME%\config\jms_client.properties
   com.deitel.advjhtp1.jms.voter.Voter
   ```

Once you have finished running the application, you can remove the connection factory with the command:

```
j2eeadmin -removeJmsFactory VOTE_FACTORY
```

To remove the topic, use the command:

```
j2eeadmin -removeJmsDestination Votes
```

To stop J2EE server, use the command:

```
j2ee -stop
```

16.4 Publish/Subscribe Messaging

The publish/subscribe messaging model (Fig. 16.10) allows multiple clients to connect to a topic on the server and send and receive messages. Once connected, the client may publish messages or subscribe to the topic. When a client publishes a message, the server sends the message to those clients that subscribe to the topic. A client may obtain two types of *subscriptions—nondurable* and *durable*. Nondurable subscriptions receive messages only while the subscriptions are active. Durable subscriptions, however, can receive messages while inactive—the server maintains messages sent to the topic while the subscription is inactive and sends those messages to the client when the client reactivates the subscription. Note that if a client specifies a message selector to filter the messages, the server maintains only those messages that satisfy the selector.

16.4.1 Weather Application: Overview

We present an example of publish/subscribe messaging that uses a nondurable subscription. The following application publishes messages to a **Weather** topic on the server. These messages contain weather information for various U. S. cities retrieved from the National Weather Service Travelers Forecast page (**iwin.nws.noaa.gov/iwin/us/ traveler.html**). Class **WeatherPublisher** (Section 16.4.2) retrieves weather updates and publishes them as messages to the topic. Class **WeatherSubscriber** (Section 16.4.3), presents a graphical user interface that allows the user to select cities for which to display weather updates. Class **WeatherSubscriber** subscribes to the **Weather** topic and receives messages corresponding to the selected cities, using a message selector. Figure 16.11 provides an overview of the application.

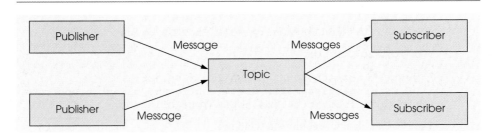

Fig. 16.10 Publish/subscribe messaging model.

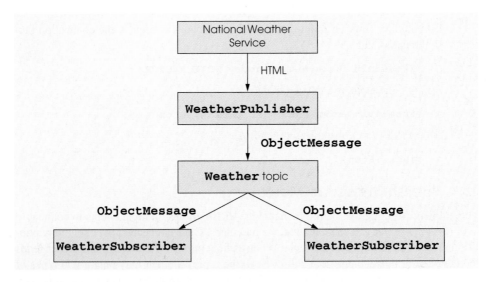

Fig. 16.11 Weather application overview.

16.4.2 Weather Application: Publisher Side

Class **WeatherPublisher** (Fig. 16.12) retrieves weather updates from the National Weather Service and publishes those updates as messages to the **Weather** topic. An **ObjectMessage** contains each city's weather conditions. The **ObjectMessage**'s **String** property **City** specifies the corresponding city. The **WeatherSubscriber** uses the **City** property in its message selector.

```
1   // WeatherPublisher.java
2   // WeatherPublisher retrieves weather conditions from the National
3   // Weather Service and publishes them to the Weather topic
4   // as ObjectMessages containing WeatherBeans. The city name is
5   // used in a String property "City" in the message header.
6   package com.deitel.advjhtp1.jms.weather;
7
8   // Java core packages
9   import java.io.*;
10  import java.net.*;
11  import java.util.*;
12
13  // Java extension packages
14  import javax.jms.*;
15  import javax.naming.*;
16
17  // Deitel packages
18  import com.deitel.advjhtp1.rmi.weather.WeatherBean;
19
20  public class WeatherPublisher extends TimerTask {
21
22     private BufferedReader in;
23     private TopicConnection topicConnection;
24
25     // WeatherPublisher constructor
26     public WeatherPublisher()
27     {
28        // update weather conditions every minute
29        Timer timer = new Timer();
30        timer.scheduleAtFixedRate( this, 0, 60000 );
31
32        // allow user to quit
33        InputStreamReader inputStreamReader =
34           new InputStreamReader( System.in );
35        char answer = '\0';
36
37        // loop until user enters q or Q
38        while ( !( ( answer == 'q' ) || ( answer == 'Q' ) ) ) {
39
40           // read in character
41           try {
42              answer = ( char ) inputStreamReader.read();
43           }
```

Fig. 16.12 WeatherPublisher class publishes messages to **Weather** topic (part 1 of 5).

```
44
45            // process IO exception
46            catch ( IOException ioException ) {
47               ioException.printStackTrace();
48               System.exit( 1 );
49            }
50
51         } // end while
52
53         // close connections
54         try {
55
56            // close topicConnection if it exists
57            if ( topicConnection != null ) {
58               topicConnection.close();
59            }
60
61            in.close();  // close connection to NWS Web server
62            timer.cancel();  // stop timer
63         }
64
65         // process JMS exception from closing topic connection
66         catch ( JMSException jmsException ) {
67            jmsException.printStackTrace();
68            System.exit( 1 );
69         }
70
71         // process IO exception from closing connection
72         // to NWS Web server
73         catch ( IOException ioException ) {
74            ioException.printStackTrace();
75            System.exit( 1 );
76         }
77
78         System.exit( 0 );
79
80      } // end WeatherPublisher constructor
81
82      // get weather information from NWS
83      public void run()
84      {
85         // connect to topic "Weather"
86         try {
87            System.out.println( "Update weather information..." );
88
89            // create JNDI context
90            Context jndiContext = new InitialContext();
91            String topicName = "Weather";
92
```

Fig. 16.12 WeatherPublisher class publishes messages to **Weather** topic (part 2 of 5).

```
93          // retrieve topic connection factory and topic
94          // from JNDI context
95          TopicConnectionFactory topicConnectionFactory =
96             ( TopicConnectionFactory )
97             jndiContext.lookup( "WEATHER_FACTORY" );
98
99          Topic topic =
100            ( Topic ) jndiContext.lookup( topicName );
101
102         // create connection, session, publisher and message
103         topicConnection =
104            topicConnectionFactory.createTopicConnection();
105
106         TopicSession topicSession =
107            topicConnection.createTopicSession( false,
108               Session.AUTO_ACKNOWLEDGE );
109
110         TopicPublisher topicPublisher =
111            topicSession.createPublisher( topic );
112
113         ObjectMessage message =
114            topicSession.createObjectMessage();
115
116         // connect to National Weather Service
117         // and publish conditions to topic
118
119         // National Weather Service Travelers Forecast page
120         URL url = new URL(
121            "http://iwin.nws.noaa.gov/iwin/us/traveler.html" );
122
123         // set up text input stream to read Web page contents
124         in = new BufferedReader(
125            new InputStreamReader( url.openStream() ) );
126
127         // helps determine starting point of data on Web page
128         String separator = "TAV12";
129
130         // locate separator string in Web page
131         while ( !in.readLine().startsWith( separator ) )
132            ;    // do nothing
133
134         // strings representing headers on Travelers Forecast
135         // Web page for daytime and nighttime weather
136         String dayHeader =
137            "CITY            WEA      HI/LO    WEA      HI/LO";
138
139         String nightHeader =
140            "CITY            WEA      LO/HI    WEA      LO/HI";
141
142         String inputLine = "";
143
```

Fig. 16.12 WeatherPublisher class publishes messages to **Weather** topic (part 3 of 5).

```
144            // locate header that begins weather information
145            do {
146               inputLine = in.readLine();
147            }
148
149            while ( !inputLine.equals( dayHeader ) &&
150               !inputLine.equals( nightHeader ) );
151
152            // create WeatherBean objects for each city's data
153            // publish to Weather topic using city as message's type
154            inputLine = in.readLine();   // get first city's info
155
156            // the portion of inputLine containing relevant data is
157            // 28 characters long. If the line length is not at
158            // least 28 characters long, done processing data.
159            while ( inputLine.length() > 28 ) {
160
161               // create WeatherBean object for city
162               // first 16 characters are city name
163               // next six characters are weather description
164               // next six characters are HI/LO temperature
165               WeatherBean weather = new WeatherBean(
166                  inputLine.substring( 0, 16 ).trim(),
167                  inputLine.substring( 16, 22 ).trim(),
168                  inputLine.substring( 23, 29 ).trim() );
169
170               // publish WeatherBean object with city name
171               // as a message property,
172               // used for selection by clients
173               message.setObject( weather );
174               message.setStringProperty( "City",
175                  weather.getCityName() );
176               topicPublisher.publish( message );
177
178               System.out.println( "published message for city: "
179                  + weather.getCityName() );
180
181               inputLine = in.readLine();   // get next city's info
182            }
183
184            System.out.println( "Weather information updated." );
185
186         } // end try
187
188         // process Naming exception from JNDI context
189         catch ( NamingException namingException ) {
190            namingException.printStackTrace();
191            System.exit( 1 );
192         }
193
```

Fig. 16.12 WeatherPublisher class publishes messages to **Weather** topic (part 4 of 5).

```
194          // process JMS exception from connection,
195          // session, publisher or message
196          catch ( JMSException jmsException ) {
197              jmsException.printStackTrace();
198              System.exit( 1 );
199          }
200
201          // process failure to connect to National Weather Service
202          catch ( java.net.ConnectException connectException ) {
203              connectException.printStackTrace();
204              System.exit( 1 );
205          }
206
207          // process other exceptions
208          catch ( Exception exception ) {
209              exception.printStackTrace();
210              System.exit( 1 );
211          }
212
213      } // end method run
214
215      // launch WeatherPublisher
216      public static void main( String args[] )
217      {
218          System.err.println( "Initializing server...\n" +
219              "Enter 'q' or 'Q' to quit" );
220
221          WeatherPublisher publisher = new WeatherPublisher();
222      }
223  }
```

Fig. 16.12 WeatherPublisher class publishes messages to Weather topic (part 5 of 5).

Class **WeatherPublisher** publishes weather information for U.S. cities to the **Weather** topic on the server. Every minute, the **WeatherPublisher** obtains the weather information from the National Weather Service and publishes an individual message for each city's weather. Figure 16.13 shows the server in progress. Method **run** (lines 83–213)—specified by class **TimerTask**—connects to the topic and publishes the messages. Line 90 creates the JNDI context, in which the WeatherPublisher looks up the **TopicConnectionFactory** and **Topic** (lines 95–100). The **TopicConnectionFactory**—which the server administrator must create—creates a **TopicConnection** (lines 103–104). The **TopicConnection** then creates a **TopicSession** (lines 106–108). Lines 110–111 obtain the **TopicPublisher** from the **TopicSession**. The **TopicSession** also creates an **ObjectMessage** (lines 113–114); the **ObjectMessage** will contain **WeatherBean** objects (see Fig. 13.3 in Chapter 13, Remote Method Invocation) that maintain the weather information for a given city. Lines 165–168 create the **WeatherBean** object with data from the National Weather Service. Method **setObject** of class **ObjectMessage** stores the **WeatherBean** object in the message. Lines 174–175 use the **setStringProperty** of class **Message** to set **String** property **City** to the city name. The subscriber can use this property to filter the messages. Finally, the **topicPublisher** publishes the message to the **topic** (line 176).

16.4.3 Weather Application: Subscriber Side

Class **WeatherSubscriber** (Fig. 16.14) subscribes to the **Weather** topic to receive weather updates for selected cities. Class **WeatherSubscriber** creates a graphical user interface, which allows the user to choose cities, and displays the resulting weather conditions.

As with the **WeatherPublisher**, the **WeatherSubscriber** uses a JNDI context to obtain the **TopicConnectionFactory** and **Topic** (lines 55–65). The **Topic-ConnectionFactory** creates a **TopicConnection** (lines 68–69), which creates a **TopicSession** (lines 72–73). Line 76 initializes the message listener for the topic receiver (created in method **getWeather**) to a new instance of the **WeatherListener** class (Fig. 16.17). Lines 90–135 set up the user interface; the weather conditions are displayed in a **WeatherDisplay** (Fig. 16.18). Figure 16.15 shows the client GUI.

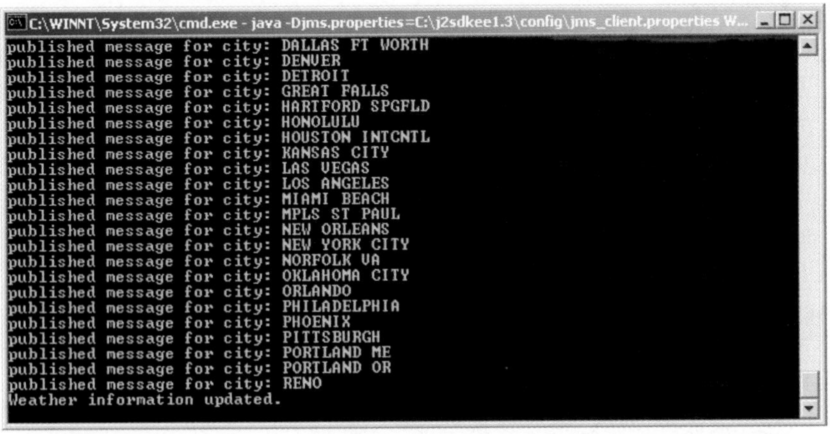

Fig. 16.13 WeatherPublisher publishing weather update messages.

```
1   // WeatherSubscriber.java
2   // WeatherSubscriber presents a GUI for the client to request
3   // weather conditions for various cities. The WeatherSubscriber
4   // retrieves the weather conditions from the Weather topic;
5   // each message body contains a WeatherBean object. The message
6   // header contains a String property "City," which allows
7   // the client to select the desired cities.
8   package com.deitel.advjhtp1.jms.weather;
9
10  // Java core packages
11  import java.awt.*;
12  import java.awt.event.*;
```

Fig. 16.14 WeatherSubscriber class allows user to receive weather updates (part 1 of 6).

```
13
14   // Java extension packages
15   import javax.swing.*;
16   import javax.naming.*;
17   import javax.jms.*;
18
19   public class WeatherSubscriber extends JFrame {
20
21      // GUI variables
22      private WeatherDisplay weatherDisplay;
23      private JList citiesList;
24
25      // cities contains cities for which weather
26      // updates are available on "Weather" topic
27      private String cities[] = { "ALBANY NY", "ANCHORAGE",
28         "ATLANTA", "ATLANTIC CITY", "BOSTON", "BUFFALO",
29         "BURLINGTON VT", "CHARLESTON WV", "CHARLOTTE", "CHICAGO",
30         "CLEVELAND", "DALLAS FT WORTH", "DENVER", "DETROIT",
31         "GREAT FALLS", "HARTFORD SPGFLD", "HONOLULU",
32         "HOUSTON INTCNTL", "KANSAS CITY", "LAS VEGAS",
33         "LOS ANGELES", "MIAMI BEACH", "MPLS ST PAUL", "NEW ORLEANS",
34         "NEW YORK CITY", "NORFOLK VA", "OKLAHOMA CITY", "ORLANDO",
35         "PHILADELPHIA", "PHOENIX", "PITTSBURGH", "PORTLAND ME",
36         "PORTLAND OR", "RENO" };
37
38      // JMS variables
39      private TopicConnection topicConnection;
40      private TopicSession topicSession;
41      private Topic topic;
42      private TopicSubscriber topicSubscriber;
43      private WeatherListener topicListener;
44
45      // WeatherSubscriber constructor
46      public WeatherSubscriber()
47      {
48         super( "JMS WeatherSubscriber..." );
49         weatherDisplay = new WeatherDisplay();
50
51         // set up JNDI context and JMS connections
52         try {
53
54            // create JNDI context
55            Context jndiContext = new InitialContext();
56
57            // retrieve topic connection factory
58            // from JNDI context
59            TopicConnectionFactory topicConnectionFactory =
60               ( TopicConnectionFactory ) jndiContext.lookup(
61                  "WEATHER_FACTORY" );
62
63            // retrieve topic from JNDI context
64            String topicName = "Weather";
```

Fig. 16.14 **WeatherSubscriber** class allows user to receive weather updates
(part 2 of 6).

```
65              topic = ( Topic ) jndiContext.lookup( topicName );
66
67              // create topic connection
68              topicConnection =
69                 topicConnectionFactory.createTopicConnection();
70
71              // create topic session
72              topicSession = topicConnection.createTopicSession( false,
73                 Session.AUTO_ACKNOWLEDGE );
74
75              // initialize listener
76              topicListener = new WeatherListener( weatherDisplay );
77           }
78
79           // process Naming exception from JNDI context
80           catch ( NamingException namingException ) {
81              namingException.printStackTrace();
82           }
83
84           // process JMS exceptions from topic connection or session
85           catch ( JMSException jmsException ) {
86              jmsException.printStackTrace();
87           }
88
89           // lay out user interface
90           Container container = getContentPane();
91           container.setLayout( new BorderLayout() );
92
93           JPanel selectionPanel = new JPanel();
94           selectionPanel.setLayout( new BorderLayout() );
95
96           JLabel selectionLabel = new JLabel( "Select Cities" );
97           selectionPanel.add( selectionLabel, BorderLayout.NORTH );
98
99           // create list of cities for which users
100          // can request weather updates
101          citiesList = new JList( cities );
102          selectionPanel.add( new JScrollPane( citiesList ),
103             BorderLayout.CENTER );
104
105          JButton getWeatherButton = new JButton( "Get Weather..." );
106          selectionPanel.add( getWeatherButton, BorderLayout.SOUTH );
107
108          // invoke method getWeather when getWeatherButton clicked
109          getWeatherButton.addActionListener (
110
111             new ActionListener() {
112
113                public void actionPerformed ( ActionEvent event )
114                {
115                   getWeather();
116                }
```

Fig. 16.14 **WeatherSubscriber** class allows user to receive weather updates (part 3 of 6).

```
117            }
118
119        ); // end call to addActionListener
120
121        container.add( selectionPanel, BorderLayout.WEST );
122        container.add( weatherDisplay, BorderLayout.CENTER );
123
124        // invoke method quit when window closed
125        addWindowListener(
126
127           new WindowAdapter() {
128
129              public void windowClosing( WindowEvent event )
130              {
131                 quit();
132              }
133           }
134
135        ); // end call to addWindowListener
136
137     } // end WeatherSubscriber constructor
138
139     // get weather information for selected cities
140     public void getWeather()
141     {
142        // retrieve selected indices
143        int selectedIndices[] = citiesList.getSelectedIndices();
144
145        if ( selectedIndices.length > 0 ) {
146
147           // if topic subscriber exists, method has
148           // been called before
149           if ( topicSubscriber != null ) {
150
151              // close previous topic subscriber
152              try {
153                 topicSubscriber.close();
154              }
155
156              // process JMS exception
157              catch ( JMSException jmsException ) {
158                 jmsException.printStackTrace();
159              }
160
161              // clear previous cities from display
162              weatherDisplay.clearCities();
163           }
164
165           // create message selector to retrieve specified cities
166           StringBuffer messageSelector = new StringBuffer();
167           messageSelector.append(
168              "City = '" + cities[ selectedIndices[ 0 ] ] + "'" );
```

Fig. 16.14 WeatherSubscriber class allows user to receive weather updates
(part 4 of 6).

```
169
170            for ( int i = 1; i < selectedIndices.length; i++ ) {
171               messageSelector.append( " OR City = '" +
172                  cities[ selectedIndices[ i ] ] + "'" );
173            }
174
175            // create topic subscriber and subscription
176            try {
177               topicSubscriber = topicSession.createSubscriber(
178                  topic, messageSelector.toString(), false );
179               topicSubscriber.setMessageListener( topicListener );
180               topicConnection.start();
181
182               JOptionPane.showMessageDialog( this,
183                  "A weather update should be arriving soon..." );
184            }
185
186            // process JMS exception
187            catch ( JMSException jmsException ) {
188               jmsException.printStackTrace();
189            }
190
191      } // end if
192
193   } // end method getWeather
194
195   // quit WeatherSubscriber application
196   public void quit()
197   {
198      // close connection and subscription to topic
199      try {
200
201         // close topic subscriber
202         if ( topicSubscriber != null ) {
203            topicSubscriber.close();
204         }
205
206         // close topic connection
207         topicConnection.close();
208      }
209
210      // process JMS exception
211      catch ( JMSException jmsException ) {
212         jmsException.printStackTrace();
213         System.exit( 1 );
214      }
215
216      System.exit( 0 );
217
218   } // end method quit
219
```

Fig. 16.14 WeatherSubscriber class allows user to receive weather updates (part 5 of 6).

```
220     // launch WeatherSubscriber application
221     public static void main( String args [] )
222     {
223        WeatherSubscriber subscriber = new WeatherSubscriber();
224        subscriber.pack();
225        subscriber.setVisible( true );
226     }
227  }
```

Fig. 16.14 WeatherSubscriber class allows user to receive weather updates (part 6 of 6).

Fig. 16.15 WeatherSubscriber selecting cities for weather updates.

The program invokes method **getWeather** (lines 140–193) when the user clicks the **Get Weather** button. If the method has been called previously (i.e., the user has clicked the button before), lines 149–163 close the previous **TopicSubscriber** so that a new subscriber can filter in the selected cities with a message selector. When a client specifies a message selector for a subscription, the server will only send messages satisfying that filter to the client. Lines 166–173 create a **messageSelector** so that the weather conditions for the selected cities will be displayed. The **messageSelector** syntax is based on SQL92 (see the **Message** javadoc for more details). Lines 177–178 create the **TopicSubscriber** from **TopicSession**, passing the **Topic** and **messageSelector** as parameters. The third parameter, with value **false**, indicates that the subscriber can receive messages published by its own connection. Line 179 sets the message listener for the **TopicSubscriber** to **topicListener**. A **TopicSubscriber**'s message listener handles new messages when they arrive. Finally, line 180 starts the **TopicConnection**; once the connection has started, the **TopicSubscriber** will receive messages published to the topic.

When the user closes the application window, lines 202–204 close the **TopicSubscriber** if it exists. Line 207 closes the **topicConnection**.

Class **WeatherListener** (Fig. 16.17) implements interface **MessageListener**. It therefore defines method **onMessage** (lines 26–57) to receive incoming messages. When a new message arrives, line 32 checks that it is of the appropriate message type—**ObjectMessage**. If so, method **getObject** gets the **WeatherBean** from the **ObjectMessage**. The **WeatherBean** object is then passed to the **WeatherDisplay**, which displays the corresponding information for the user. Figure 16.16 shows the application window once it has received a weather update.

Fig. 16.16 **WeatherSubscriber** having received updated weather
conditions.

```
1   // WeatherListener.java
2   // WeatherListener is the MessageListener for a subscription
3   // to the Weather topic. It implements the specified onMessage
4   // method to update the GUI with the corresponding city's
5   // weather.
6   package com.deitel.advjhtp1.jms.weather;
7
8   // Java extension packages
9   import javax.jms.*;
10  import javax.swing.*;
11
12  // Deitel packages
13  import com.deitel.advjhtp1.rmi.weather.WeatherBean;
14
15  public class WeatherListener implements MessageListener {
16
17     private WeatherDisplay weatherDisplay;
18
19     // WeatherListener constructor
20     public WeatherListener( WeatherDisplay display )
21     {
22        weatherDisplay = display;
23     }
24
25     // receive new message
26     public void onMessage( Message message )
27     {
28        // retrieve and process message
29        try {
30
31           // ensure Message is an ObjectMessage
32           if ( message instanceof ObjectMessage ) {
33
34              // get WeatherBean from ObjectMessage
35              ObjectMessage objectMessage =
36                 ( ObjectMessage ) message;
```

Fig. 16.17 **WeatherListener** class subscribes to **Weather** topic to receive
weather forecasts (part 1 of 2).

```
37              WeatherBean weatherBean =
38                 ( WeatherBean ) objectMessage.getObject();
39
40              // add WeatherBean to display
41              weatherDisplay.addItem( weatherBean );
42
43           } // end if
44
45           else {
46              System.out.println( "Expected ObjectMessage," +
47                 " but received " + message.getClass().getName() );
48           }
49
50        } // end try
51
52        // process JMS exception from message
53        catch ( JMSException jmsException ) {
54           jmsException.printStackTrace();
55        }
56
57     } // end method onMessage
58  }
```

Fig. 16.17 **WeatherListener** class subscribes to **Weather** topic to receive weather forecasts (part 2 of 2).

Class **WeatherDisplay** (Fig. 16.18) displays **WeatherBean** objects in **JList** **weatherList**. The **weatherList** uses classes **WeatherListModel** and **WeatherCellRenderer** (see Fig. 13.5 and Fig. 13.6 in Chapter 13, Remote Method Invocation) to display **WeatherBean** objects. Method **addItem** (lines 47–65) adds the specified **WeatherBean** item to the display if the corresponding city is not displayed currently. If the city is in the display already, lines 56–58 remove the city's previous **WeatherBean** object and add the updated **WeatherBean** object.

```
1   // WeatherDisplay.java
2   // WeatherDisplay extends JPanel to display results
3   // of client's request for weather conditions.
4   package com.deitel.advjhtp1.jms.weather;
5
6   // Java core packages
7   import java.awt.*;
8   import java.awt.event.*;
9   import java.util.*;
10
11  // Java extension packages
12  import javax.swing.*;
13
14  // Deitel packages
15  import com.deitel.advjhtp1.rmi.weather.*;
```

Fig. 16.18 **WeatherDisplay** displays **WeatherBean**s in a **JList** using a **WeatherCellRenderer** (part 1 of 3).

```
16
17   public class WeatherDisplay extends JPanel {
18
19       // WeatherListModel and Map for storing WeatherBeans
20       private WeatherListModel weatherListModel;
21       private Map weatherItems;
22
23       // WeatherDisplay constructor
24       public WeatherDisplay()
25       {
26          setLayout( new BorderLayout() );
27
28          ImageIcon headerImage = new ImageIcon(
29             WeatherDisplay.class.getResource(
30                "images/header.jpg" ) );
31          add( new JLabel( headerImage ), BorderLayout.NORTH );
32
33          // use JList to display updated weather conditions
34          // for requested cities
35          weatherListModel = new WeatherListModel();
36          JList weatherJList = new JList( weatherListModel );
37          weatherJList.setCellRenderer( new WeatherCellRenderer() );
38
39          add( new JScrollPane( weatherJList ), BorderLayout.CENTER );
40
41          // maintain WeatherBean items in HashMap
42          weatherItems = new HashMap();
43
44       } // end WeatherDisplay constructor
45
46       // add WeatherBean item to display
47       public void addItem( WeatherBean weather )
48       {
49          String city = weather.getCityName();
50
51          // check whether city is already in display
52          if ( weatherItems.containsKey( city ) ) {
53
54             // if city is in Map, and therefore in display
55             // remove previous WeatherBean object
56             WeatherBean previousWeather =
57                ( WeatherBean ) weatherItems.remove( city );
58             weatherListModel.remove( previousWeather );
59          }
60
61          // add WeatherBean to Map and WeatherListModel
62          weatherListModel.add( weather );
63          weatherItems.put( city, weather );
64
65       } // end method addItem
66
```

Fig. 16.18 WeatherDisplay displays WeatherBeans in a JList using a
WeatherCellRenderer (part 2 of 3).

```
67       // clear all cities from display
68       public void clearCities()
69       {
70          weatherItems.clear();
71          weatherListModel.clear();
72       }
73    }
```

Fig. 16.18 `WeatherDisplay` displays `WeatherBean`s in a `JList` using a
`WeatherCellRenderer` (part 3 of 3).

16.4.4 Weather Application: Configuring and Running

To run the application, issue the following commands at a command prompt:

1. Start J2EE server in a command window:

   `j2ee -verbose`

2. In a new command window, create the `Weather` topic:

   `j2eeadmin -addJmsDestination Weather topic`

3. Verify that the topic was created:

   `j2eeadmin -listJmsDestination`

4. Create the connection factory:

   `j2eeadmin -addJmsFactory WEATHER_FACTORY topic`

5. Start `WeatherPublisher`:

   `java -classpath %J2EE_HOME%\lib\j2ee.jar;.`
   `-Djms.properties=%J2EE_HOME%\config\jms_client.properties`
   `com.deitel.advjhtp1.jms.weather.WeatherPublisher`

6. Start `WeatherSubscriber` in a new command window:

   `java -classpath %J2EE_HOME%\lib\j2ee.jar;.`
   `-Djms.properties=%J2EE_HOME%\config\jms_client.properties`
   `com.deitel.advjhtp1.jms.weather.WeatherSubscriber`

Once you have finished running the application, you can remove the connection factory with the command:

`j2eeadmin -removeJmsFactory WEATHER_FACTORY`

To remove the topic, use the command:

`j2eeadmin -removeJmsDestination Weather`

To stop J2EE server, use the command:

`j2ee -stop`

16.5 Message-Driven Enterprise JavaBeans

Message-driven EJBs, or *message-driven beans,* are a new type of Enterprise JavaBean available in Enterprise JavaBeans version 2.0, which is part of the Java 2 Enterprise Edition version 1.3.[1] Message-driven beans are capable of processing JMS messages posted to a queue or topic. When a message is received, the EJB container uses any available instance of a particular message-driven bean to process the message. This is similar to the way an EJB container will use any instance of a stateless session EJB to handle a client request. Since any message-driven EJB instance may be used, message-driven beans are not specific to particular client and must not maintain client state information. Note that any given EJB instance may process messages from multiple clients. Unlike session and entity beans (which require developers to provide home and remote interfaces), message-driven beans require that developers to provide only the bean implementation class.

16.5.1 Voter Application: Overview

This section presents an implementation of the Voter application from Section 16.3 using a message-driven bean to tally the votes posted to the **Votes** queue. Class **Voter** (Fig. 16.4), which posts the vote messages to the queue, remains exactly the same—a benefit of loosely-coupled applications. The sender simply sends messages to the queue regardless of the receiver's implementation. The receiving end of the application (Section 16.5.2) is now a message-driven bean. Entity bean **Candidate** (Fig. 16.20, Fig. 16.21 and Fig. 16.22) represents a particular candidate for which users can vote. Entity bean **Candidate** stores the vote tallies in database **Voting**. Message-driven bean **VoteCollectorEJB** (Fig. 16.23) uses the **Candidate** EJB to update the tallies when the **Votes** queue receives a new vote message. Class **TallyDisplay** (Fig. 16.24) accesses the **Candidate** EJB to present a GUI with the current tallies from the database. Figure 16.19 provides an overview of the application.

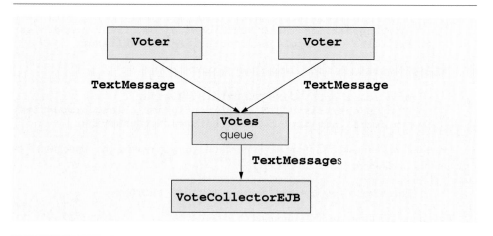

Fig. 16.19 Voter application overview.

---

[1]. At the time of this writing, the Java 2 Enterprise Edition Specification, version 1.3, was a Proposed Final Draft in the Java Community Process.

16.5.2 Voter Application: Receiver Side

The **Candidate** entity EJB represents a particular candidate for which users can vote and the total number of votes the **Candidate** has received. Home interface **Candidate-Home** (Fig. 16.20) provides methods **findByPrimaryKey** (lines 15–16) and **find-AllCandidates** (lines 19–20) to locate a particular **Candidate** or a **Collection** of all **Candidate**s, respectively. Method **create** (lines 23–24) creates a new **Candidate** EJB with the given **candidateName** and zero votes.

Remote interface **Candidate** (Fig. 16.21) provides method **incrementVote-Count** to add a new vote for the **Candidate**. Method **getVoteCount** (line 18) returns the current vote tally for the **Candidate**. Method **getCandidateName** (line 21) returns the **Candidate**'s name.

```
1   // CandidateHome.java
2   // CandidateHome is the home interface for the Candidate EJB.
3   package com.deitel.advjhtp1.jms.mdb;
4
5   // Java core libraries
6   import java.rmi.*;
7   import java.util.*;
8
9   // Java standard extensions
10  import javax.ejb.*;
11
12  public interface CandidateHome extends EJBHome {
13
14     // find Candidate with given name
15     public Candidate findByPrimaryKey( String candidateName )
16        throws RemoteException, FinderException;
17
18     // find all Candidates
19     public Collection findAllCandidates()
20        throws RemoteException, FinderException;
21
22     // create new Candidate EJB
23     public Candidate create( String candidateName )
24        throws RemoteException, CreateException;
25  }
```

Fig. 16.20 **CandidateHome** interface for **Candidate** EJB.

```
1   // Candidate.java
2   // Candidate is the remote interface for the Candidate
3   // EJB, which maintains a tally of votes.
4   package com.deitel.advjhtp1.jms.mdb;
5
6   // Java core libraries
7   import java.rmi.RemoteException;
8
```

Fig. 16.21 **Candidate** remote interface for **Candidate** EJB (part 1 of 2).

```
9    // Java standard extensions
10   import javax.ejb.EJBObject;
11
12   public interface Candidate extends EJBObject {
13
14      // place vote for this Candidate
15      public void incrementVoteCount() throws RemoteException;
16
17      // get total vote count for this Candidate
18      public Integer getVoteCount() throws RemoteException;
19
20      // get Candidate's name
21      public String getCandidateName() throws RemoteException;
22   }
```

Fig. 16.21 **Candidate** remote interface for **Candidate** EJB (part 2 of 2).

Class **CandidateEJB** (Fig. 16.22) implements the **Candidate** entity EJB. The **Candidate** EJB uses container-managed persistence for storing **Candidate** information in a database. Lines 17–18 declare container-managed fields **voteCount** and **name** for storing the **Candidate**'s total vote tally and name, respectively. Method **incrementVoteCount** (lines 21–25) increments the **Candidate**'s vote tally. Method **getName** (lines 34–37) returns the **Candidate**'s name. Method **ejbCreate** (lines 40–47) creates a new **Candidate** EJB, sets the **Candidate**'s **name** and initializes the **voteCount** to zero.

```
1    // CandidateEJB.java
2    // CandidateEJB is an entity EJB that uses container-managed
3    // persistence to persist its Candidate and its vote tally.
4    package com.deitel.advjhtp1.jms.mdb;
5
6    // Java core libraries
7    import java.rmi.RemoteException;
8
9    // Java standard extensions
10   import javax.ejb.*;
11
12   public class CandidateEJB implements EntityBean {
13
14      private EntityContext entityContext;
15
16      // container-managed fields
17      public Integer voteCount;
18      public String name;
19
20      // place vote for this Candidate
21      public void incrementVoteCount()
22      {
23         int newVoteCount = voteCount.intValue() + 1;
24         voteCount = new Integer( newVoteCount );
25      }
```

Fig. 16.22 **CandidateEJB** class to maintain candidate tallies (part 1 of 3).

```
26
27      // get total vote count for this Candidate
28      public Integer getVoteCount()
29      {
30         return voteCount;
31      }
32
33      // get Candidate's name
34      public String getCandidateName()
35      {
36         return name;
37      }
38
39      // create new Candidate
40      public String ejbCreate( String candidateName )
41         throws CreateException
42      {
43         name = candidateName;
44         voteCount = new Integer( 0 );
45
46         return null;
47      }
48
49      // do post-creation tasks when creating new Candidate
50      public void ejbPostCreate( String candidateName ) {}
51
52      // set EntityContext
53      public void setEntityContext( EntityContext context )
54      {
55         entityContext = context;
56      }
57
58      // unset EntityContext
59      public void unsetEntityContext()
60      {
61         entityContext = null;
62      }
63
64      // activate Candidate instance
65      public void ejbActivate()
66      {
67         name = ( String ) entityContext.getPrimaryKey();
68      }
69
70      // passivate Candidate instance
71      public void ejbPassivate()
72      {
73         name = null;
74      }
75
76      // load Candidate from database
77      public void ejbLoad() {}
78
```

Fig. 16.22 CandidateEJB class to maintain candidate tallies (part 2 of 3).

```
79        // store Candidate in database
80        public void ejbStore() {}
81
82        // remove Candidate from database
83        public void ejbRemove() {}
84    }
```

Fig. 16.22 CandidateEJB class to maintain candidate tallies (part 3 of 3).

To handle incoming messages from the **Votes** queue, the container uses message-driven bean class **VoteCollectorEJB** (Fig. 16.23). When **VoteCollectorEJB** receives a new vote, the container invokes method **onMessage** (lines 21–48).

```
1     // VoteCollectorEJB.java
2     // VoteCollectorEJB is a MessageDriven EJB that tallies votes.
3     package com.deitel.advjhtp1.jms.mdb;
4
5     // Java core packages
6     import java.util.*;
7     import java.rmi.*;
8
9     // Java extension packages
10    import javax.ejb.*;
11    import javax.rmi.*;
12    import javax.jms.*;
13    import javax.naming.*;
14
15    public class VoteCollectorEJB
16        implements MessageDrivenBean, MessageListener {
17
18        private MessageDrivenContext messageDrivenContext;
19
20        // receive new message
21        public void onMessage( Message message )
22        {
23            TextMessage voteMessage;
24
25            // retrieve and process message
26            try {
27
28                if ( message instanceof TextMessage ) {
29                    voteMessage = ( TextMessage ) message;
30                    String vote = voteMessage.getText();
31                    countVote( vote );
32
33                    System.out.println( "Received vote: " + vote );
34                } // end if
35
```

Fig. 16.23 VoteCollectorEJB class tallies votes from **Votes** queue (part 1 of 3).

```
36              else {
37                 System.out.println( "Expecting " +
38                    "TextMessage object, received " +
39                    message.getClass().getName() );
40              }
41
42        } // end try
43
44        // process JMS exception from message
45        catch ( JMSException jmsException ) {
46           jmsException.printStackTrace();
47        }
48     }
49
50     // add vote to corresponding tally
51     private void countVote( String vote )
52     {
53        // CandidateHome reference for finding/creating Candidates
54        CandidateHome candidateHome = null;
55
56        // find Candidate and increment vote count
57        try {
58
59           // look up Candidate EJB
60           Context initialContext = new InitialContext();
61
62           Object object = initialContext.lookup(
63              "java:comp/env/ejb/Candidate" );
64
65           candidateHome =
66              ( CandidateHome ) PortableRemoteObject.narrow(
67                  object, CandidateHome.class );
68
69           // find Candidate for whom the user voted
70           Candidate candidate =
71              candidateHome.findByPrimaryKey( vote );
72
73           // increment Candidate's vote count
74           candidate.incrementVoteCount();
75
76        } // end try
77
78        // if Candidate not found, create new Candidate
79        catch ( FinderException finderException ) {
80
81           // create new Candidate and increment its vote count
82           try {
83              Candidate newCandidate = candidateHome.create( vote );
84              newCandidate.incrementVoteCount();
85           }
86
```

Fig. 16.23 VoteCollectorEJB class tallies votes from **Votes** queue (part 2 of 3).

```
87                // handle exceptions creating new Candidate
88                catch ( Exception exception ) {
89                    throw new EJBException( exception );
90                }
91
92            } // end FinderException catch
93
94            // handle exception when looking up OrderProducts EJB
95            catch ( NamingException namingException ) {
96                throw new EJBException( namingException );
97            }
98
99            // handle exception when invoking OrderProducts methods
100           catch ( RemoteException remoteException ) {
101               throw new EJBException( remoteException );
102           }
103
104       } // end method countVote
105
106       // set message driven context
107       public void setMessageDrivenContext(
108           MessageDrivenContext context )
109       {
110           messageDrivenContext = context;
111       }
112
113       // create bean instance
114       public void ejbCreate() {}
115
116       // remove bean instance
117       public void ejbRemove() {}
118   }
```

Fig. 16.23 VoteCollectorEJB class tallies votes from **Votes** queue (part 3 of 3).

Class **VoteCollectorEJB** implements interfaces **MessageDrivenBean** and **MessageListener**. The container invokes method **ejbCreate** following instantiation of a new bean instance and method **ejbRemove** just before the instance is destroyed. Interface **MessageDrivenBean** specifies method **setMessageDrivenContext**. Note that interface **MessageDrivenBean** also specifies that the message-driven context should be stored as an instance variable (**messageDrivenContext**).

Upon receiving a message, the container invokes method **onMessage**, specified by interface **MessageListener**. Line 28 checks that the received **Message** is of type **TextMessage**. If so, line 31 invokes method **countVote** to count the received vote. Method **countVote** (lines 51–104) looks up the **Candidate** EJB (lines 60–67) and invokes method **findByPrimaryKey** of interface **CandidateHome** to locate the **Candidate** for which the user voted. If the **Candidate** is found, line 74 invokes method **incrementVoteCount** of interface **Candidate** to add a vote for the **Candidate**. If the **Candidate** is not found, lines 79–92 catch a **FinderException**.

Class **TallyDisplay** (Fig. 16.24) displays a snapshot of the candidates and corresponding tallies. Class **TallyDisplay** uses the **Candidate** EJB to retrieve the voting data. Lines 36–46 look up the **Candidate** EJB and retrieve a Collection of all Candidates.

For each **Candidate**, lines 51–58 create and add a new **TallyPanel** (Fig. 16.26), passing the candidate name and vote count as parameters to the **TallyPanel** constructor.

```
1   // TallyDisplay.java
2   // TallyDisplay displays the votes from database.
3   package com.deitel.advjhtp1.jms.mdb;
4
5   // Java core packages
6   import java.awt.*;
7   import java.awt.event.*;
8   import java.rmi.*;
9   import java.util.*;
10  import java.util.List;
11
12  // Java extension packages
13  import javax.swing.*;
14  import javax.ejb.*;
15  import javax.rmi.*;
16  import javax.naming.*;
17
18  public class TallyDisplay extends JFrame {
19
20     // TallyDisplay constructor
21     public TallyDisplay()
22     {
23        super( "Vote Tallies" );
24
25        Container container = getContentPane();
26
27        // displayPanel displays tally results
28        JPanel displayPanel = new JPanel();
29        displayPanel.setLayout( new GridLayout( 0, 1 ) );
30        container.add( new JScrollPane( displayPanel ) );
31
32        // find Candidates and display tallies
33        try {
34
35           // look up Candidate EJB
36           Context initialContext = new InitialContext();
37
38           Object object = initialContext.lookup(
39              "Candidate" );
40           CandidateHome candidateHome =
41              ( CandidateHome ) PortableRemoteObject.narrow(
42                 object, CandidateHome.class );
43
44           // find all Candidates
45           Collection candidates =
46              candidateHome.findAllCandidates();
```

Fig. 16.24 TallyDisplay displays candidate tallies from database (part 1 of 2).

```
47
48              // add TallyPanel with candidate name and
49              // vote count for each candidate
50              Iterator iterator = candidates.iterator();
51              while ( iterator.hasNext() ) {
52                  Candidate candidate = ( Candidate ) iterator.next();
53
54                  // create TallyPanel for Candidate
55                  TallyPanel tallyPanel =
56                      new TallyPanel( candidate.getCandidateName(),
57                          candidate.getVoteCount().intValue() );
58                  displayPanel.add( tallyPanel );
59              }
60
61          } // end try
62
63          // handle exception finding Candidates
64          catch ( FinderException finderException ) {
65              finderException.printStackTrace();
66          }
67          // handle exception looking up Candidate EJB
68          catch ( NamingException namingException ) {
69              namingException.printStackTrace();
70          }
71
72          // handle exception communicating with Candidate
73          catch ( RemoteException remoteException ) {
74              remoteException.printStackTrace();
75          }
76
77      } // end TallyDisplay constructor
78
79      // launch TallyDisplay application
80      public static void main( String args[] )
81      {
82          TallyDisplay tallyDisplay = new TallyDisplay();
83          tallyDisplay.setDefaultCloseOperation( EXIT_ON_CLOSE );
84          tallyDisplay.pack();
85          tallyDisplay.setVisible( true );
86      }
87  }
```

Fig. 16.24 TallyDisplay displays candidate tallies from database (part 2 of 2).

Figure 16.25 demonstrates the **TallyDisplay**. Note that the **TallyDisplay** displays only those votes already registered; the **TallyDisplay** does not update as new votes are received.

Class **TallyPanel** (Fig. 16.26) displays the name and tally for an individual candidate in a **JPanel**.

Fig. 16.25 `TallyDisplay` displays candidate tallies from database.

```
1   // TallyPanel.java
2   // TallPanel is the GUI component which displays
3   // the name and tally for a vote candidate.
4   package com.deitel.advjhtp1.jms.mdb;
5
6   // Java core packages
7   import java.awt.*;
8
9   // Java extension packages
10  import javax.swing.*;
11
12  public class TallyPanel extends JPanel {
13
14     private JLabel nameLabel;
15     private JTextField tallyField;
16     private String name;
17     private int tally;
18
19     // TallyPanel constructor
20     public TallyPanel( String voteName, int voteTally )
21     {
22        name = voteName;
23        tally = voteTally;
24
25        nameLabel = new JLabel( name );
26        tallyField =
27           new JTextField( Integer.toString( tally ), 10 );
28        tallyField.setEditable( false );
29        tallyField.setBackground( Color.white );
30
31        add( nameLabel );
32        add( tallyField );
33
34     } // end TallyPanel constructor
35
36  }
```

Fig. 16.26 `TallyPanel` class displays the name and tally for a candidate.

16.5.3 Voter Application: Configuring and Running

This section presents the steps needed to deploy and run the message-driven bean **Voter** application. Since the application relies on the Cloudscape database, the following lines must be added to the file **resource.properties** within the **config** directory under the main J2EE directory (e.g., **C:\j2sdkee1.3\config\resource.properties**):

> **jdbcDataSource.5.name=jdbc/Voting**
>
> **jdbcDataSource.5.url=jdbc:cloudscape:rmi:VotingDB;create=true**

Note that there may be several **jdbcDataSource** entries in this properties file. In the above examples, you should replace the **5** with the number of the last **jdbcDataSource** entry plus **1**. For example, if the last **jdbcDatSource** entry is number **3**, you would specify **jdbcDataSource.4.name** and **jdbcDataSource.4.url**. Once you have added these lines, start Cloudscape. Then start the J2EE server, using the command

> **j2ee -verbose**

In a new command window, create the queue and connection factory (note that these might still exist, if created in Section 16.3.4):

> **j2eeadmin -addJmsDestination Votes queue**
>
> **j2eeadmin -listJmsDestination**
>
> **j2eeadmin -addJmsFactory VOTE_FACTORY queue**

To deploy the **VoteCollector** application, start

> **deploytool**

Create a new application by selecting **File -> New Application** from the menu bar. In the dialog, click **Browse** and navigate to the directory above the **com** directory. Enter **VoteCollectorApp.ear** as the **File** name and click **New Application**. Then click **OK**.

Now, add the Candidate EJB by selecting **New Enterprise Bean** from the **File** menu. In the **EJB JAR** dialog, select the **Create new EJB File in Application** radio button, highlighting **VoteCollectorApp** from the resulting pull-down menu. Enter **VoteCollectorJAR** as the **EJB Display Name**. See Fig. 16.27 for details. Click the **Edit** button to add the class files. Inside the **Edit** dialog, specify the directory that contains the **com.deitel.advjhtp1** packages structure as the **Starting Directory**. Navigate down the tree to the **mdb** directory (**com/deitel/advjhtp1/jms/mdb**) and **Add Candidate.class**, **CandidateEJB.class** and **CandidateHome.class** (Fig. 16.28). Click **OK** to exit the **Edit** dialog. Click **Next** to proceed to the **General** dialog.

In the **General** dialog, select the **Entity** radio button as the **Bean Type**. Select **com.deitel.advjhtp1.jms.mdb.CandidateEJB** from the pull-down menu for the **Enterprise Bean Class**. Enter **Candidate** as the **Enterprise Bean Name**. In the **Remote Interfaces** section, select **com.deitel.advjhtp1.jms.mdb.CandidateHome** and **com.deitel.advjhtp1.jms.mdb.Candidate** as the **Remote Home Interface** and **Remote Interface**, respectively. (See Fig. 16.29 for details.) Click **Next** to proceed to the **Entity Settings** dialog.

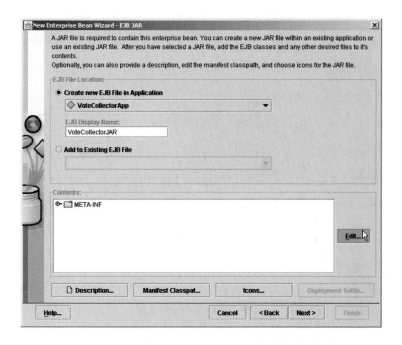

Fig. 16.27 EJB JAR settings for **VoteCollectorApp** application.

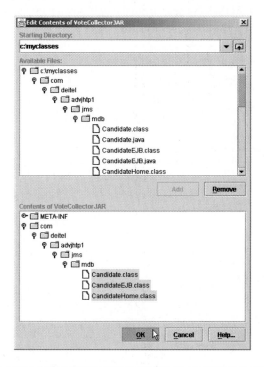

Fig. 16.28 Add class files for **Candidate** EJB.

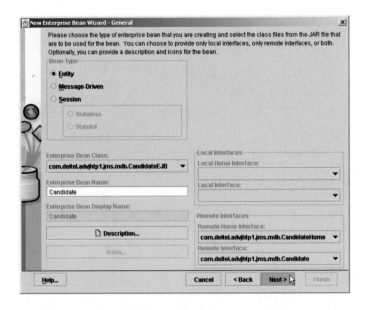

Fig. 16.29 General settings for `Candidate` EJB.

In the **Entity Settings** dialog, select radio button **Container managed persistence(1.0)**. Check both `voteCount` and `name`. Enter `java.lang.String` as the **Primary Key Class**, and select `name` from the pull-down menu under the **Primary Key Field**. See Fig. 16.30 for details. Click **Finish**.

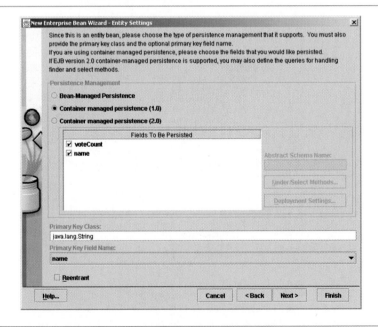

Fig. 16.30 Entity settings for `Candidate` EJB.

In the main **deploytool** window, select **Candidate** and click the **Entity** tab (Fig. 16.31). Click **Deployment Settings**. In the resulting dialog, click **Database Settings**. Enter **jdbc/Voting** as the **Database JNDI Name** (Fig. 16.32). Click **OK**. In the **Deployment Settings** dialog, click **Generate Default SQL**. A dialog will pop up, indicating **SQL Generation complete**; click **OK** (Fig. 16.33). In the **Deployment Settings** dialog, click **OK**. A warning dialog will appear that indicates there is no **WHERE** clause for method **findAllCandidates**; click **OK** to ignore the warning (Fig. 16.34).

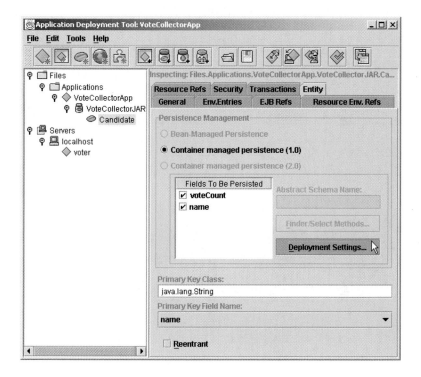

Fig. 16.31 Entity tab for **Candidate** EJB.

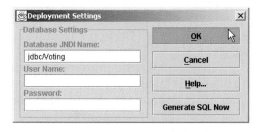

Fig. 16.32 Database settings for **Candidate** EJB.

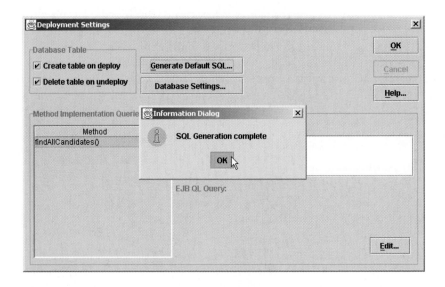

Fig. 16.33 SQL generation for **Candidate** EJB.

Fig. 16.34 SQL warning for **Candidate** EJB.

Now create the **VoteCollector** EJB by selecting **File -> New Enterprise Bean** from the menu bar. Click radio button **Add to Existing EJB File** and select **VoteCol-lectorJAR(VoteCollectorApp)** from the resulting pull-down menu (Fig. 16.35). Click **Edit** and **Add VoteCollectorEJB.class** from tree structure **com/deitel/advjhtp1/jms/mdb** (Fig. 16.36). Click **OK** to exit the **Edit** dialog. Click **Next** to proceed to the **General** dialog.

In the **General** dialog (Fig. 16.37), select **Message-Driven Bean** as the **Bean Type**. Select **com.deitel.advjhtp1.jms.mdb.VoteCollectorEJB** as the **Enterprise Bean Class**. Enter **VoteCollector** as the **Enterprise Bean Name**. Click **Next** to proceed to the **Transaction Management** dialog.

In the **Transaction Management** dialog (Fig. 16.38), select **Container-Managed**. Verify **Transaction Attribute Required** for method **onMessage**. Click **Next** to proceed to the **Message-Driven Bean Settings** dialog.

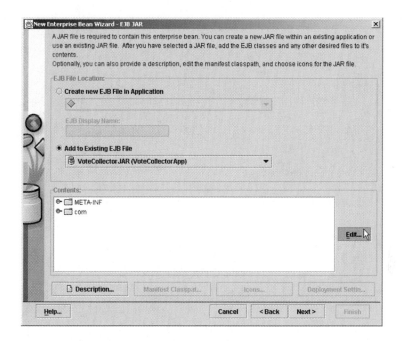

Fig. 16.35 EJB JAR settings for **VoteCollector** EJB.

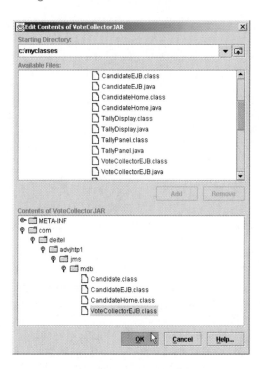

Fig. 16.36 Add class file for **VoteCollector** EJB.

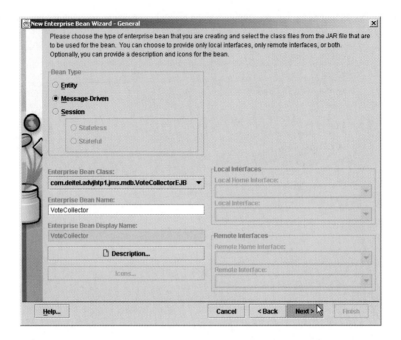

Fig. 16.37 General settings for **VoteCollector** EJB.

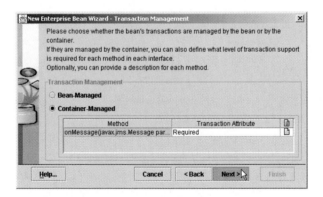

Fig. 16.38 Transaction management settings for the **VoteCollector** EJB.

In the **Message-Driven Bean** dialog, select **Queue** as the **Destination Type** (Fig. 16.39). Select **Votes** and **VOTE_FACTORY** from the pull-down menus for **Destination** and **Connection Factory**, respectively. Click **Next** to proceed to the **Environment Entries** dialog. Do not enter anything in this dialog; click **Next** again to proceed to the **Enterprise Bean References** dialog.

In the **Enterprise Bean References** dialog (Fig. 16.40), click **Add**. For the **Coded Name**, enter **ejb/Candidate**. Select **Entity** for **Type** and **Remote** for **Interfaces**. Enter **com.deitel.advjhtp1.jms.mdb.CandidateHome** and **com.deitel.advjhtp1.jms.mdb.Candidate** as the **Home Interface** and

Local/Remote Interface, respectively. Select radio button **JNDI Name** and enter **Candidate** in the corresponding text field. Click **Finish**.

In the main **deploytool** window, select **VoteCollectorApp** from the tree, and click the **JNDI Names** tab. Enter **Candidate** as the **JNDI Name** for **Candidate**. Verify that **Votes** is the **JNDI Name** for **VoteCollector** (Fig. 16.41).

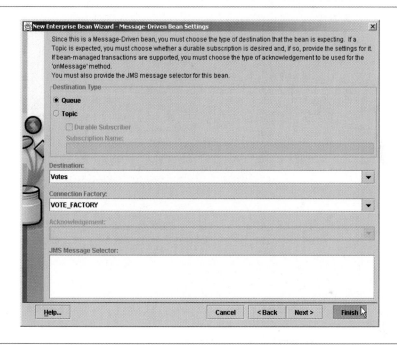

Fig. 16.39 Message-Driven Bean settings for **VoteCollector** EJB.

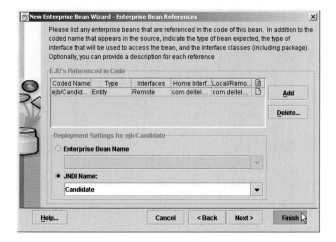

Fig. 16.40 Enterprise Bean References for **VoteCollector** EJB.

Finally, deploy the application by selecting **Deploy** from the **Tools** menu. Select **VoteCollectorApp** as the **Object to Deploy**. In the dialog, check **Return Client JAR** (Fig. 16.42). Click **Next** and verify the JNDI names. Click **Next**, then **Finish**.

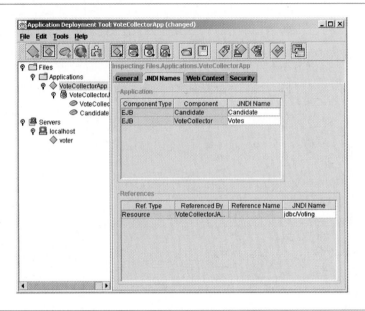

Fig. 16.41 Setting JNDI names for **VoteCollectorApp**.

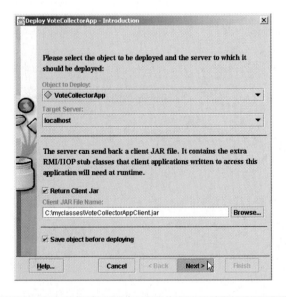

Fig. 16.42 Deploying the **VoteCollector** application.

After deploying the **VoteCollector** application, run the **Voter** client application:

```
java -classpath %J2EE_HOME%\lib\j2ee.jar;.
    -Djms.properties=%J2EE_HOME%\config\jms_client.properties
    com.deitel.advjhtp1.jms.mdb.Voter
```

To view the current vote tallies, run **TallyDisplay** (note that the client JAR must be included in the classpath)

```
java -classpath
    %J2EE_HOME%\lib\j2ee.jar;VoteCollectorAppClient.jar;.
    com.deitel.advjhtp1.jms.mdb.TallyDisplay
```

SUMMARY

- A messaging system loosely couples components.
- Messaging systems allow components to post messages for other components to read.
- There are two basic messaging system models—point-to-point and publish/subscribe. The point-to-point messaging model allows components to send messages to a message queue. A message consumer is a target component that processes the received messages.
- In the point-to-point model, exactly one client consumes a message; the server maintains messages that have not been consumed.
- The publish/subscribe messaging model allows components to publish messages to a topic. Components interested in messages published to a particular topic can subscribe to that topic.
- When a publisher publishes a message to a given topic, current subscribers receive that message.
- In the publish/subscribe model, zero or more subscribers consume a published message.
- A message consists of a header, properties (optional) and a body (also optional). The message header contains information, such as the message destination and the sending time.
- Message properties allow message receivers to select which types of messages they would like to receive; the sender of a message can set these properties. Message receivers use message selectors to filter out messages; filtering is done on the server side.
- Message-driven beans are a type of enterprise bean that integrate nicely with MOM.
- The EJB container can use any instance of a message-driven bean to process incoming messages to a given queue or topic. Using message-driven beans, a component can receive messages asynchronously.
- The Java Message Service (JMS) API. JMS standardizes enterprise messaging, providing APIs for both the point-to-point and publish/subscribe models.
- JMS provides five types of messages—**BytesMessage**s, **MapMessage**s, **ObjectMessage**s, **StreamMessage**s and **TextMessage**s.
- The server administrator creates the connection factories, queues and topics.
- A **QueueConnectionFactory** allows the client to create a **QueueConnection**.
- A **QueueConnection** creates a **QueueSession**. A **QueueSession** creates either a **QueueSender** or a **QueueReceiver**.
- When the queue receiver or topic subscriber receives a message, the message listener processes the message.
- Interface **MessageListener** declares method **onMessage** that is invoked when a new message arrives.
- A client may obtain two types of subscriptions—nondurable and durable. Nondurable subscriptions receive messages only while the subscriptions are active.

- Durable subscriptions can receive messages while inactive—the server maintains messages sent to the topic while the subscription is inactive and sends them to the client when the subscription is reactivated. Note that, if a message selector is specified for the subscription to filter the messages, the server maintains only the messages that satisfy the selector.

- A **TopicConnectionFactory**, which the server has created, creates a **TopicConnection**. A **TopicConnection** creates a **TopicSession**. A **TopicSession** creates a **TopicPublisher** or **TopicSubscriber**.

- A topic subscriber (or queue receiver) can filter messages with a message selector. When a client specifies a message selector, the server will only send messages satisfying that filter to the client. The message selector syntax is based on SQL92.

- Message-driven EJBs, or message-driven beans, are a new type of Enterprise JavaBean available in Enterprise JavaBeans version 2.0, which is part of the Java 2 Enterprise Edition version 1.3.

- Message-driven beans are capable of processing JMS messages posted to a queue or topic.

- When a message is received, the EJB container uses any available instance of a particular message-driven bean to process the message.

- Since any message-driven EJB instance may be used, message-driven beans are not specific to particular client and must not maintain client state information.

- Any given EJB instance may process messages from multiple clients.

- Unlike session and entity beans (which require interfaces), message-driven beans require only that developers to provide the bean implementation class.

- Interface **MessageDrivenBean** declares **setMessageDrivenContext** and specifies that the message-driven context should be stored as instance variable **messageDrivenContext**.

TERMINOLOGY

BytesMessage interface
durable subscription
Java Message Service (JMS)
MapMessage interface
message
message body
message consumer
message-driven bean
message header
message-oriented middleware (MOM)
message property
message selector
messaging system
nondurable subscription
ObjectMessage interface
point-to-point messaging model
publish
publish/subscribe messaging model
publisher

queue
QueueConnection interface
QueueConnectionFactory interface
QueueReceiver interface
QueueSender interface
QueueSession interface
receiver
sender
StreamMessage interface
subscribe
subscriber
subscription
TextMessage interface
topic
TopicConnection interface
TopicConnectionFactory interface
TopicPublisher interface
TopicSession interface
TopicSubscriber interface

SELF-REVIEW EXERCISES

16.1 State which of the following are *true* and which are *false*. If *false*, explain why.
   a) Messages in the point-to-point messaging model are intended for zero or more recipients.
   b) Messages in the publish/subscribe messaging model are intended for zero or one recipient.

    c) When a message selector is specified, filtering is done on the server side.

    d) The server maintains messages published to a topic while there are no subscriptions until a subscription is created.

    e) The server maintains messages sent to a queue while there is no receiver until a receiver connects.

    f) Message-driven beans maintain state for a specific client.

16.2   Fill in the blanks in each of the following:

    a) The two messaging models are _____ and _____.

    b) In the _____ messaging model, the client sends a message a _____ and intends that message for exactly one recipient.

    c) In the _____ messaging model, the client sends a message to a _____ and intends that message for zero or more recipients.

    d) The server will maintain messages for a _____ subscription while the subscription is inactive.

    e) A _____ bean is a type of enterprise bean, which integrates well with MOM.

ANSWERS TO SELF-REVIEW EXERCISES

16.1 a) False. Messages in the point-to-point messaging model are intended for exactly one recipient. b) False. Messages in the publish/subscribe messaging model are intended for zero or more recipients. c) True. d) False. If there are no current subscriptions, the server will not maintain an incoming message; note that if there is a durable subscription that is inactive, however, the server will maintain messages for that subscription. e) True. f) False. A message-driven bean instance may process messages from multiple clients; message-driven beans cannot maintain client-specific state.

16.2   a) Point-to-point, Publish/subscribe. b)Point-to-point, Queue. c) Publish/subscribe, Topic. d) Durable. e) Message-driven.

EXERCISES

16.3   What is the purpose of a messaging system?

16.4   Compare and contrast the point-to-point messaging model and the publish/subscribe messaging model. When would it be appropriate to use one over the other?

16.5   Using the point-to-point messaging model, create an application that allows a seller to receive bids on an item. The offering message should include the bidder's email address and bid price. (*Hint:* The seller should be the receiver of the offering messages, and the bidders should be the senders of the offering messages.)

16.6   Modify your solution to Exercise 16.5 to allow the seller to filter out offers lower than a certain bid price. (*Hint:* Set the bid price as a **double** property of the offering messages and use this property in a message selector.)

16.7   Create an application using the publish/subscribe messaging model that accepts orders from a client. The order should be published as a message to a **Domestic_orders** topic if the client's shipping address is domestic or an **International_orders** topic if the client's shipping address is international.

16.8   Modify your solution to Exercise 16.7 to allow subscribers of the **Domestic_orders** and **International_orders** topics to filter out product orders by category. For instance, suppose a component is responsible for book orders—allow that component to filter out all orders not of the "book" category. (*Hint:* Use a **String** property to set the order category and a message selector to filter by that property.)

17

Enterprise Java Case Study: Architectural Overview

Objectives

- To understand the Deitel Bookstore Enterprise Java case study architecture.
- To understand the decisions made in designing the Deitel Bookstore.
- To understand the Model-View-Controller (MVC) architecture in an Enterprise Java application context.
- To understand how XML and XSLT can generate content for many different client types.
- To understand the roles that servlets and EJBs play in enterprise applications.
- To understand multi-tier application design within the J2EE framework.

It is easier to go down a hill than up,
but the view is from the top.
Arnold Bennett

The universe is wider than our views of it.
Henry David Thoreau

Don't bother looking at the view—I have already composed it.
Gustav Mahler

A whole is that which has a beginning, middle and end.
Aristotle

The life of the law has not been logic: it has been experience.
Oliver Wendell Holmes, Jr.

Outline

17.1 Introduction

The technologies that comprise the Java 2 Enterprise Edition (J2EE) enable developers to build robust, scalable enterprise applications. In this case study, we build an online bookstore e-business application using several features of J2EE, including servlets and Enterprise JavaBeans, and other technologies, such as XML, XSLT, XHTML, WML and cHTML.

We used the Model-View-Controller (MVC) architecture in Chapter 5 to build a substantial drawing application. The Deitel Drawing application used MVC to separate the underlying representation of a drawing (a **Collection** of **MyShape**s) from views of that drawing (rendered using Java 2D) and input-processing logic (**MyShapeController**s and a **DragAndDropController**). In this case study, we employ the MVC architecture to separate data and business logic from presentation logic and controller logic in a Java 2 Enterprise Edition application. A relational database and entity EJBs comprise the applications model. Java servlets implement controller logic for processing user input, and XSL transformations implement the application's presentation logic.

XSLT presentation logic enables our application to present content to several client types. XSL transformations process application data (marked up with XML) to generate XHTML, WML and other presentations dynamically. We can extend the application to support additional client types and customize output for certain client types by implementing additional XSL transformations. For example, we could develop a J2ME MIDlet for handheld devices and implement a set of XSL transformations that produce output suitable for that MIDlet.

In this chapter, we present an overview of the Deitel Bookstore case study architecture. In the following chapters, we present the controller logic implementation with servlets (Chapter 18) and the business logic and data abstraction implementations with EJBs (Chapters 19 and 20). In Chapter 20, we also provide instructions for deploying the Deitel Bookstore case study on Sun Microsystems' J2EE reference implementation application server. In Chapter 21, Application Servers, we introduce three of the top J2EE-compliant commercial application servers—BEA's WebLogic, IBM's WebSphere and the iPlanet Application Server. We discuss the features of each application server, then deploy the Deitel Bookstore case study on BEA's WebLogic and IBM's WebSphere.

17.2 Deitel Bookstore

The application we develop in this case study implements a subset of the functionality that customers expect of commercial on-line stores. We provide a product catalog that customers can search or browse for available books. We also provide a shopping cart to which customers can add products to be purchased. The customer can view the shopping cart, remove products, change the quantity of any product or purchase the products.

We provide customer registration, in which customers enter billing and shipping information. We also allow customers to view the details of previous orders and recover lost passwords. Customers can access the on-line store, using standard Web browsers, Wireless Markup Language (WML) browsers and cHTML (i-mode) browsers.

17.3 System Architecture

The Deitel Bookstore is a multi-tier application. Multi-tier applications—sometimes referred to as *n*-tier applications—divide functionality into separate tiers. Each tier may be located on a separate physical computer. We use a three-tier architecture in the Deitel Bookstore. Figure 17.1 presents the basic structure of three-tier applications.

The *information tier* (also called the *data tier* or the *bottom tier*) maintains data for the application. The information tier of an enterprise application typically stores data in a relational database management system (RDBMS). In the Deitel Bookstore case study, the database contains product information, such as a description, price and quantity in stock, and customer information, such as a user name, billing address and credit-card number.

The *middle tier* implements business logic and controller logic that control interactions between application clients and application data. The middle tier acts as an intermediary between the data in the information tier and the application clients. The middle-tier controller logic processes client requests (e.g., a request to view the product catalog) and retrieves data from the database. The middle-tier presentation logic then processes data from the information tier and presents the content to the client.

> **Software Engineering Observation 17.1**
>
> *The Web server in a multi-tier application could be considered to be a separate tier, resulting in a four-tier application. We consider the Web server to be part of the middle tier in this case study, because the Web server simply delegates requests to the application server and forwards responses to the client tier.*

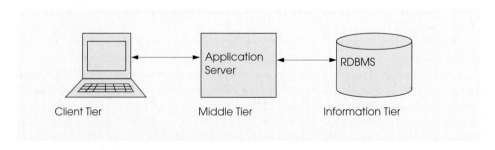

Fig. 17.1 Three-tier application model in Deitel Bookstore.

Business logic enforces *business rule*s and ensures that data are reliable before updating the database or presenting data to the user. Business rules dictate how clients of the application can and cannot access data, and how data are processed within the application. For example, an on-line store could have a business rule requiring that a customer's credit-card issuer verify the customer's credit card before the warehouse can ship the customer's order. Business logic might implement this business rule by obtaining the credit-card number, expiration date and billing address from the customer and performing the verification. If the verification is successful, the business logic would update the database to indicate that the warehouse can ship the customer's order.

The middle tier also implements the application's presentation logic. Web applications typically present information to clients as XHTML documents. With recent advances in wireless technologies, many Web applications also present information to wireless clients as WML and cHTML documents. The middle tier of the Deitel Bookstore uses XML and XSLT to generate content for different client types dynamically, enabling support for Web browsers (XHTML), WAP browsers (WML) and i-mode browsers (cHTML).

The *client tier*, or top tier, is the application's user interface. For Web applications, the client tier typically consists of a Web browser. Users view application output in the Web browser and click hyperlinks and form buttons to interact with the application. The Web browser then communicates with the middle tier to make requests and retrieve data from the information tier. The Deitel Bookstore supports Web, WML and cHTML browsers in the client tier. Developers can add support for other clients by providing XSL transformations for those other clients. Figure 17.2 presents a detailed diagram of the Deitel Bookstore enterprise application architecture. We discuss each portion of the diagram in the following sections.

17.4 Enterprise JavaBeans

Enterprise JavaBeans (EJBs) implement the Deitel Bookstore's business logic and database abstraction layer. The primary business logic component is a stateful session EJB that represents a customer's shopping cart. The entity EJBs in the Deitel Bookstore, which provide an object-based interface to the information tier, implement the Deitel Bookstore application's model. Any program that can communicate using RMI-IIOP can use the EJB business logic. For example, an administrative tool could be developed as a stand-alone Java application that uses EJB business logic to modify application data. Servlets use the EJB business logic in the Deitel Bookstore application to create an on-line store.

17.4.1 Entity EJBs

Entity EJBs provide an object-based abstraction of the application's information tier. Each entity EJB represents a particular object stored in the application's relational database. Instances of each entity EJB represent individual rows in the database. For example, a **Customer** EJB instance represents a store customer. The database stores each customer's first name, last name, billing address, shipping address and credit-card information. Each **Customer** EJB instance represents a particular customer and provides methods for retrieving and storing the customer's information.

Clients communicate with the Web server, which forwards requests to the servlets running in the application server's servlet container.

Servlets implement the application's controller and communicate with EJBs using RMI-IIOP.

The information tier and EJBs form the application's model.

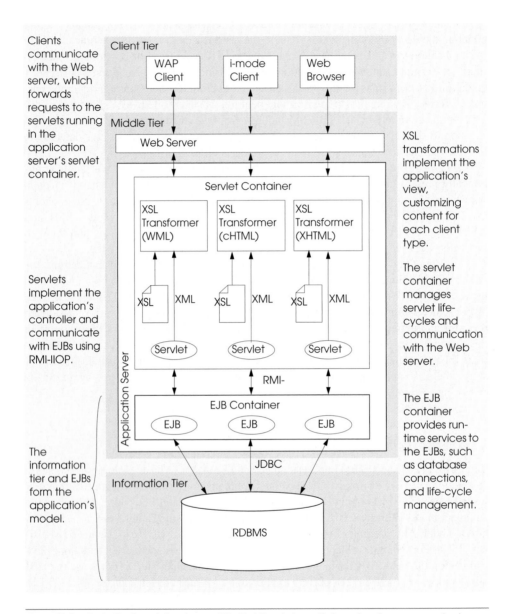

XSL transformations implement the application's view, customizing content for each client type.

The servlet container manages servlet life-cycles and communication with the Web server.

The EJB container provides run-time services to the EJBs, such as database connections, and life-cycle management.

Fig. 17.2 Detailed architecture of Deitel Bookstore Enterprise Java case study.

To facilitate transmitting data through the application, each entity EJB has a corresponding *model class* that has properties for each entity EJB property. For example, the **Product** EJB, which represents a product in the database, has a corresponding **ProductModel** class with properties for the product's ISBN, price, author, etc. Each model class implements interface **Serializable** and therefore is suitable for transmission over RMI-IIOP. Encapsulating data into model classes relieves network congestions by reducing the number of remote method calls required to obtain information from an entity EJB. For example, a servlet can invoke method **getProductModel** to obtain information about a **Product**, instead of invoking separate methods such as **getISBN**, **get-Price**, **getAuthor**, etc. Each model class also implements interface **XMLGenerator**, which declares method **getXML** for retrieving an XML representation of a particular model class instance. The servlets in the Deitel Bookstore use these XML elements to build XML documents, such as the product catalog and order history.

17.4.2 Stateful Session EJBs

The **ShoppingCart** stateful session EJB, which manages the customer's shopping cart, is the primary business-logic component in the Deitel Bookstore. Sometimes, customers browse online stores and add products to their shopping carts, then decide not to purchase those products. Such shopping carts are said to be *abandoned*. Rather than store an abandoned shopping cart in the database, the Deitel Bookstore uses a stateful session EJB to parallel more closely a user's experience in brick-and-mortar stores. When a customer abandons a shopping cart, the EJB container removes the **ShoppingCart** EJB instance.

17.5 Servlet Controller Logic

Servlets provide the middle-tier interface between the client and the EJB business logic. The servlets in the Deitel Bookstore implement the controller in the application's MVC architecture. Servlets handle client requests (via HTTP and WAP) and interact with the EJB business-logic components to fulfill those requests. The servlets then process data retrieved from the EJBs and generate XML documents that represent those data. These XML documents act as intermediate models of application data. The servlets then pass those XML documents through XSL transformations, which produce presentations for each client type.

17.6 XSLT Presentation Logic

Each servlet in the Deitel Bookstore employs an XSL **Transformer** and XSL transformations to generate appropriate presentations for each client type. The application requires a separate set of XSL transformations for each supported client type. For example, we provide one set of XSL transformations for producing XHTML, a second set for producing WML and a third set for producing cHTML. The servlets use a configuration file to determine the appropriate XSL transformation to apply for a particular client type.

  GetProductServlet obtains an XML description of a product from that product's **ProductModel**. An XSL **Transformer** uses an XSL transformation to extract data from the XML document and create a presentation for the client. If the client is a Web browser, the XSL **Transformer** uses an XSL transformation that produces XHTML. If the client is a WAP browser (e.g., running on a cell phone), the XSL **Transformer** uses an XSL transformation that produces WML.

  Figure 17.3 shows a sample XML document generated by **GetProductServlet**. This XML document marks up a product, including the product's ISBN, title, author, publisher, price, etc.

  The XSL document of Fig. 17.4 transforms **GetProductServlet**'s XML document into XHTML, which is rendered in a Web browser in Fig. 17.5. The transformation simply extracts the relevant pieces of information from the XML document and creates an appropriate XHTML representation. We discuss the structures of these XSL transformations in Chapter 18.

```
1   <?xml version="1.0" encoding="UTF-8"?>
2   <catalog>
3      <product>
4         <isbn>0130284173</isbn>
5         <publisher>Prentice Hall</publisher>
6         <author>Deitel, Deitel, Nieto, Lin &amp; Sadhu</author>
7         <title>XML How to Program</title>
8         <price>$69.95</price>
9         <pages>1200</pages>
10        <image>images/xmlhtp1.jpg</image>
11        <media>CD</media>
12        <quantity>500</quantity>
13     </product>
14  </catalog>
```

Fig. 17.3   XML file generated by **GetProductServlet**.

```
1   <?xml version = "1.0"?>
2
3   <!-- ProductDetails.xsl                                    -->
4   <!-- XSLT stylesheet for transforming content generated by -->
5   <!-- GetProductServlet into XHTML.                          -->
6
7   <xsl:stylesheet version = "1.0"
8      xmlns:xsl = "http://www.w3.org/1999/XSL/Transform">
9
10     <xsl:output method = "xml" omit-xml-declaration = "no"
11        indent = "yes" doctype-system = "DTD/xhtml1-strict.dtd"
12        doctype-public = "-//W3C//DTD XHTML 1.0 Strict//EN"/>
13
14     <!-- include template for processing error elements -->
15     <xsl:include href = "/XSLT/XHTML/error.xsl"/>
16
17     <!-- template for product element -->
18     <xsl:template match = "product">
19        <html xmlns = "http://www.w3.org/1999/xhtml"
20           xml:lang = "en" lang = "en">
21
22        <head>
23           <title>
24              <xsl:value-of select = "title"/> -- Description
25           </title>
26
27           <link rel = "StyleSheet" href = "styles/default.css"/>
28        </head>
29
30        <body>
31
32           <!-- copy navigation header into XHTML document -->
33           <xsl:for-each select =
34              "document( '/XSLT/XHTML/navigation.xml' )">
```

Fig. 17.4   XSL transformation for generating XHTML from **GetProductServlet** (part 1 of 3).

```
35              <xsl:copy-of select = "."/>
36          </xsl:for-each>
37
38          <div class = "header">
39              <xsl:value-of select = "title"/>
40          </div>
41
42          <div class = "author">
43              by <xsl:value-of select = "author"/>
44          </div>
45
46          <!-- create div element with details of Product -->
47          <div class = "productDetails">
48              <table style = "width: 100%;">
49                  <tr>
50                      <td style = "text-align: center;">
51                          <img class = "bookCover"
52                              src = "images/{image}"
53                              alt = "{title} cover image."/>
54                      </td>
55
56                      <td>
57                          <p style = "text-align: right;">
58                              Price: <xsl:value-of select = "price"/>
59                          </p>
60
61                          <p style = "text-align: right;">
62                              ISBN: <xsl:value-of select = "ISBN"/>
63                          </p>
64
65                          <p style = "text-align: right;">
66                              Pages: <xsl:value-of select = "pages"/>
67                          </p>
68
69                          <p style = "text-align: right;">
70                              Publisher:
71                              <xsl:value-of select = "publisher"/>
72                          </p>
73
74                          <!-- AddToCart button -->
75                          <form method = "post" action = "AddToCart">
76                              <p style = "text-align: center;">
77                                  <input type = "submit"
78                                      value = "Add to cart"/>
79
80                                  <input type = "hidden" name = "ISBN"
81                                      value = "{ISBN}"/>
82                              </p>
83                          </form>
84                      </td>
85                  </tr>
86              </table>
```

Fig. 17.4 XSL transformation for generating XHTML from **GetProductServlet** (part 2 of 3).

```
87                </div>
88
89            </body>
90            </html>
91        </xsl:template>
92    </xsl:stylesheet>
```

Fig. 17.4   XSL transformation for generating XHTML from **GetProductServlet**
(part 3 of 3).

```
1   <?xml version="1.0" encoding="UTF-8"?>
2   <!DOCTYPE html PUBLIC "-//W3C//DTD XHTML 1.0 Strict//EN"
3      "DTD/xhtml1-strict.dtd">
4   <html xmlns="http://www.w3.org/1999/xhtml"
5      lang="en" xml:lang="en">
6   <head>
7      <title>XML How to Program -- Description</title>
8      <link href="styles/default.css" rel="StyleSheet" />
9   </head>
10  <body>
11     <div>
12        <div class="logo">
13           <table style="width: 100%;">
14              <tr>
15                 <td style="text-align: left;">
16                    <img src="images/logotiny.gif"
17                       alt="Deitel &amp; Associates, Inc. logo." />
18                 </td>
19
20                 <td style="text-align: right;">
21                    <div style=
22                       "position: relative; bottom: -50px;">
23                       <form action="ProductSearch" method="get">
24                       <p><input type="text" size="15"
25                          name="searchString" />
26                          <input type="submit" value="Search" />
27                       </p>
28                       </form>
29                    </div>
30                 </td>
31              </tr>
32           </table>
33        </div>
34
35        <div class="navigation">
36           <table class="menu">
37              <tr>
38                 <td class="menu">
39                    <a href="GetAllProducts">Product Catalog</a>
40                 </td>
41
```

Fig. 17.5   XHTML document generated by XSLT in **GetProductServlet** (part 1 of
3).

```
42                  <td class="menu">
43                      <a href="registration.html">Create Account</a>
44                  </td>
45
46                  <td class="menu">
47                      <a href="login.html">Log in</a>
48                  </td>
49
50                  <td class="menu">
51                      <a href="ViewCart">Shopping Cart</a>
52                  </td>
53
54                  <td class="menu">
55                      <a href="ViewOrderHistory">Order History</a>
56                  </td>
57              </tr>
58          </table>
59      </div>
60
61  </div>
62  <div class="header">XML How to Program</div>
63  <div class="author">
64      by Deitel, Deitel, Nieto, Lin &amp; Sadhu</div>
65  <div class="productDetails">
66      <table style="width: 100%;">
67          <tr>
68              <td style="text-align: center;">
69                  <img alt="XML How to Program cover image."
70                      src="images/xmlhtp1.jpg"
71                      class="bookCover" /></td>
72              <td>
73                  <p style="text-align: right;">
74                  Price: $69.95</p>
75                  <p style="text-align: right;">
76                  ISBN: 0130284173</p>
77                  <p style="text-align: right;">
78                  Pages: 1100</p>
79                  <p style="text-align: right;">
80                  Publisher: Prentice Hall</p>
81
82                  <form action="AddToCart" method="post">
83                      <p style="text-align: center;">
84                          <input value="Add to cart"
85                              type="submit" />
86                          <input value="0130284173"
87                              name="ISBN" type="hidden" /></p>
88                  </form>
89              </td>
90          </tr>
91      </table>
92  </div>
93  </body>
```

Fig. 17.5   XHTML document generated by XSLT in **GetProductServlet** (part 2 of 3).

```
94    </html>
```

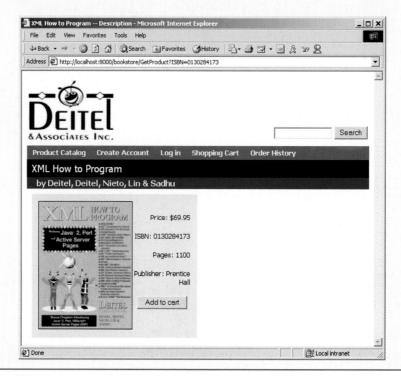

Fig. 17.5 XHTML document generated by XSLT in **GetProductServlet** (part 3 of 3).

The XSL transformation of Fig. 17.6 transforms **GetProductServlet**'s XML document into WML, which appears in a WML browser in Fig. 17.7. Note that in the WML document there is little formatting information. WML is rendered on small devices, such as cell phones, so display capabilities are limited. These devices also have limited network connections, so the amount of data sent should be kept to a minimum. For example, the WML document does not contain an image of the books cover, which would be cumbersome to download over a wireless connection.

```
1    <?xml version = "1.0"?>
2
3    <xsl:stylesheet version = "1.0"
4       xmlns:xsl = "http://www.w3.org/1999/XSL/Transform">
5
6       <xsl:output method = "xml" omit-xml-declaration = "no"
7          doctype-system = "http://www.wapforum.org/DTD/wml_1.1.xml"
8          doctype-public = "-//WAPFORUM//DTD WML 1.1//EN"/>
9
10       <xsl:include href = "/XSLT/WML/error.xsl"/>
```

Fig. 17.6 XSL transformation for generating WML from **GetProductServlet** (part 1 of 2).

```
11
12      <xsl:template match = "product">
13         <wml>
14
15            <card id = "product" title = "{title}">
16               <do type = "accept" label = "Add To Cart">
17                  <go href = "AddToCart" method = "post">
18                     <postfield name = "ISBN" value = "{ISBN}"/>
19                  </go>
20               </do>
21
22               <do type = "prev" label = "Back">
23                  <prev/>
24               </do>
25
26               <p>Description:</p>
27               <p><xsl:value-of select = "title"/></p>
28               <p>by <xsl:value-of select = "author"/></p>
29
30               <p>
31                  <table columns = "2" title = "info">
32                     <tr>
33                        <td>ISBN:
34                           <xsl:value-of select = "ISBN"/>
35                        </td>
36                        <td>Price:
37                           $<xsl:value-of select = "price"/>
38                        </td>
39                     </tr>
40                     <tr>
41                        <td>Publisher:
42                           <xsl:value-of select = "publisher"/>
43                        </td>
44                        <td>Pages:
45                           <xsl:value-of select = "pages"/>
46                        </td>
47                     </tr>
48                  </table>
49               </p>
50            </card>
51
52         </wml>
53      </xsl:template>
54   </xsl:stylesheet>
```

Fig. 17.6   XSL transformation for generating WML from **GetProductServlet**
(part 2 of 2).

```
1   <?xml version="1.0"?>
2   <!DOCTYPE wml PUBLIC "-//WAPFORUM//DTD WML 1.1//EN"
3      "http://www.wapforum.org/DTD/wml_1.1.xml">
```

Fig. 17.7   WML document generated by XSLT in **GetProductServlet** (part 1 of
2). (Image © 2001 Nokia Mobile Phones.)

```
4
5   <wml>
6     <card title="XML How to Program" id="product">
7       <do label="Add To Cart" type="accept">
8         <go method="post" href="AddToCart">
9           <postfield value="0130284173" name="ISBN"/></go>
10      </do>
11      <do label="Back" type="prev"><prev/></do>
12
13      <p>Description:</p>
14      <p>XML How to Program</p>
15      <p>by Deitel, Deitel, Nieto, Lin &amp; Sadhu</p>
16      <p>
17        <table title="info" columns="2">
18          <tr>
19            <td>ISBN: 0130284173</td>
20            <td>Price: $$69.95</td>
21          </tr>
22          <tr>
23            <td>Publisher: Prentice Hall</td>
24            <td>Pages: 1100</td>
25          </tr>
26        </table>
27      </p>
28    </card>
29  </wml>
```

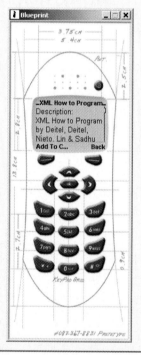

Fig. 17.7   WML document generated by XSLT in **GetProductServlet** (part 2 of 2). (Image © 2001 Nokia Mobile Phones.)

The XSL document of Fig. 17.8 transforms **GetProductServlet**'s XML document into cHTML, which appears in a cHTML browser in Fig. 17.9.

```
1    <?xml version = "1.0"?>
2
3    <xsl:stylesheet version = "1.0"
4       xmlns:xsl = "http://www.w3.org/1999/XSL/Transform">
5
6       <xsl:output method = "html"
7          omit-xml-declaration = "yes"
8          indent = "yes"
9          doctype-system =
10             "http://www.w3.org/MarkUp/html-spec/html-spec_toc.html"
11         doctype-public = "-//W3C//DTD HTML 2.0//EN"/>
12
13      <xsl:include href = "/XSLT/cHTML/error.xsl"/>
14
15      <xsl:template match = "product">
16         <html>
17
18            <head>
19               <title>
20                  <xsl:value-of select = "title"/> -- Description
21               </title>
22            </head>
23
24            <body>
25               <div class = "header">
26                  <xsl:value-of select = "title"/>
27               </div>
28
29               <div class = "author">
30                  by <xsl:value-of select = "author"/>
31               </div>
32
33               <!-- create div element with details of Product -->
34               <div class = "productDetails">
35                  <table>
36                     <tr>
37                        <td style = "text-align: center;">
38                           <img class = "bookCover"
39                              src = "images/{image}"/>
40                        </td>
41
42                        <td>
43                           <p style = "text-align: right;">
44                              Price: <xsl:value-of select = "price"/>
45                           </p>
46
47                           <p style = "text-align: right;">
48                              ISBN: <xsl:value-of select = "ISBN"/>
49                           </p>
```

Fig. 17.8   XSL transformation for generating cHTML from **GetProductServlet**
(part 1 of 2).

```
50
51                              <p style = "text-align: right;">
52                                  Pages: <xsl:value-of select = "pages"/>
53                              </p>
54
55                              <p style = "text-align: right;">
56                                  Publisher:
57                                  <xsl:value-of select = "publisher"/>
58                              </p>
59
60                              <!-- AddToCart button -->
61                              <form method="post" action="AddToCart">
62                                  <p style = "text-align: center;">
63                                      <input type = "submit"
64                                          value = "Add to cart"/>
65                                  </p>
66
67                                  <input type = "hidden" name = "ISBN"
68                                      value = "{ISBN}"/>
69                              </form>
70                          </td>
71                      </tr>
72                  </table>
73              </div>
74          </body>
75
76      </html>
77    </xsl:template>
78 </xsl:stylesheet>
```

Fig. 17.8   XSL transformation for generating cHTML from **GetProductServlet**
(part 2 of 2).

```
1  <!DOCTYPE HTML PUBLIC "-//W3C//DTD HTML 2.0//EN"
2      "http://www.w3.org/MarkUp/html-spec/html-spec_toc.html">
3  <html>
4  <head>
5     <META http-equiv="Content-Type"
6        content="text/html; charset=UTF-8">
7     <title>XML How to Program -- Description</title>
8  </head>
9  <body>
10    <div class="header">XML How to Program</div>
11    <div class="author">
12       by Deitel, Deitel, Nieto, Lin &amp; Sadhu</div>
13    <div class="productDetails">
14       <table>
15          <tr>
16             <td style="text-align: center;">
17                <img src="images/xmlhtp1.jpg" class="bookCover">
18             </td>
```

Fig. 17.9   cHTML document generated by XSLT in **GetProductServlet** (part 1 of
2). (Image courtesy of Pixo, Inc.)

```
19              <td>
20                 <p style="text-align: right;">Price: $69.95</p>
21
22                 <p style="text-align: right;">ISBN: 0130284173</p>
23
24                 <p style="text-align: right;">Pages: 1100</p>
25
26                 <p style="text-align: right;">
27                    Publisher: Prentice Hall</p>
28
29                 <form action="AddToCart" method="post">
30                    <p style="text-align: center;">
31                       <input value="Add to cart" type="submit">
32                    </p>
33                       <input value="0130284173" name="ISBN"
34                          type="hidden">
35                 </form>
36              </td>
37           </tr>
38        </table>
39     </div>
40  </body>
41  </html>
```

Fig. 17.9 cHTML document generated by XSLT in **GetProductServlet** (part 2 of 2). (Image courtesy of Pixo, Inc.)

This chapter overviewed the Deitel Bookstore case study architecture, which uses powerful enterprise Java capabilities, including servlets, EJBs, RMI, XML and XSLT. Chapters 18, 19 and 20 present the implementations of each tier. In Chapters 20–21, we provide instructions for deploying the Deitel Bookstore using the J2EE reference implementation, BEA's WebLogic and IBM's WebSphere.

SUMMARY

- The MVC design pattern, as applied in this enterprise application case study, separates data and business logic from presentation logic and controller logic.

- Multi-tier applications—sometimes referred to as *n*-tier applications—are divided into modular parts called tiers. Each tier may be located on a separate physical computer.

- The information tier, or data tier, maintains data for the application. The information tier typically stores data in a relational database management system (RDBMS). The database could contain product information, such as a description, price and quantity in stock, and customer information, such as a user name, billing address and credit-card number.

- The middle tier implements business logic and presentation logic to control interactions between application clients and application data. The middle tier acts as an intermediary between the data in the information tier and application clients.

- Middle-tier controller logic processes client requests (e.g., a request to view the product catalog) and retrieves data from the database. The middle-tier presentation logic then processes data from the information tier and presents the content to the client.

- Business logic enforces business rules and ensures that data are reliable before updating the database or presenting data to the user. Business rules dictate how clients of the application can and cannot access data and how data are processed within the application.

- The middle tier also implements the application's presentation logic. The middle tier accepts client requests, retrieves data from the information tier and presents content to clients.

- Web applications typically present information to clients as XHTML documents. Many Web applications present information to wireless clients as Wireless Markup Language (WML) documents or Compact HyperText Markup Language (cHTML) documents.

- The middle tier of the Deitel Bookstore uses XML and XSLT to generate content for different client types dynamically, enabling support for XHTML, WML, cHTML and virtually any other client type.

- The client tier is the application's user interface. Users interact directly with the application through the user interface. The client interacts with the middle tier to make requests and retrieve data from the application. The client then displays data retrieved from the middle tier to the user.

- Enterprise JavaBeans (EJBs) implement the Deitel Bookstore's business rules. The entity EJBs in the Deitel Bookstore, along with the database they represent, are the model for the Deitel Bookstore application.

- Any program that can communicate using RMI-IIOP can use EJB business logic and database abstraction objects. For example, an administrative tool could be developed as a stand-alone Java application that uses the EJB business logic to process orders.

- Entity EJBs provide an object-based representation of the application's information tier. Each entity EJB represents a particular object stored in the database. Instances of each entity EJB represent individual rows in the database.

- On-line store customers often browse the store catalog and add products to their shopping carts, but decide not to purchase the products. The shopping cart is therefore abandoned. Rather than store the abandoned shopping cart in the database, we use session EJBs to parallel more closely a user's experience in brick-and-mortar stores.

- Servlets provide the middle-tier interface between the client and the EJB business logic. The servlets in the Deitel Bookstore implement the controller of the MVC architecture. Servlets handle user requests (via HTTP and WAP) and interact with the EJB business logic.

- Servlets process data retrieved from EJBs and generate XML representations, which act as intermediate models of application data.

- XSL transformations act as the application view by transforming the XML model to appropriate formats for various client types.

- Each servlet in the Deitel Bookstore employs an XSL **Transformer** and XSL transformations to generate appropriate content for each client type. A separate set of XSL transformations generates content for each client type.

- The servlets produce XML documents to which the XSL **Transformer** applies XSL transformations to generate the appropriate content. To support additional client types, the developer can create additional sets of XSL transformations.

TERMINOLOGY

abandoned shopping cart	Enterprise JavaBean (EJB)
application server	entity EJB
bottom tier	four-tier application
brick-and-mortar store	information tier
business logic	middle tier
business rules	model-view-controller (MVC)
business-logic component	multi-tier application
client tier	*n*-tier application
Compact HyperText Markup Language (cHTML)	presentation logic
container-managed persistence	shopping cart e-commerce model
controller logic	three-tier architecture
controller-logic component	top tier
data tier	Wireless Access Protocol (WAP)
delegate	Wireless Markup Language (WML)
design patterns	XHTML
e-business	XML
e-business application	XSL transformation
e-commerce	XSL **Transformer**
e-commerce application	XSLT

SELF-REVIEW EXERCISES

17.1   What architectural pattern plays a major role in the Deitel Bookstore application architecture? What benefits does this design pattern provide?

17.2   Which part of the Deitel Bookstore application architecture could be separated into an additional tier? Why?

17.3   Section 17.3 describes a hypothetical business rule requiring credit-card verification. Describe an additional business rule appropriate for the Deitel Bookstore.

17.4   What are the controller-logic components in the Deitel Bookstore? What are the business-logic components? How do the controller-logic components in the application server communicate with the business-logic components?

17.5   What type of EJB in the Deitel Bookstore closely parallels customer experiences in brick-and-mortar stores?

17.6   How is the Deitel Bookstore application able to present content to clients of virtually any type?

17.7   How could a B2B partner (e.g., a corporate client) communicate with the Deitel Bookstore application? For example, a B2B partner may wish to order, on a periodic basis, large numbers of copies of a particular book used for training new employees. How could this B2B partner order the books programmatically?

ANSWERS TO SELF-REVIEW EXERCISES

17.1 The Deitel Bookstore application architecture uses the Model-View-Controller (MVC) architecture. MVC separates business logic from controller logic and presentation logic. Implementations of the business logic, controller logic and presentation logic can change independently of one another without requiring changes in the other components.

17.2   The Web server could be separated into a fourth tier. Separating the Web server into a fourth tier would provide a more modular design for applications that support clients using other protocols, in addition to HTTP.

17.3   An additional business rule could require customers to provide their e-mail addresses in the registration. Business logic could process the registration forms and reject registrations that do not include e-mail addresses.

17.4   Servlets are the controller-logic components in the Deitel Bookstore. Enterprise JavaBeans are the business-logic components. The servlets communicate with the EJBs through the EJB container using RMI-IIOP.

17.5   The **ShoppingCart** EJB is implemented as a stateful session EJB to simulate a shopping cart in a brick-and-mortar store.

17.6   The Deitel Bookstore application uses XSL transformations to present content for each client type. The servlets generate XML documents, and the developer supplies XSL transformations to transform the servlet XML documents for each client type.

18

Enterprise Java Case Study: Presentation and Controller Logic

Objectives

- To understand the role of presentation logic in a multitier application.
- To understand the role of controller logic in a multitier application.
- To understand the use of servlets in the middle tier of an Enterprise Java application.
- To understand how XML and XSLT can enable support for a variety of client types in a Web application.
- To understand how servlet initialization parameters can make servlets more flexible.

First come, first served.
Traditional Proverb

'Tis distance lends enchantment to the view…
Thomas Campbell

Invention is nothing more than a fine deviation from, or enlargment on a fine model…
Edward G. Bulwer-Lytton

Do not become the slave of your model.
Vincent Van Gogh

While Genius was thus wasting his strength in eccentric flights, I saw a person of a very different appearance, named Application.
Anna Letitia Barbauld

18.1 Introduction

In this chapter, we present the controller and presentation logic for the Deitel Bookstore. Controller logic in an application is responsible for processing user requests. For example, when a customer makes a request to add a book to a shopping cart, controller logic handles the request and invokes the appropriate business-logic methods to perform the requested action. The presentation logic then shows the output from the request to the user.

Java servlets in the implement the Deitel Bookstore's controller logic. After invoking business-logic methods to process client requests, the servlets generate XML documents that contain content to presented to the client. These XML documents are not specific to any particular type of client (e.g., Web browser, cell phone, etc.); they simply mark up the data that the business logic supplies. XSL transformations implement the application's presentation logic—the view in the MVC architecture—by transforming the XML documents into output suitable for each client type. For example, an XSL transformation might generate an XHTML document to present to a Web browser on a desktop computer, or a WML document to present to a WAP browser in a cell phone.

Using XSL transformations as presentation logic enable developers to extend the set of client types that the application supports without modifying the controller logic or business logic. To support a new client type, the developer simply supplies an additional set of

XSL transformations that produce appropriate output for the new client type. The developer then modifies an XML configuration file to install support for the new client type. [*Note*: The Deitel Bookstore requires the Apache Software Foundation's Xalan XSL transformer. Download Xalan version 2.1 from **xml.apache.org/dist/xalan-j** and copy **xalan.jar** and **xerces.jar** to your J2SE SDK's **jre/lib/ext** directory.]

This chapter is the first of three chapters that present the implementation of the Deitel Bookstore case study. In Chapters 19 and 20 we present the business logic and entity EJB components required for processing orders and working with the database.

18.2 **XMLServlet** Base Class

Each servlet in the Deitel Bookstore case study extends class **XMLServlet** (Fig. 18.1), which provides common initialization and utility methods. To enable support for multiple client types, each servlet in the Deitel Bookstore creates an XML document that represents raw application data retrieved from the application's business logic and information tier. An XSLT transformation processes this XML document and presents the output to the client. Class **XMLServlet** implements this common functionality.

Method **init** (lines 41–85) initializes the servlet. The servlet container provides the **ServletConfig** argument when the container initializes the servlet. Line 49 retrieves the name of the XSL transformation that will transform the servlet's content for each client type. This file name is provided as a servlet-initialization parameter, so the deployer must define this parameter when deploying the servlet. Line 52 creates a **DocumentBuilderFactory** instance, which will be used to create **DocumentBuilder**s for building XML documents. Line 55 creates a **TransformerFactory**, with which instances of **XMLServlet** perform XSL transformations. Lines 58–81 set a **URIResolver** for the **TransformerFactory** to enable its **Transformer**s to resolve relative URIs in XSL documents. For example, if an XSL document references another XSL document using element **xsl:include** with a relative URI (e.g., **/XSLT/XHTML/error.xsl**), the **Transformer** invokes method resolve of interface **URIResolver** to determine from where the **Transformer** should load the included XSL. Line 67 resolves the relative URI by invoking **ServletContext** method **getResource**, which returns a **URL**. Line 71 returns a **StreamSource** for the **URL**s **InputStream**. The **Transformer** uses this **StreamSource** to read the contents of the included XSL document.

```
1   // XMLServlet.java
2   // XMLServlet is a base class for servlets that generate
3   // XML documents and perform XSL transformations.
4   package com.deitel.advjhtp1.bookstore.servlets;
5
6   // Java core packages
7   import java.io.*;
8   import java.util.*;
9   import java.net.URL;
10
11  // Java extension packages
12  import javax.servlet.*;
13  import javax.servlet.http.*;
```

Fig. 18.1 **XMLServlet** base class for servlets in the Deitel Bookstore (part 1 of 8).

```
14    import javax.xml.parsers.*;
15    import javax.xml.transform.*;
16    import javax.xml.transform.dom.*;
17    import javax.xml.transform.stream.*;
18
19    // third-party packages
20    import org.w3c.dom.*;
21    import org.xml.sax.SAXException;
22
23    // Deitel packages
24    import com.deitel.advjhtp1.bookstore.model.*;
25
26    public class XMLServlet extends HttpServlet {
27
28       // factory for creating DocumentBuilders
29       private DocumentBuilderFactory builderFactory;
30
31       // factory for creating Transformers
32       private TransformerFactory transformerFactory;
33
34       // XSL file that presents servlet's content
35       private String XSLFileName;
36
37       // ClientModel List for determining client type
38       private List clientList;
39
40       // initialize servlet
41       public void init( ServletConfig config )
42          throws ServletException
43       {
44          // call superclass's init method for initialization
45          super.init( config );
46
47          // use InitParameter to set XSL file for transforming
48          // generated content
49          setXSLFileName( config.getInitParameter( "XSL_FILE" ) );
50
51          // create new DocumentBuilderFactory
52          builderFactory = DocumentBuilderFactory.newInstance();
53
54          // create new TransformerFactory
55          transformerFactory = TransformerFactory.newInstance();
56
57          // set URIResolver for resolving relative paths in XSLT
58          transformerFactory.setURIResolver(
59
60             new URIResolver() {
61
62                // resolve href as relative to ServletContext
63                public Source resolve( String href, String base )
64                {
65                   try {
66                      ServletContext context = getServletContext();
```

Fig. 18.1 **XMLServlet** base class for servlets in the Deitel Bookstore (part 2 of 8).

```
67                    URL url = context.getResource( href );
68
69                    // create StreamSource to read document from URL
70                    return new StreamSource( url.openStream() );
71                 }
72
73                 // handle exceptions obtaining referenced document
74                 catch ( Exception exception ) {
75                    exception.printStackTrace();
76
77                    return null;
78                 }
79              }
80           }
81       ); // end call to setURIResolver
82
83       // create ClientModel ArrayList
84       clientList = buildClientList();
85    }
86
87    // get DocumentBuilder instance for building XML documents
88    public DocumentBuilder getDocumentBuilder( boolean validating )
89    {
90       // create new DocumentBuilder
91       try {
92
93          // set validation mode
94          builderFactory.setValidating( validating );
95
96          // return new DocumentBuilder to the caller
97          return builderFactory.newDocumentBuilder();
98       }
99
100         // handle exception when creating DocumentBuilder
101         catch ( ParserConfigurationException parserException ) {
102            parserException.printStackTrace();
103
104            return null;
105         }
106
107      }  // end method getDocumentBuilder
108
109      // get non-validating parser
110      public DocumentBuilder getDocumentBuilder()
111      {
112         return getDocumentBuilder( false );
113      }
114
115      // set XSL file name for transforming servlet's content
116      public void setXSLFileName( String fileName )
117      {
118         XSLFileName = fileName;
119      }
```

Fig. 18.1   XMLServlet base class for servlets in the Deitel Bookstore (part 3 of 8).

```
120
121     // get XSL file name for transforming servlet's content
122     public String getXSLFileName()
123     {
124        return XSLFileName;
125     }
126
127     // write XML document to client using provided response
128     // Object after transforming XML document with
129     // client-specific XSLT document
130     public void writeXML( HttpServletRequest request,
131        HttpServletResponse response, Document document )
132        throws IOException
133     {
134        // get current session, create if not extant
135        HttpSession session = request.getSession( true );
136
137        // get ClientModel from session Object
138        ClientModel client = ( ClientModel )
139           session.getAttribute( "clientModel" );
140
141        // if client is null, get new ClientModel for this
142        // User-Agent and store in session
143        if ( client == null ) {
144           String userAgent = request.getHeader( "User-Agent" );
145           client = getClientModel( userAgent );
146           session.setAttribute( "clientModel", client );
147        }
148
149        // set appropriate Content-Type for client
150        response.setContentType( client.getContentType() );
151
152        // get PrintWriter for writing data to client
153        PrintWriter output = response.getWriter();
154
155        // build file name for XSLT document
156        String xslFile = client.getXSLPath() + getXSLFileName();
157
158        // open InputStream for XSL document
159        InputStream xslStream =
160           getServletContext().getResourceAsStream( xslFile );
161
162        // transform XML document using XSLT
163        transform( document, xslStream, output );
164
165        // flush and close PrintWriter
166        output.close();
167
168     } // end method writeXML
169
170     // transform XML document using provided XSLT InputStream
171     // and write resulting document to provided PrintWriter
```

Fig. 18.1 XMLServlet base class for servlets in the Deitel Bookstore (part 4 of 8).

```
172     public void transform( Document document,
173         InputStream xslStream, PrintWriter output )
174     {
175         // create Transformer and apply XSL transformation
176         try {
177
178             // create DOMSource for source XML document
179             Source xmlSource = new DOMSource( document );
180
181             // create StreamSource for XSLT document
182             Source xslSource =
183                 new StreamSource( xslStream );
184
185             // create StreamResult for transformation result
186             Result result = new StreamResult( output );
187
188             // create Transformer for XSL transformation
189             Transformer transformer =
190                 transformerFactory.newTransformer( xslSource );
191
192             // transform and deliver content to client
193             transformer.transform( xmlSource, result );
194
195         } // end try
196
197         // handle exception when transforming XML document
198         catch ( TransformerException transformerException ) {
199             transformerException.printStackTrace();
200         }
201
202     } // end method transform
203
204     // build error element containing error message
205     public Node buildErrorMessage( Document document,
206         String message)
207     {
208         // create error element
209         Element error = document.createElement( "error" );
210
211         // create message element
212         Element errorMessage =
213             document.createElement( "message" );
214
215         // create message text and append to message element
216         errorMessage.appendChild(
217             document.createTextNode( message ) );
218
219         // append message element to error element
220         error.appendChild( errorMessage );
221
222         return error;
223     }
224
```

Fig. 18.1   **XMLServlet** base class for servlets in the Deitel Bookstore (part 5 of 8).

```
225        // build list of ClientModel Objects for delivering
226        // appropriate content to each client
227        private List buildClientList()
228        {
229            // get validating DocumentBuilder for client XML document
230            DocumentBuilder builder = getDocumentBuilder( true );
231
232            // create client ArrayList
233            List clientList = new ArrayList();
234
235            // get name of XML document containing client
236            // information from ServletContext
237            String clientXML = getServletContext().getInitParameter(
238                "CLIENT_LIST" );
239
240            // read clients from XML document and build ClientModels
241            try {
242
243                // open InputStream to XML document
244                InputStream clientXMLStream =
245                    getServletContext().getResourceAsStream(
246                        clientXML );
247
248                // parse XML document
249                Document clientsDocument =
250                    builder.parse( clientXMLStream );
251
252                // get NodeList of client elements
253                NodeList clientElements =
254                    clientsDocument.getElementsByTagName( "client" );
255
256                // get length of client NodeList
257                int listLength = clientElements.getLength();
258
259                // process NodeList of client Elements
260                for ( int i = 0; i < listLength; i++ ) {
261
262                    // get next client Element
263                    Element client =
264                        ( Element ) clientElements.item( i );
265
266                    // get agent Element from client Element
267                    Element agentElement = ( Element )
268                        client.getElementsByTagName(
269                            "userAgent" ).item( 0 );
270
271                    // get agent Element's child text node
272                    Text agentText =
273                        ( Text ) agentElement.getFirstChild();
274
275                    // get value of agent Text node
276                    String agent = agentText.getNodeValue();
277
```

Fig. 18.1 **XMLServlet** base class for servlets in the Deitel Bookstore (part 6 of 8).

```
278              // get contentType Element
279              Element typeElement = ( Element )
280                 client.getElementsByTagName(
281                    "contentType" ).item( 0 );
282
283              // get contentType Element's child text node
284              Text typeText =
285                 ( Text ) typeElement.getFirstChild();
286
287              // get value of contentType text node
288              String type = typeText.getNodeValue();
289
290              // get XSLPath element
291              Element pathElement = ( Element )
292                 client.getElementsByTagName(
293                    "XSLPath" ).item( 0 );
294
295              // get Text node child of XSLPath
296              Text pathText =
297                 ( Text ) pathElement.getFirstChild();
298
299              // get value of XSLPath text node
300              String path = pathText.getNodeValue();
301
302              // add new ClientModel with userAgent, contentType
303              // and XSLPath for this client Element
304              clientList.add(
305                 new ClientModel( agent, type, path ) );
306           }
307
308        } // end try
309
310        // handle SAXException when parsing XML document
311        catch ( SAXException saxException ) {
312           saxException.printStackTrace();
313        }
314
315        // catch IO exception when reading XML document
316        catch ( IOException ioException ) {
317           ioException.printStackTrace();
318        }
319
320        // return newly creating list of ClientModels
321        return clientList;
322
323     } // end method buildClientList
324
325     // get ClientModel for given User-Agent HTTP header
326     private ClientModel getClientModel( String header )
327     {
328        // get Iterator for clientList
329        Iterator iterator = clientList.iterator();
330
```

Fig. 18.1 **XMLServlet** base class for servlets in the Deitel Bookstore (part 7 of 8).

```
331          // find ClientModel whose userAgent property is a
332          // substring of given User-Agent HTTP header
333          while ( iterator.hasNext() ) {
334             ClientModel client = ( ClientModel ) iterator.next();
335
336             // if this ClientModel's userAgent property is a
337             // substring of the User-Agent HTTP header, return
338             // a reference to the ClientModel
339             if ( header.indexOf( client.getUserAgent() ) > -1 )
340                 return client;
341          }
342
343          // return default ClientModel if no others match
344          return new ClientModel(
345             "DEFAULT CLIENT", "text/html", "/XHTML/" );
346
347     } // end method getClientModel
348 }
```

Fig. 18.1   **XMLServlet** base class for servlets in the Deitel Bookstore (part 8 of 8).

Line 84 invokes method **buildClientList**, which reads the **clients.xml** configuration file and produces a **List** of **ClientModel**s (Fig. 18.4). Instances of **XMLServlet** use these **ClientModel**s to determine which XSL transformation to apply for each client type.

Method **getDocumentBuilder** (lines 88–107) creates a **DocumentBuilder** object for parsing and creating XML documents. The **boolean** argument specifies whether method **getDocumentBuilder** should create a validating XML parser. Class **XMLServlet** stores a **DocumentBuilderFactory** in an instance variable (line 29), which prevents the need to create a new **DocumentBuilderFactory** each time a **DocumentBuilder** is needed. The overloaded **getDocumentBuilder** (lines 110–113) invokes method **getDocumentBuilder** with a **false** argument to create a non-validating XML parser.

Methods **setXSLFileName** and **getXSLFileName** (lines 116–125) are *set* and *get* methods for the **XSLFileName** property of class **XMLServlet**. The **XSLFile-Name** property specifies the name of the XSLT document that transforms the servlet's content for a particular client type. The Deitel Bookstore application separates the XSL transformations for the various client types into separate directories. For example, the file **products.xsl** in directory **/XSLT/XHTML** produces XHTML output, whereas the version of **products.xsl** in directory **/XSLT/WML** produces WML output. The **XSL-FileName** property specifies only the filename (e.g., **products.xsl**); each **ClientModel** specifies the appropriate directory for a particular client type.

Method **writeXML** (lines 130–168) determines which type of client is accessing the servlet and invokes method **transform** to perform an XSL transformation. Lines 138–139 attempt to obtain a **ClientModel** from the **HttpSession**. If the **HttpSession** does not contain a **ClientModel**, line 144 obtains the client's **User-Agent** header, which uniquely identifies the client type. Line 145 invokes method **getClientModel** to get an appropriate **ClientModel** for the given client type. Line 146 places the **Client-Model** in the **HttpSession** for later use. Line 150 obtains the content type for the client from the **ClientModel** and configure the **HttpServletResponse** object. Line 156 constructs the complete relative path for the XSL transformation by concatenating the **ClientModel**'s **XSLPath** property with the servlet's **XSLFileName** property. Lines 159–160 open an **InputStream** for the XSL transformation. Line 163 invokes method **transform** to perform the transformation and send the result to the client.

Method **transform** (lines 172–202) performs the given XSL transformation on the given XML document, and writes the result of the transformation to the given **Print-Writer**. Line 179 creates a **DOMSource** for the XML document. Lines 182–183 create a **StreamSource** for the XSL document. Line 159 creates a **StreamResult** for the **PrintWriter** to which the **Transformer** will write the results of the XSL transformation. Lines 189–190 create a **Transformer** by invoking **TransformerFactory** method **newTransformer**. Line 193 invokes **Transformer** method **transform** to perform the XSL transformation on the given **Source** object and writes the result to the given **Result** object.

Method **buildErrorMessage** (lines 205–223) is a utility method for constructing XML **Element** that contains an error message. Line 209 creates an **error Element** using the provided **document**. Lines 212–213 create a **errorMessage Element** that will contain the actual error message. Lines 189–190 create a **Text** node that contains the text of the error message and append this **Text** node to the **errorMessage Element**. Line 220 appends the **errorMessage Element** to the **error Element**, and line 223 returns the complete **error Element**.

Method **buildClientList** (lines 227–323) constructs a **List** of **Client-Model**s by reading client information from an XML configuration file (Fig. 18.2). Lines 237–238 retrieve the name of the configuration file from an initialization parameter in the servlet's **ServletContext**. The deployer must specify the value of this parameter when deploying the application. Lines 244–246 open an **InputStream** to the configuration file. Lines 249–50 parse the XML configuration file and build a **Document** object in memory. Lines 253–254 get a **NodeList** of **client Element**s from the document. Each **client Element** has a **name Attribute** and three child **Element**s—**user-Agent**, **contentType** and **XSLPath**—each of which corresponds to a **ClientModel** property. Lines 260–306 construct a **ClientModel** for each **client Element** in the XML configuration file and add those **ClientModel**s to the **List**.

Method **getClientModel** (lines 326–347) returns a **ClientModel** that matches the given **User-Agent** header. The **UserAgent** property of class **ClientModel** contains a substring of the **User-Agent** header that uniquely identifies a particular client type. For example, the **User-Agent** substring **Mozilla/4.0 (compatible; MSIE 5** uniquely identifies the Microsoft Internet Explorer version 5 client. Lines 333–341 compare the **UserAgent** property of each **ClientModel** with the given **User-Agent** header. If the **UserAgent** property is a substring of the **User-Agent** header, the **ClientModel** is a match and line 340 returns it to the caller. Lines 344–345 construct a generic XHTML **Cli-entModel** as a default if no others match the given **User-Agent** header.

Figure 18.2 presents a sample configuration file that enables application support for several popular client types. Figure 18.3 presents the DTD for this configuration file.

Class **ClientModel** (Fig. 18.4) represents a particular client type. Lines 18–23 define the **ClientModel** constructor. Lines 26–59 provide *set* and *get* methods for the **UserAgent**, **ContentType** and **XSLPath** properties.

```
1   <?xml version = "1.0" encoding = "UTF-8"?>
2   <!DOCTYPE clients SYSTEM
3      "http://www.deitel.com/advjhtp1/clients.dtd">
4
5   <!-- Client configuration file for the Deitel Bookstore -->
6
7   <clients>
8
9      <!-- Microsoft Internet Explorer version 5 client -->
10     <client name = "Microsoft Internet Explorer 5">
11        <userAgent>Mozilla/4.0 (compatible; MSIE 5</userAgent>
12        <contentType>text/html</contentType>
13        <XSLPath>/XSLT/XHTML/</XSLPath>
14     </client>
15
16     <!-- Microsoft Internet Explorer version 6 client -->
17     <client name = "Microsoft Internet Explorer 6">
18        <userAgent>Mozilla/4.0 (compatible; MSIE 6</userAgent>
19        <contentType>text/html</contentType>
20        <XSLPath>/XSLT/XHTML/</XSLPath>
21     </client>
22
23     <!-- Netscape version 4.7x client -->
24     <client name = "Netscape 4.7">
25        <userAgent>Mozilla/4.7</userAgent>
26        <contentType>text/html</contentType>
27        <XSLPath>/XSLT/XHTML/</XSLPath>
28     </client>
29
30     <!-- Mozilla/Netscape version 6 client -->
31     <client name = "Mozilla/Netscape 6">
32        <userAgent>Gecko</userAgent>
33        <contentType>text/html</contentType>
34        <XSLPath>/XSLT/XHTML/</XSLPath>
35     </client>
36
37     <!-- Phone.com WML browser client -->
38     <client name = "Openwave SDK Browser">
39        <userAgent>UP.Browser/4</userAgent>
40        <contentType>text/vnd.wap.wml</contentType>
41        <XSLPath>/XSLT/WML/</XSLPath>
42     </client>
43
44     <!-- Nokia WML browser client -->
45     <client name = "Nokia WAP Toolkit Browser">
46        <userAgent>Nokia-WAP</userAgent>
47        <contentType>text/vnd.wap.wml</contentType>
48        <XSLPath>/XSLT/WML/</XSLPath>
49     </client>
50
51     <!-- Pixo iMode browser client -->
52     <client name = "Pixo Browser">
```

Fig. 18.2   Configuration file for enabling support for various client types (**clients.xml**) (part 1 of 2).

```
53           <userAgent>Pixo-Browser</userAgent>
54           <contentType>text/html</contentType>
55           <XSLPath>/XSLT/cHTML/</XSLPath>
56      </client>
57
58  </clients>
```

Fig. 18.2 Configuration file for enabling support for various client types
(`clients.xml`) (part 2 of 2).

```
1   <!-- clients.dtd                                -->
2   <!-- DTD for specifying Bookstore client types -->
3
4   <!ELEMENT clients ( client+ )>
5
6   <!ELEMENT client ( userAgent, contentType, XSLPath )>
7   <!ATTLIST client name CDATA #REQUIRED>
8
9   <!ELEMENT userAgent ( #PCDATA )>
10  <!ELEMENT contentType ( #PCDATA )>
11  <!ELEMENT XSLPath ( #PCDATA )>
```

Fig. 18.3 DTD for `clients.xml`.

```
1   // ClientModel.java
2   // ClientModel is a utility class for determining the proper
3   // Content-Type and path for XSL files for each type of client
4   // supported by the Bookstore application.
5   package com.deitel.advjhtp1.bookstore.model;
6
7   // Java core packages
8   import java.io.*;
9
10  public class ClientModel implements Serializable {
11
12     // ClientModel properties
13     private String userAgent;
14     private String contentType;
15     private String XSLPath;
16
17     // ClientModel constructor for initializing data members
18     public ClientModel( String agent, String type, String path )
19     {
20        setUserAgent( agent );
21        setContentType( type );
22        setXSLPath( path );
23     }
24
```

Fig. 18.4 `ClientModel` for representing supported clients (part 1 of 2).

```
25    // set UserAgent substring
26    public void setUserAgent( String agent )
27    {
28       userAgent = agent;
29    }
30
31    // get UserAgent substring
32    public String getUserAgent()
33    {
34       return userAgent;
35    }
36
37    // set ContentType
38    public void setContentType( String type )
39    {
40       contentType = type;
41    }
42
43    // get ContentType
44    public String getContentType()
45    {
46       return contentType;
47    }
48
49    // set XSL path
50    public void setXSLPath( String path )
51    {
52       XSLPath = path;
53    }
54
55    // get XSL path
56    public String getXSLPath()
57    {
58       return XSLPath;
59    }
60 }
```

Fig. 18.4   ClientModel for representing supported clients (part 2 of 2).

18.3 Shopping Cart Servlets

Several e-commerce models have become common for shopping on the Web. These models include auction sites, bargain shoppers, bartering and name your own price. Our application uses the familiar shopping-cart model, in which a customer browses through the store and selects items for purchase. Each of these items is placed in a virtual shopping cart. When the customer is finished shopping, a checkout process gathers the person's billing and shipping information to complete the transaction. Maintaining the shopping cart is part of the business logic implemented in the application's EJBs.

Figure 18.5 shows the flow of client requests and responses for a new customer who orders multiple copies of a book using a Web browser. The customer enters the site at **index.html**. The customer then selects a link to view the product catalog, which is generated by **GetAllProductsServlet**. The customer then chooses a product from the product catalog, and **GetProductServlet** shows the details of the product, including a picture of the cover, the price and the author(s). The customer adds the product to the shopping cart through **AddToCartServlet**, and **ViewCartServlet** shows the shopping cart contents. The customer updates the quantity to be purchased through **UpdateCartServlet**, and **ViewCartServlet** again shows the shopping cart contents to the customer. The customer then selects a link to register as a new customer and fills out the registration form in **register.html**. The customer submits the form to **RegisterServlet**, which then invokes **LoginServlet** to log the customer into the store. The customer then selects a link to invoke **CheckoutServlet**. **CheckoutServlet** places the order and forwards the customer to **ViewOrderServlet**, which shows the details of the customer's order.

18.3.1 AddToCartServlet

As customers browse through our on-line store, they add products they wish to purchase to their shopping carts. Servlet **AddToCartServlet** (Fig. 18.6) handles each customer request to add a product to the shopping cart. Class **AddToCartServlet** extends class **XMLServlet**, which implements functionality common to all servlets in the Deitel Bookstore, such as initialization and XSL transformations.

Line 41 retrieves from the **HttpServletRequest** object the ISBN of the product the customer would like purchase. Lines 37–38 retrieve a reference to the customer's **ShoppingCart** from the servlet's **HttpSession** object. It is possible that the customer does not yet have a shopping cart, in which case the **ShoppingCart** reference will be **null**. If this is the case, line 59 creates a new **ShoppingCart** using the **ShoppingCart** home interface, and stores its reference in the servlet's **HttpSession** object (line 62) for later use. The **ShoppingCart** EJB is a stateful session bean and will therefore maintain the contents of the customer's **ShoppingCart** throughout the browsing session.

Once the servlet has a valid **ShoppingCart** reference, line 66 invokes the **ShoppingCart**'s **addProduct** business method with the product's ISBN as an argument. Line 70 invokes method **sendRedirect** of class **HttpServletResponse** to redirect the client to **ViewCartServlet**, which displays a list of products in the shopping cart.

There are three checked exceptions that could be thrown from the **try** block on lines 44–72. Lines 75–86 **catch** a **NamingException** if the **ShoppingCart** EJB is not found in the JNDI directory. Lines 89–99 **catch** a **CreateException** if there is an error creating the customer's shopping cart. Lines 102–110 **catch** a **ProductNotFoundException**, which is an application-specific exception that we present in detail in Chapter 19. A **ProductNotFoundException** indicates that a product with the given ISBN could not be found in the database.

Each of these exception handlers uses **XMLServlet** method **buildErrorMessage** to create an XML error message to present to the client. In each case, we provide a message to inform the user of the error, and print a stack trace of the exception to aid the developer in debugging the application. Invoking **XMLServlet** method **writeXML** (lines 85, 98 and 109) sends the content to the client.

18.3.2 ViewCartServlet

Once the customer has added an item to the shopping cart, **ViewCartServlet** (Fig. 18.7) displays the shopping cart's contents. This servlet is a subclass of **XMLServlet**.

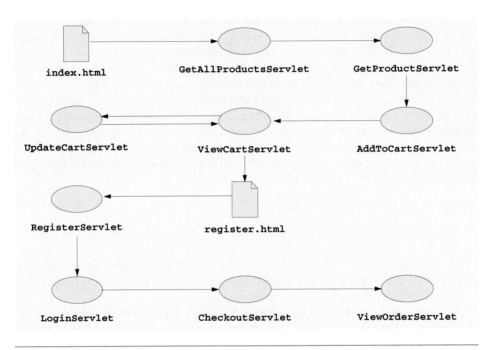

Fig. 18.5   Flow of client requests and data returned in the Deitel Bookstore for
XHTML clients.

```
1   // AddToCartServlet.java
2   // AddToCartServlet adds a Product to the Customer's
3   // ShoppingCart.
4   package com.deitel.advjhtp1.bookstore.servlets;
5
6   // Java core packages
7   import java.io.*;
8
9   // Java extension packages
10  import javax.servlet.*;
11  import javax.servlet.http.*;
12  import javax.naming.*;
13  import javax.rmi.*;
14  import javax.ejb.*;
15
16  // third-party packages
17  import org.w3c.dom.*;
18
19  // Deitel packages
20  import com.deitel.advjhtp1.bookstore.model.*;
21  import com.deitel.advjhtp1.bookstore.ejb.*;
22  import com.deitel.advjhtp1.bookstore.exceptions.*;
23
```

Fig. 18.6   AddToCartServlet for adding products to a shopping cart
(part 1 of 3).

```
24   public class AddToCartServlet extends XMLServlet {
25
26       // respond to HTTP post requests
27       public void doPost( HttpServletRequest request,
28                           HttpServletResponse response )
29           throws ServletException, IOException
30       {
31           Document document = getDocumentBuilder().newDocument();
32
33           // get HttpSession Object for this user
34           HttpSession session = request.getSession();
35
36           // get Customer's ShoppingCart
37           ShoppingCart shoppingCart =
38               ( ShoppingCart ) session.getAttribute( "cart" );
39
40           // get ISBN parameter from request Object
41           String isbn = request.getParameter( "ISBN" );
42
43           // get ShoppingCart and add Product to be purchased
44           try {
45               InitialContext context = new InitialContext();
46
47               // create ShoppingCart if Customer does not have one
48               if ( shoppingCart == null ) {
49                   Object object = context.lookup(
50                       "java:comp/env/ejb/ShoppingCart" );
51
52                   // cast Object reference to ShoppingCartHome
53                   ShoppingCartHome shoppingCartHome =
54                       ( ShoppingCartHome )
55                           PortableRemoteObject.narrow(
56                               object, ShoppingCartHome.class );
57
58                   // create ShoppingCart using ShoppingCartHome
59                   shoppingCart = shoppingCartHome.create();
60
61                   // store ShoppingCart in session
62                   session.setAttribute( "cart", shoppingCart );
63               }
64
65               // add Product to Customer's ShoppingCart
66               shoppingCart.addProduct( isbn );
67
68               // redirect Customer to ViewCartServlet to view
69               // contents of ShoppingCart
70               response.sendRedirect( "ViewCart" );
71
72           } // end try
73
74           // handle exception when looking up ShoppingCart EJB
75           catch ( NamingException namingException ) {
```

Fig. 18.6 **AddToCartServlet** for adding products to a shopping cart (part 2 of 3).

```
76              namingException.printStackTrace();
77
78              String error = "The ShoppingCart EJB was not " +
79                 "found in the JNDI directory.";
80
81              // append error message to XML document
82              document.appendChild( buildErrorMessage(
83                 document, error ) );
84
85              writeXML( request, response, document );
86           }
87
88           // handle exception when creating ShoppingCart EJB
89           catch ( CreateException createException ) {
90              createException.printStackTrace();
91
92              String error = "ShoppingCart could not be created";
93
94              // append error message to XML document
95              document.appendChild( buildErrorMessage(
96                 document, error ) );
97
98              writeXML( request, response, document );
99           }
100
101          // handle exception when Product is not found
102          catch ( ProductNotFoundException productException ) {
103             productException.printStackTrace();
104
105             // append error message to XML document
106             document.appendChild( buildErrorMessage(
107                document, productException.getMessage() ) );
108
109             writeXML( request, response, document );
110          }
111
112    } // end method doGet
113 }
```

Fig. 18.6 `AddToCartServlet` for adding products to a shopping cart
(part 3 of 3).

```
1   // ViewCartServlet.java
2   // ViewCartServlet presents the contents of the Customer's
3   // ShoppingCart.
4   package com.deitel.advjhtp1.bookstore.servlets;
5
6   // Java core packages
7   import java.io.*;
8   import java.util.*;
9   import java.text.*;
10
```

Fig. 18.7 `ViewCartServlet` for viewing contents of shopping cart (part 1 of 3).

```
11    // Java extension packages
12    import javax.servlet.*;
13    import javax.servlet.http.*;
14    import javax.rmi.*;
15
16    // third-party packages
17    import org.w3c.dom.*;
18
19    // Deitel packages
20    import com.deitel.advjhtp1.bookstore.model.*;
21    import com.deitel.advjhtp1.bookstore.ejb.*;
22
23    public class ViewCartServlet extends XMLServlet {
24
25        // respond to HTTP get requests
26        public void doGet( HttpServletRequest request,
27                           HttpServletResponse response )
28           throws ServletException, IOException
29        {
30           Document document = getDocumentBuilder().newDocument();
31           HttpSession session = request.getSession();
32
33           // get Customer's ShoppingCart from session
34           ShoppingCart shoppingCart =
35              ( ShoppingCart ) session.getAttribute( "cart" );
36
37           // build XML document with contents of ShoppingCart
38           if ( shoppingCart != null ) {
39
40              // create cart element in XML document
41              Element root = ( Element ) document.appendChild(
42                 document.createElement( "cart" ) );
43
44              // get total cost of Products in ShoppingCart
45              double total = shoppingCart.getTotal();
46
47              // create NumberFormat for local currency
48              NumberFormat priceFormatter =
49                 NumberFormat.getCurrencyInstance();
50
51              // format total price for ShoppingCart and add it
52              // as an attribute of element cart
53              root.setAttribute( "total",
54                 priceFormatter.format( total ) );
55
56              // get contents of ShoppingCart
57              Iterator orderProducts =
58                 shoppingCart.getContents().iterator();
59
60              // add an element for each Product in ShoppingCart
61              // to XML document
62              while ( orderProducts.hasNext() ) {
63                 OrderProductModel orderProductModel =
```

Fig. 18.7 `ViewCartServlet` for viewing contents of shopping cart (part 2 of 3).

```
64                        ( OrderProductModel ) orderProducts.next();
65
66              root.appendChild(
67                  orderProductModel.getXML( document ) );
68            }
69
70         } // end if
71
72         else {
73            String error = "Your ShoppingCart is empty.";
74
75            // append error message to XML document
76            document.appendChild( buildErrorMessage(
77                 document, error ) );
78         }
79
80         // write content to client
81         writeXML( request, response, document );
82
83      } // end method doGet
84   }
```

Fig. 18.7 `ViewCartServlet` for viewing contents of shopping cart (part 3 of 3).

A remote reference to the customer's **ShoppingCart** is stored in the **HttpSession** object. Lines 34–35 retrieve this remote reference. After ensuring the **Shopping-Cart** remote reference is not **null**, lines 41–42 begin building the XML document that describes the customer's shopping cart by creating element **cart**. Line 45 obtains the total price for the items in the shopping cart by invoking **ShoppingCart** method **getTotal**. Lines 48–49 format the **total** using a **NumberFormat** and append the formatted **total** to the XML document.

Lines 62–68 iterate through the **Collection** of **OrderProductModel**s in the shopping cart. Each **OrderProductModel** represents a product and the quantity of that product in the shopping cart. Line 67 invokes **OrderProductModel** method **getXML** to obtain an XML element that describes the **OrderProductModel**, including the product's ISBN and quantity. Lines 66–67 append this description to the servlet's XML document.

If the **ShoppingCart** remote reference stored in the **HttpSession** object was **null**, lines 72–78 generate an error message. Line 81 invokes method **writeXML** to transforms the XML content using XSLT and present that content to the client.

The XSL transformation of Fig. 18.8 produces XHTML for **ViewCartServlet**. Lines 6–8 set the output parameters for the transformation. Line 10 includes templates from **error.xsl** for transforming error messages. Lines 23–27 load a navigation header from an external XML document. Note that we refer to the **error.xsl** and **navigation.xml** documents with relative URIs. Recall that class **XMLServlet** creates a custom **URIResolver** that enables the XSL transformer to resolve these relative URIs. Had we not provided a custom **URIResolver**, each XSL transformation would have to specify the complete URI for these documents, which would make the application less portable. This header contains links for viewing the product catalog, creating an online account, viewing the shopping cart, etc. Lines 42–43 apply a template that populates a table with product information, including the title, author, ISBN price and quantity. The **form** on lines 51–54 enables the customer to check out from the online store to place the order. The **xsl:template** on lines 61–91 extracts each product's information from the **View-CartServlet**'s XML document and creates a table row. The **form** on lines 75–80 enables the user to change the quantity of the product in the shopping cart. The **form** on lines 84–88 enables the user to remove the product from the shopping cart.

The XSL transformation of Fig. 18.9 produces cHTML for **ViewCartServlet**. Lines 28-29 display the total cost of products in the cart. Lines 38–41 apply the **xsl:template** for **orderProduct** elements to produce an unordered list of product information. The **form** on lines 44–47 enables the customer to check out of the online store to place the order. The **form** on lines 64–69 enables the customer to update the quantity of a particular product in the shopping cart. The **form** on lines 72–76 enables the customer to remove a product from the shopping cart.

```
1    <?xml version = "1.0"?>
2
3    <xsl:stylesheet version = "1.0"
4       xmlns:xsl = "http://www.w3.org/1999/XSL/Transform">
5
6       <xsl:output method = "xml" omit-xml-declaration = "no"
7          indent = "yes" doctype-system = "DTD/xhtml1-strict.dtd"
8          doctype-public = "-//W3C//DTD XHTML 1.0 Strict//EN"/>
9
10      <xsl:include href = /XSLT/XHTML/error.xsl"/>
11
12      <xsl:template match = "cart">
13         <html xmlns = "http://www.w3.org/1999/xhtml"
14             xml:lang = "en" lang = "en">
15
16         <head>
17            <title>Your Online Shopping Cart</title>
18            <link rel = "StyleSheet" href = "styles/default.css"/>
19         </head>
20
21         <body>
22
23            <xsl:for-each select =
24               "document( '/XSLT/XHTML/navigation.xml' )">
25
26               <xsl:copy-of select = "."/>
27            </xsl:for-each>
28
29            <div class = "header">Your Shopping Cart:</div>
30
31            <table class = "cart">
32               <tr>
33                  <th>Title</th>
34                  <th>Author(s)</th>
```

Fig. 18.8   ViewCartServlet XSL transformation for XHTML browsers (**XHTML/ viewCart.xsl**) (part 1 of 3).

```
35                      <th>ISBN</th>
36                      <th>Price</th>
37                      <th>Quantity</th>
38                  </tr>
39
40                  <xsl:apply-templates
41                      select = "orderProduct"/>
42
43              </table>
44
45              <p>
46                  Your total:
47                  <xsl:value-of select = "@total"/>
48              </p>
49
50              <p>
51                  <form action = "Checkout" method = "post">
52                      <input name = "submit" type = "submit"
53                          value = "Check Out"/>
54                  </form>
55              </p>
56
57          </body>
58      </html>
59   </xsl:template>
60
61   <xsl:template match = "orderProduct">
62      <tr>
63         <td>
64            <a href = "GetProduct?ISBN={product/ISBN}">
65               <xsl:value-of select = "product/title"/></a>
66         </td>
67
68         <td><xsl:value-of select = "product/author"/></td>
69
70         <td><xsl:value-of select = "product/ISBN"/></td>
71
72         <td><xsl:value-of select = "product/price"/></td>
73
74         <td>
75            <form action = "UpdateCart" method = "post">
76               <input type = "text" size = "2"
77                  name = "{product/ISBN}"
78                  value = "{quantity}"/>
79               <input type = "submit" value = "Update"/>
80            </form>
81         </td>
82
83         <td align = "center">
84            <form action = "RemoveFromCart" method = "post">
85               <input name = "ISBN" type = "hidden"
86                      value = "{product/ISBN}"/>
```

Fig. 18.8 ViewCartServlet XSL transformation for XHTML browsers (**XHTML/viewCart.xsl**) (part 2 of 3).

```
87                        <input type = "submit" value = "Remove"/>
88                  </form>
89            </td>
90         </tr>
91      </xsl:template>
92   </xsl:stylesheet>
```

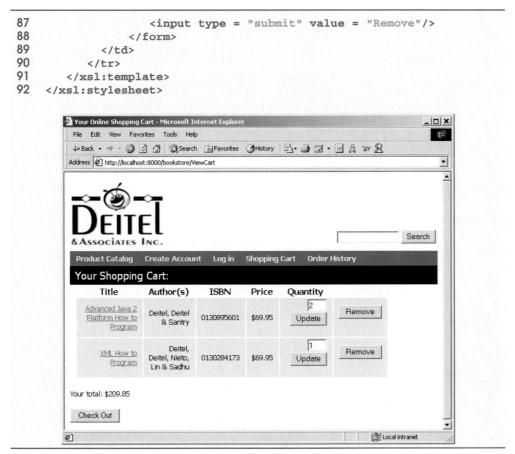

Fig. 18.8 **ViewCartServlet** XSL transformation for XHTML browsers (**XHTML/viewCart.xsl**) (part 3 of 3).

```
1    <?xml version = "1.0"?>
2
3    <xsl:stylesheet version = "1.0"
4       xmlns:xsl = "http://www.w3.org/1999/XSL/Transform">
5
6       <xsl:output method = "html"
7          omit-xml-declaration = "yes"
8          indent = "yes"
9          doctype-system =
10            "http://www.w3.org/MarkUp/html-spec/html-spec_toc.html"
11         doctype-public = "-//W3C//DTD HTML 2.0//EN"/>
12
13      <xsl:include href = "/XSLT/cHTML/error.xsl"/>
14
```

Fig. 18.9 **ViewCartServlet** XSL transformation for i-mode browsers (**cHTML/viewCart.xsl**) (part 1 of 3). (Image courtesy of Pixo, Inc.)

```
15    <xsl:template match = "cart">
16       <html>
17
18          <head>
19             <title>Your Online Shopping Cart</title>
20          </head>
21
22          <body>
23             <div class = "header">
24                Your Shopping Cart:
25             </div>
26
27             <p>
28                Your total:
29                <xsl:value-of select = "@total"/>
30             </p>
31
32             <p>Title</p>
33             <p>Author(s)</p>
34             <p>ISBN</p>
35             <p>Price</p>
36             <p>Quantity</p>
37
38             <ul>
39                <xsl:apply-templates
40                   select = "orderProduct"/>
41             </ul>
42
43             <p>
44                <form method = "post" action = "Checkout">
45                   <input type = "submit" name = "Checkout"
46                          value = "Checkout"/>
47                </form>
48             </p>
49
50          </body>
51
52       </html>
53    </xsl:template>
54
55    <xsl:template match = "orderProduct">
56       <li>
57          <a href = "GetProduct?ISBN={product/ISBN}">
58                <xsl:value-of select = "product/title"/></a>
59          <br/>
60          <p><xsl:value-of select = "product/author"/></p>
61          <p><xsl:value-of select = "product/ISBN"/></p>
62          <p><xsl:value-of select = "product/price"/></p>
63          <p>
64             <form method = "post" action = "UpdateCart">
65                <input type = "text" size = "2"
66                   name = "{product/ISBN}"
```

Fig. 18.9 ViewCartServlet XSL transformation for i-mode browsers (**cHTML/ viewCart.xsl**) (part 2 of 3). (Image courtesy of Pixo, Inc.)

```
67                    value = "{quantity}"/>
68                <input type = "submit" value = "Update"/>
69             </form>
70          </p>
71          <p>
72             <form method = "post" action = "RemoveFromCart">
73                <input type = "hidden" name = "ISBN"
74                    value = "{product/ISBN}"/>
75                <input type = "submit" value = "Remove"/>
76             </form>
77          </p>
78          <br/>
79       </li>
80    </xsl:template>
81 </xsl:stylesheet>
```

Fig. 18.9 `ViewCartServlet` XSL transformation for i-mode browsers (`cHTML/ viewCart.xsl`) (part 3 of 3). (Image courtesy of Pixo, Inc.)

The XSL transformation of Fig. 18.10 produces WML for `ViewCartServlet`. The **do** element on lines 21–23 enables the user to check out of the online store to place the order. Lines 25–49 mark up the list of products in the shopping cart. The **card** element on lines 55–64 displays information about a single product. The **card** element on lines 66–81 provides an interface for changing the quantity of a particular product in the shopping cart. [*Note*: To download the Nokia WAP Toolkit WML browser, please visit **www.nokia.com/corporate/wap/downloads.html**.]

18.3.3 RemoveFromCartServlet

Once a customer has added a product to the shopping cart, the customer may wish to remove that product. **RemoveFromCartServlet** (Fig. 18.11) processes requests to remove products from shopping carts. Line 34 retrieves from the **HttpSession** the ISBN of the product that the customer would like to remove from the shopping cart. Lines 39–40 obtain the **ShoppingCart** remote reference from the **HttpSession** object. After ensuring that the **ShoppingCart** reference is not **null**, line 44 invokes **ShoppingCart** method **removeProduct**, providing the ISBN as an argument. Line 48 redirects the client to **ViewCartServlet** to display the results of removing the product from the shopping cart. Method **removeProduct** throws a **ProductNotFoundException** if a product with the given ISBN is not found in the shopping cart. Lines 53–61 **catch** this exception and generate an error message to inform the user of the problem.

18.3.4 UpdateCartServlet

Products in a customer's shopping cart each have an associated quantity. **UpdateCartServlet** (Fig. 18.12) enables customers to change the quantities of products in their shopping carts. Lines 37–38 retrieve the customer's **ShoppingCart** from the **HttpSession** object. Line 44 retrieves an **Enumeration** of parameter names from the **HttpServletRequest** object. Each parameter name is the ISBN of a product in the customer's shopping cart. The value of each parameter is the desired quantity of the product in the shopping cart. For each product in the shopping cart, lines 50–51 obtain the **newQuantity** for that product from the **request** parameter. Lines 55–56 set the quantity for each product in the shopping cart by invoking **ShoppingCart** method **setProductQuantity**. Once all of the quantities have been updated, line 61 redirects the client to **ViewCartServlet** to show the updates to the shopping cart.

```
1   <?xml version = "1.0"?>
2
3   <xsl:stylesheet version = "1.0"
4      xmlns:xsl = "http://www.w3.org/1999/XSL/Transform">
5
6      <xsl:output method = "xml" omit-xml-declaration = "no"
7         doctype-system = "http://www.wapforum.org/DTD/wml_1.1.xml"
8         doctype-public = "-//WAPFORUM//DTD WML 1.1//EN"/>
9
10     <xsl:include href = "/XSLT/WML/error.xsl"/>
11
12     <xsl:template match = "cart">
13        <wml>
14
15           <card title = "Shopping Cart">
16              <do type = "prev">
17                 <prev/>
18              </do>
19
```

Fig. 18.10 **ViewCartServlet** XSL transformation for WML browsers (**WML/ viewCart.xsl**) (part 1 of 3). (Image © 2001 Nokia Mobile Phones.)

```
20              <do type = "accept" label = "Check Out">
21                 <go href = "Checkout" method = "post"/>
22              </do>
23
24              <p><em>Shopping Cart</em></p>
25
26              <p>
27                 Your total: $<xsl:value-of select = "@total"/>
28
29                 <table columns = "2">
30                    <tr>
31                       <td>Title</td>
32                       <td>Price</td>
33                    </tr>
34
35                    <xsl:for-each select = "orderProduct">
36                       <tr>
37                          <td>
38                             <a href = "#ISBN{product/ISBN}">
39                             <xsl:value-of select = "product/title"/>
40                             </a>
41                          </td>
42                          <td>
43                             $<xsl:value-of select = "product/price"/>
44                          </td>
45                       </tr>
46                    </xsl:for-each>
47
48                 </table>
49              </p>
50
51           </card>
52
53           <xsl:for-each select = "orderProduct" >
54              <card id = "ISBN{product/ISBN}">
55                 <do label = "OK" type = "prev"><prev/></do>
56                 <do label = "Change Quant" type = "options">
57                    <go href = "#quant{product/ISBN}"/>
58                 </do>
59                 <p><xsl:value-of select = "product/title"/></p>
60                 <p>Quantity: <xsl:value-of select = "quantity"/></p>
61                 <p><xsl:value-of select = "product/author"/></p>
62                 <p><xsl:value-of select = "product/ISBN"/></p>
63              </card>
64
65              <card id = "quant{product/ISBN}">
66                 <p>Enter new quantity
67                    <input name = "quantity" emptyok = "false"
68                       type = "text" format = "*n"/>
69                 </p>
70
```

Fig. 18.10 `ViewCartServlet` XSL transformation for WML browsers (**WML/viewCart.xsl**) (part 2 of 3). (Image © 2001 Nokia Mobile Phones.)

```
71                    <do type = "accept" label = "Update Quantity">
72                       <go href = "UpdateCart" method = "post">
73                          <postfield name = "{product/ISBN}"
74                                         value = "$quantity"/>
75                       </go>
76                    </do>
77
78                    <do type = "prev" label = "Cancel"><prev/></do>
79
80                 </card>
81              </xsl:for-each>
82
83           </wml>
84        </xsl:template>
85     </xsl:stylesheet>
```

Fig. 18.10 `ViewCartServlet` XSL transformation for WML browsers (**WML/
viewCart.xsl**) (part 3 of 3). (Image © 2001 Nokia Mobile Phones.)

```
1   // RemoveFromCartServlet.java
2   // RemoveFromCartServlet removes a Product from the Customer's
3   // ShoppingCart.
4   package com.deitel.advjhtp1.bookstore.servlets;
5
6   // Java core packages
7   import java.io.*;
```

Fig. 18.11 `RemoveFromCartServlet` for removing products from shopping cart
(part 1 of 3).

```
8
9    // Java extension packages
10   import javax.servlet.*;
11   import javax.servlet.http.*;
12
13   // third-party packages
14   import org.w3c.dom.*;
15
16   // Deitel packages
17   import com.deitel.advjhtp1.bookstore.model.*;
18   import com.deitel.advjhtp1.bookstore.ejb.*;
19   import com.deitel.advjhtp1.bookstore.exceptions.*;
20
21   public class RemoveFromCartServlet extends XMLServlet {
22
23      // respond to HTTP post requests
24      public void doPost( HttpServletRequest request,
25                          HttpServletResponse response )
26         throws ServletException, IOException
27      {
28         Document document = getDocumentBuilder().newDocument();
29
30         // remove Product from ShoppingCart
31         try {
32
33            // get ISBN of Product to be removed
34            String isbn = request.getParameter( "ISBN" );
35
36            // get Customer's ShoppingCart from session
37            HttpSession session = request.getSession();
38
39            ShoppingCart shoppingCart =
40               ( ShoppingCart ) session.getAttribute( "cart" );
41
42            // if ShoppingCart is not null, remove Product
43            if ( shoppingCart != null )
44               shoppingCart.removeProduct( isbn );
45
46            // redirect Customer to ViewCartServlet to view
47            // the contents of ShoppingCart
48            response.sendRedirect( "ViewCart" );
49
50         } // end try
51
52         // handle exception if Product not found in ShoppingCart
53         catch ( ProductNotFoundException productException ) {
54            productException.printStackTrace();
55
56            // append error message to XML document
57            document.appendChild( buildErrorMessage(
58               document, productException.getMessage() ) );
59
```

Fig. 18.11 RemoveFromCartServlet for removing products from shopping cart (part 2 of 3).

```
60                 writeXML( request, response, document );
61             }
62
63       } // end method doGet
64   }
```

Fig. 18.11 RemoveFromCartServlet for removing products from shopping cart (part 3 of 3).

```
1   // UpdateCartServlet.java
2   // UpdateCartServlet updates the quantity of a Product in the
3   // Customer's ShoppingCart.
4   package com.deitel.advjhtp1.bookstore.servlets;
5
6   // Java core packages
7   import java.io.*;
8   import java.util.*;
9
10  // Java extension packages
11  import javax.servlet.*;
12  import javax.servlet.http.*;
13
14  // third-party packages
15  import org.w3c.dom.*;
16
17  // Deitel packages
18  import com.deitel.advjhtp1.bookstore.model.*;
19  import com.deitel.advjhtp1.bookstore.ejb.*;
20  import com.deitel.advjhtp1.bookstore.exceptions.*;
21
22  public class UpdateCartServlet extends XMLServlet {
23
24      // respond to HTTP post requests
25      public void doPost( HttpServletRequest request,
26                          HttpServletResponse response )
27          throws ServletException, IOException
28      {
29          Document document = getDocumentBuilder().newDocument();
30
31          // update quantity of given Product in ShoppingCart
32          try {
33
34              // get Customer's ShoppingCart from session
35              HttpSession session = request.getSession( false );
36
37              ShoppingCart shoppingCart = ( ShoppingCart )
38                  session.getAttribute( "cart" );
39
40              // get Enumeration of parameter names
41              Enumeration parameters = request.getParameterNames();
```

Fig. 18.12 UpdateCartServlet for updating quantities of products in shopping cart (part 1 of 2).

```
42
43        // update quantity for each ISBN parameter
44        while ( parameters.hasMoreElements() ) {
45
46            // get ISBN of Product to be updated
47            String ISBN = ( String ) parameters.nextElement();
48
49            // get new quantity for Product
50            int newQuantity = Integer.parseInt(
51                request.getParameter( ISBN ) );
52
53            // set quantity in ShoppingCart for Product
54            // with given ISBN
55            shoppingCart.setProductQuantity( ISBN,
56                newQuantity );
57        }
58
59        // redirect Customer to ViewCartServlet to view
60        // contents of ShoppingCart
61        response.sendRedirect( "ViewCart" );
62
63      } // end try
64
65      // handle exception if Product not found in ShoppingCart
66      catch ( ProductNotFoundException productException ) {
67          productException.printStackTrace();
68
69          document.appendChild( buildErrorMessage(
70              document, productException.getMessage() ) );
71
72          writeXML( request, response, document );
73      }
74
75   } // end method doGet
76 }
```

Fig. 18.12 UpdateCartServlet for updating quantities of products in shopping cart (part 2 of 2).

Method **setProductQuantity** throws a **ProductNotFoundException** if the product with the given ISBN is not found in the shopping cart. Lines 66–73 handle this exception and generate an XML error message using method **buildErrorMessage**. the Method **writeXML** presents the error message to the client (line 72).

18.3.5 CheckoutServlet

Once the customer has finished browsing through the store and adding products to the shopping cart, **CheckOutServlet** (Fig. 18.13) completes the customer's **Order**.

A customer must log into the on-line store before checking out. Lines 32–33 retrieve the customer's **userID** from the **HttpSession**. Lines 39–40 then obtain a remote reference to the customer's **ShoppingCart** from the **session** object. After ensuring that neither the **ShoppingCart** nor the **userID** is **null**, line 51 invokes **ShoppingCart** method **checkout** to place the order. Method **checkout** returns a remote reference to an **Order** EJB instance, which represents the customer's order. Line 54 gets the **orderID** for the **Order** by invoking method **getPrimaryKey**. Lines 57–58 redirect the client to **ViewOrderServlet**, which displays the details of the order that was placed.

If the **userID** is **null**, lines 60–70 generates an error message indicating that the customer is not logged in. Lines 75–83 catch a **ProductNotFoundException**, which method **checkout** throws if the shopping cart is empty (i.e., contains no products).

18.4 Product Catalog Servlets

Servlets **GetAllProductsServlet** and **ProductSearchServlet** provide an online catalog. These servlets retrieve a list of products and present the list to the customer. **GetProductServlet** shows the details of a given product.

18.4.1 GetAllProductsServlet

GetAllProductsServlet (Fig. 18.14) provides a list of products available at our online store. Lines 35–44 retrieve a remote reference to the **Product** EJB, which represents a product in the store. Method **findAllProducts** of interface **ProductHome** returns a **Collection** of **Product** EJBs, each of which represents a single product (lines 47–48). Lines 58–70 iterate through the **Collection** of products to build an XML document that contains information about each product. Lines 64–65 obtain a **ProductModel** for each product and lines 68–69 retrieve each product's XML description.

```
1   // CheckOutServlet.java
2   // CheckOutServlet allows a Customer to checkout of the online
3   // store to purchase the Products in the ShoppingCart.
4   package com.deitel.advjhtp1.bookstore.servlets;
5
6   // Java core packages
7   import java.io.*;
8
9   // Java extension packages
10  import javax.servlet.*;
11  import javax.servlet.http.*;
12
13  // third-party packages
14  import org.w3c.dom.*;
15
16  // Deitel packages
17  import com.deitel.advjhtp1.bookstore.model.*;
18  import com.deitel.advjhtp1.bookstore.ejb.*;
19  import com.deitel.advjhtp1.bookstore.exceptions.*;
20
21  public class CheckoutServlet extends XMLServlet {
22
23      // respond to HTTP post requests
24      public void doPost( HttpServletRequest request,
25                          HttpServletResponse response )
```

Fig. 18.13 CheckoutServlet for placing **Order**s (part 1 of 3). (Images courtesy Pixo, Inc. or © 2001 Nokia Mobile Phones.)

```
26          throws ServletException, IOException
27      {
28          Document document = getDocumentBuilder().newDocument();
29          HttpSession session = request.getSession();
30
31          // get Customer's userID from session
32          String userID = ( String )
33              session.getAttribute( "userID" );
34
35          // get ShoppingCart and check out
36          try {
37
38              // get Customer's ShoppingCart from session
39              ShoppingCart shoppingCart = ( ShoppingCart )
40                  session.getAttribute( "cart" );
41
42              // ensure Customer has a ShoppingCart
43              if ( shoppingCart == null )
44                  throw new ProductNotFoundException( "Your " +
45                      "ShoppingCart is empty." );
46
47              // ensure userID is neither null nor empty
48              if ( !( userID == null || userID.equals( "" ) ) ) {
49
50                  // invoke checkout method to place Order
51                  Order order = shoppingCart.checkout( userID );
52
53                  // get orderID for Customer's Order
54                  Integer orderID = ( Integer ) order.getPrimaryKey();
55
56                  // go to ViewOrder to show completed order
57                  response.sendRedirect( "ViewOrder?orderID=" +
58                      orderID );
59              }
60              else {
61                  // userID was null, indicating Customer is
62                  // not logged in
63                  String error = "You are not logged in.";
64
65                  // append error message to XML document
66                  document.appendChild( buildErrorMessage( document,
67                      error ) );
68
69                  writeXML( request, response, document );
70              }
71
72          } // end try
73
74          // handle exception if Product not found in ShoppingCart
75          catch ( ProductNotFoundException productException ) {
76              productException.printStackTrace();
77
```

Fig. 18.13 CheckoutServlet for placing **Order**s (part 2 of 3). (Images courtesy Pixo, Inc. or © 2001 Nokia Mobile Phones.)

```
78              // append error message to XML document
79          document.appendChild( buildErrorMessage(
80              document, productException.getMessage() ) );
81
82          writeXML( request, response, document );
83      }
84
85   } // end method doPost
86 }
```

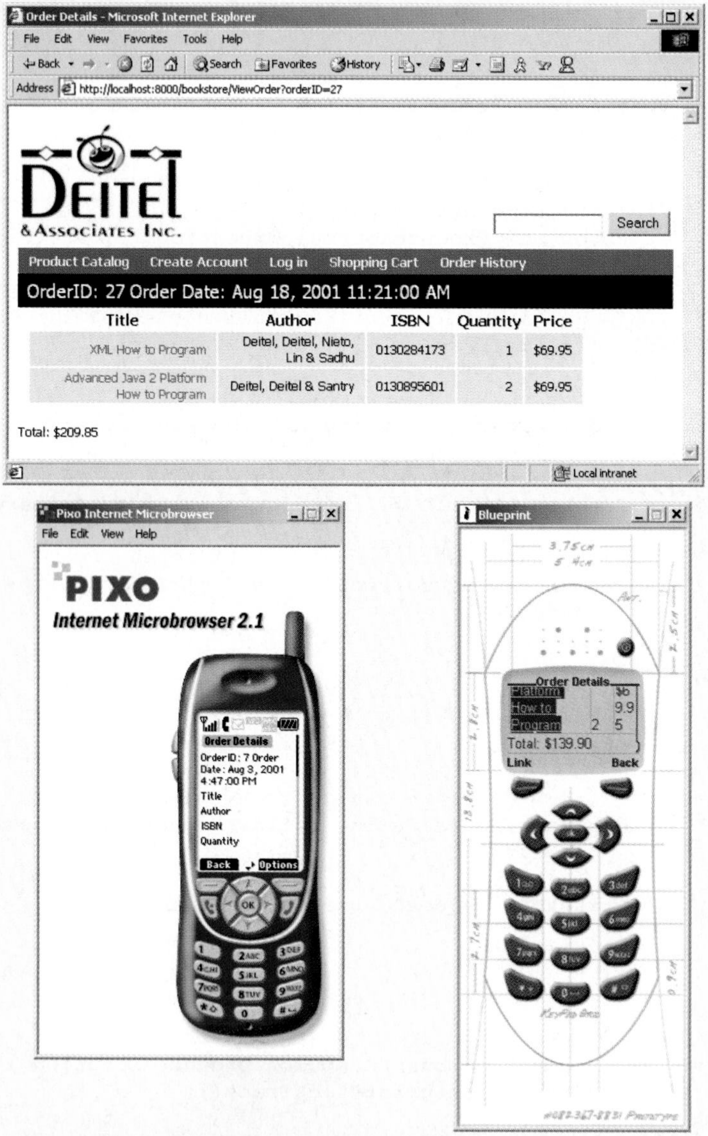

Fig. 18.13 **CheckoutServlet** for placing **Order**s (part 3 of 3). (Images courtesy Pixo, Inc. or © 2001 Nokia Mobile Phones.)

```
1    // GetAllProductsServlet.java
2    // GetAllProductsServlet retrieves a list of all Products
3    // available in the store and presents the list to the client.
4    package com.deitel.advjhtp1.bookstore.servlets;
5
6    // Java core packages
7    import java.io.*;
8    import java.util.*;
9
10   // Java extension packages
11   import javax.servlet.*;
12   import javax.servlet.http.*;
13   import javax.rmi.*;
14   import javax.naming.*;
15   import javax.ejb.*;
16
17   // third-party packages
18   import org.w3c.dom.*;
19
20   // Deitel packages
21   import com.deitel.advjhtp1.bookstore.model.*;
22   import com.deitel.advjhtp1.bookstore.ejb.*;
23
24   public class GetAllProductsServlet extends XMLServlet {
25
26      // respond to HTTP get requests
27      public void doGet( HttpServletRequest request,
28                         HttpServletResponse response )
29         throws ServletException, IOException
30      {
31         Document document = getDocumentBuilder().newDocument();
32
33         // generate Product catalog
34         try {
35            InitialContext context = new InitialContext();
36
37            // look up Product EJB
38            Object object =
39               context.lookup( "java:comp/env/ejb/Product" );
40
41            // get ProductHome interface to find all Products
42            ProductHome productHome = ( ProductHome )
43               PortableRemoteObject.narrow( object,
44                  ProductHome.class );
45
46            // get Iterator for Product list
47            Iterator products =
48               productHome.findAllProducts().iterator();
49
50            // create root of XML document
51            Element rootElement =
52               document.createElement( "catalog" );
```

Fig. 18.14 GetAllProductsServlet for viewing the product catalog (part 1 of 3). (Images courtesy Pixo, Inc. or © 2001 Nokia Mobile Phones.)

```
53
54              // append catalog Element to XML document
55              document.appendChild( rootElement );
56
57              // add each Product to the XML document
58              while ( products.hasNext() ) {
59                 Product product = ( Product )
60                    PortableRemoteObject.narrow( products.next(),
61                       Product.class );
62
63                 // get ProductModel for current Product
64                 ProductModel productModel =
65                    product.getProductModel();
66
67                 // add an XML element to document for Product
68                 rootElement.appendChild(
69                    productModel.getXML( document ) );
70              }
71
72           } // end try
73
74           // handle exception when looking up Product EJB
75           catch ( NamingException namingException ) {
76              namingException.printStackTrace();
77
78              String error = "The Product EJB was not found in " +
79                 "the JNDI directory.";
80
81              // append error message to XML document
82              document.appendChild( buildErrorMessage(
83                    document, error ) );
84           }
85
86           // handle exception when a Product cannot be found
87           catch ( FinderException finderException ) {
88              finderException.printStackTrace();
89
90              String error = "No Products found in the store.";
91
92              // append error message to XML document
93              document.appendChild( buildErrorMessage(
94                    document, error ) );
95           }
96
97           // ensure content is written to client
98           finally {
99              writeXML( request, response, document );
100          }
101
102       } // end method doGet
103    }
```

Fig. 18.14 GetAllProductsServlet for viewing the product catalog (part 2 of 3). (Images courtesy Pixo, Inc. or © 2001 Nokia Mobile Phones.)

Fig. 18.14 GetAllProductsServlet for viewing the product catalog (part 3 of 3). (Images courtesy Pixo, Inc. or © 2001 Nokia Mobile Phones.)

Method **lookup** (line 39) throws a **NamingException** if the **Product** EJB cannot be found in the JNDI directory. The corresponding **catch** block (lines 75–84) produces an XML error message indicating that the JNDI lookup of the **Product** EJB failed. Method **findAllProducts** (line 48) throws a **FinderException** if no **Product**s are found. Lines 87–95 **catch** this exception and build an XML error message that indicates there were no products found in the database. The **finally** block (lines 98–100) presents the content to the client using method **writeXML**.

18.4.2 GetProductServlet

GetAllProductsServlet presents a list of all **Product**s in the store. To view the details of a given product, the customer invokes **GetProductServlet** (Fig. 18.15). This servlet uses the application's business logic to retrieve detailed information about a given product for the customer.

```
1   // GetProductServlet.java
2   // GetProductServlet retrieves the details of a Product and
3   // presents them to the customer.
4   package com.deitel.advjhtp1.bookstore.servlets;
5
6   // Java core packages
7   import java.io.*;
8
9   // Java extension packages
10  import javax.servlet.*;
11  import javax.servlet.http.*;
12  import javax.naming.*;
13  import javax.ejb.*;
14  import javax.rmi.*;
15
16  // third-party packages
17  import org.w3c.dom.*;
18
19  // Deitel packages
20  import com.deitel.advjhtp1.bookstore.model.*;
21  import com.deitel.advjhtp1.bookstore.ejb.*;
22
23  public class GetProductServlet extends XMLServlet {
24
25     public void doGet( HttpServletRequest request,
26                        HttpServletResponse response )
27        throws ServletException, IOException
28     {
29        Document document = getDocumentBuilder().newDocument();
30
31        // get ISBN from request object
32        String isbn = request.getParameter( "ISBN" );
33
34        // generate XML document with Product details
```

Fig. 18.15 GetProductServlet for viewing product details (part 1 of 4). (Images courtesy Pixo, Inc. or © 2001 Nokia Mobile Phones.)

```
35          try {
36             InitialContext context = new InitialContext();
37
38             // look up Product EJB
39             Object object =
40                context.lookup( "java:comp/env/ejb/Product" );
41
42             // get ProductHome interface to find Product
43             ProductHome productHome = ( ProductHome )
44                PortableRemoteObject.narrow(
45                   object, ProductHome.class );
46
47             // find Product with given ISBN
48             Product product =
49                productHome.findByPrimaryKey( isbn );
50
51             // create XML document root Element
52             Node rootNode =
53                document.createElement( "bookstore" );
54
55             // append root Element to XML document
56             document.appendChild( rootNode );
57
58             // get Product details as a ProductModel
59             ProductModel productModel =
60                product.getProductModel();
61
62             // build an XML document with Product details
63             rootNode.appendChild(
64                productModel.getXML( document ) );
65
66          } // end try
67
68          // handle exception when looking up Product EJB
69          catch ( NamingException namingException ) {
70             namingException.printStackTrace();
71
72             String error = "The Product EJB was not found in " +
73                "the JNDI directory.";
74
75             document.appendChild( buildErrorMessage(
76                document, error ) );
77          }
78
79          // handle exception when Product is not found
80          catch ( FinderException finderException ) {
81             finderException.printStackTrace();
82
83             String error = "The Product with ISBN " + isbn +
84                " was not found in our store.";
85
```

Fig. 18.15 GetProductServlet for viewing product details (part 2 of 4). (Images courtesy Pixo, Inc. or © 2001 Nokia Mobile Phones.)

```
86              document.appendChild( buildErrorMessage(
87                  document, error ) );
88          }
89
90          // ensure content is written to client
91          finally {
92              writeXML( request, response, document );
93          }
94
95      } // end method doGet
96  }
```

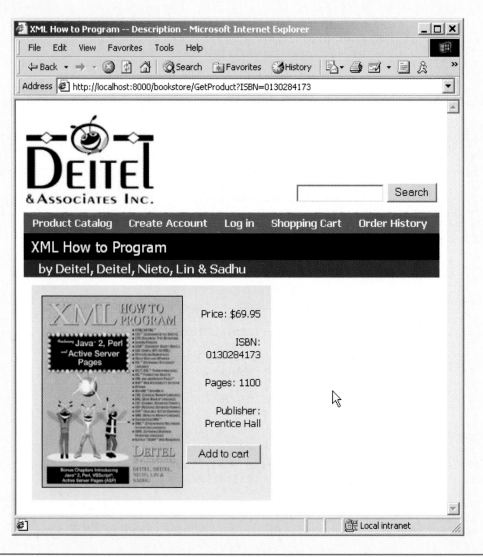

Fig. 18.15 `GetProductServlet` for viewing product details (part 3 of 4). (Images courtesy Pixo, Inc. or © 2001 Nokia Mobile Phones.)

Fig. 18.15 `GetProductServlet` for viewing product details (part 4 of 4). (Images courtesy Pixo, Inc. or © 2001 Nokia Mobile Phones.)

The **Product** EJB provides the details of a given product as a **ProductModel**. Lines 39–45 retrieve a reference to the **ProductHome** interface. Lines 48–49 invoke **ProductHome** interface method **findByPrimaryKey** to obtain the **Product** EJB for the given **ISBN**. Lines 59–64 obtain the details of the product as a **ProductModel** and use method **getXML** to generate the XML content for the client.

Lines 69–77 **catch** a **NamingException** if the **lookup** of the **ProductHome** interface fails. Lines 80–88 **catch** a **FinderException**, which is generated by the call to **findByPrimaryKey** on line 49 if a product with the given **ISBN** is not found in the database. In each **catch** block, we create an XML error message to inform the user of the error. The **finally** block on lines 91–93 ensures that the content is presented to the client, regardless of any exceptions that may be thrown.

18.4.3 ProductSearchServlet

ProductSearchServlet (Fig. 18.16) searches the database for products whose titles contain a particular keyword. Method **findByTitle** of the **Product** EJB's home interface takes a **String** as an argument and finds a product whose title contains the provided keyword. Because a search of this type may match many different products, method **findByTitle** returns a **Collection** of **Product** EJB remote references.

Lines 34–35 get the **searchString** parameter from the request object and place a wildcard character (**%**) before and after the **searchString**. The database uses this wildcard character to match titles that contains the given **searchString**. Lines 50–51 create an **Iterator** to iterate through the list of products returned by the search. Lines 58–69 add an XML representation to the XML document for each product found.

```
1    // ProductSearchServlet.java
2    // ProductSearchServlet allows a Customer to search through
3    // the store for a particular Product.
4    package com.deitel.advjhtp1.bookstore.servlets;
5
6    // Java core packages
7    import java.io.*;
8    import java.util.*;
9
10   // Java extension packages
11   import javax.servlet.*;
12   import javax.servlet.http.*;
13   import javax.naming.*;
14   import javax.ejb.*;
15   import javax.rmi.PortableRemoteObject;
16
17   // third-party packages
18   import org.w3c.dom.*;
19
20   // Deitel packages
21   import com.deitel.advjhtp1.bookstore.model.*;
22   import com.deitel.advjhtp1.bookstore.ejb.*;
23
24   public class ProductSearchServlet extends XMLServlet {
25
26      // respond to HTTP get requests
27      public void doGet( HttpServletRequest request,
28                         HttpServletResponse response )
29         throws ServletException, IOException
30      {
31         Document document = getDocumentBuilder().newDocument();
32
33         // get the searchString from the request object
34         String searchString = "%" +
35            request.getParameter( "searchString" ) + "%";
36
37         // find Product using Product EJB
38         try {
39            InitialContext context = new InitialContext();
40
41            // look up Product EJB
42            Object object =
43               context.lookup( "java:comp/env/ejb/Product" );
44
45            ProductHome productHome = ( ProductHome )
```

Fig. 18.16 ProductSearchServlet for searching product catalog (part 1 of 3). (Images courtesy Pixo, Inc. or © 2001 Nokia Mobile Phones.)

```
46              PortableRemoteObject.narrow(
47                 object, ProductHome.class );
48
49          // find Products that match searchString
50          Iterator products = productHome.findByTitle(
51             searchString ).iterator();
52
53          // create catalog document element
54          Node rootNode = document.appendChild(
55             document.createElement( "catalog" ) );
56
57          // generate list of matching products
58          while ( products.hasNext() ) {
59             Product product = ( Product )
60                PortableRemoteObject.narrow( products.next(),
61                   Product.class );
62
63             ProductModel productModel = product.getProductModel();
64
65             // append XML element to the document for the
66             // current Product
67             rootNode.appendChild(
68                productModel.getXML( document ) );
69          }
70
71       } // end try
72
73       // handle exception when looking up Product EJB
74       catch ( NamingException namingException ) {
75          namingException.printStackTrace();
76
77          String error = "The Product EJB was not found in " +
78             "the JNDI directory.";
79
80          document.appendChild( buildErrorMessage(
81                document, error ) );
82       }
83
84       // handle exception when Product is not found
85       catch ( FinderException finderException ) {
86          finderException.printStackTrace();
87
88          String error = "No Products match your search.";
89
90          document.appendChild( buildErrorMessage(
91                document, error ) );
92       }
93
94       // ensure content is written to client
95       finally {
96          writeXML( request, response, document );
97       }
```

Fig. 18.16 ProductSearchServlet for searching product catalog (part 2 of 3).
(Images courtesy Pixo, Inc. or © 2001 Nokia Mobile Phones.)

```
98
99    } // end method doGet
100   }
```

Fig. 18.16 `ProductSearchServlet` for searching product catalog (part 3 of 3). (Images courtesy Pixo, Inc. or © 2001 Nokia Mobile Phones.)

18.5 Customer Management Servlets

Online stores typically allow customers to register personal information (e.g., name, e-mail address and shipping address) with the store, for a number of purposes. Primarily, the store needs the information provided in a customer registration to bill the customer and ship products from the store. By registering, a customer will need to enter this information only once. Later, a customer can return to the store and log-in with a user name and password to retrieve previously entered billing and shipping information. Customer registrations also allow on-line stores to provide customers with personalized content and order-tracking information. Some on-line stores also can use customer registration information to help target advertisements to customers with certain preferences or within particular demographics.

RegisterServlet (Section 18.5.1) handles customer registrations for the Deitel Bookstore. Once a customer registers, **LoginServlet** allows the customer to log into the site with a user name and password. **ViewOrderHistoryServlet** allows customers to see information about orders they already have placed. **GetLostPasswordServlet** provides **Customer**s with a hint to remind them of forgotten passwords.

18.5.1 RegisterServlet

RegisterServlet (Fig. 18.17) processes the registration forms submitted by new customers. The servlet creates a **CustomerModel** instance (line 34) and uses the parameter values received from the client to populate the model with details about the customer (lines 38–125). Once the **CustomerModel** has been populated with data, line 133 looks up the **Customer** EJB, which represents a customer in the database. Lines 141–142 create a new customer registration in the database by invoking **Customer** EJB method **create** with the newly created **CustomerModel** object as an argument. After registering the customer, lines 147–157 forward the customer to **LoginServlet** to log into the store.

```
1   // RegisterServlet.java
2   // RegisterServlet processes the Customer registration form
3   // to register a new Customer.
4   package com.deitel.advjhtp1.bookstore.servlets;
5
6   // Java core packages
7   import java.io.*;
8   import java.util.*;
9
10  // Java extension packages
11  import javax.servlet.*;
12  import javax.servlet.http.*;
13  import javax.ejb.*;
14  import javax.naming.*;
15  import javax.rmi.*;
16
17  // third-party packages
18  import org.w3c.dom.*;
19
```

Fig. 18.17 RegisterServlet for registering new **Customer**s (part 1 of 5).

```
20    // Deitel packages
21    import com.deitel.advjhtp1.bookstore.model.*;
22    import com.deitel.advjhtp1.bookstore.ejb.*;
23
24    public class RegisterServlet extends XMLServlet {
25
26       // respond to HTTP post requests
27       public void doPost( HttpServletRequest request,
28                           HttpServletResponse response )
29          throws ServletException, IOException
30       {
31          Document document = getDocumentBuilder().newDocument();
32
33          // create CustomerModel to store registration data
34          CustomerModel customerModel = new CustomerModel();
35
36          // set properties of CustomerModel using values
37          // passed through request object
38          customerModel.setUserID( request.getParameter(
39             "userID" ) );
40
41          customerModel.setPassword( request.getParameter(
42             "password" ) );
43
44          customerModel.setPasswordHint( request.getParameter(
45             "passwordHint" ) );
46
47          customerModel.setFirstName( request.getParameter(
48             "firstName" ) );
49
50          customerModel.setLastName( request.getParameter(
51             "lastName" ) );
52
53          // set credit card information
54          customerModel.setCreditCardName( request.getParameter(
55             "creditCardName" ) );
56
57          customerModel.setCreditCardNumber( request.getParameter(
58             "creditCardNumber" ) );
59
60          customerModel.setCreditCardExpirationDate(
61             request.getParameter( "creditCardExpirationDate" ) );
62
63          // create AddressModel for billing address
64          AddressModel billingAddress = new AddressModel();
65
66          billingAddress.setFirstName( request.getParameter(
67             "billingAddressFirstName" ) );
68
69          billingAddress.setLastName( request.getParameter(
70             "billingAddressLastName" ) );
71
72          billingAddress.setStreetAddressLine1(
```

Fig. 18.17 RegisterServlet for registering new **Customer**s (part 2 of 5).

```
73                request.getParameter( "billingAddressStreet1" ) );
74
75            billingAddress.setStreetAddressLine2(
76                request.getParameter( "billingAddressStreet2" ) );
77
78            billingAddress.setCity( request.getParameter(
79                "billingAddressCity" ) );
80
81            billingAddress.setState( request.getParameter(
82                "billingAddressState" ) );
83
84            billingAddress.setZipCode( request.getParameter(
85                "billingAddressZipCode" ) );
86
87            billingAddress.setCountry( request.getParameter(
88                "billingAddressCountry" ) );
89
90            billingAddress.setPhoneNumber( request.getParameter(
91                "billingAddressPhoneNumber" ) );
92
93            customerModel.setBillingAddress( billingAddress );
94
95            // create AddressModel for shipping address
96            AddressModel shippingAddress = new AddressModel();
97
98            shippingAddress.setFirstName( request.getParameter(
99                "shippingAddressFirstName" ) );
100
101           shippingAddress.setLastName( request.getParameter(
102               "shippingAddressLastName" ) );
103
104           shippingAddress.setStreetAddressLine1(
105               request.getParameter( "shippingAddressStreet1" ) );
106
107           shippingAddress.setStreetAddressLine2(
108               request.getParameter( "shippingAddressStreet2" ) );
109
110           shippingAddress.setCity( request.getParameter(
111               "shippingAddressCity" ) );
112
113           shippingAddress.setState( request.getParameter(
114               "shippingAddressState" ) );
115
116           shippingAddress.setZipCode( request.getParameter(
117               "shippingAddressZipCode" ) );
118
119           shippingAddress.setCountry( request.getParameter(
120               "shippingAddressCountry" ) );
121
122           shippingAddress.setPhoneNumber( request.getParameter(
123               "shippingAddressPhoneNumber" ) );
124
125           customerModel.setShippingAddress( shippingAddress );
```

Fig. 18.17 **RegisterServlet** for registering new **Customer**s (part 3 of 5).

```
126
127         // look up Customer EJB and create new Customer
128      try {
129         InitialContext context = new InitialContext();
130
131         // look up Customer EJB
132         Object object =
133            context.lookup( "java:comp/env/ejb/Customer" );
134
135         CustomerHome customerHome = ( CustomerHome )
136            PortableRemoteObject.narrow( object,
137               CustomerHome.class );
138
139         // create new Customer using the CustomerModel with
140         // Customer's registration information
141         Customer customer =
142            customerHome.create( customerModel );
143
144         customerModel = customer.getCustomerModel();
145
146         // get RequestDispatcher for Login servlet
147         RequestDispatcher dispatcher =
148            getServletContext().getRequestDispatcher( "/Login" );
149
150         // set userID and password for Login servlet
151         request.setAttribute( "userID",
152            customerModel.getUserID() );
153         request.setAttribute( "password",
154            customerModel.getPassword() );
155
156         // forward user to LoginServlet
157         dispatcher.forward( request, response );
158
159      } // end try
160
161      // handle exception when looking up Customer EJB
162      catch ( NamingException namingException ) {
163         namingException.printStackTrace();
164
165         String error = "The Customer EJB was not " +
166            "found in the JNDI directory.";
167
168         document.appendChild( buildErrorMessage(
169               document, error ) );
170
171         writeXML( request, response, document );
172      }
173
174      // handle exception when creating Customer
175      catch ( CreateException createException ) {
176         createException.printStackTrace();
177
178         String error = "The Customer could not be created";
```

Fig. 18.17 RegisterServlet for registering new **Customer**s (part 4 of 5).

```
179
180            document.appendChild( buildErrorMessage(
181                document, error ) );
182
183            writeXML( request, response, document );
184        }
185
186    } // end method doPost
187 }
```

Fig. 18.17 RegisterServlet for registering new **Customer**s (part 5 of 5).

Lines 162–172 **catch** a **NamingException**, which indicates that the **CustomerHome** interface could not be found in the JNDI directory. Because **RegisterServlet** creates a new **Customer**, lines 175–184 **catch** a **CreateException** in case the **Customer** EJB could not be created. Each **catch** block builds an XML error message using method **buildErrorMessage** and invokes method **writeXML** to display the error message to the customer.

18.5.2 LoginServlet

To log into the store, a registered customer must provide a valid **userID** and **password**, which the client submits to **LoginServlet**. **LoginServlet** (Fig. 18.18) checks the **userID** and **password** against the **userID**s and **password**s stored in the database.

```
1   // LoginServlet.java
2   // LoginServlet that logs an existing Customer into the site.
3   package com.deitel.advjhtp1.bookstore.servlets;
4
5   // Java core packages
6   import java.io.*;
7
8   // Java extension packages
9   import javax.servlet.*;
10  import javax.servlet.http.*;
11  import javax.naming.*;
12  import javax.ejb.*;
13  import javax.rmi.*;
14
15  // third-party packages
16  import org.w3c.dom.*;
17
18  // Deitel packages
19  import com.deitel.advjhtp1.bookstore.model.*;
20  import com.deitel.advjhtp1.bookstore.ejb.*;
21
22  public class LoginServlet extends XMLServlet {
23
```

Fig. 18.18 LoginServlet for authenticating registered **Customer**s (part 1 of 4).(Images courtesy Pixo, Inc. or © 2001 Nokia Mobile Phones.)

```
24      // respond to HTTP post requests
25      public void doPost( HttpServletRequest request,
26                          HttpServletResponse response )
27         throws ServletException, IOException
28      {
29         Document document = getDocumentBuilder().newDocument();
30
31         String userID = request.getParameter( "userID" );
32         String password = request.getParameter( "password" );
33
34         // use Customer EJB to authenticate user
35         try {
36            InitialContext context = new InitialContext();
37
38            // look up Customer EJB
39            Object object =
40               context.lookup( "java:comp/env/ejb/Customer" );
41
42            CustomerHome customerHome = ( CustomerHome )
43               PortableRemoteObject.narrow( object,
44                  CustomerHome.class );
45
46            // find Customer with given userID and password
47            Customer customer =
48               customerHome.findByLogin( userID, password );
49
50            // get CustomerModel for Customer
51            CustomerModel customerModel =
52               customer.getCustomerModel();
53
54            // set userID in Customer's session
55            request.getSession().setAttribute( "userID",
56               customerModel.getUserID() );
57
58            // create login XML element
59            Element login = document.createElement( "login" );
60            document.appendChild( login );
61
62            // add Customer's first name to XML document
63            Element firstName =
64               document.createElement( "firstName" );
65
66            firstName.appendChild( document.createTextNode(
67               customerModel.getFirstName() ) );
68
69            login.appendChild( firstName );
70
71         } // end try
72
73         // handle exception when looking up Customer EJB
74         catch ( NamingException namingException ) {
75            namingException.printStackTrace();
```

Fig. 18.18 LoginServlet for authenticating registered **Customer**s (part 2 of 4).(Images courtesy Pixo, Inc. or © 2001 Nokia Mobile Phones.)

```
76
77           String error = "The Customer EJB was not found in " +
78              "the JNDI directory.";
79
80           document.appendChild( buildErrorMessage(
81              document, error ) );
82        }
83
84        // handle exception when Customer is not found
85        catch ( FinderException finderException ) {
86           finderException.printStackTrace();
87
88           String error = "The userID and password entered " +
89              "were not found.";
90
91           document.appendChild( buildErrorMessage(
92              document, error ) );
93        }
94
95        // ensure content is written to client
96        finally {
97           writeXML( request, response, document );
98        }
99
100   } // end method doPost
101 }
```

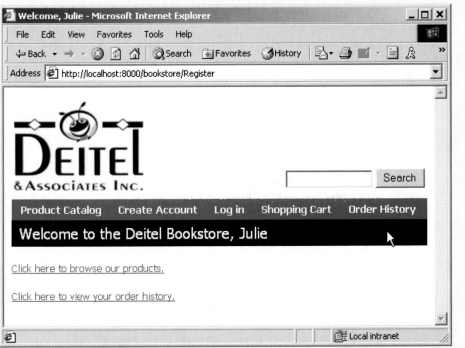

Fig. 18.18 LoginServlet for authenticating registered Customers (part 3 of 4).(Images courtesy Pixo, Inc. or © 2001 Nokia Mobile Phones.)

Fig. 18.18 **LoginServlet** for authenticating registered **Customer**s (part 4 of 4).(Images courtesy Pixo, Inc. or © 2001 Nokia Mobile Phones.)

LoginServlet uses the **Customer** EJB to validate the **userID** and password that the customer entered. Lines 39–44 obtain a reference to the **CustomerHome** interface. Lines 47–48 invoke **CustomerHome** method **findByLogin**, which returns a remote reference to the **Customer** with the **userID** and **password** that the user provided. Once the **Customer** is found, lines 59–69 build a simple XML document that indicates the customer has successfully logged into the store.

Lines 74–82 **catch** a **NamingException** if the **Customer** EJB cannot be found in the JNDI directory. If no **Customer** is found that matches the **userID** and **password** the user entered, lines 85–93 **catch** a **FinderException**. Each **catch** block builds an XML error message for the client to display. Lines 96–98 present the content to the client.

18.5.3 ViewOrderHistoryServlet

Registered customers may want to see information about orders they have placed in the past. **ViewOrderHistoryServlet** (Fig. 18.19) allows customers to see orders they have placed, along with the dates the orders were taken, the total costs of the orders and whether or not the orders were shipped from the warehouse.

```
1    // ViewOrderHistoryServlet.java
2    // ViewOrderHistoryServlet presents a list of previous Orders
3    // to the Customer.
4    package com.deitel.advjhtp1.bookstore.servlets;
5
6    // Java core packages
7    import java.io.*;
8    import java.util.*;
9
10   // Java extension packages
11   import javax.servlet.*;
12   import javax.servlet.http.*;
13   import javax.naming.*;
14   import javax.rmi.*;
15   import javax.ejb.*;
16
17   // third-party packages
18   import org.w3c.dom.*;
19
20   // Deitel packages
21   import com.deitel.advjhtp1.bookstore.model.*;
22   import com.deitel.advjhtp1.bookstore.ejb.*;
23   import com.deitel.advjhtp1.bookstore.exceptions.*;
24
25   public class ViewOrderHistoryServlet extends XMLServlet {
26
27      // respond to HTTP get requests
28      public void doGet( HttpServletRequest request,
29                         HttpServletResponse response )
30         throws ServletException, IOException
31      {
32         Document document = getDocumentBuilder().newDocument();
33
34         HttpSession session = request.getSession();
35         String userID = ( String )
36            session.getAttribute( "userID" );
37
38         // build order history using Customer EJB
39         try {
40            InitialContext context = new InitialContext();
41
42            // look up Customer EJB
43            Object object =
44               context.lookup( "java:comp/env/ejb/Customer" );
45
46            CustomerHome customerHome = ( CustomerHome )
47               PortableRemoteObject.narrow(
48                  object, CustomerHome.class );
49
50            // find Customer with given userID
51            Customer customer =
```

Fig. 18.19 `ViewOrderHistoryServlet` for viewing customer's previously placed **Order**s (part 1 of 4). (Images courtesy Pixo, Inc. or © 2001 Nokia Mobile Phones.)

```
52              customerHome.findByUserID( userID );
53
54          // create orderHistory element
55          Element rootNode = ( Element ) document.appendChild(
56              document.createElement( "orderHistory" ) );
57
58          // get Customer's Order history
59          Iterator orderHistory =
60              customer.getOrderHistory().iterator();
61
62          // loop through Order history and add XML elements
63          // to XML document for each Order
64          while ( orderHistory.hasNext() ) {
65              OrderModel orderModel =
66                  ( OrderModel ) orderHistory.next();
67
68              rootNode.appendChild(
69                  orderModel.getXML( document ) );
70          }
71      } // end try
72
73      // handle exception when Customer has no Order history
74      catch ( NoOrderHistoryException historyException ) {
75          historyException.printStackTrace();
76
77          document.appendChild( buildErrorMessage( document,
78              historyException.getMessage() ) );
79      }
80
81      // handle exception when looking up Customer EJB
82      catch ( NamingException namingException ) {
83          namingException.printStackTrace();
84
85          String error = "The Customer EJB was not found in " +
86              "the JNDI directory.";
87
88          document.appendChild( buildErrorMessage(
89                  document, error ) );
90      }
91
92      // handle exception when Customer is not found
93      catch ( FinderException finderException ) {
94          finderException.printStackTrace();
95
96          String error = "The Customer with userID " + userID +
97              " was not found.";
98
99          document.appendChild( buildErrorMessage(
100                 document, error ) );
101     }
102
```

Fig. 18.19 `ViewOrderHistoryServlet` for viewing customer's previously placed **Order**s (part 2 of 4). (Images courtesy Pixo, Inc. or © 2001 Nokia Mobile Phones.)

```
103        // ensure content is written to client
104        finally {
105            writeXML( request, response, document );
106        }
107
108    } // end method doGet
109 }
```

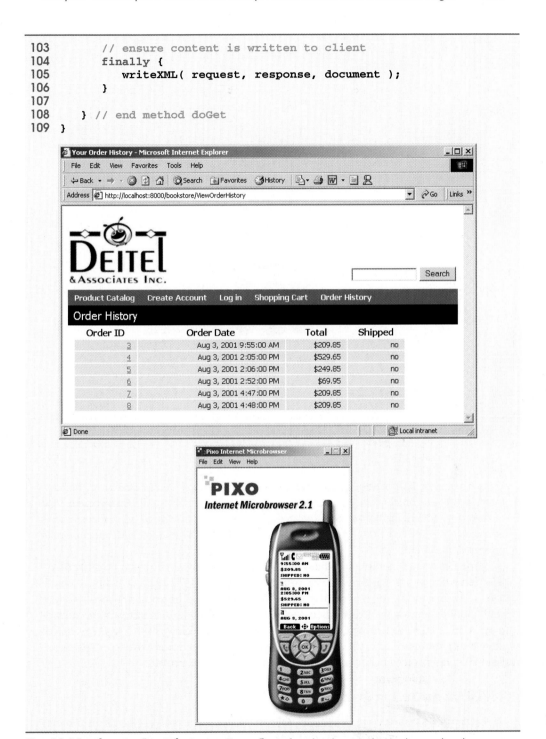

Fig. 18.19 ViewOrderHistoryServlet for viewing customer's previously placed **Order**s (part 3 of 4). (Images courtesy Pixo, Inc. or © 2001 Nokia Mobile Phones.)

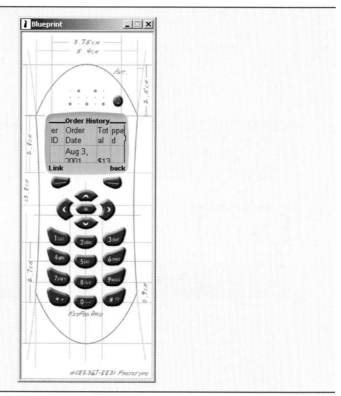

Fig. 18.19 **ViewOrderHistoryServlet** for viewing customer's previously placed **Order**s (part 4 of 4). (Images courtesy Pixo, Inc. or © 2001 Nokia Mobile Phones.)

Customer EJB method **getOrderHistory** returns a **Collection** of the customer's previous orders. Lines 51–52 obtain the **Customer** EJB for the **Customer**, who must be logged into the bookstore. Lines 59–60 retrieve an **Iterator** for the customer's order history. Lines 64–70 loop through the order history and build the XML document to present to the client.

If the customer has not placed any orders in our on-line store, method **getOrderHistory** throws a **NoOrderHistoryException**. Lines 74–79 **catch** this exception and build an error message to display to the customer. If the **CustomerHome** interface could not be found or the **Customer** could not be found in the database, a **NamingException** or **FinderException** is thrown, respectively. Lines 82–101 **catch** each of these exceptions and construct an error message, using method **buildErrorMessage**. Line 105 presents the content to the client, using method **writeXML**.

18.5.4 **ViewOrderServlet**

ViewOrderServlet (Fig. 18.20) displays the details of an order. **CheckoutServlet** forwards clients to **ViewOrderServlet** when a customer places an order. **ViewOrderHistoryServlet** forwards clients to **ViewOrderServlet** to present the details of an order that has already been placed.

Lines 39–44 obtain a reference to interface **OrderHome**. Lines 47–48 retrieve the **orderID** parameter from the **request** object. Line 51 invokes **OrderHome** method **findByPrimaryKey** to obtain a remote reference to the **Order** with the given **orderID**. Lines 54–58 get the **OrderModel** for the **Order** and append its XML representation to the XML document.

Lines 63–71 **catch** a **NamingException**, which is thrown from method **lookup** if the **Order** EJB cannot be found in the JNDI directory. Lines 74–82 **catch** a **Finder-Exception**, which is thrown by method **findByPrimaryKey** if an **Order** with the given **orderID** is not found. Line 86 presents the XML document to the client, using method **writeXML**.

```
1    // ViewOrderServlet.java
2    // ViewOrderServlet presents the contents of a Customer's
3    // Order.
4    package com.deitel.advjhtp1.bookstore.servlets;
5
6    // Java core packages
7    import java.io.*;
8
9    // Java extension packages
10   import javax.servlet.*;
11   import javax.servlet.http.*;
12   import javax.naming.*;
13   import javax.ejb.*;
14   import javax.rmi.*;
15
16   // third-party packages
17   import org.w3c.dom.*;
18
19   // Deitel packages
20   import com.deitel.advjhtp1.bookstore.model.*;
21   import com.deitel.advjhtp1.bookstore.ejb.*;
22
23   public class ViewOrderServlet extends XMLServlet {
24
25      // respond to HTTP get requests
26      public void doGet( HttpServletRequest request,
27                         HttpServletResponse response )
28         throws ServletException, IOException
29      {
30         Document document = getDocumentBuilder().newDocument();
31         Integer orderID = null;
32
33         // look up Order EJB and get details of Order with
34         // given orderID
35         try {
36            InitialContext context = new InitialContext();
37
38            // look up Order EJB
```

Fig. 18.20 **ViewOrderServlet** for viewing details of an order (part 1 of 3). (Images courtesy Pixo, Inc. or © 2001 Nokia Mobile Phones.)

```
39                  Object object =
40                     context.lookup( "java:comp/env/ejb/Order" );
41
42                  OrderHome orderHome = ( OrderHome )
43                     PortableRemoteObject.narrow(
44                        object, OrderHome.class );
45
46                  // get orderID from request object
47                  orderID = new Integer(
48                     request.getParameter( "orderID" ) );
49
50                  // find Order with given orderID
51                  Order order = orderHome.findByPrimaryKey( orderID );
52
53                  // get Order details as an OrderModel
54                  OrderModel orderModel = order.getOrderModel();
55
56                  // add Order details to XML document
57                  document.appendChild(
58                     orderModel.getXML( document ) );
59
60               } // end try
61
62               // handle exception when looking up Order EJB
63               catch ( NamingException namingException ) {
64                  namingException.printStackTrace();
65
66                  String error = "The Order EJB was not found in " +
67                     "the JNDI directory.";
68
69                  document.appendChild( buildErrorMessage(
70                     document, error ) );
71               }
72
73               // handle exception when Order is not found
74               catch ( FinderException finderException ) {
75                  finderException.printStackTrace();
76
77                  String error = "An Order with orderID " + orderID +
78                     " was not found.";
79
80                  document.appendChild( buildErrorMessage(
81                     document, error ) );
82               }
83
84               // ensure content is written to client
85               finally {
86                  writeXML( request, response, document );
87               }
88
89         } // end method doGet
90      }
```

Fig. 18.20 `ViewOrderServlet` for viewing details of an order (part 2 of 3).
(Images courtesy Pixo, Inc. or © 2001 Nokia Mobile Phones.)

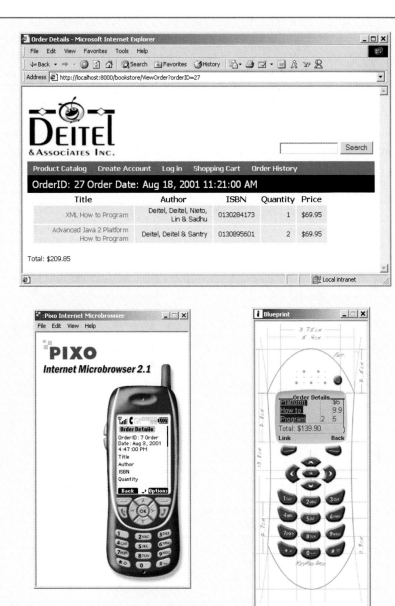

Fig. 18.20 ViewOrderServlet for viewing details of an order (part 3 of 3). (Images courtesy Pixo, Inc. or © 2001 Nokia Mobile Phones.)

18.5.5 GetPasswordHintServlet

Registered **Customer**s occasionally forget their passwords. **GetPasswordHint-Servlet** (Fig. 18.21) provides hints to help **Customer**s remember their passwords. The customer supplies the password hint as part of the registration process.

The hint is stored with other customer registration information in the **Customer** EJB. Lines 38–47 look up the **CustomerHome** interface and retrieve the **Customer** EJB remote reference. **Customer** EJB method **getPasswordHint** (line 55) returns the hint the user entered when registering on the site. Line 58 adds the hint to the XML document.

In this chapter, we presented the controller and presentation logic for the Deitel Bookstore. This controller logic provides an HTTP interface to the business logic objects we present in Chapters 18 and 19. Java servlets provide a robust and flexible controller logic implementation. XSLT presentation logic allows the Deitel Bookstore application to support many different client types without a need for changes in controller logic implementations. In Chapters 19 and 20, we present the business logic for the Deitel Bookstore, using Enterprise JavaBeans.

```java
1   // GetPasswordHintServlet.java
2   // GetPasswordHintServlet allows a customer to retrieve a
3   // lost password.
4   package com.deitel.advjhtp1.bookstore.servlets;
5
6   // Java core packages
7   import java.io.*;
8
9   // Java extension packages
10  import javax.servlet.*;
11  import javax.servlet.http.*;
12  import javax.naming.*;
13  import javax.ejb.*;
14  import javax.rmi.*;
15
16  // third-party packages
17  import org.w3c.dom.*;
18
19  // Deitel packages
20  import com.deitel.advjhtp1.bookstore.model.*;
21  import com.deitel.advjhtp1.bookstore.ejb.*;
22
23  public class GetPasswordHintServlet extends XMLServlet {
24
25     // respond to HTTP get requests
26     public void doGet( HttpServletRequest request,
27                        HttpServletResponse response )
28        throws ServletException, IOException
29     {
30        Document document = getDocumentBuilder().newDocument();
31        String userID = request.getParameter( "userID" );
32
33        // get password hint from Customer EJB
34        try {
35           InitialContext context = new InitialContext();
36
37           // look up Customer EJB
38           Object object =
```

Fig. 18.21 GetPasswordHintServlet for viewing a **Customer**'s password hint (part 1 of 3). (Images courtesy Pixo, Inc. or © 2001 Nokia Mobile Phones.)

```
39                  context.lookup( "java:comp/env/ejb/Customer" );
40
41            CustomerHome customerHome = ( CustomerHome )
42               PortableRemoteObject.narrow( object,
43                  CustomerHome.class );
44
45            // find Customer with given userID
46            Customer customer =
47               customerHome.findByUserID( userID );
48
49            // create passwordHint element in XML document
50            Element hintElement =
51               document.createElement( "passwordHint" );
52
53            // add text of passwordHint to XML element
54            hintElement.appendChild( document.createTextNode(
55               customer.getPasswordHint() ) );
56
57            // append passwordHint element to XML document
58            document.appendChild( hintElement );
59
60         } // end try
61
62         // handle exception when looking up Customer EJB
63         catch ( NamingException namingException ) {
64            namingException.printStackTrace();
65
66            String error = "The Customer EJB was not found in " +
67               "the JNDI directory.";
68
69            document.appendChild( buildErrorMessage(
70                  document, error ) );
71         }
72
73         // handle exception when Customer is not found
74         catch ( FinderException finderException ) {
75            finderException.printStackTrace();
76
77            String error = "No customer was found with userID " +
78               userID + ".";
79
80            document.appendChild( buildErrorMessage(
81                  document, error ) );
82         }
83
84         // ensure content is written to client
85         finally {
86            writeXML( request, response, document );
87         }
88
89      } // end method doGet
90   }
```

Fig. 18.21 GetPasswordHintServlet for viewing a **Customer**'s password hint (part 2 of 3). (Images courtesy Pixo, Inc. or © 2001 Nokia Mobile Phones.)

Fig. 18.21 `GetPasswordHintServlet` for viewing a **Customer**'s password hint (part 3 of 3). (Images courtesy Pixo, Inc. or © 2001 Nokia Mobile Phones.)

SELF-REVIEW EXERCISES

18.1 Which part of the MVC architecture do the servlets in the Deitel Bookstore implement? Which part of the MVC architecture do the XSL transformations implement?

18.2   Write a code snippet for looking up the **ShoppingCart** EJB in the JNDI directory and creating a new instance using interface **ShoppingCartHome**. Be sure to catch any exceptions thrown when looking up the EJB or creating a new instance.

18.3   How does **ViewOrderServlet** (Fig. 18.20) locate the **Order** that the user requested to view?

18.4   What common functionality does class **XMLServlet** (Fig. 18.1) provide for the servlets in the Deitel Bookstore? Describe the purposes of the main methods of class **XMLServlet**.

18.5   How does class **XMLServlet** determine the name of the XSLT stylesheet to use when transforming content generated by the servlet? What benefit does this strategy provide?

18.6   How does class **XMLServlet** determine the particular XSLT stylesheet to use when transforming content generated by the servlet for a particular type of client? What benefit does this strategy provide?

ANSWERS TO SELF-REVIEW EXERCISES

18.1 The servlets implement the controller in the MVC architecture, because they handle all user requests and process user input. The XSL transformations implement the view in the MVC design pattern because they produce presentations of application data.

18.2   The following code snippet looks up the **ShoppingCart** EJB in the JNDI directory and creates a new instance using interface **ShoppingCartHome**:

```
try {
    InitialContext context = new InitialContext;

    Object object = context.lookup(
        "java:comp/env/ejb/ShoppingCart" );

    ShoppingCartHome shoppingCartHome =
        ( ShoppingCartHome ) PortableRemoteObject.narrow(
            object, ShoppingCartHome.class );

    ShoppingCart shoppingCart = shoppingCartHome.create();
}

catch ( NamingException namingException ) {
    namingException.printStackTrace();
}

catch ( CreateException createException ) {
    createException.printStackTrace();
}
```

18.3   **ViewOrderServlet** uses **OrderHome** method **findByPrimaryKey** to locate the **Order**, with the **orderID** passed as a parameter to the **HttpServletRequest** object.

18.4   Class **XMLServlet** provides a common **init** method for initializing the **DocumentBuilderFactory**, **TransformerFactory** and properties each servlet uses. Class **XMLServlet** provides method **buildErrorMessage**, which creates an XML element to describe an error message. Class **XMLServlet** also provides method **writeXML**, which uses method **transform** to transform the XML content generated by each servlet using client-specific XSL transformations.

18.5   Class **XMLServlet** has property **XSLFileName** that specifies the name of the XSL file to use when transforming the servlet's content. Class **XMLServlet**'s **init** method sets the **XSLFileName** property to the value specified in the **XSL_FILE** servlet initialization parameter. Determining the file name from an initialization parameter enables the deployer to specify the file name when deploying the application. The file name can be changed later without the need to recompile the servlet.

18.6   Class **XMLServlet** uses a **ClientModel** to determine which directory contains the XSL transformation for XML content generated by the servlet. Class **XMLServlet** creates a list of **ClientModel**s from an XML configuration file when the servlet is first initialized. Each **ClientModel** specifies a **User-Agent** header that uniquely identifies the client, the **Content-Type** for sending data to the client and the directory in which the XSL transformations can be found for generating content specific to the client. This enables the developer to add support for new client types without modifying any servlet code. The developer simply provides a set of XSL transformations for the new client type and includes information about the new client type in **clients.xml**.

19

Enterprise Java Case Study: Business Logic Part 1

Objectives

- To understand the EJB data model for the Deitel Bookstore case study.
- To understand the business logic used in the Deitel Bookstore case study.
- To understand performance issues involved in transmitting objects over RMI-IIOP.
- To understand the benefits of EJBs that use container-managed persistence for database storage.
- To understand the usage of primary-key classes that represent complex primary keys.

Drive thy business, or it will drive thee.
Benjamin Franklin

Everybody's business is nobody's business, and nobody's business is my business.
Clara Barton

Outline

19.1 Introduction

In this chapter, we present the EJB business logic for the shopping-cart e-commerce model, and entity EJBs that provide an object-based interface to the store's product catalog. After reading this chapter, you will understand the use of EJBs in an e-commerce application context, as well as more advanced EJB topics, such as custom primary-key classes and many-to-many relationships.

19.2 EJB Architecture

EJBs implement the business logic of the Deitel Bookstore case study. Servlet controller logic communicates with EJB business logic to process user requests and retrieve data from the database. For example, **GetProductServlet** handles **Customer** requests to view **Product** details. **GetProductServlet** uses the JNDI directory to locate the **Product** EJB's home interface. **GetProductServlet** invokes **ProductHome** method **findByPrimaryKey** to retrieve a remote reference to the **Product** with the requested

ISBN. **GetProductServlet** must then use methods in the **Product** remote interface to retrieve information about the **Product**. Each method call on the **Product** remote interface incurs network traffic, because communication with the EJB is performed over RMI-IIOP (discussed in Chapter 27). If separate method calls were required to retrieve the **Product**'s **title**, **author**, **price** and other properties, the network overhead would severely limit the performance and scalability of the application.

The entity EJBs in the Deitel Bookstore case study alleviate this network congestion by using *models* to transmit EJB data. A model is a **Serializable** class that contains all the data for a given EJB. These classes are called models because each model class implements a piece of the model in the MVC architecture. Each entity EJB provides a *get* method that returns its model representation. For example, the **Product** EJB has method **getProductModel**, which returns a **ProductModel** containing the **ISBN**, **author**, **price** and other properties of a **Product**. Many of the entity EJBs also provide *create* methods that accept models as arguments. These *create* methods create new EJB instances and set the data in the EJB, using property values provided in the model.

Performance Tip 19.1

Aggregating entity EJB data into a model class and returning instances of this model class from EJB business methods can improve EJB performance by reducing the network traffic associated with multiple method calls over RMI-IIOP.

Figure 19.1 shows a sample communication between servlet **GetProductServlet** and the **Product** EJB. To get the details of a given **Product**, **GetProductServlet** invokes **Product** method **getProductModel**. Method **getProductModel** returns a **ProductModel** object containing data for a given **Product** and serializes the **ProductModel** over RMI-IIOP. **GetProductServlet** retrieves the **ProductModel**'s property values to build the output for the user.

19.3 ShoppingCart Implementation

Stateful session EJB **ShoppingCart** implements business logic for managing each Customer's shopping cart. The **ShoppingCart** EJB consists of a remote interface, an EJB implementation and a home interface. We implement **ShoppingCart** as a stateful session EJB so each **ShoppingCart** instance will persist throughout a customer's shopping session. Just as customers of brick-and-mortar stores use shopping carts to gather products, customers of our on-line store use **ShoppingCart** EJBs to gather products while they browse through our store.

19.3.1 ShoppingCart Remote Interface

Remote interface **ShoppingCart** (Fig. 19.2) defines business logic methods available in the **ShoppingCart** EJB. Each remote interface method must declare that it **throws RemoteException**. Each method also must declare any application-specific exceptions that may be thrown from the implementation. Method **getContents** (line 20) returns an **Collection** of **Product**s in the **ShoppingCart**. Method **addProduct** (lines 23–24) takes as a **String** argument the **ISBN** of a **Product** to add to the **ShoppingCart**. Method **addProduct** throws **ProductNotFoundException**, which is an application-specific exception that indicates the **Product** with the given **ISBN** is not in the database and therefore could not be added to the **ShoppingCart**.

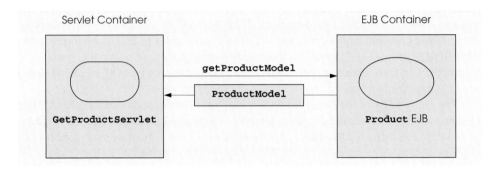

Fig. 19.1 Communication between **GetProductServlet** and **Product** EJB.

Method **removeProduct** (lines 27–28) removes the **Product** with the given **ISBN** from the **ShoppingCart**. If the **Product** with the given **ISBN** is not found in the **ShoppingCart**, method **removeProduct** throws a **ProductNotFoundException**.

Method **setProductQuantity** (lines 32–34) updates the quantity of the **Product** with the given **ISBN** in the **ShoppingCart**. For example, if there were one copy of *Advanced Java 2 Platform How to Program* in the **Customer**'s **ShoppingCart**, **setProductQuantity** could be called with the **ISBN** of *Advanced Java How to Program* and the integer **5** to purchase five copies of the book. If the **Product** with the given **ISBN** is not in the **ShoppingCart**, method **setProductQuantity** throws the application-specific **ProductNotFoundException**.

Method **checkout** (lines 37–38) places an **Order** for the **Product**s in the **Customer**'s **ShoppingCart**. Method **checkout** takes as a **String** argument the **userID** of the customer placing the **Order**. Only registered customers may place **Order**s. Method **getTotal** (line 41) returns the total cost of the **Product**s in the **Customer**'s **ShoppingCart**.

```
1   // ShoppingCart.java
2   // ShoppingCart is the remote interface for stateful session
3   // EJB ShoppingCart.
4   package com.deitel.advjhtp1.bookstore.ejb;
5
6   // Java core packages
7   import java.rmi.RemoteException;
8   import java.util.ArrayList;
9
10  // Java extension packages
11  import javax.ejb.EJBObject;
12
13  // Deitel packages
14  import com.deitel.advjhtp1.bookstore.model.*;
15  import com.deitel.advjhtp1.bookstore.exceptions.*;
```

Fig. 19.2 **ShoppingCart** remote interface for adding, removing and updating **Product**s, checking out and calculating the **Order**'s total cost (part 1 of 2).

```
16
17  public interface ShoppingCart extends EJBObject {
18
19      // get contents of ShoppingCart
20      public Collection getContents() throws RemoteException;
21
22      // add Product with given ISBN to ShoppingCart
23      public void addProduct( String isbn )
24          throws RemoteException, ProductNotFoundException;
25
26      // remove Product with given ISBN from ShoppingCart
27      public void removeProduct( String isbn )
28          throws RemoteException, ProductNotFoundException;
29
30      // change quantity of Product in ShoppingCart with
31      // given ISBN to given quantity
32      public void setProductQuantity( String isbn, int quantity )
33          throws RemoteException, ProductNotFoundException,
34              IllegalArgumentException;
35
36      // checkout ShoppingCart (i.e., create new Order)
37      public Order checkout( String userID )
38          throws RemoteException, ProductNotFoundException;
39
40      // get total cost for Products in ShoppingCart
41      public double getTotal() throws RemoteException;
42  }
```

Fig. 19.2 **ShoppingCart** remote interface for adding, removing and updating
Products, checking out and calculating the **Order**'s total cost
(part 2 of 2).

19.3.2 ShoppingCartEJB Implementation

ShoppingCart remote interface implementation **ShoppingCartEJB** (Fig. 19.3) contains an **Collection** of **OrderProductModel**s (line 24). An **OrderProductModel** (Fig. 19.25) represents an item in the **ShoppingCart**. Each **OrderProductModel** contains a **Product** and that **Product**'s quantity in the **ShoppingCart**. Method **ejbCreate** (lines 27–30) initializes the **Collection** (line 29). Method **getContents** (line 33–36) returns the contents of the **ShoppingCart** as a **Collection** of **OrderProductModel**s.

```
1  // ShoppingCartEJB.java
2  // Stateful session EJB ShoppingCart represents a Customer's
3  // shopping cart.
4  package com.deitel.advjhtp1.bookstore.ejb;
5
6  // Java core packages
7  import java.util.*;
8  import java.rmi.RemoteException;
```

Fig. 19.3 **ShoppingCartEJB** implementation of **ShoppingCart** remote
interface (part 1 of 7).

```
9    import java.text.DateFormat;
10
11   // Java extension packages
12   import javax.ejb.*;
13   import javax.naming.*;
14   import javax.rmi.PortableRemoteObject;
15
16   // Deitel packages
17   import com.deitel.advjhtp1.bookstore.model.*;
18   import com.deitel.advjhtp1.bookstore.exceptions.*;
19
20   public class ShoppingCartEJB implements SessionBean {
21      private SessionContext sessionContext;
22
23      // OrderProductModels (Products & quantities) in ShoppingCart
24      private Collection orderProductModels;
25
26      // create new ShoppingCart
27      public void ejbCreate()
28      {
29         orderProductModels = new ArrayList();
30      }
31
32      // get contents of ShoppingCart
33      public Collection getContents()
34      {
35         return orderProductModels;
36      }
37
38      // add Product with given ISBN to ShoppingCart
39      public void addProduct( String isbn )
40         throws ProductNotFoundException, EJBException
41      {
42         // check if Product with given ISBN is already
43         // in ShoppingCart
44         Iterator iterator = orderProductModels.iterator();
45
46         while ( iterator.hasNext() ) {
47            OrderProductModel orderProductModel =
48               ( OrderProductModel ) iterator.next();
49
50            ProductModel productModel =
51               orderProductModel.getProductModel();
52
53            // if Product is in ShoppingCart, increment quantity
54            if ( productModel.getISBN().equals( isbn ) ) {
55
56               orderProductModel.setQuantity(
57                  orderProductModel.getQuantity() + 1 );
58
59               return;
60            }
```

Fig. 19.3   ShoppingCartEJB implementation of **ShoppingCart** remote interface (part 2 of 7).

```
61
62         } // end while
63
64         // if Product is not in ShoppingCart, find Product with
65         // given ISBN and add OrderProductModel to ShoppingCart
66         try {
67            InitialContext context = new InitialContext();
68
69            Object object = context.lookup(
70               "java:comp/env/ejb/Product" );
71
72            ProductHome productHome = ( ProductHome )
73               PortableRemoteObject.narrow( object,
74                  ProductHome.class );
75
76            // find Product with given ISBN
77            Product product = productHome.findByPrimaryKey( isbn );
78
79            // get ProductModel
80            ProductModel productModel = product.getProductModel();
81
82            // create OrderProductModel for ProductModel and set
83            // its quantity
84            OrderProductModel orderProductModel =
85               new OrderProductModel();
86
87            orderProductModel.setProductModel( productModel );
88            orderProductModel.setQuantity( 1 );
89
90            // add OrderProductModel to ShoppingCart
91            orderProductModels.add( orderProductModel );
92
93         } // end try
94
95         // handle exception when finding Product record
96         catch ( FinderException finderException ) {
97            finderException.printStackTrace();
98
99            throw new ProductNotFoundException( "The Product " +
100              "with ISBN " + isbn + " was not found." );
101        }
102
103        // handle exception when invoking Product EJB methods
104        catch ( Exception exception ) {
105           throw new EJBException( exception );
106        }
107
108     } // end method addProduct
109
110     // remove Product with given ISBN from ShoppingCart
111     public void removeProduct( String isbn )
112        throws ProductNotFoundException
```

Fig. 19.3 ShoppingCartEJB implementation of **ShoppingCart** remote interface (part 3 of 7).

```
113     {
114         Iterator iterator = orderProductModels.iterator();
115
116         while ( iterator.hasNext() ) {
117
118             // get next OrderProduct in ShoppingCart
119             OrderProductModel orderProductModel =
120                 ( OrderProductModel ) iterator.next();
121
122             ProductModel productModel =
123                 orderProductModel.getProductModel();
124
125             // remove Product with given ISBN from ShoppingCart
126             if ( productModel.getISBN().equals( isbn ) ) {
127                 orderProductModels.remove( orderProductModel );
128
129                 return;
130             }
131
132         } // end while
133
134         // throw exception if Product not found in ShoppingCart
135         throw new ProductNotFoundException( "The Product " +
136             "with ISBN " + isbn + " was not found in your " +
137             "ShoppingCart." );
138
139     } // end method removeProduct
140
141     // set quantity of Product in ShoppingCart
142     public void setProductQuantity( String isbn,
143         int productQuantity ) throws ProductNotFoundException
144     {
145         // throw IllegalArgumentException if uantity not valid
146         if ( productQuantity < 0 )
147             throw new IllegalArgumentException(
148                 "Quantity cannot be less than zero." );
149
150         // remove Product if productQuantity less than 1
151         if ( productQuantity == 0 ) {
152             removeProduct( isbn );
153             return;
154         }
155
156         Iterator iterator = orderProductModels.iterator();
157
158         while ( iterator.hasNext() ) {
159
160             // get next OrderProduct in ShoppingCart
161             OrderProductModel orderProductModel =
162                 ( OrderProductModel ) iterator.next();
163
164             ProductModel productModel =
```

Fig. 19.3 **ShoppingCartEJB** implementation of **ShoppingCart** remote interface (part 4 of 7).

```
165              orderProductModel.getProductModel();
166
167          // set quantity for Product with given ISBN
168          if ( productModel.getISBN().equals( isbn ) ) {
169              orderProductModel.setQuantity( productQuantity );
170              return;
171          }
172
173      } // end while
174
175      // throw exception if Product not found in ShoppingCart
176      throw new ProductNotFoundException( "The Product " +
177          "with ISBN " + isbn + " was not found in your " +
178          "ShoppingCart." );
179
180  } // end method setProductQuantity
181
182  // checkout of store (i.e., create new Order)
183  public Order checkout( String userID )
184      throws ProductNotFoundException, EJBException
185  {
186      // throw exception if ShoppingCart is empty
187      if ( orderProductModels.isEmpty() )
188          throw new ProductNotFoundException( "There were " +
189              "no Products found in your ShoppingCart." );
190
191      // create OrderModel for Order details
192      OrderModel orderModel = new OrderModel();
193
194      // set OrderModel's date to today's Date
195      orderModel.setOrderDate( new Date() );
196
197      // set list of OrderProduct in OrderModel
198      orderModel.setOrderProductModels( orderProductModels );
199
200      // set OrderModel's shipped flag to false
201      orderModel.setShipped( false );
202
203      // use OrderHome interface to create new Order
204      try {
205          InitialContext context = new InitialContext();
206
207          // look up Order EJB
208          Object object = context.lookup(
209              "java:comp/env/ejb/Order" );
210
211          OrderHome orderHome = ( OrderHome )
212              PortableRemoteObject.narrow( object,
213                  OrderHome.class );
214
215          // create new Order using OrderModel and
216          // Customer's userID
```

Fig. 19.3   **ShoppingCartEJB** implementation of **ShoppingCart** remote interface (part 5 of 7).

```
217             Order order = orderHome.create( orderModel, userID );
218
219             // empty ShoppingCart for further shopping
220             orderProductModels = new ArrayList();
221
222             // return Order EJB that was created
223             return order;
224
225          } // end try
226
227          // handle exception when looking up Order EJB
228          catch ( Exception exception ) {
229             throw new EJBException( exception );
230          }
231
232       } // end method checkout
233
234       // get total cost for Products in ShoppingCart
235       public double getTotal()
236       {
237          double total = 0.0;
238          Iterator iterator = orderProductModels.iterator();
239
240          // calculate Order's total cost
241          while ( iterator.hasNext() ) {
242
243             // get next OrderProduct in ShoppingCart
244             OrderProductModel orderProductModel =
245                ( OrderProductModel ) iterator.next();
246
247             ProductModel productModel =
248                orderProductModel.getProductModel();
249
250             // add OrderProduct extended price to total
251             total += ( productModel.getPrice() *
252                orderProductModel.getQuantity() );
253          }
254
255          return total;
256
257       } // end method getTotal
258
259       // set SessionContext
260       public void setSessionContext( SessionContext context )
261       {
262          sessionContext = context;
263       }
264
265       // activate ShoppingCart EJB instance
266       public void ejbActivate() {}
267
```

Fig. 19.3   ShoppingCartEJB implementation of **ShoppingCart** remote
interface (part 6 of 7).

```
268     // passivate ShoppingCart EJB instance
269     public void ejbPassivate() {}
270
271     // remove ShoppingCart EJB instance
272     public void ejbRemove() {}
273  }
```

Fig. 19.3   **ShoppingCartEJB** implementation of **ShoppingCart** remote interface (part 7 of 7).

Method **addProduct** (lines 39–108) adds a **Product** to the **ShoppingCart**. Lines 46–62 determine if the **ShoppingCart** already contains the given **Product**. If the **Product** is found in the **ShoppingCart**, lines 56–57 increment the associated **Order-ProductModel**'s **quantity**. Otherwise, method **findByPrimaryKey** of interface **ProductHome** locates the **Product** with the given **ISBN** (line 77). Lines 84–85 create an **OrderProductModel** to store the **Product** in the **ShoppingCart**. Line 87 adds the **ProductModel** to the **OrderProductModel**, and line 88 sets the **OrderProduct-Model**'s **quantity** to **1**. Line 91 adds the **OrderProductModel** to the **Collection**, which completes the addition of the **Product** to the **ShoppingCart**.

If method **findByPrimaryKey** of interface **ProductHome** does not find the **Product** with the given primary key, lines 96–101 catch a **FinderException**. Lines 99–100 throw a **ProductNotFoundException** to indicate that a **Product** with the given **ISBN** could not be found.

Method **removeProduct** (lines 111–139) compares the **ISBN** of each **Product** in the **ShoppingCart**'s **OrderProductModel Collection** with the **ISBN** of the **Product** to be removed. If the **Product** with the given **ISBN** is found, line 127 removes the associated **OrderProductModel** from the **Collection**. If the **Product** is not found in the **ShoppingCart**, lines 135–137 throw a **ProductNotFoundException**.

Method **setProductQuantity** (lines 142–180) sets the **quantity** of an **OrderProductModel** in the **ShoppingCart**. If argument **productQuantity** is less than **0**, lines 147–148 throw an **IllegalArgumentException**. If the **pro-ductQuantity** equals **0**, line 152 removes the **Product** from the **ShoppingCart**. Lines 158–173 compare the **ISBN** of each **Product** in the **OrderProductModel Collection** with the given **ISBN**. Line 169 updates the matching **OrderProduct-Model**'s **quantity** by invoking **OrderProductModel** method **setQuantity**. If the **Product** with the given **ISBN** is not found in the **ShoppingCart**, lines 176–178 **throw** a **ProductNotFoundException**.

Method **checkout** (lines 183–232) places an **Order** for the **Products** in the **ShoppingCart**. Each **Order** must have an associated **Customer**, so method **checkout** takes the **Customer**'s **userID** as an argument. Lines 192–201 create an **OrderModel** to represent the **Order**'s details. Each **Order** has an **orderDate**, a **shipped** flag and a **Collection** of **OrderProductModel**s. Line 195 sets the date in the **OrderModel**. Line 198 invokes method **setOrderProductModels** of class **OrderModel** to add the **OrderProductModels** list to the **Order**. Line 201 sets the **shipped** flag to **false**, to indicate that the **Order** has not shipped from the warehouse. We discuss entity EJB **Order** in detail in Section 19.5.

Line 217 invokes method **create** of interface **OrderHome** to create a new **Order**. Method **create** takes as arguments an **OrderModel** containing the details of the **Order** to be created and a **String** containing the **Customer**'s **userID**. Line 220 empties the **ShoppingCart** by creating assigning a new **ArrayList** to **Collection** reference **orderProductModels**. Line 223 returns a remote reference to the newly created **Order**. Lines 228–230 catch any exceptions that occur.

Method **getTotal** (lines 235–257) iterates through the **Collection** of **OrderProductModel**s and calculates the total cost of items in the **ShoppingCart**.

19.3.3 ShoppingCartHome Interface

Interface **ShoppingCartHome** (Fig. 19.4) defines a single **create** method (lines 15–16) that creates new **ShoppingCart** EJB instances. The EJB container provides the implementation for method **create**.

Figure 19.5 and Figure 19.6 show the deployment settings for stateful session EJB **ShoppingCart**. In addition to the settings shown here, be sure to set the **Transaction Type** to **Required** for all business methods.

```
1   // ShoppingCartHome.java
2   // ShoppingCartHome is the home interface for stateful session
3   // EJB ShoppingCart.
4   package com.deitel.advjhtp1.bookstore.ejb;
5
6   // Java core packages
7   import java.rmi.RemoteException;
8
9   // Java extension packages
10  import javax.ejb.*;
11
12  public interface ShoppingCartHome extends EJBHome {
13
14     // create new ShoppingCart EJB
15     public ShoppingCart create()
16        throws RemoteException, CreateException;
17  }
```

Fig. 19.4   **ShoppingCartHome** interface for creating **ShoppingCart** EJB instances.

ShoppingCart General Deployment Settings	
Bean Type	Stateful Session
Enterprise Bean Class	com.deitel.advjhtp1.bookstore.ejb.ShoppingCartEJB

Fig. 19.5   **ShoppingCart** general deployment settings (part 1 of 2).

ShoppingCart General Deployment Settings	
Home Interface	com.deitel.advjhtp1.bookstore.ejb.ShoppingCartHome
Remote Interface	com.deitel.advjhtp1.bookstore.ejb.ShoppingCart

Fig. 19.5 **ShoppingCart** general deployment settings (part 2 of 2).

ShoppingCart EJB References	
Coded Name	ejb/Product
Type	Entity
Home	com.deitel.advjhtp1.bookstore.ejb.ProductHome
Remote	com.deitel.advjhtp1.bookstore.ejb.Product
JNDI Name	Product
Coded Name	ejb/Order
Type	Entity
Home	com.deitel.advjhtp1.bookstore.ejb.OrderHome
Remote	com.deitel.advjhtp1.bookstore.ejb.Order
JNDI Name	Order

Fig. 19.6 **ShoppingCart** EJB references.

19.4 Product Implementation

Entity EJB **Product** uses container-managed persistence to represent a **Product** in the Deitel Bookstore. The EJB container implements methods that select, insert, update and delete database data. The deployer must provide information about how the database table should be created and the SQL queries to be used for the **create**, **remove** and *finder* methods at deployment time.

19.4.1 Product Remote Interface

Remote interface **Product** (Fig. 19.7) declares method **getProductModel** (line 17–18), which returns a **ProductModel** that contains the **Product**'s details.

```
1   // Product.java
2   // Product is the remote interface for entity EJB Product.
3   package com.deitel.advjhtp1.bookstore.ejb;
```

Fig. 19.7 **Product** remote interface for modifying details of **Product** EJB instances (part 1 of 2).

```
4
5    // Java core packages
6    import java.rmi.RemoteException;
7
8    // Java extension packages
9    import javax.ejb.*;
10
11   // Deitel packages
12   import com.deitel.advjhtp1.bookstore.model.*;
13
14   public interface Product extends EJBObject {
15
16      // get Product details as ProductModel
17      public ProductModel getProductModel()
18         throws RemoteException;
19   }
```

Fig. 19.7 **Product** remote interface for modifying details of **Product** EJB instances (part 2 of 2).

19.4.2 **ProductEJB** Implementation

Product remote interface implementation **ProductEJB** (Fig. 19.8) uses container-managed persistence. The EJB container manages the synchronization of the **public** data members declared on lines 18–24 with the database. Method **getProductModel** (lines 27–43) creates a **ProductModel** that contains the **Product**'s details. Line 30 creates the **ProductModel** instance, and lines 33–39 invoke *set* methods to initialize the **ProductModel**'s data members.

```
1    // ProductEJB.java
2    // Entity EJB Product represents a Product, including the
3    // ISBN, publisher, author, title, price number of pages
4    // and cover image.
5    package com.deitel.advjhtp1.bookstore.ejb;
6
7    // Java extension packages
8    import javax.ejb.*;
9
10   // Deitel packages
11   import com.deitel.advjhtp1.bookstore.model.*;
12   import com.deitel.advjhtp1.bookstore.*;
13
14   public class ProductEJB implements EntityBean {
15      private EntityContext entityContext;
16
17      // container-managed fields
18      public String ISBN;
19      public String publisher;
20      public String author;
21      public String title;
22      public double price;
```

Fig. 19.8 **ProductEJB** implementation of **Product** remote interface (part 1 of 3).

```
23      public int pages;
24      public String image;
25
26      // get Product details as ProductModel
27      public ProductModel getProductModel()
28      {
29         // construct new ProductModel
30         ProductModel productModel = new ProductModel();
31
32         // initialize ProductModel with data from Product
33         productModel.setISBN( ISBN );
34         productModel.setPublisher( publisher );
35         productModel.setAuthor( author );
36         productModel.setTitle( title );
37         productModel.setPrice( price );
38         productModel.setPages( pages );
39         productModel.setImage( image );
40
41         return productModel;
42
43      } // end method getProductModel
44
45      // set Product details using ProductModel
46      private void setProductModel( ProductModel productModel )
47      {
48         // populate Product's data members with data in
49         // provided ProductModel
50         ISBN = productModel.getISBN();
51         publisher = productModel.getPublisher();
52         author = productModel.getAuthor();
53         title = productModel.getTitle();
54         price = productModel.getPrice();
55         pages = productModel.getPages();
56         image = productModel.getImage();
57
58      } // end method setProductModel
59
60      // create instance of Product EJB using given ProductModel
61      public String ejbCreate( ProductModel productModel )
62      {
63         setProductModel( productModel );
64         return null;
65      }
66
67      // perform any necessary post-creation tasks
68      public void ejbPostCreate( ProductModel productmodel ) {}
69
70      // set EntityContext
71      public void setEntityContext( EntityContext context )
72      {
73         entityContext = context;
74      }
75
```

Fig. 19.8   **ProductEJB** implementation of **Product** remote interface (part 2 of 3).

```
76     // unset EntityContext
77     public void unsetEntityContext()
78     {
79         entityContext = null;
80     }
81
82     // activate Product EJB instance
83     public void ejbActivate()
84     {
85         ISBN = ( String ) entityContext.getPrimaryKey();
86     }
87
88     // passivate Product EJB instance
89     public void ejbPassivate()
90     {
91         ISBN = null;
92     }
93
94     // remove Product EJB instance
95     public void ejbRemove() {}
96
97     // store Product EJB data in database
98     public void ejbStore() {}
99
100    // load Product EJB data from database
101    public void ejbLoad() {}
102 }
```

Fig. 19.8   **ProductEJB** implementation of **Product** remote interface (part 3 of 3).

Method **setProductModel** (lines 46–58) sets the **Product**'s details, using values in the given **ProductModel**. Line 50 sets the value of the **ISBN** data member to the value of the **ISBN** contained in the **ProductModel** argument. Lines 51–56 set the values of the other **ProductEJB** data members. Method **ejbCreate** (lines 61–65) accepts a **ProductModel** argument. Method **ejbCreate** invokes method **setProductModel** with the provided **ProductModel** to initialize the **Product** EJB instance (line 63).

19.4.3 ProductHome Interface

Interface **ProductHome** (Fig. 19.9) creates new **ProductEJB** instances and declares *finder* methods for finding existing **Product**s. Method **create** (lines 18–19) corresponds to method **ejbCreate** of Fig. 19.8, and provides an interface for creating a **ProductEJB** instance. Method **findByPrimaryKey** (lines 22–23) takes as a **String** argument the ISBN for a particular **Product** in the database. Method **findAllProducts** (lines 26–27) returns a **Collection** of all **Product**s in the database. Method **findByTitle** (lines 30–31) searches for **Product**s whose titles contain the given **searchString** and returns a **Collection** of **Product** remote references. The EJB container implements each *finder* method, using SQL queries the deployer must provide at deployment time.

```
1   // ProductHome.java
2   // ProductHome is the home interface for entity EJB Product.
3   package com.deitel.advjhtp1.bookstore.ejb;
4
5   // Java core packages
6   import java.rmi.RemoteException;
7   import java.util.Collection;
8
9   // Java extension packages
10  import javax.ejb.*;
11
12  // Deitel packages
13  import com.deitel.advjhtp1.bookstore.model.*;
14
15  public interface ProductHome extends EJBHome {
16
17     // create Product EJB using given ProductModel
18     public Product create( ProductModel productModel )
19        throws RemoteException, CreateException;
20
21     // find Product with given ISBN
22     public Product findByPrimaryKey( String isbn )
23        throws RemoteException, FinderException;
24
25     // find all Products
26     public Collection findAllProducts()
27        throws RemoteException, FinderException;
28
29     // find Products with given title
30     public Collection findByTitle( String title )
31        throws RemoteException, FinderException;
32  }
```

Fig. 19.9   **ProductHome** interface for finding and creating **Product** EJB instances.

19.4.4 ProductModel

Class **ProductModel** (Fig. 19.10) implements interface **Serializable**, so that instances may be serialized over RMI-IIOP. **ProductModel** has a **private** data member (lines 18–25) and *set* and *get* methods (lines 28–109) for each **Product** EJB property.

```
1   // ProductModel.java
2   // ProductModel represents a Product in the Deitel Bookstore,
3   // including ISBN, author, title and a picture of the cover.
4   package com.deitel.advjhtp1.bookstore.model;
5
6   // Java core packages
7   import java.io.*;
8   import java.util.*;
9   import java.text.*;
10
```

Fig. 19.10   **ProductModel** class for serializing **Product** data (part 1 of 4).

```
11   // third-party packages
12   import org.w3c.dom.*;
13
14   public class ProductModel implements Serializable,
15      XMLGenerator {
16
17      // ProductModel properties
18      private String ISBN;
19      private String publisher;
20      private String author;
21      private String title;
22      private double price;
23      private int pages;
24      private String image;
25      private int quantity;
26
27      // set ISBN
28      public void setISBN( String productISBN )
29      {
30         ISBN = productISBN;
31      }
32
33      // get ISBN
34      public String getISBN()
35      {
36         return ISBN;
37      }
38
39      // set publisher
40      public void setPublisher( String productPublisher )
41      {
42         publisher = productPublisher;
43      }
44
45      // get publisher
46      public String getPublisher()
47      {
48         return publisher;
49      }
50
51      // set author
52      public void setAuthor( String productAuthor )
53      {
54         author = productAuthor;
55      }
56
57      // get author
58      public String getAuthor()
59      {
60         return author;
61      }
62
```

Fig. 19.10 ProductModel class for serializing Product data (part 2 of 4).

```
63      // set title
64      public void setTitle( String productTitle )
65      {
66          title = productTitle;
67      }
68
69      // get title
70      public String getTitle()
71      {
72          return title;
73      }
74
75      // set price
76      public void setPrice( double productPrice )
77      {
78          price = productPrice;
79      }
80
81      // get price
82      public double getPrice()
83      {
84          return price;
85      }
86
87      // set number of pages
88      public void setPages( int pageCount )
89      {
90          pages = pageCount;
91      }
92
93      // get number of pages
94      public int getPages()
95      {
96          return pages;
97      }
98
99      // set URL of cover image
100     public void setImage( String productImage )
101     {
102         image = productImage;
103     }
104
105     // get URL of cover image
106     public String getImage()
107     {
108         return image;
109     }
110
111     // get XML representation of Product
112     public Element getXML( Document document )
113     {
114         // create product Element
115         Element product = document.createElement( "product" );
```

Fig. 19.10 **ProductModel** class for serializing **Product** data (part 3 of 4).

```
116
117        // create ISBN Element
118        Element temp = document.createElement( "ISBN" );
119        temp.appendChild(
120           document.createTextNode( getISBN() ) );
121        product.appendChild( temp );
122
123        // create publisher Element
124        temp = document.createElement( "publisher" );
125        temp.appendChild(
126           document.createTextNode( getPublisher() ) );
127        product.appendChild( temp );
128
129        // create author Element
130        temp = document.createElement( "author" );
131        temp.appendChild(
132           document.createTextNode( getAuthor() ) );
133        product.appendChild( temp );
134
135        // create title Element
136        temp = document.createElement( "title" );
137        temp.appendChild(
138           document.createTextNode( getTitle() ) );
139        product.appendChild( temp );
140
141        NumberFormat priceFormatter =
142           NumberFormat.getCurrencyInstance( Locale.US );
143
144        // create price Element
145        temp = document.createElement( "price" );
146        temp.appendChild( document.createTextNode(
147           priceFormatter.format( getPrice() ) ) );
148        product.appendChild( temp );
149
150        // create pages Element
151        temp = document.createElement( "pages" );
152        temp.appendChild( document.createTextNode(
153           String.valueOf( getPages() ) ) );
154        product.appendChild( temp );
155
156        // create image Element
157        temp = document.createElement( "image" );
158        temp.appendChild(
159           document.createTextNode( getImage() ) );
160        product.appendChild( temp );
161
162        return product;
163
164     } // end method getXML
165 }
```

Fig. 19.10 `ProductModel` class for serializing `Product` data (part 4 of 4).

`ProductModel` also implements interface `XMLGenerator` (Fig. 19.11), which defines a single method, `getXML`. Method `getXML` of class `ProductModel` (lines 112–

164) generates an XML **Element** for the data contained in the **ProductModel**. This method uses the **Document** argument to create XML elements for each **ProductModel** data member. However, method **getXML** does not modify the **Document**. Line 162 returns the newly created **product** element.

Figure 19.12 and Fig. 19.13 show the deployment settings for entity EJB **Product**. In addition to the settings shown here, be sure to set the **Transaction Type** to **Required** for all business methods.

```
1   // XMLGenerator.java
2   // XMLGenerator is an interface for classes that can generate
3   // XML Elements. The XML element returned by method getXML
4   // should contain Elements for each public property.
5   package com.deitel.advjhtp1.bookstore.model;
6
7   // third-party packages
8   import org.w3c.dom.*;
9
10  public interface XMLGenerator {
11
12      // build an XML element for this Object
13      public Element getXML( Document document );
14  }
```

Fig. 19.11 XMLGenerator interface for generating XML **Element**s for **public** properties.

Product General Deployment Settings	
Bean Type	**Entity**
Enterprise Bean Class	`com.deitel.advjhtp1.bookstore.ejb.ProductEJB`
Home Interface	`com.deitel.advjhtp1.bookstore.ejb.ProductHome`
Remote Interface	`com.deitel.advjhtp1.bookstore.ejb.Product`

Fig. 19.12 Product general deployment settings.

Product Entity and Deployment Settings	
Persistence Management	**Container-Managed Persistence**

Fig. 19.13 Product Entity and deployment settings (part 1 of 2).

Product Entity and Deployment Settings	
Primary Key Class	`java.lang.String`
Primary Key Field Name	`ISBN`
Database JNDI Name	`jdbc/Bookstore`
Method `findBy-Title` **SQL Statement**	`SELECT ISBN FROM Product WHERE title LIKE ?1`
Method `find-AllProducts` **SQL Statement**	`SELECT ISBN FROM Product WHERE 1 = 1`
Method `ejb-Store` **SQL Statement**	`UPDATE Product SET author = ?, image = ?, pages = ?, price = ?, publisher = ?, title = ? WHERE ISBN = ?`
Method `ejb-Create` **SQL Statement**	`INSERT INTO Product ( ISBN, author, image, pages, price, publisher, title ) VALUES ( ?, ?, ?, ?, ?, ?, ? )`
Method `ejb-Remove` **SQL Statement**	`DELETE FROM Product WHERE ISBN = ?`
Method `find-ByPrimaryKey` **SQL Statement**	`SELECT ISBN FROM Product WHERE ISBN = ?`
Method `ejb-Load` **SQL Statement**	`SELECT author, image, pages, price, publisher, title FROM Product WHERE ISBN = ?`
Table Create SQL Statement	`CREATE TABLE Product ( ISBN VARCHAR( 255 ), author VARCHAR( 255 ), image VARCHAR( 255 ), pages INTEGER NOT NULL, price DOUBLE PRECISION NOT NULL, publisher VARCHAR( 255 ), title VARCHAR( 255 ), CONSTRAINT pk_Product PRIMARY KEY ( ISBN ) )`
Table Delete SQL Statement	`DROP TABLE Product`

Fig. 19.13 Product Entity and deployment settings (part 2 of 2).

19.5 Order Implementation

Entity EJB **Order** represents an **Order** placed at the Deitel Bookstore. Each **Order** consists of a list of **Product**s and their associated quantities, as well as the **customerID** of the **Customer** who placed the **Order**.

19.5.1 Order Remote Interface

The **Order** EJB remote interface (Fig. 19.14) defines the business methods available in the **Order** EJB. Method **getOrderModel** (line 17) returns an **OrderModel** containing **Order** details. Method **setShipped** (lines 20–21) marks an **Order** as having been shipped from the warehouse. Method **isShipped** (line 24) returns a **boolean** that indicates whether the **Order** has been shipped.

19.5.2 OrderEJB Implementation

Order remote interface implementation **OrderEJB** (Fig. 19.15) declares **public** data members for container-manage persistence (lines 26–29). Method **getOrderModel** (lines 32–91) constructs an **OrderModel** instance that contains **Order** details. Lines 42–44 populate the **OrderModel** with the values of the **Order** EJB's data members.

```
1   // Order.java
2   // Order is the remote interface for entity EJB Order.
3   package com.deitel.advjhtp1.bookstore.ejb;
4
5   // Java core packages
6   import java.rmi.RemoteException;
7
8   // Java extension packages
9   import javax.ejb.*;
10
11  // Deitel packages
12  import com.deitel.advjhtp1.bookstore.model.*;
13
14  public interface Order extends EJBObject {
15
16     // get Order details as OrderModel
17     public OrderModel getOrderModel() throws RemoteException;
18
19     // set shipped flag
20     public void setShipped( boolean flag )
21        throws RemoteException;
22
23     // get shipped flag
24     public boolean isShipped() throws RemoteException;
25  }
```

Fig. 19.14 **Order** remote interface for modifying details of **Order** EJB instances.

```
1   // OrderEJB.java
2   // Entity EJB Order represents an Order, including the
3   // orderID, Order date, total cost and whether the Order
4   // has shipped.
5   package com.deitel.advjhtp1.bookstore.ejb;
6
```

Fig. 19.15 **OrderEJB** implementation of **Order** remote interface (part 1 of 6).

```
7    // Java core packages
8    import java.util.*;
9    import java.text.DateFormat;
10   import java.rmi.RemoteException;
11
12   // Java extension packages
13   import javax.ejb.*;
14   import javax.naming.*;
15   import javax.rmi.PortableRemoteObject;
16
17   // Deitel packages
18   import com.deitel.advjhtp1.bookstore.model.*;
19
20   public class OrderEJB implements EntityBean  {
21      private EntityContext entityContext;
22      private InitialContext initialContext;
23      private DateFormat dateFormat;
24
25      // container-managed fields
26      public Integer orderID;
27      public Integer customerID;
28      public String orderDate;
29      public boolean shipped;
30
31      // get Order details as OrderModel
32      public OrderModel getOrderModel() throws EJBException
33      {
34         // construct new OrderModel
35         OrderModel orderModel = new OrderModel();
36
37         // look up OrderProduct EJB to retrieve list
38         // of Products contained in the Order
39         try {
40
41            // populate OrderModel data members with data from Order
42            orderModel.setOrderID( orderID );
43            orderModel.setOrderDate( dateFormat.parse( orderDate ) );
44            orderModel.setShipped( shipped );
45
46            initialContext = new InitialContext();
47
48            Object object = initialContext.lookup(
49               "java:comp/env/ejb/OrderProduct" );
50
51            OrderProductHome orderProductHome =
52               ( OrderProductHome ) PortableRemoteObject.narrow(
53                  object, OrderProductHome.class );
54
55            // get OrderProduct records for Order
56            Collection orderProducts =
57               orderProductHome.findByOrderID( orderID );
58
59            Iterator iterator = orderProducts.iterator();
```

Fig. 19.15 OrderEJB implementation of **Order** remote interface (part 2 of 6).

```
60
61                // OrderProductModels to place in OrderModel
62                Collection orderProductModels = new ArrayList();
63
64                // get OrderProductModel for each Product in Order
65                while ( iterator.hasNext() ) {
66                   OrderProduct orderProduct = ( OrderProduct )
67                      PortableRemoteObject.narrow( iterator.next(),
68                         OrderProduct.class );
69
70                   // get OrderProductModel for OrderProduct record
71                   OrderProductModel orderProductModel =
72                      orderProduct.getOrderProductModel();
73
74                   // add OrderProductModel to list of
75                   // OrderProductModels in the Order
76                   orderProductModels.add( orderProductModel );
77                }
78
79                // add Collection of OrderProductModels to OrderModel
80                orderModel.setOrderProductModels( orderProductModels );
81
82             } // end try
83
84             // handle exception working with OrderProduct EJB
85             catch ( Exception exception ) {
86                throw new EJBException( exception );
87             }
88
89             return orderModel;
90
91          } // end method getOrderModel
92
93          // set shipped flag
94          public void setShipped( boolean flag )
95          {
96             shipped = flag;
97          }
98
99          // get shipped flag
100         public boolean isShipped()
101         {
102            return shipped;
103         }
104
105         // create new Order EJB using given OrderModel and userID
106         public Integer ejbCreate( OrderModel order, String userID )
107            throws CreateException
108         {
109            // retrieve unique value for primary key of this
110            // Order using SequenceFactory EJB
111            try {
112               initialContext = new InitialContext();
```

Fig. 19.15 OrderEJB implementation of **Order** remote interface (part 3 of 6).

```
113
114              Object object = initialContext.lookup(
115                 "java:comp/env/ejb/SequenceFactory" );
116
117              SequenceFactoryHome sequenceFactoryHome =
118                 ( SequenceFactoryHome )
119                    PortableRemoteObject.narrow(
120                       object, SequenceFactoryHome.class );
121
122              // find sequence for CustomerOrder table
123              SequenceFactory sequenceFactory =
124                 sequenceFactoryHome.findByPrimaryKey(
125                    "CustomerOrders" );
126
127              // get next unique orderID
128              orderID = sequenceFactory.getNextID();
129
130              // get date, cost, shipped flag and list of
131              // OrderProduct from provided OrderModel
132              orderDate = dateFormat.format( order.getOrderDate() );
133              shipped = order.getShipped();
134
135              // get OrderProductModels that comprise OrderModel
136              Collection orderProductModels =
137                 order.getOrderProductModels();
138
139              // create OrderProduct EJBs for each Product in
140              // Order to keep track of quantity
141              object = initialContext.lookup(
142                 "java:comp/env/ejb/OrderProduct" );
143
144              OrderProductHome orderProductHome =
145                 ( OrderProductHome ) PortableRemoteObject.narrow(
146                       object, OrderProductHome.class );
147
148              Iterator iterator = orderProductModels.iterator();
149
150              // create an OrderProduct EJB with Product's
151              // ISBN, quantity and orderID for this Order
152              while ( iterator.hasNext() ) {
153
154                 OrderProductModel orderProductModel =
155                    ( OrderProductModel ) iterator.next();
156
157                 // set orderID for OrderProduct record
158                 orderProductModel.setOrderID( orderID );
159
160                 // create OrderProduct EJB instance
161                 orderProductHome.create( orderProductModel );
162              }
163
164              // get customerID for customer placing Order
165              object = initialContext.lookup(
```

Fig. 19.15 OrderEJB implementation of **Order** remote interface (part 4 of 6).

```
166                      "java:comp/env/ejb/Customer" );
167
168              CustomerHome customerHome =
169                 ( CustomerHome ) PortableRemoteObject.narrow(
170                    object, CustomerHome.class );
171
172              // use provided userID to find Customer
173              Customer customer =
174                 customerHome.findByUserID( userID );
175
176              customerID = ( Integer ) customer.getPrimaryKey();
177
178           } // end try
179
180           // handle exception when looking up EJBs
181           catch ( Exception exception ) {
182              throw new CreateException( exception.getMessage() );
183           }
184
185           return null;
186
187        } // end method ejbCreate
188
189        // perform any necessary post-creation tasks
190        public void ejbPostCreate( OrderModel order, String id ) {}
191
192        // set EntityContext
193        public void setEntityContext( EntityContext context )
194        {
195           entityContext = context;
196           dateFormat = DateFormat.getDateTimeInstance(
197              DateFormat.FULL, DateFormat.SHORT, Locale.US );
198        }
199
200        // unset EntityContext
201        public void unsetEntityContext()
202        {
203           entityContext = null;
204        }
205
206        // activate Order EJB instance
207        public void ejbActivate()
208        {
209           orderID = ( Integer ) entityContext.getPrimaryKey();
210        }
211
212        // passivate Order EJB instance
213        public void ejbPassivate()
214        {
215           orderID = null;
216        }
217
218        // remove Order EJB instanceCus
```

Fig. 19.15 OrderEJB implementation of **Order** remote interface (part 5 of 6).

```
219        public void ejbRemove() {}
220
221        // store Order EJB data in database
222        public void ejbStore() {}
223
224        // load Order EJB data from database
225        public void ejbLoad() {}
226 }
```

Fig. 19.15 **OrderEJB** implementation of **Order** remote interface (part 6 of 6).

In addition to the **orderDate**, **orderID** and **shipped** flag, an **Order** contains a list of **OrderProductModel**s. The relationship between an **Order** and its associated **Products** and quantities is represented by a many-to-many relationship in the database (i.e., an **Order** can contain many **Products**, and a single **Product** can be found in many **Orders**). The **OrderProduct** EJB represents this relationship by mapping an **orderID** to the **ISBN**s of **Products** in the **Order**. For each **Order**, there are records in the **OrderProduct** table containing the **ISBN**s and quantities of each **Product** in the **Order**. For example, if a **Customer** orders one copy of *Java How to Program* and two copies of *Advanced Java 2 Platform How to Program*, there will be two records in the **OrderProduct** table. Each record will have the same **orderID**, but one will have the **ISBN** for *Java How to Program* and the **quantity 1**, and the other will have the **ISBN** for *Advanced Java 2 Platform How to Program* and the **quantity 2**.

Lines 56–57 invoke method **findByOrderID** to obtain the **OrderProduct** records for the **Order**. Method **findByOrderID** returns a **Collection** of **Order-Product** remote references. Lines 65–77 traverse the **Collection** of **OrderProducts** using an **Iterator**, and lines 71–72 retrieve an **OrderProductModel** for each **OrderProduct** record. Line 76 adds each **OrderProductModel** to a **Collection**. Line 80 adds the **OrderProductModel Collection** to the **OrderModel**, and line 89 **returns** the newly created **OrderModel**.

Method **setShipped** (lines 94–97) accepts a **boolean** argument and updates the **Order** EJB's **shipped** flag. An order-tracking application could use method **setShipped** to update the status of the **Order** when the warehouse ships the **Order**. Method **isShipped** (lines 100–103) returns the **shipped** data member's current value, indicating whether the **Order** has been shipped from the warehouse.

Method **ejbCreate** (lines 106–187) creates an **Order** EJB using data from the given **OrderModel** and **userID**. Each **Order** has an associated **orderID**, which serves as the primary key in the **Order** EJB database table. **SequenceFactory** method **getNextID** generates a unique **orderID** for the **Order** (line 128).

Lines 132–133 populate the **Order** with data from the **OrderModel**. The **OrderModel** also provides the **Products** and quantities in the **Order** as an **Collection** of **OrderProductModel**s. Lines 152–162 process the **Collection** of **OrderProductModel**s and create **OrderProduct** records for each, using interface **OrderProductHome** method **create** (line 161).

Each **Order** also must have an associated **Customer** who placed the **Order**. This is a one-to-many relationship, because one **Customer** can place many orders, but an **Order** can be associated with only one **Customer**. Lines 173–174 retrieve the **Cus-**

tomer EJB for the given **userID**. **Customer** method **getPrimaryKey** retrieves the **Customer**'s **customerID**. Line 176 sets the **customerID** for the **Order**.

19.5.3 OrderHome Interface

Interface **OrderHome** (Fig. 19.16) creates **Order** instances and finds existing **Order**s. Method **create** (lines 18–19) corresponds to method **ejbCreate** of Fig. 19.15 and creates new **Order**s, using an **OrderModel** and **userID**. Method **findByPrimaryKey** (lines 22–23) locates an existing **Order**, using its **orderID**. Method **findByCustomerID** (lines 26–27) retrieves a **Collection** of **Order**s for the given **Customer**.

19.5.4 OrderModel

Class **OrderModel** (Fig. 19.17) encapsulates the details of an **Order** EJB in a **Serializable** object suitable for delivery over RMI-IIOP. **OrderModel** has **private** data members (lines 19–22) with associated *set* and *get* methods (lines 31–102) for each **Order** EJB data member. **OrderModel** also maintains a **Collection** of **OrderProductModel**s, to keep track of the **Product**s in the **Order**. **OrderModel** implements interface **XMLGenerator** and method **getXML** to facilitate the generation of an XML representation of an **Order** (lines 105–166).

```
1   // OrderHome.java
2   // OrderHome is the home interface for entity EJB Order.
3   package com.deitel.advjhtp1.bookstore.ejb;
4
5   // Java core packages
6   import java.util.*;
7   import java.rmi.RemoteException;
8
9   // Java extension packages
10  import javax.ejb.*;
11
12  // Deitel packages
13  import com.deitel.advjhtp1.bookstore.model.*;
14
15  public interface OrderHome extends EJBHome {
16
17     // create Order using given OrderModel and userID
18     public Order create( OrderModel orderModel, String userID )
19        throws RemoteException, CreateException;
20
21     // find Order using given orderID
22     public Order findByPrimaryKey( Integer orderID )
23        throws RemoteException, FinderException;
24
25     // find Orders for given customerID
26     public Collection findByCustomerID( Integer customerID )
27        throws RemoteException, FinderException;
28  }
```

Fig. 19.16 OrderHome interface for finding and creating **Order** EJB instances.

```
1   // OrderModel.java
2   // OrderModel represents an Order and contains the order ID,
3   // date, total cost and a boolean indicating whether or not the
4   // order has shipped.
5   package com.deitel.advjhtp1.bookstore.model;
6
7   // Java core packages
8   import java.io.*;
9   import java.util.*;
10  import java.text.*;
11
12  // third-party packages
13  import org.w3c.dom.*;
14
15  public class OrderModel implements Serializable,
16     XMLGenerator {
17
18     // OrderModel properties
19     private Integer orderID;
20     private Date orderDate;
21     private boolean shipped;
22     private Collection orderProductModels;
23
24     // construct empty OrderModel
25     public OrderModel()
26     {
27        orderProductModels = new ArrayList();
28     }
29
30     // set order ID
31     public void setOrderID( Integer id )
32     {
33        orderID = id;
34     }
35
36     // get order ID
37     public Integer getOrderID()
38     {
39        return orderID;
40     }
41
42     // set order date
43     public void setOrderDate( Date date )
44     {
45        orderDate = date;
46     }
47
48     // get order date
49     public Date getOrderDate()
50     {
51        return orderDate;
52     }
53
```

Fig. 19.17 `OrderModel` class for serializing `Order` data (part 1 of 4).

```
54       // get total cost
55       public double getTotalCost()
56       {
57          double total = 0.0;
58
59          Iterator iterator = orderProductModels.iterator();
60
61          // calculate Order's total cost
62          while ( iterator.hasNext() ) {
63
64             // get next OrderProduct in ShoppingCart
65             OrderProductModel orderProductModel =
66                ( OrderProductModel ) iterator.next();
67
68             ProductModel productModel =
69                orderProductModel.getProductModel();
70
71             // add OrderProduct extended price to total
72             total += ( productModel.getPrice() *
73                orderProductModel.getQuantity() );
74          }
75
76          return total;
77       }
78
79       // set shipped flag
80       public void setShipped( boolean orderShipped )
81       {
82          shipped = orderShipped;
83       }
84
85       // get shipped flag
86       public boolean getShipped()
87       {
88          return shipped;
89       }
90
91       // set list of OrderProductModels
92       public void setOrderProductModels( Collection models )
93       {
94          orderProductModels = models;
95       }
96
97       // get OrderProductModels
98       public Collection getOrderProductModels()
99       {
100         return Collections.unmodifiableCollection(
101            orderProductModels );
102      }
103
104      // get XML representation of Order
105      public Element getXML( Document document )
106      {
```

Fig. 19.17 OrderModel class for serializing Order data (part 2 of 4).

```
107        // create order Element
108        Element order = document.createElement( "order" );
109
110        // create orderID Element
111        Element temp = document.createElement( "orderID" );
112        temp.appendChild( document.createTextNode(
113           String.valueOf( getOrderID() ) ) );
114        order.appendChild( temp );
115
116        // get DateFormat for writing Date to XML document
117        DateFormat formatter = DateFormat.getDateTimeInstance(
118           DateFormat.DEFAULT, DateFormat.MEDIUM, Locale.US );
119
120        // create orderDate Element
121        temp = document.createElement( "orderDate" );
122        temp.appendChild( document.createTextNode(
123           formatter.format( getOrderDate() ) ) );
124        order.appendChild( temp );
125
126        NumberFormat costFormatter =
127           NumberFormat.getCurrencyInstance( Locale.US );
128
129        // create totalCost Element
130        temp = document.createElement( "totalCost" );
131        temp.appendChild( document.createTextNode(
132           costFormatter.format( getTotalCost() ) ) );
133        order.appendChild( temp );
134
135        // create shipped Element
136        temp = document.createElement( "shipped" );
137
138        if ( getShipped() )
139           temp.appendChild(
140              document.createTextNode( "yes" ) );
141        else
142           temp.appendChild(
143              document.createTextNode( "no" ) );
144
145        order.appendChild( temp );
146
147        // create orderProducts Element
148        Element orderProducts =
149           document.createElement( "orderProducts" );
150
151        Iterator iterator = getOrderProductModels().iterator();
152
153        // add orderProduct element for each OrderProduct
154        while ( iterator.hasNext() ) {
155           OrderProductModel orderProductModel =
156              ( OrderProductModel ) iterator.next();
157
158           orderProducts.appendChild(
159              orderProductModel.getXML( document ) );
```

Fig. 19.17 OrderModel class for serializing **Order** data (part 3 of 4).

```
160          }
161
162          order.appendChild( orderProducts );
163
164          return order;
165
166     } // end method getXML
167 }
```

Fig. 19.17 **OrderModel** class for serializing **Order** data (part 4 of 4).

Figure 19.18, Fig. 19.19 and Fig. 19.20 show the deployment settings for entity EJB **Order**. In addition to the settings shown here, be sure to set the **Transaction Type** to **Required** for all business methods.

Order General Deployment Settings	
Bean Type	**Entity**
Enterprise Bean Class	**com.deitel.advjhtp1.bookstore.ejb.OrderEJB**
Home Interface	**com.deitel.advjhtp1.bookstore.ejb.OrderHome**
Remote Interface	**com.deitel.advjhtp1.bookstore.ejb.Order**

Fig. 19.18 Order general deployment settings.

Order Entity and Deployment Settings	
Persistence Management	**Container-Managed Persistence**
Primary Key Class	**java.lang.Integer**
Primary Key Field Name	**orderID**
Database JNDI Name	**jdbc/Bookstore**
Method **findBy-CustomerID** **SQL Statement**	**SELECT orderID FROM CustomerOrders WHERE custom-erID = ?1**

Fig. 19.19 Order entity and deployment settings (part 1 of 2).

Order Entity and Deployment Settings

Method `ejb-Store` SQL Statement	`UPDATE CustomerOrders SET customerID = ?, orderDate = ?, shipped = ? WHERE orderID = ?`
Method `ejbCreate` SQL Statement	`INSERT INTO CustomerOrders ( customerID, orderDate, orderID, shipped ) VALUES ( ?, ?, ?, ? )`
Method `ejbRemove` SQL Statement	`DELETE FROM CustomerOrders WHERE orderID = ?`
Method `findByPrimaryKey` SQL Statement	`SELECT orderID FROM CustomerOrders WHERE orderID = ?`
Method `ejbLoad` SQL Statement	`SELECT customerID, orderDate, shipped FROM CustomerOrders WHERE orderID = ?`
Table Create SQL Statement	`CREATE TABLE CustomerOrders ( customerID INTEGER, orderDate VARCHAR(255), orderID INTEGER, shipped BOOLEAN NOT NULL, CONSTRAINT pk_CustomerOrders PRIMARY KEY ( orderID ) )`
Table Delete SQL Statement	`DROP TABLE CustomerOrders`

Fig. 19.19 `Order` entity and deployment settings (part 2 of 2).

Order EJB References

Coded Name	`ejb/Product`
Type	`Entity`
Home	`com.deitel.advjhtp1.bookstore.ejb.ProductHome`
Remote	`com.deitel.advjhtp1.bookstore.ejb.Product`
JNDI Name	`Product`
Coded Name	`ejb/SequenceFactory`
Type	`Entity`
Home	`com.deitel.advjhtp1.bookstore.ejb.SequenceFactory-Home`
Remote	`com.deitel.advjhtp1.bookstore.ejb.SequenceFactory`
JNDI Name	`SequenceFactory`
Coded Name	`ejb/Customer`

Fig. 19.20 `Order` EJB references (part 1 of 2).

Order EJB References	
Type	`Entity`
Home	`com.deitel.advjhtp1.bookstore.ejb.CustomerHome`
Remote	`com.deitel.advjhtp1.bookstore.ejb.Customer`
JNDI Name	`Customer`
Coded Name	`ejb/OrderProduct`
Type	`Entity`
Home	`com.deitel.advjhtp1.bookstore.ejb.OrderProductHome`
Remote	`com.deitel.advjhtp1.bookstore.ejb.OrderProduct`
JNDI Name	`OrderProduct`

Fig. 19.20 `Order` EJB references (part 2 of 2).

19.6 `OrderProduct` Implementation

Entity EJB **OrderProduct** represents the many-to-many relationship between **Order**s and **Product**s. Each **OrderProduct** EJB includes an **orderID**, **Product ISBN** and **quantity**, and represents one line item in an **Order**.

19.6.1 `OrderProduct` Remote Interface

The **OrderProduct** remote interface (Fig. 19.21) defines the business methods for the **OrderProduct** EJB. The **OrderProduct** EJB maps **Product ISBN**s to **orderID**s and quantities. Method **getOrderProductModel** (lines 18–19) returns an **Order-ProductModel** that contains the details of an **OrderProduct** record.

```
1   // OrderProduct.java
2   // OrderProduct is the remote interface for entity EJB
3   // OrderProduct.
4   package com.deitel.advjhtp1.bookstore.ejb;
5
6   // Java core packages
7   import java.rmi.RemoteException;
8
9   // Java extension packages
10  import javax.ejb.*;
11
12  // Deitel packages
13  import com.deitel.advjhtp1.bookstore.model.*;
14
15  public interface OrderProduct extends EJBObject {
16
17      // get OrderProduct details as OrderProductModel
```

Fig. 19.21 `OrderProduct` remote interface for modifying details of `OrderProduct` EJB instances (part 1 of 2).

```
18        public OrderProductModel getOrderProductModel()
19            throws RemoteException;
20    }
```

Fig. 19.21 **OrderProduct** remote interface for modifying details of
OrderProduct EJB instances (part 2 of 2).

19.6.2 OrderProductEJB Implementation

OrderProduct remote interface implementation **OrderProductEJB** (Fig. 19.22) declares container-managed fields **ISBN**, **orderID** and **quantity** (lines 22–24). Method **getOrderProductModel** (lines 27–69) returns the details of the **OrderProduct** record as an **OrderProductModel**. Method **setOrderProductModel** (lines 72–77) sets the details of the **OrderProduct** record, using data from the **OrderProduct-Model** argument.

```
1    // OrderProductEJB.java
2    // Entity EJB OrderProductEJB represents the mapping between
3    // a Product and an Order, including the quantity of the
4    // Product in the Order.
5    package com.deitel.advjhtp1.bookstore.ejb;
6
7    // Java core packages
8    import java.rmi.RemoteException;
9
10   // Java extension packages
11   import javax.ejb.*;
12   import javax.naming.*;
13   import javax.rmi.PortableRemoteObject;
14
15   // Deitel packages
16   import com.deitel.advjhtp1.bookstore.model.*;
17
18   public class OrderProductEJB implements EntityBean {
19       private EntityContext entityContext;
20
21       // container-managed fields
22       public String ISBN;
23       public Integer orderID;
24       public int quantity;
25
26       // get OrderProduct details as OrderProductModel
27       public OrderProductModel getOrderProductModel()
28           throws EJBException
29       {
30          OrderProductModel model = new OrderProductModel();
31
32          // get ProductModel for Product in this OrderProduct
33          try {
34             Context initialContext = new InitialContext();
```

Fig. 19.22 **OrderProductEJB** implementation of **OrderProduct** remote
interface (part 1 of 3).

```
35
36              // look up Product EJB
37              Object object = initialContext.lookup(
38                 "java:comp/env/ejb/Product" );
39
40              // get ProductHome interface
41              ProductHome productHome = ( ProductHome )
42                 PortableRemoteObject.narrow( object,
43                    ProductHome.class );
44
45              // find Product using its ISBN
46              Product product =
47                 productHome.findByPrimaryKey( ISBN );
48
49              // get ProductModel
50              ProductModel productModel =
51                 product.getProductModel();
52
53              // set ProductModel in OrderProductModel
54              model.setProductModel( productModel );
55
56           } // end try
57
58           // handle exception when looking up Product EJB
59           catch ( Exception exception ) {
60              throw new EJBException( exception );
61           }
62
63           // set orderID and quantity in OrderProductModel
64           model.setOrderID( orderID );
65           model.setQuantity( quantity );
66
67           return model;
68
69        } // end method getOrderProductModel
70
71        // set OrderProduct details using OrderProductModel
72        private void setOrderProductModel( OrderProductModel model )
73        {
74           ISBN = model.getProductModel().getISBN();
75           orderID = model.getOrderID();
76           quantity = model.getQuantity();
77        }
78
79        // create OrderProduct for given OrderProductModel
80        public OrderProductPK ejbCreate( OrderProductModel model )
81        {
82           setOrderProductModel( model );
83           return null;
84        }
85
86        // perform any necessary post-creation tasks
```

Fig. 19.22 **OrderProductEJB** implementation of **OrderProduct** remote interface (part 2 of 3).

```
87      public void ejbPostCreate( OrderProductModel model ) {}
88
89         // set EntityContext
90      public void setEntityContext( EntityContext context )
91      {
92         entityContext = context;
93      }
94
95         // unset EntityContext
96      public void unsetEntityContext()
97      {
98         entityContext = null;
99      }
100
101        // activate OrderProduct EJB instance
102     public void ejbActivate()
103     {
104        OrderProductPK primaryKey =
105           ( OrderProductPK ) entityContext.getPrimaryKey();
106
107        ISBN = primaryKey.getISBN();
108        orderID = primaryKey.getOrderID();
109     }
110
111        // passivate OrderProduct EJB instance
112     public void ejbPassivate()
113     {
114        ISBN = null;
115        orderID = null;
116     }
117
118        // remove OrderProduct EJB instance
119     public void ejbRemove() {}
120
121        // store OrderProduct EJB data in database
122     public void ejbStore() {}
123
124        // load OrderProduct EJB data from database
125     public void ejbLoad() {}
126  }
```

Fig. 19.22 **OrderProductEJB** implementation of **OrderProduct** remote
interface (part 3 of 3).

The EJB container calls method **ejbCreate** (lines 80–84) to create new instances of
the **OrderProduct** EJB. The **ISBN**, **orderID** and **quantity** for the **OrderProduct**
record are provided in the **OrderProductModel** argument. Line 82 invokes method
setOrderProductModel to complete the creation of the **OrderProduct** record.

19.6.3 OrderProductHome Interface

Interface **OrderProductHome** (Fig. 19.23) provides methods for creating new **Order-
Product** EJB instances and locating existing **OrderProduct** records. Method **create**
(lines 19–20) corresponds to method **ejbCreate** of the **OrderProductEJB** implemen-

tation (Fig. 19.22). Method **findByOrderID** (lines 23–24) locates all **OrderProduct** records with the provided **orderID** and returns a **Collection** of **OrderProduct** remote references. Method **findByPrimaryKey** (lines 27–28) locates an **OrderProduct** record, using an instance of the **OrderProductPK** primary-key class.

19.6.4 OrderProductPK Primary-Key Class

OrderProductPK (Fig. 19.24) is the primary-key class for the **OrderProduct** EJB. An **orderID** and **ISBN** are required to identify a particular **OrderProduct** EJB instance uniquely. An entity EJB that has a complex primary key (i.e., a primary key that consists of multiple fields) requires a custom primary-key class. A custom primary-key class must have a **public** data member for each field in the complex primary key. The primary-key class **OrderProductPK** has two **public** data members (lines 12–13)—**ISBN** and **orderID**, which correspond to **OrderProductEJB**'s two primary-key fields (Fig. 19.22). A custom primary-key class also must override methods **hashCode** and **equals** of class **Object**. The overridden implementations of methods **hashCode** (lines 38–41) and **equals** (lines 44–57) enable the EJB container and **OrderProduct** EJB clients to determine if two **OrderProduct** EJB instances are equal by comparing their primary-key class instances.

```
1   // OrderProductHome.java
2   // OrderProductHome is the home interface for entity EJB
3   // OrderProduct.
4   package com.deitel.advjhtp1.bookstore.ejb;
5
6   // Java core packages
7   import java.util.Collection;
8   import java.rmi.RemoteException;
9
10  // Java extension packages
11  import javax.ejb.*;
12
13  // Deitel packages
14  import com.deitel.advjhtp1.bookstore.model.*;
15
16  public interface OrderProductHome extends EJBHome {
17
18     // create OrderProduct using given OrderProductModel
19     public OrderProduct create( OrderProductModel model )
20        throws RemoteException, CreateException;
21
22     // find OrderProduct for given orderID
23     public Collection findByOrderID( Integer orderID )
24        throws RemoteException, FinderException;
25
26     // find OrderProduct for given primary key
27     public OrderProduct findByPrimaryKey( OrderProductPK pk )
28        throws RemoteException, FinderException;
29  }
```

Fig. 19.23 **OrderProductHome** interface for finding and creating **OrderProduct** EJB instances.

```
1   // OrderProductPK.java
2   // OrderProductPK is a primary-key class for entity EJB
3   // OrderProduct.
4   package com.deitel.advjhtp1.bookstore.ejb;
5
6   // Java core packages
7   import java.io.*;
8
9   public class OrderProductPK implements Serializable {
10
11      // primary-key fields
12      public String ISBN;
13      public Integer orderID;
14
15      // no-argument constructor
16      public OrderProductPK() {}
17
18      // construct OrderProductPK with ISBN and orderID
19      public OrderProductPK( String isbn, Integer id )
20      {
21         ISBN = isbn;
22         orderID = id;
23      }
24
25      // get ISBN
26      public String getISBN()
27      {
28         return ISBN;
29      }
30
31      // get orderID
32      public Integer getOrderID()
33      {
34         return orderID;
35      }
36
37      // calculate hashCode for this Object
38      public int hashCode()
39      {
40         return getISBN().hashCode() ^ getOrderID().intValue();
41      }
42
43      // custom implementation of Object equals method
44      public boolean equals( Object object )
45      {
46         // ensure object is instance of OrderProductPK
47         if ( object instanceof OrderProductPK ) {
48            OrderProductPK otherKey =
49               ( OrderProductPK ) object;
50
51            // compare ISBNs and orderIDs
52            return ( getISBN().equals( otherKey.getISBN() )
```

Fig. 19.24 OrderProductPK primary-key class for OrderProduct EJB
(part 1 of 2).

```
53                    && getOrderID().equals( otherKey.getOrderID() ) );
54          }
55
56          return false;
57       }
58    }
```

Fig. 19.24 OrderProductPK primary-key class for **OrderProduct** EJB
(part 2 of 2).

19.6.5 OrderProductModel

Model class **OrderProductModel** (Fig. 19.25) represents an **OrderProduct** record. Line 18 declares a **ProductModel** reference for the **Product** associated with this **OrderProduct** record. The **quantity** (line 19) is the quantity of the **Product** in the **Order**. The **Order** is identified by its **orderID** (line 20). Method **getXML** (lines 59–76) generates an XML **Element** that represents the **OrderProductModel**.

```
1    // OrderProductModel.java
2    // OrderProductModel represents a Product and its quantity in
3    // an Order or ShoppingCart.
4    package com.deitel.advjhtp1.bookstore.model;
5
6    // Java core packages
7    import java.io.*;
8    import java.util.*;
9    import java.text.*;
10
11   // third-party packages
12   import org.w3c.dom.*;
13
14   public class OrderProductModel implements Serializable,
15      XMLGenerator {
16
17      // OrderProductModel properties
18      private ProductModel productModel;
19      private int quantity;
20      private Integer orderID;
21
22      // set ProductModel
23      public void setProductModel( ProductModel model )
24      {
25         productModel = model;
26      }
27
28      // get ProductModel
29      public ProductModel getProductModel()
30      {
31         return productModel;
32      }
```

Fig. 19.25 OrderProductModel class for serializing **OrderProduct** data
(part 1 of 2).

```
33
34        // set quantity
35        public void setQuantity( int productQuantity )
36        {
37            quantity = productQuantity;
38        }
39
40        // get quantity
41        public int getQuantity()
42        {
43            return quantity;
44        }
45
46        // set orderID
47        public void setOrderID( Integer id )
48        {
49            orderID = id;
50        }
51
52        // get orderID
53        public Integer getOrderID()
54        {
55            return orderID;
56        }
57
58        // get XML representation of OrderProduct
59        public Element getXML( Document document )
60        {
61            // create orderProduct Element
62            Element orderProduct =
63                document.createElement( "orderProduct" );
64
65            // append ProductModel product Element
66            orderProduct.appendChild (
67                getProductModel().getXML( document ) );
68
69            // create quantity Element
70            Element temp = document.createElement( "quantity" );
71            temp.appendChild( document.createTextNode(
72                String.valueOf ( getQuantity() ) ) );
73            orderProduct.appendChild( temp );
74
75            return orderProduct;
76        }
77    }
```

Fig. 19.25 **OrderProductModel** class for serializing **OrderProduct** data (part 2 of 2).

Figure 19.26, Fig. 19.27 and Fig. 19.28 show the deployment settings for entity EJB **OrderProduct**. In addition to the settings shown here, be sure to set the **Transaction Type** to **Required** for all business methods. Note that because entity EJB **Order-Product** uses a custom primary-key class, the **Primary Key Field Name** (Fig. 19.27) must be left blank.

OrderProduct General Deployment Settings	
Bean Type	**Entity**
Enterprise Bean Class	`com.deitel.advjhtp1.bookstore.ejb.OrderProductEJB`
Home Interface	`com.deitel.advjhtp1.bookstore.ejb.OrderProductHome`
Remote Interface	`com.deitel.advjhtp1.bookstore.ejb.OrderProduct`

Fig. 19.26 `OrderProduct` general deployment settings.

OrderProduct Entity and Deployment Settings	
Persistence Management	**Container-Managed Persistence**
Primary Key Class	`com.deitel.advjhtp1.bookstore.ejb.OrderProductPK`
Primary Key Field Name	N/A
Database JNDI Name	`jdbc/Bookstore`
Method `findByOrderID` **SQL Statement**	`SELECT ISBN, orderID FROM OrderProduct WHERE orderID = ?1`
Method `ejbStore` **SQL Statement**	`UPDATE OrderProduct SET quantity = ? WHERE ISBN = ? AND orderID = ?`
Method `ejbCreate` **SQL Statement**	`INSERT INTO OrderProduct ( ISBN, orderID, quantity ) VALUES ( ?, ?, ? )`
Method `ejbRemove` **SQL Statement**	`DELETE FROM OrderProduct WHERE ISBN = ? AND orderID = ?`
Method `findByPrimaryKey` **SQL Statement**	`SELECT ISBN, orderID FROM OrderProduct WHERE ISBN = ? AND orderID = ?`
Method `ejbLoad` **SQL Statement**	`SELECT quantity FROM OrderProduct WHERE ISBN = ? AND orderID = ?`

Fig. 19.27 `OrderProduct` entity and deployment settings (part 1 of 2).

OrderProduct Entity and Deployment Settings	
Table Create SQL Statement	`CREATE TABLE OrderProduct ( ISBN VARCHAR( 255 ), orderID INTEGER, quantity INTEGER NOT NULL, CONSTRAINT pk_OrderProduct PRIMARY KEY ( ISBN, orderID ) )`
Table Delete SQL Statement	`DROP TABLE OrderProduct`

Fig. 19.27 `OrderProduct` entity and deployment settings (part 2 of 2).

OrderProduct EJB References	
Coded Name	`ejb/Product`
Type	`Entity`
Home	`com.deitel.advjhtp1.bookstore.ejb.ProductHome`
Remote	`com.deitel.advjhtp1.bookstore.ejb.Product`
JNDI Name	`Product`

Fig. 19.28 `OrderProduct` EJB references.

In this chapter, we presented the business logic for managing the **Customer**'s **ShoppingCart** and the data model for **Product**s and **Order**s in our on-line store. We also discussed how **Serializable** objects can be used to reduce network traffic when communicating with EJBs. In the next chapter, we present EJBs for managing **Customer**s of the on-line store.

20

Enterprise Java Case Study: Business Logic Part 2

Objectives

- To understand the data model for **Customer** management in the Deitel Bookstore case study.
- To implement an EJB for storing billing and shipping information.
- To build an EJB for generating primary keys.
- To understand the benefits of declarative transaction semantics.
- To understand the steps necessary to deploy the Deitel Bookstore case study.

The best investment is in the tools of one's own trade.
Benjamin Franklin

Creativity is not the finding of a thing, but the making something out of it after it is found.
James Russell Lowell

Events that are predestined require but little management. They manage themselves.
Amelia Barr

All meanings, we know, depend on the key of interpretation.
George Eliot

Outline

20.1 Introduction

In this chapter, we present entity EJBs for managing customers. Maintaining information about the customers of an on-line store can make purchases more convenient, because billing and shipping information is stored on the server. The on-line store's marketing department also can use gathered data for distribution of marketing materials and analysis of demographic information.

We also present an entity EJB that generates unique IDs for the **Customer**, **Order** and **Address** EJBs. Instances of these EJBs are created when new **Customer**s register and when **Customer**s place new **Order**s. Relational databases require unique primary keys to maintain referential integrity and perform queries. We provide the **Sequence-Factory** EJB to generate these unique IDs, because not all databases can generate these primary-key values automatically. Finally, we provide instructions for deploying the Deitel Bookstore case study on Sun Microsystems' J2EE reference implementation application server.

20.2 Customer Implementation

The **Customer** entity EJB represents a customer in the underlying database. The following subsections present the EJB implementation and its corresponding model class.

20.2.1 Customer Remote Interface

The **Customer** EJB remote interface (Fig. 20.1) defines the business logic methods in the EJB. Method **getCustomerModel** (lines 19–20) builds a **Serializable** object of class **CustomerModel**, which contains the details of the **Customer**. Method **getOrderHistory** (lines 23–24) returns a **Collection** of **OrderModel**s that contains information about past **Order**s the **Customer** has placed. Method **getPasswordHint** (line 27) returns a **String** containing a hint to remind **Customer**s of forgotten passwords.

20.2.2 CustomerEJB Implementation

The **CustomerEJB** implementation (Fig. 20.2) of remote interface **Customer** (Fig. 20.1) contains instance variables for each **Customer** property (lines 25–36). These instance variables are **public**, so the EJB container can synchronize their values with the associated database table.

```
1   // Customer.java
2   // Customer is the remote interface for entity EJB Customer.
3   package com.deitel.advjhtp1.bookstore.ejb;
4
5   // Java core libraries
6   import java.rmi.RemoteException;
7   import java.util.ArrayList;
8
9   // Java standard extensions
10  import javax.ejb.*;
11
12  // Deitel Bookstore libraries
13  import com.deitel.advjhtp1.bookstore.model.*;
14  import com.deitel.advjhtp1.bookstore.exceptions.*;
15
16  public interface Customer extends EJBObject {
17
18     // get Customer data as a CustomerModel
19     public CustomerModel getCustomerModel()
20        throws RemoteException;
21
22     // get Order history for CustomerModel
23     public Collection getOrderHistory()
24        throws RemoteException, NoOrderHistoryException;
25
26     // get password hint for CustomerModel
27     public String getPasswordHint() throws RemoteException;
28  }
```

Fig. 20.1   Customer remote interface for modifying **Customer** details, getting an **Order** history and password hint.

```
1    // CustomerEJB.java
2    // Entity EJB Customer represents a Customer, including
3    // the Customer's user name, password, billing
4    // address, shipping address and credit card information.
5    package com.deitel.advjhtp1.bookstore.ejb;
6
7    // Java core packages
8    import java.util.*;
9    import java.rmi.RemoteException;
10
11   // Java extension packages
12   import javax.ejb.*;
13   import javax.naming.*;
14   import javax.rmi.PortableRemoteObject;
15
16   // Deitel packages
17   import com.deitel.advjhtp1.bookstore.model.*;
18   import com.deitel.advjhtp1.bookstore.exceptions.*;
19
20   public class CustomerEJB implements EntityBean {
21      private EntityContext entityContext;
22      private InitialContext initialContext;
23
24      // container-managed fields
25      public Integer customerID;
26      public String userID;
27      public String password;
28      public String passwordHint;
29      public String firstName;
30      public String lastName;
31      public Integer billingAddressID;
32      public Integer shippingAddressID;
33
34      public String creditCardName;
35      public String creditCardNumber;
36      public String creditCardExpirationDate;
37
38      // get CustomerModel
39      public CustomerModel getCustomerModel() throws EJBException
40      {
41         // construct new CustomerModel
42         CustomerModel customer = new CustomerModel();
43
44         // populate CustomerModel with data for this Customer
45         customer.setCustomerID( customerID );
46         customer.setUserID( userID );
47         customer.setPassword( password );
48         customer.setPasswordHint( passwordHint );
49         customer.setFirstName( firstName );
50         customer.setLastName( lastName );
51
52         // use Address EJB to get Customer billing and shipping
```

Fig. 20.2   **CustomerEJB** implementation of **Customer** remote interface
(part 1 of 6).

```
53          // Address instances
54          try {
55             initialContext = new InitialContext();
56
57             Object object = initialContext.lookup(
58                "java:comp/env/ejb/Address" );
59
60             AddressHome addressHome = ( AddressHome )
61                PortableRemoteObject.narrow( object,
62                   AddressHome.class );
63
64             // get remote reference to billing Address
65             Address billingAddress =
66                addressHome.findByPrimaryKey( billingAddressID );
67
68             // add billing AddressModel to CustomerModel
69             customer.setBillingAddress(
70                billingAddress.getAddressModel() );
71
72             // get remote reference to shipping Address
73             Address shippingAddress =
74                addressHome.findByPrimaryKey( shippingAddressID);
75
76             // add shipping AddressModel to CustomerModel
77             customer.setShippingAddress(
78                shippingAddress.getAddressModel() );
79
80          } // end try
81
82          // handle exception using Address EJB
83          catch ( Exception exception ) {
84             throw new EJBException( exception );
85          }
86
87          // set credit card information in CustomerModel
88          customer.setCreditCardName( creditCardName );
89          customer.setCreditCardNumber( creditCardNumber );
90          customer.setCreditCardExpirationDate(
91             creditCardExpirationDate );
92
93          return customer;
94
95       } // end method getCustomerModel
96
97       // get Order history for Customer
98       public Collection getOrderHistory()
99          throws NoOrderHistoryException, EJBException
100      {
101         Collection history = new ArrayList();
102
103         // use Order EJB to obtain list of Orders for Customer
104         try {
```

Fig. 20.2   CustomerEJB implementation of **Customer** remote interface
(part 2 of 6).

```
105              initialContext = new InitialContext();
106
107           Object object = initialContext.lookup(
108              "java:comp/env/ejb/Order" );
109
110           OrderHome orderHome = ( OrderHome )
111              PortableRemoteObject.narrow( object,
112                 OrderHome.class );
113
114           // find Orders for this Customer
115           Collection orders =
116              orderHome.findByCustomerID( customerID );
117
118           Iterator iterator = orders.iterator();
119
120           // use list of Orders to build Order history
121           while ( iterator.hasNext() ) {
122              Order order = ( Order ) PortableRemoteObject.narrow(
123                 iterator.next(), Order.class );
124
125              // retrieve OrderModel for the Order
126              OrderModel orderModel = order.getOrderModel();
127
128              // add each OrderModel to Order history
129              history.add( orderModel );
130           }
131
132        } // end try
133
134        // handle exception when finding Order records
135        catch ( FinderException finderException ) {
136           throw new NoOrderHistoryException( "No order " +
137              "history found for the customer with userID " +
138              userID );
139        }
140
141        // handle exception when invoking Order EJB methods
142        catch ( Exception exception ) {
143           exception.printStackTrace();
144           throw new EJBException( exception );
145        }
146
147        return history;
148
149     } // end method getOrderHistory
150
151     // get password hint for Customer
152     public String getPasswordHint()
153     {
154        return passwordHint;
155     }
156
```

Fig. 20.2   CustomerEJB implementation of **Customer** remote interface
         (part 3 of 6).

```
157     // set Customer data using CustomerModel
158     private void setCustomerModel( CustomerModel customer )
159     {
160        // set Customer data members to CustomerModel values
161        userID = customer.getUserID();
162        password = customer.getPassword();
163        passwordHint = customer.getPasswordHint();
164        firstName = customer.getFirstName();
165        lastName = customer.getLastName();
166
167        billingAddressID =
168           customer.getBillingAddress().getAddressID();
169
170        shippingAddressID =
171           customer.getShippingAddress().getAddressID();
172
173        creditCardName = customer.getCreditCardName();
174        creditCardNumber = customer.getCreditCardNumber();
175
176        creditCardExpirationDate =
177           customer.getCreditCardExpirationDate();
178
179     } // end method setCustomerModel
180
181     // create Customer EJB using given CustomerModel
182     public Integer ejbCreate( CustomerModel customerModel )
183        throws CreateException
184     {
185        // retrieve unique value for primary key using
186        // SequenceFactory EJB
187        try {
188           initialContext = new InitialContext();
189
190           // look up SequenceFactory EJB
191           Object object = initialContext.lookup(
192              "java:comp/env/ejb/SequenceFactory" );
193
194           SequenceFactoryHome sequenceFactoryHome =
195              ( SequenceFactoryHome ) PortableRemoteObject.narrow(
196                 object, SequenceFactoryHome.class );
197
198           // find sequence for Customer EJB
199           SequenceFactory sequenceFactory =
200              sequenceFactoryHome.findByPrimaryKey( "Customer" );
201
202           // retrieve next available customerID
203           customerID = sequenceFactory.getNextID();
204
205           // create Address EJBs for billing and shipping
206           // Addresses
207           object = initialContext.lookup(
208              "java:comp/env/ejb/Address" );
```

Fig. 20.2   CustomerEJB implementation of **Customer** remote interface
(part 4 of 6).

```
209
210            AddressHome addressHome = ( AddressHome )
211               PortableRemoteObject.narrow( object,
212                  AddressHome.class );
213
214            // get Customer's billing address
215            AddressModel billingAddressModel =
216               customerModel.getBillingAddress();
217
218            // create Address EJB for billing Address
219            Address billingAddress =
220               addressHome.create( billingAddressModel );
221
222            // set addressID in billing AddressModel
223            billingAddressModel.setAddressID( ( Integer )
224               billingAddress.getPrimaryKey() );
225
226            // get Customer's shipping address
227            AddressModel shippingAddressModel =
228               customerModel.getShippingAddress();
229
230            // create Address EJB for shipping Address
231            Address shippingAddress =
232               addressHome.create( shippingAddressModel );
233
234            // set addressID in shipping AddressModel
235            shippingAddressModel.setAddressID( ( Integer )
236               shippingAddress.getPrimaryKey() );
237
238            // use CustomerModel to set data for new Customer
239            setCustomerModel( customerModel );
240
241         } // end try
242
243         // handle exception when looking up, finding and using EJBs
244         catch ( Exception exception ) {
245            throw new CreateException( exception.getMessage() );
246         }
247
248         // EJB container will return a remote reference
249         return null;
250
251      } // end method ejbCreate
252
253      // perform any necessary post-creation tasks
254      public void ejbPostCreate( CustomerModel customer ) {}
255
256      // set EntityContext
257      public void setEntityContext( EntityContext context )
258      {
259         entityContext = context;
260      }
```

Fig. 20.2   CustomerEJB implementation of **Customer** remote interface
(part 5 of 6).

```
261
262     // unset EntityContext
263     public void unsetEntityContext()
264     {
265         entityContext = null;
266     }
267
268     // activate Customer EJB instance
269     public void ejbActivate()
270     {
271         customerID = ( Integer ) entityContext.getPrimaryKey();
272     }
273
274     // passivate Customer EJB instance
275     public void ejbPassivate()
276     {
277         customerID = null;
278     }
279
280     // remove Customer EJB instance
281     public void ejbRemove() {}
282
283     // store Customer EJB data in database
284     public void ejbStore() {}
285
286     // load Customer EJB data from database
287     public void ejbLoad() {}
288 }
```

Fig. 20.2   **CustomerEJB** implementation of **Customer** remote interface
(part 6 of 6).

Method **getCustomerModel** (lines 39–95) constructs a **CustomerModel** whose data members contain values from the **CustomerEJB**. **Address** EJBs maintain address information for each **Customer**. The **Customer** EJB stores the **addressID** for each **Address** (billing and shipping). Method **getCustomerModel** uses interface **AddressHome** to obtain the **Customer**'s **Address** EJBs (lines 65–78). For each **Address** EJB, method **getCustomerModel** obtains an **AddressModel** and adds it to the **CustomerModel**.

Method **getOrderHistory** (lines 98–149) builds a **Collection** that contains an **OrderModel** for each **Order** the **Customer** has placed. Method **findByCustomerID** of interface **OrderHome** returns a **Collection** of **Order**s for a given **Customer** (line 116). Lines 115–130 obtain the **Collection** of **Order**s and build an **Collection** of **OrderModel**s to represent the **Customer**'s **Order** history.

Method **setCustomerModel** (lines 158–179) is a helper method for method **ejbCreate** (lines 182–251). Method **setCustomerModel** modifies the details of the **CustomerEJB**, using data in the **CustomerModel** argument. Lines 161–177 retrieve the data members of the **CustomerModel** and set the values of the **CustomerEJB** data members.

The EJB container invokes method **ejbCreate** (lines 182–251) when creating a new instance of the **Customer** EJB. Method **ejbCreate** takes a **CustomerModel** argument, with which it invokes method **setCustomerModel** to initialize the **CustomerEJB** data members (line 239). Method **ejbCreate** uses **SequenceFactory** method **getNextID** to generate a unique **customerID** for the new **Customer** (line 203). Each **Customer** has a billing address and a shipping address, each of which is stored in an **Address** EJB. Lines 215–236 create these **Address** EJBs, using data from the **AddressModel**s given in the **CustomerModel** argument.

20.2.3 CustomerHome Interface

Interface **CustomerHome** (Fig. 20.3) provides **create** methods for creating new **Customer**s and *finder* methods for finding existing **Customer**s. Method **create** (lines 17–18) corresponds to method **ejbCreate** in the **CustomerEJB** implementation (Fig. 20.2). Method **findByLogin** (lines 21–22) returns a **Customer** remote reference for the **Customer** with the given **userID** and **password**. This method authenticates **Customer**s when they attempt to log into the store. Method **findByUserID** (lines 25–26) returns the **Customer** with the given **userID**. Method **findByPrimaryKey** (lines 29–30) returns the **Customer** with the given **customerID**. The EJB container provides implementations for these methods, using SQL queries the developer provides when deploying the application.

```
1   // CustomerHome.java
2   // CustomerHome is the home interface for entity EJB Customer.
3   package com.deitel.advjhtp1.bookstore.ejb;
4
5   // Java core libraries
6   import java.rmi.RemoteException;
7
8   // Java standard extensions
9   import javax.ejb.*;
10
11  // Deitel Bookstore libraries
12  import com.deitel.advjhtp1.bookstore.model.*;
13
14  public interface CustomerHome extends EJBHome {
15
16     // create Customer EJB using given CustomerModel
17     public Customer create( CustomerModel customerModel )
18        throws RemoteException, CreateException;
19
20     // find Customer with given userID and password
21     public Customer findByLogin( String userID, String pass )
22        throws RemoteException, FinderException;
23
24     // find Customer with given userID
25     public Customer findByUserID( String userID )
26        throws RemoteException, FinderException;
27
28     // find Customer with given customerID
```

Fig. 20.3 **CustomerHome** interface for creating and finding **Customer** EJB instances (part 1 of 2).

```
29      public Customer findByPrimaryKey( Integer customerID )
30         throws RemoteException, FinderException;
31   }
```

Fig. 20.3 **CustomerHome** interface for creating and finding **Customer** EJB instances (part 2 of 2).

20.2.4 **CustomerModel**

CustomerModel (Fig. 20.4) is a model class for the **Customer** EJB. **CustomerModel** contains **private** data members (lines 17–29) for each **public** data member in the **CustomerEJB** implementation (Fig. 20.2). Class **CustomerModel** maintains references to **AddressModel** objects for the **Customer**'s billing and shipping addresses (lines 24–25). **CustomerModel** has *set* and *get* methods for each of its properties, implements interface **XMLGenerator** and provides method **getXML** (lines 168–233), for generating an XML **Element** that describes the **Customer**.

```
1   // CustomerModel.java
2   // CustomerModel represents a Deitel Bookstore Customer,
3   // including billing, shipping and credit card information.
4   package com.deitel.advjhtp1.bookstore.model;
5
6   // Java core libraries
7   import java.io.*;
8   import java.util.*;
9
10  // third-party libraries
11  import org.w3c.dom.*;
12
13  public class CustomerModel implements Serializable,
14     XMLGenerator {
15
16     // CustomerModel properties
17     private Integer customerID;
18     private String userID;
19     private String password;
20     private String passwordHint;
21     private String firstName;
22     private String lastName;
23
24     private AddressModel billingAddress;
25     private AddressModel shippingAddress;
26
27     private String creditCardName;
28     private String creditCardNumber;
29     private String creditCardExpirationDate;
30
31     // construct empty CustomerModel
32     public CustomerModel() {}
33
34     // set customer ID
```

Fig. 20.4 **CustomerModel** for serializing **Customer** data (part 1 of 5).

```
35        public void setCustomerID( Integer id )
36        {
37           customerID = id;
38        }
39
40        // get customer ID
41        public Integer getCustomerID()
42        {
43           return customerID;
44        }
45
46        // set user ID
47        public void setUserID( String id )
48        {
49           userID = id;
50        }
51
52        // get user ID
53        public String getUserID()
54        {
55           return userID;
56        }
57
58        // set password
59        public void setPassword( String customerPassword )
60        {
61           password = customerPassword;
62        }
63
64        // get password
65        public String getPassword()
66        {
67           return password;
68        }
69
70        // set password hint
71        public void setPasswordHint( String passwordHint )
72        {
73           passwordHint = passwordHint;
74        }
75
76        // get password hint
77        public String getPasswordHint()
78        {
79           return passwordHint;
80        }
81
82        // set first name
83        public void setFirstName( String name )
84        {
85           firstName = name;
86        }
87
```

Fig. 20.4 CustomerModel for serializing **Customer** data (part 2 of 5).

```
 88     // get first name
 89     public String getFirstName()
 90     {
 91        return firstName;
 92     }
 93
 94     // set last name
 95     public void setLastName( String name )
 96     {
 97        lastName = name;
 98     }
 99
100     // get last name
101     public String getLastName()
102     {
103        return lastName;
104     }
105
106     // set billing address
107     public void setBillingAddress( AddressModel address )
108     {
109        billingAddress = address;
110     }
111
112     // get billing address
113     public AddressModel getBillingAddress()
114     {
115        return billingAddress;
116     }
117
118     // set shipping address
119     public void setShippingAddress( AddressModel address )
120     {
121        shippingAddress = address;
122     }
123
124     // get shipping address
125     public AddressModel getShippingAddress()
126     {
127        return shippingAddress;
128     }
129
130     // set name of credit card
131     public void setCreditCardName( String name )
132     {
133        creditCardName = name;
134     }
135
136     // get name of credit card
137     public String getCreditCardName()
138     {
139        return creditCardName;
140     }
```

Fig. 20.4 **CustomerModel** for serializing **Customer** data (part 3 of 5).

```
141
142      // set credit card number
143      public void setCreditCardNumber( String number )
144      {
145         creditCardNumber = number;
146      }
147
148      // get credit card number
149      public String getCreditCardNumber()
150      {
151         return creditCardNumber;
152      }
153
154      // set expiration date of credit card
155      public void setCreditCardExpirationDate( String date )
156      {
157         creditCardExpirationDate = date;
158      }
159
160      // get expiration date of credit card
161      public String getCreditCardExpirationDate()
162      {
163            return creditCardExpirationDate;
164      }
165
166      // build an XML representation of this Customer including
167      // all public properties as nodes
168      public Element getXML( Document document )
169      {
170         // create customer Element
171         Element customer =
172            document.createElement( "customer" );
173
174         // create customerID Element
175         Element temp = document.createElement( "customerID" );
176         temp.appendChild( document.createTextNode(
177            String.valueOf( getCustomerID() ) ) );
178         customer.appendChild( temp );
179
180         // create userID Element
181         temp = document.createElement( "userID" );
182         temp.appendChild(
183            document.createTextNode( getUserID() ) );
184         customer.appendChild( temp );
185
186         // create firstName Element
187         temp = document.createElement( "firstName" );
188         temp.appendChild( document.createTextNode(
189            getFirstName() ) );
190         customer.appendChild( temp );
191
192         // create lastName Element
193         temp = document.createElement( "lastName" );
```

Fig. 20.4 **CustomerModel** for serializing **Customer** data (part 4 of 5).

```
194        temp.appendChild( document.createTextNode(
195           getLastName() ) );
196        customer.appendChild( temp );
197
198        // create billingAddress Element
199        temp = document.createElement( "billingAddress" );
200        temp.appendChild( billingAddress.getXML( document ) );
201
202        // create shippingAddress Element
203        temp = document.createElement( "shippingAddress" );
204        temp.appendChild( shippingAddress.getXML( document ) );
205
206        // create creditCardName Element
207        temp = document.createElement( "creditCardName" );
208        temp.appendChild( document.createTextNode(
209           getCreditCardName() ) );
210        customer.appendChild( temp );
211
212        // create creditCardNumber Element
213        temp = document.createElement( "creditCardNumber" );
214        temp.appendChild( document.createTextNode(
215           getCreditCardNumber() ) );
216        customer.appendChild( temp );
217
218        // create creditCardExpirationDate Element
219        temp = document.createElement(
220           "creditCardExpirationDate" );
221        temp.appendChild( document.createTextNode(
222           getCreditCardExpirationDate() ) );
223        customer.appendChild( temp );
224
225        // create passwordHint Element
226        temp = document.createElement( "passwordHint" );
227        temp.appendChild( document.createTextNode(
228           getPasswordHint() ) );
229        customer.appendChild( temp );
230
231        return customer;
232
233    } // end method getXML
234 }
```

Fig. 20.4 CustomerModel for serializing **Customer** data (part 5 of 5).

Figure 20.5, Fig. 20.6 and Fig. 20.7 list the deployment settings for entity EJB **Customer**. In addition to the settings shown here, be sure to set the **Transaction Type** to **Required** for all business methods.

20.3 Address Implementation

The application maintains a billing address and a shipping address for each **Customer**. Each address contains similar information (e.g., street address, city, state and zip code), so we abstract these two address types into a single **Address** EJB. Each **Customer** EJB stores an ID for the billing address and an ID for the shipping address.

Customer General Deployment Settings

Bean Type	**Entity**
Enterprise Bean Class	`com.deitel.advjhtp1.bookstore.ejb.CustomerEJB`
Home Interface	`com.deitel.advjhtp1.bookstore.ejb.CustomerHome`
Remote Interface	`com.deitel.advjhtp1.bookstore.ejb.Customer`

Fig. 20.5 Customer general deployment settings.

Customer Entity and Deployment Settings

Persistence Management	**Container-Managed Persistence**
Primary Key Class	`java.lang.Integer`
Primary Key Field Name	`customerID`
Database JNDI Name	`jdbc/Bookstore`
Method **findBy-UserID SQL Statement**	`SELECT customerID FROM Customer WHERE userID = ?1`
Method **findBy-Login SQL Statement**	`SELECT customerID FROM Customer WHERE userID = ?1 AND password = ?2`
Method **ejb-Store SQL Statement**	`UPDATE Customer SET billingAddressID = ?, creditCardExpirationDate = ?, creditCardName = ?, creditCardNumber = ?, firstName = ?, lastName = ?, password = ?, passwordHint = ?, shippingAddressID = ?, userID = ? WHERE customerID = ?`
Method **ejb-Create SQL Statement**	`INSERT INTO Customer ( billingAddressID, creditCardExpirationDate, creditCardName, creditCardNumber, customerID, firstName, lastName, password, passwordHint, shippingAddressID, userID ) VALUES ( ?, ?, ?, ?, ?, ?, ?, ?, ?, ?, ? )`

Fig. 20.6 Customer entity and deployment settings (part 1 of 2).

Customer Entity and Deployment Settings	
Method **ejb-Remove SQL Statement**	`DELETE FROM Customer WHERE customerID = ?`
Method **find-ByPrimaryKey SQL Statement**	`SELECT customerID FROM Customer WHERE customerID = ?`
Method **ejb-Load SQL Statement**	`SELECT billingAddressID, creditCardExpirationDate, creditCardName, creditCardNumber, firstName, lastName, password, passwordHint, shippingAddressID, userID FROM Customer WHERE customerID = ?`
Table Create SQL Statement	`CREATE TABLE Customer (billingAddressID INTEGER, creditCardExpirationDate VARCHAR(255), creditCardName VARCHAR(255), creditCardNumber VARCHAR(255), customerID INTEGER, firstName VARCHAR(255), lastName VARCHAR(255), password VARCHAR(255), passwordHint VARCHAR(255), shippingAddressID INTEGER, userID VARCHAR(255), CONSTRAINT pk_Customer PRIMARY KEY (customerID))`
Table Delete SQL Statement	`DROP TABLE Customer`

Fig. 20.6 Customer entity and deployment settings (part 2 of 2).

Customer EJB References	
Coded Name	`ejb/Order`
Type	`Entity`
Home	`com.deitel.advjhtp1.bookstore.ejb.OrderHome`
Remote	`com.deitel.advjhtp1.bookstore.ejb.Order`
JNDI Name	`Order`
Coded Name	`ejb/SequenceFactory`
Type	`Entity`
Home	`com.deitel.advjhtp1.bookstore.ejb.SequenceFactoryHome`
Remote	`com.deitel.advjhtp1.bookstore.ejb.SequenceFactory`
JNDI Name	`SequenceFactory`
Coded Name	`ejb/Address`

Fig. 20.7 Customer EJB References (part 1 of 2).

Customer EJB References	
Type	`Entity`
Home	`com.deitel.advjhtp1.bookstore.ejb.AddressHome`
Remote	`com.deitel.advjhtp1.bookstore.ejb.Address`
JNDI Name	`Address`

Fig. 20.7 **Customer** EJB References (part 2 of 2).

20.3.1 Address Remote Interface

The **Address** remote interface (Fig. 20.8) has *set* and *get* methods for updating data in and retrieving data from the **Address** EJB. Method **getAddressModel** (lines 17–18) constructs an **AddressModel** that contains the details of a particular **Address** EJB.

20.3.2 AddressEJB Implementation

AddressEJB (Fig. 20.9) is the implementation of the **Address** remote interface. Class **AddressEJB** contains **public**, container-managed data members for the first and last names of the contact person at the **Address**, as well as the street address, city, state, zip code, country and phone number (lines 24–33).

```
1   // Address.java
2   // Address is the remote interface for entity EJB Address.
3   package com.deitel.advjhtp1.bookstore.ejb;
4
5   // Java core libraries
6   import java.rmi.RemoteException;
7
8   // Java standard extensions
9   import javax.ejb.*;
10
11  // Deitel Bookstore libraries
12  import com.deitel.advjhtp1.bookstore.model.*;
13
14  public interface Address extends EJBObject {
15
16      // get Address data as an AddressModel
17      public AddressModel getAddressModel()
18         throws RemoteException;
19  }
```

Fig. 20.8 **Address** remote interface for modifying **Address** details.

```
1   // AddressEJB.java
2   // Entity EJB Address represents an Address, including
3   // the street address, city, state and zip code.
```

Fig. 20.9 **AddressEJB** implementation of **Address** remote interface (part 1 of 4).

```
 4   package com.deitel.advjhtp1.bookstore.ejb;
 5
 6   // Java core packages
 7   import java.util.*;
 8   import java.rmi.RemoteException;
 9
10   // Java extension packages
11   import javax.ejb.*;
12   import javax.naming.*;
13   import javax.rmi.PortableRemoteObject;
14
15   // Deitel packages
16   import com.deitel.advjhtp1.bookstore.model.*;
17   import com.deitel.advjhtp1.bookstore.exceptions.*;
18
19   public class AddressEJB implements EntityBean {
20      private EntityContext entityContext;
21
22      // container-managed fields
23      public Integer addressID;
24      public String firstName;
25      public String lastName;
26      public String streetAddressLine1;
27      public String streetAddressLine2;
28      public String city;
29      public String state;
30      public String zipCode;
31      public String country;
32      public String phoneNumber;
33
34      // get AddressModel
35      public AddressModel getAddressModel()
36      {
37         // construct new AddressModel
38         AddressModel address = new AddressModel();
39
40         // populate AddressModel fields with Address EJB
41         // data members
42         address.setAddressID( addressID );
43         address.setFirstName( firstName );
44         address.setLastName( lastName );
45         address.setStreetAddressLine1( streetAddressLine1 );
46         address.setStreetAddressLine2( streetAddressLine2 );
47         address.setCity( city );
48         address.setState( state );
49         address.setZipCode( zipCode );
50         address.setCountry( country );
51         address.setPhoneNumber( phoneNumber );
52
53         return address;
54
55      } // end method getAddressModel
56
```

Fig. 20.9 **AddressEJB** implementation of **Address** remote interface (part 2 of 4).

```
57       // set Address data using AddressModel
58       private void setAddressModel( AddressModel address )
59       {
60          // update Address' data members using values provided
61          // in the AddressModel
62          firstName = address.getFirstName();
63          lastName = address.getLastName();
64          streetAddressLine1 = address.getStreetAddressLine1();
65          streetAddressLine2 = address.getStreetAddressLine2();
66          city = address.getCity();
67          state = address.getState();
68          zipCode = address.getZipCode();
69          country = address.getCountry();
70          phoneNumber = address.getPhoneNumber();
71
72       } // end method setAddressModel
73
74       // create Address EJB using given AddressModel
75       public Integer ejbCreate( AddressModel address )
76          throws CreateException
77       {
78          // retrieve unique value for primary key using
79          // SequenceFactory EJB
80          try {
81             Context initialContext = new InitialContext();
82
83             // look up SequenceFactory EJB
84             Object object = initialContext.lookup(
85                "java:comp/env/ejb/SequenceFactory" );
86
87             SequenceFactoryHome sequenceFactoryHome =
88                ( SequenceFactoryHome )
89                   PortableRemoteObject.narrow(
90                      object, SequenceFactoryHome.class );
91
92             // find sequence for Address EJB
93             SequenceFactory sequenceFactory =
94                sequenceFactoryHome.findByPrimaryKey( "Address" );
95
96             // retrieve next available addressID
97             addressID = sequenceFactory.getNextID();
98
99             // set addressID for Address (primary key)
100            address.setAddressID( addressID );
101
102            // use AddressModel to set data for new Address
103            setAddressModel( address );
104
105         } // end try
106
107         // handle exception using SequenceFactory EJB
108         catch ( Exception exception ) {
109            throw new CreateException( exception.getMessage() );
```

Fig. 20.9 **AddressEJB** implementation of **Address** remote interface (part 3 of 4).

```
110             }
111
112         // EJB container will return a remote reference
113         return null;
114
115     } // end method ejbCreate
116
117     // perform any necessary post-creation tasks
118     public void ejbPostCreate( AddressModel address ) {}
119
120     // set EntityContext
121     public void setEntityContext( EntityContext context )
122     {
123         entityContext = context;
124     }
125
126     // unset EntityContext
127     public void unsetEntityContext()
128     {
129         entityContext = null;
130     }
131
132     // activate Address EJB instance
133     public void ejbActivate()
134     {
135         addressID = ( Integer ) entityContext.getPrimaryKey();
136     }
137
138     // passivate Address EJB instance
139     public void ejbPassivate()
140     {
141         addressID = null;
142     }
143
144     // remove Address EJB instance
145     public void ejbRemove() {}
146
147     // store Address EJB data in database
148     public void ejbStore() {}
149
150     // load Address EJB data from database
151     public void ejbLoad() {}
152 }
```

Fig. 20.9 **AddressEJB** implementation of **Address** remote interface (part 4 of 4).

Method **getAddressModel** (lines 35–55) constructs an **AddressModel**, sets its properties to the values of the **Address** EJB's **public** data members and returns the **AddressModel** to the caller. Method **setAddressModel** (lines 58–72) is a utility method that takes an **AddressModel** argument and updates the values in the **AddressEJB**'s data members.

The EJB container invokes method **ejbCreate** (lines 75–115) to create a new **AddressEJB**. Each **Address** must have a unique **addressID** for its primary key.

SequenceFactory method **getNextID** (line 97) generates this unique **addressID**. Line 100 sets the **addressID** value in the **AddressModel**. Line 103 passes the **AddressModel** to method **setAddressModel** to complete initialization of the **AddressEJB**.

20.3.3 **AddressHome** Interface

Interface **AddressHome** (Fig. 20.10) provides methods for creating and finding **Address** EJBs. Method **create** (lines 18–19) takes an **AddressModel** argument. The EJB container invokes method **ejbCreate** (Fig. 20.9) when a client invokes method **create**. Method **findByPrimaryKey** (lines 22–23) locates an existing **Address** EJB, using its **addressID** primary key, and returns a remote reference to the **Address**.

20.3.4 **AddressModel**

Class **AddressModel** (Fig. 20.11) is a model class that implements interface **XMLGenerator** and method **getXML** to generate an XML description of an **Address**. Class **AddressModel** contains properties (lines 17–149) for each **public** data member in the **AddressEJB** implementation (Fig. 20.9). Method **getXML** (lines 152–212) builds an XML **Element** that contains child **Element**s for each of the **AddressModel**'s properties.

```
1   // AddressHome.java
2   // AddressHome is the home interface for entity EJB Address.
3   package com.deitel.advjhtp1.bookstore.ejb;
4
5   // Java core libraries
6   import java.rmi.RemoteException;
7
8   // Java standard extensions
9   import javax.ejb.EJBHome;
10  import javax.ejb.*;
11
12  // Deitel Bookstore libraries
13  import com.deitel.advjhtp1.bookstore.model.*;
14
15  public interface AddressHome extends EJBHome {
16
17     // create Address EJB using given AddressModel
18     public Address create( AddressModel address )
19        throws RemoteException, CreateException;
20
21     // find Address with given addressID
22     public Address findByPrimaryKey( Integer addressID )
23        throws RemoteException, FinderException;
24  }
```

Fig. 20.10 **AddressHome** interface for creating and finding **Address** EJB instances.

```
1   // AddressModel.java
2   // AddressModel represents a Customer's address, including
3   // street, city, state and zip code.
4   package com.deitel.advjhtp1.bookstore.model;
5
6   // Java core libraries
7   import java.io.*;
8   import java.util.*;
9
10  // third-party libraries
11  import org.w3c.dom.*;
12
13  public class AddressModel implements Serializable,
14     XMLGenerator {
15
16     // AddressModel properties
17     private Integer addressID;
18     private String firstName;
19     private String lastName;
20     private String streetAddressLine1;
21     private String streetAddressLine2;
22     private String city;
23     private String state;
24     private String zipCode;
25     private String country;
26     private String phoneNumber;
27
28     // construct empty AddressModel
29     public AddressModel() {}
30
31     // set addressID
32     public void setAddressID( Integer id )
33     {
34        addressID = id;
35     }
36
37     // get addressID
38     public Integer getAddressID()
39     {
40        return addressID;
41     }
42
43     // set first name
44     public void setFirstName( String name )
45     {
46        firstName = name;
47     }
48
49     // get first name
50     public String getFirstName()
51     {
52        return firstName;
53     }
54
```

Fig. 20.11 AddressModel for serializing **Address** EJB data (part 1 of 4).

```
55      // set last name
56      public void setLastName( String name )
57      {
58         lastName = name;
59      }
60
61      // get last name
62      public String getLastName()
63      {
64         return lastName;
65      }
66
67      // set first line of street address
68      public void setStreetAddressLine1( String address )
69      {
70         streetAddressLine1 = address;
71      }
72
73      // get first line of street address
74      public String getStreetAddressLine1()
75      {
76         return streetAddressLine1;
77      }
78
79      // set second line of street address
80      public void setStreetAddressLine2( String address )
81      {
82         streetAddressLine2 = address;
83      }
84
85      // set second line of street address
86      public String getStreetAddressLine2()
87      {
88         return streetAddressLine2;
89      }
90
91      // set city
92      public void setCity( String addressCity )
93      {
94         city = addressCity;
95      }
96
97      // get city
98      public String getCity()
99      {
100        return city;
101     }
102
103     // set state
104     public void setState( String addressState )
105     {
106        state = addressState;
107     }
108
```

Fig. 20.11 AddressModel for serializing **Address** EJB data (part 2 of 4).

```
109    // get state
110    public String getState()
111    {
112       return state;
113    }
114
115    // set zip code
116    public void setZipCode( String zip )
117    {
118       zipCode = zip;
119    }
120
121    // get zip code
122    public String getZipCode()
123    {
124       return zipCode;
125    }
126
127    // set country
128    public void setCountry( String addressCountry )
129    {
130       country = addressCountry;
131    }
132
133    // get country
134    public String getCountry()
135    {
136       return country;
137    }
138
139    // set phone number
140    public void setPhoneNumber( String phone )
141    {
142       phoneNumber = phone;
143    }
144
145    // get phone number
146    public String getPhoneNumber()
147    {
148       return phoneNumber;
149    }
150
151    // build XML representation of Customer
152    public Element getXML( Document document )
153    {
154       // create address Element
155       Element address = document.createElement( "address" );
156
157       // crate firstName Element
158       Element temp = document.createElement( "firstName" );
159       temp.appendChild(
160          document.createTextNode( getFirstName() ) );
161       address.appendChild( temp );
162
163       // create lastName Element
```

Fig. 20.11 **AddressModel** for serializing **Address** EJB data (part 3 of 4).

```
164        temp = document.createElement( "lastName" );
165        temp.appendChild(
166           document.createTextNode( getLastName() ) );
167        address.appendChild( temp );
168
169        // create streetAddressLine1 Element
170        temp = document.createElement( "streetAddressLine1" );
171        temp.appendChild(
172           document.createTextNode( getStreetAddressLine1() ) );
173        address.appendChild( temp );
174
175        // create streetAddressLine2 Element
176        temp = document.createElement( "streetAddressLine2" );
177        temp.appendChild(
178           document.createTextNode( getStreetAddressLine2() ) );
179        address.appendChild( temp );
180
181        // create city Element
182        temp = document.createElement( "city" );
183        temp.appendChild( document.createTextNode( city ) );
184        address.appendChild( temp );
185
186        // create state Element
187        temp = document.createElement( "state" );
188        temp.appendChild(
189           document.createTextNode( getState() ) );
190        address.appendChild( temp );
191
192        // create zipCode Element
193        temp = document.createElement( "zipCode" );
194        temp.appendChild(
195           document.createTextNode( getZipCode() ) );
196        address.appendChild( temp );
197
198        // create country Element
199        temp = document.createElement( "country" );
200        temp.appendChild(
201           document.createTextNode( getCountry() ) );
202        address.appendChild( temp );
203
204        // create phoneNumber Element
205        temp = document.createElement( "phoneNumber" );
206        temp.appendChild(
207           document.createTextNode( getPhoneNumber() ) );
208        address.appendChild( temp );
209
210        return address;
211
212     } // end method getXML
213 }
```

Fig. 20.11 AddressModel for serializing **Address** EJB data (part 4 of 4).

Figure 20.12, Fig. 20.13 and Fig. 20.14 show the deployment settings for entity EJB **Address**. In addition to the settings shown here, be sure to set the **Transaction Type** to **Required** for all business methods.

Address General Deployment Settings	
Bean Type	Entity
Enterprise Bean Class	`com.deitel.advjhtp1.bookstore.ejb.AddressEJB`
Home Interface	`com.deitel.advjhtp1.bookstore.ejb.AddressHome`
Remote Interface	`com.deitel.advjhtp1.bookstore.ejb.Address`

Fig. 20.12 **Address** General deployment settings.

Address Entity and Deployment Settings	
Persistence Management	Container-Managed Persistence
Primary Key Class	`java.lang.Integer`
Primary Key Field Name	`addressID`
Database JNDI Name	`jdbc/Bookstore`

Method **ejb-Store** SQL Statement	`UPDATE Address SET city = ?, country = ?,`
	`firstName = ?, lastName = ?, phoneNumber = ?,`
	`state = ?, streetAddressLine1 = ?,`
	`streetAddressLine2 = ?, zipCode = ?`
	`WHERE addressID = ?`

Method **ejb-Create** SQL Statement	`INSERT INTO Address ( addressID, city, country,`
	`firstName, lastName, phoneNumber, state,`
	`streetAddressLine1, streetAddressLine2, zipCode )`
	`VALUES ( ?, ?, ?, ?,  ?, ?, ?, ?, ?, ? )`

Method **ejb-Remove** SQL Statement	`DELETE FROM Address WHERE addressID = ?`
Method **find-ByPrimaryKey** SQL Statement	`SELECT addressID FROM Address WHERE addressID = ?`

Method **ejb-Load** SQL Statement	`SELECT city, country, firstName, lastName,`
	`phoneNumber, state, streetAddressLine1,`
	`streetAddressLine2, zipCode FROM Address`
	`WHERE addressID = ?`

Fig. 20.13 **Address** entity and deployment settings (part 1 of 2).

Address Entity and Deployment Settings	
Table Create SQL Statement	`CREATE TABLE Address (addressID INTEGER, city VARCHAR(255), country VARCHAR(255), firstName VARCHAR(255), lastName VARCHAR(255), phoneNumber VARCHAR(255), state VARCHAR(255), streetAddressLine1 VARCHAR(255), streetAddressLine2 VARCHAR(255), zipCode VARCHAR(255), CONSTRAINT pk_Address PRIMARY KEY (addressID))`
Table Delete SQL Statement	`DROP TABLE Address`

Fig. 20.13 Address entity and deployment settings (part 2 of 2).

Address EJB References	
Coded Name	`ejb/SequenceFactory`
Type	`Entity`
Home	`com.deitel.advjhtp1.bookstore.ejb.SequenceFactoryHome`
Remote	`com.deitel.advjhtp1.bookstore.ejb.SequenceFactory`
JNDI Name	`SequenceFactory`

Fig. 20.14 Address EJB references.

20.4 SequenceFactory Implementation

One of the fundamental concepts in relational databases is that of a primary key, which uniquely identifies a row in a database table. The primary key is needed to define relationships between tables in the database. For example, in our case study, each **Order** relates to a **Customer** by storing the **Customer** table's primary key—**customerID**—as a field (called a *foreign key*) in the **Order** table. The **customerID** is guaranteed to be unique, so it can be used to determine which **Customer** placed an **Order**. The **Customer**, **Order** and **Address** EJBs all have **SequenceFactory** records from which these EJBs can obtain primary keys.

20.4.1 SequenceFactory Remote Interface

Interface **SequenceFactory** (Fig. 20.15) is the remote interface for the **SequenceFactory** EJB. Method **getNextID** (line 15) returns the next available primary key.

```
 1   // SequenceFactory.java
 2   // SequenceFactory is the remote interface for the entity EJB
 3   // SequenceFactory.
 4   package com.deitel.advjhtp1.bookstore.ejb;
 5
 6   // Java core packages
 7   import java.rmi.RemoteException;
 8
 9   // Java extension packages
10   import javax.ejb.EJBObject;
11
12   public interface SequenceFactory extends EJBObject {
13
14      // get next available unique ID
15      public Integer getNextID() throws RemoteException;
16   }
```

Fig. 20.15 **SequenceFactory** remote interface for generating primary keys.

20.4.2 SequenceFactoryEJB Implementation

Figure 20.16 shows the **SequenceFactoryEJB** implementation of the **Sequence-Factory** remote interface. The EJB container manages the synchronization of the **public** data members (lines 19–22) with the database.

Method **getNextOrderID** (lines 25–31) calculates the next available unique **orderID** by incrementing the current value of the **orderID** (line 27). This new value is saved in the EJB (line 28) and returned to the caller (line 30). Method **getNextCustomerID**, (lines 34–40) increments the current value of the **customerID** field and returns the value to the caller (line 39). Method **getNextAddressID** (lines 43–49) increments the value of the **addressID** field and returns the value to the caller on line 48.

For the **SequenceFactory** EJB to calculate unique **orderID**s, **customerID**s and **addressID**s properly, there must be only one **SequenceFactory** EJB instance. If there were more than one **SequenceFactory** EJB instance, duplicate **orderID**s, **customerID**s or **addressID**s could be generated. **SequenceFactory** EJB clients should use only method **findSequenceFactory** of interface **SequenceFactory-Home** to obtain the correct **SequenceFactory** EJB instance. The deployer must specify an SQL query that will return the same **SequenceFactory** record each time a method **findSequenceFactory** is invoked.

```
 1   // SequenceFactoryEJB.java
 2   // Entity EJB SequenceFactory generates unique primary keys.
 3   package com.deitel.advjhtp1.bookstore.ejb;
 4
 5   // Java core packages
 6   import java.rmi.RemoteException;
 7   import java.util.ArrayList;
 8
 9   // Java extension packages
```

Fig. 20.16 **SequenceFactoryEJB** implementation of **SequenceFactory** remote interface (part 1 of 3).

```
10   import javax.ejb.*;
11   import javax.naming.*;
12   import javax.rmi.PortableRemoteObject;
13
14   public class SequenceFactoryEJB implements EntityBean {
15      private EntityContext entityContext;
16
17      // container-managed fields
18      public String tableName;   // table name for ID sequence
19      public Integer nextID;      // next available unique ID
20
21      // get next available orderID
22      public Integer getNextID()
23      {
24         // store nextID for returning to caller
25         Integer ID = new Integer( nextID.intValue() );
26
27         // increment ID to produce next available unique ID
28         nextID = new Integer( ID.intValue() + 1 );
29
30         return ID;
31      }
32
33      // set entity context
34      public void setEntityContext( EntityContext context )
35      {
36         entityContext = context;
37      }
38
39      // unset entity context
40      public void unsetEntityContext()
41      {
42         entityContext = null;
43      }
44
45      // activate SequenceFactory EJB instance
46      public void ejbActivate()
47      {
48         tableName = ( String ) entityContext.getPrimaryKey();
49      }
50
51      // passivate SequenceFactory EJB instance
52      public void ejbPassivate()
53      {
54         tableName = null;
55      }
56
57      // remove SequenceFactory EJB instance
58      public void ejbRemove() {}
59
60      // store SequenceFactory EJB data in database
61      public void ejbStore() {}
```

Fig. 20.16 **SequenceFactoryEJB** implementation of **SequenceFactory** remote interface (part 2 of 3).

```
62
63      // load SequenceFactory EJB data from database
64      public void ejbLoad() {}
65   }
```

Fig. 20.16 **SequenceFactoryEJB** implementation of **SequenceFactory**
remote interface (part 3 of 3).

20.4.3 SequenceFactoryHome Interface

Interface **SequenceFactoryHome** (Fig. 20.17) is the home interface for the **Se-quenceFactory** EJB. Method **findByPrimaryKey** (lines 15–16) returns a remote reference to the **SequenceFactory** EJB for the database table with the given name.

Figure 20.18 and Fig. 20.19 show the deployment settings for entity EJB **Sequence-Factory**. In addition to the settings shown here, be sure to set the **Transaction Type** to **Required** for all business methods.

```
1    // SequenceFactoryHome.java
2    // SequenceFactoryHome is the home interface for entity EJB
3    // SequenceFactory.
4    package com.deitel.advjhtp1.bookstore.ejb;
5
6    // Java core packages
7    import java.rmi.RemoteException;
8
9    // Java extension packages
10   import javax.ejb.*;
11
12   public interface SequenceFactoryHome extends EJBHome {
13
14       // find SequenceFactory with given primary key
15       public SequenceFactory findByPrimaryKey( String tableName )
16           throws RemoteException, FinderException;
17   }
```

Fig. 20.17 **SequenceFactoryHome** interface for finding
SequenceFactory EJB instances.

SequenceFactory General Deployment Settings	
Bean Type	Entity
Enter-prise Bean Class	com.deitel.advjhtp1.bookstore.ejb.SequenceFactoryEJB

Fig. 20.18 **SequenceFactory** general deployment settings (part 1 of 2).

SequenceFactory General Deployment Settings	
Home Interface	com.deitel.advjhtp1.bookstore.ejb.SequenceFactoryHome
Remote Interface	com.deitel.advjhtp1.bookstore.ejb.SequenceFactory

Fig. 20.18 SequenceFactory general deployment settings (part 2 of 2).

SequenceFactory Entity and Deployment Settings	
Persistence Management	**Container-Managed Persistence**
Primary Key Class	java.lang.String
Primary Key Field Name	tableName
Database JNDI Name	jdbc/Bookstore
Method ejb-Store SQL Statement	UPDATE SequenceFactory SET nextID = ? WHERE tableName = ?
Method ejb-Create SQL Statement	INSERT INTO SequenceFactory (nextID, tableName) VALUES (?, ?)
Method ejb-Remove SQL Statement	DELETE FROM SequenceFactory WHERE tableName = ?
Method find-ByPrimaryKey SQL Statement	SELECT tableName FROM SequenceFactory WHERE tableName = ?
Method ejb-Load SQL Statement	SELECT nextID FROM SequenceFactory WHERE tablename = ?
Table Create SQL Statement	CREATE TABLE SequenceFactory (nextID INTEGER, tableName VARCHAR(255), CONSTRAINT pk_SequenceFactory PRIMARY KEY (tableName))
Table Delete SQL Statement	DROP TABLE SequenceFactory

Fig. 20.19 SequenceFactory entity and deployment settings.

20.5 Deitel Bookstore Application Deployment with J2EE

Deploying the components of the Deitel Bookstore on the Java 2 Enterprise Edition (J2EE) Reference Implementation requires the use of the **Application Deployment Tool**. The following steps walk through the process of deploying the **Order** EJB. The deployment process for the other entity EJBs is similar. For general instructions on deploying stateful session EJBs, such as the **ShoppingCart** EJB, please refer to Chapter 14, Session EJBs and Distributed Transactions. For general instructions on deploying Java servlets, please refer to Chapter 11, Case Study: Servlet and JSP Bookstore.

20.5.1 Deploying Deitel Bookstore CMP Entity EJBs

To begin deploying the entity EJBs for the Deitel Bookstore, select the **New Enterprise Bean...** menu item in the **Application Deployment Tool**'s **File** menu (Fig. 20.20) to begin deploying the EJB. You then will be presented with a wizard-style interface for creating the EJB JAR file (Fig. 20.21). The **JAR Display Name** field contains the text that will appear for this EJB JAR in the **Application Deployment Tool**, but has no effect on the deployment of the application. Click the **Add...** button next to the **Contents** field to add the class files for the EJB to the JAR.

To add the EJB class files to the EJB JAR file, you must specify the **Root Directory** that contains the class' package structure (Fig. 20.22). For example, the **Order** EJB is in the package **com.deitel.advjhtp1.bookstore.ejb**. If the compiled class file is placed in the directory **D:\BookStore\com\deitel\advjhtp1\bookstore\ejb**, select **D:\BookStore** as the **Root Directory**. Click the **Browse...** button to use a file selection dialog to select the **Root Directory**.

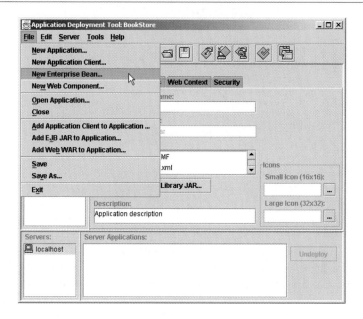

Fig. 20.20 Adding an EJB to an enterprise application.

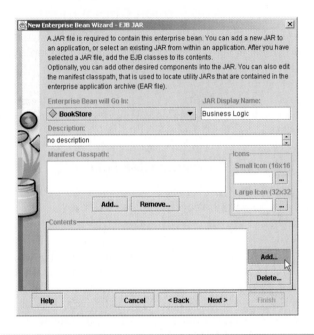

Fig. 20.21 Creating an EJB JAR file.

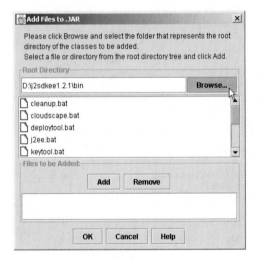

Fig. 20.22 Specifying the **Root Directory** for EJB classes.

Once you have selected the proper **Root Directory**, select the class files for the EJB remote interface, home interface, implementation and other classes that the EJB requires (e.g., **OrderModel.class**, **XMLGenerator.class**, application-specific exception classes, etc.). By holding down the *CTRL* key, you may select multiple files at once. Click the **Add** button to add the selected class files to the EJB JAR and click **OK** (Fig. 20.23). Figure 20.24 shows the results of adding the class files for the **Order** EJB to the EJB JAR file.

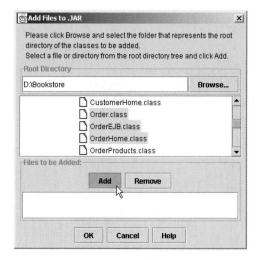

Fig. 20.23 Adding EJB classes to an EJB JAR file.

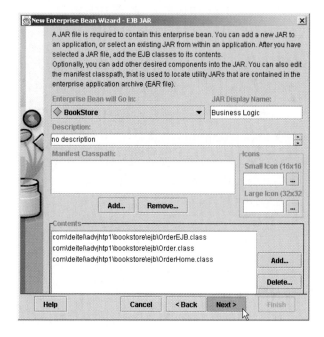

Fig. 20.24 Results of adding EJB classes to an EJB JAR file.

Once you have added the class files to the EJB JAR file, you must specify the class files that contain the remote interface, the home interface and the EJB implementation (Fig. 20.25). Select the appropriate class from the drop-down list as shown in Fig. 20.25. The **Order** EJB is an entity bean, so select the **Entity** radio button under the **Bean Type** heading (Fig. 20.26).

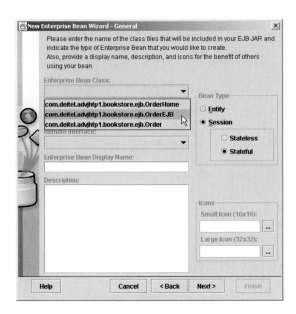

Fig. 20.25 Specifying classes for EJB, home interface and remote interface.

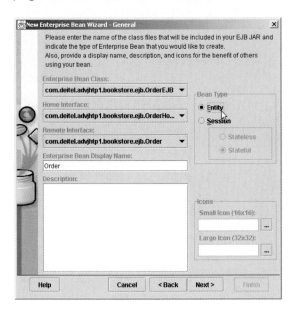

Fig. 20.26 Setting **Bean Type** to **Entity**.

The **Order** EJB uses container-managed persistence to synchronize its data with the corresponding database table. In the following step of the EJB wizard (Fig. 20.27), select the **Container-Managed Persistence** radio button and place checkmarks next to each of the container-managed fields. Specify the complete class name of the primary-key class (including its package name) in the **Primary Key Class** field. For the **Order** EJB, enter

java.lang.Integer as the primary-key class. If your EJB uses a user-defined primary-key class (e.g., the **OrderProduct** EJB), you must also specify the complete package name (e.g., **com.deitel.advjhtp1.bookstore.ejb.OrderProductPK**). Select the field that contains the primary key from the **Primary Key Field Name** drop-down list (e.g., **orderID**).

If your EJB references other EJBs in its implementation, these EJBs must be specified in the **Application Deployment Tool** (Fig. 20.28). Click the **Add** button to add a new EJB reference. The **Coded Name** column corresponds to the **String** used to locate the EJB in the JNDI directory. For example, to locate the **Product** EJB, we use the **String java:comp/env/ejb/Product**. The corresponding coded name is **ejb/Product**. Select the appropriate type for the EJB (i.e., **Session** or **Entity**) from the **Type** drop-down list. Provide the full class name (including the package name) for the home and remote interfaces in the **Home** and **Remote** columns. For example, in the **Home** column for the **Product** EJB, specify **com.deitel.advjhtp1.bookstore.ejb.ProductHome**. Enter the JNDI name for the referenced EJB in the **JNDI Name** field (e.g., **Product**).

J2EE application servers provide transaction management, the semantics of which can be specified when deploying an application. For each of the business methods, specify the appropriate **Transaction Type** (Fig. 20.29), as discussed in Chapter 15.

Figure 20.30 shows the XML descriptor that was generated by the previous steps. This XML descriptor can be used when deploying this application on any J2EE-compliant application server.

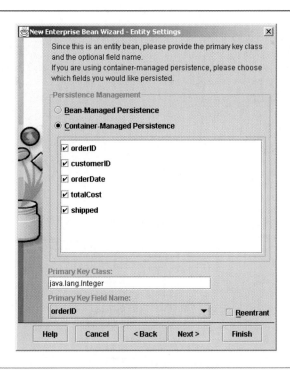

Fig. 20.27 Configuring container-managed fields and primary-key class.

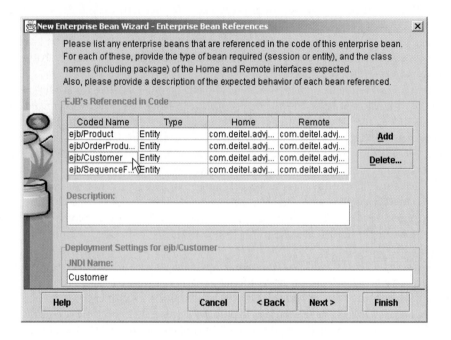

Fig. 20.28 Specifying other EJBs referenced by this EJB.

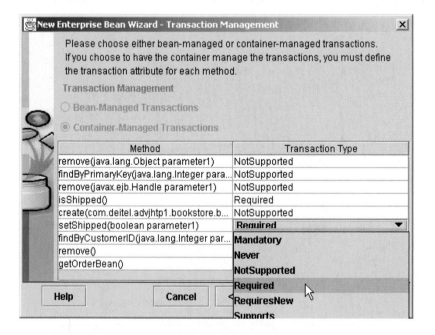

Fig. 20.29 Specifying **Container-Managed Transactions** for EJB business methods.

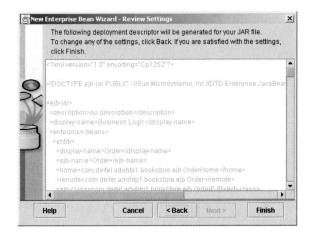

Fig. 20.30 XML descriptor generated by **Application Deployment Tool**.

You must now configure the database to which the CMP entity bean will persist its data. Click the **Deployment Settings**... button in the **Entity** tab (Fig. 20.31).

Specify the JNDI name for the database in the **Database JNDI Name** field (Fig. 20.32). In the J2EE Reference Implementation, this value corresponds to the value specified in the **default.properties** configuration file (e.g., **jdbc/BookStore**). Once you have specified the JNDI name for the database, click the **Generate SQL Now** button to create the necessary SQL statements for the EJB *finder* and *create* methods.

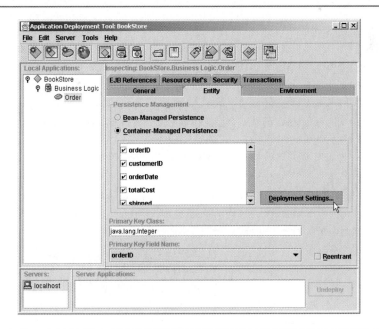

Fig. 20.31 Specifying EJB **Deployment Settings**.

Fig. 20.32 Configuring EJB **Database Settings**.

You will be prompted to provide SQL **WHERE** clauses for any custom *finder* methods specified in the EJB's home interface (Fig. 20.33). For each method listed under **EJB Method** (e.g., **findByPrimaryKey**, **ejbStore**, **Table Create**, etc.) enter the appropriate SQL query from the tables in Chapters 19–20. For example, Fig. 20.6 lists the appropriate SQL queries for the **Customer** EJB.

20.5.2 Deploying Deitel Bookstore Servlets

The servlets in the Deitel Bookstore take advantage of context and initialization parameters—which the deployer supplies when deploying the application—to facilitate the installation of new client types. Figure 20.35 lists each servlet, the value for that servlet's XSL_FILE initialization parameter and that servlet's alias.

In addition, you must set the Web Context for the servlet's WAR file to the value **bookstore** (Fig. 20.36).

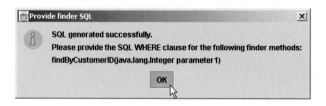

Fig. 20.33 Dialog indicating methods that require **WHERE** clauses for SQL queries.

Fig. 20.34 Specifying SQL query for method `findByCustomerID`.

Servlet	XSL_FILE Initialization Parameter Value	Servlet Alias
AddToCartServlet	error.xsl	AddToCart
RemoveFromCartServlet	error.xsl	RemoveFromCart
UpdateCartServlet	error.xsl	UpdateCart
ViewCartServlet	viewCart.xsl	ViewCart
CheckoutServlet	error.xsl	Checkout
ViewOrderServlet	viewOrder.xsl	ViewOrder
ViewOrderHistoryServlet	viewOrderHistory.xsl	ViewOrderHistory
GetAllProductsServlet	products.xsl	GetAllProducts
GetProductServlet	productDetails.xsl	GetProduct
ProductSearchServlet	products.xsl	ProductSearch
RegisterServlet	error.xsl	Register
LoginServlet	login.xsl	Login
GetPasswordHintServlet	passwordHint.xsl	GetPasswordHint

Fig. 20.35 Deployment settings for Deitel Bookstore servlets.

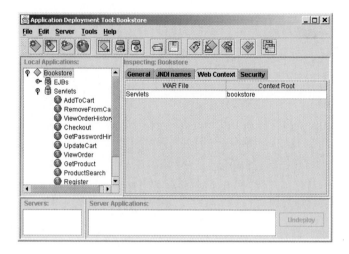

Fig. 20.36 Setting the **Context Root** for the Deitel Bookstore servlets.

Recall that the servlets in the Deitel Bookstore read client configuration information from the **CLIENT_LIST** servlet context parameter. Specify the value for this context parameter as shown in Fig. 20.37.

The servlets in the Deitel Bookstore utilize EJB business logic to maintain the customers shopping cart, create customer registrations, etc. To enable the servlets to access the EJBs, we must specify EJB references in the deployment tool. Figure 20.38 shows the necessary EJB references. Be sure to specify the JNDI name for each EJB (e.g., **Shopping-Cart**) and full class names for the home and remote interfaces.

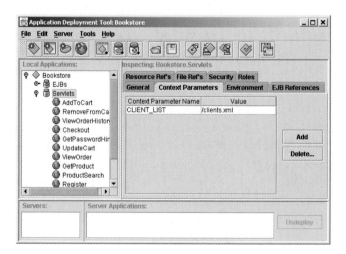

Fig. 20.37 Setting the **CLIENT_LIST Context Parameter** for the Deitel Bookstore servlets.

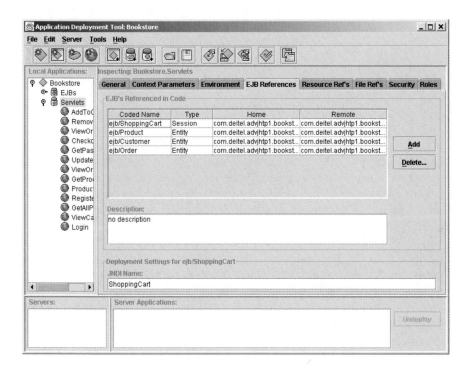

Fig. 20.38 Servlet **EJB References**.

The final step before deploying the Deitel Bookstore case study is to add the XSL transformation documents and other supporting files to the servlet WAR file. Figure 20.39 lists these supporting files, their relative paths in the servlet WAR file and a description of each.

File Name(s)	Relative Path	Description
clients.xml	/	Configuration file for enabling client support.
index.html	/	Welcome page for XHTML client.s
login.html	/	Login form for XHTML clients.
registration.html	/	Registration form for XHTML clients.
index.wml	/	Welcome page for WML clients.
login.wml	/	Login form for WML clients
default.css	/styles/	Cascading Style Sheet for XHTML clients.
*.jpg	/images/	Book cover images for bookstore products.
*.xsl	/XSLT/XHTML/	XSL transformations for XHTML clients.
navigation.xml	/XSLT/XHTML/	Navigation header for XHTML clients.

Fig. 20.39 Supporting files for inclusion in servlet WAR file (part 1 of 2).

File Name(s)	Relative Path	Description
`*.xsl`	`/XSLT/WML/`	XSL transformations for WML clients.
`*.xsl`	`/XSLT/cHTML/`	XSL transformations for cHTML clients.

Fig. 20.39 Supporting files for inclusion in servlet WAR file (part 2 of 2).

After completing the EJB and servlet configuration in the **Application Deployment Tool**, select **Deploy Application** from the **Tools** menu to deploy the application to the J2EE reference implementation application server. You can access the newly deployed application by opening the URL **http://localhost:8000/bookstore/index.html** in a Web browser or i-mode simulator, or the URL **http://localhost:8000/bookstore/index.wml** for a WML simulator.

This concludes our discussion of the Deitel Bookstore case study. This case study integrated several enterprise Java technologies into a substantial online application. In Chapter 21, Application Servers, we introduce three of the most popular J2EE-compliant commercial application servers—BEA's WebLogic, IBM's WebSphere and the iPlanet Application Server. We then discuss the steps necessary to deploy the Deitel Bookstore case study on BEA's WebLogic and IBM's WebSphere.

21

Application Servers

Objectives

- To introduce several popular commercial application servers.
- To introduce open-source alternatives to commercial application servers.
- To understand the requirements for J2EE-compliant application servers.
- To understand the differences among commercial application server implementations.
- To deploy the Deitel Bookstore Enterprise Java case study on two leading commercial application servers.

Can anything be so elegant as to have few wants, and to serve them one's self?
Ralph Waldo Emerson

"Contrariwise," continued Tweedledee, "if it was so, it might be; and if it were so, it would be; but as it isn't, it ain't. That's logic."
Lewis Carroll

Eloquence is logic on fire.
Lyman Beecher

...a pool that nobody's fathomed the depth of, and paths threaded with flowers planted by the mind.
Katherine Mansfield

Outline

21.1 Introduction

The Java 2 Enterprise Edition is a specification for enterprise runtime environments. Although Sun provides a reference implementation of this specification, real-world systems must use an application server from a commercial vendor. In this chapter, we introduce the three most popular J2EE-compliant, commercial application servers—BEA WebLogic, IBM WebSphere and iPlanet Application Server. We also introduce the JBoss open-source application server. We deploy the Deitel Bookstore application from Chapters 17–20 to demonstrate the portability of applications written for the J2EE specification. After reading this chapter you will understand the role of an Application Server in an enterprise application, and be able to deploy your own applications on commercial application servers.

21.2 J2EE Specification and Benefits

For many years, there did not exist a standard for application servers. Each application server vendor provided its own set of APIs and varying functionality. If a company wished to move its enterprise applications to a new application-server platform, that company's developers would need to rewrite large amounts of code, resulting in a complex and expensive migration process. Sun Microsystems, along with a large community of application-server vendors, developed the Java 2 Enterprise Edition specification through the Java Community Process (Appendix F, Java Community Process). J2EE defines an application server platform and supporting APIs for building enterprise applications that are portable across application servers, and, because they use Java, across platforms. J2EE extends Java's *"Write Once, Run Anywhere™"* principle to enterprise applications. J2EE facilitates portability among application servers by enabling deployers to specify server-dependant features, such as distributed transactions and database queries at deployment time. At the time of this writing, the J2EE specification was evolving through the Java Community Process. The current release is 1.2.1, and version 1.3 is in beta.

The J2EE specification can be broken down into several pieces, including API support, security, transaction management and deployment processes. An application server vendor is required to provide runtime support for the APIs of the J2EE platform. Figure 21.1 lists the specific API requirements for version 1.2 of the J2EE specification.[1]

21.3 Commercial Application Servers

To be J2EE certified, an application server must implement the minimum functionality that the J2EE specification defines. Application server vendors can provide functionality that goes beyond the J2EE specification to differentiate their products. For example, application servers can provide advanced deployment tools, enhanced security strength, higher performance, error recovery, etc. This section describes four popular application servers—BEA WebLogic, iPlanet Application Server, IBM WebSphere and JBoss.

21.3.1 BEA WebLogic 6.0

BEA Systems is currently the number one application-server provider in the world. WebLogic's popularity is largely based upon its first-to-market advantage and its reputation with current enterprises. BEA provides a general-purpose application server, balancing speed with stability and solid support for various features beyond the J2EE specification.

Required APIs	Web Containers	EJBs
Java Data Base Connectivity(JDBC) 2.0 Extension	required	required
Remote Method Invocation-Internet Inter-ORB Protocol(RMI-IIOP) 1.0	required	required
Enterprise Java Beans(EJB) 1.1	required	required
Servlets 2.2	required	N/A
Java Server Pages(JSP) 1.1	required	N/A
Java Messaging System(JMS) 1.0	required	required
Java Naming and Directory Interface(JNDI) 1.2	required	required
Java Transaction API (JTA) 1.0	required	required
JavaMail 1.1	required	required
Java Activation Framework(JAF) 1.0	required	required

Fig. 21.1 Application server required APIs.

WeLogic provides *data pools*, which eliminate the need to create new database connections for each client. Establishing database connections has considerable overhead—up to several seconds per connection for some database servers. By maintaining a pool of open connections and assigning these to clients as needed, WebLogic increases application performance. WebLogic also provides a mechanism for *"hot" deployment*. The application server continually checks a specified directory for new applications; if the application server finds a new application in that directory, WebLogic automatically deploys the application without restarting the server. WebLogic also will undeploy an application if the administrator removes that application from the deployment directory. Hot deployment increases server up time and makes deployment simpler. However, BEA does not recommend enabling hot deployment in production environments. Rather, hot deployment can be useful for developers when testing applications.

WebLogic uses *clustering* to increase availability through *failover* support for EJBs and Web components. Servers within a cluster enable redundancy—if a server conducting a transaction fails, another server can take over transparently without interrupting the transaction. This redundancy also facilitates *load balancing*. In a load-balanced environment, the application server distributes requests among several servers based on their load (i.e., how many requests each server already is handling). Load balancing helps prevent individual servers from failing under high numbers of requests.

For single-server environments, WebLogic provides *multi-pooling*—a service that distributes transactions among data sources. Whereas a connection pool is limited to a single data source; multi-pooling allows an application to access several pools, thus distributing requests among multiple data sources. Multi-pooling divides labor among data sources to provide a degree of load balancing within a single application server.

WebLogic is completely J2EE 1.2 compliant and already supports many requirements of the J2EE 1.3 beta specification. WebLogic includes a Web server, but no longer includes a graphical deployment tool, so deployers must code deployment descriptors manually. WebLogic also works with several popular Java Development environments, including JBuilder and Visual Café.

WebLogic also provides advanced security. User access and control are managed within WebLogic through *Access control list*s (ACLs)–ACLs provide an efficient method for managing users and permissions, WebLogic also includes SSL support and digital certificates.[2]

21.3.2 iPlanet Application Server 6.0

iPlanet E-Commerce Solutions is an alliance between Netscape Communications and Sun Microsystems. iPlanet has created a fully J2EE-certified application server as a replacement for Netscape's application server. iPlanet's primary goals are speed, stability and full J2EE compliance. iPlanet integrates C++ with Java to produce a fast, scalable application server. iPlanet provides failover support, connection pooling and several unique features.

The *Web connector* controls load balancing in iPlanet application server. The Web connector manages communication between the application server and the Web server. The Web connector distributes requests among server instances based on server response time. For more control, the application server may handle its own load balancing. Requests are distributed according to a specific algorithm defined by the deployer in the configuration tool. iPlanet includes support for *"sticky" load balancing*—if a components is flagged as "sticky," then the normal load-balancing algorithm will be bypassed and the component will always be executed on the "sticky" machine. "Sticky" load balancing helps in situations where the overhead of creating connections between servers for a given EJB is greater than the time saved by load balancing.

iPlanet uses the *Lightweight Directory Access Protocol* (*LDAP*) to manage security. Users may be assigned group and individual permissions to access parts of applications. Configuring LDAP permissions adds additional complexity to the server configuration process, but enables tight control over user permissions. iPlanet Application Server is integrated with, and includes, the iPlanet Directory Server and the iPlanet Web Server.

At the time of this writing, iPlanet was about to release a new version of iPlanet Application Server. To download the latest version, please visit **www.iplanet.com/ ias_deitel**. When this new version of iPlanet is available, we will provide a complete description of the iPlanet deployment process for the Deitel Bookstore application on our Web site, **www.deitel.com**

21.3.3 IBM WebSphere Advanced Application Server 4.0

IBM WebSphere is a popular application server that is approaching BEA's WebLogic in market share. Version 4.0 is a substantial improvement over previous versions, including simpler configuration options, faster response time and enhanced security. Version 4.0 provides a simple user interface for administration and deployment, and a focus on speed and scalability. WebSphere includes IBM's version of the Apache Web server, failover support, data pooling, and user-level security controls.

21.3.4 JBoss 2.2.2 Application Server

JBoss, combined with the Apache Software Foundation's Tomcat servlet container, currently is the only J2EE 1.2-compliant, open-source application server. JBoss is distributed under the Lesser General Public License (LGPL). The source code for JBoss is freely available, and can be used to serve commercial applications. JBoss aims to maintain compliance with future J2EE specifications. Currently, JBoss includes most features of commercial application servers. JBoss was one of the first application servers to support hot deployment, and it runs with a small memory footprint, which leaves more resources for applications.[3]

JBoss lacks clustering support, which may not be a concern for many small to mid-sized businesses, but prevents JBoss from competing in the commercial market. JBoss also does not provide graphical tools for deployment or configuration. Fortunately, the JBoss community consists of a large and generally helpful user base that will help with most configuration issues quickly.

21.4 Deploying the Deitel Bookstore on BEA WebLogic

Configuring an application server can be a complex task. In this section, we guide you through the steps required to install and configure BEA WebLogic for the Deitel Bookstore case study. Please refer to **e-docs.bea.com/wls/docs60/install/inst-prg.html** for installation instructions. For these configuration instructions we assume **c:\bea** as the home directory, **Deitel** as the WebLogic administration domain name, and **bookstore** as the server name. We also assume Cloudscape is installed in `c:\cloudscape_3.6` and our database is `c:\cloudscape_3.6\databas-es\Bookstore`. Depending on your security requirements you may wish to create a file named **password.ini** with the password you entered during installation. Placing **password.ini** in `c:\bea\wlserver6.0\config\deitel\` will prevent We-bLogic from asking for your password each time you start the application server.

First, we configure WebLogic to enable Cloudscape database support. Open the file `c:\bea\wlserver6.0\config\CaseStudyDS\startWebLogic.cmd` with a text editor, such as Notepad. Near the bottom of the file replace the line

```
set CLASSPATH=.;.\lib\weblogic_sp.jar;.\lib\weblogic.jar
```

with

```
set CLASSPATH=.;.\lib\weblogic_sp.jar;.\lib\weblogic.jar;
c:\cloudscape_3.6\lib\cloudscape.jar
```

which includes the Cloudscape packages in the **CLASSPATH**. The following line contains the parameters to start the server:

```
%JAVA_HOME%\bin\java -hotspot -ms64m -mx64m -classpath
%CLASSPATH% -Dweblogic.Domain=deitel
-Dweblogic.Name=bookstore -Dbea.home=C:\bea
-Djava.security.policy==C:\bea\wlserver6.0/lib/weblogic.pol-
icy -Dweblogic.management.password=%WLS_PW% weblogic.Server
```

To simplify detection of our database, we specify property **cloudscape.sys-tem.home** with value `c:/cloudscape_3.6/databases/` on the command line.

Next, run **startWeblogic.cmd** either by double clicking it, or typing its name at the console. If a console window loads, and, after a minute, presents text similar to:

```
<WebLogic Server started>
<Notice> <WebLogicServer> <SSLListenThread listening on port
7002>
<Notice> <WebLogicServer> <ListenThread listening on port
7001>
```

the application server is ready for configuration.

Use your Web browser to access **localhost:7001/console**. A window should prompt for your network password. Enter **system** under **User Name** and the password you specified during WebLogic installation. Your Web browser should display the page shown in Fig. 21.2. This is the administration console for managing most aspects of the application server.

We now configure the JDBC data pool and data source. In the main pane of the administration console, select **Connection Pools** under the **JDBC** heading. The top of the right pane should contain the link **Create new JDBC Connection Pool**. Configure the options as shown in Fig. 21.3. Specify **BookstorePool** for the pool **Name**, the **URL** **jdbc:cloudscape:Bookstore** and the **Driver Classname** COM.cloud-scape.core.JDBCDriver. Finally, set the **password** and **server** properties to **none**. After entering these values, select **Apply**. You need not restart the server until we have made a few more changes.

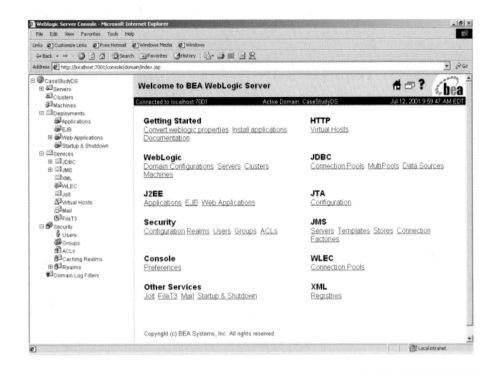

Fig. 21.2 WebLogic administration console. (Courtesy BEA Systems.)

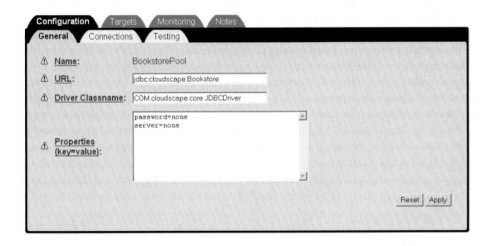

Fig. 21.3 JDBC Connection pool properties. (Courtesy of BEA Systems, Inc.)

Next, select the **Targets** tab—select **Bookstore** from available servers, click the arrow pointing right to add this connection pool to the bookstore server then click **Apply**. In the right pane select **CaseStudyDS > Services > JDBC > Data Sources** then,

Create new JDBC data source. Specify the name of the data source (e.g., **Book-storeDataSource**), enter **jdbc/Bookstore** as the JNDI name, **BookstorePool** as the pool name and select **Create**. Finally, assign **Bookstore** under the **Targets** tab and click **Apply**. Shut down the server, close the WebLogic command window and restart the server with **startWebLogic.cmd**.

We now create the deployment descriptors for our bookstore application. Extract the contents of **bookstore.ear** into a new directory. You may use any zip or jar utility to extract the files. To extract the files via the **jar** utility included with the JDK, enter the command

```
jar xvf bookstore.ear
```

Next, extract the contents of **ejb-jar-ic.jar** into a temporary directory named **ejb-jar**. Create a text file named **weblogic-ejb-jar.xml** and save it in the **ejb-jar\META-INF** directory. This file is the WebLogic-specific deployment descriptor. If you are not familiar with XML please refer to Appendix A, Creating Markup with XML.

The Deployment descriptor **weblogic-ejb-jar.xml** (Fig. 21.4) defines name caching, persistence, transaction options, and other options for the EJBs in the Deitel Bookstore. Lines 6–8 specify the DTD for the descriptor. We specify the WebLogic 5.1.0 doctype because our application uses EJB 1.1. Element **weblogic-ejb-jar** (line 11–356) contains deployment information for all EJBs in the EJB JAR. Element **weblogic-enterprise-bean** (line 13–71) contains deployment information for the **Customer** EJB. Element **ejb-name** (line 14) specifies the name of this bean. Element **ejb-name** must match the name found in **ejb-jar.xml** for WebLogic to correctly identify the current bean. Lines 17–21 contain the descriptions of caching properties. Element **max-beans-in-cache** (Line 18) defines the maximum number of active instances the container should allow. When this limit is reached, the EJB container will passivate idle EJB instances. Element **cache-strategy** (line 19) sets how EJBs should cache data. Valid values include **Read-Write** or **Read-Only**. **Read-Write**, the default value, allows clients to write information to the bean in a standard transaction, and the container invokes **ejbStore** at the completion of the transaction. **Read-Only** does not allow the **ejb-Store** method to be called, but it does allow the bean to be updated by an underlying data source periodically, for example this may be useful as a stock ticker bean. Line 19 defines this bean as a standard transaction bean. Element **read-timeout-seconds** is not used for **Read-Write** beans, if this were a **Read-Only** bean, the value specifies the number of seconds between database update intervals. When set to **0**, the Read-Only bean updates only when it is first created.

```
1    <?xml version = "1.0" encoding = "UTF-8"?>
2
3    <!-- weblogic-ejb-jar.xml deployment descriptor for bookstore -->
4    <!-- describes weblogic specific properties of each bean -->
5
6    <!DOCTYPE weblogic-ejb-jar PUBLIC
7        '-//BEA Systems, Inc.//DTD WebLogic 5.1.0 EJB//EN'
8        'http://www.bea.com/servers/wls510/dtd/weblogic-ejb-jar.dtd'>
```

Fig. 21.4 **Weblogic-ejb-jar.xml** defines WebLogic deployment properties for Bookstore case study (part 1 of 8).

```
9
10    <!-- Customer EJB weblogic descriptor -->
11    <weblogic-ejb-jar>
12
13       <weblogic-enterprise-bean>
14          <ejb-name>Customer</ejb-name>
15
16          <!-- determines caching properties -->
17          <caching-descriptor>
18             <max-beans-in-cache>100</max-beans-in-cache>
19             <cache-strategy>Read-Write</cache-strategy>
20             <read-timeout-seconds>0</read-timeout-seconds>
21          </caching-descriptor>
22
23          <!-- maps cmp types for bean -->
24          <persistence-descriptor>
25
26             <persistence-type>
27                <type-identifier>
28                   WebLogic_CMP_RDBMS
29                </type-identifier>
30                <type-version>5.1.0</type-version>
31                <type-storage>
32                   META-INF/weblogic-cmp-rdbms-jar-Customer.xml
33                </type-storage>
34             </persistence-type>
35
36             <persistence-use>
37                <type-identifier>
38                   WebLogic_CMP_RDBMS
39                </type-identifier>
40                <type-version>5.1.0</type-version>
41             </persistence-use>
42          </persistence-descriptor>
43
44          <!-- transaction paramaters -->
45          <transaction-descriptor>
46             <trans-timeout-seconds>200</trans-timeout-seconds>
47          </transaction-descriptor>
48
49          <!-- maps references to ejb names -->
50          <reference-descriptor>
51             <ejb-reference-description>
52                <ejb-ref-name>ejb/Order</ejb-ref-name>
53                <jndi-name>ejb/Order</jndi-name>
54             </ejb-reference-description>
55
56             <ejb-reference-description>
57                <ejb-ref-name>ejb/SequenceFactory</ejb-ref-name>
58                <jndi-name>ejb/SequenceFactory</jndi-name>
59             </ejb-reference-description>
60
```

Fig. 21.4 **Weblogic-ejb-jar.xml** defines WebLogic deployment properties for Bookstore case study (part 2 of 8).

```
61                 <ejb-reference-description>
62                    <ejb-ref-name>ejb/Address</ejb-ref-name>
63                    <jndi-name>ejb/Address</jndi-name>
64                 </ejb-reference-description>
65
66          </reference-descriptor>
67
68          <!-- assigns JNDI name to EJB -->
69          <jndi-name>ejb/Customer</jndi-name>
70
71    </weblogic-enterprise-bean> <!-- end customer descriptor -->
72
73    <!-- Sequence factory EJB weblogic descriptor -->
74    <weblogic-enterprise-bean>
75
76          <ejb-name>SequenceFactory</ejb-name>
77                        -
78          <!-- manages beans caching behavior -->
79          <caching-descriptor>
80             <max-beans-in-cache>100</max-beans-in-cache>
81             <idle-timeout-seconds>20</idle-timeout-seconds>
82             <cache-strategy>Read-Write</cache-strategy>
83             <read-timeout-seconds>0</read-timeout-seconds>
84          </caching-descriptor>
85
86          <!-- map bean to CMP descriptor -->
87          <persistence-descriptor>
88             <persistence-type>
89                <type-identifier>
90                   WebLogic_CMP_RDBMS
91                </type-identifier>
92                <type-version>5.1.0</type-version>
93                <type-storage>
94                   META-INF/weblogic-cmp-rdbms-jar-Sequence.xml
95                </type-storage>
96             </persistence-type>
97
98             <persistence-use>
99                <type-identifier>
100                   WebLogic_CMP_RDBMS
101                </type-identifier>
102                <type-version>5.1.0</type-version>
103             </persistence-use>
104          </persistence-descriptor>
105
106          <!-- transaction management properties -->
107          <transaction-descriptor>
108             <trans-timeout-seconds>200</trans-timeout-seconds>
109          </transaction-descriptor>
110
111          <!-- assigns JNDI name to bean -->
112          <jndi-name>ejb/SequenceFactory</jndi-name>
```

Fig. 21.4   Weblogic-ejb-jar.xml defines WebLogic deployment properties for Bookstore case study (part 3 of 8).

```
113
114    </weblogic-enterprise-bean>
115    <!-- end SequenceFactory descriptor -->
116
117    <!-- Order EJB weblogic descriptor -->
118    <weblogic-enterprise-bean>
119       <ejb-name>Order</ejb-name>
120
121       <!-- defines caching properties, set to defaults -->
122       <caching-descriptor>
123          <max-beans-in-cache>100</max-beans-in-cache>
124          <idle-timeout-seconds>20</idle-timeout-seconds>
125          <cache-strategy>Read-Write</cache-strategy>
126          <read-timeout-seconds>0</read-timeout-seconds>
127       </caching-descriptor>
128
129       <!-- maps bean to specific CMP descriptor -->
130       <persistence-descriptor>
131          <persistence-type>
132             <type-identifier>
133                WebLogic_CMP_RDBMS
134             </type-identifier>
135             <type-version>5.1.0</type-version>
136             <type-storage>
137                META-INF/weblogic-cmp-rdbms-jar-order.xml
138             </type-storage>
139          </persistence-type>
140
141          <persistence-use>
142             <type-identifier>
143                WebLogic_CMP_RDBMS
144             </type-identifier>
145             <type-version>5.1.0</type-version>
146          </persistence-use>
147       </persistence-descriptor>
148
149       <!-- defines transaction attributes -->
150       <transaction-descriptor>
151          <trans-timeout-seconds>200</trans-timeout-seconds>
152       </transaction-descriptor>
153
154       <!-- maps bean references to JNDI names -->
155       <reference-descriptor>
156          <ejb-reference-description>
157             <ejb-ref-name>ejb/SequenceFactory</ejb-ref-name>
158             <jndi-name>ejb/SequenceFactory</jndi-name>
159          </ejb-reference-description>
160
161
162          <ejb-reference-description>
163             <ejb-ref-name>ejb/OrderProduct</ejb-ref-name>
164             <jndi-name>ejb/OrderProduct</jndi-name>
```

Fig. 21.4 **Weblogic-ejb-jar.xml** defines WebLogic deployment properties for Bookstore case study (part 4 of 8).

```
165              </ejb-reference-description>
166
167          <ejb-reference-description>
168              <ejb-ref-name>ejb/Customer</ejb-ref-name>
169              <jndi-name>ejb/Customer</jndi-name>
170          </ejb-reference-description>
171
172      </reference-descriptor>
173      <jndi-name>ejb/Order</jndi-name>
174
175  </weblogic-enterprise-bean> <!-- end Order descriptor -->
176
177  <!-- Address EJB weblogic deployment descriptor -->
178  <weblogic-enterprise-bean>
179      <ejb-name>Address</ejb-name>
180
181      <!-- defines caching properties for bean -->
182      <caching-descriptor>
183          <max-beans-in-cache>100</max-beans-in-cache>
184          <idle-timeout-seconds>20</idle-timeout-seconds>
185          <cache-strategy>Read-Write</cache-strategy>
186          <read-timeout-seconds>0</read-timeout-seconds>
187      </caching-descriptor>
188
189      <!-- maps EJB to specific cmp descriptor -->
190      <persistence-descriptor>
191          <persistence-type>
192              <type-identifier>
193                  WebLogic_CMP_RDBMS
194              </type-identifier>
195              <type-version>5.1.0</type-version>
196              <type-storage>
197                  META-INF/weblogic-cmp-rdbms-jar-address.xml
198              </type-storage>
199          </persistence-type>
200
201          <persistence-use>
202              <type-identifier>
203                  WebLogic_CMP_RDBMS
204              </type-identifier>
205              <type-version>5.1.0</type-version>
206          </persistence-use>
207      </persistence-descriptor>
208
209      <!-- defines transaction properties -->
210      <transaction-descriptor>
211          <trans-timeout-seconds>200</trans-timeout-seconds>
212      </transaction-descriptor>
213
214      <!-- maps referenced to JNDI names of beans -->
215      <reference-descriptor>
216          <ejb-reference-description>
```

Fig. 21.4   Weblogic-ejb-jar.xml defines WebLogic deployment properties for Bookstore case study (part 5 of 8).

```
217              <ejb-ref-name>ejb/SequenceFactory</ejb-ref-name>
218              <jndi-name>ejb/SequenceFactory</jndi-name>
219           </ejb-reference-description>
220        </reference-descriptor>
221
222        <!-- assigns JNDI name to this bean -->
223        <jndi-name>ejb/Address</jndi-name>
224
225     </weblogic-enterprise-bean> <!-- end Address descriptor -->
226
227     <!-- OrderProduct EJB weblogic deployment descriptor -->
228     <weblogic-enterprise-bean>
229        <ejb-name>OrderProduct</ejb-name>
230
231        <!-- sets default caching properties -->
232        <caching-descriptor>
233           <max-beans-in-cache>100</max-beans-in-cache>
234           <idle-timeout-seconds>20</idle-timeout-seconds>
235           <cache-strategy>Read-Write</cache-strategy>
236           <read-timeout-seconds>0</read-timeout-seconds>
237        </caching-descriptor>
238
239        <!-- maps this bean to specific cmp descriptor -->
240        <persistence-descriptor>
241           <persistence-type>
242              <type-identifier>
243                 WebLogic_CMP_RDBMS
244              </type-identifier>
245              <type-version>5.1.0</type-version>
246              <type-storage>
247                 META-INF/weblogic-cmp-rdbms-jar-orderProduct.xml
248              </type-storage>
249           </persistence-type>
250
251           <persistence-use>
252              <type-identifier>
253                 WebLogic_CMP_RDBMS
254              </type-identifier>
255              <type-version>5.1.0</type-version>
256           </persistence-use>
257        </persistence-descriptor>
258
259        <!-- maps references to JNDI names of beans -->
260        <reference-descriptor>
261           <ejb-reference-description>
262              <ejb-ref-name>ejb/Product</ejb-ref-name>
263              <jndi-name>ejb/Product</jndi-name>
264           </ejb-reference-description>
265        </reference-descriptor>
266
267        <!-- assigns JNDI name of this bean -->
268        <jndi-name>ejb/OrderProduct</jndi-name>
```

Fig. 21.4 Weblogic-ejb-jar.xml defines WebLogic deployment properties
for Bookstore case study (part 6 of 8).

```
269
270      </weblogic-enterprise-bean>
271      <!-- end OrderProduct Descriptor -->
272
273      <!-- Product EJB weblogic deployment descriptor -->
274      <weblogic-enterprise-bean>
275         <ejb-name>Product</ejb-name>
276
277         <!-- defines caching properties for EJB -->
278         <caching-descriptor>
279            <idle-timeout-seconds>20</idle-timeout-seconds>
280            <cache-strategy>Read-Write</cache-strategy>
281            <read-timeout-seconds>0</read-timeout-seconds>
282         </caching-descriptor>
283
284         <!-- maps this bean to its CMP descriptor -->
285         <persistence-descriptor>
286            <persistence-type>
287               <type-identifier>
288                  WebLogic_CMP_RDBMS
289               </type-identifier>
290               <type-version>5.1.0</type-version>
291               <type-storage>
292                  META-INF/weblogic-cmp-rdbms-jar-product.xml
293               </type-storage>
294            </persistence-type>
295
296            <persistence-use>
297               <type-identifier>
298                  WebLogic_CMP_RDBMS
299               </type-identifier>
300               <type-version>5.1.0</type-version>
301            </persistence-use>
302         </persistence-descriptor>
303
304         <!-- defines transaction properties -->
305         <transaction-descriptor>
306            <trans-timeout-seconds>200</trans-timeout-seconds>
307         </transaction-descriptor>
308
309         <!-- assigns JNDI name -->
310         <jndi-name>ejb/Product</jndi-name>
311
312      </weblogic-enterprise-bean> <!-- end Product descriptor -->
313
314      <!-- ShoppingCart EJB weblogic deployment descriptor -->
315      <weblogic-enterprise-bean>
316         <ejb-name>ShoppingCart</ejb-name>
317
318         <!-- defines chaching properties, set to defaults -->
319         <caching-descriptor>
320            <max-beans-in-cache>100</max-beans-in-cache>
```

Fig. 21.4   `Weblogic-ejb-jar.xml` defines WebLogic deployment properties for Bookstore case study (part 7 of 8).

```
321          <idle-timeout-seconds>20</idle-timeout-seconds>
322          <cache-strategy>Read-Write</cache-strategy>
323          <read-timeout-seconds>0</read-timeout-seconds>
324       </caching-descriptor>
325
326       <!-- assigns a store directory for bean -->
327       <persistence-descriptor>
328          <stateful-session-persistent-store-dir>
329             /config/deitel/
330          </stateful-session-persistent-store-dir>
331       </persistence-descriptor>
332
333       <!-- defines transaction attributes -->
334       <transaction-descriptor>
335          <trans-timeout-seconds>200</trans-timeout-seconds>
336       </transaction-descriptor>
337
338       <!-- maps EJB references to JNDI names -->
339       <reference-descriptor>
340
341          <ejb-reference-description>
342             <ejb-ref-name>ejb/Product</ejb-ref-name>
343             <jndi-name>ejb/Product</jndi-name>
344          </ejb-reference-description>
345
346          <ejb-reference-description>
347             <ejb-ref-name>ejb/Order</ejb-ref-name>
348             <jndi-name>ejb/Order</jndi-name>
349          </ejb-reference-description>
350
351       </reference-descriptor>
352       <jndi-name>ejb/ShoppingCart</jndi-name>
353
354    </weblogic-enterprise-bean> <!-- end ShoppingCart descriptor -->
355
356 </weblogic-ejb-jar> <!-- end weblogic descriptor -->
```

Fig. 21.4   Weblogic-ejb-jar.xml defines WebLogic deployment properties for Bookstore case study (part 8 of 8).

Element **persistence-descriptor** (Lines 24–42) defines the EJBs persistence properties. The **Customer** bean uses container-managed persistence (CMP). WebLogic requires each CMP bean to have its own separate XML descriptor, thus the persistence block in this code simply identifies the name and type of persistence-management descriptor. Element **persistence-type** (lines 26–34) contains the elements **type-identifier** (line 27–29), which must be **WebLogic_CMP_RDBMS**. Element **type-version** is 5.1.0 for EJB 1.1 and 6.0 for EJB 1.2. The version number must correspond to the **weblogic-ejb-jar** DTD. Element **type-storage** (lines 31–33) specifies the location of the CMP descriptor, a file we will create next. You may define multiple **persistence-type**s, in the next block, **persistence-use** you choose which **persistence-type** to use. Lines 36–41 tell WebLogic to use the persistence given in the previous element. Currently, element **transaction-descriptor** contains only a single option—**trans-timeout-seconds** (Line 46). If a transaction lasts longer than the specified length, it will be rolled back. Element **reference-descriptor** (lines 50–66) maps each reference to the correct JNDI name. Each block contains **ejb-ref-name** and **jndi-name** elements for resolving references to other EJBs.

The descriptors for each of the other entity EJBs follow the same format as the descriptor for **Customer**. The only differences are the reference to the RDBMS persistence descriptor file and each bean's EJB references.

Stateful session EJB **ShoppingCart** (lines 315–354) requires slightly different deployment information. Stateful session beans do not require a RDBMS persistence descriptor file. Instead they simply require a location in which to store persistent sessions and a directory location in which to store passivated sessions. Element **stateful-session-persistent-store-dir** within element **persistence-descriptor** defines where the container should store passivated sessions.[4]

Figure 21.5 lists some optional elements in **weblogic-ejb-jar.xml**. For a full listing, please consult **edocs.bea.com**. If an element is not defined, WebLogic uses its default value.

The RDBMS descriptor specifies the interactions of an entity EJB with the database. The descriptor specifies a connection pool and table name, maps EJB fields to database fields, and defines custom finders for home interface methods.

Parent Element	Element	Description
caching-descriptor	max-beans-in-free-pool	Valid for stateless session EJBs, defines the maximum number of free beans to keep in the pool. The default is no limit.
caching-descriptor	initial-beans-in-free-pool	Valid for stateless session EJBs, defines the number of initial bean instances. The default is 0.
persistence-descriptor	is-modified-method-name	Method name to be called when EJB is stored, method must return a boolean value. If method returns **true** EJB is saved.

Fig. 21.5   Optional tags for **weblogic-ejb-jar.xml** not used in text (part 1 of 3).

Parent Element	Element	Description
`persistence-descriptor`	`delay-updates-until-end-of-tx`	When set to **false**, the beans database table is updated after every method. If **true** database is updated at the end of the transaction. The default is **true**.
`persistence-descriptor`	`finders-call-ejbload`	Valid for entity beans, the value **true** specifies that bean is loaded after it is first referenced with a *finder* method. Value **false** specifies that the bean is loaded when first invoked. The default is **false**.
`persistence-descriptor`	`db-is-shared`	Valid for entity beans, For value **false** bean assumes it has exclusive access to database and does not reload data. For value **true** data is reloaded before each transaction. The default is **true**.
`reference-descriptor`	`resource-descriptor`	Contains description of resource factories referenced in `ejb-jar.xml`
`resource-descriptor`	`res-ref-name`	Resource reference name found in `ejb-jar.xml`
`resource-descriptor`	`jndi-name`	Assigns a JNDI name for resource factory

Fig. 21.5   Optional tags for **weblogic-ejb-jar.xml** not used in text (part 2 of 3).

Parent Element	Element	Description
`security-role-assignment`	`role-name`	Security role name defined in ejb-jar.xml
`security-role-assignment`	`principal-name`	Maps the role name to a principal defined in WebLogic. Consult **edocs.bea.com** for valid principal names.
`weblogic-enterprise-bean`	`enable-call-by-reference`	When EJBs are on the same server arguments are passed by reference, setting this value to **false** will cause variables to be passed by value.

Fig. 21.5   Optional tags for **weblogic-ejb-jar.xml** not used in text (part 3 of 3).

Descriptor **weblogic-cmp-rdbms-jar-address.xml** (Fig. 21.6) follows the WebLogic version 5.1 DTD. Element **weblogic-rdbms-bean** (line 11) is the base element for the descriptor, there may be only one **webLogic-rdbms-bean** element per file. Element **pool-name** on line 14 must contain the name for a data pool already defined in WebLogic. The value of **table-name** must correspond to the table within the datasource that this bean uses. In our case study, EJB **Address** writes to table **Address** (line 17). Element **attribute-map** contains the mappings between EJB fields and database fields defined in **ejb-jar.xml**. In our example the database field names are the same as the EJB field names, but this is not required. Defining mappings within a deployment descriptor allows deployers to customize EJBs to particular databases without changing any EJB code. Element **object-link** (line 21–24) contains the mappings between the EJB fields and database fields for **zipCode**. The bean field and database field names are specified within **bean-field** and **dbms-column**, respectively.

```
1    <?xml version = "1.0" encoding = "UTF-8" ?>
2
3    <!-- weblogic-cmp-rdbms-jar-address.xml rdbms deployment    -->
4    <!-- descriptor for EJB Address. Defines database properties -->
5
```

Fig. 21.6   Weblogic-cmp-rdbms-jar-address.xml defines WebLogic CMP database properties for EJB **Address** (part 1 of 3).

```
 6   <!DOCTYPE weblogic-rdbms-bean PUBLIC
 7      '-//BEA Systems, Inc.//DTD WebLogic 5.1.0 EJB RDBMS Persistence/
/EN'
 8       'http://www.bea.com/servers/wls510/dtd/weblogic-rdbms-persis-
tence.dtd'>
 9
10   <!-- main block for rdbms descriptor -->
11   <weblogic-rdbms-bean>
12
13        <!-- Sets data pool to BookstorePool -->
14        <pool-name>BookstorePool</pool-name>
15
16        <!-- Sets database table to ADDRESS -->
17        <table-name>Address</table-name>
18
19        <!-- maps EJB fields to database fields -->
20        <attribute-map>
21           <object-link>
22              <bean-field>zipCode</bean-field>
23              <dbms-column>zipCode</dbms-column>
24           </object-link>
25
26           <object-link>
27              <bean-field>state</bean-field>
28              <dbms-column>state</dbms-column>
29           </object-link>
30
31           <object-link>
32              <bean-field>addressID</bean-field>
33              <dbms-column>addressID</dbms-column>
34           </object-link>
35
36           <object-link>
37              <bean-field>streetAddressLine2</bean-field>
38              <dbms-column>streetAddressLine2</dbms-column>
39           </object-link>
40
41           <object-link>
42              <bean-field>country</bean-field>
43              <dbms-column>country</dbms-column>
44           </object-link>
45
46           <object-link>
47              <bean-field>streetAddressLine1</bean-field>
48              <dbms-column>streetAddressLine1</dbms-column>
49           </object-link>
50
51           <object-link>
52              <bean-field>city</bean-field>
53              <dbms-column>city</dbms-column>
54           </object-link>
55
```

Fig. 21.6 `Weblogic-cmp-rdbms-jar-address.xml` defines WebLogic CMP database properties for EJB **Address** (part 2 of 3).

```
56            <object-link>
57                <bean-field>firstName</bean-field>
58                <dbms-column>firstName</dbms-column>
59            </object-link>
60
61            <object-link>
62                <bean-field>lastName</bean-field>
63                <dbms-column>lastName</dbms-column>
64            </object-link>
65
66            <object-link>
67                <bean-field>phoneNumber</bean-field>
68                <dbms-column>phoneNumber</dbms-column>
69            </object-link>
70          </attribute-map>
71
72     <options>
73       <use-quoted-names>false</use-quoted-names>
74     </options>
75
76  </weblogic-rdbms-bean> <!-- end Address RDBMS descriptor -->
```

Fig. 21.6 **Weblogic-cmp-rdbms-jar-address.xml** defines WebLogic CMP database properties for EJB **Address** (part 3 of 3).

WebLogic XML descriptor **weblogic-cmp-rdbms-jar-Customer.xml** (Fig. 21.7) is the database deployment descriptor for the **Customer** EJB. The database descriptors closely mirror each other in terms of structure. For each EJB you must provide field mappings, the database table name and custom queries for finder methods.

```
1   <?xml version = "1.0" encoding = "UTF-8"?>
2
3   <!-- weblogic-cmp-rdbms-jar-Customer.xml ejb descriptor for  -->
4   <!-- CustomerEJB defines rdbms properties for WebLogic -->
5
6   <!DOCTYPE weblogic-rdbms-bean PUBLIC
7       '-//BEA Systems, Inc.//DTD WebLogic 5.1.0 EJB RDBMS Persistence/
/EN'
8       'http://www.bea.com/servers/wls510/dtd/weblogic-rdbms-persis-
tence.dtd'>
9
10  <!-- element containing rdbms properties for Customer EJB -->
11  <weblogic-rdbms-bean>
12
13    <!-- assigns this bean to pool named BookstorePool -->
14    <pool-name>BookstorePool</pool-name>
15
16    <!-- assigns this bean to table named CUSTOMER -->
17    <table-name>Customer</table-name>
18
```

Fig. 21.7 **WebLogic-cmp-rdbms-jar-Customer.xml** defines WebLogic CMP database properties for EJB **CustomerEJB** (part 1 of 4).

```
19      <!-- element containing field mappings -->
20      <attribute-map>
21
22         <!-- field mapping for customerID -->
23         <object-link>
24            <bean-field>customerID</bean-field>
25            <dbms-column>customerID</dbms-column>
26         </object-link>
27
28         <!-- field mapping for creditCardExpirationDate -->
29         <object-link>
30            <bean-field>creditCardExpirationDate</bean-field>
31            <dbms-column>creditCardExpirationDate</dbms-column>
32         </object-link>
33
34         <!-- field mapping for shippingAddressID -->
35         <object-link>
36            <bean-field>shippingAddressID</bean-field>
37            <dbms-column>shippingAddressID</dbms-column>
38         </object-link>
39
40         <!-- field mapping for billingAddressID -->
41         <object-link>
42            <bean-field>billingAddressID</bean-field>
43            <dbms-column>billingAddressID</dbms-column>
44         </object-link>
45
46         <!-- field mapping for passwordHint -->
47         <object-link>
48            <bean-field>passwordHint</bean-field>
49            <dbms-column>passwordHint</dbms-column>
50         </object-link>
51
52         <!-- field mapping for creditCardName -->
53         <object-link>
54            <bean-field>creditCardName</bean-field>
55            <dbms-column>creditCardName</dbms-column>
56         </object-link>
57
58         <!-- field mapping for firstName -->
59         <object-link>
60            <bean-field>firstName</bean-field>
61            <dbms-column>firstName</dbms-column>
62         </object-link>
63
64         <!-- field mapping for password -->
65         <object-link>
66            <bean-field>password</bean-field>
67            <dbms-column>password</dbms-column>
68         </object-link>
69
```

Fig. 21.7 `WebLogic-cmp-rdbms-jar-Customer.xml` defines WebLogic CMP database properties for EJB `CustomerEJB` (part 2 of 4).

```
70          <!-- field mapping for lastName -->
71          <object-link>
72              <bean-field>lastName</bean-field>
73              <dbms-column>lastName</dbms-column>
74          </object-link>
75
76          <!-- field mapping for userID -->
77          <object-link>
78              <bean-field>userID</bean-field>
79              <dbms-column>userID</dbms-column>
80          </object-link>
81
82          <!-- field mapping for creditCardNumber -->
83          <object-link>
84              <bean-field>creditCardNumber</bean-field>
85              <dbms-column>creditCardNumber</dbms-column>
86          </object-link>
87
88      </attribute-map>
89
90      <!-- list of custom finders -->
91      <finder-list>
92
93          <!-- finder for findByUserID -->
94          <finder>
95              <method-name>findByUserID</method-name>
96              <method-params>
97                  <method-param>java.lang.String</method-param>
98              </method-params>
99
100             <!-- get fields where userID matches argument string -->
101             <finder-query>
102                 <![CDATA[( like userID $0 )]]>
103             </finder-query>
104         </finder>
105
106         <!-- finder for findByLogin -->
107         <finder>
108             <method-name>findByLogin</method-name>
109             <method-params>
110                 <method-param>java.lang.String</method-param>
111                 <method-param>java.lang.String</method-param>
112             </method-params>
113
114             <!-- fields where userID and password match arguments -->
115             <finder-query>
116                 <![CDATA[(& ( like userID $0 )( like password $1 ))]]>
117             </finder-query>
118         </finder>
119
120     </finder-list>
121
```

Fig. 21.7 `WebLogic-cmp-rdbms-jar-Customer.xml` defines WebLogic CMP database properties for EJB **CustomerEJB** (part 3 of 4).

```
122     <!-- additional options -->
123     <options>
124      <use-quoted-names>false</use-quoted-names>
125     </options>
126
127  </weblogic-rdbms-bean>
128  <!-- end rdbms descriptor for CustomerEJB -->
```

Fig. 21.7   `WebLogic-cmp-rdbms-jar-Customer.xml` defines WebLogic
CMP database properties for EJB **CustomerEJB** (part 4 of 4).

Element **finder-list** (lines 91–120) contains *finder* methods for the customer
EJB. WebLogic requires a **finder** element for each customer *finder* method in the home
interface. You must define the *finder* name, parameters, and the query to use. The value of
element **method-name** (line 95) is a string that matches a *finder* method defined in the
home interface. Element **method-params** (lines 96–98) contains element **method-
param** (line 97), which specifies the fully qualified type of any passed parameters (e.g.
java.lang.String). The **finder-query** is a query written in WebLogic Query
Language (WQL). Be sure to place WQL expressions in **CDATA** sections to escape special
characters.

Figure 21.8 lists operators and syntax examples in WQL. The operands of the expressions may be arguments, literals, **bean-fields** within this descriptor, or other expressions. The syntax **$***n* signifies that the operator is an argument and *n* corresponds to the
order of the passed arguments, beginning at 0. Literals must always be enclosed in single
quotes.   Lines 107–118 define **findByLogin**, which takes two arguments and returns
only the fields that match both.[5]

Operator	Function	Syntax example
=	equal to	(= ID $0)
<	less than	(< price $0)
>	greater than	(> quantity $0)
<=	less than or equal	(<= operand1 operand2)
>=	greater than or equal	(>= operand1 operand2)
!	not	(! (= quantity '0'))
&	and	(& (< price $0) (> quantity $1))
|	or	(| (> quantity '0') (> onOrder $0)
like	string equal to, % indi-cates wildcard	(like '%Java%')
isNull	check for null reference	(isNull bookID)
isNotNull	check if not null	(isNotNull bookID)

Fig. 21.8   Some WebLogic Query Language operations and examples (part 1 of 2).

Operator	Function	Syntax example
orderBy	order by a column name, desc indicates descending	`( like '%Java%' orderBy 'Price' )`

Fig. 21.8   Some WebLogic Query Language operations and examples (part 2 of 2).

Figure 21.9 through Fig. 21.12 contain the remaining CMP descriptors, which each follow the same basic structure.

```
1   <?xml version = "1.0" encoding = "UTF-8"?>
2
3   <!-- weblogic-cmp-rdbms-jar-order.xml ejb descriptor for  -->
4   <!-- OrderEJB defines rdbms properties for WebLogic -->
5
6   <!DOCTYPE weblogic-rdbms-bean PUBLIC
7      '-//BEA Systems, Inc.//DTD WebLogic 5.1.0 EJB RDBMS Persistence/
/EN'
8      'http://www.bea.com/servers/wls510/dtd/weblogic-rdbms-persis-
tence.dtd'>
9
10
11  <!-- element containing rdbms properties for OrderEJB -->
12  <weblogic-rdbms-bean>
13
14     <!-- assigns this bean to pool named BookstorePool -->
15     <pool-name>BookstorePool</pool-name>
16
17
18     <!-- assigns this bean to table named CUSTOMERORDERS -->
19     <table-name>CustomerOrders</table-name>
20
21     <!-- element containing field mappings -->
22     <attribute-map>
23
24
25        <!-- field mapping for orderDate -->
26        <object-link>
27           <bean-field>orderDate</bean-field>
28           <dbms-column>orderDate</dbms-column>
29        </object-link>
30
31
32        <!-- field mapping for shipped -->
33        <object-link>
34           <bean-field>shipped</bean-field>
35           <dbms-column>shipped</dbms-column>
36        </object-link>
```

Fig. 21.9   `Weblogic-cmp-rdbms-jar-order.xml` defines WebLogic CMP database properties for EJB **OrderEJB** (part 1 of 2).

```
37
38
39          <!-- field mapping for customerID -->
40          <object-link>
41              <bean-field>customerID</bean-field>
42              <dbms-column>customerID</dbms-column>
43          </object-link>
44
45          <!-- field mapping for orderID -->
46          <object-link>
47              <bean-field>orderID</bean-field>
48              <dbms-column>orderID</dbms-column>
49          </object-link>
50
51      </attribute-map>
52
53      <finder-list>
54
55          <!-- finder for findByCustomerID -->
56          <finder>
57              <method-name>findByCustomerID</method-name>
58              <method-params>
59                  <method-param>java.lang.Integer</method-param>
60              </method-params>
61
62              <!-- return enumeration where customerID = argument -->
63              <finder-query>
64                  <![CDATA[( = customerID $0 )]]>
65              </finder-query>
66          </finder>
67
68      </finder-list>
69
70      <!-- additional options -->
71      <options>
72       <use-quoted-names>false</use-quoted-names>
73      </options>
74
75  </weblogic-rdbms-bean>
76  <!-- end rdbms descriptor for OrderEJB -->
```

Fig. 21.9 `Weblogic-cmp-rdbms-jar-order.xml` defines WebLogic CMP database properties for EJB **OrderEJB** (part 2 of 2).

```
1   <?xml version = "1.0" encoding = "UTF-8"?>
2
3   <!-- weblogic-cmp-rdbms-jar-orderProduct.xml ejb descriptor for -->
4   <!-- OrderProductEJB defines rdbms properties for WebLogic -->
5
```

Fig. 21.10 `Weblogic-cmp-rdbms-jar-orderProduct.xml` defines WebLogic CMP database properties for the **OrderProduct** EJB (part 1 of 3).

```
 6   <!DOCTYPE weblogic-rdbms-bean PUBLIC
 7      '-//BEA Systems, Inc.//DTD WebLogic 5.1.0 EJB RDBMS Persistence/
/EN'
 8         'http://www.bea.com/servers/wls510/dtd/weblogic-rdbms-persis-
tence.dtd'>
 9
10   <!-- element containing rdbms properties for OrderProductsEJB -->
11   <weblogic-rdbms-bean>
12
13      <!-- assigns this bean to pool named BookstorePool -->
14      <pool-name>BookstorePool</pool-name>
15
16      <!-- assigns this bean to table named ORDERPRODUCT -->
17      <table-name>OrderProduct</table-name>
18
19      <!-- element containing field mappings -->
20      <attribute-map>
21
22         <!-- field mapping for quantity -->
23         <object-link>
24            <bean-field>quantity</bean-field>
25            <dbms-column>quantity</dbms-column>
26         </object-link>
27
28         <!-- field mapping for ISBN -->
29         <object-link>
30            <bean-field>ISBN</bean-field>
31            <dbms-column>ISBN</dbms-column>
32         </object-link>
33
34         <!-- field mapping for orderID -->
35         <object-link>
36            <bean-field>orderID</bean-field>
37            <dbms-column>orderID</dbms-column>
38         </object-link>
39
40      </attribute-map>
41
42
43      <finder-list>
44
45        <!-- finder for findByOrderID -->
46        <finder>
47            <method-name>findByOrderID</method-name>
48            <method-params>
49               <method-param>java.lang.Integer</method-param>
50            </method-params>
51
52            <!-- select fields where orderID matches argument -->
53            <finder-query>
54                <![CDATA[( like orderID $0 )]]>
```

Fig. 21.10 `Weblogic-cmp-rdbms-jar-orderProduct.xml` defines
WebLogic CMP database properties for the **OrderProduct** EJB
(part 2 of 3).

```
55              </finder-query>
56          </finder>
57
58      </finder-list>
59
60      <!-- additional options -->
61      <options>
62       <use-quoted-names>false</use-quoted-names>
63      </options>
64
65  </weblogic-rdbms-bean> <!-- end OrderProduct Descriptor -->
```

Fig. 21.10 `Weblogic-cmp-rdbms-jar-orderProduct.xml` defines WebLogic CMP database properties for the **OrderProduct** EJB (part 3 of 3).

```
1   <?xml version = "1.0" encoding = "UTF-8"?>
2
3   <!-- weblogic-cmp-rdbms-jar-product.xml ejb descriptor for  -->
4   <!-- ProductEJB defines rdbms properties for WebLogic -->
5
6   <!DOCTYPE weblogic-rdbms-bean PUBLIC
7       '-//BEA Systems, Inc.//DTD WebLogic 5.1.0 EJB RDBMS Persistence/
/EN'
8       'http://www.bea.com/servers/wls510/dtd/weblogic-rdbms-persis-
tence.dtd'>
9
10  <!-- element containing rdbms properties for ProductEJB -->
11  <weblogic-rdbms-bean>
12
13      <!-- assigns this bean to pool named BookstorePool -->
14      <pool-name>BookstorePool</pool-name>
15
16      <!-- assigns this bean to table named PRODUCT -->
17      <table-name>Product</table-name>
18
19      <!-- element containing field mappings -->
20      <attribute-map>
21
22          <!-- field mapping for pages -->
23          <object-link>
24              <bean-field>pages</bean-field>
25              <dbms-column>pages</dbms-column>
26          </object-link>
27
28          <!-- field mapping for author -->
29          <object-link>
30              <bean-field>author</bean-field>
31              <dbms-column>author</dbms-column>
32          </object-link>
```

Fig. 21.11 `weblogic-cmp-rdbms-jar-product.xml` defines WebLogic CMP database properties for the **Product** EJB (part 1 of 3).

```
33
34          <!-- field mapping for publisher -->
35          <object-link>
36             <bean-field>publisher</bean-field>
37             <dbms-column>publisher</dbms-column>
38          </object-link>
39
40          <!-- field mapping for price -->
41          <object-link>
42             <bean-field>price</bean-field>
43             <dbms-column>price</dbms-column>
44          </object-link>
45
46          <!-- field mapping for image -->
47          <object-link>
48             <bean-field>image</bean-field>
49             <dbms-column>image</dbms-column>
50          </object-link>
51
52          <!-- field mapping for ISBN -->
53          <object-link>
54             <bean-field>ISBN</bean-field>
55             <dbms-column>ISBN</dbms-column>
56          </object-link>
57
58          <!-- field mapping for title -->
59          <object-link>
60             <bean-field>title</bean-field>
61             <dbms-column>title</dbms-column>
62          </object-link>
63
64       </attribute-map>
65
66       <finder-list>
67
68          <!-- finder for findAllProducts -->
69          <finder>
70             <method-name>findAllProducts</method-name>
71
72             <!-- select fields where ISBN is not null -->
73             <finder-query>
74                <![CDATA[( isNotNull ISBN )]]>
75             </finder-query>
76          </finder>
77
78          <!-- finder for findByTitle -->
79          <finder>
80             <method-name>findByTitle</method-name>
81             <method-params>
82                <method-param>java.lang.String</method-param>
83             </method-params>
84
```

Fig. 21.11 `weblogic-cmp-rdbms-jar-product.xml` defines WebLogic CMP database properties for the **Product** EJB (part 2 of 3).

```
85              <!-- select fields that title matches argument -->
86              <finder-query>
87                  <![CDATA[( like title $0 )]]>
88              </finder-query>
89          </finder>
90
91      </finder-list>
92
93
94      <!-- additional options -->
95      <options>
96          <use-quoted-names>false</use-quoted-names>
97      </options>
98
99  </weblogic-rdbms-bean> <!-- end ProductEJB Descriptor -->
```

Fig. 21.11 `weblogic-cmp-rdbms-jar-product.xml` defines WebLogic CMP database properties for the **Product** EJB (part 3 of 3).

```
1   <?xml version = "1.0" encoding = "UTF-8"?>
2
3   <!-- weblogic-cmp-rdbms-jar-sequence.xml ejb descriptor for -->
4   <!-- SequenceFactory defines rdbms properties for WebLogic -->
5
6   <!DOCTYPE weblogic-rdbms-bean PUBLIC
7       '-//BEA Systems, Inc.//DTD WebLogic 5.1.0 EJB RDBMS Persistence/
/EN'
8       'http://www.bea.com/servers/wls510/dtd/weblogic-rdbms-persis-
tence.dtd'>
9
10  <!-- element containing rdbms properties for SequenceFactoryEJB -->
11  <weblogic-rdbms-bean>
12
13      <!-- assigns this bean to pool named BookstorePool -->
14      <pool-name>BookstorePool</pool-name>
15
16      <!-- assigns this bean to table SEQUENCEFACTORY -->
17      <table-name>SequenceFactory</table-name>
18
19      <!-- element containing field mappings -->
20      <attribute-map>
21
22          <!-- field mapping for addressID -->
23          <object-link>
24              <bean-field>tableName</bean-field>
25              <dbms-column>tableName</dbms-column>
26          </object-link>
27
```

Fig. 21.12 `Weblogic-cmp-rdbms-jar-sequence.xml` defines WebLogic CMP database properties for the **SequenceFactory** EJB (part 1 of 2).

```
28            <!-- field mapping for primaryKey -->
29            <object-link>
30               <bean-field>nextID</bean-field>
31               <dbms-column>nextID</dbms-column>
32            </object-link>
33
34      </attribute-map>
35
36      <options>
37         <use-quoted-names>false</use-quoted-names>
38      </options>
39
40   </weblogic-rdbms-bean>
```

Fig. 21.12 `Weblogic-cmp-rdbms-jar-sequence.xml` defines WebLogic CMP database properties for the **SequenceFactory** EJB (part 2 of 2).

Finally, the EJB references in the servlets must be mapped to the JNDI names for each EJB. The deployment descriptor **weblogic.xml** in Web application directory **WEB-INF** defines these mappings. Figure 21.13 contains the mappings for the Bookstore servlets. Optional element **description** provides a simple description for the web application. Element **reference-descriptor** is the only required element for our application. This element maps references defined in **web.xml** to the JNDI names of the referenced EJBs. We have named the references the same as the JNDI names, but that is not required. Each reference description is contained within element **ejb-reference-descrip-tion**. A mapping requires the **ejb-ref-name** and **jndi-name** contained within **ejb-reference-description**. Lines 22–29 map the **ShoppingCart** EJB reference to its JNDI name.

```
 1   <?xml version = "1.0" encoding = "UTF-8"?>
 2
 3   <!-- weblogic.xml Deployment descriptor for servlets -->
 4   <!-- maps ejb references to JNDI names -->
 5
 6   <!DOCTYPE weblogic-web-app PUBLIC
 7      "-//BEA Systems, Inc.//DTD Web Application 6.0//EN"
 8      "http://www.bea.com/servers/wls600/dtd/weblogic-web-jar.dtd">
 9
10   <!-- main block for descriptor -->
11   <weblogic-web-app>
12
13      <!-- optional, provides description for war file. -->
14      <description>
15         Bookstore servlets
16      </description>
17
18      <!-- block contains ejb reference maps -->
19      <reference-descriptor>
20
```

Fig. 21.13 `Weblogic.xml` Web application deployment descriptor (part 1 of 2).

```
21        <!-- individual reference map -->
22        <ejb-reference-description>
23
24           <!-- reference name defined in web.xml -->
25           <ejb-ref-name>ejb/ShoppingCart</ejb-ref-name>
26
27           <!-- JNDI name specified within weblogic-ejb-jar.xml -->
28           <jndi-name>ejb/ShoppingCart</jndi-name>
29        </ejb-reference-description>
30
31        <!-- individual reference map -->
32        <ejb-reference-description>
33           <ejb-ref-name>ejb/Product</ejb-ref-name>
34           <jndi-name>ejb/Product</jndi-name>
35         </ejb-reference-description>
36
37        <!-- individual reference map -->
38        <ejb-reference-description>
39           <ejb-ref-name>ejb/Customer</ejb-ref-name>
40           <jndi-name>ejb/Customer</jndi-name>
41        </ejb-reference-description>
42
43        <!-- individual reference map -->
44        <ejb-reference-description>
45           <ejb-ref-name>ejb/Order</ejb-ref-name>
46           <jndi-name>ejb/Order</jndi-name>
47        </ejb-reference-description>
48
49     </reference-descriptor>
50
51  </weblogic-web-app>
52  <!-- end servlet descriptor -->
```

Fig. 21.13 Weblogic.xml Web application deployment descriptor (part 2 of 2).

This completes the deployment descriptors for our case study application; you are almost ready to deploy. Our application uses Xalan version 2.1, so prepend **xalan.jar** and **xerces.jar** to the **CLASSPATH** in **startWeblogic.cmd**. Your final **classpath** entry should be:

```
set CLASSPATH=.;c:\xalan-j_2_1_0\xerces.jar;c:\xalan-
j_2_1_0\xalan.jar;.\lib\weblogic_sp.jar;.\lib\weblogic.jar;c:
\cloudscape_3.6\lib\cloudscape.jar
```

Be sure to replace **c:\xalan-j_2_1_0** with the correct path to the Xalan JAR files. Execute **startWeblogic.cmd** and open your Web browser to **localhost:7001/bookstore** to access the bookstore.

21.5 Deploying the Deitel Bookstore on IBM WebSphere

This section presents the configuration and deployment of the Deitel Bookstore application on IBM WebSphere 4.0. Consult the WebSphere documentation for specific information on installing the application server on your system. We assume that Cloudscape is installed in **C:\cloudscape_3.6**, the WebSphere application server is installed in **c:\WebSphere\AppServer** and the IBM HTTP Server (included with installation) is installed in **c:\IBM HTTP Server**. You also must copy **xalan.jar** and **xerces.jar** to **c:\WebSphere\AppServer\lib\ext**, which ensures that our application has access to the correct XML parser and XSL transformer.

Next, run the **StartServerBasic** script from the **WebSphere\AppServer\bin** directory to launch the application server. When the server completes loading, open the URL **localhost:9090/admin** in a Web browser. You may specify any user name in the login page—the name is used to track changes, not for security. To configure the JDBC driver and data source, select **Resources > JDBC Drivers** then click the **New** button from the right pane. Enter **c:\cloudscape_3.6\lib\cloudscape.jar** for the **Server Class Path**, **Bookstore** for the **Name** and **COM.cloudscape.core.LocalConnectionPoolDataSource** for the **Implementation Class Name**. After entering these values, click **OK** and save the configuration. Expand the recently created driver (**Bookstore**) and select **Data Sources**. Click the **New** button, and fill in the fields as follows. The **Name** is **Bookstore**, the **JNDI Name** is **jdbc/Bookstore**, the **Database Name** should be the full path to the database (e.g., **c:\cloudscape_3.6\databases\bookstore**). Click **OK** and save the configuration.

Next, we must generate the deployment descriptors for WebSphere. WebSphere includes a graphical tool for creating deployment descriptors. Open the **Application Assembly Tool** by executing the assembly script in the **WebSphere/AppServer/bin** directory. When the tool loads, select the **Existing** tab from the welcome window. Then, enter the full path to **bookstore.ear**, or select browse to locate the file. Click **Open** to open the file and begin deployment configuration.

In the left pane, expand **Bookstore > EJB modules > EJBs > Session Beans > Shopping Cart**. Select EJB **ShoppingCart** and choose the **Bindings** tab from the main pane (the bottom right pane). Enter **ShoppingCart** as the **JNDI Name**. Select **EJB References** from the upper right pane. Be sure **ejb/Order** is selected and use the **Link** drop-down box to select the appropriate reference. You also must select the **Bindings** tab from the main pane and enter **Order** for the reference's **JNDI Name**. Complete the same steps to map the reference **ejb/Product** to the **Product** EJB.

Select **Bookstore > EJB Modules > EJBs > Entity Beans > Address**. Select the **Bindings** tab from the main pane and enter the **JNDI Name Address**, and set the datasource **JNDI Name jdbc/Bookstore**. Select **EJB References** from the upper pane and map **ejb/SequenceFactory** to **SequenceFactory** with **JNDI Name SequenceFactory**. Configure the EJB references for the other EJBs using the same process.

After defining the JNDI names and EJB references for the **Customer** EJB select **Method Extensions**. You must define custom *finder* queries for methods **findByUserID** and **findByLogin**. To define a custom query, select each method, check the **Finder Descriptor** box and specify the appropriate **WHERE** clause (Fig. 21.14). The **WHERE** clause option will fill in the **SELECT** and **FROM** SQL statements for you—all you must define is the **WHERE** clause. WebSphere determines the table name from the EJB name, thus to specify a different table you must rename the EJB. When deploying the Deitel

Bean	method	Where clause
Customer	findByLogin	userID = ? AND password = ?
Customer	findByUserID	userID = ?
Order	findByCustomerID	customerID = ?
OrderProduct	findByOrderID	orderID = ?
Product	findAllProducts	1 = 1
Product	findByTitle	title like ?

Fig. 21.14 WHERE clauses for bookstore finder methods.

Bookstore be sure to select the **Order** EJB and change the EJB name to **Customer-Orders**, which is the table for storing order information.

To configure the servlets in WebSphere you must select **Bookstore > Web Modules > Servlets > EJB references** and map each reference as you did for each EJB. After you map the references you can generate the code for deployment. Select the **File** menu and **Generate code for deployment**. Specify the **Deployed module location** text field to the path in which to save the deployed EAR. Enter the path to **xalan.jar** and **xerces.jar** in the **Dependent Classpath** field. The **Database type** is **Generic/SQL-92**, **Database Name** is **jdbc/Bookstore** and **Schema** is **APP**. Fill in these values then select the **Generate Now** button.

You may now deploy the application in the administration tool Web page (**local-host:9090/admin**). In the left pane, select **Nodes > Computer Name > Enterprise Applications**. Click the **Install** button then use the **Browse** button to locate the deployed EAR file (e.g., **Deployed_Bookstore.ear**) and click **Next**. The following page shows the JNDI name mapping—be sure to double check each value then select **Next**. The following page shows each EJB reference. The following page verifies the database mappings. Each field must contain the value **jdbc/Bookstore**. The **Database type** must be **Generic/SQL-92** and the **Schema** name is **APP**. The next page defines the servlet mapping to **default_host**. In the following page, uncheck the option to redeploy the application. Click **Next**, confirm the values and click **Finish** to deploy. After the application is deployed, click the link at the top of the page to regenerate the Web server plug-in configuration. Save the configuration and restart the server by running the **stopServer** script followed by the **startServerBasic** script. Finally, open the URL **localhost/bookstore** to browse the Deitel Bookstore.

21.6 Internet and World Wide Web Resources

serverwatch.internet.com/appservers.html
Application server news site, also includes reviews and comparisons of popular application servers.

www.appserver-zone.com
The Application Server Zone Web site provides technical articles, product comparisons and other information related to application servers.

java.sun.com/j2ee
Sun's J2EE site, includes the J2EE specification, J2EE news and SDK download and support.

SUMMARY

- The Java 2 Enterprise Edition is a specification for enterprise runtime environments. Although Sun provides a reference implementation of this specification, real-world systems must use an application server from a commercial vendor.

- Sun Microsystems, along with a large community of application-server vendors, developed the Java 2 Enterprise Edition specification through the Java Community Process. J2EE defines an application server platform and supporting APIs for building enterprise applications that are portable across application servers, and, because they use Java, across platforms.

- The J2EE specification can be broken down into several pieces, including API support, security, transaction management and deployment processes. An application server vendor is required to provide runtime support for the APIs of the J2EE platform.

- To be J2EE certified, an application server must implement the minimum functionality that the J2EE specification defines. Application server vendors also can provide functionality that goes beyond the J2EE specification to differentiate their products.

- BEA provides a general-purpose application server, balancing speed with stability and solid support for various features beyond the J2EE specification, including data pools, "hot" deployment clustering, *failover* support for EJBs and Web components and *load balancing*.

- For single-server environments, WebLogic provides multi-pooling—a service that distributes transactions among data sources. Whereas a connection pool is limited to a single data source; multi-pooling allows an application to access several pools, thus distributing requests among multiple data sources.

- iPlanet E-Commerce Solutions is an alliance between Netscape Communications and Sun Microsystems. iPlanet's primary goals are speed, stability and full J2EE compliance. iPlanet provides failover support, connection pooling and several unique features.

- The Web connector controls load balancing in iPlanet application server. The Web connector manages communication between the application server and the Web server. The Web connector distributes requests among server instances based on server response time.

- iPlanet includes support for "sticky" load balancing—if a components is flagged as "sticky," then the normal load-balancing algorithm will be bypassed and the component will always be executed on the "sticky" machine.

- iPlanet uses the Lightweight Directory Access Protocol (LDAP) to manage security. Users may be assigned group and individual permissions to access parts of applications. Configuring LDAP permissions enables tight control over user permissions.

- IBM WebSphere is a popular application server that is approaching BEA's WebLogic in market share. Version 4.0 provides a simple user interface for administration and deployment, and a focus on speed and scalability. WebSphere includes IBM's version of the Apache Web server, failover support, data pooling, and user-level security controls.

- JBoss, combined with the Apache Software Foundation's Tomcat servlet container, currently is the only J2EE 1.2-compliant, open-source application server. JBoss aims to maintain compliance with future J2EE specifications. Currently, JBoss includes most features of commercial application servers.

TERMINOLOGY

Access Control List (ACL)
application server
attribute-map

BEA Weblogic
bean-field element
cache-strategy element

data pool

data source

dbms-column element

deployment descriptor

description element

ejb-name element

ejb-reference-description
    element

ejb-ref-name element

ejbStore method

failover

finder element

finder-list element

finder-query element

hot deployment

IBM WebSphere

iPlanet Application Server

J2EE specification

JBoss

jndi-name element

life cycle

load balancing

max-beans-in-cache element

method-name element

method-param element

method-params element

multi pool

object-link element

persistence-descriptor element

persistence-type element

persistence-use element

pool-name element

read-timeout-seconds element

reference-descriptor element

reference-descriptor element

stateful-session-persistent-
    store-dir element

sticky load balancing

table-name element

three-tier

transaction management

transaction-descriptor element

trans-timeout-seconds element

type-identifier element

type-storage element

type-version element

Web connector

WebLogic Query Language (WQL)

WebLogic_CMP_RDBMS element

weblogic-ejb-jar element

weblogic-enterprise-bean element

weblogic-rdbms-bean element

weblogic-web-app element

WORKS CITED

1.   Shannon B. "Java™ 2 Platform Enterprise Edition Specification, v1.2," 17 December 1999
<java.sun.com/j2ee/download.html>

2.   "BEA WebLogic Server® Datasheet," **<www.bea.com/products/weblogic/**
server/datasheet.shtml>

3.   "Frequently Asked Questions," **<www.jboss.org/faq.jsp>**.

4.   "Using WebLogic Server RDBMS Persistence," 2000 **<www.weblogic.com/docs51/**
classdocs/API_ejb/EJB_environment.html#1022233>.

5.   "**weblogic-cmp-rdbms-jar.xml** Properties," 2000   **<www.weblogic.com/**
docs51/classdocs/API_ejb/EJB_reference.html#1026608>.

22

Jini

Objectives

- To understand the Jini Technology Architecture.
- To be able to identify the major components of a Jini solution.
- To be able to implement Jini services and register those services with Jini lookup services.
- To be able to write a Jini client.
- To be able to use Jini helper classes to simplify service implementations.

The real voyage of discovery consists not in seeking new landscapes, but in having new eyes.
Marcel Proust

For, when with beauty we can virtue join,
We paint the semblance of a form divine.
Matthew Prior

...To tell your name the livelong day
To an admiring bog.
Emily Dickinson

...And summer's lease hath all too short a date.
William Shakespeare

Outline

22.1 Introduction

Many network devices provide *services* to network clients. For example, a network printer provides printing services to many clients by allowing them to share the printer. Similarly, a Web server provides a service by allowing many clients to access documents over a network. We can extend this idea of providing services beyond computer-based networks and into home-based networks. For example, when you arrive home, your car could use a wireless network to notify your home's lighting service to turn on the lights over the walkway, so you can walk into your home safely. Each service mentioned here has a well-defined interface. The network-printing service provides an interface that enables applications to print documents. A Web server provides an HTTP interface that enables Web browsers to download documents. Your home's lighting service provides an interface that enables other devices on the network to turn the lights on and off.

To use a service, a client must be able to discover that a service exists and must know the interface for interacting with the service. For example, your car must be able to discover that your home provides a lighting service and must know the service's interface to interact with the lighting service. However, the car need not know the implementation of the underlying lighting service.

Jini extends RMI (Chapter 13) to provide services, such as those mentioned above, to a network. Jini services are plug-and-play—clients can discover services on the network dynamically, transparently download classes required to use those services, then begin interacting with those services. Jini, like RMI, requires clients to know the interface of a service to use that service. However, RMI's dynamic class-downloading capability enables Jini clients to use services without installing special driver software for those services in advance. For Jini clients to discover and use Jini services, standardized interfaces for common services must be developed. Many such interfaces are under development now. For example, printer manufacturers are working on a standard interface for Jini-based printing services.

In this chapter, we introduce Jini technology to build plug-and-play, network-based services. We begin with Jini lookup services, which enable clients to discover other services on the network. We build a simple Jini service that provides information about fictitious professional seminars offered by Deitel & Associates, Inc. and we build a simple Jini client to use that service. The chapter ends with introductions to various Jini utility classes that facilitate discovering lookup services, registering Jini services and building Jini clients. After completing this chapter, you will be able to build simple Jini services and clients that interact with those services. [Note: The commands to execute the examples in this chapter often are quite long. For this reason, we provide batch files containing the commands. These batch files can be found with the examples on the CD that accompanies this book. You can modify these batch files as specified in the text, then use them to execute the programs.]

A new technology that is generating exceitement in the computing industry is peer-to-peer computing, which enables communication between computers without connecting through a centralized server. In Chapter 28, we use the Jini technology presented in this chapter as one means of implementing a peer-to-peer instant-messaging application.

22.2 Installing Jini

The basic software requirements for Jini include the Java 2 Standard Edition (J2SE) and the *Jini Technology Starter Kit*. If you are going to write commercial Jini services and want to test their compatibility with the Jini platform, you also need to download the *Jini Technology Core Platform Compatibility Kit* (Jini *TCK*).

The Jini Starter Kit has three components—the *Jini Technology Core Platform* (*JCP*), the *Jini Technology Extended Platform* (*JXP*) and the *Jini Software Kit* (*JSK*). The JCP contains the fundamental Jini interfaces and classes. The JXP provides helper utilities for implementing Jini services and clients. The JSK contains an implementation of the services specified in the JCP and the JXP. The JSK also includes a *JavaSpaces* technology implementation. We discuss JavaSpaces in Chapter 23.

Jini can be downloaded from Sun's Web site at:

www.sun.com/communitysource/jini/download.html

Downloading Jini requires a free registration. After completing the registration, download and extract **JINI-1.1-G-CS.zip**, which contains the Jini Technology Starter Kit. At the time of this writing, the latest version of Jini is 1.1.

22.3 Configuring the Jini Runtime Environment

To compile and execute Jini services and clients the JAR files **jini-core.jar**, **jini-ext.jar** and **sun-util.jar** must be included in the **CLASSPATH** environment variable. These three JAR files are in the **lib** directory of the Jini Starter Kit—they correspond to the Jini Technology Core Platform, the Jini Technology Extended Platform and the Jini Software Kit, respectively. To set the **CLASSPATH** environment variable on Windows platforms, enter

```
set CLASSPATH=C:\jini1_1\lib\jini-core.jar;C:\jini1_1\lib\
jini-ext.jar;C:\jini1_1\lib\sun-util.jar;%CLASSPATH%;.
```

in a command window. To set the **CLASSPATH** environment variable on most UNIX systems, enter

```
set CLASSPATH=/jini1_1/lib/jini-core.jar:/jini1_1/lib/
jini-ext.jar:/jini1_1/lib/sun-util.jar:$CLASSPATH:.

export CLASSPATH
```

in a command window. Note that you will need to do this in every command window from which you intend to use Jini unless you set the **CLASSPATH** permanently on your system. See your operating system's documentation for information on setting environment variables. These are the only Jini JAR files that should be in the **CLASSPATH**. Be sure not to include other JAR files from the Jini distribution. If you extracted the Jini files to a different directory, be sure to specify the appropriate directory name.

22.4 Starting the Required Services

Jini depends heavily on a number of network services at run time. Jini uses Java and RMI to provide facilities for downloading resources from the network and for moving Java objects from one JVM to another on demand. To achieve these capabilities, Jini provides various support services. The Jini distribution comes with three services that must be running correctly before executing Jini applications. The following required services must be started:

1. A Web server to enable Jini clients to download class files through RMI, so the clients can access Jini services dynamically.

2. The RMI activation daemon (**rmid**) to enable the RMI infrastructure that allows Jini clients to communicate with Jini services. The RMI activation daemon enables **Activatable** services to function properly.

3. A lookup service to maintain information about available Jini services, and to enable clients to discover and use those services.

Testing and Debugging Tip 22.1

*The Web server and **rmid** must be executing (they can be started in any order) before starting the lookup service.*

The Jini Technology Core Platform implementation includes the **StartService** GUI tool for launching required services. Before running the **StartService** tool, be sure to set the **CLASSPATH** environment variable properly as specified in Section 22.3. To start the GUI on Windows, enter the following at a command prompt:

```
java -classpath %CLASSPATH%;C:\jini1_1\lib\jini-examples.jar
    com.sun.jini.example.launcher.StartService
```

Figure 22.1 shows the **StartService** user interface. Jini provides a basic *property file* for configuring the **StartService** tool. For Windows, the property file is **jini1_1\example\launcher\jini11_win32.properties**. To load this property file, go to the **File** menu, select **Open Property File** and select the property file from the appropriate directory.

Configure the Web Server

To configure the Web server, select the **WebServer** panel. Figure 22.2 shows the values for configuring the Web server. If you install the Jini Starter Kit in a directory other than **C:\jini1_1**, be sure to enter the appropriate directory name. Note the **Port** number in Fig. 22.2, which is required in each of the later examples.

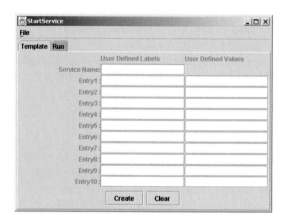

Fig. 22.1   StartService window.

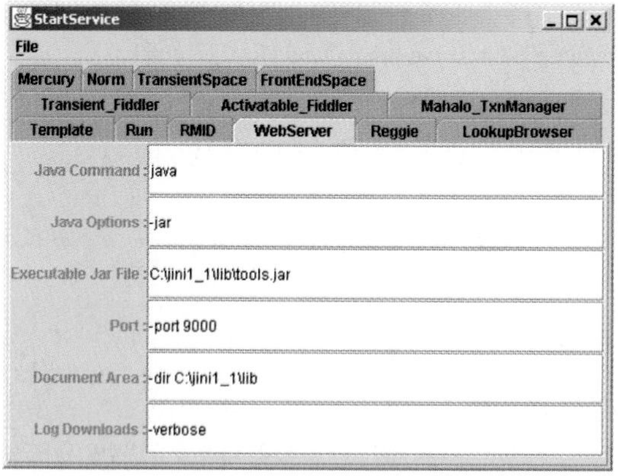

Fig. 22.2   WebServer configuration tab.

Configure the RMI Activation Daemon

To configure the RMI activation daemon (**rmid**), select the **RMID** panel. Figure 22.3 shows the default values used to configure the RMI activation daemon. If you want to use your own policy, or you want to add other options (i.e., port number or log directory), you can put all of them in the **Options** parameter. Use a single space to separate the options. Figure 22.4 shows a sample that specifies the directory in which **rmid** will write its log files.

Configure the Lookup Service

To configure the lookup service, select the **Reggie** panel. Figure 22.5 shows the configuration values. Replace *hostname* in the **Codebase** field with the name or IP address of your computer. Replace the port number (8081) with the port number you specified in the Web server's configuration (e.g., **9000**). Also, be sure to specify for **Log Directory** a directory that actually exists on your computer, or create a new directory, to avoid exceptions when running the lookup service. The **Groups** value in this example (**public**) specifies that the lookup service supports any clients on the network. You can define other values that can be used to restrict the set of clients supported by the lookup service.

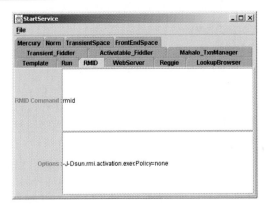

Fig. 22.3   **RMID** configuration tab.

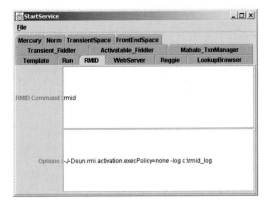

Fig. 22.4   Specifying the **RMID** log directory.

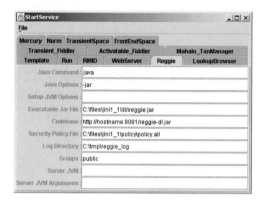

Fig. 22.5 **Reggie** lookup service configuration tab.

Common Programming Error 22.1
Specifying the local computer's name or using a `file:` *URL for the* **Codebase** *is an error. Use an* `http:` *URL with a fully qualified name or IP address.*

Common Programming Error 22.2
Starting the lookup service without creating a log directory causes exceptions at run-time. Create the log directory before starting the lookup service.

Common Programming Error 22.3
Create different log directories if you run multiple lookup service instances. Failure to do so can cause an exception that says the directory exists when trying to start a lookup service.

Starting Required Services

To run the required services, select the **Run** panel in the **StartService** window (Fig. 22.6). Click the **Start RMID** button to start the RMI activation daemon. Click the **Start WebServer** button to start the Web server. Click the **Start Reggie** button to start the lookup service. Remember to start the RMI activation daemon and the Web server before starting the lookup service.

Fig. 22.6 **Run** panel for starting and stopping Jini basic services.

22.5 Running the Jini `LookupBrowser`

After starting these services, use the Jini **LookupBrowser** to test your configuration. The following command starts the browser on Windows:

```
java -cp c:\jini1_1\lib\jini-examples.jar
    -Djava.security.policy=c:\jini1_1\example\browser\policy
    -Djava.rmi.server.codebase=http://hostname:port/
jini-examples-dl.jar
    com.sun.jini.example.browser.Browser
```

where *hostname* is the hostname running the Web server and *port* is the port number for the Web server (e.g., **9000**).

You also can start the browser via the **StartService** GUI. Select the *LookupBrowser* panel. Replace *hostname* with the name or IP address of the computer on which the Web server is running. Change the port number if you specified a different one when you started the Web server. Then go to the **Run** panel and click the *Start LookupBrowser* button. Figure 22.7 shows the **LookupBrowser** panel in the **StartService** window.

Figure 22.8 shows the result of running the **LookupBrowser** sample. This output indicates that there is one lookup service registered with **rmid**. Actually, this uses a discovery protocol to find the lookup service. If you set up two lookup services, you would see "**2 registrars, not selected**." The number of registrars found is equal to the number of lookup services. If you see "**no registrar to select**," the part of the prior configuration was performed incorrectly. In this case, check whether the lookup service started, then check that you specified the correct **Codebase** in the **Reggie** panel.

If you click the *Registrar menu*, you should see the *hostname* (or IP address) and port number on which the lookup service registered. In Fig. 22.9, the *hostname* is **DRAGONFLY**. The default port number was used, so no port number appears in this screen capture.

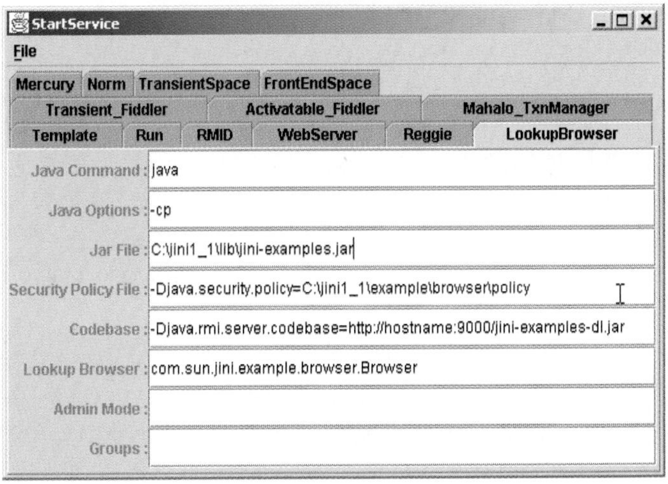

Fig. 22.7 **LookupBrowser** configuration tab.

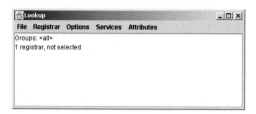

Fig. 22.8   LookupBrowser application window.

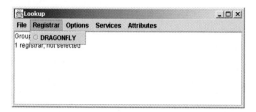

Fig. 22.9   Registrar menu for viewing computers that provide lookup services.

22.6 Discovery

The Jini lookup service is the heart of a Jini community. The process of finding the lookup services and obtaining references to them is called *discovery*. A service registers itself with one or more lookup services to make itself available to clients. To do so, the services must first discover the lookup services. Clients search the lookup services to locate the services they require. To do so, the clients must first discover the lookup services. Hence discovery is a common task for both services and clients.

Discovery distinguishes Jini technology from RMI. In RMI, you must know in advance where to register an object. In Jini, you do not need to know where—just how. The discovery process determines where, but hides the details from the developer. Discovery can be accomplished using either *unicast discovery* or *multicast discovery*.

22.6.1 Unicast Discovery

Unicast discovery, or *locator discovery*, enables a Jini service or client to discover lookup services on a specific host. The Jini service or client sends a discovery request to the computer, which responds with a remote reference to the lookup service running on that computer on the given port.

The application of Fig. 22.10 demonstrates unicast discovery. Class **UnicastDiscovery** uses class **_net.jini.core.discovery.LookupLocator_** to perform unicast discovery. Lines 17–18 import class **LookupLocator**, for discovering lookup services, and interface **ServiceRegistrar** (package **net.jini.core.lookup**), which represents a lookup service. The **UnicastDiscovery** constructor (lines 29–52) creates **JButton discoverButton** and **JTextArea outputArea**. When the user clicks **discoverButton**, line 43 invokes method **discoverLookupServices**, which displays information about discovered lookup services in **outputArea**.

```
1    // UnicastDiscovery.java
2    // UnicastDiscovery is an application that demonstrates Jini
3    // lookup service discovery for a known host (unicast).
4    package com.deitel.advjhtp1.jini.discovery;
5
6    // Java core packages
7    import java.rmi.*;
8    import java.net.*;
9    import java.io.*;
10   import java.awt.*;
11   import java.awt.event.*;
12
13   // Java extension packages
14   import javax.swing.*;
15
16   // Jini core packages
17   import net.jini.core.discovery.LookupLocator;
18   import net.jini.core.lookup.ServiceRegistrar;
19
20   public class UnicastDiscovery extends JFrame {
21
22      private JTextArea outputArea = new JTextArea( 10, 20 );
23      private JButton discoverButton;
24
25      // hostname for discovering lookup services
26      private String hostname;
27
28      // UnicastDiscovery constructor
29      public UnicastDiscovery( String host )
30      {
31         super( "UnicastDiscovery Output" );
32
33         hostname = host; // set target hostname for discovery
34
35         // create JButton to discover lookup services
36         discoverButton = new JButton( "Discover Lookup Services" );
37         discoverButton.addActionListener(
38            new ActionListener() {
39
40               // discover lookup services on given host
41               public void actionPerformed( ActionEvent event )
42               {
43                  discoverLookupServices();
44               }
45            }
46         );
47
48         Container contentPane = getContentPane();
49         contentPane.add( outputArea, BorderLayout.CENTER );
50         contentPane.add( discoverButton, BorderLayout.NORTH );
51
52      } // end UnicastDiscovery constructor
```

Fig. 22.10 UnicastDiscovery performs unicast discovery to locate Jini lookup services (part 1 of 3).

```
53
54    // discover lookup services on given host and get details
55    // about each lookup service from ServiceRegistrar
56    public void discoverLookupServices()
57    {
58       // construct Jini URL
59       String lookupURL = "jini://" + hostname + "/";
60
61       // connect to the lookup service at lookupURL
62       try {
63          LookupLocator locator = new LookupLocator( lookupURL );
64          outputArea.append( "Connecting to " + lookupURL + "\n" );
65
66          // perform unicast discovery to get ServiceRegistrar
67          ServiceRegistrar registrar =
68             locator.getRegistrar();
69
70          // print lookup service information and
71          outputArea.append( "Got ServiceRegistrar\n" +
72             "  Lookup Service Host: " + locator.getHost() + "\n" +
73             "  Lookup Service Port: " + locator.getPort() + "\n" );
74
75          // get groups that lookup service supports
76          String[] groups = registrar.getGroups();
77          outputArea.append( "Lookup service supports " +
78             + groups.length + " group(s):\n" );
79
80          // get group names; if empty, write public
81          for ( int i = 0; i < groups.length ; i++ ) {
82
83             if ( groups[ i ].equals( "" ) )
84                outputArea.append( "  public\n" );
85
86             else
87                outputArea.append( "   " + groups[ i ] + "\n" );
88          }
89       }
90
91       // handle exception if URL is invalid
92       catch ( MalformedURLException exception ) {
93          exception.printStackTrace();
94          outputArea.append( exception.getMessage() );
95       }
96
97       // handle exception communicating with ServiceRegistrar
98       catch ( RemoteException exception ) {
99          exception.printStackTrace();
100         outputArea.append( exception.getMessage() );
101      }
102
```

Fig. 22.10 UnicastDiscovery performs unicast discovery to locate Jini lookup services (part 2 of 3).

```
103        // handle ClassNotFoundException obtaining ServiceRegistrar
104        catch ( ClassNotFoundException exception ) {
105           exception.printStackTrace();
106           outputArea.append( exception.getMessage() );
107        }
108
109        // handle IOException obtaining ServiceRegistrar
110        catch ( IOException exception ) {
111           exception.printStackTrace();
112           outputArea.append( exception.getMessage() );
113        }
114
115   } // end method discoverLookupServices
116
117   // launch UnicastDiscovery application
118   public static void main( String args[] )
119   {
120      // set SecurityManager
121      if ( System.getSecurityManager() == null )
122         System.setSecurityManager(
123            new RMISecurityManager() );
124
125      // check command-line arguments for hostname
126      if ( args.length != 1 ) {
127         System.err.println(
128            "Usage: java UnicastDiscovery hostname" );
129      }
130
131      // create UnicastDiscovery for given hostname
132      else {
133         UnicastDiscovery discovery =
134            new UnicastDiscovery( args[ 0 ] );
135
136         discovery.setDefaultCloseOperation( EXIT_ON_CLOSE );
137         discovery.pack();
138         discovery.setVisible( true );
139      }
140   }
141 }
```

Fig. 22.10 UnicastDiscovery performs unicast discovery to locate Jini lookup
services (part 3 of 3).

Method **discoverLookupServices** (lines 56–115) locates services on a particular computer. Line 59 creates a **String** that represents the URL for the computer running the lookup services. This URL must specify the **jini** protocol, a hostname and, optionally, the port on which to connect (e.g., **jini://mycomputer.mydomain.com:1234**). If the URL does not specify a port, the default port **4160** is used. Class **UnicastDiscovery** reads the hostname from a command-line argument and stores it in instance variable **hostname**. Line 63 creates a new **LookupLocator** for discovering lookup services. This **LookupLocator** constructor takes as an argument the Jini URL for the computer running the lookup service. A **MalformedURLException** occurs if the URL specified does not follow the appropriate format.

Line 68 invokes method **getRegistrar** of class **LookupLocator** to perform unicast discovery. Method **getRegistrar** returns a **ServiceRegistrar**, which represents a lookup service. An overloaded version of method **getRegistrar** takes as an integer argument the maximum number of milliseconds to wait for the unicast discovery to locate a **ServiceRegistrar** before issuing a timeout.

Lines 71–88 display information about the discovered lookup service in **output-Area**. Lines 72–73 invoke methods **getHost** and **getPort** of class **LookupLocator** to retrieve the hostname and port number where the lookup service was discovered. Line 76 invokes method **getGroups** of interface **ServiceRegistrar** to retrieve an array of supported group names. An empty string indicates the **public** group.

Method **main** (lines 118–140) launches the **UnicastDiscovery** application. Lines 121–122 install an **RMISecurityManager** to enable network class loading—downloading executable code over the network. When class **UnicastDiscovery** discovers a new lookup service, the classes that implement that lookup service are loaded over the network. This class loading is a security risk, because the code will execute locally. A malicious programmer could access, modify or destroy sensitive data on the local machine. Installing a **SecurityManager** restricts downloaded code from performing tasks that are not granted explicitly in the current security policy. For more information on setting security policies, please see Chapter 7, Security. For the examples in this chapter, we use the policy file of Fig. 22.11, which grants **AllPermission** to the code in each example. This is a security risk and should not be used with production applications.

Lines 126–128 of Fig. 22.10 check the command-line arguments for a hostname and print out usage instructions if no hostname is provided. Lines 133–138 create a new **Uni-castDiscovery** instance and display the user interface.

Before executing class **UnicastDiscovery**, start **rmid**, the Web server and the Reggie lookup service (if necessary, review Section 22.4). To execute the **UnicastDiscovery** application, enter

```
java -Djava.security.policy=policy
    com.deitel.advjhtp1.jini.discovery.UnicastDiscovery host
```

where *policy* is a security file that specifies the security policy and *host* is the hostname or IP address of the computer running the lookup service. Be sure that you execute this command from the directory that contains the **com.deitel.advjhtp1** package structure, and be sure that the **CLASSPATH** environment variable includes the current directory. Figure 22.12 shows the running application.

```
1   // policy.all
2   // grant AllPermission to all code (DANGEROUS!)
3   grant {
4       permission java.security.AllPermission "", "";
5   };
```

Fig. 22.11 Policy file that grants **AllPermission** to all code.

Fig. 22.12 UnicastDiscovery application output.

22.6.2 Multicast Discovery

Multicast discovery, or *group discovery*, enables a Jini service or client to discover lookup services when the particular host running the lookup service is not known. Recall that when using unicast discovery, the Jini service or client must request lookup services from a particular host. A multicast discovery request uses network multicast to discover nearby lookup services. Lookup services, in turn, periodically issue multicast announcements to notify interested Jini services and clients that the lookup services are available.

The application of Fig. 22.13 demonstrates multicast discovery Class **Multicast-Discovery** uses class *net.jini.discovery.LookupDiscovery* to perform discovery. Class **MulticastDiscovery** implements the interface **DiscoveryListener** (line 22) to enable the class **MulticastDiscovery** to receive **DiscoveryEvent**s— notifications of discovered lookup services. Line 36 creates a **LookupDiscovery**. The **LookupDiscovery** constructor takes as an argument an array of **String**s in which each element is the name of a group. The **LookupDiscovery** object will discover all nearby lookup services that support the groups specified in this **String** array. Line 37 creates a new **String** array with an empty string as its only element. This indicates that the **LookupDiscovery** instance should discover lookup services that support the "**public**" group. Line 43 invokes method **addDiscoveryListener** of class **LookupDiscovery** to register the **MulticastDiscovery** object as the listener for **DiscoveryEvent**s.

Class **LookupDiscovery** invokes method **discovered** (lines 56–114) when **LookupDiscovery** locates new lookup services. Line 59 invokes method **getRegistrars** of class **DiscoveryEvent** to obtain an array of discovered **ServiceRegistrar**s. Lines 74–80 create a new **TextAppender** that contains information about a **discoveredServiceRegistrar**. Class **TextAppender** (lines 130–148) appends text to the **outputArea**. Lines 75–80 obtain information about the **ServiceRegistrar** and build an output string. Line 83 invokes method **invokeLater** of class **SwingUtilities** with the **TextAppender** as an argument to append the text to **outputArea**. Lines 91–97 obtain group information from the **ServiceRegistrar** and lines 100–101 append the group information to **outputArea**.

Class **LookupDiscovery** invokes method **discarded** (lines 118–126) when a lookup service should be discarded because it is no longer available or because it no longer matches the set of groups in which the Jini service or client is interested. Lines 120–121 invoke method **getRegistrars** of class **DiscoveryEvent** to obtain an array of discarded **ServiceRegistrar**s. Lines 123–125 add the number of discarded **ServiceRegistrar**s to the display.

```
1    // MulticastDiscovery.java
2    // MulticastDiscovery is an application that demonstrates Jini
3    // lookup service discovery using multicast.
4    package com.deitel.advjhtp1.jini.discovery;
5
6    // Java core packages
7    import java.rmi.*;
8    import java.io.*;
9    import java.awt.*;
10   import java.awt.event.*;
11
12   // Java extension packages
13   import javax.swing.*;
14
15   // Jini core packages
16   import net.jini.core.lookup.ServiceRegistrar;
17
18   // Jini extension packages
19   import net.jini.discovery.*;
20
21   public class MulticastDiscovery extends JFrame
22      implements DiscoveryListener {
23
24      // number of lookup services discovered through multicast
25      private int servicesFound = 0;
26
27      private JTextArea outputArea = new JTextArea( 10, 20 );
28
29      // MulticastDiscovery constructor
30      public MulticastDiscovery ()
31      {
32         super( "MulticastDiscovery" );
33
34         // discover lookup services in public group using multicast
35         try {
36            LookupDiscovery lookupDiscovery = new LookupDiscovery(
37               new String[] { "" } );
38
39            outputArea.append( "Finding lookup services for " +
40               "public group ...\n" );
41
42            // listen for DiscoveryEvents
43            lookupDiscovery.addDiscoveryListener ( this );
44         }
45
46         // handle exception discovering lookup services
47         catch ( IOException exception ) {
48            exception.printStackTrace();
49         }
50
```

Fig. 22.13 MulticastDiscovery performs multicast discovery to locate Jini lookup services (part 1 of 4).

```
51            getContentPane().add( new JScrollPane( outputArea ),
52                BorderLayout.CENTER );
53        }
54
55        // receive notification of found lookup services
56        public void discovered ( DiscoveryEvent event )
57        {
58            // get the ServiceRegistrars for found lookup services
59            ServiceRegistrar[] registrars = event.getRegistrars();
60            int order = 0;
61
62            // get the information for each lookup service found
63            for ( int i = 0; i < registrars.length ; i++ ) {
64                ServiceRegistrar registrar = registrars[ i ];
65
66                if ( registrar != null ) {
67
68                    // append information about discovered services
69                    // to outputArea
70                    try {
71                        order = servicesFound + i + 1;
72
73                        // get the hostname and port number
74                        Runnable appender = new TextAppender(
75                            "Lookup Service " + order + ":\n" +
76                            "  Host: " +
77                            registrar.getLocator().getHost() + "\n" +
78                            "\n  Port: " +
79                            registrar.getLocator().getPort() + "\n" +
80                            "  Group support: " );
81
82                        // append to outputArea on event-dispatch thread
83                        SwingUtilities.invokeLater( appender );
84
85                        // get the group(s) the lookup service served
86                        String[] groups = registrar.getGroups();
87
88                        StringBuffer names = new StringBuffer();
89
90                        // get the group names, if empty write public
91                        for ( int j = 0; j < groups.length ; j++ ) {
92
93                            if ( groups[ j ].equals( "" ) )
94                                names.append( "public\t" );
95                            else
96                                names.append( groups[ j ] + "\t" );
97                        }
98
99                        // append group names to outputArea
100                       SwingUtilities.invokeLater(
101                           new TextAppender( names + "\n" ) );
102               }
```

Fig. 22.13 MulticastDiscovery performs multicast discovery to locate Jini lookup services (part 2 of 4).

```
103
104                    // handle exception communicating with ServiceRegistrar
105                    catch ( RemoteException exception ) {
106                       exception.printStackTrace();
107                    }
108                 }
109              }
110
111           // update number of services found
112           servicesFound = order;
113
114        } // end method discovered
115
116        // receive notification of discarded lookup services that
117        // are no longer valid
118        public void discarded( DiscoveryEvent event )
119        {
120           ServiceRegistrar[] discardedRegistrars =
121              event.getRegistrars();
122
123           SwingUtilities.invokeLater(
124              new TextAppender( "Number of discarded registrars: "  +
125                 discardedRegistrars.length + "\n" ) );
126        }
127
128        // TextAppender is a Runnable class for appending
129        // text to outputArea on the event-dispatching thread.
130        private class TextAppender implements Runnable {
131
132           private String textToAppend; // text to append to outputArea
133
134           // TextAppender constructor
135           public TextAppender( String text )
136           {
137              textToAppend = text;
138           }
139
140           // append text to outputArea and scroll to bottom
141           public void run()
142           {
143              outputArea.append( textToAppend );
144              outputArea.setCaretPosition(
145                 outputArea.getText().length() );
146           }
147
148        } // end inner class TextAppender
149
150        // launch MulticastDiscovery application
151        public static void main( String args[] )
152        {
```

Fig. 22.13 MulticastDiscovery performs multicast discovery to locate Jini lookup services (part 3 of 4).

```
153        // set SecurityManager
154        if ( System.getSecurityManager() == null )
155           System.setSecurityManager(
156              new RMISecurityManager() );
157
158        MulticastDiscovery discovery = new MulticastDiscovery();
159        discovery.setDefaultCloseOperation( EXIT_ON_CLOSE );
160        discovery.pack();
161        discovery.setVisible( true );
162     }
163  }
```

Fig. 22.13 **MulticastDiscovery** performs multicast discovery to locate Jini
lookup services (part 4 of 4).

Before running this example, start several instances of the Reggie lookup service. If
there is only one lookup service running, the result is the same as the **Unicast-
Discovery** example (Fig. 22.10). To start multiple instances of the Reggie lookup service, specify a different log directory in the **Reggie** panel, then click **Start Reggie** from
the **Run** panel. Try adding new group names to some of the lookup services (e.g., "**test**"
or "**MyGroup**"). To execute **MulticastDiscovery**, enter the following at a command
prompt:

```
java -Djava.security.policy=policy
     com.deitel.advjhtp1.jini.discovery.MulticastDiscovery
```

where *policy* is an appropriate security policy. Figure 22.14 shows the output window with
several lookup services running.

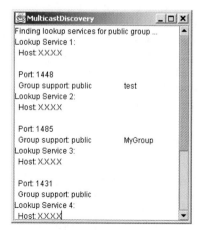

Fig. 22.14 **MulticastDiscovery** application output.

22.7 Jini Service and Client Implementations

In this section, we develop a Jini service that provides information about fictitious seminars offered at Deitel & Associates, Inc. Then, we create a client for that service. A Jini service consists of several components, each of which contributes to the flexibility and portability of the Jini architecture. A *service proxy* is an intermediary between a Jini service and its clients. The seminar service proxy implements the service's **public** interface, which declares the methods that the service provides. The service proxy communicates with the actual service implementation through the service's *back-end interface*, which defines methods in the service implementation. A separate application discovers lookup services and registers the Jini service, making the service available to Jini clients.

Software Engineering Observation 22.1

Providing a back-end interface for the service implementation is not required. However, using a back-end interface makes the Jini service more flexible, since the back-end implementation can be changed without requiring changes in the service proxy.

Software Engineering Observation 22.2

An alternative to providing a back-end interface and implementation is to implement the service's functionality in the service proxy itself.

A Jini client uses the lookup service discovery techniques presented earlier in this chapter to discover lookup services. The Jini client then uses the discovered lookup services to locate the desired Jini service. When the lookup service locates the service requested by the Jini client, the lookup service serializes the service proxy and delivers the proxy to the Jini client. The client can then invoke methods defined in the service's **public** interface directly on the service proxy, which implements that interface. The service proxy communicates with the service implementation through the back-end interface.

Our Jini service provides information about fictitious seminars offered at Deitel & Associates, Inc. Information about these seminars is stored in instances of class **Seminar** (Fig. 22.15). Interface **SeminarInterface** (Fig. 22.16) is the public interface for the Jini service. Class **SeminarProxy** (Fig. 22.18) implements interface **SeminarInterface** and communicates with the service implementation through **BackendInterface** (Fig. 22.17). Class **SeminarInfo** (Fig. 22.19) is the service implementation, which implements interface **BackendInterface**. Class **SeminarInfoService** (Fig. 22.21) discovers lookup services and registers the **SeminarInfo** Jini service. Class **UnicastSeminarInfoClient** (Fig. 22.22) is a Jini client that uses unicast discovery to discover lookup services and locate the **SeminarInfo** Jini service. This client allows a user to select a day of the week and view the seminars offered on that day.

22.7.1 Service Interfaces and Supporting Classes

Class **Seminar** (Fig. 22.15) represents a fictitious seminar, including the seminar's title and location. It implements **Serializable**, so that objects of this class can be sent from the Jini service to its clients across the network.

Line 13 explicitly specifies the **serialVersionUID** for class **Seminar**. Developers can define this **static** member in **Serializable** classes to ensure compatibility between versions of such classes. If an object of one version of a class is serialized, the object can be deserialized into an object of a newer version of the class as long as both versions use the same **serialVersionUID** (and are implemented in a compatible manner). Changing the **serialVersionUID** for a new version of the class indicates that the new version is not compatible with older versions. In this case, deserialization would not work correctly.

Interface **SeminarInterface** (Fig. 22.16) defines a single method **getSeminar**, which takes as a **String** argument a day of the week. Method **getSeminar** returns a **Seminar** object containing information about the **Seminar** offered on the given day. The service proxy must implement this interface, because Jini clients use this interface to interact with the service.

```
1   // Seminar.java
2   // Seminar represents a seminar, or lecture, including the
3   // Seminar title and location.
4   package com.deitel.advjhtp1.jini.seminar;
5
6   // Java core package
7   import java.io.Serializable;
8
9   public class Seminar implements Serializable
10  {
11      private String title;
12      private String location;
13      private static final long serialVersionUID = 20010724L;
14
15      // Seminar constructor
16      public Seminar( String seminarTitle, String seminarLocation )
17      {
18          title = seminarTitle;
19          location = seminarLocation;
20      }
21
22      // get String representation of Seminar object
23      public String toString()
24      {
25          return "Seminar title: " + getTitle() +
26              "; location: " + getLocation();
27      }
28
29      // get Seminar title
30      public String getTitle()
31      {
32          return title;
33      }
34
35      // get Seminar location
36      public String getLocation()
37      {
38          return location;
39      }
40  }
```

Fig. 22.15 Seminar maintains the location and title of a seminar.

```
1   // SeminarInterface.java
2   // SeminarInterface defines methods available from the SeminarInfo
3   // Jini service.
4   package com.deitel.advjhtp1.jini.seminar.service;
5
6   // Java core packages
7   import java.rmi.Remote;
8
9   // Deitel packages
10  import com.deitel.advjhtp1.jini.seminar.Seminar;
11
12  public interface SeminarInterface {
13
14      // get Seminar for given date
15      public Seminar getSeminar( String date );
16  }
```

Fig. 22.16 SeminarInterface defines the methods available from the
         SeminarInfo Jini service.

Interface **BackendInterface** (Fig. 22.17) defines methods that the service proxy
uses to communicate with the service implementation. The proxy invokes method **get-
Seminar** to retrieve **Seminar** information for the requested day. In this Jini service, the
seminar proxy communicates with the service implementation using RMI, although Jini
implementations may use any protocol to communicate with back-end implementations.

Software Engineering Observation 22.3

*Jini does not require that service proxies communicate with back-end implementations using
RMI. Service proxies may use RMI, TCP/IP, CORBA or any suitable protocol to connect to
back-end implementations.*

```
1   // BackendInterface.java
2   // BackendInterface defines the interface through which the
3   // service proxy communicates with the back-end service.
4   package com.deitel.advjhtp1.jini.seminar.service;
5
6   // Java core packages
7   import java.rmi.*;
8
9   // Deitel packages
10  import com.deitel.advjhtp1.jini.seminar.Seminar;
11
12  public interface BackendInterface extends Remote {
13
14      // get Seminar for given day of the week
15      public Seminar getSeminar( String day ) throws RemoteException;
16  }
```

Fig. 22.17 BackEndInterface defines methods available to the **SeminarInfo**
         service proxy.

22.7.2 Service Proxy and Service Implementations

Class **SeminarProxy** (Fig. 22.18) is a service proxy for the **SeminarInfo** Jini service. Line 12 specifies that class **SeminarProxy** implements **SeminarInterface**, which is the **public** interface for the **SeminarInfo** Jini service. The service proxy must implement this interface to enable Jini clients to communicate with the **SeminarInfo** service. The service proxy also must implement interface **Serializable** (line 13), so that instances can be delivered to the remote client over RMI. The **SeminarProxy** constructor (lines 18–21) initializes the proxy with a remote reference to the back-end implementation. Method **getSeminar** (lines 24–38) invokes the back-end implementation's **getSeminar** method to retrieve the seminar information (line 28).

```
1   // SeminarProxy.java
2   // SeminarProxy is a proxy for the SeminarInfo Jini service.
3   package com.deitel.advjhtp1.jini.seminar.service;
4
5   // Java core packages
6   import java.io.Serializable;
7   import java.rmi.*;
8
9   // Deitel packages
10  import com.deitel.advjhtp1.jini.seminar.Seminar;
11
12  public class SeminarProxy implements SeminarInterface,
13     Serializable {
14
15     private BackendInterface backInterface;
16
17     // SeminarProxy constructor
18     public SeminarProxy( BackendInterface inputInterface )
19     {
20        backInterface = inputInterface;
21     }
22
23     // get Seminar for given date through BackendInterface
24     public Seminar getSeminar( String date )
25     {
26        // get Seminar from service through BackendInterface
27        try {
28           return backInterface.getSeminar( date );
29        }
30
```

Fig. 22.18 SeminarProxy is a service proxy that clients use to communicate with the **SeminarInfo** service (part 1 of 2).

```
31          // handle exception communicating with back-end service
32          catch ( RemoteException remoteException ) {
33             remoteException.printStackTrace();
34          }
35
36          return null;
37
38       } // end method getSeminar
39    }
```

Fig. 22.18 **SeminarProxy** is a service proxy that clients use to communicate with the **SeminarInfo** service (part 2 of 2).

Class **SeminarInfo** (Fig. 22.19) is an RMI object that implements the Jini service's back-end interface. The service proxy communicates with this back-end implementation through interface **BackendInterface** using RMI. Method **getSeminar** (lines 29–91) reads seminar information from file **SeminarInfo.txt** and returns a new **Seminar** object containing **Seminar** information for the given day of the week.

File **SeminarInfo.txt** (Fig. 22.20) contains **Seminar** information that the **SeminarInfo** service provides to its clients. A semicolon separates the **Seminar** title from the **Seminar** location.

```
1    // SeminarInfo.java
2    // SeminarInfo is a Jini service that provides information
3    // about Seminars offered throughout the week.
4    package com.deitel.advjhtp1.jini.seminar.service;
5
6    // Java core packages
7    import java.io.*;
8    import java.rmi.server.UnicastRemoteObject;
9    import java.rmi.RemoteException;
10   import java.util.StringTokenizer;
11
12   // Deitel packages
13   import com.deitel.advjhtp1.jini.seminar.Seminar;
14
15   public class SeminarInfo extends UnicastRemoteObject
16      implements BackendInterface {
17
18      // Strings that represent days of the week
19      private static final String MONDAY = "MONDAY";
20      private static final String TUESDAY = "TUESDAY";
21      private static final String WEDNESDAY = "WEDNESDAY";
22      private static final String THURSDAY = "THURSDAY";
23      private static final String FRIDAY = "FRIDAY";
24
25      // SeminarInfo no-argument constructor
26      public SeminarInfo() throws RemoteException {}
27
```

Fig. 22.19 **SeminarInfo** implements the **SeminarInfo** Jini service (part 1 of 3).

```
28      // get Seminar information for given day
29      public Seminar getSeminar( String date )
30         throws RemoteException
31      {
32         String[] titles = new String[] { "", "", "", "", "" };
33         String[] locations = new String[] { "", "", "", "", "" };
34
35         // read seminar information from text file
36         try {
37            String fileName = SeminarInfo.class.getResource(
38               "SeminarInfo.txt" ).toString();
39            fileName = fileName.substring( 6 );
40
41            FileInputStream inputStream =
42               new FileInputStream( fileName );
43
44            BufferedReader reader = new BufferedReader(
45               new InputStreamReader( inputStream ));
46
47            String line = reader.readLine();
48
49            // read seminar info from the file
50            for ( int lineNo = 0; ( line != null )
51               && ( lineNo < 5 ); lineNo++ ) {
52               StringTokenizer tokenizer =
53                  new StringTokenizer( line, ";" );
54
55               titles[ lineNo ] = tokenizer.nextToken();
56               locations[ lineNo ] = tokenizer.nextToken();
57               line = reader.readLine();
58            }
59         }
60
61         // handle exception loading Seminar file
62         catch ( FileNotFoundException fileException ) {
63            fileException.printStackTrace();
64         }
65
66         // handle exception reading from Seminar file
67         catch ( IOException ioException ) {
68            ioException.printStackTrace();
69         }
70
71         // match given day of the week to available seminars
72         if ( date.equalsIgnoreCase( MONDAY ) ) {
73            return new Seminar( titles[ 0 ], locations[ 0 ] );
74         }
75         else if ( date.equalsIgnoreCase( TUESDAY ) ) {
76            return new Seminar( titles[ 1 ], locations[ 1 ] );
77         }
78         else if ( date.equalsIgnoreCase( WEDNESDAY ) ) {
79            return new Seminar( titles[ 2 ], locations[ 2 ] );
80         }
```

Fig. 22.19 SeminarInfo implements the SeminarInfo Jini service (part 2 of 3).

```
81              else if ( date.equalsIgnoreCase( THURSDAY ) ) {
82                  return new Seminar( titles[ 3 ], locations[ 3 ] );
83              }
84              else if ( date.equalsIgnoreCase( FRIDAY ) ) {
85                  return new Seminar( titles[ 4 ], locations[ 4 ] );
86              }
87              else {
88                  return new Seminar( "Empty", "Not available" );
89              }
90
91          } // end method getSeminar
92      }
```

Fig. 22.19 `SeminarInfo` implements the `SeminarInfo` Jini service (part 3 of 3).

```
1    Advanced Swing GUI Components; Deitel Seminar Room
2    Model-View-Controller Architecture; Deitel Seminar Room
3    Java 2 Enterprise Edition; Deitel Seminar Room
4    Introduction to Jini; Deitel Seminar Room
5    Java 2 Micro Edition; Deitel Seminar Room
```

Fig. 22.20 Content of `SeminarInfo.txt`.

22.7.3 Registering the Service with Lookup Services

Class **SeminarInfoService** (Fig. 22.21) discovers lookup services using multicast discovery and registers the **SeminarInfo** service with discovered lookup services. Lines 29–30 create a **LookupDiscovery** object to perform multicast discovery for the "**public**" group. Line 33 registers the **SeminarInfoService** object as a **DiscoveryListener** to receive lookup service discovery notifications. Line 42 creates an array of **Entry** objects. An **Entry** (in package **net.jini.core.entry**) describes a service, which enables Jini clients to search for services of a particular description. Line 43 creates a new **Name Entry** (in package **net.jini.lookup.entry**) and adds it to array **entries** to provide the name of the Jini service. Lines 46–47 create a new **ServiceItem** (in package **net.jini.core.lookup**) for the **SeminarInfo** Jini service. The lookup service requires a **ServiceItem** to register a Jini service. The first argument to the **ServiceItem** constructor is the Jini service's ID. The **null** argument on line 53 causes the lookup service to assign a new, unique ID to the service. To keep the services persistent, the service provider should use the previously assigned service ID when re-registering services. The second argument is an instance of the service proxy for the Jini service. The third argument is the array of **Entry** objects that describe the service.

```
1    // SeminarInfoService.java
2    // SeminarInfoService discovers lookup services and registers
3    // the SeminarInfo service with those lookup services.
4    package com.deitel.advjhtp1.jini.seminar.service;
5
```

Fig. 22.21 `SeminarInfoService` registers the `SeminarInfo` service with lookup services (part 1 of 4).

```
6    // Java core packages
7    import java.rmi.RMISecurityManager;
8    import java.rmi.RemoteException;
9    import java.io.IOException;
10
11   // Jini core packages
12   import net.jini.core.lookup.*;
13   import net.jini.core.entry.Entry;
14
15   // Jini extension packages
16   import net.jini.discovery.*;
17   import net.jini.lookup.entry.Name;
18
19   public class SeminarInfoService implements DiscoveryListener {
20
21      private ServiceItem serviceItem;
22      private final int LEASETIME = 10 * 60 * 1000;
23
24      // SeminarInfoService constructor
25      public SeminarInfoService()
26      {
27         // search for lookup services with public group
28         try {
29            LookupDiscovery discover =
30               new LookupDiscovery( new String[] { "" } );
31
32            // add listener for DiscoveryEvents
33            discover.addDiscoveryListener( this );
34         }
35
36         // handle exception creating LookupDiscovery
37         catch ( IOException exception ) {
38            exception.printStackTrace();
39         }
40
41         // create an Entry for this service
42         Entry[] entries = new Entry[ 1 ];
43         entries[ 0 ] = new Name( "Seminar" );
44
45         // set the service's proxy and Entry name
46         serviceItem = new ServiceItem(
47            null, createProxy(), entries );
48
49      } // end SeminarInfoService constructor
50
51      // receive lookup service discovery notifications
52      public void discovered( DiscoveryEvent event )
53      {
54         ServiceRegistrar[] registrars = event.getRegistrars();
55
```

Fig. 22.21 SeminarInfoService registers the **SeminarInfo** service with
lookup services (part 2 of 4).

```
56         // register service with each lookup service
57         for ( int i = 0; i < registrars.length; i++ ) {
58            ServiceRegistrar registrar = registrars[ i ];
59
60            // register service with discovered lookup service
61            try {
62               ServiceRegistration registration =
63                  registrar.register( serviceItem, LEASETIME );
64            }
65
66            // catch the remote exception
67            catch ( RemoteException exception) {
68               exception.printStackTrace();
69            }
70
71         } // end for
72
73      } // end method discovered
74
75      // ignore discarded lookup services
76      public void discarded( DiscoveryEvent event ) {}
77
78      // create the seminar service proxy
79      private SeminarInterface createProxy()
80      {
81         // get BackendInterface for service and create SeminarProxy
82         try {
83            return new SeminarProxy( new SeminarInfo() );
84         }
85
86         // handle exception creating SeminarProxy
87         catch ( RemoteException exception ) {
88            exception.printStackTrace();
89         }
90
91         return null;
92
93      } // end method discovered
94
95      // method main keeps the application alive
96      public static void main( String args[] )
97      {
98         // set SecurityManager
99         if ( System.getSecurityManager() == null )
100           System.setSecurityManager( new RMISecurityManager() );
101
102        new SeminarInfoService();
103
104        Object keepAlive = new Object();
105
```

Fig. 22.21 **SeminarInfoService** registers the **SeminarInfo** service with lookup services (part 3 of 4).

```
106          synchronized ( keepAlive ) {
107
108             // keep application alive
109             try {
110                keepAlive.wait();
111             }
112
113             // handle exception if wait interrupted
114             catch ( InterruptedException exception ) {
115                exception.printStackTrace();
116             }
117          }
118
119       } // end method main
120    }
```

Fig. 22.21 **SeminarInfoService** registers the **SeminarInfo** service with lookup services (part 4 of 4).

Method **discovered** (lines 52–73) receives notifications of discovered lookup services. For each discovered lookup service, line 62 invokes method **register** of interface **ServiceRegistrar** to register the Jini service's **serviceItem** with the lookup service. Method **register** takes as arguments a **serviceItem**, which contains the service proxy and a *lease time*. The lease time specifies the length of time for which the service should be available from the lookup service. For this example, the lease time is 10 minutes. The **LEASETIME** specified in method **register** is the service requested lease time. In fact, Sun's implementation limits it to 5 minutes. This means the desired lease time is not necessarily granted. After 10 minutes or even less, the Jini service's lease expires and the service is no longer available through the lookup service. It is the service provider's responsibility to store the **ServiceRegistation** (line 62) returned by method **register** and use it to periodically renew the lease. We discuss leasing and how to manage leases in Section 22.8.3.

Method **createProxy** (lines 79–93) creates a new **SeminarProxy** service proxy for our Jini service. Line 83 creates a new instance of the **SeminarInfo** back-end implementation. Line 84 returns a new **SeminarProxy** service proxy for the **SeminarInfo** service back-end implementation.

Method **main** (lines 95–118) launches the **SeminarInfoService** application. Line 99 sets a **SecurityManager** and line 101 creates a new instance of class **SeminarInfoService**, which discovers lookup services and registers the **SeminarInfo** service. Lines 103–115 create an **Object** named **keepAlive**. The **synchronized** block (lines 105–116) prevents the **main** thread from terminating, which would cause the **SeminarInfoService** application to terminate, thus shutting down the **SeminarInfo** service. Clients then would be unable to access **Seminar** information.

22.7.4 Jini Service Client

Class **UnicastSeminarInfoClient** (Fig. 22.22) is a Jini client that uses the **SeminarInfo** service to retrieve information about **Seminar**s available on a given day. Class **UnicastSeminarInfoClient** performs unicast discovery to discover lookup services. The **UnicastSeminarInfoClient** constructor (lines 44–82) initializes the application GUI.

Line 51 creates a **JButton** that the user can click to begin the discovery process and retrieve **Seminar** information. Line 61 invokes method **discoverLookupServices** to discover lookup services using unicast discovery. Lines 63–64 obtain a remote reference to the **SeminarInfo** service's service proxy by invoking method **lookupSeminarService**. Lines 66–69 prompt the user for the day of the week for which the user would like **Seminar** information. Line 71 invokes method **showSeminars** to display the **Seminar** information for the selected day.

```
1   // UnicastSeminarInfoClient.java
2   // UnicastSeminarInfoClient uses unicast discovery to locate
3   // lookup services for the SeminarInfo service.
4   package com.deitel.advjhtp1.jini.seminar.client;
5
6   // Java core packages
7   import java.awt.*;
8   import java.awt.event.*;
9   import java.io.*;
10  import java.rmi.*;
11  import java.net.*;
12  import java.util.*;
13
14  // Java extension packages
15  import javax.swing.*;
16
17  // Jini core packages
18  import net.jini.core.discovery.LookupLocator;
19  import net.jini.core.lookup.*;
20  import net.jini.core.entry.Entry;
21
22  // Jini extension packages
23  import net.jini.lookup.entry.Name;
24
25  // Deitel packages
26  import com.deitel.advjhtp1.jini.seminar.Seminar;
27  import com.deitel.advjhtp1.jini.seminar.service.SeminarInterface;
28
29  public class UnicastSeminarInfoClient extends JFrame {
30
31     // Strings representing the days of the week on which
32     // Seminars are offered
33     private static final String[] days = { "Monday", "Tuesday",
34        "Wednesday", "Thursday", "Friday" };
35
36     // hostname and ServiceRegistrar for lookup services
37     private String hostname;
38     private ServiceRegistrar registrar;
39
```

Fig. 22.22 **UnicastSeminarInfoClient** is a client for the SeminarInfo service (part 1 of 4).

```
40      // JButton for finding Seminars
41      private JButton findSeminarButton;
42
43      // UnicastSeminarInfoClient constructor
44      public UnicastSeminarInfoClient( String host )
45      {
46         super( "UnicastSeminarInfoClient" );
47
48         hostname = host; // set target hostname for discovery
49
50         // create JButton for finding Seminars
51         findSeminarButton = new JButton( "Find Seminar" );
52         findSeminarButton.addActionListener(
53
54            new ActionListener() {
55
56               // discover lookup services, look up SeminarInfo
57               // service, prompt user for desired day of the
58               // week and display available Seminars
59               public void actionPerformed( ActionEvent event )
60               {
61                  discoverLookupServices();
62
63                  SeminarInterface seminarService =
64                     lookupSeminarService();
65
66                  String day = ( String ) JOptionPane.showInputDialog(
67                     UnicastSeminarInfoClient.this, "Select Day",
68                     "Day Selection", JOptionPane.QUESTION_MESSAGE,
69                     null, days, days[ 0 ] );
70
71                  showSeminars( seminarService, day );
72               }
73            }
74
75         ); // end call to addActionListener
76
77         JPanel buttonPanel = new JPanel();
78         buttonPanel.add( findSeminarButton );
79
80         getContentPane().add( buttonPanel, BorderLayout.CENTER );
81
82      } // end UnicastSeminarInfoClient constructor
83
84      // discover lookup services using unicast discovery
85      private void discoverLookupServices()
86      {
87         String lookupURL = "jini://" + hostname + "/";
88
89         // Get the lookup service locator at jini://hostname
90         // use default port
91         try {
```

Fig. 22.22 UnicastSeminarInfoClient is a client for the SeminarInfo service (part 2 of 4).

```
92              LookupLocator locator = new LookupLocator( lookupURL );
93
94           // return registrar
95           registrar = locator.getRegistrar();
96        }
97
98        // handle exceptions discovering lookup services
99        catch ( Exception exception ) {
100           exception.printStackTrace();
101        }
102
103     } // end method discoverLookupServices
104
105     // lookup SeminarInfo service in given ServiceRegistrar
106     private SeminarInterface lookupSeminarService()
107     {
108        // specify the service requirement
109        Class[] types = new Class[] { SeminarInterface.class };
110        Entry[] attribute = new Entry[] { new Name( "Seminar" ) };
111        ServiceTemplate template =
112           new ServiceTemplate( null, types, attribute );
113
114        // find the service
115        try {
116           SeminarInterface seminarInterface =
117              ( SeminarInterface ) registrar.lookup( template );
118           return seminarInterface;
119        }
120
121        // handle exception looking up SeminarInfo service
122        catch ( RemoteException exception ) {
123           exception.printStackTrace();
124        }
125
126        return null;
127
128     } // end method lookupSeminarService
129
130     // show Seminar in given SeminarInfo service for given
131     // day of the week
132     private void showSeminars( SeminarInterface seminarService,
133        String day )
134     {
135        StringBuffer buffer = new StringBuffer();
136
137        // get Seminar from SeminarInfo service
138        if ( seminarService != null ) {
139           Seminar seminar = seminarService.getSeminar( day );
140
141           // get subject and location from Seminar object
142           buffer.append( "Seminar information: \n" );
143           buffer.append( day + ":\n" );
```

Fig. 22.22 UnicastSeminarInfoClient is a client for the SeminarInfo service
    (part 3 of 4).

```
144          buffer.append( seminar.getTitle() + "\n" ); // title
145          buffer.append( seminar.getLocation() );      // location
146       }
147       else  // SeminarInfo service does not available
148          buffer.append(
149             "SeminarInfo service does not available. \n" );
150
151       // display Seminar information
152       JOptionPane.showMessageDialog( this, buffer );
153
154    } // end method showSeminars
155
156    // launch UnicastSeminarInfoClient application
157    public static void main ( String args[] )
158    {
159       // check command-line arguments for hostname
160       if ( args.length != 1 ) {
161          System.err.println(
162             "Usage: java UnicastSeminarInfoClient hostname" );
163       }
164
165       // create UnicastSeminarInfoClient for given hostname
166       else {
167          System.setSecurityManager( new RMISecurityManager() );
168
169          UnicastSeminarInfoClient client =
170             new UnicastSeminarInfoClient( args[ 0 ] );
171
172          client.setDefaultCloseOperation( EXIT_ON_CLOSE );
173          client.pack();
174          client.setSize( 250, 65 );
175          client.setVisible( true );
176       }
177
178    } // end method main
179 }
```

Fig. 22.22 `UnicastSeminarInfoClient` is a client for the SeminarInfo service (part 4 of 4).

Method **discoverLookupServices** (lines 85–103) performs unicast discovery to discover lookup services on a particular host, specified at the command line. Line 92 creates a **LookupLocator**, and line 95 invokes method **getRegistrar** of class **Look-upLocator** to obtain a **ServiceRegistrar** reference to the lookup service, which is stored in instance variable **registrar**.

Method **lookupSeminarService** uses the **ServiceRegistrar** discovered in method **discoverLookupServices** to obtain a **SeminarProxy** for the **Seminar-Info** service. Line 109 creates an array of **Class** objects and initializes the first element to **SeminarInterface**'s **Class** object. The **ServiceRegistrar** uses this array of **Class** objects to locate the appropriate service proxies for the Jini client. Line 110 creates an array of **Entry** objects. Recall that when we registered the **SeminarInfo** service, we provided an array of **Entry** objects to describe that service. Line 110 populates the

entries array with a single **Name Entry**. The **ServiceRegistrar** uses this array of **Entry** objects to locate the desired service. Lines 111–112 create a **ServiceTemplate** (package **net.jini.core.lookup**) that contains the **Class** and **Entry** arrays from lines 109–110. The **ServiceRegistrar** uses this **ServiceTemplate** to locate a service that matches the given set of **Class** and **Entry** objects. The first argument to the **ServiceTemplate** constructor is the service ID for the Jini service. We pass a **null** argument to indicate that we do not know the service ID for the desired service.

Lines 116–117 invoke method **lookup** of interface **ServiceRegistrar** to perform the lookup and retrieve a **SeminarProxy** service proxy. Line 117 passes the **ServiceTemplate** to method **lookup**. The **ServiceRegistrar** matches the information in the **ServiceTemplate** to the **ServiceItem**s registered in the lookup service. For a **ServiceItem** to match a **ServiceTemplate** when a **ServiceTemplate** contains a non-null service ID, the service ID must match that in the **ServiceTemplate**. Also, the service must be an instance of every class in the **Class** array in the **ServiceTemplate**. Finally, the service attributes must match one or more of the attributes in the **Entry** array in the **ServiceTemplate**. Line 118 returns a reference to the **SeminarProxy** returned by method **lookup**.

Method **showSeminars** (lines 132–154) takes as arguments a **SeminarInterface** and a **String** containing the day of the week for which the user would like **Seminar** information. Line 139 invokes method **getSeminar** of interface **SeminarInterface** and passes as an argument the day. Recall that **SeminarInterface** is the **public** interface for the **SeminarInfo** Jini service and defines all methods available for that service. Line 152 displays the **Seminar** information in a **JOptionPane** message dialog.

Method **main** (lines 157–178) launches the **UnicastSeminarInfoClient** application. Lines 160–163 ensure that the user enters the hostname on which to perform lookup service discovery. Lines 167–175 set a **SecurityManager** and start **UnicastSeminarInfoClient**.

Running the Service and Client
Clients and services typically run on different computers. To mimic this configuration on a single computer, we must separate the class files for the Jini client, the class files for the Jini service and the downloadable Jini service class files. In this example, we package the service's class files in a JAR file named **SeminarService.jar**. Figure 22.23 shows the contents of **SeminarService.jar**.

Class File	Directory in **SeminarService.jar**
Seminar.class	
	com\deitel\advjhtp1\jini\seminar\
SeminarInterface.class	
	com\deitel\advjhtp1\jini\seminar\service\
SeminarProxy.class	
	com\deitel\advjhtp1\jini\seminar\service\

Fig. 22.23 **SeminarService.jar** contents (part 1 of 2).

Class File	Directory in `SeminarService.jar`

`BackendInterface.class`

    `com\deitel\advjhtp1\jini\seminar\service\`

`SeminarInfo.class`

    `com\deitel\advjhtp1\jini\seminar\service\`

`SeminarInfo_Stub.class`

    `com\deitel\advjhtp1\jini\seminar\service\`

`SeminarInfoService.class`

    `com\deitel\advjhtp1\jini\seminar\service\`

Fig. 22.23 `SeminarService.jar` contents (part 2 of 2).

Recall that class **SeminarInfo** is an RMI remote object from which the **Seminar-Proxy** retrieves **Seminar** information. This requires that we use the RMI stub compiler (**rmic**) to compile a stub file for class **SeminarInfo** and place this stub file (**SeminarInfo_Stub.class**) in **SeminarService.jar**.

We place our Jini client's class files in JAR file **SeminarClient.jar**. To access the **SeminarInfo** Jini Service, the client needs the class file for the service's **public** interface, as well as any supporting classes that used by methods in the **public** interface. **SeminarClient.jar** contains **Seminar.class** and **SeminarInterface.class**, which contains the service's **public** interface. Figure 22.24 shows the contents of **SeminarClient.jar**.

When the client requests the **SeminarInfo** service from a lookup service, the client uses network class loading to load the service proxy class into memory and execute methods on the Jini service. Therefore, we must package the necessary class files for the Jini client to download. The client requires the service proxy's class file and class files for objects that the service proxy references. Recall that the client interacts with the service proxy through interface **SeminarInterface**. The client does not know about the service proxy **SeminarProxy** or its supporting classes. Therefore, the client must download the **SeminarProxy** class file and its supporting class files at run time using network class loading. The download classes include **BackendInterface.class** and **Seminar-Info_Stub.class**, which the service proxy uses to communicate with the **Seminar-Info** remote object. We package these files in **SeminarServiceDownload.jar** (Fig. 22.25) and publish this JAR file on a Web server for the client to download.

After creating these JAR files, start **rmid**, a Web server and the Reggie lookup service (if necessary, review Section 22.4 for detailed instructions). Configure and start an additional Web server to enable clients to download the service proxy and supporting files. Place **SeminarServiceDownload.jar** in the **Document Area** directory specified in this additional Web server's configuration (e.g., **C:\Jini\seminar\service**). Figure 22.26 shows a sample Web server configuration that uses port 9090. We specify this port number in the **java.rmi.server.codebase** command-line property when we launch the **SeminarInfo** service.

Class File	Directory in `SeminarClient.jar`

`Seminar.class`

        `com\deitel\advjhtp1\jini\seminar\`

`SeminarInterface.class`

        `com\deitel\advjhtp1\jini\seminar\service\`

`UnicastSeminarInfoClient.class`

        `com\deitel\advjhtp1\jini\seminar\client\`

`UnicastSeminarInfoClient$1.class`

        `com\deitel\advjhtp1\jini\seminar\client\`

`UnicastSeminarInfoClient$2.class`

        `com\deitel\advjhtp1\jini\seminar\client\`

Fig. 22.24 `SeminarClient.jar` contents.

Class File	Directory in `SeminarServiceDownload.jar`

`SeminarProxy.class`

        `com\deitel\advjhtp1\jini\seminar\service\`

`BackendInterface.class`

        `com\deitel\advjhtp1\jini\seminar\service\`

`SeminarInfo_Stub.class`

        `com\deitel\advjhtp1\jini\seminar\service\`

Fig. 22.25 `SeminarServiceDownload.jar` contents.

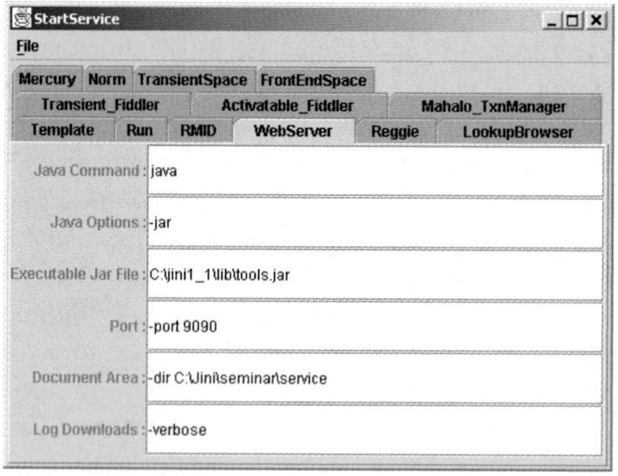

Fig. 22.26 Web server configuration for `SeminarInfo` service.

Start the **SeminarInfo** service by launching **SeminarInfoService**. Be sure that **jini-core.jar**, **jini-ext.jar** and **sun-util.jar** are in your **CLASS-PATH**, and enter the following command at the command prompt:

```
java -classpath %CLASSPATH%;SeminarService.jar
    -Djava.security.policy=policy
    -Djava.rmi.server.codebase=http://hostname:9090/
SeminarServiceDownload.jar
    com.deitel.advjhtp1.jini.seminar.service.SeminarInfoService
```

where *policy* is an appropriate security policy and *hostname* is the hostname on which the Web server for downloading the Jini service proxy is running. Be sure to specify the proper port number for the Web server that serves **SeminarServiceDownload.jar** (e.g., **9090**).

Start the **SeminarInfo** Jini client by launching **UnicastSeminarInfoService**. Ensure that **jini-core.jar**, **jini-ext.jar** and **sun-util.jar** are in your **CLASSPATH**, and that none of the **SeminarInfo** service class files are in your **CLASSPATH**. Type the following from a command prompt:

```
java -classpath %CLASSPATH%;SeminarClient.jar
    -Djava.security.policy=policy
    com.deitel.advjhtp1.jini.seminar.client.
UnicastSeminarInfoClient hostname
```

where *policy* is an appropriate security policy and *hostname* is the hostname of the computer providing lookup services. Figure 22.27 shows the **UnicastSeminarInfoClient** application output.

 Common Programming Error 22.4

*Placing the JAR file or classes for the **SeminarInfo** service in the Jini client's **CLASS-PATH** prevents the client from downloading the class files at runtime using network class loading.*

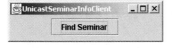

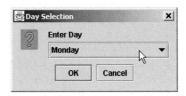

Fig. 22.27 **UnicastSeminarInfoClient** application output.

22.8 Introduction to High-Level Helper Utilities

One can build a complete Jini-aware service using previously introduced technology. However, Jini helper utilities simplify the process of developing the Jini applications. These helper utilities provide high-level management capabilities. As we proceed, you will see how these utilities make developing and using Jini services easier.

22.8.1 Discovery Utilities

As you now know, before a client or a server can interact with a lookup service, it must first discover the lookup service. Figure 22.13 introduced a low-level discovery utility, **LookupDiscovery**. This section discusses two high-level discovery utilities—class **net.jini.discovery.LookupLocatorDiscovery** and class **net.jini.discovery.LookupDiscoveryManager**.

LookupLocatorDiscovery Utility
In the **UnicastDiscovery** example (Fig. 22.10), we used class **LookupLocator** to discover lookup services on a known host. Using that technique to discover lookup services located on several known hosts would require several **LookupLocator**s—one for each host that provides lookup services. Class **LookupLocatorDiscovery** enables a Jini service or client to discover lookup services on multiple known hosts more easily. Class **LookupLocatorDiscovery** uses **DiscoveryEvent**s to notify the Jini service or client of discovered lookup services. This is similar to the task class **LookupDiscovery** performs for multicast discovery.

Class **UnicastDiscoveryUtility** (Fig. 22.28) uses class **LookupLocatorDiscovery** to perform unicast lookup-service discovery on multiple known hosts. Class **UnicastDiscoveryUtility** implements interface **DiscoveryListener** to receive **DiscoveryEvent**s from the **LookupLocatorDiscovery** object.

The **UnicastDiscoveryUtility** constructor (lines 31–62) takes a **String** array as an argument containing a list of **jini:** URLs on which to perform unicast discovery. Lines 42–43 create an array of **LookupLocator**s and lines 49–50 create a **LookupLocator** object for each URL in array **urls**. Line 53 registers the **UnicastDiscoveryUtility** object as a **DiscoveryListener** for the **LookupLocatorDiscovery** object.

```
1   // UnicastDiscoveryUtility.java
2   // Demonstrating how to locate multiple lookup services
3   // using LookupLocatorDiscovery utility
4   package com.deitel.advjhtp1.jini.utilities.discovery;
5
6   // Java core packages
7   import java.rmi.*;
8   import java.io.*;
9   import java.awt.*;
10  import java.awt.event.*;
11  import java.net.*;
```

Fig. 22.28 **UnicastDiscoveryUtility** uses class **LookupLocatorDiscovery** to facilitate lookup service discovery (part 1 of 4).

```
12
13    // Java swing package
14    import javax.swing.*;
15
16    // Jini core packages
17    import net.jini.core.lookup.ServiceRegistrar;
18    import net.jini.core.discovery.LookupLocator;
19
20    // Jini extension packages
21    import net.jini.discovery.LookupLocatorDiscovery;
22    import net.jini.discovery.DiscoveryListener;
23    import net.jini.discovery.DiscoveryEvent;
24
25    public class UnicastDiscoveryUtility extends JFrame
26       implements DiscoveryListener {
27
28       private JTextArea outputArea = new JTextArea( 10, 20 );
29
30       // UnicastDiscoveryUtility constructor
31       public UnicastDiscoveryUtility( String urls[] )
32       {
33          super( "UnicastDiscoveryUtility" );
34
35          getContentPane().add( new JScrollPane( outputArea ),
36             BorderLayout.CENTER );
37
38          // discover lookup services using LookupLocatorDiscovery
39          try {
40
41             // create LookupLocator for each URL
42             LookupLocator locators[] =
43                new LookupLocator[ urls.length ];
44
45             for ( int i = 0; i < locators.length ; i++ )
46                locators[ i ] = new LookupLocator( urls[ i ] );
47
48             // create LookupLocatorDiscovery object
49             LookupLocatorDiscovery locatorDiscovery =
50                new LookupLocatorDiscovery( locators );
51
52             // register DiscoveryListener
53             locatorDiscovery.addDiscoveryListener( this );
54
55          } // end try
56
57          // handle invalid Jini URL
58          catch ( MalformedURLException exception ) {
59             exception.printStackTrace();
60          }
61
62       } // end UnicastDiscoveryUtility constructor
63
```

Fig. 22.28 `UnicastDiscoveryUtility` uses class `LookupLocatorDis-
covery` to facilitate lookup service discovery (part 2 of 4).

```
64      // receive notification of found lookup services
65      public void discovered( DiscoveryEvent event )
66      {
67         // get the proxy registrars for those services
68         ServiceRegistrar[] registrars = event.getRegistrars();
69
70         // display information for each lookup service found
71         for ( int i = 0; i < registrars.length ; i++ )
72            displayServiceDetails( registrars[ i ] );
73
74      } // end method discovered
75
76      // display details of given ServiceRegistrar
77      private void displayServiceDetails( ServiceRegistrar registrar )
78      {
79         try {
80            final StringBuffer buffer = new StringBuffer();
81
82            // get the hostname and port number
83            buffer.append( "Lookup Service: " );
84            buffer.append( "\n   Host: " +
85               registrar.getLocator().getHost() );
86            buffer.append( "\n   Port: " +
87               registrar.getLocator().getPort() );
88            buffer.append( "\n   Group support: " );
89
90            // get lookup service groups
91            String[] groups = registrar.getGroups();
92
93            // get group names; if empty write public
94            for ( int i = 0; i < groups.length ; i++ ) {
95
96               if ( groups[ i ].equals( "" ) )
97                  buffer.append( "public," );
98
99               else
100                  buffer.append( groups[ i ] + "," );
101            }
102
103            buffer.append( "\n\n" );
104
105            // append information to outputArea
106            SwingUtilities.invokeLater(
107
108               // create Runnable for appending text
109               new Runnable() {
110
111                  // append text and update caret position
112                  public void run()
113                  {
114                     outputArea.append( buffer.toString() );
```

Fig. 22.28 UnicastDiscoveryUtility uses class **LookupLocatorDiscovery** to facilitate lookup service discovery (part 3 of 4).

```
115                         outputArea.setCaretPosition(
116                            outputArea.getText().length() );
117                      }
118                   }
119
120               ); // end call to invokeLater
121
122            } // end try
123
124            // handle exception communicating with lookup service
125            catch ( RemoteException exception ) {
126               exception.printStackTrace();
127            }
128
129      } // end method displayServiceDetails
130
131      // ignore discarded lookup services
132      public void discarded( DiscoveryEvent event ) {}
133
134      // launch UnicastDiscoveryUtility application
135      public static void main( String args[] )
136      {
137         // set SecurityManager
138         if ( System.getSecurityManager() == null )
139            System.setSecurityManager( new RMISecurityManager() );
140
141         // check command-line arguments for hostnames
142         if ( args.length < 1 ) {
143            System.err.println(
144               "Usage: java UnicastDiscoveryUtility " +
145               "jini://hostname:port [ jini://hostname:port ] ..." );
146         }
147
148         // launch UnicastDiscoveryUtility for set of hostnames
149         else {
150            UnicastDiscoveryUtility unicastUtility =
151               new UnicastDiscoveryUtility( args );
152
153            unicastUtility.setDefaultCloseOperation( EXIT_ON_CLOSE );
154            unicastUtility.setSize( 300, 300 );
155            unicastUtility.setVisible( true );
156         }
157
158      } // end method main
159 }
```

Fig. 22.28 `UnicastDiscoveryUtility` uses class **`LookupLocatorDis-`**
`covery` to facilitate lookup service discovery (part 4 of 4).

Class **LookupLocatorDiscovery** invokes method **discovered** (lines 65–74)
when it discovers new lookup services. Line 68 retrieves an array of **ServiceRegis-**
trars from the **DiscoveryEvent** object and line 72 invokes method **displaySer-**
viceDetails to show information about each discovered lookup service. Method
displayServiceDetails (lines 77–129) places host, port and group information

about a **ServiceRegistrar** in a **StringBuffer** (lines 83–103) and appends the text in that **StringBuffer** to **outputArea** (lines 106–120).

To demonstrate the **UnicastDiscoverUtility** application on a single computer, start multiple instances of the Jini lookup service. Remember that you must specify a different log directory for each Reggie instance. After starting several Reggie instances, run the **MulticastDiscovery** application of Fig. 22.13 to obtain the various port numbers on which **Reggie**s are running. Recall that **UnicastDiscoverUtility** uses unicast discovery, therefore you must specify the hostnames and port numbers for the computers running the lookup services. Using the **MulticastDiscovery** application is an easy way to determine these hostnames and port numbers for testing class **UnicastDiscoveryUtility**. Figure 22.29 shows sample output from application **Multicast-Discovery** with four lookup services running on the local machine. Note that each lookup service uses a different port number. We use these port numbers when specifying **jini:** URLs for application **UnicastDiscoveryUtility**.

After running the **MulticastDiscovery** application to find the available lookup services, enter the following to launch **UnicastDiscoveryUtility**:

```
java -Djava.security.policy=policy
    com.deitel.advjhtp1.jini.utilities.discovery.
UnicastDiscoveryUtility
    jini://hostname:3249 jini://hostname:3257 jini://hostname:3240
jini://hostname:4160
```

where *policy* is an appropriate security policy and *hostname* is the hostname running the lookup services. Remember to replace the port numbers in the preceding command with the port numbers that application **MulticastDiscovery** found on your computer. Figure 22.30 shows the **UnicastDiscoveryUtility** application output.

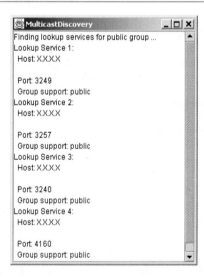

Fig. 22.29 Using **MulticastDiscovery** to obtain sample data for testing **UnicastDiscoveryUtility**.

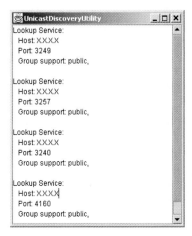

Fig. 22.30 `UnicastDiscoveryUtility` application output.

LookupDiscoveryManager Utility

Class **LookupDiscoveryManager** provides flexible lookup service discovery by enabling Jini applications and clients to perform both unicast and multicast lookup service discovery using a single class. Class **LookupDiscoveryManager** combines the functionality provided in classes **LookupLocatorDiscovery** (for unicast discovery) and **LookupDiscovery** (for multicast discovery).

Class **GeneralDiscoveryUtility** (Fig. 22.31) performs unicast and multicast discovery using class **LookupDiscoveryManager**. Lines 38–51 create and lay out two **JTextArea**s—one for displaying unicast discovery notifications and one for displaying multicast discovery notifications. Lines 55–60 create an array of **LookupLocator**s and populate the array with **jini:** URLs from the command-line arguments. Lines 63–64 create a new **LookupDiscoveryManager**. The **LookupDiscoveryManager** constructor takes as its first argument an array of group names for performing multicast discovery. The constant **DiscoveryGroupManagement.ALL_GROUPS** specifies that the **LookupDiscoveryManager** should discover all lookup services. This constant is equivalent to passing **null** as the first argument. If the first argument is an empty **String** array, no multicast discovery is performed. The second argument to the **LookupDiscoveryManager** constructor is an array of **LookupLocator**s for performing unicast discovery. If the **LookupLocator** array is **null** or empty, no unicast discovery is performed. The final argument is the **DiscoveryListener** to which discovery notifications should be sent.

Method **discovered** (lines 80–101) receives discovery notifications from the **LookupDiscoveryManager**. Line 83 retrieves an array of discovered **ServiceRegistrars** from the **DiscoveryEvent** object. Line 89 invokes method **getFrom** of class **LookupDiscoveryManager** to determine which form of discovery—unicast or multicast—discovered the given **ServiceRegistrar**. Constant **LookupDiscoveryManager.FROM_GROUP** (line 90) identifies **ServiceRegistrar**s discovered through multicast, or group, discovery. If the **ServiceRegistrar** was discovered through multicast discovery, lines 92–93 invoke method **displayServiceDetails** to display information about the **ServiceRegistrar** in **multicastArea**. If the **ServiceRegistrar** was not discovered through multicast discovery, line 98 invokes method **displayServiceDetails** to display the **ServiceRegistrar** information in **unicastArea**.

```
1   // GeneralDiscoveryUtility.java
2   // GeneralDiscoveryUtility demonstrates using class
3   // LookupDiscoveryManager for performing multicast
4   // and unicast discovery.
5   package com.deitel.advjhtp1.jini.utilities.discovery;
6
7   // Java core packages
8   import java.rmi.*;
9   import java.io.*;
10  import java.awt.*;
11  import java.awt.event.*;
12  import java.net.*;
13
14  // Java standard extensions
15  import javax.swing.*;
16  import javax.swing.border.*;
17
18  // Jini core packages
19  import net.jini.core.lookup.ServiceRegistrar;
20  import net.jini.core.discovery.LookupLocator;
21
22  // Jini extension packages
23  import net.jini.discovery.*;
24
25  public class GeneralDiscoveryUtility extends JFrame
26     implements DiscoveryListener {
27
28     private LookupDiscoveryManager lookupManager;
29     private JTextArea multicastArea = new JTextArea( 15, 20);
30     private JTextArea unicastArea = new JTextArea( 15, 20 );
31
32     // GeneralDiscoveryUtility constructor
33     public GeneralDiscoveryUtility( String urls[] )
34     {
35        super( "GeneralDiscoveryUtility" );
36
37        // lay out JTextAreas
38        JPanel multicastPanel = new JPanel();
39        multicastPanel.setBorder(
40           new TitledBorder( "Multicast (Group) Notifications" ) );
41        multicastPanel.add( new JScrollPane( multicastArea ) );
42
43        JPanel unicastPanel = new JPanel();
44        unicastPanel.setBorder(
45           new TitledBorder( "Unicast (Locator) Notifications" ) );
```

Fig. 22.31 GeneralDiscoveryUtility uses class **LookupDiscoveryManager** to perform both unicast and multicast lookup service discovery (part 1 of 4).

```
46            unicastPanel.add( new JScrollPane( unicastArea ) );
47
48            Container contentPane = getContentPane();
49            contentPane.setLayout( new FlowLayout() );
50            contentPane.add( unicastPanel );
51            contentPane.add( multicastPanel );
52
53            // get LookupLocators and LookupDiscoveryManager
54            try {
55               LookupLocator locators[] =
56                  new LookupLocator[ urls.length ];
57
58               // get array of LookupLocators
59               for ( int i = 0; i < urls.length ; i++ )
60                  locators[ i ] = new LookupLocator( urls[ i ] );
61
62               // instantiate a LookupDiscoveryManager object
63               lookupManager = new LookupDiscoveryManager(
64                  DiscoveryGroupManagement.ALL_GROUPS, locators, this );
65            }
66
67            // handle invalid Jini URL
68            catch ( MalformedURLException exception ) {
69               exception.printStackTrace();
70            }
71
72            // handle exception creating LookupDiscoveryManager
73            catch ( IOException exception ) {
74               exception.printStackTrace();
75            }
76
77         } // end GeneralDiscoveryUtility constructor
78
79         // receive notifications of discovered lookup services.
80         public void discovered( DiscoveryEvent event )
81         {
82            // get the proxy registrars for those services
83            ServiceRegistrar[] registrars = event.getRegistrars();
84
85            // display information for each lookup service found
86            for ( int i = 0; i < registrars.length ; i++ ) {
87
88               // display multicast results in multicastArea
89               if ( lookupManager.getFrom( registrars[ i ] ) ==
90                  LookupDiscoveryManager.FROM_GROUP ) {
91
92                  displayServiceDetails( registrars[ i ],
93                     multicastArea );
94               }
95
```

Fig. 22.31 GeneralDiscoveryUtility uses class **LookupDiscoveryManager** to perform both unicast and multicast lookup service discovery (part 2 of 4).

```
96              // display unicast results in unicastArea
97              else
98                  displayServiceDetails( registrars[ i ], unicastArea );
99          }
100
101     } // end method discovered
102
103     // display details of given ServiceRegistrar
104     private void displayServiceDetails(
105         ServiceRegistrar registrar, final JTextArea outputArea )
106     {
107         try {
108             final StringBuffer buffer = new StringBuffer();
109
110             // get hostname and port number
111             buffer.append( "Lookup Service: " );
112             buffer.append( "\n   Host: " +
113                 registrar.getLocator().getHost() );
114             buffer.append( "\n   Port: " +
115                 registrar.getLocator().getPort() );
116             buffer.append( "\n   Group support: " );
117
118             // get lookup service groups
119             String[] groups = registrar.getGroups();
120
121             // get group names; if empty write public
122             for ( int i = 0; i < groups.length ; i++ ) {
123
124                 if ( groups[ i ].equals( "" ) )
125                     buffer.append( "public," );
126
127                 else
128                     buffer.append( groups[ i ] + "," );
129             }
130
131             buffer.append( "\n\n" );
132
133             // append information to outputArea
134             SwingUtilities.invokeLater(
135
136                 // create Runnable for appending text
137                 new Runnable() {
138
139                     // append text and update caret position
140                     public void run()
141                     {
142                         outputArea.append( buffer.toString() );
143                         outputArea.setCaretPosition(
144                             outputArea.getText().length() );
145                     }
146                 }
```

Fig. 22.31 `GeneralDiscoveryUtility` uses class `LookupDiscoveryManager` to perform both unicast and multicast lookup service discovery (part 3 of 4).

```
147
148            ); // end call to invokeLater
149
150         } // end try
151
152         // handle exception communicating with lookup service
153         catch ( RemoteException exception ) {
154            exception.printStackTrace();
155         }
156
157      } // end method displayServiceDetails
158
159      // receive discarded lookup service notifications
160      public void discarded( DiscoveryEvent event ) {}
161
162      // launch GeneralDiscoveryUtility application
163      public static void main( String[] args )
164      {
165         // set SecurityManager
166         if ( System.getSecurityManager() == null )
167            System.setSecurityManager( new RMISecurityManager() );
168
169         // launch GeneralDiscoveryUtility for set of hostnames
170         GeneralDiscoveryUtility utility =
171            new GeneralDiscoveryUtility( args );
172         utility.setDefaultCloseOperation( EXIT_ON_CLOSE );
173         utility.pack();
174         utility.setVisible( true );
175
176      } // end method main
177   }
```

Fig. 22.31 **GeneralDiscoveryUtility** uses class **LookupDiscoveryManager** to perform both unicast and multicast lookup service discovery (part 4 of 4).

Method **displayServiceDetails** (lines 104–159) takes as arguments a **ServiceRegistrar** and a **JTextArea** in which to display that **ServiceRegistrar**'s information. Lines 111–131 append the **ServiceRegistrar**'s information to a **StringBuffer**. Lines 134–148 invoke **static** method **invokeLater** of class **SwingUtilities** to append the **ServiceRegistrar** information to the appropriate **JTextArea**.

Method **main** (lines 163–176) installs an **RMISecurityManager** (line 167) and creates a new **GeneralDiscoveryUtility** instance, passing the array of command-line arguments to the constructor (lines 170–171). If the user does not supply any **jini:** URLs as command-line arguments, **GeneralDiscoveryUtility** will not perform unicast discovery. To execute **GeneralDiscoveryUtility**, enter the following at a command prompt:

```
java -Djava.security.policy=policy
   com.deitel.advjhtp1.jini.utilities.discovery.
GeneralDiscoveryUtility jini://hostname:4160
```

where *policy* is an appropriate security policy, *hostname* is the hostname for a known computer running a lookup service and **4160** is the default lookup service port number. Figure 22.32 shows the output from **GeneralDiscoveryUtility** with several lookup services running on the local machine.

22.8.2 Entry Utilities

Entry attributes specify characteristics of Jini services. We used the **Name Entry** in Fig. 22.21 to provide a name for the **SeminarInfo** Jini service. **Entry** attributes help clients identify Jini services. By attaching attributes to services, service providers can publish services with detailed information, such as the service location and the functionality of the service. Jini provides seven common attributes (Fig. 22.33).

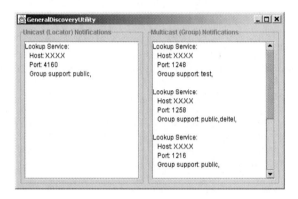

Fig. 22.32 **GeneralDiscoveryUtility** application output.

Attribute	Description
Address	Specifies the physical location of a service. (e.g., the city and street address of an Automated Teller Machine).
Comment	Provides general descriptive comments about a service.
Location	Provides more detailed location information, such as floor, suite and room number.
Name	Provides the service's name, suitable for use by people to identify a service (e.g., "BankABC ATM").
ServiceInfo	Provides basic information about a service. For example, the manufacturer and model number of a printer.
ServiceType	Provides a human-understandable description of the service type (e.g., "Print Queue").
Status	Describes the current status of the service in varying levels of severity.

Fig. 22.33 Standard Jini **Entry** attributes.

Developers also can create custom attributes for Jini services. Class **Seminar-Provider** (Fig. 22.34) is an **Entry** attribute that gives the name of the company that provides **Seminar**s for a given **SeminarInfo** service. Class **SeminarProvider** extends class **AbstractEntry** and implements interface **ServiceControlled**. **AbstractEntry** is a basic implementation of interface **Entry**. By implementing interface **ServiceControlled**, class **SeminarProvider** indicates that the service itself controls the **SeminarProvider** attribute.

An **Entry** class must supply a no-argument constructor (line 12). Also, instance variables must be **public** references to **Serializable** objects, so clients can perform searches using these instance variables. Line 12 declares **public String** reference **providerName**, which contains the name of the organization providing the **Seminar**s.

To use the **SeminarProvider** attribute for our **SeminarInfo** Jini service, we need to modify class **SeminarInfoService**, which registers the **SeminarInfo** service with **ServiceRegistrar**s. Replace line 43 of Fig. 22.21 with the line

```
entries[ 0 ] = new
    com.deitel.advjhtp1.jini.utilities.entry.SeminarProvider(
        "Deitel" );
```

We also must modify **UnicastSeminarInfoClient** to search for the **SeminarInfoService**s using the new **SeminarProvider** attribute. Replace line 110 of Fig. 22.22 with the line

```
Entry[] attribute = new Entry[] { new
    com.deitel.advjhtp1.jini.utilities.entry.SeminarProvider(
        "Deitel" ) };
```

```
1   // SeminarProvider.java
2   // SeminarProvider is an Entry object for the SeminarInfo service.
3   package com.deitel.advjhtp1.jini.utilities.entry;
4
5   // Jini extension package
6   import net.jini.entry.*;
7   import net.jini.lookup.entry.*;
8
9   public class SeminarProvider extends AbstractEntry
10      implements ServiceControlled
11  {
12      public String providerName = "";
13
14      // no-argument constructor
15      public SeminarProvider() {}
16
17      // SeminarProvider constructor for specifying providerName
18      public SeminarProvider( String provider )
19      {
20          providerName = provider;
21      }
22  }
```

Fig. 22.34 SeminarProvider subclass of **Entry** for describing the **Seminar** provider as a Jini attribute.

Compile and run the Jini service and **UnicastSeminarInfoClient** to locate the **SeminarInfo** service using the new **SeminarProvider** attribute. Be sure to include **SeminarProvider.class** in the service and client JAR files.

22.8.3 Lease Utilities

Jini uses *leasing* to ensure integrity in distributed systems built with Jini. Recall that Jini services register with lookup services to make the Jini service's functionality available to other members in the Jini community. If all goes well, other members of the Jini community use the service and the service stays up and running perpetually. However, in reality, services fail for many reasons. Network outages can make a service unreachable. A physical device associated with a service (e.g., a printer) might need repairs. The service itself could encounter an unrecoverable exception. In these and many other situations, a service could become unavailable and that service might not be able to unregister itself from lookup services to prevent other clients from attempting to use that service.

One goal of Jini technology is to make Jini communities "self-healing" and able to recover from common problems, such as network outages, hardware failures and software failures. Therefore, when a Jini service registers with a lookup service, the registration is not permanent. The registration is leased for a specific amount of time, after which the lookup service revokes the registration. This prevents problematic services from disrupting the entire Jini community. If a Jini service fails, the Jini service's lease eventually expires, and lookup services will no longer provide the failed Jini service to clients.

The leasing strategy that Jini employs is strict—if a Jini service does not renew its lease, the lookup service terminates the registration when the lease expires and the service becomes unavailable to clients. Therefore, developers must ensure that their Jini services manage registration leases to ensure that services do not lose their registrations prematurely.

Our **SeminarInfo** Jini service does not perform any lease maintenance. After the **SeminarInfo** service's first lease expires (i.e., 10 minutes), the **SeminarInfo** service is no longer available to clients. The service itself continues executing, but the lookup services with which the service registered will have terminated the registrations.

Class **LeaseRenewalManager** is a Jini utility class that enables services to manage their leases to ensure that the service's leases do not expire prematurely. Class **SeminarInfoLeaseService** (Fig. 22.35) uses class **LeaseRenewalManager** to manage leases for the **SeminarInfo** service. Class **SeminarInfoLeaseService** is similar to class **SeminarInfoService** (Fig. 22.21), so we concentrate only on lease management in this example.

```
1   // SeminarInfoLeaseService.java
2   // SeminarInfoLeaseService discovers lookup services, registers
3   // the SeminarInfo service, and creates a LeaseRenewalManager
4   // to maintain the SeminarInfo service lease.
5   package com.deitel.advjhtp1.jini.utilities.leasing;
6
7   // Java core packages
8   import java.rmi.RMISecurityManager;
```

Fig. 22.35 **SeminarInfoLeaseService** uses class **LeaseRenewalManager** to manage **SeminarInfo** service leasing (part 1 of 4).

```
 9   import java.rmi.RemoteException;
10   import java.io.IOException;
11
12   // Jini core packages
13   import net.jini.core.lookup.*;
14   import net.jini.core.entry.Entry;
15   import net.jini.core.lease.Lease;
16
17   // Jini extension packages
18   import net.jini.discovery.*;
19   import net.jini.lookup.entry.Name;
20   import net.jini.lease.LeaseRenewalManager;
21
22   // Deitel packages
23   import com.deitel.advjhtp1.jini.seminar.service.*;
24   import com.deitel.advjhtp1.jini.utilities.entry.SeminarProvider;
25
26   public class SeminarInfoLeaseService implements DiscoveryListener {
27
28      private LookupDiscovery discover;
29      private ServiceItem item;
30      private static final int LEASETIME = 10 * 60 * 1000;
31
32      // SeminarInfoLeaseService constructor
33      public SeminarInfoLeaseService()
34      {
35         // search for lookup services with public group
36         try {
37            discover = new LookupDiscovery( new String[] { "" } );
38
39            // register DiscoveryListener
40            discover.addDiscoveryListener( this );
41         }
42
43         // handle exception creating LookupDiscovery
44         catch ( IOException exception ) {
45            exception.printStackTrace();
46         }
47
48         // create and set Entry name for service
49         Entry[] entries = new Entry[ 1 ];
50         entries[ 0 ] = new SeminarProvider( "Deitel" );
51
52         // specify the service's proxy and entry
53         item = new ServiceItem( null, createProxy(), entries );
54
55      } // end SeminarInfoLeaseService constructor
56
57      // receive notifications of discovered lookup services
58      public void discovered ( DiscoveryEvent event )
59      {
60         ServiceRegistrar[] registrars = event.getRegistrars();
```

Fig. 22.35 SeminarInfoLeaseService uses class LeaseRenewalManager
to manage SeminarInfo service leasing (part 2 of 4).

```
61
62          // register the service with the lookup service
63          for ( int i = 0; i < registrars.length; i++ ) {
64
65             ServiceRegistrar registrar = registrars[ i ];
66
67             // register the service with the lookup service
68             try {
69                ServiceRegistration registration =
70                   registrar.register( item, LEASETIME );
71
72                // create LeaseRenewalmanager
73                LeaseRenewalManager leaseManager =
74                   new LeaseRenewalManager();
75
76                // renew SeminarInfo lease indefinitely
77                leaseManager.renewUntil( registration.getLease(),
78                   Lease.FOREVER, null );
79
80             }   // end try
81
82             // handle exception registering ServiceItem
83             catch ( RemoteException exception ) {
84                exception.printStackTrace();
85             }
86
87          } // end for
88
89       } // end method discovered
90
91       // ignore discarded lookup services
92       public void discarded( DiscoveryEvent event ) {}
93
94       // create seminar service proxy
95       private SeminarInterface createProxy()
96       {
97          // get BackendInterface reference to SeminarInfo
98          try {
99             BackendInterface backInterface = new SeminarInfo();
100
101            return new SeminarProxy( backInterface );
102         }
103
104         // handle exception creating SeminarProxy
105         catch ( RemoteException exception ) {
106            exception.printStackTrace();
107         }
108
109         return null;
110
111      } // end method createProxy
112
```

Fig. 22.35 SeminarInfoLeaseService uses class LeaseRenewalManager to manage SeminarInfo service leasing (part 3 of 4).

```
113    // launch SeminarInfoLeaseService
114    public static void main( String args[] )
115    {
116       // set SecurityManager
117       if ( System.getSecurityManager() == null ) {
118          System.setSecurityManager( new RMISecurityManager() );
119       }
120
121       SeminarInfoLeaseService service =
122          new SeminarInfoLeaseService();
123
124       Object keepAlive = new Object();
125
126       // wait on keepAlive Object to keep service running
127       synchronized ( keepAlive ) {
128
129          // keep application alive
130          try {
131             keepAlive.wait();
132          }
133
134          // handle exception if wait interrupted
135          catch ( InterruptedException exception ) {
136             exception.printStackTrace();
137          }
138
139       } // end synchronized block
140
141    } // end method main
142 }
```

Fig. 22.35 **SeminarInfoLeaseService** uses class **LeaseRenewalManager** to manage **SeminarInfo** service leasing (part 4 of 4).

In method **discovered**, lines 69–70 register the **SeminarInfo** service's **ServiceItem** with the discovered **ServiceRegistrar**. Lines 73–74 create a new **LeaseRenewalManager**, which class **SeminarInfoLeaseService** uses to manage the **SeminarInfo** service's lease. Lines 77–78 invoke method **renewUntil** of class **LeaseRenewalManager**. Method **renewUntil** takes as its first argument the **Lease** object to be renewed. In this example, we obtain the **Lease** object by invoking method **getLease** of class **ServiceRegistration**. The second argument specifies the desired expiration time (in milliseconds) for renewed **Lease**s. Line 78 specifies the constant **Lease.FOREVER** to request a **Lease** that never expires. This does not guarantee that the lookup service will provide an everlasting **Lease**—the lookup service is free to grant a lease that is shorter than the requested length. The third argument to method **renewUntil** is the **LeaseListener**, to notify of problems encountered when renewing the **Lease**. We pass **null** as the third argument to disregard such notifications.

To run the **SeminarInfo** Jini service with lease management, create a new JAR file named **SeminarServiceWithLeasing.jar**. Figure 22.36 shows the contents of **SeminarServiceWithLeasing.jar**. Note that this JAR file replaces **SeminarInfoService.class** with **SeminarInfoLeaseService.class**. Note also that this JAR file includes **SeminarProvider.class**, which is our custom **Entry** object for the **SeminarInfo** service.

After packaging the classes in **SeminarServiceWithLeasing.jar**, run the new version of the service by typing the following command at a command prompt:

```
java -classpath %CLASSPATH%;SeminarServiceWithLeasing.jar
   -Djava.security.policy=policy
   -Djava.rmi.server.codebase=http://hostname:9090/
SeminarServiceDownload.jar
   com.deitel.advjhtp1.jini.utilities.leasing.
SeminarInfoLeaseService
```

where *policy* is an appropriate security policy and *hostname* is the hostname where the Web server for downloading the **SeminarInfo** service proxy is running. The **LeaseRenewalManager** will renew the **SeminarInfo** service's lease to maintain the service's lookup service registrations.

22.8.4 **JoinManager** Utility

As we have seen, making a Jini service available in a Jini community requires several steps. The service must discover lookup services, register with discovered lookup services and maintain registration leases. Class **JoinManager** is a utility class that facilitates the process of deploying a Jini service by performing lookup discovery, service registration and lease management in a single class.

Class File	Directory in **SeminarServiceWithLeasing.jar**
Seminar.class	com\deitel\advjhtp1\jini\seminar\
SeminarInterface.class	com\deitel\advjhtp1\jini\seminar\service\
SeminarProxy.class	com\deitel\advjhtp1\jini\seminar\service\
BackendInterface.class	com\deitel\advjhtp1\jini\seminar\service\
SeminarInfo.class	com\deitel\advjhtp1\jini\seminar\service\
SeminarInfo_Stub.class	com\deitel\advjhtp1\jini\seminar\service\
SeminarProvider.class	com\deitel\advjhtp1\jini\utilities\entry\
SeminarInfoLeaseService.class	com\deitel\advjhtp1\jini\utilities\leasing\

Fig. 22.36 **SeminarServiceWithLeasing.jar** contents.

Class **SeminarInfoJoinService** (Fig. 22.37) uses class **JoinManager** to deploy the **SeminarInfo** service. Lines 38–40 create a **LookupDiscoveryManger** that the **JoinManager** will use to discover lookup services. We pass as the first argument to the **LookupDiscoveryManager** constructor a **String** array with a single element, which is an empty **String**. This argument specifies that the **LookupDiscoveryManager** should perform multicast discovery for lookup services that support the "**public**" group. For the second and third arguments, line 40 passes the value **null**. These arguments disable unicast discovery and specify a **null DiscoveryListener**, respectively. The **JoinManager** handles the discovery process, so class **SeminarInfoJoinService** need not handle **DiscoveryEvent**s.

Lines 43–44 create a new **Entry** array with a single **SeminarProvider** element that specifies the provider of **Seminar**s for the **SeminarInfo** service. Lines 47–49 create a new instance of class **JoinManager** to discover lookup services, register the service and maintain the service's registration leases. Line 47 invokes method **createProxy** to create a **SeminarProxy** for the **SeminarInfo** service. The second argument to the **JoinManager** constructor is the array of **Entry** attributes that describe the service. The third argument is a reference to a **ServiceIDListener**. When the **JoinManager** registers the Jini service with a lookup service, the **JoinManager** notifies the **ServiceIDListener** of the service ID that the lookup service assigns to the Jini service. The fourth argument is a **DiscoveryManagement** object for discovering lookup services. For this example, we pass the **LookupDiscoveryManager** created on lines 38–40. The final argument to the **JoinManager** constructor is a **LeaseRenewalManager** for maintaining the service's registration leases.

```
1   // SeminarInfoJoinService.java
2   // SeminarInfoJoinService uses a JoinManager to find lookup
3   // services, register the Seminar service with the lookup
4   // services and manage lease renewal.
5   package com.deitel.advjhtp1.jini.utilities.join;
6
7   // Java core packages
8   import java.rmi.RMISecurityManager;
9   import java.rmi.RemoteException;
10  import java.io.IOException;
11
12  // Jini core packages
13  import net.jini.core.lookup.ServiceID;
14  import net.jini.core.entry.Entry;
15
16  // Jini extension packages
17  import net.jini.lookup.entry.Name;
18  import net.jini.lease.LeaseRenewalManager;
19  import net.jini.lookup.JoinManager;
20  import net.jini.discovery.LookupDiscoveryManager;
21  import net.jini.lookup.ServiceIDListener;
22
```

Fig. 22.37 **SeminarInfoJoinService** uses class **JoinManager** to facilitate registering the **SeminarInfo** service and manage its leasing (part 1 of 3).

```
23   // Deitel packages
24   import com.deitel.advjhtp1.jini.seminar.service.*;
25   import com.deitel.advjhtp1.jini.utilities.entry.*;
26
27   public class SeminarInfoJoinService implements ServiceIDListener {
28
29      // SeminarInfoJoinService constructor
30      public SeminarInfoJoinService()
31      {
32         // use JoinManager to register SeminarInfo service
33         // and manage lease
34         try {
35
36            // create LookupDiscoveryManager for discovering
37            // lookup services
38            LookupDiscoveryManager lookupManager =
39               new LookupDiscoveryManager( new String[] { "" },
40                  null, null );
41
42            // create and set Entry name for service
43            Entry[] entries = new Entry[ 1 ];
44            entries[ 0 ] = new SeminarProvider( "Deitel" );
45
46            // create JoinManager
47            JoinManager manager = new JoinManager( createProxy(),
48               entries, this, lookupManager,
49               new LeaseRenewalManager() );
50         }
51
52         // handle exception creating JoinManager
53         catch ( IOException exception ) {
54            exception.printStackTrace();
55         }
56
57      } // end SeminarInfoJoinService constructor
58
59      // create seminar service proxy
60      private SeminarInterface createProxy()
61      {
62         // get SeminarProxy for SeminarInfo service
63         try {
64            return new SeminarProxy( new SeminarInfo() );
65         }
66
67         // handle exception creating SeminarProxy
68         catch ( RemoteException exception ) {
69            exception.printStackTrace();
70         }
71
72         return null;
73
74      } // end method createProxy
```

Fig. 22.37 SeminarInfoJoinService uses class JoinManager to facilitate registering the SeminarInfo service and manage its leasing (part 2 of 3).

```
75
76      // receive notification of ServiceID assignment
77      public void serviceIDNotify( ServiceID serviceID )
78      {
79          System.err.println( "Service ID: " + serviceID );
80      }
81
82      // launch SeminarInfoJoinService
83      public static void main( String args[] )
84      {
85          // set SecurityManager
86          if ( System.getSecurityManager() == null ) {
87              System.setSecurityManager( new RMISecurityManager() );
88          }
89
90          // create SeminarInfoJoinService
91          new SeminarInfoJoinService();
92      }
93  }
```

```
Service ID: 0084d3a0-4bbe-4b76-aa0b-f73294738fec
```

Fig. 22.37 `SeminarInfoJoinService` uses class `JoinManager` to facilitate registering the `SeminarInfo` service and manage its leasing (part 3 of 3).

Method **serviceIDNotify** (lines 77–80) is required by interface **Service-IDListener**. The **JoinManager** invokes method **serviceIDNotify** to notify a **ServiceIDListener** that a lookup service has assigned a service ID to the Jini service. Line 79 simply prints out the service ID.

Method **main** (lines 83–92) sets the **RMISecurityManager** and launches the **SeminarInfoJoinService** application. Note that method **main** does not use a **keepAlive Object** to keep the application running, as was required in previous examples. The **JoinManager** keeps the application alive.

To run the **SeminarInfo** service using the **JoinManager**, create the JAR file **SeminarServiceJoinManager.jar** with the contents listed in Figure 22.38.

Class File	Directory in **SeminarServiceJoinManager.jar**

Seminar.class

    com\deitel\advjhtp1\jini\seminar\

SeminarInterface.class

    com\deitel\advjhtp1\jini\seminar\service\

SeminarProxy.class

    com\deitel\advjhtp1\jini\seminar\service\

Fig. 22.38 `SeminarServiceJoinManager.jar` contents (part 1 of 2).

Class File	Directory in `SeminarServiceJoinManager.jar`

`BackendInterface.class`

        `com\deitel\advjhtp1\jini\seminar\service\`

`SeminarInfo.class`

        `com\deitel\advjhtp1\jini\seminar\service\`

`SeminarInfo_Stub.class`

        `com\deitel\advjhtp1\jini\seminar\service\`

`SeminarProvider.class`

        `com\deitel\advjhtp1\jini\utilities\entry\`

`SeminarInfoJoinService.class`

        `com\deitel\advjhtp1\jini\utilities\join\`

Fig. 22.38 `SeminarServiceJoinManager.jar` contents (part 2 of 2).

After packaging the classes in **`SeminarServiceJoinManager.jar`**, run the new version of the service by typing the following at a command prompt:

```
java -classpath %CLASSPATH%;SeminarServiceJoinManager.jar
   -Djava.security.policy=policy
   -Djava.rmi.server.codebase=http://hostname:9090/
SeminarServiceDownload.jar
   com.deitel.advjhtp1.jini.utilities.join.
SeminarInfoJoinService
```

where *policy* is an appropriate security policy and *hostname* is the hostname where the Web server for downloading the **`SeminarInfo`** service proxy is running. Figure 22.37 shows a sample service ID output from application **`SeminarInfoJoinService`**.

22.8.5 Service Discovery Utilities

Complex Jini clients often have specific requirements for the Jini services they employ. To satisfy these requirements, the Jini client often must work with sets of Jini services. The client searches through these services to locate the particular service that can satisfy the client's needs. For example, a Jini client that provides users with information about printers available in a given office needs a set of services for the available printers. This printer-monitoring program would need to be aware of the status of each printer to know when a new printer has been added. The service also should be able to search among the printers for particular features (color support, print quality, capacity, speed etc.).

Class **`net.jini.lookup.ServiceDiscoveryManager`** provides Jini clients with a richer set of service and lookup-service management features than interface **`ServiceRegistrar`** provides. Class **`ServiceDiscoveryManager`** facilitates discovering available services and enables clients to perform finer-grained searches than are possible with the **`ServiceRegistrar`** interface. Jini clients also can use class **`ServiceDiscoveryManager`** to enhance application performance by maintaining a local cache of services. There are three primary ways in which Jini clients use class **`ServiceDiscoveryManager`**—creating a local cache of services, receiving event notifications when services become available or unavailable and performing detailed searches not possible with simple **ServiceTemplate**s.

Class **ServiceDiscoveryManager** can enhance Jini-client performance by creating a local cache of discovered services. This local cache—implemented as a *net.jini.lookup.LookupCache*—enables the client to perform additional service lookups without incurring the network overhead of a remote call to a lookup service. When the client needs a particular service that is in the **LookupCache**, the client simply invokes method **lookup** of interface **LookupCache** to retrieve the service from the local cache.

Jini clients also can use a **LookupCache** retrieved from a **ServiceDiscovery-Manager** to receive notifications related to a set of services. By implementing interface **ServiceDiscoveryListener** and registering with a **LookupCache**, a Jini client can receive events indicating when a particular service has been discovered, when a service's attributes have changed and when the service is removed from the **LookupCache**. This event notification is particularly useful for Jini clients that monitor available resources, such as our printer-monitoring example.

Class **ServiceDiscoveryManager** also provides an enhanced interface that enables Jini clients to search for services using more specific search criteria. Jini clients can use class **ServiceDiscoverManager** with implementations of interface **Service-ItemFilter** to locate services whose attribute values fall within a particular range. For example, a Jini client could use a **ServiceItemFilter** to locate all automated teller machines in the area whose service charge is less than two dollars. Such a specific query is not possible using the standard **ServiceTemplate** matching available through interface **ServiceRegistrar**.

For more information on class **ServiceDiscoveryManager**, please see the Jini API documentation included with the Jini Technology Core Platform.

22.9 Internet and World Wide Web Resources

www.jini.org
Home of the Jini community.

www.sun.com/jini/specs/jini1.1html/coreTOC.html
The site for *Jini Technology Core Platform Specification*.

www.sun.com/jini/specs/jini1.1html/collectionTOC.html
This site contains a collection of *Jini Technology Helper Utilities and Services Specifications*.

www.sun.com/jini/specs/jini1.1html/jsTOC.html
This site provides *JavaSpaces Service Specification*.

developer.java.sun.com/developer/products/jini/installation.index.html
This site provides installation instructions for Jini technology.

SUMMARY

- Many network devices provide services to network clients.

- Each service has a well-defined interface.

- To use a service, a client must be able to discover that a service exists and must know the interface for interacting with the service.

- Jini extends RMI to provide services to a network.

- Jini services are plug-and-play—clients can discover services on the network dynamically, transparently download classes required to use those services, then begin interacting with those services.
- RMI's dynamic class-downloading capability enables Jini clients to use services without installing special driver software for those services in advance.
- For Jini clients to discover and use Jini services, standardized interfaces for common services must be developed.
- The basic software requirements for Jini include the Java 2 Standard Edition (J2SE) and the Jini Technology Starter Kit. If you are going to write commercial Jini services and want to test their compatibility with the Jini platform, you also need to download the Jini Technology Core Platform Compatibility Kit (Jini TCK).
- The Jini Starter Kit has three components—the Jini Technology Core Platform (JCP), the Jini Technology Extended Platform (JXP) and the Jini Software Kit (JSK). The JCP contains the fundamental Jini interfaces and classes. The JXP provides helper utilities for implementing Jini services and clients. The JSK contains an implementation of the services specified in the JCP and the JXP.
- To compile and execute Jini services and clients the JAR files **jini-core.jar**, **jini-ext.jar** and **sun-util.jar** must be included in the **CLASSPATH** environment variable. These three JAR files are in the **lib** directory of the Jini Starter Kit—they correspond to the Jini Technology Core Platform, the Jini Technology Extended Platform and the Jini Software Kit, respectively.
- The Jini distribution comes with three services that must be running correctly before executing Jini applications—a Web server to enable Jini clients to download class files through RMI, so the clients can access Jini services dynamically; the RMI activation daemon (**rmid**) to enable the RMI infrastructure that allows Jini clients to communicate with Jini services; and a lookup service to maintain information about available Jini services, and to enable clients to discover and use those services. The Web server and **rmid** must be executing (they can be started in any order) before starting the lookup service.
- The Jini Technology Core Platform implementation includes the **StartService** GUI tool for launching required services.
- The Jini lookup service is the heart of a Jini community. The process of finding the lookup services and obtaining references to them is called discovery.
- Discovery distinguishes Jini technology from RMI. In RMI, you must know in advance where to register an object. In Jini, you do not need to know where—just how. The discovery process determines where, but hides the details from the developer.
- Discovery can be accomplished using either unicast discovery or multicast discovery.
- Unicast discovery, or locator discovery, enables a Jini service or client to discover lookup services on a specific host.
- Method **getRegistrar** of class **LookupLocator** performs unicast discovery. The method returns a **ServiceRegistrar**, which represents a lookup service. An overloaded version of method **getRegistrar** takes as an integer argument the maximum number of milliseconds to wait for the unicast discovery to locate a **ServiceRegistrar** before issuing a timeout.
- Methods **getHost** and **getPort** of class **LookupLocator** retrieve the hostname and port number where a lookup service was discovered.
- Multicast discovery, or group discovery, enables a Jini service or client to discover lookup services when the particular host running the lookup service is not known. A multicast discovery request uses network multicast to discover nearby lookup services. Lookup services periodically issue multicast announcements to notify interested Jini services and clients that the lookup services are available.
- Class **net.jini.discovery.LookupDiscovery** performs multicast discovery.
- Implementing interface **DiscoveryListener** enables an object of a class to receive **DiscoveryEvent**s—notifications of discovered lookup services.

- Class **LookupDiscovery** invokes method **discovered** when **LookupDiscovery** locates new lookup services.
- Method **getRegistrars** of **DiscoveryEvent** obtains an array of **ServiceRegistrar**s.
- Class **LookupDiscovery** invokes method **discarded** when a lookup service should be discarded because it is no longer available or because it no longer matches the set of groups in which the Jini service or client is interested.
- A Jini service consists of several components, each of which contributes to the flexibility and portability of the Jini architecture. A service proxy is an intermediary between a Jini service and its clients. The service proxy communicates with the actual service implementation through the service's back-end interface, which defines methods in the service implementation. A separate application discovers lookup services and registers the Jini service, making the service available to Jini clients.
- A Jini client uses the lookup service discovery techniques to discover lookup services. The Jini client then uses the discovered lookup services to locate the desired Jini service. When the lookup service locates the service requested by the Jini client, the lookup service serializes the service proxy and delivers the proxy to the Jini client. The client can then invoke methods defined in the service's **public** interface directly on the service proxy, which implements that interface. The service proxy communicates with the service implementation through the back-end interface.
- An **Entry** (package **net.jini.core.entry**) describes a service, which enables Jini clients to search for services of a particular description.
- The lookup service requires a **ServiceItem** (package **net.jini.core.lookup**) to register a Jini service.
- Jini helper utilities simplify the process of developing the Jini applications. These helper utilities provide high-level management capabilities.
- Class **LookupLocatorDiscovery** enables a Jini service or client to discover lookup services on multiple known hosts. Class **LookupLocatorDiscovery** uses **DiscoveryEvent**s to notify the Jini service or client of discovered lookup services.
- Class **LookupDiscoveryManager** provides flexible lookup service discovery by enabling Jini applications and clients to perform both unicast and multicast lookup service discovery using a single class.
- **Entry** attributes specify characteristics of Jini services. By attaching attributes to services, service providers can publish services with detailed information, such as the service location and the functionality of the service. Developers also can create custom attributes for Jini services. Class **AbstractEntry** provides a basic implementation of interface **Entry**.
- An **Entry** class must supply a no-argument constructor. Also, instance variables must be **public** references to **Serializable** objects.
- One goal of Jini technology is to make Jini communities "self-healing" and able to recover from common problems, such as network outages, hardware failures and software failures. Therefore, when a Jini service registers with a lookup service, the registration is not permanent. The registration is leased for a specific amount of time, after which the lookup service revokes the registration. This prevents problematic services from disrupting the entire Jini community.
- The leasing strategy that Jini employs is strict—if a Jini service does not renew its lease, the lookup service terminates the registration when the lease expires, making the service unavailable to clients.
- Class **LeaseRenewalManager** is a Jini utility class that enables services to manage their leases to ensure that the service's leases do not expire prematurely.
- Class **JoinManager** is a utility class that facilitates the process of deploying a Jini service by performing lookup discovery, service registration and lease management in a single class.
- Complex Jini clients often have specific requirements for the Jini services they employ. To satisfy these requirements, the Jini client often must work with sets of Jini services. The client searches

through these services to locate the particular service that can satisfy the client's needs. Class **ServiceDiscoveryManager** facilitates discovering available services and enables clients to perform finer-grained searches than are possible with the **ServiceRegistrar** interface.

- There are three primary ways in which Jini clients use class **ServiceDiscoveryManager**— creating a local cache of services, receiving event notifications when services become available or unavailable and performing detailed searches not possible with simple **ServiceTemplate**s.

- Class **ServiceDiscoveryManager** can enhance Jini-client performance by creating a local cache of discovered services. This local cache—implemented as a **LookupCache**.

TERMINOLOGY

serviceAdded method of **ServiceDiscoveryListener**	**LeaseRenewalManager** class
AbstractEntry class	locator discovery
createLookupCache method of **ServiceDiscoveryManager**	**lookup** method of **ServiceDiscoveryManager**
discovery	**lookup** method of **ServiceDiscoveryManager**
DiscoveryEvent class	**lookup** method of **LookupCache**
DiscoveryListener interface	lookup service
DiscoveryManagement class	**LookupCache** interface
Entry interface	**LookupDiscovery** class
getFrom method of **LookupDiscoveryManager**	**LookupDiscoveryManager** class
getGroups method of **LookupDiscovery**	**LookupLocator** class
getHost method of class **LookupLocator**	**LookupLocatorDiscovery** class
getPort method of class **LookupLocator**	multicast discovery
getRegistrar method of class **LookupLocator**	**Name** class
getRegistrars method of class **LookupDiscovery**	plug and play
group discovery	Reggie lookup service
Jini	**renewFor** method of **LeaseRenewalManager**
Jini client	**renewUntil** method of **LeaseRenewalManager**
Jini Software Kit	**ServiceDiscoveryListener** interface
Jini Technology Core Platform Compatibility Kit	**ServiceDiscoveryManager** class
Jini Technology Starter Kit	**ServiceID** class
Jini transaction manager service	**serviceIDNotify** method of **ServiceIDListener**
jini: URL	**ServiceItem** class
join protocol	**ServiceItemFilter** interface
JoinManager class	**ServiceRegistrar** interface
Lease class	**serviceRemoved** method in **ServiceDiscoveryListener**
lease renewal service	**ServiceTemplate** class
Lease.FOREVER constant	unicast discovery
LeaseListener interface	

SELF-REVIEW EXERCISES

22.1 Fill in the blanks in each of the following statements:
   a) Name three required services for running Jini services and clients: _____, _____ and _____.
   b) Two ways to discover lookup services are _____ and _____.

   c) To generate the stub file for a remote object, use _____.

   d) A service proxy that is exported to the remote client must implement interface _____.

   e) Service providers use _____ to describe a service. Jini clients use _____ to find a matching service.

22.2 State whether each of the following is *true* or *false*. If *false*, explain why.

   a) Unicast discovery is also known as locator discovery.

   b) The **JoinManager** can discover lookup services, register a service and renew a service's lease.

   c) Class **LookupDiscoveryManager** can perform only unicast discovery.

   d) Jini requires only the RMI activation daemon (**rmid**) and a Web server.

   e) Jini clients must have all the **.class** files for a Jini service in the local **CLASSPATH**.

ANSWERS TO SELF-REVIEW EXERCISES

22.1 a) the HTTP Web server, the **rmi** activation daemon, the lookup service. b) unicast discovery, multicast discovery. c) **rmic**. d) **Serializable**. e) **ServiceItem**, **ServiceTemplate**.

22.2 a) True. b) True. c) False. Class **LookupDiscoveryManager** performs both unicast and multicast discovery. d) False. Jini also requires lookup services to enable clients to locate Jini services. e) False. Jini clients require that only the public interface and supporting classes be in the local **CLASSPATH**. Having the Jini service's **.class** files in the client's **CLASSPATH** prevents network class loading.

EXERCISES

22.3 Modify class **MulticastDiscovery** (Fig. 22.13) to perform multicast discovery for lookup services that support any group, not just the public group. Can you use **null** for a wildcard match?

22.4 Create an application to find all services that are registered with local lookup services.

22.5 Write a currency exchange service using Jini technology. This currency exchange service simply does one function: It exchanges the currency of one country to the currency of another country. The exchange rate can be dynamically loaded from an on-line resource or can be just statically loaded from a file. Create the public interface, service proxy, back-end interface and service implementation.

22.6 Register the currency exchange service with the lookup services on the local machine using **JoinManager**.

22.7 Create a Jini client that allows a user to use the exchange service. Search the currency exchange service with the lookup service on the local machine, and use the found service to exchange one currency into another currency.

22.8 Modify Exercise 22.6 to add a set of **Entry** attributes to the service. The attributes should include the name of the exchange service, the address of the exchange service and any other attributes you want to add to the service. Use part or all of the attributes set to find a matching service.

BIBLIOGRAPHY

Edwards, W. K. *Core Jini (Second Edition)*, Upper Saddle River, NJ: Prentice Hall, Inc., 2001.

Li, S. *Professional Jini*, Birmingham, U.K.: Wrox Press Ltd., 2000.

Newmarch, J., *A Programer's Guide to Jini Technology*, New York, NY: Springer-Verlag New York, Inc., 2000.

Oaks, S., and Wong, H. *Jini in a Nutshell* Sebastopol, CA: O'Reilly & Associates, Inc., 2000.

JavaSpaces

Objectives

- To be able to use the JavaSpaces service for building distributed applications.
- To understand the operations available in a JavaSpaces service.
- To be able to match entries in a JavaSpaces service against templates.
- To understand the use of transactions in JavaSpaces services.
- To be able to use notifications to build event-driven JavaSpaces applications.

The world is a book, and those who do not travel read only a page.
Saint Augustine

Write what you like; there is no other rule.
O. Henry

Take nothing on its looks: take everything on evidence. There's no better rule.
Charles Dickens

Believe nothing, no matter where you read it, or who said it, no matter if I have said it, unless it agrees with your own reason and your own common sense.
Buddha

23.1 Introduction

Objects that take part in distributed systems must be able to communicate with one another and share information. Thus far we have introduced several mechanisms by which Java objects in distributed systems can communicate. Java servlets (Chapter 9) enable Java objects (and non-Java objects) to communicate using the HTTP protocol. RMI (Chapter 13) enables Java objects running in separate virtual machines to invoke methods on one another as if those objects were in the same virtual machine. The Java Message Service (Chapter 16) enables Java objects (and non-Java objects) to communicate by publishing and consuming simple messages.

The *JavaSpaces service* is a Jini service that implements a simple, high-level architecture for building distributed systems. The JavaSpaces service enables Java objects to communicate, share objects and coordinate tasks using an area of shared memory.[1] A JavaSpaces service provides three fundamental operations—*write*, *take* and *read*. The write operation places an object—called an *entry*—into the JavaSpaces service. The take operation specifies a *template* and removes from the JavaSpaces service an entry that matches the given template. The read operation is similar to the take operation, but does not remove the matching entry from the JavaSpaces service. In addition to the three basic operations, JavaSpaces services support transactions through the Jini transaction manager, and a notification mechanism that notifies an object when an entry that matches a given template is written to the JavaSpaces service.

In the first half of this chapter, we present fundamental JavaSpaces technology concepts and use simple examples to demonstrate operations, transactions and notifications. The case study at the end of this chapter uses JavaSpaces services to build a distributed image-processing application. This image-processing application uses JavaSpaces services to distribute the work of applying filters to images across many programs (normally on separate computers).

23.2 JavaSpaces Service Properties

JavaSpaces technology eases the design and development of distributed systems. A JavaSpaces service has five major properties:[2]

1. A JavaSpaces service is a Jini service.

1. Multiple processes can access a JavaSpaces service concurrently.

2. An entry stored in a JavaSpaces service will remain in the JavaSpaces service until its lease expires or until a program takes the entry from the JavaSpaces service.

3. A JavaSpaces service locates objects by comparing those objects to a template. The template specifies the search criteria against which the JavaSpaces service compares each entry. When one or more entries match the template, the JavaSpaces service returns a single matching entry.

4. JavaSpaces services use the Jini transaction manager to ensure operations execute atomically.

5. Objects in a JavaSpaces service are shared. Programs can read and take entries from the JavaSpaces service, modify the **public** fields in those entries and write them back to the JavaSpaces service for other programs to use.

23.3 JavaSpaces Service

The JavaSpaces service provides distributed, shared storage for Java objects. Any Java-compatible client can put shared objects into the storage. However, several restrictions apply to these Java objects. First, any object stored in the JavaSpaces service must implement interface **Entry** (package **net.jini.core.entry**). JavaSpaces service **Entry**s adhere to the Jini **Entry** contract defined in the Jini Core Specification (see Chapter 22, Jini). An **Entry** can have multiple constructors and as many methods as required. Other requirements include a **public** no-argument constructor, **public** fields and no-primitive type fields. The JavaSpaces service proxy uses the no-argument constructor to instantiate the matching **Entry** during the deserialization process. All fields that will be used as the template matching fields in an **Entry** must be **public** (for more information on template matching fields, see Section 23.8). As defined by the Jini Core Specification, an **Entry** cannot have primitive-type fields. The object field requirement simplifies the model for template matching because primitive types cannot have **null** values, which are used as wildcards in templates.

JavaSpaces technology, like Jini, requires several underlying services. The JavaSpaces service depends on the Jini lookup service (for more information on Jini services, see Chapter 22, Jini). When transactions are required, the Jini transaction service (Section 23.11.2) must be started. JavaSpaces services also depend on a Web server and **rmid** (for more information on starting these services, see Chapter 22, Jini). Section 23.6 explains the relationships between JavaSpaces services and these Jini services. Section 23.11 demonstrates using the Transaction service with the JavaSpaces service. To use the JavaSpaces service, we need to start **outrigger**, which is Sun's implementation of the JavaSpaces service. Two versions of the JavaSpaces service are available. One is the *transient JavaSpaces service* (nonactivatable). The other is the *persistent JavaSpaces service* (activatable). The transient JavaSpaces service does not require the RMI activation daemon (**rmid**), because the transient JavaSpaces service is not activatable. Once the transient JavaSpaces service terminates, all state information is lost and **rmid** is unable to restart the service. The persistent JavaSpaces service is activatable, and therefore requires the RMI activation daemon. If the persistent JavaSpaces service terminates, all of its state information is stored in a log file and **rmid** can restart the service at a later time.

To start the transient JavaSpaces service enter the following a command prompt

```
java -Djava.security.policy=policy
    -Djava.rmi.server.codebase=
      http://hostname:port/outrigger-dl.jar
    -jar c:\files\jini1_1\lib\transient-outrigger.jar public
```

where *policy* is the path to an appropriate policy file, *hostname* is the name of the machine on which the Web server is running and *port* specifies the port number on which the Web server will accept connections. The argument **public** specifies to which group this service belongs.

The following command starts the persistent JavaSpaces service:

```
java -jar c:\files\jini1_1\lib\outrigger.jar
    http://hostname:port/outrigger-dl.jar
    policy log_path public
```

where *hostname* is the name of the machine on which the Web server is running, *port* specifies the port number from which the Web server will accept connections, *policy* is the full path of the policy file and *log_path* is the location where the **outrigger** log will be created.

An additional parameter is useful in systems where two or more JavaSpaces services operate. The parameter is

```
-Dcom.sun.jini.outrigger.spaceName=name
```

where *name* defines the **String** with which the JavaSpaces service will register itself in the Jini lookup service. The default name for the JavaSpaces service is **"JavaSpace"**. When searching for a specific JavaSpaces service in the Jini lookup service, you must use a **Name Entry** (package **net.jini.lookup.entry**) and initialize it to the **String** specified in the previous parameter. While this is a necessary parameter for systems with two or more JavaSpaces services, the examples in this chapter assume that only one JavaSpaces service exists in the system. The examples introduce a simple by which clients can locate the JavaSpaces service from the Jini lookup service.

You can start either a transient or persistent JavaSpaces service from the **StartSer-vice** GUI tool included in the Jini distributions. Start the GUI as in Chapter 21, then choose the **TransientSpace** tab (for a transient JavaSpaces service) or the **FrontEnd-Space** (for a persistent JavaSpaces service). Go to the **Run** tab and click the **Start Tran-sientSpace** button to run the transient service or click the **Start FrontEndSpace** button to run the persistent service.

23.4 Discovering the JavaSpaces Service

Upon initialization, each JavaSpaces service registers itself with local Jini lookup services. We assume that you already know how to start a Web server and RMI activation daemon from Chapter 22. The following is an example of a command that starts the persistent JavaSpaces service. Replace *hostname* with the name or IP address of your computer and *port* with the port number on which the Web server is listening.

```
java -jar C:\files\jini1_1\lib\outrigger.jar
    http://hostname:port/outrigger-dl.jar
    C:\files\jini1_1\policy\policy.all
    C:\tmp\outrigger_log public
```

Class **JavaSpaceFinder** (Fig. 23.1) shows how to obtain access to a JavaSpaces service. (We use this class in the example of Fig. 23.3.) The application performs unicast discovery to find the Jini lookup service on the hostname that the user specifies. Lines 35–36 get the **LookupLocator** at a user-specified Jini URL and obtain its **ServiceRegistrar**. Lines 55-68 look for all JavaSpaces services registered in the lookup service. Lines 55–57 specify a **ServiceTemplate** object (package **net.jini.core.lookup**). Lines 61–62 use the **ServiceTemplate** to search for all matching services in the lookup service and obtain a **JavaSpace**. Method **getJavaSpace** (lines 77–80) returns the discovered **JavaSpace**. For more information on how to use the Jini lookup service, please refer to Chapter 22, Jini.

```
1   // JavaSpaceFinder.java
2   // This application unicast discovers the JavaSpaces service.
3   package com.deitel.advjhtp1.javaspace.common;
4
5   // Jini core packages
6   import net.jini.core.discovery.LookupLocator;
7   import net.jini.core.lookup.*;
8   import net.jini.core.entry.Entry;
9
10  // Jini extension package
11  import net.jini.space.JavaSpace;
12
13  // Java core packages
14  import java.io.*;
15  import java.rmi.*;
16  import java.net.*;
17
```

Fig. 23.1   Discovering a JavaSpaces service (part 1 of 3).

```
18    // Java extension package
19    import javax.swing.*;
20
21    public class JavaSpaceFinder {
22
23       private JavaSpace space;
24
25       public JavaSpaceFinder( String jiniURL )
26       {
27          LookupLocator locator = null;
28          ServiceRegistrar registrar = null;
29
30          System.setSecurityManager( new RMISecurityManager() );
31
32          // get lookup service locator at "jini://hostname"
33          // use default port and registrar of the locator
34          try {
35             locator = new LookupLocator( jiniURL );
36             registrar = locator.getRegistrar();
37          }
38
39          // handle exception invalid jini URL
40          catch ( MalformedURLException malformedURLException ) {
41             malformedURLException.printStackTrace();
42          }
43
44          // handle exception I/O
45          catch ( java.io.IOException ioException ) {
46             ioException.printStackTrace();
47          }
48
49          // handle exception finding class
50          catch ( ClassNotFoundException classNotFoundException ) {
51             classNotFoundException.printStackTrace();
52          }
53
54          // specify the service requirement
55          Class[] types = new Class[] { JavaSpace.class };
56          ServiceTemplate template =
57             new ServiceTemplate( null, types, null );
58
59          // find service
60          try {
61             space =
62                ( JavaSpace ) registrar.lookup( template );
63          }
64
65          // handle exception getting JavaSpaces service
66          catch ( RemoteException remoteException ) {
67             remoteException.printStackTrace();
68          }
69
```

Fig. 23.1 Discovering a JavaSpaces service (part 2 of 3).

```
70          // if does not find any matching service
71          if ( space == null ) {
72             System.out.println( "No matching service" );
73          }
74
75       } // end JavaSpaceFinder constructor
76
77       public JavaSpace getJavaSpace()
78       {
79          return space;
80       }
81    }
```

Fig. 23.1   Discovering a JavaSpaces service (part 3 of 3).

23.5 JavaSpace Interface

Clients access objects in a JavaSpaces service through interface **JavaSpace** (package **net.jini.space**). Interface **JavaSpace** provides several methods—**notify**, **read**, **readIfExists**, **take**, **takeIfExists**, **write** and **snapshot**. The purpose of each method is as follows:[3]

1. **write**—This method implements the **write** operation. The **write** operation inserts an **Entry** into a JavaSpaces service. If an identical **Entry** already exists in the JavaSpaces service, this operation does not overwrite the existing **Entry**. Instead, the **write** operation places a copy of the **Entry** into the JavaSpaces service. JavaSpaces services may contain multiple copies of the same **Entry**. Section 23.7 demonstrates how to use the **write** operation.

2. **read**, **readIfExists**—These two methods implement the **read** operation, which attempts to read an **Entry** that matches an **Entry** template from a JavaSpaces service. If no matching **Entry** exists in the JavaSpaces service, this operation returns **null**. If multiple matching **Entry** exist in the JavaSpaces service, the **read** operation arbitrarily picks one among the matching **Entry**s. Method **read** blocks until a matching **Entry** is found in the JavaSpaces service or until a time-out occurs. Method **readIfExists** checks to see if a matching **Entry** exists within the JavaSpaces service. If an **Entry** does not exist in the JavaSpaces service, method **readIfExists** should return **null** immediately. Method **readIfExists** does not block unless the matching **Entry** is a participant in an uncommitted transaction. For information on transactions, see Section 23.11. Section 23.8.1 demonstrates the **read** and **readIfExists** operations.

3. **take**, **takeIfExists**—These two methods implement the **take** operation, which attempts to remove an **Entry** that matches an **Entry** template from a JavaSpaces service. This operation works like the **read** operation, except that the **take** operation removes the matching **Entry** from the JavaSpaces service. Method **take** blocks until a matching **Entry** is found in the JavaSpaces service or until a time-out occurs. Method **takeIfExists** checks to see if a matching **Entry** exists within the JavaSpaces service. If an **Entry** does not exist in the JavaSpaces service, method **takeIfExists** should return **null** immediately.

Method **takeIfExists** does not block unless the matching **Entry** is part of an uncommitted transaction. Section 23.8.2 demonstrates the **take** and **take-IfExists** operations.

4. **notify**—This method implements the **notify** operation, which requests that the JavaSpaces service sends a notification to a listener object when a client writes a matching **Entry** into the JavaSpaces service. With this method, an application does not need to check repeatedly for an **Entry** in a JavaSpaces service. Section 23.9 demonstrates the **notify** operation.

5. **snapshot**—This method increases performance when a program must serialize one **Entry** repeatedly. Each time a program transfers an **Entry** into a JavaSpaces service (e.g., by writing that **Entry** or by using that **Entry** as a template), that **Entry** must be serialized. If a program transfers the same **Entry** to a JavaSpaces service many times, the serialization process can be time consuming. Invoking method **snapshot** serializes the **Entry** once and reuses this serialized **Entry** for future transfers. Section 23.10 demonstrates how to use method **snapshot**.

23.6 Defining an Entry

The following sections and subsections create an application for managing registrations for fictitious seminars offered at Deitel & Associates, Inc. For each seminar, an administration tool writes an **AttendeeCounter** (Fig. 23.2) into the JavaSpaces service. Each **AttendeeCounter** keeps track of the number of attendees registered for a particular seminar. We implement the complete application one step at a time to demonstrate the mechanics of each of each JavaSpaces service operation.

AttendeeCounter (Fig. 23.2) is an **Entry** that represents a count of the number of people attending a seminar. Recall that **Entry**s require non-primitive type, **public** fields (lines 9–10) and an empty constructor (line 13). The **AttendeeCounter** constructor on lines 16–19 takes as a **String** argument the day of the week for which this **AttendeeCounter** tracks attendee registrations.

Common Programming Error 23.1

*Including primitive fields in an **Entry** does not cause an error during compilation. However, an **IllegalArgumentException** does occur during serialization.*

```
1   // Fig. 23.2: AttendeeCounter.java
2   // This class defines the AttendeeCounter Entry.
3   package com.deitel.advjhtp1.javaspace.common;
4
5   import net.jini.core.entry.Entry;
6
7   public class AttendeeCounter implements Entry {
8
9       public String day;
10      public Integer counter;
11
```

Fig. 23.2   **AttendeeCounter** is an **Entry** for keeping track of registrations for a seminar on a particular day (part 1 of 2).

```
12        // empty constructor
13        public AttendeeCounter() {}
14
15        // constructor has a single String input
16        public AttendeeCounter( String seminarDay )
17        {
18            day = seminarDay;
19        }
20    }
```

Fig. 23.2   **AttendeeCounter** is an **Entry** for keeping track of registrations for a seminar on a particular day (part 2 of 2).

Software Engineering Observation 23.1

Use wrapper classes rather than primitive types in **Entry** *fields.*

23.7 Write Operation

The write operation places an **Entry** in a JavaSpaces service. Method **write** takes three arguments—an **Entry**, a **Transaction** object and a **long** value that requests an amount of time for which the JavaSpaces service should keep the **Entry**. The **long** value represents the lease length for the **Entry**. Normally, the JavaSpaces service grants each written **Entry** a lease time of 5 minutes. The JavaSpaces service will not keep the **Entry** beyond the lease time granted. A developer can extend the life of an **Entry** by renewing its lease before it expires. Method **write** returns a **net.jini.lease.Lease** object that contains the time that the JavaSpaces service granted to the **Entry**. Method **write** throws two exceptions. Method **write** throws a **RemoteException** (package **java.rmi**) when a network failure occurs or a variety of other errors occur on the server. When a **write** operation takes place under an invalid transaction, method **write** throws a **TransactionException** (package **net.jini.core.transaction**). For information on transactions, see Section 23.11.

The **WriteOperation** application (Fig. 23.3) uses class **AttendeeCounter** (Fig. 23.2) and class **JavaSpaceFinder** (Fig. 23.1) to demonstrate writing an **Entry** into a JavaSpaces service. In this example, a seminar administrator would use the **WriteOperation** application to place **AttendeeCounter Entry**s for each available seminar in the JavaSpaces service. The constructor (lines 30–36) takes a **JavaSpace** as an argument. Method **writeEntry** (lines 39–62) writes an **Entry** into the JavaSpaces service. Lines 44–45 initialize an **Entry** by setting the number of people who register for the seminar to zero. Line 46 writes the **Entry** into the JavaSpaces service. The first argument (**counter**) specifies the **Entry** to write into the JavaSpaces service. The second argument (**null**) indicates that the **write** operation does not use a **Transaction**. When the write operation completes, the written **Entry** is ready for a **read** or **take** operation. If a **Transaction** object is specified, the **write** operation uses that **Transaction** to ensure that a series of operations completes successfully. This means that until the transaction completes successfully, other clients cannot **read** or **take** the **Entry** from the JavaSpaces service. The third argument (**Lease.FOREVER**) specifies how long the JavaSpaces service should keep the **Entry**. Although we request that the JavaSpaces service keep our **Entry** forever, Sun's implementation limits the lease to 5 minutes. Programs can use the Jini lease-renewal mechanism to maintain **Lease**s for **Entry**s. After the lease expires, the JavaSpaces service removes and destroys the object.

Method **showOutput** (lines 65–75) displays the results. In method **main**, lines 81–85 check the user-specified hostname. Lines 88–90 ask user to choose a particular day to write. Figure 23.4 shows the results of running the **WriteOperation** application.

```
1   // WriteOperation.java
2   // This application initializes an new Entry,
3   // and puts this Entry to the JavaSpace.
4   package com.deitel.advjhtp1.javaspace.write;
5
6   // Jini core packages
7   import net.jini.core.lease.Lease;
8   import net.jini.core.transaction.TransactionException;
9
10  // Jini extension package
11  import net.jini.space.JavaSpace;
12
13  // Java core package
14  import java.rmi.RemoteException;
15
16  // Java extension package
17  import javax.swing.*;
18
19  // Deitel package
20  import com.deitel.advjhtp1.javaspace.common.*;
21
22  public class WriteOperation {
23
24     private JavaSpace space;
25     private static final String[] days = { "Monday", "Tuesday",
26        "Wednesday", "Thursday", "Friday" };
27     private String output = "\n";
28
29     // WriteOperation constructor
30     public WriteOperation( String hostname )
31     {
32        // get JavaSpace
33        String jiniURL = "jini://" +  hostname;
34        JavaSpaceFinder findtool = new JavaSpaceFinder( jiniURL );
35        space = findtool.getJavaSpace();
36     }
37
38     // deposit new Entry to JavaSpace
39     public void writeEntry( String day )
40     {
41        // initialize AttendeeCounter Entry and deposit
42        // Entry in JavaSpace
43        try {
44           AttendeeCounter counter = new AttendeeCounter( day );
45           space.write( counter, null, Lease.FOREVER );
46
```

Fig. 23.3   Writing an **Entry** into a JavaSpaces service (part 1 of 2).

```
47              output += "Initialize the Entry: \n";
48              output += "   Day: " + day + "\n";
49              output += "   Count: 0\n";
50           }
51
52           // handle exception network failure
53           catch ( RemoteException exception ) {
54              exception.printStackTrace();
55           }
56
57           // handle exception invalid transaction
58           catch ( TransactionException exception ) {
59              exception.printStackTrace();
60           }
61        }
62
63        // show output
64        public void showOutput()
65        {
66           JTextArea outputArea = new JTextArea();
67           outputArea.setText( output );
68           JOptionPane.showMessageDialog( null, outputArea,
69              "WriteOperation Output",
70              JOptionPane.INFORMATION_MESSAGE );
71
72           // terminate program
73           System.exit( 0 );
74        }
75
76        // method main
77        public static void main( String args[] )
78        {
79           // get hostname
80           if ( args.length != 1 ) {
81              System.out.println(
82                 "Usage: WriteOperation hostname" );
83              System.exit( 1 );
84           }
85
86           // get user input day
87           String day = ( String ) JOptionPane.showInputDialog(
88              null, "Select Day", "Day Selection",
89              JOptionPane.QUESTION_MESSAGE, null, days, days[ 0 ] );
90
91           // write Entry
92           WriteOperation write = new WriteOperation( args[ 0 ] );
93           write.writeEntry( day );
94
95           write.showOutput();
96
97        } // end method main
98     }
```

Fig. 23.3   Writing an **Entry** into a JavaSpaces service (part 2 of 2).

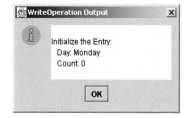

Fig. 23.4   Results of running the **WriteOperation** application.

This application takes a command-line argument that specifies the hostname of a computer that has the JavaSpaces service running. The following steps compile and execute the **WriteOperation** application. Ensure that your **CLASSPATH** includes **jini-core.jar**, **jini-ext.jar** and **sun-util.jar**. Compile the java files in the **com\deitel\advjhtp1\javaspace\common** directory. Run **WriteOperation** by specifying the hostname of the Jini lookup service. Do not forget to specify to the JVM the policy file with the proper permissions.

23.8 Read and Take Operations

The **read** and the **take** operations retrieve **Entry**s from a JavaSpaces service. A client can read or take an **Entry** from the JavaSpaces service by supplying a template **Entry** against which to compare the **public** fields of **Entry**s in the JavaSpaces service. The template indicates which fields to use for comparison purposes.

The retrieval process uses a *template-matching mechanism* to match **Entry**s according to the values of their **public** fields. Each **Entry** in the JavaSpaces service requires its **public** fields to be object references, so each field is either **null** or a reference to an object. Fields in the template with non-**null** values must match with their **Entry** counterparts in the JavaSpaces service exactly. Fields in the template that are set to **null** act as wildcards. If a set of **Entry**s of the same type exist within a JavaSpaces service, only those fields which equal those of the template are used to match an **Entry** or a set of **Entry**s contained in the JavaSpaces service. Fields in the template set to **null** can have their matching counterparts in the JavaSpaces service have any value in the corresponding field(s).

23.8.1 Read Operation

The **read** operation obtains **Entry**s without removing them from the JavaSpaces service. Methods **read** and **readIfExists** perform the read operation. Each method takes three arguments—an **Entry** that specifies the template to match, a **Transaction** object and a **long** value. The **long** value has different meanings in methods **read** and **readIfExists**. Method **read** specifies a period of time for which the read operation should block before simply returning **null**. Method **readIfExists** is a non-blocking version of method **read**. If there are no matching **Entry**s, **readIfExists** returns **null** immediately. Method **readIfExists** blocks only if the developer specifies a period of time for which the **readIfExists** waits if, at first, the matching **Entry** is a part of an incomplete transaction. If the matching **Entry** is not involved in any transaction, then the **read** operation returns the matching **Entry** immediately. Both the **read** and **readIfExists** methods return only one **Entry**. If multiple **Entry**s match the template, the **read** operation picks one arbitrarily. These methods throw four exception types—**RemoteException**, **TransactionException**, **UnusableEntryException** and **InterruptedException**. The first two are the same as in method **write**. If the matching **Entry** cannot be deserialized, these methods throw an **UnusableEntryException** (package **net.jini.core.entry**).

The **ReadOperation** application (Fig. 23.5) uses class **AttendeeCounter** (Fig. 23.2) and class **JavaSpaceFinder** (Fig. 23.1) to demonstrate reading an **Entry** from a JavaSpaces service. A seminar administrator or prospective attendee could use this application to determine the current enrollment for a particular seminar. Line 47 specifies the matching template against which to compare **Entry**s. Users must specify the day for which they would like to see attendee registrations.

```java
1   // ReadOperation.java
2   // This application reads an Entry from the JavaSpace and
3   // displays the Entry information.
4   package com.deitel.advjhtp1.javaspace.read;
5
6   // Jini core packages
7   import net.jini.core.transaction.TransactionException;
8   import net.jini.core.entry.UnusableEntryException;
9
10  // Jini extension package
11  import net.jini.space.JavaSpace;
12
13  // Java core packages
14  import java.rmi.RemoteException;
15  import java.lang.InterruptedException;
16
17  // Java extension package
18  import javax.swing.*;
19
20  // Deitel package
21  import com.deitel.advjhtp1.javaspace.common.*;
22
23  public class ReadOperation {
24
25     private JavaSpace space;
26     private static final String[] days = { "Monday", "Tuesday",
27        "Wednesday", "Thursday", "Friday" };
28     private String output = "\n";
29
30     // constructor gets JavaSpace
31     public ReadOperation( String hostname )
32     {
33        // get JavaSpace
34        String jiniURL = "jini://" +  hostname;
35        JavaSpaceFinder findtool = new JavaSpaceFinder( jiniURL );
36        space = findtool.getJavaSpace();
37     }
38
```

Fig. 23.5   Reading an **Entry** from JavaSpaces service (part 1 of 3).

```
39      // read Entry from JavaSpace
40      public void readEntry( String day )
41      {
42          // specify matching template, read template
43          // from JavaSpace and output Entry information
44          try {
45
46              // read Entry from JavaSpace
47              AttendeeCounter counter = new AttendeeCounter( day );
48              AttendeeCounter resultCounter = ( AttendeeCounter )
49                  space.read( counter, null, JavaSpace.NO_WAIT );
50
51              if (resultCounter == null) {
52                  output += "Sorry, cannot find an Entry for "
53                      + day + "!\n";
54              }
55              else {
56
57                  // get Entry information
58                  output += "Count Information:\n";
59                  output += "   Day: " + resultCounter.day;
60                  output += "\n";
61                  output += "   Count: "
62                      + resultCounter.counter.intValue() + "\n";
63              }
64          }
65
66          // handle exception network failure
67          catch ( RemoteException exception ) {
68              exception.printStackTrace();
69          }
70
71          // handle exception invalid transaction
72          catch ( TransactionException exception ) {
73              exception.printStackTrace();
74          }
75
76          // handle exception unusable Entry
77          catch ( UnusableEntryException exception ) {
78              exception.printStackTrace();
79          }
80
81          // handle exception interrupting
82          catch ( InterruptedException exception ) {
83              exception.printStackTrace();
84          }
85
86      } // end method readEntry
87
88      // show output
89      public void showOutput()
90      {
91          JTextArea outputArea = new JTextArea();
```

Fig. 23.5 Reading an `Entry` from JavaSpaces service (part 2 of 3).

```
92              outputArea.setText( output );
93              JOptionPane.showMessageDialog( null, outputArea,
94                 "ReadOperation Output",
95                 JOptionPane.INFORMATION_MESSAGE );
96
97              // terminate program
98              System.exit( 0 );
99           }
100
101       // method main
102       public static void main( String args[] )
103       {
104          // get hostname
105          if ( args.length != 1 ) {
106             System.out.println(
107                "Usage: ReadOperation hostname" );
108             System.exit( 1 );
109          }
110
111          // get user input day
112          String day = ( String ) JOptionPane.showInputDialog(
113             null, "Select Day", "Day Selection",
114             JOptionPane.QUESTION_MESSAGE, null, days, days[ 0 ] );
115
116          // read an Entry
117          ReadOperation read = new ReadOperation( args[ 0 ] );
118          read.readEntry( day );
119
120          read.showOutput();
121
122       } // end method main
123    }
```

Fig. 23.5   Reading an **Entry** from JavaSpaces service (part 3 of 3).

The first argument to method **read** (lines 48–49) specifies an **Entry** that the template-matching mechanism will use. The second argument (**null**) indicates that this **read** operation does not use a **Transaction**. The third argument (**JavaSpace.NO_WAIT**) specifies the period for which the read operations wait for the read operation to find a matching **Entry** before simply returning **null**. Our example sets the method **read** to **JavaSpace.NO_WAIT**, which equals zero. If the template-matching mechanism does not locate a matching **Entry**, the **read** operation returns **null** immediately. Figure 23.6 shows the results of running the **ReadOperation** application.

This application takes a command-line argument that specifies the hostname of a machine that has the JavaSpaces service service running. The following steps compile and execute the **ReadOperation** application. Ensure that your **CLASSPATH** includes **jini-core.jar**, **jini-ext.jar** and **sun-util.jar**. Compile the java files in the **com\deitel\advjhtp1\javaspace\read** directory. Run **ReadOperation** by specifying the hostname of the Jini lookup service. Do not forget to specify to the JVM the policy file with the proper permissions.

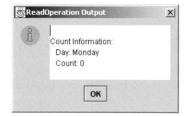

Fig. 23.6   Results of running the **ReadOperation** application.

*The **read** operation returns only a single matching **Entry**. If multiple matching **Entry**s exist, the **read** operation may return different matching objects each time.*

23.8.2 Take Operation

The **take** operation obtains an **Entry** and removes it from the JavaSpaces service. Methods **take** and **takeIfExists** perform the take operation. Methods **take** and **take-IfExists** are similar to methods **read** and **readIfExists**. The only difference is that the matching **Entry** returned by a **take** or **takeIfExists** operation is removed from the JavaSpaces service.

The **TakeOperation** application (Fig. 23.7) uses class **AttendeeCounter** (Fig. 23.2) and class **JavaSpaceFinder** (Fig. 23.1) to demonstrate taking an **Entry** from a JavaSpaces service. This application is similar to the **ReadOperation** application. The only difference is that this application calls method **take** (lines 46–47) of interface **JavaSpace** to remove the **AttendeeCounter** from the JavaSpaces service. A seminar administrator could use this application to remove from the JavaSpaces service an **AttendeeCounter** for a seminar that has already been given or for a seminar that was cancelled. Figure 23.8 shows the results of running the **TakeOperation** application.

This application takes a command-line argument that specifies the hostname of a machine that has the JavaSpaces service running. The following steps compile and execute the **TakeOperation** application. Ensure that your **CLASSPATH** includes **jini-core.jar**, **jini-ext.jar** and **sun-util.jar**. Compile the java files in the **com\deitel\advjhtp1\javaspace\take** directory. Run **TakeOperation** by specifying the hostname of the Jini lookup service. Do not forget to specify to the JVM the policy file with the proper permissions.

```
1   // TakeOperation.java
2   // This application removes an Entry from the JavaSpace.
3   package com.deitel.advjhtp1.javaspace.take;
4
5   // Jini core packages
6   import net.jini.core.transaction.TransactionException;
7   import net.jini.core.entry.UnusableEntryException;
8
```

Fig. 23.7   Taking an **Entry** from a JavaSpaces service (part 1 of 4).

```
 9    // Jini extension package
10    import net.jini.space.JavaSpace;
11
12    // Java core packages
13    import java.rmi.RemoteException;
14
15    // Java extension package
16    import javax.swing.*;
17
18    // Deitel package
19    import com.deitel.advjhtp1.javaspace.common.*;
20
21    public class TakeOperation {
22
23       private JavaSpace space = null;
24       private static final String[] days = { "Monday", "Tuesday",
25          "Wednesday", "Thursday", "Friday" };
26       private String output = "\n";
27
28       // constructor gets JavaSpace
29       public TakeOperation( String hostname )
30       {
31          // get JavaSpace
32          String jiniURL = "jini://" +  hostname;
33          JavaSpaceFinder findtool = new JavaSpaceFinder( jiniURL );
34          space = findtool.getJavaSpace();
35       }
36
37       // remove Entry from JavaSpace
38       public void TakeAnEntry( String day )
39       {
40          AttendeeCounter resultCounter = null;
41
42          // specify matching template, remove template
43          // from JavaSpace
44          try {
45             AttendeeCounter count = new AttendeeCounter( day );
46             resultCounter = ( AttendeeCounter ) space.take( count,
47                null, JavaSpace.NO_WAIT );
48
49             if ( resultCounter == null) {
50                output += "No Entry for " + day
51                   + " is available from the JavaSpace.\n";
52             }
53             else {
54                output += "Entry is taken away from ";
55                output += "the JavaSpace successfully.\n";
56             }
57          }
58
```

Fig. 23.7 Taking an **Entry** from a JavaSpaces service (part 2 of 4).

```
59          // handle exception network failure
60          catch ( RemoteException exception ) {
61             exception.printStackTrace();
62          }
63
64          // handle exception invalid transaction
65          catch ( TransactionException exception ) {
66             exception.printStackTrace();
67          }
68
69          // handle exception unusable entry
70          catch ( UnusableEntryException exception ) {
71             exception.printStackTrace();
72          }
73
74          // handle exception interrupt
75          catch ( InterruptedException exception ) {
76             exception.printStackTrace();
77          }
78
79       } // end method TakeAnEntry
80
81       // show output
82       public void showOutput()
83       {
84          JTextArea outputArea = new JTextArea();
85          outputArea.setText( output );
86          JOptionPane.showMessageDialog( null, outputArea,
87             "TakeOperation Output",
88             JOptionPane.INFORMATION_MESSAGE );
89
90          // terminate program
91          System.exit( 0 );
92       }
93
94       public static void main( String args[] )
95       {
96          // get hostname
97          if ( args.length != 1 ) {
98             System.out.println(
99                "Usage: WriteOperation hostname" );
100            System.exit( 1 );
101         }
102
103         // get user input day
104         String day = ( String ) JOptionPane.showInputDialog(
105            null, "Select Day", "Day Selection",
106            JOptionPane.QUESTION_MESSAGE, null, days, days[ 0 ] );
107
108         // take Entry
109         TakeOperation take = new TakeOperation( args[ 0 ] );
110         take.TakeAnEntry( day );
111
```

Fig. 23.7 Taking an `Entry` from a JavaSpaces service (part 3 of 4).

```
112            take.showOutput();
113
114       } // end method main
115  }
```

Fig. 23.7   Taking an **Entry** from a JavaSpaces service (part 4 of 4).

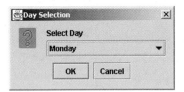

Fig. 23.8   Results of running the **TakeOperation** application.

Software Engineering Observation 23.3

*The take operation returns only a single matching **Entry**. If multiple matching **Entry**s exist, the take operation can remove only one **Entry** from the JavaSpaces service each time. To take all the matching **Entry**s away from the JavaSpaces service, execute the **TakeOperation** application repeatedly until the **TakeOperation** application returns a message that says "No Entry is available from the JavaSpaces service".*

23.9 Notify Operation

The **notify** operation asks the JavaSpaces service to send a notification to a listener when a client writes a matching **Entry** into the JavaSpaces service. Method **notify** takes five parameters—an **Entry** that specifies the matching template, a **Transaction** object, a listener that implements interface **RemoteEventListener** (package **net.jini.core.event**), a **long** value that specifies the lease time for the registration of the listener and a **MarshalledObject** (package **java.rmi**) that the JavaSpaces service will pass to the remote listener as part of a notification. This method may throw exceptions of type **RemoteException** and **TransactionException**. A **RemoteException** occurs due to a network failure. A **TransactionException** occurs when a notify operation takes place as part of an invalid transaction.

Class **EntryListener** (Fig. 23.9) defines a listener that the JavaSpaces service will notify when an **Entry** matching the given template is written to the JavaSpaces service. The **EntryListener** listens on the JavaSpaces service for a matching **Entry** written into the JavaSpaces service. This listener must implement interface **RemoteEventListener** (line 14). A person interested in attending a seminar on a particular day could use this application to be notified when an **AttendeeCounter** is added for a seminar on a particular day. The constructor takes one argument—a **RemoteEventListener** and exports the listener to the JavaSpaces service so that when a client writes a matching **Entry** into the JavaSpaces service, the JavaSpaces service will call **notify**. Method **notify** (lines 35–40) forwards the notification to the **NotifyOperation** application (Fig. 23.10).

```
1    // EntryListener.java
2    // This class defines the listener for the NotifyOperation
3    // application.
4    package com.deitel.advjhtp1.javaspace.notify;
5
6    // Jini core packages
7    import net.jini.core.event.*;
8
9    // Java core packages
10   import java.rmi.RemoteException;
11   import java.rmi.server.UnicastRemoteObject;
12   import java.io.Serializable;
13
14   public class EntryListener implements RemoteEventListener {
15
16      private RemoteEventListener eventListener;
17
18      // EntryListener constructor
19      public EntryListener( RemoteEventListener listener )
20      {
21         eventListener = listener;
22
23         // export stub object
24         try {
25            UnicastRemoteObject.exportObject( this );
26         }
27
28         // handle exception exporting stub
29         catch ( RemoteException remoteException ) {
30            remoteException.printStackTrace();
31         }
32      }
33
34      // receive notifications
35      public void notify( RemoteEvent remoteEvent )
36         throws UnknownEventException, RemoteException
37      {
38         // forward notifications to NotifyOperation application
39         eventListener.notify( remoteEvent );
40      }
41   }
```

Fig. 23.9 **EntryListener** for **NotifyOperation** application.

The **NotifyOperation** application (Fig. 23.10) demonstrates how to write a program that receives a notification when a matching **Entry** is written into a JavaSpaces service. Lines 30–36 define the constructor, which gets a JavaSpaces service. In method **notifyEntry** (lines 39–61), line 42 gets an **EntryListener** that listens on the JavaSpaces service for matching **Entry**s. This **EntryListener** will be passed to method **notify** of interface **JavaSpace**. Line 48 creates the matching template. Lines 50–51 define the object to send to the listener when a notification occurs. Lines 52–53 call the **notify** method of the **JavaSpace** interface. The first argument (**counter**) specifies an **Entry** that is used as a matching template. The second argument (**null**) indicates that the **notify** operation does not occur within a transaction. The third argument (**listener**) is an instance of the **EntryListener** class. The fourth argument (**600000**) specifies the number of milliseconds requested for the lease. After the expiration of the listener's granted lease, the listener will cease to be active. The last argument (**handback**—a reference to a **MarshalledObject**) is an object that the JavaSpaces service provides to the remote listener as part of the notification.

```
1   // NotifyOperation.java
2   // This application receives a notification when a matching entry
3   // is written to the JavaSpace.
4   package com.deitel.advjhtp1.javaspace.notify;
5
6   // Jini core packages
7   import net.jini.core.transaction.TransactionException;
8   import net.jini.core.lease.Lease;
9   import net.jini.core.event.*;
10
11  // Jini extension package
12  import net.jini.space.JavaSpace;
13
14  // Java core packages
15  import java.rmi.*;
16
17  // Java standard extensions
18  import javax.swing.*;
19
20  // Deitel packages
21  import com.deitel.advjhtp1.javaspace.common.*;
22
23  public class NotifyOperation implements RemoteEventListener
24  {
25     private JavaSpace space;
26     private static final String[] days = { "Monday", "Tuesday",
27        "Wednesday", "Thursday", "Friday" };
28
29     // constructor gets JavaSpace
30     public NotifyOperation( String hostname )
31     {
32        // get JavaSpace
33        String jiniURL = "jini://" + hostname;
34        JavaSpaceFinder findtool = new JavaSpaceFinder( jiniURL );
35        space = findtool.getJavaSpace();
36     }
37
38     // call notify method of JavaSpace
39     public void notifyEntry( String day )
40     {
41        // get Entry listener
42        EntryListener listener = new EntryListener( this );
43
```

Fig. 23.10 Receiving notifications when matching **Entry**s are written into **JavaSpace** (part 1 of 3).

```
44          // specify matching template, asks JavaSpace to
45          // send notification when matching entry is written
46          // to JavaSpace
47          try {
48             AttendeeCounter counter = new AttendeeCounter( day );
49
50             MarshalledObject handback = new MarshalledObject(
51                "JavaSpace Notification" );
52             space.notify(
53                counter, null, listener, 10 * 60 * 1000, handback );
54          }
55
56          // handle exception notifying space
57          catch ( Exception exception ) {
58             exception.printStackTrace();
59          }
60
61       } // end method notifyEntry
62
63       // show output
64       public void showOutput( String output )
65       {
66          JTextArea outputArea = new JTextArea();
67          outputArea.setText( output );
68          JOptionPane.showMessageDialog( null, outputArea,
69             "NotifyOperation Output",
70             JOptionPane.INFORMATION_MESSAGE );
71       }
72
73       // receive notifications
74       public void notify( RemoteEvent remoteEvent )
75       {
76          String output = "\n";
77
78          // prepare output
79          try {
80             output += "id: " + remoteEvent.getID() + "\n";
81             output += "sequence number: "
82                + remoteEvent.getSequenceNumber() + "\n";
83             String handback = ( String )
84                remoteEvent.getRegistrationObject().get();
85             output += "handback: " + handback + "\n";
86
87             // display output
88             showOutput( output );
89          }
90
91          // handle exception getting handback
92          catch ( Exception exception ) {
93             exception.printStackTrace();
94          }
95       }
```

Fig. 23.10 Receiving notifications when matching **Entry**s are written into
JavaSpace (part 2 of 3).

```
96
97      // method main
98      public static void main( String args[] )
99      {
100        // get hostname
101        if ( args.length != 1 ) {
102           System.out.println(
103              "Usage: NotifyOperation hostname" );
104           System.exit( 1 );
105        }
106
107        // get user input day
108        String day = ( String ) JOptionPane.showInputDialog(
109           null, "Select Day", "Day Selection",
110           JOptionPane.QUESTION_MESSAGE, null, days, days[ 0 ] );
111
112        // notify Entry
113        NotifyOperation notifyOperation =
114           new NotifyOperation( args[ 0 ] );
115
116        notifyOperation.notifyEntry( day );
117
118     } // end method main
119   }
```

Fig. 23.10 Receiving notifications when matching **Entry**s are written into **JavaSpace** (part 3 of 3).

The following steps execute the **NotifyOperation** application. Ensure that your **CLASSPATH** includes **jini-core.jar**, **jini-ext.jar** and **sun-util.jar**. Compile the source files in the **com\deitel\advjhtp1\javaspace\notify** directory. Start a Web server. Generate a stub for class **EntryListener** (Fig. 23.9). Create a **JAR** file for **EntryListener_Stub.class** and place it in the Web server's document directory. Run **NotifyOperation** by specifying the hostname of the Jini lookup service. Do not forget to specify to the JVM the codebase and the policy file with the proper permissions.

Figure 23.11 shows sample outputs of this application. To test this application, execute several **WriteOperation** applications.

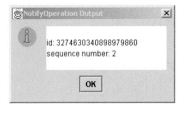
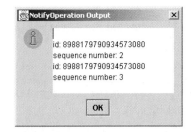

Fig. 23.11 NotifyOperation Output samples.

JavaSpaces service notifications are not guaranteed to be delivered, as network problems may interfere with notification delivery.

23.10 Method `snapshot`

Method **snapshot** optimizes interactions with a JavaSpaces service by reducing the overhead of continually serializing **Entry**s. Every time we pass a matching template to methods in the **JavaSpace** interface, the template must be serialized before it is moved to the JavaSpaces service. When the same template is passed to a JavaSpaces service repeatedly, it is preferable to avoid multiple serializations of the same **Entry**. Fortunately, method **snapshot** provides such a mechanism. Method **snapshot** takes a matching template and returns a specialized representation of the **Entry** (a *snapshot* **Entry**). This snapshot **Entry** can be used only in the JavaSpaces service that generated it. For example, to remove all the seminar **Entry**s for Monday from the JavaSpaces service, we call the **snapshot** method to create a snapshot **Entry**, then pass this snapshot **Entry** to the **take** method repeatedly.

The **SnapshotUsage** application (Fig. 23.12) removes **Entry**s from the JavaSpaces service and uses method **snapshot** to avoid repeated serialization of the matching template. Line 49 defines the original matching template. We do not pass this original template to method **take**. Instead, we pass the snapshot to the **take** method. Line 50 calls method **snapshot** to get the snapshot **Entry** of the original template.

```
1   // SnapshotUsage.java
2   // This application removes entries from the JavaSpace using
3   // method snapshot.
4   package com.deitel.advjhtp1.javaspace.snapshot;
5
6   // Jini core packages
7   import net.jini.core.transaction.TransactionException;
8   import net.jini.core.entry.UnusableEntryException;
9   import net.jini.core.entry.Entry;
10
11  // Jini extension package
12  import net.jini.space.JavaSpace;
13
14  // Java core packages
15  import java.rmi.RemoteException;
16
17  // Java extension package
18  import javax.swing.*;
19
20  // Deitel packages
21  import com.deitel.advjhtp1.javaspace.common.*;
22
23  public class SnapshotUsage {
24
25      private JavaSpace space;
```

Fig. 23.12 Removing entries from JavaSpaces service using method **snapshot** (part 1 of 3).

```
26        private static final String[] days = { "Monday", "Tuesday",
27           "Wednesday", "Thursday", "Friday" };
28        private String output = "\n";
29
30        // constructor gets JavaSpace
31        public SnapshotUsage( String hostname )
32        {
33           // get JavaSpace
34           String jiniURL = "jini://" +  hostname;
35           JavaSpaceFinder findtool = new JavaSpaceFinder( jiniURL );
36           space = findtool.getJavaSpace();
37        }
38
39        // create snapshot Entry, pass this object as
40        // Entry parameter to take method
41        public void snapshotEntry( String day )
42        {
43           // specify matching template, snapshot template
44           // and remove matching entries from JavaSpace using
45           // snapshot entry
46           try {
47              AttendeeCounter counter = new AttendeeCounter( day );
48              Entry snapshotentry = space.snapshot( counter );
49              AttendeeCounter resultCounter = ( AttendeeCounter )
50                 space.take( snapshotentry, null, JavaSpace.NO_WAIT );
51
52              // keep removing entries until no more entry exists
53              // in space
54              while ( resultCounter != null ) {
55                 output += "Removing an entry ... \n";
56                 resultCounter = ( AttendeeCounter ) space.take(
57                    snapshotentry, null, JavaSpace.NO_WAIT );
58              }
59
60              output += "No more entry to remove!\n";
61           }
62
63           // handle exception network failure
64           catch ( RemoteException remoteException ) {
65              remoteException.printStackTrace();
66           }
67
68           // handle exception invalid transaction
69           catch ( TransactionException transactionException ) {
70              transactionException.printStackTrace();
71           }
72
73           // handle exception unusable entry
74           catch ( UnusableEntryException unusableEntryException ) {
75              unusableEntryException.printStackTrace();
76           }
77
```

Fig. 23.12 Removing entries from JavaSpaces service using method **snapshot** (part 2 of 3).

```
78             // handle exception interrupt
79             catch ( InterruptedException interruptedException ) {
80                 interruptedException.printStackTrace();
81             }
82
83         } // end method snapshotEntry
84
85         // show output
86         public void showOutput()
87         {
88             JTextArea outputArea = new JTextArea();
89             outputArea.setText( output );
90             JOptionPane.showMessageDialog( null, outputArea,
91                 "SnapshotUsage Output",
92                 JOptionPane.INFORMATION_MESSAGE );
93
94             // terminate program
95             System.exit( 0 );
96         }
97
98         // method main
99         public static void main( String args[] )
100        {
101            // get hostname
102            if ( args.length != 1 ) {
103                System.out.println(
104                    "Usage: SnapshotUsage hostname" );
105                System.exit( 1 );
106            }
107
108            // get user input day
109            String day = ( String ) JOptionPane.showInputDialog(
110                null, "Select Day", "Day Selection",
111                JOptionPane.QUESTION_MESSAGE, null, days, days[ 0 ] );
112
113            // snapshot Entry
114            SnapshotUsage snapshot = new SnapshotUsage( args[ 0 ] );
115            snapshot.snapshotEntry( day );
116
117            snapshot.showOutput();
118
119        } // end method main
120 }
```

Fig. 23.12 Removing entries from JavaSpaces service using method **snapshot** (part 3 of 3).

The only argument of method **snapshot** (line 48) specifies the template to serialize. Method **snapshot** returns a snapshot **Entry** that represents the matching template. Lines 49–51 call method **take** to remove the **Entry**s that match the template from the JavaSpaces service. Lines 54–58 remove all matching **Entry**s in the JavaSpaces service. Figure 23.13 shows the output of running the **SnapshotUsage** application. This output indicates that there are three matching **Entry**s in the JavaSpaces service. The take operation removes all three matching **Entry**s from the JavaSpaces service.

Fig. 23.13 SnapshotUsage Output window.

The following steps compile and execute the **SnapshotUsage** application. Make sure your **CLASSPATH** includes **jini-core.jar**, **jini-ext.jar** and **sun-util.jar**. Compile the java files in the **com\deitel\advjhtp1\javaspace\snapshot** directory. Run **SnapshotUsage** by specifying the hostname of the Jini lookup service. Do not forget to specify to the JVM the policy file with the proper permissions.

Software Engineering Observation 23.5

Using the snapshot **Entry** *is equivalent to using the original* **Entry**, *as long as all operations take place on the same JavaSpaces service that generated the snapshot.*

23.11 Updating Entries with Jini Transaction Service

We cannot modify an **Entry** in a JavaSpaces service directly. Instead, we must take the **Entry** away from the JavaSpaces service, change the values of the **Entry** fields, then place the **Entry** back into the JavaSpaces service. To ensure that the JavaSpaces service does not lose the **Entry** when a process takes that **Entry** away, we can perform the take, update and write processes in a transaction. If all these processes succeed, the transaction completes. Otherwise, the transaction fails and the JavaSpaces service returns the **Entry** to its state prior to the transaction.

Assume a distributed system in which dedicated nodes take **Entry**s from a JavaSpaces service, process each **Entry**, and **write** them back to the JavaSpaces service when finished. What happens if a problem occurs and one of the dedicated nodes never returns a processed **Entry**? The information that node processed could be permanently lost. Furthermore, because the processing node removed the **Entry** from the JavaSpaces service, the unprocessed **Entry** is also lost. The use of a transaction manager protects a JavaSpaces service from these situations. When a transaction fails, the transaction manager restores the **Entry** to its previous state—as if the client never took the **Entry**.

Our next example demonstrates how to update an **Entry** in a JavaSpaces service. The application takes an **AttendeeCounter Entry** from the JavaSpaces service, updates the count variable and reinserts the **Entry** back into the JavaSpaces service. A seminar administrator could use this application to register a new attendee for a seminar and update the appropriate **AttendeeCounter**. We have to ensure that if a client takes an **Entry** from the JavaSpaces service, it will write the **Entry** back into the JavaSpaces service later. In this example, we use the Jini transaction manager to guarantee that only one client at a time can update a seminar **Entry**. Otherwise, one client potentially could overwrite a previously written **Entry**, thus corrupting the proper count of the number of people who will attend a seminar.

23.11.1 Defining the User Interface

This section defines the user interface for the application. To update an **Entry**, the program must know which **AttendeeCounter** to update and the number to add to the counter. Class **UpdateInputWindow** (Fig. 23.14) prompts the user for the day of the week to update and the number of people who will attend the seminar on that day.

```
1   // UpdateInputWindow.java
2   // This application is an user interface used
3   // to get the input data.
4   package com.deitel.advjhtp1.javaspace.update;
5
6   // Java extension package
7   import javax.swing.*;
8
9   // Java core packages
10  import java.awt.*;
11  import java.awt.event.*;
12
13  public class UpdateInputWindow extends JFrame {
14
15     private String[] dates = { "Monday", "Tuesday",
16        "Wednesday", "Thursday", "Friday" };
17     private JButton okButton;
18     private JComboBox dateComboBox;
19     private JLabel firstLabel;
20     private JTextField numberText;
21     private String date = "Monday";
22     private int count = 0;
23     private String hostname;
24
25     public UpdateInputWindow( String name )
26     {
27        super( "UpdateInputWindow" );
28        Container container = getContentPane();
29
30        hostname = name;
31
32        // define center panel
33        JPanel centerPanel = new JPanel();
34        centerPanel.setLayout( new GridLayout( 2, 2, 0, 5 ) );
35
36        // add label
37        firstLabel = new JLabel( "Please choose a date:",
38           SwingConstants.CENTER );
39        centerPanel.add( firstLabel );
40
41        // add combo box
42        dateComboBox = new JComboBox( dates );
43        dateComboBox.setSelectedIndex( 0 );
44        centerPanel.add( dateComboBox );
45
```

Fig. 23.14 UpdateInputWindow user interface (part 1 of 3).

```
46        // install listener to combo box
47        dateComboBox.addItemListener(
48
49           new ItemListener() {
50
51              public void itemStateChanged( ItemEvent itemEvent )
52              {
53                 date = ( String )dateComboBox.getSelectedItem();
54              }
55           }
56        );
57
58        // add label
59        JLabel numberLabel = new JLabel(
60           "Please specify a number:", SwingConstants.CENTER );
61        centerPanel.add( numberLabel );
62
63        // add text field
64        numberText = new JTextField( 10 );
65        centerPanel.add( numberText );
66
67        // install listener to text field
68        numberText.addActionListener(
69
70           new ActionListener() {
71
72              public void actionPerformed( ActionEvent event )
73              {
74                 count = Integer.parseInt(
75                    event.getActionCommand() );
76              }
77           }
78        );
79
80        // define button panel
81        JPanel buttonPanel = new JPanel();
82        buttonPanel.setLayout( new GridLayout( 1, 1, 0, 5 ) );
83
84        // add OK button
85        okButton = new JButton( "OK" );
86        buttonPanel.add( okButton );
87
88        // add listener to OK button
89        okButton.addActionListener(
90
91           new ActionListener() {
92
93              public void actionPerformed( ActionEvent event )
94              {
95                 // get user input
96                 count = Integer.parseInt( numberText.getText() );
97
```

Fig. 23.14 UpdateInputWindow user interface (part 2 of 3).

```
98                       if ( count == 0 ) {
99                           System.out.println(
100                              "Please Specify a Number" );
101                      }
102
103                      else {
104                          UpdateOperation update = new UpdateOperation();
105                          String jiniURL = "jini://" +  hostname;
106                          update.getServices( jiniURL );
107                          update.updateEntry( date, count );
108
109                          setVisible( false );
110                          update.showOutput();
111                      }
112                   }
113                }
114            );
115
116            // put everything together
117            container.add( centerPanel, BorderLayout.CENTER );
118            container.add( buttonPanel, BorderLayout.SOUTH );
119
120            // set window size and display it
121            setSize( 320, 130 );
122            setVisible( true );
123
124        } // end updateInputWindow constructor
125 }
```

Fig. 23.14 **UpdateInputWindow** user interface (part 3 of 3).

23.11.2 Discovering the **TransactionManager** Service

Creating a transaction, requires a transaction manager. In our example, we use Jini's **TransactionManager** service to obtain a transaction manager. We assume that you already know how to start the Web server and the RMI activation daemon from Chapter 22.

```
java -jar
    -Dcom.sun.jini.mahalo.managerName=TransactionManager
    c:\files\jini1_1\lib\mahalo.jar
    http://hostname:port/mahalo-dl.jar
    c:\files\jini1_1\policy\policy.all
    c:\mahalo\txn_log public
```

Class **TransactionManagerFinder** (Fig. 23.15) demonstrates the **TransactionManager** service. This application performs unicast discovery to find the Jini lookup service, through which we can get a reference to the **TransactionManager**. The application looks for a **TransactionManager** in the lookup service. Lines 40–43 specify a **ServiceTemplate** object with which lines 46–47 search the lookup service. Method **getTransactionManager** (lines 72–75) returns a **Transaction Manager**.

```
1    // TransactionManagerFinder.java
2    // This application unicast discovers the
3    // TransactionManager service.
4    package com.deitel.advjhtp1.javaspace.common;
5
6    // Jini core packages
7    import net.jini.core.discovery.LookupLocator;
8    import net.jini.core.lookup.*;
9    import net.jini.core.entry.Entry;
10   import net.jini.core.transaction.server.TransactionManager;
11
12   // Java core packages
13   import java.io.*;
14   import java.rmi.RMISecurityManager;
15   import java.net.*;
16
17   // Java extension package
18   import javax.swing.*;
19
20   public class TransactionManagerFinder {
21
22      private TransactionManager transactionManager = null;
23
24      public TransactionManagerFinder( String jiniURL )
25      {
26         LookupLocator locator = null;
27         ServiceRegistrar registrar = null;
28
29         System.setSecurityManager( new RMISecurityManager() );
30
31         // get lookup service locator at "jini://hostname"
32         // use default port
33         try {
34            locator = new LookupLocator( jiniURL );
35
36            // get registrar for the locator
37            registrar = locator.getRegistrar();
38
39            // specify service requirement
40            Class[] types = new Class[] {
41               TransactionManager.class };
42            ServiceTemplate template =
43               new ServiceTemplate( null, types, null );
44
45            // find service
46            transactionManager =
47               (TransactionManager) registrar.lookup( template );
48         }
49
50         // handle exception invalid jini URL
51         catch ( MalformedURLException malformedURLException ) {
52            malformedURLException.printStackTrace();
53         }
```

Fig. 23.15 Finding Jini **TransactionManager** (part 1 of 2).

```
54
55        // handle exception I/O
56        catch ( IOException ioException ) {
57            ioException.printStackTrace();
58        }
59
60        // handle exception finding class
61        catch ( ClassNotFoundException classNotFoundException ) {
62            classNotFoundException.printStackTrace();
63        }
64
65        // does not find any matching service
66        if ( transactionManager == null ) {
67            System.out.println( "No matching service" );
68        }
69
70     } // end TransactionManagerFinder constructor
71
72     public TransactionManager getTransactionManager()
73     {
74         return transactionManager;
75     }
76  }
```

Fig. 23.15 Finding Jini **TransactionManager** (part 2 of 2).

23.11.3 Updating an **Entry**

We now have the user interface (class **UpdateInputWindow**), the transaction manager (class **TransactionManagerFinder**) and the JavaSpaces service (class **JavaSpaceFinder**) ready for use. The next step is to put everything together to build an application for updating **AttendeeCounter**s.

The **UpdateOperation** application (Fig. 23.16) demonstrates updating an **Entry** within a transaction. The **main** method constructs an **UpdateInputWindow** to allow the user to select a day and enter a count for the **AttendeeCounter** to update. Method **getServices** (lines 40–50) obtains a reference to the JavaSpaces service.

Method **updateEntry** (lines 53–136) updates an **AttendeeCounter** in the context of a transaction. Lines 67–68 create a transaction by passing the transaction manager and the lease duration to **TransactionFactory** method **create**, which returns a **Transaction.Created** object. Lines 69–70 specify the lease time for the transaction. Line 85 creates an **AttendeeCounter** template that will match all **AttendeeCounter**s in the JavaSpaces service. Lines 86–87 take an **Entry** from the JavaSpaces service using **transactionCreated.transaction**. If **UpdateOperation** retrieves an **AttendeeCounter** successfully, then it modifies the **AttendeeCounter** with the day and count information (lines 98–102) and writes it back to the JavaSpaces service. If **UpdateOperation** finds no **AttendeeCounter**, then it does nothing. Lines 115–116 commit the transaction, thus finalizing the transaction and ending the transaction's lease. If an exception occurs at any time, lines 126–127 abort the transaction and end the transaction's lease.

```
1    // UpdateOperation.java
2    // This application removes an Entry from the JavaSpace,
3    // changes the variable's value in the returned Entry and
4    // deposits the updated Entry into the JavaSpace. All these
5    // operations are occurred within a transaction.
6    package com.deitel.advjhtp1.javaspace.update;
7
8    // Jini core package
9    import net.jini.core.lease.Lease;
10   import net.jini.core.transaction.*;
11   import net.jini.core.entry.UnusableEntryException;
12   import net.jini.core.transaction.server.TransactionManager;
13
14   // Jini extension package
15   import net.jini.space.JavaSpace;
16   import net.jini.lease.*;
17
18   // Java core packages
19   import java.rmi.RemoteException;
20
21   // Java extension packages
22   import javax.swing.*;
23
24   // Deitel packages
25   import com.deitel.advjhtp1.javaspace.common.*;
26
27   public class UpdateOperation {
28
29      private JavaSpace space;
30      private TransactionManager transactionManager;
31      private static String hostname = "";
32      private static String day = "";
33      private static int inputCount = 0;
34      private static String output = "\n";
35
36      // default constructor
37      public UpdateOperation() {}
38
39      // constructor gets JavaSpace and TransactionManager
40      public void getServices( String jiniURL )
41      {
42         // get JavaSpace and TransactionManager
43         JavaSpaceFinder findtool =
44            new JavaSpaceFinder( jiniURL );
45         space = findtool.getJavaSpace();
46         TransactionManagerFinder findTransaction =
47            new TransactionManagerFinder( jiniURL );
48         transactionManager =
49            findTransaction.getTransactionManager();
50      }
51
```

Fig. 23.16 Updating an **Entry** using Jini **TransactionManager** (part 1 of 4).

```
52        // update Entry
53        public void updateEntry( String inputDay, int countNumber )
54        {
55            day = inputDay;
56            inputCount = countNumber;
57
58            AttendeeCounter resultCounter = null;
59            Transaction.Created transactionCreated = null;
60            LeaseRenewalManager manager = new LeaseRenewalManager();
61
62            int oldCount = 0;
63            int newCount = 0;
64
65            // create transaction and renew transaction's lease
66            try {
67                transactionCreated = TransactionFactory.create(
68                    transactionManager, Lease.FOREVER );
69                manager.renewUntil(
70                    transactionCreated.lease, Lease.FOREVER, null );
71            }
72
73            // handle exception creating transaction and renewing lease
74            catch ( Exception exception ) {
75                exception.printStackTrace();
76            }
77
78            // specify matching template, remove template
79            // from JavaSpace in transaction, change
80            // variable's value and write updated template back
81            // to JavaSpace within a transaction
82            try {
83
84                // take Entry away from JavaSpace
85                AttendeeCounter count = new AttendeeCounter( day );
86                resultCounter = ( AttendeeCounter ) space.take( count,
87                    transactionCreated.transaction, JavaSpace.NO_WAIT );
88
89                // if no matching entry
90                if ( resultCounter == null ) {
91
92                    // set output message
93                    output += " No matching Entry is available!\n";
94                }
95                else { // if find a matching entry
96
97                    // update value
98                    oldCount = resultCounter.counter.intValue();
99                    newCount = oldCount + inputCount;
100
101                    // put updated Entry back to JavaSpace
102                    resultCounter.counter = new Integer( newCount );
103                    space.write( resultCounter,
104                        transactionCreated.transaction, Lease.FOREVER );
```

Fig. 23.16 Updating an `Entry` using Jini `TransactionManager` (part 2 of 4).

```
105
106            // output result if transaction completes
107            output += "Count Information:\n";
108            output += "   Day: ";
109            output += resultCounter.day + "\n";
110            output += "   Old Count: " + oldCount + "\n";
111            output += "   New Count: " + newCount + "\n";
112          }
113
114       // commit transaction and release lease
115       transactionCreated.transaction.commit();
116       manager.remove( transactionCreated.lease );
117
118    } // end try
119
120    // handle exception updating Entry
121    catch ( Exception exception ) {
122       exception.printStackTrace();
123
124       // revert change and release lease
125       try {
126          transactionCreated.transaction.abort();
127          manager.remove( transactionCreated.lease );
128       }
129
130       // handle exception reverting change
131       catch ( Exception abortException ) {
132          abortException.printStackTrace();
133       }
134    }
135
136 } // end method updateEntry
137
138 // show output
139 public void showOutput()
140 {
141    JTextArea outputArea = new JTextArea();
142    outputArea.setText( output );
143    JOptionPane.showMessageDialog( null, outputArea,
144       "UpdateOperation Output",
145       JOptionPane.INFORMATION_MESSAGE );
146
147    // terminate program
148    System.exit( 0 );
149 }
150
151 public static void main( String args[] )
152 {
153    // get hostname
154    if ( args.length != 1 ) {
155       System.out.println(
156          "Usage: UpdateOperation hostname" );
```

Fig. 23.16 Updating an `Entry` using Jini `TransactionManager` (part 3 of 4).

```
157            System.exit( 1 );
158         }
159         else
160            hostname = args[ 0 ];
161
162         // get user input day
163         UpdateInputWindow input = new UpdateInputWindow( hostname );
164
165      } // end method main
166 }
```

Fig. 23.16 Updating an `Entry` using Jini `TransactionManager` (part 4 of 4).

Figure 23.17 and Fig. 23.18 show the results of running the update **Entry** application. The **WriteOperation Output** window in Fig. 23.17 is the result of running the **Write-Operation** application. We initialize the **Entry** for Wednesday. The **Update-InputWindow** in Fig. 23.17 is the interface for the user to provide the update information, such as the number of attendees for a seminar on a given day. In that window, we want to send 15 people to attend Wednesday's seminar. The **UpdateOperation Output** window in Fig. 23.18 shows the result of running the **UpdateOperation** application. The **ReadOperation Output** window in Fig. 23.18 shows the result of reading Wednesday's **Entry** via the **ReadOperation** application.

To execute this application a Web server, the RMI activation daemon, the Jini lookup service, the JavaSpaces service and the **TransactionManager** service should be running. The following steps compile and execute the **UpdateOperation** application. Ensure that your **CLASSPATH** includes **jini-core.jar**, **jini-ext.jar** and **sun-util.jar**. Compile the java files in the **com\deitel\advjhtp1\javaspace\common** and **com\deitel\advjhtp1\javaspace\update** directories. Run application **UpdateOperation** by specifying the hostname of the Jini lookup service. Do not forget to specify a policy file with the proper permissions.

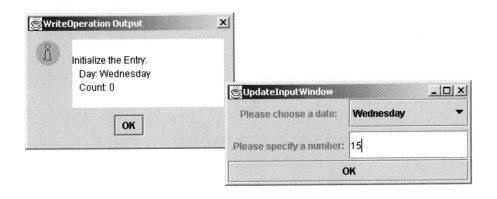

Fig. 23.17 WriteOperation Output and UpdateInputWindow user interface.

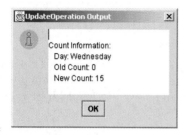 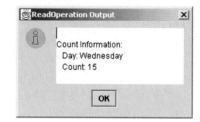

Fig. 23.18 UpdateOperation Output and ReadOperation Output.

23.12 Case Study: Distributed Image Processing

Image processing can be a time-consuming task, especially for large images. In this case study, we use JavaSpaces services to build a distributed image-processing system for applying filters to images (e.g., blur, sharpen, etc.). We define class **ImageProcessorClient** to partition a large image into smaller pieces and write these pieces into a JavaSpaces service. Multiple **ImageProcessor**s run in parallel to process the smaller images by applying appropriate filters, then write the processed images back into the JavaSpaces service. The **ImageProcessorClient** then takes the processed subimages from the JavaSpaces service and builds the complete, processed image. Figure 23.19 shows the basic structure of the **ImageProcessor** application.

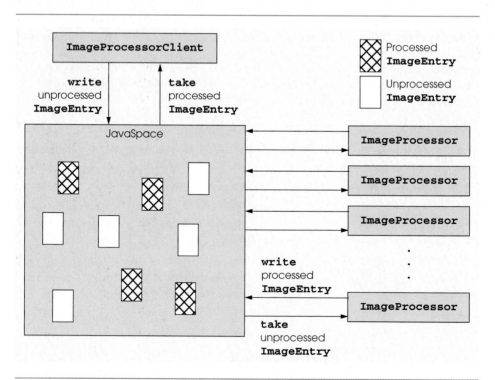

Fig. 23.19 Structure of the **ImageProcessor** distributed application.

23.12.1 Defining an Image Processor

In this case study, the distributed infrastructure consists of a set of dedicated image-processor nodes that retrieve **Entry**s from a JavaSpaces service. Each of these nodes processes an **Entry** and writes it back to the JavaSpaces service. The image processors have four filters—blur, color, invert and sharpen. A blur filter blurs an image. A color filter alters the RGB color bands of an image. An invert filter inverts an image's RGB color values. A sharpen filter sharpens the edges of an image. Each image-processor node in this distributed system polls the JavaSpaces service constantly looking for **Entry**s to process.

Applications can use the distributed system to process images. The application in our case study is **ImageProcessorClient** (Fig. 23.23). **ImageProcessorClient** will prompt the user for a file name and the number of pieces in which to divide the original image. **ImageProcessorClient** then writes the pieces to the JavaSpaces service. **ImageProcessorClient** will then poll the JavaSpaces service until it retrieves all of the processed pieces. Finally, the application will assemble the image and display the results to the user.

Class **ImageEntry** (Fig. 23.20) defines the **Entry**s that the application can store in the JavaSpaces service. Lines 16–20 define the **public** fields of the **Entry**. Line 23 defines the required empty constructor. Lines 26–34 define a constructor that initializes all fields in **ImageEntry**. Lines 37–41 define a constructor that initializes the **name** and **processed** fields. Lines 44–47 define a constructor that initializes the **name** field.

Class **ImageProcessor** (Fig. 23.21) represents each node of the image-processing distributed system that is capable of processing images. Each **ImageProcessor** node polls the JavaSpaces service for **ImageEntrys**. When a client writes an unprocessed **ImageEntry** into the JavaSpaces service, the first **ImageProcessor** node to retrieve that **Entry** will process it. Each **ImageProcessor** node creates a transaction for each **Entry** it retrieves and doesn't commit the transaction until it successfully writes the processed **ImageEntry** back to the JavaSpaces service, so if an **ImageProcessor** were to fail, the **ImageEntry** would not be lost.

```
1    // Fig. 23.20 ImageEntry.java
2    // This class defines the Entry for the image.
3    package com.deitel.advjhtp1.javaspace.ImageProcessor;
4
5    // Java core packages
6    import java.util.*;
7
8    // Java standard extension
9    import javax.swing.ImageIcon;
10
11   // Jini core packages
12   import net.jini.core.entry.Entry;
13
14   public class ImageEntry implements Entry {
15
16       public String name;
17       public String filter;
```

Fig. 23.20 **ImageEntry** defines the **Entry**s to store in the JavaSpaces service (part 1 of 2).

```
18        public Integer number;
19        public Boolean processed;
20        public ImageIcon imageIcon;
21
22        // empty constructor
23        public ImageEntry() {}
24
25        // ImageEntry constructor
26        public ImageEntry( String imageName, String imageFilter,
27           int order, boolean done, ImageIcon icon )
28        {
29           name = imageName;
30           filter = imageFilter;
31           number = new Integer( order );
32           processed = new Boolean( done );
33           imageIcon = icon;
34        }
35
36        // ImageEntry constructor
37        public ImageEntry( String imageName, boolean done )
38        {
39           name = imageName;
40           processed = new Boolean( done );
41        }
42
43        // ImageEntry constructor
44        public ImageEntry( String imageName )
45        {
46           name = imageName;
47        }
48     }
```

Fig. 23.20 `ImageEntry` defines the `Entry`s to store in the JavaSpaces service (part 2 of 2).

```
1    // Fig. 23.21 ImageProcessor.java
2    // Takes entries from the JavaSpace, applies a filter to
3    // the image piece, and writes processed entry back to JavaSpace.
4    package com.deitel.advjhtp1.javaspace.ImageProcessor;
5
6    // Java standard extensions
7    import javax.swing.*;
8
9    // Jini core packages
10   import net.jini.core.lease.Lease;
11   import net.jini.core.transaction.*;
12   import net.jini.core.transaction.server.TransactionManager;
13   import net.jini.core.entry.*;
14   import net.jini.core.transaction.*;
15   import net.jini.lease.*;
16
```

Fig. 23.21 Image processing node that uses the JavaSpaces service (part 1 of 4).

```
17   // Jini extension package
18   import net.jini.space.JavaSpace;
19
20   // Deitel packages
21   import com.deitel.advjhtp1.javaspace.common.*;
22
23   public class ImageProcessor {
24
25      private JavaSpace space;
26      private TransactionManager manager;
27
28      // ImageProcessor constructor
29      public ImageProcessor ( String hostname )
30      {
31         // get the JavaSpace
32         String jiniURL = "jini://" +  hostname;
33         JavaSpaceFinder finder =
34            new JavaSpaceFinder( jiniURL );
35         space = finder.getJavaSpace();
36
37         // get the TransactionManager
38         TransactionManagerFinder findTransaction =
39            new TransactionManagerFinder( jiniURL );
40         manager =
41            findTransaction.getTransactionManager();
42      }
43
44      // wait for unprocessed image
45      public void waitForImage()
46      {
47         LeaseRenewalManager leaseManager =
48            new LeaseRenewalManager();
49
50         while ( true ) {
51
52            // get unprocessed image and process it
53            try {
54               Transaction.Created transactionCreated =
55                  TransactionFactory.create(
56                     manager, Lease.FOREVER );
57
58               // renew transaction's lease
59               leaseManager.renewUntil(
60                  transactionCreated.lease, Lease.FOREVER, null );
61
62               ImageEntry template = new ImageEntry( null, false );
63               ImageEntry entry = ( ImageEntry ) space.take(
64                  template, transactionCreated.transaction,
65                  Lease.FOREVER );
66
```

Fig. 23.21 Image processing node that uses the JavaSpaces service (part 2 of 4).

```
67              if ( entry != null ) {
68
69                  // get image icon
70                  ImageIcon imageIcon = entry.imageIcon;
71
72                  Filters filters = new Filters( imageIcon );
73
74                  if ( entry.filter.equals( "BLUR" ) )
75                      filters.blurImage();
76
77                  else if ( entry.filter.equals( "COLOR" ) )
78                      filters.colorFilter();
79
80                  else if ( entry.filter.equals( "INVERT" ) )
81                      filters.invertImage();
82
83                  else if ( entry.filter.equals( "SHARP" ) )
84                      filters.sharpenImage();
85
86                  // update the fields of result entry
87                  entry.imageIcon = filters.getImageIcon();
88                  entry.processed = new Boolean( true );
89
90                  // put the updated Entry back to JavaSpace
91                  Lease writeLease = space.write( entry,
92                      transactionCreated.transaction,
93                      Lease.FOREVER );
94                  leaseManager.renewUntil(
95                      writeLease, Lease.FOREVER, null );
96
97              } // end if
98
99                  // commit the transaction and release the lease
100                 transactionCreated.transaction.commit();
101                 leaseManager.remove( transactionCreated.lease );
102
103         } // end try
104
105             // handle exception
106         catch ( Exception exception ) {
107             exception.printStackTrace();
108         }
109
110     } // end while
111
112 } // end method wait for images
113
114 public static void main( String[] args )
115 {
116     // get the hostname
117     if ( args.length != 1 ) {
118         System.out.println(
119             "Usage: ImageProcessor hostname" );
```

Fig. 23.21 Image processing node that uses the JavaSpaces service (part 3 of 4).

```
120              System.exit( 1 );
121          }
122
123          ImageProcessor processor =
124              new ImageProcessor( args[ 0 ] );
125
126          // wait for image
127          processor.waitForImage();
128
129      } // end method main
130  }
```

Fig. 23.21 Image processing node that uses the JavaSpaces service (part 4 of 4).

Constructor **ImageProcessor** (lines 29–42) gets a JavaSpaces service and a **TransactionManager** service from the user-specified hostname. Classes **Java-SpaceFinder** and **TransactionManagerFinder** are defined in Fig. 23.1 and Fig. 23.15 respectively. Method **waitForImage** (lines 45–112) waits for an unprocessed image. Lines 50–110 cycle indefinitely to process **Entry**s from the JavaSpaces service. Line 62 defines the **Entry** template that **ImageProcessor** will use to retrieve unprocessed **ImageEntry** from the JavaSpaces service. Lines 63–65 retrieve an object from the JavaSpaces service. If the **Entry** retrieved from the JavaSpaces service is not **null**, lines 70–84 apply a filter to the image. Lines 87–88 set fields in the **ImageEntry** with values that will identify the **ImageEntry** as a processed **Entry**. Lines 91-91-93 write the processed **ImageEntry** back to the JavaSpaces service. Line 100 commits the transaction. Line 101 expires the lease on the transaction.

Method **main** (lines 114–129) gets the user-specified hostname and calls **ImageProcessor** constructor. Method **waitForImage** starts polling the JavaSpaces service for an unprocessed image.

Class **Filters** (Fig. 23.22) filters an image. It provides four types of filters—blur, sharpen, invert and color. These four filters can be found in the Chapter 4 package **com.deitel.advjhtp.java2d**. The **Filters** constructor (lines 26–40) takes an **ImageIcon** and converts the **ImageIcon** to the **BufferedImage**. Method **blurImage** (lines 43–46) applies a blur filter to the **BufferedImage**. Method **sharpenImage** (lines 49–53) applies a sharpen filter to the **BufferedImage**. Method **invertImage** (lines 56–60) applies an invert filter to the **BufferedImage**. Method **colorFilter** (lines 63–67) applies a color filter to a **BufferedImage**. Method **getImageIcon** (lines 70–73) returns the filtered image as an **ImageIcon**.

```
1  // Fig. 23.22: Filters.java
2  // Applies blurring, sharpening, converting, modifying on images.
3  package com.deitel.advjhtp1.javaspace.ImageProcessor;
4
5  // Java core packages
6  import java.awt.*;
7  import java.awt.image.*;
8
```

Fig. 23.22 Class **Filters** applies a Java 2D filter to an image (part 1 of 3).

```
9    // Java standard extensions
10   import javax.swing.*;
11
12   // Deitel packages
13   import com.deitel.advjhtp1.java2d.*;
14
15   public class Filters {
16
17      Java2DImageFilter blurFilter;
18      Java2DImageFilter sharpenFilter;
19      Java2DImageFilter invertFilter;
20      Java2DImageFilter colorFilter;
21
22      BufferedImage bufferedImage;
23
24      // constructor method initializes ImageFilters and pulls
25      // BufferedImage out of ImageIcon
26      public Filters( ImageIcon icon )
27      {
28         blurFilter = new BlurFilter();
29         sharpenFilter = new SharpenFilter();
30         invertFilter = new InvertFilter();
31         colorFilter = new ColorFilter();
32
33         Image image = icon.getImage();
34         bufferedImage = new BufferedImage(
35            image.getWidth( null ), image.getHeight( null ),
36            BufferedImage.TYPE_INT_RGB );
37
38         Graphics2D gg = bufferedImage.createGraphics();
39         gg.drawImage( image, null, null );
40      }
41
42      // apply BlurFilter to bufferedImage
43      public void blurImage()
44      {
45         bufferedImage = blurFilter.processImage( bufferedImage );
46      }
47
48      // apply SharpenFilter to bufferedImage
49      public void sharpenImage()
50      {
51         bufferedImage = sharpenFilter.processImage(
52            bufferedImage );
53      }
54
55      // apply InvertFilter to bufferedImage
56      public void invertImage()
57      {
58         bufferedImage = invertFilter.processImage(
59            bufferedImage );
60      }
61
```

Fig. 23.22 Class **Filters** applies a Java 2D filter to an image (part 2 of 3).

```
62        // apply ColorFilter to bufferedImage
63        public void colorFilter()
64        {
65           bufferedImage = colorFilter.processImage(
66              bufferedImage );
67        }
68
69        // constructs and returns an ImageIcon from bufferedImage
70        public ImageIcon getImageIcon()
71        {
72           return ( new ImageIcon( bufferedImage ) );
73        }
74     }
```

Fig. 23.22 Class **Filters** applies a Java 2D filter to an image (part 3 of 3).

23.12.2 Partitioning an Image into Smaller Pieces

To parallelize the task of filtering a large image, we can partition the image into smaller pieces and let multiple **ImageProcessor**s concurrently filter the smaller images. Then, we can combine the processed pieces to create the complete, processed image. Class **ImageProcessorClient** (Fig. 23.23) prompts the user for an image file to process and partitions the large image. **ImageProcessorClient** wraps the image pieces in **ImageEntry**s and write them into the JavaSpaces service. Once **ImageProcessorClient** writes all image pieces into the JavaSpaces service, it reads back all processed **ImageEntry**s.

The **ImageProcessorClient** constructor (lines 42–192) defines the user interface to get the user input data. Lines 66–81 display a **JChooserPanel** when a user presses the **Choose file to process** button to prompt the user for an image file. Lines 90–111 define a **JLabel** and a **JTextfield** which obtains the user-specified number of subimages. Lines 114–135 create a label and a drop-down box that allows the user to specify the filter to apply on the image. Lines 142–186 add an **OK** button to the window. Lines 152–186 define the action when the user clicks the **OK** button. The application first checks whether the user specified the image name and partition number. If so, the application passes the user specified data to the **ImageSeparator** (Fig. 23.24) constructor and calls methods **partitionImage** and **storeImage** of class **ImageSeparator** to partition the image and store the sub images in a JavaSpaces service, respectively. Method **collect** obtains a reference to the JavaSpaces service (lines 198–201). Lines 211–212 verify that the user input number divides evenly between columns and rows. If the user-input number does not divide evenly, then the image will be broken into 4 pieces. Line 215 creates a template that will match all processed image pieces. Line 218 creates a snapshot of the template. Lines 221–225 retrieve all processed **ImageEntry**s from the JavaSpaces service. Lines 251–265 reassemble the image and display the resulting image in a separate window. Lines 267–274 display an error message if the file was not found. Method **main** (lines 278–294) gets the user-specified hostname from the command line and displays the GUI.

Class **ImageSeparator** (Fig. 23.24) partitions an image into smaller pieces and places the subimages into a JavaSpaces service. The constructor (lines 33–39) gets the image name, number of subimages and this filter to be apply to the image. Method **partitionImage** (lines 42–50) gets the **ImageIcon** from the image file (lines 44–45) and calls method **parseImage** of class **ImageParser** (Fig. 23.25) to partition the image into smaller pieces. Method **displayImage** (lines 53–60) creates a **ImageDisplayer** (Fig. 23.26) to display the original image. Method **storeImage** (lines 63–101) writes the subimages into a JavaSpaces service. Lines 77–88 write each image into the JavaSpaces service and renew the image's lease to **Lease.FOREVER**.

```java
1    // Fig. 23.23 ImageProcessingClient.java
2    // The application asks for user-specified image file, image
3    // filter type and image partition number, filters the image
4    // and displays the processed image.
5    package com.deitel.advjhtp1.javaspace.ImageProcessor;
6
7    // Java core packages
8    import java.awt.*;
9    import java.awt.event.*;
10   import java.util.*;
11   import java.io.*;
12
13   // Java extension packages
14   import javax.swing.*;
15
16   // Jini core packages
17   import net.jini.core.lease.Lease;
18   import net.jini.core.entry.*;
19   import net.jini.core.transaction.*;
20   import net.jini.core.transaction.server.TransactionManager;
21
22   // Jini extension packages
23   import net.jini.space.JavaSpace;
24
25   // Deitel packages
26   import com.deitel.advjhtp1.javaspace.common.*;
27
28   public class ImageProcessingClient extends JFrame {
29
30      private String[] operations = { "BLUR", "COLOR",
31         "INVERT", "SHARP" };
32      private JButton okButton;
33      private JComboBox operationComboBox;
34      private JTextField imageText;
35      private JTextField numberText;
36
37      private static String hostname = "";
38      private String imageName;
39      private String operation = "BLUR";
40      private int partitionNumber = 0;
41
42      public ImageProcessingClient( String host )
43      {
44         super ( "ImageProcessInput" );
45
46         hostname = host;
47         Container container = getContentPane();
```

Fig. 23.23 Image-processing distributed system client (part 1 of 6).

```
48
49        // define the center panel
50        JPanel centerPanel = new JPanel();
51        centerPanel.setLayout( new GridLayout( 3, 2, 0, 5 ) );
52
53        // add image label
54        JLabel imageLabel = new JLabel( "Image File:",
55           SwingConstants.CENTER );
56        centerPanel.add( imageLabel );
57
58        JButton openFile = new JButton(
59           "Choose file to process" );
60        openFile.addActionListener(
61
62           new ActionListener() {
63
64              public void actionPerformed( ActionEvent event )
65              {
66                 JFileChooser fileChooser = new JFileChooser();
67
68                 fileChooser.setFileSelectionMode(
69                    JFileChooser.FILES_ONLY );
70                 int result = fileChooser.showOpenDialog( null );
71                 File file;
72
73                 // user clicked Cancel button on dialog
74                 if ( result == JFileChooser.CANCEL_OPTION )
75                    file = null;
76                 else {
77                    file = fileChooser.getSelectedFile();
78                    imageName = file.getPath();
79                 }
80
81              } // end method actionPerformed
82
83           } // end ActionListener constructor
84
85        ); // end addActionListener
86
87        centerPanel.add( openFile );
88
89        // add number label
90        JLabel numberLabel = new JLabel( "Partition Number:",
91           SwingConstants.CENTER );
92        centerPanel.add( numberLabel );
93
94        // add number text field
95        numberText = new JTextField( 10 );
96        centerPanel.add( numberText );
97
98        // install a listener to the number text field
99        numberText.addActionListener(
100
```

Fig. 23.23 Image-processing distributed system client (part 2 of 6).

```
101            new ActionListener() {
102
103                // get the text when the user feeds a return
104                // character in the text field
105                public void actionPerformed( ActionEvent event )
106                {
107                    partitionNumber = Integer.parseInt(
108                        event.getActionCommand() );
109                }
110            }
111        );
112
113        // add operation label
114        JLabel operationLabel = new JLabel( "Operation Type:",
115            SwingConstants.CENTER );
116        centerPanel.add( operationLabel );
117
118        // add a combo box
119        operationComboBox = new JComboBox( operations );
120        operationComboBox.setSelectedIndex( 0 );
121        centerPanel.add( operationComboBox );
122
123        // install a listener to the combo box
124        operationComboBox.addItemListener(
125
126            new ItemListener() {
127
128                // an operation other than BLUR is selected
129                public void itemStateChanged( ItemEvent itemEvent )
130                {
131                    operation =
132                        ( String ) operationComboBox.getSelectedItem();
133                }
134            }
135        );
136
137        // define the button panel
138        JPanel buttonPanel = new JPanel();
139        buttonPanel.setLayout( new GridLayout( 1, 1, 0, 5 ) );
140
141        // add the OK button
142        okButton = new JButton( "OK" );
143        buttonPanel.add( okButton );
144
145        // add a listener to the OK button
146        okButton.addActionListener(
147
148            new ActionListener() {
149
```

Fig. 23.23 Image-processing distributed system client (part 3 of 6).

```
150                     // partition image file into number of pieces user
151                     // specified
152                     public void actionPerformed( ActionEvent event )
153                     {
154                         // get user inputs
155                         partitionNumber = Integer.parseInt(
156                             numberText.getText() );
157
158                         // check whether the user
159                         // fills in both text fields
160                         if ( ( partitionNumber == 0 )
161                             || ( imageName == null ) ) {
162                             JOptionPane.showMessageDialog( null,
163                                 "Either image name or partition number "
164                                 + "is not specified!", "Error",
165                                 JOptionPane.ERROR_MESSAGE );
166                         }
167
168                         else {
169                             setVisible( false );
170
171                             // partition the image into smaller pieces
172                             // and store the sub images into a JavaSpace
173                             ImageSeparator imageSeparator =
174                                 new ImageSeparator(
175                                     imageName, operation, partitionNumber );
176                             imageSeparator.partitionImage();
177                             imageSeparator.storeImage( hostname );
178                             imageSeparator.displayImage();
179                             collect();
180                         }
181
182                     } // end method actionPerformed
183
184                 } // end ActionListener constructor
185
186         ); // end addActionListener
187
188         // put everything together
189         container.add( centerPanel, BorderLayout.CENTER );
190         container.add( buttonPanel, BorderLayout.SOUTH );
191
192     } // end ImageProcessingClient constructor
193
194     // collect processed images
195     public void collect()
196     {
197         // get the JavaSpace
198         String jiniURL = "jini://" + hostname;
199         JavaSpaceFinder findtool =
200             new JavaSpaceFinder( jiniURL );
201         JavaSpace space = findtool.getJavaSpace();
202
```

Fig. 23.23 Image-processing distributed system client (part 4 of 6).

```
203            Vector unOrderedImages = new Vector();
204            Vector orderedImages = null;
205
206            // removes all images in the JavaSpace
207            // that have the specified name
208            try {
209                double squareRoot = Math.sqrt( partitionNumber );
210
211                if ( Math.floor( squareRoot ) != ( squareRoot ) )
212                    partitionNumber = 4;
213
214                // specify the matching template
215                ImageEntry template = new ImageEntry( imageName, true );
216
217                // snapshot the template
218                Entry snapshotEntry = space.snapshot( template );
219
220                // collect images
221                for ( int i = 0; i < partitionNumber ; i++ ) {
222                    ImageEntry remove = ( ImageEntry ) space.take(
223                        snapshotEntry, null, Lease.FOREVER );
224                    unOrderedImages.add( remove );
225                }
226
227                int imageCount = unOrderedImages.size();
228                orderedImages =
229                    new Vector( imageCount );
230
231                // initialize the Vector
232                for ( int i = 0; i < imageCount; i++ )
233                    orderedImages.add( null );
234
235                // order the sub images
236                for ( int i = 0; i < imageCount; i++ ) {
237                    ImageEntry image =
238                        ( ImageEntry ) unOrderedImages.elementAt( i );
239                    orderedImages.setElementAt(
240                        image.imageIcon, image.number.intValue() );
241                }
242
243            } // end try
244
245            // handle exception collecting images
246            catch ( Exception exception ) {
247                exception.printStackTrace();
248            }
249
250            // put images together and display the result image
251            if ( orderedImages.size() > 0 ) {
252                ImageParser imageParser = new ImageParser();
253
254                ImageIcon icon = imageParser.putTogether(
255                    orderedImages );
```

Fig. 23.23 Image-processing distributed system client (part 5 of 6).

```
256
257              ImageDisplayer imageDisplayer =
258                 new ImageDisplayer( icon );
259
260              imageDisplayer.setSize( icon.getIconWidth() + 50,
261                 icon.getIconHeight() + 50 );
262              imageDisplayer.setVisible( true );
263              imageDisplayer.setDefaultCloseOperation(
264                 JFrame.EXIT_ON_CLOSE );
265           }
266
267           else {
268              JOptionPane.showMessageDialog( null,
269                 "Invalid image name", "Error",
270                 JOptionPane.ERROR_MESSAGE);
271
272              // terminate program
273              System.exit( 0 );
274           }
275
276        } // end method collect
277
278        public static void main( String[] args )
279        {
280           // get the hostname
281           if ( args.length != 1 ) {
282              System.out.println(
283                 "Usage: ImageProcessingClient hostname" );
284              System.exit( 1 );
285           }
286
287           ImageProcessingClient processor =
288              new ImageProcessingClient( args[ 0 ] );
289
290           // set the window size and display it
291           processor.setSize( 350, 150 );
292           processor.setVisible( true );
293
294        } // end method main
295     }
```

Fig. 23.23 Image-processing distributed system client (part 6 of 6).

```
1   // Fig. 23.24 ImageSeparator.java
2   // This class partitions the image into smaller pieces evenly
3   // and stores the smaller images into a JavaSpace.
4   package com.deitel.advjhtp1.javaspace.ImageProcessor;
5
6   // Java core packages
7   import java.util.*;
8   import java.rmi.*;
```

Fig. 23.24 Partitioning an image into smaller pieces and storing subimages in a JavaSpaces service (part 1 of 3).

```
9
10   // Java standard extensions
11   import javax.swing.*;
12
13   // Jini core packages
14   import net.jini.core.lease.Lease;
15   import net.jini.core.transaction.TransactionException;
16
17   // Jini extension packages
18   import net.jini.space.JavaSpace;
19   import net.jini.lease.*;
20
21   // Deitel packages
22   import com.deitel.advjhtp1.javaspace.common.*;
23
24   public class ImageSeparator {
25
26      private String imageName;
27      private String filterType;
28      private int partitionNumber;
29      private Vector imagePieces;
30      private ImageIcon icon;
31
32      // ImageSeparator constructor
33      public ImageSeparator(
34         String name, String type, int number )
35      {
36         imageName = name;
37         filterType = type;
38         partitionNumber = number;
39      }
40
41      // partition the image into smaller pieces evenly
42      public void partitionImage()
43      {
44         ImageParser imageParser = new ImageParser();
45         icon = new ImageIcon( imageName );
46
47         // partition the image
48         imagePieces = imageParser.parseImage(
49            icon, partitionNumber );
50      }
51
52      // display the image
53      public void displayImage(  )
54      {
55         ImageDisplayer imageDisplayer =
56            new ImageDisplayer( icon );
57         imageDisplayer.setSize( icon.getIconWidth() + 50,
58            icon.getIconHeight() + 50 );
59         imageDisplayer.setVisible( true );
60      }
```

Fig. 23.24 Partitioning an image into smaller pieces and storing subimages in a JavaSpaces service (part 2 of 3).

```
61
62      // write image pieces into a JavaSpace
63      public void storeImage( String hostname )
64      {
65          // get the JavaSpace
66          String jiniURL = "jini://" +  hostname;
67          JavaSpaceFinder findtool =
68              new JavaSpaceFinder( jiniURL );
69          JavaSpace space = findtool.getJavaSpace();
70
71          LeaseRenewalManager leaseManager =
72              new LeaseRenewalManager();
73
74          // write sub images to JavaSpace
75          try {
76
77              for ( int i = 0; i < imagePieces.size(); i++ ) {
78                  ImageIcon subImage =
79                      ( ImageIcon ) imagePieces.elementAt( i );
80
81                  ImageEntry imageEntry = new ImageEntry(
82                      imageName, filterType, i, false, subImage );
83
84                  Lease writeLease = space.write(
85                      imageEntry, null, Lease.FOREVER );
86                  leaseManager.renewUntil(
87                      writeLease, Lease.FOREVER, null );
88              }
89          }
90
91          // if a network failure occurs
92          catch ( RemoteException remoteException ) {
93              remoteException.printStackTrace();
94          }
95
96          // if write operates under an invalid transaction
97          catch ( TransactionException transactionException ) {
98              transactionException.printStackTrace();
99          }
100
101     } // end method storeImage
102 }
```

Fig. 23.24 Partitioning an image into smaller pieces and storing subimages in a JavaSpaces service (part 3 of 3).

Class **ImageParser** (Fig. 23.25) partitions an image into smaller pieces and puts subimages together to reform a large image. Method **parseImage** (lines 25–66) partitions an image into smaller pieces. If the number of subimages specified by the user does not divide evenly between the number of rows and columns, then the default number 4 is used (lines 29–35). Lines 42–62 partition the image. The resulting subimages are stored in a **Vector**. Method **putTogether** (lines 71–106) puts subimages back together. Lines 93–102 get the subimages from the input **Vector** and piece them together into a **BufferedImage** to form a complete image. Line 104 returns the image as an **ImageIcon**.

Class **ImageDisplayer** (Fig. 23.26) is a **JFrame** subclass for displaying an image.
The constructor (lines 15–30) gets an **ImageIcon** and displays it in a **JLabel**.

```
1   // Fig. 23.25: ImageParser.java
2   // This class partitions an image into smaller pieces.
3   package com.deitel.advjhtp1.javaspace.ImageProcessor;
4
5   // Java core packages
6   import java.awt.image.*;
7   import java.net.URL;
8   import java.awt.*;
9   import java.lang.*;
10  import java.util.Vector;
11  import java.awt.geom.*;
12
13  // Java standard extensions
14  import javax.swing.*;
15
16  public class ImageParser  {
17
18     ImageIcon image;
19
20     public ImageParser() {}
21
22     // pass parseImage an ImageIcon on the number of piece
23     // you want it split into the number of piece must be a
24     // perfect square - this can be extended later
25     public Vector parseImage(
26        ImageIcon imageIcon, int numberPieces )
27     {
28        Vector vector = new Vector();
29        double squareRoot = Math.sqrt( numberPieces );
30
31        if ( Math.floor( squareRoot ) != ( squareRoot ) ) {
32           System.out.println( "This is not a square number,"
33              + " setting to default...");
34           numberPieces = 4;
35        }
36
37        // get number of rows and columns
38        int numberRows = ( int ) Math.sqrt( numberPieces );
39        int numberColumns = ( int ) Math.sqrt( numberPieces );
40
41        // retrieve Image from BufferedImage
42        Image image = imageIcon.getImage();
43        BufferedImage bufferedImage = new BufferedImage(
44           image.getWidth( null ), image.getHeight( null ),
45           BufferedImage.TYPE_INT_RGB );
46
47        Graphics2D g2D = bufferedImage.createGraphics();
48        g2D.drawImage( image, null, null );
49
```

Fig. 23.25 Partitioning and reforming an image (part 1 of 3).

```
50          // get size of each piece
51          int width = bufferedImage.getWidth() / numberColumns;
52          int height = bufferedImage.getHeight() / numberRows;
53
54          // make each of images
55          for ( int x = 0; x < numberRows; x++ ) {
56
57             for ( int y = 0; y < numberColumns; y++ ) {
58                vector.add( new ImageIcon(
59                   bufferedImage.getSubimage(
60                      x * width, y * height, width, height ) ) );
61             }
62          }
63
64          return vector;
65
66       } // end method parseImage
67
68       // takes a vector of image icons (must be a square number)
69       // of elements and returns an image icon with the images
70       // put back together again
71       public ImageIcon putTogether( Vector vector )
72       {
73          double size = vector.size();
74          int numberRowColumn = ( int ) Math.sqrt( size );
75
76          // step 1, get first Image
77          Image tempImage =
78             ( ( ImageIcon ) vector.get( 0 ) ).getImage();
79
80          // get total size of one piece
81          int width = tempImage.getWidth( null );
82          int height = tempImage.getHeight( null );
83
84          // create buffered image
85          BufferedImage totalPicture = new BufferedImage(
86             width * numberRowColumn, height * numberRowColumn,
87             BufferedImage.TYPE_INT_RGB );
88
89          // create Graphics for BufferedImage
90          Graphics2D graphics = totalPicture.createGraphics();
91
92          // draw images from the vector into buffered image
93          for ( int x = 0; x < numberRowColumn; x++ ) {
94
95             for ( int y = 0; y < numberRowColumn; y++ ) {
96                Image image = ( ( ImageIcon ) vector.get(
97                   y + numberRowColumn * x ) ).getImage();
98                graphics.drawImage( image,
99                   AffineTransform.getTranslateInstance(
100                     x * width, y * height ), null );
101            }
102         }
```

Fig. 23.25 Partitioning and reforming an image (part 2 of 3).

```
103
104          return new ImageIcon( totalPicture );
105
106     } // end method putTogether
107 }
```

Fig. 23.25 Partitioning and reforming an image (part 3 of 3).

```
1   // Fig. 23.26: ImageDisplayer.java
2   // This application is an user interface used
3   // to display an image.
4   package com.deitel.advjhtp1.javaspace.ImageProcessor;
5
6   // Java extension packages
7   import javax.swing.*;
8
9   // Java core packages
10  import java.awt.*;
11  import java.awt.event.*;
12
13  public class ImageDisplayer extends JFrame {
14
15     public ImageDisplayer( ImageIcon icon )
16     {
17        super( "ImageDisplay" );
18        Container container = getContentPane();
19
20        // define the center panel
21        JPanel centerPanel = new JPanel();
22
23        // add display label
24        JLabel imageLabel = new JLabel(
25           icon, SwingConstants.LEFT );
26        centerPanel.add( imageLabel );
27
28        container.add( centerPanel, BorderLayout.CENTER );
29
30     } // end ImageDisplayer constructor
31  }
```

Fig. 23.26 Displaying an image.

23.12.3 Compiling and Running the Example

Before compiling the sample code, ensure that **jini-core.jar**, **jini-ext.jar** and **sun-util.jar** are included in the **CLASSPATH**. To execute the example, start:

1. a Web server,
2. the RMI activation daemon,
3. the Jini lookup service,
4. the JavaSpaces service, and
5. the Jini **Transaction** service.

On a second computer, perform the following tasks:

1. compile all java files in directory **com\deitel\advjhtp1\java-space\ImageProcessor**, and

2. start the **ImageProcessorClient** application by specifying the hostname of the computer running the Jini lookup service (you also must specify an appropriate policy file).

On at least one other machine, start an **ImageProcessor** node and specify the hostname of the computer running the Jini lookup service (you also must specify an appropriate policy file).

One important thing to note in this example is that doubling the number of **ImageProcessor** nodes that retrieve **Entry**s from the JavaSpaces service doubles the processing power of the application. If you do not have multiple computers, you can run the entire application on a single computer. Although this defeats the purpose of a distributed system, running the application on a single computer can be useful for testing and debugging the application. Figure 23.27 displays the GUI for the **ImageProcessorClient** application

Fig. 23.28 displays the image on the left-hand side before application **ImageProcessorClient** distributes the image to the **ImageProcessor** nodes. The **ImageProcessor** nodes apply the blur filter to the image. The image on the right-hand side shows the resulting image after **ImageProcessorClient** assembles the processed pieces.

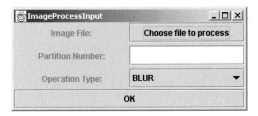

Fig. 23.27 GUI from **ImageProcessorMain** and **ImageCollector** applications.

Fig. 23.28 Images before and after blurring.

23.13 Internet and World Wide Web Resources

www.sun.com/jini/specs/js1_1.pdf
This site provides the Jini JavaSpaces service Specification.

www.javaworld.com/jw-11-1999/jw-11-jiniology.html
www.javaworld.com/jw-01-2000/jw-01-jiniology.html
www.javaworld.com/jw-03-2000/jw-03-jiniology.html
www.javaworld.com/jw-04-2000/jw-0421-jiniology.html
www.javaworld.com/jw-06-2000/jw-0623-jiniology.html
These JavaWorld online magazine URLs represent a series of articles that introduce JavaSpaces technology, including the available operations, transactions and leasing.

www.byte.com/documents/s=146/BYT19990921S0001/index.htm
This article provides an overview of JavaSpaces technology and introduces its basic concepts.

SUMMARY

- A JavaSpaces service is a Jini service that implements a simple, high-level architecture for building distributed systems. The JavaSpaces service enables Java objects to communicate, share objects and coordinate tasks using an area of shared memory.

- A JavaSpaces service provides three fundamental operations—write, take and read. The write operation places an object—called an entry—into the JavaSpaces service.

- The take operation specifies a template and removes from the JavaSpaces service an entry that matches the given template. The read operation is similar to the take operation, but does not remove the matching entry from the JavaSpaces service.

- In addition to the three basic operations, JavaSpaces services support transactions through the Jini transaction manager, and a notification mechanism that notifies an object when an entry that matches a given template is written to the JavaSpaces service.

- An entry stored in a JavaSpaces service will remain in the JavaSpaces service until its lease expires or until a program takes the entry from the JavaSpaces service.

- A JavaSpaces service locates objects by comparing those objects to a template. The template specifies the search criteria against which the JavaSpaces service compares each entry. When one or more entries match the template, the JavaSpaces service returns a single matching entry.

- JavaSpaces services can use the Jini transaction manager to ensure operations execute atomically.

- Objects in a JavaSpaces service are shared. Programs can read and take entries from the JavaSpaces service, modify the **public** fields in those entries and write them back to the JavaSpaces service for other programs to use.

- Any object stored in the JavaSpaces service must implement interface **Entry** (package **net.jini.core.entry**). JavaSpaces services **Entry**s adhere to the Jini **Entry** contract defined in the Jini Core Specification.

- An **Entry** can have multiple constructors and as many methods as required. Other requirements include a **public** no-argument constructor, **public** fields and no-primitive type fields. The JavaSpaces service proxy uses the no-argument constructor to instantiate the matching **Entry** during the deserialization process.

- All fields that will be used as the template matching fields in an **Entry** must be **public** (for more information on template matching fields, see Section 23.8). As defined by the Jini Core Specification, an **Entry** cannot have primitive-type fields.

- JavaSpaces technology, like Jini, requires several underlying services. The JavaSpaces service depends on the Jini lookup service. When transactions are required, the Jini transaction service must be started. JavaSpaces services also depend on a Web server and **rmid**

- Two versions of JavaSpaces services are available. One is the transient JavaSpaces service (non-activatable). The other is the persistent JavaSpaces service (activatable).

- The transient JavaSpaces service does not require the RMI activation daemon (**rmid**), because the transient JavaSpaces service is not activatable. Once the transient JavaSpaces service terminates, all state information is lost and **rmid** is unable to restart the service.

- The persistent JavaSpaces service is activatable, and therefore requires the RMI activation daemon. If the persistent JavaSpaces servicee terminates, all of its state information is stored in a log file and **rmid** can restart the service at a later time.

- Upon initialization, each JavaSpaces service registers itself with local Jini lookup services.

- Clients access objects in a JavaSpaces service through interface **JavaSpace** (package **net.jini.space**). Interface **JavaSpace** provides several methods—**notify**, **read**, **readIfExists**, **take**, **takeIfExists**, **write** and **snapshot**.

- The **write** operation inserts an **Entry** into a JavaSpaces service. If an identical **Entry** already exists in the JavaSpaces service, this operation does not overwrite the existing **Entry**. Instead, the **write** operation places a copy of the **Entry** into the JavaSpaces service.

- The **read** operation attempts to read an **Entry** that matches an **Entry** template from a JavaSpaces service. If no matching **Entry** exists in the JavaSpaces service, this operation returns **null**. If multiple matching **Entry** exist in the JavaSpaces service, the **read** operation arbitrarily picks one among the matching **Entry**s. Method **read** blocks until a matching **Entry** is found in the JavaSpaces service or until a time-out occurs.

- Method **readIfExists** checks to see if a matching **Entry** exists within the JavaSpaces service. If an **Entry** does not exist in the JavaSpaces service, method **readIfExists** should return **null** immediately. Method **readIfExists** does not block unless the matching **Entry** is a participant in an uncommitted transaction.

- The **take** operation attempts to remove an **Entry** that matches an **Entry** template from a JavaSpaces service. This operation works like the **read** operation, except that the **take** operation removes the matching **Entry** from the JavaSpaces service.

- Method **take** blocks until a matching **Entry** is found in the JavaSpaces service or until a time-out occurs.

- Method **takeIfExists** checks to see if a matching **Entry** exists within the JavaSpaces service. If an **Entry** does not exist in the JavaSpaces service, method **takeIfExists** should return **null** immediately. Method **takeIfExists** does not block unless the matching **Entry** is part of an uncommitted transaction.

- The **notify** operation requests that the JavaSpaces service sends a notification to a listener object when a client writes a matching **Entry** into the JavaSpaces service. With this method, an application does not need to check repeatedly for an **Entry** in a JavaSpaces service.

- Method **snapshot** increases performance when a program must serialize one **Entry** repeatedly. Each time a program transfers an **Entry** into a JavaSpaces service (e.g., by writing that **Entry** or by using that **Entry** as a template), that **Entry** must be serialized. Invoking method **snapshot** serializes the **Entry** once and reuses this serialized **Entry** for future transfers.

- Method **write** takes three arguments—an **Entry**, a **Transaction** object and a **long** value that requests an amount of time for which the JavaSpaces service should keep the **Entry**. The **long** value represents the lease length for the **Entry**.

- The **read** and the **take** operations retrieve **Entry**s from a JavaSpaces service. A client can read or take an **Entry** from the JavaSpaces service by supplying a template **Entry** against which to compare the public fields of **Entry**s in the JavaSpaces service. The template indicates which fields should be used for comparison purposes.

- The retrieval process is based on the a template-matching mechanism, which matches **Entry**s according to the values of their **public** fields. Fields in the template with non-**null** values must match with their **Entry** counterparts in the JavaSpaces service exactly. Fields in the template that are set to **null** act as wildcards.

- If a set of **Entry**s of the same type exist within a JavaSpaces service, only those fields which equal those of the template are used to match an **Entry** or a set of **Entry**s contained in the JavaSpaces service. Fields in the template set to **null** can have their matching counterparts in the JavaSpaces service have any value in the corresponding field(s).

- The **read** operation obtains **Entry**s without removing them from the JavaSpaces service. Methods **read** and **readIfExists** perform the read operation. Each method takes three arguments—an **Entry** that specifies the template to match, a **Transaction** object and a **long** value.

- Method **read** specifies a period of time for which the read operation should block before simply returning **null**. Method **readIfExists** is a non-blocking version of method **read**. If there are no matching **Entry**s, **readIfExists** returns **null** immediately.

- Method **readIfExists** blocks only if the developer specifies a period of time for which the **readIfExists** waits if, at first, the matching **Entry** is a part of an incomplete transaction. If the matching **Entry** is not involved in any transaction, then the **read** operation returns the matching **Entry** immediately.

- Both the **read** and **readIfExists** methods return only one **Entry**. If multiple **Entry**s match the template, the **read** operation picks one arbitrarily.

- The **take** operation obtains an **Entry** and removes it from the JavaSpaces service. Methods **take** and **takeIfExists** perform the take operation. Methods **take** and **takeIfExists** are similar to methods **read** and **readIfExists**. The only difference is that the matching **Entry** returned by a **take** or **takeIfExists** operation is removed from the JavaSpaces service.

- The **notify** operation asks the JavaSpaces service to send a notification to a listener when a client writes a matching **Entry** into the JavaSpaces service. Method **notify** takes five parameters—an **Entry** that specifies the matching template, a **Transaction** object, a listener that implements interface **RemoteEventListener** (package **net.jini.core.event**), a **long** value that specifies the lease time for the registration of the listener and a **MarshalledObject** (package **java.rmi**) that the JavaSpaces service will pass to the remote listener as part of a notification.

- Method **snapshot** takes a matching template and returns a specialized representation of the **Entry** (a snapshot **Entry**). This snapshot **Entry** can be used only in the JavaSpaces service that generated it.

TERMINOLOGY

abort method of class **Transaction**
commit method of class **Transaction**
Entry class (**net.jini.core.entry**)
JavaSpace interface (**net.jini.space**)
JavaSpaces service
notify method of **JavaSpace**
outrigger JavaSpace implementation
persistent JavaSpaces service
read method of interface **JavaSpace**
readIfExists method of interface
     JavaSpace
RemoteEventListener interface
     (**net.jini.core.event**)

snapshot method of **JavaSpace**
take method of **JavaSpace**
takeIfExists method of **JavaSpace**
template matching mechanism
transaction
Transaction.Created class
Transaction.Created.transaction
     interface
TransactionException class
TransactionManager service
transient JavaSpaces service
UnusableEntryException class
write method of **JavaSpace**

SELF-REVIEW EXERCISES

23.1 Fill in the blanks in each of the following statements:
a) The JavaSpaces technology is an _____ queue.
b) Objects placed in the JavaSpaces service must implement the _____ interface.
c) Two methods of the **JavaSpace** interface that read an **Entry** from the JavaSpaces service are _____ and _____.
d) Creating a transaction, requires a _____.
e) Method _____ can be used to avoid unnecessary serializations of an **Entry**.

23.2 State whether each of the following is *true* or *false*. If *false*, explain why.
a) **Entry**s may have **private** fields that are used for template matching.
b) Method **take** can remove all matching **Entry**s from the JavaSpaces service.
c) To modify an **Entry** in a JavaSpaces service, we need to take the **Entry** away from the JavaSpaces service, change the values of the **Entry** and put the **Entry** back to the JavaSpaces service.
d) Objects stored in a JavaSpaces service cannot have primitive type fields.
e) When writing an **Entry** to a JavaSpaces service, if the **Entry** already exists, the new **Entry** overwrites the old **Entry**.

ANSWERS TO SELF-REVIEW EXERCISES

23.1 a) object-based message-oriented. b) **Entry**. c) **read**, **readIfExists**. d) transaction manager. e) **snapshot**.

23.2 a) False. The fields in an **Entry** used for template matching must be **public** because the JavaSpaces service needs to access these fields. b) False. If multiple **Entry**s match the template, method **take** removes only one. c) True. d) True. e) False. JavaSpaces services can have multiple copies of the same **Entry**. No matter whether an **Entry** exist, the write operation puts the **Entry** into the JavaSpaces service, unless an exception occurs during the write process.

EXERCISES

23.3 Describe the difference between method **take** and method **takeIfExists** in the **JavaSpace** interface.

23.4 Start a JavaSpaces service with a name other than the default name and find this JavaSpaces service with Jini lookup service using a **Name Entry**.

23.5 In the **WriteOperation** application (Fig. 23.3), the **Entry**s written into the JavaSpaces service are kept in the JavaSpaces service for at most 5 minutes. Using **LeaseRenewalManager**, rewrite the application so that the written **Entry**s are kept in the JavaSpaces service forever.

23.6 Write a program that uses method **take** to remove all **Entry**s that match a specific template. Compare the speed of running this application with the speed of running the **SnapshotEntry** application.

23.7 Write a program that uses method **notify** to track all **Entry**s written into a JavaSpaces service. Can you tell whether there are any **Entry**s that the listener does not track?

23.8 In our examples, we use class **JavaSpaceFinder** to find a JavaSpaces service and class **TransactionManagerFinder** to find a transaction manager. These two classes are similar. Write a program called **ServiceFinder** that takes the **Class** object (i.e., **JavaSpace.class**) as input and returns the service object (i.e., **JavaSpace** object). Does **ServiceFinder** return the same **JavaSpace** object if you have multiple JavaSpaces services running? If not, how can you fix it so that **ServiceFinder** always returns the JavaSpaces service you wanted. [*Hint:* set the name for each JavaSpaces service instance using the **com.sun.jini.outrigger.spaceName** property when running the JavaSpaces service from the commandline. This property will register the corresponding **JavaSpace** stub in the Jini lookup service with the **Name Entry** set to the value specified.

23.9   Write a program that reads all matching **Entry**s from a JavaSpaces service without removing them from the JavaSpaces service.

WORKS CITED

1.   **<java.sun.com/products/javaspaces/faqs/jsfaq.html>**.

2.   **<www.javaworld.com/javaworld/jw-11-1999/jw-11-jiniology_p.html>**.

3.   **<www.javaworld.com/javaworld/jw-11-1999/jw-11-jiniology_p.html>**.

BIBLIOGRAPHY

Freeman, E., S. Hupfer, and K. Arnold. *JavaSpaces Principles, Patterns, and Practice*. Reading, MA: Addison Wesley Publishing, 1999.

Edwards, W. K. *Core Jini (Second Edition)*. Upper Saddle River, NY: Prentice-Hall, Inc., 2001.

Li, S. *Professional Jini*. Birmingham, UK: Wrox Press Ltd. 2000.

Newmarch, J. *A Programmer's Guide to Jini Technology*. New York, NY: Springer-Verlag New York, Inc., 2000.

Oaks, S., and H. Wong. *Jini in a Nutshell*. Sebastopol, CA: O'Reilly & Associates, Inc., 2000.

24

Java Management Extensions (JMX)

Objectives

- To understand the JMX technology architecture.
- To understand the design pattern of the standard MBeans.
- To make a resource manageable by defining a management interface for the resource and exposing this interface through MBeans.
- To understand the JMX agent architecture.
- To be able to design and develop management agents to expose MBeans.
- To be able to develop management applications to interact with management agents.

Chapter 24 is included on the CD that accompanies this book in printable Adobe® Acrobat® PDF format. The chapter includes pages 1319–1363.

25

Jiro

Objectives

- To understand the Jiro technology architecture.
- To be able to locate static services.
- To understand how the controller service, event service, log service, scheduling service and transaction service work.
- To be able to deploy dynamic services.
- To be able to instantiate dynamic services.

Chapter 25 is included on the CD that accompanies this book in printable Adobe® Acrobat® PDF format. The chapter includes pages 1364–1434.

26

Common Object Request Broker Architecture (CORBA): Part 1

Objectives

- To introduce CORBA (Common Object Request Broker Architecture).
- To introduce the Interface Definition Language (IDL).
- To use CORBA to develop push-model and pull-model applications.
- To understand distributed exceptions.
- To implement the Deitel Messenger application using CORBA.
- To compare CORBA to other technologies for building distributed systems.

Chapter 26 is included on the CD that accompanies this book in printable Adobe® Acrobat® PDF format. The chapter includes pages 1435–1507.

27

Common Object Request Broker Architecture (CORBA): Part 2

Objectives

- To introduce the Dynamic Invocation Interface (DII).
- To understand the differences among BOAs, POAs and TIEs.
- To introduce CORBAservices, including Naming, Security, Object Transaction and Persistent State services.
- To understand the differences between RMI and CORBA.
- To introduce RMI-IIOP for integrating RMI with CORBA.

Chapter 27 is included on the CD that accompanies this book in printable Adobe® Acrobat® PDF format. The chapter includes pages 1508–1547.

28

Peer-to-Peer Applications and JXTA

Objectives

- To understand peer-to-peer application architectures.
- To understand how various popular peer-to-peer applications work.
- To create a complete P2P instant-messenger application using RMI and Jini technologies.
- To create a complete P2P instant-messenger application using Multicast Sockets and RMI.
- To introduce the emerging JXTA peer-to-peer technology.

No! let me taste the whole of it, fare like my peers,
The heroes of old,
Bear the brunt, in a minute pay glad life's arrears
Of pain, darkness, and cold.
Robert Browning

If we do not lay out ourselves in the service of mankind whom should we serve?
John Adams

We are as much as we see...
Henry David Thoreau

Good counselors lack no clients.
William Shakespeare

Outline

28.1 Introduction

Instant-messaging systems and document-sharing applications such as AOL Instant Messenger™ and Gnutella have exploded in popularity, transforming the way users interact with one another over networks. In a *peer-to-peer (P2P) application*, each node performs both client and server functions. Such applications distribute processing responsibilities and information to many computers, thus reclaiming otherwise wasted computing power and storage space, and eliminating central points of failure.

In this chapter, we introduce the fundamental concepts of peer-to-peer applications. Using Jini (Chapter 22), RMI (Chapter 13) and multicast sockets, we present two peer-to-peer application case studies. We first implement an instant-messaging application with Jini and RMI to demonstrate a more substantial Jini application and show the benefits of integrating Jini with other technologies. We then implement the same instant-messaging application using multicast sockets and RMI. Finally, we introduce JXTA (short for "juxtapose")—a new open-source technology from Sun Microsystems™ that defines common protocols for implementing peer-to-peer applications.

28.2 Client/Server and Peer-to-Peer Applications

Many network applications operate on the principle that computers should be segregated by function. Some computers—called *servers*—offer common stores of programs and data. Other computers—called *clients*—access the data provided by the servers. The Yahoo!™ search engine (**www.yahoo.com**) is an example of a *client/server application*. Client send queries to the central servers, which have pre-compiled catalogs of the Internet. The central servers refer to their databases and respond with the requested information.

P2P applications are different than client/server applications. Instead of segregating computers by function, all computers act as both clients and servers. P2P applications are similar to the telephone system—a single user can both speak (send information) and listen (receive information).[1] Figure 28.1 lists some common peer-to-peer applications.

28.3 Centralized vs. Decentralized Network Applications

An application that uses a *centralized server* exemplifies the client/server relationship. One major weakness of this centralized system is the dependency on the central server. If the central node (i.e., server) fails, the entire application also fails. The server's capabilities limit the application's overall performance. For instance, Web sites can fail when malicious users overload the Web server(s) with an excessive number of requests. However, centralized architectures also have advantages, such as simplifying management tasks (e.g., monitoring user access by providing single points of network control).

True P2P applications are completely decentralized and do not suffer from the same deficiencies as applications that depend on centralized servers. If nodes in a P2P application fail, well-designed P2P applications continue to function. P2P applications often leverage distributed computational power. *Freenet*, for instance, allows users to share documents in a way that precludes censorship. Peer-to-peer architectures allow real-time searches that return up-to-date results. Centralized search engines today are slow to incorporate recently created Web data into these catalogs. Peer-to-peer searches accurately reflect the network status at the time of the query.[2]

Distributed Applications	Description
Gnutella	A P2P technology that does not use any central servers. There is no authentication, and peers search for files via a distributed-search mechanism.
KaZaA	A file-sharing application that is a hybrid between Gnutella and centralized applications. A central server authenticates all users. Certain peers serve as *search hubs*, which catalog the files of peers connected to them. Searches are distributed to each search hub, which then respond with results that allow direct connections for file transfers.
Instant Messengers	Peer-to-peer applications that enable users to send short text messages and files to one another. Most instant messengers use central servers that authenticate all users and route messages between peers.
Telephone System	A peer-to-peer application that enables users to conduct voice conversations remotely.

Fig. 28.1   Common P2P applications.

1. E. Harold, *JAVA Network Programming*. Sebastopol: O'Relly & Associates, Inc., 1997: 26–27.
2. S. Waterhouse, "JXTA Search: Distributed Search for Distributed Networks," May, 2001. `search.jxta.org/JXTAsearch.pdf`

Peer-to-peer applications have disadvantages as well. Anyone with the appropriate software can join the network of peers and often remain anonymous—for this reason, determining who is on the network at any instant is difficult. Also, the lack of a central server hinders the enforcement of copyright and intellectual-property laws. Real-time searches can be slow and increase network traffic, because every query must propagate throughout the entire network.

True client/server applications are completely centralized, whereas true peer-to-peer applications are completely decentralized. Many applications adopt aspects of both to achieve specific goals. For example, some file-sharing applications are not true peer-to-peer applications, because they use central servers to authenticate users and index each peer's shared files. However, peers connect directly to one another to transfer files. In such a system, centralization increases search performance but makes the network dependent on a central server. Performing file transfers between peers decreases the load on the central server.

28.4 Peer Discovery and Searching

Peer discovery is the act of finding peers in a P2P application. Decentralizing an application often slows peer discovery and information searching. Gnutella presents one approach for circumventing these problems. Gnutella is a true peer-to-peer technology that enables distributed information storage and retrieval. Users can search for and download files from any peer on the network. Users first join a Gnutella network by specifying the network address of a known Gnutella peer. Without knowing of at least one peer on the network, a user cannot join the network. Each user's Gnutella software functions as a server and uses the HTTP protocol to search for and transfer files.

To perform a search, a peer sends search criteria to several nearby peers. Those peers then propagate the search throughout the network of peers. If a particular peer can satisfy the search, that peer passes this information back to the originator. The originator then connects directly to the target peer and downloads the information. The peer that made the original query loses anonymity only when it connects directly to the peer with the requested file to begin file transfer.

In the *Freenet* P2P application, files also propagate throughout the network of peers. Each peer that uses Freenet forwards search requests to only one other peer. If the search fails, the peer that received the request forwards the request to the next known peer. If we view the searching peer as the root of a hierarchical structure that represents the Gnutella network, each search request traverses in a breadth-first fashion, because peers forward each search request to several peers at once. Freenet works essentially like Gnutella, except that each search request traverses depth-first.

Searches conducted in both Gnutella and Freenet are called *distributed searches*. Distributed searches make networks more robust by removing single points of failure, such as central servers. Information found via distributed searches is current because it reflects the current state of the network. Not only can peers find information in this way, but peers can search for other peers via distributed searches as well.

28.5 Case Study: Deitel Instant Messenger

In the next several sections, we present a peer-to-peer application that allows users to send instant messages to one other. The Deitel Instant Messenger application uses Jini to *boot-*

strap—or register—users onto the peer-to-peer network. Jini lookup services store remote references to peers on the network. Peers use RMI to connect to one another directly and converse. Although we sometimes refer to an instance of the application as a client, each application instance is both a client and a server.

The application's main window (Fig. 28.2, left-side image) displays a list of peers running Deitel Instant Messenger on the local network. To send an instant message, the user selects a name and clicks the **Connect** button. The conversation window (Fig. 28.2, right-side image) appears with the selected peer's name as the title. The user can type a message, then send it by clicking **Send**.

Deitel Instant Messenger uses Sun's Jini technology, which requires at least one lookup service. However, with only one lookup service, the application acts as a hybrid between P2P and client/server applications. The lookup service is centralized to enable peers to find other peers easily. Peers use RMI to connect to one another directly. A setup with only one lookup service is similar to the setup that many instant messaging applications use today.

For Deitel Instant Messenger to be truly peer-to-peer, each node must run its own lookup service. However, running a lookup service on each peer is inefficient and could generate extensive network traffic. Thus, a compromise between using only one lookup service and using a lookup service for every nod balances both reliability and robustness with speed and efficiency.

If a node does not run a lookup service, that node depends on the existing lookup services on the network—this results in centralization. Each client consists of a Jini-service proxy and an RMI object that enables the peer-to-peer communication. The application registers with all known lookup services, which includes those found through both multicast and unicast discovery. Users can add lookup services to the program by selecting the **Add Locator** item in the **File** menu and supplying the lookup service's URL.

After registering the client's proxy with the lookup service, the Deitel Instant Messenger client retrieves all other proxies in the Jini lookup service. These proxies represent all known peers. To send messages, a client must hold a remote reference to the other peer. Therefore, to begin a conversation, a client sends a reference to itself through the service proxy to the other peer. The other peer responds by sending a remote reference back to the peer that initiated the conversation. When each party has a reference to the other, they can both send and receive messages.

Fig. 28.2 Sample windows of Deitel Instant Messenger.

The major steps in this example are as follows:

1. define a *service interface* that contains a remote reference to the service implementation,

2. define the service implementation,

3. provide methods for bootstrapping the service into the peer group and

4. compile and run the P2P application.

We discuss each step in detail in the next several sections, as we implement the Deitel Instant Messenger application.

28.6 Defining the Service Interface

The first step in the example is to define the service interface—**IMService** (Fig. 28.3). Method **connect** (lines 16–17) enables remote users to send a remote reference to an **IMPeer** (the instant-messenger peer). A remote reference enables one-way communication. To establish two-way communication, each client must have a remote reference to the other client's **IMPeer** objects.

IMPeer (Fig. 28.4) specifies the interface for communicating between peers. Method **connect** (line 16) takes as an argument an **IMPeer** and returns an **IMPeer** reference. Remote interface **IMPeer** describes the basic methods for interacting with an **IMPeer**.

```
1   // IMService.java
2   // IMService interface defines the methods
3   // through which the service proxy
4   // communicates with the service.
5   package com.deitel.advjhtp1.jini.IM.service;
6
7   // Java core packages
8   import java.rmi.*;
9
10  // Deitel packages
11  import com.deitel.advjhtp1.jini.IM.IMPeer;
12
13  public interface IMService extends Remote {
14
15      // return RMI reference to a remote IMPeer
16      public IMPeer connect( IMPeer sender )
17         throws RemoteException;
18  }
```

Fig. 28.3   Interface **IMService** specifies how service proxy interacts with the service.

```
1   // IMPeer.java
2   // Interface that all Peer to Peer apps must implement
3   package com.deitel.advjhtp1.jini.IM;
4
```

Fig. 28.4   Interface **IMPeer** specifies interaction between peers (part 1 of 2).

```
5   //java core packages
6   import java.rmi.*;
7   import java.util.*;
8
9   public interface IMPeer extends Remote
10  {
11     // posts Message to peer
12     public void sendMessage( Message message )
13        throws RemoteException;
14
15     // information methods
16     public String getName() throws RemoteException;
17  }
```

Fig. 28.4   Interface **IMPeer** specifies interaction between peers (part 2 of 2).

In line 9, **IMPeer** extends interface **java.rmi.Remote**, because **IMPeer**s are remote objects. The Deitel Instant Messenger client sends a message to a peer by calling that peer's **sendMessage** method (line 12–13) and passing a **Message** object as an argument. Class **Message** (Fig. 28.5) represents a message that **IMPeer**s can send to one another.

```
1   // Message.java
2   // Message represents an object that can be sent to an IMPeer;
3   // contains the sender and content of the message.
4   package com.deitel.advjhtp1.jini.IM;
5
6   // Java core package
7   import java.io.Serializable;
8
9   public class Message implements Serializable
10  {
11     private static final long SerialVersionUID = 20010808L;
12     private String from;
13     private String content;
14
15     // Message constructor
16     public Message( String messageSenderName,
17        String messageContent )
18     {
19        from = messageSenderName;
20        content = messageContent;
21     }
22
23     // get String representation
24     public String toString()
25     {
26        return from + ": " + content + "\n";
27     }
28
```

Fig. 28.5   Class **Message** defines an object for sending and receiving messages between peers (part 1 of 2).

```
29      // get Message sender's name
30      public String getSenderName()
31      {
32         return from;
33      }
34
35      // get Message content
36      public String getContent()
37      {
38         return content;
39      }
40   }
```

Fig. 28.5 Class **Message** defines an object for sending and receiving messages between peers (part 2 of 2).

In the upcoming exercises, we ask you to extend this class to allow more complex types of communication. Line 10 specifies that class **Message** implements interface **Serializable**, because **Message**s must be serialized for delivery over RMI. The **Message** constructor (lines 16–21) takes as arguments the sender's name and the content of the message.

28.7 Defining the Service implementation

The second step in the example is defining the service implementation—**IMService-Impl** (Fig. 28.6), which implements interface **IMService**. Lines 18–19 declare that class **IMServiceImpl** extends **UnicastRemoteObject**, which facilitates exporting the **IMServiceImpl** as a remote object.

```
1    // IMServiceImpl.java
2    // IMServiceImpl implements IMService interface
3    // is service side of IM application
4    package com.deitel.advjhtp1.jini.IM.service;
5
6    // Java core packages
7    import java.io.*;
8    import java.rmi.server.UnicastRemoteObject;
9    import java.rmi.RemoteException;
10   import java.util.StringTokenizer;
11
12   // Deitel packages
13   import com.deitel.advjhtp1.jini.IM.IMPeer;
14   import com.deitel.advjhtp1.jini.IM.IMPeerImpl;
15   import com.deitel.advjhtp1.jini.IM.Message;
16   import com.deitel.advjhtp1.jini.IM.client.IMPeerListener;
17
18   public class IMServiceImpl extends UnicastRemoteObject
19      implements IMService, Serializable {
20
```

Fig. 28.6 **IMServiceImpl** service implementation for our case study (part 1 of 2).

```
21    private static final long SerialVersionUID = 20010808L;
22    private String userName = "Anonymous";
23
24    // IMService no-argument constructor
25    public IMServiceImpl() throws RemoteException{}
26
27    // IMService constructor takes userName
28    public IMServiceImpl( String name ) throws RemoteException
29    {
30       userName = name;
31    }
32
33    // sets serviceís userName
34    public void setUserName( String name )
35    {
36       userName = name;
37    }
38
39    // return RMI reference to an IMPeer on the receiver side
40    public IMPeer connect( IMPeer sender )
41       throws RemoteException
42    {
43       // Make a GUI and IMPeerImpl to be sent to remote peer
44       IMPeerListener listener =
45          new IMPeerListener( userName );
46
47       IMPeerImpl me = new IMPeerImpl( userName );
48       me.addListener( listener );
49
50       // add remote peer to my GUI
51       listener.addPeer( sender );
52
53       //send my IMPeerImpl to him
54       return me;
55
56    }  // end method connect
57 }
```

Fig. 28.6   **IMServiceImpl** service implementation for our case study (part 2 of 2).

The second constructor (lines 28–31) takes as a **String** argument the user's name. This name appears in the **PeerList** window. Lines 40–56 implement method **connect**.

For two peers to communicate, each peer requires a remote reference to the other peer. The following steps summarize the connection process:

1. Peer A sends a reference to itself to peer B by invoking **IMService** method **connect**.

2. Peer B stores that reference (line 51) to peer A for use when conversation starts.

3. Peer B returns a reference to itself (line 54) to peer A.

The Deitel Instant Messenger creates an object of class **IMPeerListener** (Fig. 28.7)—the GUI that starts the peer communication. The upper text area outputs messages sent via the remote reference to an **IMPeer**. The bottom text area contains text to be sent via a remote method call.

```
1   // IMPeerListener.java
2   // IMPeerListener extends JFrame and provides GUI for
3   // conversations with other peers
4   package com.deitel.advjhtp1.jini.IM.client;
5
6   // Java core packages
7   import java.awt.*;
8   import java.awt.event.*;
9   import java.rmi.RemoteException;
10
11  // Java extension packages
12  import javax.swing.*;
13  import javax.swing.text.*;
14  import javax.swing.border.*;
15
16  // Deitel Packages
17  import com.deitel.advjhtp1.jini.IM.IMPeer;
18  import com.deitel.advjhtp1.jini.IM.Message;
19
20  public class IMPeerListener extends JFrame {
21
22     // JTextAreas for displaying and inputting messages
23     private JTextArea messageArea;
24     private JTextArea inputArea;
25
26     // Actions for sending messages, etc.
27     private Action sendAction;
28
29     // userName to add to outgoing messages
30     private String userName = "";
31
32     // IMPeer to send messages to peer
33     private IMPeer remotePeer;
34
35     // constructor
36     public IMPeerListener( String name )
37     {
38        super( "Conversation Window" );
39
40        // set user name
41        userName = name;
42
43        // init sendAction
44        sendAction = new SendAction();
45
46        // create JTextArea for displaying messages
47        messageArea = new JTextArea( 15, 15 );
48
49        // disable editing and wrap words at end of line
50        messageArea.setEditable( false );
51        messageArea.setLineWrap( true );
52        messageArea.setWrapStyleWord( true );
```

Fig. 28.7 Class **IMPeerListener** is the GUI that starts peer communication (part 1 of 4).

```
53
54          JPanel panel = new JPanel();
55          panel.setLayout( new BorderLayout( 5, 5 ) );
56          panel.add( new JScrollPane( messageArea ),
57             BorderLayout.CENTER );
58
59          // create JTextArea for entering new messages
60          inputArea = new JTextArea( 4, 12 );
61          inputArea.setLineWrap( true );
62          inputArea.setWrapStyleWord( true );
63
64          // map Enter key in inputArea area to sendAction
65          Keymap keyMap = inputArea.getKeymap();
66          KeyStroke enterKey = KeyStroke.getKeyStroke(
67             KeyEvent.VK_ENTER, 0 );
68          keyMap.addActionForKeyStroke( enterKey, sendAction );
69
70          // lay out inputArea and sendAction JButton in Box
71          Box box = Box.createVerticalBox();
72          box.add( new JScrollPane( inputArea ) );
73          box.add( new JButton( sendAction ) );
74
75          panel.add( box, BorderLayout.SOUTH );
76
77          // lay out components
78          Container container = getContentPane();
79          container.add( panel, BorderLayout.CENTER );
80
81          setSize( 200, 400 );
82          setVisible( true );
83       }
84
85       // Action for sending messages
86       private class SendAction extends AbstractAction {
87
88          // configure SendAction
89          public SendAction()
90          {
91             putValue( Action.NAME, "Send" );
92             putValue( Action.SHORT_DESCRIPTION,
93                "Send Message" );
94             putValue( Action.LONG_DESCRIPTION,
95                "Send an Instant Message" );
96          }
97
98          // send message and clear inputArea
99          public void actionPerformed( ActionEvent event )
100         {
101            // send message to server
102            try {
103               Message message = new Message( userName,
104                  inputArea.getText() );
```

Fig. 28.7 Class **IMPeerListener** is the GUI that starts peer communication (part 2 of 4).

```
105
106                    // use RMI reference to send a Message
107                    remotePeer.sendMessage( message );
108
109                    // clear inputArea
110                    inputArea.setText( "" );
111                    displayMessage( message );
112                 }
113
114                 // catch error sending message
115                 catch( RemoteException remoteException ) {
116                    JOptionPane.showMessageDialog( null,
117                       "Unable to send message." );
118
119                    remoteException.printStackTrace();
120                 }
121           } // end method actionPerformed
122
123        } // end sendAction inner class
124
125        public void displayMessage( Message message )
126        {
127           // displayMessage uses SwingUntilities.invokeLater
128           // to ensure thread-safe access to messageArea
129           SwingUtilities.invokeLater(
130              new MessageDisplayer(
131                 message.getSenderName(), message.getContent() ) );
132        }
133
134        // MessageDisplayer displays a new message by appending
135        // the message to the messageArea JTextArea. This Runnable
136        // object should be executed only on the event-dispatch
137        // thread, as it modifies a live Swing component.
138        private class MessageDisplayer implements Runnable {
139
140           private String fromUser;
141           private String messageBody;
142
143           // MessageDisplayer constructor
144           public MessageDisplayer( String from, String body )
145           {
146              fromUser = from;
147              messageBody = body;
148           }
149
150           // display new message in messageArea
151           public void run()
152           {
153              // append new message
154              messageArea.append( "\n" + fromUser + "> " +
155                 messageBody );
156
```

Fig. 28.7 Class **IMPeerListener** is the GUI that starts peer communication (part 3 of 4).

```
157             // move caret to end of messageArea to ensure new
158             // message is visible on screen
159             messageArea.setCaretPosition(
160                messageArea.getText().length() );
161          }
162
163       }  // end MessageDisplayer inner class
164
165       // addPeer takes IMPeer as arg
166       // associates IMPeer with sendAction to send messages
167       public void addPeer( IMPeer peer ) throws RemoteException
168       {
169          remotePeer = peer;
170
171          // change title of window to name of peer
172          setTitle( remotePeer.getName() );
173       }
174 }
```

Fig. 28.7   Class **IMPeerListener** is the GUI that starts peer communication (part 4 of 4).

In Fig. 28.6, line 48 adds an **IMPeerListener** object to an **IMPeerImpl** object using method **addListener**. **IMPeerImpl** method **sendMessage** sends **Message** objects to the **IMPeerListener**.

Line 51 calls method **addPeer** to add a reference to a remote **IMPeer** object to the **IMPeerListener**. This allows the **IMPeerListener** to send messages to the remote peer. Notice the symmetry: **IMPeerListener** is also client/server, because the application itself is client/server. Just as each peer must provide a reference to itself and store references to the remote party, so must the **IMPeerListener**. **IMPeerListener** mediates between the two peers.

IMPeerListener (Fig. 28.7) is the GUI for communication between peers. Method **addPeer** (lines 167–173) stores a reference to the remote **IMPeer** and sets the title of the conversation window to the name of the remote **IMPeer**. When the user presses the **JButton** on the GUI, line 107 calls method **sendMessage** of the remote **IMPeer**, passing the contents of **inputArea** as the argument. This is how the client sends messages to remote peers. On the receiving end, the remote **IMPeerImpl** (Fig. 28.8) calls **IMPeerListener** method **displayMethod** to display the message.

```
1   // IMPeerImpl.java
2   // Implements the IMPeer interface
3   package com.deitel.advjhtp1.jini.IM;
4
5   // Java core packages
6   import java.io.*;
7   import java.net.*;
8   import java.rmi.*;
9   import java.rmi.server.*;
10  import java.util.*;
```

Fig. 28.8   Class **IMPeerImpl** is the **IMPeer** implementation (part 1 of 2).

```
11
12   // Deitel Packages
13   import com.deitel.advjhtp1.jini.IM.Message;
14   import com.deitel.advjhtp1.jini.IM.client.IMPeerListener;
15
16
17   public class IMPeerImpl extends UnicastRemoteObject
18      implements IMPeer {
19
20      private String name;
21      private IMPeerListener output;
22
23      // No argument constructor
24      public IMPeerImpl() throws RemoteException
25      {
26         super();
27         name = "anonymous";
28      }
29      // constructor takes userName
30      public IMPeerImpl( String myName ) throws RemoteException
31      {
32         name = myName;
33      }
34
35      public void addListener( IMPeerListener listener )
36      {
37         output = listener;
38      }
39
40      // send message to this peer
41      public void sendMessage( Message message )
42         throws RemoteException
43      {
44         output.displayMessage( message );
45      }
46
47      // accessor for name
48      public String getName() throws RemoteException
49      {
50         return name;
51      }
52   }
```

Fig. 28.8 Class **IMPeerImpl** is the **IMPeer** implementation (part 2 of 2).

Class **IMPeerImpl** implements the **IMPeer** interface. An **IMPeerImpl** instance represents each peer in conversations with other peers and allows peers to communicate with one another. Lines 17–18 declare that **IMPeerImpl** extends **UnicastRemoteObject**, to facilitate exporting the **IMPeerImpl** as a remote object. Method **addListener** (lines 35–38) adds an object of type **IMPeerListener** that will display the **IMPeerImpl**'s actions. Method **sendMessage** (lines 41–45) calls method **displayMessage** of interface **IMPeerListener** to display the message.

28.8 Registering the Service

The third step in the example is registering (bootstrapping) the service with the peer group. Class **IMServiceManager** (Fig. 28.9) takes the user's name as a **String** argument and uses the Jini's **JoinManager** class to register the service with all known lookup services. The code is similar to the **JoinManager** version of the **SeminarInfo** program in Chapter 22. One difference is that the constructor (lines 33–65) takes a **String** that specifies the **Name Entry** for the service.

```
1   // IMServiceManager.java
2   // IMServiceManager uses JoinManager to find Lookup services,
3   // registers the IMService with the Lookup services,
4   // manages lease renewal
5   package com.deitel.advjhtp1.jini.IM;
6
7   // Java core packages
8   import java.rmi.RMISecurityManager;
9   import java.rmi.RemoteException;
10  import java.io.IOException;
11
12  // Jini core packages
13  import net.jini.core.lookup.ServiceID;
14  import net.jini.core.entry.Entry;
15
16  // Jini extension packages
17  import net.jini.lookup.entry.Name;
18  import net.jini.lease.LeaseRenewalManager;
19  import net.jini.lookup.JoinManager;
20  import net.jini.discovery.LookupDiscoveryManager;
21  import net.jini.lookup.ServiceIDListener;
22
23  // Deitel packages
24  import com.deitel.advjhtp1.jini.IM.service.*;
25
26  public class IMServiceManager implements ServiceIDListener {
27
28      JoinManager manager;
29      LookupDiscoveryManager lookupManager;
30      String serviceName;
31
32      // constructor takes name of the service
33      public IMServiceManager( String screenName )
34      {
35          System.setSecurityManager( new RMISecurityManager() );
36
37          // sets the serviceName of this service
38          serviceName = screenName;
39
```

Fig. 28.9   Class **IMServiceManager** registers **IMServiceImpl** with lookup services (part 1 of 3).

```
40        // use JoinManager to register SeminarInfo service
41        // and manage lease
42        try {
43
44           // create LookupDiscoveryManager for discovering
45           // lookup services
46           lookupManager =
47              new LookupDiscoveryManager( new String[] { "" },
48                 null, null );
49
50           // create and set Entry name for service
51           // name used from constructor
52           Entry[] entries = new Entry[ 1 ];
53           entries[ 0 ] = new Name( serviceName );
54
55           // create JoinManager
56           manager = new JoinManager( createProxy(),
57           entries, this, lookupManager,
58              new LeaseRenewalManager() );
59        }
60
61     // handle exception creating JoinManager
62     catch ( IOException exception ) {
63        exception.printStackTrace();
64     }
65  } // end SeminarInfoJoinService constructor
66
67  // return the LookupDiscoveryManager created by JoinManager
68  public LookupDiscoveryManager getDiscoveryManager()
69  {
70     return lookupManager;
71  }
72
73  // create service proxy
74  private IMService createProxy()
75  {
76     // get SeminarProxy for SeminarInfo service
77     try {
78        return( new IMServiceImpl( serviceName  ) );
79     }
80
81     // handle exception creating SeminarProxy
82     catch ( RemoteException exception ) {
83        exception.printStackTrace();
84     }
85
86     return null;
87
88  } // end method createProxy
89
```

Fig. 28.9 Class **IMServiceManager** registers **IMServiceImpl** with lookup
services (part 2 of 3).

```
90      // receive notification of ServiceID assignment
91      public void serviceIDNotify( ServiceID serviceID )
92      {
93         System.err.println( "Service ID: " + serviceID );
94      }
95
96      // informs all lookup services that service is ending
97      public void logout()
98      {
99         manager.terminate();
100     }
101  }
```

Fig. 28.9 Class **IMServiceManager** registers **IMServiceImpl** with lookup services (part 3 of 3).

28.9 Find Other Peers

Class **PeerList** (Fig. 28.10)—the main window of the Deitel Instant Messenger—lists peers to whom the user can send instant messages. Line 264 creates a new **IMService-Manager**, passing **String userName** as an argument to the **IMServiceManager** constructor to name the peer.

IMPeer (Fig. 28.4) specifies the interface for communicating between peers. Method **connect** (line 16) takes as an argument an **IMPeer** and returns an **IMPeer** reference. Remote interface **IMPeer** describes the basic methods for interacting with an **IMPeer**.

A **LookupCache** also allows an application to respond to services being added, removed, or changed without constantly polling lookup services. The Peer List uses a **LookupCache** to determine when other peers join and leave the network. To use this functionality, an application must pass a **ServiceDiscoveryListener** object to method **createLookupCache**. **PeerList** implements **ServiceDiscoveryListener** (lines 33–34), so line 276 passes the **this** reference to method **createLookupCache**. **ServiceDiscoveryManager** uses remote events registered with lookup services to implement asynchronous notification of **ServiceDiscoveryEvent**s. Therefore, we must provide lookup services with a way to download the stub class files for the **RemoteEvent** handlers. Section 28.10 explains how to do this.

```
1    // PeerList.java
2    // Initializes ServiceManager, starts service discovery
3    // and lists all IM services in a window
4    package com.deitel.advjhtp1.jini.IM;
5
6    // Java core packages
7    import java.awt.*;
8    import java.awt.event.*;
9    import java.net.MalformedURLException;
10   import java.util.*;
11   import java.util.List;
12   import java.io.IOException;
13   import java.rmi.*;
```

Fig. 28.10 Class **PeerList** is the GUI for finding peers (part 1 of 7).

```
14
15   // Java extension packages
16   import javax.swing.*;
17   import javax.swing.event.*;
18
19   // Jini core packages
20   import net.jini.core.lookup.ServiceItem;
21   import net.jini.core.lookup.ServiceTemplate;
22   import net.jini.lookup.*;
23   import net.jini.discovery.LookupDiscoveryManager;
24   import net.jini.lease.LeaseRenewalManager;
25   import net.jini.lookup.entry.Name;
26   import net.jini.core.entry.Entry;
27   import net.jini.core.discovery.LookupLocator;
28
29   // Deitel Packages
30   import com.deitel.advjhtp1.jini.IM.service.IMService;
31   import com.deitel.advjhtp1.jini.IM.client.IMPeerListener;
32
33   public class PeerList extends JFrame
34      implements ServiceDiscoveryListener {
35
36      private DefaultListModel peers;
37      private JList peerList;
38      private List serviceItems;
39      private ServiceDiscoveryManager serviceDiscoveryManager;
40      private LookupCache cache;
41      private IMServiceManager myManager;
42      private LookupDiscoveryManager lookupDiscoveryManager;
43
44      // initialize userName to anonymous
45      private String userName = "anonymous";
46
47      // method called when ServiceDiscoveryManager finds
48      // IM service adds service proxy to serviceItems
49      // adds Service name to ListModel for JList
50      public void serviceAdded( ServiceDiscoveryEvent event )
51      {
52         // get added serviceItem
53         ServiceItem item = event.getPostEventServiceItem();
54         Entry attributes[] = item.attributeSets;
55
56         // iterates through attributes to find name
57         for( int i = 0; i < attributes.length; i++ )
58
59            if ( attributes[ i ] instanceof Name ) {
60               System.out.println( "Added: " + item );
61               serviceItems.add( item.service );
62               peers.addElement(
63                  ( ( Name )attributes[ i ] ).name );
64               break;
65            }
66      } // end method serviceAdded
```

Fig. 28.10 Class **PeerList** is the GUI for finding peers (part 2 of 7).

```
67
68      // empty method ignores seviceChanged event
69      public void serviceChanged( ServiceDiscoveryEvent event )
70      {}
71
72      // removes services from PeerList GUI and data structure
73      // when serviceRemoved event occurs
74      public void serviceRemoved( ServiceDiscoveryEvent event )
75      {
76         // getPreEvent because item has been removed
77         // getPostEvent would return null
78         ServiceItem item = event.getPreEventServiceItem();
79         Entry attributes[ ] = item.attributeSets;
80
81         // debug
82         System.out.println( "Remove Event!" );
83
84         // remove from arraylist and DefaultListModel
85         int index = serviceItems.indexOf( item.service );
86
87         // print name of person removed
88         if ( index >= 0 )
89         {
90            System.out.println( "Removing from List:" +
91               serviceItems.remove( index ));
92
93            System.out.println( "Removing from DefList" +
94               peers.elementAt( index ) );
95
96            peers.removeElementAt( index );
97         }
98      } // end method ServiceRemoved
99
100     // constructor
101     public PeerList()
102     {
103        super( "Peer List" );
104
105        System.setSecurityManager( new RMISecurityManager() );
106
107        // get desired userName
108        userName = JOptionPane.showInputDialog(
109           PeerList.this, "Please enter your name: " );
110
111        // change title of window
112        setTitle( userName + "'s Peer List Window" );
113
114        // Init Lists
115        serviceItems = new ArrayList();
116
117        Container container = getContentPane();
118        peers = new DefaultListModel();
119
```

Fig. 28.10 Class **PeerList** is the GUI for finding peers (part 3 of 7).

```
120          // init components
121          peerList = new JList( peers );
122          peerList.setVisibleRowCount( 5 );
123          JButton connectButton = new JButton( "Connect" );
124
125          // do not allow multiple selections
126          peerList.setSelectionMode(
127             ListSelectionModel.SINGLE_SELECTION );
128
129          // set up event handler for connectButton
130          connectButton.addActionListener(
131             new ActionListener() {
132
133                public void actionPerformed( ActionEvent event )
134                {
135                   int itemIndex = peerList.getSelectedIndex();
136
137                   Object selectedService =
138                      serviceItems.get( itemIndex );
139                   IMService peerProxy =
140                      ( IMService )selectedService;
141
142                   // send info to remote peer
143                   // get RMI reference
144                   try {
145
146                      // set up gui and my peerImpl
147                      IMPeerListener gui =
148                         new IMPeerListener( userName );
149                      IMPeerImpl me =
150                         new IMPeerImpl( userName );
151                      me.addListener( gui );
152
153                      // Connect myGui to remote IMPeer object
154                      IMPeer myPeer = peerProxy.connect( me );
155                      gui.addPeer( myPeer );
156                   }
157
158                   // connecting may cause RemoteException
159                   catch( RemoteException re ) {
160                      JOptionPane.showMessageDialog
161                         ( null, "Couldn't Connect" );
162                      re.printStackTrace();
163                   }
164                }
165             }
166          ); // end connectButton actionListener
167
168          // set up File menu
169          JMenu fileMenu = new JMenu( "File" );
170          fileMenu.setMnemonic( 'F' );
171
```

Fig. 28.10 Class **PeerList** is the GUI for finding peers (part 4 of 7).

```
172          // about Item
173          JMenuItem aboutItem = new JMenuItem( "About..." );
174          aboutItem.setMnemonic( 'A' );
175          aboutItem.addActionListener(
176             new ActionListener() {
177                public void actionPerformed( ActionEvent event )
178                {
179                   JOptionPane.showMessageDialog( PeerList.this,
180                   "Deitel Instant Messenger" ,
181                   "About", JOptionPane.PLAIN_MESSAGE );
182                }
183             }
184          );
185
186          fileMenu.add( aboutItem );
187
188          // AddLocator item
189          JMenuItem federateItem =
190             new JMenuItem( "Add Locators" );
191          federateItem.setMnemonic( 'L' );
192          federateItem.addActionListener(
193
194             new ActionListener() {
195                public void actionPerformed( ActionEvent event )
196                {
197                   // get LookupService url to be added
198                   String locator =
199                      JOptionPane.showInputDialog(
200                         PeerList.this,
201                         "Please enter locator in this" +
202                         "form: jini://host:port/" );
203
204                   try {
205                      LookupLocator newLocator =
206                         new LookupLocator( locator );
207
208                      // make one element LookupLocator array
209                      LookupLocator[] locators = { newLocator };
210
211                      // because addLocators takes array
212                      lookupDiscoveryManager.addLocators( locators );
213                   }
214
215                   catch( MalformedURLException urlException) {
216
217                      JOptionPane.showMessageDialog(
218                         PeerList.this, "invalid url" );
219                   }
220                }
221             }
222          );
223          fileMenu.add( federateItem );
224
```

Fig. 28.10 Class **PeerList** is the GUI for finding peers (part 5 of 7).

```
225          // set up JMenuBar and attach File menu
226          JMenuBar menuBar = new JMenuBar();
227          menuBar.add ( fileMenu );
228          setJMenuBar( menuBar );
229
230          // handow window closing event
231          addWindowListener(
232             new WindowAdapter(){
233                public void windowClosing( WindowEvent w )
234                {
235                   System.out.println( "CLOSING WINDOW" );
236
237                   // disconnects from lookup services
238                   myManager.logout();
239                   System.exit( 0 );
240                }
241             }
242          );
243
244          // lay out GUI components
245          peerList.setFixedCellWidth( 100 );
246          JPanel inputPanel = new JPanel();
247          inputPanel.add( connectButton );
248
249          container.add( new JScrollPane( peerList ) ,
250             BorderLayout.NORTH );
251          container.add( inputPanel, BorderLayout.SOUTH );
252
253          setSize( 100, 170 );
254          setVisible( true );
255
256          // peer list displays only other IMServices
257          Class[] types = new Class[] { IMService.class };
258          ServiceTemplate IMTemplate =
259             new ServiceTemplate( null, types, null );
260
261          // Initialize IMServiceManager, ServiceDiscoveryManager
262          try {
263             myManager = new IMServiceManager( userName );
264
265             // store LookupDiscoveryManager
266             // generated by IMServiceManager
267             lookupDiscoveryManager = myManager.getDiscoveryManager();
268
269             // ServiceDiscoveryManager uses lookupDiscoveryManager
270             serviceDiscoveryManager =
271                new ServiceDiscoveryManager( lookupDiscoveryManager,
272                   null );
273
274             // create a LookupCache
275             cache = serviceDiscoveryManager.createLookupCache(
276                IMTemplate, null, this );
277          }
```

Fig. 28.10 Class **PeerList** is the GUI for finding peers (part 6 of 7).

```
278
279        // catch all exceptions and inform user of problem
280        catch ( Exception managerException) {
281          JOptionPane.showMessageDialog( null,
282            "Error initializing IMServiceManger" +
283            "or ServiceDisoveryManager" );
284          managerException.printStackTrace();
285        }
286     }
287
288     public static void main( String args[] )
289     {
290        new PeerList();
291     }
292  }
```

Fig. 28.10 Class **PeerList** is the GUI for finding peers (part 7 of 7).

The methods required to implement **ServiceDiscoveryListener** are **serviceAdded** (lines 50–66), **serviceChanged** (lines 69–70) and **serviceRemoved** (lines 74–98). Method **ServiceAdded** calls method **getPostEventServiceItem** of the **ServiceDiscoveryEvent** to obtain a **ServiceItem** that represents the added service. Lines 57–65 cycle through all the attributes of the **ServiceItem**. If line 59 finds a **Name** entry, line 61 adds the service proxy to a **List**, and lines 62–63 add the service **Name** to a **DefaultListModel**. Method **serviceChanged** is an empty method, because we are not concerned whether services change their attributes. Method **serviceRemoved** invokes method **getPreEventServiceItem** of the **ServiceDiscoveryEvent** to obtain a **ServiceItem** that represents the removed service.

The **ActionListener** (lines 130–167) of the **connectButton** object gets the index of the selected item in the **JList** and retrieves the **IMService** proxy associated with that index from **List serviceItems** (lines 138–141). Lines 147–148 create an **IMPeerListener** object, and lines 149–150 create an **IMPeerImpl** object. Line 151 adds the **IMPeerListener** to the **IMPeerImpl**. The **IMPeerImpl** will post all messages sent by the remote peer to the **IMPeerListener**. Using method **connect** of the **IMService**, line 154 sends a remote reference to the **IMPeerImpl** to the remote peer. Line 155 adds the returned **IMPeer** remote reference to the **IMPeerListener**—this allows the local peer to send messages to remote peer. If this sequence of events throws a **RemoteException**, lines 160–162 inform the user of the error. If the connection succeeds, the service returns an **IMPeer**, and communication occurs as described in earlier sections.

Lines 189–223 create the **Add Locator** menu item in the **File** menu. Selecting this menu item launches a dialog box that prompts the user for the URL of a Jini lookup service to add via unicast discovery. Lines 204–213 add this URL to the list of **LookupLocator**s—this results in the client's registering with the newly added lookup service, and the **PeerList** window lists all other peers registered with the new lookup service.

28.10 Compiling and Running the Example

Finally, we can compile and run the peer-to-peer application. This requires several steps. First, compile the classes using **javac**.

Next, compile the remote classes **IMServiceImpl** and **IMPeerImpl** using the **rmic** *compiler* to produce stub classes (see Chapter 13). Next, place the RMI stub classes that need to be available to other Deitel Instance Messenger clients and lookup services (**IMServiceImpl_Stub** and **IMPeerImpl_Stub**) in a JAR file (e.g., **DIM_dl.jar**) with the proper package structure.

For lookup services to notify our application when services are added or removed, the **ServiceDiscoveryManager** needs to upload a remote-event listener. Change to the root directory of your Web server and execute the following command lines:

```
jar xvf C:\jini1_1\lib\jini-ext.jar net\jini\lookup\Service-
DiscoveryManager$LookupCacheImpl$LookupListener_Stub.class

jar xvf C:\jini1_1\lib\jini-core.jar
net\jini\core\event\RemoteEventListener.class
```

This creates a **net** subdirectory in your Web server's root directory.

To use the Deitel Instant Messenger, first start the RMI activation daemon, an HTTP Server, and a lookup service (see Chapter 22). To start Deitel Instant Messenger, change to the directory that contains the application's package structure and execute the following command line:

```
java -Djava.security.policy=policy.all
-Djava.rmi.server.codebase=http://host:port/DIM_dl.jar
com.deitel.advjhtp1.jini.IM.PeerList
```

Substitute the appropriate values for the *host*, *port* and JAR file name (e.g., **DIM_dl.jar**). The codebase provides the location of the JAR file which contains the RMI stub files that remote peers and lookup services must download.

28.11 Improving Deitel Instant Messenger

The Deitel Instant Messenger Jini implementation does not address issues of security and scalability. The **ServiceDiscoveryManager** downloads proxies for every user listed on every known lookup service. As more users and lookup services join the network, network overhead becomes overwhelming. The lack of security and authentication mechanisms forces anonymity on clients, because there is no absolute way of verifying that users are who they claim to be.

There are various ways to address these problems. Filters can limit the number of service proxies that the **ServiceDiscoveryManager** downloads. Lookup services can limit the number of services they manage. The application also could use distributed searches to locate peers (see Section 28.4). This involves sending a request to a known search service, which forwards the request if unable to find the user. The ubiquitous use of digital signatures and public and private keys can enable security and authentication—however, this does not solve the problem of having duplicate user names in a large-scale peer-to-peer network. These solutions are incomplete.

28.12 Deitel Instant Messenger with Multicast Sockets

The Deitel Instant messenger uses Jini's **JoinManager** and **ServiceDiscovery-Manager** to advertise the existence of each peer and discover other peers. With Jini, a few lines of code implemented this functionality. To adhere to a true peer-to-peer architecture, each peer must run a lookup service. Lookup services require significant amounts of memory and processor time. Because of these performance and memory concerns, we introduce an improved implementation of the Deitel Instant Messenger that uses multicast sockets and a simple, text-based protocol to advertise and find peers in the network.

28.12.1 Registering the Peer

In the Jini implementation of the Deitel Instant Messenger, Jini provided the mechanism that allowed peers to sign onto the network and find other peers. If a peer loses its connection without explicitly disconnecting (e.g., by calling method **terminate** of a **Join-Manager** instance), the Jini lookup services remove the peer after the service's lease expires. When a peer's lease expires, the Jini lookup service removes the peer's service from the registry—in the Deitel Instant Messenger, the peer disappears from the Peer-List window. Because we are removing Jini from this application, we must implement these mechanisms ourselves.

The first mechanism we implement is class **MulticastSendingThread** (Fig. 28.11). **MulticastSendingThread** multicasts a peer's presence. **MulticastSendingThread** periodically sends multicast packets throughout the network to notify other peers that this peer is still available. Each peer on the receiving end renew's the lease for the multicasting peer. In the event that the multicasting peer stops advertising its presence (e.g., the user quits the peer application), that peer's lease expires. Essentially, the peer ceases to exist on the network.

```
1   // MulticastSendingThread.java
2   // Sends a multicast periodically containing a remote reference
3   // to the IMServiceImpl object
4   package com.deitel.advjhtp1.p2p;
5
6   // Java core packages
7   import java.net.MulticastSocket;
8   import java.net.*;
9   import java.rmi.*;
```

Fig. 28.11 MulticastSendingThread broadcasts **DatagramPacket**s (part 1 of 4).

```
10   import java.rmi.registry.*;
11   import java.io.*;
12
13   // Deitel core packages
14   import com.deitel.advjhtp1.jini.IM.service.IMServiceImpl;
15   import com.deitel.advjhtp1.jini.IM.service.IMService;
16
17   public class MulticastSendingThread extends Thread
18      implements IMConstants {
19
20      // InetAddress of group for messages
21      private InetAddress multicastNetAddress;
22
23      // MulticastSocket for multicasting messages
24      private MulticastSocket multicastSocket;
25
26      // Datagram packet to be reused
27      private DatagramPacket multicastPacket;
28
29      // stub of local peer
30      private IMService peerStub;
31
32      // flag for terminating MulticastSendingThread
33      private boolean keepSending = true;
34
35      private String userName;
36
37      // MulticastSendingThread constructor
38      public MulticastSendingThread( String myName )
39      {
40         // invoke superclass constructor to name Thread
41         super( "MulticastSendingThread" );
42
43         userName = myName;
44
45         // create a registry on default port 1099
46         try {
47            Registry registry =
48               LocateRegistry.createRegistry( 1099 );
49            peerStub = new IMServiceImpl( userName );
50            registry.rebind( BINDING_NAME, peerStub );
51         }
52         catch ( RemoteException remoteException ) {
53            remoteException.printStackTrace();
54         }
55
56         try {
57
58            // create MulticastSocket for sending messages
59            multicastSocket =
60               new MulticastSocket ( MULTICAST_SENDING_PORT );
61
```

Fig. 28.11 MulticastSendingThread broadcasts DatagramPackets (part 2 of 4).

```
62              // set TTL for Multicast Socket
63              multicastSocket.setTimeToLive( MULTICAST_TTL );
64
65              // use InetAddress reserved for multicast group
66              multicastNetAddress = InetAddress.getByName(
67                 MULTICAST_ADDRESS );
68
69              // create greeting packet
70              String greeting = new String( HELLO_HEADER + userName );
71
72              multicastPacket = new DatagramPacket(
73                 greeting.getBytes(), greeting.getBytes().length,
74                 multicastNetAddress, MULTICAST_LISTENING_PORT );
75           }
76
77           // MULTICAST_ADDRESS IS UNKNOWN HOST
78           catch ( java.net.UnknownHostException unknownHostException )
79           {
80              System.err.println( "MULTICAST_ADDRESS is unknown" );
81              unknownHostException.printStackTrace();
82           }
83
84           // any other exception
85           catch ( Exception exception )
86           {
87              exception.printStackTrace();
88           }
89        }
90
91        // deliver greeting message to peers
92        public void run()
93        {
94           while ( keepSending ) {
95
96              // deliver greeting
97              try {
98
99                 // send greeting packet
100                multicastSocket.send( multicastPacket );
101
102                Thread.sleep( MULTICAST_INTERVAL );
103             }
104
105             // handle exception delivering message
106             catch ( IOException ioException ) {
107                ioException.printStackTrace();
108                continue;
109             }
110             catch ( InterruptedException interruptedException ) {
111                interruptedException.printStackTrace();
112             }
113
```

Fig. 28.11 MulticastSendingThread broadcasts DatagramPackets
(part 3 of 4).

```
114              } // end while
115
116          multicastSocket.close();
117
118      } // end method run
119
120      // send goodbye message
121      public void logout()
122      {
123          String goodbye = new String( GOODBYE_HEADER + userName );
124          System.out.println( goodbye );
125          multicastPacket = new DatagramPacket(
126              goodbye.getBytes(), goodbye.getBytes().length,
127              multicastNetAddress, MULTICAST_LISTENING_PORT );
128
129          try {
130              multicastSocket.send( multicastPacket );
131
132              Naming.unbind( BINDING_NAME );
133          }
134
135          // error multicasting
136          catch ( IOException ioException ) {
137              System.err.println("Couldn't Say Goodbye");
138              ioException.printStackTrace();
139          }
140
141          // unbinding may cause many possible exceptions
142          catch ( Exception unbindingException ) {
143              unbindingException.printStackTrace();
144          }
145
146          keepSending = false;
147
148      }
149  }
```

Fig. 28.11 **MulticastSendingThread** broadcasts **DatagramPacket**s
          (part 4 of 4).

MulticastSendingThread extends class **Thread**. Lines 47–48 calls method
createRegistry of class **LocateRegistry** to instantiate an RMI registry on port
1099—the port that **rmiregistry** application normally uses. Line 49 creates a new
IMServiceImpl object. Line 50 **rebind**s the **IMServiceImpl** object to the RMI
registry, using **BINDING_NAME**—one of many constants defined in interface **IMConstants** (Fig. 28.12), which class **MulticastSendingThread** implements.
Figure 28.12 shows the interface **IMConstants**, which defines all the constants used by
Deitel Instant Messenger.

```
1  // IMConstants.java
2  // contains constants used by IM application
```

Fig. 28.12 Interface **IMConstants** defines Deitel-Instant-Messenger constants
          (part 1 of 2).

```
3   package com.deitel.advjhtp1.p2p;
4
5   public interface IMConstants {
6
7       public static final String MULTICAST_ADDRESS = "228.5.6.10";
8
9       public static final int MULTICAST_TTL = 30;
10
11      // port on local machine for broadcasting
12      public static final int MULTICAST_SENDING_PORT = 6800;
13
14      // port on local machine for receiving broadcasts
15      public static final int MULTICAST_RECEIVING_PORT = 6789;
16
17      // port on multicast ip address to send packets
18      public static final int MULTICAST_LISTENING_PORT = 6789;
19
20      public static final String HELLO_HEADER = "HELLOIM: ";
21
22      public static final String GOODBYE_HEADER = "GOODBYE: ";
23
24      // time in milliseconds to wait between each multicast
25      public static final int MULTICAST_INTERVAL = 10000;
26
27      // how many MUTLICAST_INTERVALS before LEASE EXPIRATION
28      public static final int PEER_TTL = 5;
29
30      public static final int MESSAGE_SIZE = 256;
31
32      public static String BINDING_NAME = "IMSERVICE";
33
34  }
```

Fig. 28.12 Interface **IMConstants** defines Deitel-Instant-Messenger constants (part 2 of 2).

Lines 59–60 of Fig. 28.11 create a **MulticastSocket** on the port number that constant **MULTICAST_SENDING_PORT** defines. Line 63 sets the default *Time To Live* (*TTL*) for **DatagramPacket**s sent through the **MulticastSocket**. Lines 66–67 create an **InetAddress** with the multicast IP address specified by constant **MULTICAST_ADDRESS**.

Lines 70–74 create a **DatagramPacket** that contains a **String** with the peer's name. **HELLO_HEADER** informs all peers listening on the multicast port that this peer can receive messages. **MULTICAST_LISTENING_PORT** specifies the port on the multicast IP address on which all peers listen. Lines 78–82 catch an **UnknownHostException** if **MULTICAST_ADDRESS** is an invalid multicast IP address.

Line 100 multicasts the **MulticastPacket** that the constructor generated. Line 102 specifies that the thread should wait **MULTICAST_INTERVAL** milliseconds between each multicast. Line 116 closes the **MulticastSocket** when the user exits the application.

Lines 123–127 create a **DatagramPacket** that contains a **String** with the **GOODBYE_HEADER** and the peer's user name. **GOODBYE_HEADER** indicates that the peer is leaving the network. Lines 130–133 send this **DatagramPacket** and **unbind** the

IMServiceImpl associated with **BINDING_NAME** from the RMI registry. Line 146 sets **boolean keepSending** to **false** to terminate the thread.

28.12.2 Finding Other Peers

In the Jini implementation of the Deitel Instant Messenger, the Jini lookup service listed new peers and removed peers that left the network. Class **ServiceDiscoveryManager** updated the application when peers were either added or removed. To implement these mechanisms, we create class **MulticastReceivingThread** (Figure 28.13), which listens for **DatagramPacket**s that contain notifications of peers joining and leaving the network.

Lines 48–55 create a **MulticastSocket** on port **MULTICAST_RECEIVING_PORT** and join the multicast group. Line 58 specifies that the **MulticastSocket** should time out receiving a packet takes longer than five seconds. Lines 69–71 start the **LeasingThread** as a daemon thread. We explain **LeasingThread** in greater detail later in this section.

Line 89 receives a **DatagramPacket** from the **MulticastSocket** using by invoking method **receive**. If the call to **receive** times out, lines 93–97 catch the **InterruptedIOException** that is thrown. Lines 106–107 retrieve the message **String** stored in the received **DatagramPacket**.

```
1   // MulticastReceivingThread.java
2   // Receive and process multicasts from multicast group
3   package com.deitel.advjhtp1.p2p;
4
5   // Java core packages
6   import java.net.MulticastSocket;
7   import java.net.*;
8   import java.io.*;
9   import java.util.*;
10
11  // Deitel packages
12  import com.deitel.advjhtp1.p2p.PeerDiscoveryListener;
13
14  public class MulticastReceivingThread extends Thread
15     implements IMConstants {
16
17     // HashMap containing peer names and time to live
18     // used to implement leasing
19     private HashMap peerTTLMap;
20
21     // LeasingThread reference
22     private LeasingThread leasingThread;
23
24     // object that will respond to peer added or removed events
25     private PeerDiscoveryListener peerDiscoveryListener;
26
```

Fig. 28.13 Class **MulticastReceivingThread** uses threads to add and remove peers (part 1 of 6).

```
27        // MulticastSocket for receiving broadcast messages
28        private MulticastSocket multicastSocket;
29
30        // InetAddress of group for messages
31        private InetAddress multicastNetAddress;
32
33        // flag for terminating MulticastReceivingThread
34        private boolean keepListening = true;
35
36        // MulticastReceivingThread constructor
37        public MulticastReceivingThread( String userName,
38           PeerDiscoveryListener peerEventHandler )
39        {
40           // invoke superclass constructor to name Thread
41           super( "MulticastReceivingThread" );
42
43           // set peerDiscoveryListener
44           peerDiscoveryListener = peerEventHandler;
45
46           // connect MulticastSocket to multicast address and port
47           try {
48              multicastSocket =
49                 new MulticastSocket( MULTICAST_RECEIVING_PORT );
50
51              multicastNetAddress =
52                 InetAddress.getByName( MULTICAST_ADDRESS );
53
54              // join multicast group to receive messages
55              multicastSocket.joinGroup( multicastNetAddress );
56
57              // set 5 second time-out when waiting for new packets
58              multicastSocket.setSoTimeout( 5000 );
59           }
60
61           // handle exception connecting to multicast address
62           catch( IOException ioException ) {
63              ioException.printStackTrace();
64           }
65
66           peerTTLMap = new HashMap();
67
68           // create Leasing thread which decrements TTL of peers
69           leasingThread = new LeasingThread();
70           leasingThread.setDaemon( true );
71           leasingThread.start();
72
73        } // end MulticastReceivingThread constructor
74
75        // listen for messages from multicast group
76        public void run()
77        {
```

Fig. 28.13 Class **MulticastReceivingThread** uses threads to add and remove peers (part 2 of 6).

```
78              while( keepListening ) {
79
80                  // create buffer for incoming message
81                  byte[] buffer = new byte[ MESSAGE_SIZE ];
82
83                  // create DatagramPacket for incoming message
84                  DatagramPacket packet = new DatagramPacket( buffer,
85                     MESSAGE_SIZE );
86
87                  // receive new DatagramPacket (blocking call)
88                  try {
89                     multicastSocket.receive( packet );
90                  }
91
92                  // handle exception when receive times out
93                  catch ( InterruptedIOException interruptedIOException ) {
94
95                     // continue to next iteration to keep listening
96                     continue;
97                  }
98
99                  // handle exception reading packet from multicast group
100                 catch ( IOException ioException ) {
101                    ioException.printStackTrace();
102                    break;
103                 }
104
105                 // put message data into String
106                 String message = new String( packet.getData(),
107                    packet.getOffset(), packet.getLength() );
108
109                 // ensure non-null message
110                 if ( message != null ) {
111
112                    // trim extra whitespace from end of message
113                    message = message.trim();
114
115                    System.out.println( message );
116
117                    // decide if goodbye or hello
118                    if ( message.startsWith( HELLO_HEADER ) ) {
119                       processHello(
120                          message.substring( HELLO_HEADER.length() ),
121                          packet.getAddress().getHostAddress()
122                       );
123                    }
124
125                    else if ( message.startsWith( GOODBYE_HEADER ) )
126                       processGoodbye( message.substring(
127                          GOODBYE_HEADER.length() ) );
128
129                 } // end if
```

Fig. 28.13 Class **MulticastReceivingThread** uses threads to add and remove peers (part 3 of 6).

```
130
131          } // end while
132
133          // leave multicast group and close MulticastSocket
134          try {
135             multicastSocket.leaveGroup( multicastNetAddress );
136             multicastSocket.close();
137          }
138
139          // handle exception leaving group
140          catch ( IOException ioException ) {
141             ioException.printStackTrace();
142          }
143
144       } // end run
145
146       // process hello message from peer
147       public void processHello( String peerName,
148          String registryAddress  )
149       {
150          registryAddress += ( "/" + BINDING_NAME );
151          synchronized( peerTTLMap )
152          {
153
154             // if it is a new peer, call peerAdded event
155             if ( !peerTTLMap.containsKey( peerName ) ) {
156                peerDiscoveryListener.peerAdded( peerName,
157                   registryAddress);
158             }
159
160             // add to map or if present, refresh TTL
161             peerTTLMap.put( peerName, new Integer( PEER_TTL ) );
162
163          }
164       }
165
166       // process goodbye message from peer
167       public void processGoodbye( String peerName )
168       {
169          synchronized( peerTTLMap )
170          {
171             System.out.println( "Removing peer" + peerName );
172             if ( peerTTLMap.containsKey( peerName ) ) {
173                peerDiscoveryListener.peerRemoved( peerName );
174                peerTTLMap.remove( peerName );
175             }
176          }
177       }
178
179       // periodically decrements the TTL of peers listed
180       private class LeasingThread extends Thread
181       {
```

Fig. 28.13 Class **MulticastReceivingThread** uses threads to add and remove peers (part 4 of 6).

```
182        public void run()
183        {
184           while ( keepListening )
185           {
186              // sleep
187              try {
188                 Thread.sleep( MULTICAST_INTERVAL );
189              }
190
191              // InterruptedException may interrupt Thread Sleep
192              catch ( InterruptedException interruptedException ) {
193                 interruptedException.printStackTrace();
194              }
195
196              // lock hashmap while decrementing TTL values
197              synchronized( peerTTLMap ) {
198
199                 // decrement peers
200                 Iterator peerIterator =
201                    peerTTLMap.entrySet().iterator();
202
203                 while ( peerIterator.hasNext() ) {
204                    // make new TTL of peer
205                    Map.Entry tempMapEntry =
206                       ( Map.Entry ) peerIterator.next();
207
208                    Integer tempIntegerTTL =
209                       ( Integer ) tempMapEntry.getValue();
210                    int tempIntTTL = tempIntegerTTL.intValue();
211
212                    // decrement TTL
213                    tempIntTTL--;
214
215                    // if lease expired, remove peer
216                    if ( tempIntTTL < 0 ) {
217                       peerDiscoveryListener.peerRemoved(
218                          ( String ) tempMapEntry.getKey() );
219                       peerIterator.remove();
220                    }
221
222                    // otherwise set TTL of peer to new value
223                    else
224                       tempMapEntry.setValue(
225                          new Integer( tempIntTTL ) );
226
227                 } // end while iterating through peers
228
229              } // end synchronized
230
231           } // end while in run method
232
233        } // end run method
```

Fig. 28.13 Class `MulticastReceivingThread` uses threads to add and remove peers (part 5 of 6).

```
234
235        } // end class LeasingThread
236
237        // stop listening for multicasts
238        public void logout()
239        {
240           // terminate thread
241           keepListening = false;
242        }
243  }
```

Fig. 28.13 Class **MulticastReceivingThread** uses threads to add and remove peers (part 6 of 6).

Lines 118–123 call method **processHello** (lines 147–164) if the message **String** begins with constant **HELLO_HEADER**. Lines 125–127 call method **processGoodbye** (lines 167–177) if the message starts with **GOODBYE_HEADER**. When the **while** loop terminates, lines 134–187 unsubscribe from the multicast group and close the socket.

Method **processHello** handles messages that contain the **HELLO_HEADER**. Line 150 appends **BINDING_NAME** to the given **String** containing the IP address of the peer that sent the "hello" message. This forms an RMI URL with which the peer can connect to the newly joined peer. Line 151 synchronizes object **HashMap peerTTLMap**, to prevent other threads from accessing and modifying **peerTTLMap**. This **HashMap** stores peer names as keys and stores the peer lease-expiration times as values. Line 155 tests if the peer name specified in the "hello" message is in **peerTTLMap**. If the peer is not in **peerT-TLMap**, line 156 calls method **peerAdded** of the **peerDiscoveryListener** object. Each **MulticastReceivingThread** contains a reference of an object that implements interface **PeerDiscoveryListener** (Fig. 28.14).

Methods **peerAdded** (line 8) and **peerRemoved** (line 11) inform the **PeerDiscoveryListener** implementation that a peer has entered, or has been removed from, the multicast group, respectively. Line 161 of class **MulticastReceivingThread** **put**s an entry into **peerTTLMap** that contains the peer's name and TTL (specified by **PEER_TTL**). If the peer is already in **peerTTLMap**, line 161 replaces the pre-existing entry with a new entry, which renews the peer's lease by resetting its Time to Live (TTL). Line 174 of class **MulticastReceivingThread** removes a peer from **peerTTLMap**. Because every peer continuously multicasts "hello" packets, datagram packets may be duplicated. Therefore, line 172 first checks if the given peer is in **peerTTLMap** before attempting to remove it. Line 173 calls method **peerRemoved** on the registered **PeerDiscoveryListener** to inform it that a peer has left the multicast group.

```
1    // PeerDiscoveryListener.java
2    // Interface for listening to peerAdded or peerRemoved events
3    package com.deitel.advjhtp1.p2p;
4
5    public interface PeerDiscoveryListener {
6
```

Fig. 28.14 Interface **PeerDiscoveryListener** listens for when peers are added and removed from peer groups (part 1 of 2).

```
7       // add peer with given name and ip address
8       public void peerAdded( String name, String peerStubAddress );
9
10      // remove peer with given name
11      public void peerRemoved( String name );
12
13   }
```

Fig. 28.14 Interface `PeerDiscoveryListener` listens for when peers are added and removed from peer groups (part 2 of 2).

Lines 180–235 define inner class **LeasingThread**. A single-leasing-thread instance periodically decrements the TTL of each peer in the **peerTTLMap**. Line 197 synchronizes **peerTTLMap** to prevent modification conflicts between threads trying to access **peerTTLMap** concurrently. Lines 200–201 obtain an **Iterator** object of **peerTTLMap**'s entries. Lines 203–227 decrement the TTL of each entry in **peerTTLMap**. Lines 208–210 obtains an **int** that contains a peer's TTL—line 213 decrements the TTL value. Line 216 checks if the modified TTL is less than zero, which indicates that the peer's lease has expired. Lines 217–218 then pass the expired peer's name as an argument to method **peerRemoved** of the **PeerDiscoveryListener** object. Line 219 calls **Iterator** method **remove**, which removes the current entry from **peerTTLMap**. If the modified TTL is greater than (or equal to) zero, the peer's lease is still active, so lines 224–225 set the peer's TTL to the newly decremented value. Method **logout** (lines 238–242) enables an outside object to terminate the **MulticastReceivingThread**.

To use classes **MulticastReceivingThread** and **PeerDiscoveryListener** in the Deitel Instant Messenger, we had to modify class **PeerList** from our Instant Messenger Jini implementation. Figure 28.15 contains the modified **PeerList** listing.

```
1    // PeerList.java
2    // Starts broadcasting and receiving threads
3    // and lists all IM peers in a window
4    package com.deitel.advjhtp1.p2p;
5
6    // Java core packages
7    import java.awt.*;
8    import java.awt.event.*;
9    import java.net.MalformedURLException;
10   import java.util.*;
11   import java.util.List;
12   import java.io.IOException;
13   import java.rmi.*;
14
15   // Java extension packages
16   import javax.swing.*;
17   import javax.swing.event.*;
18
```

Fig. 28.15 Modified **PeerList** enables the use of classes **MulticastReceivingThread** and **PeerDiscoveryListener** in the Deitel Instant Messenger (part 1 of 6).

```
19   // Deitel Packages
20   import com.deitel.advjhtp1.jini.IM.service.IMService;
21   import com.deitel.advjhtp1.jini.IM.client.IMPeerListener;
22   import com.deitel.advjhtp1.jini.IM.IMPeerImpl;
23   import com.deitel.advjhtp1.jini.IM.IMPeer;
24
25   public class PeerList extends JFrame
26      implements PeerDiscoveryListener, IMConstants {
27
28      // initialize userName to anonymous
29      private String userName = "anonymous";
30      private MulticastSendingThread multicastSender;
31      private MulticastReceivingThread multicastReceiver;
32
33      // list variables
34      private DefaultListModel peerNames;     // contains peer names
35      private List peerStubAddresses;         // contains peer stubs
36      private JList peerJList;
37
38      // add peer name and peer stub to lists
39      public void peerAdded( String name, String peerStubAddress )
40      {
41         // add name to peerNames
42         peerNames.addElement( name );
43
44         // add stub to peerStubAddresses
45         peerStubAddresses.add( peerStubAddress );
46
47      } // end method peerAdded
48
49
50      // removes services from PeerList GUI and data structure
51      public void peerRemoved( String name )
52      {
53         // remove name from peerNames
54         int index = peerNames.indexOf( name );
55         peerNames.removeElementAt( index );
56
57         // remove stub from peerStubAddresses
58         peerStubAddresses.remove( index );
59
60      } // end method peerRemoved
61
62      // constructor
63      public PeerList()
64      {
65         super( "Peer List" );
66
67         // get desired userName
68         userName = JOptionPane.showInputDialog(
69            PeerList.this, "Please enter your name: " );
```

Fig. 28.15 Modified **PeerList** enables the use of classes
MulticastReceivingThread and **PeerDiscoveryListener**
in the Deitel Instant Messenger (part 2 of 6).

```
70
71          // change title of window
72          setTitle( userName + "'s Peer List Window" );
73
74          // Init List data structures
75          peerNames = new DefaultListModel();
76          peerStubAddresses = new ArrayList();
77
78          // init components
79          Container container = getContentPane();
80          peerJList = new JList( peerNames );
81          peerJList.setVisibleRowCount( 5 );
82          JButton connectButton = new JButton( "Connect" );
83
84          // do not allow multiple selections
85          peerJList.setSelectionMode(
86              ListSelectionModel.SINGLE_SELECTION );
87
88          // set up event handler for connectButton
89          connectButton.addActionListener(
90              new ActionListener() {
91
92                  public void actionPerformed( ActionEvent event )
93                  {
94                      int itemIndex = peerJList.getSelectedIndex();
95
96                      String stubAddress =
97                          ( String ) peerStubAddresses.get( itemIndex );
98
99                      // get RMI reference to IMService and IMPeer
100                     try {
101
102                         IMService peerStub =
103                             ( IMService ) Naming.lookup( "rmi://" +
104                                 stubAddress );
105
106                         // set up gui and my peerImpl
107                         IMPeerListener gui =
108                             new IMPeerListener( userName );
109                         IMPeerImpl me =
110                             new IMPeerImpl( userName );
111                         me.addListener( gui );
112
113                         // Connect myGui to remote IMPeer object
114                         IMPeer myPeer = peerStub.connect( me );
115                         gui.addPeer( myPeer );
116                     }
117
```

Fig. 28.15 Modified **PeerList** enables the use of classes
MulticastReceivingThread and **PeerDiscoveryListener**
in the Deitel Instant Messenger (part 3 of 6).

```
118            // malformedURL passed to lookup
119            catch( MalformedURLException exception ) {
120               JOptionPane.showMessageDialog
121                 ( null, "Stub address incorrectly formatted" );
122               exception.printStackTrace();
123            }
124
125
126            // Remote object not bound to remote registry
127            catch ( NotBoundException notBoundException ) {
128               JOptionPane.showMessageDialog
129                 ( null, "Remote object not present in Registry" );
130               notBoundException.printStackTrace();
131            }
132
133            // connecting may cause RemoteException
134            catch ( RemoteException remoteException ) {
135               JOptionPane.showMessageDialog
136                  ( null, "Couldn't Connect" );
137               remoteException.printStackTrace();
138            }
139
140         } // end method ActionPerformed
141
142      } // end ActionListener anonymous inner class
143
144   ); // end connectButton actionListener
145
146   // set up File menu
147   JMenu fileMenu = new JMenu( "File" );
148   fileMenu.setMnemonic( 'F' );
149
150   // about Item
151   JMenuItem aboutItem = new JMenuItem( "About..." );
152   aboutItem.setMnemonic( 'A' );
153   aboutItem.addActionListener(
154      new ActionListener() {
155         public void actionPerformed( ActionEvent event )
156         {
157            JOptionPane.showMessageDialog( PeerList.this,
158            "Deitel Instant Messenger" ,
159            "About", JOptionPane.PLAIN_MESSAGE );
160         }
161      }
162   );
163
164   fileMenu.add( aboutItem );
165
166   // set up JMenuBar and attach File menu
167   JMenuBar menuBar = new JMenuBar();
168   menuBar.add ( fileMenu );
```

Fig. 28.15 Modified **PeerList** enables the use of classes
MulticastReceivingThread and **PeerDiscoveryListener**
in the Deitel Instant Messenger (part 4 of 6).

```
169          setJMenuBar( menuBar );
170
171          // handow window closing event
172          addWindowListener(
173
174             new WindowAdapter(){
175
176                public void windowClosing( WindowEvent w )
177                {
178                   System.out.println( "CLOSING WINDOW" );
179
180                   // disconnects from lookup services
181                   multicastSender.logout();
182                   multicastReceiver.logout();
183
184                   // join threads
185                   try {
186                      multicastSender.join();
187                      multicastReceiver.join();
188                   }
189                   catch( InterruptedException interruptedException ) {
190                      interruptedException.printStackTrace();
191                   }
192
193                   System.exit( 0 );
194                }
195             }
196          );
197
198          // lay out GUI components
199          peerJList.setFixedCellWidth( 100 );
200          JPanel inputPanel = new JPanel();
201          inputPanel.add( connectButton );
202
203          container.add( new JScrollPane( peerJList ) ,
204             BorderLayout.NORTH );
205          container.add( inputPanel, BorderLayout.SOUTH );
206
207          // Initialize threads
208          try {
209
210             multicastReceiver =
211                new MulticastReceivingThread( userName, this );
212             multicastReceiver.start();
213
214             multicastSender =
215                new MulticastSendingThread( userName );
216             multicastSender.start();
217
218          }
219
```

Fig. 28.15 Modified **PeerList** enables the use of classes
MulticastReceivingThread and **PeerDiscoveryListener**
in the Deitel Instant Messenger (part 5 of 6).

```
220        // catch all exceptions and inform user of problem
221        catch ( Exception managerException ) {
222           JOptionPane.showMessageDialog( null,
223              "Error initializing MulticastSendingThread" +
224              "or MulticastReceivingThread" );
225           managerException.printStackTrace();
226        }
227     }
228
229     public static void main( String args[] )
230     {
231        PeerList peerlist = new PeerList();
232        peerlist.setSize( 100, 170 );
233        peerlist.setVisible( true );
234     }
235  }
```

Fig. 28.15 Modified **PeerList** enables the use of classes
MulticastReceivingThread and **PeerDiscoveryListener**
in the Deitel Instant Messenger (part 6 of 6).

Class **PeerList** implements interface **PeerDiscoveryListener**—the Jini version implemented interface **ServiceDisoveryListener**. Lines 210–211 create a **MulticastReceivingThread** and passes the **this** reference as a **PeerDiscoveryListener**—line 212 starts this thread. Lines 214–215 create a **MulticastSendingThread** specifying the user name—line 216 starts this thread.

Lines 39–47 implement method **PeerAdded**, which takes two **String**s—**name** and **peerStubAddress**. Parameter **name** specifies the peer's name. Parameter **peerStubAddress** is a URL-formatted **String** that contains the information needed to make a **Naming.lookup** call on the remote peer. The **Naming.lookup** call obtains an **IMService** remote reference. Lines 42–45 store the **IMService** remote reference.

Lines 51–60 implement method **peerRemoved**. Lines 54–58 remove the information of the given peer from **peerNames** and **peerStubAddresses**.

Lines 89–141 specify the **ActionListener** for the **JButton** that we use to connect peers. Line 96–97 obtains the **peerStubAddress** of the selected peer in the **JList**. Lines 102–104 calls method **Naming.lookup** to obtain a reference to the remote peer's **IMService** object from the RMI registry. The code in lines 106–140 works similarly to that of the previous Deitel Instant Messenger implementation.

Lines 176–194 specify instructions to execute when the user closes the **PeerList** window. Lines 180–181 terminate each thread by calling method **logout**. Lines 186–187 **join** each thread, thereby blocking until each thread terminates. Line 193 exits the program.

28.13 Introduction to JXTA

Sun Microsystems, Inc. created Project JXTA[3] as a response to the growing popularity of peer-to-peer applications. Project JXTA strives to create a standard, low-level, platform and language-independent protocol that promotes interoperability among peer-to-peer applications. The current JXTA implementation is written in Java, but developers can imple-

---

3. For more information, see **www.jxta.org**.

ment JXTA in any programming language. JXTA provides a foundation from which developers can build any type of P2P application.

JXTA attempts to solve the following problems of peer-to-peer applications:

1. Security/Authentication—Large peer-to-peer network applications, such as AOL Instant Messenger and MSN Instant Messenger, use central servers to bootstrap users onto the network. This bootstrapping ensures, to some degree, that the same person uses a particular online identity.

2. Peer Discovery—Without a central server, it is difficult to realize the presence of other peers on the network. Multicasting, as used by Jini, is not a viable solution outside the LAN setting.

3. Network Incompatibility—Currently, each popular peer-to-peer application yields a set of proprietary protocols that prevent compatibility with other peer-to-peer networks. For example, the millions of users on the AIM platform cannot communicate with Yahoo Instant Messenger users. Most new users opt for the peer-to-peer application with the largest following.

4. Platform Incompatibility—Software developers must rewrite the low-level core aspects of their peer-to-peer applications for each platform they wish to support. Wireless phones and other mobile devices usually have a limited selection of P2P applications, if any.

JXTA attempts to solve these problems by standardizing the low-level protocols that govern peer-to-peer applications. JXTA is designed to be a general infrastructure, rather than a special-purpose one. Therefore, developers can use JXTA to implement virtually any type of P2P application. Because all JXTA-based P2P applications use identical low-level protocols, they will be compatible with one another.

Networks built with the JXTA protocols consist of three basic types of entities—*peer/peer groups*, *advertisements* and *pipes/messages*. Each JXTA runtime environment associates each entity's name and network address with a unique 128-bit identifier.

A *peer* is any entity that uses JXTA protocols (Fig. 28.16) to communicate with other peers. Each peer need support only some of the protocols, so devices with low processing power and memory can participate in JXTA networks (albeit with limited functionality). *Peer groups* are logical constructs that represent sets of peers. JXTA specifies only two rules regarding peer groups

1. peers can join or leave groups

2. the group administrator, if the group has one, controls access to the group.

All peers are part of the World Peer Group. Membership in the World Peer Group does not imply that each peer can discover and communicate with every other peer on the network.

Advertisements are XML documents that perform a function similar to that of multicast packets in Jini. An entity in the JXTA network advertises itself to notify others of its existence by sending XML documents formatted according to JXTA specifications.

At the simplest level, *pipes* are unreliable one-way communication channels. More sophisticated pipes may be reliable and multi-directional. Earlier in the chapter, we mentioned that an RMI peer reference allows one-way communication with that peer. Pipes perform similarly. Two peers communicate by configuring two pipes that "flow" in opposite directions. Each peer communicates by sending *Messages* to the other peer through the pipe. JXTA specifies the Messages' structure. The most recent JXTA implementation uses XML Messages. The developers of JXTA use XML because of its portability. However, JXTA does not restrict the Message format to XML.

JXTA is still in development and has not yet resolved all of the problems with peer-to-peer applications. The implementation of peer discovery and security measures continues to progress. JXTA suggests that peer discovery use a combination of *LAN-based discovery, discovery through invitation, cascaded discovery* and *rendezvous discovery*. Jini illustrates one means of LAN-based discovery. In LAN-based discovery, peers in a local network discover each other automatically by multicasting. Discovery through invitation occurs when a peer receives a message from a previously unknown peer. Cascaded discovery is a distributed-search mechanism—similar to that of Gnutella. Rendezvous discovery is the creation of certain well-known sites that provide network addresses of many users on the network to bootstrap new users.

For further information on the current state of JXTA and other P2P technologies, see the resources provided in Section 28.14.

28.14 Internet and World Wide Web Resources

www.openp2p.com
openp2p.com is a Web site that is part of the O'Reilly Network. This online resource provides articles and links about peer-to-peer technologies.

www.clip2.com
This site provides information and statistics regarding the popular and upcoming peer-to-peer technologies. This site also provides columns that explain how various peer-to-peer protocols work.

www.peer-to-peerwg.org
This page is published by the peer-to-peer working group.

Protocol	Function
Peer Discovery	Peers use this protocol to find other entities in the JXTA network by searching for advertisements.
Peer Resolver	Peers that help a search process (e.g., higher bandwidth, capacity storage, etc.) implement this protocol.
Peer Information	Peers obtain information about other peers via this protocol.
Peer Membership	Peers use this protocol to learn about the requirements of groups, how to apply for membership, how to modify their membership and how to quit a group. Authentication and security are implemented through this protocol.
Pipe Binding	Peers can connect pipes to one another, via advertisements, through this protocol.
Endpoint Routing	Peer routers implement this protocol to provide other routing services to other peers (e.g., tunneling through a firewall).

Fig. 28.16 JXTA low-level protocols.

www.jxta.org
This is the official Web site for Project JXTA and contains the newest downloads of the source code and opportunities to participate in developing JXTA.

www.peerintelligence.com
This Web site publishes columns that discuss how peer-to-peer technologies are being developed into enterprise solutions. This site focuses on how businesses can use peer-to-peer applications.

www.peertal.com
This site presents columns that discuss peer-to-peer technologies.

SUMMARY

- In a peer-to-peer (P2P) network architecture, each node can perform both client and server functions. Such networks distribute processing and information to many computers, thus reclaiming otherwise wasted computing power and storage space and eliminating central points of failure.

- Developers may implement P2P applications using various technologies, such as multicast sockets.

- Many networks operate on the principle that computers should be segregated by function.

- Instead of segregating computers by function, in P2P networks all computers act as both clients and servers.

- The concept of P2P applications is similar to that of the telephone system—a single user can both speak (send information) and listen (receive information).

- Many network applications do not fall neatly into either client/server or peer-to-peer categories.

- One major weakness of this centralized system is the dependency on the central server. If the central node (i.e., server) fails, so does the entire application.

- The capabilities of the server limit the overall performance of the application.

- Centralized architectures simplify management tasks, such as monitoring user access, by providing single points of network control.

- True P2P applications are completely decentralized and do not suffer from the same deficiencies as applications that depend on centralized servers.

- Some P2P applications leverage distributed computational power.

- Peer-to-peer architectures allow real-time searches that return up-to-date results.

- Peer-to-peer searches reflect the status of the network at the time of the query.

- In peer-to-peer networks determining who is on the network at any instant is difficult.

- Real-time searches are slower and increase network traffic, because every query must propagate throughout the entire network.

- A true client/server network is completely centralized, whereas a true peer-to-peer application is completely decentralized.

- Many applications adopt aspects of both networking styles to achieve specific goals.

- Peer discovery is the act of finding peers in a P2P application.

- Decentralizing an application makes peer discovery and searching for information difficult.

- Distributed searches make networks more robust by removing single points of failure, such as central servers.

- Information found via distributed searches is up-to-date because it reflects the current state of the network.

TERMINOLOGY

authentication	P2P (peer-to-peer) application
bootstrapping	peer
central server	peer discovery
centralization	peer group
client/server computing	pipe
decentralization	proxy
distributed search	real-time search
Freenet	Remote Method Invocation (RMI)
Gnutella	search engine
Jini	search hub
JXTA	Time to Live (TTL)
lookup service	unicast discovery
multicast socket	

SELF-REVIEW EXERCISES

28.1 Fill in the blanks in each of the following statements:

a) For the Deitel Instant Messenger to send a message to a remote peer, it must hold a _____ to the remote peer.

b) Pipes are _____ one-way communication channels.

c) Large peer-to-peer networks, such as AOL Instant Messenger and MSN Instant Messenger, use _____ to bootstrap users onto the network.

d) Peer discovery is the act of _____ and _____ with other peers.

e) Class _____ can be used to cache proxies of all services listed in known lookups ervices.

28.2 State whether each of the following is *true* or *false*. If *false*, explain why.

a) In a peer-to-peer application, each peer performs both client and server functions.

b) One remote reference provides one-way communication.

c) Jini is the best tool for designing peer-to-peer applications.

d) Client/Server network architecture is the most efficient way of organizing groups of computers.

e) The **ServiceDiscoveryManager** needs to export certain classes to asynchronously notify **ServiceDiscoveryListener**s of **ServiceDiscoveryEvent**s.

f) Broadcasting is a viable solution to the problem of discovering other peers on a large-scale peer-to-peer network.

g) All network applications are either peer-to-peer or client/server.

ANSWERS TO SELF-REVIEW EXERCISES

28.1 a) reference.   b) unreliable.   c) central servers.   d) finding, connecting.
e) **ServiceDiscoveryManager**.

28.2 a) True.

b) True.

c) False. Implementing authentication, security and large-scale networks is difficult in Jini. There is no automatic means of peer discovery by distributed search.

d) False. Client/server computing wastes the unused processing power and storage space of the client computers.

e) True.

    f) False. Broadcasting is an inefficient way for computers to announce their existence in a large network. As the number of computers in a network grow, broadcasting creates too much network traffic to be a viable solution.

    g) False. Many applications include elements of both peer-to-peer applications and client/server applications.

EXERCISES

28.3   Modify Deitel Instant Messenger so that it can be used to send image files and display them on the remote computer.

28.4   Modify Deitel Instant Messenger so that it plays a user-selected sound file when an incoming message is received.

28.5   Deitel Instant Messenger can create multiple conversations with the same person. Modify Deitel Instant Messenger so that it will not allow multiple conversations with the same person simultaneously.

28.6   Modify Deitel Instant Messenger so that peers notify any peers with whom they are speaking when they close the conversation window. Remote peers will reconnect to continue sending messages.

28.7   Expand Deitel Instant Messenger so that users can have a user profile. Enable users to search for users with keywords.

29

Introduction to Web Services and SOAP

Objectives

- To understand the Simple Object Access Protocol (SOAP) and how it uses XML.
- To understand the structure of a SOAP message.
- To be able to write Java applications that send and receive SOAP messages.

Nothing happens until something is sold.
Arthur H. Motley

Men are going to have to learn to be managers in a world where the organization will come close to consisting of all chiefs and one Indian. The Indian, of course, is the computer.
Thomas L. Whisler

…it is always the simple that produces the marvelous.
Amelia Barr

Resemblance reproduces the formal aspect of objects…
Ching Hao

…if the simple things of nature have a message that you understand, rejoice, for your soul is alive…
Eleonora Duse

Outline

29.1 Introduction

Interoperability, or seamless communication and interaction between different software systems, is a primary goal of many businesses and organizations that rely heavily on computers and electronic networks. Many applications use the Internet to transfer data. Some of these applications run on client systems with little processing power, so they invoke method calls on remote machines to process data. Many applications use proprietary data specifications, which makes communication with other applications difficult, if not impossible. The majority of applications also reside behind *firewalls*—security barriers that restrict communication between networks. The *Simple Object Access Protocol* (*SOAP*) is a protocol that addresses these problems. Combining the powers of HTTP and XML, it provides a fully extensible mode of communication between software systems.

Web Services are an emerging area of distributed computing. Sun Microsystems' *Open Net Environment (ONE)* and Microsoft Corporation's *.NET* initiative are frameworks for writing and deploying Web services. There are several definitions of a Web service. A Web service can be any Web-accessible application, such as a Web page with dynamic content. A narrower definition of a Web service is an application that exposes a public interface usable by other applications over the Web. Sun's ONE requires Web services to be accessible through HTTP and other Web protocols, to communicate with XML-based messages and to be available through lookup services. SOAP provides the XML communication in many Web services. Web services can provide great interoperability between diverse systems.[1]

A hypothetical Web service designed for the Sun ONE architecture might take a form in which a service registry publishes a description of the Web service as a *Universal Description, Discovery and Integration (UDDI)* document. The client, such as a Web browser or Java GUI client, searches a directory service for a needed Web service. The client uses the information it receives through the lookup service to send an XML message via HTTP to the Web server hosting the Web service. A servlet processes the client request. The servlet then accesses an application server that provides Enterprise Java Beans. The EJBs in turn access a database that stores the Web service's information. After accessing the database, the EJB responds to the servlet with the requested information. The servlet formats the information for the client (e.g. creates a JavaServer Page). The HTTP server sends an XML response back to the client. The client then parses the response and displays the information for the user.[1]

The great potential of Web services does not lie with the technology used to create them. HTTP, XML and the other protocols used by Web services are not new. The interoperability and scalability of Web services means developers can rapidly create large applications and larger Web services from small Web services. Sun's Open Net Environment describes an architecture for creating *smart Web services*. Smart Web services share a common operating environment with one another. By sharing context, smart Web services can perform common authentication for financial transactions, provide location-specific recommendations and directions, etc., among e-businesses. At the time of this writing, there are two major obstacles in the way of developing smart Web services. There do not yet exist widely accepted standards for sharing context between Web services or ensuring the security and privacy of Web-service transactions.

29.2 Simple Object Access Protocol (SOAP)

IBM, Lotus Development Corporation, Microsoft, DevelopMentor and Userland Software developed and drafted SOAP, which is an HTTP-XML-based protocol that enables applications to communicate over the Internet, by using XML documents called *SOAP messages*. SOAP is compatible with any object model, because it includes only functions and capabilities that are absolutely necessary for defining a communication framework. Thus, SOAP is both platform and software independent, and any programming language can implement it. SOAP supports transport using almost any conceivable protocol. For example, SOAP binds to HTTP and follows the HTTP request–response model. SOAP also supports any method of encoding data, which enables SOAP-based applications to send virtually any type information (e.g., images, objects, documents, etc.) in SOAP messages.

A SOAP message contains an *envelope*, which describes the content, intended recipient and processing requirements of a message. The optional **header** *element* of a SOAP message provides processing instructions for applications that receive the message. For example, for implementations that support transactions, the header could specify details of that transaction. The header also can incorporate routing information. Through the header, more complex protocols can be built onto SOAP. Header entries can modularly extend the message for purposes such as authentication, transaction management and payment. The body of a SOAP message contains application-specific data for the intended recipient of the message.

SOAP has the ability to make a *Remote Procedure Call* (*RPC*), which is a request made to another machine to run a task. The RPC uses an XML vocabulary to specify the method to be invoked, any parameters the method takes and the Universal Resource Identifier (URI) of the target object. An RPC call naturally maps to an HTTP request, so an HTTP **post** sends the message. A SOAP-response message is an HTTP-response document that contains the results of the method call (e.g., returned values, error messages, etc.). SOAP also supports *asynchronous RPC*, in which program that invokes the RPC does not wait for a response from the remote procedure.

At the time of this writing, SOAP is still under development, and many of the technologies that build on it are in the early stages of development. To realize the benefits of SOAP, industry must establish higher-level specifications and standards that use this technology. Nevertheless, SOAP is the leading industry standard for an XML-distributed computing infrastructure, providing previously nonexistent extensibility and interoperability.

Figure 29.1–Fig. 29.4 present a SOAP example using Apache's SOAP implementation API, version 2.2 (available at **xml.apache.org/soap**). The SOAP RPC requires a servlet engine, such as Tomcat (**jakarta.apache.org**) and Apache's Xerces parser for Java (available at **xml.apache.org/xerces-j/index.html**). The SOAP documentation (**docs/install/index.html**) includes installation instructions for both the server and the client.

Figure 29.1 shows class **SimpleService**, which resides on the server and contains method **getWelcome**. The Java application in Fig. 29.4 invokes this method using an RPC.

```
1   // Fig. 29.1: SimpleService.java
2   // Implementation for the requested method on the server
3
4   public class SimpleService {
5
6      public String getWelcome( String message ) throws Exception
7      {
8         String text =
9            "Welcome to SOAP!\nHere is your message: " + message;
10
11        return text;    // response
12     }
13  }
```

Fig. 29.1 Class **SimpleService**.

Method **getWelcome** (lines 6–12) returns a **String** when invoked. To make this method available to clients (i.e., to facilitate RPC), we need to provide the server with the name of the method that processes the request—i.e., we must *deploy the service*.

To deploy the service, first copy the **SimpleService.class** file into the **jakarta-tomcat/classes** directory. If you created a Java Archive (JAR) file, copy the JAR file into the **jakarta-tomcat/lib** directory. Create the **classes** or **lib** directories if they do not exist. Jakarta-Tomcat includes files in these directories in the **CLASSPATH**.

Deploy the service with the XML-SOAP administration tool included in the SOAP package (located in the directory **webapps/soap**). To run this application, type the URL **localhost:8080/soap/admin** into a Web browser. Figure 29.2 and Fig. 29.3 show the administration tool that allows you to deploy, remove and list services. The *ID field* in Fig. 29.2 contains a URI (**urn:xml-simple-message**) that identifies the service to the client. This URI is programmer defined. If one service has the same URI as another, the client cannot differentiate between them; consequently, errors may occur. The *Scope field* specifies the lifetime of the object created (on the server) for serving the SOAP request. The object can exist for the duration of the **Request**, **Session** or **Application**. **Request** denotes that the server deletes the object after it sends the response, **Session** indicates that the object persists for the duration of the client's session with the server. **Application** signifies that the object is available for all requests throughout the lifetime of the application. The *Methods field* (Fig. 29.2) specifies the methods available for a SOAP request—in this case, method **getWelcome**. The *Provider Type* field specifies the service implementation language. Languages supported include Java, JavaScript, Perl and Bean Markup Language (BML). For the examples in this chapter, we use Java. In the **Provider Class** field we specify the class that implements the service—**SimpleService**. The **Script Language**, **Script File** and **Script** fields are used only for services implemented in a supported scripting language. The **Type Mapping** field allows manual mapping of Java types to XML. The Apache SOAP implementation provides default mappings for most Java types and for Java classes that follow the JavaBeans design patterns. After completing the form, click the **Deploy** button on the bottom of the form to deploy the service. Click the **List** button, which lists the services, to confirm that the service deployed successfully (Fig. 29.3). Instructions for other methods of deployment (such as using the command line) are provided in **docs\guide\index.html**.

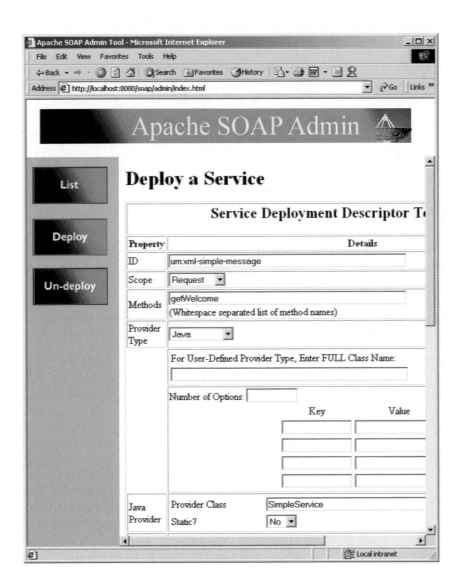

Fig. 29.2   SOAP package administration tool.

Figure 29.4 lists the client-side code for the RPC. When executed, the program sends a SOAP request to the server, which in our case is the same machine, the local host. The client sends a message as a parameter to the remote method. (This message can be from the command line; by default, the application uses the message **Thanks!**) When the server invokes the method, it sends back the message

```
Welcome to SOAP!
Here is your message: Thanks!
```

Fig. 29.3   Description of deployed service.

```
1   // Fig. 29.4 : GetMessage.java
2   // Program that makes a SOAP RPC
3
4   // import Java packages
5   import java.io.*;
6   import java.net.*;
7   import java.util.*;
8
9   // import third-party packages
10  import org.apache.soap.*;
11  import org.apache.soap.rpc.*;
12
13  public class GetMessage {
14
15     // main method
16     public static void main( String args[] ) {
17        String encodingStyleURI = Constants.NS_URI_SOAP_ENC;
18        String message;
```

Fig. 29.4   Client making a SOAP request (part 1 of 3).

```
19
20          if ( args.length != 0 )
21            message = args[ 0 ];
22          else
23            message = "Thanks!";
24
25          // attempt SOAP remote procedure call
26          try {
27             URL url = new URL(
28                "http://localhost:8080/soap/servlet/rpcrouter" );
29
30             // build call
31             Call remoteMethod = new Call();
32             remoteMethod.setTargetObjectURI(
33                "urn:xml-simple-message" );
34
35             // set name of remote method to be invoked
36             remoteMethod.setMethodName( "getWelcome" );
37             remoteMethod.setEncodingStyleURI( encodingStyleURI );
38
39             // set parameters for remote method
40             Vector parameters = new Vector();
41
42             parameters.addElement( new Parameter( "message",
43                String.class, message, null ) );
44             remoteMethod.setParams( parameters );
45             Response response;
46
47             // invoke remote method
48             response = remoteMethod.invoke( url, "" );
49
50             // get response
51             if ( response.generatedFault() ) {
52                Fault fault = response.getFault();
53
54                System.err.println( "CALL FAILED:\nFault Code = "
55                   + fault.getFaultCode()+ "\nFault String = "
56                   + fault.getFaultString() );
57             }
58
59             else {
60                Parameter result = response.getReturnValue();
61
62                // display result of call
63                System.out.println( result.getValue() );
64             }
65          }
66
67          // catch malformed URL exception
68          catch ( MalformedURLException malformedURLException ) {
69             malformedURLException.printStackTrace();
70             System.exit( 1 );
71          }
```

Fig. 29.4   Client making a SOAP request (part 2 of 3).

```
72
73          // catch SOAPException
74          catch ( SOAPException soapException ) {
75              System.err.println( "Error message: " +
76                  soapException.getMessage() );
77              System.exit( 1 );
78          }
79      }
80  }
```

```
java GetMessage
Welcome to SOAP!
Here is your message: Thanks!
```

```
java GetMessage "my message"
Welcome to SOAP!
Here is your message: my message
```

Fig. 29.4 Client making a SOAP request (part 3 of 3).

Line 10 **import**s the SOAP package that provides the API for the SOAP implementation. The package **org.apache.soap.rpc** in line 11 provides the implementation for RPC using SOAP. Line 17 specifies the encoding style used for the message. SOAP, which has no default encoding style, supports many encoding styles—we use the standard RPC encoding (**WS_URI_SOAP_ENC**). Lines 27–28 specify the server-side URL to which the client sends **message**'s value, **rpcrouter**. This document, a Java servlet, receives the SOAP envelope through the HTTP **post** method. Using the URI specified in the SOAP message, it looks up the services deployed on the server in order to instantiate the appropriate object, in this case a **SimpleService** object.

Objects of *class* **Call** invoke remote methods. Line 31 instantiates a **Call** object and assigns it to reference **remoteMethod**, and lines 32–33 set the remote method's URI. Line 36 specifies the name of the method to be invoked, **getWelcome**. We then set the encoding style for the message on line 37. Lines 40–44 build the parameters passed to the remote method for processing. Each parameter must be in its own object, and the parameter objects must be placed in a **Vector**.

Lines 42–43 build a new parameter for the method by constructing a *Parameter object*. The first constructor argument is the name of the variable or reference (**message**), the second argument is the class to which the **Parameter** object belongs (**String**), the third argument is the value of the parameter (the object **message**) and the fourth argument specifies the parameter's encoding. (**null** specifies the application's default encoding.) *Method* **setParams** in line 44 sets the parameters of the **remoteMethod** object.

We invoke the remote method by calling method **invoke** in line 48. It takes two arguments: the server URL to which the SOAP message is being sent and the value of the **SOAPAction** header, which specifies the intent of the request. The second argument can take a **null** string if a **SOAPAction** header is not being used. Method **invoke** throws a *SOAPException* (lines 74–78) if any network error occurs while the SOAP request is being sent. Once the method is invoked on the server, the result is sent back to the client and stored in the object referenced by **response** (line 48). This object receives an error message if a server error, such as a failure to locate the appropriate services, occurs. Lines 51–57 determine whether the received message is an error message. Lines 59–64 print the output if no error has been received.

29.3 SOAP Weather Service

This section describes a simple Web service implemented with Java and SOAP. The Web service is a modified version of the weather service implemented with RMI in Chapter 13. The weather service now uses SOAP RPC instead of Java RMI to send information from the server to the client. The required software components are the same as the previous section.

The SOAP weather service uses classes **WeatherBean**, **WeatherCellRenderer**, **WeatherItem** and **WeatherListModel** from the RMI weather service without modification. SOAP RPC does not require a Java interface like RMI, so this example does not use interface **WeatherService** and class **WeatherServiceImpl**. For this example, class **WeatherService** uses most of **WeatherServiceImpl**'s code and exposes method **getWeatherInformation** via SOAP. Class **WeatherServiceClient** now uses SOAP RPC instead of Java RMI.

Class **WeatherService** (Fig. 29.5) provides method **getWeatherInformation** that class **WeatherServiceClient** calls through a SOAP RPC. **WeatherService** must be in the **classes** directory of the Tomcat servlet engine for the call to be successful. The RMI version of method **getWeatherInformation** returns a **List** of **WeatherBean** objects. SOAP does not support direct transmission of these Java objects, so the SOAP RPC version of **getWeatherInformation** returns a **Vector** of **String**s. Lines 66–71 add the **String**s parsed from the *Traveler's Forecast* Web page to **Vector weatherInformation** (line 13). Line 99 returns **Vector weatherInformation**. The rest of class **WeatherService** is identical to class **WeatherServiceImpl** from Chapter 13.

```
1   // Fig. 29.5: WeatherService.java
2   // WeatherService provides a method to retrieve weather
3   // information from the National Weather Service.
4   package com.deitel.advjhtp1.soap.weather;
5
6   // Java core packages
7   import java.io.*;
8   import java.net.URL;
9   import java.util.*;
10
11  public class WeatherService {
12
13     private Vector weatherInformation;   // WeatherBean objects
14
15     // get weather information from NWS
16     private void updateWeatherConditions()
17     {
18        try {
19           System.out.println( "Update weather information..." );
```

Fig. 29.5 SOAP implementation of class **WeatherService** (part 1 of 3).

```
20
21          // National Weather Service Travelers Forecast page
22          URL url = new URL(
23             "http://iwin.nws.noaa.gov/iwin/us/traveler.html" );
24
25          // set up text input stream to read Web page contents
26          BufferedReader in = new BufferedReader(
27             new InputStreamReader( url.openStream() ) );
28
29          // helps determine starting point of data on Web page
30          String separator = "TAV12";
31
32          // locate separator string in Web page
33          while ( !in.readLine().startsWith( separator ) )
34             ;     // do nothing
35
36          // strings representing headers on Travelers Forecast
37          // Web page for daytime and nighttime weather
38          String dayHeader =
39             "CITY            WEA     HI/LO   WEA     HI/LO";
40          String nightHeader =
41             "CITY            WEA     LO/HI   WEA     LO/HI";
42
43          String inputLine = "";
44
45          // locate header that begins weather information
46          do {
47             inputLine = in.readLine();
48          } while ( !inputLine.equals( dayHeader ) &&
49                    !inputLine.equals( nightHeader ) );
50
51          weatherInformation = new Vector(); // create Vector
52
53          // create WeatherBeans containing weather data and
54          // store in weatherInformation Vector
55          inputLine = in.readLine();  // get first city's data
56
57          // The portion of inputLine containing relevant data
58          // is 28 characters long. If the line length is not at
59          // least 28 characters long, then done processing data.
60          while ( inputLine.length() > 28 ) {
61
62             // Prepare strings for WeatherBean for each city.
63             // First 16 characters are city name. Next, six
64             // characters are weather description. Next six
65             // characters are HI/LO or LO/HI temperature.
66             weatherInformation.add(
67                inputLine.substring( 0, 16 ) );
68             weatherInformation.add(
69                inputLine.substring( 16, 22 ) );
70             weatherInformation.add(
71                inputLine.substring( 23, 29 ) );
72
```

Fig. 29.5   SOAP implementation of class **WeatherService** (part 2 of 3).

```
73                  inputLine = in.readLine();   // get next city's data
74              }
75
76              in.close();   // close connection to NWS Web server
77
78              System.out.println( "Weather information updated." );
79          }
80
81          // process failure to connect to National Weather Service
82          catch( java.net.ConnectException connectException ) {
83              connectException.printStackTrace();
84              System.exit( 1 );
85          }
86
87          // process other exceptions
88          catch( Exception exception ) {
89              exception.printStackTrace();
90              System.exit( 1 );
91          }
92      }
93
94      // implementation for WeatherService interface method
95      public Vector getWeatherInformation()
96      {
97          updateWeatherConditions();
98
99          return weatherInformation;
100     }
101 }
```

Fig. 29.5   SOAP implementation of class **WeatherService** (part 3 of 3).

Class **WeatherServiceClient** (Fig. 29.6) makes a SOAP remote procedure call to method **getWeatherInformation** of class **WeatherService**. Lines 14–15 **import** the Apache SOAP packages. Lines 31–32 set the SOAP service's URL. Line 35 creates a new **Call** object, which stores information needed to perform the remote procedure call. Lines 36–37 set the URI that uniquely identifies the weather service in the servlet engine. Lines 40–41 specify the method name for the RPC. Lines 42–43 set the encoding for the call. Line 46 creates a **Response** object and calls method **invoke** on the **Call** object with a URL as an argument. The **Response** object holds the response to the remote procedure call. Line 49 determines if the response generates a **Fault**. If a **Fault** occurs, lines 52–54 print the error code. If no **Fault** occurs, line 58 gets the object returned by the remote procedure call. Lines 60–61 cast the **Object** to a **Vector**. Lines 64–65 create a **List** and call method **createBeans** (lines 95–107) with the **Vector** of **String**s as a parameter. Method **createBeans** turns the **Vector** of **String**s into a **List** of **WeatherBeans**. Lines 68–69 create a **ListModel** of the **List** of **WeatherBean**s. Lines 73–77 create a **JList** of the information obtained from the remote procedure call and display the **JList** in a **JFrame**.

The weather service deploys in the same manner as the simple message service. Start the Tomcat servlet engine and go to the SOAP administration tool (**localhost:8080/ soap/admin**) as shown in Fig. 29.7. Click **Deploy** and fill in the information in the form

```
1   // Fig. 29.6: WeatherServiceClient.java
2   // WeatherServiceClient accesses the WeatherService remote
3   // object via SOAP to retrieve weather information.
4   package com.deitel.advjhtp1.soap.weather;
5
6   // Java core packages
7   import java.util.*;
8   import java.net.*;
9
10  // Java extension packages
11  import javax.swing.*;
12
13  // third-party packages
14  import org.apache.soap.*;
15  import org.apache.soap.rpc.*;
16
17  // Deitel packages
18  import com.deitel.advjhtp1.rmi.weather.*;
19
20  public class WeatherServiceClient extends JFrame {
21
22     // WeatherServiceClient constructor
23     public WeatherServiceClient( String server )
24     {
25        super( "SOAP WeatherService Client" );
26
27        // connect to server and get weather information
28        try {
29
30           // URL of remote SOAP object
31           URL url = new URL( "http://" + server + ":8080/soap/"
32              + "servlet/rpcrouter" );
33
34           // build SOAP RPC call
35           Call remoteMethod = new Call();
36           remoteMethod.setTargetObjectURI(
37              "urn:xml-weather-service" );
38
39           // set name of remote method to be invoked
40           remoteMethod.setMethodName(
41              "getWeatherInformation" );
42           remoteMethod.setEncodingStyleURI(
43              Constants.NS_URI_SOAP_ENC );
44
45           // invoke remote method
46           Response response = remoteMethod.invoke( url, "" );
47
48           // get response
49           if ( response.generatedFault() ) {
50              Fault fault = response.getFault();
51
```

Fig. 29.6 SOAP implementation of class **WeatherServiceClient**. (part 1 of 3)

```
52              System.err.println( "CALL FAILED:\nFault Code = "
53                 + fault.getFaultCode() + "\nFault String = "
54                 + fault.getFaultString() );
55           }
56
57           else {
58              Parameter result = response.getReturnValue();
59
60              Vector weatherStrings = ( Vector )
61                 result.getValue();
62
63              // get weather information from result object
64              List weatherInformation = createBeans(
65                 weatherStrings );
66
67              // create WeatherListModel for weather information
68              ListModel weatherListModel =
69                 new WeatherListModel( weatherInformation );
70
71              // create JList, set its CellRenderer and add to
72              // layout
73              JList weatherJList = new JList( weatherListModel );
74              weatherJList.setCellRenderer( new
75                 WeatherCellRenderer() );
76              getContentPane().add( new
77                 JScrollPane( weatherJList ) );
78           }
79
80        } // end try
81
82        // handle bad URL
83        catch ( MalformedURLException malformedURLException ) {
84           malformedURLException.printStackTrace();
85        }
86
87        // handle SOAP exception
88        catch ( SOAPException soapException ) {
89           soapException.printStackTrace();
90        }
91
92     } // end WeatherServiceClient constructor
93
94     // create List of WeatherBeans from Vector of Strings
95     public List createBeans( Vector weatherStrings )
96     {
97        List list = new ArrayList();
98        for ( int i = 0; ( weatherStrings.size() - 1 ) > i;
99           i += 3 ) {
100          list.add( new WeatherBean(
101             ( String ) weatherStrings.elementAt( i ),
102             ( String ) weatherStrings.elementAt( i + 1 ),
103             ( String ) weatherStrings.elementAt( i + 2 ) ) );
104       }
```

Fig. 29.6   SOAP implementation of class **WeatherServiceClient**. (part 2 of 3)

```
105
106        return list;
107    }
108
109    // execute WeatherServiceClient
110    public static void main( String args[] )
111    {
112        WeatherServiceClient client = null;
113
114        // if no server IP address or host name specified,
115        // use "localhost"; otherwise use specified host
116        if ( args.length == 0 )
117            client = new WeatherServiceClient( "localhost" );
118        else
119            client = new WeatherServiceClient( args[ 0 ] );
120
121        // configure and display application window
122        client.setDefaultCloseOperation( JFrame.EXIT_ON_CLOSE );
123        client.pack();
124        client.setResizable( false );
125        client.setVisible( true );
126    }
127 }
```

Fig. 29.6 SOAP implementation of class **WeatherServiceClient**. (part 3 of 3)

as it appears in Fig. 29.8. Be sure to enter the fully qualified package name of **WeatherService**. Once the service is deployed, run **WeatherServiceClient**. The remote procedure call retrieves the weather information and, the client displays it (Fig. 29.9).

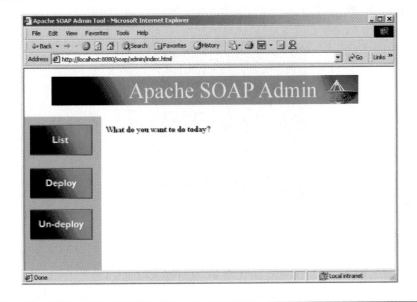

Fig. 29.7 **Apache SOAP Admin** page.

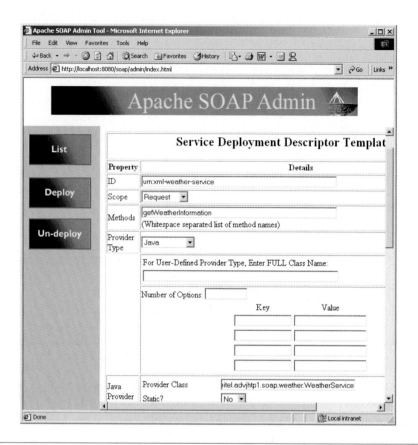

Fig. 29.8 Apache SOAP **Service Deployment Descriptor Template**.

Fig. 29.9 SOAP WeatherService Client.

29.4 Internet and World Wide Web Resources

www.sun.com/software/sunone/index.html
This is Sun Microsystem's site for the Open Net Environment Web services architecture.

xml.apache.org/soap

Apache's SOAP implementation can be downloaded from this site, which also provides information and documentation.

xml.apache.org/xerces-j/index.html

Apache's Xerces parser for Java can be downloaded from this site, along with documentation.

jakarta.apache.org

Web site for Apache's Jakarta-Tomcat servlet engine.

SUMMARY

- A Web service can be any Web-accessible application, such as a Web page with dynamic content.

- A narrower definition of a Web service is an application that exposes a public interface usable by other applications over the Web.

- Sun's ONE requires a Web service to be accessible through HTTP and other Web protocols, to communicate using XML-based messages and to be registered with a lookup service.

- Web services can provide great interoperability between diverse systems. The interopability and scalability of Web services means developers can rapidly create large applications and larger Web services from small Web services.

- Sun's Open Net Environment describes an architecture for creating *smart Web services*. According to Sun, smart Web services share a common operating environment with other services.

- SOAP is an HTTP–XML-based protocol that allows applications to communicate over the Internet, using XML documents called SOAP messages.

- SOAP is both platform and software independent and can be implemented in any programming language. SOAP supports transport using almost any conceivable protocol.

- A SOAP message contains an envelope, which describes the content, intended recipient and processing requirements of a message. The optional **header** element of a SOAP message specifies additional processing information for applications that receive the SOAP message.

- Through the header, more complex protocols can be built onto SOAP. The body of a SOAP message contains application-specific data for the intended recipient of the message.

- SOAP can be used to make a Remote Procedure Call (RPC), which is a request made to another machine to run a task. The RPC uses an XML vocabulary to specify the method to be invoked, any parameters the method takes and the URI of the target object.

- Because businesses use different platforms, applications and data specifications, exchanging data can be difficult. Business partners therefore establish protocols and data formats to engage in electronic commerce.

TERMINOLOGY

application-to-application (A2A) integration
asynchronous RPC
Call class
deploying a service
distributed object architecture
Fault class
firewall
Hypertext Transfer Protocol (HTTP)
invoke method of class **Call**
loosely coupled messaging

messaging
org.apache.soap.rpc
Parameter class
Remote Procedure Call (RPC)
request–response
schema
setMethodName method of class **Call**
setParams method of class **Call**
Simple Object Access Protocol (SOAP)
Sun Open Net Environment

synchronous RPC
Universal Description, Discovery and
    Integration (UDDI)

Web services
XML-SOAP admin tool

SELF-REVIEW EXERCISES

29.1   State whether each of the following is *true* or *false*. If *false*, explain why.
   a)   SOAP is a technology for facilitating data transfer across a network.
   b)   SOAP must be bound to HTTP in order to work.
   c)   In order to communicate with SOAP, software systems must have the same distributed object architecture.
   d)   The body of a SOAP message can contain a Remote Procedure Call.

29.2   Fill in the blanks in each of the following statements:
   a)   A SOAP RPC requires the name of the method being called, its parameters and _____.
   b)   A SOAP _____ contains information that describes the content, recipient and processing requirements of a SOAP message.
   c)   SOAP can pass through most firewalls because _____ is its transport mechanism.
   d)   SOAP RPCs use the HTTP _____ model.

ANSWERS TO SELF-REVIEW EXERCISES

29.1   a) True. b) False. SOAP can be bound to other protocols. c) False. SOAP is platform independent. d) True.

29.2   a) the processing requirements of the message. b) envelope. c) HTTP. d) request–response.

EXERCISES

29.3   Write a server-side class with a **sort** method that can sort given numbers. Write a client-side program that can make SOAP RPC invoke the **sort** method by sending a set of unsorted numbers. Display the results of sorting on the client.

29.4   Rewrite class **WeatherServiceClient** to update its information at a user-defined interval. Change the settings of Tomcat to make the **WeatherService** object persistent. This make the updates more efficient.

29.5   Write a client and server with a similar architecture to the weather service, but that obtains pricing information from a price-comparison site, such as **shopper.cnet.com**.

29.6   Write a server-side class that stores and retrieves **String**s. Deploy the class so it is persistent on the server. Then write a client that stores and retrieves **String**s from the server.

29.7   Write a simple peer-to-peer instant-messaging service. Write a server class with a method that opens a window with a text message when it is called by a client. The client allows the user to enter a text message and call the method on the server class to display the message on the other machine.

WORKS CITED

1.   D. Savarese, "ONEWeb to Rule Them ALL." Java Pro August 2001: p. 58.

Creating Markup with XML

Objectives

- To create custom markup using XML.
- To understand the concept of an XML parser.
- To use elements and attributes to mark up data.
- To understand the difference between markup text and character data.
- To understand the concept of a well-formed XML document.
- To understand the concept of an XML namespace.
- To be able to use **CDATA** sections and processing instructions.

Appendix A is included on the CD that accompanies this book in printable Adobe® Acrobat® PDF format. The appendix includes pages 1611–1626.

Document Type Definition (DTD)

Objectives

- To understand what a DTD is.
- To be able to write DTDs.
- To be able to declare elements and attributes in a DTD.
- To understand the difference between general entities and parameter entities.
- To be able to use conditional sections with entities.
- To be able to use **NOTATION**s.
- To understand how an XML document's whitespace is processed.

Appendix B is included on the CD that accompanies this book in printable Adobe® Acrobat® PDF format. The appendix includes pages 1627–1651.

Document Object Model (DOM™)

Objectives

- To understand what the Document Object Model is.
- To understand and be able to use the major DOM features.
- To use Java to manipulate an XML document.
- To become familiar with DOM-based parsers.

Appendix C is included on the CD that accompanies this book in printable Adobe® Acrobat® PDF format. The appendix includes pages 1652–1675.

XSL: Extensible Stylesheet Language Transformations (XSLT)

Objectives

- To understand what the Extensible Stylesheet Language is and how it relates to XML.
- To understand what an Extensible Stylesheet Language Transformation (XSLT) is.
- To be able to write XSLT documents.
- To be able to write templates.
- To be able to iterate through a node set.
- To be able to sort.
- To be able to perform conditional processing.
- To be able to declare variables.

Appendix D is included on the CD that accompanies this book in printable Adobe® Acrobat® PDF format. The appendix includes pages 1676–1698.

E

Downloading and Installing J2EE 1.2.1

Appendix E is included on the CD that accompanies this book in printable Adobe® Acrobat® PDF format. The appendix includes pages 1699–1700.

Java Community
Process^{SM} (JCP)

Appendix F is included on the CD that accompanies this book in printable Adobe® Acrobat® PDF format. The appendix includes pages 1701–1704.

Java Native Interface (JNI)

Objectives

- To become familiar with basic JNI concepts.
- To create simple JNI applications.
- To convert C++ and JNI types.
- To learn how to interact with Java objects natively.
- To learn native exception handling.

Appendix G is included on the CD that accompanies this book in printable Adobe® Acrobat® PDF format. The appendix includes pages 1705–1737.

Career Opportunities

Objectives

- To explore the various online career services.
- To examine the advantages and disadvantages of posting and finding jobs online.
- To review the major online career services Web sites available to job seekers.
- To explore the various online services available to employers seeking to build their workforces.

Appendix H is included on the CD that accompanies this book in printable Adobe® Acrobat® PDF format. The appendix includes pages 1738–1761.

Unicode®

Objectives

- To become familiar with Unicode.
- To discuss the mission of the Unicode Consortium.
- To discuss the design basis of Unicode.
- To understand the three Unicode encoding forms: UTF-8, UTF-16 and UTF-32.
- To introduce characters and glyphs.
- To discuss the advantages and disadvantages of using Unicode.
- To provide a brief tour of the Unicode Consortium's Web site.

Appendix I is included on the CD that accompanies this book in printable Adobe® Acrobat® PDF format. The appendix includes pages 1762–1773.

Index

End User License Agreements

SUN MICROSYSTEMS, INC.
BINARY CODE LICENSE AGREEMENT

READ THE TERMS OF THIS AGREEMENT AND ANY PROVIDED SUPPLEMENTAL LICENSE TERMS (COLLECTIVELY "AGREEMENT") CAREFULLY BEFORE OPENING THE SOFTWARE MEDIA PACKAGE. BY OPENING THE SOFTWARE MEDIA PACKAGE, YOU AGREE TO THE TERMS OF THIS AGREEMENT. IF YOU ARE ACCESSING THE SOFTWARE ELECTRONICALLY, INDICATE YOUR ACCEPTANCE OF THESE TERMS BY SELECTING THE "ACCEPT" BUTTON AT THE END OF THIS AGREEMENT. IF YOU DO NOT AGREE TO ALL THESE TERMS, PROMPTLY RETURN THE UNUSED SOFTWARE TO YOUR PLACE OF PURCHASE FOR A REFUND OR, IF THE SOFTWARE IS ACCESSED ELECTRONICALLY, SELECT THE "DECLINE" BUTTON AT THE END OF THIS AGREEMENT.

1. LICENSE TO USE. Sun grants you a non-exclusive and non-transferable license for the internal use only of the accompanying software and documentation and any error corrections provided by Sun (collectively "Software"), by the number of users and the class of computer hardware for which the corresponding fee has been paid.

2. RESTRICTIONS. Software is confidential and copyrighted. Title to Software and all associated intellectual property rights is retained by Sun and/or its licensors. Except as specifically authorized in any Supplemental License Terms, you may not make copies of Software, other than a single copy of Software for archival purposes. Unless enforcement is prohibited by applicable law, you may not modify, decompile, or reverse engineer Software. You acknowledge that Software is not designed, licensed or intended for use in the design, construction, operation or maintenance of any nuclear facility. Sun disclaims any express or implied warranty of fitness for such uses. No right, title or interest in or to any trademark, service mark, logo or trade name of Sun or its licensors is granted under this Agreement.

3. LIMITED WARRANTY. Sun warrants to you that for a period of ninety (90) days from the date of purchase, as evidenced by a copy of the receipt, the media on which Software is furnished (if any) will be free of defects in materials and workmanship under normal use. Except for the foregoing, Software is provided "AS IS". Your exclusive remedy and Sun's entire liability under this limited warranty will be at Sun's option to replace Software media or refund the fee paid for Software.

4. DISCLAIMER OF WARRANTY. UNLESS SPECIFIED IN THIS AGREEMENT, ALL EXPRESS OR IMPLIED CONDITIONS, REPRESENTATIONS AND WARRANTIES, INCLUDING ANY IMPLIED WARRANTY OF MERCHANTABILITY, FITNESS FOR A PARTICULAR PURPOSE OR NON-INFRINGEMENT ARE DISCLAIMED, EXCEPT TO THE EXTENT THAT THESE DISCLAIMERS ARE HELD TO BE LEGALLY INVALID.

5. LIMITATION OF LIABILITY. TO THE EXTENT NOT PROHIBITED BY LAW, IN NO EVENT WILL SUN OR ITS LICENSORS BE LIABLE FOR ANY LOST REVENUE, PROFIT OR DATA, OR FOR SPECIAL, INDIRECT, CONSEQUENTIAL, INCIDENTAL OR PUNITIVE DAMAGES, HOWEVER CAUSED REGARDLESS OF THE THEORY OF LIABILITY, ARISING OUT OF OR RELATED TO THE USE OF OR INABILITY TO USE SOFTWARE, EVEN IF SUN HAS BEEN ADVISED OF THE POSSIBILITY OF SUCH DAMAGES. In no event will Sun's liability to you, whether in contract, tort (including negligence), or otherwise, exceed the amount paid by you for Software under this Agreement. The foregoing limitations will apply even if the above stated warranty fails of its essential purpose.

6. Termination. This Agreement is effective until terminated. You may terminate this Agreement at any time by destroying all copies of Software. This Agreement will terminate immediately without notice from Sun if you fail to comply with any provision of this Agreement. Upon Termination, you must destroy all copies of Software.

7. Export Regulations. All Software and technical data delivered under this Agreement are subject to US export control laws and may be subject to export or import regulations in other countries. You agree to comply strictly with all such laws and regulations and acknowledge that you have the responsibility to obtain such licenses to export, re-export, or import as may be required after delivery to you.

8. U.S. Government Restricted Rights. If Software is being acquired by or on behalf of the U.S. Government or by a U.S. Government prime contractor or subcontractor (at any tier), then the Government's rights in Software and accompanying documentation will be only as set forth in this Agreement; this is in accordance with 48 CFR 227.7201 through 227.7202-4 (for Department of Defense (DOD) acquisitions) and with 48 CFR 2.101 and 12.212 (for non-DOD acquisitions).

9. Governing Law. Any action related to this Agreement will be governed by California law and controlling U.S. federal law. No choice of law rules of any jurisdiction will apply.

10. Severability. If any provision of this Agreement is held to be unenforceable, this Agreement will remain in effect with the provision omitted, unless omission would frustrate the intent of the parties, in which case this Agreement will immediately terminate.

11. Integration. This Agreement is the entire agreement between you and Sun relating to its subject matter. It supersedes all prior or contemporaneous oral or written communications, proposals, representations and warranties and prevails over any conflicting or additional terms of any quote, order, acknowledgment, or other communication between the parties relating to its subject matter during the term of this Agreement. No modification of this Agreement will be binding, unless in writing and signed by an authorized representative of each party.

JAVA™ 2 SOFTWARE DEVELOPMENT KIT (J2SDK), STANDARD EDITION, VERSION 1.3 SUPPLEMENTAL LICENSE TERMS

These supplemental license terms ("Supplemental Terms") add to or modify the terms of the Binary Code License Agreement (collectively, the "Agreement"). Capitalized terms not defined in these Supplemental Terms shall have the same meanings ascribed to them in the Agreement. These Supplemental Terms shall supersede any inconsistent or conflicting terms in the Agreement, or in any license contained within the Software.

1. Software Internal Use and Development License Grant. Subject to the terms and conditions of this Agreement, including, but not limited to Section 4 (Java™ Technology Restrictions) of these Supplemental Terms, Sun grants you a non-exclusive, non-transferable, limited license to reproduce internally and use internally the binary form of the Software complete and unmodified for the sole purpose of designing, developing and testing your Java applets and applications intended to run on the Java platform ("Programs").

2. License to Distribute Software. Subject to the terms and conditions of this Agreement, including, but not limited to Section 4 (Java ™ Technology Restrictions) of these Supplemental Terms, Sun grants you a non-exclusive, non-transferable, limited license to reproduce and distribute the Software in binary code form only, provided that (i) you distribute the Software complete and unmodified and only bundled as part of, and for the sole purpose of running, your Programs, (ii) the Programs add significant and primary functionality to the Software, (iii) you do not distribute additional software intended to replace any component(s) of the Software, (iv) you do not remove or alter any proprietary legends or notices contained in the Software, (v) you only distribute the Software subject to a license agreement that protects Sun's interests consistent with the terms

contained in this Agreement, and (vi) you agree to defend and indemnify Sun and its licensors from and against any damages, costs, liabilities, settlement amounts and/or expenses (including attorneys' fees) incurred in connection with any claim, lawsuit or action by any third party that arises or results from the use or distribution of any and all Programs and/or Software.

3. License to Distribute Redistributables. Subject to the terms and conditions of this Agreement, including but not limited to Section 4 (Java Technology Restrictions) of these Supplemental Terms, Sun grants you a non-exclusive, non-transferable, limited license to reproduce and distribute the binary form of those files specifically identified as redistributable in the Software "README" file ("Redistributables") provided that: (i) you distribute the Redistributables complete and unmodified (unless otherwise specified in the applicable README file), and only bundled as part of Programs, (ii) you do not distribute additional software intended to supersede any component(s) of the Redistributables, (iii) you do not remove or alter any proprietary legends or notices contained in or on the Redistributables, (iv) you only distribute the Redistributables pursuant to a license agreement that protects Sun's interests consistent with the terms contained in the Agreement, and (v) you agree to defend and indemnify Sun and its licensors from and against any damages, costs, liabilities, settlement amounts and/or expenses (including attorneys' fees) incurred in connection with any claim, lawsuit or action by any third party that arises or results from the use or distribution of any and all Programs and/or Software.

4. Java Technology Restrictions. You may not modify the Java Platform Interface ("JPI", identified as classes contained within the "java" package or any subpackages of the "java" package), by creating additional classes within the JPI or otherwise causing the addition to or modification of the classes in the JPI. In the event that you create an additional class and associated API(s) which (i) extends the functionality of the Java platform, and (ii) is exposed to third party software developers for the purpose of developing additional software which invokes such additional API, you must promptly publish broadly an accurate specification for such API for free use by all developers. You may not create, or authorize your licensees to create, additional classes, interfaces, or subpackages that are in any way identified as "java", "javax", "sun" or similar convention as specified by Sun in any naming convention designation.

5. Trademarks and Logos. You acknowledge and agree as between you and Sun that Sun owns the SUN, SOLARIS, JAVA, JINI, FORTE, STAROFFICE, STARPORTAL and iPLANET trademarks and all SUN, SOLARIS, JAVA, JINI, FORTE, STAROFFICE, STARPORTAL and iPLANET-related trademarks, service marks, logos and other brand designations ("Sun Marks"), and you agree to comply with the Sun Trademark and Logo Usage Requirements currently located at http://www.sun.com/policies/trademarks. Any use you make of the Sun Marks inures to Sun's benefit.

6. Source Code. Software may contain source code that is provided solely for reference purposes pursuant to the terms of this Agreement. Source code may not be redistributed unless expressly provided for in this Agreement.

7. Termination for Infringement. Either party may terminate this Agreement immediately should any Software become, or in either party's opinion be likely to become, the subject of a claim of infringement of any intellectual property right.

For inquiries please contact: Sun Microsystems, Inc. 901 San Antonio Road, Palo Alto, California 94303 (LFI#83838/Form ID#011801)

JAVA™ MEDIA FRAMEWORK (JMF) 2.1.1 BINARY CODE LICENSE AGREEMENT

READ THE TERMS OF THIS AGREEMENT AND ANY PROVIDED SUPPLEMENTAL LICENSE TERMS (COLLECTIVELY "AGREEMENT") CAREFULLY BEFORE OPENING THE SOFTWARE MEDIA PACKAGE. BY OPENING THE SOFTWARE MEDIA PACKAGE, YOU AGREE TO THE TERMS OF THIS AGREEMENT. IF YOU ARE ACCESSING THE SOFTWARE ELECTRONICALLY, INDICATE YOUR ACCEPTANCE OF THESE TERMS BY SELECTING THE "ACCEPT" BUTTON AT THE END OF THIS AGREEMENT. IF YOU DO NOT AGREE TO ALL THESE TERMS, PROMPTLY RETURN THE UNUSED SOFTWARE TO YOUR PLACE OF PURCHASE FOR A REFUND OR, IF THE SOFTWARE IS ACCESSED ELECTRONICALLY, SELECT THE "DECLINE" BUTTON AT THE END OF THIS AGREEMENT.

1. License to Use. Sun Microsystems, Inc. ("Sun") grants you a non-exclusive and non-transferable license for the internal use only of the accompanying software and documentation and any error corrections provided by

Sun (collectively "Software"), by the number of users and the class of computer hardware for which the corresponding fee has been paid.

2.   Restrictions. Software is confidential and copyrighted. Title to Software and all associated intellectual property rights is retained by Sun and/or its licensors. Except as specifically authorized in any Supplemental License Terms, you may not make copies of Software, other than a single copy of Software for archival purposes. Unless enforcement is prohibited by applicable law, you may not modify, decompile, or reverse engineer Software. You acknowledge that Software is not designed or intended for use in the design, construction, operation or maintenance of any nuclear facility. Sun disclaims any express or implied warranty of fitness for such uses. No right, title or interest in or to any trademark, service mark, logo or trade name of Sun or its licensors is granted under this Agreement.

3.   Limited Warranty. Sun warrants to you that for a period of ninety (90) days from the date of purchase, as evidenced by a copy of the receipt, the media on which Software is furnished (if any) will be free of defects in materials and workmanship under normal use. Except for the foregoing, Software is provided "AS IS". Your exclusive remedy and Sun's entire liability under this limited warranty will be at Sun's option to replace Software media or refund the fee paid for Software.

4.   DISCLAIMER OF WARRANTY. UNLESS SPECIFIED IN THIS AGREEMENT, ALL EXPRESS OR IMPLIED CONDITIONS, REPRESENTATIONS AND WARRANTIES, INCLUDING ANY IMPLIED WARRANTY OF MERCHANTABILITY, FITNESS FOR A PARTICULAR PURPOSE OR NON-INFRINGEMENT ARE DISCLAIMED, EXCEPT TO THE EXTENT THAT THESE DISCLAIMERS ARE HELD TO BE LEGALLY INVALID.

5.   LIMITATION OF LIABILITY. TO THE EXTENT NOT PROHIBITED BY LAW, IN NO EVENT WILL SUN OR ITS LICENSORS BE LIABLE FOR ANY LOST REVENUE, PROFIT OR DATA, OR FOR SPECIAL, INDIRECT, CONSEQUENTIAL, INCIDENTAL OR PUNITIVE DAMAGES, HOWEVER CAUSED REGARDLESS OF THE THEORY OF LIABILITY, ARISING OUT OF OR RELATED TO THE USE OF OR INABILITY TO USE SOFTWARE, EVEN IF SUN HAS BEEN ADVISED OF THE POSSIBILITY OF SUCH DAMAGES. In no event will Sun's liability to you, whether in contract, tort (including negligence), or otherwise, exceed the amount paid by you for Software under this Agreement. The foregoing limitations will apply even if the above stated warranty fails of its essential purpose.

6.   Termination. This Agreement is effective until terminated. You may terminate this Agreement at any time by destroying all copies of Software. This Agreement will terminate immediately without notice from Sun if you fail to comply with any provision of this Agreement. Upon Termination, you must destroy all copies of Software.

7.   Export Regulations. All Software and technical data delivered under this Agreement are subject to US export control laws and may be subject to export or import regulations in other countries. You agree to comply strictly with all such laws and regulations and acknowledge that you have the responsibility to obtain such licenses to export, re-export, or import as may be required after delivery to you.

8.   U.S. Government Restricted Rights. If Software is being acquired by or on behalf of the U.S. Government or by a U.S. Government prime contractor or subcontractor (at any tier), then the Government's rights in Software and accompanying documentation will be only as set forth in this Agreement; this is in accordance with 48 C.F.R. 227.7202-4 (for Department of Defense (DOD) acquisitions) and with 48 CFR 2.101 and 12.212 (for non-DOD acquisitions).

9.   Governing Law. Any action related to this Agreement will be governed by California law and controlling U.S. federal law. No choice of law rules of any jurisdiction will apply.

10.   Severability. If any provision of this Agreement is held to be unenforceable, this Agreement will remain in effect with the provision omitted, unless omission would frustrate the intent of the parties, in which case this Agreement will immediately terminate.

11.   Integration. This Agreement is the entire agreement between you and Sun relating to its subject matter. It supersedes all prior or contemporaneous oral or written communications, proposals, representations and warranties and prevails over any conflicting or additional terms of any quote, order, acknowledgment, or other communication between the parties relating to its subject matter during the term of this Agreement. No modification of this Agreement will be binding, unless in writing and signed by an authorized representative of each party.

JAVA™ MEDIA FRAMEWORK (JMF) 2.1.1
SUPPLEMENTAL LICENSE TERMS

These supplemental license terms ("Supplemental Terms") add to or modify the terms of the Binary Code License Agreement (collectively, the "Agreement"). Capitalized terms not defined in these Supplemental Terms shall have the same meanings ascribed to them in the Agreement. These Supplemental Terms shall supersede any inconsistent or conflicting terms in the Agreement, or in any license contained within the Software.

1.   Software Internal Use and Development License Grant. Subject to the terms and conditions of this Agreement, including, but not limited to Section 3 (Java™ Technology Restrictions) of these Supplemental Terms, Sun grants you a non-exclusive, non-transferable, limited license to reproduce internally and use internally the binary form of the Software, complete and unmodified, for the sole purpose of designing, developing and testing your Java applets and applications ("Programs").

2.   License to Distribute Software. In addition to the license granted in Section 1 (Software Internal Use and Development License Grant) of these Supplemental Terms, subject to the terms and conditions of this Agreement, including but not limited to, Section 3 (Java™ Technology Restrictions) of these Supplemental Terms, Sun grants you a non-exclusive, non-transferable, limited license to reproduce and distribute the Software in binary code form only, provided that you:

   i.   distribute the Software complete and unmodified, except that you may omit those files specifically identified as "optional" in the Software "README" file, which include samples, documents, and bin files, or that are removable by using the Software customizer tool provided, only as part of and for the sole purpose of running your Program into which the Software is incorporated;

   ii.   do not distribute additional software intended to replace any components of the Software;

   iii.   do not remove or alter any proprietary legends or notices contained in the Software;

   iv.   only distribute the Software subject to a license agreement that protects Sun's interests consistent with the terms contained in this Agreement; and

   v.   agree to defend and indemnify Sun and its licensors from and against any damages, costs, liabilities, settlement amounts or expenses, including attorneys' fees, incurred in connection with any claim, lawsuit or action by any third party that arises or results from the use or distribution of any and all Programs or Software.

3.   Java™ Technology Restrictions. You may not modify the Java Platform Interface ("JPI", identified as classes contained within the "java" package or any subpackages of the "java" package), by creating additional classes within the JPI or otherwise causing the addition to or modification of the classes in the JPI. In the event that you create an additional class and associated API's, which:

   i.   extends the functionality of the Java platform, and

   ii.   is exposed to third party software developers for the purpose of developing additional software which invokes such additional API, you must promptly publish broadly an accurate specification for such API for free use by all developers. You may not create, or authorize your licensees to create additional classes, interfaces, packages or subpackages that are in any way identified as "java", "javax", "sun" or similar convention as specified by Sun in any class file naming convention designation.

4.   Java™ Runtime Availability. Refer to the appropriate version of the Java™ Runtime Environment binary code license (currently located at http://www.java.sun.com/jdk/index.html) for the availability of runtime code which may be distributed with Java™ applets and applications.

5.   Trademarks and Logos. You acknowledge and agree as between you and Sun that Sun owns the SUN, SOLARIS, JAVA, JINI, FORTE, STAROFFICE, STARPORTAL and iPLANET trademarks and all SUN, SOLARIS, JAVA, JINI, FORTE, STAROFFICE, STARPORTAL and IPLANET-related trademarks, service marks, logos and other brand designations ("Sun Marks"), and you agree to comply with the Sun Trademark and Logo Usage Requirements currently located at http://www.sun.com/policies/trademarks. Any use you make of the Sun Marks inures to Sun's benefit.

6.   Source Code. Software may contain source code that is provided solely for reference purposes pursuant to the terms of this Agreement. Source code may not be redistributed unless expressly provided for in this Agreement.

7.   Termination for Infringement. Either party may terminate this Agreement immediately should any Software become, or in either party's opinion be likely to become, the subject of a claim of infringement of any intellectual property right.

For inquiries please contact: Sun Microsystems, Inc. 901 San Antonio Road, Palo Alto, California 94303 LFI# 81806/Form ID#011801 01/23/2001

JAVA™ PLUG-IN HTML CONVERTER, VERSION 1.3 BINARY CODE LICENSE

SUN MICROSYSTEMS, INC., THROUGH JAVASOFT ("SUN") IS WILLING TO LICENSE THE JAVA™ PLUG-IN HTML CONVERTER AND THE ACCOMPANYING DOCUMENTATION INCLUDING AUTHORIZED COPIES OF EACH (THE "SOFTWARE") TO LICENSEE ONLY ON THE CONDITION THAT LICENSEE ACCEPTS ALL OF THE TERMS IN THIS AGREEMENT.

PLEASE READ THE TERMS CAREFULLY BEFORE CLICKING ON THE "ACCEPT" BUTTON. BY CLICKING ON THE "ACCEPT" BUTTON, LICENSEE ACKNOWLEDGES THAT LICENSEE HAS READ AND UNDERSTANDS THIS AGREEMENT AND AGREES TO BE BOUND BY ITS TERMS AND CONDITIONS.

IF LICENSEE DOES NOT ACCEPT THESE LICENSE TERMS, SUN DOES NOT GRANT ANY LICENSE TO THE SOFTWARE, AND LICENSEE SHOULD CLICK ON THE "REJECT" BUTTON TO EXIT THIS PAGE.

1. LICENSE GRANT

(A) License To Use

Licensee is granted a non-exclusive and non-transferable no fee license to download, install and internally use the binary Software. Licensee may copy the Software, provided that Licensee reproduces all copyright and other proprietary notices that are on the original copy of the Software.

(B) License to Distribute

Licensee is granted a royalty-free right to reproduce and distribute the Software provided that Licensee: (i) distributes Software complete and unmodified only as part of Licensee's value-added applet or application ("Program"), and for the sole purpose of allowing customers of Licensee to modify HTML pages to access Sun's Java™ Plug-in technology; (ii) does not distribute additional software intended to replace any component(s) of the Software; (iii) agrees to incorporate the most current version of the Software that was available 180 days prior to each production release of the Program; (iv) does not remove or alter any proprietary legends or notices contained in the Software; (v) includes the provisions of Sections 1(C), 1(D), 5, 7, 8, 9 in Licensee's license agreement for the Program; (vi) agrees to indemnify, hold harmless, and defend Sun and its licensors from and against any claims or lawsuits, including attorneys' fees, that arise or result from the use or distribution of the Program.

(C) Java Platform Interface

Licensee may not modify the Java Platform Interface ("JPI", identified as classes contained within the "java" package or any subpackage of the "java" package), by creating additional classes within the JPI or otherwise causing the addition to or modification of the classes in the JPI. In the event that Licensee creates any Java-related API and distributes such API to others for applet or application development, Licensee must promptly publish broadly, an accurate specification for such API for free use by all developers of Java-based software.

(D) License Restrictions

The Software is licensed to Licensee only under the terms of this Agreement, and Sun reserves all rights not expressly granted to Licensee. Licensee may not use, copy, modify, or transfer the Software, or any copy thereof, except as expressly provided for in this Agreement. Except as otherwise provided by law for purposes of decompilation of the Software solely for interoperability, Licensee may not reverse engineer, disassemble, decompile, or translate the Software, or otherwise attempt to derive the source code of the Software. Licensee may not rent, lease, loan, sell, or distribute the Software, or any part of the Software. No right, title, or interest in or to any trademarks, service marks, or trade names of Sun or Sun's licensors is granted hereunder.

(E) Aircraft Product and Nuclear Applications Restriction

SOFTWARE IS NOT DESIGNED OR INTENDED FOR USE IN ON-LINE CONTROL OF AIRCRAFT, AIR TRAFFIC, AIRCRAFT NAVIGATION OR AIRCRAFT COMMUNICATIONS; OR IN THE DESIGN, CONSTRUCTION, OPERATION OR MAINTENANCE OF ANY NUCLEAR FACILITY. SUN DISCLAIMS ANY EXPRESS OR IMPLIED WARRANTY OF FITNESS FOR SUCH USES. LICENSEE REPRESENTS AND WARRANTS THAT IT WILL NOT USE THE SOFTWARE FOR SUCH PURPOSES.

2. CONFIDENTIALITY

The Software is the confidential and proprietary information of Sun and/or its licensors. The Software is protected by United States copyright law and international treaty. Unauthorized reproduction or distribution is subject to civil and criminal penalties. Licensee agrees to take adequate steps to protect the Software from unauthorized disclosure or use.

3. TRADEMARKS AND LOGOS

This Agreement does not authorize Licensee to use any Sun name, trademark, or logo. Licensee acknowledges that Sun owns the Java trademark and all Java-related trademarks, logos and icons including the Coffee Cup and Duke ("Java Marks") and agrees to: (i) comply with the Java Trademark Guidelines at http://java.sun.com/trademarks.html; (ii) not do anything harmful to or inconsistent with Sun's rights in the Java Marks; and (iii) assist Sun in protecting those rights, including assigning to Sun any rights acquired by Licensee in any Java Mark.

4. TERM, TERMINATION AND SURVIVAL

(A) The Agreement shall automatically terminate 180 days after production release of the next version of the Software by Sun.

(B) Licensee may terminate this Agreement at any time by destroying all copies of the Software.

(C) This Agreement will immediately terminate without notice if Licensee fails to comply with any obligation of this Agreement.

(D) Upon termination, Licensee must immediately cease use of and destroy the Software or, upon request from Sun, return the Software to Sun.

(E) The provisions set forth in paragraphs 1 (D), 2, 5, 7, 8, 9, and 10 will survive termination or expiration of this Agreement.

5. NO WARRANTY

THE SOFTWARE IS PROVIDED TO LICENSEE "AS IS". ALL EXPRESS OR IMPLIED CONDITIONS, REPRESENTATIONS, AND WARRANTIES, INCLUDING ANY IMPLIED WARRANTY OF MERCHANTABILITY, SATISFACTORY QUALITY, FITNESS FOR A PARTICULAR PURPOSE, OR NON-INFRINGEMENT, ARE DISCLAIMED, EXCEPT TO THE EXTENT THAT SUCH DISCLAIMERS ARE HELD TO BE LEGALLY INVALID.

6. MAINTENANCE AND SUPPORT

Sun has no obligation to provide maintenance or support for the Software under this Agreement.

7. LIMITATION OF DAMAGES

TO THE EXTENT NOT PROHIBITED BY APPLICABLE LAW, SUN'S AGGREGATE LIABILITY TO LICENSEE OR TO ANY THIRD PARTY FOR CLAIMS RELATING TO THIS AGREEMENT, WHETHER FOR BREACH OR IN TORT, WILL BE LIMITED TO THE FEES PAID BY LICENSEE FOR SOFTWARE WHICH IS THE SUBJECT MATTER OF THE CLAIMS. IN NO EVENT WILL SUN BE LIABLE FOR ANY INDIRECT, PUNITIVE, SPECIAL, INCIDENTAL OR CONSEQUENTIAL DAMAGE IN CONNECTION WITH OR ARISING OUT OF THIS AGREEMENT (INCLUDING LOSS OF BUSINESS, REVENUE, PROFITS, USE, DATA OR OTHER ECONOMIC ADVANTAGE), HOWEVER IT ARISES, WHETHER FOR BREACH OR IN TORT, EVEN IF SUN HAS BEEN PREVIOUSLY ADVISED OF THE POSSIBILITY OF SUCH DAMAGE. LIABILITY FOR DAMAGES WILL BE LIMITED AND EXCLUDED, EVEN IF ANY EXCLUSIVE REMEDY PROVIDED FOR IN THIS AGREEMENT FAILS OF ITS ESSENTIAL PURPOSE.

8. GOVERNMENT USER

Rights in Data: If procured by, or provided to, the U.S. Government, use, duplication, or disclosure of technical data is subject to restrictions as set forth in FAR 52.227-14(g)(2), Rights in Data-General (June 1987); and for computer software and computer software documentation, FAR 52-227-19, Commercial Computer Software-Restricted Rights (June 1987). However, if under DOD, use, duplication, or disclosure of technical data is subject to DFARS 252.227-7015(b), Technical Data-Commercial Items (June 1995); and for computer software and computer software documentation, as specified in the license under which the computer software was procured pursuant to DFARS 227.7202- 3(a). Licensee shall not provide Software nor technical data to any third party, including the U.S. Government, unless such third party accepts the same restrictions. Licensee is responsible for ensuring that proper notice is given to all such third parties and that the Software and technical data are properly marked.

9. EXPORT LAW

Licensee acknowledges and agrees that this Software and/or technology is subject to the U.S. Export Administration Laws and Regulations. Diversion of such Software and/or technology contrary to U.S. law is prohibited. Licensee agrees that none of this Software and/or technology, nor any direct product therefrom, is being or will be acquired for, shipped, transferred, or reexported, directly or indirectly, to proscribed or embargoed countries or their nationals, nor be used for nuclear activities, chemical biological weapons, or missile projects unless authorized by the U.S. Government. Proscribed countries are set forth in the U.S. Export Administration Regulations. Countries subject to U.S. embargo are: Cuba, Iran, Iraq, Libya, North Korea, Syria, and the Sudan. This list is subject to change without further notice from Sun, and Licensee must comply with the list as it exists in fact. Licensee certifies that it is not on the U.S. Department of Commerce's Denied Persons List or affiliated lists or on the U.S. Department of Treasury's Specially Designated Nationals List. Licensee agrees to comply strictly with all U.S. export laws and assumes sole responsibility for obtaining licenses to export or reexport as may be required.

Licensee is responsible for complying with any applicable local laws and regulations, including but not limited to, the export and import laws and regulations of other countries.

10. GOVERNING LAW, JURISDICTION AND VENUE

Any action related to this Agreement shall be governed by California law and controlling U.S. federal law, and choice of law rules of any jurisdiction shall not apply. The parties agree that any action shall be brought in the United States District Court for the Northern District of California or the California superior Court for the County of Santa Clara, as applicable, and the parties hereby submit exclusively to the personal jurisdiction and venue of the United States District Court for the Northern District of California and the California Superior Court of the county of Santa Clara.

11. NO ASSIGNMENT

Neither party may assign or otherwise transfer any of its rights or obligations under this Agreement, without the prior written consent of the other party, except that Sun may assign its right to payment and may assign this Agreement to an affiliated company.

12. OFFICIAL LANGUAGE

The official text of this Agreement is in the English language and any interpretation or construction of this Agreement will be based thereon. In the event that this Agreement or any documents or notices related to it are translated into any other language, the English language version will control.

13. ENTIRE AGREEMENT

This Agreement is the parties' entire agreement relating to the Software. It supersedes all prior or contemporaneous oral or written communications, proposals, warranties, and representations with respect to its subject matter, and following Licensee's acceptance of this license by clicking on the "Accept" Button, will prevail over any conflicting or additional terms of any subsequent quote, order, acknowledgment, or any other communications by or between the parties. No modification to this Agreement will be binding, unless in writing and signed by an authorized representative of each party.

FORTE™ FOR JAVA™ RELEASE 2.0, COMMUNITY EDITION LICENSE

Copyright 2000 Sun Microsystems, Inc., 901 San Antonio Road Palo Alto, California 94043, U.S.A. All rights reserved.

This product or document is protected by copyright and distributed under licenses restricting its use, copying, distribution, and decompilation. No part of this product or related documentation may be reproduced in any form by any means without prior written authorization of Sun and its licensors, if any.

Third party software, including font technology, is copyrighted and licensed from Sun suppliers.

This product includes software developed by the Apache Software Foundation (http://www.apache.org/).

Sun, Sun Microsystems, the Sun logo, Java, Forte, NetBeans, Solaris, iPlanet, StarOffice, StarPortal, Jini, Jiro are trademarked or registered trademarks of Sun Microsystems, Inc. in the U.S. and other countries.

Federal Acquisitions: Commercial Software--Government Users Subject to Standard License Terms and Conditions.

IBM WEBSPHERE APPLICATION SERVER V4.0 (EVALUATION COPY) LICENSE AGREEMENT
INTERNATIONAL LICENSE AGREEMENT FOR EVALUATION OF PROGRAMS

Part 1 - General Terms

PLEASE READ THIS AGREEMENT CAREFULLY BEFORE USING THE PROGRAM. IBM WILL LICENSE THE PROGRAM TO YOU ONLY IF YOU FIRST ACCEPT THE TERMS OF THIS AGREEMENT. BY USING THE PROGRAM YOU AGREE TO THESE TERMS. IF YOU DO NOT AGREE

TO THE TERMS OF THIS AGREEMENT, PROMPTLY RETURN THE UNUSED PROGRAM TO IBM.

The Program is owned by International Business Machines Corporation or one of its subsidiaries (IBM) or an IBM supplier, and is copyrighted and licensed, not sold.

The term "Program" means the original program and all whole or partial copies of it. A Program consists of machine-readable instructions, its components, data, audio-visual content (such as images, text, recordings, or pictures), and related licensed materials.

This Agreement includes Part 1 - General Terms and Part 2 - Country-unique Terms and is the complete agreement regarding the use of this Program, and replaces any prior oral or written communications between you and IBM. The terms of Part 2 may replace or modify those of Part 1.

1. License

Use of the Program

IBM grants you a nonexclusive, nontransferable license to use the Program.

You may 1) use the Program only for internal evaluation, testing or demonstration purposes, on a trial or "try-and-buy" basis and 2) make and install a reasonable number of copies of the Program in support of such use, unless IBM identifies a specific number of copies in the documentation accompanying the Program. The terms of this license apply to each copy you make. You will reproduce the copyright notice and any other legends of ownership on each copy, or partial copy, of the Program.

THE PROGRAM MAY CONTAIN A DISABLING DEVICE THAT WILL PREVENT IT FROM BEING USED UPON EXPIRATION OF THIS LICENSE. YOU WILL NOT TAMPER WITH THIS DISABLING DEVICE OR THE PROGRAM. YOU SHOULD TAKE PRECAUTIONS TO AVOID ANY LOSS OF DATA THAT MIGHT RESULT WHEN THE PROGRAM CAN NO LONGER BE USED.

You will 1) maintain a record of all copies of the Program and 2) ensure that anyone who uses the Program does so only for your authorized use and in compliance with the terms of this Agreement.

You may not 1) use, copy, modify or distribute the Program except as provided in this Agreement; 2) reverse assemble, reverse compile, or otherwise translate the Program except as specifically permitted by law without the possibility of contractual waiver; or 3) sublicense, rent, or lease the Program.

This license begins with your first use of the Program and ends 1) as of the duration or date specified in the documentation accompanying the Program or 2) when the Program automatically disables itself. Unless IBM specifies in the documentation accompanying the Program that you may retain the Program (in which case, an additional charge may apply), you will destroy the Program and all copies made of it within ten days of when this license ends.

2. No Warranty

SUBJECT TO ANY STATUTORY WARRANTIES WHICH CANNOT BE EXCLUDED, IBM MAKES NO WARRANTIES OR CONDITIONS EITHER EXPRESS OR IMPLIED, INCLUDING WITHOUT LIMITATION, THE WARRANTY OF NON-INFRINGEMENT AND THE IMPLIED WARRANTIES OF MERCHANTABILITY AND FITNESS FOR A PARTICULAR PURPOSE, REGARDING THE PROGRAM OR TECHNICAL SUPPORT, IF ANY. IBM MAKES NO WARRANTY REGARDING THE CAPABILITY OF THE PROGRAM TO CORRECTLY PROCESS, PROVIDE AND/OR RECEIVE DATE DATA WITHIN AND BETWEEN THE 20TH AND 21ST CENTURIES.

This exclusion also applies to any of IBM's subcontractors, suppliers or program developers (collectively called "Suppliers").

Manufacturers, suppliers, or publishers of non-IBM Programs may provide their own warranties.

3. Limitation of Liability

NEITHER IBM NOR ITS SUPPLIERS ARE LIABLE FOR ANY DIRECT OR INDIRECT DAMAGES, INCLUDING WITHOUT LIMITATION, LOST PROFITS, LOST SAVINGS, OR ANY INCIDENTAL, SPECIAL, OR OTHER ECONOMIC CONSEQUENTIAL DAMAGES, EVEN IF IBM IS INFORMED OF THEIR POSSIBILITY. SOME JURISDICTIONS DO NOT ALLOW THE EXCLUSION OR LIMITATION OF INCIDENTAL OR CONSEQUENTIAL DAMAGES, SO THE ABOVE EXCLUSION OR LIMITATION MAY NOT APPLY TO YOU.

4. General

Nothing in this Agreement affects any statutory rights of consumers that cannot be waived or limited by contract.

IBM may terminate your license if you fail to comply with the terms of this Agreement. If IBM does so, you must immediately destroy the Program and all copies you made of it.

You may not export the Program.

Neither you nor IBM will bring a legal action under this Agreement more than two years after the cause of action arose unless otherwise provided by local law without the possibility of contractual waiver or limitation. Neither you nor IBM is responsible for failure to fulfill any obligations due to causes beyond its control. There is no additional charge for use of the Program for the duration of this license.

IBM does not provide program services or technical support, unless IBM specifies otherwise.

The laws of the country in which you acquire the Program govern this Agreement, except 1) in Australia, the laws of the State or Territory in which the transaction is performed govern this Agreement; 2) in Albania, Armenia, Belarus, Bosnia/Herzegovina, Bulgaria, Croatia, Czech Republic, Georgia, Hungary, Kazakhstan, Kirghizia, Former Yugoslav Republic of Macedonia (FYROM), Moldova, Poland, Romania, Russia, Slovak Republic, Slovenia, Ukraine, and Federal Republic of Yugoslavia, the laws of Austria govern this Agreement; 3) in the United Kingdom, all disputes relating to this Agreement will be governed by English Law and will be submitted to the exclusive jurisdiction of the English courts; 4) in Canada, the laws in the Province of Ontario govern this Agreement; and 5) in the United States and Puerto Rico, and People's Republic of China, the laws of the State of New York govern this Agreement.

Part 2 - Country-unique Terms

AUSTRALIA:

No Warranty (Section 2):

The following paragraph is added to this Section:

Although IBM specifies that there are no warranties, you may have certain rights under the Trade Practices Act 1974 or other legislation and are only limited to the extent permitted by the applicable legislation.

Limitation of Liability (Section 3):

The following paragraph is added to this Section:

Where IBM is in breach of a condition or warranty implied by the Trade Practices Act 1974, IBM's liability is limited to the repair or replacement of the goods, or the supply of equivalent goods. Where that condition or warranty relates to right to sell, quiet possession or clear title, or the goods are of a kind ordinarily acquired for personal, domestic or household use or consumption, then none of the limitations in this paragraph apply.

GERMANY:

No Warranty (Section 2):

The following paragraphs are added to this Section:

The minimum warranty period for Programs is six months.

In case a Program is delivered without Specifications, we will only warrant that the Program information correctly describes the Program and that the Program can be used according to the Program information. You have to check the usability according to the Program information within the "money-back guaranty" period.

Limitation of Liability (Section 3):

The following paragraph is added to this Section:

The limitations and exclusions specified in the Agreement will not apply to damages caused by IBM with fraud or gross negligence, and for express warranty.

INDIA:

General (Section 4):

The following replaces the fourth paragraph of this Section:

If no suit or other legal action is brought, within two years after the cause of action arose, in respect of any claim that either party may have against the other, the rights of the concerned party in respect of such claim will be forfeited and the other party will stand released from its obligations in respect of such claim.

IRELAND:

No Warranty (Section 2):

The following paragraph is added to this Section:

Except as expressly provided in these terms and conditions, all statutory conditions, including all warranties implied, but without prejudice to the generality of the foregoing, all warranties implied by the Sale of Goods Act 1893 or the Sale of Goods and Supply of Services Act 1980 are hereby excluded.

ITALY:

Limitation of Liability (Section 3):

This Section is replaced by the following:

Unless otherwise provided by mandatory law, IBM is not liable for any damages which might arise.

NEW ZEALAND:

No Warranty (Section 2):

The following paragraph is added to this Section:

Although IBM specifies that there are no warranties, you may have certain rights under the Consumer Guarantees Act 1993 or other legislation which cannot be excluded or limited. The Consumer Guarantees Act 1993 will not apply in respect of any goods or services which IBM provides, if you require the goods and services for the purposes of a business as defined in that Act.

Limitation of Liability (Section 3):

The following paragraph is added to this Section:

Where Programs are not acquired for the purposes of a business as defined in the Consumer Guarantees Act 1993, the limitations in this Section are subject to the limitations in that Act.

UNITED KINGDOM:

Limitation of Liability (Section 3):

The following paragraph is added to this Section at the end of the first paragraph:

The limitation of liability will not apply to any breach of IBM's obligations implied by Section 12 of the Sales of Goods Act 1979 or Section 2 of the Supply of Goods and Services Act 1982.

Z125-5543-01 (10/97)

LICENSE INFORMATION

The Programs listed below are licensed under the following terms and conditions in addition to those of the International License Agreement for Evaluation of Programs.

Program Name: IBM® WebSphere® Application Server, Advanced Edition, Version 4, for Windows NT® and Windows® 2000, Evaluation Copy.

Specified Operating Environment

The Program Specifications and Specified Operating Environment information may be found in documentation accompanying the Program such as the Installation/Users Guide.

Evaluation Period

The license begins on the date you first use the Program and ends after 90 days.

U.S. Government Users Restricted Rights

U.S. Government Users Restricted Rights - Use, duplication, or disclosure restricted by the GSA ADP Schedule Contract with the IBM Corporation.

IBM and WebSphere are trademarks of IBM Corporation in the United States, other countries, or both.

Microsoft and Windows are trademarks of Microsoft Corporation in the United States, other countries, or both.

PRENTICE HALL LICENSE AGREEMENT AND LIMITED WARRANTY

READ THE FOLLOWING TERMS AND CONDITIONS CAREFULLY BEFORE OPENING THIS SOFT-WARE PACKAGE. THIS LEGAL DOCUMENT IS AN AGREEMENT BETWEEN YOU AND PRENTICE-HALL, INC. (THE "COMPANY"). BY OPENING THIS SEALED SOFTWARE PACKAGE, YOU ARE AGREEING TO BE BOUND BY THESE TERMS AND CONDITIONS. IF YOU DO NOT AGREE WITH THESE TERMS AND CONDITIONS, DO NOT OPEN THE SOFTWARE PACKAGE. PROMPTLY RETURN THE UNOPENED SOFTWARE PACKAGE AND ALL ACCOMPANYING ITEMS TO THE PLACE YOU OBTAINED THEM FOR A FULL REFUND OF ANY SUMS YOU HAVE PAID.

1.   GRANT OF LICENSE: In consideration of your purchase of this book, and your agreement to abide by the terms and conditions of this Agreement, the Company grants to you a nonexclusive right to use and display the copy of the enclosed software program (hereinafter the "SOFTWARE") on a single computer (i.e., with a single CPU) at a single location so long as you comply with the terms of this Agreement. The Company reserves all rights not expressly granted to you under this Agreement.

2.   OWNERSHIP OF SOFTWARE: You own only the magnetic or physical media (the enclosed media) on which the SOFTWARE is recorded or fixed, but the Company and the software developers retain all the rights, title, and ownership to the SOFTWARE recorded on the original media copy(ies) and all subsequent copies of the SOFTWARE, regardless of the form or media on which the original or other copies may exist. This license is not a sale of the original SOFTWARE or any copy to you.

3.   COPY RESTRICTIONS: This SOFTWARE and the accompanying printed materials and user manual (the "Documentation") are the subject of copyright. The individual programs on the media are copyrighted by the authors of each program. Some of the programs on the media include separate licensing agreements. If you intend to use one of these programs, you must read and follow its accompanying license agreement. You may not copy the Documentation or the SOFTWARE, except that you may make a single copy

of the SOFTWARE for backup or archival purposes only. You may be held legally responsible for any copying or copyright infringement which is caused or encouraged by your failure to abide by the terms of this restriction.

4.   USE RESTRICTIONS: You may not network the SOFTWARE or otherwise use it on more than one computer or computer terminal at the same time. You may physically transfer the SOFTWARE from one computer to another provided that the SOFTWARE is used on only one computer at a time. You may not distribute copies of the SOFTWARE or Documentation to others. You may not reverse engineer, disassemble, decompile, modify, adapt, translate, or create derivative works based on the SOFTWARE or the Documentation without the prior written consent of the Company.

5.   TRANSFER RESTRICTIONS: The enclosed SOFTWARE is licensed only to you and may not be transferred to any one else without the prior written consent of the Company. Any unauthorized transfer of the SOFTWARE shall result in the immediate termination of this Agreement.

6.   TERMINATION: This license is effective until terminated. This license will terminate automatically without notice from the Company and become null and void if you fail to comply with any provisions or limitations of this license. Upon termination, you shall destroy the Documentation and all copies of the SOFTWARE. All provisions of this Agreement as to warranties, limitation of liability, remedies or damages, and our ownership rights shall survive termination.

7.   MISCELLANEOUS: This Agreement shall be construed in accordance with the laws of the United States of America and the State of New York and shall benefit the Company, its affiliates, and assignees.

8.   LIMITED WARRANTY AND DISCLAIMER OF WARRANTY: The Company warrants that the SOFTWARE, when properly used in accordance with the Documentation, will operate in substantial conformity with the description of the SOFTWARE set forth in the Documentation. The Company does not warrant that the SOFTWARE will meet your requirements or that the operation of the SOFTWARE will be uninterrupted or error-free. The Company warrants that the media on which the SOFTWARE is delivered shall be free from defects in materials and workmanship under normal use for a period of thirty (30) days from the date of your purchase. Your only remedy and the Company's only obligation under these limited warranties is, at the Company's option, return of the warranted item for a refund of any amounts paid by you or replacement of the item. Any replacement of SOFTWARE or media under the warranties shall not extend the original warranty period. The limited warranty set forth above shall not apply to any SOFTWARE which the Company determines in good faith has been subject to misuse, neglect, improper installation, repair, alteration, or damage by you. EXCEPT FOR THE EXPRESSED WARRANTIES SET FORTH ABOVE, THE COMPANY DISCLAIMS ALL WARRANTIES, EXPRESS OR IMPLIED, INCLUDING WITHOUT LIMITATION, THE IMPLIED WARRANTIES OF MERCHANTABILITY AND FITNESS FOR A PARTICULAR PURPOSE. EXCEPT FOR THE EXPRESS WARRANTY SET FORTH ABOVE, THE COMPANY DOES NOT WARRANT, GUARANTEE, OR MAKE ANY REPRESENTATION REGARDING THE USE OR THE RESULTS OF THE USE OF THE SOFTWARE IN TERMS OF ITS CORRECTNESS, ACCURACY, RELIABILITY, CURRENTNESS, OR OTHERWISE.

IN NO EVENT, SHALL THE COMPANY OR ITS EMPLOYEES, AGENTS, SUPPLIERS, OR CONTRACTORS BE LIABLE FOR ANY INCIDENTAL, INDIRECT, SPECIAL, OR CONSEQUENTIAL DAMAGES ARISING OUT OF OR IN CONNECTION WITH THE LICENSE GRANTED UNDER THIS AGREEMENT, OR FOR LOSS OF USE, LOSS OF DATA, LOSS OF INCOME OR PROFIT, OR OTHER LOSSES, SUSTAINED AS A RESULT OF INJURY TO ANY PERSON, OR LOSS OF OR DAMAGE TO PROPERTY, OR CLAIMS OF THIRD PARTIES, EVEN IF THE COMPANY OR AN AUTHORIZED REPRESENTATIVE OF THE COMPANY HAS BEEN ADVISED OF THE POSSIBILITY OF SUCH DAMAGES. IN NO EVENT SHALL LIABILITY OF THE COMPANY FOR DAMAGES WITH RESPECT TO THE SOFTWARE EXCEED THE AMOUNTS ACTUALLY PAID BY YOU, IF ANY, FOR THE SOFTWARE.

SOME JURISDICTIONS DO NOT ALLOW THE LIMITATION OF IMPLIED WARRANTIES OR LIABILITY FOR INCIDENTAL, INDIRECT, SPECIAL, OR CONSEQUENTIAL DAMAGES, SO THE ABOVE LIMITATIONS MAY NOT ALWAYS APPLY. THE WARRANTIES IN THIS AGREEMENT GIVE YOU SPECIFIC LEGAL RIGHTS AND YOU MAY ALSO HAVE OTHER RIGHTS WHICH VARY IN ACCORDANCE WITH LOCAL LAW.

ACKNOWLEDGMENT

YOU ACKNOWLEDGE THAT YOU HAVE READ THIS AGREEMENT, UNDERSTAND IT, AND AGREE TO BE BOUND BY ITS TERMS AND CONDITIONS. YOU ALSO AGREE THAT THIS AGREEMENT IS THE COMPLETE AND EXCLUSIVE STATEMENT OF THE AGREEMENT BETWEEN

YOU AND THE COMPANY AND SUPERSEDES ALL PROPOSALS OR PRIOR AGREEMENTS, ORAL, OR WRITTEN, AND ANY OTHER COMMUNICATIONS BETWEEN YOU AND THE COMPANY OR ANY REPRESENTATIVE OF THE COMPANY RELATING TO THE SUBJECT MATTER OF THIS AGREEMENT.

Should you have any questions concerning this Agreement or if you wish to contact the Company for any reason, please contact in writing at the address below.

Robin Short
Prentice Hall PTR
One Lake Street
Upper Saddle River, New Jersey 07458

The DEITEL & DEITEL Suite of Products...

BOOKS

e-Business & e-Commerce How to Program

BOOK / CD-ROM

©2001, 1254 pp., paper bound
w/CD-ROM (0-13-028419-X)

This innovative book explores programming technologies for developing Web-based e-business and e-commerce solutions, and covers e-business and e-commerce models and business issues. Readers learn a full range of options, from "build-your-own" to turnkey solutions. The book examines a number of the top e-businesses (such as Amazon, eBay, Priceline, Travelocity, etc.), explaining the technical details of building successful e-business and e-commerce sites and their underlying business premises. Learn how to implement the dominant e-commerce models — shopping carts, auctions, naming-your-own-price, comparison shopping and bots/ intelligent agents—by using markup languages (HTML, Dynamic HTML and XML), scripting languages (JavaScript, VBScript and Perl), server-side technologies (Active Server Pages and Perl/CGI) and database (SQL and ADO) , security and online payment technologies. Updates are regularly posted to **www.deitel.com** and the book includes a CD-ROM with software tools, source code and live links.

e-Business & e-Commerce for Managers

©2001, 794 pp., paper
(0-13-032364-0)

This comprehensive overview of building and managing an e-business explores topics such as the decision to bring a business online, choosing a business model, accepting payments, marketing strategies and security, as well as many other important issues (such as career resources). Features Web resources and online demonstrations that supplement the text and direct readers to additional materials. The book also includes an appendix that develops a complete Web-based shopping cart application using HTML, JavaScript, VBScript, Active Server Pages, ADO, SQL, HTTP, XML and XSL. Plus, company-specific sections provide "real-world" examples of the concepts presented in the book.

Internet & World Wide Web How to Program, Second Edition

BOOK / CD-ROM

©2002, 1300 pp., paper bound w/CD-ROM
(0-13-030897-8)

The world's best-selling Internet and Web programming text uses the scripting and markup languages of the Web to present traditional introductory programming concepts. Now you can learn programming fundamentals "wrapped in the metaphor of the Web." Employing the Deitels' signature "live-code™" approach, the book covers markup languages (XHTML, Dynamic HTML), client-side scripting (JavaScript) and server-side scripting (VBScript, ASP, Perl/CGI, Python, PHP, Java servlets, Java Server Pages). The book offers a thorough treatment of programming concepts, with programs that yield visible or audible results in Web pages and Web-based applications. It discusses Internet Explorer, effective Web-based design, multi-tier Web-based applications development, ActiveX® controls and introduces electronic commerce and security. Updated material on **www.deitel.com** and **www.prenhall.com/deitel** provides additional resources for instructors who want to cover Microsoft® or non-Microsoft technologies. The Web site includes an extensive treatment of Netscape® 6 and alternate versions of the code from the Dynamic HTML chapters that will work with non-Microsoft environments as well. The Second Edition also features new and updated material on XHTML, CSS, wireless Internet (WML, WMLScript), Web accessibility, career resources, Python, PHP, XML/XSLT, SVG, SMIL, Web servers, Photoshop Elements, multimedia audio, animation, Macromedia Flash, databases, Perl, CGI, Java servlets, JavaServer Pages, PWS, IIS and Apache.

Python How to Program

BOOK / CD-ROM

© 2002, 1000 pp., paper
(0-13-092361-3)

This exciting new book provides a comprehensive introduction to Python — a powerful object-oriented programming language with clear syntax and the ability to bring together various technologies quickly and easily. This book covers introductory programming techniques as well as more advanced topics such as graphical user interfaces, databases, wireless Internet programming, networking and multimedia. Readers will learn principles that are applicable to both systems development and Web programming. The book features the outstanding, consistent and applied pedagogy that the *How to Program* series is known for, including the Deitels' signature Live-Code™ Approach, with thousands of lines of code in hundreds of working programs; hundreds of valuable programming tips identified with icons throughout the text; an extensive set of exercises, projects and case studies; two-color four-way syntax coloring and much more.

Wireless Internet & Mobile Business How to Program

© 2002, 1300 pp., paper
(0-13-062226-5)

While the rapid growth of wireless technologies (such as cell phones, pagers and personal digital assistants) offers many new opportunities for businesses and programmers, it also presents numerous challenges related to issues such as security and standardization. This book offers a thorough treatment of both the management and technical aspects of this expanding area, including current practices and future trends. The first half explores the business issues surrounding wireless technology and mobile business, including an overview of existing and developing communication technologies and the application of business principles to wireless devices. It then turns to programming for the wireless Internet, exploring topics such as WAP (including 2.0), WML, WMLScript, XML, XSL, XSLT, XHTML, Wireless Java Programming, Web Clipping and more. Other topics covered include career resources, location-based services, wireless marketing, wireless payments, security, accessibility, international issues, Palm, PocketPC, Windows CE, i-Mode, Bluetooth, J2ME, MIDP, MIDlets, ASP, Perl and PHP. Also discussed are Microsoft .NET Mobile Framework, BREW, multimedia, Flash, VBScript and legal, ethical and social issues.

XML How to Program

BOOK / CD-ROM

© 2001, 934 pp., paper
(0-13-028417-3)

This book is a complete guide to programming in XML. It explains how to use XML to create customized tags and addresses standard custom markup languages for science and technology, multimedia, commerce and other fields. Concise introductions to Java, JavaServer Pages, VBScript, Active Server Pages and Perl/CGI provide readers with the essentials of these programming languages and server-side development technologies to enable them to work effectively with XML. The book also covers cutting-edge topics such as XQL and SMIL, plus a real-world e-commerce case study and a complete chapter on Web accessibility that addresses Voice XML. It also includes tips such as Common Programming Errors, Software Engineering Observations, Portability Tips and Debugging Hints. Other topics covered include XHTML, CSS, DTD, schema, parsers, DOM, SAX, XPath, XLink, namespaces, XBase, XInclude, XPointer, XSL, XSLT, XSL Formatting Objects, JavaServer Pages, XForms, topic maps, X3D, MathML, OpenMath, CML, BML, CDF, RDF, SVG, Cocoon, WML, XBRL, and BizTalk and SOAP Web resources.

Perl How to Program

BOOK / CD-ROM

© 2001, 1057 pp., paper
(0-13-028418-1)

This comprehensive guide to Perl programming emphasizes the use of the Common Gateway Interface (CGI) with Perl to create powerful dynamic Web content for e-commerce applications. The book begins with a clear and careful introduction to programming concepts at a level suitable for beginners, and proceeds through advanced topics such as references and complex data structures. Key Perl topics such as regular expressions and string manipulation are covered in detail. The authors address important and topical issues such as object-oriented programming, the Perl database interface (DBI), graphics and security. Also included is a treatment of XML, a bonus chapter introducing the Python programming language, supplemental material on career resources and a complete chapter on Web accessibility. The text also includes tips such as Common Programming Errors, Software Engineering Observations, Portability Tips and Debugging Hints.

Java How to Program
Fourth Edition

BOOK / CD-ROM

©2002, 1100 pp.,
cloth bound
w/CD-ROM
(0-13-034151-7)

The world's best-selling Java text is now even better! The Fourth Edition of *Java How to Program* now includes a new focus on object-oriented design with the UML, design patterns, full-color program listings and figures, and the most up-to-date Java coverage available.

Readers will discover key topics in Java programming, such as graphical user interface components, exception handling, multithreading, multimedia, files and streams, networking, data structures, and more. In addition, a new chapter on design patterns explains frequently recurring architectural patterns —information that can help save designers considerable time when building large systems.

The highly detailed optional case study focuses on object-oriented design with the UML and presents fully implemented working Java code.

Updated throughout, the text now includes new and revised discussions on topics such as Swing, graphics, multithreading, multimedia, Java Media Framework, streaming audio, streaming video, socket-and-packet-based networking and career resources. Three introductory chapters heavily emphasize problem solving and programming skills. The chapters on RMI, JDBC, servlets and JavaBeans have been moved to *Advanced Java 2 Platform How to Program*, where they are now covered in much greater depth. (See *Advanced Java 2 Platform How to Program*, at right.)

Advanced Java™ 2 Platform How to Program

BOOK / CD-ROM

© 2002, 1000 pp., paper
(0-13-089560-1)

Expanding on the world's best-selling Java textbook— *Java How to Program*— *Advanced Java 2 Platform How To Program* presents advanced Java topics for developing sophisticated, user-friendly GUIs; significant, scalable enterprise applications; wireless applications and distributed systems. Focusing on Java 2 Enterprise Edition (J2EE), this textbook integrates technologies such as XML, XSLT, JavaBeans, security, JDBC, JavaServer Pages (JSP), servlets, Remote Method Invocation (RMI), Enterprise JavaBeans (EJB) and design patterns into a significant enterprise case study that leverages J2EE's powerful component model. This textbook also features a case study that integrates Swing, Java2D, drag and drop, XML and design patterns to build a sophisticated drawing application. Additional topics include CORBA, Jini, JavaSpaces, Jiro, Java Management Extensions (JMX) and Peer-to-Peer networking with an introduction to JXTA. This textbook also introduces the Java 2 Micro Edition (J2ME) for building applications for handheld and wireless devices using MIDP and MIDlets. Wireless technologies covered include WAP, WML and i-mode.

C++ How to Program
Third Edition

BOOK / CD-ROM

© 2001, 1168 pp., paper
(0-13-089571-7)

The world's best-selling C++ text teaches programming by emphasizing object-oriented programming, software reuse and component-oriented software construction. This comprehensive book uses the Deitels' signature live-code™ approach, presenting every concept in the context of a complete, working C++ program followed by a screen capture showing the program's output. It also includes a rich collection of exercises and valuable insights in its set of Common Programming Errors, Software Engineering Observations, Portability Tips and Debugging Hints. The Third Edition features an extensive treatment of the Standard Template Library and includes a new case study that focuses on object-oriented design with the UML, illustrating the entire process of object-oriented design from conception to implementation. In addition, it adheres to the latest ANSI/ISO C++ standards. The accompanying CD-ROM contains Microsoft® Visual C++ 6.0 Introductory Edition software, source code for all examples in the text and hyperlinks to C++ demos and Internet resources.

C# How to Program

BOOK / CD-ROM

©2002, 1000 pp., paper (0-13-062221-4)

An exciting new addition to the *How to Program* series, *C# How to Program* provides a comprehensive introduction to Microsoft's new object-oriented language. C# builds on the skills already mastered by countless C++ and Java programmers, enabling them to create powerful Web applications and components—ranging from XML-based Web services on Microsoft's .NET™ platform to middle-tier business objects and system-level applications. Mastering C# will allow programmers to create complex systems—using fewer lines of code and reducing the chance for error. The end result is faster development at a decreased cost—and optimum adaptibility that makes it easy to keep up with the evolving Web.

Look for these related titles in the Deitels' *.NET Series:*
- *Visual Basic® .NET How to Program*
- *Visual C++ .NET How to Program*

C How to Program
Third Edition

BOOK / CD-ROM

©2001, 1253 pp., paper (0-13-089572-5)

Highly practical in approach, the Third Edition of the world's best-selling C text introduces the fundamentals of structured programming and software engineering and gets up to speed quickly. This comprehensive book not only covers the full C language, but also reviews library functions and introduces object-based and object-oriented programming in C++ and Java, as well as event-driven GUI programming in Java. The Third Edition includes a new 346-page introduction to Java 2 and the basics of GUIs, and the 298-page introduction to C++ has been updated to be consistent with the most current ANSI/ISO C++ standards. Plus, icons throughout the book point out valuable programming tips such as Common Programming Errors, Portability Tips and Testing and Debugging Tips.

Look for new Visual Studio .NET editions coming soon!

Visual Basic® 6
How to Program

BOOK / CD-ROM

©1999, 1015 pp., paper bound w/CD-ROM
(0-13-456955-5)

Getting Started with Microsoft® Visual C++™ 6
with an Introduction to MFC

BOOK / CD-ROM

©2000, 163 pp., paper (0-13-016147-0)

BOOK/MULTIMEDIA PACKAGES

Complete Training Courses

Each complete package includes the corresponding *How to Program Series* book and interactive multimedia CD-ROM. *Complete Training Courses* are perfect for anyone interested in learning Java, C++, Visual Basic, XML, Perl, Internet/World Wide Web and e-commerce programming. They are exceptional and affordable resources for college students and professionals learning programming for the first time or reinforcing their knowledge.

Each *Complete Training Course* is compatible with Windows 95, Windows 98, Windows NT and Windows 2000 and includes the following features:

Intuitive Browser-Based Interface

Whether you choose the Web-based *Complete Training Course* or the CD-ROM, you'll love the new browser-based interface, designed to be easy and accessible to anyone who's ever used a Web browser. Every *Complete Training Course* features the full text, illustrations, and program listings of its corresponding *How to Program* book—all in full color—with full-text searching and hyperlinking.

Further Enhancements to the Deitels' Signature Live-Code™ Approach

Every code sample from the main text can be found in the interactive, multimedia, CD-ROM-based *Cyber Classrooms* included in the *Complete Training Courses*. Syntax coloring of code is included for the *How to Program* books that are published in full color. Even the recent two-color books use effective four-way syntax coloring. The *Cyber Classroom* software is provided in full color for all the Deitel books.

Audio Annotations

Hours of detailed, expert audio descriptions of thousands of lines of code help reinforce concepts.

Easily Executable Code

With one click of the mouse, you can execute the code or save it to your hard drive to manipulate using the programming environment of your choice. With selected *Complete Training Courses*, you can also automatically load all of the code into a development environment such as Microsoft® Visual C++™, enabling you to modify and execute the programs with ease.

Abundant Self-Assessment Material

Practice exams test your understanding with hundreds of text questions and answers in addition to those found in the main text. Hundreds of self-review questions, all with answers, are drawn from the text; as are hundreds of programming exercises, half with answers.

Announcing New Web-Based Versions of the Deitels' *Complete Training Courses!*

The same highly acclaimed material found on the *Cyber Classroom* CD-ROMs is now available at the same price via the World Wide Web! When you order the Web-based version of a *Complete Training Course,* you receive the corresponding *How to Program* book with a URL and password that give you six months of access to the *Cyber Classroom* software via the Web.

To explore a demo of this new option, please visit
http://ptgtraining.com

www.phptr.com/phpinteractive

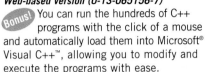

www.Deitel.InformIT.com

Deitel & Associates, Inc. is partnering with Prentice Hall's parent company, Pearson PLC, and its information technology Web site, InformIT (www.informit.com) to launch the Deitel InformIT site at www.Deitel.InformIT.com. The Deitel InformIT site is an online resource center that delivers premium IT content, adding new e-Learning offerings to the established Deitel product suite and the ability to purchase Deitel products. The site will contain information on the continuum of Deitel products, including:

 • **Free weekly Deitel Buzz e-mail newsletter**

 • **Free informational articles**

• **Deitel e-Matter**

• **Books and new e-Books**
• **Instructor-led training**
• **Web-based training**
• **Complete Training Courses/Cyber Classrooms**

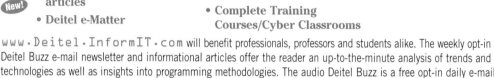

www.Deitel.InformIT.com will benefit professionals, professors and students alike. The weekly opt-in Deitel Buzz e-mail newsletter and informational articles offer the reader an up-to-the-minute analysis of trends and technologies as well as insights into programming methodologies. The audio Deitel Buzz is a free opt-in daily e-mail featuring a link to an audio-annotated code sample. One of the authors will provide a detailed walkthrough of the code, offering insights into portability issues, maximizing efficiency and other valuable tips. For more in-depth material, we are pleased to announce the launch of **Deitel e-Matter**. e-Matter consists of sections on leading-edge technologies taken from already published texts, forthcoming texts or pieces written during the Deitel research and development process.

A Sneak Peek at Deitel™ Web-Based Tutorials

Deitel & Associates, Inc. is developing a series of self-paced Web-based tutorials using content from the Cyber Classrooms in their *How to Program Series*. Eventually, it will be possible to access the same cutting-edge content via CD-ROM, the Web, or even wireless devices. New features of these innovative tutorials include:

Five-way Flash animation demonstrating looping.

Interactive Questions

Specialized Q icons are attached to particular lines of code. When clicked, the icon provides a question and—upon pressing a button—an answer relating specifically to that line of code.

Dynamic Glossary

Users click on designated keywords, phrases or programming elements, displaying small windows containing definitions.

Interactive Animations

Deitel Web-based tutorial courses take advantage of the small file sizes of vector-based graphics and advancements in the tools used to produce them such as Macromedia™ Flash®, and use cutting-edge compression techniques and streaming media to deliver abundant audio. The Deitel Java Web-based tutorial features an interactive five-way for-loop animation, as pictured above, which includes an animated flowchart, audio and a simulated output window. Future *Cyber Classrooms* will contain animations illustrating important programming concepts such as flow of control and recursion.

Web-based Labs

Gain hands-on knowledge of the concepts you read about in the text. Deitel Web-based tutorial labs present challenging programming assignments and their solutions.

Abundant Audio

The courses deliver hours of streaming audio-based lectures. All code is syntax colored to make it easier to read and comprehend. Future Cyber Classrooms will contain nearly twice the current amount of audio.

Richer Assessment Types

In addition to the true/false questions found in current *Cyber Classrooms*, future versions will contain richer assessment types including fill-in-the-blank and matching questions.

Multiple Content Paths

Future *Cyber Classrooms* will contain multiple paths through the content, optimized for different users. Students will find an abundance of pedagogy designed just for them, while corporate users will find the content arranged in a way that meets their challenging "just-in-time" learning needs.

For those interested in
Microsoft® Visual Basic .NET

Visual Basic .NET™ How to Program: This book builds on the pedagogy of the first edition, which was developed for Visual Studio 6. It has a much-enhanced treatment of developing Web-based e-business and e-commerce applications. The book includes an extensive treatment of XML and wireless applications, Web Forms and Web Services.

For those interested in
Python

Python How to Program: This book introduces the increasingly popular Python language which makes many application development tasks easier to accomplish than with traditional object-oriented languages. Many people are touting Python as a more effective first language than C++ or Java.

For those interested in
Flash

Flash 6 How to Program: Hundreds of millions of people browse Flash-enabled Web sites daily. This first book in the Deitel Multimedia series introduces the powerful features of Flash 6 and includes a detailed introduction to programming with the Flash 6 scripting language. The key to the book is that it presents a complete treatment of building Flash-centric multi-tier client/server Web-based applications.

For those interested in
Microsoft® Visual C++ .NET

Visual C++ .NET™ How to Program: This book combines the pedagogy and extensive coverage of *C++ How to Program, Third Edition* with a more in-depth treatment of Windows and Internet programming in Visual Studio .NET. We have carefully culled the best material from each of these areas to produce a solid, two-semester, introductory/intermediate level treatment.

For those interested in
C++

Advanced C++ How to Program: This book builds on the pedagogy of *C++ How to Program, Third Edition,* and features more advanced discussions of templates, multiple inheritance and other key topics. We are co-authoring this book with Don Kostuch, one of the world's most experienced C++ educators.

New & Improved Deitel™ Web Site!

Deitel & Associates, Inc. is constantly upgrading **www·deitel·com**. The new site will feature Macromedia™ Flash® enhancements and additional content to create a more valuable resource for students, professors and professionals. Features will include FAQs, Web resources, e-publications and online chat sessions with the authors. We will include streaming audio clips where the authors discuss their publications. Web-based training demos will also be available at the site.

> **Turn the page to find out more about Deitel & Associates!**

Further Notes on Software Installation

Note: On the CD-ROM that accompanies this book, the installation instructions include a table of system requirements for installing the software packages. In each of the columns of the system requirements tables for Windows and Linux, a particular row may list multiple options. Sometimes a single option or a subset of the options will meet the requirements for a given piece of software. For detailed information on any software included on this CD, please visit the Web site of the software provider.

ERRATA AND CLARIFICATIONS FOR THE MICROSOFT WINDOWS SYSTEM REQUIREMENTS

Forte for Java Release 2.0 Community Edition

This product executes on computers running the Windows 98 (or higher) operating system and the Java 2 Platform, Standard Edition, Version 1.3 (or higher).

BEA WebLogic Server™ 6.0 SP2

Only one of the versions of Java listed in the table is required to execute WebLogic. Also, WebLogic will execute without Oracle 8.1.6.

Cloudscape 6.4

For a complete list of supported Java Virtual Machines and supported platforms visit:

`http://www.cloudscape.com/support/servepage.jsp?page=fyi_cert36vms.html`

Jakarta Tomcat 3.2.2

The actual version included on the CD and used in Chapter 9, *Servlets* and Chapter 10, *Java Server Pages (JSP)* is version 3.2.3. Tomcat will execute on Windows 95 or higher, and on any platform on which Java 1.1 or later is installed. Tomcat does not require a Web server; however, it can be configured to work with those Web servers listed in the table.

ERRATA AND CLARIFICATIONS FOR THE LINUX SYSTEM REQUIREMENTS

Cloudscape 6.4

For a complete list of supported Java Virtual Machines and supported platforms visit:

`http://www.cloudscape.com/support/servepage.jsp?page=fyi_cert36vms.html`

Also, in the row "Other" the requirements indicate, "Need Administrator Password." This should read, "Need root password."

Jakarta Tomcat 3.2.2

The actual version included on the CD and used in Chapter 9, Servlets and Chapter 10, Java Server Pages (JSP) is version 3.2.3. Also, Tomcat will execute on Linux and any platform on which Java 1.1 or later is installed. Tomcat does not require the Web servers listed; however, it can be configured to work with those Web servers.

IMPORTANT
SEE THE TWO PREVIOUS PAGES
FOR IMPORTANT INFORMATION
ABOUT SOFTWARE INSTALLATION

License Agreement and Limited Warranty

The software is distributed on an "AS IS" basis, without warranty. Neither the authors, the software developers, nor Prentice Hall make any representation, or warranty, either express or implied, with respect to the software programs, their quality, accuracy, or fitness for a specific purpose. Therefore, neither the authors, the software developers, nor Prentice Hall shall have any liability to you or any other person or entity with respect to any liability, loss, or damage caused or alleged to have been caused directly or indirectly by the programs contained on the media. This includes, but is not limited to, interruption of service, loss of data, loss of classroom time, loss of consulting or anticipatory profits, or consequential damages from the use of these programs. If the media itself is defective, you may return it for a replacement. Use of this software is subject to the Binary Code License terms and conditions at the back of this book. Read the licenses carefully. By opening this package, you are agreeing to be bound by the terms and conditions of these licenses. If you do not agree, do not open the package.

Please refer to end-user license agreements on the CD-ROM for further details.

Using the CD-ROM

The contents of this CD are designed to be accessed through the interface provided in the file **AUTORUN.EXE**. If a startup screen does not pop up automatically when you insert the CD into your computer, double click on the icon for **AUTORUN.EXE** to launch the program or refer to the file **README.TXT** on the CD.

Contents of the CD-ROM

- Java™ 2 Software Development Kit Standard Edition Version 1.3.1 for Windows and Linux (Intel x86)
- Forte for Java, Release 2.0, Community Edition for all platforms
- BEA WebLogic Server™, Version 6.0 (Windows/Linux) with Service Pack 1 or 2, 30-Day Trial
- IBM® WebSphere® Application Server, Advanced Single Server Edition, Version 4.0, for Windows NT® and Windows® 2000, Evaluation Copy
- Cloudscape 3.6.4 for all platforms
- Jakarta Tomcat 3.2.3 for all platforms, from the Apache Software Foundation
- Live links to websites mentioned in this book
- Live code examples from this book
- Portions of this book's text in Adobe® Acrobat® PDF format

Software and Hardware System Requirements

- Intel Pentium 166 MHz or faster processor (Forte requires a minimum 350 MHz processor, IBM® WebSphere® Application Server v4.0 (Evaluation Copy) requires a minimum 500 MHz processor.)
- Windows 9x, Windows NT or later,
- Red Hat Linux 6.2 or later
- 128 MB of RAM (256 MB recommended; IBM® WebSphere® Application Server v4.0 (Evaluation Copy) requires a minimum of 516 MB of RAM)
- CD-ROM drive
- Internet connection and web browser